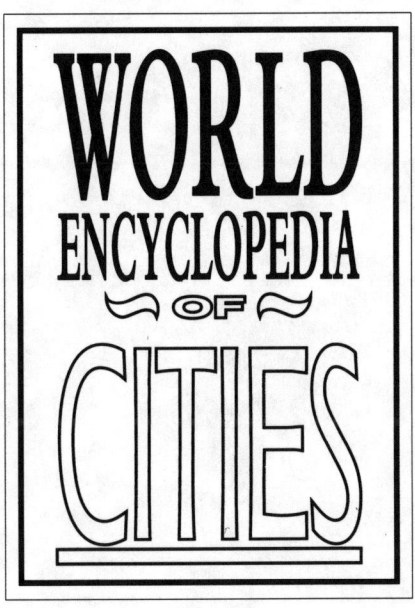

WORLD ENCYCLOPEDIA OF ~ OF ~ CITIES

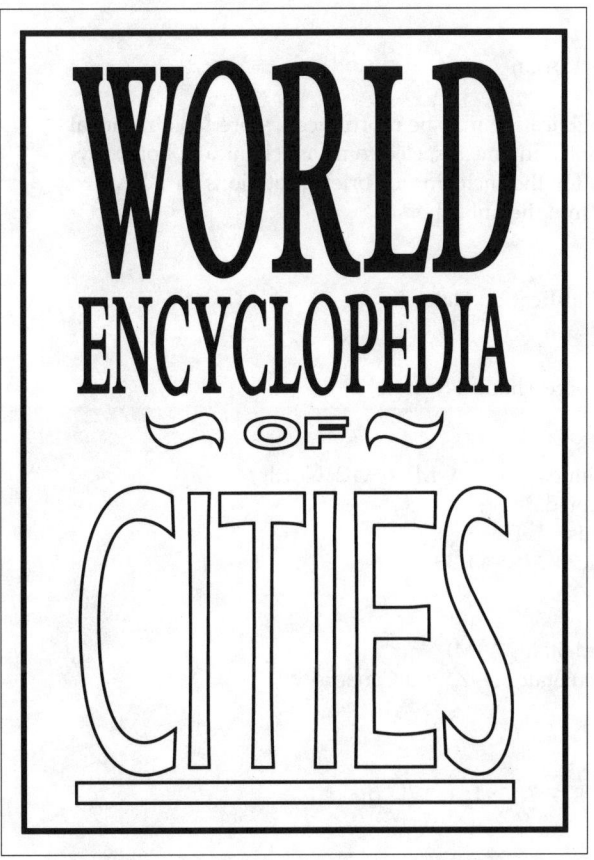

WORLD
ENCYCLOPEDIA
~ OF ~
CITIES

VOLUME I
NORTH AMERICA
(United States A–M)

George Thomas Kurian

ABC-CLIO

Library of Congress Cataloging-in-Publication Data

Kurian, George Thomas.
    World encyclopedia of cities / George Thomas Kurian.
      p. cm.
    Includes bibliographical references.
    Contents: v. 1. North America (United States A–M) — v. 2. North
America (United States N–Z and Canada)
    1. Cities and towns—Encyclopedias. I. Title.
    HT108.5.K87 1993   307.76'03—dc20   93-43133

ISBN 0-87436-650-X (Volume I, United States A–M)
ISBN 0-87436-651-8 (Volume II, United States N–Z, and Canada)
ISBN 0-87436-649-6 (set)

00 99 98 97 96 95 94 93   10 9 8 7 6 5 4 3 2 1 (hc)

ABC-CLIO, Inc.
130 Cremona Drive, P.O. Box 1911
Santa Barbara, California 93116-1911

This book is printed on acid-free paper ⊖ .
Manufactured in the United States of America

Contents

Volume I: North America
(United States A–M)

Preface

The first volumes of the *World Encyclopedia of Cities*, covering North America north of Mexico, were designed for ease-of-use and accessibility for the general researcher. Information compiled from hundreds of books, government documents, and other sources has been gathered within these volumes to provide a one-stop source of information on urban areas across the continent. Information categories vary from history and climate to public finance and parks and recreation. The data chosen reflect the various information needs of different library patrons, whether they are travelers, students, geography teachers, public officials, or simply interested laypersons. Our purpose is to provide a balanced picture of the cities, the history that has influenced and continues to shape them, and the social and economic conditions that bear on them.

The criteria for including or excluding cities in these volumes evolved during the writing and development of the work. The list of cities to be covered was originally compiled on the basis of population—all cities in North America with populations over 100,000—yet this proved to be problematic in presenting a balanced geographical reference work. For example, was the work to include many cities from one heavily populated state, yet completely exclude whole regions with generally lower populations? Should every state capital be included, even though there are other cities in the region both more populous and more economically or socially significant? Such questions eventually led to the modification of the inclusion criteria, and cities were added to help round-out and balance the work geographically.

Both statistical data and narrative information are provided for each city. The problem of gathering statistics that are both current and internally consistent was difficult and in the last analysis not entirely solvable; thus, some of the statistics boxes are sprinkled with the abbreviation *NA*, Not Available or Not Applicable. In general, the smaller the city, the larger the problem of obtaining detailed statistical information. In some cases, the only available statistics were internally inconsistent; where the inconsistencies could not be resolved but were not egregious, they were preserved as a better alternative than excluding the information altogether. Also included for each city are maps, a history narrative, and a brief chronology to assist the reader in placing a city's development in historical perspective.

Inevitably, as in any work of this scope, there will be some errors of fact and omission. The reader is invited to submit corrections or suggestions to the publisher so that such oversights might be corrected in future editions.

The statistical data summarized in the boxes that appear within the text for each city are from a variety of sources. The categories of information and their sources are listed below.

Basic Data

Information for the Name, Name Origin, Year Founded, and Status of cities is primarily from city chambers of commerce, supplemented by a variety of secondary sources. Data for Area, Elevation, Time Zone, and road mileage between cities are from the 1993 *Rand McNally Road Atlas*. The Population and Population of Metro Area statistics are from the 1992 *County and City Extra*. Sister Cities listings are from the 1992 *Directory of Sister Cities, Counties and States by State and Country*.

Environment

The Environmental Stress Index data are from the April 1991 *ZPG Reporter*. The Green Cities Index Rank and Score statistics are from the 1992 *Information Please Environmental Almanac*. The Parkland as % of Total City Area statistic is from *The Livable Cities Almanac*. Information for the % of Waste Landfilled/Recycled and the Annual Parks Expenditures per Capita statistics are provided by the National Urban League.

Weather

The weather statistics are from the National Oceanic and Atmospheric Administration and its annual publication, *Comparative Climatic Data for the United States*.

Population

Population statistics, including the information on composition of households, are compiled from the 1992 *County and City Extra*.

Ethnic Composition

Data on the ethnic composition of cities are from the 1992 *County and City Extra*.

Government

Most government information is provided courtesy of the city chambers of commerce. The City Government Employment Total and Rate per 10,000 statistics are from the 1992 *County and City Extra*.

Public Finance

The statistical data for Total Revenue, Intergovernmental Revenue–Total, Federal Revenue per Capita, % Federal Assistance, % State Assistance, Sales Tax as % of Total Revenue, Local Revenue as % of Total Revenue, City Income Tax, and Fiscal Year Begins are from the U.S. Bureau of the Census publication *Government Finances. City Government Finances: 1989-90*.

Data for Taxes Total, Taxes per Capita (Total and Property), Sales and Gross Receipts, General Expenditures–Total, General Expenditures per Capita, Capital Outlays per Capita, % of Expenditures (for Public Welfare, Highways, Education, Health and Hospitals, Police, Sewage and Sanitation, Parks and Recreation, and Housing and Community Development), Debt Outstanding per Capita, Federal Procurement Contract Awards, and Federal Grant Awards are from the 1992 *County and City Extra*.

Economy

Statistical data for Total Money Income, % of State Average, Per Capita Annual Income, and % of Population below Poverty Level are from the 1992 *County and City Extra*. The information on Fortune 500 companies is from the 19 April 1993 issue of *Fortune* magazine. The data on Banks, Passenger Autos, Electric Meters, and Gas Meters are from the 1992 *Editor & Publisher Market Guide*. Manufacturing, Wholesale Trade, Retail Trade, and Service Industries data are from the 1992 *County and City Extra*.

Labor

Data for Civilian Labor Force (including % Change), Total Unemployment (including Rate %), and Federal Government Civilian Employment are from the 1992 *County and City Extra*. Information on Work Force Distribution is from the U.S. Department of Labor publication, *Employment, Hours, and Earnings, States and Areas, Data for 1987-92*.

Education

Most of the education data are from the National Center for Education Statistics' June 1991 survey report, *Key Statistics on Public Elementary and Secondary Education Reported by State and by Regional, Locale, and Wealth Clusters, 1988-89*. The Educational Attainment (Age 25 and Over) data are from the 1992 *County and City Extra*. Information for Four-Year and Two-Year Colleges and Universities is from the 1992 *Higher Education Directory*.

Libraries

All information on libraries is from the 1991–92 *American Library Directory*.

Health

The numbers and rates for Deaths and Infant Deaths are from the 1992 *County and City Extra*. Information for Health Expenditures per Capita is from the U.S. Bureau of the Census publication, *Government Finances: City Government Finances, 1989-90*. All other health statistics are from *The Livable Cities Almanac*.

Transportation

Data for Interstate Highway Mileage, Total Urban Mileage, and Total Daily Vehicle Mileage are provided by the U.S. Department of Transportation. Information for Daily Average Commute Time and Number of Buses is from *Places Rated Almanac*. All statistics on air transportation are from the Federal Aviation Administration's 1991 publication, *Airport Activity Statistics of Certified Route Air Carriers*.

Housing

All housing data are from the 1992 *County and City Extra* except the data for Tallest Buildings, which are from the 1993 World Almanac.

Crime

Information for Police and Fire Expenditures per Capita is from the 1992 *County and City Extra*. Data for Number of Police and Police per Thousand are from the 1992 *City and County Extra*. Other statistical information for Crime is from the Federal Bureau of Investigation's publication,

Crime in the United States 1991: Uniform Crime Reports.

Religion

All statistical information on religion is from the 1992 *Churches and Church Membership in the United States.*

Media

Media data are from the *Gale Directory of Publications and Broadcast Media.*

Travel and Tourism

The statistical data on Hotel Rooms, Convention and Exhibit Space, Convention Centers, and Festivals are provided by city chambers of commerce.

Cities Listed by State or Province

UNITED STATES

Alabama
Birmingham
Mobile

Alaska
Anchorage

Arizona
Phoenix
Tucson

Arkansas
Little Rock

California
Los Angeles
Sacramento
San Diego
San Francisco
San Jose

Colorado
Colorado Springs
Denver

Connecticut
Bridgeport
Hartford
New Haven
Stamford
Waterbury

Delaware
Wilmington

Florida
Miami
St. Petersburg
Tampa

Georgia
Atlanta

Hawaii
Honolulu

Idaho
Boise

Illinois
Chicago
Peoria
Springfield

Indiana
Evansville
Fort Wayne
Indianapolis
South Bend

Iowa
Cedar Rapids
Davenport
Des Moines

Kansas
Kansas City
Topeka
Wichita

Kentucky
Lexington
Louisville

Louisiana
Baton Rouge
New Orleans

Maine
Augusta
Lewiston
Portland

Maryland
Baltimore

Massachusetts
Boston
Lowell
Springfield
Worcester

Michigan
Ann Arbor
Detroit
Grand Rapids
Lansing

Minnesota
Duluth
Minneapolis
St. Paul

Mississippi
Jackson

Missouri
Kansas City
St. Louis
Springfield

Montana
Billings

Nebraska
Lincoln
Omaha

Nevada
Las Vegas

New Hampshire
Concord
Manchester
Nashua
Portsmouth

New Jersey
Atlantic City
Jersey City
Newark
Trenton

New Mexico
Albuquerque

New York
Albany
Buffalo
New York City
Rochester
Syracuse

North Carolina
Charlotte
Greensboro

North Dakota
Fargo

Ohio
Cincinnati
Cleveland
Columbus
Dayton
Toledo

Oklahoma
Oklahoma City
Tulsa

Oregon
Eugene
Portland

Pennsylvania
Allentown
Erie
Philadelphia
Pittsburgh
Scranton

Rhode Island
Newport
Providence

South Carolina
Charleston

South Dakota
Sioux Falls

Tennessee
Knoxville
Memphis
Nashville

Texas
Austin
Dallas
Fort Worth
Houston
San Antonio

Utah
Salt Lake City

Vermont
Burlington
Montpelier
Rutland

Virginia
Richmond

Washington
Seattle
Spokane
Tacoma

Washington, D.C.

West Virginia
Charleston

Wisconsin
Green Bay
Madison
Milwaukee

Wyoming
Cheyenne

CANADA

Alberta
Calgary
Edmonton

British Columbia
Vancouver

Manitoba
Winnipeg

Newfoundland
St. John's

Nova Scotia
Halifax

Ontario
Hamilton
London
Ottawa
Toronto

Quebec
Montreal
Quebec

Saskatchewan
Regina
Saskatoon

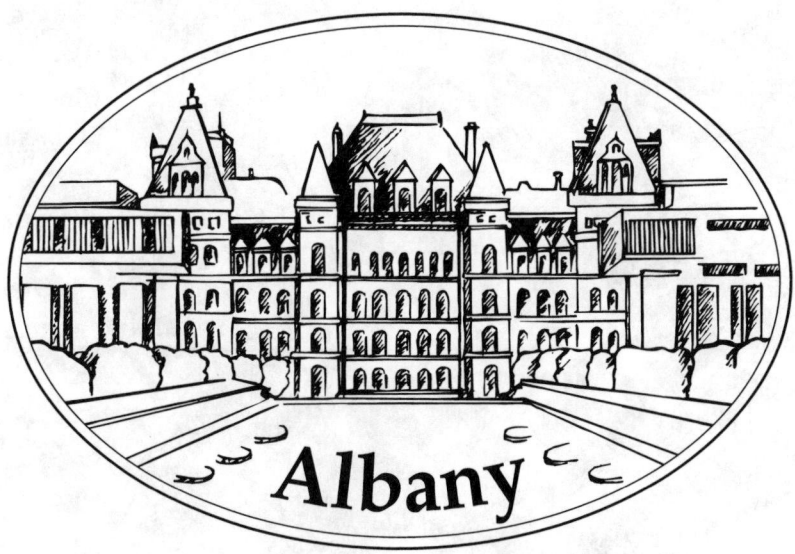

Albany

New York

Location and Topography

Albany, the capital of New York and the seat of Albany County, is in the east-central part of the state, located about 160 miles by highway north of New York City, just a few miles downstream from Troy and the confluence of the Mohawk and Hudson rivers. It is on the west bank of the Hudson River, and the city's business district, on a hill, overlooks the Hudson.

Layout of City and Suburbs

Albany's skyline was altered dramatically with the completion of the Empire State Plaza—called The Mall—in 1978.

The Mall, between State Street and Madison Avenue, is, with other public buildings and the State Capitol, at the heart of the city. From here spread prim, tree-shaded streets lined with the brownstone and brick homes of Victorian Albany interspersed with modern apartment buildings. In the Pine Hills section, along Western and Madison avenues, are large homes built by wealthy residents in the last century. The Whitehall, New Scotland, and West Albany sections were built up later. Docks, railroad terminals, and factories occupy a narrow shelf along the Hudson. Union Station, a massive rectangular building recently redesigned, occupies an entire city block on Broadway between Steuben and Columbia streets. The main shopping area is in the Broadway, Pearl, and lower State Street section.

Climate

Albany has a continental climate moderated by its proximity to the Atlantic Ocean. Nonetheless, wintertime temperatures are cold, averaging 20 to 26°F. In summer, temperatures average in the low 70s, becoming chillier overnight, with only occasional heat waves. The growing season of about 160 days, longer than other places at this latitude, lasts from late April until mid-October.

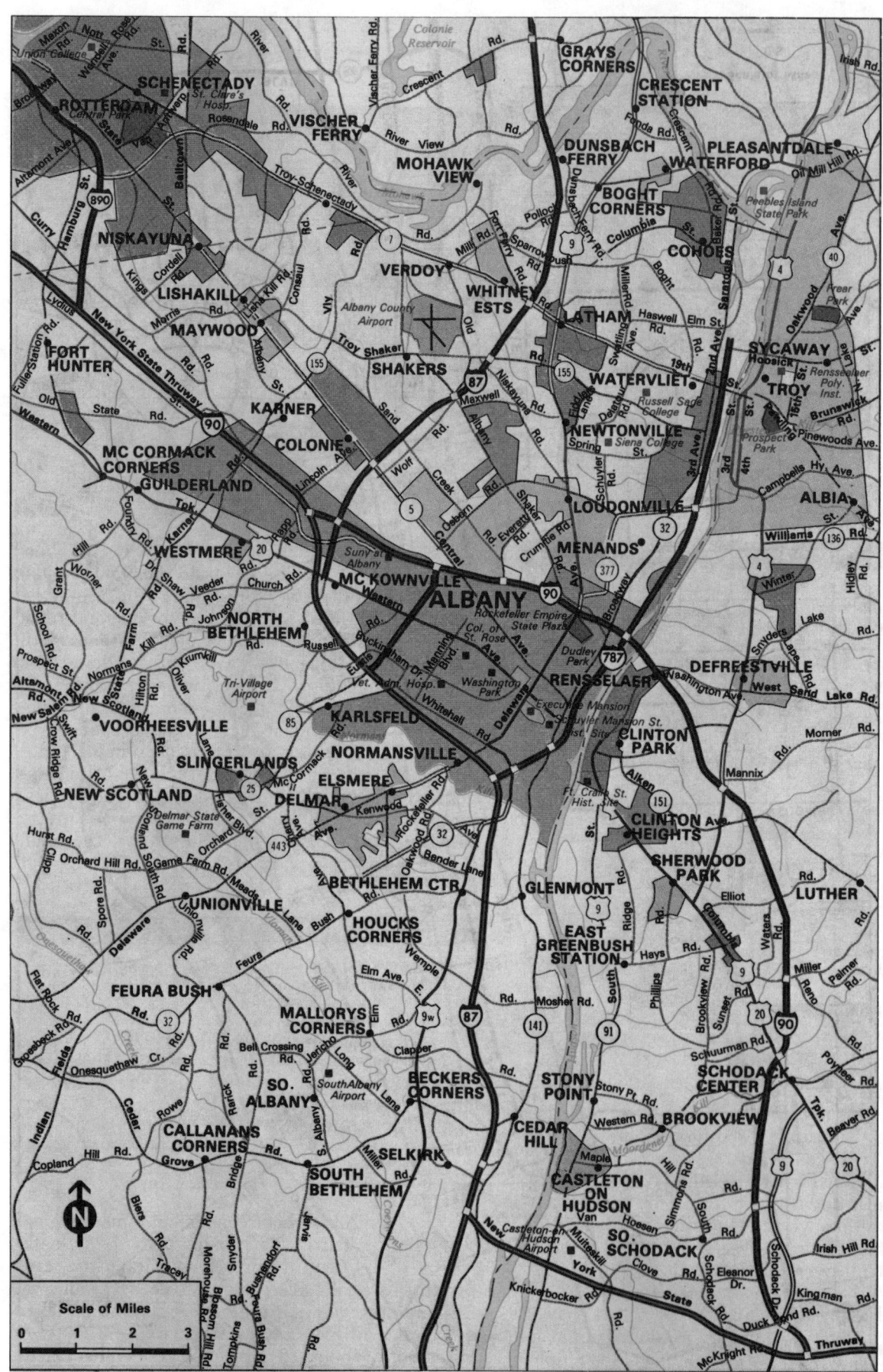

Weather

Temperature

Highest Monthly Average °F	83.9
Lowest Monthly Average °F	12.5

Annual Averages

Days 32°F or Below	155
Days above 90°F	8
Zero Degree Days	17
Precipitation (inches)	33
Snow (inches)	71
% Seasonal Humidity	71
Wind Speed (m.p.h.)	8.9
Clear Days	71
Cloudy Days	183
Storm Days	28
Rainy Days	135

Average Temperatures (°F)	High	Low	Mean
January	30.4	12.5	21.5
February	32.7	14.3	23.5
March	42.6	24.2	33.4
April	58.0	35.7	46.9
May	69.7	45.7	57.7
June	79.4	55.6	67.5
July	83.9	60.1	72.0
August	81.4	57.8	69.6
September	73.7	50.1	61.9
October	62.8	40.0	51.4
November	48.1	31.1	39.6
December	34.1	17.7	25.9

History

Mohicans had a thriving settlement on the site of present-day Albany when English explorer Henry Hudson, sailing for the Dutch East India Company, anchored his ship, the *Half Moon*, in September 1609 in shallows near the site of the present city. In 1613 Captain Adriaen Block followed Hudson's route and in 1614 built Fort Nassau on an island that is now a part of the Port of Albany. A decade later the Dutch West India Company, founded in 1621, sent the first permanent settlers to the Albany area. The party of 18 families were mostly Walloons or French-speaking Huguenots. They built a second fort near the site of the present capital and called it Fort Orange. In 1630 Amsterdam diamond merchant Kiliaen Van Rensselaer purchased a large land parcel from the Dutch West India Company and established the patroonship of Rensselaerswyck, which had Fort Orange as its approximate center and included land on both sides of the Hudson River. Immigrant settlers were obligated to pay the patroon one third of their crops as rent in a system that survived into the early nineteenth century. Peter Stuyvesant, appointed as the governor in New Amsterdam, made the settlement around Fort Orange independent of the patroonship in 1652 and renamed it Beverwyck, Dutch for "town of the beaver."

In 1664 the British took Fort Orange as well as New Amsterdam from the Dutch, renaming the settlement Albany, after James, Duke of York and Albany (later James II of England); New Amsterdam became New York. In 1686 Thomas Dongan, British governor of New York, granted Albany, now a town of three hundred, a charter and a monopoly in fur trade with the Indians for a quit-rent of one beaver skin a year payable to the king. The monopoly became less important as farming quickly replaced fur trading.

In four colonial wars between 1689 and 1763, the French with their Indian allies, and the British colonists with troops from England, contested claims in North America. Albany was a key to the British frontier and constantly faced threat of attack. In 1754, as the Pennsylvania delegate to the Albany Congress, Benjamin Franklin presented his Plan of Union, a proposal that the colonies unify against the French. The proposal was ignored, but the idea still earned Albany the nickname "Cradle of the Union." The French and Indian threat ended in 1763 with the Treaty of Paris, in which the French lost all claims in North America to the British.

At the outset of the American Revolution, the city's population rallied behind George Washington. The British campaign to capture Albany in 1777 ended with the surrender of General John Burgoyne after the Battle of Saratoga.

The city capitalized on its location as head of navigation on the Hudson and became a gateway for trade and settlement to the central and western parts of New York and beyond. A stagecoach line chartered in 1785 between Albany and New York City complemented the well-established river route transportation network. In addition to agriculture, Albany became a major shipbuilding center because it was close to the forests of the Adirondacks, which supplied timbers for masts, tar, pitch, lumber, and turpentine. Sail makers and chandlers opened shops here, as did coopers, joiners, and blacksmiths. Hatters and other clothing manufacturers also located in Albany, as did glass factories.

In 1797 Albany became the state capital after the legislature had, over the years, migrated upriver from White Plains, to Kingston, to Poughkeepsie.

Albany's golden era was as a commercial center and transportation hub to the nation's interior in the first part of the 19th century. The age of steamboats on the Hudson began when Robert Fulton and Robert Livingston's experimental vessel, the *Clermont*, steamed from New York to Albany and back to New York in five days (with stops) in August 1807. The Champlain Canal linking Albany with Lake Champlain opened in 1822, and the Erie Canal linking Albany with Buffalo on Lake Erie was completed in 1825. Access to the Great Lakes meant as many as 50 canal boats a day left Albany for the west, coinciding with waves of immigrants arriving from Europe. Railroads then enhanced Albany's role as a transportation hub.

Albany was also the country's center for the wholesale lumber trade from 1840 through the end of the Civil War in 1865. Some of the city's largest manufacturing plants were established in the 1870s and 1880s, and by 1880 the population exceeded 90,000.

Chronology

1609 English explorer Henry Hudson reaches the site of present day Albany in the *Half Moon*.

1614 Hendrick Christiansen builds Fort Nassau on an island in the Hudson River.

1624 18 Walloon and French-speaking Huguenot families reach Albany as settlers. They build a second fort, called Fort Orange

1630 Kiliaen Van Rensselaer purchases a parcel of land on both sides of the Hudson River to establish the patroonship of Rensselaerswyck.

1664 The British take over Beverwyck and rename it Albany.

1754 Benjamin Franklin presents plan at Albany Congress to unify British colonies against the French.

1763 Treaty of Paris brings to an end the French and Indian wars.

1777 British threats to the city during the Revolution end with the surrender of General John Burgoyne.

1785 A stagecoach line is chartered between New York City and Albany.

1797 Albany becomes the state capital and the site of the state legislature.

1807 *Clermont*, the first steamboat to visit Albany, arrives.

1813 Attorney Martin Van Buren starts *The Argus*, Albany's first newspaper. He later serves as New York's governor (1829) and is elected eighth president (1837–1841) of the United States.

1822 The Champlain Canal opens.

1825 The Erie Canal completed.

1880 City population exceeds 90,000.

1932 Port of Albany opens.

1978 Empire State Plaza opens on a 98-acre site in downtown.

Increasingly, politics became the business of Albany. Over the years such national figures as William H. Seward, Hamilton Fish, Theodore Roosevelt, Charles Evans Hughes, Alfred E. Smith, Franklin D. Roosevelt, Thomas E. Dewey, and Nelson A. Rockefeller served in Albany as governors of New York.

The Port of Albany opened in 1932, continuing the commercial significance of transportation to the city's economy. By the 1950s, however, the city had become more white collar than blue collar, with a substantial part of its work force employed in governmental services and lobbying. In 1978 the monumental Empire State Plaza, the downtown development program begun in 1966, was completed.

Historical Landmarks

While Empire State Plaza is architecture on a grand and modern scale, Albany still proudly displays its graceful historical architecture. The Albany Urban Cultural Park at 25 Quackenbush Square presents a summary of city history and architecture. It is also the site of a house built in 1730, the oldest house surviving from Albany's early days.

Another 18th-century landmark is the red brick, late Georgian Schuyler mansion at 32 Clinton Street, built by Philip Schuyler in 1761–1762 and now a state historic site. Built in 1787, Cherry Hill at 523 1/2 Pearl Street was home to five generations of the Philip Van Rensselaer family, who lived in the frame house until 1963. The First Dutch Reformed Church at North Pearl and Orange streets was begun in 1797 and is the second-oldest Protestant church in continuous existence. Architect Philip Hooker designed the building originally; it was extensively modified in 1858. Its oaken pulpit was carved in Holland in 1656. Abraham Ten Broeck had his mansion, at 9 Ten Broeck Place, built in 1798. This solidly built and well-preserved home is open to the public.

Philip Hooker, who designed a number of Albany buildings, also designed the Albany Academy, a private school for boys built between 1815 and 1817. The academy is now known as the Joseph Henry Memorial, honoring a pioneer in electromagnetism and the Smithsonian Institution's first secretary.

Gratitude for the wealth generated during Albany's golden era of the nineteenth century is expressed in the city's church architecture. St. Joseph's Roman Catholic Church, 10 Broeck Street, was completed in 1860 except for the spire, which was added about 1910. The Cathedral of the Immaculate Conception, dedicated in 1852, is a large Gothic Revival building of warm brownstone. St. Mary's Church, erected in 1867, is a striking example of Italian Romanesque Revival style; a weather vane depicting the Archangel Gabriel blowing his trumpet tops its tower.

The rambling Queen Anne-style Executive Mansion, 138 Eagle Street, was begun in the 1850s. Another public building, the State Capitol building, like its neighbor and successor, Empire State Plaza, took more time and many more dollars than originally planned. Begun in 1867, construction lasted until 1899. Its design was directed by five architects, each with his own idiosyncratic tastes. First architect Thomas Fuller favored Gothic, Leopold Eidlitz was enchanted by Moorish and Saracen elements, and H. H. Richardson, who also designed Albany City Hall on Eagle Street, liked Romanesque. Governor Theodore Roosevelt dedicated the capitol, then the most costly building in the United States.

Population

Albany's population in 1990 was 101,082, a slight decrease from the 1980 count of 101,727, reflecting the continuing nationwide trend of movement out of central cities into the suburbs. In contrast, the six-county region (Greene, Montgomery, Rensselaer, Saratoga, and Schenectady counties, including cities such as Schenectady and Troy) grew 4.6% during this same period, increasing from 835,880 to 874,304.

Population

	1980	1990
Central City	115,781	101,082
Rank	164	190
Metro Area	835,880	874,304
Pop. Change 1980–1990	-645	
Pop. % Change 1980–1990	-0.6	
Median Age	30.8	
% Male	46.5	
% Age 65 and Over	15.3	
Density (per square mile)	4,723	

Households

Number	42,121
Persons per Household	2.17
% Female-Headed Households	14.7
% One-Person Households	38.6
Births—Total	1,461
% to Mothers under 20	14.7
Birth Rate per 1,000	14.7

Ethnic Composition

Whites made up 75.51% of the 1990 population of 101,082, African Americans 20.65%, Hispanics 3.5%, Asian and Pacific Islanders 2.3%, and all other races less than 2%.

Ethnic Composition (as % of total pop.)

	1980	1990
White	81.93	75.51
Black	16.09	20.65
American Indian	0.16	0.27
Asian and Pacific Islander	0.93	2.3
Hispanic	1.58	3.15
Other	NA	1.27

Government

The city, divided into 15 wards, is governed by a mayor and a 16-member council that is elected for four-year terms.

Public Finance

Albany is working toward a balanced budget. General revenues totaled $130.616 million while expenditures, including expenditures for police protection and for housing and community development, totaled

Government

Year of Home Charter	1686
Number of Members of the Governing Body	19
Elected at Large	4
Elected by Wards	15
Number of Women in Governing Body	1
Salary of Mayor	$86,165
Salary of Council Members	$13,839
City Government Employment Total	1,872
Rate per 10,000	192.9

Public Finance

Total Revenue (in millions)	$130.616
Intergovernmental Revenue—Total (in millions)	$53.1
Federal Revenue per capita	$14.35
% Federal Assistance	10.98
% State Assistance	14.11
Sales Tax as % of Total Revenue	NA
Local Revenue as % of Total Revenue	69.8
City Income Tax	no
Taxes—Total (in millions)	$30.2
Taxes per capita	$
Total	311
Property	282
Sales and Gross Receipts	17
General Expenditures—Total (in millions)	$79.7
General Expenditures per capita	$822
Capital Outlays per capita	$34
% of Expenditures for:	
Public Welfare	0.2
Highways	5.1
Education	0.0
Health and Hospitals	0.2
Police	20.5
Sewerage and Sanitation	10.9
Parks and Recreation	5.8
Housing and Community Development	9.9
Debt Outstanding per capita	$1,567
% Utility	11.0
Federal Procurement Contract Awards (in millions)	$22.4
Federal Grants Awards (in millions)	$1,143.5
Fiscal Year Begins	January 1

$121.015 million. The outstanding debt at that time was $235.427 million. Cash and security holdings amounted to $196.056 million.

Economy

State government and the service sector are Albany's largest employers. Manufacturing, once a cornerstone of the city's economy, declined by nearly 14% between 1977 and 1982. National financial services companies, such as Fleet/Norstar and KeyCorp have recently

Economy

Total Money Income (in millions)	$960	
% of State Average	90.7	
Per capita Annual Income	$10,675	
% Population below Poverty Level	17.5	
Fortune 500 Companies	0	
Banks	Number	Deposits (in millions)
Commercial	20	2,362.9
Savings	12	3,670.2
Passenger Autos	165,269	
Electric Meters	75,081	
Gas Meters	48,440	

Economy (continued)

Manufacturing

Number of Establishments   106
% with 20 or More Employees   34.0
Manufacturing Payroll (in millions) $123.8
Value Added by Manufacture (in millions) $390
Value of Shipments (in millions) $616.4
New Capital Expenditures (in millions) $18.6

Wholesale Trade

Number of Establishments   270
Sales (in millions) $1,477.3
Annual Payroll (in millions) $110.313

Retail Trade

Number of Establishments   1,116
Total Sales (in millions) $964.3
Sales per capita $9,939
Number of Retail Trade Establishments with Payroll   867
Annual Payroll (in millions) $117.6
Total Sales (in millions) $951.4
General Merchandise Stores (per capita) $1,678
Food Stores (per capita) $1,381
Apparel Stores (per capita) $651
Eating and Drinking Places (per capita) $1,037

Service Industries

Total Establishments   1,082
Total Receipts (in millions) $645.4
Hotels and Motels (in millions) $20.3
Health Services (in millions) $153.5
Legal Services (in millions) $107.7

expanded here. Medical and corporate research are significant in the local economy, as are smaller advanced technology firms.

Labor

Albany's civilian work force in 1990 totaled 53,476 and the unemployment rate then was 3.3%. More than a third of the region's total number of workers are employed in state, local, and federal government. As manufacturing has declined, the white-collar labor force has grown, a trend that is expected to continue as blue-collar jobs experience a parallel drop.

Labor

Civilian Labor Force   53,476
% Change 1989–1990   0.7
Work Force Distribution
Mining   400
Construction   17,200
Manufacturing   45,200
Transportation and Public Utilities   17,100
Wholesale and Retail Trade   89,000
FIRE (Finance, Insurance, Real Estate)   25,700
Service   118,300
Government   112,800
Women as % of Labor Force   48.7
% Self-Employed   3.5
% Professional/Technical   21.4
Total Unemployment   1,790
Rate %   3.3
Federal Government Civilian Employment   4,596

Education

Albany is one school district, with one senior high school, two middle schools, and about a dozen elementary schools. Colleges and universities in Albany include the State University of New York at Albany, the Albany Law School, Albany Medical College, and Albany College of Pharmacy. There are two Roman Catholic institutions: The College of St. Rose and Maria College. There is also an evening and a junior college affiliated with Russell Sage College of Troy.

Education

Number of Public Schools   16
Special Education Schools   NA
Total Enrollment   7,700
% Enrollment in Private Schools   13.2
% Minority   NA
Classroom Teachers   NA
Pupil-Teacher Ratio   13:1
Number of Graduates   NA
Total Revenue (in millions)   NA
Total Expenditures (in millions)   NA
Expenditures per Pupil   NA
Educational Attainment (Age 25 and Over)
    % Completed 12 or More Years   66.8
    % Completed 16 or More Years   22.4
Four-Year Colleges and Universities   4
Enrollment   34,520
Two-Year Colleges   2
Enrollment   2,004

Libraries

Number   44
Public Libraries   5
Books (in thousands)   335
Circulation (in thousands)   647
Persons Served (in thousands)   NA
Circulation per Person Served   NA
Income (in millions) $2.352
Staff   81

Four-Year Colleges and Universities
    Albany Medical College
    Albany Law School
    College of St. Rose
    State University of New York at Albany

Health

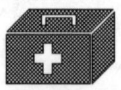

Albany has six hospitals and related health-care facilities. Among the largest is the Albany Medical Center, which recently underwent a $156 million expansion, and the

Health

Deaths—Total   1,279
Rate per 1,000   12.9
Infant Deaths—Total   20
Rate per 1,000   13.7
Number of Metro Hospitals   6
Number of Metro Hospital Beds   2,424
Rate per 100,000   2,498
Number of Physicians   1,852
Physicians per 1,000   18.5
Nurses per 1,000   NA
Health Expenditures per capita   1.06

Albany Department of Veterans Affairs Medical Center. Other area hospitals include St. Peter's Hospital, Albany Memorial Hospital, the Capital District Psychiatric Center, and Children's Hospital.

Transportation

Albany's location at the junction of several interstates enhances its long history as a transportation hub. The New York State Thruway (I-87 and I-90) connects Albany with New York City to the south, Montreal to the north, and Buffalo to the west. In Massachusetts, to the east, I-90 is the Massachusetts Turnpike, linking Albany with Boston. Just northwest of Albany, I-88 connects Schenectady with Binghamton.

The Capital District Transportation Authority's nearly 200 buses provide local public transit service.

Amtrak provides passenger rail service, while Conrail and D&H/CP provide freight service. Albany County Airport is 7 miles west of the city.

Albany remains a river city. Oceangoing vessels dock here regularly and can make their way to the Great Lakes through the New York State Barge Canal System. In 1990, the Port of Albany handled over 300,000 tons of goods.

Transportation
Interstate Highway Mileage 83
Total Urban Mileage 2,558
Total Daily Vehicle Mileage (in millions) 11.563
Daily Average Commute Time 43.3 min.
Number of Buses 192
Port Tonnage (in millions) 1.334
Airports 1
Number of Daily Flights 82
Daily Average Number of Passengers 4,462
Airlines (American carriers only)
American
Delta
Eastern
Midway
Northwest
Piedmont
Trans World
United
USAir
Westair

Housing

Housing in Albany totaled 42,000 units in 1990, of which 38.3% were occupied by the owners; the average rent paid was $388. The Albany Housing Authority, with a total of 2,047 units of federal and state-assisted housing, is the largest rental-property owner in the city, and houses almost 2% of the city's population.

Urban Redevelopment

The Empire State Plaza inspired additional renovations in the downtown area. In 1985 the Albany Strategic Planning Committee issued 32 recommendations for preparing the city for the 21st century. The Visitors Center

Housing
Total Housing Units 46,199
% Change 1980–1990 0.0
Vacant Units for Sale or Rent 2,850
Occupied Units 42,121
% with More Than One Person per Room 2.2
% Owner-Occupied 38.3
Median Value of Owner-Occupied Homes $101,800
Average Monthly Purchase Cost $290
Median Monthly Rent $388
New Private Housing Starts 162
Value (in thousands) $10,233
% Single-Family 35.2
Nonresidential Buildings Value (in thousands) $16,630

Tallest Buildings	Hgt. (ft.)	Stories
Erastus Corning II Tower	589	44
State Office Building	388	34
Agency (4 bldgs.), So. Mall	310	23

at the Albany Urban Cultural Park, 25 Quackenbush Square, was expanded to educate residents and visitors alike about historic preservation as well as economic opportunities. Another project is a riverfront nature preserve.

Crime

In 1991 the number of crimes known to police in Albany was 7,570, of which 1,202 were violent and 6,368 involved property. The city spends 13% of its budget on police protection in 1984–1985.

Crime
Violent Crimes—Total 1,202
Violent Crime Rate per 100,000 410.6
Murder 12
Rape 71
Robbery 487
Aggravated Assaults 632
Property Crimes 6,368
Burglary 1,988
Larceny 3,878
Motor Vehicle Theft 502
Arson 61
Per capita Police Expenditures $131.23
Per capita Fire Protection Expenditures $154.31
Number of Police 324
Per 1,000 3.23

Religion

More than 16 denominations are represented in the city, and churches are among the most prominent of its religious monuments.

Religion	
Largest Denominations (Adherents)	
United Methodist	9,903
Presbyterian	4,464
Episcopal	4,529
Reformed	6,269
Catholic	168,414
Black Baptist	4,888
Jewish	3,924

Media

Albany's sole daily is *The Times Union*, published mornings and Sundays. The city has 3 television stations and 9 radio stations.

Media

Newsprint
  The Times Union, daily
  Capitol District Business Review, weekly

Television
  WNYT (Channel 13)
  WTEN (Channel 10)
  WXXA (Channel 23)

Radio

WABY (AM)	WAMC (FM)
WCDB (FM)	WGNA (AM)
WGNA (FM)	WHRL (FM)
WPTR (AM)	WROW (FM)
WROW (AM)	

Sports

Knickerbocker Arena hosts both the Albany Patroons of the Continental Basketball Association and the Albany Firebirds football team. The Albany-Colonie Yankees, a baseball farm team of the New York Yankees, play home games at Heritage Park in Colonie. The Adirondack Red Wings and the Capital Islanders are local professional ice hockey teams. The Empire State Regatta, an annual 2-day rowing event, attracts crews from Canada as well as Eastern colleges. The Friehofer Run for Women, a 10-kilometer road race, attracts world-class competitors, as does the Tour de Pump.

Arts, Culture, and Tourism

Nelson A. Rockefeller, New York's governor from 1958 to 1973, dreamed of a monumental civic plaza. His dream was realized with the completion in 1978 of the Empire State Plaza, known as The Mall. The Mall's chief architect was Wallace K. Harrison. The complex includes office buildings as well as museums, galleries, and space for performances. The 14-story Cultural Education Center at the south end of The Mall houses the New York State Museum and the New York State Library and Archives. An underground concourse a quarter of a mile long and an eighth of a mile wide links it and other buildings on The Mall, including the State Capitol, the 4,200-seat Convention Center, and the distinctive oval-shaped Performing Arts Center (dubbed the Egg), home to the New

---

Travel and Tourism

Hotel Rooms 5,758
Convention and Exhibit Space (square feet) 65,000

Convention Centers
  Knickerbocker Arena

Festivals
  Tulip Festival (May)
  Imagination Celebration (May–June)

York State Theater. The 44-story Tower Building's Observation Deck offers views of the Adirondacks to the west, east across the Hudson to the Berkshires in Massachusetts, and the Catskills to the south. The Empire State Plaza Art Collection in the Tower Building includes works by Helen Frankenthaler, Claes Oldenberg, Robert Motherwell, and Alexander Calder.

The Palace Theatre is the cultural capital of the city, where events ranging from Broadway shows to rock concerts are staged. The nearby Market Theatre, run by the Capital Repertory Company, presents contemporary and classic plays during its October to May season. Complementing these institutions are community groups such as the Albany Civic Theatre, the Queens Theatre, Theater Voice, and Kids Fare. A summer season of musical theater is offered by the Park Playhouse, and the Actors Shakespeare Company performs in July and August. Additionally, the Egg presents the best of contemporary dance from all over the country. The recently relocated Albany Berkshire Ballet has brought classical dance to the city. The Albany Symphony Orchestra gives eight concert performances each year at the Palace Theater, while L'Ensemble, a local opera company, performs at various locations.

The city has dozens of art galleries, including Albany Center galleries and the Gallery at the State University of New York at Albany. The New York State Museum and the Albany Institute of History and Art hold extensive historical collections.

Parks and Recreation

The City Department of Parks and Recreation administers over 74 parks, of which the largest is the 84-acre Washington Park at State and Willett streets, site of the annual spring Tulip Festival, a tribute to the city's Dutch heritage. There are several nature preserves, including a 77-acre riverfront preserve.

Sources of Further Information

Albany Public Library
161 Washington Avenue
Albany, NY 12210
(518) 449-3380

Center for Economic Growth,
32 James Street
Albany, NY 12207
(518) 465-8975

Albany County Convention and Visitors Bureau
52 S. Pearl Street
Albany, NY 12207
(518) 434-1217

Albany County Historical Association
910 Broeck Place
Albany, NY 12210
(518) 436-9826

Albany-Colonie Regional Chamber of Commerce
14 Corporate Woods Blvd.
Albany, NY 12211
(518) 434-1214

Additional Reading

Dumbleton, Susanne, and Anne Older. *In and Around Albany: A Guide for Residents, Students, and Visitors.* 1980.

Kennedy, William. *O Albany! Improbable City of Political Wizards, Fearless Ethnics, Spectacular Aristocrats, Splendid Nobodies, and Underrated Scoundrels.* 1983.

Mulligan, Tim. *The Hudson River Valley: A History and Guide.* 1981.

Roberts, Anne F., and Marcia W. Cockrell, editors. *Historic Albany: Its Churches and Synagogues.* 1986.

Roseberry, Cecil. R. *Flashback: A Fresh Look At Albany's Past.* 1986.

Scheller, William G. *The Hudson River Valley.* 1988.

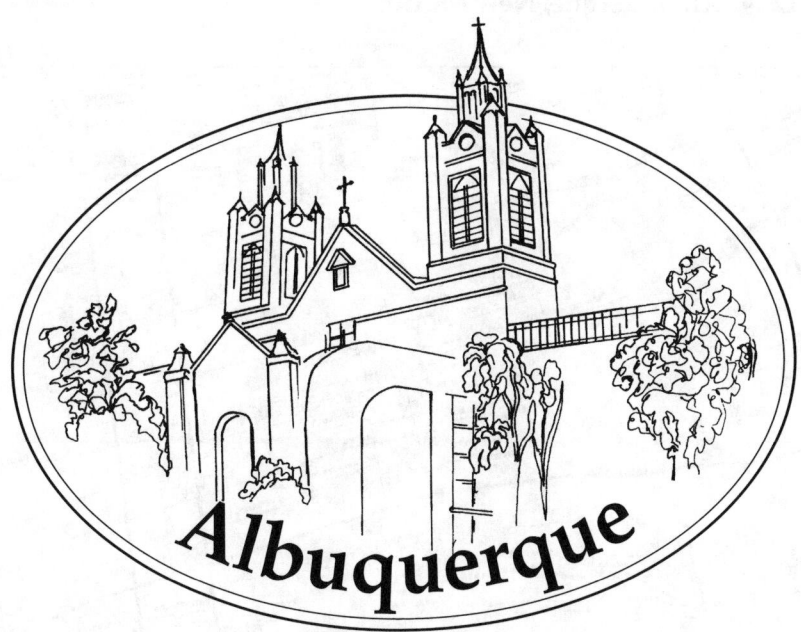

Albuquerque

New Mexico

Basic Data

Name   Albuquerque
Name Origin   From Duke of Albuquerque
Year Founded   1706 Inc. 1891
Status: State   New Mexico
      County   Seat of Bernalillo County
Area (square miles)   132.2
Elevation (feet)   4,945
Time Zone   Mountain
Population (1990)   384,736
Population of Metro Area (1990)   480,577

Sister Cities

   Ahkabad, Turkmenistan
   Chihuahua, Mexico
   Guadalajara, Mexico
   Helmstedt, Germany
   Hualien, China
   Sasebo, Japan

Distance in Miles To:

Atlanta	1,404
Boston	2,220
Chicago	1,312
Cleveland	1,585
Denver	437
Houston	853
Los Angeles	811
Miami	1,970
Minneapolis	1,219
New York	1,997
Philadelphia	1,947
Washington, DC	1,849

Location and Topography

Albuquerque, at the center of the state, is in a wide valley of the Rio Grande where the river sweeps down in a broad curve from the north. The Sandia Mountains are just east of Albuquerque, the largest city in New Mexico and seat of Bernalillo County. The city, at the south-eastern edge of the high, arid Colorado Plateau, lies at an elevation of 4,945 feet and is about 50 miles south-west of Santa Fe, the state capital. Mount Taylor, an 11,389-foot snow-capped peak, is just northwest of the city.

Layout of City and Suburbs

There are two Albuquerques: Old Albuquerque, established by the Spanish in the 18th century and called Old Town, and the century-old new Albuquerque. Central Avenue, a stretch of U.S. 66, divides the two sections. The streets of Old Town are lined with Pueblo Revival buildings. Typical of Spanish Mexico is the plaza, which served as a market, livestock corral, and the site of fiestas. Interstate 25, which runs north and south and parallels the Rio Grande, divides the city into east and west; Interstate 40, the major east-west highway, intersects I-25 and divides the city north and south. The city calls its northwest quadrant—west of I-25 and north of I-40 on both banks of the Rio Grande—North Valley; South Valley is due south. Major institutions such as the municipal building, the University of New Mexico, and Kirtland Air Force Base are in the southeast quadrant of the city, called the East Heights, or East Mesa. The main residential districts are now north of I-40 and also west, across the river.

Environment

Environmental Stress Index   3
Green Cities Index: Rank   17
             Score   23.62
Water Quality   Alkaline, hard, fluoridated
   Average Daily Use (gallons per capita)   231
   Maximum Supply (gallons per capita)   638
Parkland as % of Total City Area   1.8
% Waste Landfilled/Recycled   NA
Annual Parks Expenditures per capita   176.23

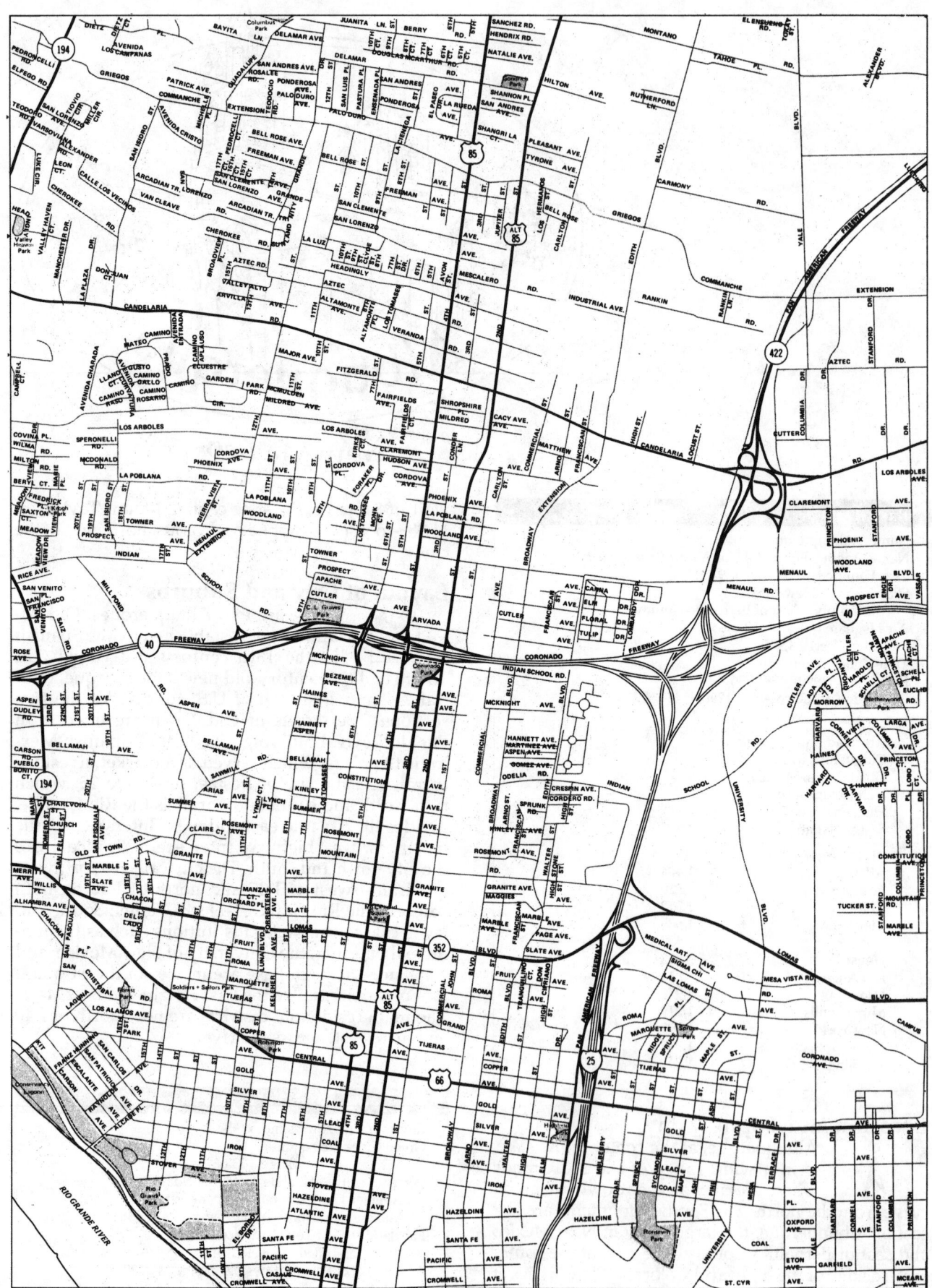

Climate

Albuquerque has an arid continental climate. An average of eight inches of rain falls annually, mostly during thunderstorms in July, August, and September. During July, the hottest month, temperatures reach 90° F almost daily but are tolerable because of low humidity and cool nights. Winters are mild, with temperatures averaging from 35 to 45° F.

Weather

Temperature

Highest Monthly Average °F 92.2
Lowest Monthly Average °F 23.5

Annual Averages

Days 32°F or Below   123
Days above 90°F   61
Zero Degree Days   1
Precipitation (inches)   7.7
Snow (inches)   11
% Seasonal Humidity   43
Wind Speed (m.p.h.)   9
Clear Days   172
Cloudy Days   82
Storm Days   43
Rainy Days   59

Average Temperatures (°F)	High	Low	Mean
January	46.9	23.5	35.2
February	52.6	27.4	40.0
March	59.2	32.3	45.8
April	70.1	41.4	55.8
May	79.9	50.7	65.3
June	89.5	54.7	74.6
July	92.2	65.2	78.7
August	89.7	63.4	76.6
September	83.4	56.7	70.1
October	71.7	44.7	58.2
November	57.1	31.8	44.5
December	47.5	24.9	36.2

History

Indian cultures flourished in the Albuquerque region for centuries. The ruins of multistory buildings of the Anasazi, ancestors of the Indians now in the area of New Mexico, still stand in many places. The first Europeans to see this part of the Rio Grande Valley may have been Spanish soldiers with Francisco Vasquez de Coronado, who was seeking cities of gold in 1540.

Nearly a century later, after the Spanish had consolidated their North American claims from centers such as Mexico City, the Aztec capital captured by Hernan Cortes in 1521, and Santa Fe, established in 1609, a few settlers established isolated ranches in the vicinity of Albuquerque. These first ranches were destroyed during the Pueblo Revolt of 1680. Twenty-six years later, in 1706, Captain General Don Francisco Cuervo y Valdez proclaimed to his superiors in Mexico City that he had founded La Villa de San Felipe de Alburquerque as a regional seat of government on the provincial road between Santa Fe and Mexico City. City plans,

dictated from Madrid, demanded that such towns have a church, a plaza, and government buildings. Fortunately for the captain general, no inspection was made to verify that Alburquerque (which eventually lost its first r), named for the then viceroy of New Spain, met the requirements for a *villa*. It did have a church, the Church of San Felipe Neri, erected in 1706, but little else. The villa had few permanent residents, and settlers only came to Albuquerque for church.

During this time the ranchers were continually attacked by nomadic Indians such as the Comanche, Navajo, and Apache, so they demanded military protection by the few troops in Santa Fe. Since this was not really feasible, it was eventually decreed in 1779 that the settlers move into a defensible village rather than remain in widely dispersed homesteads. As a result, Albuquerque began to grow, although the population at the beginning of the 19th century remained at fewer than 2,000. In 1821 New Spain declared independence from Spain, and the region of Albuquerque and Santa Fe became a province of the new nation of Mexico.

While the Spanish influence continued in Albuquerque, Anglos, mostly overland migrants and purveyors of goods coming from the eastern United States on the Santa Fe Trail, started to become an influence in the town. The process sped up considerably when U.S. troops occupied Albuquerque at the beginning of the war with Mexico in 1846.

Mexico ceded the region to the United States in 1848 with the Treaty of Guadalupe Hidalgo. The U.S. government organized New Mexico Territory in 1850, and Albuquerque continued as a military post through the Civil War and into 1867. The withdrawal of troops, which were almost a third of the population, in that year caused an economic depression that lasted more than a decade.

The territorial legislature authorized the construction of railroads in 1879, and a route from Santa Fe south to Mexico City was surveyed almost immediately by the Atchison Topeka & Santa Fe Railroad's subsidiary, the New Mexico and Southern Pacific. The right of way passed to the east of Old Town, and businesses quickly shifted east, too, causing the newer town to develop quickly and eventually absorb the old town. Residential districts, however, remained in the older section of town. The first train reached Albuquerque in April 1880. In 1883 Albuquerque became the seat of Bernalillo County, was incorporated as a town in 1885, and became a city in 1891. The Territorial University of New Mexico was founded there in 1889.

A second growth spurt occurred between 1892 and 1910 when victims of tuberculosis and other respiratory diseases came west seeking relief in Albuquerque's fresh air and sunshine. Two sanatoriums were established, and by 1910 the city's population reached 11,020. New Mexico, with Santa Fe as its capital, became the forty-seventh state in 1912.

During the Depression of the 1930s canny politicians encouraged Works Progress Administration projects such as the University of New Mexico Library,

Chronology

1706	Alburquerque is founded by Captain General Don Francisco Cuervo y Valdez. The Church of San Felipe Neri is built.
1846	Town becomes part of the United States along with the rest of New Mexico.
1880	Atchison, Topeka, and Santa Fe Railroad subsidiary, New Mexico Town Company, surveys and plats town.
1883	Albuquerque becomes seat of Bernalillo County.
1889	Territorial University of New Mexico is founded.
1891	Albuquerque is incorporated as a city.
1912	Statehood for New Mexico.
1917	Commission-manager form of government is adopted.
1928	Oxnard Field opens.
1929–1939	Works Progress Administration projects ease Albuquerque through the Depression.
1939	Army Air Corps airfield established; becomes Kirtland Field at the beginning of World War II.
1949	Sandia Laboratories established as an adjunct to Los Alamos.
1950	Population reaches 145,673.
1986	New Mexico Museum of Natural History completed.

street and sewer construction, and the building of several schools to help the city through that era of economic difficulty. Growth—spurred by World War II– related institutions and industries such as the Army Air Corps' Kirtland Field and the Sandia Laboratories, associated with new nuclear weapons research at Los Alamos—more than doubled the city's population, from 69,341 in 1940 to 145,673 in 1950.

As the railroad had shifted the center of business from Old Town to the east in the 1880s, the 1950s and 1960s saw the development of schools, shopping centers, and neighborhoods to the west, following the alignment of Interstates 25 and 40. The city continues to thrive in its role as a research center as it has since World War II.

Historical Landmarks

The heart of Albuquerque is the Old Town Plaza, the central portion of the original villa set up by Captain General Don Francisco Cuervo y Valdez in 1706. The Church of San Felipe Neri, founded by Father Moreno in 1706,

was opened at its present site in 1793, and its twin Gothic towers were added in 1868. Like many mission churches it was built like a fort; its adobe walls are 4 feet thick and its windows are 20 feet from the ground. The Casa Armijo on the east side of the plaza was built in 1840 by the influential and wealthy Armijo family. A railroad superintendent's house built in 1881 at 1023 Second SW in the Barelas neighborhood survives as a remnant of the railroad boom of the 1880s. Huning Highlands, named for 18th century, German-born developer Franz Huning, is a well-preserved neighborhood of Victorian buildings. It is also where architect Charles Whittlesey built his Norwegian-style log home in 1903, about the time that geologist W. D. Tight, then president of the territorial university, would herd cows through town for fun. The KiMo Theatre, built in 1927 in the popular Pueblo Revival style, is now a community arts center. (KiMo is a Tiwa word meaning "king of its kind.")

Population

Like most cities in the Sunbelt, Albuquerque is one of the favorite relocation destinations. Its population grew by 35.7% between 1970 and 1980, from 243,751 to 332,920, and 15.6% between 1980 and 1990 to reach 384,736.

Population	1980	1990
Central City	332,920	384,736
Rank	44	38
Metro Area	420,262	480,577
Pop. Change 1980–1990	+51,816	
Pop. % Change 1980–1990	+15.6	
Median Age	32.5	
% Male	48.5	
% Age 65 and Over	11.1	
Density (per square mile)	2,910	

Households	
Number	153,818
Persons per Household	2.46
% Female-Headed Households	12.1
% One-Person Households	28.2
Births—Total	7,207
% to Mothers under 20	13.8
Birth Rate per 1,000	20.6

Ethnic Composition

As of 1990 whites made up 78.24% of the population, Hispanics 34.49%, blacks 2.98%, American Indians 3.04%, Asians and Pacific Islanders 1.7%, and others 14%.

Ethnic Composition (as % of total pop.)	1980	1990
White	81.00	78.24
Black	2.52	2.98
American Indian	2.21	3.04
Asian and Pacific Islander	0.95	1.73
Hispanic	33.78	34.49
Other	NA	14.0

Government

Albuquerque is governed under a mayor-council form of government with a full-time mayor, nine part-time council members, all of whom are elected to four-year terms, and a chief administrative officer.

Government

Year of Home Charter   1917
Number of Members of the Governing Body   9
Elected at Large   NA
Elected by Wards   9
Number of Women in Governing Body   2
Salary of Mayor $62,483
Salary of Council Members $6,261
City Government Employment Total   6,494
Rate per 10,000   177.1

Public Finance

The annual budget for 1989–1990 consisted of revenues of $505.335 million and expenditures of $576.991 million. The debt outstanding is $1.263 billion and cash and security holdings are $929.207 million.

Public Finance

Total Revenue (in millions) $505.3
Intergovernmental Revenue—Total (in millions) $162.23
Federal Revenue per capita $52.23
% Federal Assistance   10.5
% State Assistance   19.74
Sales Tax as % of Total Revenue   11.67
Local Revenue as % of Total Revenue   61.02
City Income Tax   no
Taxes—Total (in millions) $85.4

Taxes per capita
Total   233
Property   97
Sales and Gross Receipts   124
General Expenditures—Total (in millions) $313.7
General Expenditures per capita $855
Capital Outlays per capita $237

% of Expenditures for:
  Public Welfare   0.0
  Highways   5.6
  Education   0.0
  Health and Hospitals   1.1
  Police   10.7
  Sewerage and Sanitation   21.5
  Parks and Recreation   8.4
  Housing and Community Development   3.5
Debt Outstanding per capita $2,231
  % Utility   17.6
Federal Procurement Contract Awards (in millions)
  $1,491.3
Federal Grants Awards (in millions) $80.7
Fiscal Year Begins   July 1

Economy

The factors that historically have made Albuquerque a thriving town continue to drive the economy: rich farmland irrigated by the Rio Grande, dry climate, and a strategic location on major highways. Since the end of World War II, Albuquerque has also become a transportation, trade, and manufacturing center. More than 700 firms produce a wide range of goods, from processed foods to electrical machinery. Albuquerque is in a key position along the Rio Grande Research Corridor, a collection of high-technology industries that extends from Los Alamos to Las Cruces. The corridor includes the state's largest private employer, Sandia National Laboratories, a leader in developing solar energy and laser technology. Kirtland Air Force Base is a weapons research center. The University of New Mexico and the Center of Technical Excellence and Technical Innovation are prime movers in shaping the new economy.

Economy

Total Money Income (in millions) $4,083
% of State Average   126.3
Per capita Annual Income $11,133
% Population below Poverty Level   12.4
Fortune 500 Companies   0

Banks	Number	Deposits (in millions)
Commercial	9	3,294
Savings	7	2,971

Passenger Autos   281,016
Electric Meters   160,718
Gas Meters   141,928

Manufacturing

Number of Establishments   499
% with 20 or More Employees   22.8
Manufacturing Payroll (in millions) $291.3
Value Added by Manufacture (in millions) $673.6
Value of Shipments (in millions) $1,303.3
New Capital Expenditures (in millions) $56.6

Wholesale Trade

Number of Establishments   1,031
Sales (in millions) $2,717
Annual Payroll (in millions) $250,022

Retail Trade

Number of Establishments   3,999
Total Sales (in millions) $3,205.6
Sales per capita $8,741
Number of Retail Trade Establishments with Payroll   2,653
Annual Payroll (in millions) $378.1
Total Sales (in millions) $3,141.2
General Merchandise Stores (per capita)   NA
Food Stores (per capita) $1,412
Apparel Stores (per capita)   NA
Eating and Drinking Places (per capita) $949

Service Industries

Total Establishments   3,815
Total Receipts (in millions)   NA
Hotels and Motels (in millions)   NA
Health Services (in millions) $498
Legal Services (in millions) $154.6

Labor

According to the Department of Labor, the Albuquerque area is one of the 12 fastest-growing employment markets in the nation. Services and tourism absorb about 25% of the work-force. While white collar or professional workers predominate now, the city anticipates an increase in blue-collar jobs.

Labor

Civilian Labor Force   217,036
% Change 1989–1990   0.3

Work Force Distribution
    Mining   NA
    Construction   12,000
    Manufacturing   20,700
    Transportation and Public Utilities   11,800
    Wholesale and Retail Trade   60,400
    FIRE (Finance, Insurance, Real Estate)   13,900
    Service   78,100
    Government   50,200
    Women as % of Labor Force   43.3
    % Self-Employed   5.6
    % Professional/Technical   21.7
Total Unemployment   10,237
Rate %   4.7
Federal Government Civilian Employment   8,072

Education

The Albuquerque Public Schools System supports 79 elementary schools, 23 middle schools, and 16 senior high schools. More than 80 parochial and private schools supplement the public school system. The University of New Mexico, with an enrollment of about 25,000, dominates higher education in both city and state. The city is also home to 40 vocational, technical, and business schools.

Education

Number of Public Schools   124
Special Education Schools   5
Total Enrollment   88,295
% Enrollment in Private Schools   9.8
% Minority   51.3
Classroom Teachers   4,842
Pupil-Teacher Ratio   18.2:1
Number of Graduates   4,543
Total Revenue (in millions) $292.153
Total Expenditures (in millions) $292.032
Expenditures per Pupil $3,421
Educational Attainment (Age 25 and Over)
    % Completed 12 or More Years   79.1
    % Completed 16 or More Years   24.9
Four-Year Colleges and Universities   1
Enrollment   24,600
Two-Year Colleges   1
Enrollment   11,341

Education (continued)

Libraries

Number   53
Public Libraries   13
Books (in thousands)   733
Circulation (in thousands)   2,756
Persons Served (in thousands)   508
Circulation per Person Served   5.42
Income (in millions) $5.5
Staff   114

Four-Year Colleges and Universities
    University of New Mexico

Health

Beginning in 1892, the business community began to advertise Albuquerque as a healthy climate for those suffering respiratory problems. As a result medical facilities became an important part of the economy. There are 17 hospitals, the principal ones being Lovelace Medical Center, Veterans Hospital, Presbyterian Hospital, St. Joseph Medical Center, and the University of New Mexico Medical Center.

Health

Deaths—Total   2,674
Rate per 1,000   7.6
Infant Deaths—Total   64
Rate per 1,000   8.9
Number of Metro Hospitals   17
Number of Metro Hospital Beds   2,498
Rate per 100,000   6.81
Number of Physicians   1,242
Physicians per 1,000   2.99
Nurses per 1,000   5.76
Health Expenditures per capita   16.43

Transportation

Transportation has long figured in Albuquerque's history, from its place on the El Camino Real established by the Spanish between Santa Fe and Mexico City to its location at the junction of two interstates: the north-south I-25, known in the city as the Pan American Freeway, and the east-west I-40, known as Coronado Freeway. Rail passenger service is provided by Amtrak, which runs two daily services, and rail freight services by the Santa Fe rail line. The principal airfield is Albuquerque International Airport, which is served by 16 airlines. Corporate and private aircraft use Coronado Airport.

Transportation

Interstate Highway Mileage   40
Total Urban Mileage   1,850
Total Daily Vehicle Mileage (in millions)   10.15
Daily Average Commute Time   41.6 min.
Number of Buses   89
Port Tonnage (in millions)   NA
Airports   1
Number of Daily Flights   92
Daily Average Number of Passengers   6,401

Transportation (continued)

Airlines (American carriers only)
- American
- American West
- Continental
- Delta
- Southwest
- Trans World
- USAir

Housing

The 1990 housing stock total was 166,870, of which 57.3% was owner-occupied. The median value of an owner-occupied home was $85,900 and the median monthly rent was $353.

Housing

Total Housing Units 166,870
% Change 1980–1990 20.4
Vacant Units for Sale or Rent 9,707
Occupied Units 153,818
% with More Than One Person per Room 4.9
% Owner-Occupied 57.3
Median Value of Owner-Occupied Homes $85,900
Average Monthly Purchase Cost $358
Median Monthly Rent $353
New Private Housing Starts 1,555
Value (in thousands) $116,785
% Single-Family 73
Nonresidential Buildings Value (in thousands) $44,424

Urban Redevelopment

Much of Old Albuquerque and buildings from the late 1800s fell prey to urban redevelopment during the 1960s when federal funds were available for urban renewal. One such victim was the popular Alvarado Hotel, built in 1902 and torn down in 1970. However, the $26 million spent on building projects in the following decade included a new convention center and a public library. The Museum of Natural History was completed in 1986.

Crime

The number of crimes known to police in Albuquerque in 1991 totaled 40,443, of which 5,591 were classified as violent crimes, and 34,842 involved property.

Crime

Violent Crimes—Total 5,591
Violent Crime Rate per 100,000 1,198
Murder 51
Rape 261
Robbery 1,307
Aggravated Assaults 3,972
Property Crimes 34,842

Crime (continued)

Burglary 10,348
Larceny 22,024
Motor Vehicle Theft 2,470
Arson 195
Per capita Police Expenditures $145.47
Per capita Fire Protection Expenditures $64.60
Number of Police 644
Per 1,000 1.80

Religion

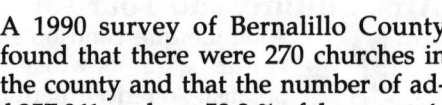

A 1990 survey of Bernalillo County found that there were 270 churches in the county and that the number of adherents totaled 257,061 or about 53.3 % of the county's population of 480,577.

Religion

Largest Denominations (Adherents)
Catholic	132,122
Southern Baptist	30,425
United Methodist	15,534
Latter-Day Saints	7,897
Presbyterian	5,242
Assembly of God	5,573
Episcopal	4,013
Jewish	4,400

Media

The Albuquerque press consists of the morning *Albuquerque Journal* and the afternoon *The Albuquerque Tribune*. The electronic media consist of 8 television stations and 22 AM and FM radio stations.

Media

Newsprint
- *Albuquerque Journal*, daily
- *The Albuquerque Tribune*, daily
- *The Albuquerque Voice*, weekly

Television
- KAZQ (Channel 32)
- KGGM (Channel 13)
- KGSW (Channel 14)
- KLUZ (Channel 41)
- KNME (Channel 5)
- KNAT (Channel 23)
- KOAT (Channel 7)
- KOB (Channel 4)

Radio
KABQ (AM)	KAMX (AM)
KDAZ (AM)	KDEF (AM)
KFLQ (FM)	KHFM (FM)
KIDI (FM)	KKIM (AM)
KKJY (FM)	KKOB (AM)
KKOB (FM)	KLYT (FM)
KMBA (AM)	KQEO (AM)
KMGA (FM)	KRZY (AM)
KRST (FM)	KUNM (FM)
KXKS (AM)	KZKL (AM)
KZRR (FM)	KZSS (AM)

Sports

Spectator sports revolve around two teams: the Albuquerque Dukes, a farm team for the Los Angeles Dodgers in baseball and the University of New Mexico Lobos in football and basketball. Hot-air ballooning is a favorite sport, enhanced by favorable wind and weather conditions. A nine-day International Balloon Fiesta is held each October.

Arts, Culture, and Tourism

Albuquerque contributes to American culture as a showcase of Indian and Spanish-American heritage. The KiMo Theater, a Pueblo-Deco landmark downtown, hosts a number of groups, such as the New Mexico Repertory Theater, New Mexico Jazz Workshop, Albuquerque Little Theater, and La Compania de Teatro de Albuquerque. Dance is represented by Southwest Ballet, which performs at KiMo Theater. The principal musical stage is Popejoy Hall, on the University of New Mexico campus, home of the New Mexico Symphony, Chamber Orchestra, and the Civic Light Opera.

The major city museums are the New Mexico Museum of Natural History, Indian Pueblo Cultural Center, National Atomic Museum on Kirtland Air Force Base, the Albuquerque Museum, KiMo Gallery, and South Broadway Cultural Center Gallery. The Art Museum, Jonson Gallery, and the Maxwell Museum of Anthropology are on the campus of the University of New Mexico.

Parks and Recreation

The municipality maintains 202 parks and 18 recreational centers. The largest are Los Altos Park, the 80-acre Rio Grande Park, and Robinson Park, the city's oldest park, founded in 1880.

Sources of Further Information

City Hall
1 Civic Plaza
Albuquerque, NM 87103
(505) 768-2000

Greater Albuquerque Chamber of Commerce
401 Second Street
Albuquerque, NM 87102
(505) 764-3700

Albuquerque Convention and Visitors Bureau
121 Tijeras St. NE
Albuquerque, NM 87102
(505) 243-3696, (800) 284-2282

Additional Reading

Alberts, Don E. *Balloons to Bombers: Aviation in Albuquerque, 1882–1945.* 1987.

Price, V. B. *A City at the End of the World.* 1992.

Smith, Carol. *Albuquerque Colors: A Close Look at the Colorful City on the Rio Grande.* 1990.

Thornton, Elizabeth. *The Ten Best of Everything in Albuquerque.* 1991.

Vance, Mary. *The Architecture of Albuquerque.* 1989.

Young, Paul. *Albuquerque: Jewel on the Rio Grande.* 1991.

Travel and Tourism	
Hotel Rooms	8,094
Convention and Exhibit Space (square feet)	NA

Convention Centers
    Albuquerque Convention Center

Festivals
    Gathering of Nations Pow Wow (April)
    San Felipe Festival (June)
    Summerfest
    Fiesta Artistica (August)
    New Mexico State Fair (September)
    International Balloon Fiesta (October)

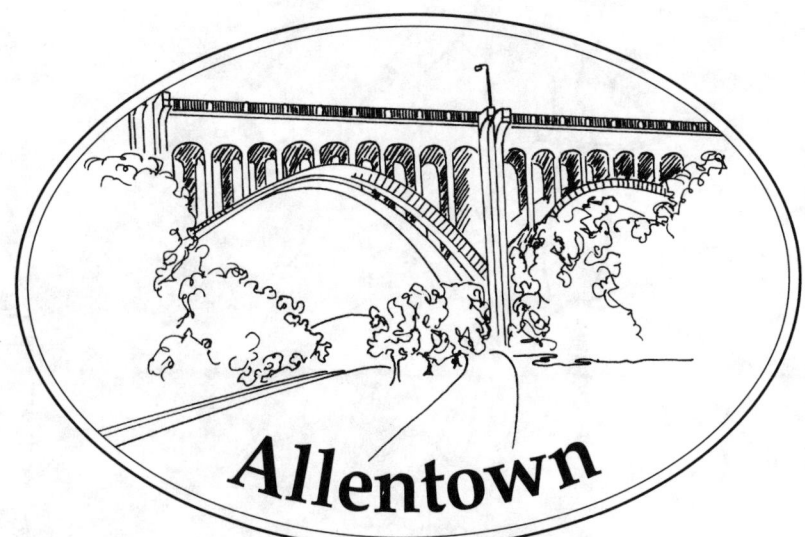

Allentown

Pennsylvania

Location and Topography

N Allentown is located in eastern Pennsylvania in the Lehigh River Valley, about 85 miles east of Harrisburg, the state capital. It is between the long mass of Blue Mountain, to the north, and South Mountain. The city and the surrounding countryside sit among rolling hills cut by many small streams.

Layout of City and Suburbs

 Allentown's business section, laid out in a grid pattern, radiates from Central Square. The principal industrial sections extend along the Lehigh River and Jordan Creek in the city's eastern part and along Lehigh Creek in the south. Older residences are located in the northern section of the city, while newer ones are found in the western areas. The Lehigh River bisects the city before it curves east. Allentown seems to blend with its neighbor just to the east, Bethlehem.

Environment

Environmental Stress Index   2.6
Green Cities Index: Rank   NA
                          Score   NA
Water Quality   Alkaline, hard
      Average Daily Use (gallons per capita)   185
      Maximum Supply (gallons per capita)   300
Parkland as % of Total City Area   NA
% Waste Landfilled/Recycled   75:25
Annual Parks Expenditures per capita $22.42

Climate

Allentown has a moderate climate, although its proximity to the Appalachian mountain range causes winter temperatures to be 10 to 15°F lower than in Philadelphia, which is closer to the moderating influences of the Atlantic Ocean. Freezing rain in winter and high humidity in summer are common. The average annual precipitation of 44 inches is adequate for farming.

Weather

Temperature

Highest Monthly Average °F   84.6
Lowest Monthly Average °F   19.5

Annual Averages

Days 32°F or Below   124
Days above 90°F   25
Zero Degree Days   0
Precipitation (inches)   44.15
Snow (inches)   32
% Seasonal Humidity   68
Wind Speed (m.p.h.)   9.2
Clear Days   93
Cloudy Days   160
Storm Days   22
Rainy Days   119

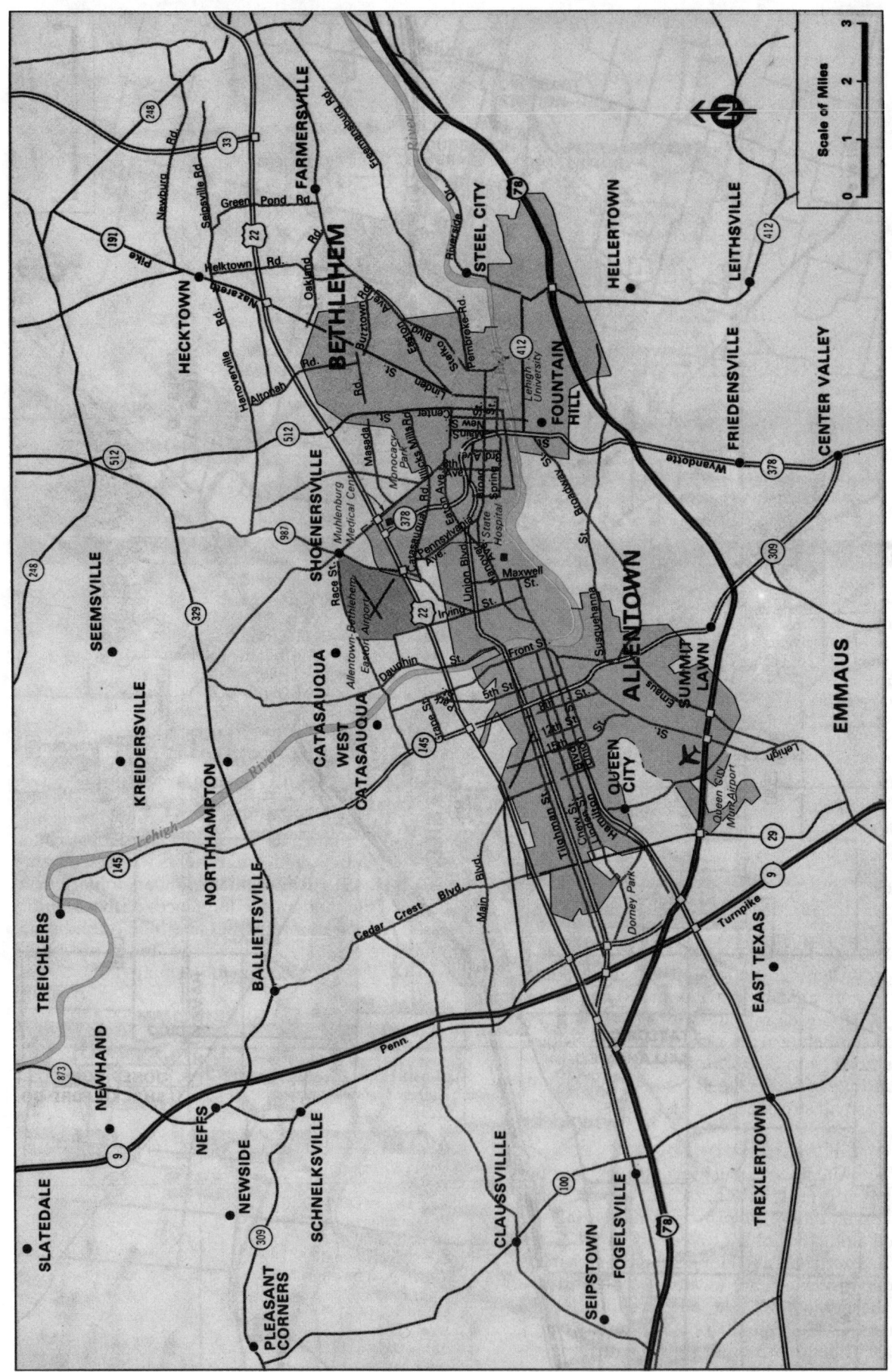

Weather (continued)			
Average Temperatures (°F)	High	Low	Mean
January	38.0	21.0	29.5
February	45.4	26.4	35.9
March	51.8	32.8	42.3
April	62.5	42.6	52.6
May	79.4	55.0	67.2
June	83.8	59.4	71.6
July	84.7	64.6	74.7
August	85.0	63.2	74.1
September	76.1	53.3	64.7
October	66.1	43.3	54.7
November	52.1	35.4	43.8
December	43.5	27.8	35.7

History

The Leni-Lenape Indians, also known as the Delaware, once lived in this area. The first Europeans to settle in the area were German immigrants who first came in 1723. In 1735 William Allen, mayor of Philadelphia and later chief justice of the State Supreme Court, acquired a large tract of land from Joseph Turner, who had obtained it from Thomas Penn in 1732. In the 1750s Allen erected a hunting and fishing lodge here; a town was not laid out until 1762, however. Known in its early days as Allen's Little Town or Northamptontown, it was then bounded by the present Fourth, 10th, Union, and Liberty streets. Its growth was slow. A local church sheltered the Liberty Bell when it was removed from Philadelphia's Independence Hall in 1777 to save it from falling into British hands during the Revolutionary War.

In 1811 the community was incorporated as a borough, and a year later it became the seat of the newly formed Lehigh County. A bridge was built across the Lehigh River in 1812 and the Lehigh Canal was completed in 1829. The town's name was changed to Allentown in 1838 to honor William Allen. In 1841 a flood swept away the Lehigh Bridge and a fire leveled a major portion of town. The iron industry was established in Allentown in 1847, and the first of a number of cement factories was built in 1850. The town's boundaries extended to the Lehigh River by 1852, and the city of Allentown was incorporated in 1867. Silk mills opened in 1882 and cotton mills in the 1890s.

Historical Landmarks

In Center Square, at Seventh and Hamilton streets (site of early taverns and trading posts), rises the soldiers' and sailors' monument, a 100-foot shaft of Barre granite topped by a figure of the Goddess of Liberty. Zion's Reformed Church on the corner of Hamilton and Church streets is a brownstone Victorian Gothic erected in 1888 on the site of a church originally built in 1773. This earlier church was the hiding place of the Liberty Bell during the Revolutionary War. Trout Hall, a colonial Georgian structure, was built in 1770 by James Allen, son of the founder of Allentown. It is now a museum and open to the public.

Population

Allentown's population increased during the 1980s, from 103,758 in 1980 to 105,090 in 1990, an increase of 1.3%.

Population		
	1980	1990
Central City	103,758	105,090
Rank	155	182
Metro Area	635,481	686,688
Pop. Change 1980–1990 +1,332		
Pop. % Change 1980–1990 +1.3		
Median Age 33.8		
% Male 47.3		
% Age 65 and Over 16.9		
Density (per square mile) 5,937		

Households
Number 42,775
Persons per Household 2.36
% Female-Headed Households 12.7
% One-Person Households 31.7
Births—Total 1,598
% to Mothers under 20 12.7
Birth Rate per 1,000 15.4

Ethnic Composition

In 1990 whites made up 86.17% of the population. Hispanics, both white and black, were the largest minority in the city with 11.68%. Blacks made up 4.98%, Asians 1.4%, American Indians 0.18%, and other races 7.33%.

Ethnic Composition (as % of total pop.)		
	1980	1990
White	93.45	86.17
Black	3.14	4.98
American Indian	0.08	0.18
Asian and Pacific Islander	0.55	1.35
Hispanic	5.14	11.68
Other	NA	7.33

Government

Allentown operates under a mayor-council form of government. The mayor and the seven councilmen are elected to four-year terms.

Government
Year of Home Charter NA
Number of Members of the Governing Body 7
Elected at Large 7
Elected by Wards NA
Number of Women in Governing Body 3
Salary of Mayor $50,000
Salary of Council Members $5,000
City Government Employment Total 961
Rate per 10,000 92.1

Chronology

1735	William Allen acquires tract of land.
1750s	Allen builds a large fishing and hunting lodge on his land.
1762	A town known as Northamptontown is laid out on Allen's land.
1777	Liberty Bell is moved from Philadelphia to Allentown to safeguard it from British troops.
1811	Northampton is incorporated as a borough.
1812	A bridge is built across the Lehigh.
1829	The Lehigh Canal is completed.
1838	Northamptontown is renamed Allentown.
1841	Flood sweeps away the Lehigh River Bridge and fire levels the town.
1850	The first cement plant opens.
1852	Allentown's eastern boundary is extended to Lehigh River.
1867	Allentown is incorporated as a city.
1882	The first silk mill opens.

Public Finance

The annual budget for 1989–1990 consisted of revenues of $70.95 million and expenditures of $63.626 million. Outstanding debt was $79.427 million, and cash and security holdings are $81.069 million.

Public Finance

Total Revenue (in millions) $70.95
Intergovernmental Revenue—Total (in millions) $6.6
Federal Revenue per capita   NA
% Federal Assistance   NA
% State Assistance   9.2
Sales Tax as % of Total Revenue   NA
Local Revenue as % of Total Revenue   69.52
City Income Tax   yes
Taxes—Total (in millions) $21.0

Taxes per capita
Total   201
Property   120
Sales and Gross Receipts   0
General Expenditures—Total (in millions) $61.2
General Expenditures per capita $586
Capital Outlays per capita $21

% of Expenditures for:
Public Welfare   0.0
Highways   10.6
Education   0.0
Health and Hospitals   1.1
Police   10.4
Sewerage and Sanitation   10.2
Parks and Recreation   4.5
Housing and Community Development   7.4

Public Finance (continued)

Debt Outstanding per capita $256
   % Utility   10.3
Federal Procurement Contract Awards (in millions) $35.4
Federal Grants Awards (in millions) $7.9
Fiscal Year Begins   January 1

Economy

Allentown, which is the industrial and commercial center of the Lehigh Valley, has three kinds of economic activity. It has long been the center of a rich farming area, and agriculture still plays a major role in the economy. Manufacturing includes such products as trucks, electrical appliances, electronic equipment, food products, and textiles. The service sector is gaining importance, as is finance, insurance, real estate, and computers.

Economy

Total Money Income (in millions) $1,103
% of State Average   102.8
Per capita Annual Income $10,575
% Population below Poverty Level   11.7
Fortune 500 Companies   1
Banks   *Number*
   Commercial   NA
   Savings   NA
Passenger Autos   160,680
Electric Meters   105,181
Gas Meters   35,962

Manufacturing

Number of Establishments   241
% with 20 or More Employees   43.6
Manufacturing Payroll (in millions) $531
Value Added by Manufacture (in millions) $1,490
Value of Shipments (in millions) $2,832.4
New Capital Expenditures (in millions) $132.6

Wholesale Trade

Number of Establishments   325
Sales (in millions)   NA
Annual Payroll (in millions)   NA

Retail Trade

Number of Establishments   1,206
Total Sales (in millions) $950
Sales per capita $9,103
Number of Retail Trade Establishments with Payroll   821
Annual Payroll (in millions) $118.3
Total Sales (in millions) $932.8
General Merchandise Stores (per capita) $932
Food Stores (per capita) $1,862
Apparel Stores (per capita) $569
Eating and Drinking Places (per capita) $868

Service Industries

Total Establishments   1,020
Total Receipts (in millions) $487
Hotels and Motels (in millions) $18.3
Health Services (in millions) $102.7
Legal Services (in millions) $34.4

Labor

The Allentown labor market encompasses part of the Lehigh Valley, and many residents commute to work in nearby Bethlehem. White-collar jobs are expected to increase and blue-collar jobs to decline as the manufacturing sector experiences a downturn. Both wages and costs of living are high. The rate of unemployment in 1990 was 6.3%. The largest employers are Bethlehem Steel, Mack Trucks, Air Products and Chemicals, Inc., and the Allentown-Lehigh Valley Hospital Centers.

Labor

Civilian Labor Force   53,673
% Change 1989–1990   +1.9

Work Force Distribution
   Mining   500
   Construction   11,300
   Manufacturing   72,200
   Transportation and Public Utilities   14,300
   Wholesale and Retail Trade   61,400
   FIRE (Finance, Insurance, Real Estate)   14,300
   Service   77,000
   Government   32,100
   Women as % of Labor Force   44.6
   % Self-Employed   4.1
   % Professional/Technical   13.2
Total Unemployment   3,399
Rate %   6.3
Federal Government Civilian Employment   465

Education

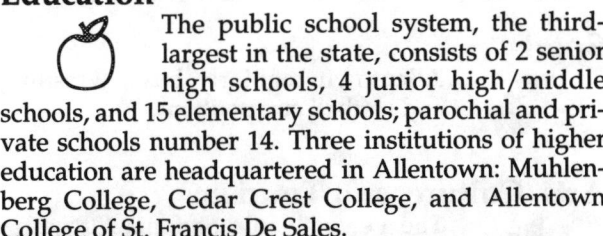

The public school system, the third-largest in the state, consists of 2 senior high schools, 4 junior high/middle schools, and 15 elementary schools; parochial and private schools number 14. Three institutions of higher education are headquartered in Allentown: Muhlenberg College, Cedar Crest College, and Allentown College of St. Francis De Sales.

Education

Number of Public Schools   21
Special Education Schools   NA
Total Enrollment   13,519
% Enrollment in Private Schools   13.4
% Minority   NA
Classroom Teachers   NA
Pupil-Teacher Ratio   24:1
Number of Graduates   NA
Total Revenue (in millions)   NA
Total Expenditures (in millions)   NA
Expenditures per Pupil   NA
Educational Attainment (Age 25 and Over)
   % Completed 12 or More Years   59.7
   % Completed 16 or More Years   10.9
Four-Year Colleges and Universities   2
Enrollment   2,552
Two-Year Colleges   3
Enrollment   945

Education (continued)

Libraries

Number   19
Public Libraries   3
Books (in thousands)   214
Circulation (in thousands)   800
Persons Served (in thousands)   109
Circulation per Person Served   7.3
Income (in millions) $1.4
Staff   43

Four-Year Colleges and Universities
   Allentown College of St. Francis De Sales
   Muhlenberg College
   Cedar Crest College

Health

There are 11 general hospitals in the region, six of which are in Allentown. The largest are the Lehigh Valley Hospital at 17th and Chew, the Lehigh Valley Hospital, Sacred Heart, Allentown Osteopathic Hospital at Cedar Crest, and Good Shepherd Rehabilitation Hospital.

Health

Deaths—Total   1,213
Rate per 1,000   11.7
Infant Deaths—Total   16
Rate per 1,000   10
Number of Metro Hospitals   6
Number of Metro Hospital Beds   1,809
Rate per 100,000   1,733
Number of Physicians   NA
Physicians per 1,000   NA
Nurses per 1,000   NA
Health Expenditures per capita $21.22

Transportation

Allentown is between U.S. 22 (called the Lehigh Valley Thruway) on the north and Interstate 78 to the south. U.S. 22 joins I-78 just west of the city. U.S. 222 connects Allentown to Reading and Lancaster, both of which are southwest of the city. The Northeast Extension of the Pennsylvania Turnpike, just west of Allentown, goes

Transportation

Interstate Highway Mileage   22
Total Urban Mileage   1,546
Total Daily Vehicle Mileage (in millions)   7.115
Daily Average Commute Time   41.4 min.
Number of Buses   58
Port Tonnage (in millions)   NA
Airports   1
Number of Daily Flights   17
Daily Average Number of Passengers   811

Airlines (American carriers only)
   American
   Continental
   Delta
   Eastern
   Northwest
   United
   USAir
   Westair

south to Philadelphia and north to Wilkes-Barre and Scranton. The regional airport, Allentown-Bethlehem-Easton Airport, is just northeast of the city off U.S. 22 and Airport Road (State 907). Allentown-Queen City Airport, a facility for small planes, is at Lehigh Street and State 309. Conrail handles rail freight.

Housing

There is very little housing activity downtown. Most new residential buildings in the suburbs consist of single-family, twins (duplexes or semiattached), and townhouses with three or more in a row. Of the 42,775 housing units occupied in 1990, 56.6% were owner-occupied. The median value was $76,600 and the median rent was $377.

Housing
Total Housing Units   45,636
% Change 1980–1990   4.1
Vacant Units for Sale or Rent   2,324
Occupied Units   42,775
% with More Than One Person per Room   3
% Owner-Occupied   56.6
Median Value of Owner-Occupied Homes $76,600
Average Monthly Purchase Cost $319
Median Monthly Rent $377
New Private Housing Starts   119
Value (in thousands) $3,491
% Single-Family   39.5
Nonresidential Buildings Value (in thousands) $5,188

Urban Redevelopment

The most recent urban redevelopment project sponsored by the Allentown Economic Development Corporation was the Downtown Renaissance Program. A second project is the ambitious Lehigh Landing riverfront development project.

Crime

Allentown ranks as the 29th-safest city in the nation, with 196 violent crimes per 100,000 people.

Crime
Violent Crimes—Total   391
Violent Crime Rate per 100,000   196.0
Murder   7
Rape   14
Robbery   164
Aggravated Assaults   206
Property Crimes   6,246
Burglary   1,371
Larceny   4,436
Motor Vehicle Theft   439
Arson   25
Per capita Police Expenditures $73.31
Per capita Fire Protection Expenditures $54.31
Number of Police   161
Per 1,000   1.56

Religion

The largest denomination is the Roman Catholic congregation. Evangelical Lutherans and United Church of Christ are also well represented.

Religion
Largest Denominations (Adherents)

Catholic	71,428
Evangelical Lutheran	41,145
United Church of Christ	31,450
Presbyterian	4,975
Jewish	4,119

Media

Allentown's daily newspaper is the *Allentown Morning Call*. Electronic media consist of one commercial television station and nine AM and FM radio stations.

Media
Newsprint
Allentown Morning Call, daily
Television
WFMZ (Channel 69)
Radio

WAEB (AM)	WAEB (FM)
WFMZ (FM)	WHOL (AM)
WKAP (AM)	WMUH (FM)
WQXA (FM)	WXKW (AM)
WZZO (FM)	

Sports

Allentown regularly hosts wrestling and softball competitions.

Arts, Culture, and Tourism

The Pennsylvania Sinfonia Orchestra holds regular performances at the Symphony Hall. The Pennsylvania Stage Company, Improvisational Music Company, Allentown Band (which calls itself the oldest municipal band in the United States), Municipal Opera Company, Muhlenberg Theatre Association, Civic Little Theatre, Allentown Contemporary Dance Theater, and Lehigh Valley Guild are all active contributors to the city's art and culture.

Travel and Tourism
Hotel Rooms   3,536
Convention and Exhibit Space (square feet)   NA
Convention Centers
Allentown Hilton
Festivals
Mayfair (May)
Das Awkscht Fescht (August)

The principal museum is the Allentown Art Museum, which houses the Samuel H. Cress Memorial Collection. Penn State at Allentown, Muhlenberg, and other colleges present regular exhibitions of paintings, sculpture, and photography. Commercial galleries include Springer Gallery, Ariel Gallery, and Open Space Gallery.

Parks and Recreation

About 13% of Allentown's area is devoted to parks, including the 124-acre Cedar Creek Park, home of the Gross Memorial Rose Gardens; 50-acre Jordan Park; 57-acre Lehigh Canal Park; 575-acre Lehigh Parkway; 90-acre South Mountain Reservoir; 142-acre Trexler Memorial Park; and the 100-acre Trout Creek Parkway.

Sources of Further Information

Lehigh Valley Convention and Visitors Bureau
International Airport Terminal Building
Lehigh Valley, PA 18001
(215) 266-0560

City Hall
Allentown, PA 18101
(215) 437-7546

Allentown Economic Development Corporation
512 Hamilton Street
Allentown, PA 18101
(215) 435-8890

Allentown-Lehigh County Chamber of Commerce
462 Walnut Street
Allentown, PA 18105
(215) 437-9661

Additional Reading

Storch, Phil H., ed. *Allentown—1950—Marking 200 Years of Growth*. 1950.

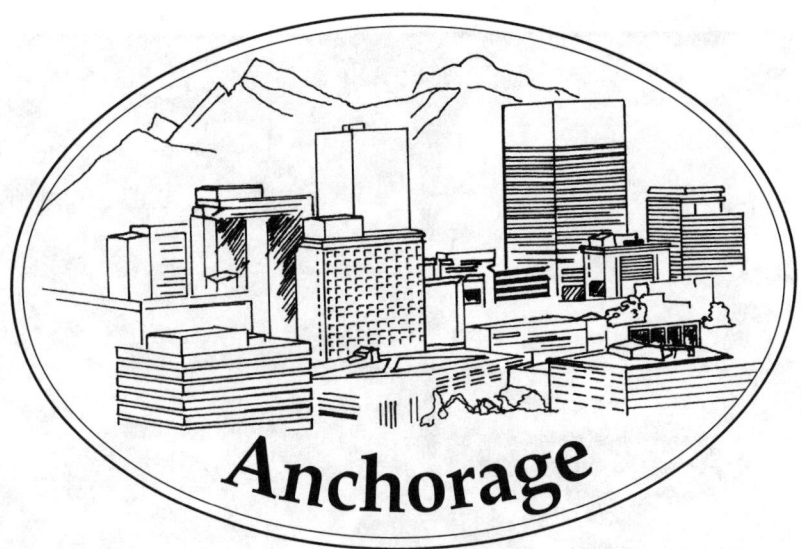

Anchorage

Alaska

Basic Data

Name   Anchorage
Name Origin   From Knik Anchorage
Year Founded   1915 Inc. 1920
Status: State   Alaska
      County   Seat of Greater Anchorage Area
Area (square miles)   1,697.7
Elevation (feet)   118
Time Zone   Alaska
Population (1990)   226,338
Population of Metro Area (1990)   226,338

Sister Cities
   Chitose, Japan
   Darwin, Australia
   Inchon, Korea
   Magadan, Russia
   Tromso, Norway
   Whitby, England

Distance in Miles To:
   Fairbanks   360

Location and Topography

N

The largest city in Alaska is on a peninsula between Knik Arm and Turnagain Arm of Cook Inlet in south-central Alaska. Rising just north of the city are the peaks of the Chugach Mountains; Mount McKinley, North America's highest mountain (20,320 feet), and other summits of the Alaska Range. The rugged wilderness country in the region of Anchorage lends substance to Alaska's claim as the "Last Frontier."

Layout of City and Suburbs

Anchorage is laid out in a grid: lettered streets run north to south and numbered streets west to east. The central business district is concentrated between 3rd and 9th avenues and the Minnesota Thruway to C Street. Most of the large hotels are in this area, as are federal and state offices and museums. Residential districts lie to the north and to the west along the coast of Turnagain Arm.

Environment

Environmental Stress Index   3.2
Green Cities Index: Rank   NA
                    Score   NA
Water Quality   Neutral, hard, fluoridated
   Average Daily Use (gallons per capita)   99
   Maximum Supply (gallons per capita)   175
Parkland as % of Total City Area   1.1
% Waste Landfilled/Recycled   NA
Annual Parks Expenditures per capita   77.35

Climate

Though Anchorage has a rigorous climate of long, cold winters, its proximity to the Pacific Ocean and sheltering mountains, such as the Alaska Range and mountains on the Kenai Peninsula, make it less harsh than inland locations such as Fairbanks, 360 road miles to the north. Temperatures average about 12°F in January and about 60 °F in July. About 70 inches of snow falls in a year and can accumulate from October into April or May. Daylight in winter is a brief 6 hours in December and as long as 19 hours in late June.

Weather

Temperature

Highest Monthly Average °F   65.6
Lowest Monthly Average °F   5.3

Annual Averages

Days 32°F or Below   192
Days above 90°F   12
Zero Degree Days   41

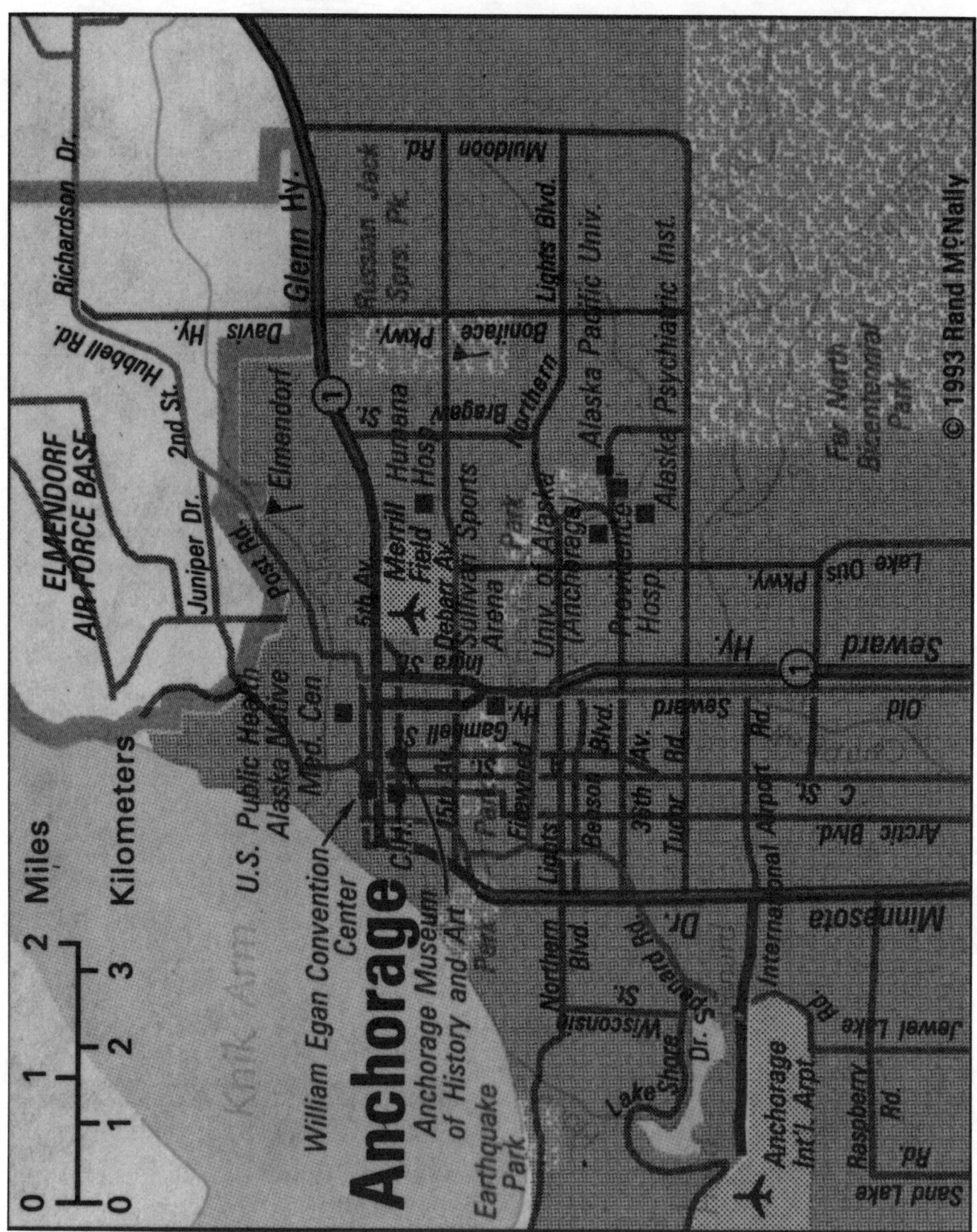

Weather (continued)

Precipitation (inches)   14
Snow (inches)   70
% Seasonal Humidity   71
Wind Speed (m.p.h.)   6.7
Clear Days   64
Cloudy Days   234
Storm Days   1
Rainy Days   113

Average Temperatures (°F)	High	Low	Mean
January	20.0	3.5	11.8
February	26.6	8.9	17.8
March	32.8	14.6	23.7
April	43.8	26.8	35.3
May	55.2	37.2	46.2
June	62.9	46.2	54.6
July	65.6	50.1	57.9
August	63.8	48.0	55.9
September	55.7	40.4	48.1
October	41.8	27.8	34.8
November	28.3	13.9	21.1
December	20.6	5.3	13.0

History

There was nothing but tidal flats, forests, pesky mosquitoes, and clear streams on the site of present-day Anchorage at the turn of the century. In 1915, however, planners for the Alaska Railroad, which was to be built between Seward and Fairbanks, chose the mouth of Ship Creek on Cook Inlet as an equipment depot for surplus steam shovels, locomotives, and derricks from construction of the Panama Canal. Lured by the promise of wages of 37-1/2 cents an hour, workers set up a tent city on the flats at Ship Creek seemingly overnight. Many of the workers were already in the area due to a 1914 gold strike in Nome. While Anchorage, as the anchorage at Ship Creek came to be called, was not known for resources such as oil, gas, timber, fisheries, or furs, it did capitalize on the business of managing and transporting the vast wealth of Alaska.

Tanaina Indians lived in the vicinity of Anchorage for generations. The Russian Vitus Bering began to explore the Alaskan coast in 1728, and English navigator Captain James Cook sailed up Cook Inlet from the Pacific in 1778. Russians established a chain of settlements and trading posts at Sitka, Kodiak, and Unalaska beginning in the 18th century. By 1867, however, the Imperial government decided that Russian America was too much of a liability and sold it to the United States for $7.2 million. Myopic U.S. citizens referred to the purchase as Seward's Folly, for William Henry Seward, President Andrew Johnson's secretary of state, who negotiated with the Russians for the territory. The former Russian administrative center at Sitka became the headquarters for the U.S. Army, which administered Alaska until 1874, after which administration shifted to the Treasury Department until 1884, when a civilian government was formed; in 1906 the government was moved to Juneau. Alaska was organized as a territory in 1912 and became the 49th state in 1959.

Anchorage incorporated as a town in 1920. The Alaska Railroad was completed to Fairbanks in 1923, the same year that the first airfield was built in Anchorage. The importance of the airplane for covering the vast distances of Alaska was quickly recognized, and Anchorage established its own airline in 1926. Private aircraft, most equipped with floats, bob on lakes around Anchorage today, seemingly as common as a second car elsewhere in the country. Merrill Field was opened in 1935.

By 1940 the population in Anchorage was 4,229, reaching about 8,000 in 1945. Alaska was a crucial location for the nation's defense during World War II, which, in turn, provided a catalyst for growth. Fort Richardson and Elmendorf Air Force Base were established near the city; and the 1,500-mile-long Alaska Highway, built between March and November 1942 to connect Alaska with British Columbia and roads south into the United States, now ended in Anchorage. Troops were stationed in the area during the war, and the military continued to be a presence throughout the cold war era.

In 1951 the International Airport opened, making Anchorage a major refueling point for transpolar flights. The population reached 44,000 in 1960, a year after Alaska became a state. On Good Friday, 27 March 1964, Anchorage, Valdez, Seward, and the rest of south-central Alaska experienced an earthquake that measured between 8.4 and 8.7 on the Richter scale. Businesses on parts of 4th Avenue dropped below street level and residences above Turnagain Arm slid toward the sea. While property damage was extensive, there were remarkably few fatalities. The city rebuilt itself, and within a few years took off on another growth trajectory. This boom was tied to the discovery in 1968 of oil in Prudhoe Bay on the North Slope. The state's sale of oil leases totaled more than $900 million in 1969. The Trans-Alaska Pipeline System was then designed to carry oil from Prudhoe Bay above the Arctic Circle south to the tanker port of Valdez. Actual construction began in 1974, and the first oil reached Valdez in 1977.

Although the fortunes of Anchorage turned when the price of oil sank to $10 a barrel in 1986, a large urban development project was initiated and completed by the end of the decade.

Historical Landmarks

The city limits extend to as far as Girdwood, 40 miles south, and twenty miles north to the largest state park in the United States—Chugach State Park, which includes most of the mountain range. The oldest building within the city limits is the St. Nicholas Russian Orthodox Church at Eklutna, built in 1848. The Swedish immigrant Oscar Anderson's house, built in 1915, survives at the north end of Elderberry Park as the city's first permanent frame building. Other historic buildings include the Old City Hall, built in 1936; the Cadastral Survey Monument, commemorating the 1915 town survey; the Leopold David House, built in 1917

Chronology

1778	Captain James Cook visits Cook Inlet.
1867	United States purchases Alaska from Russia.
1882	Gold is discovered in Alaska, bringing in thousands of prospectors, some of whom remain as residents.
1915	Ship Creek anchorage chosen as supply depot for Alaska Railroad. The site develops into the town of Anchorage.
1920	Anchorage is incorporated.
1923	Alaska Railroad is completed; the first municipal airfield is built.
1926	Anchorage establishes municipal airline.
1935	Merrill Airfield is opened.
1942	Alaska Highway is completed.
1951	International Airport opens.
1959	Alaska becomes 49th state.
1964	Earthquake on Good Friday reduces much of the city to rubble.
1968	Oil discovery at Prudhoe Bay fuels growth; leases sell for $900 million in 1969.
1975	City and borough governments merge to form Municipality of Anchorage.
1978	Anchorage embarks on an extensive redevelopment program.
1986	Oil prices sink to $10 a barrel.

for the town's first mayor; and the Boney Memorial Courthouse, decorated with native Alaskan art.

Population

The central city and the metropolitan area coincide in the case of Anchorage. The population of 226,338 represented a jump of 29.8% over the 1980 population of 174,431, despite the severe economic recession that hit the city in the late 1980s.

Ethnic Composition

In 1990 the ethnic composition was whites 80.7%, blacks 6.4%, American Indians 6.4%, Asians and Pacific Islanders 4.8%, Hispanics 4%, and others 1.6%.

Government

Anchorage is governed under a mayor-assembly form of government. The mayor and the 11 assembly members are elected to serve three-year terms.

Population

	1980	1990
Central City	174,431	226,338
Rank	78	69
Metro Area	174,431	226,338
Pop. Change 1980–1990 +51,907		
Pop. % Change 1980–1990 +29.8		
Median Age 29.8		
% Male 51.4		
% Age 65 and Over 3.6		
Density (per square mile) 133.32		

Households

Number 82,702
Persons per Household 2.68
% Female-Headed Households 10.1
% One-Person Households 22.9
Births—Total 5,194
    % to Mothers under 20 8.5
    Birth Rate per 1,000 22.9

Ethnic Composition (as % of total pop.)

	1980	1990
White	85.22	80.7
Black	5.31	6.4
American Indian	5.13	6.44
Asian and Pacific Islander	2.32	4.82
Hispanic	2.99	4.09
Other	NA	1.58

Government

Year of Home Charter 1975
Number of Members of the Governing Body 11
Elected at Large 11
Elected by Wards NA
Number of Women in Governing Body 1
Salary of Mayor $78,000
Salary of Council Members $1,500
City Government Employment Total 9,202
Rate per 10,000 391.6

Public Finance

 The annual budget consists of revenues of $762.711 million and expenditures of $736.430 million. The debt outstanding is $1.008 billion and cash and security holdings $601.192 million.

Public Finance

Total Revenue (in millions) $762.7
Intergovernmental Revenue—Total (in millions) $277.78
Federal Revenue per capita $6.61
% Federal Assistance 0.87
% State Assistance 35.6
Sales Tax as % of Total Revenue NA
Local Revenue as % of Total Revenue 48.59
City Income Tax no
Taxes—Total (in millions) $124.0

Taxes per Capita
Total 528
Property 492
Sales and Gross Receipts 14
General Expenditures—Total (in millions) $684

Public Finance (continued)

General Expenditures per capita $2,911
Capital Outlays per capita $742

% of Expenditures for:
  Public Welfare   1.0
  Highways   5.0
  Education   42.5
  Health and Hospitals   2.0
  Police   5.5
  Sewerage and Sanitation   6.8
  Parks and Recreation   1.6
  Housing and Community Development   0.0
Debt Outstanding per capita $3,202
  % Utility   23.4
Federal Procurement Contract Awards (in millions)
  $191.6
Federal Grants Awards (in millions) $151.9
Fiscal Year Begins   January 1

Economy (continued)

Service Industries

Total Establishments   2,123
Total Receipts (in millions) $1,064.1
Hotels and Motels (in millions) $85.8
Health Services (in millions) $241.6
Legal Services (in millions) $169.2

Economy

Since Anchorage is a young city, it did have an economy based on the usual Alaskan resources of fur, timber, fishing, and mining. However, with the discovery of oil on the North Slope of the Brooks Range above the Arctic Circle in 1968, Anchorage became the center of the oil industry's business. This included the Trans-Alaska Pipeline, which brought thousands of workers to the north. The oil industry went into a tailspin in the late 1980s, however. Ironically, the oil spill from the grounded tanker *Exxon Valdez* in March 1989 created a temporary boost to the economy.

Tourism is a steady and increasing source of revenue for the city. Government employment—federal, state, and local—continues as a mainstay. Known as the Air Crossroads of the World, Anchorage has two large airports. The year-round seaport also contributes significantly to the local economy.

Economy

Total Money Income (in millions) $3,646
% of State Average   113.7
Per capita Annual Income $15,517
% Population below Poverty Level   7.4
Fortune 500 Companies   NA

Banks	Number	Deposits (in millions)
Commercial	15	3,977.2
Savings	1	40.839

Passenger Autos   133,750
Electric Meters   85,558
Gas Meters   58,645

Manufacturing

Number of Establishments   146
% with 20 or More Employees   15.1
Manufacturing Payroll (in millions) $59.8
Value Added by Manufacture (in millions) $234.8
Value of Shipments (in millions) $714.1
New Capital Expenditures (in millions) $9.3

Wholesale Trade

Number of Establishments   479
Sales (in millions) $1,708.5
Annual Payroll (in millions) $146.806

Retail Trade

Number of Establishments   2,314
Total Sales (in millions) $1,994.3
Sales per capita $8,486
Number of Retail Trade Establishments with Payroll   1,403
Annual Payroll (in millions) $267
Total Sales (in millions) $1,952.5
General Merchandise Stores (per capita) $1,575
Food Stores (per capita) $1,603
Apparel Stores (per capita) $538
Eating and Drinking Places (per capita) $1,191

Labor

The 1990 unemployment rate in Anchorage was 5.2%, slightly below that of Alaska's 6.9%. Alaska was a magnet for blue-collar workers during construction of the Trans-Alaska Pipeline, and some stayed on after the project was completed in 1977. But the collapse of world crude oil prices in 1986 hit Alaska harder than most other states, causing a substantial contraction in the labor force across the board. The scaling down of the work force has had a further depressing effect on the economy.

Labor

Civilian Labor Force   117,230
% Change 1989–1990   2.6

Work Force Distribution
  Mining   NA
  Construction   NA
  Manufacturing   NA
  Transportation and Public Utilities   NA
  Wholesale and Retail Trade   NA
  FIRE (Finance, Insurance, Real Estate)   NA
  Service   NA
  Government   NA
  Women as % of Labor Force   44.4
  % Self-Employed   6.3
  % Professional/Technical   19.2
Total Unemployment   6,141
Rate %   5.2
Federal Government Civilian Employment   5,968

Education

The Anchorage School District is the largest in Alaska, with 82 schools. There are more than two dozen private and parochial schools. The University of Alaska, Anchorage and the Alaska Pacific University, as well as several

Education

Number of Public Schools 82
Special Education Schools 2
Total Enrollment 41,992
% Enrollment in Private Schools 6.0
% Minority 26.4
Classroom Teachers 2,088
Pupil-Teacher Ratio 18.9:1
Number of Graduates 2,217
Total Revenue (in millions) $247.198
Total Expenditures (in millions) $260.334
Expenditures per Pupil $5,215
Educational Attainment (Age 25 and Over)
  % Completed 12 or More Years 88.3
  % Completed 16 or More Years 23.6
Four-Year Colleges and Universities 2
Enrollment 14,908
Two-Year Colleges 1
Enrollment 500

Libraries

Number 19
Public Libraries 5
Books (in thousands) 452
Circulation (in thousands) 1,143
Persons Served (in thousands) 229
Circulation per Person Served 4.99
Income (in millions) $5.434
Staff 136

Four-Year Colleges and Universities
University of Alaska
Alaska Pacific University

smaller community and technical colleges, represent higher education in the city.

Health

The Anchorage area medical establishment consists of four major hospitals, of which the largest are Providence Hospital and Humana Hospital.

Health

Deaths—Total 704
Rate per 1,000 3.1
Infant Deaths—Total 55
Rate per 1,000 10.6
Number of Metro Hospitals 6
Number of Metro Hospital Beds 918
Rate per 100,000 417
Number of Physicians 443
Physicians per 1,000 2.32
Nurses per 1,000 2.66
Health Expenditures per capita 127.15

Transportation

Most out-of-state visitors reach Anchorage by air, arriving at Anchorage International Airport, which is about ten minutes from downtown. Domestic flights use the Anchorage Airport next door. State Route 1 connects

Transportation

Interstate Highway Mileage 42
Total Urban Mileage 1,103
Total Daily Vehicle Mileage (in millions) 3.59
Daily Average Commute Time 38.7 min.
Number of Buses 51
Port Tonnage (in millions) 2.294
Airports 2
Number of Daily Flights 89
Daily Average Number of Passengers 3,176

Airlines (American carriers only)
Alaska
American
Continental
Delta
Eastern
Northwest
Trans World
United

Anchorage to Seward 127 miles to the south and to Glennellen 187 miles to the northeast. The 360-mile drive to Fairbanks is on State Route 3. Rail passenger service to Fairbanks is provided by the Alaska Railroad, which also offers easy access to Denali National Park and Preserve in the summer. The Port of Anchorage is one of Alaska's largest and is open year-round. The city's People Mover transit company operates more than 50 buses.

Housing

Of the 82,702 occupied housing units in 1990, 52.8% were owner-occupied. The median value of owner-occupied homes was $109,700, and the median monthly rent was $528.

Housing

Total Housing Units 94,153
% Change 1980–1990 25.3
Vacant Units for Sale or Rent 6,731
Occupied Units 82,702
% with More Than One Person per Room 4.9
% Owner-Occupied 52.8
Median Value of Owner-Occupied Homes $109,700
Average Monthly Purchase Cost $671
Median Monthly Rent $528
New Private Housing Starts 399
Value (in thousands) $62,476
% Single-Family 100
Nonresidential Buildings Value (in thousands) $20,612

Urban Redevelopment

Project 80s, initiated in 1978, was Anchorage's first major urban redevelopment effort, and it changed the city's skyline. Among the major buildings constructed under the project were the George M. Sullivan Sports Arena, William A. Egan Convention and Civic Center, and

the Anchorage Performing Arts Center, completed in 1988.

Crime

Of the 29,680 crimes known to the police in 1991, 1,669 were violent and 14,017 involved property. The city employed 288 full-time officers in 1991.

Crime	
Violent Crimes—Total	1,669
Violent Crime Rate per 100,000	711.5
Murder	25
Rape	264
Robbery	542
Aggravated Assaults	709
Property Crimes	14,017
Burglary	2,489
Larceny	9,967
Motor Vehicle Theft	1,561
Arson	106
Per capita Police Expenditures	$161.87
Per capita Fire Protection Expenditures	$97.60
Number of Police	288
Per 1,000	1.25

Religion

There are some remnants of the 18th century Russian Orthodox Church in Anchorage. In 1990 about 33.5 percent of the population belonged to some of the 169 churches in Anchorage. The denominations with the most adherents were Catholic and Southern Baptist. Pentecostalism has made a strong social impact on the city through the Abbot Loop Christian Center.

Religion	
Largest Denominations (Adherents)	
Catholic	16,518
Southern Baptist	17,492
Latter Day Saints	5,611
Independent Charismatics	2,500
Black Baptist	4,093
Evangelical Lutheran	3,917
Assembly of God	3,585
United Methodist	2,484

Media

The Anchorage press consists of two dailies, *Anchorage Daily News* and *The Anchorage Times,* as well as the weekly *Tundra Times.* The electronic media consist of 6 commercial television stations and 19 AM and FM radio stations.

Sports

Anchorage is strong in hockey, and the city has two Olympic-sized hockey rinks, including the Sullivan Sports Arena. Two major basketball events for both men and women are the Great Alaska Shootout and the Northern Lights Invitational. Sled dog racing is the official state sport and the

Media

Newsprint
   *Anchorage Daily News,*daily
   *The Anchorage Times,*daily
   *Tundra Times,*weekly

Television
   KDMD (Channel 33 & 22)
   KIMO (Channel 13)
   KTBY (Channel 4)
   KTUU (Channel 2)
   KTVA (Channel 11)
   KYES (Channel 5)

Radio
KATB (FM)	KBYR (AM)
KNIK (FM)	KEAG (FM)
KENI (AM)	KBFX (FM)
KFQD (AM)	KWHL (FM)
KHAR (AM)	KKLV (FM)
KKSD (AM)	KASH (FM)
KLEF (FM)	KPXR (FM)
KSKA (FM)	KXDZ (FM)
KYAK (AM)	KGOT (FM)
KYMG (FM)	

1,000-mile Anchorage to Nome Iditarod Trail Sled Dog Race is world famous. There are numerous national and international downhill and cross-country ski events in winter. Two semi-professional baseball teams play at Mulcahy Baseball Stadium.

Arts, Culture, and Tourism

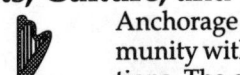

Anchorage has a flourishing arts community with more than 50 arts organizations. The centerpiece is the Performing Arts Center, completed in 1988. The Anchorage Concert Association brings international arts performers to the city. Music is represented by the Anchorage Symphony Orchestra, Anchorage Opera, the Alaska Concert Chorus, and the Alaska Chamber Singers. The Festival Theater and the Anchorage Community Theater are active in dramatic arts, and the Alaska Dance Theater represents dance.

Museums representing local history, native cultures, and wildlife include the Anchorage Wildlife and Natural History Museum, the Alaska Aviation Heritage Museum, Anchorage Museum of History and Art, and the Alaska Galleria at the Loussac Library.

Travel and Tourism	
Hotel Rooms	3,939
Convention and Exhibit Space (square feet)	NA
Convention Centers	
William A. Egan Civic and Convention Center	
George M. Sullivan Arena	
Festivals	
Fur Rondy (February)	
Iditarod Trail Sled Dog Race (March)	
Alaska Native Youth Olympics (April)	
Renaissance Festival (April)	
Basic Bach Festival Spirit Days (June)	
Alaska State Fair Alaska Scottish Highland Games (August)	
Oktoberfest, Qiana, Alaska (October)	

Parks and Recreation

Parks or designated parkland exceed more than half of the city's undeveloped land. Chugach State Park and Chugach National Forest begin at the city's edge. Delaney Park, once a firebreak for the original townsite, is now a popular recreation site. Resolution Park features a monument placed there on the 200th anniversary of Captain James Cook's exploration of the area. Goose Lake, Kincaid, and Bicentennial parks all have trails maintained for cross-country skiing in winter and biking and running in summer.

Sources of Further Information

City Hall
West 6th Street
Anchorage, AK 99501
(907) 343-4431

Anchorage Chamber of Commerce
415 F Street
Anchorage, AK 99501
(907) 272-2401

Anchorage Convention and Visitors Bureau
201 East Third Avenue
Anchorage, AK 99501
(907) 276-4118

Additional Reading

Fitch, Edwin A. *The Alaska Railroad.* 1967.
Naske, Claus M., and Herman E. Slotnick. *Alaska: A History of the 49th State.* 1987.
Oberle, Joseph G. *Anchorage.* 1990.

Ann Arbor

Michigan

The commercial district is built around Main Street, while State Street is the major thoroughfare in the university area. Nickel's Arcade, on State Street, and Kerrytown, a restored lumber-mill, feedstore, and warehouse on Fifth Avenue, are noted for their shops and galleries.

Basic Data

Name   Ann Arbor
Name Origin   From settlers Ann Rumsey and Ann Allen
Year Founded   1824 Inc. 1833
Status: State   Michigan
      County   Seat of Washtenaw County
Area (square miles)   25.9
Elevation (feet)   880
Time Zone   EST
Population (1990)   109,592
Population of Metro Area (1990)   282,937

Sister Cities

    Hikone, Japan
    Juigalpa, Nicaragua
    Peterborough, Canada
    Tubingen, Germany

Distance in Miles To:

Detroit	41
Grand Rapids	131
Lansing	63

Environment

Environmental Stress Index   2.6
Green Cities Index: Rank   NA
              Score   NA
Water Quality   Alkaline, soft, fluoridated
    Average Daily Use (gallons per capita)   147
    Maximum Supply (gallons per capita)   462
Parkland as % of Total City Area   NA
% Waste Landfilled/Recycled   75:25
Annual Parks Expenditures per capita   28.88

Location and Topography

N

Ann Arbor is on the Huron River in southeastern Michigan, about 40 miles west of Detroit and 50 miles southeast of Lansing, the state capital. The city, located at an elevation of 766 feet, is in a hilly region dotted with many lakes, remnants of glaciers that retreated some 15,000 years ago.

Layout of City and Suburbs

A commercial district and the campus of the University of Michigan occupy the center of the city. An industrial district in the north-central part of Ann Arbor parallels the railroad that follows the Huron River. The west side of the city has the air of a rural town, but the east side, under the shadow of the university, bustles with theaters, fashionable shops, libraries, and auditoriums.

Climate

Ann Arbor is in the humid continental climate zone, with hot summers, cold winters, and above-average precipitation in the form of rain and snow. Proximity to the Great Lakes helps to reduce the extremes in both winter and summer, but it also causes high humidity and cloud cover 67% of the time. The annual average snowfall is 35 inches, with an annual average rainfall of 31 inches.

Weather

Temperature

Highest Monthly Average °F   83.6
Lowest Monthly Average °F   16.8

Annual Averages

Days 32°F or Below   46
Days above 90°F   10

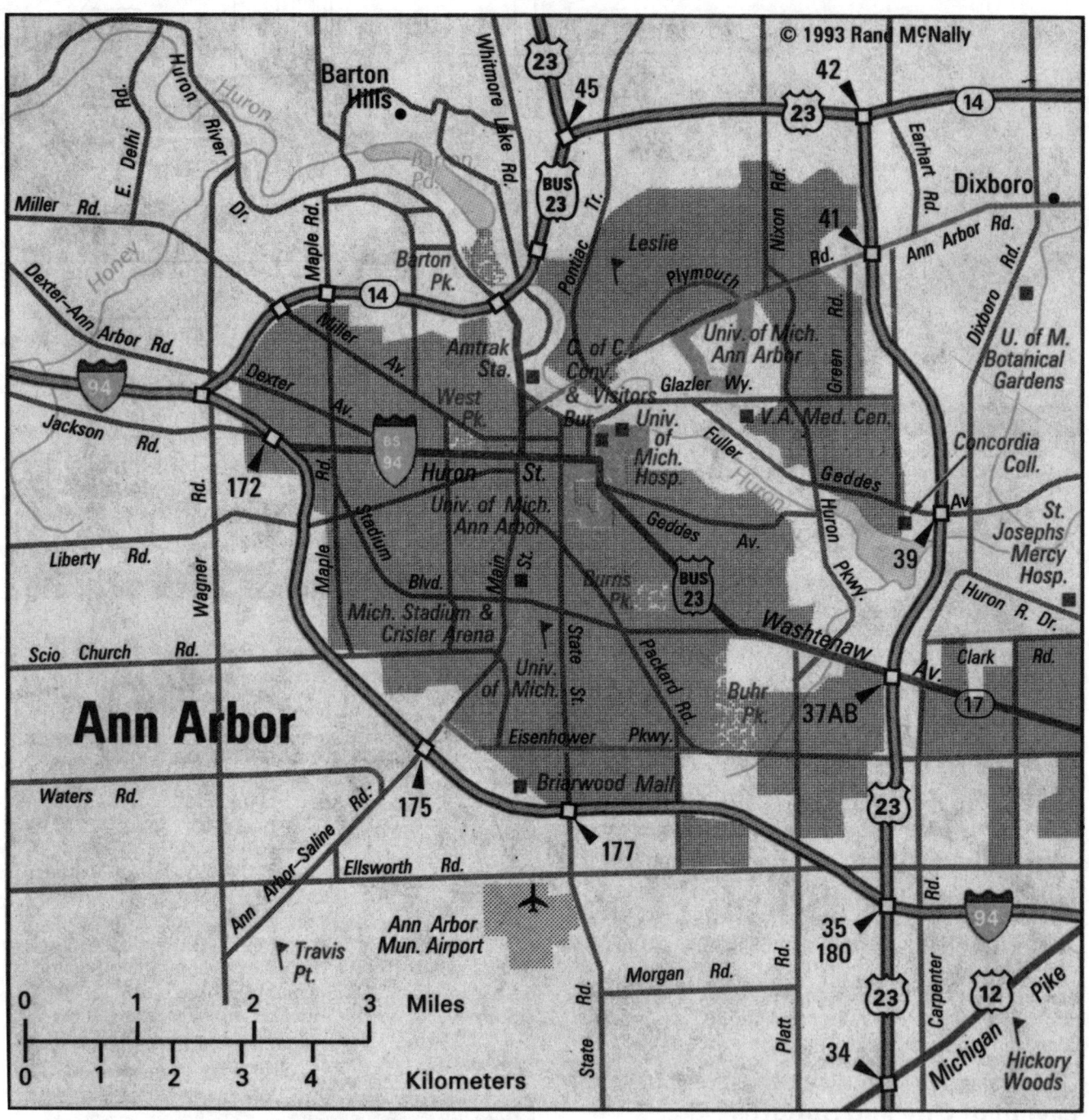

Ann Arbor

© 1993 Rand McNally

Barton Hills

Leslie

Dixboro

U. of M. Botanical Gardens

Concordia Coll.

St. Josephs Mercy Hosp.

Univ. of Mich. Ann Arbor

V.A. Med. Cen.

Univ. of Mich. Hosp.

Amtrak Sta.

West Pk.

Barton Pk.

Cty. of C. Conv. & Visitors Bur.

Univ. of Mich. Ann Arbor

Mich. Stadium & Crisler Arena

Univ. of Mich.

Buhr Pk.

Burns Pk.

Briarwood Mall

Ann Arbor Mun. Airport

Travis Pt.

Hickory Woods

0 1 2 3 Miles
0 1 2 3 4 Kilometers

Weather (continued)

Zero Degree Days 5
Precipitation (inches) 30.22
Snow (inches) 35
% Seasonal Humidity NA
Wind Speed (m.p.h.) NA
Clear Days NA
Cloudy Days NA
Storm Days NA
Rainy Days NA

Average Temperatures (°F)	High	Low	Mean
January	30.7	16.8	23.8
February	33.9	18.3	26.1
March	44.3	26.8	35.6
April	58.9	38.0	48.5
May	70.9	48.5	59.7
June	80.1	58.1	69.1
July	83.6	62.2	72.9
August	81.6	60.7	71.2
September	74.8	53.7	64.2
October	62.9	43.3	53.1
November	47.9	32.8	40.4
December	35.5	22.3	28.9

History

Ojibwa Indians criss-crossed the rivers and hills of what is now Ann Arbor. Their name for the area, Washtenaw, "the land beyond," survives as the name for Washtenaw County, of which Ann Arbor is the county seat. The founders of Ann Arbor, in 1824, were two Eastern entrepreneurs, John Allen of Virginia and Elisha Walker Rumsey of New York, both of whose wives were named Ann. They came to what was then Michigan Territory (west of what is now Detroit) to settle in a clearing in an oak forest through which a creek flowed. Rumsey and Walker named it Annarbour after their wives and for its location in the clearing. A settlement quickly developed around a tannery and general store, and Ann Arbor eventually became the seat of Washtenaw County. It grew quickly and was incorporated as a village in 1833.

When Michigan became the 26th state in 1837, Ann Arbor, now with a population of some 2,000, bid successfully to have the University of Michigan relocated from Detroit. However, in 1847, when it was decided that the state capital would be moved from Detroit, Ann Arbor lost its bid for it to Lansing. In 1851 Ann Arbor was chartered as a city.

Until 1861 Ann Arbor's city limits had been to the Huron River, but with the annexation of the Lower Town the boundaries extended across the Huron. By 1865 the University of Michigan's student body numbered 1,200, making it the largest university in the country.

The city also became an industrial center specializing in machinery. Railroads, the first of which reached Ann Arbor in 1839 from Detroit, also contributed to the city's economic wealth; in 1878 the Toledo, Ann Arbor, and Northern Michigan Railroad was built. Ann Arbor continued to grow in spurts in the 1890s and 1920s; after World War II, it nearly doubled in size

as it became the self-proclaimed "Research Capital of the Midwest."

Historical Landmarks

Ann Arbor has a number of distinctive buildings, among them St. Andrews Church and several homes dating from the early to mid-19th century. In addition to the Hill Auditorium on North University at Thayer Road, the University of Michigan also contains many architecturally significant buildings both on and near the campus. One such is the Rackham Auditorium, which covers two blocks and is made of Indiana limestone, with bronze windows and door frames, a copper-sheathed roof, and art deco interior. The Burton Memorial Tower has one of the largest carillons in the nation.

Population

Ann Arbor's population has slowly risen over the last 20 years: from 99,797 in 1970, to 107,969 in 1980, to 109,592 in 1990, a growth rate of 1.5%. The 36,306 students enrolled in the University of Michigan constitute almost one-third of the population.

Population	1980	1990
Central City	107,969	109,592
Rank	146	168
Metro Area	264,740	282,937
Pop. Change 1980–1990 +1,623		
Pop. % Change 1980–1990 +1.5		
Median Age 27.3		
% Male 49.5		
% Age 65 and Over 7.2		
Density (per square mile) 4,231		

Households		
Number 41,657		
Persons per Household 2.32		
% Female-Headed Households 8.1		
% One-Person Households 31.4		
Births—Total 1,414		
% to Mothers under 20 4.2		
Birth Rate per 1,000 13.1		

Ethnic Composition

Whites made up 81.9% of the population in 1990, blacks 9.04%, Asian and Pacific Islanders 7.7%, Hispanics 2.58%, American Indians 0.3%, and other races 0.95%. Much of the

Ethnic Composition (as % of total pop.)	1980	1990
White	85.1	81.98
Black	9.33	9.04
American Indian	0.25	0.35
Asian and Pacific Islander	3.61	7.69
Hispanic	2.08	2.58
Other	NA	0.95

Chronology

1805	Michigan, part of what was then Indiana Territory, becomes Michigan Territory.
1822	Washtenaw County is established.
1824	Two Eastern entrepreneurs, John Allen of Virginia and Elisha Walker Rumsey of New York, purchase 640 acres of land in the Huron Valley, including 170 acres covering what is the present-day intersection of Main and Huron Streets. They named the settlement Annarbour, which later becomes Ann Arbor.
1833	County Courthouse built, and Ann Arbor is incorporated as a village.
1837	University of Michigan transfers from Detroit to Ann Arbor and opens campus with nine students.
1839	Michigan Central Railroad reaches Ann Arbor.
1851	Ann Arbor is incorporated as a city.
1861	Lower Town is annexed and the city's boundaries extend south of the Huron River for the first time.
1878	The Toledo, Ann Arbor, and Northern Michigan Railroad reaches city.
1913	Hill Auditorium, designed by Albert Kahn, is completed.
1922	Olmsted Brothers draw up first Park Plan.
1930	Population reaches 26,944.
1956	Present city charter is adopted.

ethnic diversity is due to the University of Michigan, which has a varied student population.

Government

Ann Arbor's charter provides for a mayor-council form of government. Eleven council members, including a mayor, serve two-year terms. The mayor and council appoint a full-time city administrator.

Government

Year of Home Charter   1956
Number of Members of the Governing Body   11
Elected at Large   NA
Elected by Wards   11
Number of Women in Governing Body   3
Salary of Mayor $15,000
Salary of Council Members $7,000
City Government Employment Total   1,237
Rate per 10,000   114.7

Public Finance

The annual budget in 1984 and 1985 consisted of revenues of $123.4 million with expenditures of $116.7 million. The debt outstanding was $68.8 million and cash and security holdings $164.3 million.

Public Finance

Total Revenue (in millions) $123.413
Intergovernmental Revenue—Total (in millions) $27.7
Federal Revenue per capita $8.461
% Federal Assistance   6.85
% State Assistance   14.9
Sales Tax as % of Total Revenue   NA
Local Revenue as % of Total Revenue   58.19
City Income Tax   no
Taxes—Total (in millions) $25.9

Taxes per capita
Total   241
Property   232
Sales and Gross Receipts   0
General Expenditures—Total (in millions) $67.5
General Expenditures per capita $626
Capital Outlays per capita $106

% of Expenditures for:
  Public Welfare   0.1
  Highways   9.6
  Education   0.0
  Health and Hospitals   0.0
  Police   11.1
  Sewerage and Sanitation   18.1
  Parks and Recreation   4.2
  Housing and Community Development   0.1
Debt Outstanding per capita $619
  % Utility   24.7
Federal Procurement Contract Awards (in millions) $75.7
Federal Grants Awards (in millions) $117.8
Fiscal Year Begins   July 1

Economy

Education is the principal employer in Ann Arbor. Manufacturing has declined as a whole in the last 20 years and has been replaced with high technology, specifically electronics research and manufacture spurred by the University of Michigan. Ann Arbor has found a niche as the western anchor of the high-tech corridor stretching from Detroit in the east along I-94 and M-14. Ann Arbor also has developed as a printing center. Among the largest pri-

Economy

Total Money Income (in millions) $1,394
% of State Average   118.4
Per capita Annual Income $12,911
% Population below Poverty Level   14.7
Fortune 500 Companies   NA

Banks	Number	Deposits (in millions)
Commercial	9	1,534
Savings	2	7,000

Passenger Autos   156,712
Electric Meters   131,000
Gas Meters   83,231

Economy (continued)

Manufacturing

Number of Establishments 167
% with 20 or More Employees 32.9
Manufacturing Payroll (in millions) $154.9
Value Added by Manufacture (in millions) $208.8
Value of Shipments (in millions) $350.4
New Capital Expenditures (in millions) $15.1

Wholesale Trade

Number of Establishments 191
Sales (in millions) $552.5
Annual Payroll (in millions) $48.946

Retail Trade

Number of Establishments 1,111
Total Sales (in millions) $1,081.7
Sales per capita $10,033
Number of Retail Trade Establishments with Payroll 857
Annual Payroll (in millions) $143.8
Total Sales (in millions) $1,070
General Merchandise Stores (per capita) NA
Food Stores (per capita) $1,360
Apparel Stores (per capita) $895
Eating and Drinking Places (per capita) $1,191

Service Industries

Total Establishments 1,226
Total Receipts (in millions) $556.8
Hotels and Motels (in millions) $34
Health Services (in millions) $97.2
Legal Services (in millions) $35.1

vate corporations in the city are Warner-Lambert/Parke Davis (pharmaceuticals), Edwards Brothers (printing), NSK Corporation, Bearing Division (bearings), and ADP Network Services (computers).

Labor

Ann Arbor has weathered the recession of the early 1990s better than many cities. In 1990 its unemployment rate was 2.7% when that of Michigan was 7.5%. The University of Michigan and the University of Michigan Medical Center, with a total of 26,775 employees, are major stabilizing factors.

Labor

Civilian Labor Force 68,823
% Change 1989–1990 1.6
Work Force Distribution
   Mining NA
   Construction 3,600
   Manufacturing 36,400
   Transportation and Public Utilities 5,400
   Wholesale and Retail Trade 32,300
   FIRE (Finance, Insurance, Real Estate) 5,000
   Service 37,500
   Government 55,200
   Women as % of Labor Force 47.3
   % Self-Employed 4.2
   % Professional/Technical 39.2
Total Unemployment 1,876
Rate % 2.7
Federal Government Civilian Employment 2,684

Education

The public schools of Ann Arbor include 30 schools. There are also about a dozen private and parochial schools. The University of Michigan dominates city life. It is ranked among the top ten academic institutions in the nation by the American Council of Education for the breadth of its programs and its emphasis on research. The major private college is Concordia College, affiliated with the Lutheran Church–Missouri Synod.

Education

Number of Public Schools 30
Special Education Schools NA
Total Enrollment 14,190
% Enrollment in Private Schools 11.2
% Minority NA
Classroom Teachers NA
Pupil-Teacher Ratio NA
Number of Graduates NA
Total Revenue (in millions) NA
Total Expenditures (in millions) NA
Expenditures per Pupil NA
Educational Attainment (Age 25 and Over)
   % Completed 12 or More Years 90.7
   % Completed 16 or More Years 56.2
Four-Year Colleges and Universities 4
Enrollment 36,899
Two-Year Colleges 1
Enrollment 11,500

Libraries

Number 43
Public Libraries 4
Books (in thousands) 440
Circulation (in thousands) 999
Persons Served (in thousands) 128
Circulation per Person Served 7.8
Income (in millions) $3.6
Staff 80
Four-Year Colleges and Universities
   University of Michigan
   Concordia College

Health

The University of Michigan Medical Center is a large complex that includes several facilities: University Hospital, Women's Hospital, Mott Children's Hospital, Holden Perinatal Hospital, and Taubman Health Center, as well as an adult psychiatric hospital, a burn center, and

Health

Deaths—Total 489
Rate per 1,000 4.5
Infant Deaths—Total 11
Rate per 1,000 7.8
Number of Metro Hospitals 3
Number of Metro Hospital Beds 1,845
Rate per 100,000 1,711
Number of Physicians 1,657
Physicians per 1,000 NA
Nurses per 1,000 NA
Health Expenditures per capita NA

an eye-care center. Other facilities include the Catherine McAuley Health Center, which operates the Hospice of Washtenaw and home health services, and St. Joseph Mercy Hospital, which has a number of branch clinics.

Transportation

Two highways and one interstate serve Ann Arbor. U.S. 23 runs north-south along the east edge of the city, Michigan 14 runs east-west along the northern edge, and I-94 runs east-west along the southern and southwestern edge. Air transportation is provided out of Ann Arbor Municipal Airport for light passenger and recreational flights, and out of Willow Run Airport for cargo and commercial flights. The Detroit Metropolitan Airport is 11 miles to the east of Willow Run Airport. Frequent passenger rail service is provided by Amtrak, with rail freight services by Conrail. Ann Arbor Transportation Authority provides about 40 city buses.

Transportation

Interstate Highway Mileage   20
Total Urban Mileage   662
Total Daily Vehicle Mileage (in millions)   4.461
Daily Average Commute Time   41.4 min.
Number of Buses   40
Port Tonnage (in millions)   NA
Airports   NA
Number of Daily Flights   NA
Daily Average Number of Passengers   NA

Airlines (American carriers only)
   NA

Housing

Of Ann Arbor's 41,657 occupied units in 1990, 56.8% were rental units and 43.2% were owner-occupied dwellings. The median value of a home was $116,400 and the median rent $529.

Urban Redevelopment

There has been renovation and new construction in the downtown business district, as well as new construction in the

Housing

Total Housing Units   41,657
% Change 1980–1990   8.8
Vacant Units for Sale or Rent   2,051
Occupied Units   41,657
% with More Than One Person per Room   3.2
% Owner-Occupied   43.2
Median Value of Owner-Occupied Homes $116,400
Average Monthly Purchase Cost $504
Median Monthly Rent $529
New Private Housing Starts   502
Value (in thousands) $27,886
% Single-Family   15.5
Nonresidential Buildings Value (in thousands) $24,839

southern part of the city and along the Plymouth Road Corridor, where many high-tech firms are located.

Crime

There were a total of 6,991 crimes known to police in 1991, of which 613 were violent crimes, and 6,378 involved property.

Crime

Violent Crimes—Total   613
Violent Crime Rate per 100,000   694.0
Murder   2
Rape   50
Robbery   148
Aggravated Assaults   413
Property Crimes   6,378
Burglary   1,251
Larceny   4,725
Motor Vehicle Theft   402
Arson   51
Per capita Police Expenditures $97.16
Per capita Fire Protection Expenditures $57.56
Number of Police   151
Per 1,000   1.40

Religion

In 1990, Catholics accounted for the most prominent denomination with 34,376 adherents.

Religion

Largest Denominations (Adherents)

Catholic	34,376
Evangelical Lutheran	6,112
Black Baptist	10,863
United Methodist	7,503
United Church of Christ	5,627
Reformed Church	4,471
Lutheran-Missouri Synod	4,132
American Baptist	4,128
Episcopal	3,386
Jewish	4,500

Media

The city daily is *The Ann Arbor News*, which appears weekday evenings and weekend mornings. Electronic media consist of one television station and six AM and FM radio stations.

Media

Newsprint
   The Ann Arbor News, daily
Television
   WBSX (Channel 31)
Radio

WAAM (AM)	WCBN (FM)
WIQB (FM)	WPZA (AM)
WAMX (AM)	WUOM (FM)

Sports

Ann Arbor has no professional sports team but locals usually root for Detroit teams. The University of Michigan fields some fine teams. The Michigan Wolverines play football in the Big Ten conference; they won the first Rose Bowl at Pasadena in 1902 and have won it five times since then.

Arts, Culture, and Tourism

The most active cultural institutions are the Civic Theater and the Young People's Theater in drama, the Civic Ballet in dance, and the Ann Arbor Symphony Orchestra and Ann Arbor Chamber Orchestra in music. Ars Musica, specializing in baroque music, the Comic Opera Guild, and the Gilbert and Sullivan Society of the University of Michigan cater to specialized audiences. The Performance Network brings together performance artists in theater, music, dance, and film. The University of Michigan's Hill Auditorium, built in 1913, is one of the most admired performing arts facilities in the nation. The auditorium is home to the university's numerous cultural groups, one of which is its Musical Society, founded in 1879. The Power Center is an equally popular performance art facility.

The University of Michigan has many museums. Exhibit Museum is a natural history museum devoted to Michigan's prehistoric past and its flora and fauna. The Kelsey Museum of Archaeology is strong on Greek and Roman archaeology. Other outstanding museums maintained by the University of Michigan are the Museum of Art, Museum of Paleontology, Museum of Zoology, and the Stearns Collection of Musical Instruments. The city of Ann Arbor runs Kempf House, a restored Greek Revival home (1853) with period toys and antiques. The Park and Recreation Department gives tours of Cobblestone Farm, a restored pioneer homestead and barn. For children there is the privately owned Ann Arbor Hands-On Museum.

Parks and Recreation

Ann Arbor has 124 parks within its city limits, among which are the 148-acre Bird Hills Park, the city's largest; Gallup Park, the most popular, with riverside canoes and paddleboats; and Leslie Science Center, where children learn about natural science and ecology.

Sources of Further Information

Ann Arbor Area Convention and Visitors Bureau
211 East Huron Avenue, Suite 6
Ann Arbor, MI 48104
(313) 995-7281

Ann Arbor Public Library
343 South Fifth Avenue
Ann Arbor, MI 48104-2293
(313) 994-2333

City Hall
100 North Fifth Avenue
Ann Arbor, MI 48107
(313) 994-2700

Ann Arbor Area Chamber of Commerce
211 East Huron
Ann Arbor, MI 48104
(313) 665-4433

Additional Reading

An Introduction to Ann Arbor. 1991
Fitzgerald, Linda. *Ann Arbor: There's No Other City Quite Like It.* 1990
Polk's Ann Arbor City Directory. 1991

Travel and Tourism

Hotel Rooms   2,870
Convention and Exhibit Space (square feet)   NA

Convention Centers
  Michigan Union
  University of Michigan Hill Auditorium Crisler Arena
  Chrysler Center
  Towsley Center

Festivals
  Ann Arbor Film Festival (March)
  Spring Art Fair (April)
  Winter Art Fair (November)
  Summer Art Fair (July)
  May Festival (May)
  Summer Festival (June–July)
  Medieval Festival (summer)
  Ethnic Fair (August)

Atlanta

Georgia

Basic Data

Name   Atlanta
Name Origin   From Western and Atlantic Railroad
Year Founded   1837 Inc. 1847
Status: State   Capital of Georgia
   County   Seat of Fulton County
Area (square miles)   131.8
Elevation (feet)   1,050
Time Zone   EST
Population (1990)   394,017
Population of Metro Area (1990)   2,833,511

Sister Cities

 Brussels, Belgium
 Daegu, Korea
 Lagos, Nigeria
 Montego Bay, Jamaica
 Newcastle Upon Tyne, England
 Port of Spain, Trinidad
 Rio de Janeiro, Brazil
 Salzburg, Austria
 Taipei Municipality, China
 Tbilisi, Georgia
 Toulouse, France

Distance in Miles To:

Albuquerque	1,404
Boston	1,108
Chicago	708
Dallas	822
Denver	1,430
Houston	791
Indianapolis	527
Los Angeles	2,191
Minneapolis	1,121
New York	854
Philadelphia	748

Location and Topography

N

Atlanta—Georgia's capital city, seat of Fulton County, commercial giant of the southeast United States—is in northwest Georgia, just southwest of the Appalachian Mountains. The metropolitan area, at an elevation of about 1,000 feet, spreads out over hills.

Layout of City and Suburbs

Atlanta was originally laid out in a circle with a two-mile diameter, its streets radiating from the center. Rapid growth modified the plan, but the city still centers on the Five Points and Central City Park, where the main thoroughfares converge. Surrounding Five Points is the Central Business District. Peachtree Street, once Atlanta's most fashionable residential district, is now the main north-south artery, lined with skyscrapers, hotels, and apartment buildings. From Midtown north historic suburbs can be found a block or two off Peachtree Street. Lenox Square, the city's leading mall, is on Peachtree Street. The Perimeter Highway, also known as Interstate 285, has recently attracted newer malls and office clusters. The largest suburb, Sandy Springs, is due north of the city; College Park, East Point, and Forest Park are to the south, while Decatur is east and in De Kalb County; Marietta, Norcross, Roswell, and Smyrna are to the northwest.

Environment

Environmental Stress Index   2.6
Green Cities Index: Rank   29
      Score   27.08
Water Quality   Neutral, soft
 Average Daily Use (gallons per capita)   NA
 Maximum Supply (gallons per capita)   NA
Parkland as % of Total City Area   3.6
% Waste Landfilled/Recycled   NA
Annual Parks Expenditures per capita

Climate

Atlanta's elevation, not exceeded by any other U.S. city of comparable size except Denver, Colorado, accounts for its cool

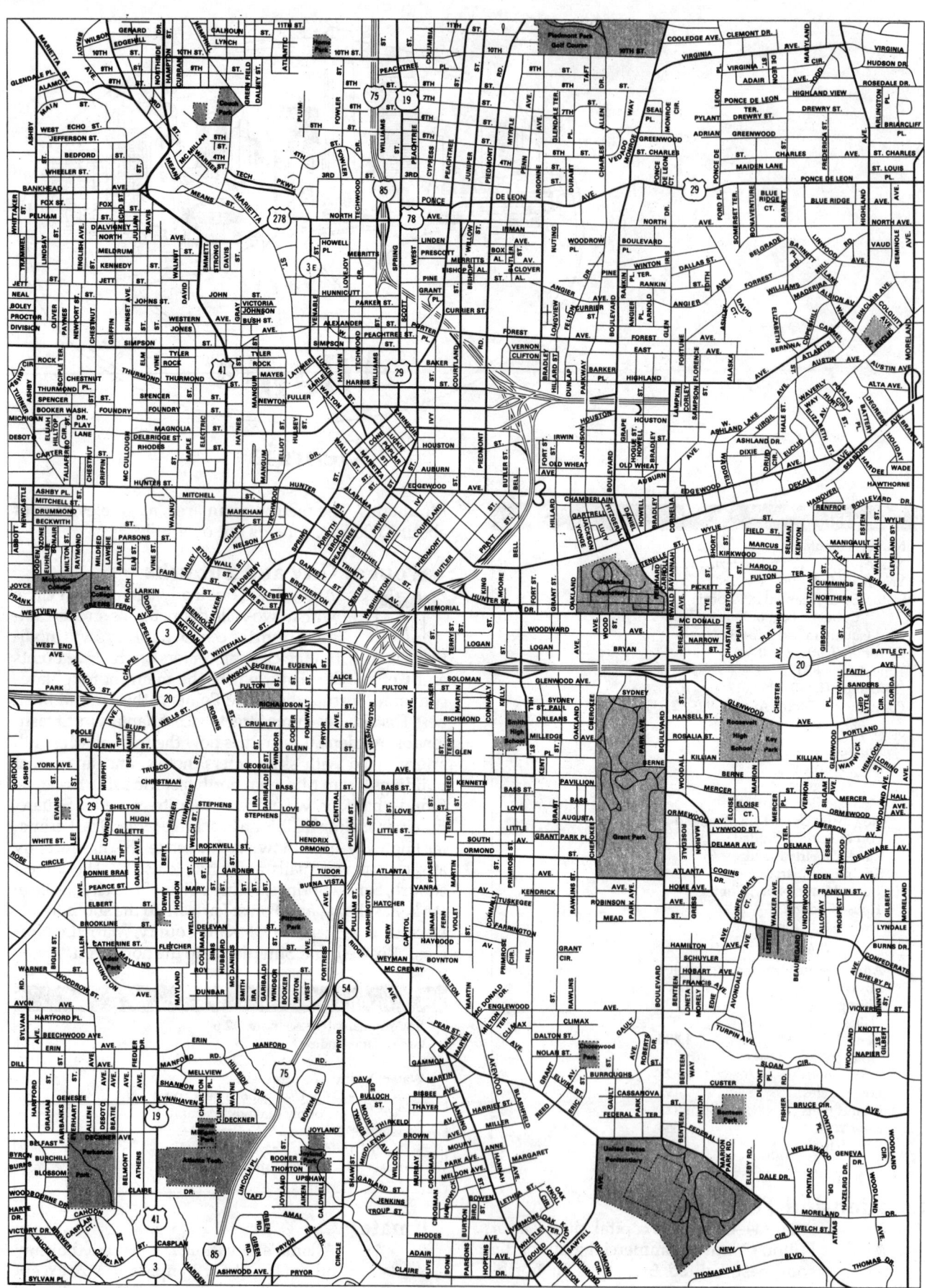

weather in summer. Its proximity to the Gulf of Mexico and the Atlantic Ocean also moderates summer temperatures, while the mountains to the north protect it from the polar air in winter. Snowfall is infrequent, usually less than two inches a year, although once every five years or so the city is visited by violent snowstorms. Tornadoes and thunderstorms are fairly frequent, especially in spring, with an average of about 50 a year. The rainiest month is March. Abundant rainfall fosters the city's ever-green look.

Weather

Temperature

Highest Monthly Average °F   87.9
Lowest Monthly Average °F   32.6

Annual Averages

Days 32°F or Below   59
Days above 90°F   19
Zero Degree Days   0
Precipitation (inches)   48
Snow (inches)   2
% Seasonal Humidity   70
Wind Speed (m.p.h.)   9.1
Clear Days   108
Cloudy Days   146
Storm Days   50
Rainy Days   116

Average Temperatures (°F)	High	Low	Mean
January	51.4	33.4	42.4
February	54.5	35.5	45.0
March	61.1	41.1	51.1
April	71.4	50.7	61.1
May	79.0	59.2	69.1
June	84.6	66.6	75.6
July	86.5	69.4	78.0
August	86.4	68.6	77.5
September	81.2	63.4	72.3
October	72.5	52.3	62.4
November	61.9	40.8	51.4
December	52.7	34.3	43.5

History

The largest city in Georgia was not known as Atlanta until 1845. Originally, the site near the Chattahoochee River that became Atlanta was called Standing Peach Tree, a Creek Indian settlement. According to legend, the Creeks won the site from the Cherokee as a prize in a series of ball games. A mention of Standing Peach Tree can be found in Revolutionary War Records of 1782. In 1813 Lieutenant George R. Gilmer was ordered to build a fort at Standing Peach Tree because of clashes between the Creeks and the Cherokee. Fort Gilmer was the first white settlement in the area. In 1821 Indian territorial claims were ceded to the state of Georgia. The Georgia legislature, urged by railroad interests, passed a law in 1836 to permit construction of the Western and Atlantic Railroad from Ross's Landing (later to become Chattanooga) in Tennessee through the mountains of northern Georgia to a proposed terminus at the Chattahoochee. Connections from other parts of the state—the Georgia Railroad from Augusta and the Central of Georgia from Savannah to Macon—were brought together at a point appropriately called Terminus (named for the engineer's final stake, the zero milepost), near what is now the southwestern corner of Wall Street and Central Avenue. Terminus became a trading center built around the railroad office. In 1843 the town Terminus was incorporated as Marthasville, after the governor's daughter. Two years later the name was changed to Atlanta. In 1847 Atlanta was incorporated as a city, and in 1853 it was made the seat of the newly formed Fulton County. In that same year the Holland Free School, the city's first public school, opened in the old Angier Academy on the southwest corner of Forsyth and Garnett streets. The next year, 1854, the Atheneum Theater opened and the first Fulton County Court House was built. The Atlanta Medical College was founded in 1855, and by the end of that year the city had gas lights. An 1859 city directory gave the population as 11,500.

Momentum was now gathering for civil war, and Georgia seceded from the Union in January 1861. Atlanta was a Confederate supply center until 22 July 1864, when the Confederate defenders under General John B. Hood engaged Union forces led by General William T. Sherman. Sherman was victorious. Bombardment of the city continued for a month, until the end of August. Sherman found that the city was not overcome by the bombardment, so, after defeating General W. J. Hardee's Confederate army, he cut all lines of supply to the city. On 2 September, the mayor surrendered the city. Within the next few days, Sherman ordered all citizens to be removed from the city, in violation of the terms of surrender. When the evacuation was completed, he ordered the city burned. All but approximately 400 of the city's 4,500 buildings were destroyed. General Sherman thereupon began his march toward the Savannah and the sea.

Atlanta was quickly rebuilt, and within two months many citizens had returned. In 1866, after Atlanta had become the headquarters for federal Reconstruction officials, the population was estimated at 20,228, almost twice what it was before the war. In 1868 the *Atlanta Constitution* was founded, and its editor, Henry W. Grady, became the voice of the New South. In 1870 the first board of education was elected and the DeGive Opera House opened. By 1873 two more railroads—the Atlanta & Charlotte Railroad and the Georgia Western—converged on the city.

Atlanta University was established in 1867, the same year that the city proposed offering free office space to the state's governing body for ten years and a capitol site if the members of the state's constitutional convention would make Atlanta the state capital. Subsequently, Atlanta became the temporary state capital in 1868, and the permanent capital in 1887.

Two major events heralding Atlanta's rise as an industrial and commercial center were the International Cotton Exposition of 1881 and the Cotton States and International Exposition of 1895. The skyline of

Chronology

1782 First documentary reference to Standing Peach Tree, a Creek settlement.

1813 Fort Gilmer is erected at Standing Peach Tree because of conflict between the Creek and Cherokee Indians.

1821 Indian territorial claims ceded to Georgia.

1836 Legislature approves plan to build Western and Atlantic rail line from Chattanooga, Tennessee, to the Chattahoochee River. Here a settlement named Terminus begins, at what is now the southwestern corner of Wall Street and Central Avenue.

1843 Terminus, now a bustling trading center, is incorporated as the town of Marthasville.

1845 Marthasville is renamed Atlanta.

1847 Atlanta is incorporated as a city.

1853 Atlanta and West Point Railroad is completed. Fulton County is created out of DeKalb County with Atlanta as its seat. The Holland Free School, the first public school, is established.

1854 Atheneum Theater opens, and City Hall is built.

1855 Atlanta Gas Light Company is chartered and the city is illuminated. The Atlanta Medical College is founded.

1861 Georgia secedes from the Union. Atlanta becomes an important Confederate railroad depot and manufacturing center.

1864 Battle of Atlanta takes place with heavy bombardment by Union forces led by General William Sherman. Atlanta is cut off from the rest of the state after the Confederate defeat at the Battle of Jonesboro. Atlanta surrenders. General Sherman orders evacuation of civilians from the city and then begins to destroy it.

1865 Rebuilding of Atlanta begins.

1866 Atlanta becomes federal headquarters for Reconstruction.

1867 The *Atlanta Constitution* newspaper is founded; the Constitutional Convention for Georgia meets in Atlanta; Atlanta University is founded.

1868 Legislature accepts proposal to name Atlanta the state capital.

1870 First board of education is elected; DeGive Opera House opens.

1881 International Cotton Exposition is held in city.

1895 Cotton States and International Exposition is held.

1917 Fire destroys nearly 2,000 buildings along North and Jackson boulevards from Decatur Street to Ponce de Leon Avenue.

1936 Publication of *Gone With the Wind*.

1947 Lochner Transportation Plan is approved and financed by a bond issue of $16.6 million.

1952 Atlanta annexes 81 square miles of surrounding land.

1957 Martin Luther King, Jr., and others found Southern Christian Leadership Conference in Atlanta.

1965 Atlanta-Fulton County Stadium is completed.

1971 Voters approve 61-mile rapid transit train system.

1973 Atlanta elects first black mayor, Maynard Jackson.

1975 Omni International Complex opens.

1973 Peachtree Center Plaza Hotel opens.

1976 World Congress Center opens.

1991 Atlanta selected to host 1996 Summer Olympic Games.

the city began to change as new multistoried buildings replaced older ones. The greatest physical catastrophe to occur since the siege of Atlanta was the blaze that started on 21 May 1917 and rapidly burned the section around North and Jackson boulevards from Decatur Street to Ponce de Leon Avenue.

Industrial growth brought about demographic changes: the slums began to fill with farm families leaving rural areas, and the well-to-do began moving to the suburbs. There was a net loss of population after the 1950s, even though Atlanta still basked in the image of itself created by author Margaret Mitchell in her 1936 novel *Gone With the Wind*. It also prospered as the headquarters of local corporations such as the Coca-Cola Company. In 1952 Atlanta annexed 81 square miles of surrounding land. During the 1960s the city came to be known as one of the most racially progressive cities in the South, since many leaders of the civil rights movement called Atlanta home. Mayor Ivan Allen, Jr., led Atlanta to a peaceful integration of public schools and other facilities. In 1973, when the first black mayor, Maynard Jackson, was voted into office, busing began in the city school system. Atlanta is scheduled to host the Summer Olympic Games in 1996, the year that its 61-mile rapid transit train system is to be completed.

Historical Landmarks

Five Points, where Peachtree, Marietta, Decatur, Edgewood, and Whitehall meet, constitutes Atlanta's downtown hub. There was an artesian well here in the 19th century. The Old Lamppost on the corner of Whitehall and Alabama streets, first lit in 1855, is a relic of the Civil War. The hole in its base is from a shell fragment that hit it during the Siege of Atlanta in 1864. The lamp was lit again at the premiere of the movie *Gone With the Wind* in 1938. The State Capitol on Washington street between Hunter and Mitchell streets was completed in 1889. The capitol dome, which rises 237 feet from the ground, is topped by a figure with a torch in one hand and a sword in the other. The State Office Building is a six-story building built of granite and marble in 1939. The Church of the Immaculate Conception at Central Avenue and King Drive is the oldest church building in the city; it was erected in 1873 to replace an earlier church. The Peace Monument at Piedmont Park and 14th Street is a bronze figure of the Goddess of Peace, created by sculptor Allen Newman and unveiled in 1911. Fort Walker, near the entrance of Grant Park, was a commanding position held by Confederate troops during the Siege of Atlanta. The Cyclorama Building, which faces the Augusta Avenue entrance of Grant Park, displays a painting of the Battle of Atlanta that is approximately 400 feet in circumference and 50 feet high. It depicts the battle as it occurred on Moreland Avenue on 22 July 1864. The Booker T. Washington Monument at the main entrance of Booker T. Washington High School represents the great black educator lifting the veil of ignorance from his race. The Martin Luther King, Jr., Historic Site honors one of Atlanta's most famous sons. The site includes King's childhood home, the Ebenezer Baptist Church, where he preached, and his tomb.

Population

Although the city of Atlanta has been steadily losing population since the end of World War II, it is still the 36th most populous city in the country. In 1990 there were 394,017 inhabitants compared to 425,022 in 1980 and 495,000 in 1970, reflecting a decrease of 14.1% during the 1970s and 7.3% during the 1980s. The greater metropolitan area of Atlanta, however, is the ninth largest metro area in the country and continues to grow with a population of 2.8 million, representing an increase of 32.5% since 1980.

Ethnic Composition

In 1990 blacks made up 67.07% of the population, with the rest of the population 31.05% white, 1.91% Hispanic, 0.14% American Indian, 0.89% Asian and Pacific Islanders, and 0.85% other.

Ethnic Composition (as % of total pop.)		
	1980	1990
White	32.44	31.05
Black	66.56	67.07
American Indian	0.10	0.14
Asian and Pacific Islander	0.47	0.89
Hispanic	1.37	1.91
Other	0.2	0.85

Government

Under its 1974 charter, Atlanta is governed by a strong mayor-council form of government. The mayor is the chief executive while the 18-member council, presided over by a council president, is the legislative arm. All are elected to four-year terms.

Government
Year of Home Charter   1974
Number of Members of the Governing Body   19
Elected at Large   7
Elected by Wards   12
Number of Women in Governing Body   6
Salary of Mayor $100,000
Salary of Council Members $18,400
City Government Employment Total   7,626
Rate per 10,000   180.7

Public Finance

The annual budget consists of revenues of $801.199 million and expenditures of $740.620 million. The debt outstanding

Population		
	1980	1990
Central City	425,022	394,017
Rank	29	36
Metro Area	2,138,143	2,833,511
Pop. Change 1980–1990 +31,005		
Pop. % Change 1980–1990 +7.3		
Median Age 31.5		
% Male 47.7		
% Age 65 and Over 11.31		
Density (per square mile) 2,989.5		

Households
Number   155,752
Persons per Household   2.4
% Female-Headed Households   23.4
% One-Person Households   35
Births—Total   7,967
% to Mothers under 20   20.7
Birth Rate per 1,000   18.7

Public Finance
Total Revenue (in millions) $801.199
Intergovernmental Revenue—Total (in millions) $165.62
Federal Revenue per capita $70.47
% Federal Assistance   8.79
% State Assistance   1.15
Sales Tax as % of Total Revenue   8.03
Local Revenue as % of Total Revenue   74.89
City Income Tax   no
Taxes—Total (in millions) $167
Taxes per capita
Total   396
Property   154

Public Finance (continued)

Sales and Gross Receipts   190
General Expenditures—Total (in millions) $417.9
General Expenditures per capita $990
Capital Outlays per capita $242

% of Expenditures for:
    Public Welfare   0.8
    Highways   4.7
    Education   3.6
    Health and Hospitals   0.1
    Police   9.2
    Sewerage and Sanitation   18.3
    Parks and Recreation   5.8
    Housing and Community Development   3.7
Debt Outstanding per capita $2,416
    % Utility   13.4
Federal Procurement Contract Awards (in millions)
    $305.5
Federal Grants Awards (in millions) $306.0
Fiscal Year Begins   January 1

is $1.068 billion, and cash and security holdings $1.401 billion.

Economy

Atlanta is the undisputed financial, distribution, and manufacturing center of the Southeast. Forty countries have consular or trade offices in Atlanta, and 28 major international banks have offices here. About 35% of Georgia's manufacturing is concentrated in and around Atlanta, although no single industry dominates the economy. Coca-Cola is perhaps the closest to being a quintessential Atlanta corporation, with its tremendous civic and financial clout. Of the top 500 industrial companies in the nation, 422 have operations in Atlanta, and nearly a dozen, including Coca-Cola, Fuqua Industries, Georgia Pacific, Gold Kist, and Scientific Atlanta, have their headquarters here.

Economy

Total Money Income (in millions) $4,353
% of State Average   101.5
Per capita Annual Income $10,341
% Population below Poverty Level   27.5
Fortune 500 Companies   6

Banks	Number	Deposits (in millions)
Commercial	64	14,000
Savings	20	8,760

Passenger Autos   336,783
Electric Meters   NA
Gas Meters   NA

Manufacturing

Number of Establishments   703
% with 20 or More Employees   39.7
Manufacturing Payroll (in millions) $1,128
Value Added by Manufacture (in millions) $2,413.3
Value of Shipments (in millions) $4,803.4
New Capital Expenditures (in millions) $191.8

Wholesale Trade

Number of Establishments   1,543
Sales (in millions) $13,590.9
Annual Payroll (in millions) $676.231

Economy (continued)

Retail Trade

Number of Establishments   3,843
Total Sales (in millions) $3,239.1
Sales per capita $7,677
Number of Retail Trade Establishments with Payroll   2,914
Annual Payroll (in millions) $499.6
Total Sales (in millions) $3,196.1
General Merchandise Stores (per capita)   NA
Food Stores (per capita) $1,035
Apparel Stores (per capita) $575
Eating and Drinking Places (per capita) $1,290

Service Industries

Total Establishments   4,913
Total Receipts (in millions) $4,344.2
Hotels and Motels (in millions)   NA
Health Services (in millions) $539.9
Legal Services (in millions) $682.1

Labor

Metropolitan Atlanta's steady growth has resulted in more than 500,000 new jobs since 1980. This growth has spared Atlanta much of the agonizing readjustment that the Northeast went through during the early 1990s recession. Interestingly, the government share of the employment market is almost as high as that of manufacturing and retail and wholesale. Trade and services together account for just over 50% of employment.

Labor

Civilian Labor Force   227,915
% Change 1989–1990   0.5

Work Force Distribution
    Mining   1,100
    Construction   59,600
    Manufacturing   171,300
    Transportation and Public Utilities   127,000
    Wholesale and Retail Trade   396,300
    FIRE (Finance, Insurance, Real Estate)   104,800
    Service   336,300
    Government   206,800
    Women as % of Labor Force   48
    % Self-Employed   4.7
    % Professional/Technical   NA
Total Unemployment   16,429
Rate %   7.2
Federal Government Civilian Employment   21,036

Education

The Atlanta City School System supports 81 elementary schools, 15 junior high/middle schools, 18 senior high schools, and 18 schools that fall into more than one category. The public school system is supplemented by more than 170 private and parochial schools and an international school. Metropolitan Atlanta has over 40 institutions of higher education, of which 6 major public and 2 private institutions are in the city itself. The most important public institutions are Georgia State University, Georgia Institute of Technology, Kennesaw College,

Education

Number of Public Schools 114
Special Education Schools NA
Total Enrollment 60,795
% Enrollment in Private Schools NA
% Minority NA
Classroom Teachers 3,829
Pupil-Teacher Ratio 15.8:1
Number of Graduates 2,814
Total Revenue (in millions) $424.171
Total Expenditures (in millions) $367.911
Expenditures per Pupil $4,987
Educational Attainment (Age 25 and Over)
   % Completed 12 or More Years 60.2
   % Completed 16 or More Years 20.5
Four-Year Colleges and Universities 14
Enrollment 56,688
Two-Year Colleges 3
Enrollment 3,149

Libraries

Number 96
Public Libraries 22
Books (in thousands) 1,451
Circulation (in thousands) 2,104
Persons Served (in thousands) 668
Circulation per Person Served 3.14
Income (in millions) $15.887
Staff 524

Four-Year Colleges and Universities
  Atlanta Christian College
  Atlanta College of Art
  Clark Atlanta University
  Clayton State College
  DeVry Institute of Technology
  Emory University
  Georgia Institute of Technology
  Georgia State University
  Kennesaw University
  Mercer University Southern School of Pharmacy
  Morehouse College
  Morehouse School of Medicine
  Morris Brown College
  Oglethorpe University
  Southern College of Technology
  Spelman College

Clayton State College, and Southern College of Technology. Of the private institutions, Emory University is the most prestigious. The Atlanta University Center is the largest consortium of black institutions in the nation, and includes the undergraduate Clark College, Morehouse College, Spelman College, and Morris Brown College, as well as the graduate school of Atlanta University. Among other institutions are Mercer University Graduate and Professional Center, Oglethorpe University, Art Institute of Atlanta, Brenau College, and DeVry Institute of Technology.

Health

Atlanta has 25 metro hospitals with a total of 5,539 beds. The premier institutions are Grady Memorial Hospital, a teaching hospital for Emory University; Emory University Hospital; Georgia Baptist Hospital and Medical Center; Piedmont Hospital; Crawford W. Long

Memorial Hospital of Emory University; Northside Hospital; and West Paces Ferry Hospital. Mental health care is available at Charter Peachford Hospital, CPC Parkwood Hospital, Charter Brook Hospital, and the Georgia Mental Health Institute; and pediatric care at Henrietta Egleston Hospital and Scottish Rite Hospital.

Health

Deaths—Total 4,721
Rate per 1,000 11.1
Infant Deaths—Total 148
Rate per 1,000 18.6
Number of Metro Hospitals 25
Number of Metro Hospital Beds 5,539
Rate per 100,000 1,313
Number of Physicians 4,963
Physicians per 1,000 1.99
Nurses per 1,000 13.64
Health Expenditures per capita NA

Transportation

Atlanta is accessible by way of three interstates, I-75, I-20, and I-85, linked by the perimeter highway I-285. Commuter traffic is heavy. Public transportation is provided by a municipal bus service and light rail service known as MARTA (Metropolitan Atlanta Rapid Transport Authority). Rail passenger service is provided by Amtrak and rail freight service by CSX and Norfolk-Southern Railway. Atlanta's Hartsfield International Airport, ten miles from downtown, is one of the busiest in the nation; it is served by more than 20 commercial airlines offering direct flights to most major cities of the world. In addition, there are 18 other small air terminals. Atlanta is a Foreign Trade Zone with special facilities for importers and exporters.

Transportation

Interstate Highway Mileage 221
Total Urban Mileage 8,765
Total Daily Vehicle Mileage (in millions) 73.733
Daily Average Commute Time 54.3
Number of Buses 664
Port Tonnage (in millions) NA
Airports 1
Number of Daily Flights 644
Daily Average Number of Passengers 55,884

Airlines (American carriers only)
  American
  American West
  Continental
  Delta
  Eastern
  Midway
  Northwest
  Trans World
  United
  USAir

Housing

Many Atlanta residents are moving to the suburbs, where housing construction is concentrated. Of the housing units available in 1990, 43.1% were owner-occupied. The median value of an owner-occupied home was $71,200, and the median monthly rent was $342. The Midtown area is high-rise and high-rent, and also contains most of the older apartment buildings. The trendy Buckhead area is also fairly high-cost.

Housing

Total Housing Units   182,754
% Change 1980–1990   2.1
Vacant Units for Sale or Rent   21,547
Occupied Units   155,752
% with More Than One Person per Room   6.5
% Owner-Occupied   43.1
Median Value of Owner-Occupied Homes $71,200
Average Monthly Purchase Cost $335
Median Monthly Rent $342
New Private Housing Starts   2,525
Value (in thousands) $145,649
% Single-Family   16.8
Nonresidential Buildings Value (in thousands) $201,365

Tallest Buildings	Hgt. (ft.)	Stories
C & S Plaza		
600 Peachtree St. (1992)	1,050	57
One Peachtree Center (1992)	880	63
Atlantic Center/IBM (1988)	828	52
191 Peachtree (1990)	770	54
Westin Peachtree Plaza (1973)	723	71
Georgia Pacific Tower (1981)	697	51
Promenade II/AT&T (1989)	691	40
Southern Bell Telephone (1980)	677	47

Urban Redevelopment

Downtown development was the order of the day in the 1960s and 1970s. The two decades saw the construction of the Merchandise Mart, Apparel Mart, and numerous hotels and office complexes. Many of these buildings were the work of architect John Portman, whose massive concrete and glass structures have come to symbolize the new Atlanta. One important trend is the shift of the town to the south, reversing the historic push to the north; most of the new infrastructure is being concentrated in the south.

Crime

In 1991 there were 11,610 violent crimes known to police and 60,109 crimes involving property.

Religion

Atlanta is the center of the Black Baptists, who constitute nearly 30% of the population. The next two largest denominations are Southern Baptists (23%) and United Methodists (16%).

Crime

Violent Crimes—Total   11,610
Violent Crime Rate per 100,000   987.9
Murder   205
Rape   638
Robbery   6,479
Aggravated Assaults   8,967
Property Crimes   60,109
Burglary   13,861
Larceny   35,237
Motor Vehicle Theft   11,011
Arson   288
Per capita Police Expenditures $161.07
Per capita Fire Protection Expenditures $87.64
Number of Police   1,278
Per 1,000   29.3

Religion

Largest Denominations (Adherents)

Catholic	29,062
Southern Baptist	90,331
United Methodist	62,725
Black Baptist	114,926
Presbyterian	28,296
Episcopal	17,860
Church of God	15,323
Jewish	14,915

Media

The Atlanta press consists of two dailies: the *Atlanta Constitution* in the morning and in the evening, the *Atlanta Journal*. The papers combine on Saturdays and Sundays. *The Atlanta Daily World*, published four times a week, and three weeklies serve the black community. The electronic media consist of 8 television stations and 22 FM and AM radio stations.

Media

Newsprint
  Atlanta, monthly
  Atlanta Business Chronicle, weekly
  Atlanta Constitution, daily
  Atlanta Daily World, 4x/wk.
  Atlanta Impressions, quarterly
  The Atlanta Inquirer, weekly
  Atlanta Journal, daily
  Atlanta Voice, weekly

Television
  WAGA (Channel 5)
  WATL (Channel 36)
  WGNX (Channel 46)
  WPBA (Channel 30)
  WSB (Channel 2)
  WTBS (Channel 17)
  WVEU (Channel 69)
  WXIA (Channel 11)

Radio

WABE (FM)	WAEC (AM)
WAOK (AM)	WVEE (FM)
WAPW (FM)	WCLK (FM)
WCNN (AM)	WGKA (AM)
WGST (AM)	WPCH (FM)
WIGO (AM)	WKHX (AM)

Media (continued)

WKHX (FM)	WKLS (FM)
WQXI (AM)	WRAS (FM)
WREK (FM)	WRFG (FM)
WSB (AM)	WSB (FM)
WYZE (AM)	WZGC (FM)

Sports

Atlanta is home to four professional sports teams: the Braves in National League baseball, the Falcons in the National Football League, the Hawks in the National Basketball Association, and the Knights in the International Hockey League. The Braves play at Atlanta-Fulton County Stadium and the Hawks and Knights play at the Omni Coliseum. The Georgia Dome is home for the Atlanta Falcons. Auto races are held at Atlanta International Raceway, about 25 miles south, and Road Atlanta, 40 miles to the north. Among other events on the sporting calendar are the Atlanta Golf Classic and the Atlanta Hunt and Steeple Chase.

Arts, Culture, and Tourism

The Woodruff Arts Center includes the High Art Museum, a collection of permanent and visiting exhibits, and the Atlanta Memorial Arts Building, with facilities for the Atlanta Symphony Orchestra, Alliance Theater, Atlanta Children's Theater, and the Atlanta College of Art. The city's oldest resident company, the Academy Theater produces dramas and musicals year-round; Skeleton Theater and Theatrical Outfit presents experimental shows, and the Theater of the Stars produces musicals. You can find Broadway-style shows at the Alliance and Fox theaters. Just Us Theater and A.T.L.A.N.T.A. are two notable black repertory companies. The Atlanta Center for Puppetry Arts presents shows for adults and children. Other professional and amateur entertainment groups include the Atlanta Ballet (one of the oldest civic ballet companies in the nation), Atlanta Community Orchestra, Choral Guild of Atlanta, Ruth Mitchell Dance Company, Phoenix Opera Company, and Atlanta Chamber Players. Mime is presented by the Great American Mime Experiment and Company Kaye. The Atlanta Arts Festival is held each fall in Piedmont Park. With a few excep-

tions most of Atlanta's art is showcased in private galleries such as Nexus Gallery. Other notable museums are the Ben W. Fortson, Jr. State Archives and Records Building, the Toy Museum, and Chastain Gallery. The Fernbank Museum of Natural History is on Clifton Road.

Parks and Recreation

Atlanta has over 5,000 acres of parks. The 185-acre Piedmont Park is the site of the annual fall arts festival. The 140-acre Grant Park is the site of Fort Walker and the Cyclorama Building. Lakewood Park on Pryot Street and Lakewood Avenue, founded in 1895, covers 366 acres.

Sources of Further Information

Atlanta Chamber of Commerce
235 International Boulevard, NW
Atlanta, GA 30303
(404) 880-9000

Atlanta Convention and Visitors Bureau
233 Peachtree Street
Atlanta, GA 30303
(404) 521-6600

City Hall
68 Mitchell Street
Atlanta, GA 30335
(404) 330-6100

Additional Reading

Garrett, Franklin M. *Atlanta and Environs: A Chronicle of Its People and Events*, 2 vols. 1982.

Hamer, Andrew Marshall, ed. *Urban Atlanta: Redefining the Role of the City.* 1980.

Kuhn, Cliff, Harlon E. Joyce, and E. Bernard West. *Living Atlanta: An Oral History of the City, 1914–1948.* 1990.

Kurtz, Wilbur G. *Atlanta and the Old South: Paintings and Drawings.* 1969.

Lankevich, George, ed. *Atlanta: A Chronological & Documentary History, 1813–1976.* 1978.

McLeod, Jonathan W. *Workers and Workplace Dynamics in Reconstruction-era Atlanta: A Case Study.* 1990.

McPheeters, Annie L. *Negro Progress in Atlanta, Georgia, 1961–1970.* 1972.

Russell, James M. *Atlanta, 1847–1890: City Building in the Old South and the New.* 1988.

Shavin, Norman. *The Atlanta Century, March 1860–May 1865*, 6th ed. 1981.

Stone, Clarence N. *Regime Politics: Governing Atlanta, 1946–1988.* 1989.

Watts, Eugene J. *The Social Bases of City Politics: Atlanta, 1865–1903.* 1978.

Williford, William Bailey. *Peachtree Street, Atlanta.* 1962.

Travel and Tourism

Hotel Rooms   20,000
Convention and Exhibit Space (square feet)   NA

Convention Centers
   Atlanta City Auditorium/Convention Hall

Festivals
   Miss America Pageant (September)
   Unlocking of the Ocean (May)
   Harbor Fest (July)
   Wedding of the Sea (August)

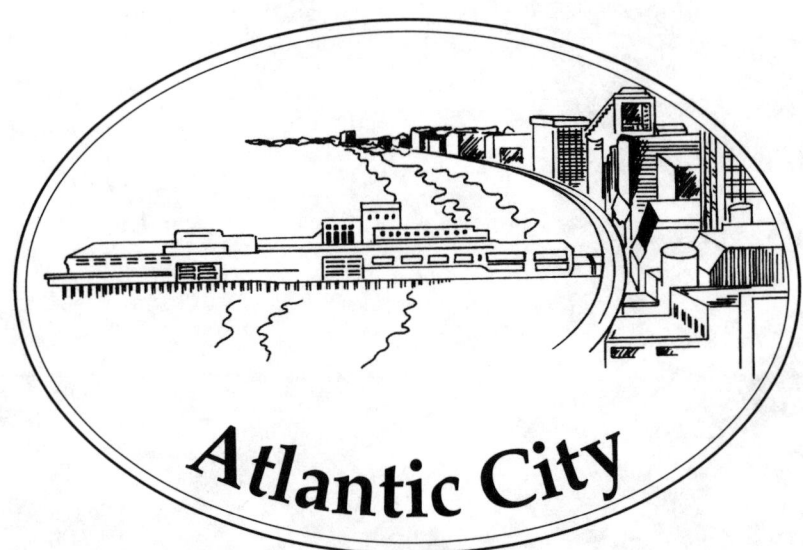

Atlantic City
New Jersey

Basic Data

Name   Atlantic City
Name Origin   From Atlantic Ocean
Year Founded   1783 Inc. 1854
Status: State   New Jersey
          County   Atlantic
Area (square miles)   11.4
Elevation (feet)   10
Time Zone   EST
Population (1990)   37,986
Population of Metro Area (1990)   319,416

Distance in Miles To:

Newark	118
Camden	59
Trenton	74
New York	41

Location and Topography

N

Atlantic City is a coastal resort city on Absecon Island, a sandy, 10-mile-long island off the southeast shore of New Jersey in Atlantic County. It is only connected to the mainland by bridges and artificial roadways. The area surrounding Atlantic City is made up of tidal flats, bays, inlets, and marshes; and the Atlantic Intracoastal Waterway passes nearby. Atlantic City rises only 10 to 20 feet above sea level.

Layout of City and Suburbs

The city is a grid of streets parallel to and at right angles to its famous Boardwalk. The Boardwalk, made of hardwood planks over concrete and steel, is 60 feet wide and 4 1/8th miles long. The shore side of the Boardwalk is lined with casino-hotels and stores, including the Ocean One mall. Inland, smaller hotels and boardinghouses crowd nar-

row streets. Chelsea is the upscale residential section, with large villas and well-tended lawns.

Environment

Environmental Stress Index   NA
Green Cities Index: Rank   NA
                    Score   NA
Water Quality   Acid, soft, 45.0 fluoridated
    Average Daily Use (gallons per capita)   NA
    Maximum Supply (gallons per capita)   NA
Parkland as % of Total City Area   NA
% Waste Landfilled/Recycled   NA
Annual Parks Expenditures per capita   NA

Climate

The moderating influence of the Atlantic Ocean's Gulf Stream is responsible for Atlantic City's generally balmy climate, which is milder than inland places at the same latitude. Summers are cooler, averaging in the low to mid-70s, while winters are milder, with temperatures generally in the 30 °F range. The city is subject to seasonal storms and hurricanes, although precipitation is moderate and distributed evenly throughout the year.

Weather

Temperature

Highest Monthly Average °F   84.7
Lowest Monthly Average °F   24.0

Annual Averages

Days 32°F or Below   15
Days above 90°F   16
Zero Degree Days   1
Precipitation (inches)   46
Snow (inches)   16
% Seasonal Humidity   73
Wind Speed (m.p.h.)   10.7

ATLANTIC CITY, NJ

From *New Jersey State Road Atlas* ©1991. Maspeth, NJ: Hagstrom Map Co.

Weather (continued)			
Clear Days 96			
Cloudy Days 161			
Storm Days 25			
Rainy Days 112			
Average Temperatures (°F)	*High*	*Low*	*Mean*
January	41.4	24.0	32.7
February	42.9	24.9	33.9
March	50.7	31.5	41.1
April	62.3	41.0	51.7
May	72.4	50.7	61.6
June	80.8	59.7	70.3
July	84.7	65.4	75.1
August	83.0	63.8	73.4
September	77.3	56.8	67.1
October	67.5	45.9	56.7
November	55.9	36.1	46.0
December	44.2	26.0	35.1

History

The first white settler was Jeremiah Leeds, a lieutenant in the colonial army who built a cabin on Absecon Island in 1783. Nearly a century later, in the early 1850s, Dr. Jonathan Pitney realized the location's potential as a health spa and resort. Pitney and a group of investors obtained a railroad charter to bring the Camden & Atlantic Railroad to the island in 1852. A year later the railroad company assigned its chief engineer, Richard B. Osborne, to lay out a city. Besides giving the city its name, he named streets at right angles to the shore for U.S. states and those parallel to the shore for oceans and seas. In 1854 the town was incorporated, held its first election (in which 18 ballots were cast), and saw the arrival of the first train. By 1877 traffic was so great that a second railroad was built to span the 50 miles between Camden and Atlantic City. A third railroad, the West Jersey & Atlantic Railroad, opened in 1880.

The first boardwalk was built in 1870, and the first pier into the Atlantic was built in 1882; by 1887 people in wicker rolling chairs, adapted from wheelchairs, were being pushed up and down the Boardwalk. Atlantic City brought the world saltwater taffy in 1883, picture postcards in 1893, and the Miss America Pageant in 1921. In 1929 the city completed an auditorium and convention hall that covered seven acres, the largest building at the time without roof posts. The board game, Monopoly, which features Atlantic City names such as Boardwalk and St. James Place, was introduced in 1929. In 1976 New Jersey citizens voted to legalize gambling, and the first casino opened two years later. Gambling, which attracts busloads of people from New York, Philadelphia, Baltimore, and Washington, D.C., has revived an economy that had been in decline in the 1960s and early 1970s.

Historical Landmarks

The Absecon Lighthouse, erected in 1854, is now a state historic site at Rhode Island and Pacific Avenues and houses a marine environmental museum. Gardner's Basin, in the northern inlet section of town, re-creates a 19th century seafarer's village. The World War II Memorial is at the corner of Ventnor and Albany avenues.

The Boardwalk is Atlantic City's best-known attraction. It is a 60-foot-wide hardwood promenade that stretches 4-1/8 miles along the shore southward into Ventnor City.

Population

The population of Atlantic City has declined over the past few decades, even though the city is now prospering as the gambling capital of the East Coast. In 1990 the population was 37,986, compared to 40,199 in 1980, a decline of 5.5%. The population in 1970 was 47,859.

Population		
	1980	*1990*
Central City	40,199	37,986
Rank	647	666
Metro Area	276,385	319,416
Pop. Change 1980–1990 -2,213		
Pop. % Change 1980–1990 -5.5		
Median Age 38.9		
% Male 43.1		
% Age 65 and Over 19.2		
Density (per square mile) 3,332.1		
Households		
Number 15,731		
Persons per Household 2.30		
% Female-Headed Households 22.8		
% One-Person Households 40.6		
Births—Total 677		
% to Mothers under 20 29.5		
Birth Rate per 1,000 18.4		

Ethnic Composition

In 1990 the majority of the city's population were black (51.3%), while there were 35.5% whites and 15.3% Hispanics (both black and white); other races make up the balance.

Ethnic Composition (as % of total pop.)		
	1980	*1990*
White	46.3	35.45
Black	49.82	51.31
American Indian	0.15	0.51
Asian and Pacific Islander	0.63	3.97
Hispanic	5.78	15.30
Other	NA	8.76

Government

Atlantic City has a mayor-council form of government. There are nine members of the governing body, three are elected at large and six are elected by wards.

Public Finance

Education accounts for 26.9% of Atlantic City's expenditures, seconded only by police expenditures, which account for 20.9% of the city's expenditures.

Chronology

1783 Jeremiah Leeds builds a cabin on Absecon Island.

1852 The Camden & Atlantic Railroad plans a spur from Camden to Absecon Island.

1853 Chief engineer Richard Osborne lays out the city and names it Atlantic City for the Camden & Atlantic Railroad.

1854 Atlantic City is incorporated; first train arrives from Camden.

1870 The Boardwalk is built, the first of its kind in the U.S.

1877 A second railroad is built to link Atlantic City with Camden.

1882 The first amusement pier is built.

1883 Saltwater taffy becomes an instant favorite of visitors after an entrepreneur promotes his candies soaked in salt water.

1887 Local hardware store owner William Hayday designs rolling wicker chairs for use on the Boardwalk.

1893 Carl M. Voelker prints the first picture postcards.

1921 The first Miss America Pageant is held in Atlantic City.

1929 The seven-acre City Auditorium and Convention Hall is built; Monopoly, a board game, makes Atlantic City features known worldwide.

1944 Hurricane causes extensive damage to beach and Boardwalk.

1976 New Jersey voters approve referendum legalizing gambling in Atlantic City.

1978 The first casino, Resorts International, opens.

Economy

Atlantic City's economy is based on tourism, including conventions, and gambling. Each year 33 million visitors come to the city. There are now 12 gambling casinos and hotels, while the city's hotel accommodations enable it to host 4,400 conventions and trade shows a year. Casinos, hotels, and conventions annually generate about $3.5 billion in business. The casino industry also generates an additional $3 billion in spinoff businesses. Over $5 billion was spent in hotel and casino construction in the 1980s.

Labor

Legalized gambling, hotels, and tourism employ 85% of Atlantic City's workers and provide 70,000 jobs. The 15 largest

Government

Year of Home Charter   NA
Number of Members of the Governing Body   9
Elected at Large   3
Elected by Wards   6
Number of Women in Governing Body   NA
Salary of Mayor   NA
Salary of Council Members   NA
City Government Employment Total   2,868
Rate per 10,000   797.1

Public Finance

Total Revenue (in millions)   NA
Intergovernmental Revenue—Total (in millions)   NA
Federal Revenue per capita   NA
% Federal Assistance   NA
% State Assistance   NA
Sales Tax as % of Total Revenue   NA
Local Revenue as % of Total Revenue   NA
City Income Tax   no
Taxes—Total (in millions) $68.2

Taxes per capita
Total   1,894
Property   1,823
Sales and Gross Receipts   NA
General Expenditures—Total (in millions) $99.7
General Expenditures per capita $2,771
Capital Outlays per capita $16

% of Expenditures for:
   Public Welfare   0.9
   Highways   3.6
   Education   26.9
   Health and Hospitals   1.6
   Police   20.9
   Sewerage and Sanitation   2.6
   Parks and Recreation   2.5
   Housing and Community Development   0.0
Debt Outstanding per capita $848
   % Utility   1.0
Federal Procurement Contract Awards (in millions) $8.1
Federal Grants Awards (in millions) $12.6
Fiscal Year Begins   January 1

Economy

Total Money Income (in millions) $331.2
% of State Average   70.1
Per capita Annual Income $9,205
% Population below Poverty Level   24.9
Fortune 500 Companies   NA

Banks	Number	Deposits (in millions)
Commercial	9	12,300
Savings	6	11,300

Passenger Autos   NA
Electric Meters   100,281
Gas Meters   49,529

Manufacturing

Number of Establishments   NA
% with 20 or More Employees   NA
Manufacturing Payroll (in millions)   NA
Value Added by Manufacture (in millions)   NA
Value of Shipments (in millions)   NA
New Capital Expenditures (in millions)   NA

Wholesale Trade

Number of Establishments   40
Sales (in millions)   NA
Annual Payroll (in millions)   NA

Economy (continued)

Retail Trade

Number of Establishments 545
Total Sales (in millions) $421.5
Sales per capita $11,715
Number of Retail Trade Establishments with Payroll 456
Annual Payroll (in millions) $54.4
Total Sales (in millions) $415.6
General Merchandise Stores (per capita) $139
Food Stores (per capita) $903
Apparel Stores (per capita) $1,149
Eating and Drinking Places (per capita) $1,750

Service Industries

Total Establishments 422
Total Receipts (in millions) $3,126.3
Hotels and Motels (in millions) $2,963.1
Health Services (in millions) $25.5
Legal Services (in millions) $39.4

Labor

Civilian Labor Force (Metro) 187,878
% Change 1989–1990 5.0

Work Force Distribution
Mining NA
Construction 6,000
Manufacturing 7,300
Transportation and Public Utilities 6,700
Wholesale and Retail Trade 34,900
FIRE (Finance, Insurance, Real Estate) 6,500
Service 77,600
Government 27,800
Women as % of Labor Force NA
% Self-Employed NA
% Professional/Technical 11.1
Total Unemployment 2,012
Rate % 7.8
Federal Government Civilian Employment 1,850

employers are casinos whose combined payroll is over $1 billion. Casino hotels employ an average of 41,000 full-time personnel. Seasonal employment swings have decreased from an average of nearly 30% in the 1970s to 4.1% in 1991. Although unemployment has declined since 1978, the unemployment rate in 1990 was 9.6% for the city while the state unemployment rate was 5.7%.

Education

The public school system consists of one senior high school, two junior high/middle schools, and eight elemen-

Education

Number of Public Schools 11
Special Education Schools NA
Total Enrollment 6,022
% Enrollment in Private Schools 13.9
% Minority NA
Classroom Teachers NA
Pupil-Teacher Ratio 25:1
Number of Graduates NA
Total Revenue (in millions) NA
Total Expenditures (in millions) NA
Expenditures per Pupil NA

Education (continued)

Educational Attainment (Age 25 and Over)
% Completed 12 or More Years 48.1
% Completed 16 or More Years 7.7
Four-Year Colleges and Universities NA
Enrollment NA
Two-Year Colleges NA
Enrollment NA

Libraries

Number 2
Public Libraries 2
Books (in thousands) 101.09
Circulation (in thousands) 131.3
Persons Served (in thousands) 40.1
Circulation per Person Served 3.27
Income (in millions) $1,471
Staff 35

Four-Year Colleges and Universities
NA

tary schools. There are no institutions of higher education within the city.

Health

The Atlantic City Medical Center, founded in 1898, is a 615-bed facility affiliated with the Hanneman University in Philadelphia. It has recently added a trauma unit. Atlantic City has one other metro hospital.

Health

Deaths—Total 772
Rate per 1,000 21.0
Infant Deaths—Total 16
Rate per 1,000 23.6
Number of Metro Hospitals 2
Number of Metro Hospital Beds 709
Rate per 100,000 1,971
Number of Physicians NA
Physicians per 1,000 NA
Nurses per 1,000 NA
Health Expenditures per capita NA

Transportation

Atlantic City is reached via the Atlantic City Expressway, which connects with the Garden State Parkway, the New Jersey Turnpike, and other interstate highways. U.S. 30 and U.S. 40/322 also lead into the city, ending in Absecon Boulevard and Albany Avenue, respectively. More than 60% of Atlantic City's visitors arrive by car. Trains arrive at the station adjacent to the Convention Center Complex; passenger service is provided by Amtrak. Thirty-five percent of Atlantic City's visitors arrive by charter bus. Numerous commercial buses use the public bus terminal at Arctic and Arkansas avenues, and New Jersey Transit operates more than 60 buses within the city. The International Airport at Pomona is nine miles west of town. Bader Field, the municipal downtown airport, handles commuter traf-

Transportation

Interstate Highway Mileage	NA
Total Urban Mileage	NA
Total Daily Vehicle Mileage (in millions)	NA
Daily Average Commute Time	44.2 min.
Number of Buses	65
Port Tonnage (in millions)	NA
Airports	2
Number of Daily Flights	NA
Daily Average Number of Passengers	NA

Airlines (American carriers only)
Trans World
TrumpAir
USAir

fic as well as charter airplane and helicopter flights; helicopters also land at the Trump heliport.

Housing

Since 1979, 5,392 housing units have been constructed in Atlantic City, and available housing has increased by 20% throughout Atlantic County. Some of the new housing was built with funds from a $654-million project directed by the Casino Reinvestment Development Authority and funded by a 1.25% tax on gross casino revenues. The building project continues. In 1990 there were 15,731 housing units, of which 30.4% were owner-occupied. The median value of a house was $73,400, and the average monthly rent was $394.

Housing

Total Housing Units	21,626
% Change 1980–1990	0.5
Vacant Units for Sale or Rent	2,456
Occupied Units	15,731
% with More Than One Person per Room	8.8
% Owner-Occupied	30.4
Median Value of Owner-Occupied Homes	$73,400
Average Monthly Purchase Cost	NA
Median Monthly Rent	$394
New Private Housing Starts	52
Value (in thousands)	$11,258
% Single-Family	57.7
Nonresidential Buildings Value (in thousands)	$314

Urban Redevelopment

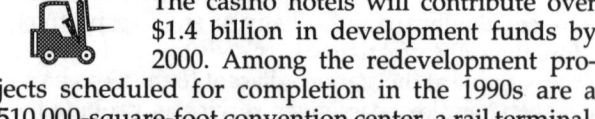

The casino hotels will contribute over $1.4 billion in development funds by 2000. Among the redevelopment projects scheduled for completion in the 1990s are a 510,000-square-foot convention center, a rail terminal, and modernization of the airport at Pomona.

Crime

Of the 29,002 crimes known to the Atlantic City police force in 1991, there were 1,406 violent crimes and 13,047 crimes involving property.

Crime

Violent Crimes—Total	1,406
Violent Crime Rate per 100,000	879.2
Murder	15
Rape	82
Robbery	636
Aggravated Assaults	673
Property Crimes	13,047
Burglary	1,737
Larceny	10,754
Motor Vehicle Theft	556
Arson	96
Per capita Police Expenditures	NA
Per capita Fire Protection Expenditures	NA
Number of Police	405
Per 1,000	104.9

Religion

Atlantic County's largest denomination is Catholic, which accounts for 20.7% of Atlantic City's metro population.

Religion

Largest Denominations (Adherents)	
Catholic	66,328
Black Baptist	9,240
United Methodist	5,492
Evangelical Lutheran	3,025
Episcopal	1,979
Presbyterian	1,601
Jewish	15,800

Media

The Press of Atlantic, a morning paper, is the city's only daily. There are five AM and FM radio stations in Atlantic City. There is no local television station, but signals are received from New York and Philadelphia.

Media

Newsprint
The Press of Atlantic, daily

Television
None

Radio

WFPG (AM)	WFPG (FM)
WMGM (FM)	WMID (FM)
WUSS (AM)	

Sports

The Atlantic City Race Course, 14 miles west of the city, presents thoroughbred racing in the summer. Some casino hotels specialize in championship boxing matches. Annual events such as the Archery Classic in late April are very popular.

Arts, Culture, and Tourism

The casino hotels regularly present big-name entertainers and performers. The Atlantic City Art Center and Atlantic

City Historical Museum, both located on Garden Pier, have recently been renovated at a cost of $5 million. The Art Center sponsors 11 fine arts shows each year.

Travel and Tourism
Hotel Rooms 20,000
Convention and Exhibit Space (square feet) NA
Convention Centers
Atlantic City Auditorium/Convention Hall
Festivals
Miss America Pageant (September)
Unlocking of the Ocean (May)
Harbor Fest (July)
Wedding of the Sea (August)

Parks and Recreation

Almost all recreational activity is concentrated in the casinos, although the Absecon Lighthouse State Historic site is nearby. The Brigantine National Wildlife Refuge is just up the coast on Great Bay.

Sources of Further Information

Atlantic City Convention and Visitors Bureau
2314 Pacific Avenue
Atlantic City, NJ 08401
(609) 348-7100

Atlantic City Free Public Library
One North Tennessee Avenue
Atlantic City, NJ 08401
(609) 345-2269

City Hall
Atlantic City, NJ 08401
(609) 347-5400

Department of Planning and Development
City Hall
Atlantic City, NJ 08401
(609) 347-5404

Additional Reading

Frommer's Atlantic City & Cape May. 1991.

Funnell, Charles E. *By the Beautiful Sea: The Rise and High Times of that Great American Resort, Atlantic City.* 1983.

Sternlieb, George and James W. Hughes. *The Atlantic City Gamble: Twentieth Century Fund Report.* 1983.

Augusta

Maine

Climate

The summers are pleasant, but the winters are relatively harsh, although moderated because of proximity to the Atlantic Ocean. Freezing temperatures are normal from early October to mid-April or early May. Precipitation is evenly distributed through the year.

Weather

Temperature

Highest Monthly Average °F   54.6
Lowest Monthly Average °F   35.6

Annual Averages

Days 32°F or Below   160
Days above 90°F   5
Zero Degree Days   15
Precipitation (inches)   41.0
Snow (inches)   74
% Seasonal Humidity   74
Wind Speed (m.p.h.)   8.8
Clear Days   107
Cloudy Days   160
Storm Days   18
Rainy Days   127

Average Temperatures (°F)	High	Low	Mean
January	31.2	11.7	21.5
February	33.3	12.5	22.9

Location and Topography

Augusta, capital of Maine and county seat of Kennebec County, lies on the Kennebec River in southwestern Maine, in an area of lakes, ponds, and low, wooded hills. It is about 35 miles inland from the Atlantic coast and 45 miles north of Portland, Maine's largest city.

Layout of City and Suburbs

Augusta rises in a series of terraces and sharp hills on both sides of the Kennebec River. Businesses, industries, and residences are so segregated that visitors seldom realize that the city is more than a pleasant residential community built around the state government center. The Capitol and the Key Bank building dominate the city skyline. The city does not have a feeling of overcrowding, and there are no slums.

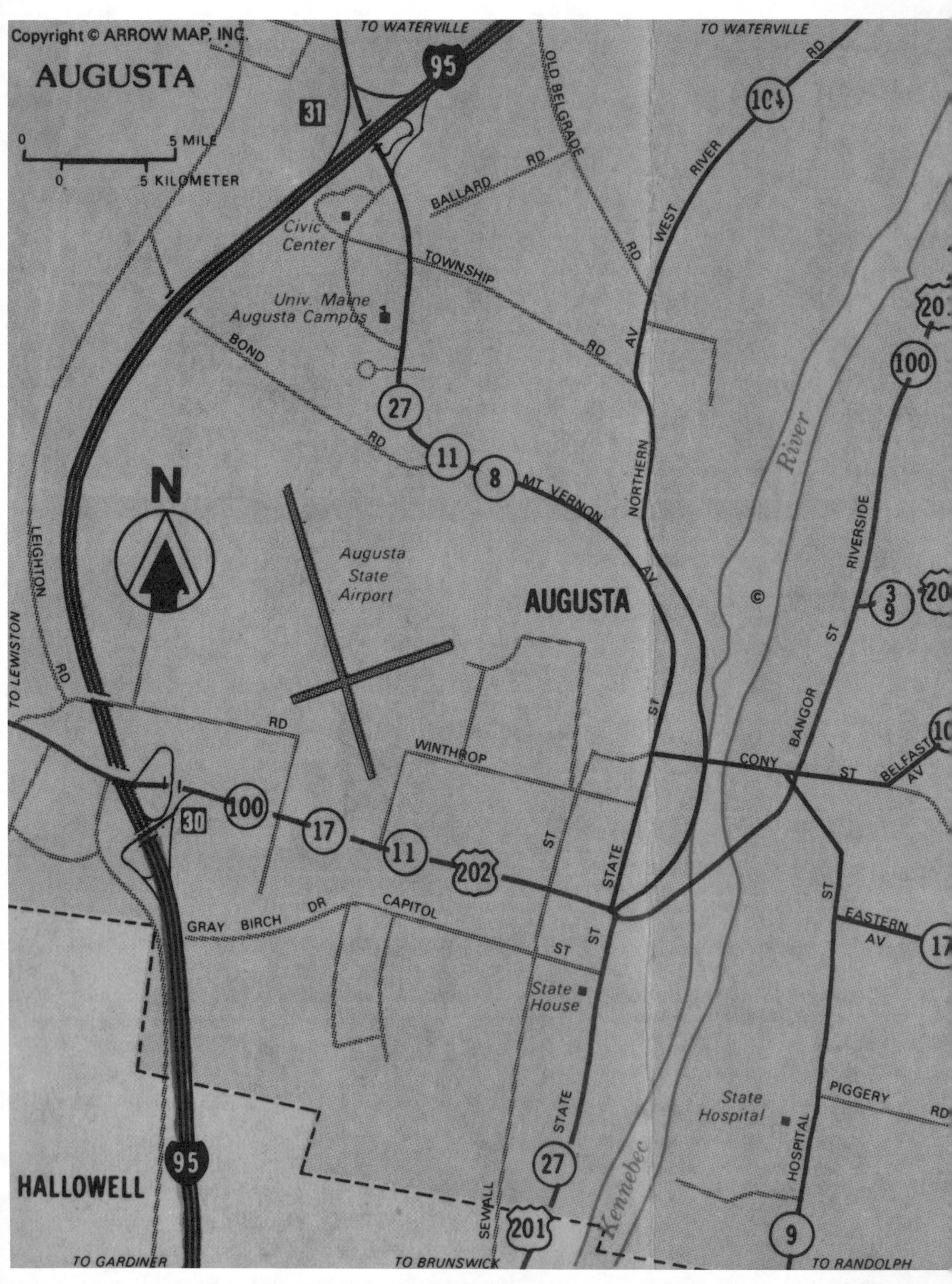

AUGUSTA

TO WATERVILLE

TO WATERVILLE

95

31

10‡

OLD BELGRADE

BALLARD RD

Civic Center

TOWNSHIP

RD

WEST RIVER RD

20

100

Univ. Maine Augusta Campus

BOND

27

11

8

MT. VERNON

NORTHERN AV

River

RIVERSIDE ST

3 9

20

N

Augusta State Airport

AUGUSTA

ST

BANGOR ST

10

RD

WINTHROP

CONY

ST

BELFAST AV

TO LEWISTON RD

30

100

17

11

202

STATE

GRAY BIRCH DR

CAPITOL

ST

ST

EASTERN AV

17

State House

LEIGHTON

Kennebec

State Hospital

PIGGERY RD

HOSPITAL ST

HALLOWELL

95

STATE

27

201

9

TO GARDINER

TO BRUNSWICK

SEWALL

TO RANDOLPH

0   5 MILE
0   5 KILOMETER

Weather (continued)

Average Temperatures (°F)	High	Low	Mean
March	40.8	22.8	31.8
April	52.8	32.5	42.7
May	63.6	41.7	52.7
June	73.2	51.1	62.2
July	79.1	56.9	68.0
August	77.6	55.2	66.4
September	69.9	47.4	58.7
October	60.2	38.0	49.1
November	47.5	29.7	38.6
December	34.9	16.4	25.7

History

The Kennebec River, or Manitou Kennebec (River God) to Algonquian-speaking Indians, has shaped the history of Augusta. The site of present-day Augusta was first inhabited by the Red Paint People, who used pigment from iron oxide to decorate themselves. The Cushnoc succeeded them. Trade with Europeans began soon after the Kennebec Patent grant was made in 1628–1629. In 1629 John Howland and John Alden (who was immortalized by Longfellow in "The Courtship of Miles Standish") established a trading post. Trading was so profitable for the pilgrims that they paid their debt to the Merchant Adventurers of London for the cost of the *Mayflower* expedition with Kennebec furs. Trade was suspended during the Indian wars.

A second attempt to colonize the Kennebec Valley followed the defeat of the French in the mid-1700s, when Forts Western, Halifax, and Shirley were built. Captain James Howard, the first and only commander of Fort Western, was Augusta's first permanent settler. The settlement of Hallowell was established a few miles south of Fort Western in 1762. Hallowell, with the addition of Fort Western, was incorporated as a town in 1771. Hallowell's population and wealth grew when the Bond Brook Sawmill opened. Rivalry between Fort Western and the town led to a split, and in 1796 Fort Western became Harrington—which Hallowell wits called Herring-town. That same year the fort's name was changed again, this time to honor Pamela Augusta Dearborn, daughter of General Henry Dearborn, member of the Continental Congress. Augusta and Hallowell eventually merged, in 1797, to become the county seat of Kennebec County.

After 1800 Augusta entered a new era that was first marked by bloody riots. The murder of surveyor Paul Chadwick in 1809 by seven squatters, and the subsequent arrest of the seven men, led to a confrontation between new settlers and old landowners, which became known in Maine history as the Malta War. The establishment of a U.S. arsenal in Augusta in 1829 contributed to the decision to make Augusta the state capital in 1832. The town's population grew to 8,225 in 1849 when a city government charter was adopted.

The town's prosperity was based on river traffic. Schooners plied the Kennebec to its mouth and south to Boston weekly. Deepwater freight was often transferred to longboats at Augusta and thence towed up-river through the rapids by ox teams. Although the arrival of the first train in 1851 eventually led to the decline of the river trade, schooners and tug-drawn barges conducted a profitable export business into the 20th century. Steamboat travel to Bath, Maine, and Boston, Massachusetts, was inaugurated in 1826.

The city experienced a brief downturn during the Civil War, and further misfortune when a fire in 1865 razed nearly all of the business district. Since then Augusta has lost some of its industrial preeminence, but as the state capital it continues to dominate Maine politics.

Historical Landmarks

On the west bank of the Kennebec River are several buildings of historical and architectural interest. The state capitol, a granite structure built in 1829 and enlarged in 1910 by architect G. Henri Desmond, is surmounted by a dome and a gold-plated statue of the goddess Minerva, which was made by W. Clark Noble to represent Augusta. The Blaine House, now the Executive Mansion, was built in 1833 in the Federalist style. It was the home of James G. Blaine, a member of Congress and presidential candidate. His daughter presented the mansion to the state in 1919 to be used as the governor's residence. The silver in the state dining room was recovered from the U.S.S. *Maine* ten years after it sank in Havana Harbor in 1898. The Kennebec County Courthouse, built in 1830, is a fine example of Greek Revival. Oblate House, designed by the noted Maine architect John Calvin Stevens, is constructed of Maine granite and St. Louis brick. The South Congregational Church, built in 1781, is the oldest of Augusta's 13 churches. The oldest Roman Catholic church dates from 1836. Fort Western is a storehouse of Augusta's history. The original garrison has been restored and furnished with colonial antiques.

Population

The population declined 2.3% between 1980 and 1990—from 21,819 in 1980 to 21,325 in 1990, making it one of the smallest state capitals in terms of population.

Ethnic Composition

Augusta is racially homogeneous, with whites, in 1990, numbering 20,965 of the 21,325 population (99.33% of the residents).

Population	1980	1990
Central City	21,819	21,325
Rank	NA	NA
Metro Area	109,899	115,904
Pop. Change 1980–1990 -494		
Pop. % Change 1980–1990 -2.3		
Median Age 36.2		
% Male 47.2		
% Age 65 and Over 17.21		
Density (per square mile) 378.7		

Chronology

1628 The Plymouth Colony is granted the Kennebec Patent, and a trading post is built by John Howland in 1629.

1634 John Alden joins Howland as co-agent of the Kennebec trading post.

1647 John Winslow is named commander of the Kennebec trading post.

1653 The British abandon the Kennebec trading post during the wars with the Indians and the French.

1754 The British return to the valley and erect Forts Western, Halifax, and Shirley along the riverbanks.

1759 General Wolfe's victory against the French makes Kennebec safe for settlers.

1762 Settlement of Hallowell is founded.

1771 Hallowell, with addition of Fort Western, is incorporated as a town.

1796 Fort Western secedes from Hallowell and incorporates itself as the town of Harrington.

1797 Hallowell and Harrington re-merge to become Augusta.

1799 Augusta becomes shire town of Kennebec County.

1809 The "Malta War" between landowners and settlers leads to widespread civil unrest.

1829 U.S. arsenal established at Augusta.

1832 Augusta becomes state capital of Maine.

1851 First train reaches Augusta.

1865 A fire razes the business district of Augusta.

Population (continued)

Households

Number 8,719
Persons per Household 2.4
% Female-Headed Households NA
% One-Person Households NA
Births—Total NA
    % to Mothers under 20 NA
    Birth Rate per 1,000 NA

Ethnic Composition (as % of total pop.)

	1980	1990
White	99.33	98.3
Black	0.67	0.3
American Indian	0.18	0.4
Asian and Pacific Islander	0.28	0.8
Hispanic	0.39	0.5
Other	NA	0.1

Government

Augusta has a city council-manager form of government. The mayor and seven council members are elected for two-year terms. The city manager is appointed by the council.

Government

Year of Home Charter 1969
Number of Members of the Governing Body 9
Elected at Large 1
Elected by Wards 8
Number of Women in Governing Body 0
Salary of Mayor NA
Salary of Council Members NA
City Government Employment Total NA
Rate per 10,000 NA

Public Finance

Total Revenue (in millions) NA
Intergovernmental Revenue—Total (in millions) NA
Federal Revenue per capita NA
% Federal Assistance NA
% State Assistance NA
Sales Tax as % of Total Revenue NA
Local Revenue as % of Total Revenue NA
City Income Tax NA
Taxes—Total (in millions) NA

Taxes per capita
    Total NA
    Property NA
    Sales and Gross Receipts NA
General Expenditures—Total (in millions) NA
General Expenditures per capita NA
Capital Outlays per capita NA

% of Expenditures for:
Highways NA
Education NA
Health and Hospitals NA
Police NA
Sewerage and Sanitation NA
Parks and Recreation NA
Housing and Community Development NA
Debt Outstanding per capita NA
    % Utility NA
Federal Procurement Contract Awards (in millions) NA
Federal Grants Awards (in millions) NA
Fiscal Year Begins NA

Economy

Augusta is primarily a government center and its economy revolves around its status as the state capital. It is home to more than 76 professional and lobbying associations, four major banks, and the regional headquarters for the state's top law firms. Medical services also generate a substantial percentage of the city's employment. Of the manufacturing plants, the Digital Equipment Company is the largest. Due to its central location in the state, the city is a wholesale and distribution center for the region. Tourism is an important source of revenue.

Economy

Total Money Income (in millions)   NA
% of State Average   NA
Per capita Annual Income $9,841
% Population below Poverty Level   NA
Fortune 500 Companies   NA

Banks	Number	Deposits (in millions)
Commercial	5	211.576
Savings	3	122.576

Passenger Autos   80,365
Electric Meters   53,528
Gas Meters   27,000

Labor

The federal, state, and city governments are the largest employers in the city, accounting for 38% of total employment. Retail and wholesale trade comes next with 20.1%, services with 17.3%, and manufacturing with 11.4%. The government share of employment is twice the state average, and thrice the share of manufacturing. Despite relatively low unemployment rates, the city has a low labor force participation rate, which means that there is considerable room for expansion.

Education

Augusta's educational system consists of one high school, two junior high/middle schools, and four elementary schools in its public system and two parochial elementary schools. The University of Maine has a campus in Augusta. Other higher education facilities include the Mid-State Business College and the Capital Area Technical Center.

Education

Number of Public Schools   7
Special Education Schools   NA
Total Enrollment   3,187
% Enrollment in Private Schools   NA
% Minority   NA
Classroom Teachers   NA
Pupil-Teacher Ratio   21:1
Number of Graduates   NA
Total Revenue (in millions)   NA
Total Expenditures (in millions)   NA
Expenditures per Pupil   NA
Educational Attainment (Age 25 and Over)
    % Completed 12 or More Years   NA
    % Completed 16 or More Years   NA
Four-Year Colleges and Universities   1
Enrollment   11,091
Two-Year Colleges   NA
Enrollment   NA

Libraries

Number   15
Public Libraries   1
Books (in thousands)   450
Circulation (in thousands)   140
Persons Served (in thousands)   22
Circulation per Person Served   6.57
Income (in millions) $3.0
Staff   64

Four-Year Colleges and Universities
    University of Maine at Augusta

Health

The primary health-care facility is the Kennebec Valley Medical Center, a 200-bed general hospital; Togus Federal Veterans Hospital and the Augusta Mental Health Institute are the other hospitals.

Health

Deaths—Total   NA
Rate per 1,000   NA
Infant Deaths—Total   NA
Rate per 1,000   NA
Number of Metro Hospitals   NA
Number of Metro Hospital Beds   NA
Rate per 100,000   NA
Number of Physicians   NA
Physicians per 1,000   NA
Nurses per 1,000   NA
Health Expenditures per capita   NA

Transportation

Augusta is the northeastern terminus of the Maine Turnpike and also is the hub of eight major interstate routes: Routes 3, 9, 11, 17, 27, 100, 201, and 202. Greyhound provides daily service to Augusta on the Portland-Bangor run. Within the city, Kennebec Valley Transit maintains bus services. Augusta State Airport, a mile southwest of the town's center, is served by a commuter airline and Northwest.

Transportation

Interstate Highway Mileage   NA
Total Urban Mileage   NA
Total Daily Vehicle Mileage (in millions)   NA
Daily Average Commute Time   NA
Number of Buses   NA
Port Tonnage (in millions)   NA
Airports   NA
Number of Daily Flights   NA
Daily Average Number of Passengers   NA

Airlines (American carriers only)
    NA

Housing

The building boom of the 1980s resulted in the expansion of housing in the suburbs, but within the city itself much of the construction was limited to office and commercial buildings. One family homes predominate in the housing market. Nearly 45% of the homes were built before 1940. Over half of the homes have three or more bedrooms. There were 9,572 housing units in Augusta in 1990.

Urban Redevelopment

The Office of Economic and Community Development oversees downtown redevelopment. With the recession of the early

Housing

Total Housing Units   9,572
% Change 1980–1990   NA
Vacant Units for Sale or Rent   NA
Occupied Units   NA
% with More Than One Person per Room   NA
% Owner-Occupied   56.6
Median Value of Owner-Occupied Homes $79,500
Average Monthly Purchase Cost   NA
Median Monthly Rent $342
New Private Housing Starts
Value (in thousands)   NA
% Single-Family   NA
Nonresidential Buildings Value (in thousands)   NA

1990s, redevelopment and building programs have slowed and are not likely to pick up for a few years.

Crime

Augusta's crime rate is comparatively low, with only a small portion of crimes attributed to violence.

Crime

Violent Crimes—Total   NA
Violent Crime Rate per 100,000   NA
Murder   1
Rape   12
Robbery   7
Aggravated Assaults   11
Property Crimes   NA
Burglary   294
Larceny   1,082
Motor Vehicle Theft   56
Arson   16
Per capita Police Expenditures   NA
Per capita Fire Protection Expenditures   NA
Number of Police   NA
Per 1,000   1.74

Religion

There are 13 churches in the city of which 3 are Roman Catholic.

Religion

Largest Denominations (Adherents)	
Catholic	32,570
American Baptist	4,035
United Methodist	4,414
United Church of Christ	1,959
Episcopal	1,447
Jewish	800

Media

The *Kennebec Journal* is published Monday through Saturday. Magazines published in Augusta deal with outdoor sports, fishing, and wildlife.

Media

Newsprint
   Kennebec Journal, daily
Television
   NA
Radio
   WFAU (AM)

Sports

Augusta has no professional sports.

Arts, Culture, and Tourism

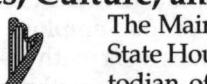

The Maine State Museum, located in the State House complex, is the principal custodian of Maine's rich cultural heritage. The Hall of Flags on the second floor of the Capitol Building displays Maine's battle flags. The University of Maine at Augusta's Forum-A brings visual and performing arts events to the city. The Augusta Civic Center, owned by the city, has an 8,000-seat auditorium.

Travel and Tourism

Hotel Rooms   NA
Convention and Exhibit Space (square feet)   NA
Convention Centers
   Augusta Civic Center
Festivals
   Great Kennebec River Whatever Race Week (Summer)

Parks and Recreation

The Capitol Park or Monument Park is a 20-acre tract between Capitol and Union streets that offers pleasant vistas and footpaths. Thousands of trees and shrubs and rustic seats and benches make the park one of the most attractive spots in the city. Maine regiments camped here during the Civil War.

Sources of Further Information

Augusta Office of Economic and Community Development
16 Cony Street
Augusta, ME 04330
(207) 626-2336

Kennebec Valley Chamber of Commerce
University Drive
Augusta, ME 04330
(207) 623-4559

Lithgow Public Library
Winthrop Street
Augusta, ME 04330
(207) 626-2415

Additional Reading

Kennebec Valley Chamber of Commerce. *The Capital Area Guide.* (occasional).

Ulrich, Laurel. *A Midwife's Tale: The Life of Martha Ballard, Based on Her Diary, 1785–1812,* 1990.

Austin

Texas

Basic Data

Name   Austin
Name Origin   From Stephen Fuller Austin
Year Founded   1838 Inc. 1839
Status: State   Capital of Texas
        County   Seat of Travis County
Area (square miles)   217.8
Elevation (feet)   505
Time Zone   Central
Population (1990)   465,622
Population of Metro Area (1990)   781,572

Sister Cities

    Adelaide, Australia
    Lima, Peru
    Maseru, Lesotho
    Oita City, Japan
    Saltillo, Mexico
    Taichung City, China

Distance in Miles To:

Dallas	195
Houston	163
San Antonio	79

Location and Topography

Austin, the capital of Texas and seat of Travis County, lies in the central part of the state on the low hills of the Balcones Escarpment. The Colorado River is west and south of the main part of the city. A chain of seven man-made lakes known as the Highland Lakes begins within the city limits and stretches 150 miles to the northwest. Elevations within the city range from 400 to 900 feet above sea level.

Layout of City and Suburbs

Congress Avenue, the principal business street, runs north and south and divides downtown into east and west. The capitol and the University of Texas Tower domi-nate the cityscape. Most of the newer residential districts are south of the river.

Environment

Environmental Stress Index	3
Green Cities Index: Rank	2
Score	16.25
Water Quality	Alkaline, soft, fluoridated
Average Daily Use (gallons per capita)	NA
Maximum Supply (gallons per capita)	NA
Parkland as % of Total City Area	7.5
% Waste Landfilled/Recycled	66:24
Annual Parks Expenditures per capita	$50.41

Climate

Austin has a subtropical climate with hot summers when temperatures can climb into the high 90s. Winters are mild, with temperatures averaging in the 50s. It rarely snows and there are only occasional cold spells, which last no more than a few days. Freezing or below-freezing temperatures are recorded an average of only 23 days a year. Rain falls throughout the year; however, precipitation is heaviest in late spring and early fall. Summer brings thunderstorms.

Weather

Temperature

Highest Monthly Average °F	95.4
Lowest Monthly Average °F	38.8

Annual Averages

Days 32°F or Below	23
Days above 90°F	101
Zero Degree Days	0
Precipitation (inches)	33
Snow (inches)	1.0
% Seasonal Humidity	67

Weather (continued)

Wind Speed (m.p.h.) 9.4
Clear Days 115
Cloudy Days 134
Storm Days 41
Rainy Days 82

Average Temperatures (°F)	High	Low	Mean
January	60.0	39.3	49.7
February	63.8	42.8	53.3
March	70.7	48.2	59.5
April	79.0	58.2	68.6
May	85.2	65.1	75.2
June	91.7	71.4	81.6
July	95.4	73.7	84.6
August	95.9	73.5	84.7
September	89.4	68.4	78.9
October	81.3	58.9	70.1
November	70.2	48.0	59.1
December	63.0	41.6	52.3

History

The first settlement on the north bank of the Colorado River was called Waterloo. In the fall of 1838 Mirabeau B. Lamar, then vice-president and later president of the Republic of Texas, camped with a party of buffalo hunters at Jacob Harrel's cabin near the Colorado River ford. In January 1839 a commission was appointed by the Texas Republic's president to locate a capital. Lamar recalled the site and recommended it to the commission. The site was chosen and its name changed to Austin in honor of Stephen F. Austin, father of the Republic of Texas. Construction on the capitol began in 1839; workmen had to be protected from Indian attack by an eight–foot-high stockade around the Hall of Congress. The town incorporated that same year with a population of 856, and its first newspaper, the *Gazette*, appeared.

In 1842 a Mexican army crossed the border and occupied San Antonio, 75 miles to the southwest. It was rumored that a detachment was headed to Austin, and the seat of government was hurriedly moved to Houston. Angry Austin citizens foiled President Sam Houston's attempt to move the republic's archives because they feared that Houston would then become the capital. After the Mexican threat ended, Austin was restored as capital. In 1845 the United States annexed Texas, and it became the 28th state.

Abolition and secession dominated Austin politics in the 1850s. The state as a whole voted for the Confederacy, although Travis County, where Austin is located, voted against it. During the Civil War Austin played a part by raising Terry's Texas Rangers. At the end of the war in 1865, Confederate soldiers, many of whom had not been paid for months, swarmed south and west. Desperate veterans and renegades traveled to Austin, and some broke into the state treasury and made off with public funds.

During Reconstruction the city began to prosper despite the political strife. In 1871 the Houston and Texas Central Railroad reached the city, followed by the International Great Northern in 1876. In 1883 the University of Texas held its first term. In 1888 the new capitol was opened. A new dam and power plant were built on the Colorado River, and partially rebuilt after they were destroyed by flood in 1900. In 1909 Austin received a charter for a commission form of government, but changed in 1926 to a city manager form, and now has a council-manager form of government.

Historical Landmarks

The oldest building in Austin is the French Legation on 8th Street, designed by Count Saligny, French *charge d'affaires* to the Republic of Texas. The Elisabet Ney Museum on the corner of Avenue H and East 44th Street is built like a medieval castle and was the workshop and home of sculptor Elisabet Ney. St. David's Episcopal Church on East 7th and San Jacinto streets is the second-oldest Protestant church in Texas, built in 1854. The Governor Elisha M. Pease home on Niles Road was built by James T. Shaw, who sold it to the governor in the 1850s.

The Texas state capitol stands at the city's center in an elevated square on 25 acres, the main front facing the north end of Congress Avenue. It is the second capitol built on this spot and was completed in 1888. The building resembles the national capitol in Washington, D.C. It is shaped like a Greek cross with a projecting center and flanks and has a rotunda and dome. The governor's mansion, built in 1855, is on Colorado Street. The capitol grounds have a number of monuments and memorials, such as the Confederate Dead Monument, the Volunteer Firemen Monument, the Texas Cowboy Monument, Terry's Texas Rangers Monument, the Alamo Monument, and Hood's Texas Brigade Monument.

Population

The population has increased by a third each census since 1920. For example, the city grew 36.3% from 251,808 in 1970 to 345,496 in 1980 and then an additional 34.6% to 465,622 in 1990.

Population	1980	1990
Central City	345,496	465,622
Rank	42	27
Metro Area	536,693	781,572
Pop. Change 1980–1990 +119,732		
Pop. % Change 1980–1990 +34.6		
Median Age 28.9		
% Male 49.9		
% Age 65 and Over 7.4		
Density (per square mile) 2,137.84		

Households

Number 192,148
Persons per Household 2.33
% Female-Headed Households 11.0
% One-Person Households 34.1
Births—Total 8,375
    % to Mothers under 20 13.6
    Birth Rate per 1,000 21.1

Chronology

1838 On the recommendation of Mirabeau B. Lamar, the settlement known as Waterloo on the Colorado River bend is chosen to be the capital of the republic of Texas.

1839 The capitol is built with an 8–foot-high protective stockade around it. The town of Austin is incorporated. The *Gazette*, Austin's first newspaper, debuts.

1841 The Republic of Texas is recognized by France, England, Holland, and the United States.

1842 Following the Mexican invasion and occupation of San Antonio, the capital is moved to Houston. In the so-called Archives War, citizens refuse to allow the transfer of official archives to Houston.

1845 Texas is annexed by the United States.

1860 Texas votes to join the Confederacy.

1871 The Houston and Texas Central Railroad reaches city.

1876 The International Great Northern Railroad reaches city.

1883 The University of Texas opens.

1900 A Colorado River flood destroys the dam and power plant.

1909 Austin receives a charter for a commission form of government.

1926 Austin adopts a city manager form of government. The first public library opens.

Ethnic Composition

In 1990 whites made up 70.56% of the population. Hispanics, both black and white, made up 23%; blacks 12.43%; Asians and Pacific Islanders 3.04%; American Indians 0.38%; and others 13.6%.

Ethnic Composition (as % of total pop.)

	1980	1990
White	75.59	70.56
Black	12.19	12.43
American Indian	0.29	0.38
Asian and Pacific Islander	1.05	3.04
Hispanic	18.75	22.95
Other	NA	13.6

Government

Austin is governed under a council-manager form of government. The mayor and six council members are elected at large for three-year terms.

Government

Year of Home Charter 1953
Number of Members of the Governing Body 7
Elected at Large 7
Elected by Wards NA
Number of Women in Governing Body 1
Salary of Mayor $35,000
Salary of Council Members $30,000
City Government Employment Total 10,445
Rate per 10,000 223.9

Public Finance

The annual budget in 1989–1990 showed revenues of $1.033 billion and expenditures of $1.011 billion. The debt outstanding in was $3.187 billion, and cash and security holdings $1.472 billion.

Public Finance

Total Revenue (in millions) $1,033.129
Intergovernmental Revenue—Total (in millions) $64.24
Federal Revenue per capita $9.11
% Federal Assistance 0.88
% State Assistance 5.31
Sales Tax as % of Total Revenue 4.56
Local Revenue as % of Total Revenue 45.46
City Income Tax no
Taxes—Total (in millions) $119.6
Taxes per capita
Total 256
Property 140
Sales and Gross Receipts 99
General Expenditures—Total (in millions) $362.0
General Expenditures per capita $776
Capital Outlays per capita $145
% of Expenditures for:
　Public Welfare 0.2
　Highways 3.0
　Education 0.2
　Health and Hospitals 24.5
　Police 10.4
　Sewerage and Sanitation 20.2
　Parks and Recreation 5.6
　Housing and Community Development 2.1
Debt Outstanding per capita $3,247
　% Utility 52.8
Federal Procurement Contract Awards (in millions) $157.2
Federal Grants Awards (in millions) $995.5
Fiscal Year Begins October 1

Economy

As the state capital, Austin's economy thrives on the public sector. Since the 1970s Austin has become one of the high-technology centers of the Southwest. High-tech corporations include IBM, Motorola, Texas Instru-

Economy

Total Money Income (in millions) $542.629
% of State Average   112.1
Per capita Annual Income $11,633
% Population below Poverty Level   15.8
Fortune 500 Companies   NA

Banks	Number	Deposits (in millions)
Commercial	54	6,394
Savings	126	4,815

Passenger Autos   457,284
Electric Meters   229,350
Gas Meters   122,338

Manufacturing

Number of Establishments   549
% with 20 or More Employees   26.0
Manufacturing Payroll (in millions) $951.3
Value Added by Manufacture (in millions) $2,212.4
Value of Shipments (in millions) $4,197.8
New Capital Expenditures (in millions) $288.5

Wholesale Trade

Number of Establishments   984
Sales (in millions)   NA
Annual Payroll (in millions)   NA

Retail Trade

Number of Establishments   5,171
Total Sales (in millions) $3,968
Sales per capita $8,505
Number of Retail Trade Establishments with Payroll   3,536
Annual Payroll (in millions) $506.3
Total Sales (in millions) $3,896.4
General Merchandise Stores (per capita)   NA
Food Stores (per capita) $1,999
Apparel Stores (per capita) $503
Eating and Drinking Places (per capita) $1,039

Service Industries

Total Establishments   4,767
Total Receipts (in millions) $2,640.5
Hotels and Motels (in millions) $147.1
Health Services (in millions) $502.1
Legal Services (in millions)   NA

Labor

Civilian Labor Force   279,528
% Change 1989–1990   0.9

Work Force Distribution
Mining   700
Construction   12,600
Manufacturing   51,000
Transportation and Public Utilities   12,600
Wholesale and Retail Trade   78,800
FIRE (Finance, Insurance, Real Estate)   23,100
Service   100,500
Government   110,400
Women as % of Labor Force   45.8
% Self-Employed   5.9
% Professional/Technical   21.3
Total Unemployment   13,344
Rate %   4.8
Federal Government Civilian Employment   7,700

---

ments, and Advanced Micro Devices. Two world-class research consortia arrived in the 1980s: SEMATECH in semiconductors and MCC in microelectronics. Overall, there are 900 manufacturers in Austin, of which 400 are in high technology. More than 95% of the businesses are small businesses (each employing fewer than 100 people). The University of Texas has a pervasive influence on the economy. Other significant economic sectors are tourism and country and western music.

Labor

More than half of the business work force is employed by small business. State, local, and federal governments combine to share more than a third of the work force. College degrees are held by 35% of the adults living in Austin, making it the most highly educated commu-

nity among American cities with populations greater than 250,000. Bergstrom Air Force Base, scheduled to close in 1993, was a major contributor to the employment market.

Education

The Austin Independent School District (AISD) supports 100 schools. The fall 1990–1991 enrollment totaled 65,885. Austin AISD is the largest urban school district in Texas. In addition, private and parochial schools

Education

Number of Public Schools   100
Special Education Schools   11
Total Enrollment   65,885
% Enrollment in Private Schools   5.9
% Minority   56.4
Classroom Teachers   4,096
Pupil-Teacher Ratio   16.1:1
Number of Graduates   3,094
Total Revenue (in millions) $279.78
Total Expenditures (in millions) $313.143
Expenditures per Pupil $4,133
Educational Attainment (Age 25 and Over)
    % Completed 12 or More Years   74.8
    % Completed 16 or More Years   30.6
Four-Year Colleges and Universities   4
Enrollment   63,263
Two-Year Colleges   2
Enrollment   18,340

Libraries

Number   79
Public Libraries   18
Books (in thousands)   924
Circulation (in thousands)   2,393
Persons Served (in thousands)   497
Circulation per Person Served   4.81
Income (in millions) $7.26
Staff   209

Four-Year Colleges and Universities
    University of Texas
    Concordia Lutheran College
    Huston-Tillotson College
    St. Edward's University

enroll about 6,000 students. Of the seven colleges and universities in the metro area, the largest is the University of Texas at Austin with almost 50,000 students; it is the third-largest public university in the nation. Its main campus consists of 232 acres on a hill behind the state capitol. The most impressive structure in the university complex is the main building's tower, which rises 27 stories to a height of 307 feet.

Austin Community College has 6 campuses and 70 instructional locations in the city, and in 1992 had 25,000 students. Another outstanding institution is St. Edward's University. Others include Southwestern University at Georgetown (north of Austin), Concordia Lutheran College, and Huston-Tillotson College. There are two seminaries, one Episcopal and one Presbyterian.

Health

Austin's medical sector consists of seven major hospitals and medical centers, of which the largest are the Seton Medical Center, St. David's Medical Center, and Brackenridge Hospital. Other facilities include Shoal Creek Hospital, a psychiatric center; Round Rock Hospital; and the Health Care Rehabilitation Center.

Health

Deaths—Total	2,377
Rate per 1,000	6.0
Infant Deaths—Total	73
Rate per 1,000	8.7
Number of Metro Hospitals	13
Number of Metro Hospital Beds	3,778
Rate per 100,000	810
Number of Physicians	1,194
Physicians per 1,000	1.87
Nurses per 1,000	3.23
Health Expenditures per capita	$55.78

Transportation

Austin is approached by one interstate: I-35 runs north-south and parallels Congress Street through downtown. U.S. highways 183 and 290 circle the city from the north to the southwest. The routes are also known in part as Research Boulevard, Anderson Lane, and Ed Bluestein Boulevard. On the west side of town is Loop 360, also called Capital of Texas Highway.

There are more than 100 city buses from the metropolitan area. Daily rail passenger service is pro-

Transportation

Interstate Highway Mileage	21
Total Urban Mileage	2,573
Total Daily Vehicle Mileage (in millions)	11.952
Daily Average Commute Time	41.8 min.
Number of Buses	112
Port Tonnage (in millions)	NA
Airports	1
Number of Daily Flights	84
Daily Average Number of Passengers	5,540

Transportation (continued)

Airlines (American carriers only)
- American
- American Eagle
- American West
- Continental
- Delta
- Northwest
- Southwest
- Trans World
- United
- USAir

vided by Amtrak, and freight service by several carriers. The principal air terminal is Robert C. Mueller Municipal Airport.

Housing

In 1990 40.6% of the 217,054 housing units were owner-occupied. The median value of an owner-occupied home was $72,600 and the median monthly rent $346.

Housing

Total Housing Units	217,054
% Change 1980–1990	32.5
Vacant Units for Sale or Rent	20,339
Occupied Units	192,148
% with More Than One Person per Room	6.8
% Owner-Occupied	40.6
Median Value of Owner-Occupied Homes	$72,600
Average Monthly Purchase Cost	$393
Median Monthly Rent	$346
New Private Housing Starts	923
Value (in thousands)	$103,114
% Single-Family	96.1
Nonresidential Buildings Value (in thousands)	$91,266

Tallest Buildings	Hgt. (ft.)	Stories
One American Center	395	32
One Congress Plaza	391	30
NCNB Tower	328	26

Urban Redevelopment

Downtown redevelopment is coordinated by a number of agencies, such as Austin Area Department of Planning and Growth Management, Austin Business and Economic Development Division, Capital Area Planning Council, and Downtown Austin Unlimited.

Crime

Of the 53,715 crimes known to police for the city of Austin in 1991, 2,968 were violent and 50,747 involved property.

Crime

Violent Crimes—Total	2,968
Violent Crime Rate per 100,000	506.9
Murder	49
Rape	276
Robbery	1,555

Crime (continued)

Aggravated Assaults   1,088
Property Crimes   50,747
Burglary   11,591
Larceny   34,417
Motor Vehicle Theft   4,739
Arson   501
Per capita Police Expenditures $96.54
Per capita Fire Protection Expenditures $65.91
Number of Police   681
Per 1,000   1.68

Religion

No single religious denomination dominates Travis County or Austin. Roman Catholics and Baptists each claim about 15% of the total population.

Religion

Largest Denominations (Adherents)

Catholic	84,424
Southern Baptist	72,367
Black Baptist	25,747
United Methodist	19,825
Evangelical Lutheran	11,412
Episcopal	9,615
Churches of Christ	7,228
Presbyterian	8,985
Lutheran-Missouri Synod	8,470
Jewish	3,687

Media

The *Austin American-Statesman* is the city's daily newspaper. The electronic media consist of 5 television stations and several AM and FM radio stations.

Sports

Media

Newsprint
Austin American-Statesman, daily
Austin Chronicle, weekly
Austin Business Journal, weekly
Austin Citizen, daily

Television
KBVO (Channel 42)
KLRU (Channel 18)
KTBC (Channel 7)
KVUE (Channel 24)
KXAN (Channel 36)

Radio
KGSR (FM)	KIXL (AM)
KKMJ (FM)	KLBJ (AM)
KLBJ (FM)	KMFA (FM)
KMOW (AM)	KEYI (FM)
KPEZ (FM)	KUT (FM)
KVET (AM)	

College sports, particularly University of Texas teams, dominate Austin. The Dallas Cowboys have their training camp at St. Edward's University.

Arts, Culture, and Tourism

Austin has named itself the live music capital of the United States because it offers more than 120 live music venues, from blues and country and western to jazz and rock and roll. The cultural scene also includes ten private theaters, the Austin Symphony, Lyric Opera, and dozens of film theaters. Ballet is represented by Ballet Austin. Numerous concerts are held at the Frank Erwin Center. Visiting entertainers perform at the lavish University of Texas at Austin Performing Arts Center.

Many museums focus on the rich historical legacy of the state. Some of these are the Daughters of the Confederacy Museum, Daughters of the Republic of Texas Museum, the O. Henry Home and Museum, and the Lyndon B. Johnson Presidential Library and Museum. Among the 35 art museums and galleries, the most noteworthy are the Laguna Gloria Art Museum, Elisabet Ney Museum, and the Art Warehouse.

Parks and Recreation

Travel and Tourism

Hotel Rooms   13,327
Convention and Exhibit Space (square feet)   NA

Convention Centers
Lester E. Palmer Auditorium
Texas Exposition and Heritage Center
Performing Arts Center
Erwin Center – University of Texas

Festivals
Austin Aqua Festival (August)
Austin Artists Harvest (November)
Yule Fest (December)
Sports Fest (March)
Livestock Show and Rodeo (March)

The city's 160 parks cover 10,000 acres. Zilker Park on Bee Cave Road in the southwest is noted for its natural beauty. Barton Creek runs through the south part of this irregular tract of 350 acres and the Colorado River through its northern section. Lake Austin Metropolitan Park, west on Bull Creek Road, covers 1,008 acres. The park has nearly three miles of riverfront and beach; Turkey Creek winds through its center.

Sources of Further Information

Austin Convention and Visitors Bureau
201 East Second Street
Austin, TX 78701
(512) 478-0098

Greater Austin Chamber of Commerce
101 Congress Avenue
Austin, TX 78701
(512) 478-9383

Mayor's Office
City Hall
124 West Eighth Street
Austin, TX 78701
(512) 499-2250

Additional Reading

Crosby, Tony. *An Austin Sketchbook*. 1978.
Endres, Clifford. *Austin City Limits*. 1987.
Hart, Katherine. *Austin & Travis County: A Pictorial History, 1839–1939*. 1975.
Zelade, Richard. *Hill Country: Discovering the Secrets of the Texas Hill Country*. 1983.

Baltimore

Maryland

Basic Data

Name   Baltimore
Name Origin   From Lord Baltimore
Year Founded   1729 Inc.1797
Status: State   Maryland
County   Baltimore
Area (square miles)   80.8
Elevation (feet)   20
Time Zone   EST
Population (1990)   736,014
Population of Metro Area (1990)   2,382,172

Sister Cities
    Cadiz, Spain
    Cbarnga, Liberia
    Genoa, Italy
    Kawasaki, Japan
    Luxor, Egypt
    Odessa, Ukraine
    Piraeus, Greece
    Rotterdam, Netherlands
    Xiamen, China

Distance in Miles To:

Philadelphia	102
Washington, DC	45
Wilmington	67
Annapolis	25
Boston	427
New York	199

Location and Topograhy

N

Baltimore, the largest city in the Middle Atlantic state of Maryland, is in the north-central part of the state. It is on the Patapsco River at its head of navigation. The Patapsco flows into Chesapeake Bay, giving Baltimore access to the Atlantic for shipping. The city, like the surrounding countryside, is hilly although the harbor and dock area is relatively flat.

Layout of City and Suburbs

Baltimore is divided roughly into four sections, with Charles Street as the east-west line and North Avenue the north-south line. The northwest sector of the city is an area of parks, golf courses, sprawling housing developments, and neat apartment buildings. Also located in this section is the Pimlico Race Course, site of the Preakness Stakes. Northeast Baltimore is more heterogeneous and more racially integrated, with a mix of small businesses and factories. Johns Hopkins University is located here. Southeast and southwest Baltimore both have areas of small homes, and the University of Maryland at Baltimore is in the southwest part of the city. South Baltimore has industries such as the Sparrows Point Plant of Bethlehem Steel and the Dundalk Marine Terminal. Baltimore still has ethnic neighborhoods but they are not as rigidly divided as in the past.

In the heart of the city, halfway between the financial/legal center and the retail district lies the 33-acre Charles Center designed by architect Mies van der Rohe in 1958. The mixed-use development was completed in 1986 at a cost of $200 million. Adjacent to the Charles Center is the Inner Harbor, a 240-acre development at the northwest end of the harbor. It includes a complex of shops and restaurants called Harborplace, the National Aquarium, Baltimore Convention Center, the 30-story World Trade Center, and the Maryland Science Center. East of this business district lies Little Italy, a thriving ethnic community with many restaurants. Southwest of this are restored row houses and to the south is a working-class neighborhood. The more run-down public housing areas are to the east, beyond the Jones Falls Expressway and west of Martin Luther King Boulevard. To the west of the Charles Center is the Baltimore Arena. Several historic

structures, including a monument to George Washington, stand near the business district. An area of run-down housing, where more than a third of the city's residents live, surrounds the business district. Several Baltimore neighborhoods outside the inner city have long stretches of red brick row houses with marble front steps.

Environment	
Environmental Stress Index	3.4
Green Cities Index: Rank	52
Score	35.93
Water Quality	NA
Average Daily Use (gallons per capita)	NA
Maximum Supply (gallons per capita)	NA
Air Quality by Federal Standards	NA
Carbon Monoxide by Federal Standards	NA
Parkland as % of Total City Area	11
% Waste Landfilled/Recycled	NA
Annual Parks Expenditures per Capita	66.9

Climate

The Appalachian Mountains to the west and proximity to the Atlantic Ocean and Chesapeake Bay to the east contribute to Baltimore's mild climate. Generally, freezing temperatures do not occur after mid-April or before the end of October; summers are humid. Rainfall is greatest in late summer and early fall, which is also the season for hurricanes and severe thunderstorms.

Weather			
Temperature			
Highest Monthly Average F	87.1		
Lowest Monthly Average F	24.3		
Annual Averages			
Days 32°F or Below	100		
Days above 90°F	31		
Zero Degree Days	0		
Precipitation (inches)	40		
Snow (inches)	22		
% Seasonal Humidity	67		
Wind Speed (m.p.h.)	9.5		
Clear Days	106		
Cloudy Days	150		
Storm Days	26		
Rainy Days	112		
Average Temperatures (°F)	*High*	*Low*	*Mean*
January	41.9	24.9	33.4
February	43.9	25.7	34.8
March	53.0	32.5	42.8
April	65.2	42.4	53.8
May	74.8	52.5	63.7
June	83.2	61.6	72.4
July	86.7	66.5	76.6
August	85.1	64.7	74.9
September	79.0	57.9	68.5
October	68.3	46.4	57.4
November	56.1	36.0	46.1
December	43.9	26.6	35.3

History

The area around Baltimore was inhabited by Piscataway and Susquehannock Indians when it was granted to George Calvert in 1632 by King Charles I. In 1659 Baltimore County was surveyed, and during the 1660s the Maryland General Assembly began granting land patents to enterprising colonists. In 1661 land on the west side of Jones Falls was taken by David Jones, while a tract on the tip of the peninsula known as Whetstone Neck was taken by Charles Gorsuch, a Quaker. Over the next 60 years numerous tracts were patented in what is now the city of Baltimore. Many of them had unusual names, such as Fell's Prospect, Gallow Bar, David's Fancy, Hale's Folly, Haphazard, Lunn's Lot, and Ridgeley's Delight. However, it was not until 1696 that a town was planned in the region. Charles and Daniel Carroll patented a thousand acres on the west side of Jones Falls, including part of an earlier patent called Cole's Harbor. By 1726 there was a gristmill on the east bank, three homes, and some tobacco houses. In 1729 tobacco farmers, looking for a customhouse and port to ship tobacco, negotiated with the Carrolls to buy 60 acres of the Carrolls' land for 600 pounds in order to establish a new town and port. Governor Benedict Leonard Calvert signed on August 8, 1729, the bill authorizing the establishment of the town. By 1730 the town had been laid out in the shape of an arrowhead, with the tip near the present intersection of Hopkins Place and Redwood Street. In 1732 neighboring Jones Town successfully petitioned the governor in Annapolis to incorporate their town; in 1745 the two towns united under the name of Baltimore. By 1752 the town's population numbered 200. There were 25 houses, one church, and two taverns, as well as one tobacco patch. In 1768 Baltimore was made the county seat and a courthouse was built. In 1773 Fell's Point was added to the town.

In 1765 Baltimore began its tradition of radicalism by hanging in effigy the stamp distributor for Maryland. In 1774 a Committee of Correspondence was appointed and a resolution passed prohibiting trade with England and the West Indies. When the Revolutionary War broke out, a company of militia was formed under Mordecai Gist. In 1776 Baltimore was host to the Congress, which had fled from Philadelphia in the face of British advances. Baltimore's greatest war effort was, however, at sea. In October 1775 the Continental Congress authorized a navy, and the Continental Marine Committee at Baltimore outfitted two cruisers. Maryland also had its own navy that dealt with Tory intruders. In 1776 Congress authorized privateers to sail against the British. Baltimoreans took the opportunity to profiteer under the guise of patriotism; between 1777 and 1783 more than two hundred privateers sailed. British merchants came to regard Baltimore as a nest of pirates.

After the war was over, a number of privately financed toll roads were built to connect the city to York in Pennsylvania and Harpers Ferry in western Virginia.

Chronology

1632	King Charles I grants George Calvert a large tract of land covering the present Baltimore County.
1656	Baltimore County planned.
1696	Charles and Daniel Carroll patent 1,000 acres on the west side of ones Falls including an earlier patent called Cole's Harbor.
1729	Sixty acres of the Carroll property are bought by local citizens and incorporated as the town of Baltimore.
1730	Baltimore is laid out in the form of an arrowhead.
1745	Jones Town and Baltimore merge to form Baltimore Town.
1755	French Acadian exiles arrive from Nova Scotia.
1768	Baltimore made county seat of Baltimore County.
1773	Baltimore annexes 80 acres that include Fell's Point.
1774	Committee of Correspondence is appointed and resolutions are passed prohibiting trade with Great Britain or West Indies. A company of militia is formed to fight against the British.
1775	Baltimore fits out two of the first cruisers of the American navy.
1776	Baltimore hosts Congress. Following Congress's authorization of privateers, Baltimore embarks on piracy against British vessels.
1796	Baltimore is incorporated as a city.
1800	U.S. census finds Baltimore's population to be 26,000, which makes it the third-largest city in the country.
1810	Population reaches 45,000.
1812	Anti-British mobs ransack newspapers opposed to the war.
1814	British under General Robert Ross attack the city at North Point but withdraw after bombardment of Fort McHenry fails. Francis Scott Key writes "Defence of Fort M'Henry," which eventually becomes the national anthem.
1815	The Washington Monument at Mount Vernon and Washington Places is begun; completed in 1829.
1827	Baltimore and Ohio Railroad is chartered.
1830	Baltimore and Ohio Railroad is completed.
1850	The Know-Nothing Party gains control of city hall and initiates a corrupt era in municipal government.
1861	Riots by pro-Confederates against Union troops leave 15 dead.
1904	Fire destroys much of Old Baltimore and causes an estimated $125 million in damage.
1967	Inner Harbor Redevelopment begins.

The roads, combined with its port, made Baltimore a gateway to the west.

In 1796 Baltimore incorporated as a city. Anti-British traditions revived during the War of 1812—newspapers that were against the war were raided and British goods destroyed. British troops marched on Baltimore after their successful attack on Washington, D.C. in August 1814. The British navy joined the assault by sailing up the Patapsco to bombard Fort McHenry. The British left, however, after their commander, General Robert Ross, was killed, and the attack on Fort McHenry ended. Washington attorney Francis Scott Key, a prisoner on board a British vessel, saw that the Stars and Stripes still flew over the fort by dawn's early light. This inspired him to write a poem that, when set to music later, became "The Star-Spangled Banner," which was adopted in 1931 as the national anthem. The Peace of Ghent ended privateering and Baltimore resumed its role as a major port, this time not only for foreign goods but for the waves of emigrants who left Europe in the first half of the 1800s.

In the early to mid-1800s, two major engineering projects enhanced Baltimore's role as a hub for transportation, despite its dominance being temporarily affected by the completion of the Erie Canal in New York in 1825. In 1827 the Baltimore and Ohio Railroad was chartered to compete with the Erie Canal; it carried its first passengers in 1830. In 1850 the city promoted the Chesapeake and Ohio Canal, which provided inexpensive transportation west as far as Cumberland in western Maryland. In the winter of 1852 the Baltimore and Ohio Railroad, which had replaced canal travel by 1842, reached the Ohio River. By the 1860s the city had also become a center for manufacturing: iron, heavy machinery, clothing, and other goods.

Baltimore was also a port for the slave trade. During the 1850s the Know-Nothing Party, which began as a reform movement, gained control of the city. During the presidential election of 1856 there was a street battle between Know-Nothings and Democrats, each side using cannon. Baltimoreans were strongly secessionist at the outbreak of the Civil War in 1861. There were riots against Union soldiers, and mobs ripped down railroad bridges and telegraph lines in an attempt to isolate Washington, D.C. from the north. Federal troops occupied the city, which was almost captured in 1864 by a Confederate force led by General Bradley T. Johnson. The city recovered from the Civil

War slowly but by the 1870s was once again thriving. It was in this era that a wealthy Quaker merchant named Johns Hopkins endowed the university bearing his name.

In 1904 the city's downtown suffered a fire that destroyed nearly all of its historic buildings. The process of rebuilding was first interrupted by World War I, then by the depression of the 1930s and World War II. Urban redevelopment has been a priority since 1945.

Historical Landmarks

Baltimore has honored a number of her own heroes as well as national heroes. The 204-foot-high Washington Monument on Mount Vernon and Washington Places was built between 1815 and 1829. The column is surmounted by a 16-foot statue of George Washington carved by Enrico Causici. Just to the south is the Lafayette Monument, a bronze equestrian statue of Lafayette as a young man. The Severn Teackle Wallis Monument, at the end of Mount Vernon Place, is an eight-foot bronze statue of a noted Baltimorean. The Taney Monument in Washington Place is a figure of Chief Justice Roger Brooke Taney in judicial robes. The Howard Monument at the north end of Washington Place is an equestrian statue of John Eager Howard, hero of the Battle of Cowpens. The Battle Monument on Calvert and Fayette Streets is a memorial to the heroes of the Battle of North Point and the defense of Fort McHenry in 1814. It is a white marble shaft on a square base surmounted by Victory wearing a crown and holding a rudder and laurel wreath. The World War Memorial on Memorial Plaza covers two city blocks at the east end of the Civic Center. Ground for the memorial was broken in 1921 by Marshal Ferdinand Foch. The building was designed by Lawrence Hall Fowler in neoclassic style with a portico of six Doric columns. The Wells-McComas Monument on Gay, Monument, and Aisquith Streets is an obelisk erected in 1871 as a memorial to Daniel Wells and Henry McComas who were killed during the Battle of North Point. The Star-Spangled Banner Monument, near the Breastworks, was erected in 1914 overlooking the harbor. The Wildey Monument on Broadway was erected by the Fraternal Order of Odd Fellows to honor their founder. The Columbus Monument, dedicated in 1792, was the first New World monument to honor America's discoverer. It is now at Harford Road and Argonne Drive in northeast Baltimore. The Confederate Women's Monument on University Parkway and Charles Street, the work of J. Maxwell Miller, was erected in 1913. The Poe Monument on 29th Street, by Moses J. Ezekiel, is a bronze figure of Edgar Allan Poe, clad in a dressing gown, listening to the muses. The Samuel Smith Monument on Charles and 29th Streets, unveiled in 1918, honors a distinguished soldier of the Revolutionary War. The Francis Scott Key Monument on Eutaw Place and Lanvale Street, is the work of Jean Marius Antonin and was unveiled in 1911. The Maryland Line Monument on Mount Royal Avenue and Cathedral Street, erected in 1901, is a high Ionic shaft bearing a bronze figure of the Goddess of Liberty holding a scroll of the Declaration of Independence to honor Maryland troops in the Revolutionary War. The Columbus Monument on Swann Drive was presented to the city by Baltimore Italians. The William Wallace Monument overlooking Druid Lake is a bronze figure of the Scottish hero given to the city by one his descendants.

Baltimore also has a number of architectural landmarks. The Peabody Institute on East Mount Vernon Place is a two-story marble building in Italian Renaissance style built as a conservatory. It honors George Peabody, who gave $1.4 million to build it. Fort McHenry, now a National Historic Site, is at the foot of the Fort Avenue on Whetstone Point overlooking the Patapsco River. The star-shaped fort, built in the 1790s, has brick walls 20 feet high and is on the site of an earlier fort. It was named for Irishman James McHenry, who served as secretary of war from 1796 to 1800.

Among Baltimore's churches, the most notable is the Cathedral of the Assumption of the Blessed Virgin Mary on Cathedral and Mulberry Streets, the first Roman Catholic cathedral in the United States. Designed by Benjamin H. Latrobe, its cornerstone was laid in 1806 by Bishop John Carroll at a time when more than half of the Catholics in the United States lived in Maryland. The building was dedicated in 1821 when Baltimore became the primatial see of the Catholic Church in America. In 1936 Pope Pius XI gave the cathedral the rank of a minor basilica, a title bestowed on churches notable for historic associations.

Other notable Baltimore churches include the Third Church of Christ Scientist on Cathedral Street; the neo-Gothic Emmanuel Protestant Episcopal Church on Cathedral and Read Streets; the First Presbyterian Church on Park Avenue and Madison Street, under construction from 1859 to 1873 in flamboyant Gothic style; the Franklin Street Presbyterian Church on the corner of Franklin and Cathedral Streets, completed in 1844 in Gothic Revival style; the First Unitarian Church on the corner of Charles and Franklin Streets, built in 1819; St. Paul's Protestant Episcopal Church on Charles and Saratoga Streets, built in 1856 although the parish was organized in 1692 and the first church built in 1739; St. Paul's Rectory on Saratoga Street, built in 1791 with funds raised by lottery; the Zion Lutheran Church on Gay and Lexington Streets, a reconstruction on the remains of an earlier edifice destroyed by fire in 1840; St. Vincent's Roman Catholic Church on Front Street; St. Mary's Seminary on Paca Street and Druid Hill Avenue, built in 1806-1808, one of the finest examples of Gothic Revival by Maximilian Godefroy; St. Stanislaus Kostka Church on Aliceanna and Ann Streets, built in 1896 and since then the center of Polish life in Baltimore; the First Methodist Church on St. Paul and 22nd Streets, designed by Stanford White; the Greek Orthodox Church on Preston Street and Maryland Avenue, a low, gray, circular granite structure of Byzantine design; the Otterbein United Brethren Church on Conway Street, built in 1785; and St. Mary's Star of the Sea on Gittings Street and Riverside Avenue, built in 1869. The Mount Vernon Place Methodist Church at the corner of Charles and Mount Vernon and Washington Places, built between 1870 and 1872, is a notable example of Victorian Gothic design with its lofty spire and turrets.

Of the historic homes in the city the largest is the Henry Barton Jacobs House, on Mount Vernon Place, the largest private dwelling designed by Stanford White in Italian Renaissance style. Others are the Randall House on Mount Vernon Place, built about 1834; the William McKim House on Park Avenue, built in 1832; and the Carroll Mansion on Lombard and Front Streets, built in 1812 and enlarged in 1820, and owned by the city since 1914. The Flag House on Albemarle and Pratt Streets, built in 1793, was the home of Mrs. Mary Pickersgill who had made the huge Star-Spangled Banner that inspired Key in 1814. Belfort on Baltimore and Central Avenues was built in 1870 by Julien Friez; this is where Ottmar Mergenthaler worked from 1876 to 1885 to perfect his linotype machine. Homewood, a stately mansion now part of Johns Hopkins University, was erected by Charles Carroll for his son in 1809 on part of a tract surveyed in 1670 for John Homewood. Other historic homes are the Wallis Warfield Home, the house in which the Duchess of Windsor was brought up; the Maryland House, a one-story frame building, part of the Maryland exhibit at the Philadelphia Centennial Exposition of 1876; Mansion House, on a hilltop south of the Memorial Grove and home of the Rogers family; the Edgar Allan Poe House on Amity Street; and the Shipley Lydecker House on McHenry and Franklintown Roads, built in 1803.

Other landmarks include the Masonic Temple on Charles Street, built in 1908 on the site of a building erected in 1866; the site of Barnum's City Hotel, built in 1825 and closed in 1889; the City Hall on Fayette and Holliday Streets and the Municipal Building on Guilford Avenue and Lexington Street; the site of the Lovely Lane Methodist Meeting House on Redwood Street, erected in 1774; the site of the Fountain Inn on Light and Redwood Streets, built in 1775, where Washington and Rochambeau stayed; the site of the Congress Hall on the corner of Baltimore and Liberty Streets, the headquarters of the Continental Congress from December 1776 through February 1777; the 104th Medical regiment Armory on Fayette Street, built about 1897; Ford's Theater on Fayette Street, built in 1871, where Edwin Booth once played; Lexington Market on Lexington Street, one of the oldest and most picturesque markets in the nation, built in 1803; and the Fifth Regiment Armory on Hoffman and Bolton Streets built in 1901 and where Woodrow Wilson received the Democratic nomination. H. L. Mencken's home, an 1880s row house, overlooks Union Square. The legendary Babe Ruth's birthplace contains mementoes of his career. Top of the World, an observatory on the 27th floor of the World Trade Center in the Inner Harbor offers panoramic views of Baltimore.

The Peale Museum, at Holliday Street near Lexington Street, opened in 1814 as the first building in the United States to be designed as a museum. Artist Rembrandt Peale had architect Robert Cary Long, Sr., design the building for him.

Docked at Pratt Street is the U.S. frigate *Constellation*, launched in 1797 from Baltimore, and the first commissioned ship of the U.S. Navy. The oldest warship afloat, it saw action against the pirates of Tripoli in 1802, in the War of 1812, and again in the Civil War; it also served as an auxiliary warship in World War II.

Population

The population of the city of Baltimore peaked at 950,000 in 1950. The city has been losing residents—mainly its middle-class—to the surrounding area ever since. Between 1970 and 1980 the population declined by 13.1%, from 905,759 to 786,741; between 1980 and 1990 it further declined by 6.4%, to 736,014. Baltimore County's population, however, increased by 5.6% from 1980 to a 1990 high of 692,134. The trend is expected to continue.

Population		
	1980	*1990*
Central City	786,741	736,014
Rank	10	13
Metro Area	2,199,947	2,382,172
Pop. Change 1980–1990 -50,727		
Pop % Change 1980–1990 -6.4		
Median Age 32.6		
% Male 46.7		
% Age 17 and Under 24.44		
% Age 65 and Over 13.7		
Density (per square mile) 9,109		

Households		
Number 276,484		
Persons per Household 2.59		
% Female-Headed Households 24.6		
% One-Person Households 30.5		
Births—Total 12,954		
% to Mothers under 20 23.7		
Birth Rate per 1,000 17		

Ethnic Composition

Baltimore has a black majority population. In 1940 blacks made up 17.6% of the population, but by 1990 they made up 59.6%. Whites made up 39.1% of the population in 1990, Hispanics 1.03 %, Asian and Pacific Islanders 1.1%, and American Indians 0.3%.

Ethnic Composition (as % of total pop.)		
	1980	*1990*
White	43.8	39.1
Black	54.8	59.2
American Indian	0.27	0.3
Asian and Pacific Islander	0.63	1.1
Other	NA	0.3
Hispanic	0.97	1.0

Government

Baltimore, like St. Louis, Missouri, is set up as an independent city rather than administered as part of a county. The City of Baltimore has a mayor-council form of government. The mayor and 19 council members—three council members from each of the six districts, plus a council president elected at large—are elected to four-year terms.

Government

Year of Home Charter 1797
Number of Members of the Governing Body 19
Elected at Large 1
Elected by Wards 18
Number of Women in Governing Body 7
Salary of Mayor $60,000
Salary of Council Members $32,000
City Government Employment Total 31,420
Rate per 10,000 417.4

Public Finance

The annual budget consists of revenues of $1.864 billion and expenditures of $1.519 billion. Debt outstanding is $1.249 billion, cash and security holdings $2.470 billion.

Public Finance

Total Revenue (in millions) $1,864.5
Intergovernmental Revenue Total (in millions) $802.2
Federal Revenue $61.4
% Federal Assistance 3.29
% State Assistance 37.52
Sales Tax as % of Total Revenue NA
Local Revenue as % of Total Revenue 47.95
City Income Tax Yes
Taxes—Total (in millions) $457.8

Taxes per Capita
   Total 608
   Property 400
   Sales and Gross Receipts 47
General Expenditures—Total (in millions) $1,178.2
General Expenditures per Capita $1,565
Capital Outlays per Capita $319

% of Expenditures for:
   Public Welfare NA
   Highways 12.8
   Education 30.8
   Health and Hospitals 3.4
   Police 9.5
   Sewerage and Sanitation 8.7
   Parks and Recreation 3.7
   Housing and Community Development 2.6
Debt Outstanding per Capita 1,378
   % Utility 5.4
Federal Procurement Contract Awards (in millions)
   $1,193.3
Federal Grants Awards (in millions) $88.5
Fiscal Year Begins July 1

Economy

The port of Baltimore's 200 berths accommodate more than 5,000 ships annually. The port consistently handles the

second- or third-greatest volume of foreign trade of any American port—more than 40 million tons of cargo a year. The port is popular with shippers because it has an advantage of at least 150 miles over competing Atlantic ports for shipments to and from Midwestern markets, and also because it has a sheltered and easily accessible harbor reached by a 50-foot wide main channel from Chesapeake Bay. Baltimore has the world's largest coastal facilities for loading and discharging bulk commodities. The port also specializes in military equipment, cars, and containerized cargoes. The Maryland Port Authority, founded in 1956, has constructed a 365-acre marine terminal to handle specialized shipments. Baltimore's industrial base eroded in the 1980s as the economy's base became more service-driven. Westinghouse, Bethlehem Steel, and Martin Marietta once sustained a large portion of the industrial sector. Of the over 2,000 factories, the largest is the Bethlehem Steel Plant at Sparrows Point, which produces steel as well as ships. Other plants produce chemicals, fabricated metal products, machinery, and food products. Growth in the 1990s has been principally in high-technology areas, particularly electronics, aerospace, and biotechnology. The Johns Hopkins University and University of Maryland have stimulated industrial research. Tourism is another contributor to the growth of construction and retail trade.

Economy

Total Money Income (in millions) $6,458.1
% of State Average 66.7
Per Capita Annual Income $8,647
% Population below Poverty Level 22.9
Fortune 500 Companies 1

Banks	Number	Deposits (in millions)
Commercial	41	NA
Savings	115	NA

Passenger Autos 450,222
Electric Meters 913,910
Gas Meters 482,538

Manufacturing

Number of Establishments 963
% with 20 or More Employees 44.5
Manufacturing Payroll (in millions) $1,252.7
Value Added by Manufacture (in millions) $4,064.2
Value of Shipments (in millions) $8,893.1
New Capital Expenditures (in millions) $193.4

Wholesale Trade

Number of Establishments NA
Sales (in millions) NA
Annual Payroll (in millions) NA

Retail Trade

Number of Establishments 5,570
Total Sales (in millions) $3,167
Sales per Capita $4,207
Number of Retail Trade Establishments with Payroll 4,096
Annual Payroll (in millions) $437.0
Total Sales (in millions) $3,091
General Merchandise Stores (per Capita) $280
Food Stores (per Capita) $333

Economy (continued)

Apparel Stores (per Capita) $289
Eating and Drinking Places (per Capita) $617

Service Industries

Total Establishments   4,414
Total Receipts (in millions) $2,499
Hotels and Motels (in millions) $137.1
Health Services (in millions)   511.9
Legal Services (in millions) $458.3

Labor

Baltimore's blue-collar tradition is being updated by new jobs in the service and high-technology sectors. The total number of manufacturing jobs has declined by over 50% in the past decade. The job loss was particularly severe in heavy industries, such as shipbuilding and steel. Nevertheless, employment has been fairly stable and unemployment rates have been consistently below national averages. One of the city's major employers is the federal government. There are several military installations nearby, such as Aberdeen Proving Ground and Fort Meade. The Johns Hopkins-University-associated research centers account for a large percentage of skilled workers

Labor

Civilian Labor Force   346,599
% Change 1989–1990   0.9

Workforce Distribution
  Mining   300
  Construction   61,900
  Manufacturing   120,200
  Transportation and Public Utilities   54,800
  Wholesale and Retail Trade   254,500
  FIRE (Finance, Insurance, Real Estate)   75,300
  Service   328,700
  Government   210,400
  Women as % of Labor Force   NA
  % Self-Employed   NA
  % Professional/Technical   NA
Total Unemployment   26,767
Rate %   7.7
Federal Government Civilian Employment   15,555

Education

The Baltimore City Public School System supports 177 schools. The Catholic diocese maintains an extensive parochial school system. Some 40,000 students attend private and parochial schools. There are a number of private schools including Gilman, McDonough, and St. Paul's for boys, Garrison Forest for girls, and the Friends School and Park School for both sexes.

In higher education, the preeminent private institution is The Johns Hopkins University, located in the northern portion of the city on the Homewood Campus; the medical school and hospital occupy a complex of new and old buildings in the eastern part of the city. The University of Maryland at Baltimore is the site of all the professional schools of the University of Maryland system, whose main campus is at College Park. Other state institutions include Towson State University at Towson, the oldest four-year college in the state; Morgan State University; and Coppin State College. Catholic-run schools are Loyola University and the College of Notre Dame (for women). Goucher College is in nearby Towson. The Maryland Institute College of Art includes the famous Rinehart School of Sculpture. The Peabody Institute, affiliated with The Johns Hopkins University, is the oldest privately endowed music school in the nation.

Education

Number of Schools   177
Special Education Schools   7
Total Enrollment   108,663
% Enrollment in Private Schools   NA
% Minority   82.3
Classroom Teachers   5,792
Pupil-Teacher Ratio   18.7:1
Number of Graduates   3,771
Total Revenue (in millions) $479.638
Total Expenditures (in millions) $408.543
Expenditures per Pupil $3,563
Educational Attainment (Age 25 and Over)
% Completed 12 or More Years   48.4
% Completed 16 or More Years   11.3
Four-Year Colleges and Universities   13
Enrollment   50,408
Two-Year Colleges   3
Enrollment   8,448

Libraries

Number   101
Public Libraries   3
Books (in thousands)   2,130,982
Circulation (in thousands)   1,493,195
Persons Served (in thousands)   763,600
Circulation per Person Served   1.95
Income (in millions) $17.014
Staff   375

Health

The medical sector includes 31 accredited hospitals, of which Johns Hopkins Hospital is one of the largest and most advanced in the nation. The University of Maryland School of Medicine also is a teaching hospital and equally prestigious. Other medical facilities include Sinai Hospital, Union Memorial Hospital, Maryland General Hospital, Greater Baltimore Medical Center, Mercy Hospital, St. Joseph Hospital, Children's Hospital, Veterans Administration Medical Center, Bon Secours Hospital, Church Hospital, Good Samaritan Hospital, South Baltimore General Hospital, and St. Agnes Hospital.

Health

Deaths—Total 9,624
Rate per 1,000 12.6
Infant Deaths—Total 217
Rate per 1,000 16.8
Number of Metro Hospitals 31
Number of Metro Hospital Beds 9,342
Rate per 100,000 1,241
Number of Physicians NA
Physicians per 1,000 3.51
Nurses per 1,000 10.9
Health Expenditures per Capita 69.08

Transportation

Baltimore is approached by four interstates: I-95 is the principal north-south route with downtown access via I-395; I-70 is the principal approach from the west; I-295 (the Baltimore-Washington Parkway) goes south to Washington D.C.; and I-83 runs north to central Pennsylvania. All of these interstates connect with the Beltway, I-695. Much north-south traffic bypasses the city by means of two under-harbor tunnels. Baltimore is connected to Boston and to Washington and points beyond by Amtrak. Pennsylvania Station is the sixth-busiest Amtrak station in the country. For commuters, the Maryland Rail Commuter Service (MARC) offers weekday rail service to Union Station in Washington, D.C., from both Pennsylvania Station and Camden Station near the Inner Harbor. Freight service is provided by CSX, Canton, Conrail, and Norfolk Southern. The principal air terminal is the Baltimore-Washington International Airport, nine miles from downtown.

Transportation

Interstate Highway Mileage 127
Total Urban Mileage 6,011
Total Daily Vehicle Mileage (in millions) $35
Daily Average Commute Time 58.3
Number of Buses 806
Port Tonnage (in millions) $42
Airports 1
Number of Daily Flights NA
Daily Average Number of Passengers NA

Airlines (American Carriers only)
    American
    American West
    Continental
    Delta
    Eastern
    Northwest
    Trans World
    United
    USAir

Housing

Baltimore housing is characterized by two features: the prevalence of row houses, a carryover from the nineteenth century, and a distaste for apartment living and a concomitant commitment to home ownership. Over the past few decades nonwhites have been moving to the western, northeastern, and northwestern parts of the city. Urban renewal has restored many areas of the city, such as Bolton Hill, Otterbein, and Federal Hill. Now the most desirable established neighborhoods in the city are Mount Vernon, Roland Park, and Homeland; newer planned communities include Cross Keys and Cold Spring; traditional middle-class neighborhoods include Hampden and Waverly. In 1990 about 48.6% (303,706) of housing stock was owner-occupied. The median value of owner-occupied housing was $54,700, and the median monthly rent was $321.

Housing

Total Housing Units 303,706
% Change 1980–1990 0.3
Vacant Units for Sale or Rent 19,025
Occupied Units 276,484
% with More Than One Person per Room 4.6
% Owner-Occupied 48.6
Median Value of Owner-Occupied Homes $54,700
Average Monthly Purchase Cost $NA
Median Monthly Rent $321
New Private Housing Starts 240
Value (in thousands) $10,764
% Single-Family 66.2
Nonresidential Buildings Value (in thousands) $91,310

Tallest Buildings:	Hgt.(ft.)	Stories
U.S. Fidelity & Guaranty Co.	529	40
Maryland National Bank Bldg.	509	34
6 St. Paul Place	493	37
World Trade Center Bldg.	395	32
Tremont Plaza Hotel	395	37
250 W. Pratt St.	360	26
Harbor Court	356	28
Blaustein Bldg.	342	30

Urban Redevelopment

The most ambitious of the downtown commercial renewal programs is the Inner Harbor Redevelopment, which began in 1967. Most of the warehouses and factories around the harbor basin were razed following the relocation of the traditional port to deeper water in the Outer Harbor at the end of World War II. The internationally recognized project involved constructing six million square feet of office space, the National Aquarium in Baltimore, Harborplace, Baltimore Convention Center and Festival Hall Exhibit Center, 2,500 new hotel rooms, and 1,500 townhouse and condominium apartment units. Also new in the area are the Charles Center, the 33-story World Trade Center, a new hotel, a new home for the Maryland Academy of Sciences, high-rise apartments, and a new convention center. Glass-enclosed shops, restaurants, and kiosks are all housed in the two-story, two-pavilion Harborplace. The Charles Center project, adjacent to Inner Harbor, is the city's most significant business redevelopment project and centers on One Charles Center, a 24-story building designed by famed architect Mies van der Rohe.

Crime

The city's violent crimes in 1991 were 19,032, while property crimes totaled 66,036.

Crime

Violent Crimes—Total   19,032
Violent Crime Rate per 100,000   1,255
Murder   304
Rape   701
Robbery   10,770
Aggravated Assaults   7,257
Property Crimes   66,036
Burglary   16,230
Larceny   39,213
Motor Vehicle Theft   10,593
Arson   601
Per Capita Police Expenditures $188.95
Per Capita Fire Protection Expenditures $101.81
Number of Police   2,965
Per 1,000   38.5

Religion

Roman Catholics make up the largest religious group with 25%. Baptists, Lutherans, and Methodists rank as the next largest groups. About 7% of the population is Jewish. Baltimore was the site of the nation's first Roman Catholic archdiocese in 1789, with the first major Catholic cathedral being dedicated in 1821.

Religion

Largest Denominations (Adherents)
Catholic   93,032
Black Baptist   86,031
Jewish   45,799
United Methodist   26,139
Evangelical Lutheran Church in America   16,091
Episcopal   14,028
American Baptist   13,704
Presbyterian   12,115

Media

The city press consists of one main daily, *The Baltimore Sun*, while *The Daily Record* is a Monday through Saturday business and legal paper. There are five weeklies. The electronic media consist of seven television stations (six commercial networks and one public) and 21 AM and FM radio stations.

Sports

The local sports heroes are the Baltimore Orioles who play baseball in Oriole Park at Camden Yards. The wins and losses of nearby college teams are also followed: the University of Maryland Terrapins at College Park, Towson's Towson State Tigers, and the Naval Academy teams at Annapolis. Lacrosse is uniquely popular in Baltimore and is played at the university level by the

Media

Newsprint
  Baltimore Business Journal, weekly
  The Baltimore Chronicle, monthly
  The Daily Record, daily
  The Baltimore Sun, daily
  Times-Herald, weekly

Television
  WBAL (Channel 11)
  WHSW (Channel 24)
  WJZ (Channel 13)
  WMAR (Channel 2)
  WMPB (Channel 67)
  WNUV (Channel 54)

Radio

WBAL-AM	WBGR-AM
WBJC-FM	WBMD-AM
WBSM-FM	WCAO-AM
WEAA-FM	WEBB-AM
WGRX-FM	WITH-AM
WIYY-FM	WJHU-FM
WLIF-FM	WPOC-FM
WQSR-FM	WRBS-FM
WWIN-AM	WWIN-FM
WXYV-FM	WYST-AM
WYST-FM	

Bluejays of Johns Hopkins. The Skip Jacks are the professional ice hockey team. Pimlico Race Course, Maryland's oldest Thoroughbred track, presents the Pimlico Cup and the Futurity Cup, as well as hosting the Preakness Stakes, the second jewel in the Triple Crown. The Maryland Hunt Cup is the grand event in the steeplechase season.

Arts, Culture, and Tourism

The cultural scene in Baltimore is rich and varied. In music, the leaders are the Baltimore Symphony Orchestra playing at the Joseph Meyerhoff Symphony Hall and the Baltimore Opera Company playing at the Lyric Opera House. The Peabody Institute provides a year-round calendar of concerts, operas, and ballets. Summer concert series are held at the Pier Six Concert Pavilion. The Eubie Blake Cultural Arts Center is dedicated to the famous Baltimore-born pianist. In theater the Morris A. Mechanic Theater and Center Stage offer an impressive repertoire of plays each season. The Arena Players is one of the foremost black theater companies, and the Theater Project represents experimental theater.

More than ten major museums make Baltimore one of the nation's most important museum centers. The Walters Art Gallery, presented to the city in 1931 by philanthropist Henry Walters, and the Baltimore Museum of Art are the largest art museums. The Maryland Historical Society's collections are held in the former residence of the nineteenth-century philanthropist Enoch Pratt. The Radcliffe Maritime Museum traces the history of Chesapeake Bay and Maryland shipbuilding. The Baltimore and Ohio Railroad Museum includes more than 80 locomotives and cars, dating from the early years of the nineteenth century.

The Baltimore Public Works Museum is located in a 1912 sewage pumping station. The Peale Museum, now part of the City Life Museums, was built in 1814 by artist-inventor Rembrandt Peale. Other museums include the Baltimore Science Center and Davis Planetarium. The National Aquarium in the Inner Harbor features exhibits of aquatic life and houses more than 5,000 creatures.

Travel and Tourism

Hotel Rooms   16,000
Convention and Exhibit Space (square feet)   300,000

Convention Centers
   Baltimore Convention Center

Festivals
   Artscape (July)
   City Fair (September)
   18 ethnic festivals

Parks and Recreation

Baltimore has over 70 parks covering 6,000 acres; Gwynns Falls Park with 686 acres is the largest. The 674-acre Druid Hill Park, which includes the City Zoo and a conservatory known as the Palm House, extends westward from the deep rocky valley of Jones Falls. Carroll Park on Washington Boulevard has Mount Clare, built as the home of Charles Carroll in 1754, at its center. The 263-acre Clifton Park on Harford Road was acquired in 1893 by the city from The Johns Hopkins University. Also on Harford Road is 572-acre Herring Run Park.

Sources of Further Information

Baltimore Area Convention and Visitors Association
100 Light Street
Baltimore, MD 21202
(410) 659-7300

Baltimore County Chamber of Commerce
102 West Pennsylvania Avenue, Suite 402
Towson, MD 21204
(410) 825-6200

Baltimore Office of Promotion
200 West Lombard Street, Suite B
Baltimore, MD 21201
(410) 752-8632

City Hall
100 North Holliday Street
Baltimore, MD 21202
(410) 396-3100

City of Baltimore Development Corporation
36 South Charles Street
Baltimore, MD 21202
(410) 752-8632

Additional Reading

Argersinger, Jo Ann. *Toward a New Deal in Baltimore: People and Government in the Great Depression.* 1988.

Beirne, Francis F. *The Amiable Baltimoreans.* 1984.

Brambilla, Roberto, and Gianni Longo. *Learning from Baltimore: What Makes Cities Livable?* 1979.

Browne, Gary. *Baltimore in the Nation, 1789–1861.* 1980.

Clayton, Ralph. *Black Baltimore, 1820–1970.* 1987.

Evans, Paul F. *City Life: A Perspective from Baltimore, 1968–1978.* 1981

Friedrichs, Jurgen, and Allen C. Goodman, with Uwe Meier. *The Changing Downtown: A Comparative Study of Baltimore and Hamburg.* 1987.

Graham, Leroy. *Baltimore: The Nineteenth Century Black Capital.* 1982.

Hicks, Mildred T. *When the Earth was Flat: Memoirs of Old Baltimore.* 1985.

Hollander, Jacob Harry. *The Financial History of Baltimore.* 1982 (first ed. 1899).

Morris, John G. *The Lords Baltimore.* 1874.

Nast, Lenora H., ed. *Baltimore, A Living Renaissance.* 1982.

Olson, Sherry H. *Baltimore: The Building of an American City.* 1980.

Spalding, Thomas W. *The Premier See: A History of the Archdiocese of Baltimore, 1789–1989.* 1989.

Vexler, Robert I., ed. *Baltimore: A Chronological and Documentary History, 1632–1970.* 1975.

Baton Rouge

Louisiana

Location and Topography

N

Baton Rouge, the capital of Louisiana, is situated along the Mississippi River in the southeastern part of the state. It is located on the Istrouma Bluff 230 miles from the mouth of the Mississippi River. The land is mainly delta coastal plain.

Layout of City and Suburbs

The city is dominated by the state capitol, adjacent to the Mississippi River. Surrounding the capitol building is a series of streets not laid out in a traditional grid pattern. The Centroplex Theatre, a 12,000-seat arena for the performing arts, is situated directly southeast of the capitol. The main streets include River Road (which runs parallel to the Mississippi River), Florida Boulevard, and Government Street. Greenwell Springs Road moves northeast toward the Comite and Amie rivers. The Baton Rouge Metro Airport lies to the

north of the city. Some of Baton Rouge's suburbs on both sides of the Mississippi River include Comite, Port Allen, College Hills, and Sunrise.

Climate

Baton Rouge has a subtropical climate free of extreme temperatures. Winters are mild with only occasional cold spells. Rainfall is ample, making the city one of the ten wettest in the nation.

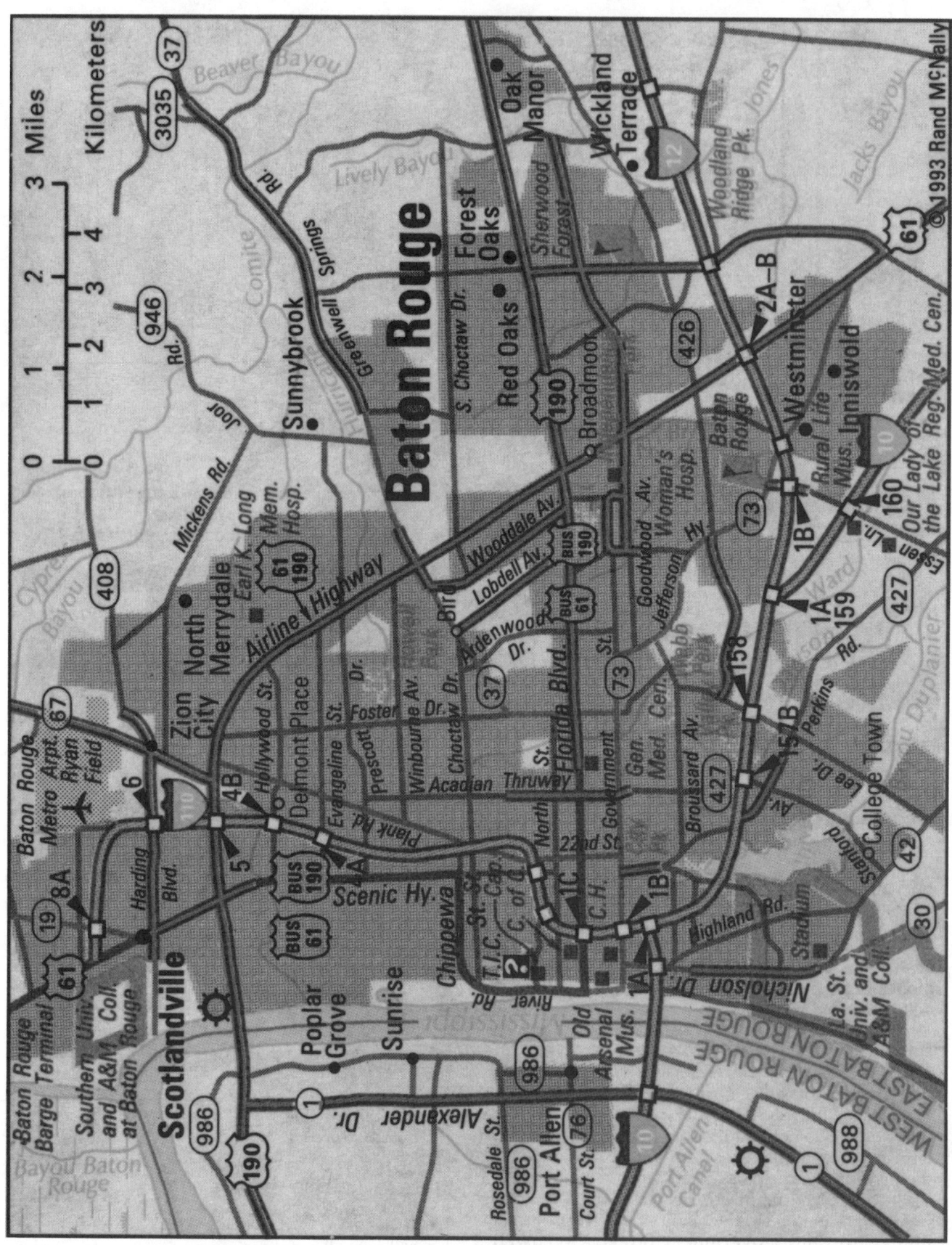

Weather (continued)

Average Temperatures (°F)	High	Low	Mean
January	59.1	42.6	50.9
February	67.8	45.5	56.7
March	73.3	52.8	63.1
April	80.0	61.8	70.9
May	84.8	69.6	77.2
June	90.9	72.2	81.6
July	92.8	74.1	83.5
August	92.2	72.0	82.1
September	87.8	67.3	77.6
October	82.4	59.0	70.7
November	68.2	43.1	55.7
December	67.3	46.9	57.1

History

American Indians have inhabited the Baton Rouge area since at least 8000 B.C. Although few records exist, there is some evidence of 16th-century European activity in the Baton Rouge area, as well as regional visits by Hernando de Soto and Rene Cavalier, Sieur de la Salle, before 1695. However, the first recorded European visitor is Pierre le Moyne, Sieur d'Iberville, who in 1699 traveled some 230 miles up the Mississippi River from the Gulf of Mexico. He discovered the Bayougoulas and Houmas Indians living on the Istrouma Bluff (*istrouma* is apparently a derivation of an Indian word for crawfish, the symbol topping Indian totem poles). The territories of their independent societies were separated by a red stick smeared with animal (possibly fish) blood. D'Iberville called this area Baton Rouge (red stick), and hence the region's name was born.

The colonization of Baton Rouge took several years. In 1712 Frenchman Antoine Crozat, who saw the agricultural potential of the area, began buying land and selling lots to wealthy Frenchmen. He eventually quit the venture, but his place was taken by Diron d'Araguette, who received a land grant from King Louis XIV. D'Araguette started a plantation on the Mississippi River about 1718, although when it was visited there by a French priest in 1721, there is scant confirmation that a man who led a number of colonists was d'Araguette. The plantation, however, was named Dironburg. By 1732 two more plantations thrived—at Pointe Coupee and Bayou Manchac.

Over the next 20 years, the Baton Rouge area was marked by an increase in the number of immigrants from the Arcadia area of Canada. French immigrants inhabited Arcadia (now Nova Scotia), but as Canada moved toward becoming a British colony, they felt more and more threatened. In 1755, as Britain and France fought for Canada, the Arcadians were required to swear allegiance to the British monarch. Instead, they fled to the United States and headed south, finally reaching French-held Louisiana and Baton Rouge. Gradually, their distinct language and customs blended into Louisiana life, making these former Canadian citizens Cajuns, a shortened version of the name of their homeland.

Not much except the political landscape changed when France gave Louisiana to Spain and then lost it completely when the British won all of Louisiana, including Baton Rouge and western Florida, as part of the Treaty of 1763, which ended the French and Indian War. The British occupied the French forts and established a semblance of command over the region. However, Spain still held some local control and began a campaign to win the territory back. On 21 September 1779, Spanish troops led by Don Bernardo de Galvez, the former Spanish governor of Louisiana, attacked British fortifications and ships in what is called the First Battle of Baton Rouge. Within three weeks, the British surrendered, reestablishing Spanish control over the city. In 1800 Spain returned Baton Rouge and the rest of Louisiana to France. Three years later, under the terms of the Louisiana Purchase, all of the territory west of the Mississippi, as well as Louisiana, was sold to the United States for $15,000,000. Alone as an outpost was Baton Rouge, which remained in Spanish hands. Americans in the city agitated to make it part of the United States. Within seven years they attacked the Spanish troops in the Second Battle of Baton Rouge on 23 September 1810 and declared the Republic of West Florida. President James Madison sent in American troops to quell the uprising, but in the process recognized the new "republic" as part of Louisiana on 7 December. Within two years Louisiana was admitted to the union as the 18th state; Baton Rouge received its city charter in 1817. In 1846 the state capital was moved to Baton Rouge, and three years later the state capitol building was completed.

The era from 1810 until 1861 was marked by the building up of Baton Rouge, most notably in architecture, and sprawling plantations became the order of the day. Fueling this economic boom were sugarcane, cotton, and slaves. By 1861 the population was over 5,000, with a third being slaves. In 1861, when the the Confederate states broke away from the Union, Louisiana was at the forefront. In 1862, Union forces seized the city. Subsequent Confederate attempts, particularly the Third Battle of Baton Rouge on 5 August 1862, to reclaim the city failed, and Baton Rouge remained in Union hands throughout most of the war. The capital was moved to several other cities before winding up in Shreveport for the duration of the war. It remained there until 1882, when it was returned to Baton Rouge.

Between the end of the war and the turn of the century, Baton Rouge sought to rebuild itself. It soon became an important commercial center and river city. The rise of Huey P. Long—known as the Kingfish—first governor, then U.S. senator, marked the early 20th century. A noted tough politician, Long was both loved and hated. His death, allegedly by an assassin's bullet, ended a major era in Louisiana politics. The Depression made a major dent in the economy, but World War II improved the picture, enabling Baton Rouge to become a leading commercial capital on the Mississippi River.

Chronology

1699 Although there have been several prior European visits to the general Louisiana area, Pierre le Moyne, Sieur d'Iberville, visits the Istrouma Bluff. Finding a stick smeared with animal blood on the bluff (separating the territories of the Bayougoulas and Houmas Indians), he calls the site Baton Rouge (red stick).

1712 Frenchman Antoine Crozat is given a land grant at Baton Rouge and begins selling plots of land to wealthy Frenchmen.

1718? Frenchman Diron d'Araguette establishes the plantation of Dironburg at Baton Rouge.

1755 Massive Arcadian migration from Canada to Louisiana begins.

1762 French king Louis XV gives possession of Louisiana to his cousin, Charles III of Spain.

1763 Under the terms of the Treaty of Paris, which ends the French and Indian War, Louisiana and western Florida are ceded to Great Britain.

1779 (21 September) Under the command of former governor Don Bernardo de Galvez, Spanish troops seize the British garrison in the First Battle of Baton Rouge.

1803 Baton Rouge is excluded as part of the Louisiana Purchase.

1810 (23 September) In the Second Battle of Baton Rouge, Americans attack the Spanish at Baton Rouge and declare the Republic of West Florida. President James Madison makes Baton Rouge part of Louisiana on 7 December.

1812 Louisiana is admitted into the Union as the 18th state.

1817 Baton Rouge receives its city charter.

1846 Baton Rouge becomes Louisiana's capital.

1861 Louisiana joins the Confederacy.

1862–1865 Baton Rouge is held by the Union. A Confederate attempt to get the city back in the Third Battle of Baton Rouge (5 August 1862) is unsuccessful. The city is destroyed, and the state capital moves to Shreveport.

1882 The state capital moves back to Baton Rouge.

1928–1935 Huey P. Long becomes a major political figure as governor and U.S. senator before being assassinated in 1935.

Historical Landmarks

The old state capitol building was originally built of cast iron and brick in 1849. Burned by invading Union forces during the Civil War, it was restored in 1882 and served as the state capitol building until 1932. It is now an art museum and veterans memorial, with educational facilities and exhibits opening in 1993. The present capitol building was built at the insistence of then-governor Huey P. Long in 1932. Its 34-story tower makes it the tallest state capitol building in the nation. The 27th floor of the tower is an observatory from which a visitor can see the Mississippi River and the surrounding suburbs for miles in every direction. Long was assassinated inside the building in 1935 and is buried on the grounds. Also on the grounds are two other important landmarks: a marker to commemorate the site of the home of Zachary Taylor, the 12th president, who lived in Baton Rouge from 1840 until his election as president in 1848, and the Old Arsenal, which was used as a military barracks and post from its construction in the 1830s until 1879. Two cannons on the site commemorate the First Battle of Baton Rouge in 1779. The old governor's mansion on North Boulevard was built during Huey Long's administration. Behind it is Beauregard Town, the outline of a village built in 1806 to resemble a quaint European city.

Population

Baton Rouge registered a slight gain in population in 1990, rising to 220,394 from 219,531 in 1980 and 166,000 in 1970. The growth rate was 32.2% in the 1970s and 0.4% in the 1980s.

Population		
	1980	*1990*
Central City	219,531	220,394
Rank	62	73
Metro Area	494,151	528,264
Pop. Change 1980–1990 +863		
Pop. % Change 1980–1990 +0.4		
Median Age 30.0		
% Male 47.3		
% Age 65 and Over 11.5		
Density (per square mile) 2,966		

Households		
Number 83,340		
Persons per Household 2.51		
% Female-Headed Households 17.7		
% One-Person Households 29.7		
Births—Total 5,210		
% to Mothers under 20 14.7		
Birth Rate per 1,000 21.8		

Ethnic Composition

Whites make up 53.9%, blacks 43.9%, American Indians 0.1%, Asians and Pacific Islanders 1.7%, Hispanics 1.6%, and others 0.3%. Descendants of the Acadians, popularly

Ethnic Composition (as % of total pop.)

	1980	1990
White	61.86	53.95
Black	36.50	43.89
American Indian	0.13	0.14
Asian and Pacific Islander	0.73	1.67
Hispanic	1.82	1.57
Other	NA	0.35

known as Cajuns, maintain a separate picturesque culture that has attracted much attention.

Government

 Baton Rouge operates under a city-parish form of government, administered by a mayor-president and a 12-member council, all elected to four-year terms.

Public Finance

The annual budget consists of revenues of $385.570 million and expenditures of $367.676 million. The outstanding debt

Government

Year of Home Charter   1949
Number of Members of the Governing Body   12
Elected at Large   NA
Elected by Wards   12
Number of Women in Governing Body   2
Salary of Mayor $81,444
Salary of Council Members $3,600
City Government Employment Total   5,344
Rate per 10,000   144.7

Public Finance

Total Revenue (in millions) $385.570
Intergovernmental Revenue—Total (in millions) $41.01
Federal Revenue per capita $18.18
% Federal Assistance   4.71
% State Assistance   5.46
Sales Tax as % of Total Revenue   19.53
Local Revenue as % of Total Revenue   80.47
City Income Tax   no
Taxes—Total (in millions) $120.5

Taxes per capita
Total   326
Property   78
Sales and Gross Receipts   225
General Expenditures—Total (in millions) $262.2
General Expenditures per capita $710
Capital Outlays per capita $96

% of Expenditures for:
Public Welfare   0.4
Highways   15.2
Education   0.0
Health and Hospitals   6.3
Police   9.2
Sewerage and Sanitation   7.6
Parks and Recreation   4.9
Housing and Community Development   2.9
Debt Outstanding per capita $1,704
% Utility   NA
Federal Procurement Contract Awards (in millions) $229.4
Federal Grants Awards (in millions) $316.1
Fiscal Year Begins   January 1

is $766.115 million, and cash and security holdings are $1.049 billion.

Economy

Baton Rouge's multitiered economy is based on government, manufacturing, commerce, and tourism. Being the capital of Louisiana plays an important part in the employment picture—nearly one out of ten workers are employed by the state government. Services employ 36%, while construction workers make up about 11%. Trade and commerce make use of the Mississippi River. Nearly half a million visitors and tourists annually contribute needed dollars to the economy.

Economy

Total Money Income (in millions) $2,311
% of State Average   118.9
Per capita Annual Income $10,505
% Population below Poverty Level   18.7
Fortune 500 Companies   NA

Banks	Number	Deposits (in millions)
Commercial	17	8,556
Savings	9	NA

Passenger Autos   267,811
Electric Meters   176,142
Gas Meters   85,122

Manufacturing

Number of Establishments   236
% with 20 or More Employees   26.7
Manufacturing Payroll (in millions) $265.3
Value Added by Manufacture (in millions) $1,059.3
Value of Shipments (in millions) $2,435.7
New Capital Expenditures (in millions) $73.4

Wholesale Trade

Number of Establishments   678
Sales (in millions) $2,047
Annual Payroll (in millions) $173.520

Retail Trade

Number of Establishments   2,515
Total Sales (in millions) $2,215.8
Sales per capita $9,189
Number of Retail Trade Establishments with Payroll   1,832
Annual Payroll (in millions) $265.2
Total Sales (in millions) $2,186.1
General Merchandise Stores (per capita)   NA
Food Stores (per capita) $2,012
Apparel Stores (per capita) $515
Eating and Drinking Places (per capita) $818

Service Industries

Total Establishments   2,483
Total Receipts (in millions) $1,077.2
Hotels and Motels (in millions) $32.7
Health Services (in millions) $297.6
Legal Services (in millions) $122.2

Labor

 Government is the largest employment sector, followed by trade, service, construction, and manufacturing, in that order. Louisiana has a right-to-work law. The efforts of the Baton Rouge Joint Labor Management

Committee have helped to maintain industrial peace for many years.

Labor	
Civilian Labor Force	121,003
% Change 1989–1990	0.1
Work Force Distribution	
Mining	900
Construction	29,800
Manufacturing	22,900
Transportation and Public Utilities	11,100
Wholesale and Retail Trade	53,000
FIRE (Finance, Insurance, Real Estate)	13,300
Service	55,200
Government	55,800
Women as % of Labor Force	44.0
% Self-Employed	4.8
% Professional/Technical	20.0
Total Unemployment	6,387
Rate %	5.3
Federal Government Civilian Employment	1,743

Education

The East Baton Rouge Parish Schools system supports 103 schools. The public school system is supplemented by over 33 parochial and private schools. Higher education is provided by two state universities: Louisiana State University and Southern University, founded in 1855 and 1880, respectively.

Education	
Number of Public Schools	103
Special Education Schools	3
Total Enrollment	61,669
% Enrollment in Private Schools	19
% Minority	57.2
Classroom Teachers	3,819
Pupil-Teacher Ratio	16.1:1
Number of Graduates	2,955
Total Revenue (in millions)	$212.6
Total Expenditures (in millions)	$181.3
Expenditures per Pupil	$3,033
Educational Attainment (Age 25 and Over)	
% Completed 12 or More Years	69.6
% Completed 16 or More Years	25.0
Four-Year Colleges and Universities	2
Enrollment	34,429
Two-Year Colleges	2
Enrollment	600

Libraries	
Number	33
Public Libraries	11
Books (in thousands)	841
Circulation (in thousands)	2,053
Persons Served (in thousands)	380
Circulation per Person Served	2.05
Income (in millions)	$7.9
Staff	133
Four-Year Colleges and Universities	
Louisiana State University	
Southern University	

Health

The medical sector consists of five hospitals and three regional medical centers. Earl K. Long Hospital (the teaching arm of the LSU Medical School), Women's Hospital, and the Medical Center of Baton Rouge are the largest hospitals. Other facilities include Our Lady of the Lake Medical Center, Lane Memorial Hospital, CPC Meadow Wood, and Parkland Psychiatric Care Unit.

Health	
Deaths—Total	1,916
Rate per 1,000	8.0
Infant Deaths—Total	71
Rate per 1,000	13.6
Number of Metro Hospitals	5
Number of Metro Hospital Beds	1,596
Rate per 100,000	432
Number of Physicians	795
Physicians per 1,000	NA
Nurses per 1,000	NA
Health Expenditures per capita	$16.70

Transportation

Baton Rouge is approached by Interstates 10, 12, and 110, as well as U.S. Highways 61 and 190. Rail service is provided by five railroads: Illinois Central Gulf, Union Pacific, Kansas City Southern, Seaboard System, and Southern Pacific. The Port of Baton Rouge is the fifth-largest deep-water port in the nation. The principal air terminus is the Baton Rouge Metropolitan Airport–Ryan Field, located about five miles north of downtown; it is served by three major airlines.

Transportation	
Interstate Highway Mileage	34
Total Urban Mileage	1,646
Total Daily Vehicle Mileage (in millions)	7.4
Daily Average Commute Time	50.2 min.
Number of Buses	55
Port Tonnage (in millions)	78.857
Airports	1
Number of Daily Flights	25
Daily Average Number of Passengers	1,170
Airlines (American carriers only)	
American	
Continental	
Delta	
Northwest	
Trans World	
United	

Housing

Housing starts declined from 2,830 in 1978 to 853 in 1990 for single-family homes, and from 1,074 to 2 for multifamily dwellings. Of the 97,115 houses, 52.8% are owner-occupied. The median value of an owner-occupied home is $67,900 and the median rent $273.

Housing

Total Housing Units	97,115
% Change 1980–1990	13.4
Vacant Units for Sale or Rent	9,376
Occupied Units	83,340
% with More Than One Person per Room	5.3
% Owner-Occupied	52.8
Median Value of Owner-Occupied Homes	$67,900
Average Monthly Purchase Cost	$309
Median Monthly Rent	$273
New Private Housing Starts	30
Value (in thousands)	$2,141
% Single-Family	63.3
Nonresidential Buildings Value (in thousands)	$46,490

Tallest Buildings	Hgt. (ft.)	Stories
State Capitol (1932)	460	34
Hancock Bank Bldg. (1974)	315	24

Urban Redevelopment

A new civic center, the Riverside Centroplex, is one of the largest post–World War II urban redevelopment projects. The Riverside Plaza is located downtown on the banks of the Mississippi River.

Crime

Baton Rouge has one of the highest crime rates among all cities. The 1991 violent crime rate per 100,000 persons was 1,286.

Crime

Violent Crimes—Total	5,452
Violent Crime Rate per 100,000	1,286
Murder	58
Rape	142
Robbery	1,139
Aggravated Assaults	4,113
Property Crimes	25,434
Burglary	6,390
Larceny	16,026
Motor Vehicle Theft	3,018
Arson	166
Per capita Police Expenditures	$107.95
Per capita Fire Protection Expenditures	$48.96
Number of Police	575
Per 1,000	2.34

Religion

In keeping with its French heritage, Baton Rouge is heavily Catholic. About 13% are Baptists and 5% Methodists.

Religion

Largest Denominations (Adherents)	
Catholic	97,051
Southern Baptist	66,033
Black Baptist	33,598
United Methodist	23,141
Episcopal	4,675
Presbyterian	4,791
Jewish	873

Media

Baton Rouge's sole daily is the *Advocate*, published seven days a week. The city's electronic media consist of four television stations (three commercial and one public) and 12 FM and AM radio stations.

Media

Newsprint
  Advocate, daily
  Greater Baton Rouge Business Report, monthly
  Baton Rouge Commerce, 2x/wk

Television
  WAFB (Channel 9)
  WBRZ (Channel 2)
  WLPB (Channel 27)
  WVLA (Channel 33)

Radio

KLSU (FM)	WBRH (FM)
WGGZ (FM)	WIBR (AM)
WJBO (AM)	WFMF (FM)
WLUX (AM)	WNDC (AM)
WTGE (FM)	WTKL (AM)
WXOK (AM)	WYNK (AM)

Sports

In the absence of a professional sports team, the Fighting Tigers of Louisiana State University (LSU) and the Jaguars of Southern University provide the best in spectator sports. Both LSU and Southern have excellent stadiums (the Tigers play at LSU Tiger Stadium and the Jaguars at Mumford Stadium) and host a number of sports events.

Arts, Culture, and Tourism

With the building of the Riverside Centroplex Theatre for the Performing Arts, a hall which includes a 12,000-seat arena, 30,000-square-foot exhibition hall, and 2,000-seat Theatre of the Performing Arts, many of the leading cultural institutions have been brought under one roof. The Centroplex houses the Baton Rouge Opera, Baton Rouge Symphony, and Baton Rouge Ballet Theater. Other arts events are performed by the Baton

Travel and Tourism

Hotel Rooms	6,034
Convention and Exhibit Space (square feet)	70,000

Convention Centers
  Riverside Centroplex
  LSU Assembly Center, LSU Union
  F. C. Clark Activity Center
  Smith-Brown Memorial Union

Festivals
  Krewe of Mystique Parade (February)
  LSU Open Livestock and Championship Rodeo
    (February)
  River City Blues Festival
  Fall Crafts Festival

Rouge Concert Band, In the Company of Dancers, and Louisiana Youth Orchestra. The museum attractions are diverse: Baker Heritage Museum, Louisiana Governor's Mansion, LSU Rural Life Museum, McHugh House Museum, and Old Arsenal Museum. The *U.S.S. Kidd* Museum is a restored World War II naval destroyer that was the subject of many Japanese kamikaze attacks.

Parks and Recreation

The Baton Rouge Recreation and Parks Commission controls and maintains 144 parks embracing some 4,100 acres. The largest include City Park and Blue Bayou Water Park.

Sources of Further Information

Baton Rouge Convention and Visitors Bureau
730 North Boulevard
Baton Rouge, LA 70802
(800) LA-ROUGE

City Hall
222 St. Louis Street
Baton Rouge, LA 70821
(504) 389-3100

Greater Baton Rouge Chamber of Commerce
564 Laurel Street
Baton Rouge, LA 70821
(504) 381-7125

Additional Reading

Jolly, Ellen R., and James Calhoun. *Pelican Guide to the Louisiana Capital.* 1980.
Kubly, Vincent. *The Louisiana Capitol: Its Art and Architecture.* 1977.

Billings

Montana

Basic Data

Name   Billings
Name Origin   From Frederick K. Billings
Year Founded   1882 Inc. 1885
Status: State   Montana
        County   Seat of Yellowstone County
Area (square miles)   32.6
Elevation (feet)   3,120
Time Zone   Mountain
Population (1990)   81,151
Population of Metro Area (1990)   113,419

Distance in Miles To:

Atlanta	1,799
Boston	2,197
Chicago	1,231
Dallas	1,421
Denver	553
Detroit	1,521
Houston	1,591
Los Angeles	1,238
Miami	2,515
New York	2,039
Philadelphia	1,983
Washington,DC	2,108

Location and Topography

N Billings is located on Clark's Fork Bottom in the Yellowstone River Valley in south-central Montana. The Yellowstone River flows along the southern and eastern boundaries of the city. To the south are the magnificent Pryor and Big Horn mountains, and to the southwest are the Beartooth Mountains. The land is mountainous, marked as one guide says "by buttes and plains." The largest city in Montana and the state's trade and commerce center, Billings is located some 220 miles southeast of the state capital at Helena.

Layout of City and Suburbs

The contour of the Yellowstone River shapes the city's southern and eastern borders. The streets downtown are predominantly in the traditional crosshatch pattern, although in the western section they cross against the pattern and are not as rigid or numerous. The southern area near the river is lined by I-90, one of two interstates to meet the city. To the north is Billings Logan International Airport. Billings's immediate suburbs include Laurel, Park City, Shepherd, and Huntley. Farther away to the southeast is Crow Agency, which borders the Little Bighorn Battlefield National Park.

Climate

Environment

Environmental Stress Index   2.2
Green Cities Index: Rank   NA
                    Score   NA
Water Quality   Alkaline; soft in spring and summer, hard
    in winter
    Average Daily Use (gallons per capita)   NA
    Maximum Supply (gallons per capita)   NA
Parkland as % of Total City Area   9
% Waste Landfilled/Recycled   NA
Annual Parks Expenditures per capita $19.99

 Billings has a typical desert climate with hot summers when the mercury hits 100°F most days, but the nights are cool because of the insulating effect of the surrounding mountains. The winters are occasionally severe, and blizzards are not uncommon. The heaviest snows come in spring or fall when temperatures may drop unexpectedly. Severe cold spells are sometimes relieved by the chinook or drainage winds, bringing warm Pacific air through the Yellowstone River Val-

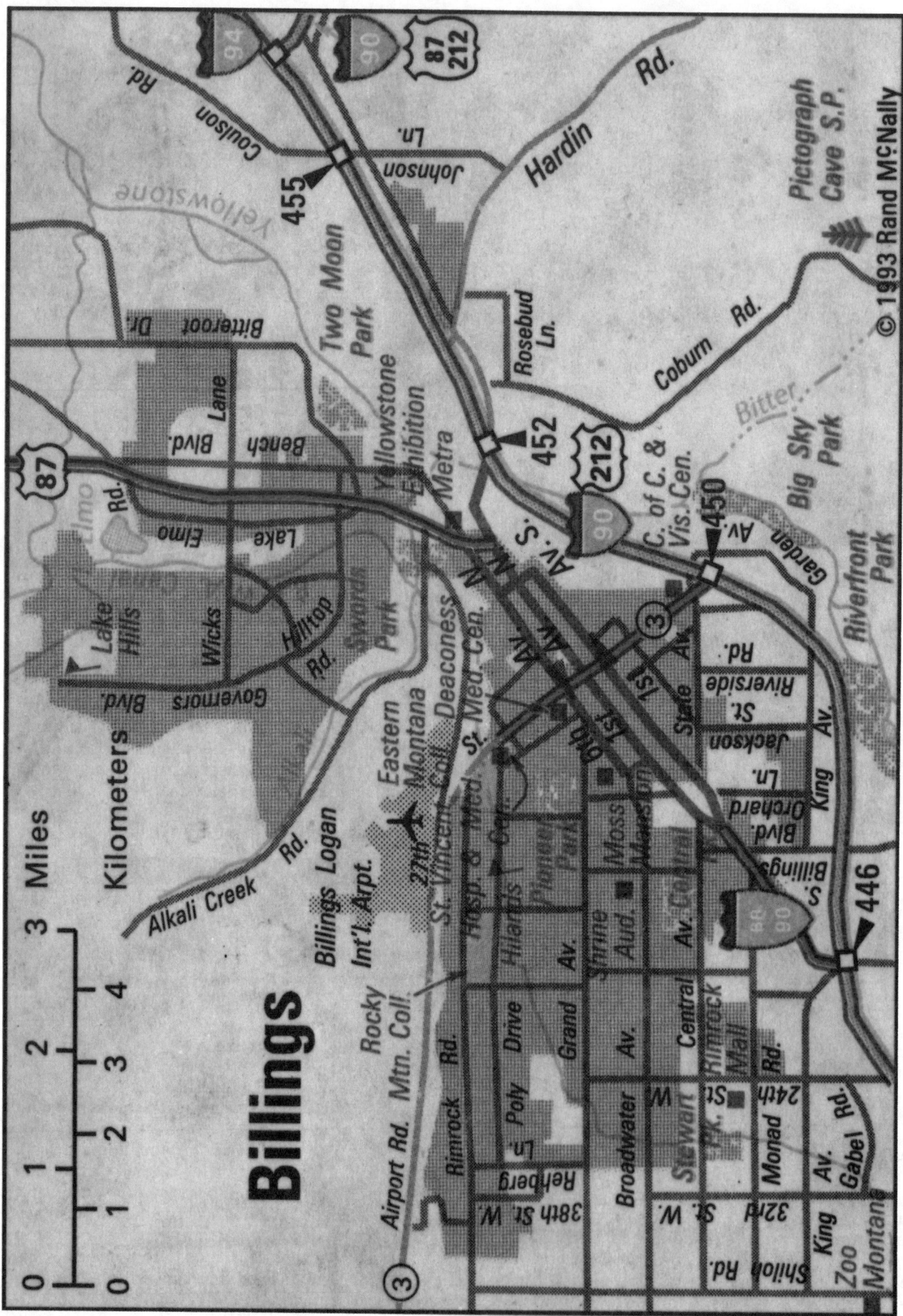

Billings

ley. About a third of the annual average rainfall of 14 inches comes during May and June.

Weather			
Temperature			
Highest Monthly Average °F 85.6			
Lowest Monthly Average °F 12.5			
Annual Averages			
Days 32°F or Below 152			
Days above 90°F 28			
Zero Degree Days 18			
Precipitation (inches) 14			
Snow (inches) 56			
% Seasonal Humidity 56			
Wind Speed (m.p.h.) 11.5			
Clear Days 90			
Cloudy Days 159			
Storm Days 29			
Rainy Days 95			
Average Temperatures (°F)	*High*	*Low*	*Mean*
January	31.2	12.5	21.9
February	37.1	17.7	27.4
March	42.1	23.1	32.6
April	55.8	33.4	44.6
May	65.7	43.3	54.5
June	73.7	51.5	62.6
July	85.6	58.0	71.8
August	83.8	56.3	70.1
September	71.3	46.5	58.9
October	61.0	37.5	49.3
November	45.0	26.4	35.7
December	35.8	17.7	26.8

History

For thousands of years the Yellowstone River Valley region was inhabited by various American Indian tribes who roamed the land freely. By the 1800s only the Absarokee, also known as the Crow, were left. Apparently the first white men who came to what is now Montana were the French fur-trading brothers Pierre and Francois de la Verendrye in 1743. In 1806 Meriwether Lewis and William Clark came to Montana on their return trip from an expedition to the western coast of the present-day United States. The two men split up at what is now Lolo, Montana. Clark explored the Yellowstone River alone, and on 25 July 1806 he visited an area just northeast of present-day Billings and carved his name on a rock called Pompey's Pillar.

The Billings area remained virtually untouched by white men until the 1850s, when the U.S. government sent inspection parties to survey the Yellowstone River Valley. On 17 September 1851, the government signed a treaty with the Crow Indians that left the entire area in the hands of the tribe. Seventeen years later, on 7 May 1868, the Crow agreed to give the U.S. government all the land north of the Yellowstone River and east of longitude 107°F. From 1864 until 1876, the Billings area remained uninhabited except for wagon trains passing by on the way to Bozeman and other points west. The Sioux were the powerful Indian tribe in the Yellowstone Valley; not until the

Battle of the Little Big Horn (southeast of Billings) was their power broken so that Billings could be settled.

In 1877 pioneer P. W. McAdow opened a trading post at Coulson, two miles downriver from where Billings would spring up. In 1882 the Northern Pacific Railroad laid its tracks north of the small town of Coulson, whose settlers hoped that it would become the railroad's main stop. Instead, the Minnesota and Montana Land Improvement Company purchased tracts of land north of the Yellowstone River and platted the town of Billings, named after the president of Northern Pacific, Frederick Billings. Within a month, 200 people settled in the new city, bringing jobs, education, and services. Cattle were also brought in, and within a year a board of trade was established, making Billings a center of commerce in the unconstructed West. In 1883 Billings became the seat of Yellowstone County, and in 1885 the city was incorporated. Several cities pushed for the construction of a rail line to Billings; the first line was completed in 1894 when the Burlington Northern built one from Sheridan, Wyoming, to Billings.

Billings's struggle to become a major city was hampered in the last years of the 19th century by three disastrous fires that destroyed most of the makeshift buildings and by the harsh winter of 1886–1887, which wiped out many of the cattle and crippled the stock business. Yet the city endeavored, and once again built itself up on a solid foundation of cattle and sugar beets. A sugar industry developed with Japanese workers at first, and later Russian-Americans, and a refinery was established in 1906. The Huntley Irrigation Project of 1907 stabilized the water supply and aided the increase of agriculture. Beet pulp was used as cattle feed, and Billings became an important horse and cattle marketing center. At one point the city was the largest inland wool-shipping point in the nation.

Billings had lost the election for state capital to Helena back in 1892, but went on to outdistance both Helena and Butte in population in the 20th century. Oil became the big business of the late 20th century when the Williston Basin was discovered in 1951, and Billings became the state headquarters of the petroleum sector. In the 1970s coal and mining helped diversify the local economy just enough that when the world oil market collapsed in the 1980s, Billings suffered economically, but not like other oil-producing towns. Today it remains a major western hub of agriculture, ranching, and trade distribution.

Historical Landmarks

Downtown Billings has many historic mansions and sites connected to its short but colorful history. The historic district, at one time the old city's business sector, contains many old buildings that have been restored and refurbished. Among these are the Rex Hotel, once a haven for passengers stopping during their travels on the Northern Pacific Railroad; Moss Mansion, built in 1903 by Preston B. Moss, a wealthy Billingsite; Western Heritage Center, formerly the city library, built in 1901

Chronology

1743 French fur-trading brothers Pierre and Francois de la Verendrye are apparently the first white men to explore the southeastern section of what is now Montana.

1806 William Clark, part of the Lewis and Clark expedition, visits an area just to the northeast of present-day Billings and carves his name on what is called Pompey's Pillar.

1851 In a treaty, the U.S. government gives all of the land that is now Billings to the Crow Indians.

1868 A new treaty signed by the Crow cedes all land north of the Yellowstone River and east of longitude 107° to the U.S. government.

1882 The Northern Pacific Railroad enters the valley and locates its tracks at the new city of Billings (named after the railroad president), which is platted by the Minnesota and Montana Land Development Company.

1883 Billings is named the seat of Yellowstone County.

1885 Billings is incorporated as a city.

1892 Billings loses an election to Helena in a contest choosing Montana's state capital.

1894 The first railroad from another western city (Sheridan, Wyoming) is constructed.

1906 First sugar beet refinery is established.

1907 The Huntley Irrigation Project stabilizes the city's water supply for the first time and aids in the growth of agriculture as a major industrial sector.

1951 The Williston Oil Basin is discovered, making Billings the center of Montana's petroleum industry.

and given to the city by Frederick Billings, Jr., son of the city's namesake; and the Northern Hotel, built in 1903 by Preston Moss and Colonel Henry W. Rowley, a Northern Pacific Railroad engineer and irrigation expert, and since restored as the Radisson Northern Hotel. About 55 miles southeast is the Little Bighorn Battlefield, commemorating the 4 July 1876 skirmish between the forces of George Armstrong Custer and the Sioux Indians. To the east is Pompey's Pillar, which famed explorer William Clark visited in 1806.

Population

Billings has become the most populous city in Montana. Its 1990 population of 81,151 was a gain of 21.5% over its 1980 population of 66,813. Earlier it had grown by 8.5% from 61,581 in 1970.

Population

	1980	1990
Central City	66,813	81,151
Rank	294	260
Metro Area	108,035	113,419
Pop. Change 1980–1990 +14,338		
Pop. % Change 1980–1990 +21.5		
Median Age 33.6		
% Male 47.7		
% Age 65 and Over 13.6		
Density (per square mile) 2,489		

Households

Number 33,181
Persons per Household 2.39
% Female-Headed Households 10.5
% One-Person Households 29.4
Births—Total 1,302
 % to Mothers under 20 9.9
 Birth Rate per 1,000 18.6

Ethnic Composition

Whites make up 94.6%, blacks 0.5%, American Indians 3.2%, Hispanics 3.06%, Asians and Pacific Islanders 0.6%, and others 1.1%.

Ethnic Composition (as % of total pop.)

	1980	1990
White	95.15	94.56
Black	0.38	0.54
American Indian	2.34	3.17
Asian and Pacific Islander	0.42	0.59
Hispanic	3.09	3.06
Other	NA	1.14

Government

Billings has a mayor-council form of government. The mayor is elected to a two-year term and the ten council members to four-year terms. The council manager is appointed by the council.

Government

Year of Home Charter 1977
Number of Members of the Governing Body 10
Elected at Large NA
Elected by Wards 10
Number of Women in Governing Body 5
Salary of Mayor NA
Salary of Council Members NA
City Government Employment Total 776
Rate per 10,000 96.6

Public Finance

The annual budget consists of revenues of $60.759 million and expenditures of $61.775 million. The debt outstanding is $89.121 million, and cash and security holdings total $83.091 million.

Public Finance

Total Revenue (in millions) $60.759
Intergovernmental Revenue—Total (in millions) $5.48
Federal Revenue per capita $0.38
% Federal Assistance   0.63
% State Assistance   8.12
Sales Tax as % of Total Revenue   NA
Local Revenue as % of Total Revenue   79.28
City Income Tax   no
Taxes—Total (in millions) $10.4

Taxes per capita
Total   129
Property   111
Sales and Gross Receipts   0.0
General Expenditures—Total (in millions) $57.4
General Expenditures per capita $715
Capital Outlays per capita $336

% of Expenditures for:
    Public Welfare   0.0
    Highways   9.3
    Education   0.0
    Health and Hospitals   0.3
    Police   6.2
    Sewerage and Sanitation   18.6
    Parks and Recreation   2.5
    Housing and Community Development   1.9
Debt Outstanding per capita $917
    % Utility   28.9
Federal Procurement Contract Awards (in millions) $5.9
Federal Grants Awards (in millions) $9.8
Fiscal Year Begins   July 1

Economy

The Billings economic picture was darkened by the collapse of world oil prices in the 1980s. Petroleum jobs dried up, causing much of the economy to falter. However, because of earlier diversification, Billings took the hit better than some oil-state cities. As a trade and commerce hub for the Mid- and Northwest, the city combines shipping by rail and truck with healthy manufacturing, agriculture, and service sectors to lead the state in economic prosperity.

Economy

Total Money Income (in millions) $883.570
% of State Average   125.3
Per capita Annual Income $11,002
% Population below Poverty Level   10.1
Fortune 500 Companies   NA

Banks	Number	Deposits (in millions)
Commercial	12	764.370
Savings	2	269.451

Passenger Autos   61,586
Electric Meters   32,786
Gas Meters   30,682

Economy (continued)

Manufacturing

Number of Establishments   119
% with 20 or More Employees   18.5
Manufacturing Payroll (in millions) $52.2
Value Added by Manufacture (in millions) $121.0
Value of Shipments (in millions) $779.5
New Capital Expenditures (in millions) $20.3

Wholesale Trade

Number of Establishments   348
Sales (in millions) $1,231.2
Annual Payroll (in millions) $85.091

Retail Trade

Number of Establishments   1,193
Total Sales (in millions) $828.5
Sales per capita $10,316
Number of Retail Trade Establishments with Payroll   806
Annual Payroll (in millions) $97.1
Total Sales (in millions) $809.5
General Merchandise Stores (per capita)   NA
Food Stores (per capita) $2,082
Apparel Stores (per capita)   NA
Eating and Drinking Places (per capita) $1,057

Service Industries

Total Establishments   996
Total Receipts (in millions) $331.9
Hotels and Motels (in millions)   NA
Health Services (in millions) $106.8
Legal Services (in millions) $38.4

Labor

Private employers claim only a small share of the employment market, which is dominated by medical services and state and city governments. Employment growth is slow, as the city is far away from the main centers of population.

Labor

Civilian Labor Force   41,492
% Change 1989–1990   0.1

Work Force Distribution
    Mining   NA
    Construction   NA
    Manufacturing   NA
    Transportation and Public Utilities   NA
    Wholesale and Retail Trade   NA
    FIRE (Finance, Insurance, Real Estate)   NA
    Service   NA
    Government   NA
    Women as % of Labor Force   43.8
    % Self-Employed   7.5
    % Professional/Technical   15.4
Total Unemployment   1,952
Rate %   4.7
Federal Government Civilian Employment   1,654

Education

The Billings School District, the largest in the state, supports 23 elementary schools, 4 junior high schools, and 3 senior high schools. There are two four-year institutions of higher education: Eastern Montana College, a public institution, and Rocky Mountain College, supported by three Christian denominations.

Education

Number of Public Schools   30
Special Education Schools   NA
Total Enrollment   15,290
% Enrollment in Private Schools   6.1
% Minority   NA
Classroom Teachers   NA
Pupil-Teacher Ratio   22:1
Number of Graduates   NA
Total Revenue (in millions)   NA
Total Expenditures (in millions)   NA
Expenditures per Pupil   NA
Educational Attainment (Age 25 and Over)
    % Completed 12 or More Years   78.1
    % Completed 16 or More Years   21.9
Four-Year Colleges and Universities   2
Enrollment   3,926
Two-Year Colleges   NA
Enrollment   NA

Libraries

Number   10
Public Libraries   1
Books (in thousands)   263.2
Circulation (in thousands)   375.9
Persons Served (in thousands)   114
Circulation per Person Served   3.29
Income (in millions) $1.038
Staff   26

Four-Year Colleges and Universities
    Eastern Montana College
    Rocky Mountain College

Health

Billings's health-care facilities include two major hospitals and two dozen clinics. The largest hospitals are St. Vincent Hospital and Health Center with 280 beds and Deaconess Medical Center with 253 beds. Smaller facilities include Billings Clinic, Billings Mental Health Center, Rivendell, and Yellowstone Treatment Center.

Health

Deaths—Total   541
Rate per 1,000   7.7
Infant Deaths—Total   10
Rate per 1,000   7.7
Number of Metro Hospitals   2
Number of Metro Hospital Beds   531
Rate per 100,000   661
Number of Physicians   241
Physicians per 1,000   NA
Nurses per 1,000   NA
Health Expenditures per capita $0.45

Transportation

Billings is mainly serviced by two interstates: I-90, which connects the city to Chicago and Seattle, and I-94, which links Billings with Minneapolis. I-25 from Denver cuts

into I-90. U.S. Highways 87, 212, and 310 also approach the city. Amtrak handles all passenger rail traffic, and rail freight service is provided by Burlington Northern and Montana Rail, Inc. The principal air terminus is Billings-Logan International Airport, two miles north of downtown.

Transportation

Interstate Highway Mileage   13
Total Urban Mileage   502
Total Daily Vehicle Mileage (in millions)   1.582
Daily Average Commute Time   35.4
Number of Buses   16
Port Tonnage (in millions)   NA
Airports   1
Number of Daily Flights   19
Daily Average Number of Passengers   599

Airlines (American carriers only)
    American
    Continental
    Delta
    Northwest
    United

Housing

Of the total housing stock, 61.2% is owner occupied. The median value of an owner-occupied home is $63,600 and the median monthly rent $294.

Housing

Total Housing Units   35,964
% Change 1980–1990   22.1
Vacant Units for Sale or Rent   2,132
Occupied Units   33,181
% with More Than One Person per Room   1.7
% Owner-Occupied   61.2
Median Value of Owner-Occupied Homes $63,600
Average Monthly Purchase Cost $385
Median Monthly Rent $294
New Private Housing Starts   144
Value (in thousands) $15,196
% Single-Family   94.4
Nonresidential Buildings Value (in thousands) $7,349

Urban Redevelopment

Urban redevelopment programs are coordinated by Billings-Yellowstone City-County Planning Board and Forward Billings Economic Development Council.

Crime

Despite its lawless past, Billings ranks above the national average in public safety, with a violent crime rate of 81.9 per 100,000 in 1991 and 3,382 property crimes the same year.

Crime

Violent Crimes—Total   81
Violent Crime Rate per 100,000   81.9
Murder   3
Rape   8
Robbery   35
Aggravated Assaults   35
Property Crimes   3,382
Burglary   573
Larceny   2,582
Motor Vehicle Theft   227
Arson   17
Per capita Police Expenditures $58.23
Per capita Fire Protection Expenditures $71.01
Number of Police   100
Per 1,000   1.42

Religion

Roman Catholics were active in the exploration of Montana, and their influence continues to dominate the religious scene. The Catholic population accounts for about half of all churchgoers. The next leading denominations are Methodists and Lutherans, who together account for about 25%.

Religion

Largest Denominations (Adherents)

Catholic	18,277
Evangelical Lutheran	6,915
Latter-Day Saints	3,952
Southern Baptist	2,640
Lutheran-Missouri Synod	3,086
United Church of Christ	2,777
United Methodist	2,702
Jewish	200

Media

The lone city daily is the *Billings Gazette*. The electronic media consist of three major commercial networks and a religious programming station as well as several AM and FM radio stations.

Media

Newsprint
  Agri-News, weekly
  Billings Gazette, daily
  The Billings Times, weekly

Television
  KTVQ (Channel 2)
  KUOS (Channel 4)
  KULR (Channel 8)

Radio
  KBLG (AM)   KRKX (FM)
  KCTR (AM)   KCTR (FM)
  KGHL (AM)   KUUS (AM)
  KYYA (FM)

Sports

Billings has no professional sports teams. The city supports rodeo and horse racing, both held at the MetraPark complex on the grounds of the Yellowstone Exhibition.

Arts, Culture, and Tourism

The hub of cultural activity in Billings is the Alberta Bair Theater for the Performing Arts, known as the ABT. The ABT is the home of the Billings Community Concert Association and the Billings Symphony and hosts plays, operas, and musical performances. Theatrical productions are held by the Billings Studio Theater, Actors Theater Montana, and Billings Children's Theater.

Museums in the area emphasize western culture and history. Among these are the Yellowstone Art Center, Western Heritage Center, Charles M. Russell Museum in Great Falls, Little Bighorn National Monument near Crow Agency, and Yellowstone County Historical Museum near Billings Logan International Airport.

Travel and Tourism

Hotel Rooms   2,425
Convention and Exhibit Space (square feet)   NA

Convention Centers
  Metrapark
  Billings Plaza Trade Center
  Alberta Bair Theater

Festivals
  Heritage of the Yellowstone Folklife Festival

Parks and Recreation

The Billings Parks and Recreation Department is the caretaker for over 40 city parks that handle various recreational activities. The largest are Two Moon, Coulson, Pioneer, Central, and South parks. ZooMontana, a 70-acre wildlife park, reserve, and botanical garden, opened in 1991 to rave reviews.

Sources of Further Information

Billings Area Chamber of Commerce
815 South 27th Street
Billings, MT 59107
(406) 245-4111

Additional Reading

Billings: Economic Handbook, 1991.
Polk's Billings City Directory, 1991.

Birmingham

Alabama

Basic Data

Name   Birmingham
Name Origin   From Birmingham, England
Year Founded   1871 Inc. 1871
Status: State   Alabama
        County   Seat of Jefferson County
Area (square miles)   148.5
Elevation (feet)   600
Time Zone   Central
Population (1990)   265,968
Population of Metro Area (1990)   907,810

Sister Cities

   Coban, Guatemala
   Hitachi, Japan

Distance in Miles To:

Atlanta	153
Boston	1,226
Chicago	657
Dallas	635
Denver	1,325
Detroit	756
Houston	701
Los Angeles	2,052
Miami	754
Minneapolis	1,068
New York	978
Washington, DC	735

Location and Topography

Birmingham is situated in the center of Alabama in the foothills of the Appalachian Mountains. The terrain is woodlands and rolling hills and marked by Red Mountain, which is topped by a statue of Vulcan, the Roman god of fire and blacksmithery.

Layout of City and Suburbs

Downtown Birmingham is laid out in a traditional grid pattern and is surrounded by highways: U.S. 31 on the east side, I-20/59 on the north, and I-65 to the west. A railroad runs through the center of the city. The University of Alabama at Birmingham is the largest structure in the southern part of the city. Birmingham's suburbs include Bessemer, Mountain Brook, Homewood, Cahaba Heights, Fairfield, and Irondale.

Environment

Environmental Stress Index   3.0
Green Cities Index: Rank   31
                    Score   28.25
Water Quality   Alkaline, soft
    Average Daily Use (gallons per capita)   115
    Maximum Supply (gallons per capita)   206
Parkland as % of Total City Area   2.4
% Waste Landfilled/Recycled   NA
Annual Parks Expenditures per capita $68.47

Climate

Birmingham has a semitropical climate with hot, humid summers and mild winters with little or no snowfall. From April through October, high temperatures are generally well into the 80s and the lows are in the 50s. Most of the summer precipitation comes in the form of thunderstorms; hurricanes are unusual.

Weather

Temperature

Highest Monthly Average °F   90.3
Lowest Monthly Average °F   34.1

Annual Averages

Days 32°F or Below   60
Days above 90°F   39
Zero Degree Days   0
Precipitation (inches)   53
Snow (inches)   1

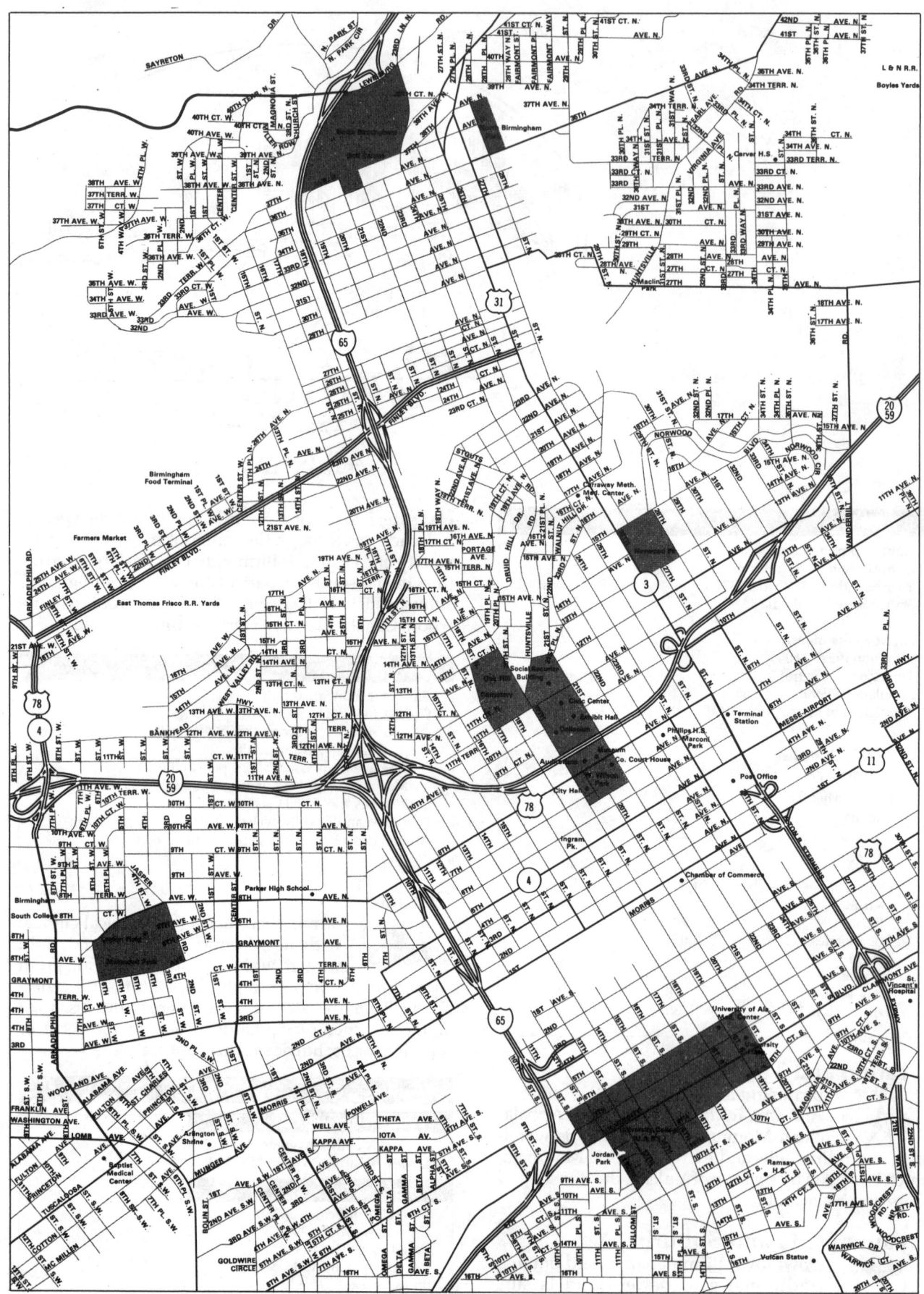

Weather (continued)

% Seasonal Humidity   72
Wind Speed (m.p.h.)   7.4
Clear Days   99
Cloudy Days   155
Storm Days   58
Rainy Days   118

Average Temperatures (°F)	*High*	*Low*	*Mean*
January	54.3	34.1	44.2
February	57.7	36.1	46.9
March	64.8	41.8	53.3
April	75.3	51.0	63.2
May	82.5	58.4	70.5
June	88.4	66.4	77.4
July	90.3	69.5	79.9
August	89.7	68.7	79.2
September	84.7	63.0	73.9
October	75.8	50.8	63.3
November	64.0	40.1	52.1
December	55.5	34.9	45.2

History

Although Birmingham is part of the Deep South, it did not become a city until after the Civil War. The region surrounding present-day Birmingham was formerly inhabited by several American Indian tribes, most notably Cherokee, Choctaw, and Chickasaw. A group of white settlers led by John Jones, veteran of numerous skirmishes with the Indians, settled at Bessemer, just west of Birmingham, and constructed Fort Jonesborough in 1813. In 1819, with the founding of Jefferson County, a small village called Carrollsville sprouted up at the western end of present-day Birmingham proper. A year later, William Ely, surveyor-general for a New England school for the deaf and dumb, arrived in the area to explore a parcel of land given to the school by the federal government. This piece of land sat two miles east of Carrollsville, and Ely intended to promote a settlement instead of a school. He called the pioneer effort that was founded two years later Elyton.

Elyton's commercial possibilities remained hidden until 1860, when iron ore was extracted from what is now called Red Mountain. During the Civil War, ore from Elyton was used for Confederate munitions until Union forces under General James H. Wilson swept into the area and captured the rifle and cannonball factories. The ore, however, remained Elyton's best economic hope for the future. This was realized in 1870 when two railroads, the South and North (later the Louisville and Nashville) and Alabama and Chattanooga (later the Alabama Great Southern) laid their tracks near the city. The junction of their meeting, two miles east of Elyton, determined the site of the village that became Birmingham. A year later, several speculators organized the Elyton Land Company and sold plots of land.

On 19 December 1871 the town of Birmingham (named after the great steel city in Great Britain) was incorporated. Although the city's first years were rocky (an almost threefold increase in the population was wiped out by cholera), the city prospered during the decades leading up to the 20th century. In 1880 coke furnaces were built by the Pratt Company, and in 1895 steel was first produced, making Birmingham one of the chief commerce centers in the South.

Birmingham flourished until the Great Depression, at which time much of the manufacturing sector failed. After the Depression, city leaders realized that reliance on one industry could lay the groundwork for another economic collapse. They began an intense effort to diversify the economy and entice new business sectors. When big steel failed in the 1970s, this diversified economy helped stabilize the city.

Birmingham was one of the major scenes of the civil rights struggle of the early 1960s. The city resisted full-scale racial integration until 1970.

Historical Landmarks

Because much of its history has been made in the last 100 years, Birmingham has fewer historical landmarks than other major cities. The Sloss Furnaces, now a historic museum, is where the Sloss-Sheffield Steel and Iron Company once produced pure iron that fed the city's steel and ore furnaces and economic engine for nearly 90 years. Overlooking the city in Vulcan Park atop Red Mountain is a statue of Vulcan, the Roman god of fire and blacksmithery, who symbolizes the city's origins. Made entirely of Birmingham ore, the statue served to represent the city at the 1904 World's Fair in St. Louis, and has stood on top of Red Mountain since 1938. Older buildings downtown are the Woodward Building, built in 1902 and now the headquarters of the National Bank of Commerce; the Brown-Marx Building; the Empire Building; and the First National Bank Building. Several historic churches, including the First Presbyterian Church, St. Paul's Cathedral, and the First United Methodist Church, were built from 1888–1893. In Bessemer, three restored pioneer homes from the 19th century are on display: the McAdory Plantation, the Sadler Plantation Home, and the Owen Plantation Home, the latter built during the mid-1830s of logs held together by wooden pegs.

Population

Birmingham reported a population of 265,968 in the 1990 census, 6.5% less than its 1980 population of 284,413. It was the second decade of demographic decline for the city, which in the 1970s suffered a 5.5% loss from a 1970 total of 301,000. Surprisingly, the decline came in the very decades when the city was showing outward signs of expansion. Despite the loss, Birmingham remains the largest city in Alabama.

Population		
	1980	*1990*
Central City	284,413	265,968
Rank	50	60
Metro Area	883,993	907,810
Pop. Change 1980–1990 -18,445		
Pop. % Change 1980–1990 -6.5		

Chronology

1813 John Jones and four associates settle in the vicinity and build Fort Jonesborough on the site of present-day Bessemer.

1819 Jefferson County is formed, with the village of Carrollsville as its seat.

1820 William Ely, a New Englander, develops a town 2 miles east of Carrollsville, known as Elyton.

1860 Iron ore in Red Mountain is extracted, making Elyton a center of manufacturing.

1861–1865 With its iron ore stocks, Elyton becomes a major munitions maker for the Confederacy.

1870 Two railroads—the South and North, and the Alabama and Chattanooga—reach an area near Elyton.

1871 Several speculators organize the Elyton Land Company, sell plots of land, and found the town of Birmingham, which is incorporated on 19 December.

1933–1941 The Great Depression strikes hard at Birmingham's economy. Steel mills close, throwing thousands out of work. The need for munitions for the American army during World War II saves the city.

1963–1965 Birmingham is a major scene of civil rights demonstrations.

Population (continued)

Median Age 32.9
% Male 45.7
% Age 65 and Over 14.8
Density (per square mile) 1,791

Households

Number 105,437
Persons per Household 2.46
% Female-Headed Households 21.7
% One-Person Households 31.9
Births—Total 4,801
   % to Mothers under 20 18.4
   Birth Rate per 1,000 17.2

Ethnic Composition

Birmingham has a majority of blacks, constituting 63.3% of the population. Whites make up 36%, American Indians 0.1%, Asians and Pacific Islanders 0.6%, Hispanics 0.4%, and others 0.1%.

Government

Birmingham's form of government changed in 1961 from mayor-commissioners to mayor-council. The mayor is elected at large every four years; the nine council

Ethnic Composition (as % of total pop.)

	1980	1990
White	43.85	35.96
Black	55.63	63.27
American Indian	0.07	0.12
Asian and Pacific Islander	0.28	0.56
Hispanic	0.78	0.39
Other	NA	0.1

Government

Year of Home Charter NA
Number of Members of the Governing Body 9
Elected at Large 9
Elected by Wards NA
Number of Women in Governing Body 2
Salary of Mayor $69,326.40
Salary of Council Members $15,000
City Government Employment Total 3,658
Rate per 10,000 131.8

members are also elected at large, but on a staggered basis in odd-numbered years.

Public Finance

The annual budget consists of revenues of $259.455 million and expenditures of $273.365 million. Debt outstanding is $730.434 million, and cash and reserve holdings are $757.899 million.

Public Finance

Total Revenue (in millions) $259.455
Intergovernmental Revenue—Total (in millions) $31.15
Federal Revenue per capita $8.11
% Federal Assistance 3.12
% State Assistance 4.74
Sales Tax as % of Total Revenue 17.66
Local Revenue as % of Total Revenue 78.89
City Income Tax yes
Taxes—Total (in millions) $105.1

Taxes per capita
Total 379
Property 67
Sales and Gross Receipts 120
General Expenditures—Total (in millions) $200.4
General Expenditures per capita $722
Capital Outlays per capita $127

% of Expenditures for:
   Public Welfare 0.0
   Highways 8.8
   Education 2.9
   Health and Hospitals 0.8
   Police 10.7
   Sewerage and Sanitation 9.4
   Parks and Recreation 10.4
   Housing and Community Development 4.9
Debt Outstanding per capita $1,571
   % Utility 0.0
Federal Procurement Contract Awards (in millions) $176.1
Federal Grants Awards (in millions) $115.6
Fiscal Year Begins July 1

Economy

$ Until the Great Depression, Birmingham was essentially a one-industry steel town. This dependence cost dearly when the Depression hit and the steel mills and iron furnaces closed down. Only during World War II did they start up again. By then, city leaders realized that a diversified economy was Birmingham's only insurance against the effects of other national economic slowdowns. Its leading employment sectors are now education, government, advanced technology, and health. The University of Alabama at Birmingham (UAB) is the largest employer in the city, with a payroll of more than 13,000 persons. Federal and state government follows. Birmingham is the site of the Southern Research Institute, a nonprofit facility that explores the areas of medicine and electronics. With 17 hospitals in the Birmingham metropolitan statistical area, the city is a leader in the health-care sector.

Economy

Total Money Income (in millions)	$2,229.79	
% of State Average	92.6	
Per capita Annual Income	$8,035	
% Population below Poverty Level	22	
Fortune 500 Companies	1	
Banks	Number	Deposits (in millions)
Commercial	26	15,970
Savings	14	2,089
Passenger Autos	477,532	
Electric Meters	306,657	
Gas Meters	176,000	

Manufacturing

Number of Establishments	442
% with 20 or More Employees	42.5
Manufacturing Payroll (in millions)	$568.9
Value Added by Manufacture (in millions)	$1,244.0
Value of Shipments (in millions)	$2,613.2
New Capital Expenditures (in millions)	$73.9

Wholesale Trade

Number of Establishments	1,030
Sales (in millions)	$6,026.0
Annual Payroll (in millions)	$413.993

Retail Trade

Number of Establishments	2,438
Total Sales (in millions)	$2,226.2
Sales per capita	$8,022
Number of Retail Trade Establishments with Payroll	1,887
Annual Payroll (in millions)	$266.3
Total Sales (in millions)	$2,199.6
General Merchandise Stores (per capita)	$884
Food Stores (per capita)	$1,186
Apparel Stores (per capita)	$581
Eating and Drinking Places (per capita)	$790

Service Industries

Total Establishments	2,428
Total Receipts (in millions)	$2,085.6
Hotels and Motels (in millions)	$52.1
Health Services (in millions)	$583.1
Legal Services (in millions)	$211.7

Labor

 The reduction of dependence on manufacturing is reflected in the fact that manufacturing employs fewer workers than services, trade, or even government. In fact, manufacturing's share of the work force dropped from 18.5% in 1980 to 13.7% in 1990. The ten top employers are all in the nonmanufacturing sector.

Labor

Civilian Labor Force	131,103
% Change 1989–1990	1.0
Work Force Distribution	
Mining	5,600
Construction	22,900
Manufacturing	55,500
Transportation and Public Utilities	32,600
Wholesale and Retail Trade	99,500
FIRE (Finance, Insurance, Real Estate)	29,700
Service	106,900
Government	67,500
Women as % of Labor Force	46.9
% Self-Employed	3.2
% Professional/Technical	15.2
Total Unemployment	9,787
Rate %	7.5
Federal Government Civilian Employment	7,581

Education

🍎 Birmingham City School District supports 85 schools. More than 50 private and parochial schools in the metro area supplement the public school system. One of the notable private schools is the Alabama School of Fine Arts. Eight institutions of higher learning are located in Birmingham. The largest is the University of Alabama at Birmingham, which ranks among the top recipients of federal research money; it also includes one of the country's leading medical schools. Other institutions include the Birmingham School of Law; Birmingham Southern College, a Methodist liberal arts college; Miles College; and Samford University, Alabama's largest private university, affiliated with the Baptist Convention. Two-year colleges include Daniel Payne College, a private school affiliated with the African Methodist Episcopal Church, Lawson State Technical College, and Jefferson State Junior College. Birmingham is home to a number of seminaries, including Southeastern Bible College and Birmingham Baptist College.

Education

Number of Public Schools	85
Special Education Schools	NA
Total Enrollment	41,710
% Enrollment in Private Schools	7.8
% Minority	88.9
Classroom Teachers	2,351
Pupil-Teacher Ratio	17.7:1
Number of Graduates	1,820
Total Revenue (in millions)	$136.695
Total Expenditures (in millions)	$112.832

Education (continued)

Expenditures per Pupil $2,483
Educational Attainment (Age 25 and Over)
    % Completed 12 or More Years   60.4
    % Completed 16 or More Years   13.0
Four-Year Colleges and Universities   4
Enrollment   22,005
Two-Year Colleges   4
Enrollment   8,990

Libraries

Number   34
Public Libraries   19
Books (in thousands)   1,137
Circulation (in thousands)   1,900
Persons Served (in thousands)   671
Circulation per Person Served   2.83
Income (in millions) $8.7
Staff   224

Four-Year Colleges and Universities
    University of Alabama at Birmingham
    Samford University
    Birmingham Southern College
    Miles College

Health

Health care is one of the more dynamic sectors of the economy. Birmingham is home to 16 hospitals with a total of 5,175 beds. The largest is the University of Alabama at Birmingham with its numerous specialized facilities and research centers. Among the 25 designated research centers at UAB are the Center for Geographic Medicine, Lister Hill Center for Health Policy, and the Center for AIDS Research. Other hospitals are Veterans Administration Medical Center, St. Vincent's Hospital, Medical Center East, Lakeshore Hospital, Hill Crest Hospital, Health South Medical Center, Eye Foundation Hospital, Children's Hospital of Alabama, Cooper Green Hospital, Carraway Methodist Medical Center, Baptist Medical Center, with two hospitals, and AMI Brookwood Medical Center.

Health

Deaths—Total   3,360
Rate per 1,000   12.0
Infant Deaths—Total   77
Rate per 1,000   16.0
Number of Metro Hospitals   16
Number of Metro Hospital Beds   5,175
Rate per 100,000   1,865
Number of Physicians   NA
Physicians per 1,000   2.71
Nurses per 1,000   NA
Health Expenditures per capita $9.57

Transportation

Birmingham lies at the intersection of Interstates 20, 59, 65, and 459, which runs just south of the city. Other roads servicing the Birmingham area include U.S. Highways

11, 31 (the Montgomery Highway), 78, and 280. Amtrak provides daily service to New York and New Orleans, as well as Mobile. Rail freight service is provided by the Burlington Northern, Birmingham Southern, Norfolk Southern, and CSX railroads. As part of the Warrior-Tombigbee river system, which empties into the Tennessee-Tombigbee waterway, Birmingham is connected by water to many major cities, including Mobile. The principal air terminus is the Birmingham Airport (located just east of the city), which is served by ten major and commuter airlines.

Transportation

Interstate Highway Mileage   112
Total Urban Mileage   4,258
Total Daily Vehicle Mileage (in millions)   17.901
Daily Average Commute Time   51.3 min.
Number of Buses   103
Port Tonnage (in millions)   NA
Airports   1
Number of Daily Flights   89
Daily Average Number of Passengers   3,176

Airlines (American carriers only)
    American
    Delta
    Eastern
    Northwest
    Southwest
    United
    USAir

Housing

An increase in multi-family housing that began in the mid-1980s has continued, particularly in South Birmingham and along U.S. 280 and U.S. 31. There are more than 20 retirement communities in the area, making it a haven for retirees. Of the total housing stock, 53.4% is owner-occupied. The median value of an owner-occupied home is $44,500 and the median monthly rent $225.

Housing

Total Housing Units   117,691
% Change 1980–1990   2.7
Vacant Units for Sale or Rent   9,178
Occupied Units   105,437
% with More Than One Person per Room   4.0
% Owner-Occupied   53.4
Median Value of Owner-Occupied Homes $44,500
Average Monthly Purchase Cost $275
Median Monthly Rent $225
New Private Housing Starts   307
Value (in thousands) $24,030
% Single-Family   46.3
Nonresidential Buildings Value (in thousands) $108,884

Tallest Buildings	Hgt. (ft.)	Stories
Southtrust Tower	454	34
Am South/Sonat Tower	390	30
South Central Bell Hdqts. Bldg.	390	30
City Federal Bldg.	325	27

Urban Redevelopment

 Redevelopment is concentrated in several pockets: downtown, UAB, and along U.S. Highways 280 and 31. Currently under way are three projects, each valued at more than $100 million: expansion of the Birmingham Airport, the Birmingham-Jefferson Civic Center, and the Kirklin Clinic, designed by I. M. Pei. Suburban projects include the Urban Center at Liberty Park, River Point Corporate Center, and the Grandview Office Park.

Crime

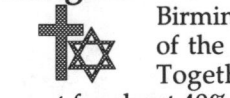 Birmingham ranks below the national average in public safety. Of the crimes known to police in 1991, there were 6,908 violent crimes and 26,987 property crimes.

Crime	
Violent Crimes—Total	6,908
Violent Crime Rate per 100,000	1,127.7
Murder	139
Rape	279
Robbery	1,861
Aggravated Assaults	4,629
Property Crimes	26,987
Burglary	7,894
Larceny	14,869
Motor Vehicle Theft	4,224
Arson	21
Per capita Police Expenditures	$115.77
Per capita Fire Protection Expenditures	$94.82
Number of Police	619
Per 1,000	2.2

Religion

 Birmingham is one of the major centers of the Baptist and Methodist churches. Together the two denominations account for about 40% of the population.

Religion	
Largest Denominations (Adherents)	
Catholic	40,830
Southern Baptist	200,570
Black Baptist	74,357
United Methodist	61,020
Am Zion	21,048
Church of God	9,335
Churches of Christ	12,538
Episcopal	11,072
Presbyterian	11,530
Jewish	3,660

Media

The press in Birmingham consists of two dailies: the *Birmingham News,* published in the afternoons and Sunday, and the *Birmingham Post-Herald,* which comes out every morning except Sunday. The electronic media consist of 6 television stations and 19 AM and FM radio stations.

Media	
Newsprint	
Birmingham Magazine, monthly	
Birmingham News, daily	
Birmingham Post-Herald, daily	
Birmingham Times, weekly	
Birmingham World, weekly	
Television	
WABM (Channel 68)	
WBMG (Channel 42)	
WBIQ (Channel 10)	
WBRC (Channel 6)	
WTTO (Channel 21)	
WVTM (Channel 13)	
Radio	
WAGG (AM)	WENN (FM)
WAPI (AM)	WAPI (FM)
WATV (AM)	WAYE (AM)
WBFR (FM)	WCEO (AM)
WDJC (FM)	WERC (AM)
WMJJ (FM)	WGIB (FM)
WJLD (AM)	WJSR (FM)
WZRR (FM)	WVSU (FM)
WYDE (AM)	WZZK (FM)
WZZK (AM)	

Sports

 Although Birmingham has no professional sports teams, it does participate in minor and collegiate team sports, including football, played by the University of Alabama Crimson Tide. Thoroughbreds race at the Birmingham Race Course from spring through midsummer. In auto racing, the Diehard 500 and Winston 500 are held at the nearby Alabama International Motor Speedway.

Arts, Culture, and Tourism

Performing arts revolve around the Birmingham-Jefferson Civic Center, a facility of nearly seven city blocks just off I-20/59. It features a 19,000-seat Coliseum, a 3,000-seat concert hall, a 1,000-seat theater, and a 220,000-square-foot exhibition hall. It is the home of the Alabama Symphony Orchestra as well as other troups that perform music, dance, and theater productions. Leading the way for the city's other dance exhibits is the State of Alabama Ballet. The Alabama Dance Theater is part of the Alabama School of Fine Arts. The Creative Dance Company has two companies: Community Dancers and Southern Danceworks. Other musical groups include the Birmingham Opera Theater, the Birmingham Chamber Music Society, and the Birmingham Music Club. The University of Alabama at Birmingham's Town & Gown Theater, the Birmingham Repertory Theater, and the Birmingham Children's Theater provide dramatic entertainment. The Birmingham Museum of Art, the largest publicly supported museum in the South, is noted for its collection of Wedgwood porcelain and Italian Renaissance art. Other museums include the Alabama Sports Hall of Fame Museum, the Red Mountain Museum, the Southern Museum of Flight (east of the Birmingham Airport), the Discovery Place, a children's museum,

Travel and Tourism	
Hotel Rooms 8,725	
Convention and Exhibit Space (square feet) 120,000	

Convention Centers
Birmingham-Jefferson Civic Center
Boutwell Auditorium
State Fair Arena

Festivals
Festival of the Arts (April)
Alabama State Fair (Fall)
Hands at Work Craftsmen's Fair (November)

and the Sloss Furnaces National Historic Landmark, a combined museum and park.

Parks and Recreation

Birmingham has more than 70 parks and 15 recreation centers. Included are Linn Park, Lane Park (which hosts the Birmingham Zoo and the Birmingham Botanical Gardens), East Lake Park, Magnolia Park, Wald Park, Ensley Park, and George Ward Park. The four-acre Vulcan Park on the top of Red Mountain features a towering statue of Vulcan, the Roman god of fire and blacksmithery, the city's symbol.

Sources of Further Information

Birmingham Area Chamber of Commerce
2027 First Avenue North
Birmingham, AL 35203
(205) 323-5461

Greater Birmingham Convention and Visitors Bureau
2200 Ninth Avenue North
Birmingham, AL 35203
(205) 252-9825

Operation New Birmingham
Massey Building
2025 Third Avenue North, Suite 300
Birmingham, AL 35203
(205) 324-8797

Additional Reading

Birmingham Area Chamber of Commerce. *Birmingham Facts and History*. 1989.

Cadwell, H. M. *History of the Elyton Land Company and Birmingham, Alabama. The Origin and Development of an American City*. 1982.

Garrow, David J. *Birmingham, Alabama, 1956–63. The Black Struggle for Civil Rights*. 1989.

Henley, John C. *This Is Birmingham: The Founding and Growth of an American City*. 1960.

Morris, Philip A., and Marjorie L. White. *Designs on Birmingham: A Landscape History of a Southern City and Its Suburbs*. 1989.

Pioneers Club. *Early Days in Birmingham*. 1968.

White, Marjorie L., and Philip A. Morris. *Cinderella Stories: Transformations of Historic Birmingham Buildings*. 1990.

Boise

Idaho

Basic Data

Name   Boise
Name Origin   From French boisé meaning "wooded"
Year Founded   1834 Inc. 1864
Status: State   Capital of Idaho
         County   Seat of Ada County
Area (square miles)   46.1
Elevation (feet)   2,740
Time Zone   Mountain
Population (1990)   125,738
Population of Metro Area (1990)   205,775

Distance in Miles To:

Atlanta	2,223
Boston	2,685
Chicago	1,711
Dallas	1,593
Denver	835
Detroit	1,978
Houston	1,823
Los Angeles	846
Miami	2,865
Minneapolis	1,476
New York	2,487
Washington, DC	2,366

Layout of City and Suburbs

Boise is shaped by the Boise River. Bordered on the south by the Boise Air Terminal and on the west by the small communities of Ustick and Meridian as well as I-84, the city is essentially cut in half by the raging river that gave the city its name. The immediate downtown area is on the east bank of the river near Julia Davis Park. Marked by the magnificent state capitol building on Jefferson Street, it includes the Morrison-Knudsen Depot, a throwback to the early days when railroads ruled the west. Other suburbs include Olson City, Garden City, and Strawberry Glen.

Environment

Environmental Stress Index   3.4
Green Cities Index: Rank   NA
                    Score   NA
Water Quality   Alkaline, soft
      Average Daily Use (gallons per capita)   199
      Maximum Supply (gallons per capita)   597
Parkland as % of Total City Area   2.7
% Waste Landfilled/Recycled   NA
Annual Parks Expenditures per capita $46.03

Location and Topography

Boise, the capital of Idaho, is located in the southwestern section of the state. The city was named for the expansive Boise River, which drains from the Snake River and virtually cuts the city in half. Known as the City of Trees, Boise stands about 2,700 feet above sea level. The land inclines upward toward the Boise Ridge on the northern border of the city; this slope is called the Boise Front.

Climate

Protected by great mountains on the north and lying in a belt of prevailing westerly winds, Boise escapes the cold blizzards from Canada and thus has relatively mild winters. Cold snaps are not uncommon but are generally relieved by warm chinook winds from the Pacific. Summers are hot and dry, with temperatures sometimes reaching 100°F, but hot spells rarely last for more than a few days. Low humidity also makes summers tolerable.

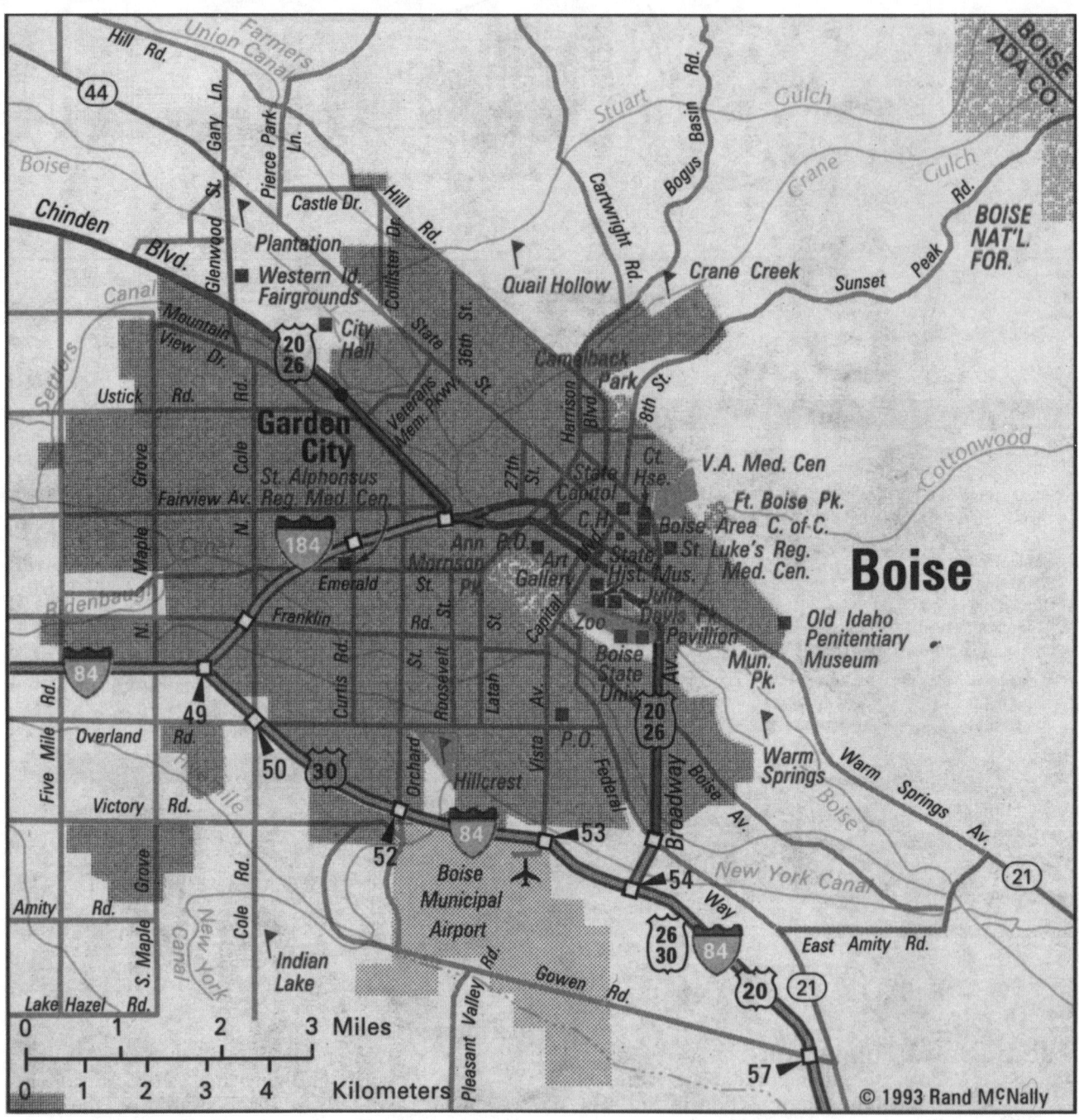

Weather

Temperature

Highest Monthly Average °F   90.5
Lowest Monthly Average °F   21.4

Annual Averages

Days 32°F or Below   124
Days above 90°F   43
Zero Degree Days   2
Precipitation (inches)   12
Snow (inches)   21
% Seasonal Humidity   57
Wind Speed (m.p.h.)   9
Clear Days   124
Cloudy Days   151
Storm Days   15
Rainy Days   91

Average Temperatures (°F)	High	Low	Mean
January	36.5	21.4	29.0
February	43.8	27.2	35.5
March	51.6	30.5	41.1
April	61.4	36.5	49.0
May	70.6	44.1	57.4
June	78.3	51.2	64.8
July	90.5	58.5	74.5
August	87.6	56.7	72.2
September	77.6	48.5	63.1
October	64.7	39.4	52.1
November	48.9	30.7	39.8
December	39.1	25.0	32.1

History

About 1811 French-Canadian explorers from John Jacob Astor's Pacific Fur Company scouted the western section of Idaho, which at that time was inhabited by the Shoshone Indians. Seeing the huge river that rushed through the wooded region, these trailblazers allegedly proclaimed it La Riviere Boise—the Wooded River. The name Boise (originally La Bois in the French) was later applied to the city that would sprawl on the river's banks.

Over the next several years Donald Mackenzie, a member of Astor's party, attempted to establish a fort on the Wooded River, but was unsuccessful because of Indian attacks. In 1834 entrepreneurs Bostonian Nathaniel J. Wyeth and Thomas McKay, an employee of the Hudson's Bay Company, founded Fort Hall and Fort Boise, respectively. In 1838 Wyeth sold Fort Hall to the Hudson's Bay Company, ushering in nearly 20 years of exclusivity by the Canadian concern.

Fort Boise soon became a way station on the Oregon Trail, even though the lucrative fur trade slowed. In 1854 Indians attacked the area, and Fort Boise was abandoned. In 1862 gold was discovered in the basin around present-day Boise, causing a tremendous gold rush and the beginning of a city on the Boise site. The following year, Congress made Idaho a U.S. territory. Towns in western Idaho sprang up as fast as gold miners could set up their pans in the rivers. A center of governmental activities for the territory was needed, and the city of Boise was organized on 7 July 1863 by several pioneers in a town meeting. Among these early settlers were Thomas Jefferson Davis and his wife Julia, whose name graces the park on which the original site of Boise City was platted.

The year 1864 was a turning point in making Boise the capital of Idaho. A huge section of the Idaho Territory was cut away to form the state of Montana, and a large building program made Boise City a commercial and trading center. On 26 July 1864 James S. Reynolds started the city's newspaper, the *Idaho Tri-Weekly Statesman*, now simply known as the *Statesman*. On 24 December 1864 Boise City was named the territorial capital.

With the end of the gold rush, Boise settled down as a major agricultural center of the western United States. By 1890 it was clear that Idaho would be admitted to the Union, and on 3 July 1890 it became the 43rd state. Owing to state government and agriculture, Boise rapidly became the largest city in Idaho and one of the leading cities in the American West.

Historical Landmarks

Much of Boise's historical architecture can be seen in the immediate downtown area. The most conspicuous landmark is the state capitol building, an imposing structure built of sandstone in 1920 and which duplicates the Capitol in Washington, D.C. A block away is Hotel Boise, completed in 1930 in art-deco style. The U.S. Assay Office on Main and Third was built in 1872 to assess, or assay, the value of gold from Boise's mines. On Capitol Boulevard is the Morrison-Knudsen Depot, a 1925 railway station that is now an Amtrak station. The O'Farrell Cabin, built in 1863 and now located in Military Reserve Park, was the city's first permanent housing structure. Downtown Boise also showcases the Egyptian Theatre, a renovated 1927 silent movies–era filmhouse; the French chateau-style Idanha Hotel, built in 1900; and the Simplot Building, named after a major agricultural entrepreneur, Jack Simplot.

Population

Boise first crossed the 100,000 threshold in the late 1970s. Between 1970 and 1980 it grew by a phenomenal 36.7% from 74,990 to 102,249. The population continued to increase in the 1980s, although at the slower rate of 23%, to reach 125,738 in 1990.

Population

	1980	1990
Central City	102,249	125,738
Rank	162	145
Metro Area	173,125	205,775
Pop. Change 1980–1990 +23,489		
Pop. % Change 1980–1990 +23		
Median Age 32.3		
% Male 48.3		
% Age 65 and Over 11.9		
Density (per square mile) 2,727		

Households

Number   50,852

Chronology

1811	French-Canadian fur trappers from John Jacob Astor's Pacific Fur Company reach the western section of Idaho. Coming upon a drainage river from the Snake River, they name the area La Riviere Boise (the Wooded River).
1834	Two members of the Hudson's Bay Company, Nathaniel Wyeth and Thomas McKay, found Fort Hall and Fort Boise, respectively.
1838	Wyeth sells Fort Hall to the Hudson's Bay Company, ushering in nearly 20 years of exclusivity by the company.
1854	Indian attacks force the settlers at Fort Boise to abandon the fort.
1862	Gold is found at Boise. The land rush causes a new settlement to spring up.
1863	(7 July) Pioneers at the new Fort Boise organize and plat Boise City.
1864	(24 December) Boise is named the territorial capital of Idaho.
1890	(3 July) Idaho is admitted to the Union as the 43rd state with Boise as the capital.

Population (continued)

Persons per Household 2.42
% Female-Headed Households 9.7
% One-Person Households 27.8
Births—Total 2,137
    % to Mothers under 20 7.9
    Birth Rate per 1,000 19.9

Ethnic Composition

Whites make up 96.4%, blacks 0.6%, American Indians 0.6%, Asians and Pacific Islanders 1.6%, Hispanics 2.72%, and others 0.8%. Boise is one of the principal Basque centers in the nation, with over 7,000 Basques, many of them descended from original settlers of the late 1800s.

Ethnic Composition (as % of total pop.)

	1980	1990
White	96.84	96.44
Black	0.50	0.58
American Indian	0.53	0.64
Asian and Pacific Islander	0.95	1.57
Hispanic	2.29	2.72
Other	NA	0.77

Government

Under its 1961 city charter, Boise is governed by a mayor-council. The mayor is elected to two-year terms and the six council members to four-year terms.

Government

Year of Home Charter 1961
Number of Members of the Governing Body 6
Elected at Large 6
Elected by Wards NA
Number of Women in Governing Body 2
Salary of Mayor $66,603
Salary of Council Members $13,860
City Government Employment Total 777
Rate per 10,000 71.7

Public Finance

The annual budget consists of revenues of $65.751 million and expenditures of $73.668 million. The debt outstanding is $30.330 million, and cash and security holdings are $26.929 million.

Public Finance

Total Revenue (in millions) $67.751
Intergovernmental Revenue—Total (in millions) $14.93
Federal Revenue per capita $9.49
% Federal Assistance 14.01
% State Assistance 7.13
Sales Tax as % of Total Revenue 1.94
Local Revenue as % of Total Revenue 78.42
City Income Tax no
Taxes—Total (in millions) $14.8

Taxes per capita
Total 137
Property 118
Sales and Gross Receipts 11
General Expenditures—Total (in millions) $44.5
General Expenditures per capita $411
Capital Outlays per capita $81

% of Expenditures for:
    Public Welfare 0.0
    Highways 0.9
    Education 0.0
    Health and Hospitals NA
    Police 13.4
    Sewerage and Sanitation 26.7
    Parks and Recreation 9.9
    Housing and Community Development 3.1
Debt Outstanding per capita $214
    % Utility 0.0
Federal Procurement Contract Awards (in millions) $25.6
Federal Grants Awards (in millions) $94.5
Fiscal Year Begins October 1

Economy

Because Boise is the state capital, its principal economic force is state government. Leaders among private concerns include the areas of agriculture, mining, lumber products, services, high technology, and service companies. Boise is the headquarters of ten major corporations, including the Albertson's supermarket chain; Morrison-Knudsen, an engineering and construction firm; Ore-Ida Foods; and Zilog, a division of Exxon. Boise-Cascade, the large timber concern, also maintains a substantial presence.

Economy

Total Money Income (in millions) $1,272.5
% of State Average 137.0
Per capita Annual Income $11,740
% Population below Poverty Level 8.8
Fortune 500 Companies 1

Banks	Number	Deposits (in millions)
Commercial	9	NA
Savings	5	NA

Passenger Autos 185,803
Electric Meters 79,000
Gas Meters 42,500

Manufacturing

Number of Establishments 189
% with 20 or More Employees 21.7
Manufacturing Payroll (in millions) $247.9
Value Added by Manufacture (in millions) $523.5
Value of Shipments (in millions) $978.2
New Capital Expenditures (in millions) $41.8

Wholesale Trade

Number of Establishments 420
Sales (in millions) $1,476.8
Annual Payroll (in millions) $95,152

Retail Trade

Number of Establishments 1,503
Total Sales (in millions) $969.2
Sales per capita $8,942
Number of Retail Trade Establishments with Payroll 1,007
Annual Payroll (in millions) $117.8
Total Sales (in millions) $948.9
General Merchandise Stores (per capita) $823
Food Stores (per capita) $1,835
Apparel Stores (per capita) NA
Eating and Drinking Places (per capita) $1,061

Service Industries

Total Establishments 1,434
Total Receipts (in millions) $516.2
Hotels and Motels (in millions) $34.7
Health Services (in millions) $143.6
Legal Services (in millions) $61.1

Labor

An exceptional quality of life, low energy and other living costs, and a good track record in job creation have helped to make Boise one of the favorite destinations of skilled workers fleeing problem-ridden large cities. More than 250 companies establish in or relocate to Boise every year.

Labor

Civilian Labor Force 72,710
% Change 1989–1990

Work Force Distribution
   Mining NA
   Construction 6,300
   Manufacturing 16,900
   Transportation and Public Utilities 6,000
   Wholesale and Retail Trade 27,500
   FIRE (Finance, Insurance, Real Estate) 8,400
   Service 25,500
   Government 20,200
   Women as % of Labor Force 44.6

Labor (continued)

   % Self-Employed 7.3
   % Professional/Technical
Total Unemployment NA
Rate % NA
Federal Government Civilian Employment 3,489

Education

The Independent School District of Boise City supports 42 schools, elementary through senior high. Thirteen private and parochial schools supplement the public school system. Boise State University is the city's only major institution of higher education.

Education

Number of Public Schools 42
Special Education Schools NA
Total Enrollment 23,394
% Enrollment in Private Schools NA
% Minority NA
Classroom Teachers NA
Pupil-Teacher Ratio NA
Number of Graduates NA
Total Revenue (in millions) $66.521
Total Expenditures (in millions) $61.311
Expenditures per Pupil $2,802
Educational Attainment (Age 25 and Over)
   % Completed 12 or More Years 83.4
   % Completed 16 or More Years 25.4
Four-Year Colleges and Universities 1
Enrollment 13,529
Two-Year Colleges 1
Enrollment 406

Libraries

Number 23
Public Libraries 1
Books (in thousands) 299
Circulation (in thousands) 724
Persons Served (in thousands) 130
Circulation per Person Served 5.56
Income (in millions) $2.2
Staff 61

Four-Year Colleges and Universities
   Boise State University

Health

The medical sector includes three major hospitals: Saint Alphonsus Regional Medical Center, St. Luke's Regional

Health

Deaths—Total 909
Rate per 1,000 8.5
Infant Deaths—Total 19
Rate per 1,000 8.9
Number of Metro Hospitals 5
Number of Metro Hospital Beds 887
Rate per 100,000 818
Number of Physicians 312
Physicians per 1,000 NA
Nurses per 1,000 NA
Health Expenditures per capita $2.58

Medical Center, and Veterans Administration Medical Center. Among the specialized treatment facilities are Mountain States Tumor Institute and CPC Intermountain Hospital.

Transportation

 Boise is approached by I-84, which reaches Idaho via Oregon, then runs south to Utah. The three state highways servicing the city are 20, 26, and 30. Rail passenger service is provided by Amtrak, while rail freight service is accommodated by Union Pacific Railroad. The Boise Air Terminal, located to the immediate south of the city and served by six major and commuter airlines, is the principal air terminus.

Transportation
Interstate Highway Mileage   15
Total Urban Mileage   808
Total Daily Vehicle Mileage (in millions)   3.173
Daily Average Commute Time   36.7 min.
Number of Buses   19
Port Tonnage (in millions)   NA
Airports   1
Number of Daily Flights   48
Daily Average Number of Passengers   1,464
Airlines (American carriers only)
Alaska Air
American
American West
Delta
United

Housing

 Of the total housing stock, 63.1% is owner-occupied. The median value of an owner-occupied home is $67,700 and the median monthly rent $346.

Housing
Total Housing Units   53,271
% Change 1980–1990   18.7
Vacant Units for Sale or Rent   1,916
Occupied Units   50,852
% with More Than One Person per Room   2.2
% Owner-Occupied   63.1
Median Value of Owner-Occupied Homes $67,700
Average Monthly Purchase Cost $373
Median Monthly Rent $346
New Private Housing Starts   1,763
Value (in thousands) $112,886
% Single-Family   59.2
Nonresidential Buildings Value (in thousands) $55,000

Urban Redevelopment

 Urban redevelopment programs have been muted since the 1980s because of growing environmental concerns. Redevelopment programs are coordinated by the Boise

Redevelopment Agency and Boise Department of Planning and Community Development.

Crime

 Boise ranks above the national average in public safety, being 123rd out of 333 cities. The number of violent crimes was 455 and the number of property crimes was 6,761 in 1991.

Crime
Violent Crimes—Total   455
Violent Crime Rate per 100,000   300.8
Murder   3
Rape   61
Robbery   46
Aggravated Assaults   345
Property Crimes   6,761
Burglary   1,211
Larceny   5,212
Motor Vehicle Theft   338
Arson   52
Per capita Police Expenditures $73.94
Per capita Fire Protection Expenditures $85.24
Number of Police   NA
Per 1,000   NA

Religion

 No religious denomination has a dominant influence in Boise. About 30% of the population are churchgoers. See box for numbers of attendees among Mormons, Catholics, Methodists, Church of Christ, Assembly of God, and the Jewish faith.

Religion	
Largest Denominations (Adherents)	
Catholic	15,583
Latter-Day Saints	32,517
United Methodist	5,783
Churchs of Christ	5,696
Assembly of God	3,154
Jews	220

Media

 The city's lone daily is the *Idaho Statesman,* although two weekly papers, the *Idaho Register* (published on Fridays) and the *Idaho Business Review* (published on Mondays), are also available. The electronic media consist of 2 major networks and 1 public network that directly serve Boise, as well as several stations from the nearby

Media
Newsprint
Idaho Register, weekly
Idaho Statesman, daily
Television
KAID (Channel 4)
KBCI (Channel 2)
KTVB (Channel 7)

Media Continued

Radio

KBOI (AM)	KQFC (FM)
KBSU (FM)	KCIX (FM)
KGEM (AM)	KJOT (FM)
KIDO (AM)	KLTB (FM)
KIZN (FM)	KKIC (AM)
KSPD (AM)	KUCL (AM)
KZMG (FM)	

---

communities of Nampa and Idaho City, and 13 Boise radio stations, excluding those from other cities.

Sports

Boise has no major professional sports teams. The Boise Hawks, a semiprofessional baseball team, play at Borah Field. The Firebird Raceway features drag racing, while Les Boise Park holds Thoroughbred and harness racing.

Arts, Culture, and Tourism

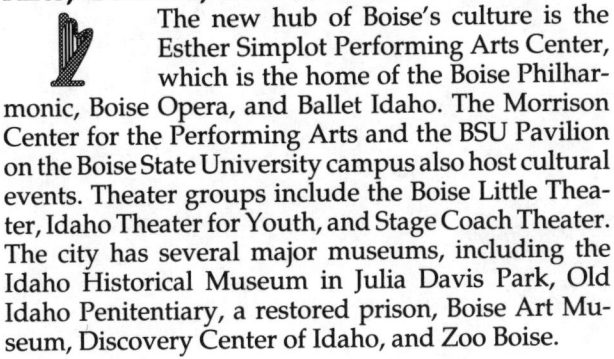

The new hub of Boise's culture is the Esther Simplot Performing Arts Center, which is the home of the Boise Philharmonic, Boise Opera, and Ballet Idaho. The Morrison Center for the Performing Arts and the BSU Pavilion on the Boise State University campus also host cultural events. Theater groups include the Boise Little Theater, Idaho Theater for Youth, and Stage Coach Theater. The city has several major museums, including the Idaho Historical Museum in Julia Davis Park, Old Idaho Penitentiary, a restored prison, Boise Art Museum, Discovery Center of Idaho, and Zoo Boise.

Travel and Tourism

Hotel Rooms   2,578
Convention and Exhibit Space (square feet)

Convention Centers
   NA

Festivals
   National Old Time Fiddlers Festival (June)

Parks and Recreation

Boise has only a few parks within the city limits. The most notable is Julia Davis Park, located on the eastern side of the river near the capitol. The 2,612,000-acre Boise National Forest east and northeast of the city offers hiking, fishing, and camping locations.

Sources of Further Information

Boise Area Chamber of Commerce
300 North Sixth Street
Boise, ID 83701
(208) 344-5515

Boise Convention & Visitors Bureau
168 North Ninth Street, Suite 200
Boise, ID 83701
(800) 635-5240

Additional Reading

Jenson, Dwight W. *Visiting Boise: A Personal Guide.* 1981.
Polk's Boise City Directory. 1991.

Boston

Massachusetts

Basic Data

Name   Boston
Name Origin   From Boston, England
Year Founded   1630 Inc. 1822
Status: State   Capital of Massachusetts
        County   Seat of Suffolk County
Area (square miles)   48.4
Elevation (feet)   21
Time Zone   EST
Population (1990)   574,283
Population of Metro Area (1990)   3,783,817

Sister Cities

Barcelona, Spain
Hargzhou, China
Kyoto, Japan
Melbourne, Australia
Padua, Italy
Strasbourg, France

Distance in Miles To:

Atlanta	1,108
Chicago	994
Dallas	1,753
Denver	1,998
Detroit	799
Houston	1,830
Los Angeles	3,017
Miami	1,520
Minneapolis	1,390
New York	222
Philadelphia	315
Washington, DC	448

Location and Topography

Boston, the capital of and the largest city in Massachusetts, is located in the central part of the state at the far eastern extreme, hugging the coast of the Atlantic Ocean. The city is twisted along the Charles River, which it shares with its immediate neighbor to the north, Cambridge. Boston was originally a hilly peninsula almost entirely separated from the mainland by marshy swamps. Over the years, the hills were partially leveled to fill in the Back Bay marshes. Today Boston's terrain is gently rolling.

Layout of City and Suburbs

Boston essentially wraps around the Charles River Basin and Boston Harbor, and is made up of nine distinct areas—North End, West End, Beacon Hill, Financial District, Back Bay, Theatre District, Chinatown, South Boston, and South End. From the west, streets such as James J. Storrow Memorial Drive, Beacon Street, Marlborough Street, Commonwealth Avenue, Newbury Street, and Boylston Street converge near the city's center at the famed Boston Common. Situated in a semicircular rather than traditional crosshatched layout, downtown thoroughfares Charles Street and Atlantic Avenue serve as borders to the wharves. Among Boston's suburbs are the aforementioned Cambridge, as well as Marblehead, Lexington, and Concord.

Environment

Environmental Stress Index   2.8
Green Cities Index: Rank   33
                    Score   29.17
Water Quality   Soft and slightly acid PH 8.7 ppm
    Average Daily Use (gallons per capita)   NA
    Maximum Supply (gallons per capita)   NA
Parkland as % of Total City Area   NA
% Waste Landfilled/Recycled   NA
Annual Parks Expenditures per capita $41.93

Climate

Boston is one of the nation's wettest cities, with frequent rain throughout spring and summer and snow in winter. It is also one of the windiest cities; Atlantic breezes

occasionally develop into full-fledged storms called northeasters. Sea breezes, however, moderate the temperature in both summer and winter.

Weather			
Temperature			
Highest Monthly Average °F	81.4		
Lowest Monthly Average °F	22.5		
Annual Averages			
Days 32°F or Below	99		
Days above 90°F	12		
Zero Degree Days	1		
Precipitation (inches)	43.43		
Snow (inches)	42		
% Seasonal Humidity	67		
Wind Speed (m.p.h.)	12.6		
Clear Days	99		
Cloudy Days	160		
Storm Days	19		
Rainy Days	128		
Average Temperatures (°F)	*High*	*Low*	*Mean*
January	35.9	22.5	29.2
February	37.5	23.3	30.4
March	44.6	31.5	38.1
April	56.3	40.8	48.6
May	67.1	50.1	58.6
June	76.6	59.3	68.0
July	81.4	65.1	73.3
August	79.3	63.3	71.3
September	72.2	56.7	64.5
October	63.2	47.5	55.4
November	51.7	38.7	45.2
December	39.3	26.6	33.0

History

Boston was founded in 1630 by the Puritans under John Winthrop and named after Boston in Lincolnshire, England. It was first called Trimountain after the three summits of Beacon Hill. In the same year it was declared the capital of the Massachusetts Bay Colony. When the colony's charter was revoked in 1684, Boston came under the direct rule of the British Crown. As the major colonial center, Boston claimed a number of firsts: It was the site of the nation's oldest school—the Boston Public School—founded in 1635, the first post office in 1639, the first bank in 1674, and the first newspaper, *Publick Occurrences Both Foreign and Domestick*, founded in 1690. Within a century of its founding, Boston became a shipping center, with shipbuilding, whaling, fishing, and trading as its main occupations.

As the birthplace of the American Revolution, Boston was the scene of the Boston Massacre of 1770 (in which five people were killed when British soldiers opened fire on an unruly crowd in front of the Old State House) and the Boston Tea Party of 1773 (in which taxable tea from the holds of three British ships was dumped into Boston Harbor). It was besieged by the Revolutionary Army under Washington (1775–1776) and evacuated by the British in 1776.

After the Revolution, Boston had a few difficult years until the opening of the China trade and worldwide commerce brought prosperity back to the city. In the last decade of the 18th century, Yankee merchant-men sailed from Boston for Europe, the Indies, and China. But the War of 1812 paralyzed the city's commerce and marked the decline of Boston's maritime supremacy. At the same time, manufacturing and industry became more important in the city's economy. Beginning in the late 1830s, railroads were built linking the city with the interior. An influx of emigrants from the British Isles, particularly Ireland, gave the city a strong labor base. In the 1830s Boston became an abolitionist center led by William Lloyd Garrison, publisher of *The Liberator*. During the late 1840s and early 1850s Boston's shipbuilders, notably Donald McKay, added a crowning chapter to Boston's maritime history with the development of clipper ships.

Boston grew rapidly in the post–Civil War decades. The Back Bay was reclaimed between 1857 and 1894, adding nearly 600 acres. Between 1868 and 1894 the independent suburbs of Roxbury, Dorchester, Charlestown, Brighton, and West Roxbury were annexed. The great fire of 1872, like the earlier fires of 1676, 1679, and 1760, did not halt the city's steady growth. During this period Boston began to achieve a new kind of eminence as the Athens of America and the Hub of the Universe. It was a time of the flowering of New England, when Boston could claim some of the most brilliant intellectuals of the age—scientists Louis Agassiz and Asa Gray; historians William Prescott, George Bancroft, John Lathrop Motley, and Francis Parkman; and writers Ralph Waldo Emerson, Nathaniel Hawthorne, Henry David Thoreau, John Greenleaf Whittier, Henry Wadsworth Longfellow, Louisa May Alcott, and Oliver Wendell Holmes.

The post–Civil War years also witnessed Boston's leadership in areas like medicine, education, and technology, a strength it has maintained to this day. Massachusetts General Hospital, Massachusetts Institute of Technology, Lowell Institute, Boston Symphony Orchestra, and Boston Museum of Fine Arts were all founded during this period.

Like other older cities, Boston began to come apart at the seams at the beginning of this century. The rise of suburbs, decentralization of industry, competition from newer cities in the South and West, and loss of population hastened Boston's eclipse, despite the fact that since World War I the city had some of the ablest mayors in its history: John Fitzgerald, James Michael Curley (elected three times despite being convicted and jailed for mail fraud), John B. Hynes, John F. Collins, Kevin White, and Raymond Flynn. The decline was not reversed until Boston established a multi-billion-dollar urban redevelopment program in the 1960s that helped stem the flight of capital and people from the city.

Historical Landmarks

Boston abounds with buildings of historical and architectural interest as well as monuments. The most conspicuous of the latter is the Bunker Hill Monument, a granite obelisk 122 feet high. The Shaw Memorial on the Common opposite the State House is the work of Augustus

Chronology

1620	Pilgrims in the *Mayflower* land at Provincetown and Plymouth.
1630	John Winthrop arrives with 11 ships and 900 settlers, and founds colony at Shawmut, later Boston.
1635	Public Latin School for Boys is founded.
1638	First printing press in the colonies is set up in Cambridge by Stephen Daye.
1642	Harvard College holds first commencement.
1674	The first bank in the colonies opens its doors in Boston.
1690	The first colonial newspaper, *Publick Occurrences Both Foreign and Domestick,* is published.
1704	*Boston NewsLetter* appears.
1742	Faneuil Hall becomes Boston's town hall and marketplace.
1770	British sentry fires on rioters near Old State House in incident known as the Boston Massacre.
1773	Irate Bostonians throw taxable tea from the holds of three British ships into Boston Harbor in incident known as the Boston Tea Party.
1775	Boston is besieged by George Washington.
1776	British General Gage evacuates Boston.
1789	The *Franklin* of Boston is the first U.S. ship to reach Japan. The *Atlantic* of Boston sails to Bombay and Calcutta.
1810	Boston Philharmonic Orchestra is founded.
1822	Boston is granted city charter.
1825	American Unitarian Association is organized in Boston. First high school for girls in the United States opens in Boston.
1831	William Lloyd Garrison founds *The Liberator.*
1832	New England AntiSlavery Society is founded in Boston.
1852	Boston Public Library opens. Donald McKay builds the clipper ship *Sovereign of the Seas.*
1865	Massachusetts Institute of Technology opens.
1867	Mary Baker Eddy founds Christian Science in Boston.
1872	The great fire of Boston guts 776 buildings.
1874	Roxbury, Jamaica Plain, and Brighton-Allston are annexed to the city.
1894	Boston and Maine Railroad opens North Station.
1897	First subway in the United States opens in Boston.
1919	Governor Calvin Coolidge puts down strike by Boston policemen and gains national prominence.
1942	Coconut Grove Nightclub fire, worst in Boston's history, claims 499 lives.
1950	Masked bandits rob the Brinks Boston office of $2.77 million.
1960	Mayor John F. Collins launches urban redevelopment project.
1990	Boston launches harbor cleanup program.

Saint-Gaudens. Thomas Ball's equestrian statue of George Washington stands in the Public Garden. A monument on Dorchester Heights commemorates the British evacuation of Boston.

Among the historic buildings are:

- The Paul Revere House, built in 1670, in the North End.
- State House on Beacon Hill, designed by Charles Bulfinch in 1795.
- Old State House at the head of State Street, built in 1748; now the Museum of the Bostonian Society.
- Faneuil Hall, the Cradle of Liberty, built in 1742.
- Old North Church, now Christ Church, built in 1723. Paul Revere hung signal lanterns from its steeple.
- King's Chapel, built in 1754 at Tremont and School streets, was the first Episcopal church in New England. In 1785 it became the nation's first Unitarian church.
- Park Street Church, at the foot of Beacon Hill, built in 1809.
- Old South Meeting House at Washington and Milk streets, first built in 1699 and rebuilt in 1730 and 1789.
- Blake House in the Dorchester District, the oldest house in the city, built in 1648.
- Louisburg Square, on Beacon Hill, with fine examples of early 19th-century architecture.
- Boston Public Library on Copley Square, opened in 1895, with notable murals by John Singer Sargent and Pierre Puvic de Chavannes.
- Trinity Church on Copley Square, completed in 1877 in the Romanesque style by architect Henry H. Richardson.

Boston is a very walkable city and many of its attractions are planned around this fact. The Freedom Trail, a 2.5-mile walking tour, begins at the Boston

Common (the oldest public park in the United States) and ends at the Bunker Hill monument. Another walking tour, the Black Heritage Trail, celebrates 350 years of Boston's black community. The city also contains the residences of such notable literary figures as Ralph Waldo Emerson, Nathaniel Hawthorne, Louisa May Alcott, and William Dean Howells. A cemetery of historic interest is the Central Burying Ground on the Common.

Population

Boston's population, like that of many older cities, has been declining since World War II, which is paradoxical because Boston has a relatively young age profile. However, many of the young people are single, reflecting the city's popularity with students and young professionals. The central city constitutes 20.4% of the metro area population and an equal percentage of the metro geographical area. Boston experiences a high rate of out-migration to the suburbs, estimated at 4.7% per annum. A continued loss of population is projected into the year 2000.

Population		
	1980	1990
Central City	562,994	574,283
Rank	20	21
Metro Area	3,662,888	3,783,817
Pop. Change 1980–1990 +11,289		
Pop. % Change 1980–1990 +2		
Median Age 30.3		
% Male 48.1		
% Age 65 and Over 11.5		
Density (per square mile) 11,865		
Households		
Number 228,464		
Persons per Household 2.37		
% Female-Headed Households 16.8		
% One-Person Households 35.5		
Births—Total 8,530		
% to Mothers under 20 13.3		
Birth Rate per 1,000 14.9		

Ethnic Composition

Boston's population was largely of English origin until the mid-1800s, when the first waves of European emigrants began to arrive. Thus came the distinction between the old elite known as Boston Brahmins or Proper Bostonians and the later arrivals. Irish peasants fleeing the Great Potato Famine settled in East Boston and Charlestown, and soon came to dominate Boston's politics. They were followed by Italians and French-Canadians. The first blacks reached Boston through the Underground Railway during the Civil War. Racial tensions surfaced during the Great Depression and continue to do so periodically. Tempers flared over court-ordered school desegregation and busing in the late 1970s. Some Boston neighborhoods have yet to be integrated.

Ethnic Composition (as % of total pop.)		
	1980	1990
White	69.97	62.84
Black	22.42	25.59
American Indian	0.23	0.33
Asian and Pacific Islander	2.69	5.29
Hispanic	6.41	10.79
Other	NA	5.95

Boston's neighborhoods retain a distinctive ethnic flavor. The stately Georgian and Regency mansions of Beacon Hill and Back Bay mainly house residents of English descent. South Boston (or Southie) and Charlestown are predominantly Irish, and North End is unmistakably Italian. Dudley and Jamaica Plain have become Hispanic in recent years. Blacks live mostly in Roxbury, Codman Square, Mattapan, and Dudley.

Government

Boston had a town-meeting form of government until 1822, when it was incorporated as a city. Since then the city charter has been altered frequently. In 1949 voters approved substitution of a 9-member city council, elected at large, for a 22-member council elected from wards. The charter provides for a strong mayor, and Boston's mayors have historically dominated city hall. The mayor is elected every four years, and city council and school committee members every two years. Elections are nonpartisan and are held in November of odd-numbered years. The mayor and council are also commissioners of Suffolk County, but the other municipalities in the county—the cities of Charles and Revere and the town of Winthrop—do not share in the expenses of governing the county.

By tradition, Boston is heavily Democratic, and Republicans constitute a permanent minority. Boston has voted Democratic in most presidential elections in this century, but voted for Reagan in 1980 and 1984.

Government
Year of Home Charter NA
Number of Members of the Governing Body 13
Elected at Large 4
Elected by Wards 9
Number of Women in Governing Body 1
Salary of Mayor $100,000
Salary of Council Members $45,000
City Government Employment Total 20,704
Rate per 10,000 360.9

Public Finance

Per capita, Boston's municipal budget is among the highest in the country. The annual budget consists of revenues of $1.805 billion and expenditures of $1.726 billion. The debt outstanding is $854.201 million, and cash and security holdings are $1.396 billion.

Boston's fiscal problem is the result of structural imbalances in the city's tax base. About 60% of city

Public Finance

Total Revenue (in millions) $1,805.126
Intergovernmental Revenue—Total (in millions) $746.33
Federal Revenue per capita $70.86
% Federal Assistance 3.92
% State Assistance 37.3
Sales Tax as % of Total Revenue 1.53
Local Revenue as % of Total Revenue 57.40
City Income Tax no
Taxes—Total (in millions) $372.6

Taxes per capita
Total 650
Property 611
Sales and Gross Receipts 14
General Expenditures—Total (in millions) $937.7
General Expenditures per capita $1,635
Capital Outlays per capita $218

% of Expenditures for:
   Public Welfare 0.2
   Highways 3.4
   Education 30.6
   Health and Hospitals 11.8
   Police 8.6
   Sewerage and Sanitation 4.6
   Parks and Recreation 1.8
   Housing and Community Development 7.3
Debt Outstanding per capita $1,073
   % Utility 1.8
Federal Procurement Contract Awards (in millions)
   $298.5
Federal Grants Awards (in millions) $751.5
Fiscal Year Begins July 1

Economy

Total Money Income (in millions) NA
% of State Average 86.1
Per capita Annual Income $10,774
% Population below Poverty Level 20.2
Fortune 500 Companies 3

Banks	Number	Deposits (in millions)
Commercial	16	18,344
Savings	12	4,045

Passenger Autos 321,019
Electric Meters 610,000
Gas Meters 163,157

Manufacturing

Number of Establishments 858
% with 20 or More Employees 35.7
Manufacturing Payroll (in millions) $1,156.0
Value Added by Manufacture (in millions) $2,517.4
Value of Shipments (in millions) $4,204.1
New Capital Expenditures (in millions) $123.6

Wholesale Trade

Number of Establishments 1,072
Sales (in millions) $8,160.6
Annual Payroll (in millions) $482.768

Retail Trade

Number of Establishments 4,837
Total Sales (in millions) $3,910.4
Sales per capita $6,817
Number of Retail Trade Establishments with Payroll 3,772
Annual Payroll (in millions) $585
Total Sales (in millions) $3,837.1
General Merchandise Stores (per capita) $687
Food Stores (per capita) $1,080
Apparel Stores (per capita) $603
Eating and Drinking Places (per capita) $1,410

Service Industries

Total Establishments 5,738
Total Receipts (in millions) $6,358.2
Hotels and Motels (in millions) NA
Health Services (in millions) $509.8
Legal Services (in millions) $1,338.6

property is tax-exempt. Further, most of the suburbs are financially independent and do not contribute toward consolidated services. There is no city tax.

Economy

 In 1990 *Fortune* magazine considered Boston's economy as among the healthiest in the nation and Boston as one of the 11 best cities in which to do business. While the traditional fishing and manufacturing sectors lost ground in recent decades, the economy became technology driven in the 1980s, generating jobs in fields that did not exist ten years before. Boston's strength in high tech is reinforced by the presence in the metro area of some of the nation's most important research centers, such as MIT. Computer, electronics, and engineering firms have sprung up along Route 128 encircling Boston. They include Raytheon, Digital Equipment, and Wang.

The Boston metro area is the largest banking, insurance, and retail trade center in the Northeast. It has the 18th largest U.S. bank (First National Boston Corporation) and two of the top insurance companies (John Hancock and New England Mutual). However, business costs are high, second only to New York. Tourism is a major revenue earner. Boston hosts 11 million tourists and conventioneers each year. Boston also is the nation's most important fishing port and wool market. Urban development is spearheaded by the Economic Development and Industrial Corporation (EDIC).

Labor

 The size of the metro labor force is estimated at 1,754,000 workers, with 591,000 in services, 290,000 in government, 385,400 in trade, 267,200 in manufacturing, 156,100 in finance, insurance, and real estate, 76,600 in transportation and utilities, and 66,900 in construc-

Labor

Civilian Labor Force 302,527
% Change 1989–1990 -0.5

Work Force Distribution
   Mining 500
   Construction 40,300
   Manufacturing 222,300
   Transportation and Public Utilities 72,500
   Wholesale and Retail Trade 340,000
   FIRE (Finance, Insurance, Real Estate) 140,900
   Service 566,900
   Government 195,000
   Women as % of Labor Force 47.6
   % Self-Employed 3.4
   % Professional/Technical 20.3

Labor (continued)

Total Unemployment 16,740
Rate % 5.5
Federal Government Civilian Employment 21,857

tion. The unemployment rate, below the national rate in the mid-1980s at 3.4%, climbed to 5.2% in 1990. The growth rate in job opportunities during the next decade is estimated at 6.33%.

Education

Boston is the birthplace of American education, being the site of the first school and first university in the United States. The Boston school district is one of the 70 largest in the nation, having 117 schools. In the 1970s the school system was embroiled in a controversy over desegregation and busing, forcing the intervention of the federal courts.

Education

Number of Public Schools 117
Special Education Schools 6
Total Enrollment 60,543
% Enrollment in Private Schools 15.5
% Minority 77.8
Classroom Teachers NA
Pupil-Teacher Ratio NA
Number of Graduates 2,812
Total Revenue (in millions) $388.625
Total Expenditures (in millions) $391.639
Expenditures per Pupil $7,078
Educational Attainment (Age 25 and Over)
   % Completed 12 or More Years 68.4
   % Completed 16 or More Years 20.3
Four-Year Colleges and Universities 10
Enrollment 88,527
Two-Year Colleges 4
Enrollment 3,139

Libraries

Number 184
Public Libraries 28
Books (in thousands) 5,992
Circulation (in thousands) 2,086
Persons Served (in thousands) NA
Circulation per Person Served NA
Income (in millions) $26.319
Staff 654

Four-Year Colleges and Universities
   Boston University
   Emerson College
   Emmanuel College
   Harvard University
   Massachusetts Institute of Technology
   Northeastern University
   Simmons College
   Suffolk University
   Wheelock College
   Wentworth Institute of Technology
   University of Massachusetts at Boston

Health

Boston has high-quality health-care service with numerous facilities, including 16 teaching hospitals, 12 cardiac rehabilitation centers, and 3 major hospices. Some of these institutions, such as Massachusetts General Hospital, Dana Farber Cancer Institute, New England Medical Center, and New England Deaconess Hospital, are world-famous pioneers in medical research.

Health

Deaths—Total 5,734
Rate per 1,000 10.0
Infant Deaths—Total 100
Rate per 1,000 11.7
Number of Metro Hospitals 31
Number of Metro Hospital Beds 9,175
Rate per 100,000 1,600
Number of Physicians NA
Physicians per 1,000 5.28
Nurses per 1,000 15.48
Health Expenditures per capita $6.46

Transportation

Each business day, more than 1 million workers and shoppers come into the city from the suburbs, making traffic congestion a major problem. Downtown Boston's narrow, winding streets are confusing to drivers unfamiliar with the city. The principal retail shopping thoroughfare, Washington Street, is extremely narrow and traffic-clogged. Other important thoroughfares are Beacon Street; Commonwealth Avenue, reaching from the Public Garden to Brookline and Brighton; Boylston Street, extending from the vicinity of the Common to Brookline; and Tremont Street, extending from the Government Center southeast into Roxbury. Highways have made the city the hub of a system of radial expressways. The Southeast Expressway leads to Cape Cod and Rhode Island; the Massachusetts Turnpike leads to the west and to New York; the Northeast Expressway goes to the North Shore and thence to New Hampshire; and Route 128 encircles the city. Within the city proper, the Central Artery carries north-south traffic over the city, and Storrow Drive carries east-west traffic along the south bank of the Charles River, paralleling Memorial Drive in Cambridge on the north. Access from the central city to the north over the Charles and Mystic rivers is provided by numerous bridges. Two toll tunnels connect the city proper and East Boston.

Bus, subway, trolley, and commuter rail service is provided throughout the Greater Boston region by the Massachusetts Bay Transportation Authority (MBTA), which operates 765 buses, 352 rapid-rail cars, 26 trolley coaches, and 2 ferry systems. Boston has the distinction of having the oldest subway system in the United States, founded in 1895. The standard MBTA fare is 60 cents.

Three rail lines converge on Boston: Boston and Maine Railroad, New York–New Haven–Hartford Line, and Boston–Albany Railroad.

Boston's international airport is at Logan in East Boston and is named after General Edward Lawrence Logan. Thirty-nine domestic and international airlines fly into Logan for a total of 536 flights each day.

Boston has one of the finest natural harbors in the world. A 40-foot channel about 7 miles long leads from the open ocean to the waterfront terminals, with 25 miles of docking space in the inner harbor. Petroleum products and sugar are the largest imports; grain, iron, and steel are the largest exports. As New England's largest port, Boston handles 20 million tons of freight each year. The docks, located in South Boston, East Boston, and Charlestown, are controlled by the Massachusetts Port Authority. The Commonwealth Pier is the world's largest fish-handling pier.

Transportation

Interstate Highway Mileage   145
Total Urban Mileage   9,398
Total Daily Vehicle Mileage (in millions)   51.641
Daily Average Commute Time   51.7 min.
Number of Buses   765
Port Tonnage (in millions)   20.641
Airports   1
Number of Daily Flights   297
Daily Average Number of Passengers   26,469

Airlines (American carriers only)
  American
  American West
  Continental
  Delta
  Eastern
  Midway
  Northwest
  Trans World
  United
  USAir

Housing

About two-thirds of Boston residents live in apartments. The city has 250,863 housing units and an additional 800,000 units in the metro area. Most of the new housing projects are concentrated in the outer counties such as Plymouth, where housing grew by more than 36% during the 1980s, compared to 4.6% in central Boston. In the late 1980s Boston had a lower vacancy rate (4.5%) than any other major city.

Urban Redevelopment

In 1957 Mayor Hynes established the Boston Redevelopment Authority and persuaded the Prudential Life Insurance Company to invest $150 million in creating a 31-acre plaza crowned by the 52-story Prudential Tower. Included in the complex, which covers twice the area of Rockefeller Center in New York, are a hotel, auditorium, twin 26-story apartment houses, 3,000-car garage, and skating rink.

The drive to restore the city's vitality continued under Mayor Collins, who hired Edward J. Logue to direct the Boston Project, the most ambitious urban revival ever authorized in New England. Logue is credited with creating a new vision of the city in four phases. First, he restored the older residential neigh-

Housing

Total Housing Units   250,863
% Change 1980–1990   3.8
Vacant Units for Sale or Rent   17,557
Occupied Units   228,464
% with More Than One Person per Room   6.9
% Owner-Occupied   30.9
Median Value of Owner-Occupied Homes $161,400
Average Monthly Purchase Cost $407
Median Monthly Rent $546
New Private Housing Starts   279
Value (in thousands) $16,120
% Single-Family   30.5
Nonresidential Buildings Value (in thousands) $81,415

Tallest Buildings	*Hgt. (ft.)*	*Stories*
John Hancock Tower	790	60
Prudential Center	750	52
Boston Co. Bldg., Court St.	605	41
Federal Reserve Bldg.	604	32
International Place, 100 Oliver St.	600	46
First National Bank of Boston	591	37
One Financial Center	590	46
Shawmut Bank Bldg.	520	38

borhoods in order to bring residents back into the city. Second, he converted 200 acres of downtown Boston into an attractive shopping mall. Third, he did away with Scollay Square and replaced it with the Government Center, including the new city hall and the John F. Kennedy Building. At the same time, Faneuil Hall and the historic houses on Union Street were preserved. Fourth, Logue converted the waterfront into a residential and public showplace.

Crime

Boston is noted for a high crime rate, and crime is a major political and social issue at election time. Overall, Boston ranks fourth in the nation in the total crime index. Of known crimes in 1991, 11, 829 were violent crimes and 50,210 were property crimes.

Crime

Violent Crimes—Total   11,829
Violent Crime Rate per 100,000   832.3
Murder   113
Rape   486
Robbery   4,784
Aggravated Assaults   6,446
Property Crimes   50,210
Burglary   10,029
Larceny   26,726
Motor Vehicle Theft   13,455
Arson   NA
Per capita Police Expenditures $272.0
Per capita Fire Protection Expenditures $151.20
Number of Police   1,829
Per 1,000   3.19

Religion

Originally a Puritan city, Boston's religious evolution has been in two almost contradictory directions. On the one hand, because of the heavy influx of Irish, Italian, and French-Canadian immigrants in the 19th century, it became heavily Catholic and now ranks third in the nation in the percentage of Catholics (55.43%). On the other, it has moved into the liberal, non-mainstream religions and now typifies some of the most heterodox traditions. In 1785 the Episcopalian King's Chapel became the first Unitarian parish in New England. The Unitarian-Universalist Association has its headquarters on Beacon Hill. In 1894 Mary Baker Eddy founded the First Church of Christ, Scientist, and Boston continues as the principal stronghold of this church.

Religion	
Largest Denominations (Adherents)	
Catholic	173,825
American Baptist	11,158
Episcopal	12,183
Black Baptist	34,183
Unitarian	4,517
Jews	40,005

Media

Boston is the birthplace of the U.S. publishing industry. However, it lost its preeminence to New York in the 19th century, and the Boston media have never quite regained their early vigor. The two major dailies, the *Boston Globe* and *Boston Herald*, are both published in the morning. The *Christian Science Monitor*, published only on weekdays, is more a national newspaper than a local one. *Boston Magazine* reports every month on Boston culture and society. Magazines of national interest published in Boston include *The Atlantic*, a respected literary institution founded in 1857. Boston is served by nine television channels and 18 radio stations.

Media
Newsprint
The Atlantic, monthly
Boston Business Journal, weekly
Boston Globe, daily
Boston Herald, daily
The Boston Tab, weekly
Television
WBZ (Channel 4)
WCVB (Channel 5)
WGBH (Channel 2)
WGBX (Channel 44)
WHDH (Channel 7)
WLVI (Channel 56)
WQTV (Channel 68)
WSBK (Channel 38)
WHLL (Channel 27)

Radio	
WBCN (FM)	WBZ (AM)
WCDJ (FM)	WERS (FM)
WEZE (AM)	WGBH (FM)
WHDH (AM)	WILD (AM)
WMEX (AM)	WMJX (FM)
WODS (FM)	WRBB (FM)
WRKO (AM)	WBMX (FM)
WROL (AM)	WUMB (FM)
WUNR (AM)	WZLX (FM)

Sports

Boston has a a major team in each of the four leading sports: the New England Patriots in football, Celtics in basketball, Bruins in hockey, and Red Sox in baseball. The principal stadiums are Fenway Park and Boston Garden. A popular annual event is the Boston Marathon, run on the third Monday in April. In the fall the most widely attended event is the Charles River regatta.

Arts, Culture, and Tourism

Boston is home to a number of major museums, a world-class symphony orchestra, and a premier dance company. The outstanding Boston Symphony Orchestra performs at Symphony Hall. Three other orchestras of note are the New England Conservatory Symphony Orchestra, Boston Conservatory Orchestra, and Boston Philharmonic Orchestra. Boston supports two opera companies; several professional troupes, such as the Boston Shakespeare Company, American Repertory Theater, Huntington Theater Company, and Boston Children's Theater; and a number of dance troupes. Major museums include the Museum of Fine Arts, Isabella Stewart Gardner Museum, Museum of Contemporary Art, and Fogg Art Museum of Harvard University.

Travel and Tourism		
Hotel Rooms 30,177		
Convention and Exhibit Space (square feet) 193,000		
Convention Centers		
John B. Hynes Veterans Convention Center		
World Trade Center		
Bayside Exposition Center		
Festivals		
St. Patrick's Day (March)		
Ancient and Honorable Artillery Parade (June)		
First Folk Festival (June)		
Harbor Fest (July)		
Boston Tea Party (December)		

The Boston Public Library system has 168 branches with 15,398,000 volumes. More than half a million books are added to the system each year.

Parks and Recreation

In the heart of the city are the celebrated Boston Common, covering 48 acres, and the 24-acre Public Garden. The beautiful Back Bay Fens, from Beacon Street to Brookline Avenue, covers 117 acres. The 223-acre Arnold Arboretum of Harvard University is famous for its woody shrubs and trees from many parts of the world. Franklin Park and Zoological Garden has 527 acres. Columbus and Marine parks on the adjoining Strandway in south Boston are seashore park developments. The Esplanade is a beautifully landscaped walk along the Charles River embankment. The Hatch Shell, where the Boston Pops Orchestra gives summer concerts, is part of the Esplanade.

Boston Common deserves special notice for its colorful history. In 1634 the town purchased the land from a settler for $150. In later years it served as a common pasture, execution ground, drill ground, football field, and open amphitheater. The Great Elm Tree, the oldest in Boston, stood here for 250 years.

Sources of Further Information

Boston Public Library
666 Boylston Street
Boston, MA 02117
(617) 536-5400

Boston Redevelopment Authority
Boston City Hall
Ninth Floor
Boston, MA 02201
(617) 722-4300

The Bostonian Society
200 Washington Street
Old State House
Boston, MA 02109
(617) 242-5610

Greater Boston Chamber of Commerce
125 High Street
Boston, MA 02110
(617) 426-1250

Greater Boston Convention and Visitors Bureau
Prudential Plaza
Boston, MA 02199
(617) 536-4100

Mayor's Office
City of Boston
One City Hall Square
Boston, MA 02108
(617) 725-3914

Metropolitan Cultural Alliance
33 Harrison Avenue
Boston, MA 02111
(617) 423-0260

Massachusetts Office of Travel and Tourism
100 Cambridge Street
Boston, MA 02202
(617) 727-3201

Additional Reading

General

American Federation of Arts. *Cultural Resources of Boston.* 1965.
Amory, Cleveland. *The Proper Bostonians.* 1984.
Garland, Joseph E. *Boston's Gold Coast: The North Shore, 1870–1929.* 1981.
Handlin, Oscar. *Boston's Immigrants: A Study of Acculturation.* 1959.
Lankevich, George. *Boston: A Chronological and Documentary History, 1602–1970.* Dobbs 1974.
McNiff, Philip J. *Twelve Mayors of Boston, 1900–1970.* 1970.
Mollenkopf, John H. *The Contested City.* 1983.
O'Connor, Thomas H. *Bibles, Brahmins and Bosses: A Short History of Boston.* 1976.
Rutman, Darett B. *Winthrop's Boston: A Portrait of a Puritan Town, 1630–49.* 1972.
Silver, Rollo G. *Publishing in Boston, 1726–1757.* 1956.
Vanderwarker, Peter. *Boston, Then and Now.* 1983.
Warner, Sam B. *Streetcar Suburbs: The Process of Growth in Boston, 1870–1900.* 1962.

Directories

Major Employers in Greater Boston. Annual. Greater Boston Chamber of Commerce.
Polk's Boston City Directory. Annual. R. L. Polk.

Guides and Gazetteers

Booth, Robert. *Boston's Freedom Trail.* 1986.
Boston in Your Pocket. 1985.
Buni, Andrew, and Alan Rogers. *Boston: City on a Hill.* 1984.
Fodor's Boston. 1986.
Frommer, Arthur. *Guide to Boston.* 1988.
I Love Boston Guide. 1983.
Lee, Mary P. *The Student-Traveler in Boston-Cambridge.* 1986.
Llewellyn, Robert. *Boston.* 1984.
Lyndon, Donlyn. *The City Observed: Boston.* 1982.
Official Guidebook to Boston. 1989.
Universal Atlas of Metropolitan Boston and Eastern Massachusetts. 1985.

Bridgeport

Connecticut

Location and Topography

N

Bridgeport is situated in the southwest section of Connecticut on Long Island Sound. Located about 50 miles southwest of the state capital at Hartford, the city is on low-lying land marked by a deep-water harbor.

Layout of City and Suburbs

The city has two harbors, Bridgeport and Black Rock. To the south lies Fairfield, to the north Trumbull, and to the west Stratford. Bridgeport is 70 miles north of New York City and 150 miles south of Boston. The New Haven Railroad crosses the city, skirting the industrial section. West from the railroad station is the cramped and congested shopping center, but in the outskirts are landscaped residential sections, more than 1,000 acres of public parks, and a shore drive of about 3 miles offering beautiful vistas of woodland and sea. Many of the streets are lined with stately elms.

Climate

As in other coastal cities in the Northeast, summers are relatively warm but tempered by sea breezes, and the winters are mild and mostly snowfree.

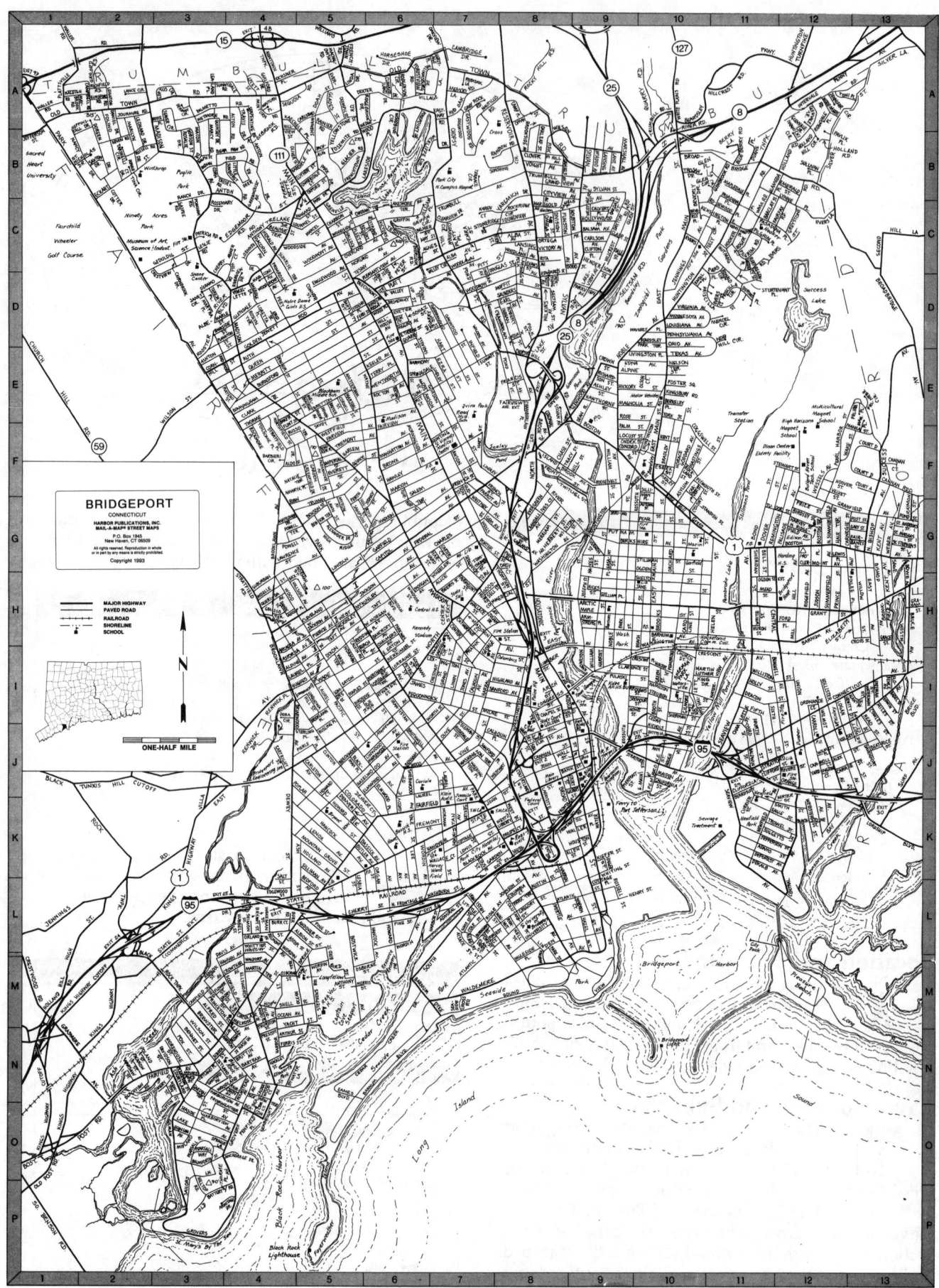

Weather (continued)

Average Temperatures (°F)	High	Low	Mean
January	39.0	24.4	31.7
February	43.9	28.4	36.2
March	49.5	34.8	42.2
April	59.9	43.7	51.8
May	74.0	54.9	64.5
June	79.4	61.1	70.3
July	83.5	67.4	75.5
August	82.9	66.6	74.8
September	73.7	56.4	65.1
October	65.0	48.4	56.7
November	52.3	39.5	45.9
December	44.3	29.0	36.7

History

Bridgeport was first settled in 1639 on the site of a Pequonnock Indian village by residents of the older towns of Fairfield and Stratford. Known first as Newfield and then as Stratford, in 1800 the area was extended by the General Assembly. The borough of Bridgeport was incorporated and named for the first drawbridge erected over the Pequonnock River. Bridgeport was incorporated as a town in 1821 and became a city in 1836. Like other New England seaport towns, Bridgeport had a lusty whaling trade, but seafaring declined in 1840 when the coming of the railroad began an industrial boom. The city soon achieved industrial preeminence, producing brass and cast-iron fittings, tools, heavy machinery, carriages, ammunition, hats, pewterware, saddles, furniture, and shirts. Bridgeport occupies a special place in U.S. industrial history as the first producer of many important commercial products: sewing machines invented by Elias Howe, gramophones produced by the American Gramophone Company (later the Columbia Phonograph Company), and one of the earliest American automobiles propelled by gasoline, produced by the Locomobile Company. From 1846 Bridgeport was the headquarters of P. T. Barnum's Greatest Show on Earth starring the midget General Tom Thumb. Barnum later became mayor and bequeathed to the city its popular Seaside Park.

Bridgeport continued to maintain its industrial leadership after the Civil War, and by 1910 claimed a population of over 100,000. Few cities in the United States had a more diversified industrial base. Nevertheless, Bridgeport was badly affected by the Great Depression. In 1933 the city elected socialist Jasper McLevy as mayor, a post he held for 25 years. During World War II the city's industries played a vital role in the war effort, and continue to be important defense contractors. In 1990 Bridgeport became the first U.S. city to declare bankruptcy in an effort to solve its chronic fiscal crises.

Historical Landmarks

Bridgeport's past is enshrined in a number of historic monuments. The most notable are Pixlee Tavern, where George Washington is believed to have stopped en route to Cambridge in 1775; Tom Thumb House; Brothwell Beach House, an early 19th-century building;

Nathaniel Wheeler Fountain, a memorial to the founder of the Wheeler and Wilson Manufacturing Company, pioneers in the development of the sewing machine; and United Congregational Church, with its tall and graceful spire. The city hall is a two-story sandstone building with heavy, fluted Ionic columns, erected in 1854–1855 and enlarged in 1905. It was the scene of an address by President Lincoln on 10 March 1860, an event commemorated by a bronze tablet.

Population

Bridgeport has been losing population in the decades since World War II, reflecting its lack of appeal to the younger generation and shortage of opportunities in growing sectors of the economy. The population in 1990 was 141,686, a decrease of 0.6%. The most severe loss was in the under-19 group. The 20-to-64 group lost moderately, and the over-65 group gained.

Population

	1980	1990
Central City	142,546	141,686
Rank	110	123
Metro Area	807,143	827,645
Pop. Change 1980–1990 -860		
Pop. % Change 1980–1990 -0.6		
Median Age 31.0		
% Male 47.5		
% Age 65 and Over 13.6		
Density (per square mile) 8,855		

Households

Number   52,328
Persons per Household   2.63
% Female-Headed Households   20.6
% One-Person Households   29.4
Births—Total   2,744
   % to Mothers under 20   20.4
   Birth Rate per 1,000   19.3

Ethnic Composition

Many races are represented in Bridgeport. Among the ethnic groups are Italians, Czechs, Hungarians, and Poles in that numerical order. Overall, whites make up 58.5% of the residents, blacks 26.6%, and other races 41.4%. The percentage of whites has decreased slightly compared to the 1980 census, and that of blacks has risen by 6%. The most dramatic increase has been of other races, whose population share grew by over 13% from 1.7% in 1980. Hispanics—both black and white—make up 26.5%.

Ethnic Composition (as % of total pop.)

	1980	1990
White	68.89	58.54
Black	20.97	26.6
American Indian	0.20	0.29
Asian and Pacific Islander	0.55	2.32
Hispanic	18.71	26.5
Other	NA	12.26

Chronology

1639	Bridgeport is founded as Newfield on the site of an Indian village.
1765	The town's residents pay the Pequonnock Indians to leave, giving them 30 bushels of Indian corn and three pounds' worth of blankets.
1821	Bridgeport is incorporated as a town.
1836	Bridgeport is incorporated as a city.
1933	Bridgeport elects socialist Jasper McLevy as mayor.
1990	Bridgeport declares bankruptcy.

Government

Bridgeport operates under a mayor-council form of government. The mayor is elected to a four-year term and the 20 council members are elected from ten districts to twoyear terms. In the early 1930s, Bridgeport was one of the first cities to elect a socialist mayor. Democrats dominate the city council.

Government

Year of Home Charter   NA
Number of Members of the Governing Body   20
Elected at Large   NA
Elected by Wards   20
Number of Women in Governing Body   6
Salary of Mayor $52,000
Salary of Council Members $250.00
City Government Employment Total   4,559
Rate per 10,000   321.4

Public Finance

The budget consists of revenues of $293.973 million and expenditures of $302.468 million. The outstanding debt is $202.108 million and cash and security holding of $61.669 million. Bridgeport declared bankruptcy in 1990, becoming the first major city to do so.

Public Finance

Total Revenue (in millions) $293.973
Intergovernmental Revenue—Total (in millions) $111.62
Federal Revenue per Capita $4.793
% Federal Assistance   1.63
% State Assistance   36.33
Sales Tax as % of Total Revenue   NA
Local Revenue as % of Total Revenue   62.03
City Income Tax   no
Taxes—Total (in millions) $94.5

Taxes per Capita
   Total $666
   Property $657
   Sales and Gross Receipts $0

Public Finance (continued)

General Expenditures—Total (in millions) $211.5
General Expenditures per Capita $1,491
Capital Outlays per Capita $138

% of Expenditures for:
   Public Welfare   6.0
   Highways   1.6
   Education   34.7
   Health and Hospitals   7.6
   Police   6.9
   Sewerage and Sanitation   4.2
   Parks and Recreation   1.8
   Housing and Community Development   3.6
Debt Outstanding per Capita $539
   % Utility   0.0
Federal Procurement Contract Awards (in millions) $27.2
Federal Grants Awards (in millions) $17.5
Fiscal Year Begins   July 1

Economy

Financial troubles notwithstanding, Bridgeport remains Connecticut's largest city and the fourth largest financial center in New England. Manufacturing and trade are the mainstays of the economy, supplemented increasingly by services. Defense contractors form the largest segment of the manufacturing sector; prominent among them are General Electric; Remington Products; Remington Arms; Textron's Sikorsky Aircraft, Lycoming, and Bridgeport Machines; and other Fortune 500 companies. Bridgeport's strategic location makes it ideally suited to exporters and importers. The city currently holds the only World Trade Center license, enabling it to penetrate offshore markets and attract foreign investment. With 11 commercial and savings banks, Bridgeport is the financial capital of southern New England.

Economy

Total Money Income (in millions) $1,337.3
% of State Average   66.9
Per Capita Annual Income $9,427
% Population below Poverty Level   20.4
Fortune 500 Companies   NA

Banks	Number	Deposits (in millions)
Commercial	8	3,238.8
Savings	8	NA

Passenger Autos   539,057
Electric Meters   109,551
Gas Meters   58,742

Manufacturing

Number of Establishments   343
% with 20 or More Employees   36.7
Manufacturing Payroll (in millions) $538.2
Value Added by Manufacture (in millions) $834.1
Value of Shipments (in millions) $1,451.9
New Capital Expenditures (in millions) $27.8

Wholesale Trade

Number of Establishments   234

Economy (continued)

Sales (in millions) $929.8
Annual Payroll (in millions) $76.967

Retail Trade

Number of Establishments   1,060
Total Sales (in millions) $698.3
Sales per Capita $4,922
Number of Retail Trade Establishments with Payroll   707
Annual Payroll (in millions) $90.4
Total Sales (in millions) $670.2
General Merchandise Stores (per capita) $392
Food Stores (per capita) $972
Apparel Stores (per capita) $219
Eating and Drinking Places (per capita) $464

Service Industries

Total Establishments   896
Total Receipts (in millions) $456.3
Hotels and Motels (in millions)   NA
Health Services (in millions) $153.2
Legal Services (in millions) $85.5

Labor

Bridgeport is one of Connecticut's ten urban enterprise zones; eligible companies locating there receive special grants and tax abatements. Of the 200,000 workers constituting the labor force, the largest sector is manufacturing, followed closely by services, and then by wholesale and retail trade. Together, manufacturing, services, and trade account for 75% of the workforce.

Labor

Civilian Labor Force   66,903
% Change 1989–1990   1.7

Work Force Distribution
   Mining   NA
   Construction   5,500
   Manufacturing   47,600
   Transportation and Public Utilities   8,400
   Wholesale and Retail Trade   40,900
   FIRE (Finance, Insurance, Real Estate)   11,400
   Service   48,500
   Government   19,300
   Women as % of Labor Force   45.6
   % Self-Employed   3.1
   % Professional/Technical   11.0
Total Unemployment   6,198
Rate %   9.3
Federal Government Civilian Employment   1,154

Education

Bridgeport's education system is considerably diversified. Its core public schools are supplemented by three alternative schools, a special-education facility, a magnet school program, an adult-education program, a parochial high school, and numerous parochial elementary schools. School enrollment has remained in the 19,000 range for a number of years. Per-pupil expenditures have climbed steadily and are now over $6,000. Nearly 62% of high school graduates pursue college education. The higher education system consists of the state-run University of Bridgeport; two Catholic universities, Sacred Heart University and the Jesuit-run Fairfield University; Fairfield Engineering Institute; and Housatonic Community College. In terms of enrollment, the largest university is Fairfield University.

Education

Number of Public Schools   38
Special Education Schools   NA
Total Enrollment   19,687
% Enrollment in Private Schools   17.9
% Minority   NA
Classroom Teachers   NA
Pupil-Teacher Ratio   17.3:1
Number of Graduates   NA
Total Revenue (in millions)   NA
Total Expenditures (in millions)   NA
Expenditures per Pupil   NA
Educational Attainment (Age 25 and Over)   NA
   % Completed 12 or More Years   50.7
   % Completed 16 or More Years   8.7
Four-Year Colleges and Universities   1
   Enrollment   4,278
Two-Year Colleges   1
   Enrollment   2,403

Libraries

Number   16
Public Libraries   5
Books (in thousands)   543
Circulation (in thousands)   398
Persons Served (in thousands)   142
Circulation per Person Served   2.8
Income (in millions) $2.936
Staff   103

Four-Year Colleges and Universities
   Fairfield University
   Sacred Heart University
   University of Bridgeport

Health

Bridgeport Hospital is one of the largest in the state, with 615 beds. Its facilities are supplemented by Park City and St. Vincent hospitals. All are teaching hospitals for Yale University's School of Medicine.

Health

Deaths—Total   1,585
Rate per 1,000   11.2
Infant Deaths—Total   45
Rate per 1,000   16.4
Number of Metro Hospitals   4
Number of Metro Hospital Beds   1,125
Rate per 100,000   793
Number of Physicians   NA
Physicians per 1,000   NA
Nurses per 1,000   NA
Health Expenditures per Capita $29.25

Transportation

Because of its strategic location between New York City and Boston, Bridgeport is a major commerce and shipping center for the northeastern United States. It is serviced by I-95, the major interstate throughway that runs along the eastern coast, as well as U.S. 1 and state roads 8, 25, and 127. Passenger rail service is provided by Amtrak and MetroNorth, while rail freight is handled by Conrail. The Bridgeport–Port Jefferson Ferry across Long Island Sound is a principal route to Long Island, eliminating the meandering inland trip toward New York City. The main airline terminus for Bridgeport is Igor Sikorsky Airport, located 4 miles east in Stratford, handling commuter and feeder airlines. Tweed/New Haven Airport is 22 miles to the east.

Transportation
Interstate Highway Mileage   19
Total Urban Mileage   1,710
Total Daily Vehicle Mileage (in millions)   7.849
Daily Average Commute Time   44.7 min.
Number of Buses   56
Port Tonnage (in millions)   2.669
Airports   1
Number of Daily Flights   0.6
Daily Average Number of Passengers   NA
Airlines (American carriers only)
Continental Express
USAir

Housing

Bridgeport has 57,224 housing units, of which 42.2% are owner occupied. The median sale price of existing homes is lower than the state average, and considerably lower than in nearby New Haven and Fairfield counties. The reason for this is that Bridgeport homes tend to be much older; nearly 47.1% were built earlier than 1939 (as against a state average of 32.0%), and only 7.8% were built after 1970 (as against a state average of 18.1%). Building permits worth over $65 million are issued annually.

Housing
Total Housing Units   57,224
% Change 1980–1990   3.4
Vacant Units for Sale or Rent   3,971
Occupied Units   52,328
% with More Than One Person per Room   6.7
% Owner-Occupied   44.2
Median Value of Owner-Occupied Homes $145,900
Average Monthly Purchase Cost $415
Median Monthly Rent $496
New Private Housing Starts   85
Value (in thousands) $3,536
% Single-Family   43.5
Nonresidential Buildings Value (in thousands) $377

Urban Redevelopment

Bridgeport's financial problems have helped to accelerate urban redeveleopment programs designed to change the stodgy image of a city that has seen its best days. Among the many projects launched during the past few years are: Schiavone Downtown Revitalization Project, incorporating 19 city blocks and 181 buildings; Price Club Plaza Mall, an $80-million project on 50 acres of waterfront property; and Harborpointe Project, a 135acre, $900-million plan to build an International Conference and Exhibition Hall on the waterfront.

Crime

Historically, Bridgeport has a higher crime rate than surrounding counties, and its index crime rate is sufficiently high to make it a major political issue. Many of the rundown areas of the city are breeding grounds for criminal activities, including drug trafficking.

Crime
Violent Crimes—Total   2,680
Violent Crime Rate per 100,000   726.1
Murder   51
Rape   82
Robbery   1,734
Aggravated Assaults   993
Property Crimes   14,528
Burglary   3,954
Larceny   4,691
Motor Vehicle Theft   5,883
Arson   133
Per Capita Police Expenditures $147.78
Per Capita Fire Protection Expenditures $140.30
Number of Police   401
Per 1,000   2.8

Religion

Reflecting its mixed ethnic heritage, Bridgeport is more Catholic than Protestant, with a substantial population following non-mainstream religions.

Religion	
Largest Denominations (Adherents)	
Catholic	347,526
Black Baptist	19,196
United Church of Christ	27,805
Episcopal	27,705
American Baptist	12,656
Presbyterian	7,625
United Methodist	18,431
Jewish	45,800

Media

The Bridgeport Post is published six days a week, and on Sundays as the *Sunday Post*. Although Bridgeport is supported by one television station, and five AM and FM radio stations, the city also receives radio and television broadcasts from New York City.

Media

Newsprint
  The Bridgeport Post, daily
  Bridgeport News, weekly

Television
  WEDW (Channel 49)

Radio
  WCUM (AM)   WDJZ (AM)
  WEZN (FM)   WICC (AM)
  WPKN (FM)

Sports

Lacking a major sports team, Bridgeport's main sporting event is jai alai, held from November through May at the Fronton downtown.

Arts, Culture, and Tourism

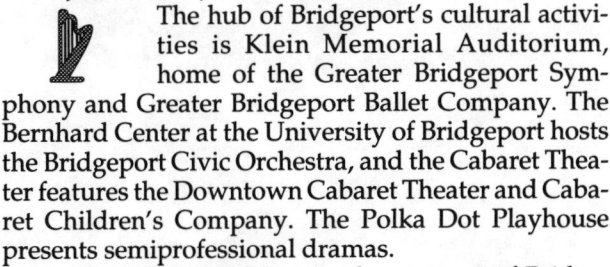

The hub of Bridgeport's cultural activities is Klein Memorial Auditorium, home of the Greater Bridgeport Symphony and Greater Bridgeport Ballet Company. The Bernhard Center at the University of Bridgeport hosts the Bridgeport Civic Orchestra, and the Cabaret Theater features the Downtown Cabaret Theater and Cabaret Children's Company. The Polka Dot Playhouse presents semiprofessional dramas.

The P. T. Barnum Museum honors one of Bridgeport's most famous citizens, and features circus memorabilia. Another important museum is the Museum of Art, Science, and Industry featuring the duPont Space Gallery and Planetarium. The Hilton Hotel Gallery and Carlson Gallery offer works by modern artists. The Housatonic Museum of Art specializes in contemporary and 19th-century European and American art.

Travel and Tourism

Hotel Rooms   6,675
Convention and Exhibit Space (square feet)   NA

Convention Centers
  Bridgeport Hilton

Festivals
  Barnum Festival and Parade (Summer)
  Long Island Sound America Festival
  Black Rock Day

Parks and Recreation

With nearly 80 parks and recreation areas totaling about 1,400 acres, Bridgeport is marked by the 181-acre Beardsley Park (which includes the Beardsley Zoological Gardens), the 370-acre Seaside Park and Barnum Field (given to the city by P. T. Barnum), and Captain's Cove Seaport, an amusement park, shopping, and restaurant area along the shore.

Sources of Further Information

Bridgeport Convention and Visitors Commission
303 State Street
Bridgeport, CT 06604
(203) 576-8494

Additional Reading

Connecticut magazine. Monthly.

Buffalo

New York

Location and Topography

Buffalo, the second-largest city in New York State and the seat of Erie County, is located in the westernmost corner of the state. It lies on the border of the United States and Canada, about 200 miles from the capital, Albany. Nicknamed the Queen City of the Lakes, it is situated on Lake Erie and is connected to Lake Ontario by the Niagara River. The terrain is level, with gently flowing hills rising to the east and south.

Layout of City and Suburbs

Bordered on the west by Lake Erie, Buffalo resembles an exposition site more than a major city. Wide, expansive thoroughfares based on those in Washington, D.C., dominate the downtown area, such as Ellicott, Washington, Pearl, and Franklin streets and Delaware Avenue. Much of the city radiates in a circular pattern from Niagara Park in the northwest section. In the eastern section is the theater district, while toward the core are important landmarks such as Erie County Hall and the Federal Building. The streets are not traditionally crosshatched, although many do cross one another. On the American side of the border, Buffalo's suburbs include Lockport and Niagara Falls. Across the border are Hamilton, St. Catherine's, and, on Lake Ontario, Toronto.

Environment

Environmental Stress Index   2.6
Green Cities Index: Rank   65
                     Score   25.14
Water Quality   Alkaline, hard, fluoridated
     Average Daily Use (gallons per capita)   171
     Maximum Supply (gallons per capita)   356
Parkland as % of Total City Area   NA
% Waste Landfilled/Recycled   NA
Annual Parks Expenditures per Capita $59.83

Climate

Despite Buffalo's notoriety for heavy snowfalls, it has a livable climate marked by mild summers and the absence of wide seasonal swings in temperature. Spring comes late primarily because of Lake Erie's cold water and ice buildup. Generally Buffalo has more sun than other cities in New York State, and thunderstorms are infrequent. Fall has long dry periods, and is frost-free until mid-October. The prevailing west winds over

Lake Erie are a natural summer air conditioner, but they serve to lengthen the winter. Buffalo usually has the nation's first and last blizzards of the season. The winter's mean temperature of 25.4° includes frequent periods of thaw; zero temperatures are unlikely to occur more than once or twice a season. The average annual rainfall of about 37.5 inches is spread almost evenly year-round.

Weather

Temperature

Highest Monthly Average °F   79.5
Lowest Monthly Average °F   17.6

Annual Averages

Days 32°F or Below   137
Days above 90°F   2
Zero Degree Days   5
Precipitation (inches)   36
Snow (inches)   90
% Seasonal Humidity   73
Wind Speed (m.p.h.)   12.3
Clear Days   55
Cloudy Days   206
Storm Days   31
Rainy Days   168

Average Temperatures (°F)	High	Low	Mean
January	29.8	17.6	23.7
February	31.0	17.7	24.4
March	39.0	25.2	32.1
April	53.3	36.4	44.9
May	64.3	45.9	55.1
June	75.1	56.3	65.7
July	79.5	60.7	70.1
August	77.6	59.1	68.4
September	70.8	52.3	61.6
October	60.2	42.7	51.5
November	46.1	33.5	39.8
December	33.6	22.2	27.9

History

The area around present-day Buffalo was inhabited by many tribes of American Indians in the 18th century. French explorers from Canada visited in the latter part of the century, but little headway was made in settlement. The first settler was Chabert Joncaire, who ran a trading post for a brief time in 1758. Joncaire may have been the man who called Buffalo Creek Beau Fleuve (Beautiful River). Eventually, the Indians shortened the name to "Boo-Flo," which became, as we know it today, Buffalo.

In 1790 the Holland Land Company, a consortium of investors from Amsterdam, bought tracts of land around Buffalo for a settlement. Ten years later, a company surveyor named Joseph Ellicott platted the new town and called it New Amsterdam. The settlers disapproved of the name and began to use the Indian mispronunciation, "Boo-Flo", or Buffalo Creek. During the War of 1812 its close proximity to Canada led Buffalo to be burned down by the British, but by 1816 the new city was organized as the first major white settlement on the eastern shore of Lake Erie.

With the construction of the Erie Canal, which opened in 1825, Buffalo became an important terminus for commerce and trade on the canal. The population of the city quadrupled from little more than 2,000 to 10,000, and in 1832 Buffalo was incorporated as a city. For the rest of the century, its geographic position led it to become one of the main centers for American trade. During the 1850s, the coming of the railroads heightened economic activity. Two 19th-century American presidents, Millard Fillmore and Grover Cleveland (who was sheriff of Erie County and mayor of Buffalo), came from Buffalo.

Buffalo's economic progress was highlighted at the 1901 Pan-American Exposition. Unfortunately, the exposition was marred by the assassination of President William McKinley by an anarchist.

Buffalo served as a commercial terminal until the late 1970s, when its economic engine began to lose steam. During the 1980s, Buffalo suffered from a serious depression, but in the 1990s the city is experiencing a renaissance of economic stability.

Historical Landmarks

Buffalo marks the presence of several presidents. The McKinley Monument, dominating Niagara Square, was erected by the state of New York in 1907 in memory of President William McKinley, who was assassinated during the Pan-American Exposition in Buffalo in 1901. The monument, of modified French Renaissance design, consists of an obelisk rising out of a series of pools decorated with crouching lions. Just to the west of the city lies the Theodore Roosevelt Inaugural National Historic Site, the location where Roosevelt was inaugurated as the nation's 26th president following the assassination of McKinley. Another president is commemorated with the site of the Millard Fillmore House on West Genesee Street and Delaware Avenue. Architect Louis Sullivan designed the Prudential Building, an 1895–1896 tower that has since been restored. Buffalo State Hospital, now Buffalo Psychiatric Center, is a twin-towered Romanesque Revival structure built between 1870 and 1896.

Population

Buffalo's population declined from 357,870 in 1980 to 328,123 in 1990, a loss of 8.3%, and its national ranking slipped from 37th to 50th. The metro area also lost population,

Population

	1980	1990
Central City	357,870	328,123
Rank	39	50
Metro Area	1,015,472	968,532
Pop. Change 1980–1990 -29,747		
Pop. % Change 1980–1990 -8.3		
Median Age 32.0		
% Male 46.6		
% Age 65 and Over 14.8		
Density (per square mile) 8,081		

Chronology

1758 French interpreter Chabert Joncaire founds a trading post within the Buffalo city limits.

1790 Investors of the Holland Land Company from Amsterdam buy plots of land around Buffalo.

1800 The land company sends surveyor Joseph Ellicott to plat the new town. Ellicott names the settlement New Amsterdam, but the locals prefer an Indian mispronunciation of a French description of the area—"boo-flo," or Buffalo.

1816 Buffalo is incorporated as a village.

1825 The opening of the Erie Canal makes Buffalo the preeminent western terminus for trade along Lake Erie.

1832 Buffalo's population quadruples in seven years, and it is incorporated as a city.

1881 Grover Cleveland is elected mayor of Buffalo.

1901 President William McKinley is assassinated during the all-important Pan-American Exposition by Leon Czolgosz, an anarchist.

1970s Recession and near-depression come to Buffalo.

1990s Buffalo, with a diversification in its economy, begins to see a revitalization.

Population (continued)

Households

Number 136,436
Persons per Household 2.33
% Female-Headed Households 20.2
% One-Person Households 35.6
Births—Total 5,757
    % to Mothers under 20 15.8
    Birth Rate per 1,000 17.0

declining from 1,015,472 to 968,532 in the same period. The population loss is likely to continue due to a soft economy.

Ethnic Composition

Buffalo's ethnic and racial composition has altered dramatically over the years. Until World War II, Buffalo was a microcosm of Europe, with sections of the city inhabited by the major European ethnic groups. The most prominent were Poles, Irish, Italians, Germans, and Hungarians. The black presence began during the Civil War, and by the turn of the century they occupied their own section in Jesse Clipper Square. They now com-

prise about 30.65% of the population, while whites make up 64.75%, and other races form the balance.

Ethnic Composition (as % of total pop.)

	1980	1990
White	70.52	64.75
Black	26.58	30.65
American Indian	0.67	0.78
Asian and Pacific Islander	0.37	0.99
Hispanic	2.65	4.92
Other	NA	2.83

Government

Under its 1927 charter, Buffalo operates under a strong mayor-council form of government. The council consists of 15 members. Nine are elected by district to two-year terms. Six members, including the council president, are elected at large to staggered four-year terms, along wth the mayor. A 1959 amendment eliminated a one-term limit on mayoral tenure, and all elected officials may now serve unlimited terms. The comptroller is elected for four years at the mayor's midterm. The chief judge and 11 associate judges of the city court are elected for ten-year terms. Buffalo is also the seat of Erie County, which has its own strong executive charter and a 20-member legislature. The county has steadily increased in budget and importance as a metropolitan-type government performing health, welfare, and other basic functions for its districts.

Government

Year of Home Charter 1922
Number of Members of the Governing Body 15
Elected at Large 6
Elected by Wards 9
Number of Women in Governing Body 0
Salary of Mayor $79,380
Salary of Council Members $41,895
City Government Employment Total 12,021
Rate per 10,000 370.1

Public Finance

The annual budget consists of revenues of $656.130 million and expenditures of $703.701 million. The outstanding debt is $383.611 million, and cash and security holdings are $171.996 million.

Public Finance

Total Revenue (in millions) $656.13
Intergovernmental Revenue—Total (in millions) $441.3
Federal Revenue per Capita $53.42
% Federal Assistance 8.14
% State Assistance 48.77
Sales Tax as % of Total Revenue 1.56
Local Revenue as % of Total Revenue 40.46

Public Finance (continued)

City Income Tax   no
Taxes—Total (in millions) $107.7

Taxes per Capita
   Total $332
   Property $294
   Sales and Gross Receipts $29
General Expenditures—Total (in millions) $530.3
General Expenditures per Capita $1,633
Capital Outlays per Capita $319

% of Expenditures for:
   Public Welfare   0.0
   Highways   5.8
   Education   41.0
   Health and Hospitals   0.2
   Police   6.0
   Sewerage and Sanitation   9.2
   Parks and Recreation   4.9
   Housing and Community Development   12.0
Debt Outstanding per Capita $782
   % Utility   7.0
Federal Procurement Contract Awards (in millions)
   $209.5
Federal Grants Awards (in millions) $106
Fiscal Year Begins   July 1

Economy

 Although Buffalo suffered a major economic slump in the early 1980s that resulted in tremendous job losses, it began to diversify its economy, which is presently on the rebound. Its centralized location along the Canadian border and the fact that 70% of the American population, as well as 62% of the Canadian population, lies just a day's drive away make Buffalo an attractive business site. The newly signed U.S.–Canada Free Trade Agreement (UCFTA) has made commerce across the border more profitable. Leading the way in job growth are service companies and health-care providers. Some of the largest companies in Buffalo are American Brass Company, Northtown Automotive, and Schmitt Sales.

Economy

Total Money Income (in millions) $2,871.4
% of State Average   75.1
Per Capita Annual Income $8,840
% Population below Poverty Level   20.7
Fortune 500 Companies   NA

Banks	Number	Deposits (in millions)
Commercial	13	6,865.7
Savings	6	8,367

Passenger Autos   547,478
Electric Meters   336,242
Gas Meters   472,873

Manufacturing

Number of Establishments   591
% with 20 or More Employees   39.3
Manufacturing Payroll (in millions) $922.4
Value Added by Manufacture (in millions) $2,339.8
Value of Shipments (in millions) $4,794.2
New Capital Expenditures (in millions) $95.7

Economy (continued)

Wholesale Trade

Number of Establishments   667
Sales (in millions) $2,729.3
Annual Payroll (in millions) $209.477

Retail Trade

Number of Establishments   2,674
Total Sales (in millions) $1,323.1
Sales per Capita $4,073
Number of Retail Trade Establishments with Payroll   1,875
Annual Payroll (in millions) $175.6
Total Sales (in millions) $1,289.2
General Merchandise Stores (per capita) $273
Food Stores (per capita) $1,249
Apparel Stores (per capita) $170
Eating and Drinking Places (per capita) $552

Service Industries

Total Establishments   2,020
Total Receipts (in millions) $1,029.3
Hotels and Motels (in millions) $18.9
Health Services (in millions) $254.1
Legal Services (in millions) $200.5

Labor

Historically the Buffalo-area work force has been inclined to function harmoniously with management. Most industrial employment is in branch plants of firms headquartered elsewhere, which tends to keep industrial relations on a professional and unemotional level. Increasing automation and closing of Bethlehem Steel and General Electric plants in the 1980s resulted in an exodus of workers from the region and a shortage of low-skilled, part-time workers. The largest employer is General Motors, whose radiator plant faces an uncertain future. Other major employers are federal, state, county, and city governments, all of which face cutbacks in the 1990s. Nevertheless, analysts expect employment growth to be strong in the service sector.

Labor

Civilian Labor Force   146,707
% Change 1989–1990   -1.2

Work Force Distribution
   Mining   300
   Construction   16,800
   Manufacturing   71,500
   Transportation and Public Utilities   22,300
   Wholesale and Retail Trade   114,200
   FIRE (Finance, Insurance, Real Estate)   27,200
   Service   125,000
   Government   75,100
   Women as % of Labor Force   45.1
   % Self-Employed   3.6
   % Professional/Technical   14.6
Total Unemployment   9,962
Rate %   6.8
Federal Government Civilian Employment   7,662

Education

 Buffalo operates the second-largest public school system in New York State, consisting of 75 schools. In addition, there are 70 private and parochial schools, including Buffalo Seminary, western New York's oldest private high school; Nichols School, noted for its outstanding college preparatory program; and Calasanctius, a nonsectarian school for gifted students. Higher education is offered in 14 public and private colleges, of which the largest are the two campuses of the State University of New York (SUNY) at Buffalo. SUNY at Buffalo is the largest unit of the New York State University System. It began in 1846 as a medical school and was known as the University of Buffalo until 1962, when it merged with the state system. The State University of New York College at Buffalo, on Elmwood Avenue, was founded in 1867 as a college for teachers. Also part of the state system is Erie Community College. Private institutions include Canisius College (founded in 1870), D'Youville College (1908), Medaille College (1875), Trocaire College (1958), Villa Maria College (1960), and Daemen College (1947). University-based and private scientific research has become a major growth industry. Among the largest defense- or industry-related research centers are Cornell Aeronautical Laboratory, Bell Aerosystems, and Hooker Chemical's central research plant. Among SUNY at Buffalo's 50 research facilities are the National Earthquake Engineering Center and the Institute on Superconductivity.

Education

Number of Public Schools   75
Special Education Schools   1
Total Enrollment   47,224
% Enrollment in Private Schools   18.8
% Minority   59.4
Classroom Teachers   3,103
Pupil-Teacher Ratio   15.2:1
Number of Graduates   2,335
Total Revenue (in millions) $294.911
Total Expenditures (in millions) $280.421
Expenditures per Pupil $6,117
Educational Attainment (Age 25 and Over)
    % Completed 12 or More Years   53.8
    % Completed 16 or More Years   11.1
Four-Year Colleges and Universities   3
    Enrollment   7,273
Two-Year Colleges   2
    Enrollment   6,434

Libraries

Number   73
Public Libraries   22
Books (in thousands)   3,705
Circulation (in thousands)   6,482
Persons Served (in thousands)   1,015
Circulation per Person Served   6.38
Income (in millions) $17.58
Staff   344

Four-Year Colleges and Universities
    Canisius College
    D'Youville College
    Medaille College
    SUNY–Buffalo

Health

 The Buffalo area has a heavy concentration of medical facilities. Among its 14 hospitals the largest is Buffalo General Hospital. Roswell Park Memorial Institute is one of the world's leading cancer research and treatment centers. Others include Children's, Millard Fillmore, Sisters of Charity Intercommunity, Mercy, Columbus, and St. Francis hospitals and the Veterans Administration Medical Center.

Health

Deaths—Total   4,574
Rate per 1,000   13.5
Infant Deaths—Total   80
Rate per 1,000   13.9
Number of Metro Hospitals   14
Number of Metro Hospital Beds   6,321
Rate per 100,000   1,946
Number of Physicians   2,321
Physicians per 1,000   2.92
Nurses per 1,000   12.19
Health Expenditures per Capita $4.76

Transportation

Transportation is one of Buffalo's historic strengths. Northeast Buffalo is linked with points east by I-90, which connects with I-290 going south along the city's eastern boundary. Northwest Buffalo is approached via I-190, which passes through the city's west side, cuts across town, and connects with I-90. The city is accessible from the south through a network of highways connecting with I-90. Buffalo is linked with Canada by four vehicular and three rail bridges. From downtown Buffalo it is only a 5-minute ride to the Peace Bridge and thence to Canada. Rail passenger service is provided by Amtrak, and freight service by over eight railroads. Buffalo has two international airports; the Greater Buffalo International Airport is only 15 minutes from downtown. The Port of Buffalo is the world's largest grain-handling center. Steamships and barges from more than 25 lines provide freight service on the St. Lawrence Seaway or the State Barge Canal System.

Transportation

Interstate Highway Mileage   72
Total Urban Mileage   3,590
Total Daily Vehicle Mileage (in millions)   17.385
Daily Average Commute Time   42.9 min.
Number of Buses   400
Port Tonnage (in millions)   1.334
Airports   1
Number of Daily Flights   82
Daily Average Number of Passengers   4,462

Airlines (American carriers only)
    American
    Continental
    Delta
    Eastern
    Midway
    Northwest
    United
    USAir

Housing

Housing		
Total Housing Units 151,971		
% Change 1980–1990 3.0		
Vacant Units for Sale or Rent 8,513		
Occupied Units 136,436		
% with More Than One Person per Room 2.1		
% Owner-Occupied 43.1		
Median Value of Owner-Occupied Homes $46,700		
Average Monthly Purchase Cost $290		
Median Monthly Rent $255		
New Private Housing Starts 128		
Value (in thousands) $7,485		
% Single-Family 59.4		
Nonresidential Buildings Value (in thousands) $17,513		

Tallest Buildings	Hgt. (ft.)	Stories
Marine Midland Center (1971)	529	40
City Hall (1926)	378	32
Rand Bldg., not incl.		
40-ft. beacon (1929)	351	29
Main Place Tower (1969)	350	26

Housing

Housing is Buffalo's weakest sector, buffeted by the anemic real estate market of the 1990s. Much of the city's housing is older than 50 years. At the same time the percentage of homeowners is high—overs 43%. Housing affordability is also relatively high compared to other cities in its class. In city spending for housing and urban development, Buffalo ranks ninth among all U.S. cities.

Urban Redevelopment

A national survey by Chicago Title and Trust ranks Buffalo first in the nation in the percentage growth rate of nonresidential construction projects. A revitalized waterfront is the showpiece of more than $2.5 billion in new development. Another is the Buffalo Place transit mall. This 18-block downtown area, considered the longest pedestrian mall in North America, offers a metro light-rail transit line that takes passengers free of charge to offices, hotels, restaurants, and shops along the 1.2-mile route. The planned Walden Galleria Mall is expected to lead expansion of retail trade in the 1990s.

Crime

Buffalo has a good record as a relatively safe city. In 1991, violent crimes totaled 6,042 and property crimes totaled 25,428.

Crime	
Violent Crimes—Total 6,042	
Violent Crime Rate per 100,000 850.0	
Murder 50	
Rape 319	
Robbery 2,705	
Aggravated Assaults 2,968	
Property Crimes 25,428	
Burglary 8,462	
Larceny 12,527	
Motor Vehicle Theft 4,439	
Arson 676	

Crime (continued)	
Per Capita Police Expenditures $147.6	
Per Capita Fire Protection Expenditures $114.63	
Number of Police 993	
Per 1,000 2.92	

Religion

The city has a Roman Catholic plurality, but its 400 places of worship represent all Christian denominations.

Religion	
Largest Denominations (Adherents)	
Catholic	572,878
United Methodist	22,311
Evangelical Lutheran	22,459
Black Baptist	22,131
American Zion	13,909
American Baptist	11,647
Assembly of God	11,210
Episcopal	13,084
Presbyterian	16,694
United Church of Christ	14,283
Jewish	18,125

Media

The demise of *The Buffalo Courier* in 1982 left Buffalo with only one daily, *The Buffalo News*, published as an all-day Monday-through-Friday edition, and in the mornings on weekends. There are 5 broadcast television stations and 16 AM and FM radio stations.

Media	
Newsprint	
Business First of Buffalo, weekly	
The Buffalo News, daily	
Buffalo Spree, quarterly	
West Side Times, weekly	
Buffalo First, weekly	
Riverside Review, weekly	
Television	
WGRZ (Channel 2)	
WIVB (Channel 4)	
WKBW (Channel 7)	
WNED (Channel 17)	
WNYB (Channel 49)	
Radio	
WBEN (AM)	WMJQ (FM)
WBFO (FM)	WBNY (FM)
WBUF (FM)	WDCX (FM)
WEBR (AM)	WGR (AM)
WGR (FM)	WHTT (AM)
WHTT (FM)	WJYE (FM)
WWKB (AM)	WXBX (AM)
WUFX (FM)	WYRK (FM)

Sports

Buffalo has recently become a major sports town in the two sports in which the city participates. The Buffalo Bills football team, which plays at the 80,000-seat Rich Stadium in Orchard Park, appeared in three straight Super Bowls in the early 1990s. The Buffalo Sabres hockey team, playing at Buffalo's Memorial Stadium, has been a major contender for the National Hockey League's prestigious Stanley Cup.

Arts, Culture, and Tourism

Buffalo's theater district, situated in the eastern section of the city from Main Street north to Delaware Avenue, features a wide variety of arts. The centerpiece is the lavish Shea's Buffalo Theatre for the Performing Arts, home of the Greater Buffalo Opera Company and a national historic landmark. Local arts and culture are supported by the Arts Council in Buffalo and Erie County, a nonprofit group. Arts sponsored by the company include the Buffalo Ensemble Theatre, Buffalo Philharmonic Orchestra at Kleinhans Music Hall, Alleyway Theatre, jazz performances at the Marquee at the Tralf (a nightclub), and Studio Arena Theatre. Museums include the Buffalo Museum of Science, Buffalo Zoological Gardens, Elbert Hubbard Museum (a private residence), and Buffalo and Erie County Historical Society.

Travel and Tourism

Hotel Rooms 5,758
Convention and Exhibit Space (square feet) 65,000

Convention Centers
  Buffalo Convention Center
  Memorial Stadium

Festivals
  Winter Fest
  St. Patrick's Day (March)
  Juneteenth Festival (June)
  Friendship Festival (July)
  Erie County Fair & Exposition (August)
  Ethnic Heritage Festival (November)
  Festival of Lights (January)

Parks and Recreation

Buffalo and its environs encompass some 101 parks totaling more than 6,000 acres. Largest are the spacious LaSalle Park along the Niagara River and the 350-acre Lincoln Parkway, designed and laid out by Frederick Law Olmstead in 1870. The 65-acre Humboldt Park on Fillmore Avenue and Best Street is the most popular park on the east side. It includes an arboretum, rose garden, and greenhouse. The Buffalo Botanical Gardens on South Park Avenue and McKinley Parkway houses rare plants.

Sources of Further Information

Greater Buffalo Convention and Visitors Bureau
107 Delaware Avenue
Buffalo, NY 14202-2801
(716) 852-0511

Metro Buffalo Alliance for Economic Development
107 Delaware Avenue
Buffalo, NY 14202-2801
(800) BUFFALO

Additional Reading

Buffalo Architectural Guidebook Corp. *Buffalo Architecture: A Guide.* 1981.
Goldman, Mark. *City on the Lake: History and the Challenge of Change in Buffalo, New York.* 1990.
Graebner, William. *Coming of Age in Buffalo: Youth and Authority in the Post-War Era.* 1989.
High Hopes: The Rise and Decline of Buffalo, New York. 1984.
Klinkenborg, Verlyn. *Last Fine Time.* 1991.

Burlington
Vermont

Basic Data

Name   Burlington
Name Origin   From Burling family
Year Founded   1763 Inc. 1865
Status: State   Vermont
          County   Seat of Chittenden County
Area (square miles)   10.6
Elevation (feet)   110
Time Zone   EST
Population (1990)   39,127
Population of Metro Area (1990)   137,079

Sister Cities
   Yaroslavl, Russia

Distance in Miles To:

Boston	224
Concord	155
Nashua	189
Portsmouth	204
New York	300
Montreal	98

Location and Topography

N

Burlington, the Queen City of Vermont, is located on three terraced slopes on the eastern shore of Lake Champlain in northern Vermont.

Layout of City and Suburbs

On the tree-covered summit, flanked by residential districts, stand the buildings of the University of Vermont. The business district occupies the middle terrace, and below it are warehouses, docks, railroad yards, and shops. With its broad streets and avenues well laid out, Burlington has the appearance of a modern city. Never having suffered from a great fire, it has preserved many of the gracious structures of an older era. The Winooski River meanders through the city, and a number of highways—15, 89, 116, 2, 7, and 189—crisscross it. The principal avenues are Main, Shelburne, Willard, Winooski, Manhattan, North, and Pine.

Environment

Environmental Stress Index   2.4
Green Cities Index: Rank   NA
                          Score   NA
Water Quality   Neutral, soft, fluoridated
   Average Daily Use (gallons per capita)   139
   Maximum Supply (gallons per capita)   427
Parkland as % of Total City Area   8.5
% Waste Landfilled/Recycled   74:26
Annual Parks Expenditures per Capita $40.94

Climate

Burlington's northerly latitude ensures the city a true New England climate. Lake Champlain, however, has a tempering effect; during the winter months, temperatures along the lakeshore run from 5° to 10° warmer than at the airport some four miles away. Summers tend to be quite pleasant, with only four 90° days per year on average. Fall is cool extending through October. Winters are cold, with intense cold snaps formed by high-pressure systems moving down from central Canada. Because of its location in the path of the St. Lawrence Valley storm track and the effects of the lake, Burlington is one of the cloudiest cities in the nation. It averages 204 cloudy days, 103 partly cloudy days, and only 58 clear days.

Weather

Temperature

Highest Monthly Average °F   80.81
Lowest Monthly Average °F   7.6

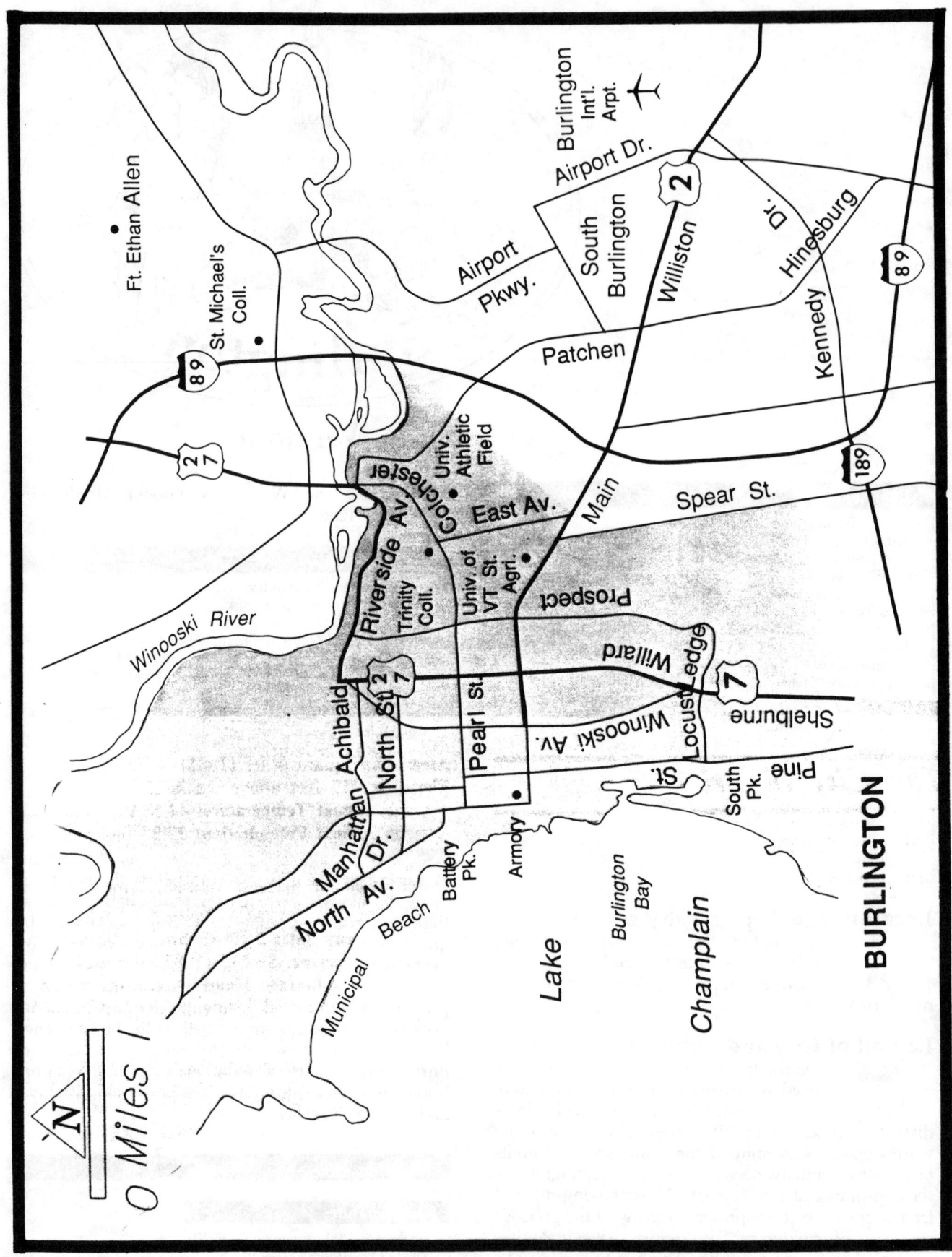

Weather (continued)

Annual Averages

Days 32°F or Below   163
Days above 90°F   5
Zero Degree Days   28
Precipitation (inches)   33.33
Snow (inches)   79
% Seasonal Humidity   71
Wind Speed (m.p.h.)   8.8
Clear Days   58
Cloudy Days   204
Storm Days   25
Rainy Days   153

Average Temperatures (°F)	High	Low	Mean
January	25.9	7.6	16.8
February	28.2	8.9	18.6
March	38.0	20.1	29.1
April	53.3	32.6	43.0
May	66.1	43.5	54.8
June	76.5	53.9	65.2
July	81.0	58.5	69.8
August	78.3	56.4	67.4
September	70.0	48.6	59.3
October	58.7	38.8	48.8
November	44.3	29.7	37.0
December	30.3	14.8	22.6

History

Burlington was chartered in 1763 by the province of New Hampshire and settled in 1773. The name derives from the Burling family of landholders. The outbreak of the Revolutionary War within a few years interrupted the settlement, and it was not until 1783 that the settlers returned. The possibilities of commercial navigation on Lake Champlain were grasped by early civic leaders such as Ira Allen (brother of Ethan Allen) and Gideon King (nicknamed Admiral of the Lake), an agent of John Jacob Astor. In 1808 the steamboat *Vermont*, the second commercially operated steamboat in the country, was built near the foot of King Street.

Since then, the history of the city has been determined by its transportation potentials. In 1823 the opening of the Champlain Canal connected the lake with the Hudson River, and a large part of the Champlain Valley commerce changed from Canada to New York. In 1826 the Champlain Transportation Company was formed. Lake travel peaked during the 1840s, then declined swiftly when Burlington was linked to Boston via two railroads, the Rutland and the Central Vermont. Railways also portended the decline of the city's industrial capacity by making available to its residents cheaper products from elsewhere. In 1865 Burlington was divided in two, the larger section forming South Burlington, while the smaller was incorporated as a city. In 1957 Burlington reappeared on the industrial map when IBM chose it as the site for a plant producing computer memory chips.

Historical Landmarks

Burlington has a number of historic districts: City Hall Park, Pearl Street, Head of Church Street, and University Green.

The city hall is a large Georgian structure. Among the more notable churches are St. Joseph's Church of 1901, the first French-Catholic parish in the United States; the Unitarian Church on Pearl Street and Elmwood Avenue, erected in 1816 with a lofty clock tower and crowning steeple; and the First Calvinistic Congregational Church, erected in 1842 to replace the 1812 building that burned down in 1839. The University of Vermont has a number of interesting buildings, such as the Ira Allen Chapel, Grassemount, the Old Mill, and Morrill Hall.

Population

The 1990 population of Burlington was 39,127, slightly higher than its 1970 population of 38,663.

Population

	1980	1990
Central City	37,712	39,127
Rank	590	644
Metro Area	15,308	137,079
Pop. Change 1980–1990 +1,415		
Pop. % Change 1980–1990 +3.8		
Median Age 26.7		
% Male 46.6		
% Age 65 and Over 10.6		
Density (per square mile) 3,691		

Households

Number   14,680
Persons per Household   2.29
% Female-Headed Households   10.2
% One-Person Households   32.1
Births—Total   466
    % to Mothers under 20   12.4
    Birth Rate per 1,000   12.3

Ethnic Composition

The population of Burlington is only slightly less homogeneous than that of other Vermont cities. Whites make up 96.8%, and blacks and others the remainder.

Ethnic Composition (as % of total pop.)

	1980	1990
White	98.52	96.8
Black	0.58	1.0
American Indian	0.18	0.3
Asian and Pacific Islander	0.38	1.4
Hispanic	0.76	1.2
Other	NA	0.4

Government

Burlington operates under a weak mayor–strong council form of government. The mayor and the 13-member board of aldermen are elected to two-year terms. Burlington is the seat of Chittenden County.

Chronology

1763	Burlington is chartered as a town in New Hampshire.
1772	Ira Allen builds the schooner *Liberty* on the Winooski River.
1773	Burlington receives its first settlers.
1776	Most settlers leave town to join the Revolutionary forces.
1789	Pioneers return to town after the war.
1797	Town of Burlington is organized.
1808	The steamboat *Vermont* is built.
1813	Guns in Battery Park beat off British ships.
1823	The Champlain Canal opens, connecting the lake with the Hudson River.
1826	The Champlain Transportation Company is chartered.
1848	The *Burlington Free Press*, the oldest daily in the state, is founded.
1849	Two rail lines are completed, linking Boston with Burlington.
1865	Burlington is split in two. The larger portion is called South Burlington, and the smaller, called Burlington, is incorporated as a city.
1957	IBM chooses the city as the site for a large plant making computer memory chips.

Government

Year of Home Charter   NA
Number of Members of the Governing Body   14
Elected at Large   1
Elected by Wards   13
Number of Women in Governing Body   1
Salary of Mayor   NA
Salary of Council Members   NA
City Government Employment Total   629
Rate per 10,000   164.2

Public Finance

The annual budget consists of revenues of $75.105 million and expenditures of $92.358 million. The total debt outstanding is $159.907 million, and cash and security holdings are $75.555 million.

Economy

The Greater Burlington area supports hundreds of small manufacturers, many of them producing small high-tech electronic components. The second-largest economic sector is tourism. One of Burlington's growth industries is the so-called captive insurance business, or wholly

Public Finance

Total Revenue (in millions) $75.105
Intergovernmental Revenue—Total (in millions) $2.24
Federal Revenue per Capita $1.83
% Federal Assistance   2.44
% State Assistance   0.56
Sales Tax as % of Total Revenue   NA
Local Revenue as % of Total Revenue   76.32
City Income Tax   no
Taxes—Total (in millions) $8.0

Taxes per Capita
   Total $208
   Property $199
   Sales and Gross Receipts $0
General Expenditures—Total (in millions) $18.9
General Expenditures per Capita $494
Capital Outlays per Capita $44

% of Expenditures for:
   Public Welfare   0.0
   Highways   6.8
   Education   0.0
   Health and Hospitals   1.4
   Police   12.3
   Sewerage and Sanitation   6.3
   Parks and Recreation   6.5
   Housing and Community Development   3.9
Debt Outstanding per Capita $2,862
   % Utility   85.2
Federal Procurement Contract Awards (in millions) $104.8
Federal Grants Awards (in millions) $32.5
Fiscal Year Begins   January 1

Economy

Total Money Income (in millions) $365.554
% of State Average   99.2
Per Capita Annual Income $9,542
% Population below Poverty Level   16.2
Fortune 500 Companies   NA

Banks	Number	Deposits (in millions)
Commercial	3	1,742.8
Savings	2	742.5

Passenger Autos   325,773
Electric Meters   13,500
Gas Meters   11,948

Manufacturing

Number of Establishments   58
% with 20 or More Employees   25.9
Manufacturing Payroll (in millions) $101.9
Value Added by Manufacture (in millions) $255.9
Value of Shipments (in millions) $361.3
New Capital Expenditures (in millions)   NA

Wholesale Trade

Number of Establishments   72
Sales (in millions) $295.7
Annual Payroll (in millions) $23.820

Retail Trade

Number of Establishments   508
Total Sales (in millions) $338.9
Sales per Capita $8,846
Number of Retail Trade Establishments with Payroll   414
Annual Payroll (in millions) $46.7
Total Sales (in millions) $336.0
General Merchandise Stores (per capita) $1,628
Food Stores (per capita) $1,216
Apparel Stores (per capita) $1,007
Eating and Drinking Places (per capita) $1,207

Economy (continued)

Service Industries

Total Establishments 459
Total Receipts (in millions) $174.3
Hotels and Motels (in millions) $10.9
Health Services (in millions) $50.1
Legal Services (in millions) $26.2

owned insurance subsidiaries of large corporations. Because of the proximity of the Canadian border, pulp and paper products are growing in importance.

Labor

Burlington is noted for its competent and highly skilled work force. There are few unions; as a result, work time lost to strikes is very low. The services, manufacturing, and trade sectors are evenly matched in number of employees. The largest employers are General Electric and IBM.

Labor

Civilian Labor Force 22,303
% Change 1989–1990 -0.2

Work Force Distribution
   Mining NA
   Construction 3,600
   Manufacturing 14,900
   Transportation and Public Utilities 3,400
   Wholesale and Retail Trade 18,600
   FIRE (Finance, Insurance, Real Estate) 4,100
   Service 20,900
   Government 12,500
   Women as % of Labor Force 48.7
   % Self-Employed 5.3
   % Professional/Technical 22.0
Total Unemployment 793
Rate % 3.6
Federal Government Civilian Employment 913

Education

The public school system consists of 1 senior high school, 2 junior high/middle schools, and 7 elementary schools. Chittenden County also has 4 parochial elementary schools, 1 parochial secondary school, and 79 other

Education

Number of Public Schools 10
Special Education Schools NA
Total Enrollment NA
% Enrollment in Private Schools NA
% Minority NA
Classroom Teachers NA
Pupil-Teacher Ratio NA
Number of Graduates NA
Total Revenue (in millions) NA
Total Expenditures (in millions) NA
Expenditures per Pupil NA
Educational Attainment (Age 25 and Over) NA
   % Completed 12 or More Years 74.6
   % Completed 16 or More Years 27.9
Four-Year Colleges and Universities 2
   Enrollment 10,807
Two-Year Colleges 1
   Enrollment 1,916

Education (continued)

Libraries

Number 11
Public Libraries 1
Books (in thousands) 118
Circulation (in thousands) 174
Persons Served (in thousands) 38
Circulation per Person Served 4.73
Income (in millions) $0.657
Staff 18

Four-Year Colleges and Universities
   University of Vermont
   Trinity College
   Burlington College

private schools. The largest institution of higher education is the University of Vermont. Although founded in 1791, General Lafayette laid the foundation stone of the Old Mill at University Place in 1825. The land for the university was a grant from Ira Allen, whose statue stands in the center of the campus. The city has three other colleges: Trinity, Champlain, and Burlington.

Health

Six of Vermont's 16 hospitals are located in Greater Burlington, which has as a result a high percentage of doctors to residents. The largest is Medical Center Hospital. The others are Fanny Allen Hospital in Colchester, Copley Hospital in Morrisville, Northwestern Medical Center, Porter Medical Center, and Central Vermont Hospital.

Health

Deaths—Total 330
Rate per 1,000 8.7
Infant Deaths—Total 7
Rate per 1,000 15
Number of Metro Hospitals 1
Number of Metro Hospital Beds 491
Rate per 100,000 1,282
Number of Physicians 529
Physicians per 1,000 NA
Nurses per 1,000 NA
Health Expenditures per Capita $13.61

Transportation

As Vermont's only port, Burlington has access by water to the Port of Montreal and the St. Lawrence Seaway to the north and the Port of New York to the south. Rail freight is handled by the Vermont Railway and Central Vermont Railway, a subsidiary of the Canadian National Railway. Amtrak runs daily trips to New York and Washington, D.C. Burlington International Airport, three miles northeast of downtown, serves all of Vermont with more than 85 flights daily, making it the third-largest airport in New England. I-89, the main highway leading to Burlington, is supplemented by U.S. Highways 2 and 7.

Transportation

Interstate Highway Mileage   21
Total Urban Mileage   531
Total Daily Vehicle Mileage (in millions)   2.54
Daily Average Commute Time   38.1 min.
Number of Buses   24
Port Tonnage (in millions)   NA
Airports   1
Number of Daily Flights   19
Daily Average Number of Passengers   975

Airlines (American carriers only)
   Continental
   United
   USAir
   Westair

Housing

Most of the new housing is in outlying areas such as Winooski and South Burlington.

Housing

Total Housing Units   15,480
% Change 1980–1990   11.1
Vacant Units for Sale or Rent   507
Occupied Units   14,680
% with More Than One Person per Room   1.9
% Owner-Occupied   40.2
Median Value of Owner-Occupied Homes $113,500
Average Monthly Purchase Cost $355
Median Monthly Rent $435
New Private Housing Starts   6
Value (in thousands) $668
% Single-Family   100
Nonresidential Buildings Value (in thousands) $5

Urban Redevelopment

In the early 1980s Burlington experienced rapid growth, as a result of which over 7,000 new jobs were created. This led to a surge in industrial and commercial construction and the building of several industrial parks. However, development has been hobbled by Vermont Act 250, which imposes strict environmental constraints on developmental projects.

Crime

The number of violent crimes known to police in 1991 totaled 104. Property crimes totaled 3,622.

Crime

Violent Crimes—Total   104
Violent Crime Rate per 100,000   10,217
Murder   2
Rape   32
Robbery   22
Aggravated Assaults   25

Crime (continued)

Property Crimes   3,622
Burglary   625
Larceny   2,630
Motor Vehicle Theft   126
Arson   NA
Per Capita Police Expenditures $104.64
Per Capita Fire Protection Expenditures $92.72
Number of Police   85
Per 1,000   2.18

Religion

Most of the Roman Catholics in the city are French-Canadians. Burlington was the earliest French-Canadian parish in the state.

Religion

Largest Denominations (Adherents)

Catholic	43,768
United Church of Christ	4,266
United Methodist	3,717
Episcopal	2,211
Jewish	2,880

Media

The city's only daily newspaper is the *Burlington Free Press*, published every morning and Sunday by the Gannett chain. The electronic media consist of three network television stations and six AM and FM radio stations.

Media

Newsprint
   Burlington Free Press, daily

Television
   WCAX (Channel 3)
   WETK (Channel 33)
   WVNY (Channel 22)

Radio

WDOT (AM)	WEZF (AM)
WIZN (FM)	WJOY (AM)
WOKO (FM)	WRUV (FM)

Sports

Burlington has no professional sports teams.

Arts, Culture, and Tourism

The University of Vermont's Royall Tyler Theater is the scene each year of the Champlain Shakespeare Festival. Summer professional theatrical performances are presented at St. Michael's Playhouse, while the Vermont Symphony Orchestra performs at the Art Deco Flynn Theater. The largest Burlington museums are the Fleming Museum of the University of Vermont, Shelburne Museum, South Hero Bicentennial Museum, and Discovery Museum of Essex.

Travel and Tourism
Hotel Rooms 2,292
Convention and Exhibit Space (square feet) NA
Convention Centers
Memorial Auditorium
Flynn Theater
Festivals
Champlain Shakespeare Festival
Vermont Mozart Festival
Discover Jazz Festival
Lake Champlain Discovery Festival
Vermont Handicrafts Fair (November)

Parks and Recreation

Ethan Allen Park, east of North Avenue, is part of what was once Allen's farm. On a nearby cliff is a stone tower memorial to Ethan Allen. Battery Park, the scene of a battle between British and American troops in 1812, offers scenic points to view the sunsets for which Burlington is noted.

Sources of Further Information

Burlington Convention Bureau
P.O. Box 453
Burlington, VT 05402
(802) 863-3489

Greater Burlington Industrial Corporation
7 Burlington Square
Burlington, VT 05402-0786
(802) 860-1899

Lake Champlain Regional Chamber of Commerce
209 Battery Street
Burlington, VT 05402-0453
(802) 863-3489

Additional Reading

Greater Burlington, Vermont: Where the Business Environment Matches the Quality of Life. 1990.
Guide to Chittenden County.

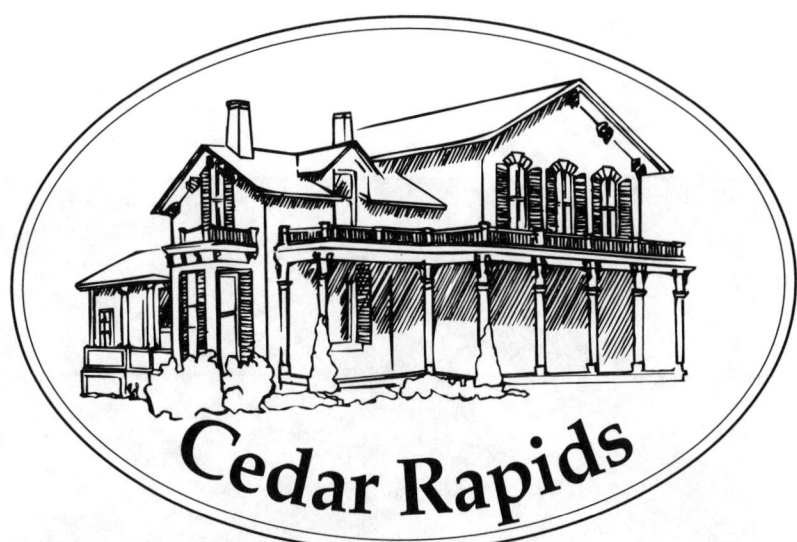

Cedar Rapids
Iowa

Location and Topography

N

Cedar Rapids, cut in half by the Cedar River, is located in eastern Iowa about 110 miles east of the state capital, Des Moines. The terrain is gently rolling prairie, and the surrounding area is laced with rivers and dotted with limestone bluffs.

Layout of City and Suburbs

The Cedar River, flowing to the southeast, divides the city neatly into east and west sides. Roads running north to south are called streets, while those that run east to west are avenues. In the middle of the Cedar River is May's Island, which houses a memorial to artist Grant Wood, the courthouse, and the county jail. Among Cedar Rapids's suburbs are the Amana Colonies to the west, West Branch (the home of President Herbert Hoover), and Iowa City.

Climate

Cedar Rapids has a four-season climate, with continental winters and an average snowfall of 34 inches, and moderate to hot summers. Cool nights make fall and spring the most pleasant seasons.

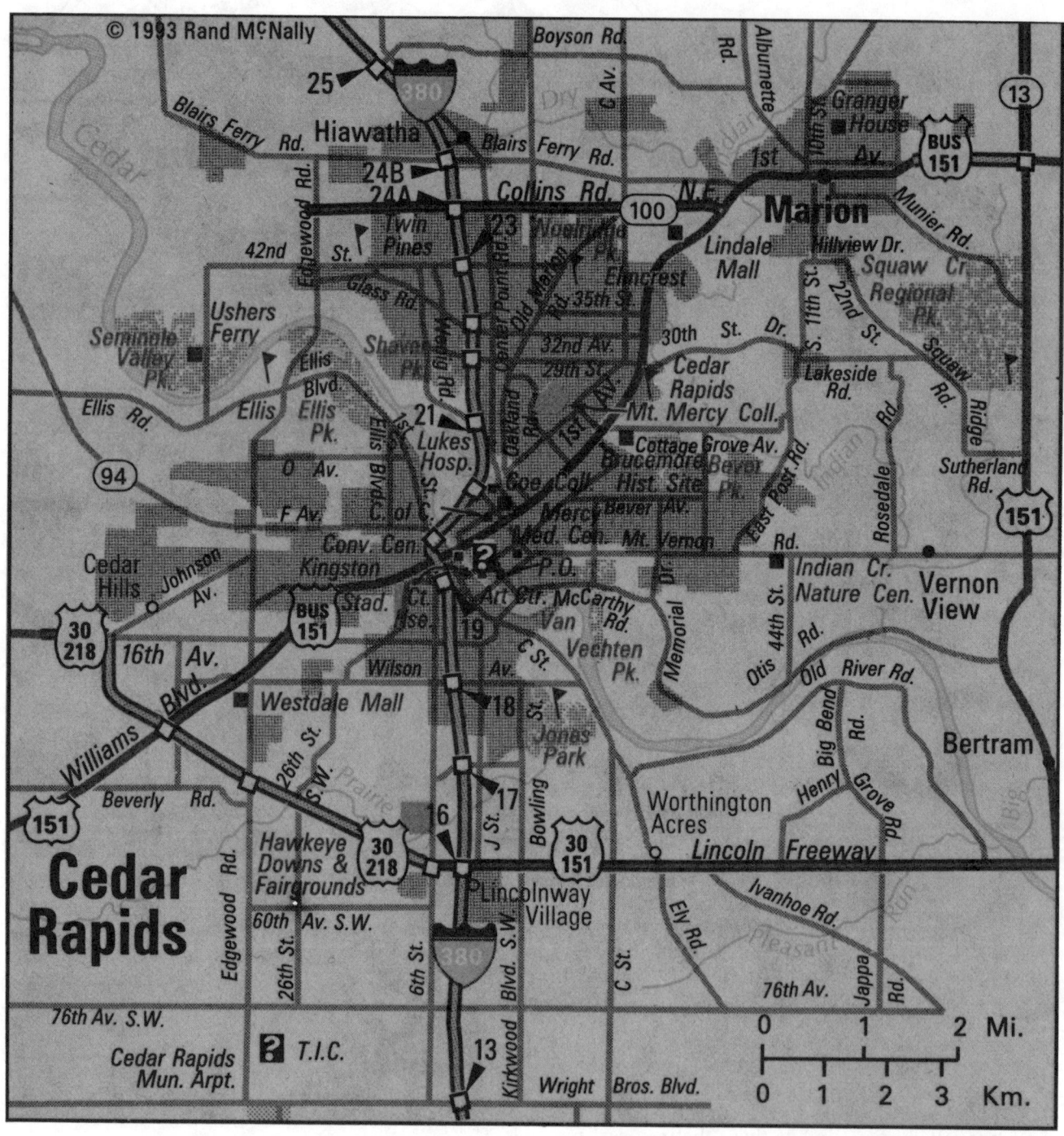

Weather (continued)			
April	61.0	38.6	49.8
May	72.9	49.6	61.3
June	81.6	59.0	70.3
July	85.3	63.2	74.3
August	83.2	61.1	72.2
September	75.4	52.5	64.0
October	64.5	41.9	53.2
November	47.3	29.1	38.2
December	33.2	17.3	25.3

History

Sac and Fox Indians once hunted and trapped in this region. In 1838 the first white settler, Osgood Shepherd, arrived and built his shack on the east side of the river at what is now First Avenue and First Street. The first survey of the city was made in 1841 by N. B. Brown, George Greene, and others who purchased squatter rights from Shepherd. These men gave the place the name of Rapids City. About this time Robert Ellis settled on the west side of the river. The first newspaper was published in 1851, and the following year David W. King laid out the town of Kingston on the west side. Early in the 1840s a dam was constructed across the Cedar River to furnish power to the grist mills and sawmills.

In 1848 the town's name was changed to Cedar Rapids. It was incorporated as a city in 1856, and the town of Kingston was annexed to Cedar Rapids in 1870. In 1858 the railroad reached the city, and river traffic was abandoned. In the 1850s Cedar Rapids became a favorite destination of Czech immigrants, and soon a Little Bohemia was established in the southwest sector. The city's industrial history began with the establishment of the T. M. Sinclair Company, a meat-packing company that later became Farmstead Foods. During the same era Quaker Oats and Cherry Burrell were founded here. Greene's Opera House was dedicated in 1880. In 1919 the county seat was changed from Marion to Cedar Rapids. In 1928 the county courthouse and the Memorial Building were built on Municipal Island (originally known as May's Island), once the home of the infamous Shepherd Gang of squatters and horse thieves.

Historical Landmarks

The Paramount Theatre, built in 1928 and renovated as the Paramount Theatre for the Performing Arts, was once a luxurious movie house. Its 1,913-seat auditorium now houses the Cedar Rapids Symphony Orchestra, among other groups. Brucemore is a 21-room Queen Anne–style mansion built by the founder of the Quaker Oats Company. The Czech Village and Immigrant Home on the banks of the Cedar River is the largest display of Czech culture and costumes outside Czechoslovakia. The Ushers Ferry Historical Village in Seminole Valley Park is a series of over 30 authentic buildings that represent a slice of Iowa pioneer life in the 19th century.

Population

Cedar Rapids lost population in the critical decades of the 1970s and 1980s. From a peak population of 111,000 in 1970, it declined to 110,243 in 1980 and 108,751 in 1990.

Population

	1980	1990
Central City	110,243	108,751
Rank	141	172
Metro Area	169,775	168,767
Pop. Change 1980–1990 -1,492		
Pop. % Change 1980–1990 -1.4		
Median Age 33.2		
% Male 48.0		
% Age 65 and Over 13.2		
Density (per square mile) 2,032		

Households

Number 43,674
Persons per Household 2.43
% Female-Headed Households 9.2
% One-Person Households 27.5
Births—Total 1,668
   % to Mothers under 20 10.1
   Birth Rate per 1,000 15.3

Ethnic Composition

Whites make up 95.5%, blacks 2.9%, Hispanics 1.1%, American Indians 0.2%, Asians and Pacific Islanders 1.0%, and others 0.4%.

Ethnic Composition (as % of total pop.)

	1980	1990
White	97.67	95.52
Black	0.91	2.88
American Indian	0.16	0.24
Asian and Pacific Islander	0.83	0.98
Hispanic	0.62	1.14
Other	NA	0.38

Government

Cedar Rapids is governed by a mayor and five-member commission elected to two-year terms.

Government

Year of Home Charter 1975
Number of Members of the Governing Body 4
Elected at Large 4
Elected by Wards NA
Number of Women in Governing Body 0
Salary of Mayor $52,000
Salary of Council Members $48,000
City Government Employment Total 1,477
Rate per 10,000 136.3

Public Finance

The annual budget consists of revenues of $110.855 million and expenditures of $107.053 million. The outstanding debt

Chronology

1838 Osgood Shepherd builds a cabin on the east side of the Cedar River.

1841 The settlement is surveyed by N. B. Brown, George Greene, and others who buy squatter rights from Shepherd and name the place Rapids City.

1848 The name of the town is changed to Cedar Rapids.

1851 The first newspaper makes its debut.

1856 Cedar Rapids is incorporated as a city.

1858 The steamer *Cedar Rapids* is launched and placed into service between St. Louis and Cedar Rapids. Railroad reaches Cedar Rapids.

1880 Greene's Opera House is dedicated.

1919 Cedar Rapids replaces Marion as county seat.

1928 Memorial Building is erected on Municipal Island.

is $131.818 million, and cash and security holdings are $230.147 million.

Public Finance

Total Revenue (in millions) $110.85
Intergovernmental Revenue—Total (in millions) $13.74
Federal Revenue per Capita $5.7
% Federal Assistance   5.14
% State Assistance   8.4
Sales Tax as % of Total Revenue   1.24
Local Revenue as % of Total Revenue   73.85
City Income Tax   No
Taxes—Total (in millions) $28.1

Taxes per Capita
    Total $259
    Property $250
    Sales and Gross Receipts $5
General Expenditures—Total (in millions) $65.7
General Expenditures per Capita $606
Capital Outlays per Capita $113

% of Expenditures for:
    Public Welfare   0.0
    Highways   14.7
    Education   0.0
    Health and Hospitals   0.0
    Police   11.2
    Sewerage and Sanitation   17.8
    Parks and Recreation   7.7
    Housing and Community Development   5.1
Debt Outstanding per Capita $1,077
    % Utility   0.0
Federal Procurement Contract Awards (in millions) $385.8
Federal Grants Awards (in millions) $5.9
Fiscal Year Begins   July 1

Economy

Historically, the economy has been based on only a few products, such as Quaker Oats, beef, and radios. Manufacturing remains the mainstay of the economy but was augmented in the 1980s by high-technology industries and transportation. The Cedar Rapids–Iowa City Corridor of Technology, catering to defense electronics, is dotted with advanced research and development laboratories. Partly because of its small population and also as a result of its technological intensity, Cedar Rapids has the largest exports per capita of any city in the nation. The city's association with electronics dates from the early years of the Collins Radio Company, started by Arthur Collins during the Great Depression. It was later sold to Rockwell, which employs over 8,000 workers in making spacecraft communications equipment, advanced navigation systems for the NASA space shuttle program, defense telecommunications systems, and NAVSTAR global positioning system equipment. The Corridor of Technology is also a vital link in the fiber optics network, in which the

Economy

Total Money Income (in millions) $1,333.0
% of State Average   121.8
Per Capita Annual Income $12,301
% Population below Poverty Level   7.6
Fortune 500 Companies   NA

Banks	Number	Deposits (in millions)
Commercial	8	1,582
Savings	5	1,406

Passenger Autos   117,698
Electric Meters   48,769
Gas Meters   44,636

Manufacturing

Number of Establishments   164
% with 20 or More Employees   46.3
Manufacturing Payroll (in millions) $640.5
Value Added by Manufacture (in millions) $1,846.4
Value of Shipments (in millions) $3,331.7
New Capital Expenditures (in millions) $106.8

Wholesale Trade

Number of Establishments   331
Sales (in millions) $1,535.8
Annual Payroll (in millions) $90.685

Retail Trade

Number of Establishments   1,208
Total Sales (in millions) $948.6
Sales per Capita $8,753
Number of Retail Trade Establishments with Payroll   846
Annual Payroll (in millions) $115.0
Total Sales (in millions) $934.0
General Merchandise Stores (per capita)   NA
Food Stores (per capita) $1,634
Apparel Stores (per capita) $376
Eating and Drinking Places (per capita) $911

Service Industries

Total Establishments   960
Total Receipts (in millions) $488.4
Hotels and Motels (in millions) $24.7
Health Services (in millions) $100.2
Legal Services (in millions) $33.5

Technology Innovation Center at the University of Iowa serves as a nucleus of planning and design.

Labor

The prominence of high technology is reflected in the composition of the work force, which is highly skilled with a productivity quota substantially above the national average and an absenteeism rate among the lowest in the nation. Data-base telemarketing is one of the emerging fields attracting experienced professionals. Import and export claims a larger share of the work force than in comparable cities. Iowa has a right-to-work law.

Labor

Civilian Labor Force   63,384
% Change 1989–1990   -0.9

Work Force Distribution
   Mining   NA
   Construction   4,700
   Manufacturing   21,500
   Transportation and Public Utilities   5,500
   Wholesale and Retail Trade   22,600
   FIRE (Finance, Insurance, Real Estate)   4,900
   Service   24,100
   Government   11,000
   Women as % of Labor Force   44.5
   % Self-Employed   3.6
   % Professional/Technical   16.1
Total Unemployment   3,221
Rate %   5.1
Federal Government Civilian Employment   859

Education

Cedar Rapids Community School District supports 33 schools. The parochial school system, with 7 elementary schools and 2 high schools, is also well developed. Coe College and Mount Mercy College are private, general, four-year colleges. Coe College, founded in 1851 and occupying eight city blocks, is a coeducational Presbyterian institution; it absorbed Leander Clark College in 1919. Kirkwood Community College serves Cedar City and seven counties offering a variety of continuing education programs as well as courses in applied science and technology and the liberal arts.

Education

Number of Public Schools   33
Special Education Schools   NA
Total Enrollment   17,003
% Enrollment in Private Schools   NA
% Minority   NA
Classroom Teachers   NA
Pupil-Teacher Ratio   NA
Number of Graduates   NA
Total Revenue (in millions)   NA
Total Expenditures (in millions)   NA
Expenditures per Pupil   NA
Educational Attainment (Age 25 and Over)   NA
   % Completed 12 or More Years   77.4

Education (continued)

   % Completed 16 or More Years   17.7
Four-Year Colleges and Universities   2
   Enrollment   2,779
Two-Year Colleges   1
   Enrollment   8,625

Libraries

Number   16
Public Libraries   3
Books (in thousands)   301.9
Circulation (in thousands)   1,242
Persons Served (in thousands)   110
Circulation per Person Served   11.2
Income (in millions) $2.87
Staff   96

Four-Year Colleges and Universities
   Coe College
   Mount Mercy College

Health

The principal medical facilities are Mercy Hospital, including the Hall Radiation Center, and St. Luke's Hospital, with a combined total of 959 beds.

Health

Deaths—Total   827
Rate per 1,000   7.6
Infant Deaths—Total   11
Rate per 1,000   6.6
Number of Metro Hospitals   2
Number of Metro Hospital Beds   959
Rate per 100,000   885
Number of Physicians   226
Physicians per 1,000   NA
Nurses per 1,000   NA
Health Expenditures per Capita $23.92

Transportation

Cedar Rapids is approached by two interstates: the north-south I-380 and the transcontinental I-80. U.S. Highways 30/218 run east to west through the southern part of the city and 151 intersects the city diagonally northeast to southwest. State roads include 150, running parallel with I-380; the east-west 94; and 1, 13, 100, and 149. Rail freight service is provided by three railroads: Cedar Rapids and Iowa City, Chicago and Northwestern, and Chicago Central and Pacific. The Cedar Rapids Municipal Airport, seven miles to the south, is served by six national and four commuter airlines.

Transportation

Interstate Highway Mileage   14
Total Urban Mileage   773
Total Daily Vehicle Mileage (in millions)   2.26
Daily Average Commute Time   36.3 min.
Number of Buses   23
Port Tonnage (in millions)   NA
Airports   1
Number of Daily Flights   22
Daily Average Number of Passengers   822

Transportation (continued)

Airlines (American carriers only)
American West
Northwest
Trans World
United

Housing

Between 1981 and 1990, 1,508 single-family homes and 254 multifamily homes were built in Cedar Rapids. The total number of housing units in the metropolitan area is 45,473, of which 67% are owner-occupied. The median value of a home is $56,900 and the median rent $318.

Housing

Total Housing Units   45,473
% Change 1980–1990   4.2
Vacant Units for Sale or Rent   1,386
Occupied Units   43,674
% with More Than One Person per Room   1.4
% Owner-Occupied   67.2
Median Value of Owner-Occupied Homes $56,900
Average Monthly Purchase Cost $356
Median Monthly Rent $318
New Private Housing Starts   331
Value (in thousands) $17,132
% Single-Family   67.4
Nonresidential Buildings Value (in thousands) $13,420

Urban Redevelopment

Large-scale commercial construction has taken place in Cedar Rapids since the 1970s. Among the major new buildings are two large malls and a downtown skywalk system.

Crime

Cedar Rapids has an above-average record of public safety. In 1991, of the crimes known to police, there were 223 violent crimes and 8,429 property crimes.

Crime

Violent Crimes—Total   233
Violent Crime Rate per 100,000   NA
Murder   2
Rape   12
Robbery   109
Aggravated Assaults   110
Property Crimes   8,429
Burglary   1,845
Larceny   6,145
Motor Vehicle Theft   390
Arson   49
Per Capita Police Expenditures $79.31
Per Capita Fire Protection Expenditures $64.55
Number of Police   158
Per 1,000   1.47

Religion

Cedar Rapids has 129 churches representing 45 denominations. The largest denominations are Catholic, United Methodist, and Evangelical Lutheran.

Religion

Largest Denominations (Adherents)

Catholic	38,980
United Methodist	13,170
Evangelical Lutheran	10,051
Presbyterian	6,440
Lutheran Missouri Synod	6,335
Christian Church Disciple	3,010
Jewish	430

Media

The city daily is the *Cedar Rapids Gazette*. The electronic media consist of 3 television stations and 10 AM and FM radio stations.

Media

Newsprint
   Cedar Rapids Gazette, daily

Television
   KCRG (Channel 9)
   KGAN (Channel 2)
   KOCR (Channel 28)

Radio

KCCK (FM)	KCRG (AM)
KHAK (AM)	KHAK (FM)
KMRY (AM)	KOJC (FM)
KQCR (FM)	KTOF (FM)
WMT (AM)	WMT (FM)

Sports

Cedar Rapids does not have a major professional sports team.

Arts, Culture, and Tourism

The renovated Paramount Theater is the home of the Cedar Rapids Symphony and Cedar Rapids Community Association, which books special cultural events. Theater Cedar Rapids stages five dramatic shows in its downtown theater. The 10,000-seat Five Seasons Center brings top entertainment talents to town. The Cedar Rapids Museum of Art, which moved into its new facility in 1969, is noted for its extensive collection of the works of Grant Wood, Marvin Cone, and Mauricio Lasansky.

Travel and Tourism

Hotel Rooms   1,881
Convention and Exhibit Space (square feet)   NA

Convention Centers
   Five Seasons Center

Travel and Tourism (continued)

Festivals
Czech Village Festival (Fall)
Buckskinner's Rendezvous (July)
Celebration of the Arts (June)
Houby Days (May)
Maple Syrup Festival (March)

Parks and Recreation

Cedar Rapids has 74 parks covering 3,600 acres. Bever Park is a thickly wooded area containing the John Vardy House, built in 1842. The Cedar Valley Nature Trail offers 52 miles of trails.

Sources of Further Information

Cedar Rapids Area Chamber of Commerce
424 First Avenue NE
Cedar Rapids, IA 52407
(319) 398-5317

Cedar Rapids Convention and Visitors Bureau
119 First Avenue SE
Cedar Rapids, IA 52406-5339
(319) 398-5009

Cedar Rapids Public Library
500 First Street SE
Cedar Rapids, IA 52406
(319) 398-5123

City Hall
50 Second Bridge Avenue
Cedar Rapids, IA 52401
(319) 273-8600

Linn County Historical Society
500 First Street SE
Cedar Rapids, IA 52406

Additional Reading

Cole's Directory for Cedar Rapids. 1991.
Polk's Cedar Rapids City Directory. 1991.

Charleston
South Carolina

Location and Topography

N

Charleston is situated on a peninsula at the junction where the Cooper, Ashley, and Wando rivers join to empty into Charleston Harbor and ultimately the Atlantic Ocean. The city is located about 100 miles southeast of the state capital, Columbia. Because of the city's low elevation, Charleston and the nearby coastal islands, together known as the Trident, are subject to tidal flooding.

Layout of City and Suburbs

Charleston is historically divided into the old city, which is the southern part of the peninsula, and "the Neck," which reaches from Calhoun Street to the northwest. Some of the principal roads are King Street, Lockwood Drive, East Bay Street, and Rutledge Avenue. The Ashley River Memorial Bridge links the city with the southern suburbs, while the Grace Memorial and Silas Pearman bridges lead north across Town Creek. Among Charleston's suburbs are Mt. Pleasant and North Charleston.

Climate

Charleston's semitropical location is tempered by the proximity of the ocean, which helps to warm winter temperatures by an average of 3° and to cool summer temperatures by as much as 15°. The summer is the city's rainiest season, accounting for about 41% of the annual precipitation, falling mostly as thundershowers and occasional storms. The Trident area is subject to severe, devastating hurricanes, nine of which were recorded in the past hundred years.

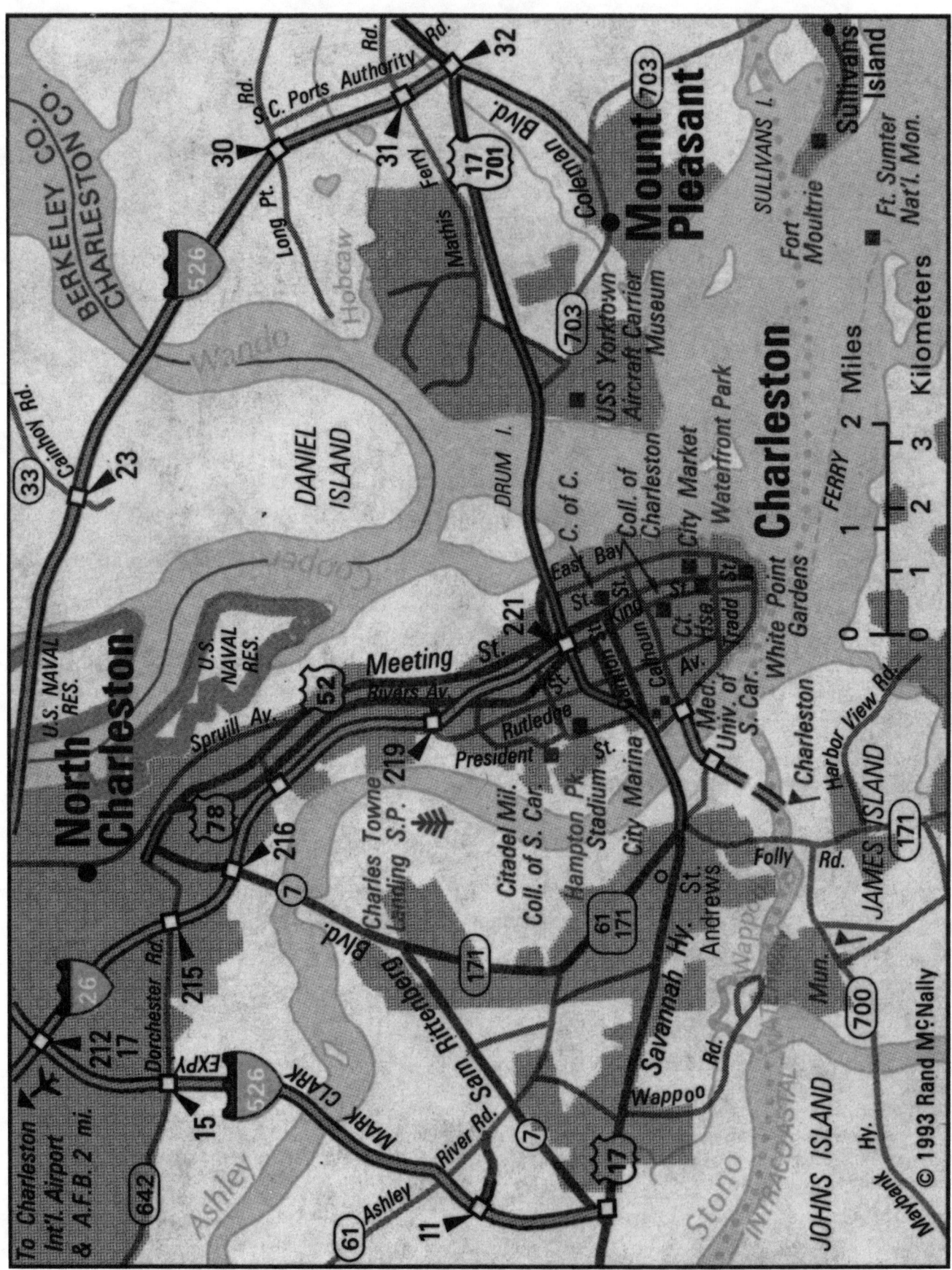

Weather			
Temperature			
Highest Monthly Average °F	89.1		
Lowest Monthly Average °F	37.3		
Annual Averages			
Days 32°F or Below	36		
Days above 90°F	47		
Zero Degree Days	0		
Precipitation (inches)	52		
Snow (inches)	0.5		
% Seasonal Humidity	76		
Wind Speed (m.p.h.)	8.8		
Clear Days	101		
Cloudy Days	151		
Storm Days	56		
Rainy Days	115		
Average Temperatures (°F)	*High*	*Low*	*Mean*
January	59.8	37.3	48.6
February	61.9	39.0	50.5
March	67.8	45.1	56.5
April	76.2	53.0	64.6
May	83.1	61.1	72.1
June	87.7	68.1	77.9
July	89.1	71.2	80.2
August	88.6	70.6	79.6
September	84.5	65.9	75.2
October	77.1	55.1	66.1
November	68.4	44.1	56.3
December	60.8	37.7	49.3

History

Charleston's beginnings originate in 1670, when English and Irish colonists on the frigate Carolina sailed into what is now Charleston Harbor. Passing the tract later known as Oyster Point (now White Point Gardens), they settled in an area just west of the Ashley River, naming it Albemarle Point. This area is now a park called Charles Towne Landing, with a plaque commemorating the event.

In 1672, on the orders of Lord Anthony Ashley Cooper, later the first Earl of Shaftesbury, and one of the True and Absolute Lords Proprietors of Carolina (a group of eight powerful Englishmen granted by the king all of the land from the Carolinas into Spanish Florida), the settlers moved across the river to Oyster Point, which became the site of a port town. In 1679 the Lords Proprietors established Oyster Point as a permanent settlement and named it Charles Town in honor of King Charles II; the settlers named the Ashley and Cooper Rivers in honor of Cooper. These early settlers depended on the growing of agricultural products, which were traded in the West Indies for rum and sugar, and, making use of the abundant forests, the manufacturing of wooden products that were shipped to England. In 1683 the village was incorporated as Charles Town.

Charles Town was a typically English village with a manorial society until French Huguenots and Catholics from Acadia began to arrive at the end of the 17th century. They were followed in the early 18th century by Scots and South Germans, North Germans, and Irish. A massive building program was under way, as evidenced today by the city's unique colonial architecture.

Charles Town was tightly tied to Mother England until the outbreak of the American Revolution. In 1775 the first provincial congress of South Carolina met in Charleston and called for the support of the new American nation. The following year, British forces under the command of Admiral Sir Peter Parker and General Sir Henry Clinton launched a massive sea assault on the fort on Sullivan's Island in Charleston Harbor. Americans led by Colonel William Moultrie repulsed the attack, but two years later on 12 May 1780 Clinton's forces successfully invaded Charleston and obtained its surrender. It was not until December 1782 that the British evacuated the city.

In 1783 Charles Town was renamed Charleston. Unrest between the Tories and Whigs continued to trouble the city. In an effort to clip the wings of any threat from British sympathizers, the state capital was moved to Columbia in 1783. With the removal of the British mercantile laws, Charleston lost its preeminence in shipping. Railroads, first introduced in 1833 with the construction of the South Carolina Railroad, helped to keep trade channels open. The economy became more and more dependent on agriculture, especially cotton.

This reliance on cotton made Charleston a key player in the secession movement after the election of Abraham Lincoln as president in 1860. On 12 April 1861, in defiance of Lincoln's command to restock the depleted Fort Sumter located in Charleston Harbor, Charleston gun and cannon batteries fired on the fort and forced its surrender. This was the opening salvo in the bloody Civil War. During the war the city was used as a port for southern blockade runners. On 17 February 1865, having endured numerous bombardments from Union soldiers, Charleston surrendered.

A massive rebuilding program was put into action, but much of what was rebuilt was destroyed in the severe earthquake of 1886, which did some $6 million in damage. In fact, Charleston was hit with a number of severe natural disasters, including hurricanes in 1893, 1911, 1928, 1938, 1952, 1959, and Hurricane Hugo in 1989, which resulted in damages of nearly $3 billion to the city alone.

Historical Landmarks

Although Charleston has endured earthquakes, fires, and hurricanes on a brutal scale over the last 200 years, its citizens have managed to preserve more than 2,800 buildings in eight architectural styles, including Colonial, Classic Revival, Italianate, and Victorian. Many of these buildings are private homes that are not open to the public; those that are, however, give a rare glimpse into this city's varied building techniques. The Thomas Elfe House on Queen Street was built in 1760 and features extensive woodworking by this English emigrant. The Heyward-Washington House was built in 1772 by Daniel Heyward, the father of Declaration of Independence signer Thomas Heyward, Jr. In 1791, when George Washington

166 • Charleston, South Carolina

Chronology

1670 English and Irish pilgrims on the frigate *Carolina* sail into Charleston Harbor and settle at Albemarle Point to the west of the Ashley River.

1672 Under instructions from Lord Anthony Ashley Cooper, later the first Earl of Shaftesbury, the settlers start a town on Oyster Point because of its higher elevation.

1679 The True and Absolute Lords Proprietors establish Oyster Point as the site of a permanent settlement. The colony is named Charles Town in honor of King Charles II of England, and the Ashley River is named in honor of Cooper.

1683 The settlement is incorporated as Charles Town in August.

1776 Americans under the command of Colonel William Moutrie repulse an offensive against Sullivan's Island by the British forces of Admiral Sir Peter Parker and General Sir Henry Clinton.

1780 Parker captures Charles Town.

1782 The British evacuate Charles Town.

1783 The city is reincorporated as Charleston.

1833 The South Carolina Railroad is completed, linking Charleston and Augusta.

1860 South Carolina secedes from the Union.

1861 Confederate batteries fire on Fort Sumter. President Lincoln orders blockade of all southern ports.

1865 Charleston surrenders after heavy federal bombardment causes damage to many sections.

1880 Work begins on construction of jetties in Charleston Harbor to aid in shipping.

1886 Earthquake causes damage estimated at $6 million.

1989 Hurricane Hugo causes massive damage to the eastern United States, particularly the Charleston area.

to sustain the town. At Middleton Place is the Middleton House (1755), home of the Middleton family, including Arthur (1742–1787), a signer of the Declaration of Independence. Fort Sumter, at the mouth of Charleston Harbor, is the site of the famous opening battle of the Civil War in 1861.

Population

After World War II Charleston was able to reverse the historic loss of population. From 66,945 in 1970, the population rose to 69,779 in 1980. In 1990 it grew by 15.2% to 80,414.

Population		
	1980	*1990*
Central City	69,779	80,414
Rank	286	263
Metro Area	430,346	506,875
Pop. Change 1980–1990 +10,635		
Pop. % Change 1980–1990 +15.2		
Median Age 30.5		
% Male 47.2		
% Age 65 and Over 12.8		
Density (per square mile) 1861		
Households		
Number 30,753		
Persons per Household 2.43		
% Female-Headed Households 17.00		
% One-Person Households 30.8		
Births—Total 1,806		
% to Mothers under 20 21.5		
Birth Rate per 1,000 26.9		

Ethnic Composition

Whites make up 57.2%, blacks 41.6%, American Indians 0.1%, Asians and Pacific Islanders 0.9%, Hispanics 0.8% and others 0.2%.

Ethnic Composition (as % of total pop.)		
	1980	*1990*
White	57.2	57.23
Black	46.49	41.58
American Indian	0.06	0.11
Asian and Pacific Islander	0.42	0.85
Hispanic	0.98	0.81
Other	NA	0.22

Government

Charleston is governed under a mayor-council form of government. The mayor and 16 aldermen of the city council are elected to four-year terms on a staggered single-district basis.

Public Finance

The annual budget consists of revenues of $109.156 million and expenditures of $131.997 million. The debt outstanding is $241.092 million, and cash and security holdings $93,876 million.

came to Charleston for an extended stay, he lived at the Heyward house, thus giving it its hypenated name. The Joseph Manigault House was built in 1803 by wealthy rice farmer Gabriel Manigault for his brother. His love of England is evidenced by this Adam-style house (named after Robert Adam, an English-Irish architect), its magnificent staircase, temple gate in back, and collection of period furniture and books. South of the city, across the Ashley River, is Charles Towne Landing, where the original settlers landed in 1670. Now a park, it also features a reproduction of an early pioneer cabin and field where crops were grown

Government

Year of Home Charter   1976
Number of Members of the Governing Body   13
Elected at Large   1
Elected by Wards   12
Number of Women in Governing Body   3
Salary of Mayor $94,000
Salary of Council Members $5,200
City Government Employment Total   1,378
Rate per 10,000   200

Public Finance

Total Revenue (in millions) $109.15
Intergovernmental Revenue—Total (in millions) $12.81
Federal Revenue per Capita $10.38
% Federal Assistance   9.51
% State Assistance   3.29
Sales Tax as % of Total Revenue   2.75
Local Revenue as % of Total Revenue   66.94
City Income Tax   no
Taxes—Total (in millions) $19.2

Taxes per Capita
   Total $279
   Property $189
   Sales and Gross Receipts $37
General Expenditures—Total (in millions) $52.3
General Expenditures per Capita $758
Capital Outlays per Capita $207

% of Expenditures for:
   Public Welfare   0.0
   Highways   5.8
   Education   0.0
   Health and Hospitals   0.0
   Police   14.7
   Sewerage and Sanitation   25.9
   Parks and Recreation   7.3
   Housing and Community Development   12.4
Debt Outstanding per Capita $1,719
   % Utility   63.9
Federal Procurement Contract Awards (in millions) $69.3
Federal Grants Awards (in millions) $34.4
Fiscal Year Begins   July 1

Economy

The economy of the Charleston-Trident region—a total of 2,600 square miles—is heavily affected by the Charleston Naval Base, tourism, the Port of Charleston, and the manufacturing sector. The Port of Charleston is the second largest on the eastern coast, tourism brings in

Economy

Total Money Income (in millions) $731.4
% of State Average   119.2
Per Capita Annual Income $10,600
% Population below Poverty Level   21.8
Fortune 500 Companies   NA

Banks	Number	Deposits (in millions)
Commercial	15	NA
Savings	6	NA

Economy (continued)

Passenger Autos   149,631
Electric Meters   165,000
Gas Meters   59,000

Manufacturing

Number of Establishments   82
% with 20 or More Employees   39.0
Manufacturing Payroll (in millions) $161.4
Value Added by Manufacture (in millions) $557.8
Value of Shipments (in millions) $1,463.5
New Capital Expenditures (in millions) $38.5

Wholesale Trade

Number of Establishments   200
Sales (in millions) $804.4
Annual Payroll (in millions) $42.491

Retail Trade

Number of Establishments   1,279
Total Sales (in millions) $997.8
Sales per Capita $14,482
Number of Retail Trade Establishments with Payroll   1,017
Annual Payroll (in millions) $127.9
Total Sales (in millions) $983.8
General Merchandise Stores (per capita) $1,972
Food Stores (per capita) $3,149
Apparel Stores (per capita) $1,220
Eating and Drinking Places (per capita) $2,010

Service Industries

Total Establishments   1,061
Total Receipts (in millions) $487.7
Hotels and Motels (in millions) $65.3
Health Services (in millions) $198.6
Legal Services (in millions) $61.6

about $850 million annually, and the city has an established and solid manufacturing sector.

Labor

Interestingly, government is the largest employment sector, even though Charleston is not the center of state government activities. Most public employment is related to the naval and air bases. Tourism accounts for the strength of the trade and service sectors. There are few major industrial corporations located in Charleston,

Labor

Civilian Labor Force   38,918
% Change 1989–1990   3.3
Work Force Distribution
   Mining   NA
   Construction   14,100
   Manufacturing   21,000
   Transportation and Public Utilities   11,000
   Wholesale and Retail Trade   50,400
   FIRE (Finance, Insurance, Real Estate)   7,700
   Service   47,8000
   Government   54,500
   Women as % of Labor Force   48.7
   % Self-Employed   6.3
   % Professional/Technical   2.31
Total Unemployment   1,313
Rate %   3.4
Federal Government Civilian Employment   15,536

but the Private Industry Council is engaged in orchestrating training programs in highly specialized skills prized by businesses.

Education

The Charleston County Public Schools support 71 schools. The city has seven institutions of higher learning. The College of Charleston, founded in the 18th century, and the Medical University of South Carolina, and the Citadel (the military college of South Carolina), founded in the 19th century, are all historic institutions. The other institutions are Webster University, a private St. Louis–based facility; Johnson and Wales College; Trident Technical College; Baptist College at Charleston; and Charleston Southern University.

Education	
Number of Public Schools	71
Special Education Schools	NA
Total Enrollment	43,637
% Enrollment in Private Schools	9.8
% Minority	57.0
Classroom Teachers	2,556
Pupil-Teacher Ratio	17:1
Number of Graduates	1,829
Total Revenue (in millions)	$158.306
Total Expenditures (in millions)	$159.219
Expenditures per Pupil	$3,351
Educational Attainment (Age 25 and Over)	
% Completed 12 or More Years	63.6
% Completed 16 or More Years	24.6
Four-Year Colleges and Universities	4
Enrollment	12,103
Two-Year Colleges	2
Enrollment	7,108

Libraries	
Number	35
Public Libraries	14
Books (in thousands)	477
Circulation (in thousands)	NA
Persons Served (in thousands)	290
Circulation per Person Served	3.15
Income (in millions)	$3.17
Staff	113

Four-Year Colleges and Universities
  Medical University of South Carolina
  Charleston Southern University
  College of Charleston
  The Citadel

Health

The Medical University Hospital of the Medical University of South Carolina was founded in 1824. The U.S. Naval Hospital serves naval personnel stationed at the base, and the Veterans Administration Medical Center serves veterans. Other institutions include Roper Hospital, the first community hospital; St. Francis Xavier Hospital, operated by the Sisters of Charity of Our Lady of Mercy; Charleston Memorial; AMI East Cooper; Trident Regional Medical Center; and Baker Hospital.

Southern Pines offers psychiatric care and the Hospice of Charleston offers home health services.

Health	
Deaths—Total	910
Rate per 1,000	13.6
Infant Deaths—Total	35
Rate per 1,000	19.4
Number of Metro Hospitals	8
Number of Metro Hospital Beds	2,239
Rate per 100,000	3,250
Number of Physicians	1,169
Physicians per 1,000	NA
Nurses per 1,000	NA
Health Expenditures per Capita	$2.06

Transportation

Charleston's two main approaches are I-526 (the Mark Clark Expressway), which intersects with U.S. 17 west of the city and heads to points east, and I-26, which comes from the north near North Charleston. U.S. 17 is an east-to-west road that utilizes the Ashley River Memorial, Grace Memorial, and Silas Pearman bridges to cross the city. Charleston is also served by U.S. Highways 52 and 701. Rail passenger service is provided by Amtrak, and rail freight service by the CSX Corporation and Norfolk Southern railroads. The Port of Charleston, one of the most efficient in the world, is served by 88 shipping lines; four major shipyards operate in Charleston. The principal air terminus is Charleston International Airport, located just north of the city in North Charleston. In addition, Charleston Air Force Base is directly north of the airport.

Transportation	
Interstate Highway Mileage	29
Total Urban Mileage	1,911
Total Daily Vehicle Mileage (in millions)	7.347
Daily Average Commute Time	48.6 min.
Number of Buses	33
Port Tonnage (in millions)	9.819
Airports	1
Number of Daily Flights	31
Daily Average Number of Passengers	1,635

Airlines (American carriers only)
  American
  Delta
  Eastern
  United
  USAir
  Westair

Housing

Of the total housing stock, 48.1% is owner-occupied. The median value of an owner-occupied home is $86,600 and the median monthly rent $341.

Urban Redevelopment

Urban redevelopment is coordinated by a number of agencies, such as the Charleston Development Board, Charleston

Housing

Total Housing Units 34,322
% Change 1980–1990 20.6
Vacant Units for Sale or Rent 2,025
Occupied Units 30,753
% with More Than One Person per Room 4.1
% Owner-Occupied 48.1
Median Value of Owner-Occupied Homes $86,600
Average Monthly Purchase Cost $388
Median Monthly Rent $341
New Private Housing Starts 391
Value (in thousands) $26,520
% Single-Family 88
Nonresidential Buildings Value (in thousands) $22,658

Department of Planning and Urban Development, and the Charleston Citywide Local Development Corporation. There have been no major urban redevelopment projects in recent years.

Crime

Charleston ranks below the national average in public safety. In 1991, of the crimes known to police, there were 1,062 violent crimes and 6,517 property crimes.

Crime

Violent Crimes—Total 1,062
Violent Crime Rate per 100,000 972.5
Murder 16
Rape 30
Robbery 308
Aggravated Assaults 708
Property Crimes 6,517
Burglary 1,215
Larceny 4,580
Motor Vehicle Theft 722
Arson NA
Per Capita Police Expenditures $130.4
Per Capita Fire Protection Expenditures $60.67
Number of Police 225
Per 1,000 3.05

Religion

South Carolina is part of the Bible Belt, where the Southern Baptist denomination, along with other conservative groups including Pentecostals and the Church of Christ, is strong. The historically dominant churches, such as the Episcopalians, Congregationalists, Methodists, and Lutherans, have been in decline in recent decades.

Religion

Largest Denominations (Adherents)
Catholics 17,271
Episcopal 10,882
Presbyterian 10,690
Southern Baptist 45,934
United Methodist 19,068
Black Baptist 28,188
Evangelical Lutheran 7,187
Jewish 2,655

Media

The Charleston city press consists of a sole daily, the *Post and Courier*, a 1991 consolidation of the *News and Courier* (founded in 1803) and the *Evening Post* (founded in 1894). The electronic media consist of 4 television stations 4 network, 1 public, and 1 independent and 7 FM and AM radio stations.

Media

Newsprint
  The Bow Hook, weekly
  The Charleston Chronicle, weekly
  Post and Courier, daily
  Moultrie News, weekly

Television
  WCIV (Channel 4)
  WCSC (Channel 5)
  WITV (Channel 7)
  WTAT (Channel 24)

Radio
  WEZL (FM)   WOKE (AM)
  WPAL (AM)   WTMA (AM)
  WWWZ (FM)   WYBB (FM)
  WXTC (FM)

Sports

Charleston has no major professional sports teams.

Arts, Culture, and Tourism

Charleston's age has allowed it to assemble a mass of arts and culture matched by few cities in the nation. The Dock Street Theatre is one such center. Built in 1800 as the Planter's Hotel and remodeled by WPA workers in the 1930s, it seats 463 people and is not a museum but a functioning, operating hub for the arts. The performing arts and theater community in Charleston is under the coordination of the League of Charleston Theatre, a group that supports the arts with funds and organization. Several symphonies were organized in the city from 1819 to 1919; the present-day Charleston Symphony Orchestra plays in the Gaillard Municipal Auditorium (on Calhoun Street), which seats 2,700 people. Other musical exhibitions are held by the Charleston Boy's Choir and the Charleston Community Band. Theater performances are given by the Charleston Theatreworks, Charleston Repertory Theatre, Opera Charleston, and the Robert Ivey Ballet, among others.

The highlight of musical productions occurs in May, when the annual Spoleto (pronounced like tomato) Festival USA takes place for two weeks. Brought to the United States in 1977 by composer Gian Carlo Menotti (who founded a similar festival in Spoleto, Italy, in 1958), it highlights opera, musical, and theatrical works. The MOJA Arts Festival in October celebrates African and Caribbean culture. The Charleston Museum, founded in 1773, is the nation's oldest museum.

In addition to its own exhibits, it owns the Aiken-Rhett House, the Joseph Manigault House, and the Heyward-Washington House, all museum-homes. The Old Exchange and Provost Dungeon on East Bay Street, built in 1771, occupies a site that has had a building on it since 1680. The Patriots Point Naval and Maritime Museum offers visitors the moored U.S.S. *Yorktown* of World War II fame; the first nuclear submarine, the *Savannah*; the destroyer *Laffey*, which participated in the D-day landings; and the World War II submarine *Clamagore*.

Travel and Tourism

Hotel Rooms 10,487

Convention and Exhibit Space (square feet) NA

Convention Centers
Gaillard Municipal Auditorium
Geodesic Dome at Charles Towne Landing
The Meeting Place
The Old Exchange
South Carolina Society Hall

Festivals
Spoleto Festival (May and June)
Moja Arts Festival (October)
International Film Festival (October–November)
Southeastern Wildlife Exposition (February)
Festival of Houses (March–April)
Fall House and Garden Candlelight Tour
Antique and Art Exposition (November)

Parks and Recreation

Charleston's Parks and Recreation Department administers numerous parks, among them the Charles Towne Landing, site of the first alighting of English settlers on the Carolinas; Hampton Park, a 65-acre reserve with a duck pond and police horse stables; Waterfront Park on the Cooper River, with a 400-foot pier; and White Point Gardens (formerly Oyster Point), site of the first Charles Town settlement.

Sources of Further Information

CharlestonTrident Chamber of Commerce
P.O. Box 975
Charleston, SC 29402
(803) 577-2510

Charleston Trident Convention and Visitors Bureau
P.O. Box 975
Charleston, SC 29402-0975
(803) 577-2510

City Hall
80 Broad Street
Charleston, SC 29401
(803) 577-6970

Additional Reading

Bell, Quentin. *Charleston: Past and Present.* 1988.
Bowes, Frederick P. *The Culture of Early Charleston.* 1978.
Burton, E. Milby. *The Siege of Charleston, 1861–1965.* 1982.
Cameron, Louisa P. *Private Gardens of Charleston.* 1991.
Fraser, Walter J. *Charleston, Charleston. The History of a Southern City.* 1989.
Goebel, Doug. *Charleston: A Unique Perspective.* 1987.
Greene, Harlan. *Charleston: City of Memory.* 1987.
Hayek, Arthur, and Gene Waddell. *Charleston in 1883.* 1984.
Miller, Ruth M., and Ann T. Andrus. *Witness to History.* 1986.
Rosen, Robert N. *A Short History of Charleston.* 1982.
Simms, William G. *The Charleston Book: A Miscellany in Prose and Verse.* 1945.
Simons, Albert, and Samuel Lapham, Jr. *The Early Architecture of Charleston.* 1990.
Stevens, Kenneth W. *Charleston Antebellum Architecture and Civic Destiny.* 1988.
Uhlendorf, Bernard A. *Siege of Charleston.* 1988.
Whitelaw, Robert N., and Alice F. Levkoff. *Charleston Come Hell or High Water: A History in Photographs.* 1988.

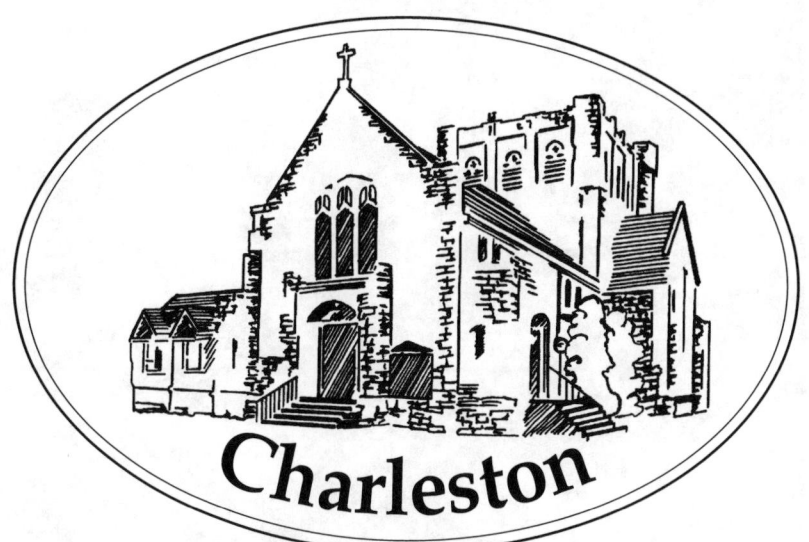

Charleston

West Virginia

Basic Data

Name   Charleston
Name Origin   From Charles Clendenin
Year Founded   1788 Inc. 1870
Status: State   Capital of West Virginia
      County   Seat of Kanawha County
Area (square miles)   29.5
Elevation (feet)   601
Time Zone   EST
Population (1990)   57,287
Population of Metro Area (1990)   250,454

Distance in Miles To:

Atlanta	501
Boston	751
Chicago	470
Dallas	1,049
Denver	1,370
Detroit	399
Houston	1,179
Los Angeles	2,411
Miami	1,008
New York	546
Philadelphia	482
Washington, DC	374

Location and Topography

N

Charleston, the capital of West Virginia and seat of Kanawha County, is in the west-central part of the state. The city is tucked into two narrow river valleys, where the Elk River flows into the Kanawha River, and on the surrounding steep slopes of the Allegheny Mountains.

Layout of City and Suburbs

Rivers and mountains shape the city's layout. While the earliest European settlement of Charleston was along the eastern section of what is now Kanawha Boulevard near its intersection with Brooks Street, the main part

Environment

Environmental Stress Index   2.6
Green Cities Index: Rank   NA
             Score   NA
Water Quality   Alkaline, soft, fluoridated
    Average Daily Use (gallons per capita)   150
    Maximum Supply (gallons per capita)   NA
Parkland as % of Total City Area   NA
% Waste Landfilled/Recycled   NA
Annual Parks Expenditures per Capita   NA

of the old town grew along what are now Kanawha and Virginia streets, east of the confluence of the Kanawha and Elk rivers. The main part of Charleston is located between the State Capitol Complex on the east and the Patrick Street Bridge on the west, and north of the South Side Bridge. To the west of the Patrick Street Bridge is the small but busy riverfront.

Climate

Charleston straddles two climatic zones and has features of both. Summers may be hot, hazy, and humid. Winters are unpredictable, depending on the intrusions of cold arctic air from Canada; annual snowfall varies widely– from 5 to 50 inches. In spring the ground warms rapidly. Most of the rain falls in summer, particularly in July, when thunderstorms are common. The peculiarities of terrain and air flow patterns combine to make Charleston one of the foggiest cities in the United States, with 111 foggy days a year.

Weather

Temperature

Highest Monthly Average °F   85.2
Lowest Monthly Average °F   23.9

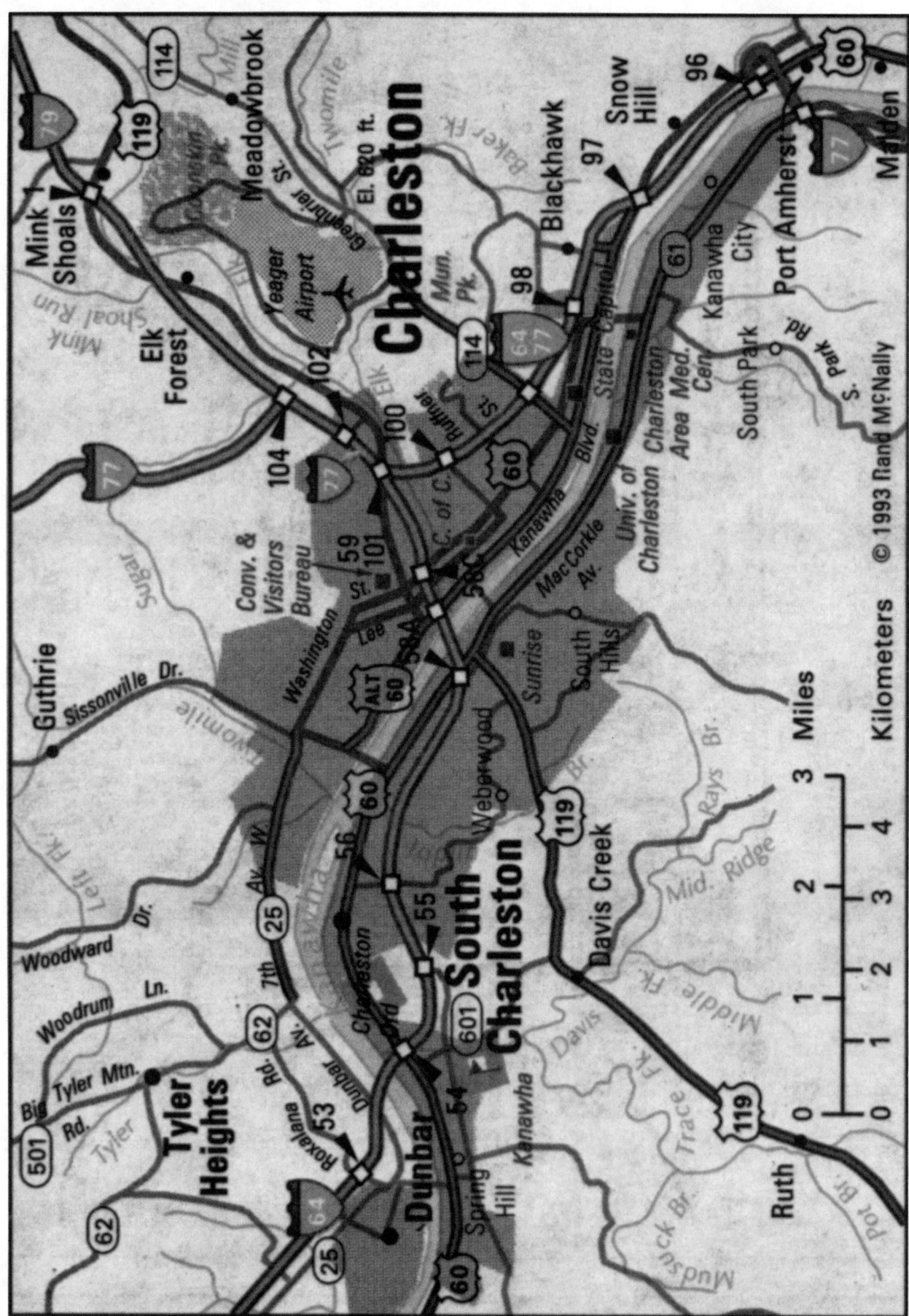

Weather (continued)

Annual Averages

Days 32°F or Below   100
Days above 90°F   21
Zero Degree Days   1
Precipitation (inches)   42.43
Snow (inches)   32.7
% Seasonal Humidity   69
Wind Speed (m.p.h.)   6.4
Clear Days   65
Cloudy Days   189
Storm Days   43
Rainy Days   149

Average Temperatures (°F)	High	Low	Mean
January	43.6	25.3	34.5
February	46.2	26.8	36.5
March	55.2	33.8	44.5
April	67.9	43.8	55.9
May	76.6	52.3	64.5
June	83.4	60.6	72.0
July	85.6	64.3	75.0
August	84.4	62.8	73.6
September	79.0	55.9	67.5
October	69.1	44.8	57.0
November	55.8	35.0	45.4
December	45.2	27.2	36.2

History

The Kanawha Valley was inhabited by an archaic culture from 10,000 to 7,000 B.C. and then by the Adena. Evidence of the Adena remains at Criel Mound, which was built in what is now South Charleston. The first whites in the area were probably the hapless Mary Ingles and Betty Draper, who had been captured by Indians during the Ingles-Draper Massacre at Draper Meadows near Blacksburg, Virginia, in 1755.

In 1775, twenty years later, Colonel Thomas Bullitt staked a claim of 1,240 acres, which included most of the area that is now the eastern side of Charleston. At the time the area was administered from Virginia's capital far to the east in Williamsburg. Bullitt's claim passed to his brother Cuthbert, who sold it to Virginia assemblyman George Clendenin for 5 shillings (87 cents) in 1787. A few weeks after the sale, Edmund Randolph, the governor of Virginia, asked Clendenin (from the new capital in Richmond) to organize a company of rangers to protect the Kanawha Valley, which was then being settled by farmers moving west from the Shenandoah Valley.

A year later, in 1788, Clendenin erected Fort Lee at the foot of the present Brooks Street. The fort became a gathering place and the nucleus of Charleston. The country was still wild enough to suit Daniel Boone, who was elected in 1789 to the Virginia assembly in Richmond in the first election held in the newly established Kanawha County. Clendenin's Settlement, as Fort Lee was commonly called, became Charles Town (after Clendenin's father) when in 1794 the Virginia Assembly authorized the establishment of a town on Clendenin's tract. In time the name was shortened to Charleston.

The need for a military outpost as a defense against Indians diminished when the northwest tribes (Delaware, Miami, Seneca, Shawnee, and Wyandot), in what would become Ohio, signed the Treaty of Greenville in 1795 with General Anthony Wayne, who had defeated them the year before at the Battle of Fallen Timbers. Battles with Indians, however, provided good stories, and in 1861 Charles Robb published *A Legend of the Kanawha*. According to Robb, English-born Ann Bailey made a desperate ride from Fort Lee to Fort Savannah at Lewisburg—a hundred miles of mountain cut by deep valleys—to bring back gunpowder.

The first post office here opened in 1801. The Kanawha Turnpike (later U.S. 60), which now has a memorable stretch of curves and hairpin turns beginning at Gauley Bridge east of Charleston and ending at Rainelle west of Lewisburg, reached the Kanawha Valley from Lewisburg in 1804. Now Charleston became a transfer point for travelers going west by way of the Ohio River.

Salt was the first of the region's natural resources to be exploited. Large-scale refining began in 1806; mining and drilling techniques developed for salt led to the discovery of both oil and natural gas, considered nuisances at the time. When competition in the Ohio Valley ended the salt industry, coal, gas, and oil became more profitable. The Chesapeake and Ohio Railroad, completed in 1873 from Charleston to the Ohio River, replaced flatboats on the Kanawha for carrying coal to the Ohio.

The sympathies of eastern Virgina were clearly with the South at the time of the Civil War, while western counties, whose economic ties were to the north rather than to the east and south, were inclined to side with the Union. When Virginia joined the Confederacy in April 1861, a government favoring the Union was organized in Wheeling. On 20 June 1863 the 50 western counties of Virginia became West Virginia. Charleston became the state capital in 1870 when political control of the state government changed from Republican to Democrat, but it only remained there for five years. The capital moved back to Wheeling in 1875. The state legislature adopted a resolution in 1877 to open the selection for a permanent state capital once again, providing for the decision to become effective in 1885. Charleston successfully won the election.

The first chemical manufacturing began in Charleston just before World War I—tetrachloride, liquid chlorine, dyes—followed by the establishment of two glass-making plants. Then the federal government established a plant to make explosives at nearby Nitro. Many of these companies have since scaled back their operations or, in the case of the glass companies, closed. The original statehouse was enlarged and an annex was built in 1902. Destroyed by fire in 1921, today's domed capitol was completed in 1932.

Until the 1960s Charleston was the second-largest city in the state. Huntington, a freight and shipping center on the Ohio River 50 miles west of Charleston, and site of an International Nickel plant and Marshall

Chronology

1775 Colonel Thomas Bullitt stakes a claim of 1,240 acres in the Kanawha Valley. Upon his death, the claim is inherited by his brother, Cuthbert Bullitt.

1787 Assemblyman George Clendenin buys the claim from Cuthbert Bullitt for five shillings (87 cents). Clendenin is designated by Governor Edmund Randolph to organize a company of rangers to protect the Kanawha Valley.

1788 Clendenin erects Fort Lee on his tract.

1789 Kanawha County is organized, with Fort Lee as its meeting place.

1794 Virginia Assembly authorizes the establishment of a town on the Clendenin tract, named Charles Town, later Charleston.

1801 Post office opens in Charleston.

1804 Kanawha Turnpike opens.

1805 First salt mill opens in nearby Malden.

1815 A pottery opens; first gas well in the area drilled.

1818 Mercer Academy opens.

1819 The town's first newspaper, the *Spectator*, debuts.

1820 Steam navigation connecting Charleston on the Kanawha River to the Ohio River is introduced; regular service begins in 1825.

1863 West Virginia admitted to the Union as the 35th state.

1870 Capital is moved from Wheeling to Charleston.

1873 Chesapeake and Ohio Railway is completed to the Ohio River.

1875 Capital returns to Wheeling.

1877 Charleston wins election to decide the permanent capital.

1885 Capital returns permanently to Charleston.

1913 The first chemical plants are built in the Kanawha Valley.

1921 The capitol burns to the ground.

1932 New capitol is dedicated.

post-colonial house with Ionic columns, was once the home of Daniel Ruffner, who bought the site of Charleston from the Clendenins. The Greek Revival home of James Craik, Elm Grove, was completed in 1834. Later sold to Colonel George S. Patton, a Confederate officer, the home is now a museum. The present capitol building, on Kanawha Boulevard, was designed in the Italian Renaissance style by Cass Gilbert and completed in 1932 at a cost of $10 million. Sunrise, a mansion built by former Governor William McCorkle in 1905, serves as a municipal museum, with a commanding view of downtown Charleston from South Hills.

Population

Charleston's population has declined during the last two decades. From 71,505 in 1970 it declined by 10.5% to 63,968 in 1980 and then by a further 10.4% to 57,287 in 1990.

Population		
	1980	*1990*
Central City	63,968	57,287
Rank	310	408
Metro Area	269,595	250,454
Pop. Change 1980–1990 -6,681		
Pop. % Change 1980–1990 -10.4		
Median Age 37.2		
% Male 45.5		
% Age 65 and Over 18.4		
Density (per square mile) 1,941		
Households		
Number 25,306		
Persons per Household 2.21		
% Female-Headed Households 13.9		
% One-Person Households 35.7		
Births—Total 723		
% to Mothers under 20 14.8		
Birth Rate per 1,000 12.2		

Ethnic Composition

Whites make up 84.1%, blacks 14.25%, Asians and Pacific Islanders 1.28%, Hispanics 0.62%, American Indians 0.19%, and others 0.18%.

Ethnic Composition (as % of total pop.)		
	1980	*1990*
White	86.57	84.1
Black	12.21	14.25
American Indian	0.10	0.19
Asian and Pacific Islander	0.77	1.28
Hispanic	0.63	0.62
Other	NA	0.18

University, was until then the larger city. Today Charleston remains the largest city in West Virginia.

Historical Landmarks

The site of Fort Lee on Kanawha Boulevard is marked by two bronze plaques. Holly Grove on Kanawha Boulevard, a

Government

Charleston has a mayor-council form of government. The mayor and members of the council are elected every 4 years.

Government

Year of Home Charter   NA
Number of Members of the Governing Body   ·27
Elected at Large   7
Elected by Wards   20
Number of Women in Governing Body   10
Salary of Mayor   NA
Salary of Council Members   NA
City Government Employment Total   1,141
Rate per 10,000   197.0

Public Finance

The annual budget in 1984–1985 consisted of revenues of $44.9 million and expenditures of $42.8 million. The debt outstanding was $53.1 million and cash and security holdings of $58.765 million.

Public Finance

Total Revenue (in millions)   NA
Intergovernmental Revenue—Total (in millions)   NA
Federal Revenue per Capita   NA
% Federal Assistance   NA
% State Assistance   NA
Sales Tax as % of Total Revenue   NA
Local Revenue as % of Total Revenue   NA
City Income Tax   no
Taxes—Total (in millions) $21.1

Taxes per Capita
   Total $364
   Property $76
   Sales and Gross Receipts $32
General Expenditures—Total (in millions) $42.8
General Expenditures per Capita $739
Capital Outlays per Capita $145

% of Expenditures for:
   Public Welfare   0.0
   Highways   7.2
   Education   0.0
   Health and Hospitals   1.1
   Police   11.2
   Sewerage and Sanitation   10.2
   Parks and Recreation   8.9
   Housing and Community Development   14.5
Debt Outstanding per Capita $917
   % Utility   0.0
Federal Procurement Contract Awards (in millions) $12.7
Federal Grants Awards (in millions) $187.5
Fiscal Year Begins   July 1

Economy

The Kanawha Valley is one of the richest regions in the nation in natural resources. Coal mining and natural gas development have been the industrial anchors, and coal-based industries gave Charleston a strong economic base at the turn of the century. The plentiful natural resources were also responsible initially for attracting chemical manufacturers to the region. Beginning in 1929 the chemical industry has provided a stable employment base for West Virginians. Almost all the chemical giants, such as Union Carbide, E.I. du Pont, Monsanto, Olin, Rhone-Poulenc, and FMC, have plants in towns near Charleston. Union Carbide also has its research and development headquarters in the Tech Center Complex in South Charleston. Other valley corporations include IBM, General Electric, Industrial Rubber Products, Kanawha Manufacturing Company, Trojan Steel Company, and West Virginia Steel Corporation. Product manufacturing has declined in recent years, but new growth in banking and insurance has added other dimensions to the economy. Charleston also has developed its transportation potential effectively, becoming a major distribution and retail center for the region. As the state capital, government services play a large role in stabilizing local employment.

Economy

Total Money Income (in millions) $748.9
% of State Average   158.8
Per Capita Annual Income $12,930
% Population below Poverty Level   12.6
Fortune 500 Companies   NA

Banks	Number	Deposits (in millions)
Commercial	33	1,811.8
Savings	15	319.8

Passenger Autos   153,860
Electric Meters   78,000
Gas Meters   19,600

Manufacturing

Number of Establishments   54
% with 20 or More Employees   29.6
Manufacturing Payroll (in millions) $83.1
Value Added by Manufacture (in millions) $81.3
Value of Shipments (in millions) $579.6
New Capital Expenditures (in millions) $14.8

Wholesale Trade

Number of Establishments   264
Sales (in millions) $884
Annual Payroll (in millions) $79.763

Retail Trade

Number of Establishments   900
Total Sales (in millions) $763.1
Sales per Capita $13,175
Number of Retail Trade Establishments with Payroll   711
Annual Payroll (in millions) $91.7
Total Sales (in millions) $755.2
General Merchandise Stores (per capita) $3,011
Food Stores (per capita) $1,724
Apparel Stores (per capita) $907
Eating and Drinking Places (per capita) $1,288

Service Industries

Total Establishments   921
Total Receipts (in millions) $429.8
Hotels and Motels (in millions) $24.6
Health Services (in millions) $145.9
Legal Services (in millions) $80.6

Labor

Although the major employers before World War II, mining companies and chemical manufacturers have shrunk in terms of employment. Services and trade are now more prominent. Government's share of the employment market has remained fairly stable over the years at about 20%. The unemployment rate in 1990 was 4.8%.

Labor

Civilian Labor Force   29,322
% Change 1989–1990   1.5

Work Force Distribution
   Mining   2,400
   Construction   5,000
   Manufacturing   10,500
   Transportation and Public Utilities   8,800
   Wholesale and Retail Trade   28,300
   FIRE (Finance, Insurance, Real Estate)   6,500
   Service   30,600
   Government   19,800
   Women as % of Labor Force   45.3
   % Self-Employed   5.2
   % Professional/Technical   20.2
Total Unemployment   1,402
Rate %   4.8
Federal Government Civilian Employment   1,484

Education

The Kanawha County Public Schools support 99 schools. More than a dozen private and parochial schools supplement the public system. The Kanawha Valley is home to four institutions of higher education, one private and three public. The private institution is the University of Charleston, on the riverfront across from the State Capitol. West Virginia State College, at Institute, eight miles west, is one of the state's largest four-year institutions. The other two public institutions are the West Virginia Institute of Technology and the College of Graduate Studies.

Education

Number of Public Schools   99
Special Education Schools   NA
Total Enrollment   34,284
% Enrollment in Private Schools   NA
% Minority   NA
Classroom Teachers   NA
Pupil-Teacher Ratio   NA
Number of Graduates   NA
Total Revenue (in millions) $126.0
Total Expenditures (in millions) $126.7
Expenditures per Pupil $3,280
Educational Attainment (Age 25 and Over)
   % Completed 12 or More Years   70.5
   % Completed 16 or More Years   23.7
Four-Year Colleges and Universities   2
   Enrollment   1,500
Two-Year Colleges   NA
   Enrollment   NA

Libraries

Number   27
Public Libraries   9
Books (in thousands)   554
Circulation (in thousands)   1,048
Persons Served (in thousands)   208.7

Education (continued)

Circulation per Person Served   5.03
Income (in millions) $2.998
Staff   83

Four-Year Colleges and Universities
   University of Charleston
   West Virginia State College

Health

Charleston has four major hospitals, the largest of which is the Charleston Area Medical Center, which has three locations within the city and is a teaching hospital for West Virginia University's School of Medicine. Thomas Memorial Hospital in South Charleston is a community hospital. St. Francis Hospital in downtown Charleston is run by the Sisters of St. Joseph. In Teas Valley, 24 miles to the west, is the Putnam General Hospital. In addition, there are a number of specialized facilities, such as the Highland Hospital, which offers psychiatric care, and the Eye and Ear Clinic.

Health

Deaths—Total   802
Rate per 1,000   13.5
Infant Deaths—Total   7
Rate per 1,000   9.7
Number of Metro Hospitals   5
Number of Metro Hospital Beds   1,425
Rate per 100,000   2,460
Number of Physicians   551
Physicians per 1,000   NA
Nurses per 1,000   NA
Health Expenditures per Capita   NA

Transportation

Three interstates (I-64, I-77, and I-79) converge at Charleston. I-64 runs east-west from the Midwest to Newport News, Virginia; I-77 links Charleston with the Great Lakes region and Cleveland to the north and south to the Carolinas; I-79 starts in Erie, Pennsylvania, and terminates in Charleston. Also serving the city are U.S. 60, 21, 35, and 119, and State Highways 4, 14, 25, and 61. Amtrak provides rail passenger service, with the Chesapeake and Ohio and Conrail providing rail freight services. Charleston is the major river port on the Kanawha; it has a navigation channel 300 feet wide and 9 feet deep. It is a U.S. Customs port of entry. The principal air terminal is Yeager Airport, 10 minutes from downtown. It was earlier known as Kanawha Airport, but in 1986 it was renamed to honor West

Transportation

Interstate Highway Mileage   38
Total Urban Mileage   749
Total Daily Vehicle Mileage (in millions)   4.345
Daily Average Commute Time   47.5 min.
Number of Buses   54

Transportation (continued)

Port Tonnage (in millions)   NA
Airports   1
Number of Daily Flights   17
Daily Average Number of Passengers   538

Airlines (American carriers only)
   USAir
   Westair

Virginia–born Air Force test pilot Charles E. (Chuck) Yeager.

Housing

In 1990, 55.5% of the total housing stock was owner occupied. The median value of an owner-occupied home was $66,100, and the median monthly rent was $261.

Housing

Total Housing Units   28,111
% Change 1980–1990   0.3
Vacant Units for Sale or Rent   1,987
Occupied Units   25,306
% with More Than One Person per Room   1.1
% Owner-Occupied   55.5
Median Value of Owner-Occupied Homes $66,100
Average Monthly Purchase Cost $347
Median Monthly Rent $261
New Private Housing Starts   85
Value (in thousands) $10,695
% Single-Family   90.6
Nonresidential Buildings Value (in thousands) $4,761

Urban Redevelopment

Since the 1983 opening of the Charleston Town Center, the largest enclosed mall in the state, a number of redevelopment projects have changed downtown. The Streetscape Project converted traditional downtown into a restored turn-of-the-century village. The Capital Plaza Theater, a 75-year-old vaudeville hall, was completely restored into a performing arts center.

Crime

In 1991, of the crimes known to police, there were 4,699 violent crimes and 6,138 property crimes.

Crime

Violent Crimes—Total   4,699
Violent Crime Rate per 100,000   372.2
Murder   12
Rape   46
Robbery   264
Aggravated Assaults   377
Property Crimes   6,138
Burglary   1,365
Larceny   4,354
Motor Vehicle Theft   419
Arson   NA

Crime (continued)

Per Capita Police Expenditures $80.87
Per Capita Fire Protection Expenditures   NA
Number of Police   149
Per 1,000   2.44

Religion

In 1990 Kanawha County had 344 churches, the largest number of which were the American Baptist Church, followed by the United Methodist Church and Roman Catholic Church

Religion

Largest Denominations (Adherents)

Catholic	8,902
American Baptist	16,627
United Methodist	14,898
Church of the Nazarene	7,091
Presbyterian	7,742
Black Baptist	5,080
Southern Baptist	3,323
Episcopal	2,209
Jewish	805

Media

The Charleston press consists of two dailies, the morning *Charleston Gazette* and the evening *Charleston Daily Mail*, which combine on Sundays as *Sunday Gazette Mail*. The electronic media consist of 9 AM and FM radio stations.

Media

Newsprint
   Charleston Daily Mail, daily
   Charleston Gazette, daily

Television
   NA

Radio

WCAW (AM)	WVAF (FM)
WCHS (AM)	WVNS (FM)
WCZR (AM)	WQBE (AM)
WQBE (FM)	WVSR (FM)
WXAF (FM)	

Sports

Charleston does not have a major professional sports team. However, the city has two professional sports franchises: Charleston Gunners in basketball and Charleston Wheelers in baseball. The city hosts a nationally prominent running event: the 15-mile Charleston Distance Run.

Arts, Culture, and Tourism

The Cultural Center is the hub of performing arts in Charleston. Located in the Capitol Complex, it houses the Great

Travel and Tourism

Hotel Rooms   3,141
Convention and Exhibit Space (square feet)   NA

Convention Centers
   Charleston Civic Center
   Coliseum
   Municipal Auditorium
   Charleston

Festivals
   Sternwheel Regatta Festival (September)
   Festival of Trees (December)
   Jazz Festival (Spring)
   Dance Festival
   Theatre Festival
   Black Cultural Festival

Hall, a 468-seat theater. The Civic Center contains a 13,500-seat Coliseum and the 750-seat Little Theater, and they provide the stage for the Kanawha Players, the oldest dramatic group and the official state theater of West Virginia. Children's Theater of Virginia also performs here. The 3,500-seat Municipal Auditorium is home to the Charleston Symphony Orchestra and the Community Chamber Music Association. Other musical groups are the Lilliput Orchestra and the Charleston Light Opera Guild. Ballet is represented by Charleston Ballet.

The Art Museum and the Children's Museum and Planetarium occupy two historic landmark buildings—Sunrise and Torquilstone in South Hills. The Cultural Center includes a museum dedicated to West Virginia history. Sunrise Museum is a privately supported nonprofit museum complex.

Parks and Recreation

The Kanawha Parks and Recreation Commission operates five regional parks, the largest of which is the 1,200-acre Coonskin Park. Other parks include Big Bend, Pioneer Regional Park at East Bank, Geary Park off I-79, and Shawnee Regional Park between Dunbar and Institute.

Sources of Further Information

Charleston Convention and Visitors Bureau
200 Civic Center Drive
Charleston, WV 25301
(304) 344-5075

Charleston Regional Chamber of Commerce and Development
106 Capitol Street
Charleston, WV 25301
(304) 345-0770

Kanawha County Department of Planning and Community Development
409 Virginia Street East
Charleston, WV 25301
(304) 357-0570

City Hall
City Building
Court and Virginia
Charleston, WV 25301
(304) 348-8174

Additional Reading

Sutphin, Gerald W., and Richard A. Andre. *Sternwheelers on the Great Kanawha River*. 1991.
Writer's Program, West Virginia. *West Virginia: A Guide to the Mountain State*. 1941.

Charlotte
North Carolina

Location and Topography

N Charlotte, the largest city in North Carolina and seat of Mecklenburg County, lies in the rolling hills of North Carolina's Piedmont, just east of the Catawba River. It is approximately 130 miles southwest of Raleigh, the state capital; 75 miles southwest of the Appalachian Mountains; and 15 miles north of the South Carolina border.

Layout of City and Suburbs

Independence Square, formed by the intersection of Trade and Tryon streets, is the city's center. A few blocks north of the square are remnants of early Charlotte, most of which have disappeared in the expansion of the business district. Neighborhoods such as East Over, Myers Park, and Dilworth are to the east and southeast, and beyond these sections are the newer suburbs. The textile mill suburbs, such as Chadwick-Hoskins and North Charlotte, are to the southeast.

Environment

Environmental Stress Index 3.0
Green Cities Index: Rank 18
                Score 24.17
Water Quality Alkaline, very soft, fluoridated
    Average Daily Use (gallons per capita) 130
    Maximum Supply (gallons per capita) NA
Parkland as % of Total City Area 2.9
% Waste Landfilled/Recycled 62:38
Annual Parks Expenditures per Capita $182.31

Climate

 Charlotte has a generally mild climate. The Appalachians moderate winter temperatures by warming air from the west and northwest. There are occasional cold spells in winter, but extreme cold is rare. Snowfall averages only once a month from December through March. Summers are long and warm, with afternoon temperatures frequently in the 90s. Nights are cooler, with temperatures dropping into the 70s even in the warmest months. Summer precipitation is primarily in the form of thundershowers, but the fall season is dry.

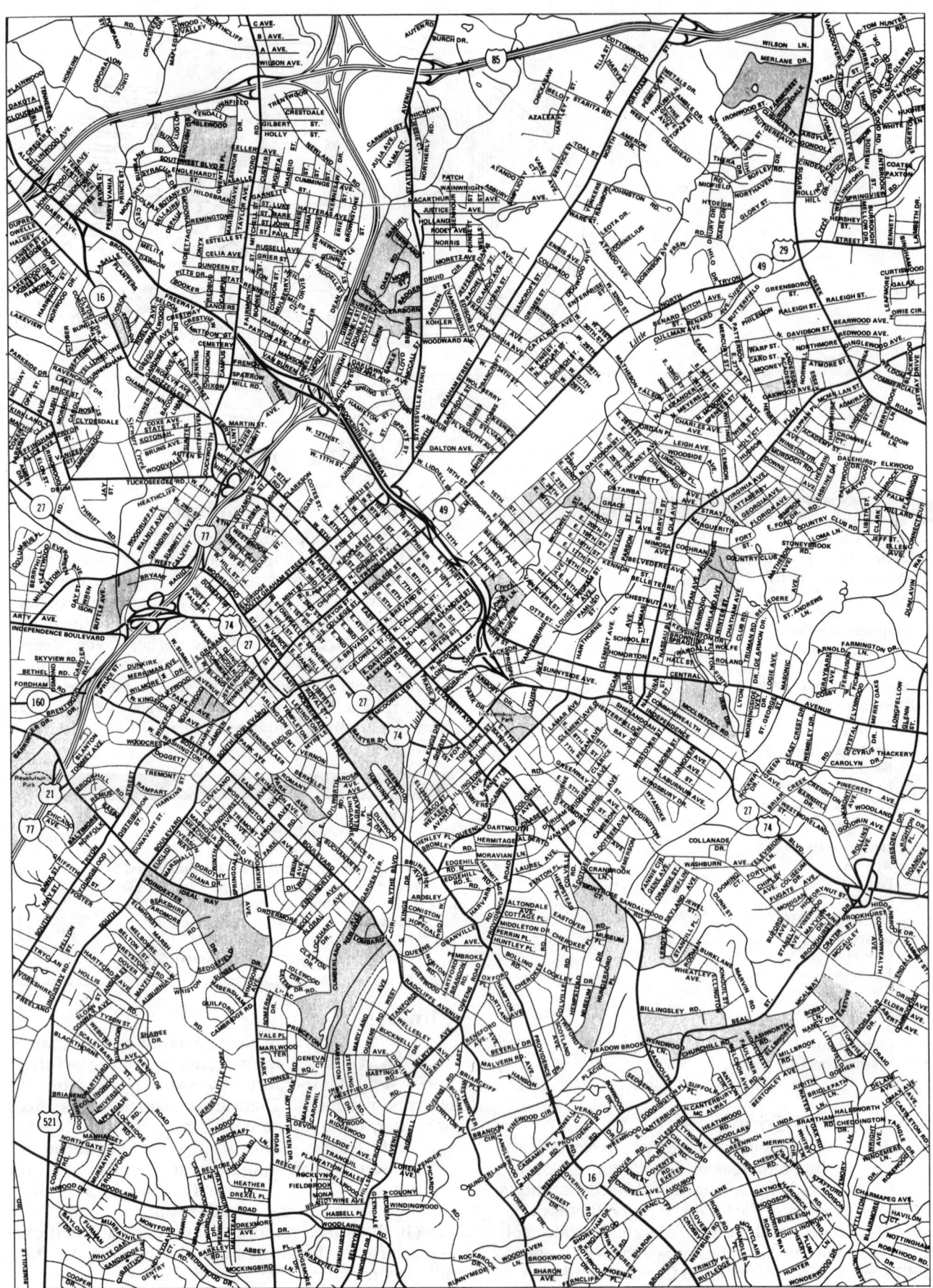

Weather

Temperature

Highest Monthly Average °F 87.4
Lowest Monthly Average °F 32.1

Annual Averages

Days 32°F or Below 71
Days above 90°F 31
Zero Degree Days 0
Precipitation (inches) 43
Snow (inches) 6
% Seasonal Humidity 69
Wind Speed (m.p.h.) 7.6
Clear Days 111
Cloudy Days 151
Storm Days 42
Rainy Days 111

Average Temperatures (°F)	High	Low	Mean
January	49.9	30.5	40.2
February	53.4	32.3	42.9
March	61.2	38.4	49.8
April	72.9	48.1	60.5
May	81.0	56.0	68.5
June	87.5	64.5	76.0
July	89.5	68.1	78.8
August	89.0	67.0	78.0
September	83.4	60.4	71.9
October	73.5	48.1	60.8
November	60.7	37.1	48.9
December	50.9	31.4	41.2

History

Catawba Indians lived in this region, which the British considered a Crown colony, in 1748—the year settlers migrated from Virginia and elsewhere to establish farms. Within two years, settlers, using Indian trails, began trade with Charleston on the coast.

Mecklenburg County was created in 1762. A log house used as a courthouse became the nucleus of Charlotte, named for English King George III's wife, Charlotte of Mecklenburg-Strelitz. A town site of 360 acres was purchased in 1767, and the town incorporated a year later. By 1774 the population numbered 200 and Charlotte was made the Mecklenburg county seat.

Independent thinkers in Charlotte opposed British rule, and on 20 May 1775 drafted a resolution declaring anyone supporting the king an enemy. This date now appears on the state flag. During the American Revolution, Lord Cornwallis occupied Charlotte for a month in 1780. He left, calling the town "a damned hornets' nest."

The first U.S. census, held in 1790, listed the county's population as 11,725. Among the residents were the parents of James K. Polk. Polk, born in 1795, became the 11th president of the United States.

Gold was discovered near Charlotte in 1799, leading to the arrival of banks, and a branch of the U.S. mint opened in 1837. By 1852 passengers could travel by rail from Charlotte to Columbia, South Carolina, and by 1856 a railroad connected Charlotte to Goldsboro.

North Carolina joined the Confederacy during the Civil War, and Charlotte was the site of Jefferson Davis's last full cabinet meeting before Robert E. Lee surrendered at Appomattox in April 1865. With the end of the war and abolition of slavery, the economic base of Piedmont North Carolina changed from agriculture to manufacturing, particularly textiles. A cotton mill opened in 1881; by 1891 the city directory listed ten cotton mills and factories as well as a furniture factory, publishing house, planing mills, and the Carolina Spoke and Handle Works. By 1903 more than half the nation's textile production was located within a 100-mile radius of Charlotte.

According to the 1920 census, Charlotte's population was 51,744. WBT Radio went on the air in 1921, and a branch of the Federal Reserve Bank opened in 1927. The Charlotte campus of the University of North Carolina opened in 1946. In 1970 the Charlotte-Mecklenburg school system became one of the first to be integrated. The 1980s brought renovation and growth to the downtown area. In 1983 the city elected its first black mayor, Harvey Gantt, and in 1987 its first woman mayor, Sue Myrick.

Historical Landmarks

The square at the intersection of Trade and Tryon streets in downtown Charlotte was once an Indian crossroads. As Charlotte grew, farmers gathered there to buy and sell goods, and Mecklenburg County's first courthouse was built there in 1762. The First Presbyterian Church, at 200 West Trade, was established in 1815. The present structure dates from 1857, with additions made in 1894 and 1895. Built in 1891 of handmade brick, St. Mary's Chapel is the last surviving structure of the Thompson Orphanage. The Old First Baptist Church, built in 1909, has been incorporated into Spirit Square at Tryon and Seventh streets. The Hezekiah Alexander Homesite, built in 1774, is considered the oldest home in Mecklenburg County. The James K. Polk Homesite, in Pineville just south of Charlotte, has reconstructed buildings and exhibits.

Population

Charlotte became the nation's 35th largest city in 1990, reflecting growth contrary to the loss pattern in most large U.S. cities during the 1980s. From 214,000 in 1970, its population burgeoned to 315,474 in 1980, and then to 395,934 in 1990. The percentage increase was 30.2% in the 1970s and 25.5% in the 1980s.

Population

	1980	1990
Central City	315,474	395,934
Rank	47	35
Metro Area	971,447	1,162,093
Pop. Change 1980–1990 +80,460		
Pop. % Change 1980–1990 +25.5		
Median Age 32.1		
% Male 47.5		

Chronology

1762	Mecklenburg County is formed; a courthouse is built that becomes the nucleus of Charlotte.
1768	Charlotte is incorporated.
1771	Liberty Hall Academy, first college in county, is established.
1774	With a population of 200, Charlotte is chosen seat of Mecklenburg County.
1775	Mecklenburg Resolutions passed.
1780	Lord Cornwallis and British troops occupy Charlotte, but evacuate after one month.
1799	Gold is discovered.
1836	U.S. mint is established in Charlotte.
1852	First passenger train arrives from South Carolina.
1865	Jefferson Davis and full cabinet of the Confederate States of Ameica meet for the last time.
1873	Grade school organized in Charlotte; first in the state.
1881	Cotton mill begins operation, presages textile industry in the Charlotte area.
1917	Camp Greene built during World War I, temporarily increasing Charlotte's population from 20,000 to 60,000.
1954	Douglas Municipal Airport completed.
1970	Schools integrate.
1971	Jefferson First Union Tower completed. Its 32 stories make it the tallest building in the Carolinas.
1982	Investments by new and expanding businesses top $300 million for the year.
1988	Charlotte Coliseum opens; first year for the Charlotte Hornets, a franchise of the National Basketball Association.

Population (continued)

% Age 65 and Over 9.80
Density (per square mile) 2,271

Households

Number 158,991
Persons per Household 2.45
% Female-Headed Households 14.0
% One-Person Households 28
Births—Total 5,021
    % to Mothers under 20 16.2
    Birth Rate per 1,000 15.2

Ethnic Composition

In 1990 whites made up 65.6% of the population, while blacks comprised 31.78%, Asians and Pacific Islanders 1.82%, Hispanics 1.41%, American Indians 0.36%, and others 0.43%.

Ethnic Composition (as % of total pop.)

	1980	1990
White	67.41	65.61
Black	31.05	31.78
American Indian	0.33	0.36
Asian and Pacific Islander	0.75	1.82
Hispanic	1.09	1.41
Other	NA	0.43

Government

Charlotte has a council-manager form of government. Voters elect the mayor and 11 members of the city council to two-year terms. The mayor may vote only to break ties in the council. The council appoints a city manager.

Government

Year of Home Charter NA
Number of Members of the Governing Body 11
Elected at Large 4
Elected by Wards 7
Number of Women in Governing Body 6
Salary of Mayor $20,000
Salary of Council Members $12,000
City Government Employment Total 4,113
Rate per 10,000 116.8

Public Finance

The annual budget consists of revenues of $422.22 million and expenditures of $507.627 million. The debt outstanding is $705.922 million, and cash and reserve holdings are $491.662 million.

Public Finance

Total Revenue (in millions) $422.22
Intergovernmental Revenue—Total (in millions) $103.68
Federal Revenue per Capita $18.99
% Federal Assistance 4.49
% State Assistance 10.5
Sales Tax as % of Total Revenue 1.18
Local Revenue as % of Total Revenue 75.63
City Income Tax no
Taxes—Total (in millions) $102.7
Taxes per Capita
    Total $292
    Property $228
    Sales and Gross Receipts $52
General Expenditures—Total (in millions) $190.0
General Expenditures per Capita $540
Capital Outlays per Capita $133

Public Finance (continued)

% of Expenditures for:
    Public Welfare   0.1
    Highways   12.4
    Education   0.0
    Health and Hospitals   0.6
    Police   12.5
    Sewerage and Sanitation   11.2
    Parks and Recreation   10.3
    Housing and Community Development   1.5
Debt Outstanding per Capita $843
    % Utility   12.8
Federal Procurement Contract Awards (in millions) $42.9
Federal Grants Awards (in millions) $17.9
Fiscal Year Begins   July 1

Economy

Once known primarily as a textile center, Charlotte has since diversified into banking and industries such as research and development.

According to a 1992 report, Charlotte was the third-largest financial center in the nation, surpassed only by New York and San Francisco in banking resources. The Charlotte bank holding companies controlled $156 billion in assets. The city is the headquarters of North Carolina National Bank, the largest bank in the Southeast.

As an inland port facility and a foreign trade zone, Charlotte attracts foreign investors looking for a foothold in the Southeast. By 1991, 260 foreign-owned companies had facilities in Charlotte.

Manufacturing is represented by 1,100 producers, including 361 of the nation's 1,000 largest industrial and service companies. In addition to textiles, the major products are chemicals, food products, printing and publishing, and machinery. The largest manufacturers are FritoLay, CocaCola, Celanese, General Tire and Rubber, and IBM.

Charlotte has developed into a major wholesale center, with the highest per capita sales in the nation.

Economy

Total Money Income (in millions) $4,316.0
% of State Average   128.8
Per Capita Annual Income $12,259
% Population below Poverty Level   12.4
Fortune 500 Companies   3

Banks	Number	Deposits (in millions)
Commercial	17	7,342.9
Savings	12	NA

Passenger Autos   288,534 (city)
Electric Meters   215,170
Gas Meters   90,912

Manufacturing

Number of Establishments   856
% with 20 or More Employees   34.6
Manufacturing Payroll (in millions) $1,114.4
Value Added by Manufacture (in millions) $2,079.0
Value of Shipments (in millions) $4,969.5
New Capital Expenditures (in millions) $172.2

Economy (continued)

Wholesale Trade

Number of Establishments   2,120
Sales (in millions) $21,127.2
Annual Payroll (in millions) $790.722

Retail Trade

Number of Establishments   4,035
Total Sales (in millions) $3,652.9
Sales per Capita $10,375
Number of Retail Trade Establishments with Payroll   2,820
Annual Payroll (in millions) $418.9
Total Sales (in millions) $3,590.8
General Merchandise Stores (per capita) $1,047
Food Stores (per capita) $1,534
Apparel Stores (per capita) $607
Eating and Drinking Places (per capita) $1,015

Service Industries

Total Establishments   3,905
Total Receipts (in millions) $2,300.9
Hotels and Motels (in millions) $166.7
Health Services (in millions) $455.7
Legal Services (in millions) $143.0

Labor

While the work force has grown by 22% since 1981, employment opportunities have grown by 23%. The number of firms locating in the city is evidence of the quality of the work force. Since 1982, 2,719 firms have selected Charlotte for new or relocated operations. As Charlotte becomes a more metropolitan community, it draws more on a regional work force. Each day more than 80,000 workers commute to Mecklenburg from outlying counties. North Carolina is a right-to-work state.

Labor

Civilian Labor Force   221,108
% Change 1989–1990   0.6

Work Force Distribution
    Mining   NA
    Construction   32,100
    Manufacturing   146,800
    Transportation and Public Utilities   49,600
    Wholesale and Retail Trade   149,900
    FIRE (Finance, Insurance, Real Estate)   39,800
    Service   122,200
    Government   71,700
    Women as % of Labor Force   46.3
    % Self-Employed   4.2
    % Professional/Technical   NA
Total Unemployment   6,855
Rate %   3.1
Federal Government Civilian Employment   2,729

Education

The Charlotte-Mecklenburg School System supports 110 schools. Thirty private and parochial schools supplement the public school system. Higher education is offered in 3 institutions, of which the largest is the University of

North Carolina at Charlotte. Others are Queens College and Johnson C. Smith University, one of the oldest historically black colleges in the nation. Eleven of the area colleges and universities are linked in a consortium.

Education

Number of Public Schools 110
Special Education Schools 2
Total Enrollment 77.069
% Enrollment in Private Schools 7.1
% Minority 43.3
Classroom Teachers 4,482
Pupil-Teacher Ratio 17.2:1
Number of Graduates 4,262
Total Revenue (in millions) $316.498
Total Expenditures (in millions) $298.881
Expenditures per Pupil $3,797
Educational Attainment (Age 25 and Over) NA
  % Completed 12 or More Years 70.1
  % Completed 16 or More Years 22.4
Four-Year Colleges and Universities 3
  Enrollment 17,094
Two-Year Colleges 1
  Enrollment 17,353

Libraries

Number 48
Public Libraries 19
Books (in thousands) 1,233
Circulation (in thousands) 2,800
Persons Served (in thousands) 518
Circulation per Person Served 5.4
Income (in millions) $10.691
Staff 279

Four-Year Colleges and Universities
John C. Smith University
Queens College
University of North Carolina at Charlotte

Health

Principal hospitals in the area include four general hospitals: Carolinas Medical Center, Mercy Hospital, Presbyterian Hospital, and University Hospital. There are seven specialty hospitals: Charlotte Rehabilitation Hospital, Amethyst Treatment Center (for substance abuse and addiction), Charter Pines Hospital, CPC Cedar Spring Hospital, Mecklenburg Mental Health Hospital, Orthopaedic Hospital, and Presbyterian Specialty Hospital for Eye, Ear, Nose, and Throat.

Health

Deaths—Total 2,549
Rate per 1,000 7.7
Infant Deaths—Total 53
Rate per 1,000 10.6
Number of Metro Hospitals 8
Number of Metro Hospital Beds 2,120
Rate per 100,000 602
Number of Physicians 1,454
Physicians per 1,000 1.41
Nurses per 1,000 8.15
Health Expenditures per Capita $6.43

Transportation

Charlotte is approached by two interstates, I-77 and I-85, that intersect in the city; I-40 is only half an hour away. Other highways serving the city are U.S. 21, 29, 74, and 521, and State Highways 16, 27, 49, 51, and 160. Norfolk Southern and CSX Transportation serve Charlotte, as does Amtrak. Charlotte/Douglas International Airport, about 20 minutes from downtown, handles domestic and international flights.

Transportation

Interstate Highway Mileage 33
Total Urban Mileage 2,144
Total Daily Vehicle Mileage (in millions) 10.58
Daily Average Commute Time 44.4 min.
Number of Buses 86
Port Tonnage (in millions) NA
Airports 1
Number of Daily Flights 311
Daily Average Number of Passengers 18,913

Airlines (American carriers only)
Air Virginia
American
Delta
Eastern
Ozark
TransWorld
United
USAir

Housing

The trend for residential growth has been to the eastern, southeastern, and southern sections, but the northeast is increasing in popularity because of the university presence. Interstate 77 is stimulating more residential development to the north and northwest. The median price for a new home was $81,300 in 1990, and the median monthly rent $377. About 55% of the total housing stock was owner-occupied. Five minutes from the center of the city is Dilworth, an area of large, traditional homes centered around Latta Park. The Fourth Ward neighborhood is being revitalized though the construction of Victorian-style homes and condominiums. The Third Ward, in the southwest quadrant, is undergoing similar development.

Housing

Total Housing Units 170,430
% Change 1980–1990 27.2
Vacant Units for Sale or Rent 9,616
Occupied Units 158,991
% with More Than One Person per Room 3.3
% Owner-Occupied 55
Median Value of Owner-Occupied Homes $81,300
Average Monthly Purchase Cost $352
Median Monthly Rent $377
New Private Housing Starts NA
Value (in thousands) NA
% Single-Family NA
Nonresidential Buildings Value (in thousands) NA

Housing (continued)		
Tallest Buildings	*Hgt. (ft.)*	*Stories*
Nations Bank Corp. Center (1992)	870	60
One First Union Center (1988)	580	42
Nations Bank Plaza (1974)	503	40
Interstate Tower (1990)	462	32
Two First Union Center (1971)	433	32
Wachovia Center (1974)	420	32
Carillon (1991)	394	24
Charlotte Plaza (1982)	388	27
First Citizens Plaza (1987)	320	23

Urban Redevelopment

 In 1961 Charlotte began the construction of the Governmental Center, an urban-renewal complex that replaced the city's worst slum. Two other major projects followed, the 25,000-seat Coliseum and 2,500-seat Oven Auditorium. Spirit Square, located in the historic 1909 First Baptist Church, has helped to revitalize uptown.

Crime

There were 8,762 incidents of violent crime known to police in 1991 and 42,140 incidents involving property.

Crime	
Violent Crimes—Total	8,762
Violent Crime Rate per 100,000	1,159.2
Murder	114
Rape	409
Robbery	2,899
Aggravated Assaults	5,340
Property Crimes	42,140
Burglary	11,615
Larceny	27,799
Motor Vehicle Theft	2,726
Arson	444
Per Capita Police Expenditures	$90.2
Per Capita Fire Protection Expenditures	$70.32
Number of Police	608
Per 1,000	1.81

Religion

Many of Charlotte's first settlers were Presbyterians at a time when the Church of England was dominant in this part of the British colonies. Not until 1771, however, were Presbyterians permitted to perform marriage ceremonies. Presbyterians remain prominent, but most other Protestant denominations, as well as Catholics, are well represented in Mecklenburg County.

Religion	
Largest Denominations (Adherents)	
Catholic	27,017
American Zion	39,794
Presbyterian	39,689
Southern Baptist	71,259
United Methodist	40,876

Religion (continued)	
Black Baptist	35,754
Episcopal	9,071
American Baptist	8,117
Evangelical Lutheran	7,896
Jewish	2,105

Media

 The city daily is the *Charlotte Observer*, whose first edition appeared in 1869. The electronic media consist of 5 television stations (3 commercial, 1 independent, 1 public), and 14 AM and FM radio stations.

Media
Newsprint
Charlotte Magazine, monthly
Charlotte Observer, daily
The Charolotte Post, weekly
Television
WBTV (Channel 3)
WCCB (Channel 18)
WCNC (Channel 36)
WSOC (Channel 9)
WTVI (Channel 42)
Radio

WAQS (AM)	WAQQ (FM)
WBT (AM)	WBT (FM)
WCNT (AM)	WFAE (FM)
WGIV (AM)	WGSP (AM)
WHVN (AM)	WRFX (FM)
WTDR (FM)	WWMG (FM)
WSOC (FM)	WYFQ (AM)

Sports

 Charlotte has one major professional sports team: the Charlotte Hornets, a franchise of the National Basketball Association. Baseball is represented by the Charlotte O's, an AA minor league team in the Baltimore Orioles farm system.

Arts, Culture, and Tourism

Performing and visual arts come together at Spirit Square in uptown, where the Charlotte Symphony and Charlotte Opera are located. The North Carolina Blumenthal Performing Arts Center opened in 1992. Theater is represented by ACE Charlotte Repertory Theater, the city's first and only resident equity theater company; Little Theater of Charlotte; Piedmont Community College's Summer Theater; and Children's Theater of Charlotte.

City museums include the Mint Museum of Art on Randolph Road, housed in the relocated and reconstructed mint that opened in Charlotte in 1835; Nature Museum, a science museum geared to children's interests; and Discovery Place on North Tryon Street, offering a rain forest, aquarium, and planetarium.

Travel and Tourism

Hotel Rooms   14,522
Convention and Exhibit Space (square feet)   134,000

Convention Centers
   Charlotte Convention Center
   Coliseum
   Owens Auditorium

Festivals
   Spring Fest
   600 Festival (May)
   Festival in Hi-Park (f all)
   Greek Yaisou Festival
   UNCC International Festival

Parks and Recreation

Charlotte has over 100 parks, of which the 9 largest cover more than 2,100 acres. The 760-acre Latta Plantation Park, northwest of town, is a nature preserve with a raptor center and Audubon sanctuary. The park takes its name from James Latta, who built a plantation there in the 1800s; the home is now a museum.

Sources of Further Information

Charlotte Chamber of Commerce
129 West Trade Street
Charlotte, NC 28202
(704) 378-1300

Charlotte Convention & Visitors Bureau
122 East Stonewall Street
Charlotte, NC 28202-2853
(704) 334-2282

Charlotte-Mecklenburg Government Center
600 East Fourth Street
Charlotte, NC 28202
(704) 336-2244

Charlotte-Mecklenburg Planning Commission
600 East Fourth Street
Charlotte, NC 28202-2853
(704) 336-2302

Additional Reading

Blythe, LeGette, and Charles Raven Brockmann. *Hornet's Nest: The Story of Charlotte and Mecklenburg County.* 1961.
Faillard, Frye. *The Dream Long Deferred.* 1988.
Kratt, Mary Norton. *Charlotte: Spirit of the New South.* 1992.

Cheyenne

Wyoming

Basic Data

Name   Cheyenne
Name Origin   From Shahiyena Indians
Year Founded   1867 Inc. 1867
Status: State   Capital of Wyoming
        County   Seat of Laramie County
Area (square miles)   18.8
Elevation (feet)   6,100
Time Zone   Mountain
Population (1990)   50,008
Population of Metro Area (1990)   73,142

Sister Cities
   Taichung City, China

Distance in Miles To:

Atlanta	1,482
Boston	1,923
Chicago	981
Dallas	881
Denver	100
Detroit	1,235
Houston	1,111
Los Angeles	1,124
Miami	2,153
New York	1,754
Philadelphia	1,763
Washington, DC	1,636

Location and Topography

N

Cheyenne is located on high plains in the southeastern corner of Wyoming, just east of the Laramie Range. The state's capital and seat of Laramie County is 10 miles north of Wyoming's border with Colorado and 30 miles west of the Nebraska border. Denver is 100 miles south of Cheyenne.

Layout of City and Suburbs

Cheyenne's streets were originally laid out to parallel the tracks of the Union Pacific, the transcontinental railroad that was constructed through the region in 1867. Union Pacific railroad tracks and the streets ran diagonal to the main compass points. Later extensions to the city were platted with regular compass points as a result of which the old and new roads seem awkward where they intersect. The heart of the city is at Warren and Central avenues. The State Capitol is on Capitol Avenue between Carey and Central avenues and 24th and 25th streets.

Environment

Environmental Stress Index   3.6
Green Cities Index: Rank   NA
                    Score   NA
Water Quality   Neutral, very soft
     Average Daily Use (gallons per capita)   224
     Maximum Supply (gallons per capita)   603
Parkland as % of Total City Area   NA
% Waste Landfilled/Recycled   NA
Annual Parks Expenditures per Capita $34.41

Climate

The Laramie Range, 30 miles west of the city, deflects winds from the northwest back to the west and then east, to produce a Chinook effect, warming the cold air in winter. Prevailing winds and Cheyenne's elevation of 6,100

Weather

Temperature

Highest Monthly Average °F   83.1
Lowest Monthly Average °F   14.8

Annual Averages

Days 32°F or Below   171
Days above 90°F   7
Zero Degree Days   8

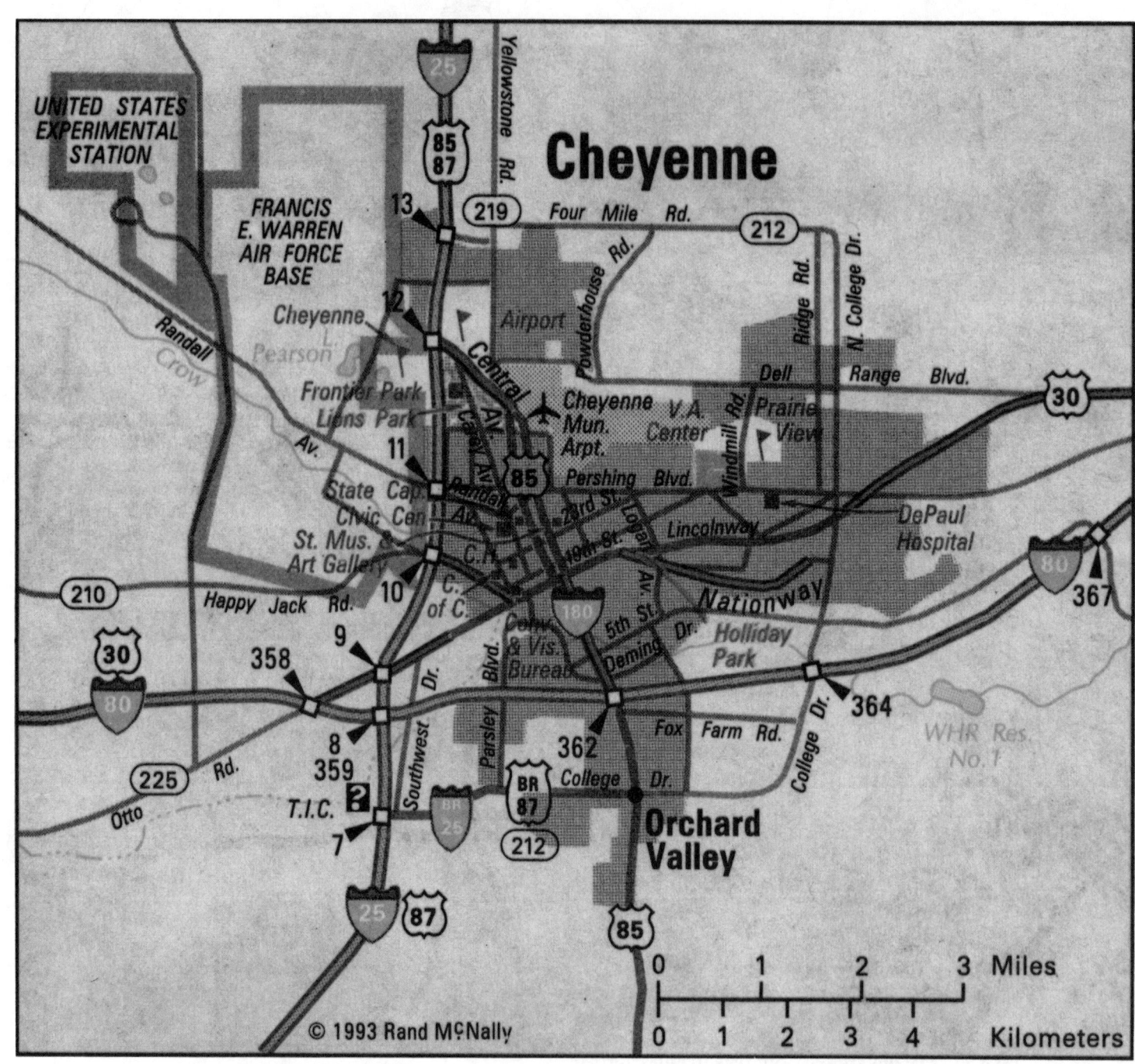

From the *Road Atlas* © 1993 by Rand McNally R.L. 93-S-92.

Weather (continued)

Precipitation (inches) 13.31
Snow (inches) 54.1
% Seasonal Humidity 54.0
Wind Speed (m.p.h.) 12.9
Clear Days 106
Cloudy Days 132
Storm Days 66
Rainy Days 122

Average Temperatures (°F)	High	Low	Mean
January	36.2	13.8	25.0
February	49.3	23.1	36.2
March	48.2	24.5	36.4
April	52.5	29.6	41.1
May	64.5	40.3	52.4
June	74.8	50.2	62.5
July	81.5	53.9	67.7
August	80.5	54.8	67.7
September	71.3	44.6	58.0
October	60.3	31.8	46.1
November	41.2	22.1	31.7
December	43.8	19.3	31.6

feet, combine to create wide daily temperature fluctuations of up to 30°F. Annual snowfall averages about 54 inches and rain about 13 inches.

History

The Cheyenne region was the domain of an Algonquian tribe of Plains Indians of the same name. Fort Laramie to the north and east had long been a stopover for wagon trains headed west on the Oregon Trail, but it was not until the late 1800s that the Cheyenne area attracted the interest of whites. Major General Grenville M. Dodge, a surveyor for the Union Pacific Railroad, passed through the Cheyenne area in 1865 while scouting a route for the transcontinental railway. In October 1867 Dodge chose the site of Cheyenne as the winter terminus for the railroad. By November there were 4,000 inhabitants and some 300 businesses. Some undesirable elements, including land sharks and gamblers, were also attracted to the tent city.

In addition to the railroad as an economic base in Cheyenne, the U.S. Army established Fort D. A. Russell just northwest of the town. Cheyenne quickly became a center for the region's rapidly growing livestock business.

Wyoming was still a part of Dakota Territory in 1867 when Cheyenne was organized. Cheyenne received its charter a year later, in January 1868. In 1869 Wyoming Territory was established with Cheyenne as its capital and the city received its second city charter.

Cheyenne earned a reputation as a wild, dangerous western town and mayhem and violence were accepted as a part of life. By the 1870s Cheyenne became noted as the center of the area's ranching business, which raised cattle for the European beef market. The discovery of gold in the Black Hills in 1874 brought more wealth as Cheyenne merchants supplied miners and prospectors with provisions and equipment.

Gentlemen ranchers established the Cheyenne Club in 1880 and members had an elegant three-story refuge occupying a block of downtown built for themselves, which had tennis courts, a restaurant, billiards, and smoking rooms.

The cattle industry was destroyed during the severe winters of 1886 and 1887 when the temperatures dropped so low most of the cattle froze to death; it was years before the industry recovered. Citizens surviving the winter decided to celebrate and held the first gathering in 1886 of what was to become Wyoming's biggest tourist event, Cheyenne Frontier Days.

In 1930 the name of Fort D. A. Russell was changed to Fort Francis A. Warren, and in 1957 it became the base for the first Atlas intercontinental ballistic missile.

Historical Landmarks

The Union Pacific was responsible for the birth of Cheyenne. Its railroad shops and yards occupy a 470-acre tract in downtown Cheyenne. The Union Pacific Depot, completed in 1886, is being renovated and will be the site of the Wyoming Transportation Museum; it is expected to be completed in 1995. St. Mary's Cathedral on the corner of Capitol Avenue and 21st Street, built in 1917, is the largest church in Wyoming. The State Capitol building is three and a half stories tall. It was designed in 1887 by D. W. Gibbs.

Population

Cheyenne has one of the smallest populations of any capital city at 50,008 in 1990. The population grew by 14.6% from 40,914 in 1970 to 47,283 in 1980 and then by a further 5.8% during the 1980s.

Population

	1980	1990
Central City	47,283	50,008
Rank	451	491
Metro Area	68,649	73,142
Pop. Change 1980–1990 +2,725		
Pop. % Change 1980–1990 +5.8		
Median Age 33.3		
% Male 48.9		
% Age 65 and Over 12.04		
Density (per square mile) 2,660		

Households

Number 20,243
Persons per Household 2.44
% Female-Headed Households 10.3
% One-Person Households 28.4
Births—Total 1,037
   % to Mothers under 20 15.8
   Birth Rate per 1,000 20.4

Ethnic Composition

In 1990 whites composed 89.61% of the population, blacks 3.12%, Hispanics, both black and white, 11.8%, Asians and Pacific Islanders 1.17%, others 5.4%, and American Indians 0.7%.

Chronology

1867 Major General Grenville M. Dodge chooses Cheyenne as winter terminus of the Union Pacific. Fort D. A. Russell is established.

1868 Cheyenne is named seat of Laramie County.

1869 Cheyenne is named capital of Wyoming Territory.

1874 Gold discovered in the Black Hills.

1882 Electric lights are installed.

1886 A day-long rodeo sets the tradition that becomes Frontier Days. Ground broken for state capitol; completed in 1890.

1890 Wyoming becomes the 44th state.

1930 Fort D. A. Russell's name is changed to Fort Francis E. Warren.

1957 The first Atlas intercontinental ballistic missile base is established.

Ethnic Composition (as % of total pop.)

	1980	1990
White	91.61	89.61
Black	2.97	3.12
American Indian	0.52	0.7
Asian and Pacific Islander	0.80	1.17
Hispanic	11.38	11.82
Other	NA	5.4

Government

Cheyenne is governed under a mayor-council form of government. The mayor and the nine council members serve four-year terms.

Government

Year of Home Charter   1971
Number of Members of the Governing Body   10
Elected at Large   1
Elected by Wards   9
Number of Women in Governing Body   1
Salary of Mayor   NA
Salary of Council Members   NA
City Government Employment Total   754
Rate per 10,000   139.7

Public Finance

The annual budget consists of revenues of $45 million and expenditures of $42.765 million. The debt outstanding is $80.241 million and cash and security holdings of $55.245 million.

Public Finance

Total Revenue (in millions) $45.0
Intergovernmental Revenue—Total (in millions) $21.57
Federal Revenue per Capita $2.67
% Federal Assistance   5.9
% State Assistance   12.9
Sales Tax as % of Total Revenue   NA
Local Revenue as % of Total Revenue   47.41
City Income Tax   no
Taxes—Total (in millions) $2.9

Taxes per Capita
   Total $54
   Property $26
   Sales and Gross Receipts $22
General Expenditures—Total (in millions) $37.8
General Expenditures per Capita $700
Capital Outlays per Capita $234

% of Expenditures for:

   Public Welfare   0.0
   Highways   9.3
   Education   0.0
   Health and Hospitals   2.2
   Police   10.0
   Sewerage and Sanitation   24.6
   Parks and Recreation   5.6
   Housing and Community Development   5.9
Debt Outstanding per Capita $1,335
   % Utility   35.4
Federal Procurement Contract Awards (in millions) $13.4
Federal Grants Awards (in millions) $53.8
Fiscal Year Begins   July 1

Economy

Cheyenne was one of the most prosperous towns in the late 19th century, but generally failed to expand beyond its agricultural and mining sectors in the 20th century. As a result it has only limited manufacturing strength, and its economy is dependent on cattle and sheep raising, the primary economic activities. The state government and Warren Air Force Base are among the largest employers. Among the manufacturing output are electronic products, precision instruments, and restaurant equipment.

Economy

Total Money Income (in millions) $584.224
% of State Average   110.7
Per Capita Annual Income $10,827
% Population below Poverty Level   7.8
Fortune 500 Companies   NA

Banks	Number	Deposits (in millions)
Commercial	7	332.2
Savings	6	289.5

Passenger Autos   51,264
Electric Meters   29,050
Gas Meters   23,691

Manufacturing

Number of Establishments   30
% with 20 or More Employees   36.7
Manufacturing Payroll (in millions)   NA
Value Added by Manufacture (in millions)   NA
Value of Shipments (in millions)   NA
New Capital Expenditures (in millions)   NA

Economy (continued)

Wholesale Trade

Number of Establishments   89
Sales (in millions) $173.7
Annual Payroll (in millions) $12.560

Retail Trade

Number of Establishments   612
Total Sales (in millions) $429.3
Sales per Capita $7,956
Number of Retail Trade Establishments with Payroll   401
Annual Payroll (in millions) $53.8
Total Sales (in millions) $420.4
General Merchandise Stores (per capita)   NA
Food Stores (per capita) $1,117
Apparel Stores (per capita)   NA
Eating and Drinking Places (per capita) $858

Service Industries

Total Establishments   461
Total Receipts (in millions) $128.6
Hotels and Motels (in millions) $20.2
Health Services (in millions) $39.2
Legal Services (in millions)   NA

Labor

 The largest employer in Cheyenne is Warren Air Force Base and the second-largest employer is the State of Wyoming. Although the population grew in the 1980s, the work force did not grow proportionately, declining by 3%. Reduction in public spending by federal and state authorities was cited as the reason for this decline.

Labor

Civilian Labor Force   26,760
% Change 1989–1990   1.9
Work Force Distribution
Mining   NA
Construction   NA
Manufacturing   NA
Transportation and Public Utilities   NA
Wholesale and Retail Trade   NA
FIRE (Finance, Insurance, Real Estate)   NA
Service   NA
Government   NA
Women as % of Labor Force   44.1
% Self-Employed   5.3
% Professional/Technical   17.6
Total Unemployment   1,318
Rate %   4.9
Federal Government Civilian Employment   1,491

Education

Laramie County School District supports 27 elementary schools, 3 junior high schools, and 3 senior high schools. Laramie County Community College in Cheyenne has a two-year degree program, and although there is no four-year college in the city, the University of Wyoming is in Laramie, 45 miles to the west.

Education

Number of Public Schools   33
Special Education Schools   NA
Total Enrollment   13,175
% Enrollment in Private Schools   NA
% Minority   NA
Classroom Teachers   NA
Pupil-Teacher Ratio   NA
Number of Graduates   NA
Total Revenue (in millions)   NA
Total Expenditures (in millions)   NA
Expenditures per Pupil   NA
Educational Attainment (Age 25 and Over)   NA
    % Completed 12 or More Years   79.6
    % Completed 16 or More Years   18.9
Four-Year Colleges and Universities   NA
    Enrollment   NA
Two-Year Colleges   1
    Enrollment   2,822

Libraries

Number   13
Public Libraries   3
Books (in thousands)   148
Circulation (in thousands)   470
Persons Served (in thousands)   73
Circulation per Person Served   6.43
Income (in millions) $1.045
Staff   29

Four-Year Colleges and Universities
    NA

Health

 The Cheyenne area has two civilian hospitals (Memorial Hospital and DePaul Hospital) and two federal hospitals (a base hospital at Warren Air Force Base and a Veterans Administration hospital). The Southeast Wyoming Mental Health Center and three smaller clinics are also located here.

Health

Deaths—Total   447
Rate per 1,000   8.8
Infant Deaths—Total   12
Rate per 1,000   11.6
Number of Metro Hospitals   4
Number of Metro Hospital Beds   487
Rate per 100,000   903
Number of Physicians   129
Physicians per 1,000   NA
Nurses per 1,000   NA
Health Expenditures per Capita $27.02

Transportation

 Cheyenne is approached from the north and south by I-25 and the east-west I-80. Amtrak has passenger rail service to Cheyenne and rail freight service is provided by Burlington Northern and Union Pacific. The principal air terminal is Cheyenne Airport.

Transportation

Interstate Highway Mileage   13
Total Urban Mileage   363
Total Daily Vehicle Mileage (in millions)   0.875
Daily Average Commute Time   31.2 min.
Number of Buses   NA
Port Tonnage (in millions)   NA
Airports   1
Number of Daily Flights   3
Daily Average Number of Passengers   14

Airlines (American carriers only)
   Continental
   Northwest
   United

Housing

 Of the total 1991 housing stock of 21,859 units, 63.9% were owner-occupied. The median value of an owner-occupied home was $68,700 and the median monthly rent was $316.

Urban Redevelopment

 Environmental concerns have dampened urban redevelopment in recent years. Development projects are coordinated by Cheyenne Development, Industrial Development Association of Cheyenne, Cheyenne Downtown Association, and Cheyenne Department of Planning.

Housing

Total Housing Units   21,859
% Change 1980–1990   10.3
Vacant Units for Sale or Rent   1,289
Occupied Units   20,243
% with More Than One Person per Room   1.8
% Owner-Occupied   63.9
Median Value of Owner-Occupied Homes $68,700
Average Monthly Purchase Cost $350
Median Monthly Rent $316
New Private Housing Starts   49
Value (in thousands) $4,366
% Single-Family   100
Nonresidential Buildings Value (in thousands) $5,573

Crime

 Despite its lawless past, Cheyenne is today one of the most law-abiding cities in the nation. In 1991 there were 98 violent crimes known to police and 3,103 crimes involving property, including 304 burglaries.

Crime

Violent Crimes—Total   98
Violent Crime Rate per 100,000   237.2
Murder   4
Rape   13
Robbery   19

Crime (continued)

Aggravated Assaults   62
Property Crimes   3,103
Burglary   304
Larceny   2,714
Motor Vehicle Theft   85
Arson   5
Per Capita Police Expenditures $77.8
Per Capita Fire Protection Expenditures $57.43
Number of Police   83
Per 1,000   1.68

Religion

 Catholics make up the largest population of Laramie County, with the balance distributed among the major Protestant denominations. As in other western states, religious institutions took a firm hold in Cheyenne only after the wild frontier days had ended.

Religion

Largest Denominations (Adherents)	
Catholic	12,692
Southern Baptist	2,760
American Baptist	2,693
Latter-Day Saints	2,648
United Methodist	2,561
Lutheran-Missouri Synod	1,839
Jewish	230

Media

 Cheyenne press consists of the *Wyoming Eagle* and the *Wyoming State Tribune*. The electronic media consist of two television stations and seven AM and FM radio stations.

Media

Newsprint
   Wyoming State Tribune, daily
Television
   KGWN (Channel 5)
   KLWY (Channel 27)
Radio
   KFBC (AM)   KFBQ (FM)
   KLEN (FM)   KRAE (AM)
   KSHY (AM)   KUUY (AM)
   KKAZ (FM)

Sports

 Cheyenne does not have any major professional sports team, but prides itself on being the home of Frontier Days, one of the biggest events on the professional rodeo circuit. The celebration of cowboy athleticism is held the last full week of each July.

Arts, Culture, and Tourism

 Theater arts flourish at the Mary Godfrey Playhouse, home of the Cheyenne Little Theater. Cheyenne Civic Center stages performances by Broadway touring companies and the Cheyenne Symphony Orchestra. Among Cheyenne's museums are the Wyoming State Museum and the Wyoming State Art Gallery located in the Barrett Building at 24th and Central avenues. Cheyenne's Frontier Days has its own museum on the grounds of the Frontier Park Arena with rodeo memorabilia from its early days. The red sandstone Union Pacific Depot, at the intersection of 15th and Capitol streets, is being renovated and will house the Wyoming Transportation Museum. The history of Fort D. A. Russell is displayed at the F. E. Warren Museum at Warren Air Force Base.

Travel and Tourism

Hotel Rooms NA

Convention and Exhibit Space (square feet) NA

Convention Centers
   NA

Festivals
   Cheyenne Frontier Days (July)
   Laramie County Fair (August)
   Cheyenne Youth Rodeo (September)
   Volksmarch (June)
   Crow Creek Rendezvous (May)

Parks and Recreation

 Cheyenne maintains 15 city parks including Lions Park, which adjoins Frontier Park on the east and includes Botanic Gardens, and Holliday Park at 17th and Morrie Avenue, which includes the Cheyenne Artist Guild.

Sources of Further Information

Cheyenne Area Convention & Visitor's Bureau
309 West Lincoln Way
Cheyenne, WY 82001
(307) 778-3133

City Hall
2101 O'Neil Avenue
Cheyenne, WY 82001
(307) 637-6300

Greater Cheyenne Chamber of Commerce
301 West 16th Street
Cheyenne, WY 82001
(307) 638-3388

Additional Reading

Adams, Judith A. *Cheyenne, City of the Blue Sky*. 1988.
Dial, Scott. *A Place to Raise Hell: Cheyenne Saloons*. 1977.
Field, Shirley Lass, ed. *History of Cheyenne, Wyoming*. 1989.
Jones, Gladys Powelson. *Cheyenne, Cheyenne, Our Blue-collar Heritage*. 1983.
Larson, T. A. *History of Wyoming*. 1978 (2d ed. rev.).

Chicago

Illinois

Basic Data

Name   Chicago
Name Origin   From Indian word *chicagou* meaning
   "strong" or "powerful"
Year Founded   1830 Inc. 1837
Status: State   Illinois
      County   Seat of Cook County
Area (square miles)   227.3
Elevation (feet)   595
Time Zone   Central
Population (1990)   2,783,726
Population of Metro Area (1990)   6,069,974

Sister Cities

   Accra, Ghana
   Casablanca
   Goteburg, Sweden
   Kiev, Ukraine
   Milan, Italy
   Osaka, Japan
   Prague, Czech and Slovak Federal Republic
   Shenyang, China
   Warsaw, Poland

Distance in Miles To:

Atlanta	708
Boston	994
Cleveland	348
Dallas	921
Denver	1,021
Detroit	279
Houston	1,091
Los Angeles	2,048
Miami	1,397
New York	809
Philadelphia	785
Washington, DC	709

Location and Topography

N The nation's third-largest city (after New York and Los Angeles), Chicago is also the seat of Cook County. Situated on the southwest shore of Lake Michigan, Chicago has a flat terrain that is only a few feet above the level of the lake. Dividing the city east and west is the Chicago River, whose direction of flow was reversed in 1900 when it was linked to the Sanitary & Ship Canal.

Layout of City and Suburbs

Chicago's Lake Michigan shoreline is 25 miles long; three-quarters of it is occupied by parks. The streets form a grid and the city's street numbering system starts downtown at the intersection of State, which runs north and south, and Madison, which runs east and west. Streets are identified east or west of State, and north or south of Madison. Lake Shore Drive runs the length of Chicago's Lake Michigan shoreline.

Downtown is known as the Loop, possibly because the area was encompassed by an elevated train built in 1897. The Loop is a rectangle stretching for 16 blocks south of the Chicago River and 8 blocks east of the south branch of the river. State Street crosses the east fringe of the Loop from north to south. North of the Chicago River, Michigan Avenue is called the Magnificent Mile because of its elegant stores, hotels, restaurants, and offices.

In contrast to downtown, North Side, stretching 9 miles north and 13 miles northwest, is almost entirely residential. The section closest to downtown is called Near North Side and includes Gold Coast, beginning at Oak Street. Northwest of Gold Coast is the high-rise apartment complex known as Carl Sandburg Village, named in honor of the poet who called Chicago the "City of the Big Shoulders." Old Town, with its elegant gift shops, night clubs, restaurants, and restored homes, is northwest of Gold Coast. Southwest of Old Town is the bleak Cabrini-Green Homes project.

To the west of Lincoln Park, Mid-North Side begins with a restored community known as New Town. There are other upscale neighborhoods in North Side, such as Edgebrook and Sauganash on the Far North-

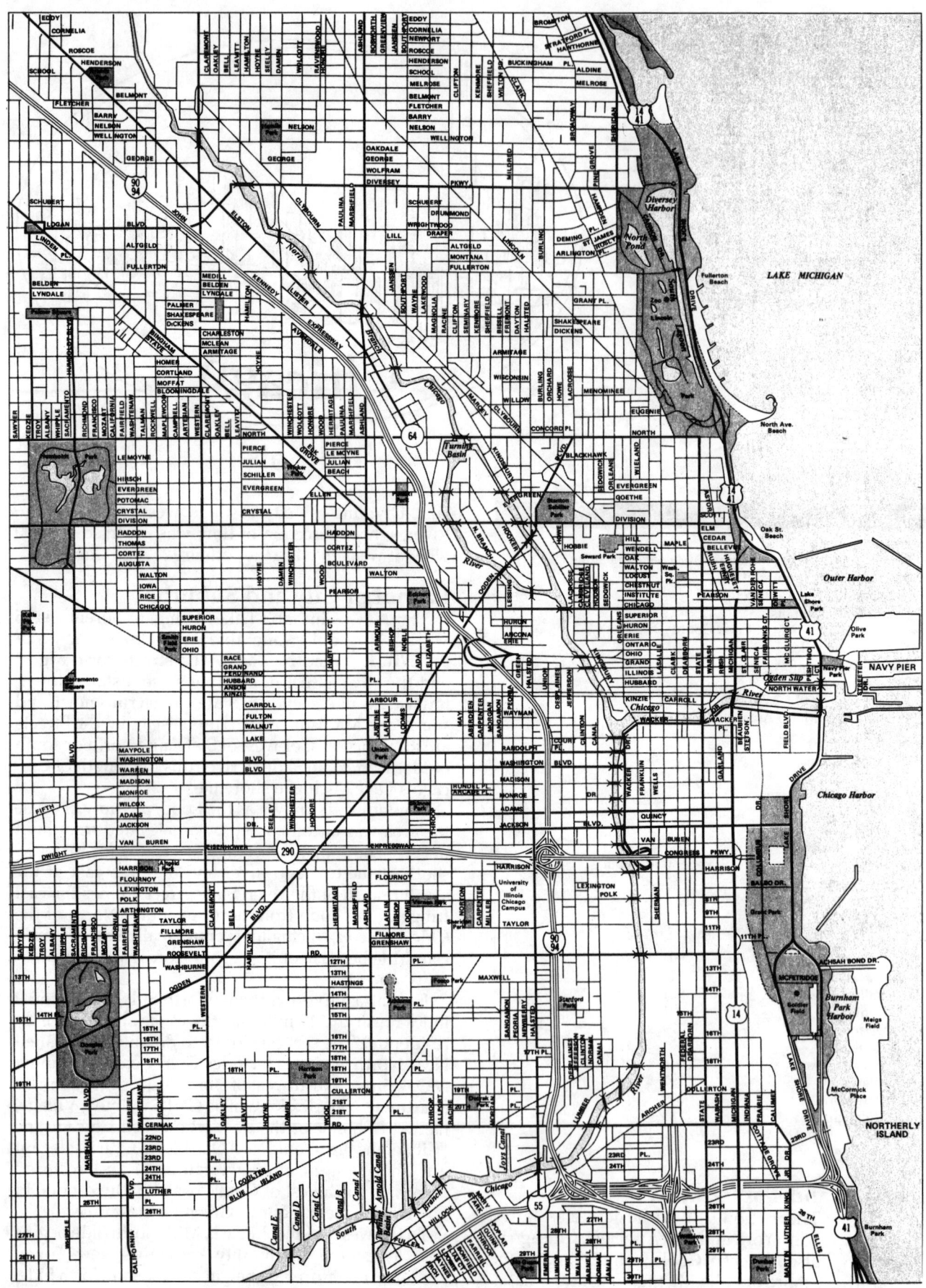

west Side. Running diagonally across North Side and into Northwest is Milwaukee Avenue, an old Indian trail. The John F. Kennedy Expressway cuts through North Side to link O'Hare International Airport in the northwest corner with the Near Northwest Side.

The West Side is west of the Loop between Grand Avenue on the north and the Chicago Sanitary & Ship Canal on the south. One of the city's principal industrial districts is along the canal; however, many factories and businesses have moved elsewhere in recent years. The Dwight D. Eisenhower Expressway (I-290) cuts through West Side between the Loop and the western suburbs. It passes through the University of Illinois at Chicago and the West Side Medical Center, the world's largest medical complex, which has seven hospitals and two medical schools.

South Side is the largest section in terms of area and population. Except for a few integrated communities such as Hyde Park, Morgan Park, and Beverly, most are segregated.

The Chicago Skyway, an elevated toll road, crosses the industrial southeast side from Dan Ryan Expressway to the Indiana border. Chinatown and Bridgeport are in the southwest; the Union Stock Yards, which closed in 1971, were also in this area.

Satellite cities form a semicircle around Chicago. The largest are (from south to north) Joliet, Aurora, Elgin, and Waukegan. Along the lakeshore north of the city are affluent suburbs from Evanston to Lake Forest.

As the city expanded, the Indiana towns of Hammond, East Chicago, and Gary became virtual suburbs of Chicago. Other towns such as Skokie, Arlington Heights, Northbrook, and Schaumburg have also come within its orbit.

Environment

Environmental Stress Index 3.0
Green Cities Index: Rank 60
                   Score 39.42
Water Quality Alkaline, fluoridated
    Average Daily Use (gallons per capita) NA
    Maximum Supply (gallons per capita) NA
Parkland as % of Total City Area 0.4
% Waste Landfilled/Recycled NA
Annual Parks Expenditures per Capita $13.81

Climate

Chicago has a continental climate. Winters are cold, with temperatures frequently dropping below freezing, and heavy snowfall occurs as cold air fronts move off Lake Michigan. Summers are relatively hot, with temperatures frequently over 95°F, but cooler along the lake's shore. Summer thunderstorms are heavy but variable. Although Chicago is called the Windy City, winds are not a regular feature. What wind there is, however, is channeled among tall buildings downtown.

Weather

Temperature

Highest Monthly Average °F   84.4
Lowest Monthly Average °F   17.0

Annual Averages

Days 32°F or Below   119
Days above 90°F   21
Zero Degree Days   7
Precipitation (inches)   34
Snow (inches)   40
% Seasonal Humidity   67
Wind Speed (m.p.h.)   10.4
Clear Days   94
Cloudy Days   168
Storm Days   40
Rainy Days   123

Average Temperatures (°F)	High	Low	Mean
January	31.5	17.0	24.3
February	34.6	20.2	27.4
March	44.6	29.0	36.8
April	59.3	40.4	49.9
May	70.3	49.7	60.0
June	80.5	60.3	70.5
July	84.4	65.0	74.7
August	83.3	64.1	73.7
September	75.8	56.0	65.9
October	65.1	45.6	55.4
November	48.1	32.6	40.4
December	35.3	21.6	28.5

History

Chicago was known as Checagou to the Indians because of the strong garlic smells from its swamps. In 1673 seven Frenchmen—Louis Jolliet, Father Jacques Marquette, and five canoeists—visited the site. Returning to Mackinac after exploring the Mississippi River as a possible route to the Pacific, they ascended the Illinois and Des Plaines rivers, portaged across swamps in the southwestern section of the present city, and paddled down the South Branch and Chicago rivers into Lake Michigan. In 1696 Father Pinet, a Jesuit, found Miami Indians living in the area as new arrivals.

In 1763 the valley passed into British hands, and the Jay Treaty of 1794 between the United States and Britain transferred control of the region to the United States. Indians who signed the 1795 Treaty of Greenville with the United States ceded, among other territories, a piece of land six miles square at the mouth of the Chicago River. Ten years passed before the new nation tried to occupy the territory.

In 1803 Captain John Whistler arrived from Detroit with his family and 69 officers and men. At the narrow bend of the river, which curved sharply before entering Lake Michigan, they built Fort Dearborn, named after President Thomas Jefferson's secretary of war, Henry Dearborn. Across the river from Fort Dearborn were four cabins, the oldest of which had been built by Frenchman Jean Baptiste Point du Sable. He had operated a flourishing trading post, which he sold in 1800 to John Kinzie, who had been hired by John Jacob Astor to buy furs from the Indians.

Chronology

1673 Louis Jolliet, Father Jacques Marquette, and others pass through "Checagou" on their return from the Mississippi Valley.

1696 Father Pinet establishes the Mission of the Guardian Angel to minister to the Miami Indians, recent arrivals in the area.

1763 Region passes into British hands.

1783 Jean Baptiste Point du Sable establishes a fur trading post near the portage of the Chicago River.

1794 Terms of the Jay Treaty between Britain and the United States include passing control of the area to the United States.

1795 By the Treaty of Greenville, Indians cede land at the mouth of the Chicago River to the U.S. government.

1803 Under orders from the War Department, Captain John Whistler and 69 officers and men build Fort Dearborn at the narrow bend of the Chicago River.

1812 On the outbreak of the war with Great Britain, Indians threaten Fort Dearborn. Americans evacuate the fort, and Indians kill 50 of them. Survivors are taken prisoner, and the Potawatomi set fire to the fort.

1818 During the passage of the bill creating the state of Illinois, Representative Nathaniel Pope successfully introduces an amendment to move the Illinois boundary with Wisconsin 40 miles to the north, thus excluding all of Chicago from Wisconsin.

1821 Lewis Cass, governor of Michigan Territory, persuades the Ottawa and Potawatomi Indians to relinquish their claims to the area.

1830 State canal commissioners file survey of a projected Illinois-Michigan Canal and offer land for sale on both sides of the Chicago River.

1831 Chicago is named the seat of Cook County.

1833 Chicago is incorporated as a town with a population of 200.

1835 State floats public debt of $500,000 for the canal.

1837 Chicago is incorporated as a city with William B. Ogden as mayor.

1847 Cyrus McCormick opens factory to manufacture his reaper.

1848 Illinois and Michigan Canal is completed, marking the beginning of Chicago's rise to greatness. The Galena and Chicago Union Railroad begins operations out of Chicago.

1860 Abraham Lincoln is the Republican National Convention nominee for president.

1864 George Pullman builds the first sleeping car.

1867 A sanitary water system is installed.

1868 City installs first blast furnace.

1870 Population numbers 300,000.

1871 Following months of severe drought, the Great Fire destroys practically every building north of Van Buren Street in downtown and the Near North Side. More than 250 people perish.

1880 Landfill along Lake Michigan shore southeast of the city becomes the U.S. Steel South Works.

1882 George Pullman moves his Palace Car Company plant to a new suburban community north of Lake Calumet named after himself.

1886 Labor strife culminates in a bomb explosion in the Haymarket, killing seven.

1889 Jane Addams opens Hull House.

1890 Population passes 1 million mark.

1892 University of Chicago is founded.

1893 Chicago holds Columbian Exposition.

1895 General Electric opens plant in suburban Cicero.

1900 Chicago Drainage Canal opens, reversing the polluting flow of the Chicago River.

1903 Fire at Iroquois Theater claims 586 lives.

1911 Mayor Carter H. Harrison closes the vice district and ends franchise of Washington Park Race Track.

1915 The corrupt administration of William Hale Thompson begins, marking the ascendancy of the Mafia in Chicago politics.

1919 First racial clash between blacks and whites claims 36 lives.

1929 St. Valentine's Day Massacre, in which seven anti–Al Capone gangsters are shot to death, shocks the nation.

1930 Federal government takes over the Chicago Drainage Canal; renamed Sanitary & Ship Canal.

1932 Al Capone is indicted on tax evasion charges and sentenced to 11 years in prison.

During the War of 1812, Indian allies of the British threatened Fort Dearborn, and on 15 August 1812 the fort was evacuated. The commander and his group started south along the lakeshore toward Fort Wayne, but a large band of Potawatomi Indians fell upon the party and killed more than half of them in an action that came to be called the Dearborn Massacre. The next day the Indians set fire to the fort.

A new fort was built in 1816, and in 1818, when Illinois became a state, the region around the fort was included within the Illinois boundary at the last minute. Representative Nathaniel Pope moved Illinois's boundary with Wisconsin 40 miles to the north, which placed Chicago within Illinois rather than Wisconsin.

In 1821 Governor Lewis Cass persuaded the Potawatomi and Ottawa Indians to move out of the area. In 1829 the state commissioned a waterway to link Lake Michigan with the Mississippi River; the northern terminus was to be at Chicago, and blocks of land on both sides of the Chicago River were offered for sale the next year.

As the state became more organized, Chicago was designated the seat of Cook County in 1831. On 5 August 1833, with a population of 200, Chicago was incorporated as a town. Just four years later it was incorporated as a city, and William B. Ogden was elected the first mayor. Chicago's population increased sixfold between 1840 and 1850, and crossed the magic 100,000 mark within another decade. By 1856 citizens anticipated the significance of Chicago history and founded the Chicago Historical Society.

In 1847 Cyrus McCormick opened a factory to produce his reaper, and the city ultimately became a leading center for the manufacture of farm implements. The canal connecting the Mississippi River to the Great Lakes at Chicago was completed in 1848. The city's future as a transportation center was further ensured with the arrival of the first railroad, the Galena and Chicago Union in 1848. Other lines entered during the 1850s, and Chicago eventually became the greatest rail junction in the nation.

Chicago also became the center of the maritime traffic on the Great Lakes. By 1869 more ships entered the Port of Chicago than New York, Philadelphia, Mobile, Baltimore, Charleston, and San Francisco combined.

Trade in grain flourished as the Midwest's agricultural potential was exploited by a burgeoning population. Since cattle and hogs were fed grain, Chicago also became a market for livestock as well as meat packing, eventually surpassing Cincinnati in this respect.

During the 1850s Chicago became the nation's principal lumber market. Further, the city became a major supplier for the railroad industry, producing the first iron rail in 1857. Although the Panic of 1857 struck the city a staggering blow, Chicago was able to attract the Republican National Convention, which nominated Abraham Lincoln for the presidency in 1860.

The Civil War helped lift Chicago out of the recession it had experienced since 1857. The demand for grain and meat rose, and by 1864 cattle merchants bought prairie southwest of the city and opened the mile-square Union Stockyards. In 1867 George Pullman opened a factory to produce railroad sleeping cars. Next year the city's first blast furnace was built. Potter Palmer, Marshall Field, and Levi Leiter began to establish their legendary fortunes as retailers.

By 1871 a large part of Chicago consisted of frame buildings. After months of drought, fire broke out on 8 October. A powerful wind spread the fire, and the heat became so intense that it was felt in Holland, Michigan, 100 miles across the lake. Three and one-third square miles of the city burned, and 250 people died. Nearly a third of the population lost their homes. Although hotels and manufacturing plants were destroyed, most businesses were spared, including lumberyards, factories, the Union Stockyards, and docks along Lake Michigan. Rebuilding began within days under stricter construction codes, and many buildings were replaced by far costlier structures.

More industries were built in Chicago in the 1880s. U.S. Steel built the South Works on landfill along Lake Michigan southeast of the city in 1880. George Pullman, who had built his first railroad sleeping car in 1864, moved his Palace Car Company to Pullman, a new town north of Lake Calumet, in 1882. Chicago annexed the town in 1889. Labor unrest accompanied industrialization. Strikes became common, and when the police tried to break up a meeting of agitators at the Haymarket on 4 May 1886, a bomb thrown into their ranks killed seven. Four labor leaders, including Albert R. Parsons, were hanged for this crime.

By 1890 the city's population exceeded 1 million, and the decade saw the establishment of the Newbery Library and Chicago Public Library, the opening of a Western Electric facility in suburban Cicero, the growth of Sears Roebuck as a mail-order firm, and the development of department stores. Chicago marked the occasion of the 400th anniversary of Columbus's discovery of America by staging the Columbian Exposition of 1893 to showcase its achievements; the exposition drew 21 million visitors.

In 1900 the Chicago Drainage Canal opened, linking the South Branch of the Chicago River with Lockport on the Des Plaines River. This reversed the flow of the Chicago River so that it no longer flowed into Lake Michigan. Instead, it drained south through a series of canals collectively called the Illinois Waterway, eventually reaching the Mississippi River.

In 1903 a fire at the Iroquois Theater took more lives than the Great Fire of 1871. A total of 596 persons died when flames swept through the audience after a stage curtain caught fire. By 1910, 2 million people lived in the city. A master plan called the Wacker Manual led to the development of the lakefront and its park and boulevard system. World War I stimulated growth, and many blacks moved from the Deep South to take advantage of jobs in the Chicago area. A clash between blacks and whites took place in 1919, resulting in 36 deaths and injuries to 537 persons.

The city also experienced growth in a different dimension. During the 1890s a large vice district had become established south of the Loop as far as 22nd Street. While evangelists, reformers, and the Anti-Saloon League attacked the development and a mayor closed the district, the underworld continued to grow and to become a powerful institution, especially during Mayor William Hale Thompson's terms of 1915 to 1923 and 1927 to 1933. His administration coincided with the years of Prohibition from 1920 to 1933. The Unione Siciliana and the Black Hand found Prohibition a fertile field for illicit operations, and rival gangs feuded among themselves. Thugs like John Torrio, Dion O'Banion, Bugs Moran, Jim Colosimo, and Al Capone corrupted judges and policemen and intimidated juries and witnesses. The St. Valentine's Day Massacre in 1929 and other atrocities, however, turned public opinion against mobsters, and Al Capone was convicted in 1932 of income-tax evasion and sentenced to 11 years in prison.

After the market crash of 1929, which hit Chicago particularly hard, the 1930s were a turbulent era for the city. Anton J. Cermak, elected mayor in 1931, was killed in 1933 by an assassin's bullet intended for President-elect Franklin D. Roosevelt. In 1933 Chicago saluted its first century with an exposition designed by noted architect Louis Skidmore, the Century of Progress, on Northerly Island. A year later, bank robber and gunman John Dillinger was shot down by FBI agents in an alley outside the Biograph Theater.

The city prospered during World War II as its factories turned to the production of war materiel. In 1942 scientists working in the city produced the first nuclear chain reaction.

Richard J. Daley was elected mayor in 1955 and held office until his death in 1976. While these years were prosperous for Chicago, Daley was insensitive to political and social changes. He was succeeded by Daleyite Jane Byrne, the city's first woman mayor. Harold Washington, the city's first black mayor, was elected in 1983 and died in office in 1987. Daley's son, Richard M. Daley, became mayor in 1989.

Historical Landmarks

Chicago's public architecture has undergone many cycles. In the late 19th and early 20th centuries, the Chicago School of Architecture, led by Daniel H. Burnham, William LeBaron Jenney, Louis Henri Sullivan, and Frank Lloyd Wright, produced such buildings as the Monadnock Building, the Rookery, Home Insurance Building, and Carson Pirie Scott Store. The 1920s saw the building of the Tribune Tower, Wrigley Building, and Merchandise Mart. In the 1930s the Ludwig Mies van der Rohe style gained the upper hand, exemplified by Crown Hall, Lake Shore Drive Apartments, Federal Center, and Civic Center. More recently the new Chicago style is represented by the twin round apartment buildings of Marina City.

Chicago has three of the world's tallest buildings. The Sears Tower, at 1,454 feet the tallest office building in the world, opened in 1973. The Amoco Building (1,136 feet) was completed in 1974, and the John Hancock Center, at 1,127 feet, was completed in 1969.

The Chicago Civic Center, which opened in 1965, is a massive rectangle of steel and glass that rises 31 stories, or 660 feet, on the north half of the block bounded by Dearborn, Clark, Randolph, and Washington streets. An eternal flame to commemorate the war dead was lighted in the Civic Plaza in 1972.

Directly on Washington Street stands a 50-foot abstract sculpture of dark brown metal made from a design by Pablo Picasso. West of it rises the 21-story office building of the Chicago Temple, which houses the First Methodist Church, founded in 1831. Across Clark Street is the City and County Building, built between 1907 and 1911. Opposite the City and County Building, at the southwest corner of Washington and La Salle streets, the Chicago Stock Exchange stood from 1894 until 1972. The facade of the building designed by Louis Sullivan has been preserved.

The Rookery on La Salle Street is a pioneer example of skyscraper construction. Built in 1886, its court on the ground floor was remodeled by Frank Lloyd Wright in 1905. The Chicago Board of Trade Building on Jackson Boulevard and La Salle Street symbolizes the city's mercantile history and might. Completed in 1930, it is topped by a statue of Ceres, the goddess of grain. The Monadnock Building on the southwest corner of Jackson Boulevard and Dearborn Street is a famous pioneer structure in modern architecture. The Marquette Building on Dearborn Street is notable for its decorations representing early historic figures and events.

At the end of Congress Parkway in Grant Park stands the Buckingham Memorial Fountain, dedicated in 1927; it was a gift to the city from Kate Buckingham. The main pool, 300 feet in diameter, contains four pairs of sea horses. In the center of the pool, three concentric basins rise to a height of 25 feet. From their outer rims spout a series of diminishing water domes. A central column of water rises almost 100 feet above the apex of the highest dome. The Auditorium Building on Michigan Avenue at Congress Parkway is a famous architectural landmark, designed by Dankmar Adler and Louis H. Sullivan. Until it became Roosevelt University in 1946, it consisted of a hotel, auditorium, and offices.

The Prairie Avenue Historic District between 18th and 21st streets became the grandest neighborhood in Chicago after the Great Fire in 1871. The Glessner House, built by the founder of International Harvester, was completed in 1885. The Kimball Mansion was built in 1887 to resemble a 16th-century Breton chateau. Other entrepreneurs who built mansions here include Marshall Field, George M. Pullman, Phillip D. Armour, and T. O. Blackstone.

McCormick Place on East 23rd and the lakefront commemorates Robert R. McCormick of the *Chicago Tribune*. First built in 1960, it burned down in 1967 and was rebuilt in 1970. It is one of the largest convention centers in the nation with three exhibition halls, nine restaurants, and a banquet hall for 20,000 people.

The Stephen A. Douglas Monument is located in a small park at the east end of 35th Street. It is a classical column rising 100 feet above the ground with a 12-foot statue of Douglas at the top. Douglas's body is buried in a marble sarcophagus in a tomb at its circular base.

The Henry B. Clarke House, now on South Indiana Avenue, is a frame building with a square cupola. The oldest building in Chicago, it was built in 1836 at Michigan Avenue and 16th Street, beyond reach of the Great Fire.

On Wacker Drive are the Merchandise Mart, one of the world's largest commercial buildings; the more modern Apparel Center; and Marina City, two circular 60-story apartment buildings. On South Wacker Drive is the 110-story Sears Tower, the world's tallest building.

The Water Tower rises 186 feet above North Michigan Avenue. Built in 1869, it was designed by W. W. Boyington to contain a standpipe 138 feet tall and 3 feet in diameter. It survived the Great Fire and was preserved as a landmark when Michigan Avenue was widened in 1928. The Water Works that it served, built in 1867, stands across the avenue. It is the oldest of the stations that pump water from Lake Michigan.

In Lincoln Park are statues of such historical figures as Robert de la Salle, Giuseppe Garibaldi, and Ulysses S. Grant, as well as the Alarm, a memorial to the Ottawa Indians.

Population

Chicago was one of the great demographic success stories in the 19th century, reaching its first million within 50 years of its founding. After World War II, its growth curve began to dip almost as dramatically. After peaking at around 3.4 million, it declined by 10.8% from 3.369 million in 1970 to 3.005 million in 1980, and then again in the 1980s to fall to 2.783 million in 1990. This loss caused Chicago to fall behind Los Angeles to the rank of third-largest city in the United States. The metro area has not fared much better. It declined slightly in the 1970s and grew by only 0.2% in the 1980s. Demographers believe that the city has reached its maximum carrying capacity and will continue to shrink well into the 21st century.

Population	1980	1990
Central City	3,005,072	2,783,726
Rank	2	3
Metro Area	6,060,401	6,069,974
Pop. Change 1980–1990	-221,346	
Pop. % Change 1980–1990	-7.4	
Median Age	31.3	
% Male	49.9	
% Age 65 and Over	11.9	
Density (per square mile)	12,246	

Households	
Number	1,025,174
Persons per Household	2.67
% Female-Headed Households	19.6
% One-Person Households	32.1
Births—Total	53,912
% to Mothers under 20	19.1
Birth Rate per 1,000	18.0

Ethnic Composition

The ethnic layers of Chicago's resident population follow geographical boundaries more closely than in comparable large cities. The North Side is 90% white, including Hispanic whites, and only 6% black. On the West Side, blacks make up 50%, Hispanics 29%, and the rest are non-Hispanic whites. The South Side is even more heavily black, accounting for 60%. The former Polish majority in the North Side has been dispersed over the suburbs, and this is also the case with the former communities of Italians, Greeks, Jews, Irish, and Ger-

Ethnic Composition (as % of total pop.)	1980	1990
White	49.59	45.39
Black	39.83	39.07
American Indian	0.20	0.25
Asian and Pacific Islander	2.30	3.74
Hispanic	14.05	19.61
Other	NA	11.54

mans. There are nearly-all-black neighborhoods such as Avalon Park, South Shore, and West Side. Overall, whites made up 45.39% of the population in 1990, blacks 39.07%, Hispanics (both black and white) 19.61%, American Indians 0.25%, Asians and Pacific Islanders 3.74%, and other races 11.5%.

Government

Under its 1971 charter, Chicago is governed by a mayor and a city council of 50 aldermen elected to four-year terms. Although Chicago has had a succession of strong mayors this century (not least memorable of whom was Richard J. Daley, who gave new meaning to the word *boss*), the city actually has a weak mayor–strong council form of government. The mayor must obtain the city council's approval on almost all important decisions and appointments. Also, many services provided by city governments in other cities are supplied by state and county governments in Chicago. Welfare services, for example, are administered by the state, and parks, education, and water are administered by semi-autonomous departments.

Government

Year of Home Charter   1971
Number of Members of the Governing Body   50
Elected at Large   NA
Elected by Wards   50
Number of Women in Governing Body   5
Salary of Mayor $80,000
Salary of Council Members $27,600
City Government Employment Total   45,260
Rate per 10,000   150.4

Public Finance

The annual budget consists of revenues of $3.776 billion and expenditures of $3.408 billion. The debt outstanding is $4.297 billion, and cash and security holdings are $6.597 billion.

Public Finance

Total Revenue (in millions) $3,776.971
Intergovernmental Revenue—Total (in millions) $752.15
Federal Revenue per Capita $265.0
% Federal Assistance   7.03
% State Assistance   10.49
Sales Tax as % of Total Revenue   22.01
Local Revenue as % of Total Revenue   62.77
City Income Tax   no
Taxes—Total (in millions) $1,160.4

Taxes per Capita
    Total $386
    Property $132
    Sales and Gross Receipts $214
General Expenditures—Total (in millions) $1,992.2
General Expenditures per Capita $662
Capital Outlays per Capita $96

% of Expenditures for:
    Public Welfare   2.8
    Highways   9.2
    Education   1.4

Health and Hospitals   2.5
Police   23.9
Sewerage and Sanitation   7.1
Parks and Recreation   0.6
Housing and Community Development   4.5
Debt Outstanding per Capita $632
    % Utility   8.3
Federal Procurement Contract Awards (in millions) $431.2
Federal Grants Awards (in millions) $902.4
Fiscal Year Begins   January 1

Economy

Chicago's economy is a product of its history and geography. The city's fortunes were founded on the Illinois-Michigan Canal and the convergence of rail systems that made it the most accessible market for prairie farmers of the Midwest. The symbol of its economic ascendancy was the Union Livestock Yard, through which millions of cattle passed. The city also was fortunate in having its economic course shepherded by some of the most daring and astute entrepreneurs:

Economy

Total Money Income (in millions) $29,022
% of State Average   85.3
Per Capita Annual Income $9,642
% Population below Poverty Level   20.3
Fortune 500 Companies   21

Banks	Number	Deposits (in millions)
Commercial	385	109,449
Savings	124	40,944

Passenger Autos   2,560,453
Electric Meters   2,676,700
Gas Meters   NA

Manufacturing

Number of Establishments   4,377
% with 20 or More Employees   40.7
Manufacturing Payroll (in millions) $5,632.9
Value Added by Manufacture (in millions) $14,333.2
Value of Shipments (in millions) $27,747.7
New Capital Expenditures (in millions) $504.8

Wholesale Trade

Number of Establishments   4,509
Sales (in millions) $32,702.1
Annual Payroll (in millions) $1,902.220

Retail Trade

Number of Establishments   19,585
Total Sales (in millions) $12,371.3
Sales per Capita $4,111
Number of Retail Trade Establishments with Payroll   12,785
Annual Payroll (in millions) $1,647.2
Total Sales (in millions) $12,021.2
General Merchandise Stores (per capita) $431
Food Stores (per capita) $792
Apparel Stores (per capita) $303
Eating and Drinking Places (per capita) $598

Service Industries

Total Establishments   17,126
Total Receipts (in millions) $13,583.1
Hotels and Motels (in millions) $695.0
Health Services (in millions) $1,434.1
Legal Services (in millions) $2,844.5

Marshall Field, Philip D. Armour, Gustavus Swift, Richard T. Crane, Julius Rosenwald, Potter Palmer, Montgomery Ward, William Butler, Charles H. Wacker, Cyrus H. McCormick, and Gordon Saltonstall. The railroads were also favorable to Chicago's expansion and helped to parlay its strategic location into enormous economic power over the Midwest.

With 14,100 industrial plants, the Chicago metro area leads the nation in the production of steel, communications equipment, office machines, diesel engines, auto accessories, surgical instruments, and radio and television receivers. It ranks second in the production of machine tools, food and confectionery products, pharmaceuticals, chemicals, petroleum products, and publishing.

The city is home to some of the best-known retailers in the country, including Sears, Montgomery Ward, Marshall Field, and Carson Pirie Scott. Overall, 4,509 wholesale firms and 19,585 retail firms operate in the city. Its financial clout is evidenced by the presence of three powerful institutions: the Chicago Board of Trade, Chicago Mercantile Exchange, and Midwest Stock Exchange. The Chicago Board of Trade, founded in 1848 and the oldest financial exchange in the nation, accounts for 45% of futures contracts and the Chicago Mercantile Exchange for 25%.

Chicago is also one of the nation's top industrial research centers, operating about 1,200 research laboratories. It has been a leader in atomic research ever since Enrico Fermi helped to produce the world's first nuclear chain reaction at the University of Chicago in 1942. Close by are the Argonne National Laboratory in Lamont and the Fermi National Accelerator Laboratory in Batavia.

Labor

The Chicago employment market ranks second only to Los Angeles–Long Beach as a magnet for job seekers. Despite the city's chronic problems with crime, jobs have been growing steadily, although much of the growth is in the suburbs, not the city. In 1950 about 80% of all jobs were in the city. Forty years later that figure was down by half. The loss of the stockyards in 1971 was a major blow to the South Side. The West Side also suffered when many employers moved their operations to the suburbs, taking thousands of jobs with them. Of the 1993 Fortune 500 industrials, 38 were located in the Chicago area, including such companies as Amoco, Sara Lee, Quaker Oats, Whitman, Inland Steel, Navistar, FMC, R. R. Donnelley, Illinois Tool Works, Brunswick, Morton International, Fruit of the Loom, Zenith, Outboard Marine, Wm. Wrigley, Pittway, Amsted, Alberto-Culver, and Helene Curtis. Thirty companies in the *Forbes* Top Private Companies list are located here, including Montgomery Ward, Marmon Group, Borg-Warner, Budget Rent-a-Car, Chicago and Northwestern Transport, Farley Industries, Wickes Lumber, Encyclopaedia Britannica, and Leo Burnett. Also located in the city are 9 of the 100 largest diversified service companies, 5 of the 100 largest commercial banks, 6 of the 50 largest diversified financial companies, 2 of the 50 largest savings institutions, 3 of the 50 largest life insurance companies, 3 of the 50 largest retailing companies, 3 of the 50 largest transportation companies, and 2 of the 50 largest utilities.

Labor	
Civilian Labor Force	1,422,230
% Change 1989–1990	0.2
Work Force Distribution	
Mining	2,100
Construction	118,500
Manufacturing	534,400
Transportation and Public Utilities	201,800
Wholesale and Retail Trade	754,600
FIRE (Finance, Insurance, Real Estate)	265,800
Service	818,700
Government	368,600
Women as % of Labor Force	44.9
% Self-Employed	3.3
% Professional/Technical	14.1
Total Unemployment	110,664
Rate %	7.7
Federal Government Civilian Employment	44,369

Education

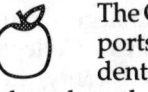

The Chicago Public Schools District supports 616 schools. About 107,000 students attend Roman Catholic parochial schools and another 25,000 go to other private schools.

The flagship of the higher education system is the University of Illinois at Chicago. The two other public schools are Northeastern Illinois University and Chicago State University. In addition, the city maintains the Chicago City Colleges with nine branches. Among private institutions, the most prestigious is the University of Chicago, founded with an endowment from John D. Rockefeller in 1891 and nursed to greatness by William Rainey Harper. The two Catholic institutions, De Paul University and Loyola University, are equally well known. The Illinois Institute of Technology owes its creation to the philanthropy of Philip Armour.

Education	
Number of Public Schools	616
Special Education Schools	43
Total Enrollment	408,830
% Enrollment in Private Schools	19.9
% Minority	88.2
Classroom Teachers	22,697
Pupil-Teacher Ratio	18.1:1
Number of Graduates	16,958
Total Revenue (in millions)	$1,812
Total Expenditures (in millions)	$1,712
Expenditures per Pupil	$3,911
Educational Attainment (Age 25 and Over)	NA
% Completed 12 or More Years	56.2
% Completed 16 or More Years	13.8
Four-Year Colleges and Universities	13
Enrollment	127,258
Two-Year Colleges	19
Enrollment	68,451

Education (continued)

Libraries

Number 369
Public Libraries 88
Books (in thousands) 11,463
Circulation (in thousands) 7,156
Persons Served (in thousands) 1,509
Circulation per Person Served 4.74
Income (in millions) $60.477
Staff NA

Four-Year Colleges and Universities
    Chicago State University
    Northeastern Illinois University
    University of Illinois at Chicago
    University of Chicago
    Columbia College
    DePaul University
    DeVry Institute of Technology
    East-West University
    Illinois Institute of Technology
    Loyola University
    Roosevelt University
    Rush University
    Saint Xavier College

Other private colleges with four-year programs are Roosevelt University, North Park College, Columbia College, Mundelein College, St. Xavier College, the Chicago campus of Northwestern University, the Chicago campus of the National College of Education, and School of the Art Institute of Chicago.

Health

Chicago has 63 hospitals with 20,000 beds and 15,000 physicians. The leading hospitals are the University of Chicago Hospitals, including Bernard Mitchell Hospital, Wyler Children's Hospital, and Chicago Lying-In Hospital; Rush-Presbyterian Hospital–St. Luke's Medical Center, affiliated with Rush Medical College; and Cook County Hospital, the largest public-operated facility.

Other institutions include Chicago Memorial Hospital, Columbus Hospital, Edgewater Hospital, Grant Hospital, Holy Cross Hospital, John F. Kennedy Medical Center, Michael Reese Hospital and Medical Center, Mercy Hospital and Medical Center, Norwegian-American Hospital, Ravenswood Hospital Medical Center, Roseland Community Hospital, Saint Joseph Hospital and Health Care Center, South

Health

Deaths—Total 28,834
Rate per 1,000 9.6
Infant Deaths—Total 887
Rate per 1,000 16.5
Number of Metro Hospitals 63
Number of Metro Hospital Beds 20,033
Rate per 100,000 666
Number of Physicians 15,279
Physicians per 1,000 1.41
Nurses per 1,000 4.81
Health Expenditures per Capita $26.52

Chicago Community Hospital, and Weiss Memorial Hospital.

Transportation

Chicago is approached by a network of interstates, expressways, toll roads, and freeways. From the northwest, I-94 merges with the John F. Kennedy Expressway leading to downtown. The Tri-State Tollway (I-294), an outer belt on the west side, joins I-80 on the south. Other approaches from the west are the East-West Tollway (State 5), which becomes I-290 (also called the Dwight D. Eisenhower Expressway); the North-West Tollway (I-90), which intersects I-290; and the Adlai Stevenson Expressway (I-55). Approaches from the south include the Calumet Expressway (I-94), Chicago Skyway (I-90), and I-57, all of which merge with the Dan Ryan Expressway leading into the city from the southeast. Interstate 80 connects with I-55, I-57, I-90, and I-94.

As a rail hub Chicago is unparalleled. Amtrak provides rail passenger services out of Union Station, one of four rail terminals in the city. Commuter railroads—the Metra, or Metropolitan Rail System—provide service from outlying points such as Aurora, Geneva, and as far north as Kenosha in Wisconsin. The Chicago Transit Authority is an elevated rail and subway system. Rail freight services are provided by Burlington Northern, Chicago and Northwestern, Illinois Central Gulf, Milwaukee Road, and Norfolk Southern.

From the mid-19th century, Chicago has been one of the busiest ports in the nation, connecting the Great Lakes with the Mississippi River system. It became a seaport in 1959 upon the opening of the St. Lawrence Seaway, which links the Great Lakes with the Atlantic Ocean. The port's main drawback is that the Great Lakes are closed in winter by ice and reopen only in April. The port has 84 terminals. Chicago is also a busy port for river barges using the Chicago Sanitary & Ship Canal.

The principal air terminal is O'Hare International Airport, the world's busiest, 17 miles northwest of downtown. O'Hare handles 800,000 flights, 56 million passengers, and 1 million tons of freight annually. Before O'Hare's rise, the city's main air terminal was Midway, 9 miles southwest of the Loop, which is still served by three commercial and two commuter carriers. A third facility is Meigs Field, built on an artificially created peninsula jutting into Lake Michigan south of Grant Park.

Transportation

Interstate Highway Mileage 370
Total Urban Mileage 19,336
Total Daily Vehicle Mileage (in millions) 126.439
Daily Average Commute Time 63.8 min.
Number of Buses 1,868
Port Tonnage (in millions) 22.893
Airports 2
Number of Daily Flights 1,039
Daily Average Number of Passengers 22,893,740

Transportation (continued)

Airlines (American carriers only)

Air Wisconsin
American
American Eagle
American West
Continental
Delta
Eastern
Midway
Northwest
Southwest
TransWorld
USAir
United

Housing

Approximately 23% of the residents live in single-family dwellings, about 34% live in buildings with two to four apartments, and 33% in very large apartment complexes. The Chicago Housing Authority, a city agency, maintains 41,000 apartments for low-income residents. As in other cities, these buildings are plagued by crime, drugs, and other urban ills. Of the total housing stock in 1990, 41.5% of the 1,139,039 units were owner occupied. The median value of an owner-occupied home was $78,700 and the median monthly rent $377.

Housing

Total Housing Units	1,133,039
% Change 1980–1990	-3.7
Vacant Units for Sale or Rent	83,759
Occupied Units	1,025,174
% with More Than One Person per Room	8.8
% Owner-Occupied	41.5
Median Value of Owner-Occupied Homes	$78,700
Average Monthly Purchase Cost	$371
Median Monthly Rent	$377
New Private Housing Starts	3,240
Value (in thousands)	$251,070
% Single-Family	17.6
Nonresidential Buildings Value (in thousands)	$666,592

Tallest Buildings	Hgt. (ft.)	Stories
Sears Tower (world's tallest –1974)	1,454	110
Amoco (1974)	1,136	80
John Hancock Center (1969)	1,127	100
311 S. Wacker (1990)	970	65
Two Prudential Plaza (1990)	901	64
AT&T Corporate Center (1989)	891	60
900 N. Michigan (1989)	871	66
Water Tower Place (1976)	859	74

Urban Redevelopment

Urban renewal had an early beginning in Chicago. In 1908 Daniel H. Burnham, one of the city's great architects, submitted a plan for urban growth for the next half century. Burnham's plan was essentially an aesthetic design involving parks, lakefronts, and forest preserves and did not anticipate the kind of urban problems that arose after World War II or deal with social and economic corollaries of development. Under Mayor Daley a comprehensive plan was developed in the mid-1960s to deal with those areas neglected by Burnham. It sought to rehabilitate the city through a series of plans for each of the city's 16 areas and attempted to coordinate social and quality-of-life factors into architectural and economic elements. The plan designated 21,400 acres in the north, south, and west parts of the city as major improvement areas. The plan was responsible for initiating such housing developments as Carl Sandburg Village, Prairie Shores, and Hyde Park–Kenwood. Nevertheless, there are still slums in Chicago.

More successful have been the commercial redevelopment programs for which Chicago is famous. The late 1980s were marked by some of the largest downtown development projects, such as NBC Tower, AT&T Corporate Center, Two Prudential Plaza, and the Leo Burnett Building. Midway Airport also underwent extensive redevelopment.

Crime

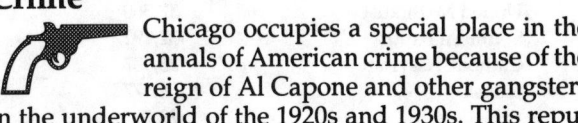

Chicago occupies a special place in the annals of American crime because of the reign of Al Capone and other gangsters in the underworld of the 1920s and 1930s. This reputation remains even as the century draws to a close. In 1991 there were 231,318 crimes involving property and 69,945 violent crimes.

Religion

Chicago has a strong Catholic as well as Protestant heritage. The Catholic legacy comes from the great migration of eastern European Poles, Croats, Slovaks, and Lithuanians, as well as Irish and Hispanics. About 40% of the population is Catholic, a percentage much higher than the national average. Among Protestants, the more prominent are Baptists (1.5%), Reformed Churches (4%), Lutherans (5%), Methodists (2.5%), and Presbyterians (1.5%). Chicago has a number of outstanding churches, including St. Peter's Roman Catholic Church on Madison Street; Old St. Mary's Roman

Crime

Violent Crimes—Total	69,945
Violent Crime Rate per 100,000	9,246
Murder	925
Rape	NA
Robbery	43,783
Aggravated Assaults	42,237
Property Crimes	231,318
Burglary	52,234
Larceny	131,688
Motor Vehicle Theft	47,396
Arson	2,069
Per Capita Police Expenditures	$179.7
Per Capita Fire Protection Expenditures	$70.53
Number of Police	11,871
Per 1,000	3.96

Catholic Church on Wabash Avenue, the city's oldest church, built in 1867, and which escaped the Great Fire; Episcopal St. James Church on Wabash Avenue at Huron Street, built in 1857 and rebuilt after the Great Fire around walls that withstood the flames; Cathedral of the Holy Name on Superior and State streets, a Victorian Gothic headquarters of the Chicago Archdiocese; Fourth Presbyterian Church on Michigan Avenue and Delaware Street, a massive edifice built in 1912 with pinnacled gables and slender spire; and Moody Church, located on Clark Street and North Avenue. Non-Christian houses of worship include Temple Sholom on Lake Shore Drive and Midwest Buddhist Temple near Lincoln Park.

Religion

Largest Denominations (Adherents)

Catholic	2,121,152
Black Baptist	290,094
Evangelical Lutheran	80,710
Lutheran-Missouri Synod	83,205
Presbyterian	40,909
United Church of Christ	55,001
United Methodist	57,560
Southern Baptist	32,192
Catholic Assyrian	25,937
Jewish	208,577
Episcopal	23,311
Assembly of God	15,886
American Baptist	21,210
Christian Reformed	12,298

Media

Chicago has two general dailies, the *Chicago Sun-Times* and *Chicago Tribune*. Both are all-day newspapers published mornings and evenings. The black community is served by the *Chicago Daily Defender*. In addition there are 40 foreign-language newspapers and about 100 neighborhood and suburban newspapers. The electronic media consist of 10 television stations, and 35 AM and FM radio stations.

Media

Newsprint
Chicago, monthly
Chicago Citizen, weekly
Chicago Independent Bulletin, weekly
Chicago Leader-Post, weekly
Chicago Metro News, weekly
Chicago Reader, weekly
Chicago Sun-Times, daily
Chicago Tribune, daily
Crains Chicago Business, weekly
New Chicago, bimonthly
The Review, weekly
Sunday Star, weekly
The Wall Street Journal (Midwest Edition), daily

Television
WBBM (Channel 2)
WCFC (Channel 38)
WCIU (Channel 26)

Media (continued)

WFLD (Channel 32)
WGN (Channel 9)
WLS (Channel 7)
WMAQ (Channel 5)
WSNS (Channel 44)
WTTW (Channel 11)
WYCC (Channel 20)

Radio

WBBM (AM)	WBBM (FM)
WBEZ (FM)	WCKG (FM)
WCRW (AM)	WEDC (AM)
WFMT (FM)	WGCI (AM)
WGCI (FM)	WGN (AM)
WHPK (FM)	WIND (AM)
WJJD (AM)	WJMK (FM)
WJPC (AM)	WKKC (FM)
WKQX (FM)	WLIT (FM)
WLS (AM)	WLS (FM)
WLUP (AM)	WLUP (FM)
WLUW (FM)	WMAQ (AM)
WMB (AM)	WNIB (FM)
WOUI (FM)	WPNT (AM)
WPNT (FM)	WSBC (AM)
WXRT (FM)	WUSN (FM)
WVON (AM)	WWBZ (FM)
WZRD (FM)	

Sports

Chicago is represented in all the major sports by at least one professional team and in baseball by two. The Chicago Cubs compete in the eastern division of the National League and play their home games at Wrigley Field. The Chicago White Sox of the western division of the American League play their home games at Comiskey Park in South Side. The Chicago Bears carry the city's hopes in football and play home games at Soldier Field in Burnham Park. The Chicago Black Hawks of the National Hockey League and Chicago Bulls of the National Basketball Association play home games at Chicago Stadium. Auto races are held at Raceway Park in Calumet Park and Santa Fe Speedway in Hinsdale. Horse racing takes place at Arlington Park, Balmoral Park, Hawthorne Race Track, Maywood Park Race Track, Sportsmans Park, and Downs Harness Racing.

Arts, Culture, and Tourism

The performing and visual arts are backed by strong public patronage and promoted by numerous institutions and organizations. There are 19 performing arts facilities, such as the Civic Opera House, Orchestra Hall, Goodman Theater, Blackstone Theater, Chicago Theater, Schubert Theater, Theater Building, and Auditorium Theater. Music is represented by the American Conservatory of Music Orchestra, Chicago Chamber Orchestra, Chicago Philharmonia, Chicago Pops Orchestra, Chicago String Ensemble, Chicago Symphony Orchestra, Chicago Youth Symphony Orchestra, Civic Orchestra of Chicago, Classical Symphony

Orchestra, Grant Park Symphony Orchestra, Music of the Baroque, and North Side Symphony Orchestra.

Chicago's contribution to the musical lexicon is the electrified urban blues sound of Muddy Waters, known as Chicago Blues. The Rosemont Horizon is a showcase for rock concerts. Opera is represented by Chicago Opera Theater and Lyric Theater of Chicago. Ballet is presented by Ballet Chicago, Elmwood Park Civic Ballet Company, Hubbard Street Dance Company, La Ballet Petit Dance Ensemble, Mordine and Company, and U.S.A. Ballet.

Chicago theater is represented by traditional companies such as Steppenwolf Theater and iconoclastic groups such as Second City. In between are such groups as Chicago Repertory Theater, Remains Theater, Body Politic Theater, Immediate Theater, Victory Gardens Theater, Wisdom Bridge Theater, Bailiwick Repertory, Center Theater, Free Street Theater, Lifeline Theater, and Organic Theater.

Among museums the name that is almost synonymous with Chicago art is the Art Institute with its incomparable holdings of French Impressionist and post-Impressionist paintings. The Field Museum of Natural History, founded in 1893, is one of the top three or four natural history museums of the world. The Museum of Contemporary Art has often provoked controversy with its bold approach to modern art. The oldest cultural institution in the city is the Chicago Historical Society; it has the largest collection of Chicagoana in the world. The huge Museum of Science and Industry, a creation of Julius Rosenwald's philanthropy, stands in Jackson Park.

Among other specialized museums are American Police Center and Museum, Chicago Maritime Society, Grand Army of the Republic Memorial Museum, Great Lakes Naval and Maritime Museum, Historic Pullman Foundation, International Museum of Surgical Sciences, Jane Addams Hull House, Mexican Fine Arts Center Museum, Morton B. Weiss Museum of Judaica, Museum of Contemporary Photography of Columbia College, Museum of Chicago Academy of Sciences, Oriental Institute Museum of the University of Chicago, Peace Museum, Printers Row Printing Museum, Spertus Museum of Judaica, Telephony Museum, and Terra Museum of American Art.

Three prominent art galleries are the David and Alfred Smart Gallery of the University of Chicago, Martin D'Arcy Gallery of Art, and State of Illinois Art Gallery.

There are 16 museums devoted to Chicago's ethnic groups. Among them are the Swedish American Museum, Balzekas Museum of Lithuanian Culture, Du Sable Museum of African American History, and Polish Museum.

Parks and Recreation

Chicago has 560 parks and playgrounds covering 7,300 acres. Grant Park, called the Front Yard of Chicago because it is between Lake Michigan and the city, extends from East Randolph Street to East 14th Boulevard. Founded as Lake Park in 1844, its name was changed in 1901. The Field Museum of Natural History, Soldier Field, and the Art Institute are all within the park's boundaries. Burnham Park, second-largest at 598 acres, begins at 14th Boulevard and the lake, and extends south to 56th Street where Jackson Park begins. It is the realization of Daniel H. Burnham's plan for a lakefront park five miles long. The 371-acre Washington Park, north from 51st Street to 60th Street and east from Martin Luther King, Jr., Drive to Cottage Grove Avenue, is the largest of Chicago's inland parks. It contains a statue of George Washington.

The 10-acre Oliver Memorial Park on Ohio Street is dedicated to a black U.S. soldier who in 1966 threw himself on a grenade in a Vietnam battlefield to save his comrades. The 1,185-acre Lincoln Park stretches along the lakeshore between North and Hollywood avenues and from Lake Michigan to Clark Street. Originally a cemetery, it was designated as a park in 1864. Union Park on Ogden Avenue contains a statue of Mayor Carter H. Harrison. Garfield Park on Central Park Avenue includes an immense conservatory. The 144-acre Columbus Park on Jackson Boulevard was landscaped by Jens Jensen. The 207-acre Humboldt Park on Augusta Boulevard has lagoons, islands, hills, and some of the most beautiful landscapes of any park. The 182-acre Douglas Park on Roosevelt Road at Sacramento Avenue has lily ponds, flower gardens, and a lake for boating. The 322-acre Marquette Park contains a red granite monument of striking design commemorating the tragic flight in 1933 from New York to Kaunas, Lithuania, by airmen Steponas Darius and Stasys Girenas.

Sources of Further Information

Chicago Convention and Tourism Bureau
McCormick Place on the Lake
Chicago, IL 60616
(312) 567-8500

Chicagoland Chamber of Commerce
200 North La Salle
Chicago, IL 60601
(312) 580-6900

Travel and Tourism	
Hotel Rooms 63,331	
Convention and Exhibit Space (square feet)	1,625,000
Convention Centers	
McCormick Place	
Expocenter/Chicago	
Rosemont/O'Hare Exposition Center	
Festivals	
Viva Chicago (June)	
Chicago International Exposition (May)	
Blues Festival (June)	
International Boat Show (June)	
Maritime Festival (June)	
Taste of Chicago (July)	
Jazz Festival (September)	
International Film Festival (October)	

City Hall
121 North La Salle Street
Chicago, IL 60602
(312) 744-4000

Additional Reading

Algren, Nelson. *Chicago: City on the Make.*
, 1983.
Bach, Ira J. *Chicago on Foot: Walking Tours of Chicago's Architecture.* 1987.
———. *Chicago's Famous Buildings.* 1980.
Cronon, William. *Nature's Metropolis: Chicago and the Great West.* 1991.
Cutler, Irving. *Chicago: Metropolis of the Mid-Continent.* 1982.
Danilov, Victor J. *Chicago's Museums.* 1987.
Pacyga, Dominic A., and Ellen Skerrett. *Chicago, City of Neighborhoods.* 1986.
Saliga, Pauline, ed. *Fragments of Chicago's Past.* 1990.
———. *The Sky's the Limit: A Century of Chicago Skyscrapers.* 1990.
Smith, Carl S. *Chicago and the American Literary Imagination, 1888–1920.* 1984.
Terkel, Studs. *Chicago.* 1986.
Viskochil, Larry. *Chicago at the Turn of the Century in Photographs.* 1984.
Zukowsky, John, ed. *Chicago Architecture, 1872–1922.* 1987.

History

Cromie, Robert. *A Short History of Chicago.* 1984.
Dedmon, Emmett. *Fabulous Chicago.* 1981.
Furer, Howard B. *Chicago: A Chronological & Documentary History, 1784–1970.* 1974.
Grossman, James R. *Land of Hope: Chicago, Black Southerners, and the Great Migration.* 1989.
Holt, Glen E., and Dominic A. Pacyga. *Chicago: A Historical Guide to the Neighborhoods.* 1979.
Joseph, Lawrence B., ed. *Creating Jobs, Creating Workers: Economic Development and Employment in Metropolitan Chicago.* 1990.
Mayer, Harold M., and Richard C. Wade. *Chicago: Growth of a Metropolis.* 1969.

Miller, Ross. *American Apocalypse: The Great Fire and the Myth of Chicago.* 1990.
Philpott, Thomas L., ed. *The Slum and the Ghetto: Immigrants, Blacks and Reformers in Chicago, 1880–1930.* 1991.
Rosenblum, Naomi, and Larry Heinemann. *Changing Chicago: A Photodocumentary.* 1989.

Politics and Society

Allswang, John M. *The Political Behavior of Chicago's Ethnic Groups, 1918–1932.* 1980.
Bowly, Devereux. *The Poorhouse: Subsidized Housing in Chicago, 1895–1976.* 1978.
Fiske, Barbara Page, ed. *Key to Government in Chicago and Suburban Cook County.* 1988.
Gosnell, Harold Foote. *Machine Politics: Chicago Model.* 1977.
Gove, Samuel K., and Louis H. Masotti, eds. *After Daley: Chicago Politics in Transition.* 1982.
Granger, Bill, and Lori Granger. *Lords of the Last Machine: The Story of Politics in Chicago.* 1987.
Green, Paul M., and Melvin G. Holli. *The Mayors: The Chicago Political Tradition.* 1987.
Guterbock, Thomas M. *Machine Politics in Transition: Party and Community in Chicago.* 1980.
Hofmeister, Rudolph A. *The Germans of Chicago.* 1976.
Holli, Melvin G., and Peter d'A. Jones. Ethnic Chicago. 1984.
Hunter, Albert. *Symbolic Communities: The Persistence and Change of Chicago's Local Communities.* 1974.
Kahn, Melvin A., and Frances J. Majors. *The Winning Ticket: Daley, the Chicago Machine, and Illinois Politics.* 1984.
Kantowicz, Edward R. *Polish-American Politics in Chicago, 1888–1940.* 1975.
Kleppner, Paul. *Chicago Divided: The Making of a Black Mayor.* 1985.
Peterson, Paul E. *School Politics, Chicago Style.* 1976.
Pinderhughes, Dianne M. *Race and Ethnicity in Chicago Politics.* 1987.
Royko, Mike. *Boss: Richard Daley of Chicago.* 1988.
Squires, Gregory D., et al. *Chicago: Race, Class, and the Response to Urban Decline.* 1987.
Zorbaugh, Harvey Warren. *Gold Coast and Slum: A Sociological Study of Chicago's Near North Side.* 1929.

Cincinnati

Ohio

Layout of City and Suburbs

One of the most picturesque U.S. cities, Cincinnati is spread out on hills that afford beautiful and scenic vistas. The city began in the Basin where the business district is now located. Some of Cincinnati's 19th-century neighborhoods, such as Over-the-Rhine and the West End, adjoin the business district. Fountain Square is at the heart of downtown, where office buildings such as the 49-story Carew Tower dominate. Neighborhoods characterized by single-family homes lie on the hills surrounding the Basin. Ribbons of white viaducts span the industrialized Mill Creek valley. Across the Ohio River, to the south, Kentucky hills stretch to the horizon.

Location and Topography

Cincinnati, the seat of Hamilton County, is in the hilly southwest corner of Ohio where Indiana, Ohio, and Kentucky meet. It is on the Ohio River's north bank, across from Covington, Kentucky. Mill Creek divides the city into east and west. The Little Miami, a national scenic river, is just east of the city.

Climate

The climate is continental, with a wide range in temperature and weather patterns, from cyclonic storms in winter and spring to summer thunderstorms. Fall is pleasant with low rainfall, an abundance of sunshine, and comfortable temperatures. Summers are generally humid, and temperatures can reach into the 90s.

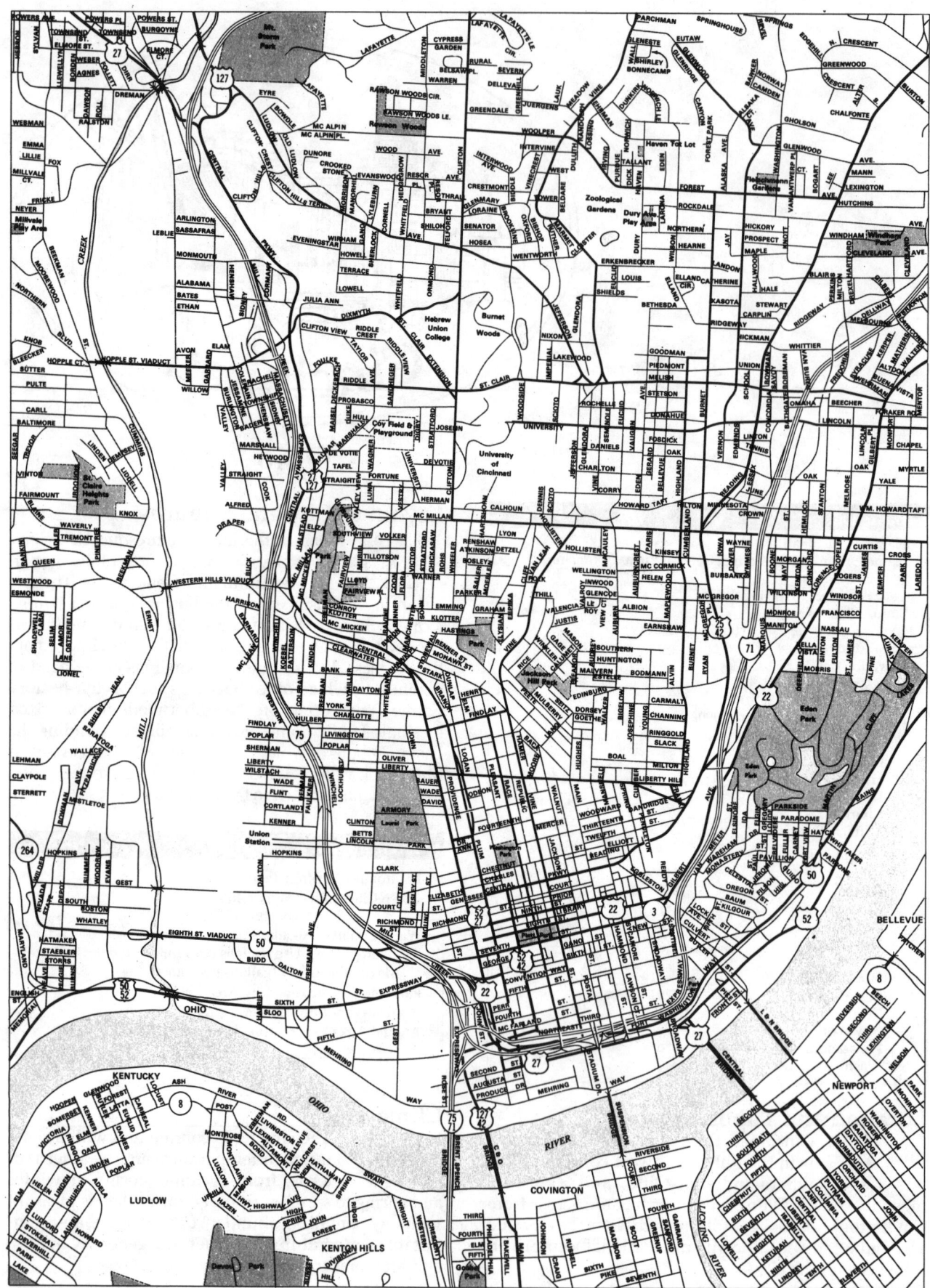

Weather

Temperature

Highest Monthly Average °F	86.6
Lowest Monthly Average °F	24.3

Annual Averages

Days 32°F or Below	98
Days above 90°F	28
Zero Degree Days	2
Precipitation (inches)	40
Snow (inches)	19
% Seasonal Humidity	70
Wind Speed (m.p.h.)	7.1
Clear Days	80
Cloudy Days	188
Storm Days	50
Rainy Days	131

Average Temperatures (°F)	High	Low	Mean
January	39.8	24.3	32.1
February	42.9	25.8	34.4
March	52.2	33.5	42.9
April	65.5	44.6	55.1
May	75.2	53.6	64.4
June	83.6	62.5	73.1
July	86.6	65.8	76.2
August	86.0	64.1	75.1
September	79.8	57.0	68.4
October	68.8	46.7	57.8
November	53.0	36.2	44.6
December	41.8	27.1	34.4

History

American Indians used what is now the site of Cincinnati as an important crossing on the Ohio River. Although European explorers visited the region from 1669 on, there was no white settlement until 1788. At that time, the area northwest of the Ohio River—the Northwest Territory—was governed by the Northwest Ordinance, passed just the year before by the Congress of the Confederation. General Arthur St. Clair was the territory's first governor. In 1788, John Cleves Symmes, a New Jersey congressman and land speculator, bought hundreds of thousands of acres east of the Great Miami River and west of the Little Miami, including the site of Cincinnati. He then sold it to three speculators who platted the Basin and brought the first settlers to the area that winter. In 1789 the settlement was named Losantiville, meaning "town opposite the mouth of the Licking," and construction began on a fort, called Fort Washington. In 1790 Governor St. Clair renamed the settlement Cincinnati and made it the town seat of Hamilton County to honor the Society of the Cincinnati, the organization for Revolutionary officers that was named after the Roman statesman Lucius Quinctius Cincinnatus.

Indians and British troops based in Canada were a constant threat. In 1791 St. Clair's forces suffered 900 casualties in a battle near present-day Fort Wayne, Indiana. Three years later, General Anthony Wayne avenged St. Clair's loss by defeating a force of Miami, Shawnee, Ottawa, Chippewa, Potawatomi, Sauk, Fox, and Iroquois at Fallen Timbers, a British fort on the Maumee River in northwest Ohio.

With the frontier secure, settlers moved west. A census in 1795 showed Cincinnati's population to be 500. In 1802, the year before Ohio became the 17th state, the settlement was large enough to be chartered as a town; in 1819 it received a city charter.

The introduction of steam-powered paddle wheelers on the Ohio River after the War of 1812 turned Cincinnati into a center of commerce and trade, and it became the largest city in Ohio. The first meat-packing plant was established in 1818, and Cincinnati was the chief meat-packing center in the country until 1860, when Chicago took the lead. While the Ohio River linked Cincinnati to the south and west as far as New Orleans, the Miami Canal from Lake Erie connected the city to the north and east. The canal passed through Ohio's rich agricultural region and the city developed a thriving food-processing industry for corn, hogs, and wheat shipped down the canal.

There has always been an ethnic and racial mix in Cincinnatti. Blacks have been prominent in Cincinnati since its founding. The city's first black church was built in 1809 and the first black school in 1825. In 1830 Germans fleeing religious and political persecution in their homeland began a mass migration to the United States. Many, passing through New York, Baltimore, or New Orleans, found themselves in Cincinnati. The ethnic mix was later enriched by the Irish escaping the potato famine. By 1840 the city's population reached 46,338.

Cincinnati flourished in the 1850s. It became the world's largest pork-packing center, and the foundations of the great Cincinnati fortunes were laid. Over 8,000 steamboats docked at the public landing. By 1859 the city's population was 160,000 and the value of its manufactured products was estimated at $112 million. The 1859 city directory listed 2 high schools and 16 elementary schools, 180 churches, 6 synagogues, 53 periodicals, and 10 insurance companies.

While river and canal links made Cincinnati great, the extension of railroads westward, especially to Chicago, diminished its primacy. Trade flourished until 1860, when Chicago became the hub of the nation's transportation system as well as the center of meat packing. However, the Civil War, from 1861 to 1865, delayed the decline. Cincinnati merchants initially complained about the loss of southern markets, but this lack was eventually replaced by government contracts for Union army supplies. River trade continued after the Civil War, and commercial ties resumed with the South and Southwest.

During the post–Civil War era there was something of a cultural boom when Cincinnati's music hall, zoo, art museum, art academy, conservatory of music, and public library were established. The city limits expanded beyond the Basin into the surrounding hills, and its population exceeded 200,000, making it one of the most crowded cities in the country. Living conditions were difficult, and there was a high rate of crime. In 1880 murders averaged one a day, riots and lynchings were common, and the courts and militia were lax in enforcing laws. The courthouse was burned down in 1883, and more than 300 were killed or injured.

Chronology

1788 Speculators buy the site of Cincinnati from John Cleves Symmes; the first settlers arrive.

1789 The settlement is named Losantiville; Fort Washington is built as a base of operations against the Indians.

1790 General Arthur St. Clair, governor of the territory northwest of the Ohio River, changes the name to Cincinnati and makes it the town seat of Hamilton County.

1794 General Anthony Wayne defeats Indians at Fallen Timbers, which ends the threat of Indian attack.

1802 Cincinnati is chartered as a town.

1803 Ohio becomes 17th state.

1819 Cincinnati is chartered as a city.

1827 The Miami Canal is completed from Lake Erie to Cincinnati.

1830 Mass migration of Germans begins.

1835 The first synagogue is built.

1852 Blacks gain the vote, locally, 18 years before the passage of the Fifteenth Amendment.

1859 City population reaches 160,000.

1867 Suspension bridge designed by John A. Roebling completed across the Ohio River to Kentucky.

1880 Cincinnati completes first city-owned railroad to the south.

1883 The courthouse is burned and more than 300 men are killed or wounded in three days of rioting and fighting between the public and the militia. Governor Joseph B. Foraker appoints George Barnsdale Cox, a tavern keeper, as head of the city's Board of Public Affairs. Cox rules as the absolute boss of both his party and city, presiding for decades over one of the most corrupt city halls in the nation.

1925 The Reform Charter party defeats the graft-ridden Cox machine and the city council passes a new charter providing for a city manager.

1931 The first black man to serve on the city council is elected.

1937 Much of the Basin is submerged by the Ohio River flood, one of the worst in history.

1989 Cincinnati celebrates its bicentennial.

Following this outbreak of violence, George Barnsdale Cox and the Republican party gained control of City Hall. A former tavern keeper, Cox set up a party machine that controlled the city for the next 28 years. Cincinnati became notorious as a hotbed of political graft and corruption. Public service contracts and franchises were given to the highest bidder, while judges did Cox's bidding. Magazine editor and muckraker Lincoln Steffens portrayed the looting of the city by Cox and thereby gave impetus to a reform movement. Cox's nominee for mayor was defeated in 1911 and, although Republican power was restored, the reformers became more influential, especially after the state legislature passed a home-rule act.

In 1925 the Reform Charter party not only defeated the old parties but also introduced the city manager form of government. The old abuses were cleaned up quickly and the city soon became known for good government.

The 1930s saw a continuation of a building boom that included the new Union Terminal, a new post office and customs house, and the massive Bell Telephone building. In 1937 the Ohio River surged to a record height, bringing much destruction.

After World War II Cincinnati embarked on an urban renewal plan intended to revitalize the inner city. Interstates, begun in the late 1950s, were finished in the 1960s. Riverfront Stadium and the Coliseum were completed in the 1970s.

Historical Landmarks

The Union Terminal was designed by Alfred Fellheimer and Stewart Wagner of New York with Paul Cret of Philadelphia as consulting architect. Completed in 1933 at a cost of $43 million, this nationally known architectural and technological showplace now houses the Cincinnati Historical Society and Natural History Museum. The Cincinnati Music Hall on the corner of Elm and West 14th streets, built in 1876, is the largest public hall in the city. The Hamilton County Memorial Building is a 2-story Beaux Arts building dedicated in 1908 as a permanent memorial to the city's pioneers, soldiers, and marines. At the foot of Broadway is the Public Landing, a granite-block bank leading down to the water's edge. Fountain Square was created in 1870; located on East Fifth Street between Vine and Walnut streets, the square is the center of the main shopping and business districts. Reconfigured in the 1960s, it is named for the Tyler Davidson Fountain, a 38-foot bronze designed by August von Kreling of Nuremburg and cast in the Royal Foundry in Munich.

The Carew Tower complex on the southwest corner of the square is one of the tallest buildings in Ohio. The Cathedral of St. Peter in Chains on the corner of West Eighth and Plum streets was built between 1840 and 1845 in the Greek Revival style. St. Francis De Sales Church on the corner of Madison Road and Woodburn Avenue contains one of the largest swinging bells in the world, weighing over 35,000 pounds. Historic homes open to the public include those of John Hauck, a 19th-century brewer; Harriet Beecher Stowe;

and William Howard Taft. Dayton Street in the West End features some restored 19th-century buildings.

Population

In 1990 the city's population was 364,040, a loss of 5.5% from its 1980 population of 385,409. The metropolitan area, however, which includes the rest of Hamilton County in Ohio as well as parts of Kentucky and Indiana, had a population of 1.47 million in 1990, an increase of 5.1% from 1980.

Population

	1980	1990
Central City	385,409	364,040
Rank	32	45
Metro Area	1,401,471	1,472,645
Pop. Change 1980–1990	-21,369	
Pop. % Change 1980–1990	-5.5	
Median Age	30.9	
% Male	46.5	
% Age 65 and Over	13.9	
Density (per square mile)	4,715	

Households

Number 154,342
Persons per Household 2.26
% Female-Headed Households 18.2
% One-Person Households 39.5
Births—Total 7,312
   % to Mothers under 20 19.2
   Birth Rate per 1,000 19.7

Ethnic Composition

In 1990 the population included 60.51% white, 37.94% black, and 1.1% Asian and Pacific Islanders. Blacks have been prominent in Cincinnati since its founding. The city's first black church was built in 1809 and the first black school in 1825. Blacks voted locally in 1852, 18 years before the passage of the Fifteenth Amendment. The first black to serve on the city council was elected in 1931, and two blacks have since served as mayors.

Ethnic Composition (as % of total pop.)

	1980	1990
White	65.15	60.51
Black	33.85	37.94
American Indian	0.11	0.18
Asian and Pacific Islander	0.57	1.11
Hispanic	0.78	0.66
Other	NA	0.26

Government

Cincinnati is governed by a nine-member city council elected every two years. The council elects one of its members as the mayor, a largely ceremonial post; another as vice-mayor; and a third as president pro tempore. The chief administrative executive is the city manager, who has a seat on the council but cannot vote.

Government

Year of Home Charter NA
Number of Members of the Governing Body 9
Elected at Large 0
Elected by Wards 9
Number of Women in Governing Body NA
Salary of Mayor $42,600
Salary of Council Members $39,100
City Government Employment Total 6,186
Rate per 10,000 167.3

Public Finance

The 1992 city budget consisted of revenues of $639.87 million and expenditures of $576.701 million. The total debt outstanding was $230.501 million, and cash and security holdings $1.243 billion.

Public Finance

Total Revenue (in millions) $639.87
Intergovernmental Revenue—Total (in millions) $100.3
Federal Revenue per Capita $38.86
% Federal Assistance 6.07
% State Assistance 6.68
Sales Tax as % of Total Revenue 0.55
Local Revenue as % of Total Revenue 62.78
City Income Tax yes
Taxes—Total (in millions) $150.2

Taxes per Capita
  Total $406
  Property $78
  Sales and Gross Receipts $4
General Expenditures—Total (in millions) $333.7
General Expenditures per Capita $902
Capital Outlays per Capita $196

% of Expenditures for:
  Public Welfare 0.0
  Highways 6.6
  Education 0.0
  Health and Hospitals 7.1
  Police 13.6
  Sewerage and Sanitation 14.6
  Parks and Recreation 7.5
  Housing and Community Development 14.6
Debt Outstanding per Capita $542
  % Utility 17.3
Federal Procurement Contract Awards (in millions) $2,948.3
Federal Grants Awards (in millions) $111.2
Fiscal Year Begins January 1

Economy

Cincinnati has a diversified economic base with strong sectors in manufacturing, trade, insurance and finance, health services, and transportation. Nationally known as the home of Procter & Gamble and U.S. Playing Cards, Cincinnati is also the headquarters of five 1993 Fortune 500 companies: Chiquita Brands, E. W. Scripps, Cincinnati Milacron, and Eagle-Picher Industries, as well as Procter & Gamble. Cincinnati has a high stake in foreign trade; more than 250 firms do business in foreign countries. Among its exports are jet engines, machine tools, computer software, and paper. The city is also a publishing and printing center.

Economy

Total Money Income (in millions)	$3,791.390	
% of State Average	98.8	
Per Capita Annual Income	$10,247	
% Population below Poverty Level	19.7	
Fortune 500 Companies	5	

Banks	Number	Deposits (in millions)
Commercial	NA	7,295
Savings	NA	6,166

Passenger Autos 529,232
Electric Meters 497,704
Gas Meters 366,287

Manufacturing

Number of Establishments 843
% with 20 or More Employees 41.2
Manufacturing Payroll (in millions) $1,722.4
Value Added by Manufacture (in millions) $3,349.8
Value of Shipments (in millions) $6,041.0
New Capital Expenditures (in millions) $167.8

Wholesale Trade

Number of Establishments 1,074
Sales (in millions) $8,680.2
Annual Payroll (in millions) $485.988

Retail Trade

Number of Establishments 3,071
Total Sales (in millions) $2,384.6
Sales per Capita $6,449
Number of Retail Trade Establishments with Payroll 2,341
Annual Payroll (in millions) $320.8
Total Sales (in millions) $2,351.2
General Merchandise Stores (per capita) $801
Food Stores (per capita) $1,509
Apparel Stores (per capita) $339
Eating and Drinking Places (per capita) $836

Service Industries

Total Establishments 3,406
Total Receipts (in millions) $2,229.9
Hotels and Motels (in millions) $89.3
Health Services (in millions) $483.2
Legal Services (in millions) $243.8

Labor

Like most U.S. cities in the early 1990s, Cincinnati has experienced higher-than-normal unemployment rates in the 5% range. Nevertheless, many of the basic industries in the area are relatively recession-proof, thus helping to avert crisis-level unemployment. The leading employer is General Electric, followed by Procter & Gamble, Kro-

Labor

Civilian Labor Force 204,491
% Change 1989–1990 1.0

Work Force Distribution
Mining 400
Construction 31,400
Manufacturing 144,900
Transportation and Public Utilities 40,600

Labor (continued)

Wholesale and Retail Trade 189,500
FIRE (Finance, Insurance, Real Estate) 43,700
Service 193,100
Government 94,000
Women as % of Labor Force 46.3
% Self-Employed 4.0
% Professional/Technical 18.5
Total Unemployment 10,646
Rate % 5.2
Federal Government Civilian Employment 10,184

ger, and Cincinnati Milacron among the private corporations. Productivity has been consistently high.

Education

Cincinnati has the third-largest school system in Ohio with 82 schools. Cincinnati also has a strong parochial school system. The flagship of higher education is the University of Cincinnati, known for its professional schools such as the Colleges of Medicine, Pharmacy, Engineering, Law, and Design, Architecture, Art, and Planning. Next in importance is Xavier University, a Jesuit institution. The Hebrew Union College–Jewish Institute of Religion is the oldest Jewish seminary in the United States, established in 1875 by Rabbi Isaac M. Wise. Colleges and universities in the metro area include Northern Kentucky University, Thomas More College, St. Thomas Institute, and the College of Mount Saint Joseph.

Education

Number of Public Schools 82
Special Education Schools 2
Total Enrollment 51,148
% Enrollment in Private Schools 18.6
% Minority 63.9
Classroom Teachers 3,073
Pupil-Teacher Ratio 16.6:1
Number of Graduates 2,190
Total Revenue (in millions) $232.969
Total Expenditures (in millions) $261.890
Expenditures per Pupil $4,777
Educational Attainment (Age 25 and Over)
    % Completed 12 or More Years 57.9
    % Completed 16 or More Years 17.6
Four-Year Colleges and Universities 3
    Enrollment 38,808
Two-Year Colleges 5
    Enrollment 6,838

Libraries

Number 195
Public Libraries 40
Books (in thousands) 3,831
Circulation (in thousands) 8,504
Persons Served (in thousands) 863.9
Circulation per Person Served 9.84
Income (in millions) $24.648
Staff 776

Four-Year Colleges and Universities
    University of Cincinnati
    Xavier University
    Union Institute

Health

Cincinnati achieved medical fame when Dr. Albert Sabin developed the first polio vaccine at the Children's Hospital Medical Center, one of the nation's largest pediatric hospitals. The first laser laboratory was founded here by Dr. Leon Goldman. The University of Cincinnati Medical Center is a respected teaching hospital. In Hamilton County there are over 30 hospitals with 9,000 beds. Among them are the Good Samaritan, Jewish, Bethesda, Christ, Deaconess, Providence, St. Elizabeth, St. Francis, St. George, and St. Luke hospitals.

Health

Deaths—Total 4,562
Rate per 1,000 12.3
Infant Deaths—Total 94
Rate per 1,000 12.9
Number of Metro Hospitals 20
Number of Metro Hospital Beds 6,753
Rate per 100,000 1,826
Number of Physicians 3,255
Physicians per 1,000 2.62
Nurses per 1,000 14.99
Health Expenditures per Capita $93.60

Transportation

Cincinnati is approached by Interstates 71, 74, and 75. Interstate connectors are 275 and 471, and the city is also served by U.S. Highways 22, 25, 27, 42, 50, 52, and 127. Passenger rail service is provided by three major railroad systems—the CSX Corporation, the Norfolk-Southern Corporation, and Conrail. Amtrak's Cardinal passenger service resumed in 1990 out of Union Terminal. In addition, the Indiana and Ohio Railroad provides service in southeastern Indiana and southwestern Ohio. More than 110 freight trains arrive in and depart from Cincinnati daily. More than 195 million tons of cargo are transported annually by Ohio River system barges; 32 barge lines link Cincinnati with the nation. Ten public river terminals are located along the 30 miles of port shoreline. The Greater Cincinnati International Airport is located 15 minutes from the city.

Transportation

Interstate Highway Mileage 139
Total Urban Mileage 3,806
Total Daily Vehicle Mileage (in millions) 26.517
Daily Average Commute Time 49.3 min.
Number of Buses 280
Port Tonnage (in millions) NA
Airports 2
Number of Daily Flights 169
Daily Average Number of Passengers 10,330

Airlines (American carriers only)

American
Continental
Delta
Northwest
Trans World
United
USAir

The airport is one of four major hubs for Delta Airlines and is home base for Comair, the Delta Connection. Twelve major national and regional airlines provide over 75 daily departures and arrivals.

Housing

Cincinnati is considered a leader in efforts to facilitate home ownership for low- and moderate-income families and first-time home buyers. Among these efforts are the Neighborhood Housing and Conservation Urban Homesteading Program, the Housing Rehabilitation Loan Program, Rental Rehabilitation Program, New Homeowner Program, Housing Implementation Program, Neighborhood Housing Services, and Home Maintenance Program. The New Housing Program was created in 1989 to promote the construction of new market-rate housing units throughout the city. The Neighborhood Development Corporation assists the housing activities of neighborhood-based non-profit development corporations. Among the new housing developments are Longworth Square, Bates Avenue Project, Baltimore Avenue Project, Storrs Street Project, townhouse developments at Park Avenue and Cedar Meadows, and Western-Southern Housing Project. Typical rehabilitation projects include Betts-Longworth Historic District Redevelopment Program, North Rhine II, Franciscan Homes, and Neave Street Project. A primary goal of the Cincinnati 2000 Plan is the development of housing to complement commercial development. Four housing projects have been completed in recent years: One Lytle Place, Fourth and Plum Apartments, Walnut Towers in the YWCA Building, and Two Garfield Place. For middle- and upper-income residents, the city has assembled four residental units downtown at Adams Landing, Garfield Place, Lombardy Building, and Central Parkway Towers.

Housing

Total Housing Units 169,088
% Change 1980–1990 -2.1
Vacant Units for Sale or Rent 11,558
Occupied Units 154,342
% with More Than One Person per Room 3.8
% Owner-Occupied 38.3
Median Value of Owner-Occupied Homes $61,900
Average Monthly Purchase Cost $332
Median Monthly Rent $283
New Private Housing Starts 528
Value (in thousands) $31,050
% Single-Family 25.8
Nonresidential Buildings Value (in thousands) $104,301

Tallest Buildings	Hgt. (ft.)	Stories
Carew Tower (1931)	568	49
Central Trust Tower	504	33
Dubois Tower		
5th & Walnut	423	32
Netherland Plaza	372	31
Central Trust Center	355	27
Atrium Two (1984)	350	30
Star Bank Center (1961)	351	26
Clarion North Tower	350	33

Of the city's 169,088 housing units in 1990, 154,342 were occupied, 38.3% by owners. The median value of an owner-occupied home was $61,900 and the median rent $283.

Urban Redevelopment

A series of comprehensive planning documents has guided Cincinnati's development since 1925. They include plans approved in 1925, 1948, and 1964, and a series of urban design plans, including the Central Business District and Central Riverfront plans, the Garfield Place Plan, the Findlay Market/Over-the-Rhine Plan, and the Queensgate II Town Center Plan. In July 1982 the city adopted the Cincinnati 2000 Plan under the direction of the City Planning Commission. The Department of Economic Development has used these plans to renovate a substantial portion of the downtown area over the past 20 years. The Central Business District Plan designated a 12-block area in the core of the business district as an urban renewal project. Fountain Square, the symbolic center of the city, was the first block to undergo development. The completed plaza has been awarded several local and national awards for design excellence. A Fountain Square Pavilion was added in 1985. Other buildings included the Clarion Hotel, the Federated Office Tower, the Federal Reserve Bank and Mercantile Center, the Fifth Race Tower, Central Trust Tower, Atrium One and Atrium Two, Saks-Hyatt and Convention Place, and Chiquita Center. Under the Cincinnati 2000 Plan, office space will be expanded by 7 million square feet, retail space by 800,000 square feet, hotel accommodations by 2,250 rooms, and housing by 6,000 units. Since 1984 the following redevelopment has taken place downtown: Cincinnati Commerce Center, Ameritrust Center, Procter & Gamble World Corporate Headquarters, Court Street Center, 800 Broadway, the Goodall Office Complex, Alms and Doepke Building, Centennial Plaza, Longworth Hall Design Center, Cincinnati Hotel, Piatt Park Office Center, Textile and Sussman Buildings, Flatiron Building, and Midland Company Headquarters. New office buildings under the redevelopment program include Centennial Plaza III, 255 Fifth Street, S&L Data Building, Society Bank Building, 312 Walnut Street, Queen City Square, 312 Elm Street, and Broadway Commons.

Crime

In 1991 there were 35,693 offenses known to Cincinnati's police force. There were 5,794 instances of violent crime and 29,899 instances of crime involving property.

Religion

Cincinnati has large Catholic and Protestant congregations attending over 1,000 churches.

Crime

Violent Crimes—Total	5,794
Violent Crime Rate per 100,000	NA
Murder	54
Rape	478
Robbery	2,315
Aggravated Assaults	2,947
Property Crimes	29,899
Burglary	8,489
Larceny	19,285
Motor Vehicle Theft	2,125
Arson	679
Per Capita Police Expenditures	$153.88
Per Capita Fire Protection Expenditures	$122.29
Number of Police	883
Per 1,000	2.39

Religion

Largest Denominations (Adherents)

Catholic	267,806
Black Baptist	62,089
United Methodist	36,358
Presbyterian	25,496
Southern Baptist	17,195
American Baptist	10,529
Church of Christ	15,503
United Church of Christ	10,045
Jewish	13,709

Media

The major newspapers are the *Cincinnati Enquirer* (mornings and Sundays) and the *Cincinnati Post* (evenings and Saturdays). The area is served by 40 community newspapers. Cincinnati is the broadcast media center for southwestern Ohio, northern Kentucky, and southeastern Indiana. Five commercial, public, and independent television stations and 18 AM and FM radio stations broadcast from the city.

Media

Newsprint
  Cincinnati Business Courier, monthly
  Cincinnati Enquirer, daily
  Cincinnati Magazine, monthly
  Cincinnati Post, daily

Television
  WCET (Channel 48)
  WCPO (Channel 9)
  WKRC (Channel 12)
  WLWT (Channel 5)
  WSTR (Channel 64)

Radio

WAIF (AM)	WAKW (FM)
WCIN (AM)	WCKY (AM)
WWEZ (FM)	WGRR (FM)
WJVS (FM)	WKRC (AM)
WKRQ (FM)	WLW (AM)
WEBN (FM)	WRRM (FM)
WSAI (AM)	WWNK (FM)
WTSJ (AM)	WUBE (AM)
WUBE (FM)	WVXU (FM)

Sports

Cincinnati supports two major professional sports teams: the Cincinnati Reds in baseball, playing their home schedule at the Riverfront Stadium, and the Cincinnati Bengals, an expansion league in the old American Football League, who have played twice in the Super Bowl. Both the University of Cincinnati and Xavier University have nationally prominent basketball teams. The Cincinnati Cyclones are in the East Coast Hockey League.

Arts, Culture, and Tourism

Art and culture have had a strong presence in Cincinnati from the 19th century on. The newly restored Music Hall is home to the Cincinnati Symphony Orchestra, Cincinnati Ballet, and Cincinnati Opera, the second-oldest opera company in the United States. Riverbend Music Center, an amphitheater designed by Michael Graves, is the summer performance headquarters for the Cincinnati Pops. Two of its popular traditions are the Matinee Musicales and the Cincinnati Chamber Music Series. The March music series presents black artists performing featured works by black composers. Cincinnati Playhouse in the Park, a professional regional theater, is housed in Eden Park. The University of Cincinnati's College Conservatory of Music presents more than 300 concerts a year. It also sponsors a summer season of musicals at Corbett Theatre on campus and at Showboat Majestic, a restored 19th-century showboat on the Ohio River Public Landing. The School for the Creative and Performing Arts also is active in offering musicals and plays. Bogarts, a rock club near the University of Cincinnati, presents rock, jazz, and blues.

Greater Cincinnati has over 100 museums, of which the oldest is the Cincinnati Art Museum on an Eden Park hilltop. The original building is a massive, turreted structure built in 1886; of the five wings since added, four are Greek style. The other major museums are the Taft Museum, built in 1820; the Contemporary Art Center; Cincinnati Museum of Natural History; Cincinnati Historical Society; and Hebrew Union College Gallery of Art and Artifacts.

Travel and Tourism

Hotel Rooms   15,097
Convention and Exhibit Space (square feet)   162,000

Convention Centers
  Dr. Albert B. Sabin Convention Center

Festivals
  Oktoberfest Zinzinnati (October)
  Greek Panegyri Festival (June)
  Taste of Cincinnati (May)
  Riverfest (September)

Parks and Recreation

Greater Cincinnati has hundreds of parks covering 4,751 acres and 195 recreation areas covering 2,395 acres. The largest is Eden Park, with 185 acres of rolling lawns, steep hills, and a miniature lake. It contains the Navigation Monument, a 30-foot granite obelisk dedicated in 1929 to commemorate the canalization of the Ohio River. Lytle Park contains a 15-foot-tall bronze statue of Abraham Lincoln, a gift of the Taft family. Garfield Park between Vine and Elm streets is one of the few green places downtown. Mount Airy Forest, begun in 1913, now contains 1,304 acres with bridle paths, nature trails, and rustic bridges. Ault Park at the end of Observatory Avenue is a beautifully landscaped park of 230 acres with nature trails and picnic groves. A popular theme park is Kings Island Amusement Park set in 1,300 acres of woodland along with the Jack Nicklaus Sports Center, College Football Hall of Fame, and Timberwolf Amphitheater. Sawyer Point on the Ohio River provides facilities for pier fishing, rowboating, skating, tennis, and volleyball.

Sources of Further Information

Cincinnati Historical Society
The Museum Center
1301 Western Avenue
Cincinnati, OH 45203
(513) 287-7030

Greater Cincinnati Chamber of Commerce
441 Vine Street, Suite 300
Cincinnati, OH 45202
(513) 579-3100

Greater Cincinnati Convention and Visitors Bureau
300 West Sixth Street
Cincinnati, OH 45202
(513) 621-2142

Public Library of Cincinnati and Hamilton County
Library Square
800 Vine Street
Cincinnati, OH 45202
(513) 369-6900

Additional Reading

Aaron, Daniel. *Cincinnati, the Queen City of the West.* 1992.

Condit, Carl W. *The Railroad and the City: A Technological and Urbanistic History of Cincinnati.* 1977.

Fairbanks, Robert B. *Making Better Citizens: Housing Reform and the Community Development Strategy in Cincinnati, 1890–1960.* 1988.

Feck, Luke. *Yesterday's Cincinnati.* 1975.

Giglierano, Geoffrey J. *The Bicentennial Guide to Greater Cincinnati: A Portrait of Two Hundred Years.* 1988.

Green, Marilyn, and Michael Bennett. *Cincinnati: A Pictorial History.* 1987.

Knue, Paul. *Cincinnati Days in History: A Bicentennial Almanac.* 1988.

Miller, Zane L. *Boss Cox's Cincinnati: Urban Politics in the Progressive Era.* 1968.

Pettigrew, Judith H. *Cincinnati Women: Jewels in the Crown.* 1988.

Regina, Karen, and Gregory L. Rhodes. *Cincinnati: An Urban History Sourcebook.* 1988.

Sarna, Jonathan D., and Nancy H. Klein. *The Jews of Cincinnati.* 1989.

Thomas, John C. *Between Citizen and City: Neighborhood Organizations and Urban Politics in Cincinnati.* 1986.

Tolzmann, Don H. *The Cincinnati Germans after the Great War.* 1987.

Vexler, Robert I. *Cincinnati: A Chronological & Documentary History, 1676–1970.* 1975.

Willoughby, Lee D. *The Making of the Cities: Cincinnati.* 1990.

Cleveland

Ohio

Location and Topography

Cleveland, seat of Cuyahoga County, is Ohio's second-largest city after Columbus. It is on a plateau about 75 feet above the south shore of Lake Erie. The surrounding terrain is generally level except for a ridge in the southeastern section that rises some 500 feet above shore level. The Cuyahoga River flows through the city.

Layout of City and Suburbs

Cleveland fans out from the Lake Erie shore, radiating from the Cuyahoga River, which divides the city into east and west sides. The industrial section is mainly along the banks of the river—an area called the Flats. Public Square is at the heart of downtown. Buildings on the square include Terminal Tower, a skyscraper completed in 1927; the Old Stone Church, built in 1855; the new BP Building; Society Center; and a striking memorial, topped by a 15-foot-tall figure of Liberty, honoring those men from Cuyahoga County who served during the Civil War. Euclid Avenue, Cleveland's most famous street, extends east from the Public Square. Once a residential street, it is now a commercial thoroughfare. Suburbs to the east, such as Cleveland Heights, University Heights, and Shaker Heights, are on higher ground than downtown Cleveland.

Climate

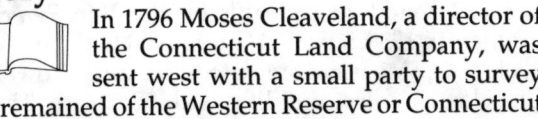

Lake Erie greatly affects Cleveland's otherwise continental climate by moderating the cold of winter and heat of summer. Nevertheless, the average annual snowfall is about 52 inches, with most falling in January. Lake breezes tend to make summers pleasant. Spring and fall, the transition seasons, are most pleasant, with daily maximum temperatures no higher than 75° and no lower than 44°.

Weather

Temperature

Highest Monthly Average °F	81.6
Lowest Monthly Average °F	20.3

Annual Averages

Days 32°F or Below	125
Days above 90°F	8
Zero Degree Days	5
Precipitation (inches)	35
Snow (inches)	52
% Seasonal Humidity	72
Wind Speed (m.p.h.)	10.8
Clear Days	70
Cloudy Days	197
Storm Days	36
Rainy Days	156

Average Temperatures (°F)	High	Low	Mean
January	33.4	20.3	26.9
February	35.0	20.8	27.9
March	44.1	28.1	36.1
April	58.0	38.5	48.3
May	68.4	48.1	58.3
June	78.2	57.5	67.9
July	81.6	61.2	71.4
August	80.4	59.6	70.6
September	74.2	53.5	63.9
October	63.6	43.9	53.8
November	48.8	34.4	41.6
December	36.4	24.1	30.3

History

In 1796 Moses Cleaveland, a director of the Connecticut Land Company, was sent west with a small party to survey what remained of the Western Reserve or Connecticut Reserve. The Western Reserve referred to lands that King Charles II of England promised to the colony of Connecticut in 1682. Connecticut had ceded most of the lands to the U.S. government in 1786, which in turn gave them to the state of Pennsylvania.

Cleaveland went as far as the Cuyahoga River and then platted township boundaries from the Cuyahoga east to Pennsylvania. Arriving at the mouth of the river, he recognized it as a likely site for a harbor and laid out a village centered on a commons. He named the site Cleaveland after himself, and the commons is now called Public Square. Somewhere in history the first "a" in his last name was lost.

One or two families from his survey party remained at the site after Cleaveland returned to Con-

necticut. In 1800 the population was only 7, but by 1830 it had reached 1,000. This boom was prompted by the 1827 completion of a section of canal ultimately linking the Ohio River and Lake Erie. By 1836 the population and economy had grown sufficiently that Cleveland was incorporated as a city. European immigrants passed through the Port of Cleveland on their way west by steamer from Buffalo to Chicago.

Railways reached Cleveland in 1851. The discovery of rich iron-ore deposits in Michigan, combined with the completion of the Sault Sainte Marie Canals in 1855, ensured Cleveland's future as a major inland port.

In the same decade William A. Otis and John A. Ford laid the foundations of Cleveland's iron industry and began building the first locomotives. The Cuyahoga Steam Furnace Company became the city's first manufacturing corporation. By 1861, with a population of 43,000, Cleveland passed Columbus to become the second-largest city in Ohio. During the Civil War, Cleveland was a militant center of antislavery sentiment and a major stop on the Underground Railway. The Civil War gave further impetus to Cleveland's industry. Cleveland Iron Company and Cleveland Cliffs Iron Company made Cleveland the iron capital. Standard Oil Company, founded by John D. Rockefeller, Henry M. Flagler, and Stephen V. Harkness, established a new industry that one day would become the largest in the nation.

Inventors flourished in the city. Charles F. Brush, originator of the carbon arc lamp, founded the Brush Electric Light and Power Company and installed arc lamps throughout the city. He also invented and manufactured the first practical storage battery. Worcester R. Warner and Ambrose Swasey perfected automotive gear improvements and designed astronomical instruments. Soon there was a Millionaire's Row on Euclid Avenue studded with mansions of the industrial barons.

The labor movement's growth paralleled the city's industrial growth. Cleveland became headquarters for the Brotherhood of Locomotive Engineers and a favorite convention city for other major unions. Labor flexed its muscles quite often and won important concessions from industry.

With prosperity came new educational, cultural, and media institutions. In education, the first was the Case School of Applied Science, followed by Western Reserve College, Adelbert College, St. Ignatius College (later John Carroll University), Notre Dame College for Women, and Fenn College. In 1856 the first public school was opened for boys; girls were admitted the next year. An opera house was erected in 1875, and three years later the *Penny Press*, forerunner of the Scripps-Howard chain, was launched. The *Plain Dealer*, the city's best-known daily, is an offspring of the *Herald*, founded in 1819.

At the turn of the century, Cleveland's history became a struggle between five-term reform mayor Thomas Loftin Johnson and his archrival, Mark A. Hanna, an equally powerful coal, iron, railroad, and

Chronology

1795 General Anthony Wayne signs Treaty of Greenville with Indians defeated the year before at the Battle of Fallen Timbers.

1796 Moses Cleaveland, agent of the Connecticut Land Company, plats a townsite at the mouth of the Cuyahoga River. Several party members remain while the rest, including Cleaveland, return to Connecticut.

1803 Ohio becomes the 17th state.

1814 Cleveland incorporates as village.

1818 The first steamboat on Lake Erie, *Walk-in-the-Water*, arrives from Buffalo.

1827 The opening of the Ohio-Erie Canal presages the rise of Cleveland as a maritime center and emporium.

1836 Cleveland is incorporated as a city. The first railroad reaches the city.

1841 *Cleveland Plain Dealer* is founded.

1850 The population is 17,034.

1854 Ohio City is annexed to Cleveland.

1855 The digging of the Soo Canal begins.

1856 The first public high school opens.

1870 The Standard Oil Company is organized.

1875 The Opera House is built.

1876 The *Penny Press*, forerunner of the Scripps-Howard chain of newspapers, is launched.

1882 Adelbert College is dedicated. J. H. Wade gives the city its first park.

1891 Federal plan of city government is adopted.

1918 Cleveland Orchestra is organized.

1924 Manager form of government is adopted.

1925 Public library opens.

1930 Manager William R. Hawkins is indicted for graft and murder; the mayoral form of government is restored. Population at highest—900,429.

1939 New Main Street High Level Bridge is built.

1967 City elects first black mayor, Carl Stokes.

1976 Cleveland declares bankruptcy.

1980 Cleveland emerges from bankruptcy.

shipping magnate. According to Lincoln Steffens, a muckraking journalist, Johnson was an upright politician under whose administration Cleveland became the best-governed city in the United States. Despite Hanna's opposition, Johnson built new streets and parks, created a municipal electric company to curb the abuses of privately owned public utilities, and introduced city-owned garbage and refuse collection. He set standards for meat and dairy products and even removed Keep Off the Grass signs from public parks. He is honored with a statue in Public Square bearing the tribute "He Left a City with a Civic Mind."

The post–World War I era witnessed the rise of the Van Sweringen brothers, Oris P. and Mantis J. Beginning as small real estate operators barely out of their teens, they initiated the Shaker Heights development. To secure rapid transit for this suburb, they acquired the Nickel Plate Railroad and eventually built it into a system of over 11,000 miles. In Cleveland they built the Terminal Tower group and Union Station. Their real estate empire collapsed in the 1930s, but meanwhile the city added other buildings. As part of Johnson's Cleveland Mall Plan, the Municipal Auditorium was built in 1920, followed by City Hall, County Courthouse, Federal Building, Board of Education, and Municipal Stadium.

In 1924 the city adopted the manager form of government, but after the administration of its first manager, William R. Hopkins, ended in his conviction on graft and murder charges, the mayoral plan of government was restored. In 1967 Cleveland became the first U.S. city to elect a black mayor, Carl B. Stokes. In 1978 Cleveland defaulted on its municipal loans and declared bankruptcy. It emerged from the bankruptcy four years later.

Historical Landmarks

When Moses Cleaveland platted the village by the Cuyahoga in 1796, he laid it out around a 10-acre commons. This remains as Public Square and is the beginning of the city's most important thoroughfares. The site of Moses Cleaveland's landing at the foot of St. Clair Avenue is marked by a bronze plaque. The Terminal Tower Building, recently renovated, is on the southwest corner of Public Square. Built by the Van Sweringen brothers in 1930, it cost $119 million. Until the 57-story Society Center was completed, Terminal Tower was Cleveland's tallest building with 52 stories. The Soldiers and Sailors Monument in Public Square was dedicated in 1894 in memory of Cuyahoga County soldiers who had served in the Civil War.

The Weddell House at the corner of Sixth Street and Frankfort Avenue, built by Peter Weddell in 1847, was in its heyday Cleveland's finest hotel. Lincoln stayed there in 1861 on his way to the inauguration. The Stadium Hotel on Sixth Street and St. Clair Avenue opened in 1854 as the Angier House, but later became the Kennard House. The Presbyterian Old Stone Church in Public Square, built in 1855, is one of the city's best-known landmarks, although it was gutted three times by fire. The Trinity Cathedral on East 22nd and Euclid avenues is the oldest Episcopal church in the county. The original Trinity Church was founded in 1816, and the cathedral, modeled after 15th-century English churches, was completed in 1907.

Population

For decades Cleveland was the largest city in Ohio, but its population base eroded over the years from a peak of 914,808 in 1950 to 506,616 in 1990. Between 1980 and 1990, the population decreased by 11.9%.

Population

	1980	1990
Central City	573,822	506,616
Rank	18	23
Metro Area	1,898,825	1,831,122
Pop. Change 1980–1990	-68,206	
Pop. % Change 1980–1990	-11.9	
Median Age	31.9	
% Male	46.9	
% Age 65 and Over	14.0	
Density (per square mile)	6,579	

Households

Number	199,787
Persons per Household	2.48
% Female-Headed Households	22.7
% One-Person Households	33.5
Births—Total	10,162
% to Mothers under 20	19.6
Birth Rate per 1,000	18.6
Deaths	6,826
Rate per 1,000	12.5
Infant Deaths	171
Rate Per 1,000	16.8

Ethnic Composition

In 1990 49.49% of Cleveland's population was white, 46.56% black, 4.59% Hispanic, 1.01% Asians and Pacific Islanders, 0.31% American Indians, and 2.63% others.

Ethnic Composition (as % of total pop.)

	1980	1990
White	53.55	49.49
Black	43.8	46.56
American Indian	0.19	0.31
Asian and Pacific Islander	0.59	1.01
Hispanic	3.10	4.59
Other	NA	2.63

Government

Cleveland is governed by a mayor and 21-member council. All are elected to four-year terms, but the mayor is elected citywide and the council members by wards. The mayor is not a member of the council. The city had Democratic mayors from the New Deal in the 1930s until 1971, when a Republican was elected to succeed the city's first black mayor.

Government

Year of Home Charter	1913
Number of Members of the Governing Body	21
Elected at Large	NA
Elected by Wards	21
Number of Women in Governing Body	3
Salary of Mayor	$82,500
Salary of Council Members	$35,683
City Government Employment Total	9,348
Rate per 10,000	174.5

Public Finance

Generally the city has operated with a balanced budget both before it entered into and after it successfully emerged from bankruptcy. The annual budget consists of revenues of $677.130 million and expenditures of $707.607 million. The debt outstanding is $712.989 million, and cash and security holdings are $454.063 million.

Public Finance

Total Revenue (in millions)	$677.13
Intergovernmental Revenue—Total (in millions)	$130.09
Federal Revenue per Capita	$73.09
% Federal Assistance	10.79
% State Assistance	8.27
Sales Tax as % of Total Revenue	0.40
Local Revenue as % of Total Revenue	57.89
City Income Tax	yes
Taxes—Total (in millions)	$208.7

Taxes per Capita
Total	$390
Property	$79
Sales and Gross Receipts	$3
General Expenditures—Total (in millions)	$392.3
General Expenditures per Capita	$732
Capital Outlays per Capita	$74

% of Expenditures for:
Public Welfare	0.3
Highways	7.2
Education	0.0
Health and Hospitals	3.1
Police	23.8
Sewerage and Sanitation	7.9
Parks and Recreation	7.1
Housing and Community Development	11.5
Debt Outstanding per Capita	$728
% Utility	35
Federal Procurement Contract Awards (in millions)	$465
Federal Grants Awards (in millions)	$220.9
Fiscal Year Begins	January 1

Economy

Cleveland is one of the earliest industrial cities in the Midwest and has established strengths in automobiles, tires, steel, oil, and electrical machinery. It has maintained these specialties even while diversifying into more technology-based industries. Cleveland entered the field of polymer plastics only within the last two decades, yet has already become a leader in this $100 billion industry. Cleveland is also a major research center, ranking fourth in the nation with some 400 laboratories. The most important of these facilities is

NASA's Lewis Research Center near Cleveland-Hopkins Airport.

Although manufacturing has declined in relation to other sectors, Cleveland remains an industrial city. Twelve Fortune 500 industrial companies for 1993 had their headquarters in Cleveland. Among the industrial leaders are the Big Three rubber companies: Goodyear, Firestone, and Goodrich, as well as two others: A. Schulman and Standard Products; four chemical companies: Sherwin-Williams, Lubrizol, M. A. Hanna, and Ferro Corporation; two electronic firms: TRW and Reliance Electric; two automotive firms: Eaton Corp and Sudbury Holding; four industrial equipment firms: Parker Hannifin, Figgie International, NAACO Industries, and Lincoln Electric; one furniture firm: Ohio Mattress; one aerospace firm: Gencorp; one publishing firm: American Greetings; and one metal products firm: Banner Industries. The city is also the divisional headquarters of BP America, LTV Steel, and Stouffers. Cleveland is the headquarters of many financial institutions, the largest of which are Society, National City Bank, First National Bank of Ohio, Bank One Cleveland, Bank One Akron, and National City Bank.

Economy

Total Money Income (in millions) $4,297.6
% of State Average   77.3
Per Capita Annual Income $8,018
% Population below Poverty Level   22.1
Fortune 500 Companies   12

Banks	Number	Deposits (in millions)
Commercial	14	NA
Savings	10	NA

Passenger Autos   849,673
Electric Meters   704,127
Gas Meters   592,789

Manufacturing

Number of Establishments   1,598
% with 20 or More Employees   36.5
Manufacturing Payroll (in millions) $2,110.4
Value Added by Manufacture (in millions) $3,974.6
Value of Shipments (in millions) $8,083.7
New Capital Expenditures (in millions) $235.6

Wholesale Trade

Number of Establishments   1,230
Sales (in millions) $5,708.2
Annual Payroll (in millions) $528,057

Retail Trade

Number of Establishments   3,956
Total Sales (in millions) $2,075.2
Sales per Capita $3,873
Number of Retail Trade Establishments with Payroll   2,952
Annual Payroll (in millions) $293
Total Sales (in millions) $2,026.7
General Merchandise Stores (per capita) $288
Food Stores (per capita) $924
Apparel Stores (per capita) $151
Eating and Drinking Places (per capita) $617

Economy (continued)

Service Industries

Total Establishments   3,488
Total Receipts (in millions) $2,600.9
Hotels and Motels (in millions) $77.1
Health Services (in millions) $315.4
Legal Services (in millions) $584.9

Labor

A long tradition of manufacturing has helped to build a skilled work force in Cleveland. The decline in the number of manufacturing jobs has been offset by a corresponding growth in service industries. The public sector is important, accounting for 13% of all jobs. Of the five largest employers, four are in the public sector, led by the federal, county, and city governments. Cleveland was the founding city for many labor unions and the scene of some of their bloodiest victories. However, since the 1930s labor relations have been mostly harmonious.

Labor

Civilian Labor Force   244,682
% Change 1989–1990   0.1

Work Force Distribution
   Mining   600
   Construction   31,200
   Manufacturing   195,800
   Transportation and Public Utilities   34,400
   Wholesale and Retail Trade   220,700
   FIRE (Finance, Insurance, Real Estate)   59,100
   Service   257,600
   Government   118,300
   Women as % of Labor Force   44.3
   % Self-Employed   2.5
   % Professional/Technical   NA
Total Unemployment   18,338
Rate %   7.5
Federal Government Civilian Employment   15,626

Education

The Cleveland City School District supports 128 schools. Alternative parochial and private schools number 30.

Cuyahoga Community College, a two-year college, had a 1990 enrollment of 24,000, making it the largest of area schools. Cleveland State University, established in 1965 when it took over the assets of Fenn College, is a four-year institution and has a law school. Western Reserve University, founded in 1820, and Case Institute of Technology, founded in 1880, merged in 1967 to become Case Western Reserve University. Saint Mary Seminary is a Roman Catholic college. Dyke College, specializing in business courses, was founded in 1848. Capital University is a small Lutheran institution. Specialized institutions include the Cleveland Institute of Art, Cleveland Institute of Music, and Ohio College of Podiatric Medicine. The Greater Cleveland area has a number of other major institutions, including John Carroll University in University Heights, Kent State University, University of Akron, Baldwin-Wallace College, Oberlin College, Ursuline College, and Hiram College.

Education

Number of Public Schools   128
Special Education Schools   NA
Total Enrollment   70,019
% Enrollment in Private Schools   NA
% Minority   79.2
Classroom Teachers   3,792
Pupil-Teacher Ratio   18.5:1
Number of Graduates   2,788
Total Revenue (in millions) $416.3
Total Expenditures (in millions) $399.1
Expenditures per Pupil $5,306
Educational Attainment (Age 25 and Over)
   % Completed 12 or More Years   50.9
   % Completed 16 or More Years   6.4
Four-Year Colleges and Universities   7
   Enrollment   36,237
Two-Year Colleges   1
   Enrollment   358

Libraries

Number   115
Public Libraries   31
Books (in thousands)   2,253
Circulation (in thousands)   5,552
Persons Served (in thousands)   505.6
Circulation per Person Served   10.98
Income (in millions) $22.131
Staff   419

Four-Year Colleges and Universities
   Case Western Reserve University
   Cleveland Institute of Art
   Cleveland State University
   Dyke College
   John Carroll University
   Notre Dame College
   Ursuline College

Health

The Cleveland area is served by more than 40 hospitals staffed by 80,000 health-care professionals. The major hospitals are Case Western Reserve University Hospital; Cleveland Clinic, known for its pioneering in kidney transplants and open-heart surgery; St. Vincent

Health

Deaths—Total   6,826
Rate per 1,000   12.5
Infant Deaths—Total   171
Rate per 1,000   16.8
Number of Metro Hospitals   21
Number of Metro Hospital Beds   8,185
Rate per 100,000   1,528
Number of Physicians   5,134
Physicians per 1,000   3.26
Nurses per 1,000   13.25
Health Expenditures per Capita   NA

Charity Hospital; and Metropolitan General Hospital. Other medical facilities include St. Luke's Hospital, Fairview General Hospital, Mount Sinai Medical Center, and Deaconess Hospital.

Transportation

Cleveland is approached by four interstates: I-80 (Ohio Turnpike) and I-90 both run east to west, while I-71 and I-77 are the principal highways from the south. I-271 skirts the city through eastern suburbs and I-480 runs through southern suburbs. Public transportation includes municipal and privately operated bus lines and two efficient rapid-transit lines, the largest of which is the municipally owned Cleveland Transit System. Amtrak provides passenger rail service and Conrail, Norfolk and Southern, and the Chesapeake and Ohio System provide rail freight services. Among U.S. ports on the Great Lakes, Cleveland ranks fifth in cargo handled and second in incoming cargo. It is the leading iron-ore port. Cleveland has two airports, both municipally owned: Cleveland Hopkins International Airport, serving international passengers, and Burke Lakefront Airport, serving domestic commuters. General aviation traffic is handled also at Cuyahoga County Airport.

Transportation

Interstate Highway Mileage   180
Total Urban Mileage   5,537
Total Daily Vehicle Mileage (in millions)   34.4
Daily Average Commute Time   51.5
Number of Buses   545
Port Tonnage (in millions)   14.5
Airports   1
Number of Daily Flights   194
Daily Average Number of Passengers   10,197

Airlines (American carriers only)
   American
   Continental
   Delta
   Eastern
   Midway
   Northwest
   Trans World
   United
   USAir

Housing

Until the Civil War, homes in Cleveland were strongly influenced by the New England origins of the early settlers, and the smaller homes were essentially farmhouses. In the late 1800s Roman and Greek Revival styles became popular for wealthier residences, and after 1900 bungalows became common. After World War II, faced with housing deterioration, the city launched a project to build thousands of low-cost homes, defraying the expense through the issue of bonds. However, overcrowding continued to be a problem. The Metropolitan Cleveland Housing Authority was set up in 1961, and during the next two decades it completed 15 housing projects to house 21,000 persons. The average price of a single-family home in Cleveland in 1990 was $40,900.

Housing

Housing		
Total Housing Units 224,311		
% Change 1980–1990 -6.8		
Vacant Units for Sale or Rent 17,358		
Occupied Units 199,787		
% with More Than One Person per Room 2.9		
% Owner-Occupied 47.9		
Median Value of Owner-Occupied Homes $40,900		
Average Monthly Purchase Cost $307		
Median Monthly Rent $237		
New Private Housing Starts 225		
Value (in thousands) $10,881		
% Single-Family 31.6		
Nonresidential Buildings Value (in thousands) $100,034		
Tallest Buildings	*Hgt. (ft.)*	*Stories*
Society Center (1991)	948	57
Terminal Tower (1930)	708	52
BP America (1985)	658	46
Plaza Tower (1985)	529	40
One Cleveland Center (1983)	450	31
Bank One Center (1991)	446	28
Justice Center (1976)	420	26
Federal Bldg. (1967)	419	32

Urban Redevelopment

During the late 1980s more than 70 development projects were completed in Cleveland, including the Cleveland Convention Center, Galleria Shopping Complex, Palace Theater, Old Broadway Market, Renaissance at Playhouse Square, Playhouse Square Hotel, Gordon Square Arcade, Cleveland State University Music and Communications Building, Nautica Phase II, Society Center, and Tower City Center. In June 1993 ground was broken for the Rock and Roll Hall of Fame.

Crime

In 1991 there were 9,341 violent crimes in Cleveland, of which 913 were rapes, and 36,269 property crimes.

Crime	
Violent Crimes—Total 9,341	
Violent Crime Rate per 100,000 669.3	
Murder 175	
Rape 913	
Robbery 5,132	
Aggravated Assaults 3,121	
Property Crimes 36,269	
Burglary 10,151	
Larceny 15,485	
Motor Vehicle Theft 10,633	
Arson 767	
Per Capita Police Expenditures $217.92	
Per Capita Fire Protection Expenditures $108.49	
Number of Police 1,742	
Per 1,000 3.19	

Religion

Catholics made up 40% of the population of Cuyahoga County in 1991. Among Protestants the strongest groups were Baptists and Methodists.

Religion	
Largest Denominations (Adherents)	
Catholic	534,785
Black Baptist	117,282
American Baptist	28,176
United Methodist	33,607
Lutheran-Missouri Synod	24,098
United Church of Christ	21,146
Presbyterian	18,110
Jewish	50,050

Media

Cleveland's daily is the *Cleveland Plain Dealer*, owned by the Newhouse Newspapers group. The electronic media consist of 22 AM and FM radio stations and five television stations.

Media	
Newsprint	
The Call & Post, weekly	
Chagrin Herald Sun, weekly	
Cleveland Magazine, monthly	
Cleveland Plain Dealer, daily	
Crain's Cleveland Business, weekly	
The News Sun, weekly	
Sun Courier, weekly	
Sun Herald, weekly	
Sun Messenger, weekly	
The Sun Press, weekly	
West Side Sun News, weekly	
Television	
WEWS (Channel 5)	
WJW (Channel 8)	
WKYC (Channel 3)	
WUAB (Channel 43)	
WVIZ (Channel 25)	
Radio	
WABQ (AM)	WCLV (FM)
WCPN (FM)	WCRF (FM)
WCSB (FM)	WDOK (FM)
WERE (FM)	WNCX (FM)
WHK (AM)	WMMS (FM)
WKNR (AM)	WGAR (FM)
WMJI (FM)	WPHR (FM)
WQAL (FM)	WRDZ (AM)
WRMR (AM)	WDOK (FM)
WRUW (FM)	WWWE (AM)
WLTF (AM)	WZAK (FM)

Sports

Four professional teams play in Cleveland. The Cleveland Indians compete in the eastern division of the Major League Baseball Association's American League and the Cleveland Browns play in the American Conference of the National Football League. Both the Indians and

Browns play home games at Cleveland Stadium. The Cleveland Cavaliers are in the National Basketball Association, and Cleveland Crunch is a professional soccer team; both teams play home games at the Coliseum. The Lumberjacks play hockey, and the Thunderbolts represent indoor football. Thoroughbred races take place at Thistledown in nearby North Randall, harness racing at Northfield Park in Northfield, and auto racing at Cloverleaf Speedway in Valley View.

Arts, Culture, and Tourism

The Cleveland Orchestra, organized in 1918, is permanently housed in Severance Hall. During summer, the orchestra plays at the Open Air Blossom Music Center, which also sponsors opera, classical, pop, jazz, rock, and folk concerts. The Cleveland Chamber Music Society, Cleveland Chamber Symphony, and Cleveland Quartet also present a full schedule of performances each year. In dance Cleveland is represented by the Cleveland Ballet performing at the State Theater from October through May, Footpath Dance Company, Dance Cleveland, and North Coast Ballet Theater. Opera Cleveland at the State Theater and Cleveland Institute of Music's Opera Theater are the two premier opera companies.

The showplace of Cleveland theater is Playhouse Square, which consists of the renovated Ohio, State, and Palace theaters in which the Cleveland Playhouse and opera and ballet companies perform. The Cleveland Playhouse is the nation's first professional residential company, founded in 1916.

University Circle, near the campus of Case Western, is the location for the Cleveland Museum of Art, Cleveland Museum of Natural History, Western Reserve Historical Society Museum, and the city's botanic gardens.

Dunham Tavern, on Euclid Avenue, was once a stagecoach stop for travelers between New York and Chicago. Completed in 1842, the structure is a historical remnant located on what was once Cleveland's most impressive residential street.

Travel and Tourism

Hotel Rooms   12,621
Convention and Exhibit Space (square feet)   NA

Convention Centers
   Cleveland Convention Center
   International Exposition Center
   Clarion Hotel and Conference Center
   Cleveland Grays Armory
   Playhouse Square Center

Festivals
   Parties in the Park
   All Nations Festival
   Flatsfest
   Ohio Valley Jazz Festival
   Cuyahoga County Fair
   National Air Show
   Apple Butter Festival

Parks and Recreation

Cleveland's Metropark system contains 19,000 acres. One of the largest is the 75-acre Wade Park on Euclid Avenue, which includes the Euclid Fine Arts Garden and the sculpture *Fountain of Waters* by Chester Beach. The 273-acre Rockefeller Park was given to the city by John Davison Rockefeller, Sr., in 1896. Within it are Rockefeller Lake and the Cleveland Cultural Gardens, a group of gardens representing foreign nations, such as the English Garden, Hebrew Garden, German Garden, and Italian Garden. The 112-acre Gordon Park on St. Clair Avenue, the 17-acre Edgewater Park on West Boulevard, the 159-acre Brookside Park, including the Cleveland Zoological Gardens, the 1,212-acre Washington Park on the brink of the Flats, Cleveland Horticultural Garden between East Ninth and West Third streets, Lakefront State Park, and Mentor Headlands State Park are among the more popular parks in the city.

Sources of Further Information

Cleveland Public Library
325 Superior Avenue
Cleveland, OH 44114-1271
(216) 623-2856

Convention and Visitors Bureau of Greater Cleveland
3100 Terminal Tower
Tower City Center
Cleveland, OH 44113
(216) 621-4110

Greater Cleveland Growth Association
200 Tower City Center
50 Public Square
Cleveland, OH 44113-2291
(216) 621-3300

New Cleveland Campaign
200 Tower City Center
Cleveland, OH 44113
(216) 621-3300

Western Reserve Historical Society
10825 East Boulevard
Cleveland, OH 44106
(216) 721-5722

Additional Reading

Barton, Josef J. *Peasants and Strangers: Italians, Rumanians, and Slovaks in an American City, 1890–1950.* 1975.

Campbell, Thomas F., and Edward M. Miggins, eds. *The Birth of Modern Cleveland, 1865–1930.* 1988.

Condon, George E. *Cleveland: The Best Kept Secret.* 1967.

The Encyclopedia of Cleveland History. 1987.

Gurwitz, Aaron S., and G. Thomas Kingsley. *The Cleveland Metropolitan Economy*. 1982.

Kusmer, Kenneth L. *A Ghetto Takes Shape: Black Cleveland, 1870–1930*. 1976.

Miller, Carol Poh, and Robert Wheeler. *Cleveland: A Concise History, 1796–1990*. 1990.

Porter, Philip W. *Cleveland: Confused City on a Seesaw*. 1976.

Rarick, Holly M. *Progressive Vision: The Planning of Downtown Cleveland, 1903–1930*. 1986.

Rose, William G. *Cleveland: The Making of a City*. 1990.

Swanstrom, Todd. *The Crisis of Growth Politics: Cleveland, Kucinich, and the Challenge of Urban Populism*. 1985.

Van Tassel, David D., and John J. Grabowski, eds. *Cleveland: A Tradition of Reform*. 1986.

Colorado

Location and Topography

Colorado Springs is located in east-central Colorado on a high, flat plain near the base of Pikes Peak. The city sits on the eastern slope of the Rocky Mountains, with flat prairie to the east and the mountain divide to the north. The land to the north slopes upward to the top of the Palmer Lake Divide, reaching an average height of 8,000 feet within 20 miles. Between the city and Pikes Peak are forested foothills and many canyons. Cheyenne Mountain looms to the southwest.

Layout of City and Suburbs

Monument Creek runs through Colorado Springs from north to south, separating the plains area of the city from the foothills. While the oldest portion of the community is west of Monument Creek (and I-25), so is much of the latest residential development. Fountain Creek flows through Ute Pass and the mineral springs at Manitou Springs to join Monument Creek in the southwestern corner of the city. The main north-south thoroughfare within the city is I-25. Midland Expressway (U.S. 24) runs east to west, becoming Platte Avenue after it crosses I-25. Other important arteries are the Garden of the Gods Road, Uintah Street, and Fillmore Street, all running east to west.

Two principal shopping centers are Citadel Mall, at Platte and Nevada avenues, and Chapel Hills Mall, at Academy and Pikes Peak avenues. The more affluent residential districts lie north of Colorado College and at Broadmoor.

Climate

Colorado Springs is noted for its mild weather, which has helped to make it a summer playground and health resort. The Rocky Mountains protect the city from hot summers, while the chinook winds warm it in winter. Precipitation is generally light, with most falling between April and September.

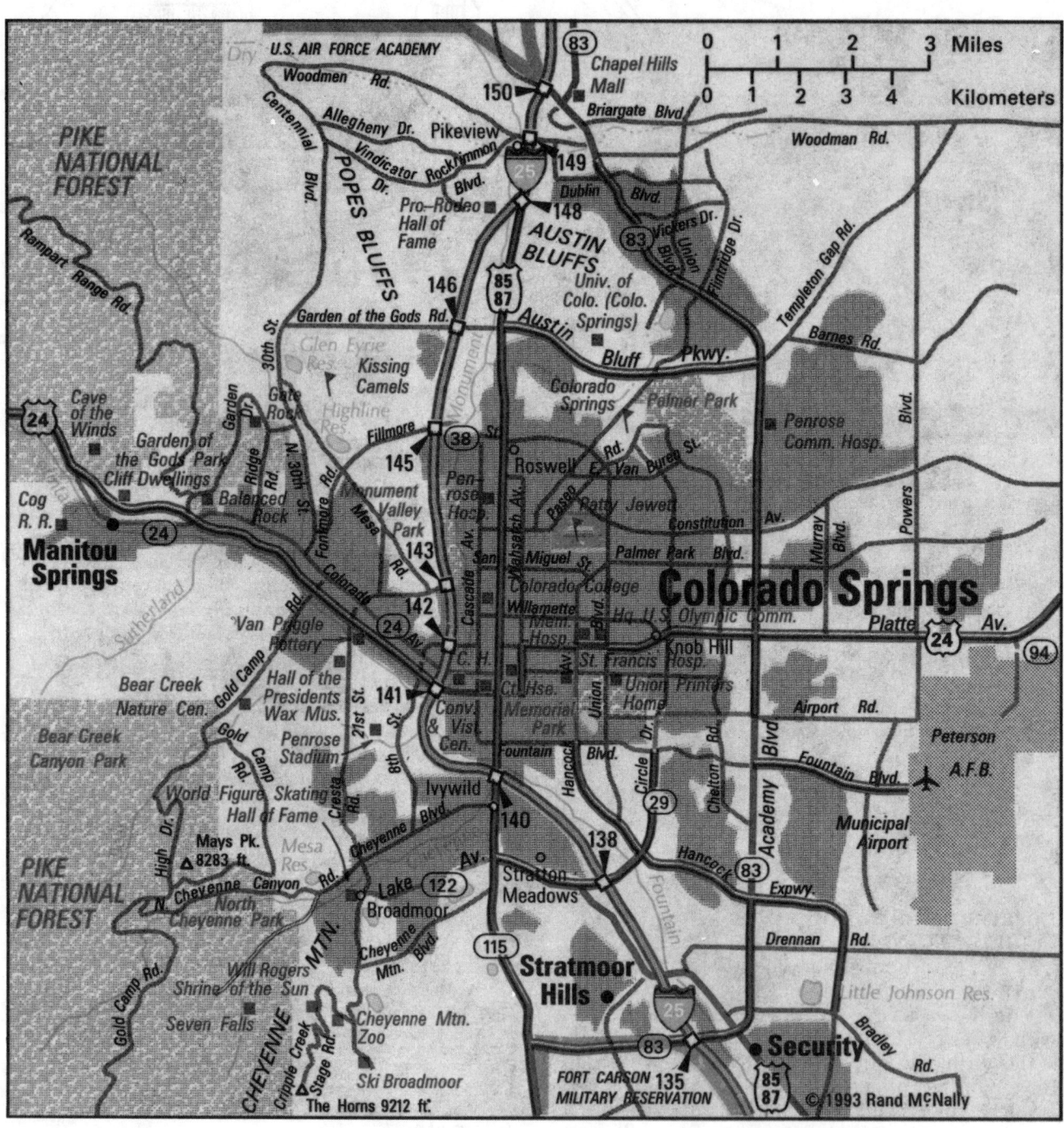

Weather

Temperature

Highest Monthly Average °F	84.9
Lowest Monthly Average °F	16.2

Annual Averages

Days 32°F or Below   162
Days above 90°F   15
Zero Degree Days   7
Precipitation (inches)   16
Snow (inches)   40
% Seasonal Humidity   49
Wind Speed (m.p.h.)   10.4
Clear Days   130
Cloudy Days   116
Storm Days   59
Rainy Days   87

Average Temperatures (°F)	High	Low	Mean
January	41.0	16.1	28.6
February	43.6	18.9	31.3
March	47.7	22.8	35.3
April	59.2	33.1	46.2
May	68.4	42.6	55.5
June	78.1	51.1	64.6
July	84.4	57.0	70.7
August	82.4	55.8	69.1
September	74.9	46.9	60.9
October	64.2	36.8	50.5
November	49.8	25.1	37.5
December	43.1	18.9	31.0

History

The site that would become Colorado Springs was initially staked out as El Dorado City, but attracted no inhabitants. In 1859, with the establishment of the Colorado City Town Company, the town of Colorado City was founded. It was settled largely by ex-miners turned merchants who supplied tools, provisions, and recreation to prospectors in the South Park region. The area was close to Pikes Peak, discovered by Lt. Zebulon Montgomery Pike in 1806, and the Garden of the Gods, considered by the Mountain Ute, Plains Arapahoe, and Cheyenne tribes to be sacred ground.

Colorado City soon degenerated into a town noted for brawls, gunfights, and saloons. Several factors combined to deal it a near death blow: the Civil War, discouraging reports from prospectors in South Park, and the Second Territorial Legislature voting to reconvene from Colorado City to Denver, subsequently making Denver the territorial capital.

Meanwhile, in 1871 the Denver and Rio Grande Western Railroad, the first narrow-gauge railroad in Colorado, came to the region. Its president, former general William Jackson Palmer, was so impressed with this site and the surrounding mountains and foothill canyons that his company purchased 10,000 acres for $30,000. The first stake was driven on 31 July 1871 at the present-day intersection of Pikes Peak and Cascade avenues. Palmer planned a resort community for men and women of sound moral character, and excluded industries and saloons. During the early years the settlement was known as the Fountain Colony, after Fountain Creek. Later it was named Colorado Springs after the mineral springs at the nearby village of Manitou. Broad thoroughfares were laid out; those running north and south were named after mountain ranges, and east-west roads after streams crossed by the Denver & Rio Grande Railroad. Lots were set aside for parks, schools, and churches, and a railroad, post office, and hotel were built within months.

Within a year, Colorado Springs supplanted Colorado City as the county seat and received national attention as a health resort and scenic worderland. In 1876 the state of Colorado was admitted to the Union. During the 1880s so many Englishmen settled there that the town was nicknamed Little London. The newcomers introduced golf, cricket, and especially polo. In 1885 the Colorado Midland Railway pushed westward from the city to become the first standard-gauge railroad to cross the Continental Divide. In 1889 the Chicago Rock Island and Pacific Railroad chose Colorado Springs as its western terminal. A cog railroad was built to the top of Pikes Peak in 1890.

The rich gold strikes at Cripple Creek temporarily put new life into Colorado City and transformed it into an industrial center. But after the mines closed, Colorado City again dwindled and was finally annexed by Colorado Springs in 1917, becoming West Colorado Springs. Colorado Springs profited from the Cripple Creek gold mines as the bonanza kings settled in the city and built elaborate mansions. In 1909 the Garden of the Gods was bequeathed to the city and added to its park system.

During World War II, Colorado Springs became an important military installation. Fort Carson was established in the early 1940s, and the U.S. Air Force Academy was completed in 1958. In 1966 the North American Air Defense Command was established in Cheyenne Mountain.

Historical Landmarks

One of Colorado City's most famous landmarks from the early days is the Broadmoor Hotel on Lake Avenue, which was a resort popular with European and Asian royalty. The site of Colorado's first capitol (now occupied by another building) is at 2526 West Colorado Avenue. A bronze equestrian statue of General William Jackson Palmer stands at the intersection of Platte and Nevada avenues.

Population

Colorado Springs has experienced phenomenal growth since World War II. From a population of 33,237 in 1940 it rose to 136,000 in 1970. The city grew by 58.8% to 215,105 in 1980 and by 30.7% to 281,140 in 1990. Colorado Springs is one of the few cities whose growth rate exceeds that of the metro area.

Chronology

1859 Colorado City Town Company founds and settles Colorado City.

1861 Colorado City briefly becomes the territorial capital.

1871 Former general William J. Palmer, president of Denver and Rio Grande Western Railroad, purchases 10,000 acres and drives the first stake for a planned resort community known as Fountain Colony. Palmer's railroad reaches the site, and a railroad station, post office, church, and school are erected.

1872 Fountain Colony is renamed Colorado Springs after the mineral springs at the nearby village of Manitou.

1873 Colorado Springs supplants Colorado City as the county seat.

1876 Colorado becomes a state in the Union.

1883 Antlers Hotel opens.

1885 The Colorado Midland Railroad pushes westward from the city.

1889 Colorado Springs is chosen as the western terminus of the Chicago Rock Island and Pacific Railroad.

1891 A cog railway is completed to the top of Pikes Peak.

1891 Gold is discovered in Cripple Creek, catapulting Colorado City into a wealthy town.

1917 Colorado City, with the depletion of the Cripple Creek mines, is absorbed by Colorado Springs.

1909 Garden of the Gods is bequeathed to the city.

1958 U.S. Air Force Academy is completed.

1978 Olympic training grounds open.

Population

	1980	1990
Central City	215,105	281,140
Rank	66	54
Metro Area	309,424	397,014
Pop. Change 1980–1990	+66,035	
Pop. % Change 1980–1990	+30.7	
Median Age	31.1	
% Male	48.9	
% Age 65 and Over	9.2	
Density (per square mile)	1,534	

Households

Number 110,862
Persons per Household 2.49
% Female-Headed Households 10.1
% One-Person Households 26.7

Population (continued)

Births—Total 5,233
    % to Mothers under 20 11.9
    Birth Rate per 1,000 21.1

Ethnic Composition

Whites make up 85.9% of the population, blacks 7%, American Indians 0.8%, Asians and Pacific Islanders 2.4%, and others 3.8%. Hispanics, both black and white, make up 9.1%.

Ethnic Composition (as % of total pop.)

	1980	1990
White	87.9	85.9
Black	5.56	7.02
American Indian	0.51	0.83
Asian and Pacific Islander	1.46	2.43
Hispanic	8.49	9.13
Other	NA	3.81

Government

Colorado Springs has a mayor-council form of government. The mayor and the members of the council are elected to four-year terms.

Government

Year of Home Charter 1921
Number of Members of the Governing Body 8
Elected at Large 4
Elected by Wards 4
Number of Women in Governing Body 3
Salary of Mayor $0.0
Salary of Council Members $0.0
City Government Employment Total 4,564
Rate per 10,000 167.4

Public Finance

The annual budget consists of revenues of $498 million and expenditures of $525.183 million. The debt outstanding

Public Finance

Total Revenue (in millions) $498.0
Intergovernmental Revenue—Total (in millions) $21.4
Federal Revenue per Capita $8.09
% Federal Assistance 1.62
% State Assistance 1.67
Sales Tax as % of Total Revenue 12.24
Local Revenue as % of Total Revenue 43.11
City Income Tax no
Taxes—Total (in millions) $62.7

Taxes per Capita
    Total $230
    Property $42
    Sales and Gross Receipts $184
General Expenditures—Total (in millions) $161.7
General Expenditures per Capita $593
Capital Outlays per Capita $177

Public Finance (continued)

% of Expenditures for:

Public Welfare   0.3
Highways   7.9
Education   0.0
Health and Hospitals   24.5
Police   10.9
Sewerage and Sanitation   25.6
Parks and Recreation   6.3
Housing and Community Development   0.4
Debt Outstanding per Capita $1,203
   % Utility   82.6
Federal Procurement Contract Awards (in millions) $328.8
Federal Grants Awards (in millions) $13.9
Fiscal Year Begins   January 1

is $429.583 million, and cash and security holdings are $341.872 million.

Economy

 The mainstay of the economy is the U.S. Department of Defense, which maintains Fort Carson, an army post; U.S. Air Force Academy; Fort Peterson Air Force Base; and North American Air Defense Command (NORAD). Together they employ one-fifth of the city's work force. Colorado Springs is also becoming a center for space research; it is headquarters for the Combined Services Space Center and Consolidated Space Operations Center. As a spillover, the aerospace sector has been able to bring in a number of electronics and high-technology firms, such as Hewlett-Packard.

The appeal of Colorado Springs as a tourist attraction has not only endured but grown over the years. The city provides a window on the grandeur of the Rocky Mountains, and Pikes Peak is one of the most visited tourist sites in the nation. Tourism generates

Economy

Total Money Income (in millions) $3,094
% of State Average   96.8
Per Capita Annual Income $11,334
% Population below Poverty Level   10.3
Fortune 500 Companies   NA

Banks	Number	Deposits (in millions)
Commercial	36	1,500
Savings	5	NA

Passenger Autos   246,171
Electric Meters   110,095
Gas Meters   90,035

Manufacturing

Number of Establishments   352
% with 20 or More Employees   25.6
Manufacturing Payroll (in millions) $509.6
Value Added by Manufacture (in millions) $1,046.7
Value of Shipments (in millions) $1,954.1
New Capital Expenditures (in millions) $92.7

Wholesale Trade

Number of Establishments   468
Sales (in millions) $864.8
Annual Payroll (in millions) $78,905

Economy (continued)

Retail Trade

Number of Establishments   3,212
Total Sales (in millions) $2,221.4
Sales per Capita $8,147
Number of Retail Trade Establishments with Payroll   2,141
Annual Payroll (in millions) $276.7
Total Sales (in millions) $2,172.8
General Merchandise Stores (per capita)   NA
Food Stores (per capita) $1,324
Apparel Stores (per capita) $349
Eating and Drinking Places (per capita) $803

Service Industries

Total Establishments   2,818
Total Receipts (in millions) $1,014.0
Hotels and Motels (in millions) $95.7
Health Services (in millions) $263.4
Legal Services (in millions)   NA

over half a billion dollars a year, sustaining a vigorous hotel and service industry.

Labor

Depending less on private corporations and more on the federal government and tourist services, Colorado Springs has been insulated from the downscaling aspects of the national economy. Colorado Springs also offers businesses a relatively union-free environment. The city has a skilled labor force as a result of training programs offered by businesses in cooperation with local schools.

Labor

Civilian Labor Force   142,865
% Change 1989–1990   0.8
Work Force Distribution
Mining   NA
Construction   NA
Manufacturing   NA
Transportation and Public Utilities   NA
Wholesale and Retail Trade   NA
FIRE (Finance, Insurance, Real Estate)   NA
Service   NA
Government   NA
Women as % of Labor Force   45.4
% Self-Employed   7.3
% Professional/Technical   30.4
Total Unemployment   8,780
Rate %   6.1
Federal Government Civilian Employment   1,760

Education

Colorado Springs Public Schools District 11 supports 56 schools. The city has 3 institutions of higher education: U.S. Air Force Academy, University of Colorado at Colorado Springs, and the private Colorado College. There are also a number of business and technical schools, including Colorado Technical College.

Education

Number of Public Schools   56
Special Education Schools   NA
Total Enrollment   30,009
% Enrollment in Private Schools   NA
% Minority   NA
Classroom Teachers   NA
Pupil-Teacher Ratio   NA
Number of Graduates   NA
Total Revenue (in millions) $116.821
Total Expenditures (in millions) $122.362
Expenditures per Pupil $3,732
Educational Attainment (Age 25 and Over)
    % Completed 12 or More Years   82.3
    % Completed 16 or More Years   22.4
Four-Year Colleges and Universities   2
    Enrollment   7,868
Two-Year Colleges   3
    Enrollment   1,240

Libraries

Number   33
Public Libraries   12
Books (in thousands)   772.9
Circulation (in thousands)   2,115
Persons Served (in thousands)   382
Circulation per Person Served   5.53
Income (in millions) $8.415
Staff   247

Four-Year Colleges and Universities
    University of Colorado at Colorado Springs
    Colorado College

Health

 The Colorado Springs medical sector consists of six hospitals Memorial Hospital, Penrose Community Hospital, Doctors Hospital, St. Francis Hospital, Langstaff Brown Emergency Medical Center, and Emergicare Medical Center. Special facilities include Penrose Cancer Hospital; Surgery, Ltd.; and Cedar Springs, a psychiatric center.

Health

Deaths—Total   1,565
Rate per 1,000   6.3
Infant Deaths—Total   62
Rate per 1,000   11.8
Number of Metro Hospitals   6
Number of Metro Hospital Beds   1,387
Rate per 100,000   509
Number of Physicians   475
Physicians per 1,000   1.35
Nurses per 1,000   NA
Health Expenditures per Capita $1.51

Transportation

 Colorado Springs is approached by the north-south I-25 and east-west I-70, the north-south U.S. 85/87 and 24, and State Highways 83 and 115. Rail freight service is provided by Rock Island, Denver & Rio Grande, and Sante Fe railroads. The principal air terminal is the Colorado Springs Municipal Airport.

Transportation

Interstate Highway Mileage   32
Total Urban Mileage   1,377
Total Daily Vehicle Mileage (in millions)   5.568
Daily Average Commute Time   38.7 min.
Number of Buses   42
Port Tonnage (in millions)   NA
Airports   1
Number of Daily Flights   39
Daily Average Number of Passengers   1,642

Airlines (American carriers only)
    American
    American West
    Continental
    Delta
    TransWorld
    United

Housing

 Of the total housing stock, 54.6% is owner-occupied. The median value of an owner-occupied home is $81,900 and the median monthly rent $360.

Housing

Total Housing Units   124,442
% Change 1980–1990   29.1
Vacant Units for Sale or Rent   11,451
Occupied Units   110,862
% with More Than One Person per Room   2.8
% Owner-Occupied   54.6
Median Value of Owner-Occupied Homes $81,900
Average Monthly Purchase Cost $372
Median Monthly Rent $360
New Private Housing Starts   NA
Value (in thousands)   NA
% Single-Family   NA
Nonresidential Buildings Value (in thousands)   NA

Urban Redevelopment

 Most urban redevelopment has been directed toward construction of hotels and other tourist facilities. Development programs are coordinated by Colorado Springs Economic Development Council and Old Colorado City Development Company.

Crime

 Colorado Springs ranks below the national average in public safety. Of the crimes known to police in 1991, there were 1,345 violent crimes and 20,059 property crimes.

Crime	
Violent Crimes—Total	1,345
Violent Crime Rate per 100,000	422.4
Murder	25
Rape	231
Robbery	387
Aggravated Assaults	742
Property Crimes	20,059
Burglary	3,865
Larceny	15,000
Motor Vehicle Theft	1,194
Arson	89
Per Capita Police Expenditures	$107.04
Per Capita Fire Protection Expenditures	$62.32
Number of Police	386
Per 1,000	1.53

Religion

 About 35% of the population belong to churches. The leading denominations are Baptists and Catholics, followed by Methodists, Presbyterians, and Lutherans.

Religion	
Largest Denominations (Adherents)	
Catholic	48,052
Southern Baptist	19,528
Latter-Day Saints	8,188
United Methodist	11,360
Black Baptist	7,839
Presbyterian	8,297
Evangelical Lutheran	7,084
Assembly of God	3,150
United Church of Christ	4,012
Jewish	1,500

Media

 The city daily is the *Colorado Springs Gazette Telegraph* The electronic media consist of 3 television stations and 19 FM and AM radio stations.

Media	
Newsprint	
Colorado Springs Gazette Telegraph, daily	
Television	
KKTV (Channel 11)	
KRDO (Channel 13)	
KXRM (Channel 21)	
Radio	
KATM (FM)	KCMN (AM)
KDZA (AM)	KEPC (FM)
KHII (FM)	KIKX (FM)

Media (continued)	
KILO (FM)	KKCS (AM)
KKCS (FM)	KKFM (FM)
KKLI (FM)	KRCC (FM)
KRDO (AM)	KRDO (FM)
KSSS (AM)	KTLF (FM)
KVOR (AM)	KSPZ (FM)
KWYD (AM)	

Sports

 The Sky Sox, a minor league Triple A baseball team affiliated with the Colorado Rockies, play in Colorado Springs. In college football, Colorado Springs residents root for the Air Force Academy. Other popular sports include golf and greyhound racing.

Arts, Culture, and Tourism

 Pikes Peak Center is the home of the Colorado Springs Symphony Orchestra, which gives free summer concerts at Antler Park. Operas are also staged at the Pike Peaks Center. Colorado Springs has a number of specialized museums, including the Museum of the American Numismatic Association, Pioneers Museum, Pro-Rodeo Hall of Fame, Will Rogers Shrine of the Sun, May Natural History Museum, Hall of Presidents Wax Museum, World Figure Skating Hall of Fame and Museum, Western Museum of Mining and Industry, Peterson Space Command Museum, and the Fine Arts Center, which houses the Taylor Collection of American Indian and Hispanic art.

Travel and Tourism	
Hotel Rooms 7,181	
Convention and Exhibit Space (square feet) NA	
Convention Centers	
City Auditorium	
Julie Penrose Center	
Fine Arts Center	
Pikes Peak Center	
Festivals	
Pikes Peak Rodeo (August)	

Parks and Recreation

 Colorado Springs is a planned city with adequate space devoted to public parks. Among the larger ones are Palmer, Memorial, Bear Creek Canyon, North Cheyenne, and Valley parks, as well as the Garden of the Gods, ceded to the city in 1909.

Sources of Further Information

City Administration Building
30 South Nevada Street
Colorado Springs, CO 80903
(719) 578-6600

Colorado Springs Chamber of Commerce
Holly Sugar Building
Colorado Springs, CO 80901
(719) 635-1551

Colorado Springs Convention and Visitors Bureau
104 South Cascade Street, Suite 104
Colorado Springs, CO 80903
(719) 635-7506

The Greater Colorado Springs Economic
Development Corporation
2 North Cascade Avenue
Colorado Springs, CO 80903
(719) 471-8183

Additional Reading

Hetzler, Rosemary, and John Hetzler. *Colorado Springs and Pikes Peak Country*. 1989.

Skolout, Patricia Farris. *Colorado Springs History A to Z*. 1992.

Sprague, Marshall. *Newport in the Rockies: The Life and Good Times of Colorado Springs*. 4th rev. ed. 1987.

Columbus

Ohio

Basic Data

Name Columbus
Name Origin From Christopher Columbus
Year Founded 1797 Inc. 1834
Status: State Capital of Ohio
        County Seat of Franklin County
Area (square miles) 190.9
Elevation (feet) 780
Time Zone EST
Population (1990) 632,910
Population of Metro Area (1990) 1,377,419

Sister Cities
    Odense, Denmark
    Genoa, Italy
    Hefei, China
    Sevilla, Spain
    Tainan City, China

Distance in Miles To:

Atlanta	585
Boston	801
Chicago	358
Dallas	1,049
Denver	1,241
Detroit	193
Houston	1,166
Los Angeles	2,242
Miami	1,171
New York	568
Philadelphia	477
Washington, DC	427

Location and Topography

Columbus is in central Ohio, near the geographic center of the state, on the Scioto and Olentangy rivers, both in the drainage area of the Ohio River. The terrain is rolling, without any prominent features.

Layout of City and Suburbs

The Scioto and Olentangy rivers join near the Ohio State Penitentiary, forming a great oxbow through the heart of the city. Alum and Big Walnut creeks also run through the city. Columbus grew along two principal streets: Broad and High. High Street is a long commercial corridor crossed by Broad Street at the State House. East of High was formerly the residential section. Other major sections of the city include the 77-acre U.S. Army Reservation, Fort Hayes, the state capitol area, the university area, and the commercial district. Metropolitan Columbus includes a number of suburbs, the principal ones being Grandview Heights, Upper Arlington, Worthington, Bexley, and Whitehall.

Environment

Environmental Stress Index 3.2
Green Cities Index: Rank 43
              Score 32.09
Water Quality Alkaline, medium soft
    Average Daily Use (gallons per capita) NA
    Maximum Supply (gallons per capita) NA
Parkland as % of Total City Area 9.7
% Waste Landfilled/Recycled NA
Annual Parks Expenditures per Capita $53.19

Climate

Columbus has a four-season climate. The weather is changeable, influenced by air masses from central and southwest Canada in winter and spring, and air masses from the Gulf of Mexico in summer and fall. The city's four rivers contribute to the formation of shallow ground fog at daybreak in summer and fall.

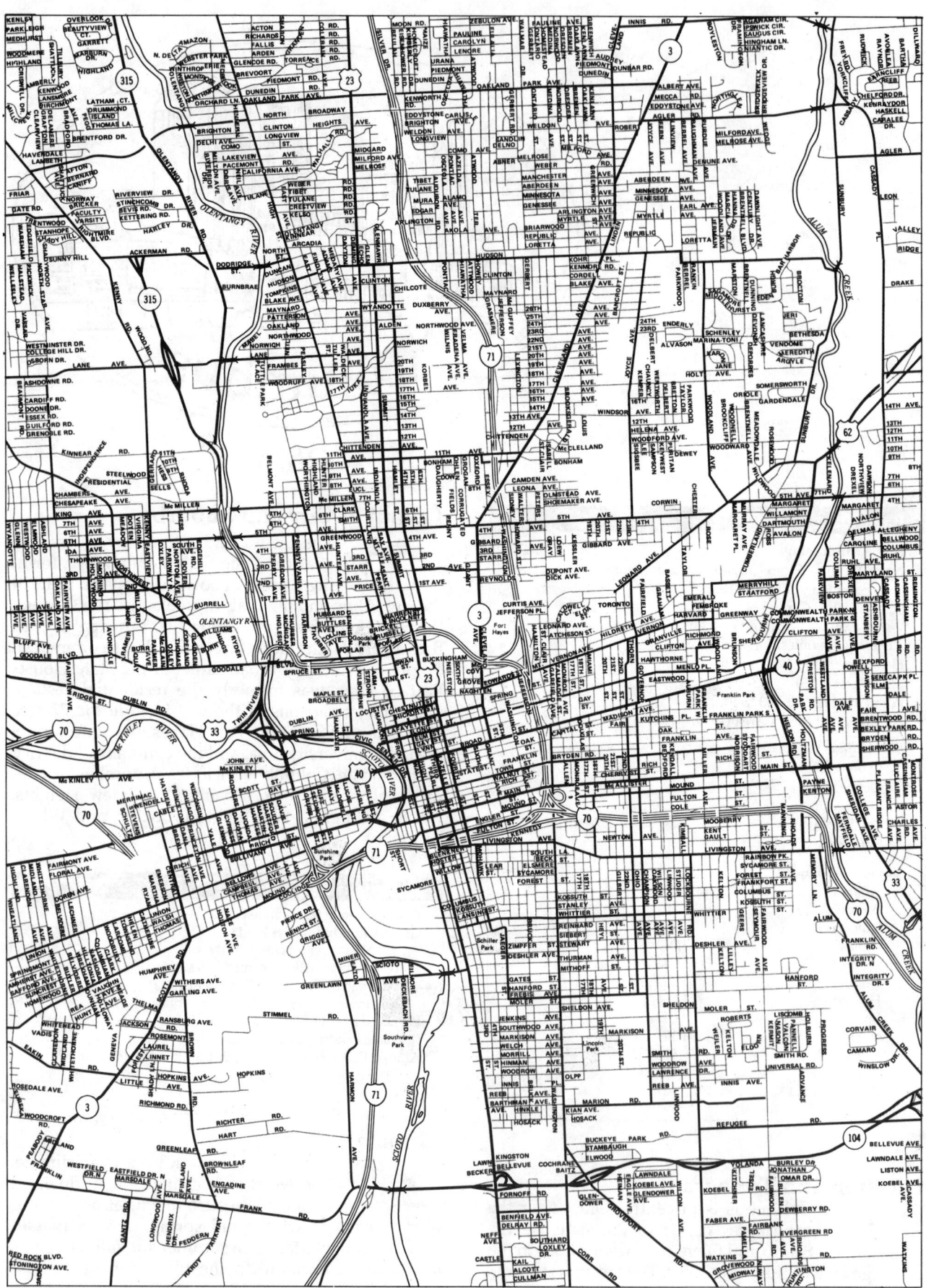

Weather

Temperature

Highest Monthly Average °F   84.4
Lowest Monthly Average °F   19.4

Annual Averages

Days 32°F or Below   122
Days above 90°F   15
Zero Degree Days   4
Precipitation (inches)   37
Snow (inches)   28
% Seasonal Humidity   70
Wind Speed (m.p.h.)   8.7
Clear Days   75
Cloudy Days   184
Storm Days   42
Rainy Days   136

Average Temperatures (°F)	High	Low	Mean
January	36.4	20.4	28.4
February	39.2	21.4	30.3
March	49.3	29.1	39.2
April	62.8	39.5	51.2
May	72.9	49.3	61.1
June	81.9	58.9	70.4
July	84.8	62.4	73.6
August	83.7	60.1	71.9
September	77.6	52.7	65.2
October	66.4	42.0	54.2
November	50.9	32.4	41.7
December	38.7	22.7	30.7

History

In 1797 Franklinton was established as one of the first villages in the Northwest Territory by Lucas Sullivant, a U.S. government surveyor. Sullivant's site, at the fork of two major waterways, was a stopover point on a major American Indian trail from the Ohio River to Lake Erie. In 1812 a group of local businessmen subdivided 1,200 acres east of the Scioto River and offered 20 acres to the state of Ohio for construction of a statehouse and penitentiary. At the suggestion of General Joseph Foos, the village was named Columbus in honor of Christopher Columbus. Within a year the population grew to 300. The construction of a temporary capitol building, delayed by the War of 1812, was completed in 1816. In the first municipal election, Jarvis Pike was elected mayor.

As Columbus grew, it absorbed Franklinton, from which the county seat was moved to the east side of the river in 1824. A series of fever and cholera epidemics checked population growth until the swamps in the center of the town were drained. Transportation needs were met by the construction of a canal and turnpike, and in 1831 a feeder canal was built connecting the city with the Ohio and Erie Canal. Two years later the National Road reached Columbus.

Columbus officially became a city in 1834 after 22 turbulent years of floods, epidemics, and a dispute over the city's designation as state capital. Construction of the current capitol building, or statehouse, began in 1839 and was completed in 1861. In 1850 the city entered the railroad age when a steam engine pulling a few flatcars chugged out of Columbus. The Columbus and Xenia Railroad made its 54-mile maiden trip to Xenia in 3 hours and 5 minutes. By 1872 five railroads were in operation.

On the eve of the Civil War the population reached 20,000. The Ohio State University was created initially as the Ohio Agricultural and Mechanical College in 1873. By the 1880s, the population grew to 50,000. The city experienced the worst strike in its history in 1910 and its worst flood in 1913. Freeway construction began in the 1950s. This, plus post–World War II housing policies favoring new construction, laid the foundation for the modern Columbus neighborhoods.

Historical Landmarks

The state capitol, one of the country's outstanding examples of Greek Revival style, stands in a 10-acre park bounded by High, Broad, State, and Third streets. Several blocks south of the capitol is the German Village, a restored community in a 50-block area. My Jewels Monument on the northwest corner of the capitol is a group of bronze statues of Ohio soldiers and statesmen—Ulysses S. Grant, William T. Sherman, Philip H. Sheridan, Edwin M. Stanton, James A. Garfield, Salmon P. Chase, and Rutherford B. Hayes. The McKinley Memorial forms an arc with a central pedestal surmounted by a bronze statue of the assassinated president. Fort Hayes on Cleveland Avenue and Buckingham Street has been a military post since 1863. The Governor's Mansion on Broad Street was a fomerly private residence purchased by the state in 1919.

Population

Columbus was one of the largest gainers in population in the 1980s. Its population rose 12% from 565,032 in 1980 to 632,910 in 1990. During the 1970s it had grown by 4.6% from 540,000 in 1970. As a result, Columbus's national rank has risen from 20th to 16th.

Population

	1980	1990
Central City	565,032	632,910
Rank	19	16
Metro Area	1,243,827	1,377,419
Pop. Change 1980–1990 +67,878		
Pop. % Change 1980–1990 +12.0		
Median Age 29.4		
% Male 48.3		
% Age 65 and Over 9.2		
Density (per square mile) 3,315		

Households

Number   256,996
Persons per Household   2.38
% Female-Headed Households   14.2
% One-Person Households   31.3
Births—Total   10,406
    % to Mothers under 20   14.4
    Birth Rate per 1,000   18.4

Chronology

1797 Lucas Sullivant, a surveyor, establishes a frontier settlement on the Scioto River called Franklinton.

1812 Ohio state legislature approves a plan to build a capitol on the high east bank of the Scioto River directly opposite Franklinton. The town is christened Columbus.

1816 The temporary capitol is completed. In the first municipal election, Jarvis Pike is elected mayor.

1824 Franklinton is absorbed by Columbus.

1831 The first boats make the trip from Lake Erie to Columbus and are welcomed in the city with parades, speeches, and banquets.

1833 National Road reaches Columbus.

1834 Columbus officially becomes a city.

1839 Permanent state house construction begins.

1873 Ohio State University is founded as Ohio Agricultural and Mechanical College.

1910 A violent streetcar strike, lasting all summer, leads to rioting and death.

1913 The Scioto River goes on a rampage and floods the valley, leaving 100 dead and 20,000 homeless.

Ethnic Composition

Whites make up 74.4%, blacks 22.6%, American Indians 0.2%, Asians and Pacific Islanders 2.4%, and others 0.4%.

Ethnic Composition (as % of total pop.)		
	1980	1990
White	76.24	74.42
Black	22.11	22.55
American Indian	0.16	0.23
Asian and Pacific Islander	0.83	2.37
Hispanic	0.82	1.07
Other	NA	0.42

Government

Columbus is governed by a city manager and a council of seven members elected at large to four-year terms.

Public Finance

The annual budget consists of revenues of $546.737 million and expenditures of $596.674 million. The debt outstanding is $1.072 billion, and cash and security holdings are $317.833 million.

Government

Year of Home Charter   NA
Number of Members of the Governing Body   7
Elected at Large   7
Elected by Wards   0
Number of Women in Governing Body   2
Salary of Mayor $77,000
Salary of Council Members $25,000
City Government Employment Total   6,784
Rate per 10,000   119.9

Public Finance

Total Revenue (in millions) $546.737
Intergovernmental Revenue—Total (in millions) $72.48
Federal Revenue per Capita $26.29
% Federal Assistance   4.81
% State Assistance   7.86
Sales Tax as % of Total Revenue   1.03
Local Revenue as % of Total Revenue   74.35
City Income Tax   yes
Taxes—Total (in millions) $168.7

Taxes per Capita
Total $298
Property $24
Sales and Gross Receipts $5
General Expenditures—Total (in millions) $333.5
General Expenditures per Capita $589
Capital Outlays per Capita $98
% of Expenditures for:
Public Welfare   0.0
Highways   8.5
Education   0.0
Health and Hospitals   4.2
Police   17.9
Sewerage and Sanitation   21.2
Parks and Recreation   5.2
Housing and Community Development   3.6
Debt Outstanding per Capita $1,330
% Utility   48.9
Federal Procurement Contract Awards (in millions) $330.6
Federal Grants Awards (in millions) $542.5
Fiscal Year Begins   January 1

Economy

Columbus has a well-balanced economy in which the government, services, trade, and manufacturing sectors are equally strong. The city has additional strengths in computer information, telecommunications, retailing, health care, and defense. Home to more than 74 insurance companies, Columbus ranks among the insurance capitals of the nation. The city is the corporate headquarters for several national firms, such as Ashland Chemicals, Adria Laboratories, Borden, Chemlawn, Compuserve, Consolidated Stores, Crane Plastics, Honda of America, Lennox Industries, Merrill Publishing, Ohio Bell Telephone, O. M. Scott & Sons, Toledo Scale, Wendy's, White Castle, and Worthington Industries. Among the largest financial institutions are BancOhio National Bank, Bank One Columbus, Chase Bank, Society Bank, Star Bank, Beneficial Management, and TransOhio Savings Bank. Columbus is the site of two military installations: Defense Construction Supply Center and Aerospace Guidance and Metrology Center. The Columbus Aircraft Division of Rockwell International is involved in a diverse range of defense-related projects. The 1,087 manufacturing establishments, with 69,602 workers and a payroll of $1.878 billion, are most concentrated in printing and publishing, fabricated metal products, machinery, and food processing. Columbus is the headquarters of several computer information services such as Chemical Abstracts Service and Online Computer Library Center. Research centers include Battelle Memorial Institute, the largest independent nonprofit research laboratory in the world.

Economy

Total Money Income (in millions)	$5,608.5	
% of State Average	95.5	
Per Capita Annual Income	$9,909	
% Population below Poverty Level	16.5	
Fortune 500 Companies	1	
Banks	*Number*	*Deposits (in millions)*
Commercial	13	17,619
Savings	18	495.7
Passenger Autos	624,922	
Electric Meters	422,000	
Gas Meters	330,000	

Manufacturing

Number of Establishments	747
% with 20 or More Employees	40.2
Manufacturing Payroll (in millions)	$1,309.8
Value Added by Manufacture (in millions)	$3,353.0
Value of Shipments (in millions)	$6,228.2
New Capital Expenditures (in millions)	$180.6

Wholesale Trade

Number of Establishments	1,322
Sales (in millions)	NA
Annual Payroll (in millions)	NA

Retail Trade

Number of Establishments	4,710
Total Sales (in millions)	$4,764.7
Sales per Capita	$8,418
Number of Retail Trade Establishments with Payroll	3,452
Annual Payroll (in millions)	$611
Total Sales (in millions)	$4,711.6
General Merchandise Stores (per capita)	$1,289
Food Stores (per capita)	$1,128
Apparel Stores (per capita)	NA
Eating and Drinking Places (per capita)	NA

Service Industries

Total Establishments	4,517
Total Receipts (in millions)	$2,876.0
Hotels and Motels (in millions)	$126.3
Health Services (in millions)	$609.6
Legal Services (in millions)	$319.0

Labor

 A high share of public employment, low unionization, and a high percentage of technical and scientific jobs are some of the peculiarities of the Columbus employment market. Worker productivity has grown at a rate significantly above the national average, and several sectors have shown employment gains despite the national downturn. The state of Ohio, Ohio State University, Columbus Public Schools, and the city of Columbus account for 8% of total employment.

Labor

Civilian Labor Force	340,774
% Change 1989–1990	0.7
Work Force Distribution	
Mining	800
Construction	26,300
Manufacturing	102,800
Transportation and Public Utilities	31,000
Wholesale and Retail Trade	180,800
FIRE (Finance, Insurance, Real Estate)	61,200
Service	184,000
Government	131,600
Women as % of Labor Force	45.6
% Self-Employed	3.6
% Professional/Technical	17.2
Total Unemployment	15,398
Rate %	4.5
Federal Government Civilian Employment	5,853

Education

The Columbus City School District supports 139 schools. In addition to the Catholic parochial school system, there are 13 private schools. Ohio State University (OSU), founded in 1873, is one of the largest university systems in the nation with an enrollment of 54,300. In addition to its Columbus campus, the university maintains four regional campuses. The system includes 8 schools and 18 colleges with 108 departments teaching 11,700 courses. Its main campus occupies 400 acres out of a total area of 1,600 acres. The main entrance is at 15th Avenue and High Street. With a budget of $1.23 billion, a payroll of $640.7 million, and a work force of 19,100, OSU is a major force in the Columbus economy. Among its noted centers are the Wexner Center for the Arts, featuring four art galleries and several auditoriums and theaters, and the Ohio Supercomputer Center. A city within a city, OSU operates its own power plant and airport. Other institutions of higher learning include Capital University, the city's oldest educational institution, founded in 1830 and affiliated with the Evangelical Lutheran Church; Columbus College of Art and Design, founded in 1879; Denison University, founded in 1831 in Granville; Franklin University, founded in 1902 by the YMCA; Ohio Dominican College, founded in 1911 as College of St. Mary of the Springs; Ohio Wesleyan University, founded by the United Methodist Church in 1842; and Otterbein College, founded in 1947 by the United Methodist Church.

Education

Number of Public Schools 139
Special Education Schools 1
Total Enrollment 64,280
% Enrollment in Private Schools 9.0
% Minority 50.4
Classroom Teachers 3,800
Pupil-Teacher Ratio 16.9:1
Number of Graduates 3,852
Total Revenue (in millions) $319.104
Total Expenditures (in millions) $331.585
Expenditures per Pupil $4,936
Educational Attainment (Age 25 and Over)
    % Completed 12 or More Years 68.9
    % Completed 16 or More Years 18.6
Four-Year Colleges and Universities 8
    Enrollment 73,101
Two-Year Colleges 1
    Enrollment 13,194

Libraries

Number 86
Public Libraries 22
Books (in thousands) 1,113
Circulation (in thousands) 5,506
Persons Served (in thousands) 688.8
Circulation per Person Served 7.99
Income (in millions) $32.319
Staff 474

Four-Year Colleges and Universities
    Ohio State University
    Capital University
    Columbus College of Art and Design
    DeVry Institute of Technology
    Franklin University
    Ohio Dominican College
    Pontifical College Josephinum

Health

The metropolitan Columbus area is served by 11 hospitals. The largest is Ohio State University Hospital, which includes the Ohio State University Comprehensive Cancer Center. Other facilities are Central Ohio Psychiatric Hospital, Children's Hospital, Columbus Community Hospital, Doctors Hospital North and West, Grant Medical Center, Harding Hospital, Mount Carmel Medical Center, Park Medical Center

Health

Deaths—Total 4,588
Rate per 1,000 8.1
Infant Deaths—Total 100
Rate per 1,000 9.6
Number of Metro Hospitals 9
Number of Metro Hospital Beds 4,959
Rate per 100,000 876
Number of Physicians 2,524
Physicians per 1,000 2.18
Nurses per 1,000 7.69
Health Expenditures per Capita $35.27

and Riverside Medical Hospitals, and St. Ann's Hospital.

Transportation

Two interstate highways—the north-south I-71 and east-west I-70—intersect in the city. I-270 serves as a bypass, and I-670 is a downtown inner belt. U.S. Highways include the east-west 40 and the northeast-southwest 62. North-south U.S. 23 bisects downtown, intersecting east-west 40. State highways include north-south 315, northeast-southwest 3, east-west 161, and northeast 16. Five railroads provide rail freight services: Norfolk & Western, Conrail, Chessie, Burlington Northern, and Union Pacific. The principal air terminus is the Port Columbus International Airport, 15 minutes east of downtown Columbus, served by 17 scheduled commercial airlines. General aviation facilities are available at Don Scott and Bolton fields. An important link in the commercial shipping network is the Rickenbacker Industrial Air Park run by the Flying Tigers, designated as a free-trade zone.

Transportation

Interstate Highway Mileage 108
Total Urban Mileage 3,194
Total Daily Vehicle Mileage (in millions) 20.664
Daily Average Commute Time 45.8 min.
Number of Buses 292
Port Tonnage (in millions) NA
Airports 1
Number of Daily Flights 77
Daily Average Number of Passengers 4,554

Airlines (American carriers only)
    American
    American West
    Continental
    Delta
    Eastern
    Northwest
    United
    USAir

Housing

The total number of residential units is 278,084, of which 46.6% are owner-occupied; 45.1% are single units. In 1960 Columbus became the first city to build apartment projects for the aged that included special recreational facilities. Housing choices range from new apartments in the Brewery District downtown to sprawling acreage in Jefferson Township. Neighborhoods such as Colonial Hills in Worthington offer homes in the range of $90,000 to $100,000. New executive homes in Powell and New Albany start at $250,000. The upscale neighborhoods are Berwick, Clintonville/Beechwold, Far East, German Village, Hilltop, Indian Village, Linden, Northland, Northwest and Far Northwest, Olde Town East and Newer East Side, South, University Area, Victorian Village and Harrison West, and Westland.

Housing

Total Housing Units   278,084
% Change 1980–1990   14.9
Vacant Units for Sale or Rent   16,781
Occupied Units   256,996
% with More Than One Person per Room   2.3
% Owner-Occupied   46.6
Median Value of Owner-Occupied Homes $66,000
Average Monthly Purchase Cost $333
Median Monthly Rent $348
New Private Housing Starts   4,676
Value (in thousands) $204,696
% Single-Family   45.1
Nonresidential Buildings Value (in thousands) $254,707

Tallest Buildings	Hgt. (ft.)	Stories
James A. Rhodes		
(State Office Tower)	629	41
LeVeque Tower, 50 W. Broad	555	47
Ohio Bureau of Worker's		
Compensation & Ind. Comm.	530	33
Huntington Center, 41 S. High St.	512	37
Verne-Riffe State Office Tower	503	33
One Nationwide Plaza	482	40
One Riverside Plaza	456	31
Borden Bldg., 180 E. Broad	438	34

Urban Redevelopment

Columbus is one of the fastest-growing cities in the nation. In the 1980s more than $1 billion was invested in downtown development. Principal projects included the State Office Tower, Ohio Center Convention Complex, Columbus City Center Retail Mall, and development of the Scioto riverfront.

Crime

Columbus has a below-average standing in public safety. Of the crimes known to police in 1991, there were 7,221 violent crimes and 57,557 property crimes.

Crime

Violent Crimes—Total   7,221
Violent Crime Rate per 100,000   720.8
Murder   138
Rape   650
Robbery   3,747
Aggravated Assaults   2,686
Property Crimes   57,557
Burglary   16,398
Larceny   32,983
Motor Vehicle Theft   8,176
Arson   837
Per Capita Police Expenditures $155.15
Per Capita Fire Protection Expenditures $99.77
Number of Police   1,223
Per 1,000   2.16

Religion

Columbus has over 600 Christian congregations. They are represented in the Metropolitan Area Church Board, which is involved in a number of projects directed against racial disharmony, juvenile delinquency, and poverty.

Religion

Largest Denominations (Adherents)

Catholic	114,514
United Methodist	51,135
Black Baptist	51,677
Evangelical Lutheran	27,887
Presbyterian	20,365
Southern Baptist	23,408
United Church of Christ	10,430
American Baptist	12,851
Church of Christ	12,434
Jewish	10,488

Media

The city dailies are the *Columbus Dispatch* and *The Daily Reporter*. Electronic media consist of 4 television stations (commercial, independent, and public) and 14 AM and FM radio stations.

Media

Newsprint
The Booster, weekly
Business First, weekly
Columbus Dispatch, daily
Columbus Monthly, monthly
The Daily Reporter, daily

Television
WBNS (Channel 10)
WCMH (Channel 4)
WOSU (Channel 34)
WSYX (Channel 6)

Radio

WBNS (AM)	WBNS (FM)
WCOL (FM)	WCOL (AM)
WMNI (AM)	WMGG (FM)
WNCI (FM)	WOSU (AM)
WOSU (FM)	WRFD (AM)
WTVN (AM)	WLVQ (FM)
WVKO (AM)	WSNY (FM)

Sports

Columbus has no major professional sports team. Fans watch the Ohio State Buckeyes football team play at the 90,000-seat Ohio Stadium and the Columbus Clippers, a Triple A affiliate of baseball's New York Yankees, play a 70-game home schedule at Cooper Stadium. The Columbus 500 is part of the Camel GT Sports Prototype Endurance Racing Series. The Columbus Marathon is held on the second Sunday in November. May to mid-September is the season for harness racing at Scioto Downs.

Arts, Culture, and Tourism

Performing arts revolve around two theaters. The renovated Palace Theater, which opened in 1926, is now the home of both Opera Columbus and Jazz Arts Group. The Ohio Theater, a restored 1928 movie theater that is the official theater for the state of Ohio, is the home of the Columbus Symphony Orchestra, BalletMet, and performances sponsored by the Columbus Association for Performing Arts. Columbus also has a chamber orchestra, ProMusica. The Martin Luther King, Jr., Center for Performing and Cultural Arts showcases Afro-American cultural events. OSU's Wexner Center for the Arts has a busy schedule throughout the year in Mershon Auditorium and Weigel Hall. Columbus's only professional equity theater company is Player's Theater Columbus (formerly a community theater), housed in the Riff Center for Government and the Arts. An adjunct group is Players Youth Theater Columbus. Two companies that often handle controversial or experimental material are Contemporary American Theater Company and Reality Theater. A much older group—in fact, the oldest community theater company in central Ohio—is Gallery Players, which is associated with the Leo Yassenoff Jewish Community Center. Center Stage Theater, a black community theater, holds its productions at the Martin Luther King Center. The OSU Theater Company and the drama department of Otterbein College also have theater seasons. Thanks largely to the exceptional dance program at OSU, Columbus has a strong dance tradition. Among the companies performing regularly are the Stuart Pimsler Dance and Theater, Van Pelt Dance Ensemble, and BalletMet. The Wexner Center for the Arts also hosts dance performances.

Newly decorated and reorganized, the Columbus Museum of Art is acknowledged to be one of the leading museums in the nation. The Wexner Center for the Arts is the newest art showplace with exhibitions emphasizing the latest art trends.

Parks and Recreation

The city of Columbus operates 166 recreational parks covering 5,431 acres. Franklin Park is the largest, with 200 acres of picnic groves and a small lake. It is the site of AmeriFlora 92, commemorating the voyage of Christopher Columbus. Schiller Park is a 23-acre park bounded by Jaeger Street and Deshler, Reinhard, and City Park avenues.

Sources of Further Information

City Hall
90 West Broad Street
Columbus, OH 43215
(614) 645-7671

Columbus Area Chamber of Commerce
37 North High Street
Columbus, OH 43215
(614) 221-1321

Greater Columbus Convention and Visitors Bureau
10 West Broad Street
Columbus, OH 43215
(614) 221-6623

Ohio Historical Society
1985 Velma Avenue
Columbus, OH 43211
(614) 297-2300

Public Library of Columbus and Franklin County
28 South Hamilton Road
Columbus, OH 43213
(614) 864-8050

Additional Reading

McKenzie, Roderick Duncan. *Neighborhood: A Study of Local Life in the City of Columbus, Ohio.* 1923.
Monkkonen, Eric H. *The Dangerous Class: Crime and Poverty in Columbus, Ohio, 1860–1885.* 1975.

Travel and Tourism

Hotel Rooms   13,405
Convention and Exhibit Space (square feet)   90,000

Convention Centers
Ohio Center Complex
Battelle Hall
Franklin County Veterans Memorial
Ohio Expositions Center
Aladdin Temple
Palace Theater

Festivals
Ohio State Fair (August)
Columbus Arts Festival (Summer)
Hot Ribs and Cool Jazz Festival (July)
Oktoberfest (September)
Columbus International Festival (October)

Concord

New Hampshire

Basic Data

Name   Concord
Name Origin   From Concord MA
Year Founded   1725 Inc. 1853
Status: State   Capital of New Hampshire
         County   Seat of Merrimack County
Area (square miles)   64.1
Elevation (feet)   290
Time Zone   EST
Population (1990)   36,006
Population of Metro Area (1990)   120,005

Distance in Miles To:

Boston	74
Portsmouth	46
Burlington	155
Nashua	36

Environment

Environmental Stress Index   NA
Green Cities Index: Rank   NA
                    Score   NA
Water Quality   Neutral, very soft, fluoridated
    Average Daily Use (gallons per capita)   NA
    Maximum Supply (gallons per capita)   NA
Parkland as % of Total City Area   NA
% Waste Landfilled/Recycled   NA
Annual Parks Expenditures per Capita   NA

Climate

Northwesterly winds provide cool, dry air all year long. Temperatures are moderate in both summer and winter. The average snowfall is 65 inches, and the growing season is short.

Weather

Temperature

Highest Monthly Average °F   82.6
Lowest Monthly Average °F   9.0

Annual Averages

Days 32°F or Below   174
Days above 90°F   17
Zero Degree Days   10
Precipitation (inches)   36.53
Snow (inches)   64.3
% Seasonal Humidity   67.5
Wind Speed (m.p.h.)   6.7
Clear Days   82
Cloudy Days   164
Storm Days   19
Rainy Days   124

Average Temperatures (°F)	High	Low	Mean
January	31.2	9.1	20.2
February	38.5	18.0	28.3
March	45.5	26.5	36.0

Location and Topography

Concord is situated in south-central New Hampshire on the west bank of the Merrimack River in Merrimack County. The terrain is hilly, with many wooded areas, ponds, and streams.

Layout of City and Suburbs

Concord has a small business district grouped within an area of seven blocks between State and Main streets. In the center is a spacious government section filled with imposing granite buildings and wide lawns. The skyline is mostly low, broken only by church steeples and the State House Tower, especially a focal point when floodlit at night. The residential districts lie mainly on the west and north.

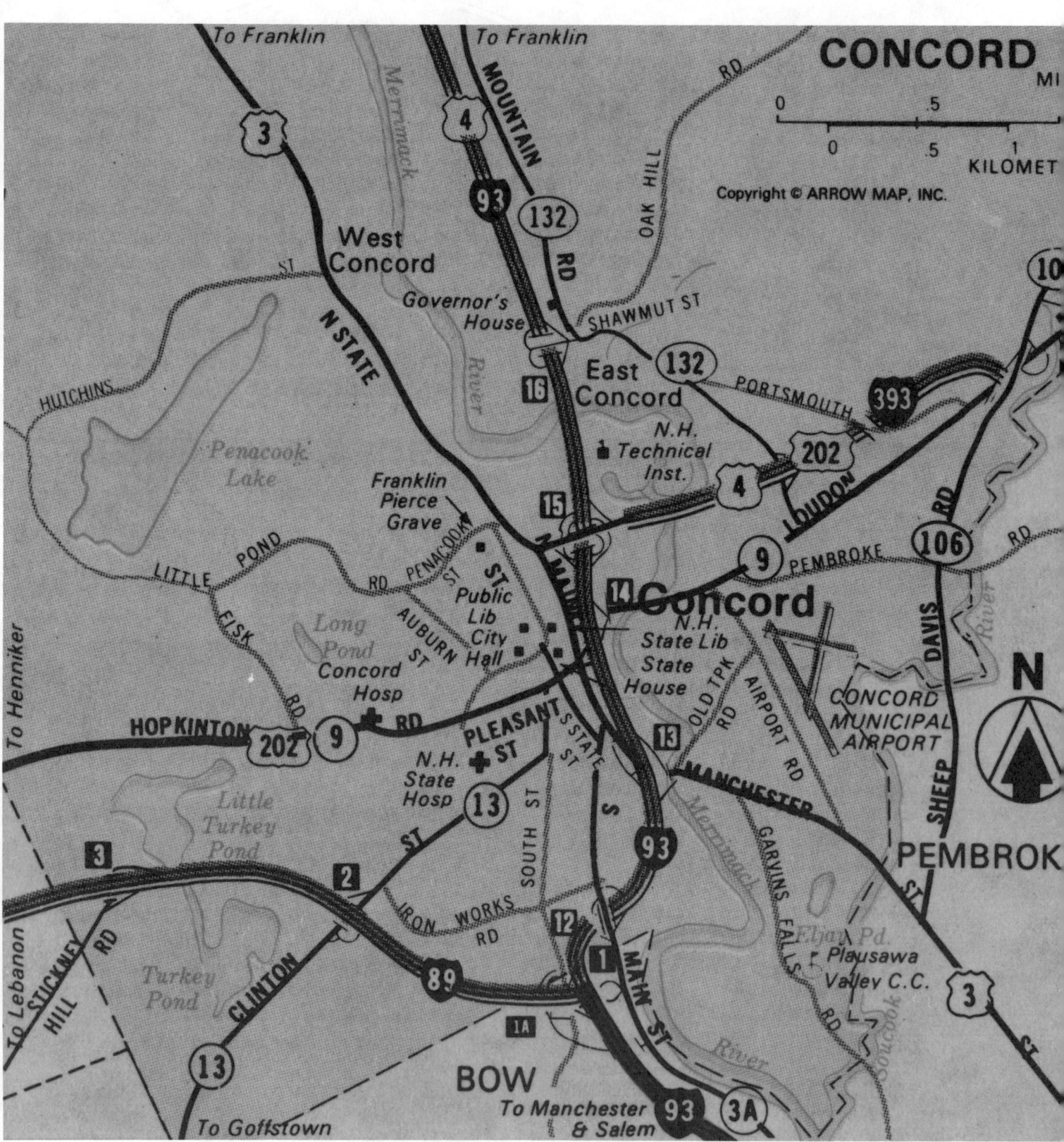

Weather (continued)

April	61.5	33.6	47.6
May	75.1	45.3	60.2
June	79.7	51.4	65.6
July	82.8	55.6	69.2
August	82.6	57.1	69.9
September	71.3	44.1	57.7
October	63.8	37.7	50.8
November	48.5	30.8	39.7
December	35.8	15.1	25.5

History

The site of present-day Concord was the home of the Pennacook tribe, who called the area Penna Cook, meaning "crooked place," or "bend in the river." The early white settlers corrupted the name to Penny Cook, and the place was called the Plantation of Penny Cook in a 1659 grant by the Massachusetts Bay Colony to Richard Waldron. In 1725 it was regranted to a group that included Ebenezer Eastman. In 1726 the first settlers arrived at Penny Cook after a long trek from their home in Haverhill. Settlement began in 1727 on the fertile west bank of the Merrimack. In 1733 the town was incorporated in Massachusetts as Rumford, then reincorporated in New Hampshire in 1765 as Concord.

The friendliness of the neighboring Indians made Concord's early history relatively peaceful. Concorders took an active role in the French and Indian wars and the American Revolution. The tradition continued during the Civil War when the First New Hampshire Regiment was the first regiment of volunteers to go to the front in 1861 in response to President Lincoln's call. In 1808 Concord was chosen as the capital of New Hampshire over Portsmouth.

Two major factors in Concord's growth were the opening of the Middlesex Canal in 1815 and the opening of the steam railroad to Boston in 1842. Concord's industrial history began in 1813 when wheelwright Lewis Downing opened his wagon-building business in the city. The Concord stagecoach became the vehicle of choice for the Wells Fargo Company, and from 1826 to 1900 Downing and his coach builder Stephen Abbot built more than 3,000 coaches. Another notable Concord business was Rumford Press, at one time the third largest printer in the country, printing more than 50 national magazines. Granite quarrying also flourished in Concord, and granite from its quarries can be found in some of the most imposing edifices in the country. Two of the most famous Concorders were Franklin Pierce, the only New Hampshire statesman elected to the Oval Office, and Mary Baker Eddy, founder of Christian Science.

Historical Landmarks

Capitol Square contains most of Concord's public buildings, including the state capitol (the nation's oldest), built of New Hampshire granite and Vermont marble. Among the statues and historical markers in the square flanking the capitol is the Memorial Arch, erected in 1891. Pierce Manse, the Concord home of President Franklin Pierce, was built in 1838.

Population

Concord is one of the smallest state capitals in the United States, with a population that has remained near the 36,000 mark for a number of decades. However, city population is expected to reach 53,000 in 2000 and 69,000 in 2010.

Population

	1980	1990
Central City	30,400	36,006
Rank	NA	700
Metro Area	115,020	120,005
Pop. Change 1980–1990 +5,606		
Pop. % Change 1980–1990 +18.4		
Median Age 33.2		
% Male 48.5		
% Age 65 and Over 14.0		
Density (per square mile) 561		

Households

Number 14,222
Persons per Household 2.35
% Female-Headed Households 9.9
% One-Person Households 30.4
Births—Total 451
  % to Mothers under 20 8.0
  Birth Rate per 1,000 14.6

Ethnic Composition

Like many cities in the Northeast, Concord is 98% white. Blacks, Asians, American Indians, and others together constitute about 1.5%.

Ethnic Composition (as % of total pop.)

	1980	1990
White	99.0	98.18
Black	0.27	0.63
American Indian	0.13	0.28
Asian and Pacific Islander	0.27	0.67
Hispanic	0.56	0.99
Other	NA	0.24

Government

Concord operates under a council-manager form of government. Seven councillors are elected at large and eight by wards. The at-large councillors serve four-year terms and the ward councillors two-year terms. The council appoints a professional city manager who is a civil servant.

Government

Year of Home Charter 1949
Number of Members of the Governing Body 15
Elected at Large 7

Government (continued)

Elected by Wards   8
Number of Women in Governing Body   5
Salary of Mayor   NA
Salary of Council Members   NA
City Government Employment Total   486
Rate per 10,000   148.3

Chronology

1659   The Plantation of Penny Cook is granted to Richard Waldron.

1725   The settlement is regranted to Ebenezer Eastman.

1726   The first settlers reach the west bank of the Merrimack near the present-day site of Concord.

1733   The town is incorporated as Rumford by Massachusetts.

1765   The town is reincorporated in New Hampshire as Concord.

1808   Concord is chosen as the capital of New Hampshire.

1815   The Middlesex Canal opens, linking Concord with major markets in the Northeast.

1827   Wheelwright Lewis Downing and coach-builder Stephen Abbot team to produce the celebrated Concord stagecoaches that helped to win the American West.

1936   Concord suffers heavy losses in a flood of the Merrimack River.

Public Finance

The available details of the Concord city budget are set forth below.

Economy

The economic core of Concord is its status as the capital of New Hampshire. Nevertheless, the city was a major industrial and distribution center in the Northeast long before it became the capital, and has continued to build on its historic strengths in trade and commerce. About 20% of the work force is employed in industry, but during the latter part of the 1980s and early 1990s, the city began losing industrial jobs. This loss is partly offset by growth in the retail and professional services sector. The completion of the Steeplegate Mall in 1990 reestablished Concord as the major retail center for the state north

Public Finance

Total Revenue (in millions)   NA
Intergovernmental Revenue—Total (in millions)   NA
Federal Revenue per Capita   NA
% Federal Assistance   NA
% State Assistance   NA
Sales Tax as % of Total Revenue   NA
Local Revenue as % of Total Revenue   NA
City Income Tax   no
Taxes—Total (in millions) $8.3

Taxes per Capita
   Total $253
   Property $242
   Sales and Gross Receipts $0
General Expenditures—Total (in millions) $21.7
General Expenditures per Capita $661
Capital Outlays per Capita $66
   % of Expenditures for:
   Public Welfare   2.5
   Highways   10.7
   Education   0.0
   Health and Hospitals   0.8
   Police   9.9
   Sewerage and Sanitation   17.8
   Parks and Recreation   4.8
   Housing and Community Development   0.0
Debt Outstanding per Capita $1,244
   % Utility   15.6
Federal Procurement Contract Awards (in millions) $2.3
Federal Grants Awards (in millions) $71.3
Fiscal Year Begins   NA

Economy

Total Money Income (in millions) $373.1
% of State Average   100
Per Capita Annual Income $11,662
% Population below Poverty Level   9.0
Fortune 500 Companies   NA

Banks	Number	Deposits (in millions)
Commercial	5	NA
Savings	4	NA

Passenger Autos   93,829
Electric Meters   14,050
Gas Meters   5,000

Manufacturing

Number of Establishments   74
% with 20 or More Employees   37.8
Manufacturing Payroll (in millions) $106.4
Value Added by Manufacture (in millions) $196.0
Value of Shipments (in millions) $360.8
New Capital Expenditures (in millions) $13.0

Wholesale Trade

Number of Establishments   86
Sales (in millions)   NA
Annual Payroll (in millions)   NA

Retail Trade

Number of Establishments   527
Total Sales (in millions) $542.5
Sales per Capita $16,555
Number of Retail Trade Establishments with Payroll   384
Annual Payroll (in millions) $57.8
Total Sales (in millions) $534.7
General Merchandise Stores (per capita) $1,633
Food Stores (per capita) $3,427
Apparel Stores (per capita) $674
Eating and Drinking Places (per capita) $1,198

Economy (continued)

Service Industries

Total Establishments   446
Total Receipts (in millions) $205.1
Hotels and Motels (in millions) $7.6
Health Services (in millions) $57.5
Legal Services (in millions) $37.4

of Manchester. The opening of the Christa McAuliffe Planetarium has helped to create a strong tourist attraction for Concord. With several new office and commercial buildings, downtown is faring quite well.

Labor

The size of the labor force, estimated at 56,000, shows a high degree of labor participation. The largest sector is government, followed by services, wholesale and retail trade, manufacturing, and FIRE (finance, insurance, and real estate). The state and city are the largest employers, followed by two medical institutions. Among private employers, the largest are the Sprague Electric Company and Chubb Insurance. Concord is the headquarters of 6 insurance companies and 12 banks.

Labor

Civilian Labor Force   19,603
% Change 1989–1990   5.7

Work Force Distribution
   Mining   NA
   Construction   NA
   Manufacturing   NA
   Transportation and Public Utilities   NA
   Wholesale and Retail Trade   NA
   FIRE (Finance, Insurance, Real Estate)   NA
   Service   NA
   Government   NA
   Women as % of Labor Force   46.3
   % Self-Employed   5.4
   % Professional/Technical   19.9
Total Unemployment   1,040
Rate %   5.3
Federal Government Civilian Employment   484

Education

The Concord School District consists of one senior high school, one junior high/middle school and nine elementary schools. The parochial system includes one elementary school, one junior high school, and Bishop Brady High School. Its Episcopal school, St. Paul's, is noted as a feeder school for Ivy League universities.

Health

As the capital, Concord is the hub of the state's medical system. Its two major hospitals are Concord Hospital, affiliated with the Dartmouth College Medical School, and New Hampshire Hospital, which specializes in psychiatric care.

Education

Number of Public Schools   11
Special Education Schools   NA
Total Enrollment   NA
% Enrollment in Private Schools   NA
% Minority   NA
Classroom Teachers   NA
Pupil-Teacher Ratio   NA
Number of Graduates   NA
Total Revenue (in millions)   NA
Total Expenditures (in millions)   NA
Expenditures per Pupil   NA
Educational Attainment (Age 25 and Over)   NA
   % Completed 12 or More Years   76.7
   % Completed 16 or More Years   21.5
Four-Year Colleges and Universities   NA
   Enrollment   NA
Two-Year Colleges   NA
   Enrollment   NA

Libraries

Number   19
Public Libraries   2
Books (in thousands)   146
Circulation (in thousands)   338
Persons Served (in thousands)   37
Circulation per Person Served   9.13
Income (in millions) $0.963
Staff   27

Four-Year Colleges and Universities
   0

Health

Deaths—Total   372
Rate per 1,000   12.0
Infant Deaths—Total   4
Rate per 1,000   8.9
Number of Metro Hospitals   2
Number of Metro Hospital Beds   768
Rate per 100,000   2,344
Number of Physicians   NA
Physicians per 1,000   NA
Nurses per 1,000   NA
Health Expenditures per Capita   NA

Transportation

Concord is accessed by a number of highways. I-93 is the major north-south artery, and I-89 branches to the northwest, as do highways 3 and 4. Running east-west are Highways 106 and 202. State Highways running through or near the city include 3A, 9, 13, 36, 103, and 106. Seven

Transportation

Interstate Highway Mileage   NA
Total Urban Mileage   NA
Total Daily Vehicle Mileage (in millions)   NA
Daily Average Commute Time   NA
Number of Buses   NA
Port Tonnage (in millions)   NA
Airports   1
Number of Daily Flights   14
Daily Average Number of Passengers   627

Airlines (American carriers only)
   Continental
   United
   USAir

bus lines serve the city. Concord is a walkable city, and its main business district occupies only a seven-block area. The Concord Municipal Airport is used only by local air carriers. Full international and domestic service is available at Logan, 75 miles to the southeast. The Boston and Maine Railroad runs through the city and provides passenger service. Freight is handled by the Southern New England Railroad.

Housing

The average Concord house is about 44 years old, but over half have three or more bedrooms. Housing costs are slightly above the national average, and so are property taxes. Heating and cooling costs also are higher because of the climate.

Housing	
Total Housing Units	15,697
% Change 1980–1990	22.7
Vacant Units for Sale or Rent	1,261
Occupied Units	14,222
% with More Than One Person per Room	1.2
% Owner-Occupied	52.3
Median Value of Owner-Occupied Homes	$112,400
Average Monthly Purchase Cost	$410
Median Monthly Rent	$485
New Private Housing Starts	99
Value (in thousands)	$5,732
% Single-Family	85.9
Nonresidential Buildings Value (in thousands)	$2,195

Urban Redevelopment

Concord has undergone considerable rebuilding, particularly downtown. The largest of the redevelopment projects are the Civic Center, with a 10,000-seat arena, 40,000 square feet of exhibition area, and a 10,000-square-foot ballroom; and the Steeplegate Mall, which has revitalized downtown. Three new shopping malls were approved in 1991.

Crime

Concord has one of the lowest crime rates in the state and nation.

Crime	
Violent Crimes—Total	57
Violent Crime Rate per 100,000	4,960
Murder	4
Rape	24
Robbery	21
Aggravated Assaults	18
Property Crimes	1,787
Burglary	315
Larceny	1,352
Motor Vehicle Theft	76
Arson	7
Per Capita Police Expenditures	NA
Per Capita Fire Protection Expenditures	NA
Number of Police	64
Per 1,000	1.98

Religion	
Largest Denominations (Adherents)	
Catholic	20,627
United Church of Christ	5,214
United Methodist	1,998
Episcopal	2,426
American Baptist	4,074
Jewish	450

Religion

Concord remained a predominantly Congregational and Episcopalian stronghold well into this century. With emigration from Canada, Ireland, and Italy, Catholicism became a dominant force. The city also has substantial Greek Orthodox and Jewish minorities. Concord is famous as the home of Mary Baker Eddy, founder of Christian Science.

Media

The *Concord Monitor* is the city's only daily newspaper; it is published weekday evenings and Saturday mornings. The major weekly is the *Concord Item*. Concord receives eight commercial television channels from Boston and Manchester. In addition, there are two local channels, one commercial and the other educational. Radio broadcasting originates in six AM and FM stations, including a National Public Radio affiliate.

Media	
Newsprint	
Concord Monitor, daily	
Television	
WNHT (Channel 21)	
Radio	
WEVO (FM)	WJYY (FM)
WKXL (AM)	WKXL (FM)
WNNH (FM)	WSPS (FM)

Sports

Concord has two excellent sports facilities: the Everett Arena, with its indoor ice rink, and Memorial Field, which hosts football, baseball, and track meets.

Arts, Culture, and Tourism

Resident professional groups are the New Hampshire Philharmonic Orchestra, Community Players of Concord, Youth Symphony, and Concord Chorale. They generally perform at the City Auditorium. The Historic Nevers 2nd Regiment Band, a semiprofessional performing band, plays at parks and theaters throughout the state.

The largest museum is the New Hampshire Historical Museum. The massive sculpture above the entrance, depicting the progress of history, was carved from a 22-ton block of Concord granite by Daniel Chester French. The League of New Hampshire

Craftsmen showcases goods made by local artisans, and the Phoenix Gallery exhibits works of local visual artists.

Travel and Tourism
Hotel Rooms   NA
Convention and Exhibit Space (square feet)   NA
Convention Centers
NA
Festivals
New Hampshire Folk Festival (August)
Summer Band Festival (June-August)
Concord Antiques Fair (April)
Coach and Carriage Festival (June)

Parks and Recreation

The city has more than 300 acres of well-equipped parks and playgrounds, as well as one public and two private golf courses. The city is only an hour's drive to the Atlantic Ocean and an hour and a half to the White Mountains.

Sources of Further Information

City Hall
41 Green Street
Concord, NH 03301
(603) 225-8570

City of Concord Economic Development Department
41 Green Street
Concord, NH 03301
(603) 225-8595

Greater Concord Chamber of Commerce
244 North Street
Concord, NH 03301
(603) 224-2508

New Hampshire Historical Society
30 Park Street
Concord, NH 03301
(603) 225-3381

Additional Reading

Concord: The Heart of a Healthy New Hampshire.
   Biennial.
The Concord Guide. Annual.

Dallas

Texas

Basic Data

Name   Dallas
Name Origin   From George Mifflin Dallas
Year Founded   1841 Inc. 1856
Status: State   Texas
        County   Seat of Dallas County
Area (square miles)   342.4
Elevation (feet)   435
Time Zone   Central
Population (1990)   1,006,877
Population of Metro Area (1990)   2,553,362

Sister Cities

Brno, Czech and Slovak Federal Republic
Dijon, France
Riga, Latvia

Distance in Miles To:

Atlanta	822
Boston	1,753
Chicago	921
Cleveland	1,189
Denver	784
Houston	246
Los Angeles	1,399
Minneapolis	949
New York	1,559
Philadelphia	1,443
Washington, DC	1,307

Location and Topography

The northeast Texas city of Dallas, the state's financial center, is located on the Trinity River at the southeastern edge of the Great Plains. Dallas, with nearby Arlington and Fort Worth, had a population in 1990 of 3.8 million.

Layout of the City and Suburbs

The Trinity River divides the city into North Dallas and southern Dallas. The central business district is just east of the river in North Dallas. Downtown streets run east-west

and north-south. Reunion Boulevard, a wide boulevard west of the Trinity ends at Reunion Tower, a 262-foot-high office building topped by a lighted globe. Upscale neighborhoods, with mostly white residents, include Highland Park and University Park in North Dallas. Much of the city's Hispanic and black population live south of the Trinity.

Environment

Environmental Stress Index   3.2
Green Cities Index: Rank   25
                    Score   25.86
Water Quality   Alkaline, soft, fluoridated
    Average Daily Use (gallons per capita)   228
    Maximum Supply (gallons per capita)   512
Parkland as % of Total City Area   8.3
% Waste Landfilled/Recycled   NA
Annual Parks Expenditures per Capita   95.91

Climate

The climate is subtropical and humid. Temperatures in summer frequently reach daytime highs in the 90s. Winters are mild, although occasional "northers" may bring cold masses from the Great Plains and Rocky Mountains. Snowfall is light, without accumulation. Most of

Weather

Temperature

Highest Monthly Average °F   96.1
Lowest Monthly Average °F   33.9

Annual Averages

Days 32°F or Below   39
Days above 90°F   88
Zero Degree Days   0

Weather (continued)

Precipitation (inches) 32
Snow (inches) 3
% Seasonal Humidity 67
Wind Speed (m.p.h.) 11
Clear Days 138
Cloudy Days 132
Storm Days 46
Rainy Days 79

Average Temperatures (°F)	High	Low	Mean
January	55.7	33.9	44.8
February	59.8	37.6	48.7
March	66.6	43.3	55.0
April	76.3	54.1	65.2
May	82.8	62.1	72.5
June	90.8	70.3	80.6
July	95.5	74.0	84.8
August	96.1	73.7	84.9
September	88.5	66.8	77.7
October	79.2	56.0	67.6
November	67.5	44.1	55.8
December	58.7	37.0	47.9

---

the rain falls during April and May. Thunderstorms and hail are experienced two or three times a year.

History

The Trinity River region was long inhabited by the Anadarkos, a tribe of Caddo Indians who farmed. Frenchmen from Louisiana traded with the Indians early in the 18th century. The region was controlled by Spain and then by Mexico until 1836, when Texans won independence and formed the Texas Republic. Arkansan entrepreneur John Neely Bryan visited the area in 1839 when it was rumored that the Republic of Texas was to build a military highway through the area. Bryan put in a land claim and eventually established a trading post and ferry. The village that sprang up at the ferry crossing grew up to become a town known as Dallas, perhaps to honor George Mifflin Dallas, who was President James Polk's vice-president at the time of Texas statehood in 1845. Platted in 1846, the town became the Dallas County seat in 1849.

The town incorporated in 1856; population increased when the nearby utopian community of La Reunion failed in 1858. Many of the French, Swiss, and German imigrants who had come to La Reunion were artisans, doctors, millers, brewers, and other professionals; they chose to stay in Dallas when the community failed.

Dallas, far from the battlefields of the Civil War, prospered during the 1860s. Thousands of Confederate soldiers came to Texas and Dallas following the war. The first train reached Dallas in 1872 on the Houston and Texas Central line; the Texas and Pacific railroad reached the city the next year. By 1886 six railroads connected Dallas with the rest of the nation, and the city's population neared 35,000.

Although there is no oil in Dallas County, the city prospered following the 1901 discovery of oil at Spindletop, near Beaumont in southeast Texas. Dollars from oilmen and related oil industry businesses flowed into the city's coffers. In 1910 the Chamber of Commerce hired city planner George E. Kessler, who widened streets, moved railroad tracks, and "straightened" the Trinity River to avoid a repeat of the floods in 1908 that had caused some $2 million in damage. In 1926 the City and County of Dallas Levee Improvement District began a five-year plan of flood control and reclamation that ultimately regained nearly 10,600 acres of land from the Trinity River.

Dallas was brought dramatically into national prominence with the assassination there of President John Fitzgerald Kennedy on November 22, 1963. While the city still lives with the terrible memory of the assassination, it moves toward the millenium with a diversified economy of oil, livestock, agriculture, and tourism. The long-running television program *Dallas* also brought the city to the world's attention.

Historical Landmarks

Dallas has fewer historical landmarks than most cities of its size. A reproduction of John Neely Bryan's log cabin stands in the Founder's Plaza. The Praetorian Building, built in 1907 as Dallas's first skyscraper (15 stories), is on Main Street. In Dealey Plaza, visitors can see the site of the assassination of President John F. Kennedy, and can view artifacts of the event on the sixth floor of the Texas School Book Depository, the area from which the alleged assassin's shots originated. The Adolphus Hotel on Commerce Street, built by beer magnate Adolphus Busch in 1912, was restored in 1981. The Dallas Farmer's Market on the two sides of the Pearl Expressway mark the site where the Pearl and Cadiz Street Produce Markets sprang up in the early 1900s.

Population

Dallas passed the 1 million mark in population in the 1980s after growing by 11.3%, from 904,599 in 1980 to 1,006,877

Population		
	1980	*1990*
Central City	904,599	1,006,877
Rank	7	8
Metro Area	1,957,430	2,553,362
Pop. Change 1980–1990 +102,278		
Pop. % Change 1980–1990 +11.3		
Median Age 30.6		
% Male 49.2		
% Age 65 and Over 9.7		
Density (per square mile) 2,940		

Households
Number 402,060
Persons per Household 2.46
% Female-Headed Households 13.9
% One-Person Households 34.2
Births—Total 19,274
% to Mothers under 20 19.1
Birth Rate per 1,000 19.8
Deaths Total 7,823
Rate per 1,000 8
Infant Deaths 226
Rate Per 1,000 11.7

Chronology

1839 Arkansan John Neely Bryan visits the area of the Trinity River that today is Dallas and makes a claim. He returns in 1841 to start a trading post and becomes a rancher.

1842 Three families move into Bryan's settlement. The town is christened Dallas.

1845 Texas becomes the 28th state.

1846 Dallas is surveyed and platted. John Bryan is named postmaster.

1849 The first newspaper appears in Dallas. A conflict with the nearby settlement of Hord's Ridge (now Oak Cliff) leads to the organization of Dallas County, and Dallas being named the county seat.

1855 About a dozen followers of the French socialist Charles Fourier settle three miles from Dallas and found the utopian colony of La Reunion. They decide to stay in Dallas when colony fails in 1858, increasing population.

1856 Dallas is incorporated. The town attracts buffalo hunters and trappers.

1886 Six railroads now reach Dallas; population nears 35,000.

1893 The Trinity River Navigation and Improvement Company runs a 116-foot-long steamboat on the Trinity from Dallas to Galveston in a little more than a month.

1901 The oil discovery at Spindletop in southeast Texas causes a financial boom in Dallas.

1907 The city's first skyscraper, the Praetorian Building, is constructed.

1910 City planner George E. Kessler proposes widening streets, removing railroad tracks from downtown, and "straightening" the Trinity River.

1928– 1931 Work by the City and County of Dallas Levee Improvement District to unite two sections of the Trinity River results in the reclamation of some 10,600 acres of land for industrial use.

1945 Following World War II, Dallas becomes a center for banking and insurance.

1963 President John F. Kennedy assassinated.

1980s Although the state is hit by a recession due to downturn in the oil industry, tourism and other diversified businesses keep Dallas afloat financially.

in 1990. Earlier, it had grown by 7.1%, from 844,000 in 1970 and 679,684 in 1960.

Ethnic Composition

In 1990 whites made up 55.3%, blacks 29.5%, American Indians 0.5%, Asians and Pacific Islanders 2.2%, and others 12.6%. Hispanics, both black and white, make up 20.9%.

Ethnic Composition (as % of total pop.)		
	1980	*1990*
White	61.42	55.3
Black	29.38	29.5
American Indian	0.41	0.48
Asian and Pacific Islander	0.85	2.18
Hispanic	12.29	20.88
Other	NA	12.55

Government

Dallas is governed under its 1931 charter by a council-manager form of government, and is the largest city in the nation with a city manager. The council is composed of 11 members, 8 of whom are elected in single member constituencies; 3 members, including the mayor, are elected at large in nonpartisan elections.

Government
Year of Home Charter   1913
Number of Members of the Governing Body   11
Elected at Large   3
Elected by Wards   8
Number of Women in Governing Body   3
Salary of Mayor $50
Salary of Council Members $50
City Government Employment Total   14,912
Rate per 10,000   148.6

Public Finance

The annual budget consists of revenues of $1.120 billion and expenditures of $989.309 million. The debt outstanding is $1.569 billion, and cash and security holdings are $1.964 billion.

Public Finance
Total Revenue (in millions) $1,120.17
Intergovernmental Revenue—Total (in millions) $38.05
Federal Revenue per Capita $18.7
% Federal Assistance   1.67
% State Assistance   0.86
Sales Tax as % of Total Revenue   9.41
Local Revenue as % of Total Revenue   69.94
City Income Tax   no
Taxes—Total (in millions) $376.4
Taxes per Capita
Total $375
Property $197
Sales and Gross Receipts $166
General Expenditures—Total (in millions) $585.1

Public Finance (continued)

General Expenditures per Capita $583
Capital Outlays per Capita $133

% of Expenditures for:
    Public Welfare 0.0
    Highways 7.9
    Education 0.0
    Health and Hospitals 1.3
    Police 19.2
    Sewerage and Sanitation 13.1
    Parks and Recreation 12.0
    Housing and Community Development 2.3
Debt Outstanding per Capita $897
    % Utility 20.6
Federal Procurement Contract Awards (in millions)
    $1,181.9
Federal Grants Awards (in millions) $107.4
Fiscal Year Begins October 1

Economy

 Diversity characterizes the city's economy. Some of its marketing and retail firms are nationally known, such as Neiman-Marcus, Sanger-Harris, and the Dallas Market Center. Dallas remains, as it was in the 19th century, one of the nation's largest inland cotton markets. It has also become a fashion as well as an important convention center. Its prominence as a financial center began in the first decade of the 20th century with the discovery of oil in East Texas. Dallas is headquarters for more than 450 companies associated with the petroleum industry, the 11th district of the Federal Reserve Bank, and 40 large commercial banks and the majority of Texas insurance companies. In manufacturing, the city has concentrated on leading-edge high technology fields such as biomedicine, aerospace, computers, and electronics. The city ranks third among wholesale markets in apparel, gifts, and furniture. Dallas is also the fifth-largest distribution center for commercial motion pictures and the leading printing, publishing, and advertising center in the Southwest. State and federal government contribute to the city's economy. Dallas and Fort Worth share a trade zone based in the

Economy

Total Money Income (in millions) $12,854
% of State Average 123.6
Per Capita Annual Income $12,816
% Population below Poverty Level 14.2
Fortune 500 Companies 12

Banks	Number	Deposits (in millions)
Commercial	77	44,800
Savings	26	82,500

Passenger Autos 1,543,301
Electric Meters 407,077
Gas Meters 375,371

Manufacturing

Number of Establishments 2,105
% with 20 or More Employees 32.8
Manufacturing Payroll (in millions) $2,871.4
Value Added by Manufacture (in millions) $6,023.1
Value of Shipments (in millions) $10,626.5
New Capital Expenditures (in millions) $403

Economy (continued)

Wholesale Trade

Number of Establishments 4,422
Sales (in millions) NA
Annual Payroll (in millions) NA

Retail Trade

Number of Establishments 11,137
Total Sales (in millions) $8,820.9
Sales per Capita $8,790
Number of Retail Trade Establishments with Payroll 7,327
Annual Payroll (in millions) $1,109.1
Total Sales (in millions) $8,631.7
General Merchandise Stores (per capita) $1,088
Food Stores (per capita) NA
Apparel Stores (per capita) $640
Eating and Drinking Places (per capita) $1,060

Service Industries

Total Establishments 11,554
Total Receipts (in millions) NA
Hotels and Motels (in millions) NA
Health Services (in millions) $1,476.6
Legal Services (in millions) $1,122.3

Dallas-Fort Worth International Airport that helps generate billions of dollars in exports.

Labor

The Dallas-Fort Worth metropolitan area forms the largest manpower pool in the state and as such is an important economic asset. Further distribution of the labor force shows strength in all areas. The job market slump of the late 1980s was the result of a shakeout in traditional manufacturing industries, and it led to a restructuring of occupational patterns. The gainers appear to be computers, services, and high technology.

Labor

Civilian Labor Force 638,035
% Change 1989–1990 0.8

Work Force Distribution
    Mining 18,300
    Construction 45,500
    Manufacturing 214,000
    Transportation and Public Utilities 84,100
    Wholesale and Retail Trade 354,400
    FIRE (Finance, Insurance, Real Estate) 127,600
    Service 368,900
    Government 164,500
    Women as % of Labor Force 45.2
    % Self-Employed 5.7
    % Professional/Technical NA
Total Unemployment 38,333
Rate % 6.0
Federal Government Civilian Employment 18,411

Education

Dallas falls within a number of school districts. The Dallas Independent School District administers schools in five different municipalities. It supports 130 elementary schools, 28 junior high/middle schools, 33 senior high schools, and 4 special education schools. The Catholic Diocese runs 43 parochial schools, and there are 27 other private and parochial schools.

Of the city's institutions of higher education, the University of Dallas is located in Irving and the University of Texas at Dallas in Richardson. Most of the other institutions are church-related, such as Southern Methodist University, Dallas Bible College, Dallas Christian College, Dallas Theological Seminary, Dallas Baptist University, and Bishop College. Two institutions provide medical education: University of Texas Health Science Center and Baylor College of Dentistry.

Education

Number of Public Schools   196
Special Education Schools   4
Total Enrollment   135,000
% Enrollment in Private Schools   NA
% Minority   83.0
Classroom Teachers   8,616
Pupil-Teacher Ratio   15.7:1
Number of Graduates   5,530
Total Revenue (in millions) $496.89
Total Expenditures (in millions) $531.33
Expenditures per Pupil $3,511
Educational Attainment (Age 25 and Over)
    % Completed 12 or More Years   68.5
    % Completed 16 or More Years   22
Four-Year Colleges and Universities   6
    Enrollment   13,650
Two-Year Colleges   4
    Enrollment   26,005

Libraries

Number   113
Public Libraries   20
Books (in thousands)   2,229
Circulation (in thousands)   4,617
Persons Served (in thousands)   1,006
Circulation per Person Served   4.58
Income (in millions) $16.793
Staff   444

Four-Year Colleges and Universities
    Criswell College
    Dallas Baptist University
    Dallas Christian College
    Paul Quinn College
    Southern Methodist University
    University of Texas Southwestern Medical Center at
        Dallas

Health

Thirty-seven full medical and surgical hospitals operate in Dallas County, with a total of nearly 11,000 beds. The largest of these facilities are Parkland Memorial Hospital, the principal teaching hospital for the University of Texas Health Science Center; Baylor University Medical Center, with five hospitals and a teaching and research hospital; Presbyterian Hospital; Veterans Administra-

tion Medical Center; St. Paul Hospital; Humana of Texas; the Children's Medical Center; and Methodist Hospital of Dallas.

Health

Deaths—Total   7,823
Rate per 1,000   8
Infant Deaths—Total   226
Rate per 1,000   11.7
Number of Metro Hospitals   30
Number of Metro Hospital Beds   7,375
Rate per 100,000   735
Number of Physicians   4,564
Physicians per 1,000   2.07
Nurses per 1,000   6.01
Health Expenditures per Capita   NA

Transportation

Dallas is approached by four interstates: the east-west I-20; the north-south I-35 (the R. L. Thornton Freeway) and its connection, the north-east-west I-30; and the southern I-45 (the Julius Schepps Freeway). These highways are linked by two loops: the Lyndon B. Johnson Freeway, which is connected to I-20, and the inner Loop 12. A third loop encircles the central business district. Dallas is also served by U.S. Highways 67, 75, 77, 80, and 175; and State Highways 78, 114, 183, 289, and 342. Rail passenger service is provided by the Amtrak railway located at the Union Railway Station at the Reunion Tower. The principal air terminal for the area is the Dallas-Fort Worth International Airport (DFW), about 17 miles from downtown. Before this airport was built in 1974, Dallas was served by Love Field. This airport, located at the northwestern end of Loop 12, remains a general aviation, commuter, and commercial air facility.

Transportation

Interstate Highway Mileage   273
Total Urban Mileage   16,731
Total Daily Vehicle Mileage (in millions)   76.6
Daily Average Commute Time   52.8 min.
Number of Buses   1,422
Port Tonnage (in millions)   NA
Airports   2
Number of Daily Flights   696
Daily Average Number of Passengers   69,580

Airlines (American carriers only)
    American
    American West
    Continental
    Delta
    Eastern
    Midway
    Northwest
    Southwest
    Trans World
    United

Housing

Of the total housing stock, 44.1% is owner-occupied. The median value of an owner-occupied home is $78,800, and the median monthly rent is $375.

Housing		
Total Housing Units 465,600		
% Change 1980–1990 16.1		
Vacant Units for Sale or Rent 50,329		
Occupied Units 402,060		
% with More Than One Person per Room 9.8		
% Owner-Occupied 44.1		
Median Value of Owner-Occupied Homes $78,800		
Average Monthly Purchase Cost $338		
Median Monthly Rent $375		
New Private Housing Starts 2,756		
Value (in thousands) $162,804		
% Single-Family 52.4		
Nonresidential Buildings Value (in thousands) $71,310		
Tallest Buildings	*Hgt. (ft.)*	*Stories*
National Bank Plaza	939	73
Bank One Center	787	60
Texas Commerce Tower	738	55
First Interstate Bank Tower	721	60
Renaissance Tower	710	56
Trammell Crow Tower	686	50
First City Center	655	50

Urban Redevelopment

Dallas experienced a redevelopment boom in the 1970s and early 1980s. It was followed by the bust phase of the cycle in the late 1980s and early 1990s, which placed many planned construction projects on hold. Redevelopment projects are coordinated by the city's Urban Planning Department as well as the Dallas Department of Planning and Development and the Central Dallas Association.

Crime

Dallas ranks near the bottom in public safety. Of the crimes known to police in 1991, there were 26,411 violent crimes and 128,518 property crimes.

Crime	
Violent Crimes—Total 26,411	
Violent Crime Rate per 100,000 1,333	
Murder 500	
Rape 1,208	
Robbery 11,254	
Aggravated Assaults 13,449	
Property Crimes 128,518	
Burglary 31,513	
Larceny 71,920	
Motor Vehicle Theft 25,085	
Arson 1,527	
Per Capita Police Expenditures $142.53	
Per Capita Fire Protection Expenditures $72.67	
Number of Police 2,170	
Per 1,000 2.18	

Religion

Dallas has no wild-frontier-town tradition. From the beginning it was noted as a town with a large churchgoing population, nearly 80% of which is Protestant. Baptists make up nearly one-half of church membership. The principal denominations are Southern Baptist, Catholics Black Baptists. Some congregations—for example, the First Baptist Church—have memberships running into the several thousands.

Religion	
Largest Denominations (Adherents)	
Catholic	207,535
Southern Baptist	321,341
Black Baptist	154,548
Presbyterian	35,022
United Methodist	112,771
Church of Christ	47,468
Assembly of God	27,900
Jewish	24,672

Media

The Dallas press has two dailies: *The Dallas Morning News* and the *Dallas Times Herald*. The electronic media consists of 7 television stations and 24 AM and FM radio stations.

Media	
Newsprint	
Business Monthly, monthly	
Dallas/Fort Worth Business, weekly	
Dallas/Fort Worth Business Journal, weekly	
Dallas/Ft. Worth Living, bimonthly	
Dallas/Fort Worth Home/Garden, monthly	
Dallas Life Magazine, weekly	
Dallas Magazine, monthly	
The Dallas Morning News, daily	
Dallas North Carrollton News, monthly	
Dallas Observer, biweekly	
Dallas Park Cities News, weekly	
Dallas Suburban Tribune, weekly	
Dallas Times Herald, daily	
Dallas Today Magazine, quarterly	
Dallas White Rocker News, weekly	
Development Announcements Report, quarterly	
Oak Cliff Advertizer, weekly	
Oak Cliff Tribune, weekly	
Television	
KDAF (Channel 33)	
KDFI (Channel 27)	
KDFW (Channel 4)	
KDTX (Channel 58)	
KERA (Channel 13)	
KXTX (Channel 39)	
KFAA (Channel 8)	
Radio	
KAAM (AM)	KZPS (FM)
KCBI (FM)	KCMZ (AM)
KDGE (FM)	KDMX (FM)
KERA (FM)	KGGR (AM)
KJMZ (FM)	KKDA (FM)
KLIF (AM)	KLRX (FM)
KLUV (FM)	KNON (FM)

Media (continued)

KODZ (FM)	KPBC (AM)
KRLD (AM)	KRSM (FM)
KRSR (FM)	KSKY (AM)
KSSA (AM)	KUII (AM)
KVTT (FM)	WRR (FM)

Sports

Dallas is the home of the legendary Dallas Cowboys, Super Bowl champions in 1993, who play their home games at Texas Stadium in Irving. In 1980 professional basketball came to town with the Dallas Mavericks, who play in the downtown Reunion Arena. The Texas Rangers baseball team plays at Arlington Stadium. The Cotton Bowl Stadium at Fair Park is the site of the annual Cotton Bowl on New Year's Day. The famed Mesquite Championship Rodeo is held every Friday night from the first week in April through the last week in September.

Arts, Culture, and Tourism

Much of Dallas's art and culture reside in the Arts District, a 60-acre tract in the northern section of the city (near the Woodall Rogers Freeway) that is being developed with public and private investment. The Dallas Theater Center resides here, as does the Myerson Symphony Center, home of the Dallas Symphony Orchestra, and the Trammell Crow Center, a focal point for folk art and traveling exhibits. In the eastern section of the city is Deep Ellum, the area for new wave and rock music clubs. In June, in accordance with the celebration of Juneteenth (a combination of June 19, 1865, the date when Texas slaves found out they had been freed), the week-long Benson and Hedges Blues Festival takes place.

Among the city's museums, the most outstanding is the Dallas Museum of Art, which opened in 1984 in the Arts District on North Harwood Street. Fair Park houses the Dallas Museum of Natural History, the Dallas Aquarium, the Age of Steam Railroad Museum, and Science Place I and the Science Place II, twin structures dedicated to science through the use of a planetarium and traveling scientific exhibits. Other museums include the Museum of African-American Culture in the WRR Building at Fair Park; The Biblical Arts Center six miles north of the city; the Meadows Museum of Art, a donation of art collector Alger Meadows; and the Sixth Floor, a commemoration at the Texas School Book Depository from where President John F. Kennedy was shot.

Parks and Recreation

Dallas has a number of different kinds of parks, including the International Wildlife Park, amusement parks such as Six Flags Over Texas and Penny Whistle Park, the Dallas Zoo, the Trinity River Greenbelt, and Mountain Creek Lake Park. The State Fair of Texas is held at the 277-acre Fair Park. Other popular recreational areas include Dallas Nature Center, the Civic Garden Center, the 50-acre Marsalis Park, the 2,314-acre White Rock Lake Park, the Robert E. Lee Park on Hall Street and Turtle Creek Boulevard, the Cottonwood Creek Preserve at Wilmer, and the Dallas Arboretum and Botanical Gardens.

Sources of Further Information

City Hall
1500 Marilla Street
Dallas, TX 75201
(214) 670-4054

Dallas Convention and Visitors Bureau
1507 Pacific Avenue
Dallas, TX 75201
(214) 954-1111

Dallas Chamber of Commerce
1507 Pacific Avenue
Dallas, TX 75201
(214) 954-1450

Additional Reading

Acheson, Sam. *Dallas Yesterday.* 1977.
Beautiful Dallas. 1980.
Cummings, Joe, *Texas Handbook.* 1992.
Dallas, U.S.A. 1984.
Dooley, Kirk. *Hidden Dallas: What You Don't Know About Your Own Backyard.* 1987.
Greene A. C. *Dallas, the Deciding Years: A Historical Portrait.* 1973.
McAlester, Virginia, and Lee McAlester. *Discover Dallas.* 1988.
Thomas, Gail. *Imagining Dallas.* 1982.
Tomlinson, Doug and David Dillon. *Dallas Architecture, 1936–1986.* 1985.

Travel and Tourism

Hotel Rooms 41,505
Convention and Exhibit Space (square feet) 600,000

Convention Centers
Dallas Convention Center
Loews Anatole Hotel
Dallas Market Center

Festivals
Cotton Bowl Festival and Parade
Shakespeare Festival
City Fest
State Fair

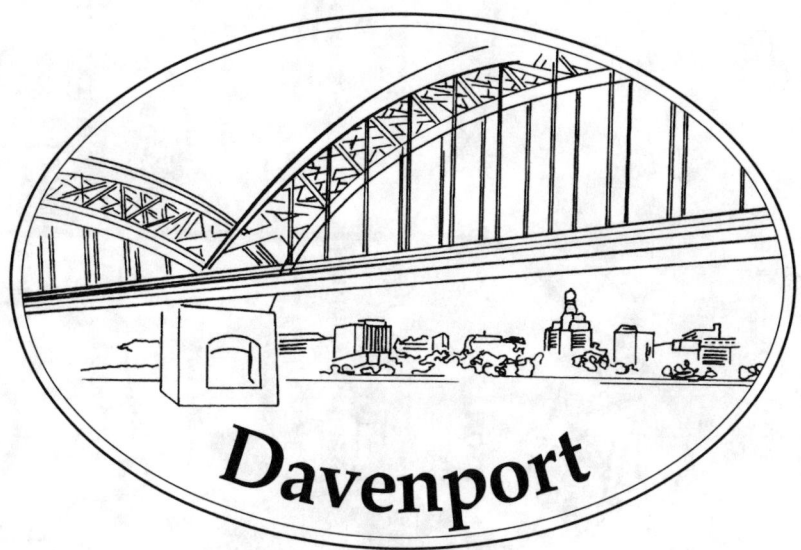

Davenport

Iowa

Basic Data

Name   Davenport
Name Origin   From Colonel George Davenport
Year Founded   1836 Inc. 1851
Status: State   Iowa
         County   Seat of Scott County
Area (square miles)   61.4
Elevation (feet)   590
Time Zone   Central
Population (1990)   95,333
Population of Metro Area (1990)   350,861

Sister Cities
    Kaiserslautern, Germany

Distance in Miles To:

Cedar Rapids	82
Des Moines	168
Dubuque	70
Kansas City, MO	359
Omaha	300
Chicago	183

Location and Topography

N   Davenport, in easternmost Iowa, is situated on bluffs overlooking a bend of the Mississippi River just west of Moline and Rock Island in Illinois. The Scott County seat, it is 168 miles east of Des Moines, the state capital.

Layout of City and Suburbs

   The main streets in Davenport include River Drive, Locust Street, Wisconsin Avenue, and Rockingham Road. The city's plan is a traditional grid that hugs the Mississippi. The older residential area of Davenport is located on a bluff overlooking the river.

Environment

Environmental Stress Index   NA
Green Cities Index: Rank   NA
                    Score   NA
Water Quality   Neutral, hard, fluoridated
    Average Daily Use (gallons per capita)   146
    Maximum Supply (gallons per capita)   230
Parkland as % of Total City Area   NA
% Waste Landfilled/Recycled   NA
Annual Parks Expenditures per Capita $56.31

Climate

Davenport has a continental climate marked by sharp temperature variations. Summers are hot, but short, and winters are severe with snowfall averaging 30 inches. Proximity to major storm tracks brings frequent weather changes. Every year the temperature goes above 90°F for 22 days a year and goes below zero about 20 days.

Weather

Temperature

Highest Monthly Average °F   83.8
Lowest Monthly Average °F   21.5

Annual Averages

Days 32°F or Below   136
Days above 90°F   22
Zero Degree Days   16
Precipitation (inches)   36
Snow (inches)   30
% Seasonal Humidity   70
Wind Speed (m.p.h.)   9.9
Clear Days   101
Cloudy Days   163
Storm Days   47
Rainy Days   112

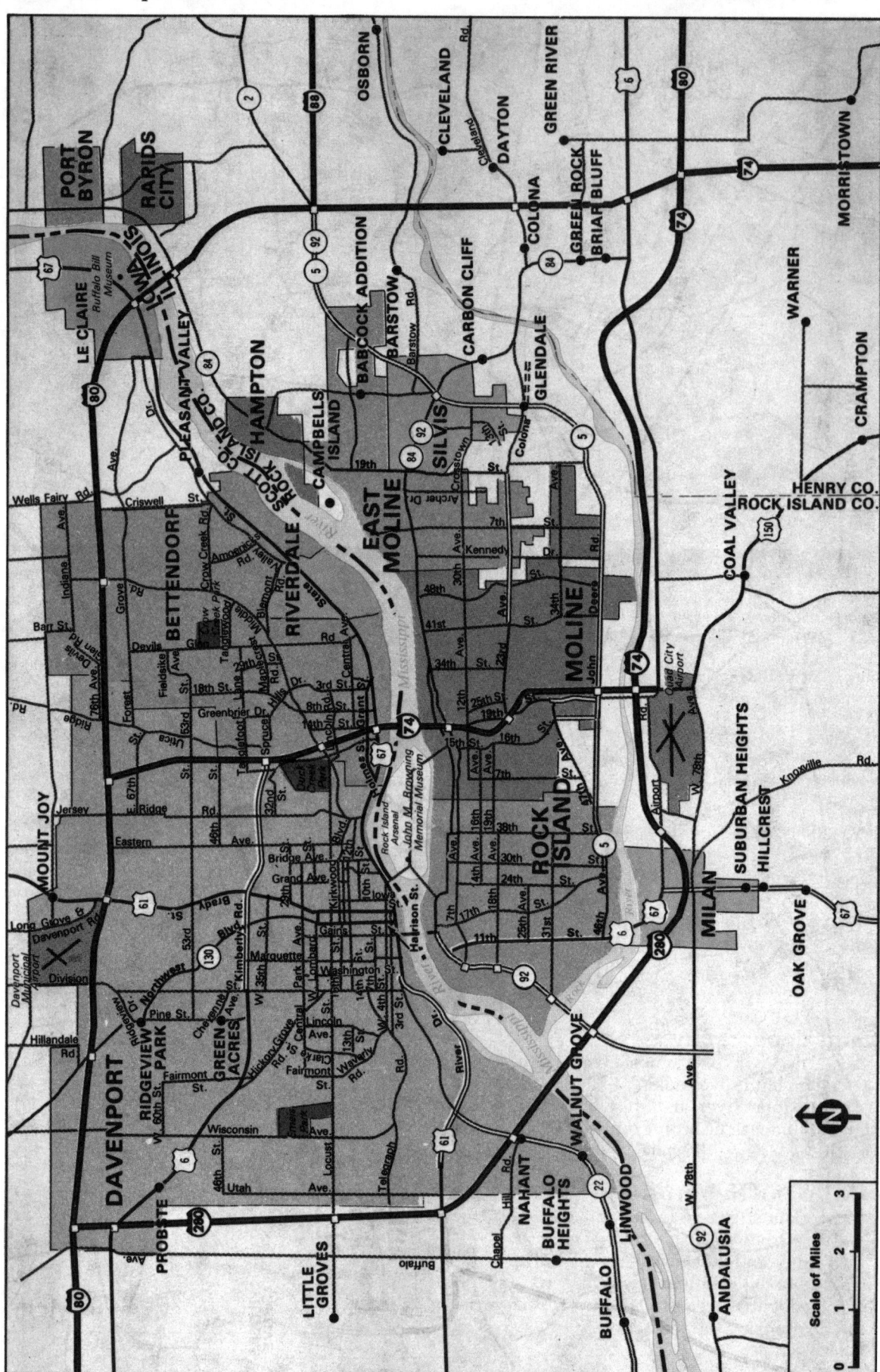

Weather (continued)

Average Temperatures (°F)	High	Low	Mean
January	30.0	13.0	21.5
February	34.3	17.0	25.7
March	45.0	26.4	35.7
April	61.3	39.8	50.6
May	72.0	50.2	61.1
June	81.4	60.2	70.8
July	85.2	63.8	74.5
August	83.8	62.0	72.9
September	76.0	53.2	64.6
October	66.0	42.8	54.4
November	48.1	30.2	39.2
December	34.6	18.5	26.6

History

The central Mississippi Valley was the home of various Indian tribes for several hundred years before European explorers arrived. These tribes included the Fox, the Mesquakie, and the Sauk. Trade began to flourish during the mid-17th century between Indians and explorers. Companies such as Hudson's Bay, Missouri Valley Fur Company, and the American Fur Company all utilized the region's resources. The region that became Iowa was included in the sale of land in 1803 by France to the United States known as the Louisiana Purchase. The end of the War of 1812 opened much of the continent to American adventurers and pioneers, which made the creation of settlements in the Davenport area necessary. Fort Armstrong in Illinois Territory was established on the east bank of the Mississippi in 1816, at Rock Island, by Colonel George Davenport. In 1832 General Winfield Scott negotiated a treaty with the native Indians while he was stationed at Fort Armstrong. French-Indian Antoine LeClaire helped with translations. In return for LeClaire's services, the government gave him a tract of land across from Rock Island. Four years later, in 1836, LeClaire sold a piece of land in the south of his claim to Colonel Davenport and some associates.

Iowa Territory was organized in 1838, and Davenport was named the county seat of Scott County (named for General Winfield Scott, who had negotiated the treaty with which LeClaire had been involved). The following year, the village was granted a charter, with a second charter given in 1843. Davenport did not live to see his town become a city; he was murdered by bandits on 4 July 1845.

Iowa became the 29th state in 1846. A decade later, in 1856, the first bridge to be built across the Mississippi was completed at Davenport. The first train crossed the bridge that year. During the Civil War, two prisoner of war camps were established near Davenport: Camp McClellan and Camp Roberts. The Rock Island Arsenal on Rock Island in the Mississippi made weapons for the Union.

After the war Davenport based its economy on limestone quarries and such companies as John Deere, the Rock Island Plow Company, Weyerhauser, Denkman Lumber, and International Harvester.

Historical Landmarks

The George Davenport home on Rock Island is a restored version of the 1833 home that Davenport built for himself. The Village of East Davenport, a restored historical village that includes Fort McClellan, is located just east of downtown Davenport. Rock Island has a tour of the Rock Island Arsenal, the Davenport home, the site of Fort Armstrong, and the Rock Island National Cemetery, which contains the remains of more than 14,000 Civil War veterans.

Population

Davenport which had reached a population of 103,264 in 1980, dropped to 95,333 in 1990, a decrease of 7.7%. Of the three large cities in Iowa, the loss of population was the most severe in Davenport.

Population

	1980	1990
Central City	103,264	95,333
Rank	158	210
Metro Area	384,794	350,861
Pop. Change 1980–1990 -7,931		
Pop. % Change 1980–1990 -7.7		
Median Age 31.8		
% Male 47.9		
% Age 65 and Over 12.7		
Density (per square mile) 1,552		

Households

Number 37,205
Persons per Household 2.50
% Female-Headed Households 12.9
% One-Person Households 28.0
Births—Total 1,876
   % to Mothers under 20 13.2
   Birth Rate per 1,000 18.4

Ethnic Composition

Whites make up 89.3%, Blacks 7.9%, American Indians 0.4%, Asian and Pacific Islanders 1%, and others 1.5% of the population.

Ethnic Composition (as % of total pop.)

	1980	1990
White	91.65	89.3
Black	6.10	7.89
American Indian	0.25	0.41
Asian and Pacific Islander	0.53	1.05
Hispanic	2.77	3.46
Other	NA	1.53

Government

Davenport is governed by a council-mayor form of government. The mayor and the ten aldermen—eight elected by ward and two at large—serve two-year terms.

Chronology

1816 Fort Armstrong is built on Rock Island.

1832 General Winfield Scott, assisted by Antoine LeClaire as translator, concludes treaty with Indians at Fort Armstrong. LeClaire is given a piece of land across the river from Rock Island that today is the northern part of Davenport.

1836 LeClaire sells a portion of his land to Davenport and others.

1838 Davenport is selected as the seat of the newly established Scott County.

1839 Davenport receives its first charter.

1843 Davenport receives its second charter.

1856 The first train crosses the Mississippi at Davenport.

1861– 1865 The Davenport area is used for two prisoner of war camps; the Rock Island Arsenal opens on Rock Island to supply the Union army with firearms.

Government

Year of Home Charter   1851
Number of Members of the Governing Body   10
Elected at Large   2
Elected by Wards   8
Number of Women in Governing Body   0
Salary of Mayor $36,400
Salary of Council Members $10,400
City Government Employment Total   1,038
Rate per 10,000   105.1

Public Finance

The annual budget consists of revenues of $92.690 million and expenditures of $80.915 million. The debt outstanding is $223.937 million, and cash and security holdings are $242.999 million.

Public Finance

Total Revenue (in millions) $92.690
Intergovernmental Revenue—Total (in millions) $16.88
Federal Revenue per Capita $4.41
% Federal Assistance   4.75
% State Assistance   13.46
Sales Tax as % of Total Revenue   10.04
Local Revenue as % of Total Revenue   76.86
City Income Tax   no
Taxes—Total (in millions) $25.1

Taxes per Capita
   Total $254
   Property $239
   Sales and Gross Receipts $6
General Expenditures—Total (in millions) $58.9
General Expenditures per Capita $596
Capital Outlays per Capita $76

Public Finance (continued)

% of Expenditures for:
   Public Welfare   0.0
   Highways   11.8
   Education   0.0
   Health and Hospitals   2.6
   Police   13.9
   Sewerage and Sanitation   12.5
   Parks and Recreation   2.6
   Housing and Community Development   7.7
Debt Outstanding per Capita $2,036
   % Utility   NA
Federal Procurement Contract Awards (in millions) $36.2
Federal Grants Awards (in millions) $5.7
Fiscal Year Begins   July 1

Economy

Davenport and Bettendorf in Iowa and the Illinois cities of Moline and Rock Island comprise the Quad Cities. The forces that drive the Quad City economic engine include retail, machinery production, agricultural goods, food products, and tourism. John Deere and Company, maker of tractors and other farm implements, has its world headquarters in Moline, Illinois. International Harvester has helped the area to become first in the production of farming equipment. The new push for tourism dollars includes use of riverboats that double as casinos and ply the Mississippi River.

Economy

Total Money Income (in millions) $1,119.6
% of State Average   112.3
Per Capita Annual Income $11,338
% Population below Poverty Level   9.9
Fortune 500 Companies   NA

Banks	Number	Deposits (in millions)
Commercial	36	2,154.8
Savings	8	2,555.5

Passenger Autos   103,022
Electric Meters   111,085
Gas Meters   161,860

Manufacturing

Number of Establishments   117
% with 20 or More Employees   37.6
Manufacturing Payroll (in millions) $257.1
Value Added by Manufacture (in millions) $696.0
Value of Shipments (in millions) $1,704
New Capital Expenditures (in millions)   NA

Wholesale Trade

Number of Establishments   284
Sales (in millions) $1,064.7
Annual Payroll (in millions) $72.643

Retail Trade

Number of Establishments   1,024
Total Sales (in millions) $774.7
Sales per Capita $7,845
Number of Retail Trade Establishments with Payroll   765
Annual Payroll (in millions) $95
Total Sales (in millions) $764.1

Economy (continued)

General Merchandise Stores (per capita) $1,092
Food Stores (per capita) $1,420
Apparel Stores (per capita) $391
Eating and Drinking Places (per capita) $755

Service Industries

Total Establishments   790
Total Receipts (in millions) $284.6
Hotels and Motels (in millions) $12.9
Health Services (in millions) $97.5
Legal Services (in millions) $19.7

Labor

Although the city work force is not large, Davenport draws on the labor pool of the larger Quad City area. Within this area, trade is the largest employment sector, followed by manufacturing, services, and government.

Labor

Civilian Labor Force   51,845
% Change 1989–1990   2.5

Work Force Distribution
   Mining   NA
   Construction   NA
   Manufacturing   NA
   Transportation and Public Utilities   NA
   Wholesale and Retail Trade   NA
   FIRE (Finance, Insurance, Real Estate)   NA
   Service   NA
   Government   NA
   Women as % of Labor Force   42.3
   % Self-Employed   4.7
   % Professional/Technical   14.5
Total Unemployment   2,895
Rate %   5.6
Federal Government Civilian Employment   352

Education

The Davenport Community School District supports 36 schools. Of the four major institutions of higher education, two are affiliated with the Catholic Church: Marycrest and St. Ambrose Universities.   The Palmer College of Chiropractic is associated with the founder of chiropractic medicine. The Eastern Iowa Community College awards associate degrees.

Education

Number of Public Schools   36
Special Education Schools   NA
Total Enrollment   17,846
% Enrollment in Private Schools   NA
% Minority   NA
Classroom Teachers   NA
Pupil-Teacher Ratio   NA
Number of Graduates   NA
Total Revenue (in millions)   NA
Total Expenditures (in millions)   NA

Education (continued)

Expenditures per Pupil   NA
Educational Attainment (Age 25 and Over)
   % Completed 12 or More Years   71.8
   % Completed 16 or More Years   18.2
Four-Year Colleges and Universities   2
   Enrollment   5,431
Two-Year Colleges   1
   Enrollment   728

Libraries

Number   11
Public Libraries   2
Books (in thousands)   355
Circulation (in thousands)   669
Persons Served (in thousands)   94.8
Circulation per Person Served   7.05
Income (in millions) $1.824
Staff   46

Four-Year Colleges and Universities
   St. Ambrose University
   Teikyo Marycrest University

Health

Davenport has three important medical facilities: the Davenport Medical Center, St. Lukes Hospital, and Mercy Hospital. The Palmer College of Chiropractic operates four clinics. Other medical facilities within commuting distance are the Franciscan Medical Center in Rock Island, and the United Medical Center in Moline.

Health

Deaths—Total   902
Rate per 1,000   8.8
Infant Deaths—Total   22
Rate per 1,000   11.7
Number of Metro Hospitals   3
Number of Metro Hospital Beds   653
Rate per 100,000   661
Number of Physicians   429
Physicians per 1,000   NA
Nurses per 1,000   NA
Health Expenditures per Capita $12.91

Transportation

Davenport is approached by three interstates: I-280 links east-west I-80 and north-south I-74 just west of the city. I-80 passes the city to the north near Davenport Municipal Airport and I-74 splits Davenport from neighboring Bettendorf. Three U.S. routes also serve the area: the north-south U.S. 61 from Minneapolis–St. Paul; U.S. 67, extending south to St. Louis; and the east-west U.S. 6, which is also I-80. The state highways are 122, 22, and 74. Rail freight service is provided by six railroads: the Davenport, Rock Island, Northwestern, Burlington Northern, Soo Lines, and Iowa Interstate railroads. Because of its location on the Mississippi, Davenport, as well as the other Quad Cities, is a vital

Transportation

Interstate Highway Mileage   56
Total Urban Mileage   1,489
Total Daily Vehicle Mileage (in millions)   5.089
Daily Average Commute Time   38.1 min.
Number of Buses   67
Port Tonnage (in millions)   NA
Airports   NA
Number of Daily Flights   34
Daily Average Number of Passengers   803

Airlines (American carriers only)
   NA

Crime

Violent Crimes—Total   940
Violent Crime Rate per 100,000   6,944
Murder   3
Rape   80
Robbery   168
Aggravated Assaults   689
Property Crimes   7,702
Burglary   1,914
Larceny   5,430
Motor Vehicle Theft   276
Arson   82
Per Capita Police Expenditures $80.93
Per Capita Fire Protection Expenditures $71.56
Number of Police   145
Per 1,000   1.43

port area. The principal air terminus is the Quad City Airport, across the river just south of Rock Island. Davenport Municipal Airport, just to the north of Davenport, serves smaller aircraft.

Housing

Residential districts developed between 1940 and 1970 make up the bulk of housing in Davenport. Cost of housing is well below the national average. Restoration of historic homes has helped the revival of old neighborhoods in East Davenport, the Gold Coast northwest of the central business district, Prospect Terrace, Riverview Terrace, Vanderveer Park, and McClellan Heights. Most of the larger upscale homes are found in Bettendorf, Pleasant Valley, and LeClaire; condominium communities are found in Ridgecrest Village and Luther Towers. The median price of a single-family home is $48,800.

Housing

Total Housing Units   40,343
% Change 1980–1990   0.1
Vacant Units for Sale or Rent   2,137
Occupied Units   37,205
% with More Than One Person per Room   2.0
% Owner-Occupied   61.2
Median Value of Owner-Occupied Homes $48,800
Average Monthly Purchase Cost $363
Median Monthly Rent $283
New Private Housing Starts   136
Value (in thousands) $12,721
% Single-Family   100
Nonresidential Buildings Value (in thousands) $31,105

Urban Redevelopment

Davenport has an Urban Revitalization Area zoned for industrial use. Its projects are coordinated with the Quad City Development Group.

Crime

Davenport ranks above average in public safety. In 1991, of crimes known to police, there were 940 violent crimes, and 7,702 property crimes.

Religion

Davenport has over 319 churches, of which 28 are Catholic, 16 Lutheran, 11 Methodist, and 244 other Protestant. Through the Churches United, church leaders representing 97 congregations meet bimonthly to address issues of economic, social, and spiritual revival. The city has a number of 19th-century churches of architectural importance, such as the Trinity Cathedral, built on the site of the first Episcopal outpost west of the Mississippi.

Religion

Largest Denominations (Adherents)

Catholic	30,718
Evangelical Lutheran	13,690
United Methodist	6,001
Presbyterian	4,620
Lutheran Missouri Synod	4,552
Black Baptist	2,708
Jewish	538

Media

The city dailies are the *Downtown News* and the *Quad-City Times*. Because Davenport picks up the radio and television signals of the other Quad Cities, there are a total of 5 television stations (network and public) and 19 AM and FM radio stations.

Media

Newsprint
   Downtown News, daily
   Quad-City Times, daily
Television
   KLJB (Channel 18)
   KWQC (Channel 6)
Radio
   KALA (FM)
   KFQC (AM)
   KRVR (FM)
   KSTT (AM)
   WOC (AM)
   KUUL (FM)

Sports

Davenport has no major professional sports team.

Arts, Culture, and Tourism

The Adler Theatre in Davenport was recently renovated and presently exhibits theater performances and musical presentations. In addition, the Quad Cities area offers the Playcrafters Barn Theatre in Moline, and the Circa '21 Dinner Playhouse in Rock Island. Among the museums that serve the area are the Davenport Museum of Art and the Putnam Museum of History and Natural Science in Davenport, as well as the Children's Museum in Bettendorf, the Rock Island Arsenal Museum at the Rock Island Arsenal, and the Buffalo Bill Museum just upriver from Davenport in LeClaire.

Parks and Recreation

Davenport's many parks include the Vanderveer Park Rose Garden and Conservatory, which features tropical and semitropical flower exhibits; the Fejervary Park and Zoo on 12th Street; and Scott County Park, nine miles north of Davenport.

Sources of Further Information

Quad Cities USA Convention and Visitors Bureau
1900 Third Avenue
Rock Island, IL, 61204
(309) 788-7800

Davenport Chamber of Commerce
112 East 3rd Street
Davenport, IL 52801
(319) 322-1706

Additional Reading

Polk's Davenport City Directory. 1991.
Cole's Directory for Davenport. 1991.

Travel and Tourism
Hotel Rooms   3,606
Convention and Exhibit Space (square feet)   NA
Convention Centers
River Center
Festivals
Great River Ramble (July)
Mississippi Valley Blues Festival (July)
Great American Celebration (May)
Bix Beiderbecke Memorial Jazz Festival (July)
Civil War Muster and Mercantile Exposition (September)

Dayton

Ohio

Location and Topography

Dayton is located in the southwestern section of Ohio 75 miles from the capital, Columbus. The city is situated near the center of the Miami River Valley on a flat plain 50 to 100 feet below the elevation of the surrounding countryside. Flowing from the northwest, the Great Miami River is joined within city limits by its three tributaries: Mad River, Stillwater River, and Wolf Creek. Stillwater River flows from the north and joins the Great Miami half a mile above the Main Street Bridge; Mad River flows from the east and joins the Great Miami four blocks from the Main Street Bridge; and Wolf Creek comes in from the west and northwest, converging with the Great Miami a few blocks down from the

bridge. Restrained by levees 20 feet high, the Great Miami then sweeps through the city in a wide S curve.

Layout of City and Suburbs

Dayton is located on a valley floor. The business district is clustered in the mile-long loop of the Great Miami. From this loop the city spreads out over the valley floor to the wooded hills. To the north is the city of Vandalia, to the south is Oakwood, to the east is Wright-Patterson Air Force Base, and to the north is Dayton International Airport. Dayton is a city of bridges, 20 of which cross the four rivers.

Climate

Dayton has comfortable and moderate temperatures, but summers are humid. The rainfall is evenly distributed. Cold polar air from the Great Lakes produces cloudiness and snow in winter.

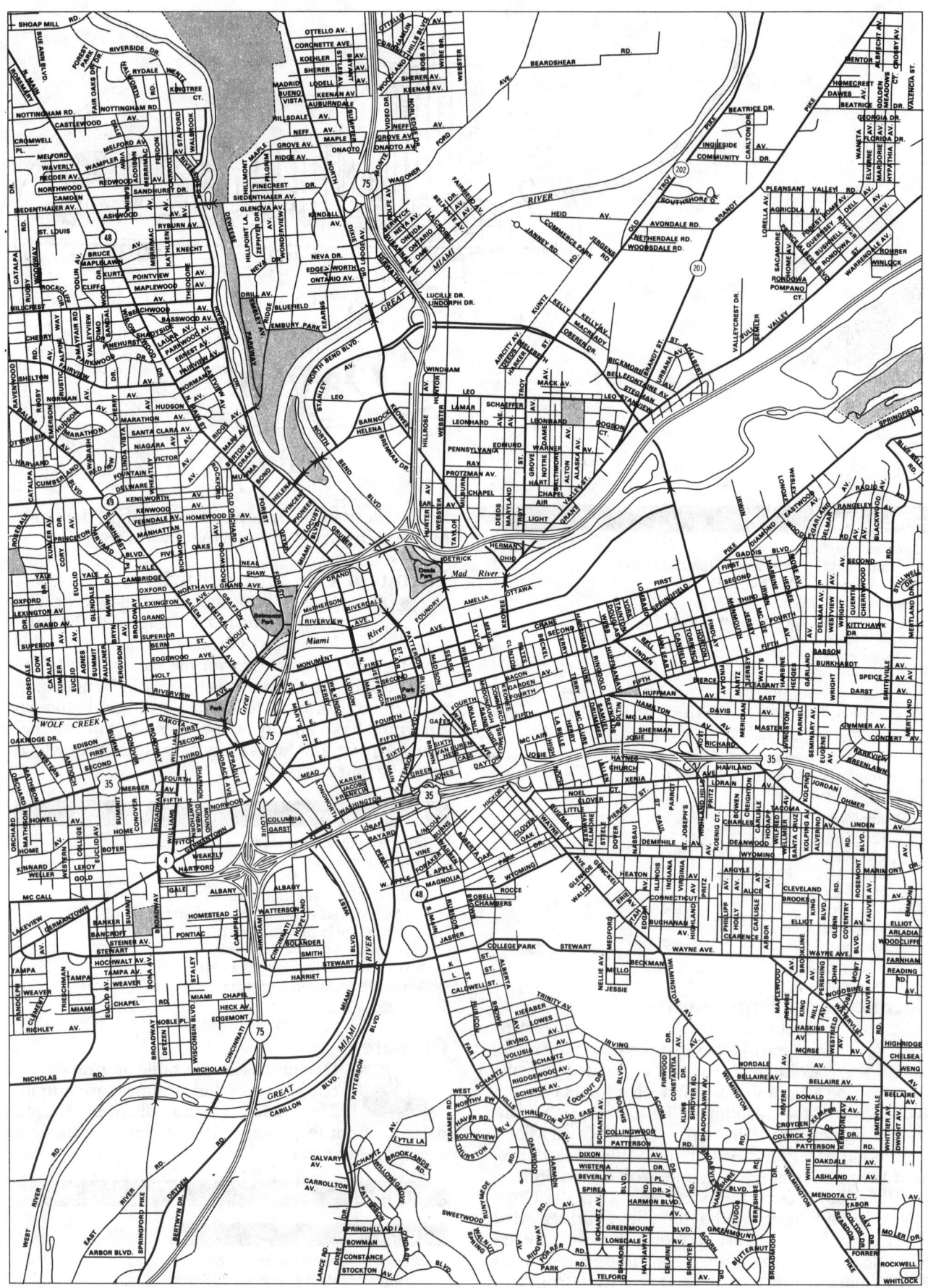

Weather (continued)

Annual Averages

Days 32°F or Below   117
Days above 90°F   27
Zero Degree Days   0
Precipitation (inches)   34.71
Snow (inches)   28.6
% Seasonal Humidity   70
Wind Speed (m.p.h.)   10.1
Clear Days   78
Cloudy Days   187
Storm Days   38
Rainy Days   126

Average Temperatures (°F)	High	Low	Mean
January	34.8	21.3	28.1
February	43.1	26.7	34.9
March	51.8	34.0	42.9
April	64.2	45.8	55.0
May	79.0	59.6	69.3
June	86.2	63.1	74.2
July	87.3	65.3	76.3
August	84.8	62.6	73.7
September	77.7	54.3	66.0
October	67.2	46.2	56.7
November	47.4	31.0	39.2
December	42.4	26.8	34.6

History

The Miami River Valley was a notable center of American Indian life and a thoroughfare on their seasonal journeys from Lake Erie to Kentucky. After the Revolutionary War, Judge John Cleves Symmes purchased the entire valley. In 1795 a group headed by General Jonathan Dayton and including General Arthur St. Clair, General James Wilkinson, and Colonel Israel Ludlow bought 60,000 acres from Symmes with the purpose of founding a settlement. Ludlow platted the town the same year.

The first settlers, led by Samuel Thompson, arrived in 1796. The newcomers were not deterred by warnings from friendly Indians against floods at the junction of the rivers. By 1799 Dayton was a cluster of nine cabins, a blockhouse that served as a school, distillery, sawmill, lime kiln, and Presbyterian church. When Ohio became a state in 1803, Dayton became the seat of Montgomery County; two years later, it was incorporated. In 1805 Dayton opened a public library, the first in the state. In the same year the town experienced its first flood, against which levees were built. Work on the Ohio canal system between Dayton and Cincinnati began in 1825, and the first section of the Miami and Erie Canal was completed in 1829. In 1851 the Mad River Lake Erie Railroad was opened to Dayton. In 1847 the telegraph came to town. The first high school was completed in 1850 and the population reached 11,000. In 1854 the Dayton and Springfield and Dayton and Western railroads were completed.

During the Civil War years, the city was polarized between pro-Union forces and the anti-Union Copperheads, the latter led by Congressman Clement L. Vallandingham. In 1863 Vallandingham was arrested and banished to the south. After the Turner Opera House fire in 1869, a waterworks system was installed.

In 1879 James Ritty invented "the money drawer," as cash registers were originally called. In 1884 John Patterson, a native Daytonian, bought the cash register patent for $6,500; the next day he tried, unsuccessfully, to sell it back to Ritty for half the price. Stuck with the patent, Patterson decided to make the best of the situation. Two years later, he built a new factory with 80% glass windows, recruited fine craftsmen, renamed the company National Cash Register (NCR), and soon became the largest manufacturer in Dayton.

Just after the turn of the century, Dayton's greatest inventors appeared on the scene. Working in their bicycle shop, Wilbur and Orville Wright laid the foundations of the modern aviation industry. Their fragile flying machine became the first successful heavier-than-air craft at Kitty Hawk, North Carolina, on 17 December 1903. In 1911 the Wright brothers established the world's first airplane factory in Dayton. Fresh from college in 1906, an engineer named Charles F. Kettering was hired to do research for NCR. Three years later he quit this job and retired to a woodshed to fashion a gadget that became the automobile self-starter. In 1910 Kettering started the Dayton Engineering Laboratories Company (Delco), which in 1919 became part of General Motors. Another local inventor, L. E. Custer, built an electric runabout in 1899.

The Main Street Bridge, one of the first concrete bridges, spanned the Miami in 1903. In 1913 disaster struck when, following a five-day downpour, the Great Miami rose over the levees in the most disastrous flood in the city's history. The flood took 361 lives and caused damage to property estimated at over $100 million. To avoid a recurrence, a comprehensive plan of flood protection (the first of its kind anywhere and the model for the TVA system) was drawn up and completed in 1922 at a cost of $32 million.

In 1919 Dayton became the first American city to adopt the commission-manager form of government. During World War I, two important government airfields were established at McCook Field and Fairfield. The Dayton-Wright Airplane Company developed the DeHavilland DH4 airplane as part of its war effort. After the war, the Frigidaire Division, established in the city, became the largest division of General Motors; the Wright and Patterson fields were built; and the Art Institute was completed.

Historical Landmarks

The Westminster Presbyterian Church on First Street, organized in 1799, is the city's oldest church. The present structure was built in 1926. The Old Courthouse on the corner of Third and Main streets, completed in 1850, is considered the finest example of Greek Revival architecture in the country. The Newcom Tavern in Van Cleve Park is a log cabin 22.5 by 48 feet with a stone fireplace. Built in 1796 by Colonel George Newcom, one of the pioneers, it is the oldest log structure in the city. In the earliest days it served as a courthouse, school, church, post office, and inn. It withstood the 1913 flood. The home of African-American

Chronology

1795	Four Revolutionary War leaders—General Arthur St. Clair, General James Wilkinson, Colonel Israel Ludlow, and Senator Jonathan Dayton—buy 60,000 acres at a place where the Mad River flows into the Great Miami. Ludlow surveys and plats the land.
1796	The first party of settlers arrive and are warned by Indians of flood danger at the junction of the rivers.
1803	Ohio becomes a state and Dayton the seat of Montgomery County.
1805	Dayton is incorporated as a town. The public library, first in the state, is built. Settlers experience the first of many devastating floods.
1825	Work begins on the Ohio canal between Cincinnati and Dayton.
1829	The Miami-Erie Canal opens.
1850	The city's first high school opens its doors.
1851	The Mad River and Lake Erie Railroad opens.
1854	The Dayton and Springfield and Dayton and Western railroads are completed.
1863	Clashes break out between pro-Union forces and the pro-slavery Copperheads. Copperhead leader Clement L. Vallandingham is arrested and banished.
1869	The Turner Opera House burns down.
1879	James Ritty invents the mechanical money drawer.
1884	John Patterson buys Ritty's cash register company for $6,500 and renames it National Cash Register.
1886	NCR builds a new daylight factory with 80% glass windows.
1896	Dayton celebrates its centenary.
1899	L. E. Custer builds an electric runabout.
1903	Two local inventors, Wilbur and Orville Wright, successfully fly the world's first heavier-than-air craft at Kitty Hawk. Main Street Bridge is built over the Great Miami.
1910	Charles F. Kettering, inventor of the automobile self-starter, and E. A. Deeds start the Dayton Engineering Laboratories Company (Delco).
1911	Wright brothers establish an experimental airplane factory.
1913	Following a five-day downpour, the Great Miami breaches its banks in the worst flood in Dayton's history. Bridges and houses are swept away. The toll is estimated at 361 lives and $100 million.
1914	Dayton becomes the first large American city to adopt the commission-manager form of government.
1916	Delco is acquired by General Motors.
1919	The manufacture of Frigidaires begins in Dayton.
1920	Dayton's James M. Cox, governor of Ohio, is the unsuccessful Democratic candidate for the presidency.
1922	A comprehensive plan of flood protection is completed at a cost of $32 million.
1927	Wright and Patterson airfields are established.
1928	Art Institute is built.

poet Paul Laurence Dunbar is open to the public. The Wright Memorial commemorates the spot where the brothers first tested their airplane.

Population

 Dayton has been losing population to the suburbs at a more rapid rate than comparable cities. Its 1990 population of 182,044 was 5.9% less than its 1980 population of 193,536, 25% less than its 1970 population of 243,000, and is not much higher than its 1930 population of 150,000. Its rank among U.S. cities has fallen from 79th to 83rd.

Population		
	1980	*1990*
Central City	193,536	182,044
Rank	73	89
Metro Area	942,083	951,270
Pop. Change 1980–1990 -11,492		
Pop. % Change 1980–1990 -5.9		
Median Age 31.0		
% Male 47.1		
% Age 65 and Over 13.1		
Density (per square mile) 3,309		
Households		
Number 72,670		
Persons per Household 2.41		
% Female-Headed Households 20.6		
% One-Person Households 33.4		
Births—Total 3,535		
% to Mothers under 20 21.7		
Birth Rate per 1,000 19.5		

Ethnic Composition

 Whites make up 58.4%; blacks 40.4%; American Indians 0.23%; Hispanics, both white and black 0.74%; and other races 0.34%.

Ethnic Composition (as % of total pop.)		
	1980	*1990*
White	62.05	58.37
Black	36.80	40.43
American Indian	0.15	0.23
Asian and Pacific Islander	0.43	0.64
Hispanic	0.86	0.74
Other	NA	0.34

Government

Dayton is governed by a five-member council and a mayor elected by the community. Council members are elected for four-year terms.

Government

Year of Home Charter   1913
Number of Members of the Governing Body   5
Elected at Large   5
Elected by Wards   NA
Number of Women in Governing Body   0
Salary of Mayor $33,810
Salary of Council Members $25,357
City Government Employment Total   2,785
Rate per 10,000   155.7

Public Finance

The total annual budget is $259.014 million. Total expenditures amount to $294.937 million. Debt outstanding is

Public Finance

Total Revenue (in millions) $259.01
Intergovernmental Revenue—Total (in millions) $32.87
Federal Revenue per Capita $17.52
% Federal Assistance   6.77
% State Assistance   5.5
Sales Tax as % of Total Revenue   NA
Local Revenue as % of Total Revenue   75.8
City Income Tax   yes
Taxes—Total (in millions) $79.6

Taxes per Capita
   Total $445
   Property $64
   Sales and Gross Receipts $2
General Expenditures—Total (in millions) $126.7
General Expenditures per Capita $708
Capital Outlays per Capita $51

% of Expenditures for:
   Public Welfare   0.0
   Highways   7.2
   Education   0.0
   Health and Hospitals   0.0
   Police   14.3
   Sewerage and Sanitation   10.0
   Parks and Recreation   5.6
   Housing and Community Development   7.0
Debt Outstanding per Capita $938
   % Utility   25.5
Federal Procurement Contract Awards (in millions) $248.2
Federal Grants Awards (in millions) $33.2
Fiscal Year Begins   January 1

$350.596 million, and cash and security holdings are $367.873 million.

Economy

The four pillars of Dayton's economy are: historical manufacturing companies like NCR and General Motors (GM); Wright-Patterson Air Force Base and its defense-related units; new high-technology firms; and foreign and multinational firms. GM is the largest manufacturing firm in terms of output and employment, as it has been since the early decades of this century. Other large manufacturers are Mead Corporation, Standard Register, Robbins and Myers, Huffy, Philips Industries, Reynolds and Reynolds, Duriron, PMI Food Equipment Group, EG&G Mound Applied Technology Division, Acustar, Hobart Brothers, and Amcast.

Wright-Patterson Air Base and its affiliated divisions account for 10% of the state of Ohio's economy. The base is the headquarters for Air Force Material Command, Center for Artificial Intelligence Applications, and Aeronautical Systems Center, among 100 other DoD divisions. Wright-Patterson has been responsible for attracting scores of research and development firms into the area. High technology has been the cutting edge of Dayton's growth. More than 800 high-technology and aerospace companies work in the Dayton area, many of them housed in the 1,500-acre Miami Valley Research Park. More recently many

Economy

Total Money Income (in millions) $1,543
% of State Average   83.1
Per Capita Annual Income $8,621
% Population below Poverty Level   20.8
Fortune 500 Companies   3

Banks	Number	Deposits (in millions)
Commercial	14	NA
Savings	12	NA

Passenger Autos   371,559
Electric Meters   239,177
Gas Meters   173,129

Manufacturing

Number of Establishments   466
% with 20 or More Employees   42.3
Manufacturing Payroll (in millions) $1,155.6
Value Added by Manufacture (in millions) $1,935.1
Value of Shipments (in millions) $3,589.1
New Capital Expenditures (in millions) $119.9

Wholesale Trade

Number of Establishments   401
Sales (in millions) $3,099.5
Annual Payroll (in millions) $168.623

Retail Trade

Number of Establishments   1,277
Total Sales (in millions) $1,056.4
Sales per Capita $5,904
Number of Retail Trade Establishments with Payroll   982
Annual Payroll (in millions) $129.5
Total Sales (in millions) $1,046.1
General Merchandise Stores (per capita) $807
Food Stores (per capita) $1,057

Economy (continued)

Apparel Stores (per capita) $137
Eating and Drinking Places (per capita) $634

Service Industries

Total Establishments   1,443
Total Receipts (in millions) $908.8
Hotels and Motels (in millions) $25.4
Health Services (in millions) $256.8
Legal Services (in millions) $89.8

multinationals, particularly Japanese firms, have moved into Dayton. Among them are AGA, Marconi, Avionics, Honda, Fujitech, and Pioneer Electronics.

Labor

Total nonagricultural employment in the Dayton area is 443,000, a figure estimated to rise by 10.4% to 482,300. The share of manufacturing in employment dropped from 35% to 25%, while the share of services gained correspondingly. Within the latter category, the share of government dropped from 18.3% in 1975 to 15.6% in 1991. The share of white males in the labor force is expected to decline, as is the total male share. The percentage of women, both white and nonwhite, is expected to increase. Unemployment rates in the Dayton area are slightly lower than both the Ohio and national rates. The fastest growing industries are business, legal, and health services, while the declining sectors are government, transportation, and agriculture.

Labor

Civilian Labor Force   89,823
% Change 1989–1990   -0.4

Work Force Distribution
   Mining   400
   Construction   14,000
   Manufacturing   98,200
   Transportation and Public Utilities   17,400
   Wholesale and Retail Trade   101,300
   FIRE (Finance, Insurance, Real Estate)   17,600
   Service   117,800
   Government   76,600
   Women as % of Labor Force   46.9
   % Self-Employed   3.0
   % Professional/Technical   14.8
Total Unemployment   7,060
Rate %   7.9
Federal Government Civilian Employment   4,126

Education

The Dayton City School System supports 49 schools. The largest public university is Wright State University with its schools of medicine, pharmacy, and nursing. The University of Dayton, founded in 1880, is a Catholic institution noted for its engineering and law schools. In nearby Yellow Springs is Antioch University, founded by Horace Mann in 1852. Specialized institutions include United Theological Seminary, affiliated with the United Methodist Church, and Sinclair Community College, offering courses in business, arts, medicine, and robotics. The Air Force Institute of Technology, although primarily a graduate school for military personnel, also accepts civilians.

Education

Number of Public Schools   49
Special Education Schools   NA
Total Enrollment   28,000
% Enrollment in Private Schools   NA
% Minority   NA
Classroom Teachers   NA
Pupil-Teacher Ratio   NA
Number of Graduates   NA
Total Revenue (in millions)   NA
Total Expenditures (in millions)   NA
Expenditures per Pupil   NA
Educational Attainment (Age 25 and Over)
   % Completed 12 or More Years   59.3
   % Completed 16 or More Years   10.4
Four-Year Colleges and Universities   2
   Enrollment   27,787
Two-Year Colleges   5
   Enrollment   20,506

Libraries

Number   50
Public Libraries   20
Books (in thousands)   1,559
Circulation (in thousands)   5,886
Persons Served (in thousands)   573
Circulation per Person Served   10.2
Income (in millions) $11.748
Staff   297

Four-Year Colleges and Universities
   University of Dayton
   Wright State University

Health

With its eight general and surgical hospitals, four of which are teaching hospitals, Dayton is the primary health-care center for southwestern Ohio. The largest are Miami Valley Hospital; Good Samaritan Hospital and Health Center; St. Elizabeth Hospital, Dayton's oldest hospital, founded in 1878; Children's Medical Center; Grandview Hospital; Dartmouth Hospital; Dayton Mental Health Center; and Veterans Administration

Health

Deaths—Total   2,083
Rate per 1,000   11.5
Infant Deaths—Total   55
Rate per 1,000   15.6
Number of Metro Hospitals   8
Number of Metro Hospital Beds   4,766
Rate per 100,000   2,664
Number of Physicians   1,552
Physicians per 1,000   1.84
Nurses per 1,000   16.10
Health Expenditures per Capita $1.74

Medical Center. In nearby Kettering is the Kettering Medical Center with its Kettering Memorial Hospital and Sycamore Hospital.

Transportation

Dayton is approached by two major interstates: east-west I-70 and north-south I-75. I-675, a bypass completed in 1987, connects these highways and provides through access to Columbus and Cincinnati. Extending east-west through the southern part of Dayton is U.S. 35. State routes leading into Dayton are 4, 202, 48, and 49. Rail freight service is provided by three railroads: CSX Transportation, Conrail, and Grand Trunk Western Railroad Company. Because of its central location, Dayton is a major distribution and warehousing center. The principal airport is Dayton International Airport, north of the city. It is served by 13 commercial airlines and 4 freight carriers.

Transportation

Interstate Highway Mileage 64
Total Urban Mileage 2,639
Total Daily Vehicle Mileage (in millions) 13.918
Daily Average Commute Time 42.2 min.
Number of Buses 137
Port Tonnage (in millions) NA
Airports 2
Number of Daily Flights 104
Daily Average Number of Passengers 5,707

Airlines (American carriers only)
   American
   Delta
   Northwest
   Trans World
   United
   USAir
   Westair

Housing

Eighty percent of the area homes are single-family dwellings. The historic Oregon District, settled in the early 1800s, has many homes that have been faithfully restored. St. Anne's Hill District, east of the Oregon District, contains excellent examples of late-Victorian architecture. South Dayton District, south of the central business district, displays a mix of Colonial, Victorian, and Gothic architecture. Each of its 226 structures is listed in the National Register of Historic Places. Other older residential areas include South Park District; Dayton View District, which was developed on a hilltop following the flood of 1913; and McPherson Town District, developed in the mid-1800s following construction of the first bridge across the Great Miami. Since World War II, construction of interstate highways has encouraged home building in Montgomery and Greene counties and other suburbs. The most rapidly growing communities are Centerville, Huber Heights, Englewood, Miamisburg, Kettering, Oakwood, Bellbrook, Xenia, Beaverbrook, Fairborn, and Yellowsprings.

Housing

Total Housing Units 80,370
% Change 1980–1990 8
Vacant Units for Sale or Rent 5,699
Occupied Units 72,670
% with More Than One Person per Room 3.0
% Owner-Occupied 51.0
Median Value of Owner-Occupied Homes $43,200
Average Monthly Purchase Cost $283
Median Monthly Rent $253
New Private Housing Starts 66
Value (in thousands) $5,208
% Single-Family 59.1
Nonresidential Buildings Value (in thousands) $19,278

Tallest Buildings	Hgt. (ft.)	Stories
Kettering Tower,	405	30
Dayton Arcade Centre	400	20
Mead World Hqtrs,	385	28

Urban Redevelopment

Urban redevelopment efforts are coordinated by the Dayton Development Council. Downtown Dayton revitalization continues through the efforts of Downtown Dayton Partnership. Recent additions include the Main Street Beautification Project; Packard Museum, near downtown; and two office/retail towers. The National Aviation Hall of Fame will open a 52,000-square-foot learning center in downtown Dayton in the near future. The Dayton Hara Complex underwent a $1.2 million expansion in 1988. The Erwin J. Nutter Center, a sports and entertainment facility at Wright State University, opened in 1990. The Fraze Pavilion was added to the Performing Arts in Kettering in 1992.

Crime

In 1991 the crimes known to police were 3,558 violent crimes and 18,044 property crimes.

Crime

Violent Crimes—Total 3,558
Violent Crime Rate per 100,000 692.3
Murder 54
Rape 316
Robbery 1,667
Aggravated Assaults 1,511
Property Crimes 18,044
Burglary 4,808
Larceny 9,906
Motor Vehicle Theft 3,330
Arson 284
Per Capita Police Expenditures $158.73
Per Capita Fire Protection Expenditures $128.59
Number of Police 440
Per 1,000 2.43

Religion

The largest denomination in Dayton is Roman Catholic, with all major Protestant denominations also represented.

Religion	
Largest Denominations (Adherents)	
Catholic	92,390
United Methodist	31,297
Black Baptist	34,453
Southern Baptist	29,853
Evangelical Lutheran	14,706
Assembly of God	7,306
American Baptist	6,477
Church of Nazarene	4,100
Presbyterian	5,801
Jewish	2,000

Media

Dayton's daily newspaper is the *Dayton Daily News*, one of the oldest newspapers in the country, founded in 1808. It merged with the *Journal Herald* in 1988. The electronic media consist of 5 television stations (4 commercial and 1 public) and 11 AM and FM radio stations.

Media	
Newsprint	
Dayton Daily News, daily	
Television	
WDTN (Channel 2)	
WHIO (Channel 7)	
WKEF (Channel 22)	
WPTD (Channel 16)	
WRGT (Channel 45)	
Radio	
WDAO (AM)	WDPR (FM)
WDPS (FM)	WGXM (FM)
WHIO (AM)	WHKO (FM)
WING (AM)	WONE (AM)
WTUE (FM)	WWSN (FM)
WWSU (FM)	

Sports

Dayton supports the Cincinnati Reds in baseball and Cincinnati Bengals in football. Dayton's two professional sports teams are the Dayton Dynamos of the American Indoor Soccer Association, who play home games at the Wright State Nutter Center, and the Dayton Bombers of the East Coast Hockey League, who play at the Hara Complex. The University of Dayton Flyers and Wright State Raiders are successful basketball teams.

Arts, Culture, and Tourism

Dayton's theatrical heritage is carried on at the Victoria Theatre, which opened in 1866 and was rebuilt in 1989 under the auspices of the Arts Center Foundation. Other major theaters include Dayton Playhouse; Human Race, the city's only resident theater company; and Dayton Theater Guild. Wright State University, University of Dayton, Sinclair Community College, and

Antioch College stage performances regularly. The Dayton Music Club is over 100 years old, having been founded in 1888. The Dayton Philharmonic Orchestra, founded in 1933, plays at Memorial Hall. Dayton Opera, founded in 1960, annually presents three operas at Memorial Hall. Dayton Ballet and Dayton Contemporary Dance Company are the major troupes in dance. The former is the second oldest regional dance company.

The Dayton Art Institute on Riverview Avenue is the principal city museum. Designed in the style of an Italian villa, it was completed in 1928 at a cost of $1.3 million. The historic St. Anne's Hill District is home to the Dayton Society of Painters and Sculptors. Art exhibitions are held regularly at Wright State University's Creative Arts Center, Rosewood Art Center, and Riverbend Art Center. Among the large museums are the U.S. Air Force Museum at Wright-Patterson Air Force Base; Dayton Museum of Natural History, which maintains Sunwatch, an 800-year-old Indian village; Kettering-Moraine Museum, which houses the artifacts of Charles Kettering and the Wright brothers; and the National Afro-American Museum and Cultural Center. The city has numerous Wright brothers memorabilia, including their cycle shop and print shop. Dayton will create the Dayton Aviation Heritage National Park following the passage of legislation by the U.S. Congress. The park will tie together four aviation-related sites and will be operated jointly by local officials and the National Park Service. The Montgomery County Historical Society also owns and administers the Patterson Homestead, home of the founder of NCR.

Travel and Tourism	
Hotel Rooms 7,703	
Convention and Exhibit Space (square feet) 77,000	
Convention Centers	
Dayton Convention Center	
Hara Arena Conference and Exhibition Center	
Ervin J. Nutter Center	
Festivals	
Dayton River Festival (May)	
World A' Fair (June)	
International Air Show	
Oktoberfest (September)	
Art in the Park (May)	
Dayton Art Expo	

Parks and Recreation

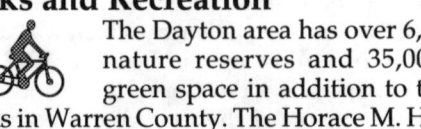

The Dayton area has over 6,400 acres of nature reserves and 35,000 acres of green space in addition to three theme parks in Warren County. The Horace M. Huffman, Jr., River Corridor Bikeway stretches for 24 miles along the Miami River. Kings Island offers seven theme areas. The 20-acre Aullwood Audubon Center and Farm and the Cox Arboretum are popular attractions. Carillon Park on the Great Miami River contains a 40-bell carillon and more than 30 historic buildings brought in from other locations and restored.

Sources of Further Information

Dayton Area Chamber of Commerce
1 Chamber Plaza
Fifth and Main
Dayton, OH 45402-2400
(513) 226-1444

Dayton/Montgomery County Convention
and Visitors Bureau
1 Chamber Plaza
Fifth and Main
Dayton, OH 45402-2400
(800) 221-8235

Dayton and Montgomery County Public Library
215 East Third Street
Dayton, OH 45402-2103
(513) 227-9500

Montgomery County Historical Society
5 North Main Street
Dayton, OH 45402
(513) 228-6271

Additional Reading

Cornelisse, Diana Good. *Remarkable Journey: The Wright Field Heritage in Photographs.* 1991.
Eckert, Allan W. *A Time of Terror: The Great Dayton Flood.* 1965.
Sealander, Judith. *Grand Plans: Business Progressivism and Social Change in Ohio's Miami Valley, 1890–1929.* 1988.

Denver

Colorado

Location and Topography

N

Denver is located on the plains in north-central Colorado at the eastern edge of the Rocky Mountains. Known as the Queen City of the Plains and as the Mile High City, because its elevation is 5,280 feet, it is at the confluence of the South Platte River and Cherry Creek.

Layout of City and Suburbs

The Rockies form a spectacular back-drop for the city and make it easy for visitors to orient themselves: the mountains are due west and run north and south, and the plains are to the east. The main business district is a triangle bounded by Broadway, Colfax Avenue, and Larimer Street, just below where Cherry Creek flows into the South Platte.

Streets in the business district run at a 45° angle to those leading to residential sections. Broadway, the principal north-south street, extends south to split the Civic Center, the park at the heart of the city, which is bracketed by the state capitol on high ground to the east and the City & County Building to the west. Also on the park are the Denver Art Museum, the Denver Public Library, the Greek Theater, and the Voorhies Memorial. The Colorado State Historical Society's museum is one block south on Broadway and the U.S. Mint is one block west on Colfax. Seventeenth Street, known as the Wall Street of the West, runs from Union Station south to Broadway, and a pedestrian mall stretches for 14 blocks along 16th Street from Cleveland Place north to Market Street.

Long, tree-lined avenues of residential areas stretch out from the business district. The City Auditorium and

Environment

Environmental Stress Index   2.4
Green Cities Index: Rank   39
                Score   30.64
Water Quality   Alkaline
    Average Daily Use (gallons per capita)   303
    Maximum Supply (gallons per capita)   704
Parkland as % of Total City Area   5.6
% Waste Landfilled/Recycled   NA
Annual Parks Expenditures per Capita $101.54

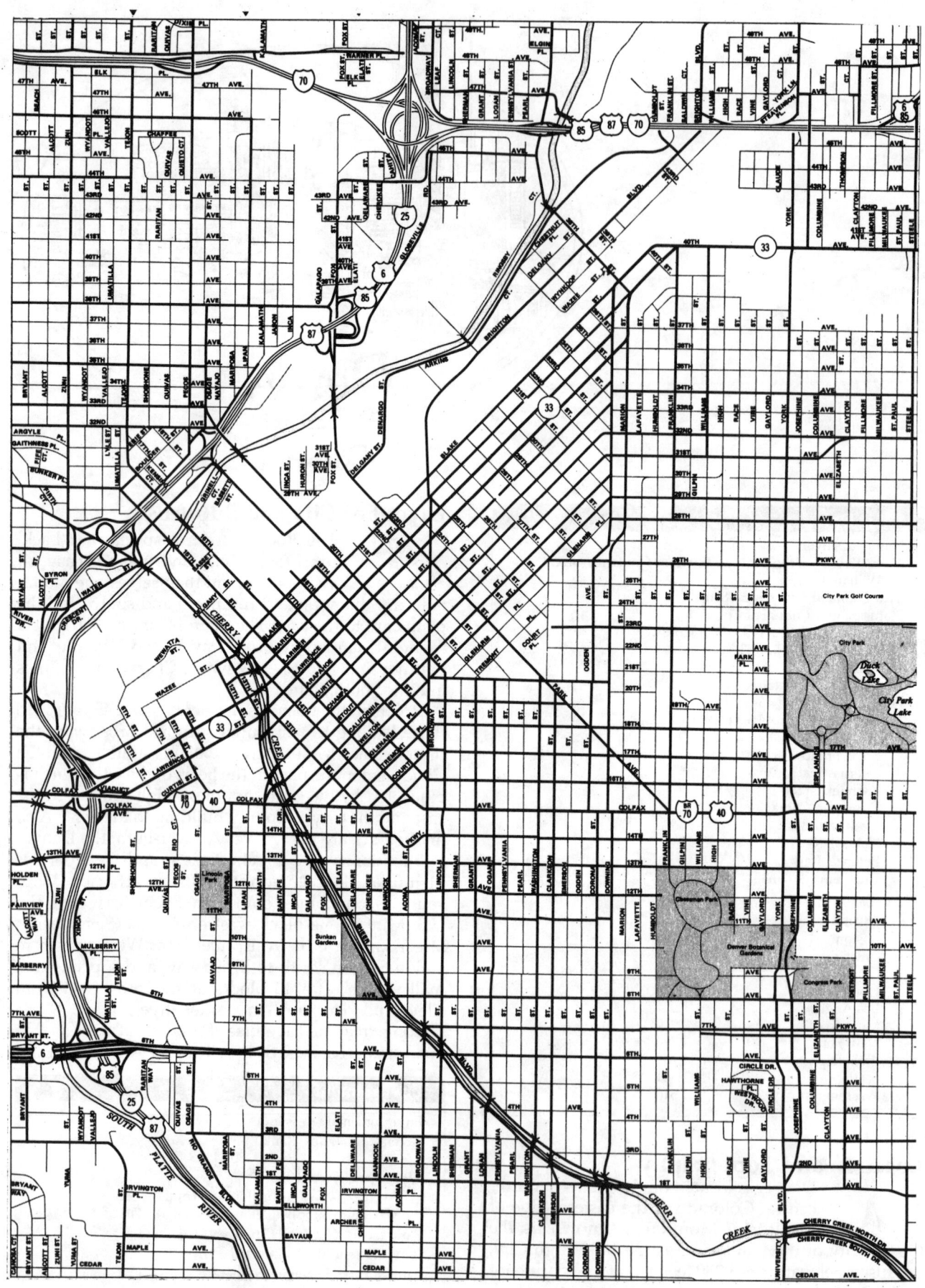

Theater, Mile High Stadium, and Currigan Exhibition Hall are west of the business district. Development and redevelopment begun in the 1950s changed the Denver skyline. Now skyscrapers, such as Republic Plaza, the Mountain Bell Center, and United Bank of Denver dominate the downtown skyline.

Climate

 Denver is noted for its salubrious mild and dry climate and its skies can be unusually clear. The average temperature in July, the warmest month, is 73°F, and the average temperature in January, the coldest month, is 29°F. Annual precipitation is only 16 inches and the city has an average of 250 clear or partly clear days, more sunny days than either Miami or San Diego. Humidity is also low. In winter the invasion of cold air from the north can be abrupt.

Weather

Temperature

Highest Monthly Average (°F)	88
Lowest Monthly Average (°F)	15.9

Annual Averages

Days 32°F or Below	163
Days below 0°F	10
Days above 90°F	32
Zero Degree Days	10
Precipitation (inches)	16
Snow (inches)	60
% Seasonal Humidity	53
Wind Speed (m.p.h.)	9.1
Clear Days	115
Cloudy Days	119
Storm Days	41
Rainy Days	88

Average Temperatures (°F)	High	Low	Mean
January	43.5	16.2	29.0
February	46.2	19.4	32.8
March	50.1	23.8	37.0
April	61.0	33.9	47.5
May	70.3	43.6	57.0
June	80.1	51.9	66.0
July	87.4	58.6	73.0
August	85.8	57.4	71.6
September	77.7	47.8	62.8
October	66.8	37.2	52.0
November	53.3	25.4	39.4
December	46.2	18.9	32.6

History

The Spanish are believed to have explored what is now the Denver region in the seventeenth century. In 1832 trader Louis Vasquez built a fur trading post north of what is now the city at the junction of the South Platte River and Clear Creek. He is believed to be the first nonnative settler.

Full-scale settlement did not begin until nearly 30 years later, in 1858, when a party of prospectors from Lawrence, Kansas, led by Charles Nichols, was drawn to the area by reports of gold along the South Platte. The Kansans built a number of log cabins along the east bank of the river at what is now East Evans Avenue, naming their settlement Montana City. Other miners started the short-lived settlement of St. Charles on the east bank of the Cherry Creek near its confluence with the Platte, and a party of gold-seekers, including miners from Georgia, laid out a third townsite and called it Auraria.

Meanwhile, Montana City residents abandoned their site and St. Charles was overrun by a party from Leavenworth led by William H. Larimer. On November 22, 1858, Larimer's party organized the Denver City Town Company, naming it for James W. Denver, who had resigned as Kansas Territory's governor after Larimer had left Leavenworth.

By the end of the year Denver City, still competing with Auraria, had some 20 cabins, including the first saloon. In 1859 the town had an all-important stagecoach connection, its first school, its first hospital, its first hotel, its first bank, and its first church service, held in a room above the gambling hall. That same year the *Rocky Mountain News* brought out its first edition. While gold fever brought people into town, there was no gold strike comparable to those in California, and disgruntled miners were so lawless and boisterous that Horace Greeley, visiting in 1859, wrote that he found there "more brawls, more pistol shots with criminal intent in this log city of 150 dwellings, nor three-fourths of them completed, nor two thirds of them inhabited, nor one-third fit to be, than in any community of equal numbers on earth."

In 1860 Denver and Auraria consolidated under the name of Denver City, and the federal government created Colorado Territory. The outbreak of the Civil War found Denver on the side of the Union, and in 1862 a regiment of Denver volunteers marched 400 miles in 13 days to win an engagement against a Confederate force at Glorieta Pass in New Mexico, the westernmost engagement of the war. In 1864, the same year that a fire and the flooding of Cherry Creek ravaged Denver, troops massacred Indians at Sand Creek.

In 1867, the territorial legislature, meeting at Golden, selected Denver as the territory's capital. Local promoters, recognizing the value of a rail link with the newly completed transcontinental railroad that passed through Cheyenne, Wyoming, financed the construction of the Denver and Pacific Railroad; its first train pulled into town in 1870. Two months later the Kansas Pacific Railroad reached town. English traveler Isabella Bird, passing through Denver in 1872, called it "the great braggart city."

In 1876, the nation's centennial year, Colorado was admitted to the Union, becoming the 38th state. Silver discoveries poured wealth into the town—enough for Horace Tabor to open the Tabor Grand Opera House in 1881. A pattern of boom and bust lent an element of risk to Denver growth.

Denver County was created in 1901, and the city and county were consolidated in 1902. In the same year, a state constitutional amendment gave Denver and other cities the right to manage their own affairs.

Chronology

1832	Louis Vasquez, a fur trader, builds post in the vicinity.
1858	Traces of gold lure prospectors to establish camps called Montana City, St. Charles, and Auraria at the junction of the South Platte River and Cherry Creek in what was then Kansas Territory.
1860	Denver, named for a former territorial governor, and Auraria are consolidated as Denver City; Colorado Territory formed.
1864	Cherry Creek in flood destroys many sections of town.
1867	Territorial legislature in Golden chooses Denver as territorial capital.
1870	Denver and Pacific Railroad is completed and first train steams into town. The Kansas Pacific Railroad reaches Denver two months later.
1876	Colorado becomes 38th state with Denver its capital.
1881	Tabor Grand Opera House opens.
1890	Denver becomes the third largest city west of the Missouri, after Omaha and San Francisco.
1901	Denver County is created from parts of Adams and Arapahoe Counties.
1902	Denver City and Denver County are consolidated. State legislature grants autonomy to Colorado cities.
1927	Moffat Tunnel is completed, linking Denver and Salt Lake City by rail providing winter access by train to Winter Park for skiing.
1958	Denver Urban Renewal Authority is charged to eliminate slums and blight.
1989	Ground is broken for Denver International Airport.
1990	Denver Performing Arts Complex is completed.

Robert W. Speer, the first mayor under the home rule amendment, instituted a broad program of urban improvements called The City Beautiful. He approved landscaping that helped to transform the naturally treeless plains into a city of tree-lined streets and boulevards and expanded the park system. An ambitious school building program begun in 1920 complemented other civic improvements.

Just before World War II Denver became one of the largest regional centers of the federal government when offices opened for the Geological Survey and the Bureau of Land Management. World War II brought prosperity as local companies adapted to wartime demands—a ski company won a contract for snowshoes and a tent and awning company made parachutes. John Gunther, in his 1947 book *Inside USA*, described Denver as an "Olympian, impassive and inert . . . self-sufficient, isolated, and self-contained." The city's boom brought people who liked the small-town atmosphere and easy access to mountain recreation. Boomers encouraged a bid for the 1976 winter Olympics, which voters, wanting to control development, rejected in 1972. Still, the pattern of boom and bust continued through the 1980s, and the populations of surrounding counties grew at Denver's expense.

Historical Landmarks

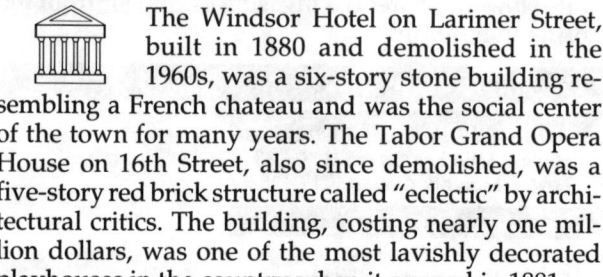

The Windsor Hotel on Larimer Street, built in 1880 and demolished in the 1960s, was a six-story stone building resembling a French chateau and was the social center of the town for many years. The Tabor Grand Opera House on 16th Street, also since demolished, was a five-story red brick structure called "eclectic" by architectural critics. The building, costing nearly one million dollars, was one of the most lavishly decorated playhouses in the country when it opened in 1881.

The Palace Theater Building on Blake Street was for many years one of the most infamous gambling and drinking houses. It opened in 1873, ostensibly as a theater, and was often denounced as a den of vice and corruption. A marker at Blake Street Bridge across Cherry Creek indicates the site of the Elephant Corral on Blake Street between 14th and 15th streets and extending to Wazee Street. Named for its size, the corral began as a log hotel. Known in 1859 as the Denver House and as the "Astor House of the Gold Fields," it became a major campground for pioneers. Its saloons were filled with gamblers. Killings were not uncommon and the victims were buried at the expense of the house. It was destroyed by fire in 1863. On this site also stood the first cabin of the St. Charles Township, built in 1858, and later the home of General William Larimer.

The U.S. Mint on West Colfax Avenue is the successor to the Denver Mint which began operating in 1869, after the federal government purchased the private mint of Clark, Gruber and Company. The elegant Brown Palace hotel, on Broadway at Tremont, completed in 1892, shifted attention from lower downtown toward the state capitol; it is considered by many the finest hotel in the city. The Daniels and Fisher Tower at 16th and Arapahoe, built in 1902, is a copy of the Campanile of St. Mark's in Venice. The City & County Building on Bannock Street, completed in 1932, represents the joint efforts of 35 leading Denver architects. The four-story granite building with Doric columns has a large central portico surmounted by a slender clock tower. "The Pioneer Monument" on the corner of Broadway and West Colfax Avenue marks the terminus of the Old Smoky Hill Trail. A bronze equestrian figure of Kit Carson surmounts the memorial, and around the rim of the fountain are three reclining bronze figures: "The Hunter," "The Prospector," and "The Pioneer Mother."

The State Capitol, on rising ground at the eastern side of the Civic Center's 15-acre tract on Broadway between East Colfax and East 14th avenues extending to Grant Street, dominates the city. The work of E. E. Myers, who also designed the Michigan and Texas state capitols, the building was completed in 1896 at a cost of $2.6 million. The three-story granite structure features a high, gold leaf–covered dome. On the steps of the west portico is a brass plate with the inscription, "One Mile Above Sea Level." The floor plan of the building is in the form of a Greek cross. At the western entrance to the Capitol is the Soldiers Monument, a bronze figure of a Union soldier flanked with two Civil War cannons. On the east lawn is the bronze figure of an Indian, known as "The Closing Era."

Population

After growing steadily for a number of decades, Denver began to lose population beginning in the 1970s while the metropolitan area as a whole continued to grow. From a peak of 514,678 in 1970, Denver's population dropped 4.3% to reach 492,365 in 1980 and then dropped an additional 5.1% to reach 467,610 in 1990.

Population		
	1980	1990
Central City	492,365	467,610
Rank	24	26
Metro Area	1,428,836	1,622,980
Pop. Change 1980–1990 -24,755		
Pop. % Change 1980–1990 -5.1		
Median Age 33.9		
% Male 48.7		
% Age 17 and Under 22.0		
% Age 65 and Over 13.86		
Density (per square mile in 1990) 3,050.7		

Households (1990)
Number 210,952
Persons per Household 2.17
% Female-Headed Households 11.5
% One-Person Households 40.4
Births—Total 8,959
% to Mothers under 20 14.4
Birth Rate per 1,000 17.5

Ethnic Composition

Whites make up 72.1% of the population, blacks 12.8%, American Indians 1.2%, Asians and Pacific Islanders 2.4%, and others 0.1%. Hispanics, both black and white, make up 23%.

Government

Denver has a consolidated city-county government under a mayor and council. The 1902 charter vests the mayor with strong executive powers. The mayor and 13 members of the council are elected to four-year terms.

Ethnic Composition (as % of total pop.)		
	1980	1990
White	76.29	72.1
Black	12.00	12.8
American Indian	0.88	1.2
Asian and Pacific Islander	1.81	2.4
Hispanic	18.74	23.0
Other	.03	0.1

Government
Year of Home Charter 1902
Number of Members of the   Governing Body 13
Elected at Large 2
Elected by Wards 11
Number of Women in Governing Body 8
Salary of Mayor $90,00
Salary of Council Members $32,400
City Government Employment Total 24,887
Rate per 10,000 491.4

Public Finance

The budget in 1984–1985 consisted of general revenues of $738.6 million while expenditures for the year totaled $675.1

Public Finance
General Revenue (in millions) $738.6
Intergovernmental Revenue—Total (in millions) $140.5
Federal Revenue per Capita $50.47
% Federal Assistance 2.61
% State Assistance 74.1
Sales Tax as % of Total Revenue 21.36
Local Revenue as % of Total Revenue 81.46
City Income Tax no
Taxes—Total (in millions) $280.1
Taxes per Capita
Total $555
Property 170.00
Sales and Gross Receipts $337
General Expenditures—Total (in millions) $675.1
General Expenditures per Capita $1,337
Capital Outlays per Capita $248
% of Expenditures for:
Public Welfare 11.7
Highways 4.2
Education NA
Health and Hospitals 15.6
Police 11.5
Sewerage and Sanitation 7.9
Parks and Recreation 6.8
Housing and Community Development 11.5
Debt Outstanding per Capita 1,327
% Utility 42
Federal Procurement Contract Awards (in millions) $1,375.9
Federal Grants Awards (in millions) $418.6
Fiscal Year Begins January 1

Economy

Denver is the financial and commercial capital of the Rocky Mountain region and its downtown banking district is known as the Wall Street of the West. Although founded as a mining town, mining plays only a small role in the economy. The only sector that has survived from its pioneer days is cattle and stock raising. The manufacturing sector is strong, with over 1,500 companies in such diverse areas as food processing, energy, and transportation equipment. The state and federal governments are major contributors to the economy. Denver is the national or regional headquarters of more federal agencies than any other city except Washington, D.C. Of the 250 federal offices and agencies, the more important ones are the Denver Federal Center, the U.S. Mint, and the Denver branch of the Federal Reserve Bank of Kansas City. More than 100 research and development installations, both public and private, are based in Denver. Oil refining was introduced in 1945. Denver's strategic location makes it an ideal transportation hub and the city broke ground in 1989 for a new airport. Both United Airlines and Continental Airlines maintain a substantial presence in the city.

Labor

Work force distribution is typical of most U.S. cities, with trade and services making up over 50%, followed by government and manufacturing. Among the largest employers are U.S. West, Martin Marietta, and A.T. & T. Federal and state government employees account for a sizable chunk of the work force.

Economy

Total Money Income (in millions)	$5,840	
% of State Average	106.6	
Per Capita Annual Income	$12,890	
% Population below Poverty Level	13.7	
Fortune 500 Companies	2	

Banks	Number	Deposits (in millions)
Commercial	182	NA
Savings	8	12,264

Passenger Autos	310,870
Electric Meters	990,600
Gas Meters	865,400

Manufacturing

Number of Establishments	1,146
% with 20 or More Employees	26.9
Manufacturing Payroll (in millions)	$935.9
Value Added by Manufacture (in millions)	$2,034.8
Value of Shipments (in millions)	$3,798.2
New Capital Expenditures (in millions)	$109.1

Wholesale Trade

Number of Establishments	2,028
Sales (in millions)	$11,108
Annual Payroll (in millions)	$685.406

Retail Trade

Number of Establishments	5,115
Total Sales (in millions)	$3,300.8
Sales per Capita	$6,536
Number of Retail Trade Establishments with Payroll	3,527
Annual Payroll (in millions)	$506.0
Total Sales (in millions)	$3,224
General Merchandise Stores (per capita)	$681
Food Stores (per capita)	$1,437
Apparel Stores (per capita)	$361
Eating and Drinking Places (per capita)	$1,069

Service Industries

Total Establishments	6,471
Total Receipts (in millions)	$3.928
Hotels and Motels (in millions)	$261.6
Health Services (in millions)	$695.7
Legal Services (in millions)	$619.4

Labor

Civilian Labor Force	266,954
% Change 1989–1990	2.8
Work Force Distribution	
Mining	13,000
Construction	31,500
Manufacturing	95,800
Transportation and Public Utilities	60,200
Wholesale and Retail Trade	203,700
FIRE (Finance, Insurance, Real Estate)	65,300
Service	198,900
Government	129,000
Women as % of Labor Force	45.4
% Self-Employed	5.7
Total Unemployment	14,482
Rate %	5.4
Federal Government Civilian Employment	11,537

Education

The Denver Public Schools system supports 78 elementary schools, 18 middle schools, and 10 senior high schools. Sixty church-supported schools supplement the public school system. Higher education is offered at six four-year institutions of which the largest are the University of Denver, the University of Colorado, based in Boulder but with a branch in Denver, Metropolitan State College of Denver, and Regis University. Denver has three theological institutions—St. Thomas Seminary, Conservative Baptist Theological Seminary, and the

Education

Number of Public Schools	106
Special Education Schools	NA
Total Enrollment	58,279
% Enrollment in Private Schools	65.4
% Minority	77
Classroom Teachers	3,706
Pupil-Teacher Ratio	16
Number of Graduates	2,685
Total Revenue (in millions)	$312.1
Total Expenditures (in millions)	$270.7
Expenditures per Pupil	$5,671
Educational Attainment (Age 25 and Over)	
% Completed 12 or More Years	74.7
% Completed 16 or More Years	24.8
Four-Year Colleges and Universities	6
Enrollment	49,144
Two-Year Colleges	4
Enrollment	7,517

Education (continued)

Libraries

Number 108
Public Libraries 22
  Books (in thousands) 1,939
  Circulation (in thousands) 3,873
  Persons Served (in thousands) 495
  Circulation per Person Served NA
  Income (in millions) $14.8
  Staff 101

Four-Year Colleges and Universities:
  Colorado Christian College
  Metropolitan State College of Denver
  Regis University
  University of Colorado at Denver
  University of Colorado Health Sciences Center
  University of Denver

Iliff School of Theology (Methodist). Nontraditional education is offered at the Denver Free University.

Health

There are more than 20 hospitals in the city, which has emerged as the medical center of the Rocky Mountain region. Among the major hospitals are the University of Colorado Health Sciences Center, AMC Cancer Research Center, Denver General Hospital, Swedish Medical Center, Colorado Psychiatric Hospital, St. Anthony Hospital System, Fitzsimons Army Medical Center, Children's Medical Center, and the National Jewish Center for Immunology and Respiratory Medicine. The Rose Medical Center offers a comprehensive range of services through its Arthritis Center, Kidney Stone Center, Center for Heart Disease, and Institute for Sports Medicine.

Health

Deaths—Total (1984) 4,629
Rate per 1,000 9.2
Infant Deaths—Total 106
Rate per 1,000 11.9
Number of Metro Hospitals 22
Number of Metro Hospital Beds 5,424
Rate per 100,000 1,074
Number of Physicians 3771
Physicians per 1,000 2.76
Nurses per 1,000 7.90
Health Expenditures per Capita 81.79

Transportation

Denver is one of the most centrally located metropolitan centers and is the hub of a vast network of roads and railways. Five major interstates intersect in the city: the north-south I-25, I-225, and I-270 and the east-west I-70 and I-76. The city is also served by U.S. Highways 6, 36 (the Denver-Boulder Turnpike), 40, 285, and 287, state highways 8, 58, and 121. Denver is a major point on Amtrak with six trains daily. Rail freight service is provided by Union Pacific, Denver and Rio Grande Western, Burlington Northern, Santa Fe, and Colorado

and Eastern. Denver's streets are divided north and south by Ellsworth Avenue and east and west by Broadway. In general, east-west roads are called avenues and north-south ones are called streets. Above Ellsworth the avenues are numbered and below it they are named. Stapleton International Airport on the eastern edge of the city is to be replaced by Denver International Airport scheduled to open in 1994.

Transportation

Interstate Highway Mileage 92
Total Urban Mileage 5,885
Total Daily Vehicle Mileage (in millions) 27.211
Daily Average Commute Time 48.6 min
Number of Buses 651
Port Tonnage (in millions) NA
Airports 1
Number of Daily Flights 447
Daily Average Number of Passengers 77,494

Airlines (American carriers only)
  American
  American West
  Continental
  Delta
  Northwest
  Trans World
  USAir
  United

Housing

Many high-rises have been built in the Capitol Hill area. A successfully integrated neighborhood in northeast Denver is Park Hill, originally platted by a former Prussian officer in the 1880s as a residential alternative to the Capitol Hill neighborhood. Denver still has some of the old ethnic neighborhoods of the nineteenth-century. Of the total housing stock 41.2% is owner-occupied. The median value of an owner-occupied home is $79,000 and the median monthly rent is $339.

Housing

Total Housing Units 239,636
% Change 1980–1990 5.2
Vacant Units for Sale or Rent 28,684
Occupied Units 210,952
% with More Than One Person per Room 4.2
% Owner-Occupied 41.2
Median Value of Owner-Occupied Homes $79,000
Average Monthly Purchase Cost $749
Median Monthly Rent $386
New Private Housing Starts (1992) 505
Value (in thousands) $37,300
% Single-Family Detached Homes (1992) 47.6
Nonresidential Buildings Value (in thousands) $799,500

Tallest Buildings:	Hgt. (ft.)	Stories
Republic Plaza	714	56
Mountain Bell Center	709	54
United Bank of Denver	698	52
1999 Broadway	544	43
Arco Tower	527	41
Anaconda Tower	507	40
Amoco Bldg.	448	36
17th Street Plaza	438	35

Urban Redevelopment

The Denver Urban Renewal Authority (DURA) was charged, beginning in 1958, to eliminate slums and blight from the city. The Auraria Campus on the south bank of Cherry Creek replaced a Hispanic neighborhood and became the site for Metropolitan State College of Denver, the University of Colorado at Denver, and Denver Community College. Larimer Square at the north end of the business district barely survived as a remnant of old Denver. DURA instituted the decade-long Skyline Project, begun in the 1970s, which replaced and restored old buildings downtown. Completed in the early 1980s, the project included offices, apartment buildings, and Sakura Square, a Japanese cultural center. The Denver Performing Arts Complex was completed in 1990. The Denver Technological Center, an office complex located southeast of the city, houses over 1,000 companies.

Crime

In 1991, of the crimes known to police, there were 3,572 violent and 34,500 property crimes.

Crime

Violent Crimes—Total   3,572
Violent Crime Rate per 100,000   55
Murder   325
Rape   1,267
Robbery   1,925
Aggravated Assaults   1,925
Property Crimes   34,500
Burglary   10,280
Larceny   18,172
Motor Vehicle Theft   6,626
Arson   422
Per Capita Police Expenditures $184.26
Per Capita Fire Protection Expenditures $1,349
Number of Police (1985)   1,349
Per 1,000   2.63

Religion

Catholics make up 15%, Baptists 4%, Reformed churches 3%, Lutherans 4%, Methodists 3%, Presbyterians 2% and Churches of Christ 1%. Denver has some old magnificent churches, including the Episcopal Cathedral of St. John in the Wilderness on 14th Avenue between Washington and Clarkson streets, designed in fifteenth-century English Gothic style in Indiana limestone with two square towers flanking the main entrance. The cathedral contains some fine examples of stained glass. It is the third church of that name, replacing an older cathedral destroyed by fire in 1903 and an earlier log cabin church built in the 1860s. The principal Roman Catholic church is the Basilica of the Immaculate Conception, a French Gothic structure with twin spires, completed in 1912 and located at the corner of East Colfax Avenue at Logan Street.

Religion

Largest Denominations	(Adherents)
Catholic	83,614
Black Baptist	15,624
Episcopal	12,782
American Baptist	10,951
United Methodist	10,729
Southern Baptist	8,214
Presbyterian	7,240
Jewish	11,385

Media

The major Denver newspapers are the *Denver Post* and the *Rocky Mountain News*; the latter, founded in 1859, is the city's oldest. Electronic media consist of seven television channels and 21 AM and FM radio stations.

Media

Newsprint
  The Colorado Statesman, Weekly
  Denver Business, Monthly
  Denver Herald-Dispatch, Weekly
  Denver Living, Bimonthly
  Denver Magazine, Monthly
  Denver Post, Daily
  Rocky Mountain News, Daily
  Metro Denver, Monthly

Television
  KBDI (Channel 12)
  KCNC (Channel 4)
  KCEC (Channel 50)
  KDVR (Channel 31)
  KMGH (Channel 7)
  KRMA (Channel 6)
  KUSA (Channel 9)

Radio
KBNO (AM)	KBPI (FM)
KCFR (FM)	KLZ (AM)
KAZY (FM)	KMJI (FM)
KNUS (AM)	KOA (AM)
KRFX (FM)	KOSI (FM)
KPOF (AM)	KRKS (AM)
KRXY (AM)	KRXY (FM)
KUVO (FM)	KVOD (FM)
KXKL (AM)	KYBG (AM)
KYGO (AM)	KYGO (FM)
KHOW (FM)	

Sports

Denver's professional sports teams are the Denver Broncos in football, the Denver Nuggets in basketball, and the new National League baseball team, the Colorado Rockies.

Arts, Culture, and Tourism

Dance, theater, and music come together at the Denver Performing Arts Complex, which encompasses four city blocks and includes the Boettcher Concert Hall, highly regarded as the home of the Colorado Symphony Orchestra; the Helen G. Bonfils Theater Complex, which has its own repertory company; the Temple Buell Theatre, which hosts Broadway stage productions; and the Auditorium Theatre. Other prominent orchestras in the city are the Denver Chamber Orchestra and the Denver Young Artists Orchestra. Opera is represented by Opera Colorado. Germinal Stage Denver, the Changing Scene, and Denver Center Theater Company regularly stage productions. Ballet is represented by Ballet Denver, the Colorado Ballet, Colorado Contemporary Dance, David Taylor Dance Theatre, and the Premiere Dance Arts Company.

The Denver Art Museum, founded in 1893, is home to some eminent art collections especially art of the Americas, including pre-Columbian and Native American collections. The Museum of Western Art is a restored gambling hall and brothel. The Trianon Museum and Art Gallery displays nineteenth-century European masterpieces. The Museum of Outdoor Arts is a museum without walls. The Denver Botanic Gardens and its associated facilities offer an extensive range of exhibits, events, and educational programs. The Denver Museum of Natural History, with exhibits of Rocky Mountain flora and fauna, also has the Gates Planetarium and an IMAX theater. Other museums include the Children's Museum, the Forney Transportation Museum, the Hall of Life, the Mizel Museum of Judaica, the Molly Brown House Museum, the State Historical Society of Colorado Museum, and the Turner Museum.

Travel and Tourism

Hotel Rooms (downtown)   4,000
Convention and Exhibit Space (square feet)   400,000

Convention Centers
    Colorado Convention Center
    Currigan Exhibition Hall
    Denver Merchandise Mart and Exposition Center
    Denver Performing Arts Complex
    McNichols Arena
    National Western Stock Show Complex

Festivals
    National Western Stock Show and Rodeo (January)
    Colorado Indian Market (January)
    Cinco de Mayo
    Cherry Creek Arts Festival (July)
    Colorado Renaissance Festival (summer)

Parks and Recreation

The city maintains about 210 parks, covering 4,000 acres in the city and another 14,000 acres in 17 mountain parks west of the city. In addition to 130 miles of off-street trails, including a greenway with paved trails along Cherry Creek and the South Platte River, there is the 8.3-acre Overland Park, designed in the 1920s to attract new residents to the city by having the country's first car-camping area, as well as a golf course and an exposition

center supported by 30 counties. Eighty-acre Cheesman Park was, until 1890, a cemetery. The 317-acre City Park on 17th Avenue between York Street and Colorado Boulevard has a golf course, the Denver Zoo, and one of the best views of the city from the west side of the Denver Museum of Natural History. Elitch Gardens, an amusement park, has been in business since 1890.

Sources of Further Information

City Hall
350 City and County Building
Denver, CO 80202
(303) 640-2721

The Greater Denver Chamber of Commerce
1445 Market Street
Denver, CO 80202
(303) 534-8500

Denver Metro Convention and Visitors Bureau
225 West Colfax Avenue
Denver, CO 80202
(303) 892-1112

Denver Regional Council of Governments
2480 W. 26th Avenue, Suite 200B
Denver, CO 80211
(303) 445-1000

Additional Reading

Barth, Gunther. *Instant Cities: Urbanization and the Rise of San Francisco and Denver.* 1988.
Brettell, Richard R. *Historic Denver: The Architects and Architecture, 1858–1893.* 1979.
Brey, Virginia D. *Uniquely Denver: A Discovery Guide to the Mile High City for Those over 50.* 1991.
Goodstein, Phil. *Denver's Capitol Hill: One Hundred Years of a Vibrant Urban Neighborhood.* 1988.
Koropp, Robert. *Denver: The City Rises.* 1989.
Leonard, Stephen J., and Thomas J. Noel. *Denver: Mining Camp to Metropolis.* 1990.
Noel, Thomas J., and Barbara S. Norgren. *The City and the Saloon: Denver 1858–1916.* 1982.
———. *Denver: The City Beautiful and its Architects, 1893–1941.* 1987.
———. *Denver's Larimer Street: Main Street Skid Row and Urban Renaissance.* 1981.
Peters, Bette D. *Denver's City Park.* 1985.
Roberts, Edwards. *The City of Denver.* 1976.
Spies, Karen. *Denver.* 1988.
West, William A. *Curtis Park: A Denver Neighborhood.* 1980.

Des Moines

Iowa

Location and Topography

N Des Moines, the capital of Iowa and county seat of Polk County, is located in south-central Iowa at the confluence of the Des Moines and Raccoon rivers. The surrounding land is gently rolling, with large wooded areas and great stretches of fertile farmland.

Layout of City and Suburbs

The main geographical feature is the Des Moines River, flowing south through the heart of the city. The river bisects the city at the Civic Center, a loose configuration of government buildings, performing arts center, library, and convention center. Toward the east, the East Side business center, a small city in itself, borders on a hill where the gold-domed capitol building towers above the metropolis. Beyond the hill's park area, businesses and residences spread out widely over the level land, with an industrial area to the south. West of the Civic Center loom the skyscrapers of the downtown business district. To the northwest is Drake University and a residential area interspersed with small shopping centers. West of the business district are the stately old homes of Grand Avenue. Overall, Des Moines gives the appearance of roominess and airiness.

Climate

 Des Moines has a continental climate characterized by rather long and cold winters, hot summers, and short springs and falls. Seasonal changes occur both in temperature and precipitation. During winter, snowfall averages

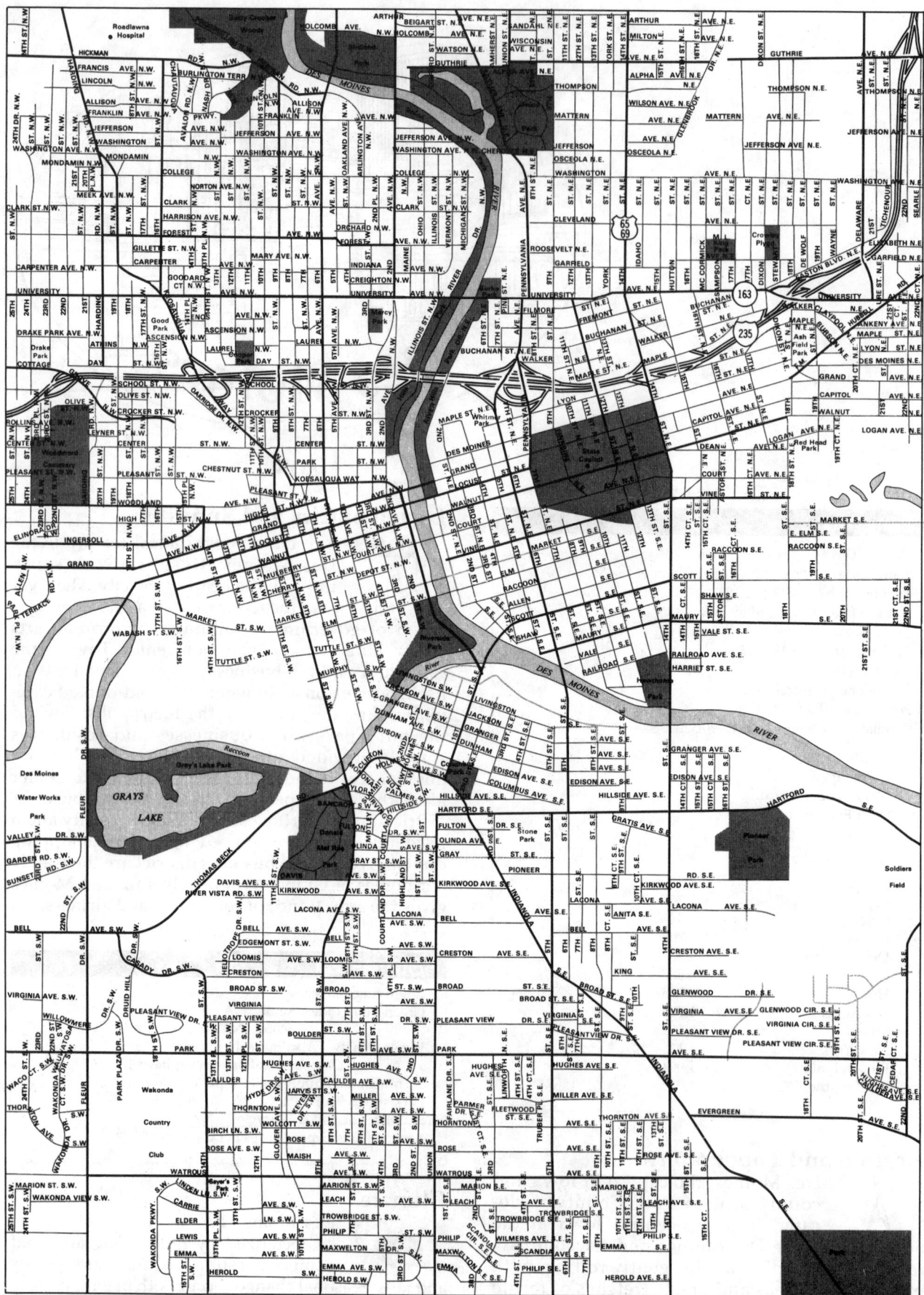

33 inches, and the cold is intensified by bitter winds that sweep over the flat land. The growing season extends from early May to early October, and 60% of the rain falls during this time, with the maximum in late May and June. Fall is generally sunny and dry.

Weather			
Temperature			
Highest Monthly Average °F 86.2			
Lowest Monthly Average °F 10.1			
Annual Averages			
Days 32°F or Below 137			
Days above 90°F 21			
Zero Degree Days 16			
Precipitation (inches) 31			
Snow (inches) 33			
% Seasonal Humidity 69			
Wind Speed (m.p.h.) 11.9			
Clear Days 103			
Cloudy Days 166			
Storm Days 50			
Rainy Days 106			
Average Temperatures (°F)	*High*	*Low*	*Mean*
January	27.5	11.3	19.4
February	32.5	15.8	24.2
March	42.5	25.2	33.9
April	59.7	39.2	49.5
May	70.9	50.9	60.9
June	79.8	51.1	70.5
July	84.9	65.3	75.1
August	83.2	63.4	73.3
September	74.6	54.0	64.3
October	64.9	43.6	54.3
November	46.4	29.2	37.8
December	32.8	17.2	25.0

History

The region around present-day Des Moines was inhabited by Mound Builders when the first French voyagers visited. The Indians called the Des Moines River *Moingwena* (River of the Mounds), and the French called it La Rivière des Moines or La Rivière de Moingona, shortened in the course of time to Des Moines. The Raccoon Fork of the Des Moines River first received mention in official records in 1834 when John Dougherty, Indian agent at Fort Leavenworth, proposed setting up a military post there. The territory was explored in 1835 by Stephen W. Kearny and in 1841 by John C. Frémont. The proposed military garrison was established in 1843 under the command of Captain James Allen.

After the Sac and Fox relinquished their rights in 1845, the territory was thrown open to white settlers, who rushed in to take the land and stake out their claims. In March 1846, Captain Allen vacated the fort, and Wilson Alexander Scott purchased 500 acres of land on the east side of the Des Moines River. He operated the first ferry the following year, and later built the first bridge across the river.

In 1846 Iowa was admitted to statehood. That same year, Fort Des Moines became the seat of Polk County. The town's first newspaper, the *Star*, appeared in the summer of 1849. With the adoption of a city charter in 1857, the word Fort was dropped from the name. Des Moines became the state capital in 1858. The next year, the first steamboats dropped anchor. The city played an active role in furnishing soldiers for the Union side in the Civil War, although Copperheads (Southern sympathizers) contended fiercely for public opinion. After the war, the first train steamed into Des Moines on the Des Moines Valley Railroad. In 1884 the new State Capitol building was dedicated. In 1894, an interesting footnote to the city's history occurred when 1,000 unemployed men (among them, author Jack London) known as Kelly's Army descended on the city on their way to Washington, D.C. The group was led by Charles T. Kelly, nicknamed King of the Commons. The townspeople not only fed the men but furnished them boats to sail downriver to Keokuk on the next leg of their journey. In 1907 the Des Moines Plan, one of the first of its kind, was adopted as a system of municipal government.

Historical Landmarks

The site of the first ferry, at the junction of the Des Moines and Raccoon rivers, is marked by a bronze tablet. The site of Fort Des Moines, at West Riverbank and Elm streets, has a marker to commemorate the spot where Captain Allen and his soldiers established their garrison. The site of the first public school on the corner of Ninth and Locust streets is indicated by a plaque. The State Capitol, between Grand Avenue and East Walnut Street, is designed on the model of the Hotel des Invalides in Paris. The height of the dome is 275 feet, and the grand rotunda under the dome is 64 feet in diameter. The Soldiers and Sailors Monument on Walnut Street, directly south of the capitol, was erected in 1897 in honor of veterans of the Civil War. The monument, designed by Harriet A. Ketcham of Mount Pleasant, has a heroic feminine figure symbolizing Iowa. The grave of Wilson Alexander Scott, the first settler, is on the capitol grounds. The Pioneers on the west terrace of the capitol building is a bronze group designed and modeled by Carl Gerhardt. Salisbury House on Tonawanda Drive, once owned by Carl Weeks, was built in the form of a 16th-century English manor. Hoyt Sherman Place on Woodland Avenue was built in 1877 by Major Hoyt Sherman, brother of William Tecumseh Sherman.

The House of Seven Gables on Dean Avenue was built in 1867 as the home of the Herbert S. Redhead family. Terrace Hill, home of the Iowa governors, was designed by W. W. Boyington; it is considered one of the finest examples of Second Empire architecture.

Population

Des Moines registered moderate growth in the 1980s. Its 1990 population was 193,187, an increase of 1.1% from its 1980 population of 191,003. Its national rank has dropped from 74th to 80th.

Chronology

1834 John Dougherty, Indian agent, recommends establishment of a military post at Raccoon Fork on the Des Moines River.

1841 John C. Fremont surveys the Des Moines River area.

1843 Captain James Allen and his company of First Dragoons set up military garrison, known first as Fort Raccoon and later as Fort Des Moines. Wilson Alexander Scott becomes first settler, raising corn and hay for the garrison.

1845 The Sac and Fox relinquish their rights, and the territory is thrown open to white settlers.

1846 Fort Des Moines is vacated by its garrison. Scott purchases 500 acres of land on the east side of the Des Moines River.

1847 Scott operates ferry across the Des Moines River. Fort Des Moines is chosen as seat of Polk County.

1849 The first newspaper, the *Star*, appears.

1857 The word Fort is dropped as city receives charter.

1858 Des Moines becomes the state capital.

1859 First steamboats drop anchor.

1866 The first train reaches Des Moines.

1884 New state capitol building is dedicated.

1894 Kelly's Army stops over in Des Moines on way to Washington, D.C.

1906 Polk County Courthouse built.

1907 General Assembly approves Des Moines plan of government.

1911 Des Moines City Hall completed.

1979 Des Moines Civic Center opens.

1985 Des Moines Convention Center completed.

1993 The great 100-year flood of the Mississippi River causes major damage to property and farmland in the Midwest; in Des Moines, 250,000 people go without running water when the city's water system fails.

Population

	1980	1990
Central City	191,003	193,187
Rank	74	80
Metro Area	367,561	392,928
Pop. Change 1980–1990 +2,184		
Pop. % Change 1980–1990 +1.1		
Median Age 32.3		
% Male 47.1		

Population (continued)

% Age 65 and Over 13.40
Density (per square mile) 2,565

Households

Number 78,453
Persons per Household 2.38
% Female-Headed Households 11.9
% One-Person Households 30.7
Births—Total 3,638
    % to Mothers under 20 11.9
    Birth Rate per 1,000 19.1

Ethnic Composition

 Whites make up 89%, blacks 7%, and others 0.9%.

Ethnic Composition (as % of total pop.)

	1980	1990
White	90.37	89.25
Black	6.83	7.11
American Indian	0.29	0.36
Asian and Pacific Islander	0.84	2.38
Hispanic	1.84	2.4
Other	NA	0.89

Government

 Des Moines is governed under a city manager/council form of government, first devised in 1907. The council is comprised of seven members, including the mayor; the city manager serves an indefinite term at the council's pleasure.

Government

Year of Home Charter NA
Number of Members of the Governing Body 6
Elected at Large 4
Elected by Wards 2
Number of Women in Governing Body 2
Salary of Mayor $19,335
Salary of Council Members $12,890
City Government Employment Total 2,250
Rate per 10,000 117.2

Public Finance

 The annual budget consists of revenues of $198.535 million and expenditures of $205.360 million. The debt outstanding is $306.133 million, and cash and security holdings are $341.451 million.

Economy

Des Moines has a mixed economy in which government dominates but all other sectors are equally active. Manufacturing is a relatively small sector in terms of employment, but is significant because most of the products are exported outside the city and some

Public Finance

Total Revenue (in millions) $198.535
Intergovernmental Revenue—Total (in millions) $19.93
Federal Revenue per Capita $4.14
% Federal Assistance   2.08
% State Assistance   7.86
Sales Tax as % of Total Revenue   NA
Local Revenue as % of Total Revenue   73.8
City Income Tax   no
Taxes—Total (in millions) $54.2

Taxes per Capita
   Total $282
   Property $250
   Sales and Gross Receipts $25
General Expenditures—Total (in millions) $156.2
General Expenditures per Capita $813
Capital Outlays per Capita $229

% of Expenditures for:
   Public Welfare   0.0
   Highways   14.5
   Education   0.0
   Health and Hospitals   0.0
   Police   10.8
   Sewerage and Sanitation   7.7
   Parks and Recreation   14.3
   Housing and Community Development   7.2
Debt Outstanding per Capita $901
   % Utility   4.7
Federal Procurement Contract Awards (in millions) $42.8
Federal Grants Awards (in millions) $189.0
Fiscal Year Begins   July 1

Economy

Total Money Income (in millions) $2,329.7
% of State Average   120.2
Per Capita Annual Income $12,134
% Population below Poverty Level   10.6
Fortune 500 Companies   NA

Banks	Number	Deposits (in millions)
Commercial	8	2,216
Savings	7	2,551

Passenger Autos   228,496
Electric Meters   165,586
Gas Meters   106,358

Manufacturing

Number of Establishments   272
% with 20 or More Employees   36.0
Manufacturing Payroll (in millions) $419.0
Value Added by Manufacture (in millions) $1,153.5
Value of Shipments (in millions) $3,097.7
New Capital Expenditures (in millions) $67.0

Wholesale Trade

Number of Establishments   577
Sales (in millions) $2,754.3
Annual Payroll (in millions) $173.817

Retail Trade

Number of Establishments   2,069
Total Sales (in millions) $1,619.2
Sales per Capita $8,431
Number of Retail Trade Establishments with Payroll   1,496
Annual Payroll (in millions) $195.8
Total Sales (in millions) $1,595.9
General Merchandise Stores (per capita) $1,195
Food Stores (per capita) $1,722
Apparel Stores (per capita) $429
Eating and Drinking Places (per capita) $889

Economy (continued)

Service Industries

Total Establishments   1,726
Total Receipts (in millions) $965.5
Hotels and Motels (in millions) $43.8
Health Services (in millions) $219.4
Legal Services (in millions) $112.1

overseas. Manufacturing also helps to generate secondary jobs. Headquarters to nearly 60 insurance companies and the regional offices of more than 100, Des Moines is the third largest international insurance center after London, England, and Hartford, Connecticut. Other major industries are health care, biotechnology, and fiber-optics communications.

Labor

As the state capital, government is the largest employer. Des Moines is one of the few cities where the FIRE (financial, insurance, and real estate) sector employs more people than manufacturing. Worker productivity is above and unemployment below the national average. Among the largest private employers are Armstrong Rubber Company, Firestone Tire and Rubber Company, Meredith Corporation, Northwestern Bell, Communications Data Services, Dahl's Food Markets, Des Moines Register, Employers Mutual Company, Hy-Vee Food Stores, R. R. Donnelly & Sons, Norwest Bank of Des Moines, and Principal Financial Group.

Labor

Civilian Labor Force   122,241
% Change 1989–1990   0.4

Work Force Distribution
   Mining   NA
   Construction   9,200
   Manufacturing   26,100
   Transportation and Public Utilities   12,300
   Wholesale and Retail Trade   61,000
   FIRE (Finance, Insurance, Real Estate)   32,900
   Service   62,500
   Government   32,200
   Women as % of Labor Force   47.0
   % Self-Employed   4.2
   % Professional/Technical   14.5
Total Unemployment   4,676
Rate %   3.8
Federal Government Civilian Employment   4,690

Education

The Des Moines Public School District supports 62 schools. There are four private and parochial school districts, including the Diocese of Des Moines Catholic Schools. The largest center for higher education is Iowa State University, followed by Des Moines Area Community College. The private Drake University was founded in 1881. Grand View College is a private liberal arts school offering cross-registration with Drake University.

Other institutions include Simpson College and the University of Osteopathic Medicine.

Education

Number of Public Schools   62
Special Education Schools   2
Total Enrollment   30,888
% Enrollment in Private Schools   9.3
% Minority   18.2
Classroom Teachers   1,720
Pupil-Teacher Ratio   17.6:1
Number of Graduates   1,729
Total Revenue (in millions) $120.631
Total Expenditures (in millions) $124.373
Expenditures per Pupil $4,010
Educational Attainment (Age 25 and Over)
   % Completed 12 or More Years   74.8
   % Completed 16 or More Years   16.6
Four-Year Colleges and Universities   5
   Enrollment   9,529
Two-Year Colleges   3
   Enrollment   1,564

Libraries

Number   35
Public Libraries   6
Books (in thousands)   554
Circulation (in thousands)   1,203
Persons Served (in thousands)   192.9
Circulation per Person Served   6.2
Income (in millions) $3.707
Staff   82

Four-Year Colleges and Universities
   Drake University
   Grand View College
   University of Osteopathic Medicine and Health Sciences

Health

Des Moines has eight hospitals, including two general, one veterans, one investor-owned, one osteopathic, and three church-related, with a total of 2,416 beds. The largest is the Iowa Methodist Medical Center, a complex that includes Blank Memorial, a children's hospital, and Younkers Rehabilitation Center. Mercy Hospital Medical Center and Veterans Hospital provide general care. Des Moines General Hospital specializes in osteopathic treatment. Broadlawn Medical Center and Iowa Lutheran Hospital are both general and psychiatric hospitals.

Health

Deaths—Total   1,884
Rate per 1,000   9.9
Infant Deaths—Total   39
Rate per 1,000   10.7
Number of Metro Hospitals   8
Number of Metro Hospital Beds   2,416
Rate per 100,000   1,258
Number of Physicians   584
Physicians per 1,000   1.76
Nurses per 1,000   10.88
Health Expenditures per Capita $5.04

Transportation

Des Moines is approached by two interstates intersecting northeast of the city—east-west I-80 and north-south I-35—as well as U.S. routes 6 and 69. Downtown is laid out in a grid pattern; however, in the northeast, streets near the Des Moines River follow the river. North-south streets are numbers and east-west routes are names. Des Moines is noted for its three-mile skywalk consisting of climate-controlled, glass-enclosed bridges connecting the major downtown and retail complexes. Passenger rail service is provided by Amtrak at Osceola, 45 minutes south of the city, and freight rail services by a variety of carriers. The destination for most commercial flights is Des Moines International Airport.

Transportation

Interstate Highway Mileage   36
Total Urban Mileage   1,385
Total Daily Vehicle Mileage (in millions)   5.177
Daily Average Commute Time   37.8 min.
Number of Buses   73
Port Tonnage (in millions)   NA
Airports   1
Number of Daily Flights   38
Daily Average Number of Passengers   1,833

Airlines (American carriers only)
   Air Wisconsin
   American
   American West
   Midway
   Northwest
   Trans World
   United
   USAir

Housing

In a *New York Times* study conducted in 1990, out of 150 housing markets Des Moines ranked fifth in terms of affordability and percentage of income required to meet home mortgage payments. The median cost of a single-family detached home in Des Moines is $74,000, nearly $30,000 less than the national average. Sixty-two percent of the homes are owner-occupied.

Housing

Total Housing Units   83,289
% Change 1980–1990   4.1
Vacant Units for Sale or Rent   3,450
Occupied Units   78,453
% with More Than One Person per Room   2.7
% Owner-Occupied   62.0
Median Value of Owner-Occupied Homes $49,500
Average Monthly Purchase Cost $341
Median Monthly Rent $346
New Private Housing Starts   491

Housing (continued)

Value (in thousands) $34,200
% Single-Family   55.4
Nonresidential Buildings Value (in thousands) $39,763

Tallest Buildings	Hgt. (ft.)	Stories
Principal Financial Group Bldg. (1990)	630	44
Ruan Center (1974)	457	35
Financial Center 7th & Walnut (1973)	345	25
Marriott Hotel 700 Grand Ave. (1981)	340	33
Plaza, 3rd & Walnut (1984)	340	25

Urban Redevelopment

During the 1980s Des Moines underwent extensive development as a result of a ten-year plan created in 1980 by the Des Moines Development Commission. Over $1 billion has been invested in redevelopment programs, including a civic performing arts center, office and retail buildings, and renovation of historic buildings. The historic Rock Island Depot was converted to office space and the Court Avenue District revitalized.

Crime

Des Moines ranks below the national average in public safety. Of crimes known to police in 1991, 1,283 were violent crimes and 16,581 were property crimes.

Crime

Violent Crimes—Total   1,283
Violent Crime Rate per 100,000   10,569
Murder   12
Rape   76
Robbery   355
Aggravated Assaults   840
Property Crimes   16,581
Burglary   2,751
Larceny   12,863
Motor Vehicle Theft   740
Arson   227
Per Capita Police Expenditures $92.29
Per Capita Fire Protection Expenditures $75.64
Number of Police   332
Per 1,000   1.76

Religion

Des Moines has nearly 300 churches representing 79 denominations.

Religion

Largest Denominations (Adherents)

Catholic	55,214
Evangelical Lutheran	21,883
Christ Church (Disciples)	9,764
United Methodist	18,988
Presbyterian	8,346
Black Baptist	4,904
Lutheran-Missouri Synod	5,717

Religion (continued)

Assembly of God	6,060
United Church of Christ	5,130
Jewish	2,164

Media

The daily newspaper is the Des Moines Register. The electronic media consist of 6 television stations (3 commercial, 1 public, and 2 independent) and 14 AM and FM radio stations.

Media

Newsprint
  Des Moines Register, daily
  Des Moines Tribune, daily

Television
  KBTV (Channel 63)
  KCCI (Channel 8)
  KDIN (Channel 11)
  KDSM (Channel 17)
  WHO (Channel 13)
  WOI (Channel 5)

Radio

KDFR (FM)	KDMI (FM)
KDPS (FM)	KGGO (AM)
KGGO (FM)	KIOA (AM)
KRNT (AM)	KRNQ (FM)
KSO (AM)	KJJY (FM)
KUCB (FM)	KWKY (AM)
WHO (AM)	KLYF (FM)

Sports

Des Moines has no major professional sports team. The focal point of sports is the Drake Relays, held in the Jim Duncan Stadium of Drake University the last week of April. The Iowa Cubs, the Chicago Cubs farm team, compete in baseball's AAA international league.

Arts, Culture, and Tourism

The Des Moines Symphony, Des Moines Metro Opera, and Des Moines Ballet perform at the Civic Center. The main drama season is presented by Des Moines Playhouse as well as Theater in the Ground and Theater for Young People. The Des Moines Art Center, the pride of the city, was designed by Eliel

Travel and Tourism

Hotel Rooms   6,384
Convention and Exhibit Space (square feet)   NA

Convention Centers
  Des Moines Convention Center
  Veterans Memorial Auditorium
  Civic Center
  Iowa State Fairgrounds

Festivals
  Carp Festival (May)
  Festival of Trees (November)

Saarinen, I. M. Pei, and Richard Meier, and houses modern art. Nollen Plaza, adjacent to the Civic Center, is a block-square amphitheater and park noted for its sculptures, waterfall, peace garden, and reflecting pool.

Parks and Recreation

Metropolitan Des Moines has over 100 parks, with the city proper having 51. The 1,500-acre Waterworks Park, on 21st Street extending south to Valley Drive and Park Avenue and west to city limits, contains a bird sanctuary and horseback and hiking trails.

Sources of Further Information

City Hall
400 East First Street
Des Moines, IA 50309
(515) 283-4500

Greater Des Moines Chamber of Commerce
601 Locust Street, Suite 100
Des Moines, IA 50309
(515) 286-4950

Greater Des Moines Convention and Visitors Bureau
601 Locust Street, Suite 222 (on the skywalk)
Des Moines, IA 50309
(515) 286-4960

Polk County Historical Society
317 Southwest 42nd Street
Des Moines, IA 50312
(515) 255-6657

Public Library of Des Moines
100 Locust Street
Des Moines, IA 50309
(515) 283-4152

Additional Reading

Cole's Directory for Des Moines. 1991.
Polk's Des Moines City Directory. 1991.

Detroit

Michigan

Basic Data

Name   Detroit
Name Origin   From French="Strait"
Year Founded   1701 Inc. 1802
Status: State   Michigan
         County   Seat of Wayne County
Area (square miles)   138.7
Elevation (feet)   585
Time Zone   EST
Population (1990)   1,027,974
Population of Metro Area (1990)   4,382,299

Sister Cities
   Kitwe, Zambia
   Mensk, Belarus
   Nassau, Bahamas
   Toyota, Japan

Distance in Miles To:

Atlanta	732
Boston	799
Chicago	279
Dallas	1,156
Denver	1,283
Houston	1,276
Los Angeles	2,288
Miami	1,385
Minneapolis	685
New York	649
Philadelphia	609
Washington, DC	516

Location and Topography

N

Detroit is situated in the southeastern corner of Michigan, across the Detroit River from Windsor, Ontario. It lies on the important waterway that connects Lake Huron to Lake Erie. The land is nearly flat and slopes gently northwest from the water's edge for about 10 miles. The terrain gives way to increasingly rolling countryside, and then to the Irish Hills, about 40 miles northwest.

Layout of City and Suburbs

The city is shaped like a half-circle. Two independent cities, Highland Park and Hamtramck, lie entirely within Detroit's boundaries. Skyscrapers rise along the riverfront downtown and cluster near Woodward Avenue, the main highway northward from the city. Nearby, on the river, is the Detroit Civic Center, including Cobo Hall, Convention Arena, Joe Louis Arena, Veterans Memorial, and Ford Auditorium. The 73-story Detroit Plaza Hotel, centerpiece of the Renaissance Center on the riverfront, opened in 1977. Here too is the Detroit-Windsor vehicular tunnel entrance, and the Ambassador Bridge is 1.5 miles west. Streets in the downtown section radiate from Grand Circus Park. In addition to Woodward, the principal thoroughfares are Fort Street and Michigan, Grand River, Gratiot, and Jefferson avenues. Grand Boulevard traverses almost every midtown section. Beginning at the Detroit River, three miles west of Woodward Avenue, it swings in a wide loop through the city, and returns to the river about three miles east of Woodward. After fire destroyed the original Detroit village in 1805, Judge Augustus B. Woodward drew up a new city plan laid out in the form of connecting hexagons, following the Washington, D.C., model. At the center of each hexagon would be a circular park with streets radiating from it. Only half of one hexagon was ever completed; it survives in the semicircular Grand Circus Park downtown. The gridiron pattern was superimposed on the original plan in many areas, resulting in some confusion about the directions of routes, especially in the center of the city. Almost three miles north of downtown Detroit is the New Center area, built in the 1920s. In this center are located the General Motors headquarters and the ornate Fisher building with its famous theater. Other major avenues are Jefferson, which parallels Lake St. Clair and the

Detroit River in the northeast, and Michigan Avenue and Fort Street running southwest and west, respectively. But the major city traffic is carried on its expressways: Edsel Ford (I-94), Chrysler (I-75), Jeffries (I-96), John C. Lodge (state highway 10), and Southfield (state highway 39).

Environment	
Environmental Stress Index 3.4	
Green Cities Index: Rank 51	
Score 35.71	
Water Quality Alkaline, soft	
Average Daily Use (gallons per capita)	172
Maximum Supply (gallons per capita)	427
Parkland as % of Total City Area NA	
% Waste Landfilled/Recycled NA	
Annual Parks Expenditures per Capita	$118.69

Climate

Detroit's climate is influenced by the city's location near the Great Lakes and in the path of a storm track, modified by the heat generated from its factories. Winter storms often bring rain, snow, freezing rain, sleet, and snow. In summer, thunderstorms alternate with warm, humid weather. The area is quite cloudy, especially in winter. Proximity to the Great Lakes gives Detroit a milder climate than would be expected in its latitude.

Weather			
Temperature			
Highest Monthly Average °F 83.1			
Lowest Monthly Average °F 16.1			
Annual Averages			
Days 32°F or Below 139			
Days above 90°F 11			
Zero Degree Days 7			
Precipitation (inches) 32.0			
Snow (inches) 39.0			
% Seasonal Humidity 72			
Wind Speed (m.p.h.) 10.4			
Clear Days 75			
Cloudy Days 180			
Storm Days 33			
Rainy Days 133			
Average Temperatures (°F)	*High*	*Low*	*Mean*
January	31.9	17.3	24.6
February	34.3	18.8	26.6
March	43.8	26.7	35.3
April	58.1	37.3	47.7
May	69.1	47.0	58.1
June	79.4	57.2	68.3
July	83.4	61.1	72.3
August	82.0	59.5	70.8
September	74.8	52.3	63.6
October	64.1	42.1	53.1
November	47.8	32.3	40.1
December	35.4	21.5	28.5

History

Detroit was founded on 24 July 1701 by Antoine de la Mothe Cadillac, an explorer in the service of Louis XIV of France. Cadillac and his men built Fort Pontchartrain, and a palisaded riverfront village grew up nearby. Cadillac named the village Ville Detroit, or City of the Strait, later shortened to Detroit. Control of the settlement changed three times during the 18th century, but it was eventually ceded to the British by the treaty that ended the French and Indian War. Under Henry Hamilton, the British governor, American Indians were encouraged to scalp frontier settlers for rewards, earning him the nickname Hair Buyer of Detroit. The British continued to hold Detroit after the Revolutionary War, despite a provision to the contrary in the Peace of Paris. Only after Major General Anthony Wayne defeated the Indians at the Battle of Fallen Timbers did the British relinquish all claims to the territory. On 11 July 1796, Captain Moses Porter raised the Stars and Stripes over Detroit.

At that time there were about 300 dwellings in the village, all in ramshackle condition owing to 20 years of continuous warfare. Incorporated as a town in 1802, Detroit suffered a new misfortune three years later when it was razed by fire. In the same year, Detroit became the capital of the newly created Michigan territory, and the government passed into the hands of a governor and three judges in accordance with the provisions of the Ordinance of 1787. During the War of 1812, Governor William Hull turned over Detroit to the British without firing a single shot. The United States regained control over the town in 1813 following Oliver H. Perry's victory in the Battle of Lake Erie.

In 1815 Detroit was incorporated as a city, but for the next two decades it grew slowly. One reason for the town's backwardness was its distance from the Ohio River, then the mainstream of immigration. Another was the widely circulated report of the U.S. surveyor general that Michigan land was all sandy and swampy, and would not admit of cultivation. The first public stage did not leave Detroit until 1822, coinciding with the arrival of the *Superior*, the second steamboat on the Great Lakes.

By 1837, when the capital of Michigan was moved to Lansing, there were 10,000 residents in Detroit. The city was then poised on a period of great expansion. Factories were established; three newpapers, a monthly, and five weeklies were launched; a library was built; and the first public schools opened. In 1838 a 12-mile stretch of the Detroit and Pontiac Railroad was put into service. By 1843 the line extended to Pontiac, and by 1858 to Milwaukee. Detroit was linked to New York in 1854, Toledo in 1856, and Lansing in 1871. Just before the Civil War, Detroit was an important antislavery center and a terminal of the Underground Railway. Nevertheless, antiblack riots were not unknown.

Although Detroit became a manufacturing city after the Civil War, producing railroad cars, stoves,

Chronology

1701 Antoine Loumet de la Mothe Cadillac and 100 Frenchmen establish a village on the Detroit River named Ville Detroit.

1718 Fort Pontchartrain is built.

1760 The French surrender Fort Pontchartrain to the British.

1763 Chief Pontiac leads unsuccessful Indian assault on the fort.

1791 Detroit and Michigan become part of Upper Canada.

1796 Detroit is occupied by American troops following General Anthony Wayne's victory against the Indians in the Battle of Fallen Timbers.

1802 Detroit is incorporated as a town.

1805 Fire reduces Detroit to ruins. Judge Augustus Woodward designs new city in the shape of a series of hexagons. Detroit is made capital of Michigan.

1806 Solomon Sibley is appointed first mayor.

1812 Detroit is surrendered to the British.

1813 Americans regain Detroit following the Battle of Lake Erie.

1815 Detroit is incorporated as a city.

1824 Under new city charter, Detroit's first elected mayor, John R. Williams, takes office. The Common Council is created.

1825 The Erie Canal opens.

1835 The *Daily Free Press* is established.

1837 Michigan becomes a state, with Detroit as capital.

1838 The 12-mile Detroit and Pontiac Railroad begins operations. The first public schools open.

1839 City is divided into wards and aldermen are elected.

1842 The Detroit Board of Education is formed.

1847 The capital of Michigan is moved from Detroit to Lansing.

1854 Detroit and New York are linked by rail.

1868 Wayne University opens.

1869 Black children are first admitted to public schools.

1870 Blacks are permitted to vote for the first time. New city hall opens on Woodward Avenue.

1873 The *Evening News* is established.

1877 University of Detroit is founded.

1896 Charles Brady King drives first horseless carriage through the city. The last horsedrawn streetcar is taken out of service.

1907 General Motors is organized.

1908 Ford Motor Company begins producing Model T cars. First mile of concrete road in the nation is laid on Woodward Avenue.

1912 Livingstone Channel in the Detroit River is opened.

1918 A new city charter is adopted and the first nonpartisan elections are held. The ward system is replaced by a citywide election for a nine-person Common Council.

1920 Detroit population passes the 1 million mark.

1921 WWJ radio station begins commercial broadcasting.

1923 The first Chrysler automobile rolls off the assembly line.

1929 The Ambassador Bridge to Windsor, Canada, is opened.

1930 The Detroit-Windsor tunnel is opened for traffic.

1943 Black-white riots break out, killing 34 people. Federal troops are called in to restore order.

1955 Ford Auditorium opens.

1959 Cobo Hall opens.

1962 City imposes 1% income tax.

1967 Race riots leave 44 dead and hundreds of buildings gutted.

1971 The Renaissance Center project is announced by Ford Motor Land Development Company.

1973 City elects first black mayor in history—Coleman A. Young. Voters approve new city charter. Common Council is renamed City Council. City is hit by heaviest snowfall of the century—19 inches.

1979 Three new additions to the Civic Center—Hart Plaza, Dodge Memorial Fountain, and Joe Louis Arena—are completed.

1984 Riverfront Chene Park opens.

<table>
<tbody><tr><td>Chronology (continued)</td></tr>
</tbody></table>

1987 People Mover begins operating on a 2.9-mile, 13-station route above the streets in downtown Detroit.

1988 Fox Theater is restored and reopens.

1990 Construction begins on One Detroit Center, the tallest office building in the city.

furniture, shoes, steel, pharmaceuticals, and bicycles, it was the rise of the automobile industry that transformed it into one of the major industrial capitals of the nation. Detroit's automobile era began when Charles B. King drove a horseless carriage on the city streets in 1896. He was soon joined by automotive pioneers such as Henry Ford, W. C. Durant, Walter P. Chrysler, Ransom Olds, Henry Leland, and the Dodge brothers, who laid the foundation of the companies that emerged as the Big Three automakers in the 20th century: Ford, General Motors, and Chrysler. The automobile also affected Detroit in other ways. It brought thousands of immigrants during the 1920s, which added to social tension and occasionally to race riots, as in 1943 and 1967.

The automobile also led to the rise of militant trade unionism under Walter Reuther and his United Automobile Workers (UAW). Through violence-marred strikes, Reuther won solid gains for the labor movement. The unionization of auto workers also wrought profound social changes. Hitherto, the population had been a shifting one, but with a closed shop, a seniority system developed and workers stayed on the job much longer. By 1880 the city's neighborhoods were well defined, with Corktown on the lower west side, Dutchtown on the east, and Kentucky below Dutchtown; the Poles lived east of Dutchtown. The richer people lived west of Woodward and north of Grand River.

During the years of transformation from small town to automobile capital, the city was guided by three able mayors: Hazen S. Pingree (1890–1901), James Couzens (1919–1923), and Frank Murphy (1930–1933). By 1970 Detroit, along with the automobile industry, was beginning to decline. Although the Renaissance Center was built during the 1970s as an act of confidence in the city's future, Detroit was choking on its fiscal and social problems. The election in 1973 of Coleman A. Young as Detroit's first black mayor only served to polarize the city further and trigger an exodus of whites.

Historical Landmarks

Few buildings survived the disastrous 1805 fire. Subsequent urban renewal and industrial expansion also took a heavy toll. However, Detroit has a number of architectural monuments and houses reflecting its association with automobiles. Some of the mansions built by automobile industry founders are now open to the public. Meadow Brook Hall, a 100-room mansion on a 1,400-

acre estate, was built by John Dodge in 1926. Henry Ford's home, the 56-room Fairlane, is located in Dearborn. The Edsel and Eleanor Ford House overlooks Lake St. Clair in Grosse Point Shores. The Fisher mansion on the Detroit River has more than 200 ounces of pure gold and silver leaf on the ceilings and moldings.

Detroit has a number of historical churches. Among them are Mariners Church on Woodward Avenue, the second oldest church, built in 1849; St. Aloysius Church on Washington Boulevard, built in 1930; Central Methodist Church on Woodward and Adams avenues, built in 1867; St. Paul's Cathedral on Woodward Avenue, completed in 1919; Sts. Peter and Paul's Church on East Jefferson Avenue, the oldest church in the city, dedicated in 1844; Fort Street Presbyterian Church, built in 1855 on Fort and Third; St. Anne's Shrine, built in 1886 but going back to St. Anne's Church, a log structure built in 1701 by Cadillac; and Blessed Sacrament Cathedral on Woodward and Belmont avenues, built in 1938.

Other historic structures include the Sibley House and Pewabic Pottery. Fort Wayne is said to be the best-preserved pre–Civil War fort in the Midwest. Greenfield Village, built by Henry Ford in 1929, contains 100 reproductions or restorations of historic buildings.

Population

Detroit ranks as the seventh largest city in the United States with a population of 1,207,974 in 1990. In 1940 it was the fourth largest, with 1.618 million residents. In 1950 Detroit's population peaked at 1.838 million, but it dropped to fifth place behind Philadelphia. By 1970 the population declined to 1.512 million, and by 1980 to 1.203 million. Between 1980 and 1990 it lost 14.6% of its population, the largest percentage drop among the top 50 cities. The decline of the automobile industry, exodus of whites to the suburbs following Mayor Coleman Young's election, and an increasing incidence of crime are cited as the reasons for Detroit's falling population.

Population	1980	1990
Central City	1,203,368	1,207,974
Rank	6	7
Metro Area	4,888,024	4,382,299
Pop. Change 1980–1990 +4,606		
Pop. % Change 1980–1990 +.38		
Median Age 30.8		
% Male 46.4		
% Age 65 and Over 12.2		
Density (per square mile) 7,449		

Households
Number 374,057
Persons per Household 2.71
% Female-Headed Households 30.3
% One-Person Households 29.8
Births—Total 18,523
% to Mothers under 20 20.4
Birth Rate per 1,000 17.0

Ethnic Composition

Detroit ranks next to Washington, D.C., as the city with the largest percentage of blacks in the United States. Blacks make up 76% of the population and whites 22%. Race relations have been unmarred by riots since 1967 and the election of the first black mayor in 1973, but they continue to be a major political irritant during election times.

Ethnic Composition (as % of total pop.)		
	1980	1990
White	34.38	21.63
Black	63.07	75.67
American Indian	0.28	0.36
Asian and Pacific Islander	0.55	0.82
Hispanic	2.41	2.77
Other	NA	1.52

Government

Detroit is governed by a mayor and a nine-member council elected on a non-partisan basis for four-year renewable terms. Under the 1973 charter the mayor has broad powers, including the appointment of top officials and veto of council legislation.

Government
Year of Home Charter   1974
Number of Members of the Governing Body   9
Elected at Large   9
Elected by Wards   NA
Number of Women in Governing Body   3
Salary of Mayor $125,300
Salary of Council Members $63,000
City Government Employment Total   20,332
Rate per 10,000   187.2

Public Finance

The annual budget consists of revenues of $2.021374 billion and expenditures of $1.945584 billion. Debt outstanding is $1,450264 billion, and cash and security holdings are $3.934 billion.

Public Finance
Total Revenue (in millions) $2,021.374
Intergovernmental Revenue—Total (in millions) $673.25
Federal Revenue per Capita $113.09
% Federal Assistance   5.59
% State Assistance   26.34
Sales Tax as % of Total Revenue   NA
Local Revenue as % of Total Revenue   43.13
City Income Tax   yes
Taxes—Total (in millions) $484.6
Taxes per Capita
Total $446
Property $163
Sales and Gross Receipts $47
General Expenditures—Total (in millions) $1,144.6
General Expenditures per Capita $1,054

Public Finance (continued)
Capital Outlays per Capita $103
% of Expenditures for:
Public Welfare   0.0
Highways   10.5
Education   0.6
Health and Hospitals   6.0
Police   16.3
Sewerage and Sanitation   15.3
Parks and Recreation   7.0
Housing and Community Development   9.2
Debt Outstanding per Capita $861
% Utility   15.5
Federal Procurement Contract Awards (in millions) $368.4
Federal Grants Awards (in millions) $319.5
Fiscal Year Begins   July 1

Economy

Detroit's economy is automobile-driven, as it has been throughout this century. However, the share of automobiles in the gross city product is declining, reflecting the industry's problems. The slack has been taken up by the service sector, such as accounting, law, financial services, and computer services, in which 70% of the labor force is currently employed. More than 600 foreign firms are represented in the Detroit area, along with 19 of the Fortune 500 companies, including some of the largest: General Motors, Ford, Chrysler, and K-Mart. Detroit remains a robust retail market. There are 18 enclosed regional or superregional malls with over 18 million square feet of retail space. Since 1980, 14 smaller retail shopping centers have been added. Detroit has a current surplus of office space with a supply of 100 million square feet, approximately 48% of it in smaller buildings. However, the economic downturn and a high crime rate have created a national negative image of Detroit. To combat this, the Greater Detroit/Southeast Michigan Business Attraction and Expansion Council (BAEC) was established in 1980 to assist other agencies with research and marketing.

Economy		
Total Money Income (in millions) $9,613.272		
% of State Average 81.2		
Per Capita Annual Income $8,852		
% Population below Poverty Level 21.9		
Fortune 500 Companies 2		
Banks	*Number*	*Deposits (in millions)*
Commercial	23	69,000
Savings	17	NA
Passenger Autos 1,102,612		
Electric Meters 1,391,197		
Gas Meters 643,405		

Manufacturing
Number of Establishments   1,255
% with 20 or More Employees   36.2
Manufacturing Payroll (in millions) $3,519.1
Value Added by Manufacture (in millions) $4,829.0
Value of Shipments (in millions) $14,334.9
New Capital Expenditures (in millions) $257.8

Wholesale Trade

Number of Establishments   1,176
Sales (in millions) $10,210.0
Annual Payroll (in millions) $447.435

Retail Trade

Number of Establishments   5,202
Total Sales (in millions) $3,159.5
Sales per Capita $2,909
Number of Retail Trade Establishments with Payroll   3,847
Annual Payroll (in millions) $387.4
Total Sales (in millions) $3,094.5
General Merchandise Stores (per capita) $117
Food Stores (per capita) $681
Apparel Stores (per capita) $119
Eating and Drinking Places (per capita) $426

Service Industries

Total Establishments   3,734
Total Receipts (in millions) $2,580.7
Hotels and Motels (in millions) $82.3
Health Services (in millions) $513.0
Legal Services (in millions) $479.6

Labor

 Manufacturing, services, and trade each account for about 25% of the labor market, with the remainder distributed among small sectors. This represents a long-term trend toward diversification that began with the first oil shock in 1973. It also is significant that of the top 21 employers, 18 are unrelated to the automobile industry. Seven are health-care organizations, three are banks, and three are public utilities. Detroit is the headquarters of the UAW and historically the scene of some of the biggest trade union victories.

Labor

Civilian Labor Force   450,341
% Change 1989–1990   -1.6

Work Force Distribution
Mining   800
Construction   58,000
Manufacturing   421,600
Transportation and Public Utilities   85,800
Wholesale and Retail Trade   456,500
FIRE (Finance, Insurance, Real Estate)   109,200
Service   502,600
Government   234,500
Women as % of Labor Force   449
% Self-Employed   2.7
% Professional/Technical   12.9
Total Unemployment   49,285
Rate %   10.9
Federal Government Civilian Employment   12,861

Education

The Detroit public school system supports 298 schools. The Merrill-Palmer School and Cranbrook Schools are nationally acclaimed private schools in the area. Higher education is led by Wayne State University, one of the nation's largest urban universities, with 13 colleges; University of Detroit, a Jesuit school with two campuses within the city; three additional Roman Catholic institutions—Marygrove College, Mercy College of Detroit, and Sacred Heart Seminary; and three specialized institutions: Lawrence Institute of Technology, Detroit College of Business, and Detroit College of Law.

Education

Number of Public Schools   298
Special Education Schools   13
Total Enrollment   168,956
% Enrollment in Private Schools   12.9
% Minority   91.6
Classroom Teachers   NA
Pupil-Teacher Ratio   NA
Number of Graduates   NA
Total Revenue (in millions) $785.684
Total Expenditures (in millions) $804.313
Expenditures per Pupil $4,016
Educational Attainment (Age 25 and Over)
    % Completed 12 or More Years   54.2
    % Completed 16 or More Years   8.3
Four-Year Colleges and Universities   5
    Enrollment   43,181
Two-Year Colleges   2
    Enrollment   12,839

Libraries

Number   115
Public Libraries   26
Books (in thousands)   2,760
Circulation (in thousands)   1,203
Persons Served (in thousands)   1,027
Circulation per Person Served   0.99
Income (in millions) $20.988
Staff   426

Four-Year Colleges and Universities
    Wayne State University
    University of Detroit
    Marygrove College
    Sacred Heart Major Seminary

Health

 Detroit is the primary medical treatment and referral center for southeastern Michigan. Detroit Medical Center, the largest health-care facility, is affiliated with Wayne State University. It is a complex comprising Chil-

Health

Deaths—Total   12,907
Rate per 1,000   11.9
Infant Deaths—Total   387
Rate per 1,000   20.9
Number of Metro Hospitals   25
Number of Metro Hospital Beds   7,880
Rate per 100,000   725
Number of Physicians   7,989
Physicians per 1,000   2.10
Nurses per 1,000   7.32
Health Expenditures per Capita $87.16

dren's, Grace, Harper, and Hutzel hospitals as well as the Rehabilitation Institute. Henry Ford Hospital operates several suburban centers and clinics. Mercy Hospitals and Health Services of Detroit operate Mount Carmel Mercy Hospital, Mercy Family Care, and Samaritan Health Center. In addition, there are a number of suburban hospitals in the Detroit metro area.

Transportation

Greater Detroit is served by six interstate highways and expressways. The principal artery, I-75, with its northern terminus in Michigan's upper peninsula, runs through the city north to southwest. North of downtown it is called Chrysler Freeway and southwest of downtown it is called the Fisher Freeway, both connected by I-375. East-west I-94, known as the Ford Freeway, leads to the Detroit Metropolitan Airport. The west-northwest I-96, the Jeffries Freeway, leads to Grand Rapids, Muskegon, and Lansing. Interstate 696, the Walter Reuther Freeway, is the main east-west route across the northern suburbs in Macomb and Oakland counties. Interstate 275 is a north-south bypass on the city's west side, linking I-75 and I-96. Other major routes leading into Detroit are the north-west U.S. 10 (Lodge Freeway) and the north-south state route 39 (Southfield Freeway). Canadian highway 401 enters Detroit from Windsor via the Windsor/Detroit International Tunnel and the Ambassador Bridge.

The city is served by two public transportation systems: Detroit Department of Transportation (D-DOT) and Suburban Mobility Authority for Regional Transport (SMART). The People Mover provides travel to major downtown sites from 13 stations. Old-time trolleys still run shuttle routes between Grand Circus Park and Cobo Conference and Exhibition Center and the Renaissance Center. City streets suffer from severe congestion during rush hours. The Port of Detroit, one of the busiest on the Great Lakes, has direct access to the Atlantic through the St. Lawrence Seaway System. The port has seven privately owned terminals with 13 berths on the Detroit and Rouge rivers. Ice is sometimes a problem on the Great Lakes. The Detroit Metropolitan Airport is situated 15 miles from downtown in Romulus. It is the major hub for Northwest Airlines. Private and charter air traffic is handled by Willow Run and Oakland-Pontiac airports. Amtrak provides passenger-rail transportation into Detroit.

Housing

Detroit is a city of homeowners. About 80% of the dwelling units are single-family homes, and owners occupy over 50% of the dwellings. However, housing has deteriorated in many sections of the city. Rehabilitation of impoverished residential districts began in 1946, expanding when the National Housing Act of 1949 provided federal assistance. The Detroit Housing Commission is the official urban-renewal agency for the city. It operates more than 8,000 permanent, low-rent public-housing units. Typical of the redevelopment projects is the Gratiot Project, completed in 1966. Before the ground was cleared in 1954, it was a slum area where 1,958 families and 989 individuals lived in deplorable conditions. Today, Gratiot has 1,700 tower and townhouse apartments in eight residential developments with 4,000 residents. The city runs additional conservation projects. These voluntary neighborhood projects have grass-roots leadership, but work closely with Keep Detroit Beautiful, Inc., and the Mayor's Committee for Neighborhood Conservation and Improved Housing.

Transportation

Interstate Highway Mileage   207
Total Urban Mileage   12,675
Total Daily Vehicle Mileage (in millions)   79.381
Daily Average Commute Time   51.3 min.
Number of Buses   569
Port Tonnage (in millions)   11.433
Airports   2
Number of Daily Flights   380
Daily Average Number of Passengers   27,627

Airlines (American carriers only)
American
Continental
Delta
Eastern
Midway
Northwest
Piedmont
Southwest
Trans World
United
USAir

Housing

Total Housing Units   410,027
% Change 1980–1990   -15.0
Vacant Units for Sale or Rent   23,665
Occupied Units   374,057
% with More Than One Person per Room   5.4
% Owner-Occupied   52.9
Median Value of Owner-Occupied Homes $25,600
Average Monthly Purchase Cost $320
Median Monthly Rent $265
New Private Housing Starts   633
Value (in thousands) $48,115
% Single-Family   0.0
Nonresidential Buildings Value (in thousands) $199,472

Tallest Buildings	Hgt. (ft.)	Stories
Westin Hotel	720	71
Penobscot Bldg.	557	47
1 Detroit Center	491	40
Guardian	485	40
Renaissance Center (4 bldgs.)	479	39
Book Tower	472	35
150 W. Jefferson Bldg.	470	29
Prudential 3000 Town Center	448	32

Urban Redevelopment

In 1970 the city launched a concerted effort to arrest its decline through rebuilding. Out of this effort came Cobo Hall, Renaissance Center, restoration of the Fox Theater, and construction of the 3-million-square-foot riverfront office complex. New industrial and research parks were built, bringing the overall total to more than 380.

Crime

Detroit has achieved a certain notoriety for its high crime rates in recent years. It ranks 323rd, or well near the bottom in public safety with a reported 28,262 violent crimes and 98,818 reported property crimes in 1991.

Crime	
Violent Crimes—Total	28,262
Violent Crime Rate per 100,000	1,001.2
Murder	615
Rape	1,427
Robbery	13,569
Aggravated Assaults	12,651
Property Crimes	98,818
Burglary	26,059
Larceny	44,019
Motor Vehicle Theft	28,740
Arson	1,524
Per Capita Police Expenditures	$277.1
Per Capita Fire Protection Expenditures	$75.07
Number of Police	4,640
Per 1,000	4.25

Religion

French-Canadian influences and the composition of emigrants in the last century made Roman Catholicism the strongest religious tradition in Detroit. Catholics make up about 25% of the population. Among the Protestants, Lutherans and Baptists are strongly represented.

Religion	
Largest Denominations (Adherents)	
Catholic	778,340
Black Baptist	219,448
American Zion	41,873
American Baptist	26,658
Church of Christ	10,034
Episcopal	15,284
Evangelical Lutheran	24,474
Lutheran-Missouri Synod	36,873
Prebyterian	28,751
Southern Baptist	13,211
United Methodist	24,601
Jewish	45,296

Media

Detroit is a two-newspaper city, with the *Detroit News* and *Detroit Free Press* as competing dailies. *Detroit Monthly* is the major city magazine. The electronic media consist of 6 television stations (3 national network affiliates, 1 independent, 1 public, and 1 Canadian) and 17 FM and AM radio stations.

Media
Newsprint
Crain's Detroit Business, weekly
Metro Times, weekly
Detroit Monthly, monthly
Detroit News, daily
The Detroiter, monthly
Metro Times, weekly
Michigan Chronicle, weekly
New Center News, weekly
Television
CBET (Channel 9)
WDIV (Channel 4)
WGPR (Channel 62)
WJBK (Channel 2)
WTVS (Channel 56)
WXON (Channel 20)
Radio
WHYT (FM)   WJOI (FM)
WCXI (AM)   WWWW (FM)
WDET (FM)   WDIV (FM)
WDTR (FM)   WGPR (FM)
WJLB (FM)   WJR (AM)
WJZZ (FM)   WKQI (FM)
WMUZ (FM)   WNZK (AM)
WOMC (FM)   WQBH (AM)
WRIF (FM)

Sports

Detroit is represented in all four major sports: Detroit Tigers in baseball, Detroit Lions in football, Detroit Pistons in basketball, and Detroit Red Wings in hockey. The Detroit Tigers, the city's oldest team, play their home games in Tiger Stadium and compete in the eastern division of the American League. The Detroit Lions play their home games in the Pontiac Silverdome and compete in the central division of the National Football League. The Detroit Pistons play their home games in the Palace of Auburn Hills and compete in the eastern division of the National Basketball Conference. The Detroit Red Wings play their home games in Joe Louis Arena and compete in the Norris Division of Clarence Campbell Conference of the National Hockey League. Detroit also hosts the Detroit Grand Prix, the nation's only Formula One race, and the Spirit of Detroit–Budweiser Thunderboat Championship, held each June on the Detroit River.

Arts, Culture, and Tourism

The Detroit Symphony, Michigan Opera Theater, and Detroit Concert Band are the bellwethers on the music scene. The Detroit Symphony plays September through May at Ford Auditorium and Orchestra Hall, but during summer moves to Meadowbrook, an outdoor amphitheater in Rochester. The Michigan Opera Theater holds its fall season at Fisher Theater and its spring season at the Masonic Temple. The city's oldest professional company is Detroit Repertory Theater. The Attic Theater has a resident professional company specializing in plays by new playwrights. Detroit has two noted theaters: Fox Theater, the largest movie theater in the nation (built in 1928 and renovated in the 1970s) and Fisher Theater, which sponsors Broadway plays. In addition, the city has numerous active playhouses: Music Hall Center for the Performing Arts, Birmingham Theater, Meadowbrook Theater at Oakland University, Hilberry and Bonstelle theaters at Wayne State University, Cranbrook Performing Arts Theater in Bloomfield Hills, Detroit Youtheater at the Detroit Institute of Arts, Masonic Temple, Music Hall for the Peforming Arts, Detroit Center for the Performing Arts, Oakland University Center for the Arts, and Palace of Auburn Hills.

Detroit Institute of the Arts, with more than 100 galleries, is one of the finest art museums in the country. Among its prized treasures is the four-wall mural *Detroit Industry* by Mexican artist Diego Rivera. The 12-acre Henry Ford Museum houses one of the largest collections of automobiles in the world. The 240-acre Greenfield Village, also founded by Henry Ford in 1929, is an outdoor museum exhibiting historic American homes and workplaces. Among them are Noah Webster's Connecticut home, the Wright brothers' bicycle shop, and Thomas Edison's Menlo Park laboratory. Other city museums include the Detroit Historical Museum, founded in 1928; Children's Museum; and Detroit Science Center.

Travel and Tourism

Hotel Rooms   25,424
Convention and Exhibit Space (square feet)   700,000

Convention Centers
  Detroit Civic Center
  Joe Louis Arena
  Cobo Arena
  Cobo Conference/Exhibition Center
  Henry and Edsel Ford Auditorium
  Veterans Memorial Building

Festivals
  International Auto Show (January)
  Detroit Boat Show (February)
  Annual Heritage Fair (June)
  International Freedom Festival (July)
  French Festival (July)
  Michigan State Fair (August)
  Stroh's Montrex Jazz Festival (October)
  Festival of Trees (November)

Parks and Recreation

Of the 56 city parks, the largest and most popular is Belle Isle Park. It occupies the whole of Belle Isle, an island in the Detroit River about a half-mile offshore. It was purchased by the city in 1879 for $200,000. At the time it contained 786 acres, but through reclamation the area increased to 985 acres. Two miles long, the island has 20 miles of shore and intra-island driveways, 5 miles of gravel walkways, and 2 miles of bridle paths. Also in the Detroit River, near the entrance to Lake Erie, is Boblo Island, a popular amusement park. The second largest park is River Rouge Park, bounded on the north by Fullerton Avenue, on the south by Warren Avenue, on the west by Outer Drive, and on the east by Burt Road. It is the city's largest indoor playground. Capitol Park on State and Griswold streets, a half-acre triangular plot converted into a park in 1893, is the site of Michigan's first capitol. Grand Circus Park is one of four original parks created under the Governor and Judges Plan of 1806. Semicircular in form, the park is divided into two quarter-circles by Woodward Avenue. Governor Richard Park adjoins the east side of the Belle Isle Bridge approach. The 287-acre Palmer Park on Woodward Avenue is the city's third largest park, while the 112-acre Waterworks Park on East Jefferson Avenue is a favorite summer playground for children.

Sources of Further Information

Detroit Department of Public Information
City/County Building, Room 608
2 Woodward Avenue
Detroit, MI 48226
(313) 224-3755

Detroit Economic Growth Corporation
150 West Jefferson
Detroit, MI 48226
(313) 963-2940

Detroit Historical Society
5401 Woodward Avenue
Detroit, MI 48202
(313) 833-7934

Detroit Main Public Library
5201 Woodward Avenue
Detroit, MI 48202-4093
(313) 833-1000

Greater Detroit Chamber of Commerce
600 West Lafayette Boulevard
Detroit, MI 48226
(313) 964-4000

Metropolitan Detroit Convention & Visitors Bureau
100 Renaissance Center, Suite 1900
Detroit, MI 48243-1056
(313) 259-4333

Additional Reading

Darden, Joe T. *Detroit: Race and Uneven Development.* Philadelphia. 1987.
Davis, Donald Finlay. *Conspicuous Production: Automobiles and Elites in Detroit, 1899–1933.* 1988.
Detroit Historical Society. *Cadillac and the Founding of Detroit.* 1976.

Ewen, Lynda Ann. *Corporate Power and Urban Crisis in Detroit.* 1988.

Farmer, Silas. *History of Detroit and Wayne County and Early Michigan: A Chronological Encyclopedia.* 1969.

Ferry, W. Hawkins. *The Buildings of Detroit, a History.* 1980.

Hyde, Charles I. *Detroit: An Industrial History Guide.* 1980.

Katzman, David M. *Before the Ghetto: Black Detroit in the Nineteenth Century.* 1973.

Lochbiler, Don. *Detroit's Coming of Age, 1873–1973.* 1973.

Lutz, William. *The News of Detroit; How a Newspaper and a City Grew Together.* 1973.

Ripps, Rae Elizabeth, ed. *Detroit in Its World Setting: A 250-Year Chronology, 1701–1951.* 1953.

Vexler, Robert. *Detroit: A Chronological and Documentary History, 1701–1976.* 1977.

Woodford, Arthur M. *Detroit: American Urban Renaissance: A Pictorial and Entertaining Commentary on the Growth and Development of Detroit, Michigan.* 1979.

Woodford, Frank B., and Arthur M. Woodford. *All Our Yesterdays: A Brief History of Detroit.* 1969.

Duluth

Minnesota

Basic Data

Name Duluth
Name Origin From Sieur Du Lhuth
Year Founded 1856 Inc. 1870
Status: State Minnesota
      County Seat of St. Louis County
Area (square miles) 67.6
Elevation (feet) 610
Time Zone Central
Population (1990) 85,493
Population of Metro Area (1990) 239,971

Sister Cities

    Ohara, Japan
    Petrozavodsk, Russia
    Vaxjo, Sweden
    Thunder Bay, Canada

Distance in Miles To:

St. Paul	150
Minneapolis	156
Rochester, MN	232

Location and Topography

N

Duluth is located on a natural harbor at the western tip of Lake Superior. It sits at the base of a range of hills overlooking the St. Louis River, rising on rock bluffs 600 to 800 feet above lake level.

Layout of City and Suburbs

Duluth has a very unusual setting provided by hills in the background and Lake Superior in the foreground. From northeast to southwest, Duluth extends 27 miles along the edge of Lake Superior with a width of sometimes less than 1 mile and never exceeding 4 miles. Occasionally the hills slope gently to the waterline, but more often the highlands rise into abrupt cliffs and ledges. The residential sections are built on these high elevations. Many of the avenues ascend at steep angles, requiring good brakes and nerves for winter driving. To the east, spanning the Ship Canal, the Aerial Lift Bridge rises against the sky, and Minnesota Point curves out into the bay toward Wisconsin, separating the lake from the river. To the west and south, the St. Louis River winds among many densely wooded islands on its way to the lake. On the opposite shore is the city of Superior, Wisconsin.

Environment

Environmental Stress Index	NA
Green Cities Index: Rank	NA
Score	NA
Water Quality	Neutral, very soft, fluoridated
Average Daily Use (gallons per capita)	148
Maximum Supply (gallons per capita)	272
Parkland as % of Total City Area	NA
% Waste Landfilled/Recycled	35:18
Annual Parks Expenditures per Capita	$154.79

Climate

Duluth is known as the air-conditioned city because the easterly winds from the lake, blocked by the high hills in the background, circulate freely over the lakefront city. Winters are long and cold, and snow remains on the ground until April. Although Lake Superior is the coldest of the Great Lakes, it never freezes over. Summer temperatures are cooler and winter temperatures warmer than in similarly situated cities with a continental climate. Severe storms occasionally occur, but are moderated by the proximity of the lake. Thus Lake Superior has a profound effect on Duluth's climate.

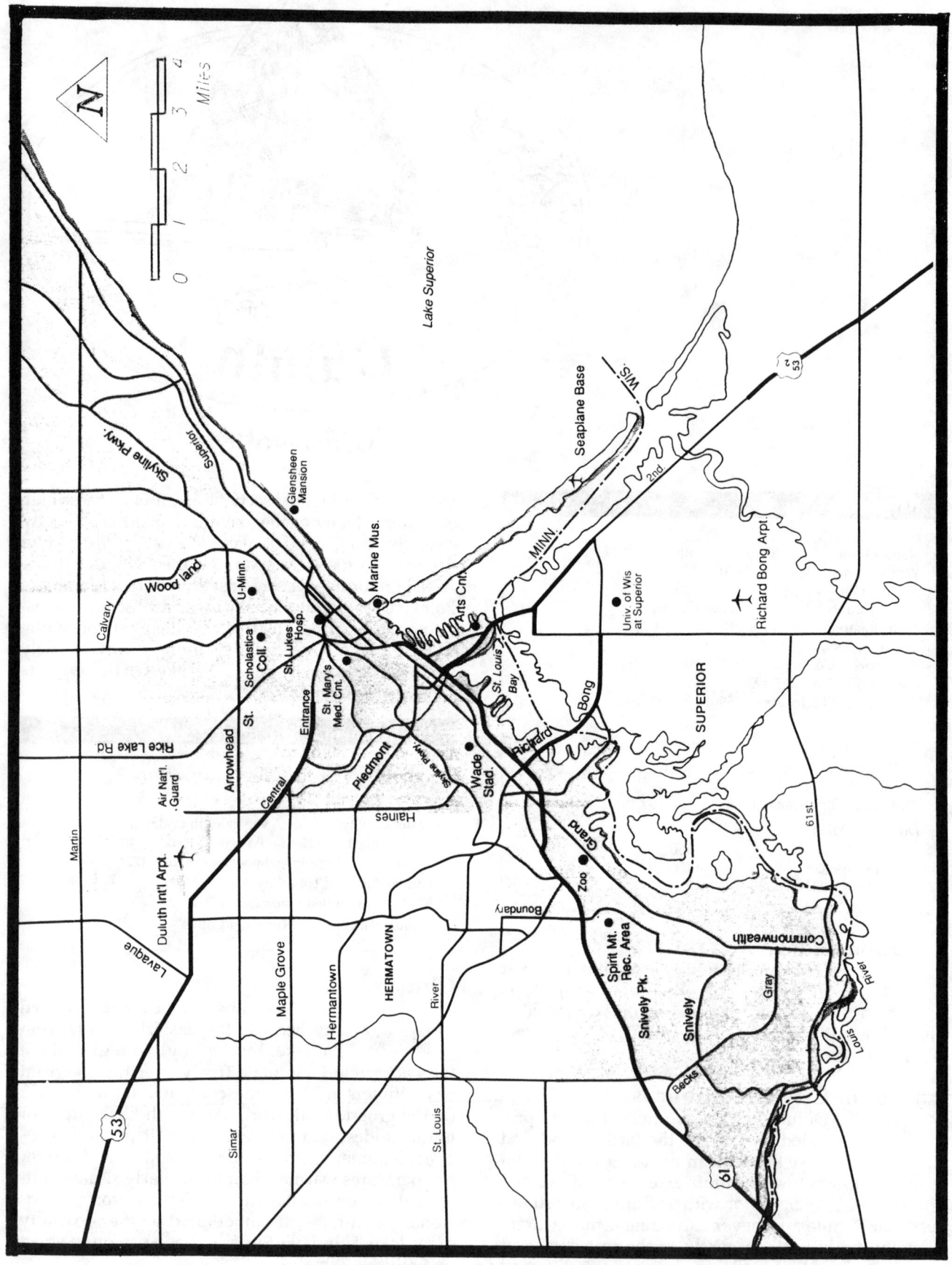

Weather

Temperature

Highest Monthly Average °F 76.4
Lowest Monthly Average °F 2.9

Annual Averages

Days 32°F or Below 185
Days above 90°F 2
Zero Degree Days 51
Precipitation (inches) 29.68
Snow (inches) 77.1
% Seasonal Humidity 71.5
Wind Speed (m.p.h.) 11.1
Clear Days 77
Cloudy Days 187
Storm Days 35
Rainy Days 134

Average Temperatures (°F)	High	Low	Mean
January	17.6	0.6	8.5
February	22.1	2.0	12.1
March	32.6	14.4	23.5
April	47.8	29.3	38.6
May	60.0	38.8	49.4
June	69.7	48.3	59.0
July	76.4	54.7	65.6
August	74.4	53.7	64.1
September	64.0	44.8	54.4
October	54.3	36.2	45.3
November	35.3	21.4	28.4
December	22.5	6.3	14.4

History

The site of Duluth was occupied by the Ojibwa Indians before the coming of Europeans. Pierre Esprit Radisson and Sieur d'Medart Chouart Groseilliers are believed to be the first white persons to visit the area in 1654–1660, followed by Father Allouez ten years later. Daniel Greysolon, Sieur du Luth, after whom the city is named, made his first visit in 1679 when he tried to make peace between the Ojibwa and Sioux tribes. Other than fur-trading posts, the region remained unsettled until 1852 when George P. Stuntz came to the region as a surveyor. Stuntz liked the wilderness so much that he returned the next year to remain permanently; he is considered the city's first inhabitant.

In 1856 the village was named Duluth and made the seat of St. Louis County. But almost immediately, the village's economy was wiped out in the Panic of 1857 and its population depleted by a scarlet fever epidemic. In 1858, Minnesota entered the Union as the 32nd state. Only a couple of houses remained in the town after the end of the Civil War. The town's fortunes soon mended when geologists found iron ore and gold-bearing quartz at nearby Lake Vermilion. Later, Duluth was selected as the northern terminus of the Lake Superior and Mississippi Railroad. A flourishing lumber industry was established, and Duluth was well on its way. In 1870 Duluth was granted its first charter, and J. B. Culver was elected the first

mayor. But it experienced another economic crisis, forcing a return to village status.

The city was once again rescued by its lumber industry, and in 1886 the legislature gave Duluth permission to call itself a city. In 1873 the U.S. government assumed control of Duluth Harbor and 20 years later renamed it Duluth-Superior Harbor. By the end of the century, six original lakeshore communities were absorbed into Greater Duluth. In 1912 the present charter providing for a commission form of government was adopted.

Historical Landmarks

The site of the Old Vermilion Trail on Washington Avenue and First Street is marked by a bronze plaque. The Civic Center on First Street consists of the central courthouse, with the federal building on the left and the city hall on the right. The site of an Ojibwa village at the foot of 133rd Avenue is marked by a bronze plaque. Here in 1826 the first Minnesota Ojibwa Treaty was signed; du Luth stopped here in 1679 and an Astor trading post was established in 1817. Union Depot is a renovated railroad depot housing the St. Louis County Heritage and Arts Center. Glensheen, a Great Lakes estate owned by the University of Minnesota, is a Jacobean-style mansion with original furnishings. The Aerial Lift Bridge connecting Minnesota Point with the mainland, built in 1930, is the world's fastest lift bridge.

Population

Duluth had a population of 85,493 in the 1990 census, a loss of 12.77% over its 1980 population of 92,811. The city estimated the population to be more than 89,000 in 1992.

Population

	1980	1990
Central City	92,811	85,493
Rank	184	240
Metro Area	266,650	239,971

Pop. Change 1980–1990 -7,318
Pop. % Change 1980–1990 -7.9
Median Age 33.9
% Male 47.1
% Age 65 and Over 17.1
Density (per square mile) 1,264

Households

Number 34,563
Persons per Household 2.36
% Female-Headed Households 11.1
% One-Person Households 31.7
Births—Total 1,298
    % to Mothers under 20 11.2
    Birth Rate per 1,000 15.2

Ethnic Composition

Whites make up 95.9%, blacks 0.9%, American Indians 2.1%, Asians and Pacific Islanders 0.9%, and others 0.2%.

Ethnic Composition (as % of total pop.)

	1980	1990
White	96.98	95.89
Black	0.83	0.87
American Indian	1.45	2.15
Asian and Pacific Islander	0.45	0.9
Hispanic	0.45	0.6
Other	NA	0.19

Chronology

1654–1660	Radisson and Groseillier explore the southern shore of Lake Superior.
1679	Daniel Greysolon, Sieur du Luth, makes first visit.
1852	George P. Stuntz, a surveyor, becomes first settler.
1856	The settlement, consisting of 14 houses, is named Duluth and made the seat of St. Louis County.
1857	The town's economy is ruined by a recession.
1858	On 11 May, Minnesota enters the Union as the 32nd state.
1859	Scarlet fever strikes town and nearly wipes out the population.
1865	Geologists report finding iron ore and gold-bearing quartz at Lake Vermilion. Duluth is made northern terminus of Jay Cooke's Lake Superior and Mississippi Railroad, stimulating a new wave of immigration.
1871	Canal is built, providing entry into the lake through Minnesota Point.
1873	City faces extinction as Jay Cooke's railroad empire collapses.
1877	Duluth lapses into bankruptcy and village status.
1893	Federal government assumes control of Duluth Harbor and renames it Duluth Superior Harbor.
1912	Charter providing for commission form of government is adopted.

Government

The city charter provides for a strong mayor–weak council form of government. The mayor and nine council members are elected to four-year terms.

Government

Year of Home Charter   1921
Number of Members of the Governing Body   10
Elected at Large   4
Elected by Wards   6
Number of Women in Governing Body   3
Salary of Mayor $1,922
Salary of Council Members $625
City Government Employment Total   1,321
Rate per 10,000   160.4

Public Finance

The annual budget consists of revenues of $125.992 million and expenditures of $129.277 million. The debt outstanding is $160.808 million, and cash and security holdings are $118.117 million.

Public Finance

Total Revenue (in millions) $125.992
Intergovernmental Revenue—Total (in millions) $30.4
Federal Revenue per Capita $4.41
% Federal Assistance   3.5
% State Assistance   19.99
Sales Tax as % of Total Revenue   5.27
Local Revenue as % of Total Revenue   49.12
City Income Tax   no
Taxes—Total (in millions) $19.1

Taxes per Capita
   Total $232
   Property $146
   Sales and Gross Receipts $82
General Expenditures—Total (in millions) $74.6
General Expenditures per Capita $905
Capital Outlays per Capita $136

% of Expenditures for:
   Public Welfare   0.0
   Highways   13.4
   Education   0.0
   Health and Hospitals   0.0
   Police   8.7
   Sewerage and Sanitation   8.3
   Parks and Recreation   8.4
   Housing and Community Development   4.2
Debt Outstanding per Capita $1,631
   % Utility   13.3
Federal Procurement Contract Awards (in millions) $27.7
Federal Grants Awards (in millions) $9.3
Fiscal Year Begins   January 1

Economy

The principal economic sectors are tourism, manufacturing, medical, and retail. Duluth also serves as a regional headquarters for financial institutions. The tourism industry exceeds $100 million annually, and generates other support services. There are large shopping facilities such as Miller Hill Mall and Fitgers on the Lake, a popular shopping and dining establishment in east downtown. There is a flourishing fishing and cold-storage industry, based on Lake Superior's fishing resources, and a lumber industry supported by the forests of northern Minnesota. A key part of the economy is the Port of Duluth-Superior, a foreign-trade zone that, despite being landlocked during hard winters, is among the top ten U.S. ports.

Economy

Total Money Income (in millions) $827.2
% of State Average 89.9
Per Capita Annual Income $10,051
% Population below Poverty Level 12
Fortune 500 Companies NA

Banks	Number	Deposits (in millions)
Commercial	9	661.644
Savings	3	292.355

Passenger Autos 107,086
Electric Meters 42,000
Gas Meters 19,504

Manufacturing

Number of Establishments 87
% with 20 or More Employees 32.2
Manufacturing Payroll (in millions) $98.9
Value Added by Manufacture (in millions) $198.1
Value of Shipments (in millions) $331.1
New Capital Expenditures (in millions) NA

Wholesale Trade

Number of Establishments 173
Sales (in millions) $734
Annual Payroll (in millions) $45.726

Retail Trade

Number of Establishments 989
Total Sales (in millions) $660.5
Sales per Capita $8,018
Number of Retail Trade Establishments with Payroll 710
Annual Payroll (in millions) $77.7
Total Sales (in millions) $646.2
General Merchandise Stores (per capita) $1,629
Food Stores (per capita) $1,444
Apparel Stores (per capita) $400
Eating and Drinking Places (per capita) $752

Service Industries

Total Establishments 656
Total Receipts (in millions) $212.4
Hotels and Motels (in millions) $19.0
Health Services (in millions) $57.8
Legal Services (in millions) $18.9

Labor

The work force is not large compared to other major cities, and its manpower distribution also shows less emphasis on manufacturing than on services, government, and trade. Among the top ten employers two are governments, four are medical institutions, two are educational institutions, one is retail, and one a public utility.

Labor

Civilian Labor Force 40,400
% Change 1989–1990 3.1

Work Force Distribution
Mining 5,300
Construction 3,700
Manufacturing 8,200
Transportation and Public Utilities 6,200
Wholesale and Retail Trade 25,300
FIRE (Finance, Insurance, Real Estate) 3,400
Service 25,500
Government 21,500
Women as % of Labor Force 44.0
% Self-Employed 4.3
% Professional/Technical 19.5
Total Unemployment 2,098
Rate % 5.2
Federal Government Civilian Employment 1,215

Education

The Duluth Public School Systems Independent School District #709 supports 26 schools. The Port Area Catholic Education (PACE) runs 6 elementary schools, and there is 1 independent public school. The largest institution of higher education is the University of Minnesota–Duluth, one of four campuses of the University of Minnesota. The College of Saint Scholastica is a coeducational Benedictine liberal arts college. Duluth Community College and Duluth Technical College are smaller institutions.

Education

Number of Public Schools 26
Special Education Schools NA
Total Enrollment 15,363
% Enrollment in Private Schools NA
% Minority NA
Classroom Teachers NA
Pupil-Teacher Ratio NA
Number of Graduates NA
Total Revenue (in millions) NA
Total Expenditures (in millions) NA
Expenditures per Pupil NA
Educational Attainment (Age 25 and Over) NA
  % Completed 12 or More Years 72.3
  % Completed 16 or More Years 18.4
Four-Year Colleges and Universities 2
  Enrollment 9,885
Two-Year Colleges NA
  Enrollment NA

Libraries

Number 16
Public Libraries 3
Books (in thousands) 357
Circulation (in thousands) 1,303
Persons Served (in thousands) 85.4
Circulation per Person Served 15.25
Income (in millions) $2.6
Staff 66

Four-Year Colleges and Universities
  University of Minnesota–Duluth
  College of Saint Scholastica

Health

Duluth has three hospitals and numerous clinics providing specialty services. The three hospitals are St. Mary's Medical Center, St. Luke's Hospital, and Miller-Dwan Medical Center, which administers a large mental-health program as well. The city clinics include Duluth Clinic, Northland Medical Center, and Polinsky Medical Rehabilitation Center.

Health	
Deaths—Total	1,025
Rate per 1,000	12.0
Infant Deaths—Total	14
Rate per 1,000	10.8
Number of Metro Hospitals	3
Number of Metro Hospital Beds	744
Rate per 100,000	903
Number of Physicians	377
Physicians per 1,000	NA
Nurses per 1,000	NA
Health Expenditures per Capita	NA

Transportation

Duluth is the northern terminus of I-35, running from the Mexican border to the Canadian border. Duluth also is approached by U.S. highways 2, 53, and 61, as well as state routes 23, 39, and 194. Duluth is one of the ten largest U.S. ports, containing 19 square miles of water at an average depth of 27 feet. It has 113 docks and nearly 50 miles of commercial waterfront. Grain is the principal export, and the port has one of the largest grain-handling facilities in the world. Duluth also is served by five railroads–Burlington Northern; Duluth, Missabe and Iron Range; Chicago and Northwestern; Duluth, Winnipeg and Pacific; and Soo Line. Duluth International Airport, about 6 miles from downtown, is the principal air terminal. An airport on Minnesota Point serves commuters.

Transportation	
Interstate Highway Mileage	12
Total Urban Mileage	862
Total Daily Vehicle Mileage (in millions)	2.425
Daily Average Commute Time	38.9 min.
Number of Buses	74
Port Tonnage (in millions)	40
Airports	1
Number of Daily Flights	5
Daily Average Number of Passengers	292
Airlines (American carriers only)	
Northwest Airlink	

Housing

The city housing has a fascinating variety, ranging from the mansions of wealthy 19th-century lumber and mining barons to late-1980 condos. A housing boom oc-

curred in the 1980s, but vacancy rates remain a low 5%. The median home cost is $59,700.

Housing	
Total Housing Units	36,022
% Change 1980–1990	-3.0
Vacant Units for Sale or Rent	947
Occupied Units	34,563
% with More Than One Person per Room	1.3
% Owner-Occupied	64.4
Median Value of Owner-Occupied Homes	$46,300
Average Monthly Purchase Cost	$355
Median Monthly Rent	$287
New Private Housing Starts	127
Value (in thousands)	$9,707
% Single-Family	85.8
Nonresidential Buildings Value (in thousands)	$5,081
None	

Urban Redevelopment

Over $1.2 billion has been invested in urban redevelopment since 1985. Among the largest investments was the construction of a $400-million paper mill by Lake Superior Paper Industries. Others include Miller Hall and the Duluth Entertainment Convention Center. Another spectacular project is the renovation of the historic waterfront, in which over $225 million has been invested. The DeWitt Seitz Marketplace is a renovated turn-of-the-century warehouse converted into a waterfront mall. Crowning the waterfront is Bayfront Festival Park with its brightly colored canopy.

Crime

Duluth is the 31st safest city in the nation. In 1991, of known crimes, 92 were violent crimes and 3,628 were property crimes. Strict enforcement of laws, mandatory arrest in domestic violence cases, and an extensive neighborhood-watch program have brought the crime rate down by 19.6% over the last ten years.

Crime	
Violent Crimes—Total	273
Violent Crime Rate per 100,000	180.6
Murder	3
Rape	25
Robbery	56
Aggravated Assaults	189
Property Crimes	4,613
Burglary	877
Larceny	3,443
Motor Vehicle Theft	293
Arson	18
Per Capita Police Expenditures	$98.83
Per Capita Fire Protection Expenditures	$96.54
Number of Police	129
Per 1,000	1.41

Religion

Catholics are the largest single denomination. Constituting the majority of church members are Protestants, divided into five major denominations: Baptists, Lutherans, Methodists, Presbyterians, and Episcopalians.

Religion	
Largest Denominations (Adherents)	
Catholic	48,383
Evangelical Lutheran	27,750
United Methodist	6,875
Lutheran-Missouri Synod	4,327
Presbyterian	3,977
Assembly of God	2,562
Episcopal	2,105

Media

The city daily is the *Duluth News-Tribune.* The electronic media consist of 4 television stations (3 commercial and 1 public) and AM and 11 FM radio stations.

Media	
Newsprint	
Duluth Budgeteer, weekly	
Duluth News-Tribune, daily	
The Duluthian, bimonthly	
Television	
KBJR (Channel 6)	
KDLH (Channel 3)	
WDIO (Channel 10)	
WDSE (Channel 8)	
Radio	
KDAL (AM)	KDAL (FM)
KQDS (FM)	KQDS (AM)
KUMD (FM)	WAKX (FM)
WEBC (AM)	WIRR (FM)
WNCB (FM)	WSCD (FM)
WWJC (AM)	

Sports

Duluth is home to the semiprofessional baseball team Duluth Dukes. Duluth has a strong hockey team in the University of Minnesota–Duluth. It also is the home of the John Beargrease Sled Dog Marathon, a 500-mile wilderness race in January from Duluth to Grand Portage and back. The Duluth Winter Sports Festival is the major event in January. Labor Day weekend is the occasion for sailboat races and an Arabian horse show.

Arts, Culture, and Tourism

Almost all the major performing arts and cultural institutions are located at the Depot. The Duluth-Superior Symphony Orchestra presents seven concerts a season as well as three Pops performances and an annual holiday concert. The Matinee Musicale is Duluth's oldest cultural institution, and has been instrumental in the rise of many young musicians. The Duluth Playhouse, founded in 1914, is one of the oldest in the region. The Duluth Ballet, founded in 1965, is a professional troupe offering three performance series annually. The premier art facilities are the Duluth Art Institute and Tweed Museum of Art. Other local museums include Glensheen, a 122-acre historic estate built by Chester and Clara Congdon between 1905 and 1908 on the lakeshore; Canal Park Marine Museum, next to the Aerial Bridge, operated by the U.S. Army Corps of Engineers; Lake Superior Museum of Transportation; St. Louis County Historical Society; and A. M. Chisholm Museum.

Travel and Tourism
Hotel Rooms 2,553
Convention and Exhibit Space (square feet) NA
Convention Centers
Duluth Entertainment Convention Center
Festivals
International Folk Festival (August)
Taste North Food Festival (August)

Parks and Recreation

The city maintains 3,264 acres in 105 parks and playgrounds. The 38-acre Lincoln Park borders Millers Creek between high, wooded hills. The 47-acre Lester Park on Snively Boulevard is the starting point for the Skyline Parkway. The 108-acre Chester Park begins at the Chester Park Bowl. Amity Park is a roadside park that began in 1926 as a reforestation project. The 330-acre Enger Park includes the Twin Lakes and Enger Peak with its 40-foot observation tower. Major parks include Chambers Grove, Fairmont, Irving, Memorial, Wheeler, Park Point, Leif Erickson, Woodland, Portland Square, Portman Square, Brighton Beach, Wade Stadium, and Bayfront Festival.

Sources of Further Information

City Hall
411 West First Street
Duluth, MN 55802
(218) 723-3300

Duluth Area Chamber of Commerce
118 East Superior Street
Duluth, MN 55802
(218) 722-5501

Duluth Convention and Visitors Bureau
100 Lake Place Drive
Duluth, MN 55802
(218) 722-4011 or (800) 4DULUTH (438-5884)

Duluth Public Library
520 West Superior Street
Duluth, MN 55802
(218) 723-3802

Additional Reading

Raimo, David. *Duluth: Profile of Progress*. Annual.
Steinners, Donald N., and Glenn O. Gronseth.
 Duluth Business Indicators. Monthly.

Erie

Pennsylvania

Location and Topography

N Erie, the northernmost city in Pennsylvania and its only port on the Great Lakes, is located on the southeast shore of Lake Erie. Presque Isle, a peninsula seven miles long, curves around its harbor. The city lies on a plain 113 feet above the level of Lake Erie. The terrain is gently rolling.

Layout of City and Suburbs

Laid out on a modification of the plan of Washington, D.C., Erie gives the impression of spaciousness with wide, tree-lined streets, broad lawns, and the general absence of very tall buildings. Even in the business district, the skyline is low, with only a few buildings over ten stories. The residential section is characterized by the same spaciousness. The waterfront presents a scene of activity when the lake, ice-locked during the winter, opens for navigation. The streets follow a grid system as in the nation's capital; many, such as 12th, run for ten miles straight.

Environment

Environmental Stress Index   3.2
Green Cities Index: Rank   NA
                    Score   NA
Water Quality   Alkaline, hard, fluoridated
    Average Daily Use (gallons per capita)   NA
    Maximum Supply (gallons per capita)   NA
Parkland as % of Total City Area   NA
% Waste Landfilled/Recycled   NA
Annual Parks Expenditures per Capita $16.88

Climate

 Although the waters of Lake Erie are relatively warm, in the winter cold air masses moving south from Canada produce frequent snows, and the temperature variance between air and water produces cloudiness. Spring is usually cloudy and cool. Summer is pleasant, with cooling breezes from the lake, and fall is typically dry, with long periods of sunshine. Rainfall is well distributed throughout the year. Erie receives 60% to 70% of possible summer sunshine and 30% of winter sunshine. Snowfall ranges from 60 inches in the west to 87 to 90 inches in the east. The growing season averages 180 days along the shore.

Weather

Temperature

Highest Monthly Average °F   78.2
Lowest Monthly Average °F   18.0

Weather (continued)

Annual Averages

Days 32°F or Below   128
Days above 90°F   6
Zero Degree Days   0
Precipitation (inches)   39.39
Snow (inches)   85.8
% Seasonal Humidity   72.5
Wind Speed (m.p.h.)   11.2
Clear Days   64
Cloudy Days   206
Storm Days   32
Rainy Days   165

Average Temperatures (°F)	High	Low	Mean
January	33.9	22.2	28.1
February	38.9	26.5	32.7
March	47.7	30.3	39.0
April	58.8	44.2	51.5
May	73.9	55.7	64.8
June	79.6	60.9	70.3
July	82.3	64.0	73.2
August	81.0	64.1	72.6
September	72.9	54.6	63.8
October	64.4	47.2	55.8
November	47.9	34.7	41.3
December	41.3	27.8	34.6

History

The Erie area, once the habitat of the Erie Indians, was settled by the French in 1753 when they built Fort Presque Isle. The French abandoned the fort to the English, who lost it to the Indians at the beginning of Pontiac's rebellion in 1763. The Indians captured the second Fort Presque Isle, which Colonel Henry Bouquet built on the site of the original French stronghold, and burned it to the ground.

In a 1784 treaty with the Six Nations, Pennsylvania acquired all the land in the northwestern part of the state, but this did not include the triangular tract fronting on Lake Erie. Congress, taking up Pennsylvania's plea for access to Lake Erie, persuaded New York, Ohio, and Massachusetts to relinquish their claims to the territory. It was thereupon deeded to the U.S. government, who in turn sold it to the commonwealth for 75 cents an acre. However, the Indians continued to resist the European advance until General Anthony Wayne launched a vigorous campaign and won the Battle of Fallen Timbers. Wayne made a treaty with the western tribes in 1795 and with the Six Nations the following November. That same year, the town of Erie was laid out by Major Andrew Ellicott and General William Irvine. It grew slowly; in 1805, when it was incorporated as a borough, it had only 100 houses. In the War of 1812, Erie played a prominent role, entering history books as the base of Commodore Oliver Hazard Perry. With ships built in Erie, Perry beat the British lake fleet off Sandusky. From then on Erie made rapid strides, helped by the opening of the Erie and Pittsburgh Canal in 1844 and the advent of the railroads in the 1850s. It was incorporated as a city in 1851.

Historical Landmarks

Erie's showpiece is the historic West Sixth Street, noted for its fine Victorian and early–20th-century Period Revival houses. It was the city's most eminent residential neighborhood from the Civil War to the Great Depression. Nearly all the landmarks are private residences except for the Cathedral of St. Paul, built in 1866, and the Presbyterian Church of the Covenant. The Charles Hamot Strong Mansion, a 46-room, $1 million house, was the wedding gift of prominent Erie industrialist and politician William L. Scott to his daughter. Other homes include the Hoskinson Double House; Clarks Olds House (1884); Ross Pier Wright House (1855); Davenport Galbraith House (1892); Alexander Jarecki House (1913); Robert Jarecki House (1909); George Black House (1896); Hall Streuber House (1875); Julius Siegel House; William Spencer House (1876) and Spencer Double House (1875), now a bed-and-breakfast inn; Otto Becker House (1918); Adrian Collins House (1923); Frank Connell House (1890); Addison Leech House (1872), the most outstanding Second Empire House in the district; Watson/Kurtze Mansion (1892), now home to the Erie Historical Museum and Planetarium; Wood/Morrison House (1858); John Hill House (1836–1854); and Charles M. Reed Mansion (1849), erected by Erie magnate Charles Manning Reed, owner of extensive real estate, railroad, and shipping interests. Among the nonresidential landmarks the most important are the Old Customs House (1839) on State Street; the legendary Dickson Tavern on French Street, the oldest surviving building in Erie; Cashiers House (1839); the Perry Monument; and the flagship Niagara, the last remaining vessel of the War of 1812's Battle of Lake Erie.

Population

Erie has been losing population since World War II. Since 1970, when the population was 129,000, the population has shrunk to 119,123 in 1980 and to 108,718 in 1990.

Population

	1980	1990
Central City	119,123	108,718
Rank	130	173
Metro Area	279,780	275,572

Pop. Change 1980–1990   -10,405
Pop. % Change 1980–1990   -8.7
Median Age   32.5
% Male   47.2
% Age 65 and Over   16.1
Density (per square mile)   4,941

Households

Number   42,131
Persons per Household   2.47
% Female-Headed Households   15.6
% One-Person Households   30.8
Births—Total   2,110
   % to Mothers under 20   14.5
   Birth Rate per 1,000   18.0

Chronology

1753 A French force under Sieur Marin builds a fort on Presque Isle, but abandons it within a few years under pressure from the British.

1763 On the outbreak of Pontiac's War, Indians invade Presque Isle and burn the fort to the ground.

1784 Pennsylvania acquires by treaty with the Six Nations all land in the northwestern part of the state excluding the triangle abutting Lake Erie.

1787 Pennsylvania becomes the second state to adopt the Constitution.

1792 Pennsylvania buys the Erie triangle from the U.S. government for 75 cents an acre.

1795 General Anthony Wayne defeats the Indians in the Battle of Fallen Timbers and signs treaties with them. Major Andrew Elliott and General William Irvine lay out the town of Erie.

1812 In the War of 1812, Erie-built ships help Commodore Oliver Hazard Perry beat back British threats.

1844 The Erie and Pittsburgh Canal opens.

1851 Erie is incorporated as a city.

Ethnic Composition

Whites make up 86% of the population and blacks 12%.

Ethnic Composition (as % of total pop.)

	1980	1990
White	89.16	86.05
Black	9.71	12.04
American Indian	0.14	0.21
Asian and Pacific Islander	0.33	0.47
Hispanic	1.15	2.4
Other	NA	1.23

Government

Erie has a mayor-council form of government, with the mayor and seven council members elected to four-year terms. Erie also is the seat of Erie County.

Public Finance

The annual budget consists of revenues of $65.327 million and expenditures of $67.633 million. The outstanding debt is $14.964 million, and cash and security holdings are $36.372 million.

Government

Year of Home Charter   NA
Number of Members of the Governing Body   7
Elected at Large   7
Elected by Wards   NA
Number of Women in Governing Body   1
Salary of Mayor $42,000
Salary of Council Members $6,000
City Government Employment Total   1,171
Rate per 10,000   101.6

Public Finance

Total Revenue (in millions) $65.327
Intergovernmental Revenue—Total (in millions) $12.69
Federal Revenue per Capita   NA
% Federal Assistance   NA
% State Assistance   18.55
Sales Tax as % of Total Revenue   NA
Local Revenue as % of Total Revenue   62.46
City Income Tax   yes
Taxes—Total (in millions) $21.8

Taxes per Capita
    Total $189
    Property $141
    Sales and Gross Receipts $0
General Expenditures—Total (in millions) $47.6
General Expenditures per Capita $413
Capital Outlays per Capita $58

% of Expenditures for:
    Public Welfare   0.0
    Highways   13.1
    Education   0.0
    Health and Hospitals   0.0
    Police   15.8
    Sewerage and Sanitation   18.8
    Parks and Recreation   3.3
    Housing and Community Development   10.8
Debt Outstanding per Capita $195
    % Utility   46.3
Federal Procurement Contract Awards (in millions) $35.2
Federal Grants Awards (in millions) $12.4
Fiscal Year Begins   January 1

Economy

Historically, the Erie economy was based primarily on manufacturing and secondarily on agriculture. In recent decades, services, trade, and tourism emerged as major sectors. Manufacturing still is important; nearly 500 industrial plants are located in the county, producing primarily metals, metal products, and plastics. Major industries include General Electric, International Paper, Lord Corporation, Riley Stoker, and Zurn Industries. Retail establishments number over 2,000. There are ten financial institutions with 70 branch offices.

Economy

Total Money Income (in millions) $1,036.8
% of State Average   87.4
Per Capita Annual Income $8,995
% Population below Poverty Level   13.4
Fortune 500 Companies   0

Banks	Number	Deposits (in millions)
Commercial	12	NA
Savings	NA	NA
Passenger Autos	137,563	

Economy (continued)

Electric Meters   81,201
Gas Meters   73,741

Manufacturing

Number of Establishments   238
% with 20 or More Employees   42.0
Manufacturing Payroll (in millions) $353.9
Value Added by Manufacture (in millions) $658.6
Value of Shipments (in millions) $1,307.6
New Capital Expenditures (in millions) $53.5

Wholesale Trade

Number of Establishments   224
Sales (in millions) $490.8
Annual Payroll (in millions) $51.241

Retail Trade

Number of Establishments   1,069
Total Sales (in millions) $650.4
Sales per Capita $5,642
Number of Retail Trade Establishments with Payroll   739
Annual Payroll (in millions) $72.9
Total Sales (in millions) $632.7
General Merchandise Stores (per capita) $494
Food Stores (per capita) $1,479
Apparel Stores (per capita) $183
Eating and Drinking Places (per capita) $596

Service Industries

Total Establishments   868
Total Receipts (in millions) $478.7
Hotels and Motels (in millions) $12.0
Health Services (in millions) $166.8
Legal Services (in millions) $26.9

Labor

Erie's labor market is unusual because of the high rate of manufacturing employment. Although the city has lost population, the labor market has not been seriously affected because most of the residents have merely moved from the city to the county.

Labor

Civilian Labor Force   54,270
% Change 1989–1990   1.9

Work Force Distribution
Mining   200
Construction   3,500
Manufacturing   35,400
Transportation and Public Utilities   4,000
Wholesale and Retail Trade   26,000
FIRE (Finance, Insurance, Real Estate)   5,700
Service   30,800
Government   13,600
Women as % of Labor Force   43.4
% Self-Employed   3.8
% Professional/Technical   13.6
Total Unemployment   3,517
Rate %   6.5
Federal Government Civilian Employment   1,071

Education

The public school system consists of 4 senior high schools, 4 junior high/middle schools, and 15 elementary schools. The parochial system consists of 5 high schools and 24 elementary schools. The principal institutions of higher education are Penn State University–Erie Campus, known as Behrend College; Gannon University; and Mercyhurst College. Specialized institutions include the Hamot Medical Center Medical School Campus, Nursing School of Saint Vincent Health Center, Erie Institute of Technology, and Erie Business Center.

Education

Number of Public Schools   23
Special Education Schools   NA
Total Enrollment   12,287
% Enrollment in Private Schools   20.9
% Minority   NA
Classroom Teachers   NA
Pupil-Teacher Ratio   25:1
Number of Graduates   NA
Total Revenue (in millions)   NA
Total Expenditures (in millions)   NA
Expenditures per Pupil   NA
Educational Attainment (Age 25 and Over)   NA
   % Completed 12 or More Years   64.8
   % Completed 16 or More Years   11.3
Four-Year Colleges and Universities   3
   Enrollment   6,662
Two-Year Colleges   NA
   Enrollment   NA

Libraries

Number   22
Public Libraries   7
Books (in thousands)   415
Circulation (in thousands)   1,507
Persons Served (in thousands)   253.4
Circulation per Person Served   5.94
Income (in millions) $2.425
Staff   76

Four-Year Colleges and Universities
   Gannon University
   Mercyhurst College

Health

The largest medical facility is the Saint Vincent Health Center with 584 beds. With more than 300 staff physicians, Saint Vincent offers care in more than 35 medical specialties and subspecialties. It also is a teaching hospital with an attached School of Nursing. The Veterans Affairs Medical Center is a 178-bed medical and surgical facility including a 40-bed nursing home. Hamot Medical Center is a 560-bed teaching hospital and regional referral center. Other medical facilities include Metro Health Center, Great Lakes Rehabilitation Hospital, Lake Erie Institute of Rehabilitation, Millcreek Community Hospital, and Shriners Hospital for Crippled Children.

Health

Deaths—Total   1,299
Rate per 1,000   11.1
Infant Deaths—Total   22
Rate per 1,000   10.4
Number of Metro Hospitals   7
Number of Metro Hospital Beds   1,663
Rate per 100,000   1,443
Number of Physicians   426
Physicians per 1,000   NA
Nurses per 1,000   NA
Health Expenditures per Capita   NA

Transportation

Erie is approached by three highways: I-79 (which links with I-90) and U.S. highways 20 and 19. Rail services are provided by six railroads: Amtrak, Conrail, Penn Central, East Erie Commercial Railway, Norfolk and Western Railway, and Bessemer and Lake Erie Railroad. Erie International Airport is located six miles from downtown and is served by two commercial airlines. Erie has one of the world's finest landlocked harbors. The navigation season is eight and a half months a year, from 1 April to around 15 December.

Transportation

Interstate Highway Mileage   7
Total Urban Mileage   665
Total Daily Vehicle Mileage (in millions)   2.196
Daily Average Commute Time   37.6 min.
Number of Buses   58
Port Tonnage (in millions)   1.00
Airports   1
Number of Daily Flights   8
Daily Average Number of Passengers   284

Airlines (American carriers only)
   USAir

Housing

As in many other cities in the Northeast, housing activity spurted in the 1980s, mostly in the suburbs. Housing remains

Housing

Total Housing Units   45,424
% Change 1980–1990   3.1
Vacant Units for Sale or Rent   2,064
Occupied Units   42,131
% with More Than One Person per Room   2.1
% Owner-Occupied   56.6
Median Value of Owner-Occupied Homes $43,300
Average Monthly Purchase Cost $315
Median Monthly Rent $231
New Private Housing Starts   24
Value (in thousands) $1,399
% Single-Family   58.3
Nonresidential Buildings Value (in thousands) $6,618

Tallest Buildings	Hgt. (ft.)	Stories
None		

affordable, but maintenance costs are high because of long and severe winters.

Urban Redevelopment

Erie's most ambitious development project is Perry's Landing, approved in 1987, which includes a $120-million condominium. Niagara Place is a $17-million redevelopment that includes a hotel, shopping mall, and sports complex. The area closest to the waterfront has experienced the most extensive redevelopment.

Crime

Erie ranks as the 50th safest city in regard to crime. Of crimes known to police in 1991, 814 were violent crimes and 5,001 were property crimes.

Crime

Violent Crimes—Total   814
Violent Crime Rate per 100,000   374.2
Murder   7
Rape   96
Robbery   335
Aggravated Assaults   376
Property Crimes   5,001
Burglary   1,158
Larceny   3,413
Motor Vehicle Theft   430
Arson   60
Per Capita Police Expenditures $84.87
Per Capita Fire Protection Expenditures $75.33
Number of Police   203
Per 1,000   1.74

Religion

There are 171 churches and 2 synagogues in the city representing all denominations. Erie is the See City for the Roman Catholic Diocese and the Cathedral City for the Episcopal Diocese.

Religion

Largest Denominations (Adherents)	
Catholic	95,190
United Methodist	17,026
Evangelical Lutheran	13,701
Presbyterian	9,194
Black Baptist	3,478
American Baptist	3,572
Assembly of God	3,254
Jewish	800

Media

Erie has two daily newspapers: the *Erie Daily Times*, published weekday evenings, and the *Morning News*, published weekday mornings, and on Saturdays as the *Weekender*. The newspapers jointly publish the *Times News* on Sundays. There is also a weekly newspaper, the *Millcreek Sun*. The electronic media consist of 5 television stations and 4 AM and 5 FM radio stations. The television stations carry the three major networks, public broadcasting, and the Fox network (on a Gannon University–affiliated station). The radio stations carry a full complement of formats, including news/talk, public, Christian, and all types of music.

Media
Newsprint
Erie Daily Times, daily
Millcreek Sun, weekly
Television
WETG (Channel 66)
WICU (Channel 12)
WJET (Channel 24)
WQLN (Channel 54)
WSEE (Channel 35)
Radio
WERG (FM)   WEYZ (AM)
WJET (FM)   WLKK (AM)
WMXE (FM)   WPSE (AM)
WQLN (FM)   WRIE (AM)
WXKC (FM)

Sports

The Erie Sailors, an affiliate of the Texas Rangers, play professional baseball at Ainsworth Field from June through September. They plan to move into a new downtown stadium adjacent to the Civic Center for the 1994 season.

Arts, Culture, and Tourism

The Erie Arts Council is made up of the Erie Philharmonic, Erie Civic Music Association, Erie Playhouse, Erie Art Center, Dance Theater, Erie Civic Theater, and Lake Erie Ballet Company. Concerts and plays are presented regularly at the Civic Center, Warner Theater, Lincoln Theater, Studio 29, and local college theaters.

The Erie region has over ten museums. The largest is the Erie Arts Museum, located in the historic Old

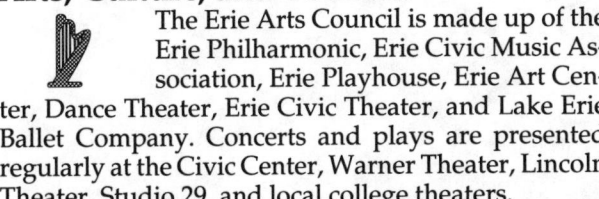

Travel and Tourism
Hotel Rooms   1,803
Convention and Exhibit Space (square feet)   NA
Convention Centers
Civic Center Complex
Festivals
Summer Festival of the Arts (June)
Wattsburg Fair (September)

Customs House. The Mad Anthony Wayne Memorial Blockhouse Museum, located on the grounds of the Soldiers and Sailors Home, is a replica of the blockhouse where the general died in 1796. Other major museums include the Firefighters Historical Museum, Erie Historical Museum and Planetarium, and Lake Shore Railway Museum.

Parks and Recreation

The 3,200-acre Presque Isle State Park is one of the most popular tourist attractions in Pennsylvania, drawing over 4 million tourists annually. There are 54 other parks and playgrounds, including Waldameer Park and Water World, the Millcreek parks (Asbury, Scott, Belle Valley, and Zuck), and Gravel Pit, Grotto, Raccoon Creek, Six-Mile Creek, Glenwood, W. L. Scott, and Turnwald parks.

Sources of Further Information

City Hall
626 State Street
Erie, PA 16501
(814) 870-1234

Economic Development Corporation of Erie County
2103 East 33rd Street
Erie, PA 16510
(814) 899-6022

Erie Area Chamber of Commerce
1006 State Street
Erie, PA 16501-1862
(814) 454-7191

Erie County Historical Society
417 State Street
Erie, PA 16501
(814) 454-1813

Erie Tourist and Convention Bureau
1006 State Street
Erie, PA 16501
(814) 454-7191

Additional Reading

Heathcliff, G. M., and Alvin K. Traz. *Memories of the Erie.* 1991.

Eugene

Oregon

Location and Topography

Eugene is located in the Willamette River Valley in the center of western Oregon, halfway between the Pacific Ocean and the Cascade Mountains. To the north the valley widens and levels out. The Coast Range begins about 5 miles to the west and rises to about 2,000 feet, while the Cascades, 75 miles to the east, rise to 10,000 feet. The Willamette River curves around the northwest corner of the city.

Layout of City and Suburbs

Eugene is a university town, dominated by the University of Oregon. The university campus occupies a tract of 100 acres between 11th and 18th streets and Alder and Agate streets. The city, like the university, has a parklike appearance with long rows of shade trees bordering its streets. Interstate 5 forms the eastern boundary of the city and Beltline Road its northern boundary. Pacific Highway and River Road enter the city from the northwest. In addition to the Willamette, a number of other rivers and creeks intersect the valley.

Environment

Environmental Stress Index   2.2
Green Cities Index: Rank   NA
                 Score   NA
Water Quality   Neutral, very soft
    Average Daily Use (gallons per capita)   176
    Maximum Supply (gallons per capita)   422
Parkland as % of Total City Area   NA
% Waste Landfilled/Recycled   NA
Annual Parks Expenditures per Capita $115.45

Climate

Eugene has a mild maritime climate. Temperatures rarely fall below 20°F or rise above 95°F. Seasonal change is gradual, and fall and spring last as long as summer and winter. Winters are warmed by prevailing winds from the southwest, and summers are cooled by northwestern winds. Most of the rain falls from October to May.

Weather

Temperature

Highest Monthly Average °F   82.6
Lowest Monthly Average °F   33.8

Annual Averages

Days 32°F or Below   54
Days above 90°F   15
Zero Degree Days   0
Precipitation (inches)   43
Snow (inches)   7.0
% Seasonal Humidity   77
Wind Speed (m.p.h.)   7.6

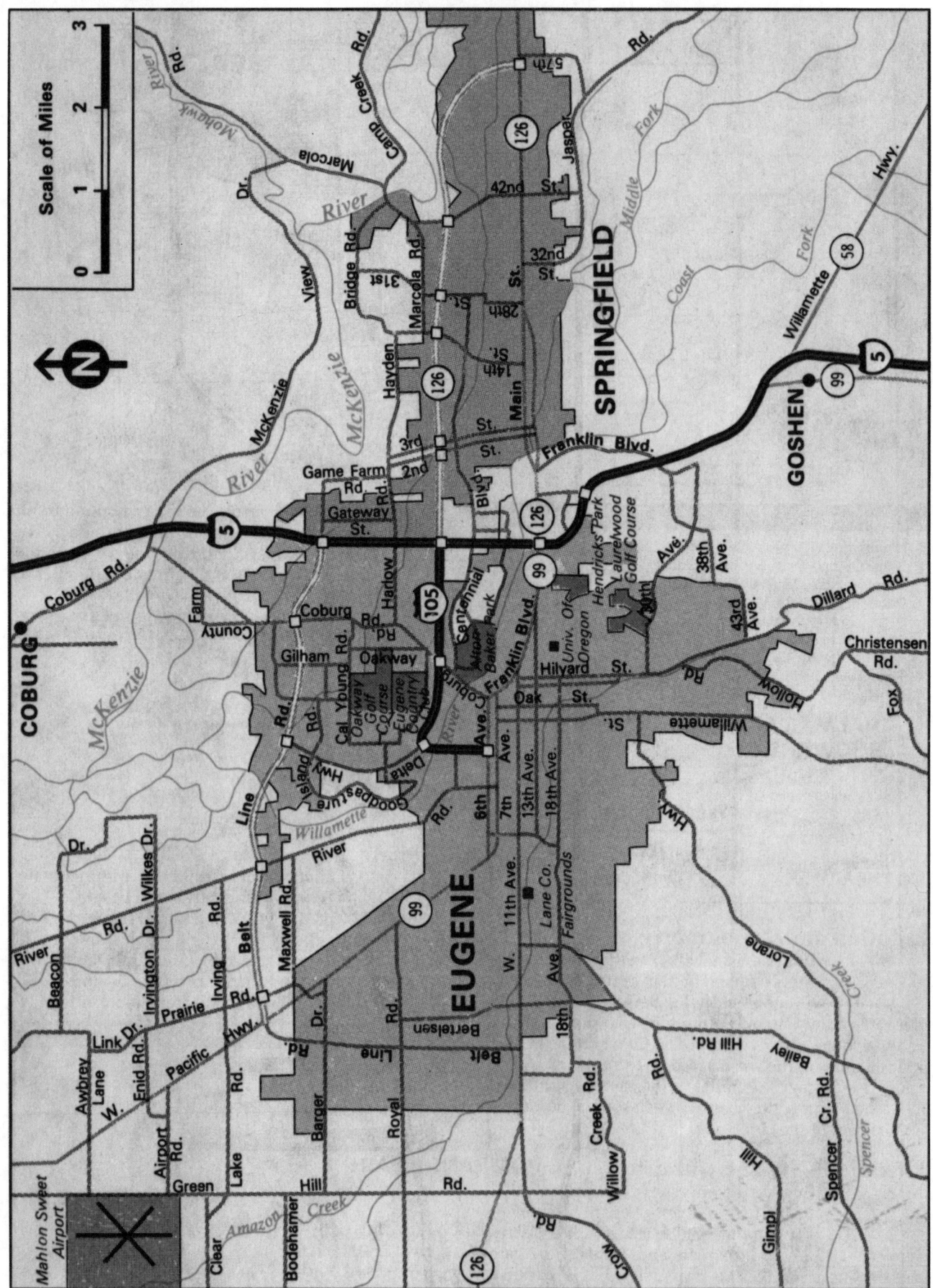

Weather (continued)			
Clear Days 77			
Cloudy Days 207			
Storm Days 5			
Rainy Days 137			
Average Temperatures (°F)	*High*	*Low*	*Mean*
January	45.6	33.1	39.4
February	51.7	35.2	43.5
March	55.2	36.5	45.9
April	61.2	39.4	50.3
May	67.8	43.7	55.8
June	74.1	48.7	61.4
July	82.6	51.1	66.9
August	81.3	50.9	66.1
September	76.5	47.4	62.0
October	64.0	42.3	53.2
November	53.1	38.1	45.6
December	47.4	35.6	41.5

History

Eugene was founded by Eugene F. Skinner in 1846. Skinner built a crude log cabin at the foot of a small peak called Ya-po-ah by the Indians, and Skinners Butte by later settlers. The small settlement that grew up at its base was first known as Skinners. The first building within the present city limits was that of Judge D. M. Risdon, erected in 1851. Skinner operated a ferry near the present Ferry Street Bridge and, with Risdon, platted a townsite in 1852. The first term of the U.S. District Court was held in 1852 in a bunkhouse originally built for loggers. By 1853 the town had a post office and schoolhouse. James Huddleston opened the first store. In the same year, the town was named the seat of newly formed Lane County, and Skinner donated 40 acres for the county offices.

The city, now renamed Eugene, was incorporated in 1862. Eugene was a candidate to become the state capital, but lost to Salem. In 1856 the Presbyterians decided to build Columbia College here. The next year, the *James Clinton* became the first steamer to ascend the Willamette River to Eugene. The town had no newspaper until 1862, when the *State Republican* began publication, followed by the *Democratic Register*. In 1871 the Oregon and California Railroad was completed. In 1872 the University of Oregon was founded, and the first class graduated in 1876. Lumbering became the principal economic activity, and the city buzzed with the sound of sawmills, shingle mills, planing mills, and box factories.

Historical Landmarks

A stone monument on Second Street marks the site of the first cabin, built by Eugene F. Skinner in 1846. A bronze marker at 11th Street marks the site of the first schoolhouse.

Population

Eugene has experienced a healthy growth since the end of World War II. During the 1970s, it grew by 33.7% from 79,000 in 1970 to 105,664 in 1980, crossing the magic 100,000 threshold in the late 1970s. Eugene continued to grow, although at a more modest pace of 6.6%, to reach 112,669 in 1990.

Population

	1980	1990
Central City	105,664	112,669
Rank	151	158
Metro Area	275,226	282,912
Pop. Change 1980–1990 +7,005		
Pop. % Change 1980–1990 +6.6		
Median Age 32.2		
% Male 48.1		
% Age 65 and Over 12.7		
Density (per square mile) 2,964		

Households

Number 46,274
Persons per Household 2.30
% Female-Headed Households 9.2
% One-Person Households 31
Births—Total 1,483
    % to Mothers under 20 6.5
    Birth Rate per 1,000 14.6

Ethnic Composition

Whites make up 93.4%, blacks 1.3%, American Indians 0.9%, Asians and Pacific Islanders 3.5%, and others 1%.

Ethnic Composition (as % of total pop.)

	1980	1990
White	94.56	93.43
Black	1.12	1.25
American Indian	0.80	0.89
Asian and Pacific Islander	1.94	3.46
Hispanic	2.08	2.71
Other	NA	0.97

Government

Under its 1905 charter, Eugene has a council-manager form of government with a mayor and eight council members elected every four years. The council appoints the city manager.

Government

Year of Home Charter 1905	
Number of Members of the Governing Body 8	
Elected at Large NA	
Elected by Wards 8	
Number of Women in Governing Body 3	
Salary of Mayor $0.0	
Salary of Council Members $0.0	
City Government Employment Total 1,500	
Rate per 10,000 142.3	

Chronology

1846 Eugene F. Skinner builds a crude log cabin at the foot of a mountain called Ya-po-ah.

1851 Judge D. M. Risdon becomes the first to build a dwelling in the settlement now known as Skinners.

1852 Skinner and Risdon plat a town. U.S. District Court holds first session in town.

1853 Skinners is renamed Eugene and designated seat of newly formed Lane County. Post office and school are established.

1856 Eugene loses to Salem in the race to be named state capital. Columbia College is founded by Presbyterians.

1857 *James Clinton* becomes first steamer to ascend the Willamette River to Eugene.

1862 Eugene is incorporated and the town's first two newspapers—the *State Republican* and the *Democratic Register*—are founded.

1871 The Oregon and California Railroad reaches town.

1872 University of Oregon is founded.

Public Finance

The annual budget consists of revenues of $241.291 million and expenditures of $244.329 million. Its outstanding debt is $638.812 million, and cash and securities holdings are $469.140 million.

Public Finance

Total Revenue (in millions) $241.292
Intergovernmental Revenue—Total (in millions) $15.21
Federal Revenue per Capita $3.74
% Federal Assistance   1.55
% State Assistance   2.44
Sales Tax as % of Total Revenue   NA
Local Revenue as % of Total Revenue   35.03
City Income Tax   no
Taxes—Total (in millions) $27.3

Taxes per Capita
  Total $259
  Property $236
  Sales and Gross Receipts $14
General Expenditures—Total (in millions) $77.3
General Expenditures per Capita $733
Capital Outlays per Capita $161

% of Expenditures for:
  Public Welfare   0.0
  Highways   19.7
  Education   0.0
  Health and Hospitals   0.0
  Police   9.8
  Sewerage and Sanitation   8.6

Public Finance (continued)

  Parks and Recreation   8.1
  Housing and Community Development   3.4
Debt Outstanding per Capita $2,313
  % Utility   80.6
Federal Procurement Contract Awards (in millions) $7.3
Federal Grants Awards (in millions) $54.2
Fiscal Year Begins   July 1

Economy

$ Eugene equals lumber in the industrial lexicon. Lumber, including plywood, is the largest industry and employs thousands of workers. Equally important is the agricultural sector, with the fertile Willamette Valley producing a variety of cash crops. More recently, manufacturing on a small scale has developed with strengths in metal fabrication.

Economy

Total Money Income (in millions) $1,086.2
% of State Average   103.8
Per Capita Annual Income $10,305
% Population below Poverty Level   14.7
Fortune 500 Companies   NA

Banks	Number	Deposits (in millions)
Commercial	11	NA
Savings	6	NA

Passenger Autos   237,045
Electric Meters   55,710
Gas Meters   14,500

Manufacturing

Number of Establishments   336
% with 20 or More Employees   23.2
Manufacturing Payroll (in millions) $180.3
Value Added by Manufacture (in millions) $346.8
Value of Shipments (in millions) $848.6
New Capital Expenditures (in millions) $17.7

Wholesale Trade

Number of Establishments   379
Sales (in millions) $1,324.4
Annual Payroll (in millions) $89.670

Retail Trade

Number of Establishments   1,507
Total Sales (in millions) $1,077.1
Sales per Capita $10,218
Number of Retail Trade Establishments with Payroll   1,103
Annual Payroll (in millions) $130.6
Total Sales (in millions) $1,060.9
General Merchandise Stores (per capita) $1,764
Food Stores (per capita) $1,551
Apparel Stores (per capita) $541
Eating and Drinking Places (per capita) $950

Service Industries

Total Establishments   1,475
Total Receipts (in millions) $461.8
Hotels and Motels (in millions) $18.3
Health Services (in millions) $152.3
Legal Services (in millions) $47.8

Labor

The environmental lobby has hurt Oregon's lumber industry, and Eugene is affected because of its dependence on lumber. Nevertheless, Eugene has a solid record in job creation and is expected to ride out the current recession by expanding into non-lumber sectors.

Labor

Civilian Labor Force   61,013
% Change 1989–1990   1.1

Work Force Distribution
    Mining   200
    Construction   4,000
    Manufacturing   19,000
    Transportation and Public Utilities   4,400
    Wholesale and Retail Trade   30,100
    FIRE (Finance, Insurance, Real Estate)   6,100
    Service   27,700
    Government   24,400
    Women as % of Labor Force   44.2
    % Self-Employed   8.6
    % Professional/Technical   22.8
Total Unemployment   2,942
Rate %   4.8
Federal Government Civilian Employment   1,170

Education

The Eugene School District supports 44 schools. Eugene also has a strong private and parochial school system. The

Education

Number of Public Schools   44
Special Education Schools   NA
Total Enrollment   17,904
% Enrollment in Private Schools   5.1
% Minority   NA
Classroom Teachers   NA
Pupil-Teacher Ratio   19:1
Number of Graduates   NA
Total Revenue (in millions)   NA
Total Expenditures (in millions)   NA
Expenditures per Pupil   NA
Educational Attainment (Age 25 and Over)   NA
    % Completed 12 or More Years   85.3
    % Completed 16 or More Years   33.7
Four-Year Colleges and Universities   2
    Enrollment   18,406
Two-Year Colleges   1
    Enrollment   8,762

Libraries

Number   12
Public Libraries   1
Books (in thousands)   253
Circulation (in thousands)   NA
Persons Served (in thousands)   NA
Circulation per Person Served   NA
Income (in millions) $2,225
Staff   52

Four-Year Colleges and Universities
    University of Oregon
    Northwest Christian College

University of Oregon has been the city's most distinguished institution since its founding in 1876, and has a pervasive influence that goes beyond the walls of academe. The other major four-year institution is Northwest Christian College.

Health

Three large hospitals serve Eugene. The premier facility is Sacred Heart General Hospital, with 422 beds. The other two are McKenzie Willamette Hospital and Eugene Clinic.

Health

Deaths—Total   807
Rate per 1,000   7.9
Infant Deaths—Total   10
Rate per 1,000   6.7
Number of Metro Hospitals   2
Number of Metro Hospital Beds   454
Rate per 100,000   431
Number of Physicians   421
Physicians per 1,000   NA
Nurses per 1,000   NA
Health Expenditures per Capita   NA

Transportation

Eugene is approached by the major West Coast interstate 5, which runs from Canada to Mexico. It is also served by U.S. highways 99 and 126 and state highways 36, 38, and 58. Rail passenger service is provided by Amtrak, and rail freight service by Burlington Northern and Southern Pacific. The principal air terminus is Mahlon Sweet Airport, nine miles north of the city.

Transportation

Interstate Highway Mileage   9
Total Urban Mileage   1,132
Total Daily Vehicle Mileage (in millions)   3.282
Daily Average Commute Time   38.7 min.
Number of Buses   57
Port Tonnage (in millions)   NA
Airports   1
Number of Daily Flights   26
Daily Average Number of Passengers   657

Airlines (American carriers only)
    American
    Horizon Air
    United
    Westair

Housing

Of the total stock of housing, 50.7% is owner-occupied. The median value of an owner-occupied home is $73,200 and the median monthly rent $375.

Housing

Total Housing Units 47,991
% Change 1980–1990 6.4
Vacant Units for Sale or Rent 1,315
Occupied Units 46,274
% with More Than One Person per Room 2.6
% Owner-Occupied 50.7
Median Value of Owner-Occupied Homes $73,200
Average Monthly Purchase Cost $390
Median Monthly Rent $375
New Private Housing Starts 1,434
Value (in thousands) $86,779
% Single-Family 31.7
Nonresidential Buildings Value (in thousands) $15,210

Urban Redevelopment

 Major urban redevelopment projects since the 1970s are the Downtown Mall, with over 180 retail outlets; Hult Center for the Performing Arts; Lane County Convention Center; and Eugene Conference Center. Urban redevelopment programs are coordinated by the Eugene Department of Development and Eugene Downtown Commission.

Crime

 Eugene ranks above the national average in public safety, with only 379 violent crimes known to police in 1991, and 8,673 property crimes in that same year.

Crime

Violent Crimes—Total 379
Violent Crime Rate per 100,000 298.4
Murder 3
Rape 59
Robbery 186
Aggravated Assaults 134
Property Crimes 8,673
Burglary 1,629
Larceny 6,630
Motor Vehicle Theft 414
Arson 106
Per Capita Police Expenditures $96.11
Per Capita Fire Protection Expenditures $72.90
Number of Police 132
Per 1,000 1.29

Religion

 About 27% of the population are church members, although not all are active.

Religion

Largest Denominations (Adherents)
Catholic 12,439
Latter-Day Saints 7,537
Evangelical Lutheran 4,356
Four-Square Gospel 4,946

Media

 The city daily is the *Register-Guard*. The electronic media consist of 3 television stations (commercial and independent) and 14 AM and FM radio stations.

Media

Newsprint
  Register-Guard, daily
Television
  KSCB (Channel 59)
  KEZI (Channel 9)
  KVAL (Channel 13)
Radio

KAVE (FM)	KDUK (AM)
KLCX (FM)	KEED (AM)
KHNN (AM)	KKXO (AM)
KMGE (FM)	KLCC (FM)
KPNW (AM)	KPNW (FM)
KRVM (FM)	KUGN (AM)
KUGN (FM)	KZEL (FM)

Sports

 The city's colors are carried in baseball by the Eugene Emeralds, a minor league team. The University of Oregon has strong teams in virtually every sport.

Arts, Culture, and Tourism

 The Hult Center for the Performing Arts is the venue for most cultural activities. Theater is represented by Mainstage Theater, Oregon Repertory Theater, and Second Season Theater. Dance is represented by the Eugene Ballet Company and music by the Eugene Symphony Orchestra, Eugene Opera, and Eugene Festival of Music Theater. Summer concerts are held at Cuthbert Amphitheater in Alton Baker Park.

The major museums are the Lane County Historical Museum, University of Oregon Museum of Art, and Willamette Science and Technology Center. The Maude Kerns Art Center showcases local artists.

Travel and Tourism

Hotel Rooms 3,550
Convention and Exhibit Space (square feet) NA
Convention Centers
  Lane County Convention Center
  Eugene Conference Center
  Hult Center for the Performing Arts
Festivals
  Oregon Bach Festival (June-July)

Parks and Recreation

 The Willamette riverbanks are lined with miles of scenic parks and picnic areas such as the Owens Memorial Rose Garden and Hendricks Park Rhododendron Garden.

Sources of Further Information

City Hall
777 Pearl Street
Eugene, OR 97401
(503) 687-5010

Eugene Area Chamber of Commerce
1401 Willamette Street
Eugene, OR 97401
(503) 484-1314

Eugene-Springfield Convention and Vistors Bureau
305 West Seventh Street
Eugene, OR 97401
(503) 484-5307

Additional Reading

Eugene-Springfield, Oregon. Cross-Reference Directory.
  1991.

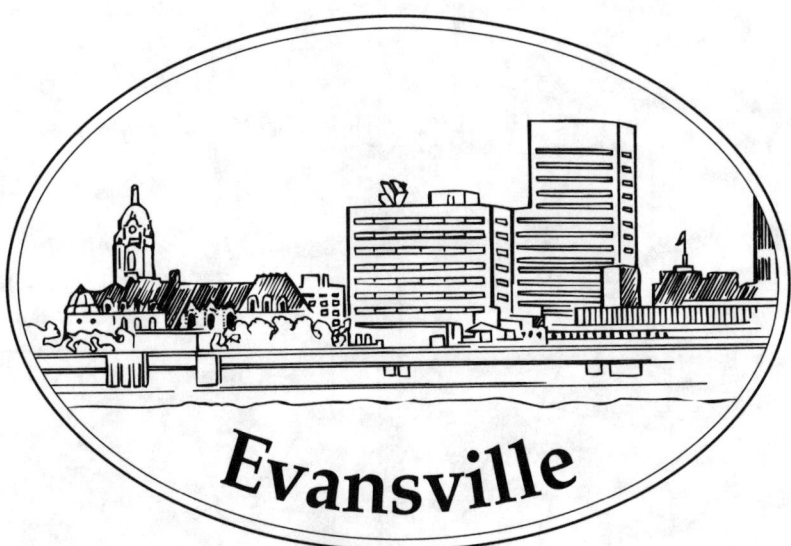

Evansville

Indiana

Basic Data

Name   Evansville
Name Origin   From General Robert Evans
Year Founded   1818 Inc. 1819
Status: State   Indiana
        County   Seat of Vanderburgh County
Area (square miles)   40.7
Elevation (feet)   385
Time Zone   EST
Population (1990)   126,272
Population of Metro Area (1990)   278,990

Sister Cities
    Osnabruck,Germany

Distance in Miles To:
Indianapolis	186
St. Louis	174
Nashville	151
Louisville	112
Fort Wayne	318

Location and Topography

N

Evansville is located at the mouth of Pigeon Creek on the north bank of the Ohio River halfway between the Falls of the Ohio and the Ohio River's estuary, in a shallow valley at the southwestern tip of Indiana. The valley opens on to the river to the south, but to the north, east, and west the flat rolling terrain is surrounded by low hills.

Layout of City and Suburbs

Evansville is a river town, and it has one of the best harbors on inland waterways. The city's terrain is level except for the hills in the northwest. The Evansville-Henderson Bridge in the southeast and the Forest Hills section in the west afford a panoramic view of the great horseshoe bend

of the waterfront. The center of the business district is on Main Street for about ten blocks back from the river. A second mercantile area is on Franklin Street—the only through east-west street—across the Pigeon Creek Bridge. Streets in the small downtown section run northwest to southeast and southwest to northeast parallel and at right angles to the northeast segment of the horseshoe curve of the river. This is the original Evansville. As the city grew, later streets were laid out north-south and east-west. The colonial mansions of early Evansville are along southeast Second Avenue.

Environment

Environmental Stress Index   2.6
Green Cities Index: Rank   NA
               Score   NA
Water Quality   Alkaline, hard, fluoridated
    Average Daily Use (gallons per capita)   NA
    Maximum Supply (gallons per capita)   NA
Parkland as % of Total City Area   NA
% Waste Landfilled/Recycled   NA
Annual Parks Expenditures per Capita $69.37

Climate

Although Evansville is 550 miles from the Gulf of Mexico, its weather is determined primarily by moisture-bearing low-pressure formations that move across the area from the western Gulf region northeastward across the Mississippi and Ohio valleys to the Great Lakes. Strong cold winds sometimes blow from the north and northwest following cold fronts. When the high-pressure systems move by, the wind backs around again from the south. Snowfall varies from year to year, but accumulation is rare. Wind damage and hail are common but severe storms and tornadoes are infrequent.

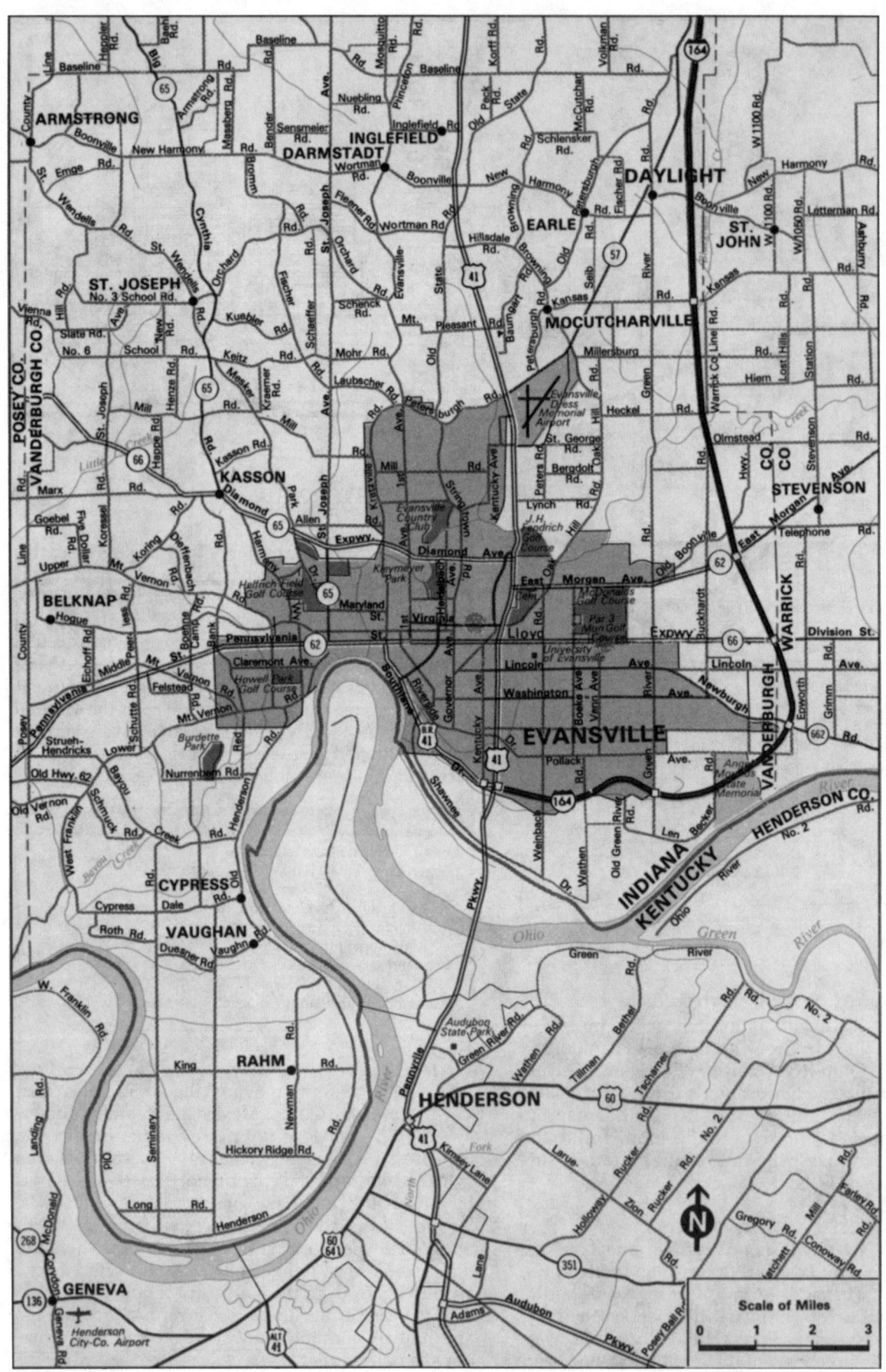

Weather

Temperature

Highest Monthly Average °F   88.8
Lowest Monthly Average °F   21.9

Annual Averages

Days 32°F or Below   103
Days above 90°F   39
Zero Degree Days   3
Precipitation (inches)   42
Snow (inches)   13.0
% Seasonal Humidity   70
Wind Speed (m.p.h.)   8.3
Clear Days   103
Cloudy Days   162
Storm Days   45
Rainy Days   114

Average Temperatures (°F)	High	Low	Mean
January	41.5	23.7	32.6
February	45.4	26.4	35.9
March	54.6	34.0	44.3
April	67.9	45.5	56.7
May	77.0	54.4	65.7
June	86.0	63.4	74.7
July	88.9	66.7	77.8
August	88.0	64.4	76.2
September	81.4	56.7	69.1
October	71.2	45.2	58.2
November	55.2	34.5	44.9
December	44.0	26.5	35.3

History

The first settler on the great U-bend of the Ohio River where Evansville is located was Colonel Hugh McGary who built his cabin at the foot of present-day Main Street. He started a ferry at this point, primarily so he could visit his wife's relatives in Henderson (then Red Banks). In 1814 the settlement became the seat of Warrick County, but lost the honor almost immediately. In 1818 McGary sold the settlement to General Robert Evans and James W. Jones, selling the section above Main Street to the former. The town was then replatted, named Evansville, and made the seat of the newly created Vanderburgh County. When the town was incorporated in 1819 it had a population of 200. The coming of the steamboat opened a golden age for Evansville. The Robert Fulton invention first appeared here in 1809; by 1822 the steamboats had displaced the earlier flatboats for river traffic. Nevertheless, the city experienced a number of reverses, such as the depression of 1824–1829, milk sickness and cholera epidemics, and the freezing winter of 1831–1832 when the Ohio River froze to a depth of 22 inches, followed by disastrous spring floods. In 1832, Colonel McGary, the town's founding father, was charged with horse stealing and forced to flee town. New prosperity followed the construction of the Wabash and Erie Canal, of which Evansville was the southern terminus. By 1848 when Evansville was incorporated as a city, its population had grown to 4,000. Although the canal itself was a financial failure, canal trade led to the establishment of numerous factories, foundries, flour mills, and saw mills in Evansville. In 1853 the first railroad arrived from Princeton. After the Civil War Evansville became a manufacturing and transportation center for southern Indiana. The population reached 50,756 in 1890 and 85,000 in 1920. The city again suffered floods in 1884, 1913, and 1937. After the 1937 flood, which covered almost half of the town, huge levees were erected to prevent a recurrence.

Historical Landmarks

The Willard Carpenter Homestead on the corner of Third, Ingle, and Carpenter streets is a fine example of Georgian architecture, built in 1848. The Willard Library was a gift to the city by Willard Carpenter. The Old Vanderburgh County Courthouse has dominated Evansville's skyline since its completion in 1890. It currently serves as the home of the Evansville Dance Theater, the Repertory People, several art galleries, an antique mall, and offices. The Soldiers and Sailors Memorial Coliseum on NW Fourth and Court streets is a tribute to the men of Vanderburgh County who fought in the Civil and Spanish-American wars. The Old Post Office and Customshouse on Second Street is a Ruskinian Gothic built in 1875–1879. It was vacated by the federal government in 1969 and now houses offices, shops, restaurants, and bars. The John Augustus Reitz Home on First and Chestnut streets, built in 1871, is one of Evansville's grandest Victorian houses. It was for many years the residence of the bishop of the Evansville Archdiocese. St. Mary's Catholic Church on Cherry Street, built in 1867, has been the center of downtown parish life for over a century.

Population

Evansville's population in 1990 was 126,272, a decline of 3.2% from its 1980 population of 130,496. The decline continued a trend that began in 1970, when the population was 139,000, but the rate of decline has slowed from the 1970s.

Population

	1980	1990
Central City	130,496	126,272
Rank	121	144
Metro Area	276,252	278,990
Pop. Change 1980–1990 -4,224		
Pop. % Change 1980–1990 -3.2		
Median Age 34.5		
% Male 46.4		
% Age 65 and Over 17.2		
Density (per square mile) 3,157		

Households

Number   52,948
Persons per Household   2.30
% Female-Headed Households   12.8
% One-Person Households   32.9
Births—Total   1,954
    % to Mothers under 20   14.8
    Birth Rate per 1,000   15.0

Chronology

1812 Colonel Hugh McGary builds cabin at the foot of present-day Main Street and starts a ferry across the river.

1814 Settlement is made seat of Warrick County but is almost immediately stripped of that status.

1818 McGary sells section above Main Street to General Robert Evans, who replats the town and names it after himself. Evansville is made seat of newly formed Vanderburgh County.

1819 Evansville is incorporated as a town.

1831–1832 Ohio River freezes to a depth of 22 inches, resulting in a disastrous flood when the snow and ice melted. Colonel McGary, charged with horse stealing, is forced to leave town.

1848 Evansville is chartered as a city.

1853 The first train arrives as well as the first canal boat from Petersburg.

1937 Evansville suffers another disastrous flood, after which huge levees are erected along riverfront.

Ethnic Composition

Whites make up 89.6%, blacks 9.5%, American Indians 0.2%, Asian and Pacific Islanders 0.6%, and others 0.1% of the population.

Ethnic Composition (as % of total pop.)	1980	1990
White	90.36	89.56
Black	8.83	9.53
American Indian	0.14	0.19
Asian and Pacific Islander	0.41	0.57
Hispanic	0.49	0.58
Other	NA	0.16

Government

Evansville is governed by a mayor and a Common Council, the nine members of which are elected to four-year terms, six from wards and three at large. The mayor, who is not a member of the council, is the chief executive officer. Appointed boards oversee all municipal operations.

Public Finance

The annual budget consists of revenues of $73.108 million and expenditures of $84.589 million. The debt outstanding is $63.082 million, and cash and security reserves are $53.589 million.

Government

Year of Home Charter   1982
Number of Members of the Governing Body   9
Elected at Large   3
Elected by Wards   6
Number of Women in Governing Body   2
Salary of Mayor $53,141
Salary of Council Members $10,001
City Government Employment Total   1,300
Rate per 10,000   100.4

Public Finance

Total Revenue (in millions) $73.108
Intergovernmental Revenue—Total (in millions) $16.29
Federal Revenue per Capita $3.93
% Federal Assistance   5.38
% State Assistance   15.94
Sales Tax as % of Total Revenue   NA
Local Revenue as % of Total Revenue   61.37
City Income Tax   no
Taxes—Total (in millions) $16.8

Taxes per Capita
    Total $130
    Property $127
    Sales and Gross Receipts $0
General Expenditures—Total (in millions) $53.0
General Expenditures per Capita $410
Capital Outlays per Capita $37

% of Expenditures for:
    Public Welfare   NA
    Highways   9.6
    Education   0.0
    Health and Hospitals   2.7
    Police   12.4
    Sewerage and Sanitation   14.0
    Parks and Recreation   6.1
    Housing and Community Development   10.9
Debt Outstanding per Capita $357
    % Utility   10.8
Federal Procurement Contract Awards (in millions) $15.3
Federal Grants Awards (in millions) $10.0
Fiscal Year Begins   January 1

Economy

Evansville is the primary industrial and transportation center for a 36-county region in the three states of Indiana, Kentucky, and Illinois. Originally a farming center, Evansville still remains a marketing and distribution center for a wide variety of agricultural products from the Midwest farm belt. Its industrial history has gone through many phases. The closure of the old Servel and Chrysler factories in the 1950s has been made up

Economy

Total Money Income (in millions) $1,296.2
% of State Average   100.7
Per Capita Annual Income $10,048
% Population below Poverty Level   12.2
Fortune 500 Companies   NA

Banks	Number	Deposits (in millions)
Commercial	3	1,982.9
Savings	6	1,179.9

Passenger Autos   95,436
Electric Meters   81,836
Gas Meters   58,315

Economy (continued)

Manufacturing

Number of Establishments 220
% with 20 or More Employees 39.1
Manufacturing Payroll (in millions) $554.2
Value Added by Manufacture (in millions) $1,915.6
Value of Shipments (in millions) $3,056.8
New Capital Expenditures (in millions) NA

Wholesale Trade

Number of Establishments 415
Sales (in millions) $1,702.0
Annual Payroll (in millions) $122.887

Retail Trade

Number of Establishments 1,620
Total Sales (in millions) $1,303.2
Sales per Capita $10,065
Number of Retail Trade Establishments with Payroll 1,173
Annual Payroll (in millions) $162.0
Total Sales (in millions) $1,285.3
General Merchandise Stores (per capita) NA
Food Stores (per capita) $1,724
Apparel Stores (per capita) NA
Eating and Drinking Places (per capita) $1,102

Service Industries

Total Establishments 1,213
Total Receipts (in millions) $516.0
Hotels and Motels (in millions) NA
Health Services (in millions) $171.1
Legal Services (in millions) $27.5

for by the arrival of Whirlpool, GE Plastics, ALCOA, and Bristol-Myers Squibb. Older privately held firms like Koch and Karges Furniture remain strong. Evansville also is located in the heart of an oil basin and rich coal fields. Nearly 150 oil companies and oil-related firms are located in the city. There is a strong financial sector led by American General Finance.

Labor

Manufacturing, services, and trade are the three largest employment sectors, with Whirlpool and Bristol-Myers Squibb as the largest employers. However, manufacturing em-

Labor

Civilian Labor Force 66,851
% Change 1989–1990 -1.0

Work Force Distribution
Mining 2,100
Construction 7,400
Manufacturing 30,800
Transportation and Public Utilities 6,800
Wholesale and Retail Trade 34,400
FIRE (Finance, Insurance, Real Estate) 5,800
Service 35,000
Government 13,700
Women as % of Labor Force 44.5
% Self-Employed 4.1
% Professional/Technical 12.9
Total Unemployment 3,995
Rate % 6.0
Federal Government Civilian Employment 769

ployment is on a falling curve while employment in trade and services is on a rising curve, reflecting a national trend.

Evansville is a union town with a high degree of unionization.

Education

The Evansville-Vanderburgh School Corporation supports 38 schools. Alternative education is offered by 18 private and parochial schools. Two universities provide higher education: the University of Evansville, a Methodist-affiliated private institution founded in 1854; and the University of Southern Indiana, a public institution. In addition, IVY Tech, ITT Technical Institute, and Lockyear College offer technical and industrial training.

Education

Number of Public Schools 38
Special Education Schools NA
Total Enrollment 22,918
% Enrollment in Private Schools 13.3
% Minority 14.6
Classroom Teachers 1,365
Pupil-Teacher Ratio 16.9:1
Number of Graduates 1,454
Total Revenue (in millions) $84.1
Total Expenditures (in millions) $88.3
Expenditures per Pupil $3,724
Educational Attainment (Age 25 and Over)
    % Completed 12 or More Years 61.1
    % Completed 16 or More Years 11.2
Four-Year Colleges and Universities 2
    Enrollment 9,531
Two-Year Colleges 1
    Enrollment 2,525

Libraries

Number 26
Public Libraries 9
Books (in thousands) 587
Circulation (in thousands) NA
Persons Served (in thousands) NA
Circulation per Person Served NA
Income (in millions) $4.293
Staff 134

Four-Year Colleges and Universities
    University of Evansville
    University of Southern Indiana

Health

The health-care sector includes five hospitals, with 2,024 beds and 465 physicians. St. Mary's Medical Center is an acute care facility; Welborn Baptist Hospital, a comprehensive care facility; and Deaconess Hospital, a tertiary care facility. Other facilities include Evansville Psychiatric Children's Center, Evansville State Hospital, and Southwest Indiana Mental Health Center.

Health

Deaths—Total   1,678
Rate per 1,000   12.9
Infant Deaths—Total   21
Rate per 1,000   10.7
Number of Metro Hospitals   5
Number of Metro Hospital Beds   2,024
Rate per 100,000   1,563
Number of Physicians   465
Physicians per 1,000   NA
Nurses per 1,000   NA
Health Expenditures per Capita $14.43

Transportation

There are six highway systems leading to and from Evansville: the eastwest I-64 provides access to Louisville and St. Louis; the north-south U.S. 41 connects with I-64 and the Kentucky Parkway System; I-164 connects I-64 and Indiana 57 with U.S. 41 south of Evansville; Indiana 62 and State Road 66 provide east-west access; and Indiana 57 provides access to the northeast. Rail freight service is provided by CSX Transportation, Conrail, Norfolk Southern Corporation, and Indiana Hi-Rail. Valley Terminal transships goods between railroad cars and trucks to river barges. Evansville was a major river port in the 19th century and, although river traffic has diminished in importance, it still contributes to the role of Evansville as a distribution center. There are five barge lines and two barge terminals: Southwind, 15 miles to the west at Mt. Vernon, and Valley Terminal. The principal air terminal is the Evansville Regional Airport, serviced by six airlines with more than 40 flights a day.

Transportation

Interstate Highway Mileage   9
Total Urban Mileage   969
Total Daily Vehicle Mileage (in millions)   2.998
Daily Average Commute Time   40.9
Number of Buses   20
Port Tonnage (in millions)   NA
Airports   1
Number of Daily Flights   8
Daily Average Number of Passengers   344

Airlines (American carriers only)
  Trans World
  USAir

Housing

The housing stock consists of 52,948 owner-occupied dwellings, 25,435 renter-occupied ones, and 310 condominiums; 32% of the houses were built before 1949 and 7% between 1975 and 1980. Rent for a two-bedroom apartment is $320–$385. Housing costs are nearly 10% below the national average.

Housing

Total Housing Units   58,188
% Change 1980–1990   6.8
Vacant Units for Sale or Rent   3,865
Occupied Units   52,948
% with More Than One Person per Room   2.0
% Owner-Occupied   59.0
Median Value of Owner-Occupied Homes $45,500
Average Monthly Purchase Cost $273
Median Monthly Rent $264
New Private Housing Starts   104
Value (in thousands) $6,708
% Single-Family   100
Nonresidential Buildings Value (in thousands) $15,386

Urban Redevelopment

Evansville has been investing millions of dollars in refurbishing downtown. Construction at the new Crosse Point Commerce Center, a 183-acre mixed-use development, began in 1990. Medical facilities are contributing heavily to redevelopment with an $8.1-million expansion of the Welborn Hospital, begun in 1991; a $3-million new building for St. Mary's Medical Center, begun in 1991; and a $15–$30-million new medical complex for the Deaconess Hospital, begun in 1992. Spearheading the redevelopment programs is Vision 2000, a unique coalition of private and public interests that is charting a new course for the future of Evansville.

Crime

Evansville ranks high in public safety. In 1991 the violent crimes known to police were 788 and the property crimes were 6,870.

Crime

Violent Crimes—Total   788
Violent Crime Rate per 100,000   584.9
Murder   12
Rape   45
Robbery   139
Aggravated Assaults   592
Property Crimes   6,870
Burglary   1,638
Larceny   4,776
Motor Vehicle Theft   456
Arson   54
Per Capita Police Expenditures $69.14
Per Capita Fire Protection Expenditures $70.18
Number of Police   231
Per 1,000   1.77

Religion

The religious community comprises 325 churches, one synagogue, and one mosque. The Christian churches are represented in the Evansville Area Council of Churches.

Religion	
Largest Denominations (Adherents)	
Catholic	29,867
Southern Baptist	20,630
United Church of Christ	8,711
United Methodist	8,596
Black Baptist	4,055
Lutheran-Missouri Synod	3,543
Presbyterian	2,478
American Baptist	1,997
Evangelical Lutheran	1,842
Jewish	520

Media

The Evansville press consists of the morning *Evansville Courier*, the evening *Evansville Press*, and the *Sunday Courier*. The electronic media consist of 6 television stations (3 commercial network, 2 public, and 1 independent) and 10 AM and FM stations.

Media	
Newsprint	
Evansville Courier, daily	
Evansville Press, daily	
Television	
WEVV (Channel 44)	
WFIE (Channel 14)	
WTVW (Channel 7)	
Radio	
WGBF (FM)	WIKY (AM)
WIKY (FM)	WNIN (FM)
WPSR (FM)	WSWI (AM)
WUEV (FM)	WVHI (AM)
WWOK (AM)	WYNG (FM)

Sports

Evansville is not represented by a team in any major professional sport. The major sports for the spectator here are horse racing (Ellis Park and Riverside Downs) and hydroplane racing on the Ohio River (during the Freedom Festival).

Arts, Culture, and Tourism

Theatrical productions are presented by two theatrical groups: the Repertory People, performing at the Old Courthouse, and the Evansville Civic Theater. Musical entertainment is offered by the Philharmonic Orchestra, Philharmonic Chorus, Symphonic Band, Master Chorale, and Phi Mu Alpha Sinfonia Fraternity. The Dance Theater and the Childrens Theater are also active.

The Evansville Museum of Arts and Science is located on the Ohio riverfront. It includes Rivertown

U.S.A. and a complete steam railroad exhibit. Angel Mound is a large prehistoric American Indian town dating from 1300. Occupied formerly by Middle Mississippian Indians, the Central Mound site is one of the largest prehistoric structures in the nation. Historic New Harmony was a religious utopian community founded in 1814 and sold to Robert Owen in 1824. The John James Audubon Museum is five miles south of Evansville.

Travel and Tourism	
Hotel Rooms 2,401	
Convention and Exhibit Space (square feet) NA	
Convention Centers	
Vanderburgh Auditorium Convention Center	
Robert E. Green Convention Center	
Roberts Stadium	
Festivals	
Freedom Festival (July)	

Parks and Recreation

Evansville has 2,000 acres of parkland at 60 sites throughout the city. The most popular is the 212-acre Mesker Municipal Park. The 145-acre Burdette Park offers a multitude of recreational activities. The 20-acre Wesselman Woods Nature Preserve is located within city limits.

Sources of Further Information

City Hall
1 NW Martin Luther King Boulevard
Evansville, IN 47708
(812) 426-5581

Evansville Convention and Visitors Bureau
715 Locust Street
Evansville, IN 47708
(812) 425-5402

Evansville-Vanderburgh County Public Library
22 SE Fifth Street
Evansville, IN 47708
(812) 428-8200

Metropolitan Evansville Chamber of Commerce
100 West Second Street
Evansville, IN 47708
(812) 425-8147

Additional Reading

Evansville Cross Reference Directory. 1991.
Polk's Evansville City Directory. 1991.

Fargo

North Dakota

Location and Topography

Fargo is located on the eastern boundary of North Dakota, about 180 miles east of Bismarck, the capital, along the Red River of the North in the Red River Valley. The Red River, part of the Hudson Bay drainage area, flows between the so-called twin cities of Fargo and Moorhead, Minnesota. Fargo's terrain, once an icebed called Lake Agassiz, is now flat and open.

Layout of City and Suburbs

The Red River of the North is the boundary between Fargo and Moorhead, Minnesota. Thus, much of Fargo's contour depends on this curved, winding border. The city is oblong-shaped, ranging from a wide, expansive southern periphery to a semitriangle at its northern end, this last dictated by the confines of the Burlington Northern Railroad's tracks and Hector International Airport. The downtown area is cut in half by I-94 and U.S. 52, and is edged on the west by I-29. In addition to West Fargo and Moorhead in Minnesota, Fargo's suburbs include Gardner and Casselton.

Climate

Summers in Fargo are generally comfortable, with the few days of hot and humid weather being offset by cool nights. Winter is cold and dry with maximum temperatures rising above freezing only about six times a month. At night the temperature drops below zero half the time. Snowfall is light, typically 36 inches a year. However, the strong winds that blow unimpeded across the flat terrain cause Fargo's legendary blizzards, even when snowfall is light. Rainfall is concentrated in the growing season from April through

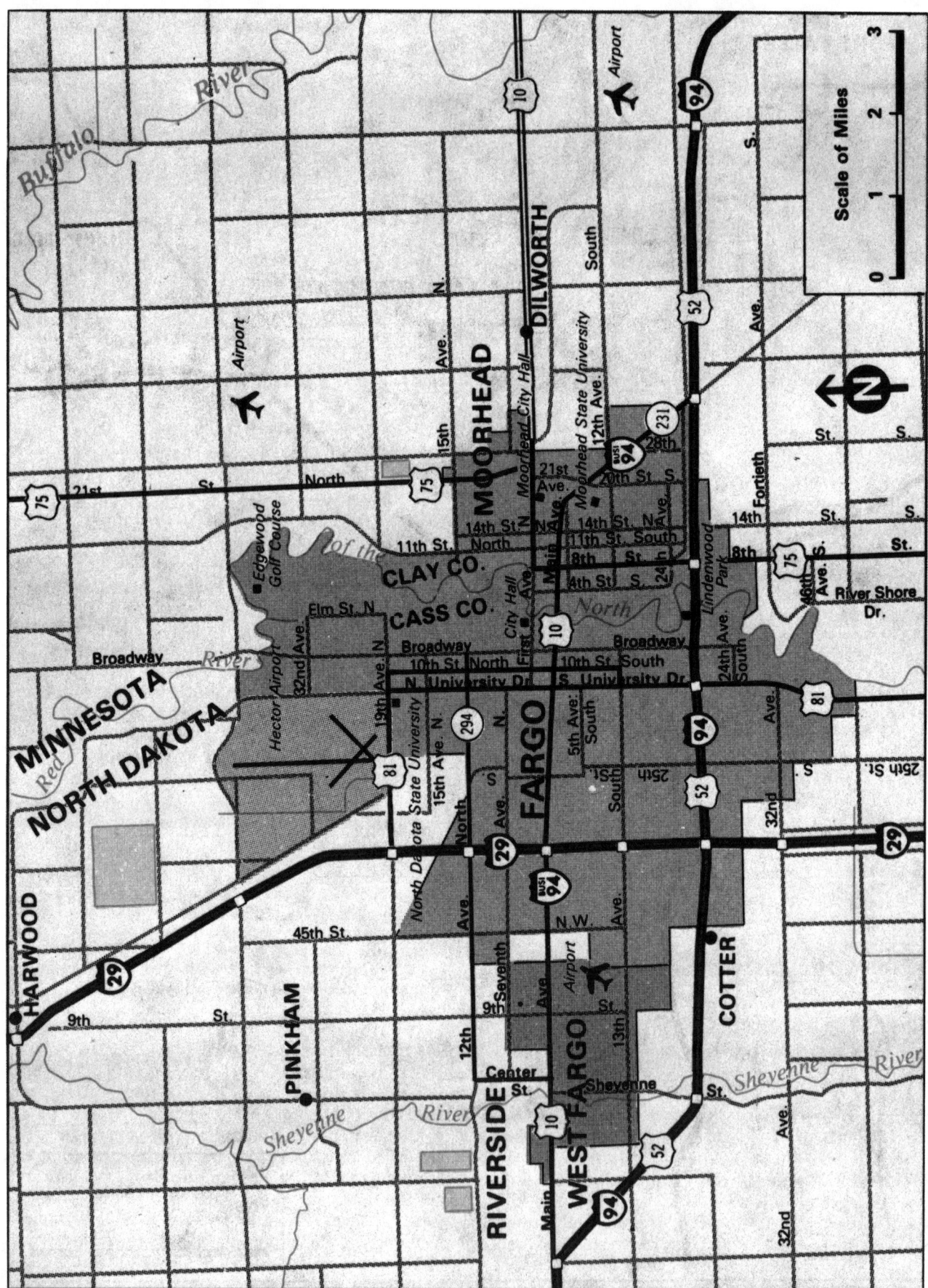

Weather

Temperature

Highest Monthly Average °F 82.7
Lowest Monthly Average °F 5.1

Annual Averages

Days 32°F or Below 179
Days above 90°F 15
Zero Degree Days 54
Precipitation (inches) 19.59
Snow (inches) 35.9
% Seasonal Humidity 72
Wind Speed (m.p.h.) 12.4
Clear Days 88
Cloudy Days 168
Storm Days 33
Rainy Days 102

Average Temperatures (°F)	High	Low	Mean
January	15.4	3.6	5.9
February	20.6	0.8	10.7
March	33.5	14.9	24.2
April	52.6	31.9	42.3
May	66.8	42.3	54.6
June	75.9	53.4	64.7
July	82.8	58.6	70.7
August	81.6	56.8	69.2
September	69.6	46.2	57.9
October	58.4	35.5	47.0
November	37.2	20.0	28.6
December	21.9	4.1	13.0

September. Thunderstorms and squalls are common then.

History

The first Europeans to investigate the Red River of the North area that is now Fargo apparently were several men who set out in 1820 from the settlement at Lower Fort Garry (now Winnipeg, Manitoba) to purchase grain. Led by Thomas Douglas, the Fifth Earl of Selkirk, they explored the Fargo portion of the Red River during their travels. Little more was done in the area until the St. Paul, Minnesota, Chamber of Commerce offered $2,000 to anyone who could open a successful ferry along the Red River. The challenge was taken up in 1859 by one Anson Northrup, whose boat (which was named after him) traveled up the Red River from Georgetown (presently just north of Moorhead, Minnesota) to Fort Garry and back in 16 days. Although Northrup's feat earned him the prize, the area that is now Fargo was not opened up for settlement, even though no Indian tribes lived there. In 1864 Congress commissioned the Northern Pacific Railway, and it began to make its way across the continent. By 1871, it had reached the area that is now Fargo. On 6 June 1872, the first train crossed the tracks of the Northern Pacific into what was then the Dakota Territory. A settlement was started and named after William Garroway Fargo, one of the directors of the Northern Pacific and later a founder of the Wells-Fargo Express Company.

For its first decade, Fargo was little more than a train stop. In 1873, the Northern Pacific had failed and for a time it seemed that the new settlement would die

out. In 1879, General George Cass revived the Northern Pacific and began an all-out program to attract settlers to the Red River area. These pioneers worked on small farms extracting wheat and other commodities from the soil. By 1880, the population of Fargo was 2,693.

Fargo experienced a building boom in the last two decades of the 19th century, but much of that was destroyed in the Great Fire of 1893, which wiped out much of the business district and northeast section of the city. Although the damage was estimated at $4 million, rebuilding was soon under way, this time using brick instead of wood for building.

In the 20th century, Fargo became a leading center for agribusiness. The North Dakota Agricultural College (now North Dakota State University) was opened in 1890 as part of an effort to teach new methods of farming. In 1917, the Equity Cooperative Exchange opened as a forum for agriculture while operating as a packing plant. The location of the Exchange led to the growth of the suburb of West Fargo.

Historical Landmarks

Fargo's downtown landmarks are all embraced in a tour called the Discovery Walk. Along the tour is the Northern Pacific Railway Depot, deLendrecie's Department Store, the Gothic Luger Department Store, the Victorian Masonic Block, and the Classic Revivalist Watkins Block. Also on the tour are the headquarters building of the Burlington Northern Railroad and the Black Building, the tallest structure in the downtown historic district. Among houses of worship, the First United Methodist Church and St. Mary's Cathedral rank among the oldest.

Population

The population of Fargo in 1990 was 74,111, a gain of 20.7% over its 1980 population of 61,383.

Population

	1980	1990
Central City	61,383	74,111
Rank	329	294
Metro Area	137,574	153,296
Pop. Change 1980–1990 +12,728		
Pop. % Change 1980–1990 +20.7		
Median Age 29.4		
% Male 49.6		
% Age 65 and Over 10.1		
Density (per square mile) 2,486		

Households

Number 30,149
Persons per Household 2.32
% Female-Headed Households 7.7
% One-Person Households 31.4
Births—Total 1,053
  % to Mothers under 20 4.7
  Birth Rate per 1,000 16.0

Chronology

1820 European explorers from the settlement at Lower Fort Garry (now Winnipeg, Manitoba) traverse the Red River of the North along the area of present-day Fargo.

1859 Responding to a challenge, Captain Anson Northrup sails his self-named ship from Georgetown (just north of Fargo) to Fort Garry and back in 16 days to win $2,000.

1872 The first train from the Northern Pacific Railway crosses into Dakota Territory on the site of Fargo. The settlement that is started there is named after William Garroway Fargo, a director of the Northern Pacific.

1873 The Northern Pacific Railway goes out of business. Fargo seems destined to fail as a community.

1879 General George Cass sees the railroad out of receivership and begins pitching Fargo as an ideal place for settlers.

1880 The population of Fargo reaches 2,693.

1890 A year after the Enabling Act of 1889, the North Dakota Agricultural College (now North Dakota State University) starts classes.

1893 Fire wipes out large sections of the city with damage estimated at $4 million.

1917 The Equity Cooperative Exchange begins as a packing plant. The town of West Fargo eventually springs up around it.

Ethnic Composition

Whites make up 97.1%, blacks 0.4%, American Indians 1.1%, Asian and Pacific Islanders 1.3%, and others 0.2%.

Ethnic Composition (as % of total pop.)		
	1980	1990
White	98.13	97.11
Black	0.19	0.35
American Indian	0.65	1.07
Asian and Pacific Islander	0.53	1.25
Hispanic	0.60	0.73
Other	NA	0.21

Government

Fargo is governed under a mayor/commission system. The commission consists of five members, one of whom serves as the mayor. Commissioners are elected at large to four-year terms. Each commissioner is responsible for a portfolio of departments.

Government	
Year of Home Charter	1970
Number of Members of the Governing Body	5
Elected at Large	5
Elected by Wards	NA
Number of Women in Governing Body	0
Salary of Mayor	NA
Salary of Council Members	NA
City Government Employment Total	534
Rate per 10,000	78.5

Public Finance

The annual budget consists of revenues of $48.421 million and expenditures of $37.004 million. The debt outstanding is $112.625 million, and cash and security reserves are $65.862 million.

Public Finance	
Total Revenue (in millions)	$48.421
Intergovernmental Revenue—Total (in millions)	$6.57
Federal Revenue per Capita	$1.48
% Federal Assistance	3.07
% State Assistance	7.79
Sales Tax as % of Total Revenue	4.54
Local Revenue as % of Total Revenue	74.27
City Income Tax	no
Taxes—Total (in millions)	$7.1
Taxes per Capita	
Total	$104
Property	$76
Sales and Gross Receipts	$19
General Expenditures—Total (in millions)	$37
General Expenditures per Capita	$543
Capital Outlays per Capita	$198
% of Expenditures for:	
Public Welfare	0.1
Highways	9.5
Education	0.0
Health and Hospitals	3.7
Police	9.9
Sewerage and Sanitation	13.6
Parks and Recreation	0.4
Housing and Community Development	5.7
Debt Outstanding per Capita	$1,416
% Utility	6.3
Federal Procurement Contract Awards (in millions)	$14.8
Federal Grants Awards (in millions)	$11.2
Fiscal Year Begins	January 1

Economy

The Red River Valley contains some of the richest farmland in the nation. Naturally, then, agricultural production is the mainstay of the city's, as well as the area's, economy. In 1988, North Dakota led the nation in the production of durum wheat, spring wheat, flaxseed, and sunflowers, and was second in barley, pinto beans, and navy beans. The Fargo area is also ripe for agriculture-related industries, such as government science studies, most notably the Red River Valley Agricultural Research Center (headquartered in Fargo), an arm of the U.S. Department of Agriculture. Anheuser-Busch owns Busch Agricultural Resources, Inc., a seed and elevator operation for potatoes and barley, both used in the company's products.

Economy

Total Money Income (in millions) $781.753
% of State Average 119.3
Per Capita Annual Income $11,493
% Population below Poverty Level 9.7
Fortune 500 Companies NA

Banks	Number	Deposits (in millions)
Commercial	6	492.9
Savings	5	1,675.3

Passenger Autos 62,467
Electric Meters 42,850
Gas Meters 15,110

Manufacturing

Number of Establishments 79
% with 20 or More Employees 34.2
Manufacturing Payroll (in millions) $59.3
Value Added by Manufacture (in millions) $176.7
Value of Shipments (in millions) $386.7
New Capital Expenditures (in millions) $6.8

Wholesale Trade

Number of Establishments 282
Sales (in millions) $1,483.3
Annual Payroll (in millions) $104.122

Retail Trade

Number of Establishments 798
Total Sales (in millions) $791.5
Sales per Capita $11,636
Number of Retail Trade Establishments with Payroll 596
Annual Payroll (in millions) $88.1
Total Sales (in millions) $783.3
General Merchandise Stores (per capita) NA
Food Stores (per capita) $1,804
Apparel Stores (per capita) $538
Eating and Drinking Places (per capita) $1,137

Service Industries

Total Establishments 671
Total Receipts (in millions) $336.7
Hotels and Motels (in millions) $27.0
Health Services (in millions) $149.2
Legal Services (in millions) NA

Labor

Fargo ranks 6th in the nation in labor costs and 14th in unionization. Manufacturing employs 7% of the work force, government employs 20%, and trade and services each employ 29%. The three largest employers—with over 1,000 workers each—are North Dakota State University, the Fargo Public School District, and St. Luke's Hospital.

Labor

Civilian Labor Force 45,279
% Change 1989–1990 0.6
Work Force Distribution
  Mining NA
  Construction 3,800
  Manufacturing 6,000
  Transportation and Public Utilities 4,600
  Wholesale and Retail Trade 23,100
  FIRE (Finance, Insurance, Real Estate) 4,900
  Service 22,300
  Government 14,900
  Women as % of Labor Force 45.4
  % Self-Employed 5.0
  % Professional/Technical 19.9
Total Unemployment 1,032
Rate % 2.3
Federal Government Civilian Employment 1,760

Education

The Fargo Public School District supports 13 elementary schools, 2 junior high schools and 3 senior high schools. There are three parochial secondary and five elementary schools. The principal institution of higher education is the North Dakota State University, with an enrollment of 9,500. Other institutions in the Fargo-Moorhead area are Concordia College, Moorhead State University, Tri-College University, Moorhead Technical College, and Interstate Business College.

Education

Number of Public Schools 18
Special Education Schools NA
Total Enrollment 9,723
% Enrollment in Private Schools 8.3
% Minority NA
Classroom Teachers NA
Pupil-Teacher Ratio NA
Number of Graduates NA
Total Revenue (in millions) NA
Total Expenditures (in millions) NA
Expenditures per Pupil NA
Educational Attainment (Age 25 and Over)
  % Completed 12 or More Years 80.0
  % Completed 16 or More Years 25.6
Four-Year Colleges and Universities 1
  Enrollment 10,422
Two-Year Colleges NA
  Enrollment NA

Libraries

Number 12
Public Libraries 1
Books (in thousands) 146
Circulation (in thousands) NA
Persons Served (in thousands) 110
Circulation per Person Served 4.26
Income (in millions) $0.912
Staff 40

Four-Year Colleges and Universities
  North Dakota State University

Health

The largest medical facility is St. Luke's Hospital's Meritcare, comprising a general hospital, a neurosciences hospital, and a children's hospital. The other large hospitals include St. John's Hospital with 360 beds, Dakota Hospital with 206 beds, and the Veterans Administration Hospital with 165 beds.

Health

Deaths—Total	472
Rate per 1,000	7.2
Infant Deaths—Total	5
Rate per 1,000	4.7
Number of Metro Hospitals	4
Number of Metro Hospital Beds	1,037
Rate per 100,000	1,525
Number of Physicians	341
Physicians per 1,000	NA
Nurses per 1,000	NA
Health Expenditures per Capita	$23.31

Transportation

Fargo is approached by the east-west I-94 running through the southern sector of the city and intersecting the north-south I-29. U.S. routes are the east-west U.S. 10 and 52, and the north-south U.S. 75 and 81. State routes are the east-west 20 and 294. The Burlington Northern Railroad Company headquarters its Dakota division in Fargo. The Amtrak Empire Builder provides passenger service on its Chicago to Seattle run. Two trains arrive and depart daily. The principal air terminal for Fargo and the surrounding area is Hector International Airport, ten minutes north of downtown; it is served by two commercial airlines.

Transportation

Interstate Highway Mileage	14
Total Urban Mileage	521
Total Daily Vehicle Mileage (in millions)	1.714
Daily Average Commute Time	31.5 min.
Number of Buses	18
Port Tonnage (in millions)	NA
Airports	1
Number of Daily Flights	7
Daily Average Number of Passengers	518

Airlines (American carriers only)
  Northwest
  United

Housing

Prices for existing homes range from around $35,000 to $500,000. Fargo is currently experiencing housing construction growth in a south-southwesterly direction, but new highway construction may cause that movement to change to a more westerly direction. Some 36% of the residents live in apartments. Rents start at $300 and are among the most affordable in the nation.

Housing

Total Housing Units	31,711
% Change 1980–1990	20.5
Vacant Units for Sale or Rent	1,338
Occupied Units	30,149
% with More Than One Person per Room	1.7
% Owner-Occupied	48.1
Median Value of Owner-Occupied Homes	$70,300
Average Monthly Purchase Cost	$457
Median Monthly Rent	$321
New Private Housing Starts	717
Value (in thousands)	$34,421
% Single-Family	32.4
Nonresidential Buildings Value (in thousands)	$12,542

Urban Redevelopment

Most of the recent redevelopment has occurred on the North Dakota State University campus and at the area's hospitals where facilities are being expanded.

Crime

Fargo, along with Moorhead, ranks very high in public safety. In 1991, violent crimes known to police were 111 and known property crimes were 3,589.

Crime

Violent Crimes—Total	111
Violent Crime Rate per 100,000	NA
Murder	NA
Rape	23
Robbery	26
Aggravated Assaults	62
Property Crimes	3,589
Burglary	456
Larceny	2,961
Motor Vehicle Theft	164
Arson	8
Per Capita Police Expenditures	$52.11
Per Capita Fire Protection Expenditures	$48.78
Number of Police	86
Per 1,000	1.35

Religion

Among the major Christian denominations represented in Fargo are Assembly of God, Baptist, Catholic, Christian and Missionary Alliance, Church of God, Episcopal, Lutheran, Mennonite, Methodist, Moravian, Nazarene, Orthodox, and Presbyterian.

Religion

Largest Denominations (Adherents)

Catholic	21,488
Evangelical Lutheran	30,188
Lutheran-Missouri Synod	2,921
United Methodist	3,134
Presbyterian	2,723
Assembly of God	1,888
United Church of Christ	1,095
Jewish	333

Media

The lone city daily is the *Fargo Forum*. The electronic media consist of 5 television stations (3 commercial, 1 public, and 1 independent) and 10 AM and FM radio stations.

Media
Newsprint
Fargo Forum, daily
Television
KFME (Channel 13)
KTHI (Channel 11)
KVRR (Channel 15)
KXJB (Channel 4)
KDAY (Channel 6)

Radio	
KDSU (FM)	KFGO (AM)
KFGO (FM)	KFNW (AM)
KFNW (FM)	KQWB (AM)
KQWB (FM)	KSMM (FM)
WDAY (AM)	WDAY (FM)

Sports

Fargo has no major professional sports teams.

Arts, Culture, and Tourism

Fargo's outstanding performing arts center is the Fargo Theater, built in 1926 and recently renovated. Distinguished by its Wurlitzer pipe organ, it upholds the look of a depression-era movie house. The Fargo-Moorhead Community Theater (FMCT) stages its productions at the Emma K. Herbst Playhouse in Island Park. Other performing groups are the Fargo-Moorhead Symphony Orchestra, the Fargo-Moorhead Civic Opera, the Red River Dance and Performing Company, and the Mahkahta Dance Theater. Every June, the twin cities hold the annual Scandinavian Hjemkomst Festival, which features Scandinavian folk art and traditions. Bonanzaville USA, located in West Fargo at the Red River Valley Fairgrounds, is a pioneer village of 45 restored buildings, vintage automobiles, and farm machinery. Trollwood Park is a cultural arts center that features various ethnic exhibits and displays. The Children's Museum at Yunker Farm is a hands-on science center for children and adults.

Travel and Tourism
Hotel Rooms 2,134
Convention and Exhibit Space (square feet) NA
Convention Centers
Civic Memorial Auditorium
Festivals
Pioneer Review Days (August)
Red River Street Fair (July)

Parks and Recreation

Fargo has 35 regional, city, and neighborhood parks, as well as a dozen other recreational centers. The largest regional parks include the 106-acre M. B. Johnson Park, the 56-acre Centennial Park, the 12-acre Viking Ship Park, and the 52-acre Gooseberry Mound Park.

Sources of Further Information

Fargo Chamber of Commerce
321 Fourth Street North
Fargo, ND 58108-2443
(701) 237-5678

Fargo-Moorhead Convention and Visitors Bureau
1220 Main Avenue
Fargo, ND 58107
(701) 237-6134

Moorhead Economic Development Authority
1001 Center Avenue, Suite K
Moorhead, MN 56560
(218) 299-5441

Additional Reading

Polk's Fargo-Moorhead City Directory. 1991.

Fort Wayne

Indiana

Basic Data

Name   Fort Wayne
Name Origin   From Anthony Wayne
Year Founded   1794 Inc. 1829
Status: State   Indiana
       County   Seat of Allen County
Area (square miles)   62.7
Elevation (feet)   790
Time Zone   EST
Population (1990)   173,072
Population of Metro Area (1990)   363,811

Sister Cities
   Plock, Poland
   Takaoka, Japan

Distance in Miles To:

Louisville	234
Evansville	318
Indianapolis	132
South Bend	91
Gary	134
Chicago	158
Detroit	161
Toledo	105

Location and Topography

Fort Wayne is located in the northeastern section of Indiana, at the convergence of the St. Mary's River, which flows from the west, and the St. Joseph River, which travels from the north. The two rivers join in the center of the city to form the Maumee River, which then heads east. The terrain is generally level south and east of the city, while to the southwest and west the land is somewhat rolling; to the northwest and north it becomes slightly hilly.

Layout of City and Suburbs

Fort Wayne is divided into three parts by the St. Mary's, St. Joseph, and Maumee rivers. The three rivers measure a total of ten miles and are spanned by a dozen bridges. Clinton Street, which runs from the north and south through the city, is the commercial and business center, while Calhoun Street is another important but lesser business street. Principal lanes are Clinton, Calhoun, Main, Superior, Berry, Wayne, Washington, Jefferson, and Fairfield streets, and Ewing, Barr, and Lafayette streets. The center of the city is the Italian Renaissance Courthouse located at a square on Clinton, Main, and Berry streets.

Environment

Environmental Stress Index   2.6
Green Cities Index: Rank   NA
               Score   NA
Water Quality   Alkaline, soft, fluoridated
   Average Daily Use (gallons per capita)   135
   Maximum Supply (gallons per capita)   318
Parkland as % of Total City Area   4.5
% Waste Landfilled/Recycled   90:10
Annual Parks Expenditures per Capita $72.08

Climate

Fort Wayne's climate can be described as continental, with mildly-hot summers and cold winters. The humidity is high, due to the proximity of the rivers, and the annual precipitation is 36 inches.

Weather

Temperature

Highest Monthly Average °F   84.1
Lowest Monthly Average °F   15.8

Annual Averages

Days 32°F or Below   134
Days above 90°F   14
Zero Degree Days   10

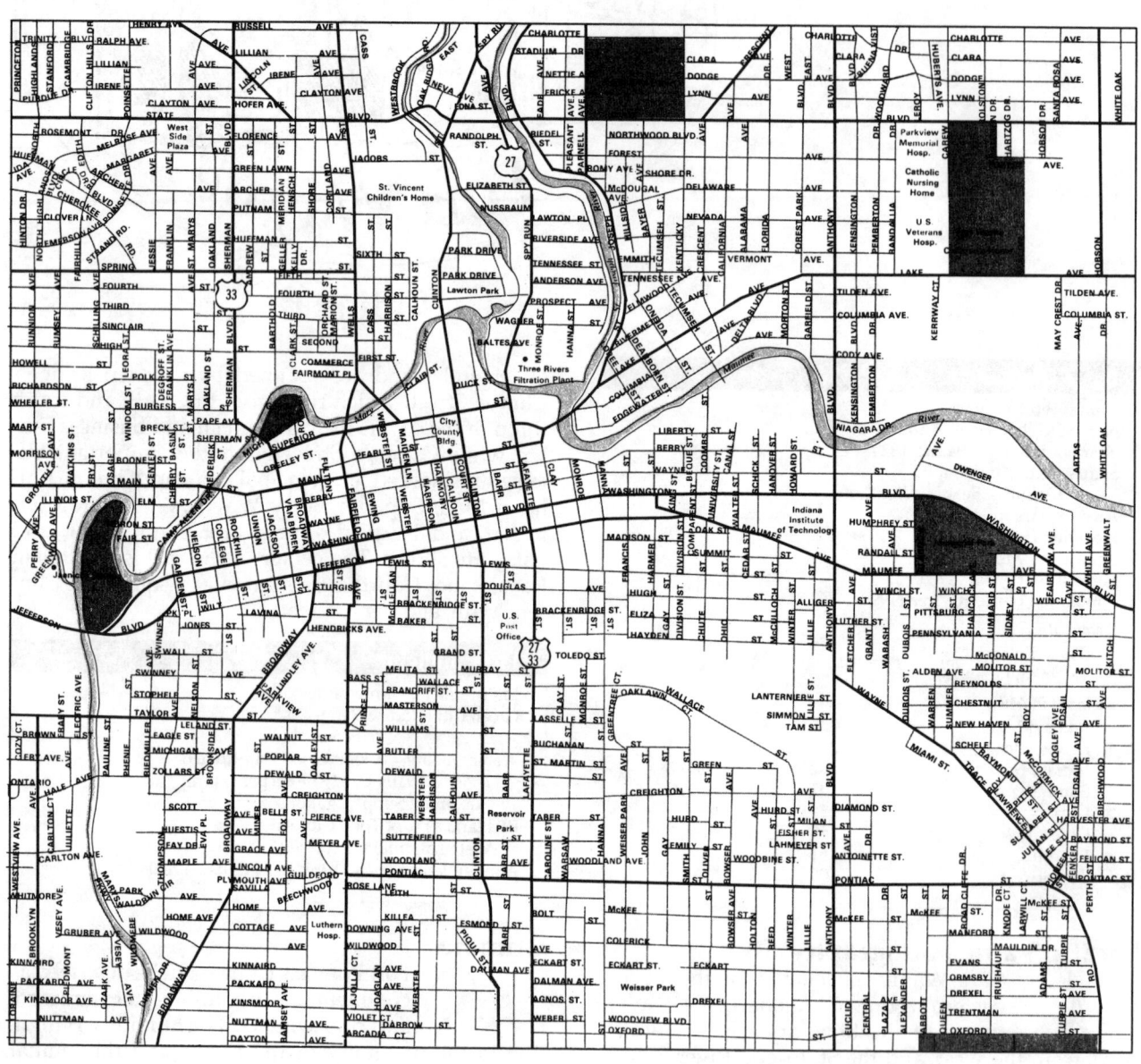

Weather (continued)

Precipitation (inches) 36.0
Snow (inches) 31.0
% Seasonal Humidity 72.0
Wind Speed (m.p.h.) 10.3
Clear Days 77
Cloudy Days 183
Storm Days 41
Rainy Days 131

Average Temperatures (°F)	High	Low	Mean
January	32.6	17.9	25.3
February	35.5	19.7	27.6
March	45.1	27.9	36.5
April	59.5	39.0	49.3
May	70.2	48.9	59.6
June	80.1	58.8	69.5
July	83.6	62.4	73.0
August	82.2	60.4	71.3
September	75.9	53.0	64.5
October	64.6	42.5	53.6
November	48.3	32.0	40.2
December	35.7	21.4	28.6

History

The site of Fort Wayne was for centuries the domain of the Miami Indians, who called the area now occupied by Fort Wayne Kekionga, or Miamitown. The French explorers Samuel de Champlain and Rene-Robert Cavelier Sieur de La Salle are purported to have visited the area before 1670, but there is little proof of a visit. Fur trappers and traders who came to the area around 1690 called a nearby stockade on the east bank of the St. Mary's River Post Miami. This settlement later became known as Frenchtown, or Miamitown. It was occupied by the French until 1748, when it was burned by Indians. Repaired in 1750, it was later abandoned for a site on the east bank of the St. Joseph River. It stayed in French hands until 1760, when the British took control of it during the French and Indian War, but it was taken over by Indians under the command of Chief Pontiac. Although the British recaptured the fort, it was eventually abandoned. A marker on the St. Joseph River now indicates the site of Old Fort Miami.

Miamitown remained, however, the third-largest trading town in the Northwest Territory (after Detroit and Vincennes, Indiana), but it continued under the eye of Chief Little Turtle. In 1780 Little Turtle massacred a French contingent led by Colonel Auguste de la Balme. A scouting party sent by General Josiah Harmar and led by Major John P. Wyllys in 1790 met with military defeat at the hands of Little Turtle. Another party in 1791 led by General Arthur St. Clair met with a similar fate. Washington then sent General "Mad" Anthony Wayne in 1794 to do battle with Little Turtle. Two engagements—at Fort Recovery and Fallen Timbers—both ended with defeat for the Indians. Wayne then marched his troops up the Maumee River and established a stockade across the river from Miamitown. Wayne turned the fort over to Colonel John Hamtramck on 21 October 1794. Hamtramck named it Fort Wayne the next day; this day, October 22, 1794, is considered the city's official founding date. The two key players in the early history of Fort Wayne were Little Turtle and William Wells, a white man who had been kidnapped as a child by the Indians and brought up as one of them. Wells and Little Turtle signed the Treaty of Greenville in 1795, which opened up to settlement half of Ohio and a strip of eastern Indiana. Soon after, Wells was appointed the government's Indian agent. In 1805 Wells and Governor General William Henry Harrison, the future president, met with the chiefs of the Delaware, Miami, and Potawatomi Indians to negotiate the purchase of 3 million acres of western land for settlement. In 1809 Wells was dismissed as Indian agent and Harrison again negotiated for land, opening another 33 million acres for white settlers, an agreement that led to the Battle of Tippecanoe (1811). On 14 July 1812, Little Turtle died at Wells's home in Fort Wayne; only a month later Wells himself was killed at Fort Dearborn in the fighting to save that besieged fort. Soon after the deaths of the two men, the Potawatomi Indians attacked Fort Wayne, and it was only the last-minute arrival of Harrison that assured Fort Wayne's survival. The Indians last attacked Fort Wayne in 1813, when troops led by Major Joseph Jenkinson were ambushed and killed at a bend in the St. Mary's River.

With no further Indian resistance to white rule, the military left Fort Wayne; civil authority was restored when Benjamin F. Stickney was appointed as Indian agent in 1819. That same year Judge Samuel Hanna reached Fort Wayne with his brother-in-law, James Barnett, and built the town's first gristmill. Called the "builder of the city," Hanna initiated construction of the city's first transportation system, the Wabash and Erie Canal. Fur traders who settled in the city over the next several years (including Alexis Coquillard, who later founded South Bend, Indiana) accounted for much of its growth. On 1 April 1824, several of the city's elders, including Samuel Hanna's brother Hugh, made Fort Wayne the county seat of Allen County. Five years later the city, then with a population of about 300, was incorporated. By the 1840s, Fort Wayne was a thriving industrial center with boatbuilders, tanneries, distilleries, sawmills, and gristmills. In 1846 the remaining Indians in the area were removed to Kansas and Oklahoma, and the last of the Indian territory was sold to the government by Chief Jean Baptiste Richardville, the half-Indian ruler of the Miami Indians.

After 1850, Fort Wayne became an even larger industrial center, due mainly to railroad connections to such cities as Chicago and Pittsburgh. In 1853 the Brass Foundry and Machine Company was founded; it became the largest manufacturer of railroad car wheels. The city prospered during the post–Civil War economic boom; 1871, for example, saw the opening of the Horton Manufacturing Company, a maker of electric-powered washing machines, by inventor Theodore Horton. Other inventors also worked and lived in Fort Wayne; the Fort Wayne Jenney Electric Light Company, founded by arc light inventor James Jenney,

Chronology

c. 1614 –1670 French explorers de Champlain and Cavelier, Sieur de La Salle, are purported to visit the area of Fort Wayne.

c. 1690 French fur trappers and traders establish Post Miami and become the first white men to inhabit the present-day Fort Wayne area.

1760 The French surrender the fort to the British at the conclusion of the French and Indian Wars.

1763 Indians capture the fort and hold it briefly.

1780 Miami Indians under Little Turtle massacre French Colonel Auguste de la Balme and his troops.

1790 Indians repulse the first American expedition to Miamitown under the command of General Josiah Harmar.

1791 Little Turtle defeats a second American army, this time led by General Arthur St. Clair.

1794 Little Turtle is beaten at the battles of Fort Recovery and Fallen Timbers by General "Mad" Anthony Wayne. Wayne builds a fort at Miamitown, which he turns over to Colonel John Hamtramck, who names it Fort Wayne.

1795 Little Turtle and William Wells sign the Treaty of Greenville.

1799 Wells becomes Indian agent at Fort Wayne.

1805 Wells and Governor General William Henry Harrison negotiate purchase of 3 million acres of western land for settlement.

1809 Harrison purchases another 33 million acres of land from Indian tribes for white settlement. William Wells is dismissed as Indian agent.

1811 Battle of Tippecanoe.

1812 Fort Wayne is saved by General William Henry Harrison after it is besieged by the Potawatomi Indians.

1813 Major Joseph Jenkinson and his men are ambushed and massacred in the last Indian fighting around Fort Wayne.

1819 Judge Samuel Hanna and his brother-in-law James Barnett build a log-cabin trading post and the town's first gristmill.

1820 Francis Comparet and Alexis Coquillard establish the city as a fur-trading station.

1823 John T. Barr and John McCorkle buy most of what is now downtown for $1.25 an acre. Founding city fathers Hugh Hanna, William Rockhill, Joseph Holman, Jesse L. Williams, and Allen Hamilton set up various business firms.

1824 Allen County is organized and Fort Wayne is named as county seat.

1829 Fort Wayne is incorporated as a city.

1832 The Wabash and Erie Canal is begun.

1850 The Wabash and Erie Canal is completed.

1853 The Brass Foundry and Machine Company, the city's first major factory, is founded.

1854 The first railroad, the Ohio and Indiana, reaches Fort Wayne.

1856 The Fort Wayne and Chicago Railroad reaches Fort Wayne.

1871 Inventor Theodore Horton opens his factory, which eventually produces the first electric-powered washing machine.

1928 Magnavox Company relocates to Fort Wayne.

1982 Fort Wayne experiences the worst floods in city history.

later went on to become the General Electric Corporation.

In the 1920s Fort Wayne emerged as a financial center because of its regionally important banks, such as the Lincoln Bank, and the Lincoln National Life Insurance Company. The Lincoln Bank built the Lincoln Tower, the tallest building in Fort Wayne when constructed; and the Lincoln National Life Insurance Company completed the Louis A. Warren Lincoln Library and Museum. Today, Fort Wayne, an important industrial center, is the home of such corporations as ITT Aerospace, General Motors, General Electric, Magnavox, and the B. F. Goodrich Tire Company.

Historical Landmarks

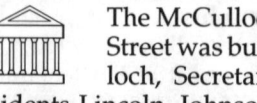

The McCulloch Homestead on Superior Street was built in 1838 by Hugh McCulloch, Secretary of the Treasury under presidents Lincoln, Johnson, and Arthur. The site of Post Miami is immediately to the north of the Old Aqueduct on the west bank of the St. Mary's River. The fort was burned by the Indians in the Chief Nicholas Conspiracy of 1748. The Old Ewing Homestead that stood on the corner of Berry and Ewing streets was built in 1854 by Judge William G. Ewing, son of Alexander Ewing, one of the pioneer settlers; it was torn down in the 1960s. The site of the first American fort is designated by a marker on the corner of Clay and Berry streets. This fort was built in 1794 by General

Anthony Wayne. The site of the Wyllys Massacre on the north bank of the Maumee River is designated by a marker at Edgewater Avenue and Dearborn Street. Here in 1790 Major John Wyllys and 60 regulars were killed by Indians under Little Turtle. The site of Fort Miami is on the east bank of the St. Joseph River at Delaware Avenue and St. Joseph Boulevard. Built by the French and surrendered to the British in 1760, it fell to the Indians in the Pontiac War of 1763. The Anthony Wayne Monument on the corner of Hayden Park, Harmar Street, and Maumee Avenue is an equestrian statue of the general after whom the city is named. The Samuel Hanna Memorial that was on the corner of Lewis and Gray streets was a brick house, the former home of Judge Samuel Hanna, the "Builder" of Fort Wayne; it is now a baseball diamond. The Allen County Courthouse, Fort Wayne's first civic building, was constructed between 1897 and 1900.

Population

The population of Fort Wayne grew by 681 persons, or 0.4%, to 173,072 in 1990 from 172,391 in 1980, thus reversing the earlier decline of 3.4% between 1970 and 1980. However, its national ranking among U.S. cities has dropped from 80th to 99th.

Population	1980	1990
Central City	172,391	173,072
Rank	80	99
Metro Area	354,156	363,811
Pop. Change 1980–1990 +681		
Pop. % Change 1980–1990 +0.4		
Median Age 31.6		
% Male 47.6		
% Age 65 and Over 13.3		
Density (per square mile) 2,760		

Households

Number 69,627
Persons per Household 2.43
% Female-Headed Households 13.8
% One-Person Households 31.0
Births—Total 3,166
   % to Mothers under 20 14.6
   Birth Rate per 1,000 19.1

Ethnic Composition

Whites make up 80.5%, blacks 16.7%, American Indians 0.3%, Asian and Pacific Islanders 1.0%, and others 1.5% of the population.

Ethnic Composition (as % of total pop.)	1980	1990
White	83.24	80.45
Black	14.55	16.67
American Indian	0.20	0.32
Asian and Pacific Islander	0.44	1.01
Hispanic	2.2	2.7
Other	NA	1.46

Government

Fort Wayne is governed by a mayor and a nine-member council. The mayor, who is elected to a four-year term, is not a member of the council. The nine members of the council also are elected—six by wards and three at large—for four-year terms.

Government

Year of Home Charter 1981
Number of Members of the Governing Body 9
Elected at Large 3
Elected by Wards 6
Number of Women in Governing Body 2
Salary of Mayor $61,750
Salary of Council Members $11,274
City Government Employment Total 1,801
Rate per 10,000 104.2

Public Finance

The annual budget consists of revenues of $103.234 million and expenditures of $97.601 million. The debt outstanding is $63.082 million, and cash and security holdings are $53.589 million.

Public Finance

Total Revenue (in millions) $103.234
Intergovernmental Revenue—Total (in millions) $21.08
Federal Revenue per Capita $4.16
% Federal Assistance 4.03
% State Assistance 15.32
Sales Tax as % of Total Revenue NA
Local Revenue as % of Total Revenue 59.73
City Income Tax no
Taxes—Total (in millions) $22.7

Taxes per Capita
  Total $131
  Property $129
  Sales and Gross Receipts $0
General Expenditures—Total (in millions) $70.2
General Expenditures per Capita $406
Capital Outlays per Capita $63

% of Expenditures for:
  Public Welfare 0.0
  Highways 7.3
  Education 0.0
  Health and Hospitals 0.9
  Police 15.0
  Sewerage and Sanitation 16.7
  Parks and Recreation 8.6
  Housing and Community Development 8.8
Debt Outstanding per Capita $454
  % Utility 28.4
Federal Procurement Contract Awards (in millions) $250.3
Federal Grants Awards (in millions) $9.7
Fiscal Year Begins January 1

Economy

The three pillars of Fort Wayne's economy are insurance, agribusiness, and industrial companies. Manufacturing makes up nearly 25% of the work force, with such companies as ITT Aerospace, Magnavox, General Electric, and Navistar employing the bulk of workers. General Motors has one of its largest assembly factories in the United States in Fort Wayne. In the area of agribusiness, the Central Soya Company, with its headquarters in Fort Wayne, is the leader. It was this innovative company that in the early years of this century staked its fortune on a new and at the time untested crop—soybeans. Today, soybeans are touted as the cure-all for the world's hunger problem, and they make up a substantial portion of human and animal protein. Lincoln National Corporation made its mark at the turn of the century in the field of insurance, and today it is Fort Wayne's largest employer with almost 5,300 employees.

Economy

Total Money Income (in millions) $1,777.7
% of State Average   103.0
Per Capita Annual Income $10,276
% Population below Poverty Level   11.0
Fortune 500 Companies   2

Banks	Number	Deposits (in millions)
Commercial	6	7,050
Savings	NA	NA

Passenger Autos   187,074
Electric Meters   147,000
Gas Meters   90,000

Manufacturing

Number of Establishments   357
% with 20 or More Employees   40.3
Manufacturing Payroll (in millions) $740.5
Value Added by Manufacture (in millions) $1,348.9
Value of Shipments (in millions) $2,887.7
New Capital Expenditures (in millions) $89.6

Wholesale Trade

Number of Establishments   607
Sales (in millions) $4,782.7
Annual Payroll (in millions) $230.211

Retail Trade

Number of Establishments   2,070
Total Sales (in millions) $1,885.4
Sales per Capita $10,905
Number of Retail Trade Establishments with Payroll   1,494
Annual Payroll (in millions) $224.7
Total Sales (in millions) $1,856.0
General Merchandise Stores (per capita) $1,708
Food Stores (per capita) $1,483
Apparel Stores (per capita) $523
Eating and Drinking Places (per capita) $1,101

Service Industries

Total Establishments   1,695
Total Receipts (in millions) $785.1
Hotels and Motels (in millions) $25.1
Health Services (in millions) $243.6
Legal Services (in millions) $47.1

Labor

 Manufacturing is the largest single employment sector, accounting for over 25%. Trade and services are also strong, but government share of employment is a modest 10%.

Labor

Civilian Labor Force   98,933
% Change 1989–1990   0.8

Work Force Distribution

Mining   NA
Construction   9,000
Manufacturing   40,900
Transportation and Public Utilities   12,800
Wholesale and Retail Trade   50,300
FIRE (Finance, Insurance, Real Estate)   13,100
Service   44,800
Government   19,300
Women as % of Labor Force   45.3
% Self-Employed   3.4
% Professional/Technical   13.9
Total Unemployment   5,844
Rate %   5.9
Federal Government Civilian Employment   1,688

Education

The Fort Wayne Community Schools System supports 35 elementary schools, 1 special education school, 11 middle schools, and 6 senior high schools. Two institutions stand out in higher education: the Indiana-Purdue University of Fort Wayne, the city's leading university, and Saint Francis College, a private liberal arts institution. Concordia Theological Seminary and Fort Wayne Bible College reflect Fort Wayne's strong Christian heritage. Technical education is available at three institutions: Indiana Technical Vocational College, ITT Technical Institute, and Indiana Institute of Technology.

Education

Number of Public Schools   53
Special Education Schools   1
Total Enrollment   31,611
% Enrollment in Private Schools   16.5
% Minority   26.7
Classroom Teachers   1,628
Pupil-Teacher Ratio   19.6
Number of Graduates   2,032
Total Revenue (in millions) $106.8
Total Expenditures (in millions) $119.5
Expenditures per Pupil $3,621
Educational Attainment (Age 25 and Over)
  % Completed 12 or More Years   68.7
  % Completed 16 or More Years   13.3
Four-Year Colleges and Universities   2
  Enrollment   12,850
Two-Year Colleges   1
  Enrollment   3,209

Libraries

Number   40
Public Libraries   14
Books (in thousands)
  2,094
Circulation (in thousands)   3,150
Persons Served (in thousands)   300
Circulation per Person Served   10.5
Income (in millions) $8.5
Staff   336

Four-Year Colleges and Universities
  Indiana Institute of Technology
  St. Francis College

Health

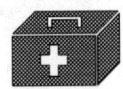

Health care is Fort Wayne's largest sector, with three large hospitals: Parkview Memorial, Lutheran Hospital, and St. Joseph's Medical Center. Among other medical facilities are the Veterans Administration Medical Center and Charter Beacon Hospital.

Health

Deaths—Total 1,669
Rate per 1,000 10.1
Infant Deaths—Total 41
Rate per 1,000 13.0
Number of Metro Hospitals 5
Number of Metro Hospital Beds 2,407
Rate per 100,000 1,392
Number of Physicians 521
Physicians per 1,000 1.62
Nurses per 1,000 8.64
Health Expenditures per Capita $7.58

Transportation

Fort Wayne is approached by I-69 running from Port Huron, Michigan, south to Indianapolis. Major highways passing through the Fort Wayne area are the north-south U.S. 27 and Indiana state roads 1 and 3, the east-west U.S. 24 and 30, and Indiana State Highway 14. Amtrak's Broadway Limited makes two daily stops in Fort Wayne. Rail freight service is provided by Conrail and Norfolk and Western. The destination for most air traffic into Fort Wayne is the Fort Wayne International Airport, which is located just south of the city and is served by nine commercial carriers. Smith Field, to the northwest of the city, is a secondary airport mainly for private air traffic.

Transportation

Interstate Highway Mileage 11
Total Urban Mileage 1,079
Total Daily Vehicle Mileage (in millions) 4.475
Daily Average Commute Time 40.3 min.
Number of Buses 52
Port Tonnage (in millions) NA
Airports 1
Number of Daily Flights 21
Daily Average Number of Passengers 747

Airlines (American carriers only)
    American
    Delta
    Northwest
    United
    USAir

Housing

Of the total housing stock, about 60% is owner-occupied. Median value of an owner-occupied home is $47,800, and median monthly rent is $312.

Housing

Total Housing Units 77,166
% Change 1980–1990 8.5
Vacant Units for Sale or Rent 5,408
Occupied Units 69,627
% with More Than One Person per Room 2.2
% Owner-Occupied 59.6
Median Value of Owner-Occupied Homes $47,800
Average Monthly Purchase Cost $276
Median Monthly Rent $312
New Private Housing Starts 392
Value (in thousands) $23,686
% Single-Family 49.5
Nonresidential Buildings Value (in thousands) $37,040

Tallest Buildings	Hgt. (ft.)	Stories
One Summit Square (1981)	442	26
Ft. Wayne Natl. Bank (1970)	339	26

Urban Redevelopment

Within the last decade, a number of new industrial plants have located in Fort Wayne. They include GM, Chuo Kagaku, Coca-Cola, and General Electric. Sixteen projects have been completed as part of the downtown revitalization program. The centerpiece of the program is Midtowne Crossing, a complex of renovated historic buildings. Other projects were the Standard Federal Plaza, a $2.8-million YMCA facility, Transit Mall, Barr Street Market, Grand Wayne Civic Center, and the Landing Condominiums in the historic commercial district. Downtown rejuvenation has centered very largely on the arts. When the retail trade in the central city shifted to the suburbs in the 1960s, many buildings along East Main and East Columbia streets were razed. In their place was erected Freimann Square, which became the site of many outdoor art events. The Performing Arts Center, the last building to be designed by Louis Kahn, was built next to the Square in 1973, and next to it the Fort Wayne Museum of Art was built in 1984.

Crime

Fort Wayne ranks high in public safety. In 1991 the violent crimes known to police were 1,098 and known property crimes were 16,006.

Crime

Violent Crimes—Total 1,098
Violent Crime Rate per 100,000 371.1
Murder 23
Rape 114
Robbery 573
Aggravated Assaults 388
Property Crimes 16,006
Burglary 2,726
Larceny 11,354
Motor Vehicle Theft 1,926
Arson 191
Per Capita Police Expenditures $123.13
Per Capita Fire Protection Expenditures $78.63
Number of Police 308
Per 1,000 1.86

Religion

In the early days Fort Wayne was known as the City of Churches. The Germans were among the first to organize congregations. In 1831 Stephen Badin, the first priest to be ordained in America, built the first Catholic church, in Cathedral Square. In 1857 the Diocese of Fort Wayne was created, with Henry Luers as bishop. The Presbyterians, under James Chute, were the next to organize. They built their first church in 1837 with Alexander Rankin as minister. Lutheranism also took hold of the new community through the efforts of Henry Rudisill, Jesse Hoover, and Friedrich Wyneken. Wyneken was one of the moving spirits behind the creation of the Missouri Synod of the Lutheran Churches in 1844. Methodists had been meeting in a rural log cabin since the 1820s, but by 1847 they were strong enough to open a college for women (which eventually became Taylor University in Upland, Indiana). The Baptists and Episcopalians were organized by the mid-1840s. Another early religious group was the first Jewish congregation west of the Appalachians. It was organized in 1848 as The Society for Visiting the Sick and Burying the Dead; it later adopted the title Achduth Veshalom (Unity and Peace).

Religion	
Largest Denominations (Adherents)	
Catholic	51,000
Evangelical Lutheran	13,653
Lutheran-Missouri Synod	25,455
United Methodist	17,434
Black Baptist	10,273
Independent Charismatics	6,100
Presbyterian	4,664
Missionary Church	4,225
United Church of Christ	3,612
Jewish	910

Media

The Fort Wayne press consists of two daily newspapers: The *Journal Gazette*, published on weekday mornings and Sundays, and the *News Sentinel*, published on weekday evenings. The electronic media consists of 5 television stations (3 commercial, 1 public, and 1 independent) and 13 FM and AM radio stations.

Media
Newsprint
Journal-Gazette, daily
News-Sentinel, daily
Metronet
Television
WANE (Channel 15)
WFFT (Channel 55)
WFWA (Channel 39)
WKJG (Channel 33)
WPTA (Channel 21)

Media *(continued)*	
Radio	
WAJI (FM)	WBCL (FM)
WBNI (FM)	WBTU (FM)
WFCV (AM)	WGL (AM)
WLAB (FM)	WLYV (AM)
WOWO (AM)	WOWO (FM)
WQHK (AM)	WMEE (FM)
WXKE (FM)	

Sports

Fort Wayne has no major professional sports teams.

Arts, Culture, and Tourism

From the Embassy Theatre, a 1930s historical landmark that is the home of the Fort Wayne Philharmonic and the Festival of Trees, to The Lincoln Museum on South Clinton Street, which contains the largest collection of Lincolniana in the nation, Fort Wayne is the home of many facets of culture that explore its rich history and highlight its present. In the area of the arts, Arts United is a group of organizations that promotes the arts in the city. Much of this is seen in the Fort Wayne Ballet, the Fort Wayne Civic Theatre, and the Fort Wayne Museum of Art, the last being founded in 1888. As to museums, the history of the city is on display at the Allen County–Fort Wayne Historical Museum on East Berry Street. Other attractions include the Firefighter's Museum, the reconstructed Historic Fort Wayne, and the Jack D. Diehm Wildlife Museum of Natural History.

Travel and Tourism
Hotel Rooms   3,155
Convention and Exhibit Space (square feet)   NA
Convention Centers
Grand Wayne Center
Allen County War Memorial Coliseum
Performing Arts Center
Scottish Rite Masonic Auditorium
Festivals
Three Rivers Festival (July)
Forte Festival (May)
Germanfest (June)
Johnny Appleseed Festival (September)

Parks and Recreation

In its total 56 square miles, Fort Wayne offers much in the way of parks. The park system, dating back to the mid-1850s, includes the Lakeside Rose Garden, located in the midst of Lakeside Park on Lake Avenue. The garden is one of America's largest, exhibiting some 2,000 rose bushes of more than 150 varieties. Also in the city is Fox Island, a nature sanctuary of some 448 acres; Foster Park, which contains a replica of the log cabin where Abraham Lincoln was born; the 282-acre Francke Park, which houses the Fort Wayne Children's Zoo; and the Foellinger-Freimann Botanical Conservatory, which displays plant species from around the world in their natural surroundings.

Sources of Further Information

Allen County Public Library
900 Webster Street
Fort Wayne, IN 46801-2270
(219) 424-7241

City Hall, City-County Building
Fort Wayne, IN 46902
(219) 427-1111

Fort Wayne Convention and Visitors Bureau
1021 South Calhoun Street
Fort Wayne, IN 46802
(219) 424-3700 or (800) 767-7752

Greater Fort Wayne Chamber of Commerce
826 Ewing Street
Fort Wayne, IN 46802
(219) 424-1435

Additional Reading

Fort Wayne Economic Development Data Book. 1991.
Hawfield, Michael C. *Here's Fort Wayne, Past and Present: A Historical Perspective.* 1992.
Indiana: A Works Projects Administration Guide to the Hoosier State. 1973.
1992 Mobil Travel Guide: Great Lakes Edition. 1992.
Polk's Fort Wayne Directory. 1991.

Fort Worth

Texas

Basic Data

Name   Fort Worth
Name Origin   From William Jenkins Worth
Year Founded   1849 Inc. 1907
Status: State   Texas
        County   Seat of Tarrant County
Area (square miles)   281.1
Elevation (feet)   670
Time Zone   Central
Population (1990)   447,619
Population of Metro Area (1990)   1,332,053

Sister Cities

    Bandung, Indonesia
    Budapest, Hungary
    Nagaoka, Japan
    Reggio Emilia, Italy
    Trier, Germany

Distance in Miles To:

Austin	190
Corpus Christi	405
Dallas	30
Houston	266
San Antonio	269

Location and Topography

N Fort Worth is located in north-central Texas, along the shores of the Trinity River, about 30 miles from its sister city of Dallas. The Trinity in fact splits in the western section of the city into West and Clear forks. Fort Worth is part of the Metroplex area of Texas, containing the cities of Dallas, Fort Worth, Arlington, Irving, and Grand Prairie.

Layout of City and Suburbs

Fort Worth is connected to Dallas by I-30, but it is connected to the rest of the state by I-35 and I-35W and is ringed by I-820. Downtown Fort Worth is bordered by the Trinity River on the north and west, the Dallas–Fort Worth Turnpike on the south, and I-35W on the east. To the extreme west of the city, the Trinity separates into the Clear and West forks. Dallas–Fort Worth International Airport is 17 miles to the east, while the new all-commercial Alliance Airport is to the immediate south. The city streets are done in a routine cross-hatching manner, and the downtown area is marked by the Tarrant County Convention Center and the Fort Worth Water Gardens.

Environment

Environmental Stress Index   3.0
Green Cities Index: Rank   51
                    Score   21.0
Water Quality   Alkaline, hard, fluoridated
    Average Daily Use (gallons per capita)   156
    Maximum Supply (gallons per capita)   216
Parkland as % of Total City Area   6.4
% Waste Landfilled/Recycled   NA
Annual Parks Expenditures per Capita $60.89

Climate

 Fort Worth has a hot continental and subtropical climate. It is one of the hottest and most humid cities in the nation. However, there are wide variations in the annual weather conditions.

Weather

Temperature

Highest Monthly Average °F   97.8
Lowest Monthly Average °F   33.9

Annual Averages

Days 32°F or Below   41
Days above 90°F   88

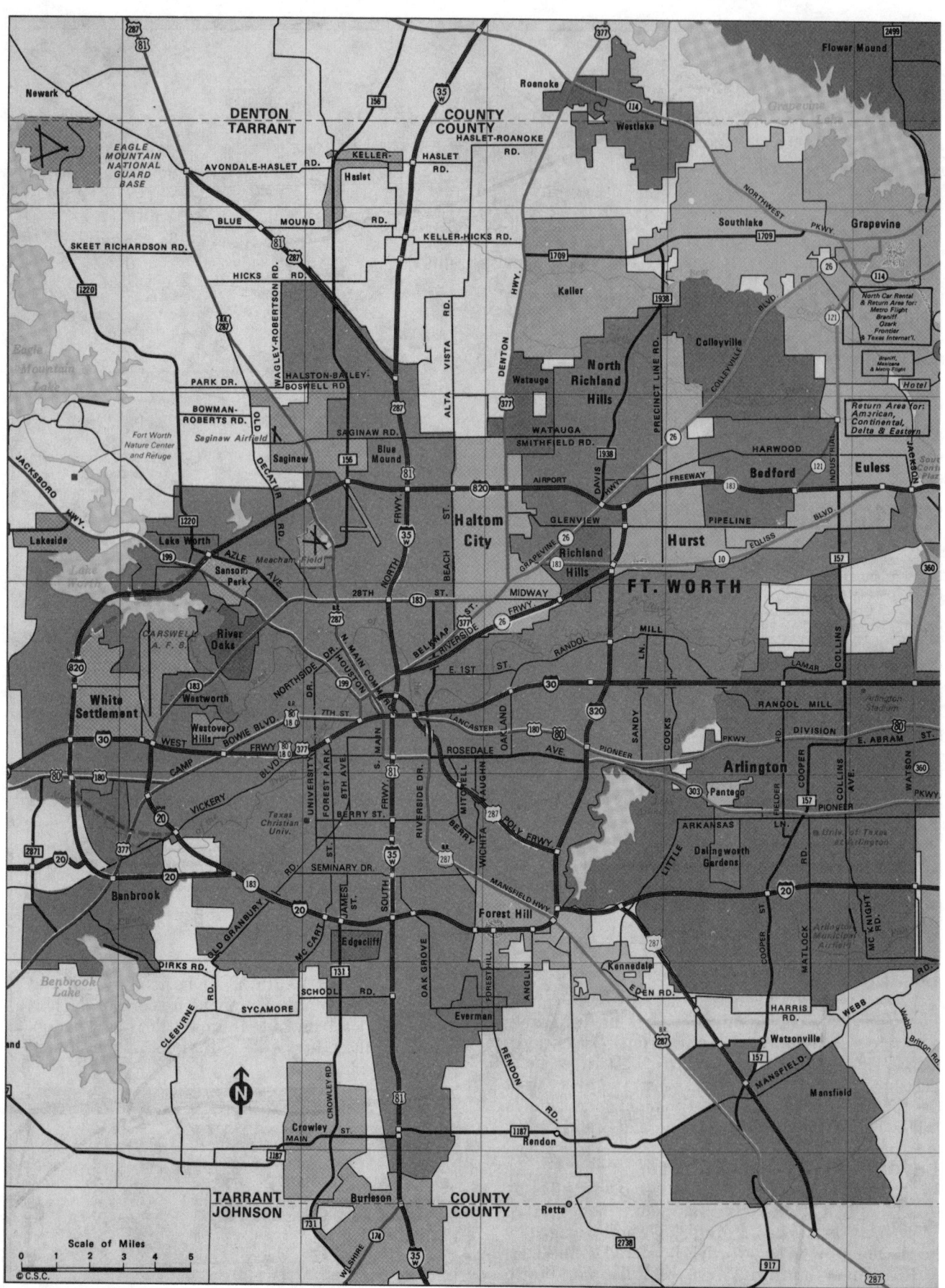

Weather (continued)

Zero Degree Days 0
Precipitation (inches) 29.46
Snow (inches) 3.0
% Seasonal Humidity 69.0
Wind Speed (m.p.h.) 10.8
Clear Days 137
Cloudy Days 130
Storm Days 46
Rainy Days 78

Average Temperatures (°F)	High	Low	Mean
January	55.7	33.9	44.8
February	59.8	37.6	48.7
March	66.6	43.3	55.0
April	76.3	54.1	65.2
May	82.8	62.1	72.5
June	90.8	70.3	80.6
July	95.5	74.0	84.8
August	96.1	73.7	84.9
September	88.5	66.8	77.7
October	79.2	56.0	67.6
November	67.5	44.1	55.8
December	58.7	37.0	47.9

History

The site of present-day Fort Worth was inhabited by the Comanche Indians when white settlers began to explore the area around 1820. In 1841, one Jonathan Bird set up Bird's Fort on the Trinity River, now located just to the north of present-day Arlington and to the west of where Fort Worth would be located. When Texas declared its independence from Mexico in 1845, the need for new outposts for travelers became evident. Four years later, Brevet Major Ripley Arnold and 42 soldiers under his command in Company F of the Army's Second Dragoons established, on the banks of the Trinity River, Camp Worth, which he named in honor of General William Jenkins Worth, a commander in the War of 1812 and a hero of the recent Mexican War. On November 14, 1849, Arnold moved the camp to a bluff at the convergence of the Clear and West forks of the Trinity and renamed it Fort Worth (although no real fort was ever built there). This date is considered to be that of the city's founding.

By the mid-1850s, Indian raids on the area had decreased, so more settlers began to arrive in Fort Worth. Among them was John Peter Smith, who set up the city's first school, and Captain Ephraim Dagget, who opened the first hotel. In 1856, Fort Worth was designated the county seat of Tarrant County. The Civil War did not have a great effect on Fort Worth, and after the war the city became the so-called last civilized stop on the Chisholm Trail. Because it was used as such a waystation, Fort Worth eventually became known as "Cowtown." In 1873 the city was incorporated, and Dr. W. P. Burts was named the first mayor. In 1875, in order to finish a bankrupt railroad that was being constructed near the city, the Tarrant County Construction Company was founded. A year later, on 19 July 1876, the first train entered town.

With the coming of the railroad, it did not take Fort Worth long to become a major area of industry and commerce, particularly beginning in the first years of the 20th century. Two industries brought prosperity to Fort Worth. In 1902, the nation's two largest meat-packers—Swift and Armour—opened large plants in the city. After 1910, and particularly 1917, when oil was struck at the nearby Ranger Field, oil became the cottage industry of this section of Texas. During World War II, Fort Worth Army Airfield became a major western depot for the housing of military hardware; after the war, it became Carswell Air Force Base. During the war, the Consolidated Vultee Aircraft Corporation (Convair) built 3,000 B-24 bombers and employed 35,000 people.

Although the city takes a back seat to its larger sister city, Dallas, Fort Worth, because of Dallas–Fort Worth International Airport, Alliance Airport, and the construction of the Superconducting Supercollider just south of the city, has become a major international center of industry and commerce.

Historical Landmarks

Known as "The City Where the West Begins," Fort Worth, along the Heritage Trail especially, is rich in landmarks that reflect its history. Log Cabin Village demonstrates the life of early pioneers of Fort Worth and how they lived. Fire Station No. 1, located at Second and Commerce streets, was the city's first fire station and contains an exhibit highlighting 150 years of city history. North of the city is the famed Stockyards Historic District, marking the place where one of the city's largest industries was born. Downtown is Sundance Square, named after the outlaw The Sundance Kid; here one can see restored saloons and hotels where The Kid and his partner Butch Cassidy hid out when evading the law.

Population

After a decade of decline in the 1970s—its population dropped from 393,000 in 1970 to 385,164 in 1980—Fort Worth picked up steam again in the 1980s, growing by 16.2% to 447,619 in 1990.

Population	1980	1990
Central City	385,164	447,619
Rank	33	28
Metro Area	973,138	1,332,053
Pop. Change 1980–1990	+62,455	
Pop. % Change 1980–1990	+16.2	
Median Age	30.3	
% Male	49.2	
% Age 65 and Over	11.2	
Density (per square mile)	1,592	

Households

Number 168,274
Persons per Household 2.58
% Female-Headed Households 13.3
% One-Person Households 29.0
Births—Total 9,069
   % to Mothers under 20 19.3
   Birth Rate per 1,000 21.9

Chronology

1841 Jonathan Bird establishes Bird's Fort along the banks of the Trinity River.

1849 Major Ripley Arnold and 42 soldiers set up Camp Worth along the banks of the Trinity to fight Indian raids. On 14 November, he moves the camp to the confluence of the Clear and West forks of the Trinity and founds Fort Worth, although a real fort was never constructed there.

1856 Fort Worth becomes the county seat of Tarrant County.

1866 Fort Worth earns the nickname "Cowtown" as it becomes the last major stop going west on the Chisholm Trail.

1872 City's first newspaper, the *Fort Worth Democrat*, is established.

1873 Fort Worth is incorporated and elects its first mayor, Dr. W. P. Burts.

1875–1876 Tarrant County Construction Company is formed to finish a rail line to Fort Worth. The first train enters the city on 19 July 1876.

1890 Census figures show that the city's population has reached 23,076, having been 6,663 in 1880.

1902 Armour and Swift companies open large meatpacking plants in the city, making meatpacking one of the city's two major industries.

1917 Oil discoveries at nearby Ranger Field pour money into Fort Worth.

1942 Fort Worth Army Airfield (later Carswell Air Force Base) becomes a major military depot.

1973 Dallas–Fort Worth International Airport, the largest such terminus in the nation at that time, opens just east of Fort Worth.

1990 Alliance Airport, a creation of financier H. Ross Perot, opens near Fort Worth.

Ethnic Composition

Whites make up 63.8%, blacks 22%, American Indians 0.4%, Asians and Pacific Islanders 2%, and others 11.8% of the population. Hispanics make up 19.5%.

Ethnic Composition (as % of total pop.)

	1980	1990
White	68.92	63.79
Black	22.78	22.01
American Indian	0.32	0.43
Asian and Pacific Islander	0.61	1.99
Hispanic	12.64	19.51
Other	NA	11.78

Government

Fort Worth has a council-manager form of government. The mayor and six members of the council are elected to two-year terms, but serve without salary. The appointed city manager is the chief executive.

Government

Year of Home Charter   1965
Number of Members of the Governing Body   6
Elected at Large   6
Elected by Wards   NA
Number of Women in Governing Body   2
Salary of Mayor $75.00
Salary of Council Members $75.00
City Government Employment Total   5,273
Rate per 10,000   122.8

Public Finance

The annual budget consists of revenues of $501.109 million and expenditures of $246.1 million. Debt outstanding is $3.176 billion, and cash and reserve holdings are $2.773 billion.

Public Finance

Total Revenue (in millions) $501.109
Intergovernmental Revenue—Total (in millions) $80.09
Federal Revenue per Capita $50.05
% Federal Assistance   9.98
% State Assistance   2.80
Sales Tax as % of Total Revenue   7.47
Local Revenue as % of Total Revenue   67.28
City Income Tax   no
Taxes—Total (in millions) $120.2

Taxes per Capita
  Total $280
  Property $156
  Sales and Gross Receipts $113
General Expenditures—Total (in millions) $246.1
General Expenditures per Capita $573
Capital Outlays per Capita $136

% of Expenditures for:
  Public Welfare   0.0
  Highways   11.5
  Education   0.0
  Health and Hospitals   1.8
  Police   12.4
  Sewerage and Sanitation   13.7
  Parks and Recreation   8.8
  Housing and Community Development   6.0
Debt Outstanding per Capita $1,199
  % Utility   15.6
Federal Procurement Contract Awards (in millions) $4,622.3
Federal Grants Awards (in millions) $25.4
Fiscal Year Begins   October 1

Economy

Fort Worth possesses a strongly diverse economy in several important commercial and industrial areas. Industrial capacity is created by General Dynamics (formerly Convair), Bell Helicopter-Textron (the largest maker of helicopters in the world), and the Tandy Corporation (computers and electronic products). The Automation and Robotics Research Institute, opened in 1987, trains companies in how to automate their facilities. In the service industry, the Dallas–Fort Worth Metroplex is the home of American Airlines and Delta Airlines, which together employ nearly 35,000 people. Now that oil is vanishing as a "cash crop" and the stockyards are just a museum, Fort Worth has expanded its economic base in the areas of transportation (Alliance Airport) and science (the Superconducting Supercollider).

Economy

Total Money Income (in millions) $4,516.7
% of State Average 101.4
Per Capita Annual Income $10,515
% Population below Poverty Level 13.9
Fortune 500 Companies NA

Banks	Number	Deposits (in millions)
Commercial	47	4,887.9
Savings	18	3,445.0

Passenger Autos 1,014,686
Electric Meters 482,609
Gas Meters 225,555

Manufacturing

Number of Establishments 907
% with 20 or More Employees 37.7
Manufacturing Payroll (in millions) $2,069.1
Value Added by Manufacture (in millions) $4,616.4
Value of Shipments (in millions) $8,646.9
New Capital Expenditures (in millions) $247.1

Wholesale Trade

Number of Establishments 1,022
Sales (in millions) $4,608.4
Annual Payroll (in millions) $325.563

Retail Trade

Number of Establishments 4,694
Total Sales (in millions) $3,271.4
Sales per Capita $7,616
Number of Retail Trade Establishments with Payroll 3,089
Annual Payroll (in millions) $389.4
Total Sales (in millions) $3,190.0
General Merchandise Stores (per capita) $847
Food Stores (per capita) $1,209
Apparel Stores (per capita) $376
Eating and Drinking Places (per capita) $825

Service Industries

Total Establishments 3,789
Total Receipts (in millions) $1,703.4
Hotels and Motels (in millions) $53.2
Health Services (in millions) $511.0
Legal Services (in millions) $193.0

Labor

Population growth during the 1980s has created a large labor pool, but job creation has kept pace. New jobs are mostly in manufacturing, especially in such advanced high-technology areas as robotics. Among service companies, American Airlines and Delta Airlines are the largest.

Labor

Civilian Labor Force 278,970
% Change 1989–1990 1.2

Work Force Distribution
Mining 4,400
Construction 21,100
Manufacturing 108,200
Transportation and Public Utilities 57,900
Wholesale and Retail Trade 149,000
FIRE (Finance, Insurance, Real Estate) 28,500
Service 141,800
Government 76,400
Women as % of Labor Force 43.9
% Self-Employed 5.7
% Professional/Technical 14.8
Total Unemployment 18,164
Rate % 6.5
Federal Government Civilian Employment 8,689

Education

The Fort Worth Independent School District supports 122 schools. The public school system is supplemented by 50 private and parochial schools. Higher education is paced by one public institution, the University of Texas at Arlington, and two private Christian institutions: the Texas Christian University and the Texas Wesleyan College. Other institutions include the Arlington Baptist College.

Education

Number of Public Schools 122
Special Education Schools 17
Total Enrollment 69,163
% Enrollment in Private Schools 6.9
% Minority 65.9
Classroom Teachers 3,728
Pupil-Teacher Ratio 18.6:1
Number of Graduates 3,154
Total Revenue (in millions) $227.067
Total Expenditures (in millions) $256.372
Expenditures per Pupil $2,893
Educational Attainment (Age 25 and Over)
% Completed 12 or More Years 62.2
% Completed 16 or More Years 17.3
Four-Year Colleges and Universities 3
Enrollment 8,241
Two-Year Colleges 1
Enrollment 27,999

Libraries

Number 47
Public Libraries 10
Books (in thousands) 1,219
Circulation (in thousands) 3,708
Persons Served (in thousands) 451.9

Education (continued)

Circulation per Person Served   8.2
Income (in millions) $6.882
Staff   NA

Four-Year Colleges and Universities
   Texas Christian University
   Texas Wesleyan College
   Texas College of Osteopathic Medicine

Transportation (continued)

   Eastern
   Northwest
   Pan Am
   Southwest
   Trans World
   USAir
   United

Health

Fort Worth is home to 17 hospitals, including a children's hospital and an osteopathic hospital. The largest facilities are Harris Hospital/Methodist with nearly 600 beds, All Saints Episcopal Hospital, and St. Joseph Hospital.

Health

Deaths—Total   4,154
Rate per 1,000   10.0
Infant Deaths—Total   129
Rate per 1,000   14.2
Number of Metro Hospitals   17
Number of Metro Hospital Beds   3,029
Rate per 100,000   705
Number of Physicians   1,593
Physicians per 1,000   1.33
Nurses per 1,000   7.50
Health Expenditures per Capita $20.22

Transportation

Fort Worth is approached by four interstates: the east-to-west I-20, the north-to-south I-35, the northeast-to-west I-30, and the southern I-45. Rail freight is provided by ten railroads, including the Burlington Northern, Missouri-Kansas-Texas, Missouri Pacific, Santa Fe, Texas and Pacific, The Rock, Conrail Freight, Cotton Belt, Kansas City Southern, and Union Pacific. The principal commercial and civilian air terminal is the Dallas–Fort Worth International Airport, located 17 miles east of downtown. In addition, the Alliance Airport, built by the Perot Group, is an industrial airport solely for use by industrial and manufacturing firms. Other facilities include Meacham and Spinks airports.

Transportation

Interstate Highway Mileage   273
Total Urban Mileage   16,731
Total Daily Vehicle Mileage (in millions)   76.6
Daily Average Commute Time   48.4 min.
Number of Buses   100
Port Tonnage (in millions)   NA
Airports   2
Number of Daily Flights   696
Daily Average Number of Passengers   69,580

Airlines (American carriers only)
   American
   American West
   Continental
   Delta

Housing

Of the total housing stock, 54.5% is owner-occupied. The median value of an owner-occupied home is $59,900 and the median monthly rent $337.

Housing

Total Housing Units   194,429
% Change 1980–1990   19.7
Vacant Units for Sale or Rent   19,335
Occupied Units   168,274
% with More Than One Person per Room   7.9
% Owner-Occupied   54.5
Median Value of Owner-Occupied Homes $59,900
Average Monthly Purchase Cost $280
Median Monthly Rent $337
New Private Housing Starts   1,104
Value (in thousands) $80,578
% Single-Family   70.7
Nonresidential Buildings Value (in thousands) $224,494

Tallest Buildings	Hgt. (ft.)	Stories
City Center Tower II (1984)	546	38
Burnett Plaza (1983)	538	40
Continental Plaza (1982)	520	40
1st City Bank Tower (1982)	475	33
Team Bank-Ft. Worth (1974)	457	37
Texas Bldg. (1955)	420	31

Urban Redevelopment

Fort Worth has received a face-lift in recent years through a number of redevelopment projects. It has two 40-story buildings: City Center II on the Continental Plaza and the InterFirst Bank Tower. The Fort Worth Convention Center covers 14 city blocks between Houston and Commerce streets.

Crime

Fort Worth has a high crime rate. In 1991 the crimes known to police consisted of 8,914 violent crimes and 68,681 property crimes.

Crime

Violent Crimes—Total   8,914
Violent Crime Rate per 100,000   992.3
Murder   195
Rape   442
Robbery   3,426
Aggravated Assaults   4,851
Property Crimes   68,681
Burglary   16,878
Larceny   38,333

Crime (continued)
Motor Vehicle Theft 13,470
Arson 386
Per Capita Police Expenditures $114.26
Per Capita Fire Protection Expenditures $72.94
Number of Police 771
Per 1,000 1.82

Religion

Fort Worth is a stronghold of Southern Baptists, but Methodists and Presbyterians also have large congregations. Pentecostals have gained substantial numbers since the 1970s.

Religion
Largest Denominations (Adherents)

Catholic	100,077
Southern Baptist	239,563
United Methodist	83,135
Black Baptist	59,210
Church of Christ	30,636
Assembly of God	19,748
Lutheran-Missouri Synod	9,272
Presbyterian	12,909
Christian Church (Disciples)	14,431
Jewish	4,392

Media

The city's only daily is the *Fort Worth Star-Telegram*. The electronic media consist of 5 television stations and 14 AM and FM radio stations.

Media
Newsprint
   Dallas/Fort Worth Business Journal, weekly
   Fort Worth Star-Telegram, daily
Television
   KTVT (Channel 11)
   KTXA (Channel 21)
   KXAS (Channel 5)
Radio

KFJZ (AM)	WBAP (AM)

Sports

In sports, Fort Worth is considered to be in tandem with Dallas, and teams with the name of that city are adopted by Fort Worth's sports fans as their own. These teams are the Dallas Cowboys in football, Dallas Mavericks in basketball, and Texas Rangers in baseball, although the Rangers play in Arlington.

Arts, Culture, and Tourism

The Arts Council of Fort Worth and Tarrant County is an umbrella organization that funds the city's major cultural organizations. Areas of activity include the Will Rogers Memorial Center, home of the 1936 Texas Centennial

Travel and Tourism
Hotel Rooms 12,188
Convention and Exhibit Space (square feet) NA
Convention Centers
   Tarrant County Convention Center
   Will Rogers Memorial Center
Festivals
   Southwestern Exposition and Livestock Show (January)
   Arts Festival (April)
   Chisholm Trail Roundup (June)
   Pioneer Days (September)

and today a center of exhibits and shows dealing with the once-thriving cattle industry; Casa Mañana, a theatre-in-the-round dome where Broadway plays are staged; and the Omni Theatre at the Fort Worth Museum of Science and History, where film and music performances dealing with science are shown.

Culture abounds in the Fort Worth Cultural District, located just two miles from downtown, where are found such museums as the Amon Carter Museum, which houses the art and pictorial collection of Carter, the founder of the Fort Worth Star-Telegram; the Kimbell Art Museum; the Cattleman's Museum; the Fort Worth Museum of Science and History, with its histories of medicine, computers, and Texas; and the restored Log Cabin Village.

Parks and Recreation

Fort Worth's parks and recreation areas are among the state's most attractive; they include the 114-acre Fort Worth Botanic Gardens; the Fort Worth Japanese Garden, which showcases the flower style of oriental gardens; Benbrook Lake; the Fort Worth Nature Center and Refuge; and Six Flags Over Texas, one of the nation's many Six Flags amusement parks.

Sources of Further Information

Fort Worth Convention and Visitors Bureau
Water Gardens Place
100 East 15th Street
Fort Worth, TX 76102
(817) 336-8791 or (800) 433-5747

Additional Reading

Cohen, Judith S. *Cowtown Moderne: Art Deco Architecture of Fort Worth, Texas.* 1988.
Cummings, Joe. *Texas Handbook.* 1992.
Knight, Oliver, and Cissy S. Lale. *Fort Worth: Outpost on the Trinity.* 1990.
Pate, J. Nell. *Livestock Legacy: The Fort Worth Stockyards.* 1988.
Patterson, R. Michael. *Fort Worth: New Frontiers in Excellence.* 1990.
Schmidt, Ruby. *Fort Worth and Tarrant County: A Historical Guide.* 1984.

Grand Rapids

Michigan

Location and Topography

N   Grand Rapids, located on both banks of the Grand River, is about 25 miles east of Lake Michigan. The river valley is fairly level and has no prominent features.

Layout of City and Suburbs

Grand Rapids is a planned city. Except for the remnants of two earlier town plats, made by rival land speculators, and the winding drives of the Ottawa Hills section, streets run east and west and avenues north and south. Riverbanks are lined by factories and warehouses. The residential areas reflect their ethnic origin. The Dutch, the largest ethnic group, are scattered throughout the city but are found primarily in five sections: on the west side, Oakdale Park in the southeast, Brickyard in the eastern section, Chicken Town, and along Grandville Avenue. The Polish are found in the parishes of St. Adelbert, St. Isidore, and Sacred Heart. The Lithuanians are found in St. Adelbert's parish, blacks south of Fulton Street, and Italians near Division and Franklin streets.

Climate

The climate is continental modified by the proximity of the Great Lakes, which help to moderate the cold in winter and heat in summer, and also regulate frost in the early spring and fall. Seasonal extremes are infrequent except for about three hot weeks in summer, which occasionally produce drought conditions. Winters are moderate but snow cover remains on the ground for most of the season. The Grand River has a tendency to flood during winter thaws, but the floods do not cause much damage.

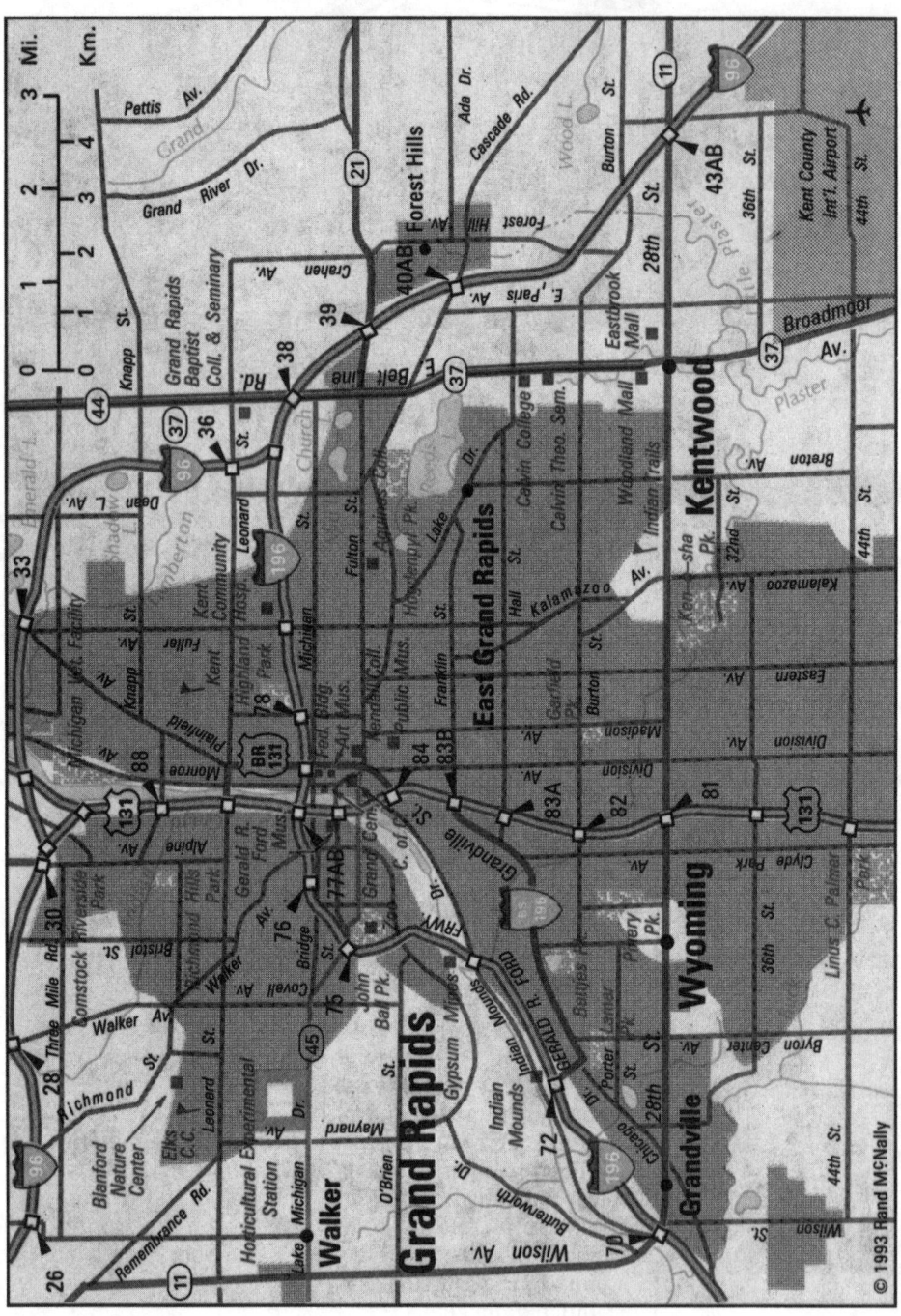

Weather (continued)

Annual Averages

Days 32°F or Below 149
Days above 90°F 11
Zero Degree Days 8
Precipitation (inches) 32.0
Snow (inches) 77.0
% Seasonal Humidity 73.0
Wind Speed (m.p.h.) 9.9
Clear Days 67
Cloudy Days 202
Storm Days 37
Rainy Days 144

Average Temperatures (°F)	High	Low	Mean
January	30.3	16.0	23.2
February	32.6	16.4	24.5
March	42.0	24.2	33.1
April	57.3	35.6	46.5
May	68.8	45.4	57.1
June	79.1	55.6	67.4
July	83.3	59.6	71.5
August	81.9	58.1	70.0
September	73.9	50.8	62.4
October	63.1	40.8	52.0
November	46.2	31.1	38.7
December	33.9	20.8	27.4

History

The Grand River Valley was occupied by the Ottawa tribes before the white man moved in. A Baptist mission was the first to colonize the area in 1824, and active mission work among the Ottawa was begun in 1826. The same year, a fur trader named Louis Campau settled in the Grand River Valley, and in 1827 he established a fur-trading post at what is now the foot of Huron Street. In 1831 he bought a large tract of land on the river—now bounded by Michigan and Fulton streets and Division Avenue—that later became the center of town. Meanwhile, Campau's rival, Lucius Lyon, purchased land north of Campau's townsite and called it Kent. The rivalry, which extended through the platting of their towns, produced unusual street configurations, unused spaces, and dead ends. Grand Rapids was incorporated in 1838, but the name was only officially recognized in 1842; it was incorporated as a city in 1850.

The city's first industry was shipbuilding. Steamboats began regular runs on the river between Grand Rapids and Grand Haven in 1837. The town first began building river steamboats and later hulls for vessels plying the Great Lakes. River traffic declined after the first railroad reached the city in 1858, but by 1854 logging had replaced shipbuilding as the most important industry. Huge quantities of logs were floated down the river to the mills in Grand Rapids, generally under the direction of river drivers, men who literally rode the pitching logs downstream. As the number of lumbermen grew, so did the number of town establishments serving them, such as brothels, bars, and gambling houses.

The river at times has brought destruction—ice and logjams sometimes caused backwaters and serious floods, as in 1838, 1852, and 1883. On the last occasion 150 million feet of logs broke away from the booms after heavy rains; the runaway logs brought down three railway bridges and left a trail of wreckage throughout the city. And in 1904 more than 1,500 houses were flooded. But the Grand River is more often a source of blessing than of distress. In 1881 the Midwest's first hydroelectric plant was built on it.

From logging to furniture making was only a short step. Furniture had been manufactured in Grand Rapids as early as 1838 using timber that came floating down the river. But the industry gained national prominence at the Philadelphia Centennial Exposition in 1876. Two years later the first of the city's furniture marts was held, and since then Grand Rapids has come to be known as the Furniture Town. However, there were periodic troubles in this business, due to using cheap immigrant labor in the furniture factories and then paying them substandard wages. A bloody but unsuccessful 17-week strike by furniture workers in 1911 helped to bring their grievances to national attention. Grand Rapids also developed as a printing center in the 1920s and 1930s.

Historical Landmarks

Campau Square, a small V-shaped space formed by the intersection of Monroe Avenue and Pearl Street, is the site of the trading post and log house built in 1827 by Louis Campau, founder of Grand Rapids. The Fountain Street Baptist Church on Fountain Street is of Italian Romanesque design. Leavitt House on Lyon Street and Ransom Avenue was built in 1858. Heritage Hill, a historic district near downtown, contains structures built in 60 different architectural styles.

Population

Grand Rapids is a growing city with a growth rate of 4.0% in the 1980s. Its 1990 census population was 189,126, an addition of 7,283 inhabitants over its 1980 total of 181,843.

Population

	1980	1990
Central City	181,843	189,126
Rank	75	83
Metro Area	601,680	688,399
Pop. Change 1980–1990 +7,283		
Pop. % Change 1980–1990 +4		
Median Age 29.8		
% Male 47.5		
% Age 65 and Over 13.1		
Density (per square mile) 4,269		

Households

Number 69,029
Persons per Household 2.60
% Female-Headed Households 16.1
% One-Person Households 27.2
Births—Total 3,937
  % to Mothers under 20 15.1
  Birth Rate per 1,000 21.5

Chronology

1824 Baptist missionaries select Grand Rapids as the site for a mission to the Ottawa Indians.

1826 Louis Campau establishes a fur-trading post on the riverbank.

1831 Campau buys a large tract of land on the river and plats a townsite called Grand Rapids.

1838 Grand Rapids is incorporated as a village but under the name of Kent. Town is completely submerged under floodwaters.

1842 The name of Grand Rapids is restored to the village.

1850 Grand Rapids is incorporated as a city.

1852 Floodwaters submerge town.

1854 Grand Rapids becomes logging center.

1858 First railroad reaches Grand Rapids.

1876 Philadelphia furniture makers gain national attention during Philadelphia Centennial Exposition.

1881 First hydroelectric plant is built on Grand River.

1883 After heavy rains, 150 million feet of logs break away from booms, wreck bridges, and cause enormous damage.

1904 More than 1,500 houses are destroyed in a massive flood.

1911 Furniture workers go on unsuccessful 17-week strike.

However, its overall rank among U.S. cities has dropped from 75th in 1980 to 83rd in 1990.

Ethnic Composition

Whites make up 76.4% of the population, blacks 18.5%, American Indians 0.8%, Asian and Pacific Islanders 1.1%, Hispanics 5.0%, and other races 3.1%.

Ethnic Composition (as % of total pop.)		
	1980	*1990*
White	80.93	76.39
Black	15.73	18.54
American Indian	0.69	0.83
Asian and Pacific Islander	0.62	1.14
Hispanic	3.16	4.97
Other	NA	3.09

Government

Grand Rapids is governed under a commission-manager system. The seven members of the Council are elected to four-year terms, and they in turn select a mayor from among themselves. The city manager is appointed.

Government
Year of Home Charter   1916
Number of Members of the Governing Body   6
Elected at Large   NA
Elected by Wards   6
Number of Women in Governing Body   2
Salary of Mayor $32,760
Salary of Council Members $17,212
City Government Employment Total   2,083
Rate per 10,000   111.7

Public Finance

The annual budget consists of revenues of $204.476 million and expenditures of $194.778 million. The debt outstanding is $238.288 million, and cash and security holdings are $485.900 million.

Public Finance
Total Revenue (in millions) $204.476
Intergovernmental Revenue—Total (in millions) $36.07
Federal Revenue per Capita $10.6
% Federal Assistance   5.19
% State Assistance   12.19
Sales Tax as % of Total Revenue   NA
Local Revenue as % of Total Revenue   53.65
City Income Tax   yes
Taxes—Total (in millions) $37.3
Taxes per Capita
Total $200
Property $92
Sales and Gross Receipts $0
General Expenditures—Total (in millions) $100.2
General Expenditures per Capita $537
Capital Outlays per Capita $50
% of Expenditures for:
Public Welfare   0.0
Highways   8.5
Education   0.0
Health and Hospitals   0.0
Police   14.3
Sewerage and Sanitation   7.5
Parks and Recreation   5.8
Housing and Community Development   3.1
Debt Outstanding per Capita $242
% Utility   17.6
Federal Procurement Contract Awards (in millions) $137.1
Federal Grants Awards (in millions) $16.0
Fiscal Year Begins   July 1

Economy

Grand Rapids is historically a manufacturing town, with a strong base in furniture, but it is expanding rapidly into modern high-technology sectors. It still is the home of five of the world's largest furniture makers: Herman Miller, Haworth, American Seating, Westinghouse, and Steelcase. The manufacturing sector consists of over 1,100 firms, employing one-third of the work force, and covering almost all primary industries. The sector leaders are General Motors and Amway, the latter based in Grand Rapids. More recently the city has been able to attract a number of foreign manufacturers, such as Yamaha musical instruments, Leitz woodcutting tools, and Leon Plastics. The majority of the manufacturers are small or family-owned businesses. Some of the family firms have grown over the years into nationally recognized firms, such as Bissell, makers of carpet cleaners; Howard Miller Clock Company; and Wolverine World Wide, makers of Hush Puppy shoes. Ninety percent of the local businesses employ fewer than 50 workers. In the nonmanufacturing sector, the leading industry is printing, sixth largest in the nation. Tourism also is a major revenue earner. Agricultural products for which Kent County is noted include Christmas trees, fruits, vegetables, and nursery products.

Economy

Total Money Income (in millions) $1,799.8
% of State Average   88.3
Per Capita Annual Income $9,625
% Population below Poverty Level   13.5
Fortune 500 Companies   NA

Banks	Number	Deposits (in millions)
Commercial	23	2,362.2
Savings	4	604.3

Passenger Autos   292,450
Electric Meters   157,795
Gas Meters   111,375

Manufacturing

Number of Establishments   489
% with 20 or More Employees   42.1
Manufacturing Payroll (in millions) $979.8
Value Added by Manufacture (in millions) $2,145.8
Value of Shipments (in millions) $3,759.7
New Capital Expenditures (in millions) $201.6

Wholesale Trade

Number of Establishments   577
Sales (in millions) $3,148.5
Annual Payroll (in millions) $218.216

Retail Trade

Number of Establishments   1,677
Total Sales (in millions) $1,297.5
Sales per Capita $6,956
Number of Retail Trade Establishments with Payroll   1,186
Annual Payroll (in millions) $161.0
Total Sales (in millions) $1,274.7
General Merchandise Stores (per capita) $841
Food Stores (per capita) $993
Apparel Stores (per capita) $344
Eating and Drinking Places (per capita) $712

Service Industries

Total Establishments   1,618
Total Receipts (in millions) $894.7
Hotels and Motels (in millions) $46.4
Health Services (in millions) $213.8
Legal Services (in millions) $134.4

Labor

 The share of the work force in manufacturing is higher than the national average at 30%. The region is noted for a strong work ethic. The labor force is expected to grow to 284,200 by 1995, a growth rate of 21.3% over the decade.

Labor

Civilian Labor Force   108,337
% Change 1989–1990   1.1

Work Force Distribution
Mining   NA
Construction   15,600
Manufacturing   100,400
Transportation and Public Utilities   13,500
Wholesale and Retail Trade   94,900
FIRE (Finance, Insurance, Real Estate)   15,900
Service   70,300
Government   32,500
Women as % of Labor Force   54.2
% Self-Employed   4.5
% Professional/Technical   15.0
Total Unemployment   8,230
Rate %   7.6
Federal Government Civilian Employment   1,968

Education

The Grand Rapids Public School System supports 71 schools. Nonpublic schools enroll 18,000 students. The higher education sector is notable for the strong presence of religious institutions. Of six four-year colleges, three are denominational: Aquinas College, Calvin College, and Grand Rapids Bible College. In addition there are five Bible colleges and seminaries: Grace Bible College, Grand Rapids School of Bible and Music, Reformed Bible College, Calvin Theological Seminary, and Grand Rapids Baptist Seminary. Public institutions of higher education include Grand Valley State University, Davenport College of Business, and Kendall College of Art and Design. In addition, three state

Education

Number of Public Schools   71
Special Education Schools   4
Total Enrollment   26,871
% Enrollment in Private Schools   21.5
% Minority   47.1
Classroom Teachers   2,268
Pupil-Teacher Ratio   11.8:1
Number of Graduates   1,065
Total Revenue (in millions) $163.2
Total Expenditures (in millions) $131.7
Expenditures per Pupil $3,937
Educational Attainment (Age 25 and Over)
% Completed 12 or More Years   67.1
% Completed 16 or More Years   16.4
Four-Year Colleges and Universities   5
Enrollment   12,284
Two-Year Colleges   2
Enrollment   15,883

Education (continued)

Libraries

Number 32
Public Libraries 6
Books (in thousands) 1,040
Circulation (in thousands) 1,018
Persons Served (in thousands) 189.1
Circulation per Person Served 5.38
Income (in millions) $3.691
Staff 106

Four-Year Colleges and Universities
Aquinas College
Calvin College
Davenport College of Business
Grand Rapids Baptist College and Seminary
Kendall School of Design

universities—Ferris State University, Michigan State University, and Western Michigan University—maintain campuses in Grand Rapids.

Health

Grand Rapids has nine hospitals in addition to mental health facilities, nursing homes, emergency medical centers, and rehabilitative clinics. The largest are Butterworth Hospital and Blodgett Memorial Medical Center. The other major medical facilities are Ferguson Hospital, Forest View Psychiatric Hospital, Kent Community Hospital, Mary Free Bed Hospital and Rehabilitation Center, Metropolitan Hospital, Pine Rest Christian Hospital, and St. Mary's Health Services.

Health

Deaths—Total 1,944
Rate per 1,000 10.6
Infant Deaths—Total 50
Rate per 1,000 12.7
Number of Metro Hospitals 9
Number of Metro Hospital Beds 2,524
Rate per 100,000 1,353
Number of Physicians NA
Physicians per 1,000 1.79
Nurses per 1,000 12.45
Health Expenditures per Capita NA

Transportation

Grand Rapids is accessed by Interstates 96, 196, and 296; U.S. 16 and 131; and state highways 11, 44, 50, 21, and 37. Rail passenger service is provided by Amtrak and rail freight service by CSX Transportation and Conrail.

Transportation

Interstate Highway Mileage 41
Total Urban Mileage 1,735
Total Daily Vehicle Mileage (in millions) 8.607
Daily Average Commute Time 37.6 min.
Number of Buses 79
Port Tonnage (in millions) NA

Transportation (continued)

Airports 1
Number of Daily Flights 33
Daily Average Number of Passengers 1,778

Airlines (American carriers only)
American
Delta
Northwest
United
USAir

Kent County International Airport, Michigan's second-largest airport, is located southeast of downtown Grand Rapids and is served by five commuter services and five airlines.

Housing

Grand Rapids has 73,716 housing units, of which 59.9% are owner occupied. The median value of an owner-occupied dwelling is $58,300 and the median monthly rent is $346. Continued population growth has resulted in a spurt of housing construction activity, most of it in the suburbs.

Housing

Total Housing Units 73,716
% Change 1980–1990 5.2
Vacant Units for Sale or Rent 3,316
Occupied Units 69,029
% with More Than One Person per Room 2.8
% Owner-Occupied 59.9
Median Value of Owner-Occupied Homes $58,300
Average Monthly Purchase Cost $315
Median Monthly Rent $346
New Private Housing Starts 449
Value (in thousands) $22,206
% Single-Family 48.3
Nonresidential Buildings Value (in thousands) $25,671

Urban Redevelopment

Urban redevelopment activity began in earnest in the 1960s. Major projects completed in the 1980s include the City Centre Mall, the Campau Square Plaza Building, the Calder Plaza Building, and the Grand Valley State University downtown campus.

Crime

Grand Rapids ranks below national average in crime rates. In 1991 the crimes known to police consisted of 3,278 violent crimes, and 14,216 property crimes.

Crime

Violent Crimes—Total 3,278
Violent Crime Rate per 100,000 645.8
Murder 22
Rape 370
Robbery 771

Aggravated Assaults   2,115
Property Crimes   14,216
Burglary   4,270
Larceny   8,675
Motor Vehicle Theft   1,271
Arson   113
Per Capita Police Expenditures $101.38
Per Capita Fire Protection Expenditures $75.86
Number of Police   259
Per 1,000   1.41

Religion

 Grand Rapids is closely identified with the Dutch Reformed Church, reflecting the influx of Dutch and Friesian immigrants into the area in the 19th century. Many of the largest Christian Reformed institutions, publishing houses, and churches are located here. The Baptists, who also are strong, maintain a seminary and college as do the Catholics.

Religion	
Largest Denominations (Adherents)	
Catholic	86,135
Christian Reformed	43,473
Assembly of God	9,021
Evangelical Lutheran	8,246
Reformed Church in America	20,738
Black Baptist	14,821
United Methodist	11,143
United Church of Christ	10,043
Lutheran-Missouri Synod	7,351
Jewish	1,090

Media

 The city daily is the *Grand Rapids Press.* The electronic media consist of 5 television stations (3 commercial networks, and 1 public and 1 independent network) and 18 AM and FM radio stations.

Media	
Newsprint	
Grand Rapids Business Journal, weekly	
Grand Rapids Magazine, monthly	
Grand Rapids Press, daily	
Television	
WGVU (Channel 35)	
WGVK (Channel 52)	
WOTV (Channel 8)	
WXMI (Channel 17)	
WZZM (Channel 13)	
Radio	
WBMX (AM)	WBYW (FM)
WBYY (AM)	WCSG (FM)
WCUZ (AM)	WCUZ (FM)
WFUR (AM)	WFUR (FM)
WGRD (AM)	WGRD (FM)
WJFM (FM)	WLAV (AM)
WLAV (FM)	WLHT (FM)
WMAX (AM)	WOOD (AM)
WOOD (FM)	WVGR (FM)

Sports

 Grand Rapids has no professional sports team. There are two semiprofessional teams, one basketball and one baseball. The local colleges field teams in many competitive sports.

Arts, Culture, and Tourism

Grand Rapids has over 54 large and small performing arts associations. In music the leaders are Opera Grand Rapids, the Grand Rapids Symphony Orchestra, the Grand Rapids Symphonic Band, and the St. Cecilia Music Society. In dance the Civic Ballet presents two performances each year. In drama, the Broadway Theater Guild brings first-class plays to the De Vorss Hall. Community Circle Theater presents stage productions from May through September at the John Ball Park Pavilion. The Grand Rapids Civic Theater presents six stage productions and six children's plays annually. Spectrum Theater, located downtown at Grand Rapids Junior College, is the home of the Actors Theater, Robeson Players, and Grand Rapids Players.

Grand Rapids Art Museum, built in 1913 and renovated in 1981, is the largest art museum between Chicago and Detroit. The Urban Institute for Contemporary Arts is an exhibition and performance center recognized for its innovation. The Gerald R. Ford Museum houses the memorabilia of the 38th president of the United States. The Grand Rapids Public Museum includes a 19th-century gaslight village and Native American artifacts. The Grand Rapids Furniture Museum displays American furniture from colonial times to the present.

Travel and Tourism	
Hotel Rooms 5,315	
Convention and Exhibit Space (square feet) NA	
Convention Centers	
Welsh Auditorium and Grand Center	
Festivals	
Arts Festival (June)	
Celebration on the Grand (September)	

Parks and Recreation

 The 143-acre Blandford Nature Center was an old farmstead with a schoolhouse. Recreational facilities include 21 inland lakes.

Sources of Further Information

City Hall
300 Monroe NW
Grand Rapids, MI 49503
(616) 456-3166

Grand Rapids Area Chamber of Commerce
17 Fountain Street NW
Grand Rapids, MI 49503
(616) 459-7221

Grand Rapids Historical Society
60 Library Plaza NE
Grand Rapids, MI 49503
(616) 456-3640

Grand Rapids Public Library
60 Library Plaza NE
Grand Rapids, MI 49503-3093
(616) 456-3600

Greater Grand Rapids Convention and Visitors Bureau
245 Monroe Avenue NW
Grand Rapids, MI 49503
(616) 456-3922

Additional Reading

Hinshaw, Candace W., and Jane B. Henderson. *Enjoying Grand Rapids and Surrounding Environs.* 1981.

Silvey, Kitty, and Marie Flagg. *Renaissance on the Grand.* 1982.

Tuttle, Charles R. *History of Grand Rapids.* 1974.

VanVulpen, James. *Grand Rapids, Then and Now.* 1988.

Green Bay

Wisconsin

Location and Topography

N

The city of Green Bay is located at the western edge of a peninsula on Lake Michigan's Green Bay, which separates a portion of eastern Wisconsin from the rest of the state. The city itself is split in two by the Fox River, a tributary of Lake Winnebago, which runs into Green Bay. An offshoot of the Fox River is the East River, which cuts into the northern part of the city. The city's name is derived from the lush green vegetation that at one time covered the bay area—*La Baye Verte*, hence Green Bay. Positioned about 140 miles northeast of the state capital of Madison, Green Bay's strategic location for the fur trade led it to become the first settlement in the state. It continues to be a major port city to the present day.

Layout of City and Suburbs

Because Green Bay is essentially two cities located on both banks of the Fox River, it has six bridges that tie it together. The main streets of both sides of the city include Mason, Walnut, and Main streets. Laid out in the traditional grid pattern of most major cities, north and south streets are named after early American presidents. It shares much of the southern Green Bay area with the suburbs of Ashwaubenon, De Pere, Duck Creek, Cormier, and Howard.

Climate

Green Bay's weather is determined by the lakes that it faces, modifying the continental climate. Although long winters with snowstorms are common, winter extremes are not severe. Snowfall averages 43 inches a year. The proximity of the lakes and the limited hours of sunshine because of cloudiness produce a narrow temperature range. Three-fifths of the total annual rainfall comes during the growing season, promoting lush vegetation.

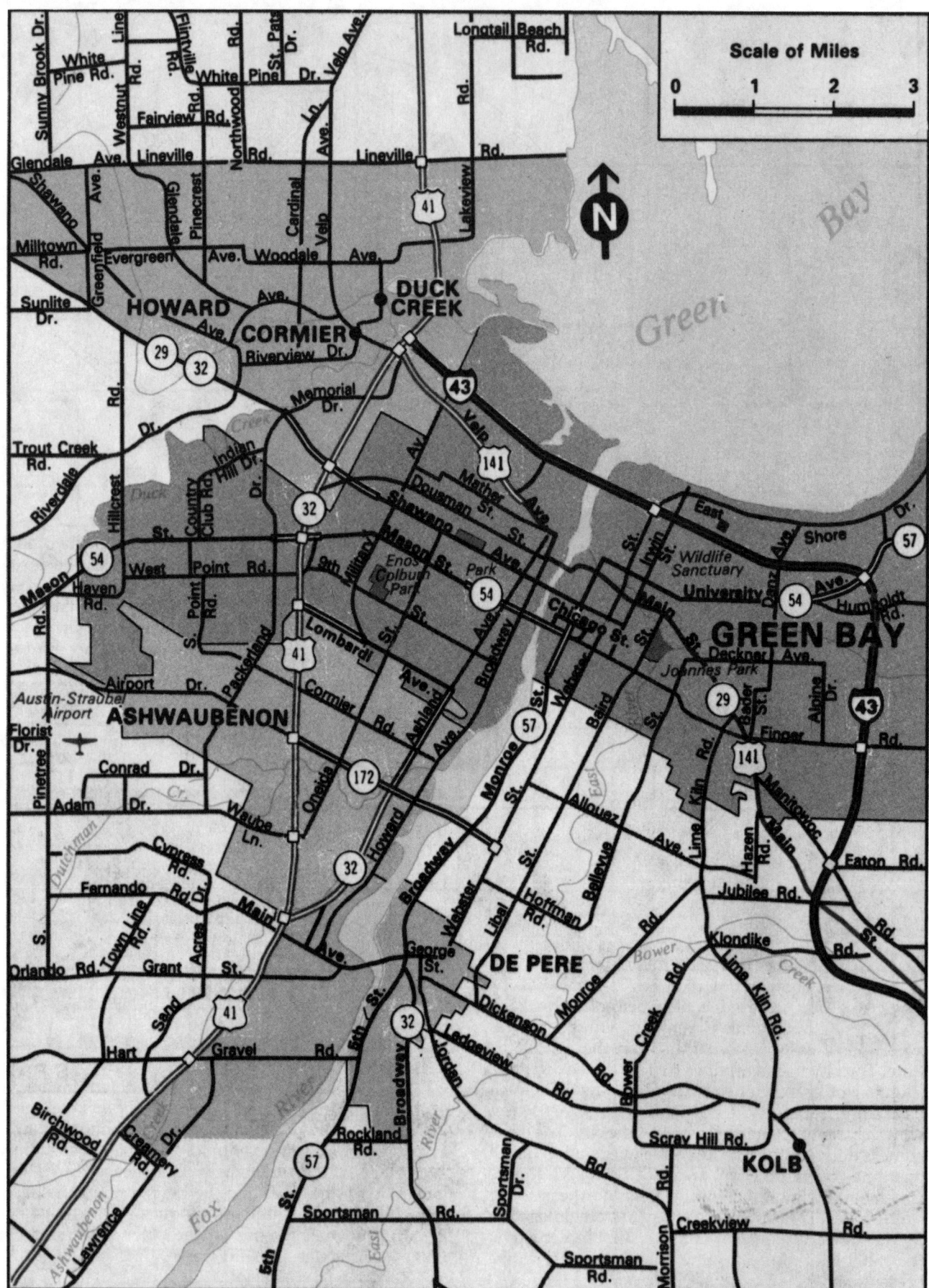

Weather			
Temperature			
Highest Monthly Average °F 80.9			
Lowest Monthly Average °F 5.4			
Annual Averages			
Days 32°F or Below 163			
Days above 90°F 7			
Zero Degree Days 29			
Precipitation (inches) 27.0			
Snow (inches) 43.0			
% Seasonal Humidity 73.0			
Wind Speed (m.p.h.) 10.2			
Clear Days 90			
Cloudy Days 173			
Storm Days 35			
Rainy Days 120			
Average Temperatures (°F)	*High*	*Low*	*Mean*
January	23.9	6.9	15.4
February	27.2	8.8	18.0
March	37.1	20.1	28.6
April	54.1	33.5	43.8
May	65.8	43.1	54.5
June	75.8	53.2	64.5
July	80.7	57.7	69.2
August	79.1	56.3	67.7
September	69.8	48.0	58.9
October	59.6	38.7	49.2
November	41.8	26.4	34.1
December	28.6	13.2	20.9

History

In 1634 Jean Nicolet landed at Red Banks on the shore of present-day Green Bay. An emissary of Samuel de Champlain, the governor of New France (Canada), Nicolet was sent to negotiate a peace treaty with the local Winnebago tribe, the so-called People of the Sea, and ally them with France. The landing area, called Baye de Puans, is now distinguished by a historical marker. The Winnebagos were impressed when Nicolet waded onto shore, claimed the land for the French empire, and fired his "thunder" (guns) into the air. They presented the newcomer with six beaver pelts. Nicolet wrote back to Champlain that such pelts would bring great profits to the empire. For the next 30 years, however, little attention was paid to Nicolet's advice.

In 1669 Father Claude Allouez established the first Jesuit fort—the Mission of St. Francis, at the site of Green Bay, which was then named La Baye. In 1673 the French explorers Father Jacques Marquette and Louis Jolliet started their exploration of the Mississippi River. Beginning at the mouth of the Fox River, they traced the waterway to New Orleans, thus opening up a trading route from Montreal, the capital of New France, to New Orleans.

For almost a hundred years, the French battled to start a colony at La Baye to exploit the fur trade. The Fox Indian Wars began in 1703 and took up precious time and manpower that the French had allocated for colonizing. Fort La Baye was built in 1717 both as a strategic outpost and as a means to continue the fur trade. The Second Fox War broke out in 1728, and the

French had to abandon and destroy the fort. In 1733, after a French general was killed by the Foxes, the fort was again reestablished. The French finally succeeded in finishing off the Foxes in 1740. This outcome allowed Fort La Baye to become a commercial and trading center.

About 1745, five years after the end of the Second Fox War, Frenchman Augustin de Langlade brought his family from Mackinac in what is now Michigan and settled around Fort La Baye. They were apparently the first white family to settle on the Fox River. Under the protection of the French, his trade prospered. However, in 1754 the French and Indian Wars began against British infringement in the middle western section of the United States known as the Northwest Territory. Within seven years, the French lost control of their colonies in Wisconsin and the British took over as a fundamental force.

In 1761, Fort La Baye was occupied by British forces under the command of Lieutenant James Gorrell. The remains of the old fort were restored, new portions added, and it was renamed Fort Edward Augustus. During the Pontiac uprising of 1763, the fort was abandoned. After the conflict, the British troops did not reoccupy it, essentially leaving it to the French pioneers who had settled there. The British influence, thus, was short. Within 20 years, the American Revolution had snatched the holding from the British and given it to the Americans, who began to transfer the power of the region's commercial activity to the new government. The work, however, was tough, and they did not fully share in the fur trade until after the War of 1812.

Just before Americans fully integrated the area under their control, John Jacob Astor's American Fur Company was organized in 1808 and secured dominance over the area's fur commerce. Astor asked for the construction of two forts for the protection of the trade. The U.S. government acceded and built Fort Howard at Green Bay and Fort Crawford at Prairie du Chien in 1816.

The Erie Canal's culmination in 1825 and the subjugation of the Black Hawk tribe in 1832 combined to draw settlers into the Green Bay region. With the backing of pioneers Daniel Whitney and Astor, who platted various sections of the settlement from 1829 to 1835, the city was chartered with the name of Green Bay in 1838. Incorporated in 1854, it was the largest city in Wisconsin, which became the 30th state on 29 May 1848.

Statehood provided a lure to Green Bay. Lithuanian and Irish workers came to the city with the railroads in the 1850s. German, Dutch, and Danish farmers plowed the land and made the state famous for its dairies. Norwegians came out of desire for religious freedom. Immigration dropped off in the late 19th century, and the main industry changed from furs to logging and then farming. The paper industry sprang up, making Green Bay at one point "the Tissue Capital of the World." Today its main industries include retail trade, health care, and farming. From 1880 until his

Chronology

1634 Jean Nicolet, an emissary of Samuel de Champlain, Governor of New France in Montreal, lands at the Baye de Puans near present-day Green Bay and claims the region in the name of the King of France. His introduction to beaver pelts serves to recognize the region for its eventual prosperity.

1669 Father Claude Allouez, a Jesuit missionary, founds the Mission of St. Francis at the area called La Baye.

1673 French explorers Father Jacques Marquette and Louis Jolliet penetrate the entire length of the Fox River and discover the upper reaches of the Mississippi, leading to a continuous route from Montreal to New Orleans.

1703 The outbreak of the First Fox Indian War leads to the French being bogged down in a shooting war.

1717 Fort La Baye is established as a strategic outpost and trading station.

1728 With the start of the Second Fox War, Fort La Baye is abandoned and destroyed by the French.

1733 The death of French officer Coulon de Villiers leads to the construction of a second Fort La Baye.

1745 Augustin de Langlade, a Frenchman from Mackinac, builds a trading post on the east bank of the Fox River and soon monopolizes the fur trade.

1754–1761 The French and Indian Wars leave the Northwest Territory and Fort La Baye in the hands of the British.

1761 British troops under the command of Lieutenant James Gorrell rebuild Fort La Baye and rename it Fort Edward Augustus.

1808 John Jacob Astor organizes the American Fur Company and dominates the Green Bay fur market.

1816 The U.S. government acts to protect Astor's business and builds Fort Howard at Green Bay and Fort Crawford at Prairie du Chien.

1825 The Erie Canal is completed.

1829–1835 Pioneers Daniel Whitney and Astor plat various parts of Green Bay, leading to the town's founding.

1838 Green Bay is chartered as a city.

1880 The population reaches 4,666.

1880–1926 Robert LaFollette becomes the most powerful politician in the state, serving as governor, senator, and presidential candidate (1924).

1900 The population reaches 18,684.

1967–1968 The Green Bay Packers football team wins Super Bowls I and II.

death in 1926, Robert LaFollette became the most powerful politician in the state, serving as governor, U.S. senator, and presidential candidate (1924). The state's recent fame is derived not by its history or economics but by sports, with the late 1960s success of Vince Lombardi and his Green Bay Packers football team.

Historical Landmarks

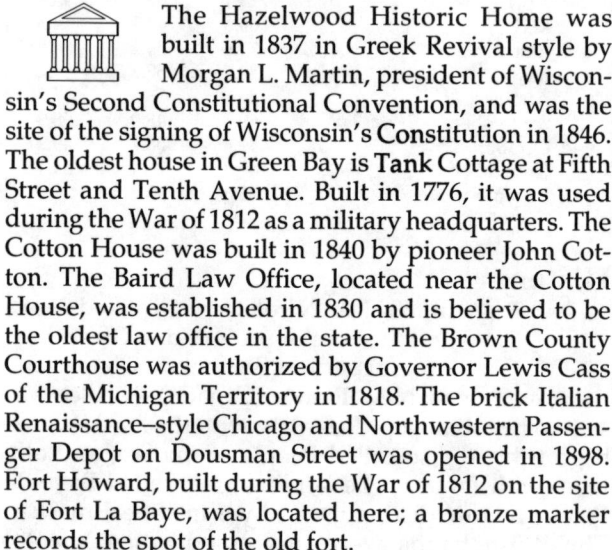

The Hazelwood Historic Home was built in 1837 in Greek Revival style by Morgan L. Martin, president of Wisconsin's Second Constitutional Convention, and was the site of the signing of Wisconsin's Constitution in 1846. The oldest house in Green Bay is Tank Cottage at Fifth Street and Tenth Avenue. Built in 1776, it was used during the War of 1812 as a military headquarters. The Cotton House was built in 1840 by pioneer John Cotton. The Baird Law Office, located near the Cotton House, was established in 1830 and is believed to be the oldest law office in the state. The Brown County Courthouse was authorized by Governor Lewis Cass of the Michigan Territory in 1818. The brick Italian Renaissance–style Chicago and Northwestern Passenger Depot on Dousman Street was opened in 1898. Fort Howard, built during the War of 1812 on the site of Fort La Baye, was located here; a bronze marker records the spot of the old fort.

Population

Although it is Wisconsin's oldest settlement, Green Bay never became a population center like Milwaukee, and it is still outside the list of large cities with over 100,000 residents. Its population in 1990 was 96,466, up from 87,899 in 1980 and 87,809 in 1970. Given the present tempo of growth and strong immigration rates, it may cross the 100,000 mark in the next decade.

Population		
	1980	*1990*
Central City	87,899	96,466
Rank	200	203
Metro Area	175,280	194,594
Pop. Change 1980–1990 +8,567		
Pop. % Change 1980–1990 +9.7		
Median Age 31.5		
% Male 47.8		
% Age 65 and Over 12.6		
Density (per square mile) 2,201		

Population (continued)

Households

Number 38,383
Persons per Household 2.45
% Female-Headed Households 10.8
% One-Person Households 29.1
Births—Total 1,542
    % to Mothers under 20 9.2
    Birth Rate per 1,000 17.1

Ethnic Composition

 Whites make up 94% of the population. American Indians are the largest minority with 2%.

Ethnic Composition (as % of total pop.)

	1980	1990
White	97.25	94.22
Black	0.25	0.47
American Indian	1.53	2.54
Asian and Pacific Islander	0.43	2.32
Hispanic	0.68	1.1
Other	NA	0.46

Government

 Green Bay is governed by a mayor and a council of 23 aldermen. The mayor is elected for a four-year term and the aldermen, who also serve as Brown County supervisors, for two-year terms.

Government

Year of Home Charter 1854
Number of Members of the Governing Body 23
Elected at Large NA
Elected by Wards 23
Number of Women in Governing Body 3
Salary of Mayor $51,000
Salary of Council Members $5,150
City Government Employment Total 1,198
Rate per 10,000 128.2

Public Finance

 The annual budget consists of revenues of $85.809 million and expenditures of $87.885 million. The debt outstanding is $61.288 million, and cash and security holdings $130.139 million.

Economy

Green Bay's leading employment sector is papermaking. Two of the top ten employers are involved in this industry: the Fort Howard Corporation, the largest private employer in the city, and Proctor & Gamble Paper Products. The second leading industrial sector is food products, revolving around Wisconsin's dairy industry. Retail sales are strong in Green Bay, making the city the predominant market for such services in the state.

Public Finance

Total Revenue (in millions) $85.809
Intergovernmental Revenue—Total (in millions) $31.03
Federal Revenue per Capita $1.9
% Federal Assistance 2.25
% State Assistance 33.19
Sales Tax as % of Total Revenue 0.57
Local Revenue as % of Total Revenue 57.35
City Income Tax no
Taxes—Total (in millions) $16.6

Taxes per Capita
    Total $177
    Property $170
    Sales and Gross Receipts $2
General Expenditures—Total (in millions) $70.2
General Expenditures per Capita $751
Capital Outlays per Capita $157

% of Expenditures for:
    Public Welfare 1.3
    Highways 19.4
    Education 0.0
    Health and Hospitals 1.3
    Police 12.4
    Sewerage and Sanitation 19.7
    Parks and Recreation 7.6
    Housing and Community Development 1.9
Debt Outstanding per Capita $904
    % Utility 9.7
Federal Procurement Contract Awards (in millions) $115.3
Federal Grants Awards (in millions) $6.5
Fiscal Year Begins January 1

Economy

Total Money Income (in millions) $996.577
% of State Average 103.5
Per Capita Annual Income $10,662
% Population below Poverty Level 9.6
Fortune 500 Companies 3

Banks	Number	Deposits (in millions)
Commercial	7	1,688
Savings	6	563

Passenger Autos 100,021
Electric Meters 73,220
Gas Meters 55,860

Manufacturing

Number of Establishments 183
% with 20 or More Employees 45.9
Manufacturing Payroll (in millions) $457.9
Value Added by Manufacture (in millions) $1,233.7
Value of Shipments (in millions) $3,711.9
New Capital Expenditures (in millions) $54.7

Wholesale Trade

Number of Establishments 273
Sales (in millions) $1,190.9
Annual Payroll (in millions) $79,982

Retail Trade

Number of Establishments 1,100
Total Sales (in millions) $817.0
Sales per Capita $8,741

Economy (continued)

Number of Retail Trade Establishments with Payroll   780
Annual Payroll (in millions) $97.4
Total Sales (in millions) $802.0
General Merchandise Stores (per capita) $1,486
Food Stores (per capita) $1,623
Apparel Stores (per capita) $386
Eating and Drinking Places (per capita) $832

Service Industries

Total Establishments   744
Total Receipts (in millions) $299.1
Hotels and Motels (in millions) $14.2
Health Services (in millions) $108.2
Legal Services (in millions) $15.7

Labor

Green Bay's job growth rate is second only to La Crosse in Wisconsin. Manufacturing is the largest employment sector, with 315 employers and over 50,000 workers. Trade and services form the second and third largest sectors, respectively. The labor force is expected to grow throughout the 1990s at 1% annually.

Labor

Civilian Labor Force   57,197
% Change 1989–1990   0.3

Work Force Distribution
   Mining   NA
   Construction   4,800
   Manufacturing   24,100
   Transportation and Public Utilities   7,900
   Wholesale and Retail Trade   26,700
   FIRE (Finance, Insurance, Real Estate)   6,400
   Service   26,400
   Government   12,100
   Women as % of Labor Force   43.7
   % Self-Employed   3.9
   % Professional/Technical   13.8
Total Unemployment   3,155
Rate %   5.5
Federal Government Civilian Employment   695

Education

The Green Bay Area Public School District (covering Green Bay as well as Allouez, Scott, and four other towns) supports 33 schools. Catholics and Lutherans run 20 parochial schools. Green Bay is one of the campuses of the giant University of Wisconsin system. The major private institution is St. Norbert College, a liberal four-year college.

Health

Green Bay is served by three hospitals: St. Vincent Hospital; Bellin Memorial Hospital and its affiliate, the Bellin College of Nursing; and St. Mary's Hospital. The Brown County Mental Health Center also is located in Green Bay.

Education

Number of Public Schools   33
Special Education Schools   NA
Total Enrollment   18,048
% Enrollment in Private Schools   19.9
% Minority   NA
Classroom Teachers   NA
Pupil-Teacher Ratio   NA
Number of Graduates   NA
Total Revenue (in millions)   NA
Total Expenditures (in millions)   NA
Expenditures per Pupil   NA
Educational Attainment (Age 25 and Over)
   % Completed 12 or More Years   71.5
   % Completed 16 or More Years   13.0
Four-Year Colleges and Universities   1
   Enrollment   4,800
Two-Year Colleges   1
   Enrollment   5,057

Libraries

Number   23
Public Libraries   9
Books (in thousands)   399
Circulation (in thousands)   1,547
Persons Served (in thousands)   193.8
Circulation per Person Served   7.98
Income (in millions) $3.809
Staff   NA

Four-Year Colleges and Universities
   University of Wisconsin–Green Bay
   St. Norbert College

Health

Deaths—Total   761
Rate per 1,000   8.5
Infant Deaths—Total   19
Rate per 1,000   12.3
Number of Metro Hospitals   3
Number of Metro Hospital Beds   1,120
Rate per 100,000   1,198
Number of Physicians   264
Physicians per 1,000   NA
Nurses per 1,000   NA
Health Expenditures per Capita $13.94

Transportation

Green Bay is linked to the rest of the state by I-43, which is coupled to U.S. 41 on the west side of the city. Other major roads in the area are U.S. 141 and state highways 29, 32, 54, and 57. Rail freight is handled by the Green Bay and Western, Wisconsin Central Limited, Chicago and Northwestern, Fox River Valley, Escambia, and Lake Superior railroads. Austin Straubel Airport, located just south of Green Bay in the community of Ashwaubenon, serves one major airline and five commuter airlines with over 40 flights a day. The Port of Green Bay is a major commerce and shipping harbor.

Transportation

Interstate Highway Mileage   11
Total Urban Mileage   852
Total Daily Vehicle Mileage (in millions)   3.588
Daily Average Commute Time   33.4 min.
Number of Buses   26
Port Tonnage (in millions)   1.640
Airports   1
Number of Daily Flights   17
Daily Average Number of Passengers   520

Airlines (American carriers only)
   Air Wisconsin
   Northwest

Housing

Wisconsin has affordable housing; the average home sells for $55,500 and a deluxe three-bedroom home for $85,000. Over 56% of the homes are owner-occupied.

Housing

Total Housing Units   39,726
% Change 1980–1990   13.3
Vacant Units for Sale or Rent   1,065
Occupied Units   38,383
% with More Than One Person per Room   2.2
% Owner-Occupied   56.6
Median Value of Owner-Occupied Homes $55,500
Average Monthly Purchase Cost $355
Median Monthly Rent $314
New Private Housing Starts   289
Value (in thousands) $25,451
% Single-Family   63.3
Nonresidential Buildings Value (in thousands) $28,729

Urban Redevelopment

Urban redevelopment is coordinated by Green Bay Advance, which has set up Business Development Center to facilitate construction of new business buildings. Among its major projects are the Interstate 43 Business Center and Madison Square, adjacent to Port Plaza Mall.

Crime

Green Bay is among the 100 safest cities in the nation, ranking 59th in public safety. Overall, in 1991, violent crime rate reached 344 known cases and property crime reached 4,638 known cases.

Crime

Violent Crimes—Total   344
Violent Crime Rate per 100,000   225.8
Murder   2
Rape   22
Robbery   37
Aggravated Assaults   283
Property Crimes   4,638
Burglary   623
Larceny   3,809

Crime (continued)

Motor Vehicle Theft   206
Arson   10
Per Capita Police Expenditures $118.18
Per Capita Fire Protection Expenditures $126.82
Number of Police   164
Per 1,000   1.82

Religion

Green Bay has 90 churches representing 26 denominations. Roman Catholicism has strong historical roots in the city.

Religion

Largest Denominations (Adherents)

Catholic	105,905
Evangelical Lutheran	13,302
Wisconsin Evangelical Lutheran Synod	4,939
United Methodist	4,542
Lutheran-Missouri Synod	7,825
Episcopal	2,848
Assembly of God	1,095
Presbyterian	1,957
Jewish	260

Media

Green Bay's press consists of two competing dailies: the *Green Bay-Press Gazette*, which is published in the evenings, Saturdays, and Sunday mornings, and the *Green Bay News-Chronicle*, published every morning except Sundays. The electronic media include five television stations (four network affiliates and one public) and six FM and AM radio stations.

Media

Newsprint
   Green Bay News-Chronicle, daily
   Green Bay Press-Gazette, daily

Television
   WBAY (Channel 2)
   WFRV (Channel 5)
   WGBA (Channel 26)
   WLUK (Channel 11)
   WPNE (Channel 38)

Radio
   WDUZ (AM)   WKFX (FM)
   WQLH (FM)   WGBW (FM)
   WIXX (FM)   WNFL (AM)

Sports

Green Bay's pride is the Green Bay Packers. The oldest modern professional football team, they have made the town famous throughout the nation. The team competes in the midwest division of the National Conference of the National Football League and plays in Lambeau Field.

Arts, Culture, and Tourism

The leading cultural institutions include the Weidner Center for the Performing Arts, which highlights theater and dance exhibitions; the Albert Pennings Hall of Fine Arts; the Brown County Memorial Arena, the site of rock concerts; and the Orpheum Theatre, built in 1903. Theatrical performances are handled by the Green Bay Community Theatre and the Next Door Theatre. Dance productions are held by Dance Company, Inc., and the New Dance troupe. Musical presentations are performed by the Green Bay Symphony Orchestra, the Civic Music Association, the Green Bay Boy's Choir, and the Pamiro Opera Company. The Neville Public Museum of Brown County displays Wisconsin and Green Bay historical exhibits. The Oneida Nation Museum is a showcase of the Oneida Nation's artifacts, including a reconstructed longhouse.The Heritage Hill Living History Museum is a replica of a pioneer community that endured at Green Bay for more than 300 years. The Green Bay Packer Hall of Fame highlights the history of the football team once coached by Vince Lombardi.

Parks and Recreation

Among Green Bay's parks are the 356-acre Baird Creek Parkway, the Bay Beach Wildlife Sanctuary, Ho-Nis-Ra Park, Fort Howard Park, and the Euers Nature Area.

Sources of Further Information

Green Bay Area Visitor and Convention Bureau
1901 South Oneida Street
Green Bay, WI 54307-0596
(800) 236-3976

Green Bay Economic Development
100 North Jefferson Street
Green Bay, WI 54301
(414) 448-3400

Additional Reading

Brody, Polly, *Discovering Wisconsin*. 1973.
Foley, Betsey. *Green Bay: Gateway to the Great Waterway*. 1983.

Travel and Tourism

Hotel Rooms   2,107
Convention and Exhibit Space (square feet)   NA

Convention Centers
  Brown County Expo Center Complex
  Brown County Veterans Memorial Arena

Festivals
  Artstreet

Greensboro
North Carolina

Location and Topography

Greensboro is in the rolling hills and thick forests of the Piedmont region of central North Carolina. About 80 miles west of Raleigh, the state capital, it is a third, with Winston-Salem and High Point, of the Triad.

Layout of City and Suburbs

The two main thoroughfares in Greensboro are Elm Street, which runs north and south, and Market Street, which runs east to west. Downtown is marked notably by the campus of the university of North Carolina at Greensboro. The city's streets are in a grid, with the Southern Railway cutting across the city just south of the university. Greensboro is surrounded by the suburbs of Pomona, Friendship, Pleasant Garden, Sedgefield, and Groometown.

Environment

Environmental Stress Index	3.4
Green Cities Index: Rank	75
Score	33.20
Water Quality Alkaline, soft	
Average Daily Use (gallons per capita)	183
Maximum Supply (gallons per capita)	333
Parkland as % of Total City Area	5.0
% Waste Landfilled/Recycled	NA
Annual Parks Expenditures per Capita	$111.22

Climate

Shielded from the cold winds from the north and west by mountains, Greensboro enjoys a relatively mild climate. While freezing temperatures occur over half of winter, zero-degree days are virtually unknown. Occasionally snowstorms may bring more than an inch of snow; during some seasons 15 to 20 inches are not uncommon. Summer temperatures are more uncertain, varying according to thunderstorm activity and cloud cover.

Weather

Temperature

Highest Monthly Average °F	87.4
Lowest Monthly Average °F	27.3

Annual Averages

Days 32°F or Below	85
Days above 90°F	39
Zero Degree Days	0
Precipitation (inches)	42.47
Snow (inches)	9.0
% Seasonal Humidity	69.0
Wind Speed (m.p.h.)	7.5

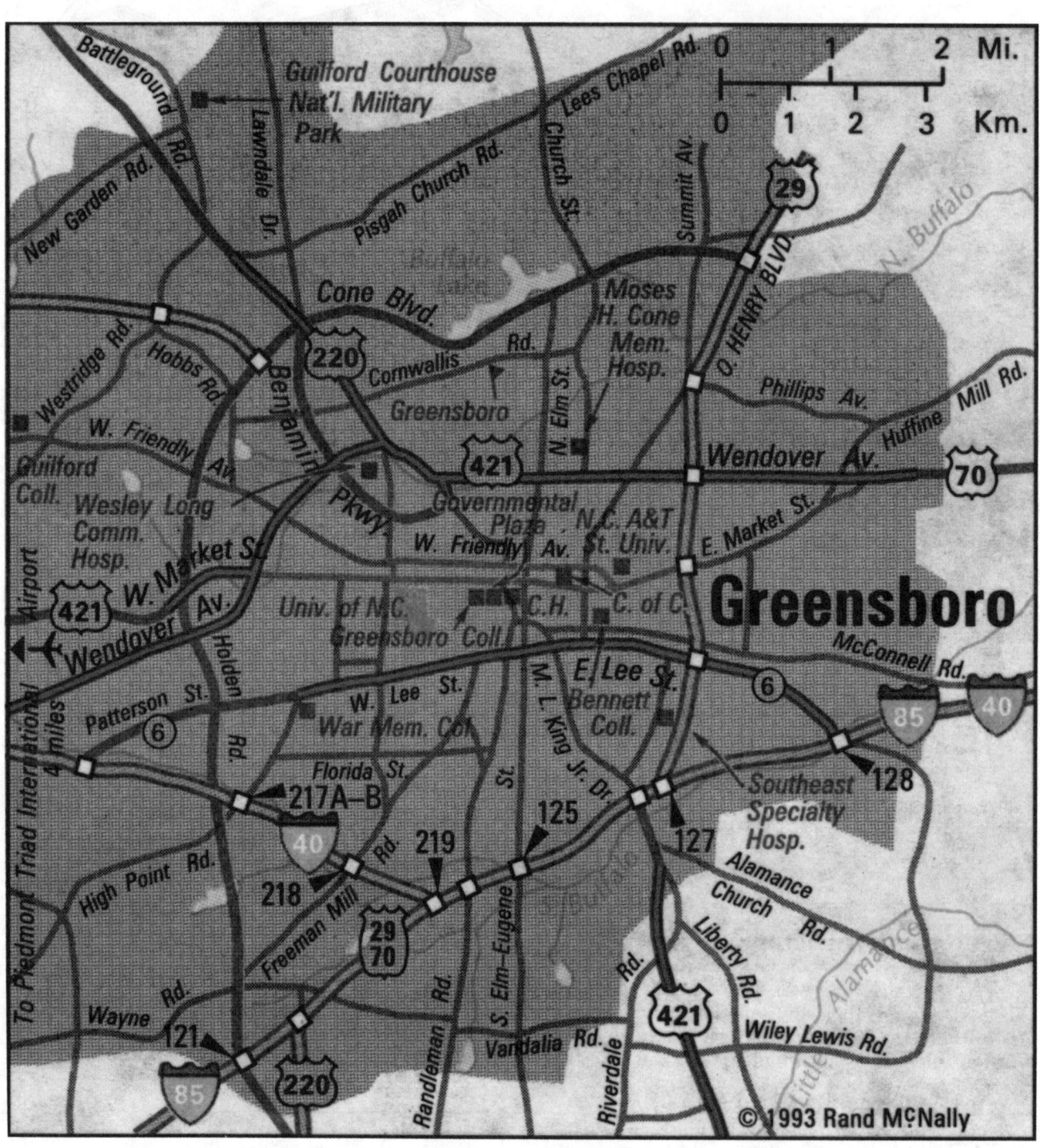

Weather (continued)

Clear Days   110
Cloudy Days   148
Storm Days   42
Rainy Days   109

Average Temperatures (°F)	High	Low	Mean
January	49.6	32.0	40.8
February	56.7	33.6	45.2
March	62.7	42.1	52.4
April	71.3	50.0	60.7
May	81.0	61.9	71.5
June	85.5	64.5	75.0
July	88.7	70.2	79.5
August	85.4	67.0	76.2
September	81.2	59.9	70.6
October	73.2	47.4	60.3
November	59.7	37.2	48.5
December	55.6	34.1	44.9

History

In 1749, the area now occupied by Greensboro was settled with a grant from John Carteret, the Earl of Grandville, to the Nottingham Company to settle Germans, Quakers of English and Welsh extraction, and others of Scotch-Irish ancestry who arrived from the more northern colonies. Five miles northwest of present-day Greensboro, a small courthouse was built in 1774 and named after Lord North, later the Earl of Guilford; a village named Guilford Courthouse sprang up around it. In 1781, this area was the site of the pivotal Battle of Guilford Courthouse during the American Revolutionary War, when the forces of American General Nathanael Greene defeated those of the British general Lord Cornwallis. After the Revolution, this settlement became known as Martinville, after Alexander Martin, a governor of North Carolina. In the first years of the 19th century, the counties of Rockingham and Randolph were carved out of Guilford County. Eventually, because of Martinville's remote location, the new state legislature in 1807 saw the need to create a more centrally located seat of county government for the citizens of Guilford County. The following year, a 42-acre plot was mapped, $98 was paid for it, and the town of Greensborough, named for Nathanael Greene, was founded.

Education and industry contributed to Greensboro's (the name was shortened in 1895) expansion and rise in population. In 1767, Dr. David Caldwell set up a Quaker log cabin school for teachers that today is Guilford College, the first co-educational school in the South. In 1828, the first steam-driven cotton mill was built by Henry Humphreys. A former student of Caldwell's school, John Motley Morehead (later to become a governor of the state), successfully lobbied to have the North Carolina railroad routed through Greensboro. The tracks reached the city in 1856. Because of the railroad, Greensboro became an arms depot during the Civil War. After General Robert E. Lee's surrender at Appomattox in 1865, Confederate president Jefferson Davis fled south to avoid capture, passing through Greensboro on his way.

Union troops occupied Greensboro for a time after the Civil War. Yardley Warner, a Quaker from the North, purchased 34 acres to create Warnerville, a village for freedmen, which eventually became part of the city. Greensboro gradually regained its prewar economic momentum. In 1895, Mose and Caesar Cone built the Southern Finishing and Warehouse Company, a textile finishing mill that later became Cone Mills. Eventually, Blue Bell and Burlington Industries moved to Greensboro, giving the city three of the world's largest textile manufacturing companies.

During World War II Greensboro became the site of a training center for army recruits. This training facility in 1944 was turned into the Overseas Replacement Depot (ORD) for the U.S. army in the eastern section of the United States. In 1960, Greensboro was the first city in which black students staged sit-ins at segregated dining facilities. These sit-ins began the civil rights movement against Jim Crow laws across the South.

Historical Landmarks

The site of Old Greensborough is now a renovated district that highlights the earliest of the city's architectural and cultural heritage. Guilford Courthouse, just north of the city, is a national military park that commemorates the Battle of Guilford Courthouse in 1781. The Colonial Heritage Center and Hoskins House at Tannenbaum Park is a Revolutionary War display showing the site of the British troop encampment. The Charlotte Hawkins Brown Memorial State Historic Site, the first site in the state to honor an black woman, is in the former Brown's Palmer Memorial Institute, a preparatory school for blacks that operated from 1902 until 1971. The Blandwood Mansion, a lavish Italian villa, was once the home of North Carolina governor John Motley Morehead and is now a National Historic Landmark.

Population

Like many southern cities, Greensboro has consistently gained population since the end of World War II. Between 1970 and 1980 it grew by 8%, from 144,000 to 155,642; between 1980 and 1990 it grew by 17.9%, to 183,521.

Population

	1980	1990
Central City	155,642	183,521
Rank	100	88
Metro Area	851,444	942,091
Pop. Change 1980–1990 +27,879		
Pop. % Change 1980–1990 +17.9		
Median Age 32.2		
% Male 46.4		
% Age 65 and Over 11.8		
Density (per square mile) 2,299		

Chronology

1749 The Nottingham Company receives a land grant near the present site of Greensboro from John Carteret, Earl of Grandville to settle German, Welsh and English Quaker, and Scotch-Irish immigrants.

1767 Dr. David Caldwell founds the first co-educational school for the instruction of teachers in the South; school later becomes Guilford College.

1774 A courthouse is built northwest of present-day Greensboro, and a small community called Guilford Courthouse springs up around it.

1781 Guilford Courthouse is the site of a major Revolutionary War battle between American forces under General Nathanael Greene and British General Lord Cornwallis; American forces win.

1807 Guilford County divided into three counties. Guilford County citizens ask the state legislature to create a more centrally located county seat.

1808 State legislature orders that 42 acres east of Guilford Courthouse be bought, mapped, and settled as Greensborough, named in honor of General Nathanael Greene.

1828 Henry Humphreys opens the first steam-driven cotton mill in Greensborough.

1856 Governor John Motley Morehead gets the North Carolina Railroad to lay its tracks to Greensborough.

1861–1865 Greensborough is a Confederate weapons depot. As the war ends, Confederate president Jefferson Davis passes through the town as he flees from capture. Union forces eventually occupy the city.

1895 The town name of Greensborough is shortened to its present form. Mose and Caesar Cone open the Southern Finishing and Warehouse Company, which later becomes Cone Mills.

1941–1944 Greensboro becomes a training center for American troops. In 1944 the training facility is turned into the Overseas Replacement Depot (ORD) for the U.S. army for the eastern United States.

1960 Greensboro is the site of the first sit-in demonstration by black students from North Carolina A&T University protesting segregation.

Population (continued)

Households

Number 74,905
Persons per Household 2.33
% Female-Headed Households 13.8
% One-Person Households 30.5
Births—Total 2,060
    % to Mothers under 20 14.2
    Birth Rate per 1,000 12.9

Ethnic Composition

Whites make up 63.9%, blacks 33.9%, American Indians 0.5%, Asian and Pacific Islanders 1.4%, and others 0.3% of the population.

Ethnic Composition (as % of total pop.)		
	1980	1990
White	65.74	63.88
Black	33.01	33.95
American Indian	0.49	0.46
Asian and Pacific Islander	0.44	1.43
Hispanic	0.77	0.96
Other	NA	0.27

Government

Greensboro adopted a council-manager form of government in 1921. The council consists of a mayor and eight members, all elected on a nonpartisan ballot. The city manager is appointed by the council as the city's chief executive.

Government
Year of Home Charter   NA
Number of Members of the Governing Body   8
Elected at Large   3
Elected by Wards   5
Number of Women in Governing Body   3
Salary of Mayor $12,500
Salary of Council Members $9,500
City Government Employment Total   2,935
Rate per 10,000   166.1

Public Finance

The annual budget consists of revenues of $154.020 million and expenditures of $170.035 million. Debt outstanding is $87.055 million, and cash and reserve holdings are $83.830 million.

Economy

The service industry and manufacturing push the engine of Greensboro's economy. Service companies include AT&T, American Express, and Sears Roebuck. Manufacturing of textiles, represented by Burlington Industries, Cone Mills, and Guilford Mills, is one of the largest in the nation. Lorillard, one of the nation's largest cigarette producers, manufactures cigarettes. The Guil-

Public Finance

Total Revenue (in millions) $154.020
Intergovernmental Revenue—Total (in millions) $44.79
Federal Revenue per Capita $1.88
% Federal Assistance 1.22
% State Assistance 15.05
Sales Tax as % of Total Revenue 0.29
Local Revenue as % of Total Revenue 67.42
City Income Tax no
Taxes—Total (in millions) $31.6

Taxes per Capita
   Total $179
   Property $166
   Sales and Gross Receipts $0
General Expenditures—Total (in millions) $82.2
General Expenditures per Capita $465
Capital Outlays per Capita $34

% of Expenditures for:
   Public Welfare 0.0
   Highways 9.6
   Education 0.0
   Health and Hospitals 0.0
   Police 18.6
   Sewerage and Sanitation 17.7
   Parks and Recreation 15.6
   Housing and Community Development 4.2
Debt Outstanding per Capita $120
   % Utility 15.3
Federal Procurement Contract Awards (in millions) $408.7
Federal Grants Awards (in millions) $14.1
Fiscal Year Begins July 1

Economy

Total Money Income (in millions) $2,064.3
% of State Average 122.8
Per Capita Annual Income $11,686
% Population below Poverty Level 12.8
Fortune 500 Companies 4

Banks	Number	Deposits (in millions)
Commercial	13	746.262
Savings	10	763.834

Passenger Autos 214,472
Electric Meters 104,020
Gas Meters 30,600

Manufacturing

Number of Establishments 396
% with 20 or More Employees 43.4
Manufacturing Payroll (in millions) $656.1
Value Added by Manufacture (in millions) $2,258.8
Value of Shipments (in millions) $3,679.9
New Capital Expenditures (in millions) $71.4

Wholesale Trade

Number of Establishments 742
Sales (in millions) $4,353.8
Annual Payroll (in millions) $278.640

Retail Trade

Number of Establishments 2,281
Total Sales (in millions) $2,042.0
Sales per Capita $11,560
Number of Retail Trade Establishments with Payroll 1,651
Annual Payroll (in millions) $250.2
Total Sales (in millions) $2,008.0
General Merchandise Stores (per capita) $1,534
Food Stores (per capita) $1,760
Apparel Stores (per capita) $731
Eating and Drinking Places (per capita) $1,168

Economy (continued)

Service Industries

Total Establishments 1,867
Total Receipts (in millions) $849.2
Hotels and Motels (in millions) $59.1
Health Services (in millions) $207.5
Legal Services (in millions) $52.6

ford County school system is the third-largest employer, followed by the Mose H. Cone Hospital.

Labor

Greensboro's demographic growth is matched by the growth in employment opportunities. Its manufacturing base is so strong that the manufacturing work force is double that employed in services and 50% more than in trade. The largest employers are Sears, Roebuck, AT&T Technologies, Cone Mills, P. Lorillard, American Express, Gilbarco, Guilford Mills, Jefferson Pilot Insurance Company, and AMP. Forty-five foreign companies are located here including 11 from Germany, 9 from Japan, and 8 from the United Kingdom. The unemployment rate, currently 4.0%, has been below the national rate for a number of years.

Labor

Civilian Labor Force 93,241
% Change 1989–1990 0.0

Work Force Distribution
   Mining NA
   Construction 22,200
   Manufacturing 143,400
   Transportation and Public Utilities 26,500
   Wholesale and Retail Trade 114,000
   FIRE (Finance, Insurance, Real Estate) 23,900
   Service 104,700
   Government 55,100
   Women as % of Labor Force 47.6
   % Self-Employed 4.2
   % Professional/Technical 16.4
Total Unemployment 3,755
Rate % 4.0
Federal Government Civilian Employment 2,730

Education

Greensboro has 40 public schools. The public school system is complemented by a dozen private and parochial schools. The city also operates the Weaver Education Center, which offers vocational, specialized, and advanced courses. The University of North Carolina at Greensboro is the largest of the higher education facilities in the city. The North Carolina Agricultural and Technical State University was founded in 1891 as a land grant institution offering agricultural and mechanical training to blacks. The city's three private institutions were all founded in the 19th century and, though smaller than public institutions, enjoy considerable prestige. Guilford College, the oldest, was incorporated as a college in 1834 by the Quakers, and it is the third oldest co-educational college in the nation. Greensboro College, founded by the Methodists a year later, is the third college chartered for women in the nation; it is located in the historic College Hill area. Bennett College opened in 1873 as a normal school for children of former slaves; it became a women's college in 1926. It also is affiliated with the Methodist Church. Other institutions include the Guilford Technical Community College and Rutledge College.

Education

Number of Public Schools 40
Special Education Schools 2
Total Enrollment 24,575
% Enrollment in Private Schools 6.7
% Minority 54.5
Classroom Teachers 1,274
Pupil-Teacher Ratio 16:1
Number of Graduates 1,398
Total Revenue (in millions) $91.840
Total Expenditures (in millions) $85.824
Expenditures per Pupil $3,993
Educational Attainment (Age 25 and Over)
   % Completed 12 or More Years 68.6
   % Completed 16 or More Years 24.6
Four-Year Colleges and Universities 4
   Enrollment 15,110
Two-Year Colleges NA
   Enrollment NA

Libraries

Number 30
Public Libraries 8
Books (in thousands) 57.5
Circulation (in thousands) 1,687
Persons Served (in thousands) 345
Circulation per Person Served 4.88
Income (in millions) $4.532
Staff 101

Four-Year Colleges and Universities
   Bennett College
   Greensboro College
   Guilford College
   University of North Carolina at Greensboro

Health

The largest medical facilities are Mose H. Cone Hospital, founded by the Cone Family Trust; Wesley Long Community Hospital, founded by John Wesley Long; Humana Hospital; and L. Richardson Memorial Hospital, named in honor of the founder of Vicks products. Specialty hospitals include Charter Hill Psychiatric Hospital and Southeastern Eye Center.

Health

Deaths—Total 1,358
Rate per 1,000 8.5
Infant Deaths—Total 28
Rate per 1,000 13.6
Number of Metro Hospitals 6
Number of Metro Hospital Beds 1,128
Rate per 100,000 639
Number of Physicians 1,759
Physicians per 1,000 2.16
Nurses per 1,000 6.92
Health Expenditures per Capita $2.37

Transportation

Greensboro is approached and intersected by two interstates: I-40 and I-85. These highways provide access to other interstates, such as I-77, I-75, I-81, and I-95. The city is also served by U.S. 29, 70, 220, and 421, and state roads 6, 22, 61, 62, 68, and 150. Rail service is provided by the Norfolk-Southern Railroad. The principal air terminus is the Piedmont Triad International Airport centrally located between Greensboro, Winston-Salem, and High Point.

Transportation

Interstate Highway Mileage 20
Total Urban Mileage 1,034
Total Daily Vehicle Mileage (in millions) 5.287
Daily Average Commute Time 40.5 min.
Number of Buses 71
Port Tonnage (in millions) NA
Airports 1
Number of Daily Flights 58
Daily Average Number of Passengers 2,450

Airlines (American carriers only)
   Air Wisconsin
   American
   Continental
   Delta
   United
   USAir

Housing

Of the total housing stock, 53.7% is owner-occupied. The median value of an owner-occupied home is $78,500, and the median monthly rent is $358.

Housing

Total Housing Units 80,411
% Change 1980–1990 25.6
Vacant Units for Sale or Rent 4,297
Occupied Units 74,905
% with More Than One Person per Room 2.4
% Owner-Occupied 53.7
Median Value of Owner-Occupied Homes $78,500
Average Monthly Purchase Cost $345
Median Monthly Rent $358
New Private Housing Starts 748

Housing (continued)	
Value (in thousands)	$44,221
% Single-Family	73.5
Nonresidential Buildings Value (in thousands)	$49,533

Urban Redevelopment

Most new urban redevelopment projects are concentrated on the corridor off I-40 leading to the Piedmont Triad International Airport. Many corporate offices located in Greensboro in the 1980s, which caused a boom in industrial and office construction. Since 1985 6.2 million square feet of office space and 15.4 million square feet of industrial space have been built.

Crime

Greensboro ranks slightly below the national average in public safety. In 1991, crimes known to police consisted of 1,799 violent crimes and 14,970 property crimes.

Crime

Violent Crimes—Total	1,799
Violent Crime Rate per 100,000	732.9
Murder	35
Rape	114
Robbery	594
Aggravated Assaults	1,056
Property Crimes	14,970
Burglary	3,379
Larceny	10,768
Motor Vehicle Theft	823
Arson	81
Per Capita Police Expenditures	$130.43
Per Capita Fire Protection Expenditures	$73.36
Number of Police	366
Per 1,000	2.26

Religion

Greensboro has over 350 Protestant churches, 4 Catholic churches, 1 Greek Orthodox church, and 1 Jewish synagogue. Among Protestants the largest denominations are Southern Baptists, Black Baptists, and United Methodists.

Religion

Largest Denominations (Adherents)	
Catholic	10,339
Southern Baptist	52,832
Black Baptist	23,833
United Methodist	42,083
Presbyterian	16,851
American Zion	16,014
Friends	4,445
Wesleyan	4,451
Episcopal	4,874
Evangelical Lutheran	4,417
Jewish	1,162

Media

Greensboro's lone city daily newspaper is the *Greensboro News and Record*. The city's electronic media consist of two television stations (one network and one religious) and two others picked up from the cities of Winston-Salem; ten AM and FM radio stations directly serve the city, while other stations are picked up from Winston-Salem and High Point.

Media

Newsprint
A & T Register, weekly
Greensboro News and Record, daily

Television
WFMY (Channel 2)
WEJC (Channel 20)
WGGT (Channel 48)
WLXI (Channel 61)

Radio

WJMH (FM)	WKEW (AM)
WKRR (FM)	WNAA (FM)
WPET (AM)	WKSI (FM)
WQFS (FM)	WQMG (AM)
WQMG (FM)	WWMY (FM)

Sports

Greensboro has no major professional sports team. The closest to a local favorite in sports is the Hornets, a farm team of the New York Yankees, who play their home games at the War Memorial Stadium. Other semi-professional teams include the Monarchs, a member of the East Coast Hockey League, and the Dynamos, part of the United States Interregional Soccer League (USISL). The University of North Carolina at Greensboro fields a strong soccer team, the Spartans, and North Carolina Agricultural and Technical State University has a strong basketball team that plays at the 17,500-seat Aggie Stadium.

Arts, Culture, and Tourism

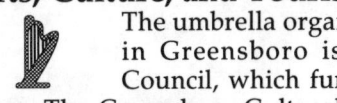

The umbrella organization for the arts in Greensboro is the United Arts Council, which funds eight organizations. The Greensboro Cultural Center at Festival Park is a five-building complex housing 25 arts organizations, including the Green Hill Center for North Carolina Art, the Guilford Native American

Travel and Tourism

Hotel Rooms 11,478
Convention and Exhibit Space (square feet) NA

Convention Centers
Greensboro Coliseum
Carolina Theater

Festivals
Jazzfest (June)
Eastern Music Festival (June)

Gallery, the Greensboro Artists League Gallery, the African American Art Gallery, and the African Heritage Center Gallery. In music, the Greensboro Symphony performs at the War Memorial Coliseum, and the Piedmont Blues Preservation Society sponsors a blues festival every May. Jazzfest, a summer program of jazz performances, takes place at the Carolina Theatre, a restored 1927 movie house. Plays are held at the Carolina as well as at the Broach Theatre by Corson Productions.

Parks and Recreation

The Greensboro city park system takes care of over 100 parks and recreational areas. Among the largest are Emerald Point, a massive 45-acre amusement park; the Bryan Park complex located next to Lake Townsend, which sports two golf courses; and the Barber, Bur-Mil, and Oka T. Hester parks.

Sources of Further Information

Greensboro Area Chamber of Commerce
125 South Elm Street
Greensboro, NC 27401
(919) 275-8675

Greensboro City Hall
P.O. Box 3136
Greensboro, NC 27402-3136
(919) 373-2000

Greensboro Area Convention and Visitors Bureau
317 South Greene Street
Greensboro, NC 27401-2615
(800) 344-2282

Additional Reading

Polk's Greensboro City Directory. 1991.
Greensboro Cross-Reference Directory. 1991.
Turner, Ginny, ed. *North Carolina Traveler: A Vacationer's Guide to the Mountains, Coast and Piedmont.* 1991.

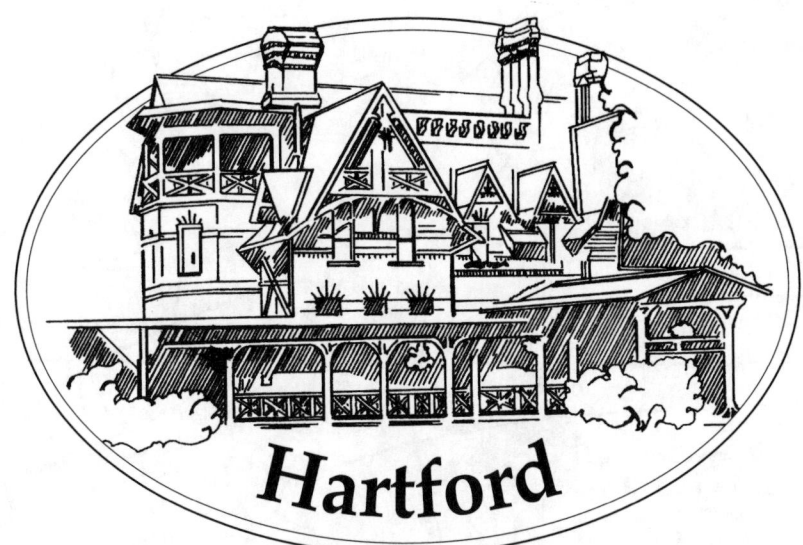

Hartford

Connecticut

Basic Data

Name   Hartford
Name Origin   From Hartford, England
Year Founded   1635 Inc. 1784
Status: State   Capital of Connecticut
     County   Seat of Hartford County
Area (square miles)   17.3
Elevation (feet)   40
Time Zone   EST
Population (1990)   139,739
Population of Metro Area (1990)   1,123,678

Sister Cities

    Caguas, Puerto Rico
    Florida, Italy
    Freetown, Sierra Leone
    Morant Bay, Jamaica
    Ocotal, Nicaragua
    Thessaloniki, Greece

Distance in Miles To:

Atlanta	959
Boston	107
Chicago	908
Dallas	1,691
Denver	1,997
Detroit	728
Houston	1,731
Los Angeles	2,899
Miami	1,416
New York	119
Philadelphia	225
Washington, DC	359

Location and Topography

N Hartford is located in Hartford County in the Connecticut River Valley on the west side of the Connecticut River. The terrain is gently rolling with extensive level areas. Through the center of the city meanders the narrow Park River, but the Connecticut River is hidden behind dikes and a railway embankment.

Layout of City and Suburbs

 The city's hub is a slight rise known as Capitol Hill on which there is a group of county and state buildings. The business district is dominated by the great insurance companies: Travelers, Aetna, The Hartford, Phoenix Mutual, and Cigna. In a central triangular plot on Main Street is the Old State House, next to which is The Pavilion, a sleek art deco–inspired office and retail complex. To the south is the pink granite (J. Pierpont) Morgan Memorial and the Center Church, of which Thomas Hooker was once pastor in the 17th century. Main Street is only 40 feet above sea level; Front Street is much lower, and only Capitol Hill and points to the west are higher than the main thoroughfare. Ever conscious of the flood hazard, the city has built an extensive system of dikes. The better residential sections are farther back from the river. Some 22% of the city consists of municipal parks or squares.

Environment

Environmental Stress Index   2.4
Green Cities Index: Rank   NA
              Score   NA
Water Quality   Acid, very soft, fluoridated
    Average Daily Use (gallons per capita)   147
    Maximum Supply (gallons per capita)   NA
Parkland as % of Total City Area   NA
% Waste Landfilled/Recycled   NA
Annual Parks Expenditures per Capita $144.13

Climate

Hartford enjoys a moderate New England climate with few extremes of heat or cold. The warmest month is July, when the average temperature is 75°F, and winters are generally moderate. There are some stretches of very cold weather, usually in January or February, when

temperatures stay in the teens or low 20s and drop into single digits at night. Snowfall may average 12 inches in February and 9.5 inches in March. Annual snowfall averages 48.8 inches. Autumn foliage is very colorful in the area. Rainfall averages between 3.8 and 4.4 inches in autumn and between 3.2 and 3.8 inches in summer. Storms moving from the Berkshire Mountains, a northern branch of the Appalachian chain, account for the frequent thunderstorms in summer, while the Atlantic Ocean is the source of the rain storms known as northeasters.

Weather

Temperature

Highest Monthly Average °F	84.8
Lowest Monthly Average °F	16.7

Annual Averages

Days 32°F or Below	136
Days above 90°F	20
Zero Degree Days	6
Precipitation (inches)	44.39
Snow (inches)	48.8
% Seasonal Humidity	64.5
Wind Speed (m.p.h.)	8.5
Clear Days	81
Cloudy Days	175
Storm Days	22
Rainy Days	128

Average Temperatures (°F)	High	Low	Mean
January	33.4	16.1	24.8
February	35.7	17.9	26.8
March	44.6	26.6	35.6
April	58.9	36.5	47.7
May	70.3	46.2	58.3
June	79.5	56.0	67.8
July	84.1	61.2	72.7
August	81.9	58.9	70.4
September	74.5	51.0	62.8
October	64.3	40.8	52.6
November	50.6	31.9	41.3
December	36.8	19.6	28.2

History

The first white man to land in Hartford was Jacob van Curler, who in 1633 built a fort and mounted two guns at Suckiage, under orders from the governor of New Amsterdam. The Dutch called the place The House of Hope, and today the site is known as the Dutch Point. The first permanent English settlement was made in 1635 when John Steele and 60 pioneers from New Towne in Massachusetts settled in October 1635, followed by the Reverend Thomas Hooker and his company in the spring of 1636. At first called Newtown, the settlement was renamed Hartford in 1637. When the colonists discovered that they were no longer under the jurisdiction of Massachusetts, representatives of the river settlements met at Hartford to draw up a plan of government. The constitution, written by Roger Ludlow, was adopted in 1639. Hartford County was organized in 1635, but the city and town were not incorporated until 1784. The British proved better colonizers than the Dutch; their Windsor, Wethersfield, and Hartford settlements cut off the Dutch trade with the Indians to such an extent that The House of Hope garrison abandoned the fort. The Colonial Court met in 1654 and the fort was occupied in the name of England without a shot being fired. By 1662 the Hartford Colony consisted of 14 towns; it was united with the 6 New Haven settlements in 1665, and by decree of the General Court, the legislature was ordered to meet in Hartford. In practice, however, the legislature met alternately in New Haven and Hartford until 1875. Hartford became an independent colony in 1662 with a charter signed by Charles II. In 1685 James II made Sir Edmund Andros governor of all New England. In 1687 Andros tried to induce Connecticut to relinquish its very liberal charter. But instead of surrendering the document when asked to do so, the colonists hid it in the hollow of a large oak tree on the property of Samuel Wyllys; this tree thereupon became known as the Charter Oak. The Andros government only lasted two years and Connecticut returned to its charter form of government.

Hartford took an active part in the Revolutionary War and the Civil War. Its later history, though, is concerned more with its growth as a financial and commercial center, and its contributions to industry and transportation. The first woolen mill in New England was established in Hartford in 1799; it wove the cloth for George Washington's inaugural suit. Other Hartford firsts include the publication of the first juvenile book in 1789 and the first cookbook in 1796, the first use of dental gold in 1812, establishment of the first school for the deaf in 1817, invention of the revolver in 1836, manufacture of oilcloth in 1837, machine-made watches in 1838, use of nitrous oxide as an anesthetic in 1844, the opening of the nation's first public art museum in 1844, the first accident life insurance policy in 1863, the first bicycle plant in 1877, invention of the friction clutch in 1885, the first standard measuring machine accurate to .00001 inch (developed by Pratt & Whitney), the first pay telephone in 1895, the first automobile insurance policy in 1897, and in 1901 the first legislation in the country regulating motor vehicle speed. The growth of the insurance industry dates from 1794 when a fire insurance policy was issued by the Hartford Fire Insurance Company. Hartford also was known as the industry leader in other, more unusual areas, such as pipe-organ building and gold-beating.

After World War II, the city experienced considerable social unrest. Ghettoes on the old east side were the scenes of riots by blacks. In response, a massive urban renewal program was launched that resulted in, among other things, the building of Constitution Plaza and Bushnell Plaza. In 1981 Thirman L. Milner became the city's first black mayor, and in the same decade Carrie Saxon Perry became the city's first black woman mayor.

Chronology

1633 Jacob van Curler builds a Dutch fort called The House of Hope under orders from the Governor of New Amsterdam.

1635 John Steel and 60 pioneers from New Towne, Massachusetts, settle here, followed a year later by the Reverend Thomas Hooker and company.

1639 Representatives of the river settlements meet at Hartford and draw up the Fundamental Orders as their constitution.

1654 The Dutch abandon their House of Hope fort, which is seized by the Colonial Court in the name of England.

1665 Hartford County is organized and later the colony merges with the New Haven settlements.

1662 King Charles II grants independence to Connecticut under a liberal charter.

1687 King James II sends Sir Edmund Andros as governor of New England; Andros is ordered to revoke and seize the liberal charter of 1662, but fails when the colonists hide the charter within the hollow of an oak tree, later called Charter Oak.

1689 Andros government falls and Connecticut returns to its charter form of government.

1764 The *Hartford Courant* newspaper begins publication.

1772 Hartford welcomes George Washington on his way to Cambridge.

1784 The city of Hartford is incorporated.

1789 *The Children's Magazine*, the first juvenile publication in the United States, begins publication.

1794 Hartford Fire Insurance Company issues its first policy.

1836 Samuel Colt begins manufacture of Colt revolvers.

1844 The Wadsworth Atheneum, the nation's first public museum, opens.

1875 Hartford becomes the sole capital of the state.

1878 The State Capitol is erected.

1894 The first pneumatic tires are built in a Hartford plant.

1901 Hartford passes first legislation in nation regulating speed of cars.

1964 The Constitution Plaza is completed.

1968 City's first racial riots experienced over death of Martin Luther King, Jr.

1975 The Hartford Civic Center opens.

1981 Thirman L. Milner becomes city's first black mayor.

Historical Landmarks

The centerpiece of the city is the State Capitol, designed by Richard Upjohn in 1878. The architecture might be considered Gothic from the profusion of crockets, finials, and niches that rise above the pointed arches to the elongated dome. Two lofty, 5-story wings at the east and west facades of the main building culminate in a 12-sided gilded dome topped by a winged figure of the Genius of Connecticut by Randolph Rogers. The State Office Building between Washington and West streets, erected in 1930–1931, is of more modern design. The State Library and Supreme Court Building, opposite the capitol, was built in 1910 from designs by Donn Barber; it is of Italian Renaissance design. The Bushnell Memorial Hall on Capitol Avenue at Trinity Street, a redbrick and limestone building designed by Harvey Corbett, contains a 3,227-seat auditorium. The Old State House, on Main Street at Central Row, was designed by Charles Bulfinch in 1796, and is considered one of the finest examples of Federal-style public buildings. Its dominant feature is arched windows over the doors.

Among Hartford's churches, the most famous are the South Congregational Church, organized in 1670 and built in 1827; the First Church of Christ on Main Street, built in 1632 and the oldest in the state; the Episcopal Christ Church Cathedral on Main Street, a dark, ornate building built in 1829; and St. Justin's Roman Catholic Church, built in 1931, which is the most interesting modern church in the city.

As the insurance capital of America, Hartford is the headquarters of a number of national insurance companies whose buildings each have their own distinctive architectural history. One such building is the Phoenix Mutual Life Insurance Company Building on Elm Street, built in 1917, a dark-green ornamental brick structure with a Spanish tile roof. Then there is the 34-story Travelers Insurance Company Building—at 527 feet the tallest building in New England—built of pink Westerly granite on the site of the Zachary Sanford Tavern, where the Colonial General Assembly used to meet. Above its pyramidal roof is a metal cupola, in fact a great 81-foot lantern constructed of copper and covered with gold leaf whose beacon is visible for many miles. Other interesting buildings include the Connecticut Mutual Life Insurance Company Building on Garden Street, the Hartford Fire Insurance Company Building on Asylum Street, the Caledonia Insurance Company Building on Cogswell

Street, and the Aetna Life Insurance Company Building. This last building, designed by James Gamble Rogers in Georgian style in 1929, is on 28 acres of landscaped grounds at the center of the city on Farmington Avenue. The main building, approached by a semicircular courtyard, is 6 stories in height and is topped by a lofty square cupola with a 250-foot New England belfry above it.

Among the historical monuments are the Charter Oak Memorial, a large granite column at the junction of Charter Oak Avenue and Charter Oak Place; the Morgan Memorial, built in 1910 of Tennessee pink granite; and the Wadsworth Atheneum on Main Street. The Atheneum was designed in 1842 by Ithiel Town in Gothic Revival and covers one city block; it also includes the Hartford Public Library and the Connecticut Historical Society.

Hartford is home to two of the most cherished literary landmarks in the United States. The Mark Twain House is an ornate Victorian Gothic mansion where he lived from 1874 to 1891. The nearby Harriet Beecher Stowe House is a small cottage. Both are located in the Nook Farm area. Also in Hartford are a number of historic homes, such as the Butler McCook Homestead of 1782; the 1854 Isham-Terry House, a fine example of Italianate architecture; the Richardson (formerly Cheney) Building on Main Street, built in 1877; and the Goodwin Building near the Hartford Civic Center.

Population

In 1990 Hartford reported a population of 139,739, an increase of 2.4% over the 1980 population of 136,392.

Population

	1980	1990
Central City	136,392	139,739
Rank	117	127
Metro Area	1,051,606	1,123,678
Pop. Change 1980–1990 +3,347		
Pop. % Change 1980–1990 +2.5		
Median Age 28.4		
% Male		
47.7% Age 65 and Over 9.9		
Density (per square mile) 8,077		

Households

Number 51,464
Persons per Household 2.55
% Female-Headed Households 27.6
% One-Person Households 32.8
Births—Total 2,776
   % to Mothers under 20 23.6
   Birth Rate per 1,000 20.5

Ethnic Composition

Hartford has a rich ethnic history, blending Italians, Jews, Slavs, blacks, and others. Each of these groups congregate in certain neighborhoods: the Italians on Front

Street, blacks on Windsor Avenue, Slavs on Park Street, and Jews on Albany and Blue Hills avenues. Hartford is reputed to have more Jewish people than any other American city except New York. Whites have ceased to be the majority in the city, now accounting for about 40% of the population, and blacks make up 39%.

Ethnic Composition (as % of total pop.)

	1980	1990
White	50.30	39.98
Black	33.86	38.89
American Indian	0.20	0.32
Asian and Pacific Islander	0.62	1.45
Hispanic	20.45	31.69
Other	NA	19.36

Government

Hartford operates under a mayor-council form of government. The eight council members and mayor are elected every two years in partisan elections.

Government

Year of Home Charter   NA
Number of Members of the Governing Body   9
Elected at Large   9
Elected by Wards   NA
Number of Women in Governing Body   2
Salary of Mayor $30,000
Salary of Council Members $15,000
City Government Employment Total   7,075
Rate per 10,000   512.8

Public Finance

Hartford's annual budget consists of revenues of $488.406 million and expenditures of $481.578 million. Total outstanding debt is $143.765 million and cash and security holdings are $539.127 million.

Public Finance

Total Revenue (in millions) $488.406
Intergovernmental Revenue—Total (in millions) $212.4
Federal Revenue per Capita $30.7
% Federal Assistance   6.28
% State Assistance   36.84
Sales Tax as % of Total Revenue   NA
Local Revenue as % of Total Revenue   48.93
City Income Tax   no
Taxes—Total (in millions) $114.9

Taxes per Capita
   Total $833
   Property $813
   Sales and Gross Receipts $0
General Expenditures—Total (in millions) $284.5
General Expenditures per Capita $2,062
Capital Outlays per Capita $171

Public Finanace (continued)

% of Expenditures for:
- Public Welfare 8.8
- Highways 2.3
- Education 38.1
- Health and Hospitals 1.8
- Police 6.2
- Sewerage and Sanitation 1.0
- Parks and Recreation 5.1
- Housing and Community Development 8.6

Debt Outstanding per Capita $600
- % Utility 0.0

Federal Procurement Contract Awards (in millions) $102.9

Federal Grants Awards (in millions) $146.3

Fiscal Year Begins July 1

Economy

The city is renowned as the insurance capital of the nation, with 25 insurance companies headquartered here, including the six largest: Aetna Life and Casualty, Travelers Insurance, Cigna, Hartford Insurance Group, Connecticut Mutual Life Insurance, and Phoenix Mutual Life Insurance. Many financial institutions also are located here, including: Connecticut Bank and Trust, Connecticut National Bank, and Northeast Savings. The insurance and banking services have grown appreciably since federal deregulation of those industries. Hartford's financial stature, however, obscures the fact that it remains one of the major manufacturing centers in the country, with headquarters of such companies as United Technologies and its subsidiaries, Pratt & Whitney, Hamilton Standard, and Otis Elevator. Together, these divisions employ over 27,500 workers. Other major manufacturers include Stanley (tools and hardware), Kaman (aerospace components), Colt (firearms), Heublein (liquor and wine), and Loctite (adhesives). Hartford also is a major retail center for southern New England; four retail giants— G. Fox, J.C. Penney, Sage-Allen, and D&L Venture— have large operations here, and several new malls and shopping districts have been built in the city in recent years. Hartford has a reputation as a high-tech center, and it is one of the largest producers of mainframe computers. One ancient tradition that persists is the production of cigars from locally grown tobacco.

Economy

Total Money Income (in millions) $1,197.2		
% of State Average 61.6		
Per Capita Annual Income $8,677		
% Population below Poverty Level 25.2		
Fortune 500 Companies 2		
Banks	*Number*	*Deposits (in millions)*
Commercial	15	19,041
Savings	33	11,412
Passenger Autos 517,610		
Electric Meters 52,500		
Gas Meters 32,453		

Manufacturing

- Number of Establishments 162
- % with 20 or More Employees 40.7
- Manufacturing Payroll (in millions) $236.1
- Value Added by Manufacture (in millions) $468.0
- Value of Shipments (in millions) $749.1
- New Capital Expenditures (in millions) $31.8

Wholesale Trade

- Number of Establishments 288
- Sales (in millions) $1,804.2
- Annual Payroll (in millions) $157.669

Retail Trade

- Number of Establishments 1,091
- Total Sales (in millions) $725.0
- Sales per Capita $5,254
- Number of Retail Trade Establishments with Payroll 856
- Annual Payroll (in millions) $111.6
- Total Sales (in millions) $704.2
- General Merchandise Stores (per capita) $604
- Food Stores (per capita) $484
- Apparel Stores (per capita) $334
- Eating and Drinking Places (per capita) $874

Service Industries

- Total Establishments 1,410
- Total Receipts (in millions) $1,166.3
- Hotels and Motels (in millions) $44.3
- Health Services (in millions) $251.4
- Legal Services (in millions) $254.0

Labor

United Technologies is the largest employer in the city, with the state government the second largest, although state employment has been hard hit by recent budgetary problems. Four other institutions employ over 5,000 workers each: Aetna, Travelers, Signa, and Connecticut Bank and Trust, all financial services. According to the Labor Department, retailing, FIRE (finance, insurance, real estate), tourism, and legal and professional services are the growth areas in the city. Services and trade account for over 45% of all city jobs while manufacturing accounts for 18%.

Labor

- Civilian Labor Force 64,988
- % Change 1989–1990 3.0
- *Work Force Distribution*
  - Mining NA
  - Construction 19,800
  - Manufacturing 77,700
  - Transportation and Public Utilities 18,200
  - Wholesale and Retail Trade 95,600
  - FIRE (Finance, Insurance, Real Estate) 72,900
  - Service 108,600
  - Government 64,200
  - Women as % of Labor Force 47.8
  - % Self-Employed 2.1
  - % Professional/Technical 13.1
- Total Unemployment 5,677
- Rate % 8.7
- Federal Government Civilian Employment 3,788

Education

The public school system, the second largest in New England, is governed by a board of nine members publicly elected in nonpartisan contests. It consists of 31 schools. There are also many noted prep schools, such as Miss Porter's School in Farmington and the Watkinson School in West Hartford.

Higher education is offered at the University of Hartford; a campus of the University of Connecticut; one Graduate Center affiliated with the Rensselaer Polytechnic Institute in New York; one religious institution, the Hartford Seminary; four colleges, Charter Oak, Saint Joseph, Trinity, and the Hartford College for Women; three community colleges, Asnuntuck at Enfield, Greater Hartford, and Manchester; and one technical college, the Hartford State Technical College. The University of Connecticut School of Medicine and Dentistry is located 7 miles west of Hartford.

Education

Number of Public Schools   31
Special Education Schools   1
Total Enrollment   25,418
% Enrollment in Private Schools   11.3
% Minority   91.7
Classroom Teachers   1,671
Pupil-Teacher Ratio   14.8:1
Number of Graduates   817
Total Revenue (in millions) $154.109
Total Expenditures (in millions) $147.263
Expenditures per Pupil $5,669
Educational Attainment (Age 25 and Over)
   % Completed 12 or More Years   50.8
   % Completed 16 or More Years   11.9
Four-Year Colleges and Universities   3
   Enrollment   11,578
Two-Year Colleges   2
   Enrollment   3,977

Libraries

Number   36
Public Libraries   10
Books (in thousands)   527
Circulation (in thousands)   473
Persons Served (in thousands)   133
Circulation per Person Served   3.55
Income (in millions) $4.367
Staff   126

Four-Year Colleges and Universities
   St. Joseph College
   Trinity College
   University of Hartford

Health

Health care is provided by six institutions with 2,700 beds among them: the Hartford Hospital, Mount Sinai, and Saint Francis, all of them affiliated with the University of Connecticut School of Medicine. The Institute of Living is a comprehensive psychiatric hospital with 400 beds.

Transportation

The Greater Hartford region is bisected by two major interstate highways: I-91 running north-south and connecting with the Massachusetts Turnpike to the north and the Connecticut Turnpike to the south, and the I-84 run-

Health

Deaths—Total   1,352
Rate per 1,000   10.0
Infant Deaths—Total   55
Rate per 1,000   19.8
Number of Metro Hospitals   6
Number of Metro Hospital Beds   2,723
Rate per 100,000   1,973
Number of Physicians   2,849
Physicians per 1,000   4.47
Nurses per 1,000   NA
Health Expenditures per Capita $39.66

Transportation

Interstate Highway Mileage   62
Total Urban Mileage   2,407
Total Daily Vehicle Mileage (in millions)   14.019
Daily Average Commute Time   44.4 min.
Number of Buses   224
Port Tonnage (in millions)   NA
Airports   1
Number of Daily Flights   84
Daily Average Number of Passengers   6,219

Airlines (American carriers only)
   American
   Continental
   Delta
   Eastern
   Midway
   Northwest
   Trans World
   USAir
   United

ning east and west. A new configuration will connect these two main arteries in a direct loop in all directions. Local bus service is provided by Connecticut Transit. Commuter express service includes free suburban parking. Area employers sponsor a scooter bus service downtown. Long-distance bus service is provided by Greyhound and Continental Trailways, with the Union Station as the hub.

Rail passenger service is provided by Amtrak from Union Station, a century-old brownstone structure that recently underwent a $15.8 million renovation. Rail freight is handled by Conrail, Central Vermont, and Providence and Worcester railroads.

Hartford is the uppermost navigable point on the Connecticut River for oceangoing vessels. Goods are transported directly to ports on the Long Island Sound.

Bradley International Airport, located minutes north of Hartford at Windsor Locks, is serviced by 18 major and commuter airlines. Within city limits is the Hartford-Brainard Airport for smaller aircraft.

Housing

Of the 56,098 housing units in the Hartford region, 23.6% are owner-occupied. In the depressed housing market of the 1990s a typical house in the region cost $156,000, down from $183,000 in 1988.

Housing

Total Housing Units 56,098
% Change 1980–1990 1.5
Vacant Units for Sale or Rent 4,053
Occupied Units 51,464
% with More Than One Person per Room 9.2
% Owner-Occupied 23.6
Median Value of Owner-Occupied Homes $133,800
Average Monthly Purchase Cost $377
Median Monthly Rent $443
New Private Housing Starts 333
Value (in thousands) $11,135
% Single-Family 2.7
Nonresidential Buildings Value (in thousands) $13,253

Tallest Buildings	Hgt. (ft.)	Stories
City Place	535	38
Travelers Ins. Co. Bldg.	527	34
Goodwin Square	522	30
Hartford Plaza	420	22
Hartford Natl. Bank & Trust	360	26
One Commercial Plaza	349	27
Bushnell Tower	349	27

Urban Development

Among Hartford's recent development projects are retail and office complexes like the Pavilion, mentioned above. The 1980s were characterized by an unprecedented level of construction activity. Over 3 million square feet of office space were added to city real estate between 1960 in suburbs such as Enfield, Middletown, Simsbury, Windsor, and Windsor Locks. The retail core of the city is composed of the Civic Center shops connected to the Richardson Mall, and the G. Fox and Sage-Allen department stores near the Pearl shopping district and Asylum and Pratt streets. Pratt Street underwent a major revitalization in 1989. Most housing projects are in the suburbs in the Greater Hartford area.

Crime

Hartford ranks high in crime. In 1991, the crimes known to police consisted of 3,576 violent crimes and 17,659 property crimes. The suburbs have much lower crime rates.

Crime

Violent Crimes—Total 3,576
Violent Crime Rate per 100,000 648.4
Murder 24
Rape 181
Robbery 1,607
Aggravated Assaults 1,764
Property Crimes 17,659
Burglary 4,690
Larceny 9,710
Motor Vehicle Theft 3,259
Arson 224
Per Capita Police Expenditures $215.04
Per Capita Fire Protection Expenditures $176.66
Number of Police 501
Per 1,000 3.67

Religion

Hartford is a Catholic archdiocese. More than 20 Protestant denominations are represented in the city.

Religion

Largest Denominations (Adherents)	
Catholic	382,719
United Church of Christ	39,603
Black Baptist	20,569
United Methodist	14,721
Episcopal	17,628
Evangelical Lutheran	13,523
American Baptist	14,885
Lutheran	4,644
Jewish	26,200

Media

The city's only daily, the *Hartford Courant*, is one of the nation's oldest continuously operated newspapers; it was founded by Thomas Green in 1764. Two independent stations, including an ABC affiliate, provide television service. The region has 13 AM and FM radio stations.

Media

Newsprint
  Hartford Courant, daily
Television
  WEDH (Channel 24)
  WFSB (Channel 3)
  WHCT-TV (Channel 18)
  WTIC-TV (Channel 61)
  WVIT (Channel 30)
Radio

WCCC (AM)	WCCC (FM)
WDRC (AM)	WEDW (FM)
WHCN (FM)	WIOF (FM)
WLAT (AM)	WNPR (FM)
WPKT (FM)	WQTQ (FM)
WRTC (FM)	WTIC (FM)
WZMX (FM)	

Sports

Professional sports have become a more prominent part of city life since the renovation of the 16,000-seat Coliseum in the Hartford Civic Center. The Hartford Whalers are the city's standard-bearers in hockey. World Jai-alai plays at the Hartford Fronton February through August, and the Canon-Sammy Davis, Jr./Greater Hartford Open is held in July in nearby Cromwell.

Arts, Culture, and Tourism

Hartford ranks first among U.S. cities in corporate contributions to the arts. As a result the city boasts some of the finest musical and performing arts groups. The Greater Hartford Symphony Orchestra, founded in 1944, is considered to be among the top 20 orchestras in the country. It plays in the Bushnell Memorial Hall in downtown Hartford. Other musical groups include the Hartford Chamber Orchestra, Hartford Pops, and Hartford Jazz Society. Summer musical events include chamber and carillon concerts at Trinity College and the Hartford Festival of Jazz at Bushnell Park.

The Connecticut Opera Association performs at Bushnell Memorial Hall. The Hartt College of Music presents several semiprofessional opera productions each year. The city's resident company is the Hartford Stage Company playing at the Huntington Theater. Other theater groups include Company One, the Producing Guild, and Theater Works. The state's foremost dance company is the Hartford Ballet. The Works Contemporary Dance, Connecticut Jazz Dance Company, and the Hartford Conservatory Modern Dance Ensemble present contemporary offerings. Real Art Ways features experimental theater and innovative multimedia performances.

Foremost among Hartford's museums is the Wadsworth Atheneum, the country's oldest art museum, founded in 1842. The Pump House Gallery located in the southeast corner of Bushnell Park on Pulaski Circle features changing exhibits of local artists housed in a Tudor Pump House. The Aetna Institute Gallery contains the largest art exhibit space in Hartford. The Matrix Gallery at the Wadsworth Atheneum and the Hartford Art Center (encompassing Real Art Ways/Art Works Gallery and the Craftery Gallery) also exhibit contemporary art. The Museum of Connecticut History contains the state's 1662 royal charter and a collection of Colt firearms. The Historical Museum of Medicine and Dentistry features a historical collection of medical instruments. The Hartford Exhibit located at the Hartford Insurance Group and the Travelers Museum at the Batterson Hall of Travelers Insurance Tower are dedicated to the history of insurance. Greater Hartford contains other fine museums, such as Trinity College's Austin Arts Center, the University of Hartford's Joseloff Gallery, the Museum of American Art in New Britain, and the Farmington Valley Arts Center and Hill-Stead Museum in Farmington.

Travel and Tourism

Hotel Rooms 8,024
Convention and Exhibit Space (square feet) 90,000

Convention Centers
    Hartford Civic Center
    The Armory

Festivals
    New England Fiddle Contest (May)
    River Festival (July)
    Festival of Jazz (July-August)
    Festa Italiana (September)
    Connecticut Antiques Show (October)

Parks and Recreation

 Bushnell Park, adjacent to the State Capitol, is the country's first public park to use natural landscaping rather than a village green. It contains the Soldiers and Sailors Memorial Arch, built in 1886, commemorating Hartford residents who fought for the Union in the Civil War. The park's Stein and Goldstein Carousel, built in 1914, features a giant Wurlitzer band organ, 48 hand-carved horses, and two chariots. The Elizabeth Park Rose Gardens contain thousands of rare plants. Close to the city are the McLean Game Refuge in Granby, Roaring Brook Nature Center in Canton, Rocky Hill Dinosaur State Park, and Talcott Mountain State Park. Hartford's 50 public parks and squares cover over 27,000 acres.

Sources of Further Information

Downtown Council
250 Constitution Plaza
Hartford, CT 06103
(203) 728-3089

Greater Hartford Arts Council
214 Farmington Avenue
Hartford, CT 06105
(203) 525-8629

Greater Hartford Chamber of Commerce
250 Constitution Plaza
Hartford, CT, 06103
(203) 525-4451

Greater Hartford Convention and Visitors Bureau
One Civic Center
Hartford, CT 06103
(203) 738-6789

Hartford Public Library
500 Main Street
Hartford, CT 06103
(203) 525-9121

Additional Information

Andrews, Charles M. *The River Towns of Connecticut: A Study of Wethersfield, Hartford and Windsor.* 1889.

Andrews, Gregory E., and David F. Ransom. *Structures & Styles: Guided Tours of Hartford Architecture.* 1988.

Close, F. Perry. *The History of Hartford Streets.* 1969.

Grant, Ellsworth S., and Marion H. Grant. *The City of Hartford, 1784–1984: An Illustrated History.* 1986.

Grant, Marion H. *In and About Hartford: Tours and Tales.* 1977.

United Way. *Forces of Change: The Next Decade.* 1984.

Honolulu

Hawaii

Basic Data

Name   Honolulu
Name Origin   From Hawaiian for "protected bay"
Year Founded   1795 Inc. 1907
Status: State   Hawaii
        County   Seat of Honolulu County
Area (square miles)   82.8
Elevation (feet)   21
Time Zone   2 hours behind Pacific
Population (1990)   365,272
Population of Metro Area (1990)   836,231

Sister Cities
    Bombay, India
    Bruyeres, France
    Cebu, Philippines
    Funchal, Portugal
    Hainan, China
    Hiroshima, Japan
    Kaohsiung County, China
    Manila, Philippines
    Laoag, Philippines
    Naha, Japan
    Seoul, Korea
    Tokyo, Japan

Distance in Miles To:
    San Francisco   2,091

Location and Topography

Honolulu is situated along the southern coast of Oahu, the third-largest (behind the islands of Hawaii and Maui) of the Hawaiian Islands. The city lies on a narrow plain on the ocean, with the Koolau Mountains serving as a backdrop. Honolulu is the only major city on the island of Oahu, and although there are several smaller towns—among them Kahuku to the north, Waianae to the west, and Waikiki to the east—the rest of the island is considered part of greater Honolulu.

Layout of City and Suburbs

Honolulu is located on Mamala Bay, several miles east of Hickam Air Force Base and Pearl Harbor. It is fronted on the north by the Lunalilo (or H-1) Freeway, and to the south by the Nimitz Highway, which traces the perimeter of Honolulu Harbor. The layout of the city is not unlike that of other American cities, although the names of the streets are ethnic Hawaiian, for example, Kukui Street and Pali Highway. Chinatown, where the ethnic Chinese live, occupies the western section of the city; to the east is the administrative area, encompassing such structures as the State Capitol, the Iolani Palace, the Aliiolani Hale (now the State Judiciary Building), and the Kawaiahao Church, as well as the grand statue of King Kamehameha the Great at the corner of King and Mililani streets. Merchant Street in downtown Honolulu is the oldest street in the city. Greater Honolulu extends west to Pearl Harbor, taking in the suburbs of Kalihi and Kapalama, north to Pacific Heights and Makiki Heights, and east to the famous Diamond Head crater and Kahala.

Environment

Environmental Stress Index   3.0
Green Cities Index: Rank   1
                    Score   10.50
Water Quality   Alkaline, soft
    Average Daily Use (gallons per capita)   170
    Maximum Supply (gallons per capita)   171.2
Parkland as % of Total City Area   2.5
% Waste Landfilled/Recycled   43:10
Annual Parks Expenditures per Capita $82.99

Climate

Although it is in a semitropical zone, Honolulu has a perpetual spring, except when the *kona*—or southerly winds—

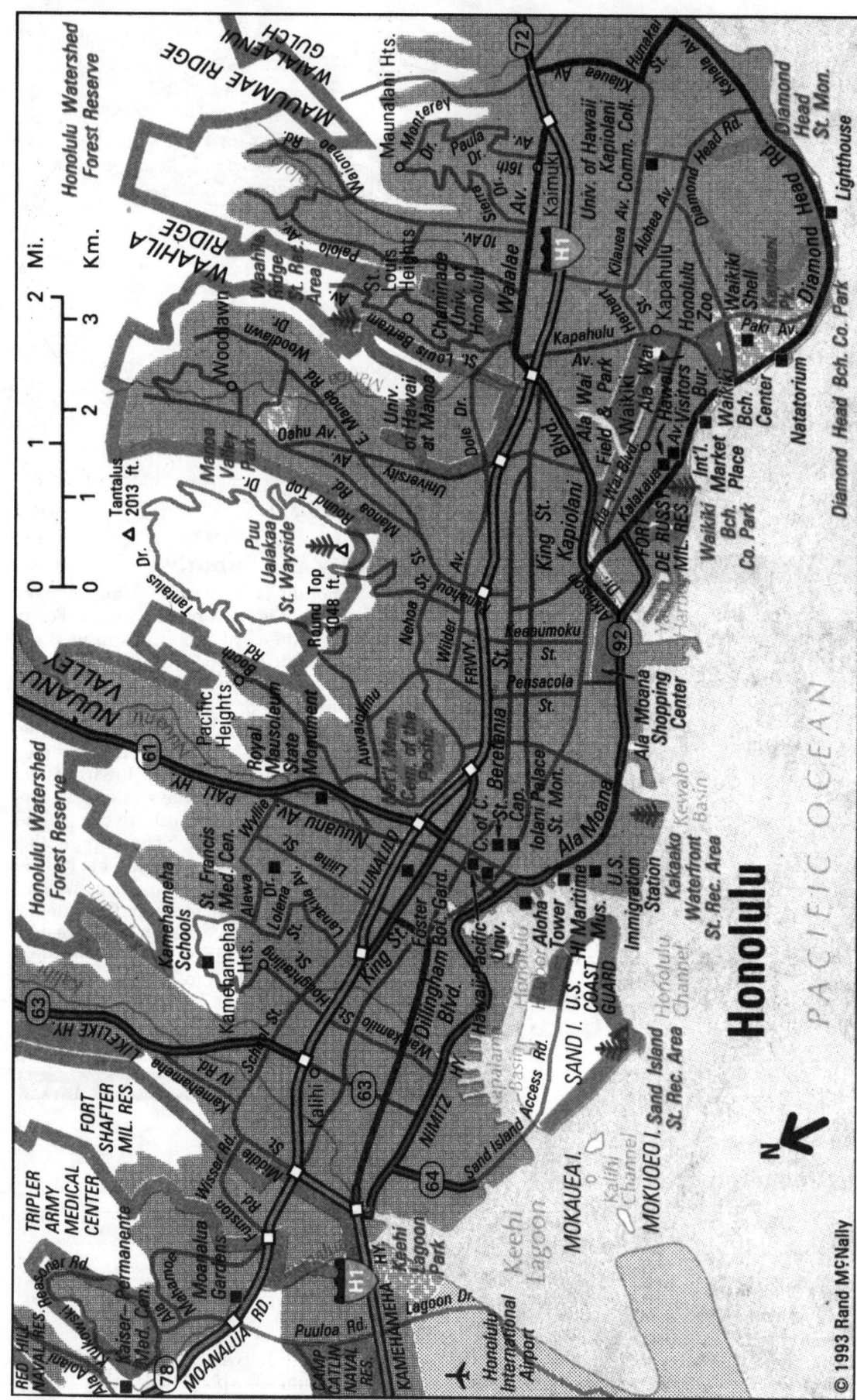

blow for a few weeks in the summer. Honolulu has the least seasonal change of any U.S. city, with a difference of only a few degrees between winter and summer. It has no snow, fog, or freezing weather; only about nine days a year have temperatures over 90 degrees, and there are no more than seven thunderstorms a year.

Weather

Temperature

Highest Monthly Average °F   87.1
Lowest Monthly Average °F   65.3

Annual Averages

Days 32°F or Below   0
Days above 90°F   9
Zero Degree Days   0
Precipitation (inches)   23.0
Snow (inches)   0.0
% Seasonal Humidity   67.0
Wind Speed (m.p.h.)   11.8
Clear Days   90
Cloudy Days   101
Storm Days   7
Rainy Days   102

Average Temperatures (°F)	High	Low	Mean
January	79.3	65.3	72.3
February	79.2	65.3	72.3
March	79.7	66.3	73.0
April	81.4	68.1	74.8
May	83.6	70.2	76.9
June	85.6	72.2	78.9
July	86.8	73.4	80.1
August	87.4	74.0	80.7
September	87.4	73.4	80.4
October	85.8	72.0	78.9
November	83.2	69.8	76.5
December	80.3	67.1	73.7

History

Although there is no set date that the first people set foot on the Hawaiian islands, historians estimate that the first deliberate migrations by Polynesian natives started about 500 to 800 A.D. The first white man to sight Oahu was Captain James Cook in 1778, when he landed with his flagship H.M.S. *Resolution* at Waimeia on the big island of Hawaii; he christened the islands the Sandwich Islands. Over the next several years, expeditions from France and America sailed to the various islands in the group. In 1795 King Kamehameha I unified the islands under his rule after defeating the king of Oahu. He settled at Waikiki, and established a dynasty based on the divine right of kings. Honolulu became a flourishing whaling port with an extensive trade in sandalwood. It came under a series of European occupations: Russia in 1816, Britain in 1843, and France in 1849, yet each time the occupiers left Hawaii as a sovereign nation. Meanwhile, missionaries began arriving from America in 1820. Among these families were the Binghams, the Judds, the Cookes, and the Chamberlains. They established schools, which are now tourist attractions, and also functioned as advisers to the monarchs. By

1845 Honolulu had become the capital of a constitutional kingdom. When the growing of sugar, which had started on the island of Maui in 1849, replaced whaling as the principal economic activity, the white merchants began controlling the economy under a paternalistic plantation system. Since the United States was the major market for Hawaiian sugar, economic ties between the two countries became stronger. In 1875 the Reciprocity Act was passed by Congress, admitting Hawaiian sugar duty-free to the United States in exchange for giving the United States long-term access to Pearl Harbor. As happened with the American Indians, contact with whites served to destroy much of the Hawaiian native culture and the people themselves. By the 1870s nearly 80% of the original inhabitants had been wiped out by disease. On 17 January 1893 Queen Liliuokalani was deposed by a group of American businessmen and marines, and a republic was declared. This government was headed by businessman Sanford B. Dole, who owned much of the pineapple plantation system in Hawaii. On 7 July 1898 the islands were formally annexed by the United States by order of President William McKinley. Honolulu remained the capital when Hawaii became a territory in 1900. The city/county of Honolulu was created in 1909. Fifty years later Hawaii became a state, with Honolulu as the state capital.

Pearl Harbor had been dredged and established as a major naval base through the efforts of Prince Jonah Kuhio Kalanianaole. Known as "Pearl," it was attacked by Japanese bombers on 7 December 1941, becoming the only U.S. city to be bombed in the twentieth century, and setting off American involvement in World War II. The history of the city after that war has been marked by the rise of Americans of Japanese descent in Hawaiian politics and government. Following statehood, Japanese investment in the islands increased, to the point where the Japanese are now the prevailing economic force on the islands.

Historical Landmarks

The remains of royal rule are seen in a number of historical buildings. The impressive Iolani Palace, built by King David Kalahua in 1862, and the place where Queen Liliuokalani was imprisoned, is on South King Street and is the only royal palace in the United States. Across the street from the palace is the Aliiolani Hale, now the State Judiciary Building, which was completed in 1874 and once housed the Hawaiian parliament. The city's first church, the Kawaiahao Church on South King and Punchbowl streets, was built in 1841 from blocks of coral and pieces of timber. A popular tourist attraction is the summer palace of Queen Emma, consort of King Kamehameha I. Located on the Pali Highway out of town, it was originally built in Boston. Wo Fat, Honolulu's oldest restaurant—founded in 1882—is in Chinatown. The Hawaii Maritime Center on Pier 7 of the Honolulu waterfront features the Falls of Clyde, a four-masted sailing vessel, built in 1878 in Scotland,

Chronology

1778	Captain James Cook sights Oahu and names the islands the Sandwich Islands.
1794	Captain James Brown enters Honolulu Harbor.
1795	King Kamehameha I unifies the Hawaiian Islands under his rule.
1803	Honolulu becomes the royal capital.
1811	King Kamehameha I dies.
1816	Russia occupies Hawaii.
1820	First U.S. missionaries arrive on island.
1843	Great Britain occupies Hawaii.
1845	Honolulu becomes the capital of a constitutional monarchy.
1849	France occupies Hawaii.
1875	The Reciprocity Treaty is concluded; admits Hawaiian sugar duty-free into the United States in exchange for rights to Pearl Harbor.
1893	Queen Liliuokalani is deposed by a U.S.-backed group, and a republic is proclaimed.
1898	The United States annexes Hawaii.
1900	Hawaii becomes a U.S. territory with Honolulu as the capital.
1909	The city of Honolulu is incorporated.
1941	Japanese bombers attack and destroy the U.S. naval fleet at Pearl Harbor, dragging the United States into World War II.
1959	Hawaii is admitted as the 50th state.

that used to sail the ocean between Hawaii and San Francisco.

Population

The limited physical size of the island places an inescapable limit on population growth. Nevertheless, Honolulu grew by 12.4% in the 1970s, from 324,871 in 1970, to 365,048 in 1980. The population remained virtually unchanged in the 1980s, growing by only 224 persons over the 1980 figure, to 365,272.

Ethnic Composition

Asians and Pacific Islanders are the dominant majority with 70.5%, followed by whites with 26.7%. The remaining

Population

	1980	1990
Central City	365,048	365,272
Rank	36	44
Metro Area	762,565	836,231
Pop. Change 1980–1990 +224		
Pop. % Change 1980–1990 +0.1		
Median Age 36.9		
% Male 49.4		
% Age 65 and Over 16.0		
Density (per square mile) 4,411		

Households

Number 134,563	
Persons per Household 2.63	
% Female-Headed Households 11.0	
% One-Person Households 27.4	
Births—Total 5,911	
% to Mothers under 20 7.6	
Birth Rate per 1,000 15.8	

Ethnic Composition (as % of total pop.)

	1980	1990
White	28.68	26.7
Black	1.16	1.32
American Indian	0.21	0.31
Asian and Pacific Islander	65.83	70.51
Hispanic	5.24	4.57
Other	NA	1.16

2.8% is made up of African Americans with 1.3%, American Indians at 0.3%, and others 1.2%. About one-fourth of the population is Japanese and about one-sixth native Hawaiian or part Hawaiian. More than one-fourth have mixed ancestry. Servicemen and their families make up 15% of the population.

Government

Honolulu is governed by a mayor-council form of government. The mayor and the nine council members serve four-year terms.

Government

Year of Home Charter NA	
Number of Members of the Governing Body 9	
Elected at Large NA	
Elected by Wards 9	
Number of Women in Governing Body 2	
Salary of Mayor $84,725	
Salary of Council Members $35,000	
City Government Employment Total NA	
Rate per 10,000 NA	

Public Finance

The annual budget consists of revenues of $1.095 billion and expenditures of $903.508 million. The debt outstanding is $804.916 million, and cash and securities holdings are $26.929 million.

Economy

The four pillars of Honolulu's economy are tourism, military bases, transportation, and agriculture. One-fifth of

Public Finance

Total Revenue (in millions) $1,095.025
Intergovernmental Revenue—Total (in millions)   NA
Federal Revenue per Capita $66.07
% Federal Assistance   6.03
% State Assistance   4.47
Sales Tax as % of Total Revenue   4.96
Local Revenue as % of Total Revenue   82.5
City Income Tax   no
Taxes—Total (in millions) $387.414

Taxes per Capita
   Total $462.03
   Property $360.35
   Sales and Gross Receipts   NA
General Expenditures—Total (in millions) $726.484
General Expenditures per Capita $1,083.49
Capital Outlays per Capita $317.49

% of Expenditures for:
   Public Welfare   0.0
   Highways   5.46
   Education   0.0
   Health and Hospitals   1.13
   Police   13.19
   Sewerage and Sanitation   8.81
   Parks and Recreation   9.58
   Housing and Community Development   9.76
Debt Outstanding per Capita $959.95
   % Utility   6.76
Federal Procurement Contract Awards (in millions)   NA
Federal Grants Awards (in millions)   NA
Fiscal Year Begins   July 1

Economy

Total Money Income (in millions) $1,182.8
% of State Average   NA
Per Capita Annual Income   NA
% Population below Poverty Level   10
Fortune 500 Companies   0

Banks	Number	Deposits (in millions)
Commercial	9	NA
Savings	7	NA

Passenger Autos   489,925
Electric Meters   216,063
Gas Meters   28,539

Manufacturing

Number of Establishments   628
% with 20 or More Employees   22.8
Manufacturing Payroll (in millions) $256.8
Value Added by Manufacture (in millions) $768.3
Value of Shipments (in millions) $1,812.9
New Capital Expenditures (in millions) $41.2

Wholesale Trade

Number of Establishments   1,293
Sales (in millions) $3,816.7
Annual Payroll (in millions) $297.270

Retail Trade

Number of Establishments   5,538
Total Sales (in millions) $4,544.1
Sales per Capita $12,205
Number of Retail Trade Establishments with Payroll   3,644
Annual Payroll (in millions) $559.4
Total Sales (in millions) $4,451.5
General Merchandise Stores (per capita) $2,470
Food Stores (per capita) $1,681
Apparel Stores (per capita) $953
Eating and Drinking Places (per capita) $2,169

Economy (continued)

Service Industries

Total Establishments   4,529
Total Receipts (in millions) $2,848.9
Hotels and Motels (in millions) $828.4
Health Services (in millions) $473.4
Legal Services (in millions) $276.5

the economy is devoted to cultivation of two primary products that have played a large part in the island's economic history: pineapples and sugarcane. Honolulu also is a major source of exotic flowers and plants, which are shipped by air to the mainland. Maritime transportation is based on Honolulu's strategic location. It is also located a short distance east of the large American naval stations at Hickam Field and Pearl Harbor, as well as south of the Fort Shafter Army Reservation, all of which bring needed dollars into the economy through jobs and spending by those posted there. Tourism, of course, is the mainstay of the economy, and since the rise of Japan as an economic power, Japanese tourists have become more numerous than those from the United States. In fact, the huge rate of Japanese investment has become a controversial subject in the last few years. And foreign tourism is beginning to be a serious threat to the island's environmental integrity, despite the tourist dollars. Research and development is an advanced sector, especially in areas where Hawaii provides unequaled facilities, as in oceanography. Manufacturing is the smallest sector, hampered as it is by transportation and other costs and the small local retail market.

Labor

 The labor market has not been particularly attractive to mainlanders. Its growth potential is limited by physical size and its economic base is not diversified. Services, trade, and government are the three main sectors. The unemployment rate has remained low compared to the mainland.

Labor

Civilian Labor Force   391,387
% Change 1989–1990   2.0

Work Force Distribution
   Mining   —
   Construction   25,300
   Manufacturing   15,200
   Transportation and Public Utilities   35,400
   Wholesale and Retail Trade   102,200
   FIRE (Finance, Insurance, Real Estate)   30,600
   Service   116,700
   Government   90,000
   Women as % of Labor Force   47.3
   % Self-Employed   5.8
   % Professional/Technical   16.2
Total Unemployment   9,999
Rate %   2.6
Federal Government Civilian Employment   6,004

Education

The Honolulu School District supports 32 high schools, 28 middle schools, and 163 primary schools. Honolulu's flagship university is the University of Hawaii at Manoa, which includes the East-West Center, an institute that attempts to bridge cultures of East and West through research and publications. There are two private colleges: Society of Mary's Chaminade University and Hawaii Pacific College.

Education

Number of Public Schools   223
Special Education Schools   2
Total Enrollment   159,285
% Enrollment in Private Schools   20.1
% Minority   77.4
Classroom Teachers   9,108
Pupil-Teacher Ratio   15.4:1
Number of Graduates   10,325
Total Revenue (in millions) $709.591
Total Expenditures (in millions) $630.273
Expenditures per Pupil $3,324
Educational Attainment (Age 25 and Over)
   % Completed 12 or More Years   74.5
   % Completed 16 or More Years   24.0
Four-Year Colleges and Universities   3
   Enrollment   27,176
Two-Year Colleges   2
   Enrollment   10,654

Libraries

Number   113
Public Libraries   53
Books (in thousands)   2,095
Circulation (in thousands)   6,521
Persons Served (in thousands)   1,082
Circulation per Person Served   6.02
Income (in millions) $17.928
Staff   737

Four-Year Colleges and Universities
   Chaminade University
   Hawaii Pacific College
   University of Hawaii at Manoa

Health

Honolulu is served by ten hospitals, of which the largest are the Queen Medical Center, the teaching hospital for the John A. Burns School of Medicine at the University of

Health

Deaths—Total   2,468
Rate per 1,000   6.6
Infant Deaths—Total   60
Rate per 1,000   10.2
Number of Metro Hospitals   10
Number of Metro Hospital Beds   2,549
Rate per 100,000   NA
Number of Physicians   1,717
Physicians per 1,000   2.41
Nurses per 1,000   5.48
Health Expenditures per Capita $9.77

Hawaii; Kaukini Medical Center; Tripler Army Base Medical Center; and St. Francis Hospital.

Transportation

Within the island five main highways lead into Honolulu: the east-west H-1 Freeway; S.R. 92, known as the Nimitz Highway; the west-southeast Ala Moana Boulevard, which moves east to Waikiki; the north-south S.R. 63, known as the Likelike Highway, which heads north to Kaneohe; and the north-south S.R. 61, the Pali Highway, which heads north to Kailua. The Port of Honolulu is one of the major ports in the Pacific-to-America route. The principal air terminal is Honolulu International Airport near Hickam Field.

Transportation

Interstate Highway Mileage   34
Total Urban Mileage   863
Total Daily Vehicle Mileage (in millions)   10.953
Daily Average Commute Time   49.7 min.
Number of Buses   380
Port Tonnage (in millions)   10.654
Airports   1
Number of Daily Flights   242
Daily Average Number of Passengers   24,502

Airlines (American carriers only)
   Aloha
   American
   American West
   American Trans Air
   Continental
   Delta
   Eastern
   Hawaiian
   Trans World
   World Airways
   United

Housing

Of the total stock of housing, 47% is owner-occupied. The median value of an owner-occupied home is $353,900, and the median monthly rent is $582.

Housing

Total Housing Units   145,796
% Change 1980–1990   2.4
Vacant Units for Sale or Rent   6,669
Occupied Units   134,563
% with More Than One Person per Room   16.2
% Owner-Occupied   47.0
Median Value of Owner-Occupied Homes $353,900
Average Monthly Purchase Cost $500
Median Monthly Rent $582
New Private Housing Starts   NA
Value (in thousands)   NA
% Single-Family   NA
Nonresidential Buildings Value (in thousands)   NA

Tallest Buildings	*Hgt. (ft.)*	*Stories*
Waterfront Towers (1990)	400	46
Ala Moana Hotel	396	38
Pacific Tower	350	30
Franklin Towers	350	41

Housing (continued)

Tallest Buildings	Hgt. (ft.)	Stories
Honolulu Tower	350	40
Discovery Bay	350	42
Hyatt Regency Waikiki	350	39
Maile Court Hotel	350	43

Urban Redevelopment

 Urban redevelopment has peaked and is now under attack from environmentalists. Much of the construction since World War II has been commercial hotels and shopping centers, like the Ala Moana Center, and has been financed with a heavy infusion of Japanese money. Fort Street has been converted into a pedestrian mall. Cultural Plaza embodies the city's ethnic diversity.

Crime

 In 1991, the crimes known to police consisted of 2,058 violent crimes and 48,974 property crimes.

Crime

Violent Crimes—Total   2,058
Violent Crime Rate per 100,000   240.3
Murder   29
Rape   275
Robbery   860
Aggravated Assaults   894
Property Crimes   48,974
Burglary   9,905
Larceny   36,019
Motor Vehicle Theft   3,050
Arson   NA
Per Capita Police Expenditures $114.26
Per Capita Fire Protection Expenditures $47.73
Number of Police   1,639
Per 1,000   2.01

Religion

 Roman Catholicism is the principal denomination, but many Protestant denominations and Buddhism and Confucianism are also represented.

Religion

Largest Denominations (Adherents)

Catholic	172,563
Southern Baptist	16,447
United Church of Christ	15,961
Latter-Day Saints	26,754
Episcopal	7,527
United Methodist	6,934
Black Baptist	6,862
Assembly of God	8,648
Evangelical Lutheran	3,419
Jewish	NA

Media

Of the city dailies, one is in Chinese, one in Korean, and one in Japanese. The two English-language dailies are the morning *Honolulu Advertiser* and the evening *Honolulu Hawaii Star Bulletin*. Electronic media consist of eight television stations and 25 AM and FM radio stations.

Media

Newsprint
Hawaii Business, monthly
Honolulu Advertiser, daily
Honolulu Hawaii Star Bulletin, daily

Television
KBFD (Channel 32)
KFVE (Channel 5)
KGMB (Channel 9)
KHAI (Channel 20)
KHET (Channel 11)
KHON (Channel 2)
KITV (Channel 4)
KWHE (Channel 14)

Radio
KAIM (AM)	KAIM (FM)
KCCN (AM)	KCCN (FM)
KGU (AM)	KHHH (FM)
KHPR (FM)	KHVH (AM)
KHHH (FM)	KIKI (AM)
KIKI (FM)	KIPO (FM)
KKUA (FM)	KLHT (AM)
KNDI (AM)	KOHO (AM)
KPOI (FM)	KQMQ (AM)
KQMQ (FM)	KSSK (AM)
KSSK (FM)	KTUT (FM)
KUMU (FM)	KWAI (AM)
KZOO (AM)	

Sports

 Honolulu has no major professional sports team. Two major sports facilities are Aloha Stadium and the Blaisdell Memorial Center.

Arts, Culture, and Tourism

The main cultural venues in Honolulu are the Neal S. Blaisdell Center, home of the Hawaii Opera Theater and the Honolulu Symphony, the Honolulu Community Theater, the Hawaii Performing Arts Company, and

Travel and Tourism

Hotel Rooms   37,776
Convention and Exhibit Space (square feet)   NA

Convention Centers
Neal S. Blaisdell Center
Polynesian Cultural Center

Festivals
Narcissus Festival (January–March)
Cherry Blossom Festival (January–March)
Lei Day (May)
Hawaii State Fair (May–June)
King Kamehameha Celebration (June)
Japan Festival (July)
Hula Festival (August)
Aloha Week Festival (September)
International Film Festival (November)

the Kennedy Theater at the University of Hawaii. The Waikiki Shell is the site of a Summer Pops series.

The Bernice Pauahi Bishop Museum, or the State Museum of Natural and Cultural History, which opened in 1889, is the city's oldest museum. The Honolulu Academy of Arts on South Beretania Street displays Western and Oriental art. The Mission Houses Museum is composed of the three oldest American buildings in Hawaii, including the Frame House, built in 1821.

Parks and Recreation

Honolulu has many unusual parks. Ala Moana and Kapiolani parks offer a variety of recreational facilities. At Punchbowl Crater, the National Memorial Cemetery of the Pacific can be seen, as well as Puu Ualakaa Park, which overlooks the city. Trained dolphins perform at Sea Life Park near Makapuu Beach. The nine-acre Foster Botanical Garden on North Vineyard Boulevard features rare flowers and trees.

Sources of Further Information

Chamber of Commerce of Hawaii
735 Bishop Street
Honolulu, HI 96813
(808) 522-8800

City Hall
530 S. King Street
Honolulu, HI 96813
(808) 523-4141

Honolulu Visitors Bureau
2270 Kalakaua Avenue
Honolulu, HI 96815
(808) 923-1811

Additional Reading

Bisignani, J. D. *Hawaii Handbook.* 1990.
Carter, Francis. *Exploring Honolulu's Chinatown.* 1988.
Johnson, Donald D. *The City and the County of Hawaii: A Governmental Chronicle.* 1991.
Riegert, Ray. *Hidden Honolulu: From the Good Life to the Great Outdoors.* 1991.
Simpson, William P. *Diggers Pearl: Wartime Honolulu.* 1990.
Stone, Scott C. *Honolulu: Heart of Hawaii.* 1983.

Houston

Texas

Location and Topography

N Houston lies near the Gulf of Mexico, spreading westward from the shores of Galveston Bay on the coastal prairie of eastern Texas. It straddles a coastal river system that includes the San Jacinto River—part of which is the artificial Houston Ship Channel—and a network of creeks and bayous, of which the largest are Buffalo Bayou, and Bray's Bayou. The terrain is low and flat.

Layout of City and Suburbs

Downtown Houston lies near the center of the city. It boasts more skyscrapers than perhaps any other city in the South, including the 75-story Texas Commerce Tower (the tallest in the state), the elegant 50-story One Shell Plaza, the 44-story Humble Oil Building, Tenneco Building, Gulf Building, First City Tower, Bank of the Southwest, and Southwest Tower. About a dozen buildings, including City Hall, make up the Houston Civic Center. Buffalo Bayou cuts through Houston from west to east, flowing past the northern end of downtown to become the Houston Ship Channel. The Turning Basin is at the western end of the Ship Channel. Several universities and the Texas Medical Center are also located downtown. The Astrodomain Complex—comprising the Astrodome, the Astrohall Convention Center, Astroworld, and Waterworld—lies farther south. The Lyndon B. Johnson Space Center is at the southeastern end. Residential areas spread out in all directions.

Environment

Environmental Stress Index   3.4
Green Cities Index: Rank   45
                Score   32.58
Water Quality   Alkaline, hard
   Average Daily Use (gallons per capita)   NA
   Maximum Supply (gallons per capita)   NA
Parkland as % of Total City Area   7.8
% Waste Landfilled/Recycled   98.5:1.5
Annual Parks Expenditures per Capita $32.97

Climate

The climate is predominantly semitropical and marine. Temperatures are modified by gulf winds. Winters are mild although polar air penetrates the area frequently enough to bring some variety. Occasionally temperatures in winter dip below freezing but rarely stay there too long. As a result the growing season is year-long. Summers are hot and humid; in 1983 the mercury remained above 90 for over 30 days at a stretch. Houston has experienced numerous hurricanes, the worst of which were Carla in 1960 and Alicia in 1983.

Weather

Temperature

Highest Monthly Average °F   93.6
Lowest Monthly Average °F   40.8

Annual Averages

Days 32°F or Below   24
Days above 90°F   81
Zero Degree Days   0
Precipitation (inches)   48.0
Snow (inches)   0
% Seasonal Humidity   77.0
Wind Speed (m.p.h.)   6.1
Clear Days   94
Cloudy Days   162
Storm Days   69
Rainy Days   107

Average Temperatures (°F)	High	Low	Mean
January	62.6	41.5	52.1
February	66.0	44.6	55.3
March	71.8	49.8	60.8
April	79.4	59.3	69.4
May	85.9	65.6	75.8
June	91.3	70.9	81.1
July	93.8	72.8	83.3
August	94.3	72.4	83.4
September	90.1	68.2	79.2
October	83.5	58.3	70.9
November	73.0	49.1	61.1
December	65.8	43.4	54.6

History

Houston, like many other cities founded in the 19th century, was the result of a real estate venture by land speculators. The site of the city was inhabited by cannibalistic Indians of the Atakapan and Karankawa tribes at the time the Spaniards first visited the region. Because the area was a breeding ground for malaria and the Indians were so hostile, the upper gulf coast remained largely unsettled. Following the War of 1812 the Galveston area became home to many pirates, such as Jean Lafitte. In the 1820s settlers from Tennessee and the Carolinas began to spill over into Texas, among them John Richardson Harris, who arrived in the Galveston area in 1823 as one of Stephen F. Austin's party. In 1824 Harris obtained title to a tract of land at the confluence of the Buffalo and Bray's bayous, then head of navigation. Within two years the settlement

had become an active maritime trading post. Called Harrisburg, it began shipping lumber to New Orleans and Mexican ports in Harris's fleet of ships.

In 1836, when Texas faced the threat of a Mexican invasion under General Santa Anna, the capital of the Republic of Texas was moved from Washington on the Brazos to Harrisburg, but within a month Santa Anna's forces captured the city and razed it. Within a week, Sam Houston's forces routed the Mexicans at the San Jacinto River, near present-day Houston, thus freeing Texas from Mexico. At this point, two brothers, John K. and Augustus C. Allen, land speculators from New York who had arrived in the region in 1832, decided to found a new town to replace Harrisburg. Paddling up the bayou in a pirogue, they reached the highest point of navigation for medium-draft boats. Disembarking here, John Allen sat on a grass-covered bank, and using his hat for a table, drew a sketch of the proposed city on a scrap of paper. He bought the land from William T. Austin and T. F. L. Parrott for $1 an acre. The Allens platted a town, named it after Sam Houston, and placed the 62 town sites on the market after setting aside a square for a capitol and congressional building. Sam Houston, by then the first president of the Republic of Texas, moved his capital from Columbia to the town named in his honor. Houston, with a population of 1,200, was incorporated as a city in 1837, but in 1839 President Lamar, a bitter enemy of Houston, moved the capital to Austin. Even after it ceased to be the capital, Houston began to grow by leaps and bounds as a result of shrewd nationwide advertising praising the upstart settlement on the bayou in extravagant terms. In 1839 the town's first newspaper, the *Morning Star*, made its debut. Sternwheel steamboats began to make regular calls, and the first local dock was constructed in 1840. A city ordinance in 1841 established the Port of Houston. In 1856 the first train steamed into town.

Houston's natural handicaps did slow its development for years, though. Drainage was poor and rainfall was heavy. The city suffered floods and disastrous fires in 1859 and 1860, and there were also serious epidemics of yellow fever and occasional outbreaks of cholera. The first efforts to widen the bayou and make it navigable for larger ships were begun in 1869 but were not successful until 1914. The first public wharf was built in 1915, and a regular New York–Houston service was established. Thereafter shipping zoomed and the Port of Houston became the largest on the Gulf of Mexico. Two other events in the 20th century contributed to Houston's phenomenal rise to become the fourth-largest metropolis in the nation. The first was the discovery of oil at Spindletop, near Houston, in 1901. This discovery enabled Houston to become the largest petrochemical center in the state. The other event was the choice of Houston by NASA in 1961 as the site of its new Manned Spacecraft Center. Eight years later *Houston* became the first name spoken from the surface of a heavenly body beyond the earth when the astronauts announced, "Houston, Tranquillity Base here, the Eagle has landed." For almost two

Chronology

1824 John Richardson Harris obtains title to a tract of land at the confluence of Buffalo and Bray's bayous and founds the settlement of Harrisburg.

1836 Threatened by Santa Anna's Mexican forces, the capital of the Republic of Texas is moved to Harrisburg, but Santa Anna captures Harrisburg and razes it. Sam Houston inflicts a crushing defeat on the Mexicans at the San Jacinto River, near present-day Houston, and captures Santa Anna. Real estate speculators John K. and Augustus C. Allen found a new town at the highest point of navigation on the Buffalo Bayou. Town is platted, named for Sam Houston, and 62 blocks are placed on the market. Sam Houston moves his capital from Columbia to Houston.

1837 Houston is incorporated. The *Laura* is the first steamship to visit town.

1839 President Lamar moves the state capital from Houston to Austin. Town's first newspaper, *Morning Star*, appears.

1840 First local dock is built.

1841 City ordinance establishes Port of Houston.

1853 The first railroad—Buffalo Bayou, Brazos, and Colorado—reaches Houston.

1859 Business district is wiped out by fire.

1866 First National Bank is founded.

1877 First free public school is established.

1887 Sisters of Charity of the Incarnate Word open first hospital, St. Joseph's Infirmary, now St. Joseph's Hospital.

1901 Oil is discovered at Spindletop, near Houston, ushering in a new age of prosperity as the oil and petrochemical capital of the nation.

1912 Rice Institute, later Rice University, is founded.

1913 Houston Symphony opens its doors.

1914 Work is completed on a project to widen the Buffalo Bayou and to construct a world-class harbor.

1927 Houston Junior College, now University of Houston, is founded.

1934 Intercoastal Canal links Houston to Mississippi River navigation system.

1943 Texas Medical Center is established.

1948 Annexation increases city's land area from 74.4 to 216 square miles.

1955 Houston's population crosses 1 million mark.

1961 NASA chooses Houston as the site of the Manned Spacecraft Center.

1965 First event is held in Astrodome.

1969 Houston Intercontinental Airport opens for business.

1990 Houston hosts 16th Economic Summit of Industrialized Nations.

1991 City Council adopts zoning regulations for first time in history.

decades after that, and especially after the Arab oil embargo of 1973, Houston continued to be a demographic magnet. It was not until the recession of the late 1980s that the city experienced its first slump in half a century.

Historical Landmarks

 The site of the capitol of the Republic of Texas on Main Street is marked by a plaque. A hotel was built on the actual site after the capital was moved to Austin. A plaque marking the site of the White House of the Republic of Texas also appears nearby. Christ Church Cathedral on Texas Avenue is a Gothic structure on a site donated by the Allen brothers in 1860. The Church of the Annunciation on Crawford Street was completed in 1871. Historic Houston in Sam Houston Park is a collection of houses and stores dating from 1837 to 1868. It includes Long Row on Bagby Street, San Felipe Cottage (1837), Noble House (1847), Rice-Cherry House, and Pilot House (1868). The San Jacinto State Historical Park features the world's tallest masonry structure. Also of historical interest is the Herbert Douglas Plantation Home.

Population

 Houston overtook Philadelphia in the 1980s to become the fourth-largest city in the nation. The population grew by 29.3% from 1.234 million in 1970 to 1.595 million in

Population		
	1980	*1990*
Central City	1,595,138	1,630,553
Rank	5	4
Metro Area	2,734,617	3,301,937
Pop. Change 1980–1990 +35,415		
Pop. % Change 1980–1990 +2.2		
Median Age 30.4		
% Male 49.6		
% Age 65 and Over 8.3		
Density (per square mile) 3,020		

Households		
Number 616,877		
Persons per Household 2.60		
% Female-Headed Households 14.6		

Population (continued)

% One-Person Households   31.0
Births—Total   37,685
    % to Mothers under 20   16.2
    Birth Rate per 1,000   22.1

1980, and then by a further 2.2% to reach 1.631 million in 1990.

Ethnic Composition

 Whites make up 52.7%, blacks 28.1%, American Indians 0.3%, Asians and Pacific Islanders 4.1%, and others 14.9%. Hispanics make up 27.6%.

Ethnic Composition (as % of total pop.)		
	1980	1990
White	61.33	52.69
Black	27.61	28.09
American Indian	0.20	0.25
Asian and Pacific Islander	2.07	4.12
Hispanic	17.64	27.63
Other	NA	14.86

Government

 Houston has a mayor-council form of government. The mayor and 14 members of the council are elected concurrently to two-year terms.

Government
Year of Home Charter   1905
Number of Members of the Governing Body   14
Elected at Large   5
Elected by Wards   9
Number of Women in Governing Body   5
Salary of Mayor $130,875
Salary of Council Members $34,900
City Government Employment Total   21,405
Rate per 10,000   123.8

Public Finance

 The annual budget consists of revenues of $1.701 billion and expenditures of $1.660 billion. The debt outstanding is

Public Finance
Total Revenue (in millions) $1,701.737
Intergovernmental Revenue—Total (in millions) $57.14
Federal Revenue per Capita $31.12
% Federal Assistance   1.82
% State Assistance   0.59
Sales Tax as % of Total Revenue   17.4
Local Revenue as % of Total Revenue   73.72
City Income Tax   no
Taxes—Total (in millions) $597.7
Taxes per Capita
Total $346
Property $195
Sales and Gross Receipts $142

Public Finance (continued)
General Expenditures—Total (in millions) $1,024.2
General Expenditures per Capita $592
Capital Outlays per Capita $109
% of Expenditures for:
Public Welfare   0.0
Highways   6.5
Education   0.0
Health and Hospitals   2.8
Police   17.9
Sewerage and Sanitation   17.8
Parks and Recreation   6.0
Housing and Community Development   1.0
Debt Outstanding per Capita $1,352
% Utility   25.1
Federal Procurement Contract Awards (in millions) $1,034.6
Federal Grants Awards (in millions) $314.9
Fiscal Year Begins   July 1

$3.610 billion and cash and securities holdings $3.558 billion.

Economy

Houston is a good barometer of the Texas economy. Its economy is a microcosm of the forces that drive the state economy: oil, cattle, aerospace, medicine, and petrochemicals. Houston's economic course was determined in 1901 when oil gushed out of Spindletop. The discovery coincided with the construction of the Houston Ship Channel, providing the right climate for the growth of the petrochemical industry. Houston's golden economy enjoyed an unbroken upward curve for the first eight decades of this century. At the beginning of the 1980s, Houston was the headquarters of eight of the ten largest energy companies, and some 5,000 businesses related to energy were located in the city and surrounding areas. The chemical industry in Houston accounted for almost 50% of the total U.S. production capacity, with more than 200 refining and processing plants. However, by the mid-1980s the bottom fell out of the economy as the oil boom burst. But by then the city had already embarked on the next phase of its economic growth. The twin props of the next phase were aerospace and medical sciences. Not only is Houston the home of the Johnson Space Center, but the federal government program to build a space station and place it in orbit by 1996 is a massive boost for the local economy. In addition, the center has embarked on a major building program to construct a Disneylike facility around the space theme that is designed to attract three million visitors per year.

The Texas Medical Center, the Institute of Biosciences and Technology of Texas A&M University, and the Texas Center for Superconductivity at the University of Houston are the anchors of Houston's technological leadership and are instrumental in pushing the city into the 21st century. The Port of Houston has survived the downturn and sustains Houston's expanding role in foreign trade. Houston is a major corporate center and the corporate headquarters of 17 Fortune 500 companies, 21 Forbes 500 companies, 6 of the Fortune 100 Fastest Growing Companies, and 11 of the Fortune Service 500 companies. Houston is also the primary U. S. location for 429 foreign companies. A center for international finance, Houston leads the Southwest in number of foreign banks, with 50 from seven nations. Forty-five foreign governments maintain consular offices in the city, and 25 maintain trade and commercial offices. Houston dominates U.S. gas and oil exploration and production, accounting for 23.4% of all jobs in crude petroleum and natural gas extraction, 13.5% of jobs in oil and gas field services, and 37.8% of jobs in oil and gas field machinery manufacturing.

Economy

Total Money Income (in millions) $209,457.4
% of State Average 116.8
Per Capita Annual Income $12,115
% Population below Poverty Level 12.7
Fortune 500 Companies 13

Banks	Number	Deposits (in millions)
Commercial	63	23,079.6
Savings	58	20,444.6

Passenger Autos 2,227,094
Electric Meters 1,217,594
Gas Meters 628,863

Manufacturing

Number of Establishments 3,142
% with 20 or More Employees 29.5
Manufacturing Payroll (in millions) $3,264.5
Value Added by Manufacture (in millions) $7,192.9
Value of Shipments (in millions) $16,814.4
New Capital Expenditures (in millions) $374.9

Wholesale Trade

Number of Establishments 5,981
Sales (in millions) NA
Annual Payroll (in millions) NA

Retail Trade

Number of Establishments 18,531
Total Sales (in millions) $14,049.1
Sales per Capita $8,126
Number of Retail Trade Establishments with Payroll
   11,502
Annual Payroll (in millions) $1,666.3
Total Sales (in millions) $13,693.1
General Merchandise Stores (per capita) $992
Food Stores (per capita) $1,534
Apparel Stores (per capita) $543
Eating and Drinking Places (per capita) $863

Service Industries

Total Establishments 17,003
Total Receipts (in millions) NA
Hotels and Motels (in millions) $418.6
Health Services (in millions) NA
Legal Services (in millions) $1,530.0

Labor

Houston's work force is the largest labor pool in the Southwest. It is also one of the youngest work forces in any metropolitan area, with a median age of 29. The labor force was hit hard in the recession of the late 1980s and early 1990s, as the unemployment rate hit the double digits.

Employment in the oil industry dropped from 14% in 1982 to less than 9% by 1990. Nevertheless, it is expected that the oil sector will continue to dominate the employment market for many decades to come. Future job growth appears to be in medicine, aerospace, and finance, with both professional and clerical workers benefiting from an economic recovery.

Labor

Civilian Labor Force 1,022,979 (metro)
% Change 1989–1990 2.3

Work Force Distribution
   Mining 70,300
   Construction 114,300
   Manufacturing 182,500
   Transportation and Public Utilities 114,700
   Wholesale and Retail Trade 382,000
   FIRE (Finance, Insurance, Real Estate) 100,200
   Service 458,600
   Government 213,800
   Women as % of Labor Force 42.0
   % Self-Employed 5.2
   % Professional/Technical 16.7
Total Unemployment 57,272
Rate % 5.6
Federal Government Civilian Employment 17,218

Education

The Houston Independent School District is the seventh largest in the nation and supports 31 high schools, 36 middle schools, 171 elementary schools. Houston has a very low high school dropout rate of 3%, compared to 40% in New York City; and 62% of high school graduates go on to Houston's 30 colleges and universities. The oldest institution is Rice University, and the largest is the University of Houston, with three campuses. Texas Southern University is also one of the most prestigious institutions. Baylor College of Medicine and the University of Texas Health Science Center are the most outstanding institutions in medicine, as the South Texas College of Law is in law. Other institutions include the Houston Baptist University, Dominican College, and St. Thomas University.

Education

Number of Public Schools 238
Special Education Schools 4
Total Enrollment 194,000
% Enrollment in Private Schools 5.9
% Minority 85.6
Classroom Teachers 10,530
Pupil-Teacher Ratio 18.4:1
Number of Graduates 7,741
Total Revenue (in millions) $652.5
Total Expenditures (in millions) $639.6
Expenditures per Pupil $2,902
Educational Attainment (Age 25 and Over)
   % Completed 12 or More Years 68.4
   % Completed 16 or More Years 23.1
Four-Year Colleges and Universities 9
   Enrollment 71,042
Two-Year Colleges 5
   Enrollment 54,034

Education (continued)

Libraries

Number   155
Public Libraries   34
Books (in thousands)   3,787
Circulation (in thousands)   6,284
Persons Served (in thousands)   1,698
Circulation per Person Served   3.70
Income (in millions) $20.228
Staff   436

Four-Year Colleges and Universities
    University of Houston (3 campuses)
    Texas Southern University
    University of Texas Health Science Center
    Baylor College of Medicine
    Houston Baptist University
    Rice University
    South Texas College of Law
    University of St Thomas

Health

Houston has 45 hospitals, including 4 teaching hospitals within city limits, while Harris County has 65. The Texas Medical Center ranks among the world's great hospital complexes, with 38 special facilities within the center and another 98 throughout the area. They include St. Luke's Episcopal Hospital, where in 1969 Dr. Denton A. Cooley performed the first transplant of an artificial heart; Methodist Hospital, the city's largest; Ben Taub General Hospital; Shriners Hospital for Crippled Children; Texas Institute for Rehabilitation and Research; M. D. Anderson Hospital and Tumor Institute; and Houston Speech and Hearing Center. Other major facilities include the Hermann Hospital and Veterans Administration Hospital.

Health

Deaths—Total   11,714
Rate per 1,000   6.9
Infant Deaths—Total   449
Rate per 1,000   11.9
Number of Metro Hospitals   45
Number of Metro Hospital Beds   13,601
Rate per 100,000   787
Number of Physicians   6,747
Physicians per 1,000   2.39
Nurses per 1,000   5.82
Health Expenditures per Capita $28.97

Transportation

Houston is approached by two interstates, the north-south I-45 and east-west I-10; U.S. Highways 59, 75, 90, and 290; and State Highways 35, 73, 225, and 288. Within Houston proper, there are 12 freeways linked by three loops. The innermost is I-610, followed by Beltway 8 and State Highway 6. The two major north-south arteries are the Gulf Freeway, which feeds traffic north to Dallas and south to Galveston; and U.S. 59, which leads northeast to Arkansas and south to Corpus Christi. The major east-west artery is I-10, linking Houston with Austin, San Antonio, and New Orleans. Amtrak passenger service is available three times weekly. Rail freight service is provided by Santa Fe, Southern Pacific, MKT, Burlington Northern, Union Pacific, and Galveston Houston & Henderson. The Port of Houston with over 100 wharves is the third largest in total tonnage and the second largest in foreign tonnage handled. It is connected with Galveston Bay by the Houston Ship Channel. The port is the largest Foreign Trade Zone in the nation, the world's largest petroleum equipment and machinery and wheat exporter, and a leading cattle and rice exporter. More than half the export tonnage consists of agricultural products. Houston has two principal air terminals: the Intercontinental Airport on the north side of the city for international flights and the William P. Hobby Airport, about 15 minutes away from downtown, for domestic flights.

Transportation

Interstate Highway Mileage   140
Total Urban Mileage   14,743
Total Daily Vehicle Mileage (in millions)   70.1
Daily Average Commute Time   58.5 min.
Number of Buses   747
Port Tonnage (in millions)   124.886
Airports   2
Number of Daily Flights   436
Daily Average Number of Passengers   30,020

Airlines (American carriers only)
    Alaska
    American
    American West
    Continental
    Delta
    Eastern
    Northwest
    Southwest
    USAir
    Trans World
    United

Housing

Housing in general is extremely attractive in Houston. As a result of overbuilding during the oil boom, there is a buyer's market in housing, with single-family homes costing less than the national average. The metropolitan area includes dozens of bedroom communities, ten of them within city limits: Bellaire, Bunker Hill, Hedwig Village, Hilshire Village, Humble, Hunters Creek Village, Piney Point Village, Southside Place, Spring Valley, and West University Place. Large suburban communities outside Houston include Baytown, Deer Park, La Porte, Missouri City, and Pasadena. There are many mixed-use developments, like Galleria–Post Oak on West Loop and Greenway Plaza on Southwest Freeway. Most Mexican Americans live north of the downtown area and along both banks of the Houston Ship Channel in the east. The once elegant Montrose and Heights areas are now home to the elderly. Most blacks live within the Freeway Loop and in the downtown area. Many million-dollar homes are found in River Oaks. Of the total housing stock 44.6% is owner-occupied. The median value of an owner-occupied home is $58,000, and the median monthly rent is $328. Houston is the 13th most affordable housing market in the nation.

Housing

Total Housing Units	726,435
% Change 1980–1990	6.6
Vacant Units for Sale or Rent	84,106
Occupied Units	616,877
% with More Than One Person per Room	11.7
% Owner-Occupied	44.6
Median Value of Owner-Occupied Homes	$58,000
Average Monthly Purchase Cost	$378
Median Monthly Rent	$328
New Private Housing Starts	2,156
Value (in thousands)	$195,651
% Single-Family	56.8
Nonresidential Buildings Value (in thousands)	$124,108

Tallest Buildings	Hgt. (ft.)	Stories
Texas Commerce Tower	1,002	75
Allied Bank Plaza	992	71
Transco Tower	901	64
RepublicBank Center	780	56
Heritage Plaza	762	53
InterFirst Plaza	744	55
1600 Smith St.	729	54
Gulf Towers	725	52

Urban Redevelopment

Houston went through a construction boom in the 1970s and 1980s, which caused it to be hit hard when the real estate market crashed in the late 1980s and early 1990s. The city skyline has not changed much since 1985. Urban redevelopment is coordinated by a number of organizations, including Central Houston and Houston-Galveston Area Local Development Corporation.

Crime

Houston ranks low in public safety. In 1991, the crimes known to police consisted of 26,651 violent crimes and 153,657 property crimes.

Religion

Houston is a city of more than 1,200 churches representing some 40 denominations and religions. Church membership continues to grow, although not in pace with population. The Union Baptist Association of Houston has the largest membership, with 200 churches; Roman Catholics, constituting 14% of the population, have some 125 parishes; and the United Methodist Church has about 130 churches. The first church to be established in Houston was the Presbyterian Church in 1841. It was followed by a Roman Catholic church in 1842, a Methodist church in 1844, Episcopalian and Baptist churches in 1847, and a Jewish synagogue in 1870.

Crime

Violent Crimes—Total	26,651
Violent Crime Rate per 100,000	1,076
Murder	608
Rape	1,213
Robbery	13,883
Aggravated Assaults	10,947
Property Crimes	153,657
Burglary	39,726
Larceny	73,769
Motor Vehicle Theft	40,162
Arson	1,877
Per Capita Police Expenditures	$140.40
Per Capita Fire Protection Expenditures	$77.60
Number of Police	4,363
Per 1,000	2.5

Religion

Largest Denominations (Adherents)	
Catholic	524,251
Assembly of God	25,892
Church of Christ	33,931
Episcopal	35,705
Southern Baptist	395,152
United Methodist	165,055
Black Baptist	230,194
Presbyterian	38,385
Lutheran-Missouri Synod	32,537
Evangelical Lutheran	17,967
Jewish	36,061

Media

The city dailies consist of the *Houston Chronicle,* and the *Houston Post.* The electronic media consist of 11 television stations, including 7 independents, 1 public, and 3 commercial networks; and 38 AM and FM radio stations.

Media

Newsprint
The Advocate, weekly
Houston Business Journal, weekly
Houston Chronicle, daily
Houston City Magazine, monthly
Houston Forward Times, weekly
Houston Informer, weekly
Houston Post, daily
Houston Sun, weekly
The Leader, weekly
Northeast News, weekly

Sports

The hub of the Houston sports scene is the Dome, as the Astrodome is popularly called, where the Oilers, the professional football team, and the Astros, the professional baseball team, play their home games. The Houston Rockets of the National Basketball Association play their home games at the Summit. Almost all the major universities and colleges have their own sports and

Media (continued)

Television

KETH (Channel 14)
KHOU (Channel 11)
KHTV (Channel 39)
KPRC (Channel 2)
KRIV (Channel 26)
KTFH (Channels 49, 53)
KDMD (Channel 48)
KTRK (Channel 13)
KTXH (Channel 20)
KUHT (Channel 8)

Radio

KACO (AM)	KCOH (AM)
KEYH (AM)	KHCB (AM)
KHMX (FM)	KHYS (FM)
KIKK (AM)	KIKK (FM)
KILT (AM)	KILT (FM)
KJOJ (FM)	KKBQ (AM)
KKBQ (FM)	KLAT (AM)
KLDE (FM)	KLTR (FM)
KLVL (AM)	KMJQ (FM)
KMPO (AM)	KNUZ (AM)
KQUE (FM)	KQQT (FM)
KODA (FM)	KPFT (FM)
KPRC (AM)	KRBE (AM)
KRBE (FM)	KTRH (AM)
KLOL (FM)	KRTS (FM)
KSEV (AM)	KTEK (AM)
KTRH (AM)	KTRU (FM)
KTSU (FM)	KUHF (FM)
KYOK (AM)	KZFX (FM)

athletic teams. Horse racing is held at the Delta Downs Race Track.

Arts, Culture, and Tourism

Houston's performing arts facilities are on the same magnificent scale as its other institutions. They include the Wortham Theater Center, a $75 million complex housing Houston Grand Opera and Houston Ballet; Jesse H. Jones Hall for the Performing Arts, home to the Houston Symphony and the Society for the Performing Arts; Music Hall, home to Theater Under the Stars; Cynthia Woods Mitchell Pavilion; Alley Theater; Arena Theater; and Miller Outdoor Theater. Founded in 1913, the Houston Symphony presents a full season of subscription concerts in Jones Hall, free summer concerts in Miller Theater, and concerts on tour. The Houston Grand Opera is one of the five largest opera companies in the nation. Other symphony ensembles include the Houston Youth Symphony, Houston Civic Symphony, and Houston Pops. The Theater Under the Stars offers lavish musicals in free summer productions and in a winter subscription season. Other musical groups include the Houston Harpsichord Society, Houston Oratorio Society, Gilbert and Sullivan Society, Houston Chamber Ensemble, and Houston Friends of Music. The Houston Ballet, founded in 1955 and established as a professional company in 1969, is one of several dance companies; others are the Allegro Dance Group, City Ballet of Houston, Cookie Joe and the Jazz Company, Discovery Dance Group, Generating Company, Joan Karff New Dance Group,

Della Stewart Dance Company, Roberta Stokes Dance Company, and Chrysalis Repertory Dance Company. The major theatrical attraction is the Nina Vance Alley Theater, one of the three oldest resident companies in the nation. A summer Shakespeare Festival produced by the University of Houston in English and Spanish is held annually in Miller Theater. Stages Repertory Company offers experimental productions of classics and revivals. Nonequity professional companies include Main Street Theater, Chocolate Bayou Theater Company, A. D. Players, Actors Workshop, and the Ensemble, a black theater.

The Museum of Fine Arts, with a collection of 27,000 pieces, is the largest in the Southwest. Other museums include the Bayou Bend Museum of Americana, Contemporary Arts Museum, The Menil Collection, Farish Gallery and Sewall Art Gallery on the Rice Campus and the Sarah Campbell Blaffer Gallery at the University of Houston, Houston Museum of Natural Science, Museum of Texas History (operated by the Harris County Heritage Society), San Jacinto Museum of History, Houston Fire Museum, Museum of American Architectural and Decorative Arts, Museum of Art of the American West, Children's Museum of Houston, Confederate Museum, Houston Center for Photography, and African American Heritage Museum. The Johnson Space Center has permanent displays of spacecraft. Its $60 million Visitor Center opened in 1992.

Parks and Recreation

Houston's 334 municipal parks cover 20,124 land acres and 12,236 acres of water. Among the most popular are the 10,532-acre Cullen Park, largest in the United States; Hermann Park, including the Houston Zoo and a children's zoo and the Miller Outdoor Theater; Memorial Park; Eisenhower Park on the San Jacinto River; Keith-Weiss Park; the 717-acre Herman Brown Park;

Travel and Tourism

Hotel Rooms 35,993
Convention and Exhibit Space (square feet) 470,500

Convention Centers

George R. Brown Convention Center
Astrodome
Astrodomain
Astroarena
Houston Civic Center (Albert Thomas Convention Center and Sam Houston Coliseum)

Festivals

Houston Livestock Show and Rodeo (winter)
Houston International Festival (spring)
Westheimer Art Festival (spring, fall)
Oktoberfest (September–November)
Texas Renaissance Festival (October)
Greek Festival (October)

Sam Houston Park, the city's oldest; Tranquillity Park in the Civic Center; Allen's Landing Park; Sesquicentennial Park; and a lineal park along Buffalo Bayou. In addition, Harris County maintains 89 parks covering 18,780 acres, including Adair Park on Clear Creek,

Armand Bayou Park and Nature Center, Clear Lake Park, Alexander Deussen Park, Mercer Arboretum and Botanical Garden, Bear Creek Park, Bay Area Park, Jesse H. Jones Park and Nature Center, and Tom Bass Regional Park. The Cypress Creek Park Project is a series of 29 park sites totaling 2,700 acres along Spring and Cypress Creeks.

Sources of Further Information

City Hall
901 Bagby Street
Houston, TX 77002
(713) 247-2200

Greater Houston Convention and Visitors Council
3300 Main Street
Houston, TX 77002
(713) 523-5050

Houston Chamber of Commerce
1100 Milam Building
Houston, TX 77002
(713) 658-2470

Additional Reading

Apple, Max. *Liquid City: Houston Writers on Houston.* 1987.
Buchanan, J. E. *Houston: A Chronological and Documentary History.* 1975.
Bullard, Robert D. *Invisible Houston: The Black Experience in Boom and Bust.* 1987.
Davenport, John C. *Houston.* 1985.
Davis, John L. *Houston: A Historical Portrait.* 1983.
De Leon, Arnoldo. *Ethnicity in the Sunbelt: A History of Mexican-Americans in Houston.* 1989.
Feagin, Joe R. *Free Enterprise City: Houston in Economic and Political Perspective.* 1988.
Fox, Stephen. *Houston Architectural Guide.* 1990.
Harrison, Joanne. *Houston: The Texas Monthly Guidebook.* 1989.
Lewis, Elizabeth W. *Houston: Star of the Republic, 1836–1846.* 1985.
Lipartito, Kenneth J., and Joseph A. Pratt. *Baker & Botts in the Development of Modern Houston.* 1991.
McAshan, Mary P. *A Houston Legacy.* 1985.
McComb, David G. *Houston: A History.* 1981.
MacManus, Susan A. "Federal Aid to Houston." 1983.
Marchiafava, Louis J. *The Houston Police, 1878–1948.* 1977.
Milburn, Douglas. *Houston: A Self-Portrait.* 1986.
Miller, Ray. *Houston.* 1984.
Rosales, Francisco A., and Barry J. Kaplan. *Houston: A Twentieth Century Urban Frontier.* 1983.
van der Mehden, Fred R. *The Ethnic Groups of Houston.* 1984.
Winningham, Geoff, and Al Reinert. *A Place of Dreams: Houston, An American City.* 1986.
Young, Dale. *A Marmac Guide to Houston.* 1988.

Indianapolis

Indiana

Basic Data

Name   Indianapolis
Name Origin   From Indiana + *polis*, Greek for "city"
Year Founded   1820 Inc. 1832
Status: State   Capital of Indiana
          County   Seat of Marion County
Area (square miles)   361.7
Elevation (feet)   710
Time Zone   EST
Population (1990)   731,327
Population of Metro Area (1990)   1,249,822

Sister Cities
   Cologne, Germany
   Scarborough, Canada
   Taipei Municipality, China

Distance in Miles To:
Atlanta	527
Boston	929
Chicago	185
Dallas	892
Denver	1,063
Detroit	284
Houston	995
Los Angeles	2,063
Miami	1,186
New York	731
Philadelphia	659
Washington, D.C	575

Location and Topography

Indianapolis, the capital of Indiana, is a large metropolitan area located in the center of the state. The largest American city not situated on navigable water, it is an agricultural (grain) and commercial center for the central region. From Indianapolis International Airport, seven miles southwest of the city, to the famed Indianapolis Speedway west of the metropolis, the terrain slopes down gradually to the capital, then upward past the city to the east.

Layout of City and Suburbs

Indianapolis, the nation's 12th-largest city, is located on what were once rolling woodlands. Selected by a group of ten businessmen to be the state capital in 1820, it was patterned after Washington, D.C., its streets purposefully planned in the national capital's style. Several great avenues intersect downtown to form, at the city's core, the Soldiers' and Sailors' Monument. Among these major thoroughfares are Washington Street, Virginia Avenue, Pennsylvania Street, Indiana Avenue, Ohio Street, and Massachusetts Avenue. Washington Street (I-40) is the main thoroughfare, running in an east-to-west course. Meridian Street, which intersects Washington just below the Soldiers' and Sailors' Monument and runs north to south, is an important route of commerce and industry.

Environment

Environmental Stress Index   2.4
Green Cities Index: Rank   67
                    Score   27.44
Water Quality   Alkaline, hard, fluoridated
   Average Daily Use (gallons per capita)   157
   Maximum Supply (gallons per capita)   257
Parkland as % of Total City Area   3.6
% Waste Landfilled/Recycled   65:35
Annual Parks Expenditures per Capita $29.74

Climate

Indianapolis has a temperate climate with no pronounced wet or dry seasons. Summers are generally warm with periods of muggy weather, although air masses from the Gulf of Mexico are soon replaced by cooler air from the northern plains and the Great Lakes. Sometimes hot, dry winds from the southwest prevail. In winter, in-

cursions of polar air from the north may produce occasional frigid temperatures. Snowfall may be no more than two or three times a year for a total of less than 21 inches. Late spring and fall are the most pleasant seasons. Rainfall is adequate and well distributed throughout the year.

Weather			
Temperature			
Highest Monthly Average °F 85.2			
Lowest Monthly Average °F 17.8			
Annual Averages			
Days 32°F or Below 122			
Days above 90°F 15			
Zero Degree Days 7			
Precipitation (inches) 39.0			
Snow (inches) 21.0			
% Seasonal Humidity 73.0			
Wind Speed (m.p.h.) 9.7			
Clear Days 90			
Cloudy Days 174			
Storm Days 45			
Rainy Days 122			
Average Temperatures (°F)	*High*	*Low*	*Mean*
January	36.0	19.7	27.9
February	39.3	22.1	30.7
March	49.0	30.3	39.7
April	62.8	41.8	52.3
May	72.9	51.5	62.2
June	82.3	61.1	71.7
July	85.4	64.6	75.0
August	84.0	62.4	73.2
September	77.7	54.9	66.3
October	67.0	44.3	55.7
November	50.5	32.8	41.7
December	38.7	23.1	30.9

History

Indiana already had its capital at Corydon (in the southern section of the state, west of Louisville, Kentucky) when the state legislature met in January 1820 to select a more central capital. Ten state commissioners were chosen to conduct the search. A month later, what would become the site of Indianapolis began as a small settlement called Fall Creek, populated in its earliest years mainly by American Indians and two white families, the Pogues and the McCormicks. On 7 June 1820 Fall Creek was selected as the new capital, and settlers began to arrive and colonize it. In 1821, after E. P. Fordham mapped the city into a one mile-square area, the legislature approved the site and followed the recommendation of State Supreme Court Justice Jeremiah Sullivan in naming the city Indianapolis (Indiana, plus the Greek *polis*, meaning city). Alexander Ralston, chief assistant to Pierre L'Enfant, who had platted Washington, D.C., was hired to plan Indianapolis. Ralston outlined a city that was one mile square (although the commissioners had called for a four mile-square city) based on the Washington, D.C., formula of spacious thoroughfares emanating from a central circle where government would be located.

Plots of land were sold for $10 each, and buildings constructed, but Indianapolis seemed unable to grow from a small town of ramshackle houses. Even the governor, James Brown Ray, and his wife refused to live in what they perceived as an ugly governor's mansion.

But these were only growing pains. In 1821 Marion County was organized with Indianapolis as the county seat. The following year the first newspaper, the *Gazette*, appeared. The settlers that arrived during and after this period were a mixed lot of Germans, Irish, Italians, and other Europeans. They laid down their roots in various portions of the city and set up communities, churches, and synagogues that were exclusively ethnic. This is why Indianapolis is known as the "City of Churches." In 1825 the legislature met here for the first time, and in 1836 the city was incorporated.

Two projects in the beginning and ending years of the 1830s led to tremendous growth in Indianapolis. In 1830 the National Road, known as U.S. 40, was built through Indianapolis, making the city an important link to other cities in the state as well as to the ever-expanding American West. In 1839 the Central Canal on the White River was constructed, making industrial activity easier and more efficient. With train lines meeting at Indianapolis in 1847, the city became an important trade and commercial center.

During the 1840s and 1850s, Germans became the largest ethnic group in the city, at one point making up 12% of the total population. Several German business owners, including the Vonneguts (a descendant, Kurt Vonnegut, is an internationally known author), Libers, Mauses, and Schmidts (who formed one of the city's largest breweries), made their mark in commerce. Although the city was an important center of munitions during the Civil War, commercial prosperity came in the years afterward when streets were paved, gas lights installed, and the overall business atmosphere became more conducive to success. In 1894 the city was the site of the invention of the first gasoline automobile, by Charles H. Black. In fact, such activity in the automobile industry led the city to become the home of the Indianapolis Speedway, which held its first race in 1911.

On 1 January 1970, by an act of the state legislature, city and county governments were consolidated in a unique program of government called Unigov. In the last three decades, Indianapolis has become an important hub for agriculture, livestock, and meat processing. In 1987 it was recognized as a growing sports arena when it hosted the Pan American Games. Future industrial growth is governed by a regional center plan, drawn up by city leaders in 1980.

Historical Landmarks

Indianapolis's long history provides a number of historical landmarks. The Athenaeum was originally designed by Bernhard Vonnegut, grandfather of the author, and built in 1892 as a sort of social club for the German populace. Originally named the Das Deutsche Haus,

Chronology

1820 State legislators at Corydon establish a ten-member commission to find a more centrally located state capital. White settlers John McCormick and George Pogue and their families build cabins in the woods at Fall Creek, on the site of present-day Indianapolis. Fall Creek is selected as the new state capital.

1821 Fall Creek is renamed Indianapolis. Surveyor E. P. Fordham lays out broad city details; city planner Alexander Ralston plots the city to model Washington, D.C. Marion County is organized and Indianapolis is named as the county seat.

1822 First city newspaper, the *Gazette*, makes its debut.

1824 State courthouse, which doubles as the state legislature, is built.

1825 State legislature meets for the first time in new capital.

1830 The National Road (U.S. 40) is built through Indianapolis.

1836 Indianapolis is incorporated as a city.

1839 The Central Canal on the White River is completed.

1847 Train lines connect Indianapolis with the rest of the nation, making it an important commercial center.

1886 The City Market is established. Added to the National Register of Historic Places in 1974, it was renovated four years later and remains a landmark in the city.

1888 The Indiana State House is completed.

1911 The first Indianapolis 500 road race is held at the Speedway.

1968 Richard G. Lugar starts serving an eight-year term as mayor of Indianapolis. He is later elected as a U.S. senator.

1970 Indianapolis city government is merged with that of surrounding Marion County to form the unique government experiment called Unigov.

1980 City devises a regional center plan to plot growth in the downtown area until the year 2000.

the name was changed because of anti-German feeling during World War I. The oldest house of worship in the city is the Christ Church Cathedral, built in 1857 and renovated in 1989. This massive stone structure reflects what one guide calls "the English Gothic country church style of architecture." The famed City Market was founded in 1886; with renovations in the 1970s, it remains a lively center of agricultural commerce. The Benjamin Harrison Home, residence of the nation's 23rd president, is located in the neighborhood known as the Old Northside, a 190-acre area of Victorian residences now added to the National Register of Historic Places. Union Station, situated at Louisiana Street, is a combination hotel–train depot–mall located at the site of the first railway depot in the United States. Abraham Lincoln gave a speech at the original depot, which was replaced in 1888. The imposing statehouse, built of Indiana limestone in 1888, was renovated in 1988 and is located just two blocks from the center of the city. Standing at the city's nucleus is the Soldiers' and Sailors' Monument, a 284-foot statue erected in 1902 to honor those men of Indiana who served in the Civil War.

Population

The consolidated city of Indianapolis (including Marion County) ranked 13th in population in 1990 with 731,327 inhabitants. It registered a growth rate of 4.4% from its 1980 population of 700,807.

Population		
	1980	*1990*
Central City	700,807	731,327
Rank	12	13
Metro Area	1,166,575	1,249,822
Pop. Change 1980–1990 +30,520		
Pop. % Change 1980–1990 +4.4		
Median Age 31.7		
% Male 47.5		
% Age 65 and Over 11.4		
Density (per square mile) 2,021		

Households
Number   291,946
Persons per Household   2.46
% Female-Headed Households   14.1
% One-Person Households   29.4
Births—Total   12,812
% to Mothers under 20   16.6
Birth Rate per 1,000   18.0

Ethnic Composition

Whites make up 75.8%, blacks 22.64%, American Indians 1.1%, Asian and Pacific Islanders 0.94%, and others 0.40%.

Ethnic Composition (as % of total pop.)		
	1980	*1990*
White	77.10	75.81
Black	21.78	22.64
American Indian	0.14	0.22
Asian and Pacific Islander	0.54	0.94
Hispanic	0.88	1.05
Other	NA	0.40

Government

In 1970 Indianapolis and Marion County consolidated governmental functions to form Unigov, whose jurisdiction includes all of Marion County except the town of Speedway and the cities of Lawrence, Southport, and Beechgrove. The mayor and the 29 members of the city/county council serve 4 years. The mayor heads a six-department city government. The council members are elected both at large and by district.

Government

Year of Home Charter   NA
Number of Members of the Governing Body   29
Elected at Large   4
Elected by Wards   25
Number of Women in Governing Body   6
Salary of Mayor $78,873
Salary of Council Members $9,600
City Government Employment Total   12,183
Rate per 10,000   169.3

Public Finance

The annual budget consists of revenues of $891.533 million and expenditures of $952.330 million. The debt outstanding is $952.927 million, and cash and security holdings are $610.379 million.

Public Finance

Total Revenue (in millions) $891.533
Intergovernmental Revenue—Total (in millions) $256.9
Federal Revenue per Capita $71.3
% Federal Assistance   8.0
% State Assistance   20.68
Sales Tax as % of Total Revenue   1.82
Local Revenue as % of Total Revenue   68.4
City Income Tax   yes
Taxes—Total (in millions) $197.9

Taxes per Capita
   Total $275
   Property $250
   Sales and Gross Receipts $16
General Expenditures—Total (in millions) $511.4
General Expenditures per Capita $710
Capital Outlays per Capita $99

% of Expenditures for:
   Public Welfare   10.4
   Highways   6.0
   Education   0.3
   Health and Hospitals   20.9
   Police   9.3
   Sewerage and Sanitation   9.9
   Parks and Recreation   3.0
   Housing and Community Development   3.5
Debt Outstanding per Capita $600
   % Utility   2.8
Federal Procurement Contract Awards (in millions)
   $1,052.4
Federal Grants Awards (in millions) $339.6
Fiscal Year Begins   January 1

Economy

As the capital of Indiana, Indianapolis has state government as one of the main tiers of its economy. Heavy industry and services are also widely represented in the city's economic pool. In 1990, 24% of the work force was in the service sector, 16% in manufacturing, and 15% in government services. Such firms as Eli Lilly and Company (pharmaceuticals), Allison Gas and Turbine (builder of gas engines), Allison Transmissions (manufacturer of transmissions), and the Associated Group (insurance) have their corporate headquarters here. In 1983 public and private sectors formed the Indianapolis Economic Development Corporation (IEDC) to expand current business and attract new business.

Economy

Total Money Income (in millions) $7,801.9
% of State Average   108.6
Per Capita Annual Income $10,836
% Population below Poverty Level   11.5
Fortune 500 Companies   2

Banks	Number	Deposits (in millions)
Commercial	7	9,924.748
Savings	7	2,405.187

Passenger Autos   480,054
Electric Meters   356,348
Gas Meters   220,809

Manufacturing

Number of Establishments   1,186
% with 20 or More Employees   36.4
Manufacturing Payroll (in millions) $2,257.1
Value Added by Manufacture (in millions) $5,268.9
Value of Shipments (in millions) $10,270.9
New Capital Expenditures (in millions) $352.6

Wholesale Trade

Number of Establishments   1,952
Sales (in millions) $14,059.5
Annual Payroll (in millions) $724.195

Retail Trade

Number of Establishments   6,894
Total Sales (in millions) $6,692.3
Sales per Capita $9,297
Number of Retail Trade Establishments with Payroll   4,760
Annual Payroll (in millions) $754.3
Total Sales (in millions) $6,592.1
General Merchandise Stores (per capita)   NA
Food Stores (per capita) $1,245
Apparel Stores (per capita) $397
Eating and Drinking Places (per capita) $963

Service Industries

Total Establishments   5,723
Total Receipts (in millions) $3,270.8
Hotels and Motels (in millions) $196.9
Health Services (in millions) $814.1
Legal Services (in millions) $241.5

Labor

Indianapolis has a balanced labor distribution with no sector employing more than 25% of the work force. The total number of jobs has been growing since the end of World War II, and reached 670,000 in 1991. The largest sector is trade, followed by services and manufacturing, in that order. The FIRE sector makes a strong showing, employing nearly 48,000 people. Federal, state, and city governments account for a substantial share of employment in services. The payroll for the entire U.S. Army is prepared at Fort Benjamin Harrison.

Labor

Civilian Labor Force	397,234
% Change 1989–1990	-3.3

Work Force Distribution
- Mining 800
- Construction 32,900
- Manufacturing 106,200
- Transportation and Public Utilities 38,600
- Wholesale and Retail Trade 169,800
- FIRE (Finance, Insurance, Real Estate) 48,900
- Service 148,100
- Government 95,700
- Women as % of Labor Force 45.3
- % Self-Employed 4.1
- % Professional/Technical 15.1

Total Unemployment 18,073
Rate % 4.5
Federal Government Civilian Employment 11,951

Education

The Indianapolis Public Schools System supports 68 elementary schools, 10 junior high schools, 7 senior high schools, and 7 special education schools. In addition, there is a strong private school system, including 41 parochial schools and 2 private high schools.

Indianapolis is home to 19 institutions of higher education. The largest is the Indiana University–Purdue University with an enrollment of over 27,000. Other schools include the private University of Indianapolis and Butler University, Marian College, Indiana Vocational Technical College (IVY Tech), and Martin Center College.

Education

Number of Public Schools	92
Special Education Schools	7
Total Enrollment	48,140
% Enrollment in Private Schools	9.9
% Minority	52.3
Classroom Teachers	3,018
Pupil-Teacher Ratio	15.9:1
Number of Graduates	1,693
Total Revenue (in millions)	$227.0
Total Expenditures (in millions)	$222.8
Expenditures per Pupil	$3,756

Educational Attainment (Age 25 and Over)
- % Completed 12 or More Years 66.7
- % Completed 16 or More Years 16.4

Four-Year Colleges and Universities 5
- Enrollment 36,549

Two-Year Colleges 3
- Enrollment 5,500

Education (continued)

Libraries

Number	82
Public Libraries	22
Books (in thousands)	1,644
Circulation (in thousands)	5,376
Persons Served (in thousands)	NA
Circulation per Person Served	NA
Income (in millions)	$16.095
Staff	358

Four-Year Colleges and Universities
- Indiana University-Purdue University
- University of Indianapolis
- Butler University
- Marian College
- Martin Center College

Health

Indianapolis claims the world's largest university medical center and the second largest medical school in the nation. The Indiana University Medical Center contains three hospitals, including University Hospital, Long Hospital, and Whitcomb Riley Hospital for Children. St. Vincents Hospital and Health Care Center specializes in surgery, and Winona Memorial Hospital has a sleep disorder clinic. A leader in sports medicine, the city is the national headquarters for the American College of Sports Medicine.

Health

Deaths—Total	6,390
Rate per 1,000	9.0
Infant Deaths—Total	170
Rate per 1,000	13.3
Number of Metro Hospitals	14
Number of Metro Hospital Beds	5,269
Rate per 100,000	732
Number of Physicians	2,917
Physicians per 1,000	2.70
Nurses per 1,000	NA
Health Expenditures per Capita	$36.80

Transportation

Commerce usually flows in and out of a state capital. Thus, Indianapolis is well served by several major roadways. Interstate 465 forms a sort of beltway as it rings the city; I-65 runs from Chicago in the northwest to Louisville in the southeast; I-74 leads west to Peoria and east to Cincinnati; I-70 connects the city to Pittsburgh and St. Louis; and U.S. 31, 36, 40, and 52 bracket the confines of Marion County. Rail service is provided by the Consolidated Rail Corporation, the Norfolk Southern Corporation, the CSX Corporation, the Indiana Railroad Company, and Amtrak out of the renovated Union Station downtown. Situated about 12 minutes southwest of downtown, the Indiana International Airport serves 13 airlines and handles more than 6 million passengers a year.

Transportation

Interstate Highway Mileage   114
Total Urban Mileage   3,830
Total Daily Vehicle Mileage (in millions)   20.828
Daily Average Commute Time   46.9 min.
Number of Buses   225
Port Tonnage (in millions)   NA
Airports   1
Number of Daily Flights   131
Daily Average Number of Passengers   6,912

Airlines (American carriers only)
   American
   American Trans Air
   Continental
   Delta
   Eastern
   Midway
   Northwest
   Trans World
   United
   USAir

Housing

The ratio of new houses to population is higher in Indianapolis than in any other midwestern city. The city has a variety of residential neighborhoods, including the downtown historical districts of Lockerbie Square, Chatham Arch, the Old Northside, Woodruff Place, and Herron-Morton Place. Some of the most expensive homes are found in the Meridan-Kessler nighborhood. The upscale suburbs are Greenwood to the south and Carmel or Noblesville to the north. The total number of housing units in 1990 was 319,980, of which 53,490 were built in the last 10 years. The average sale price of a single-family home was $82,864.

Housing

Total Housing Units   319,980
% Change 1980–1990   11.5
Vacant Units for Sale or Rent   20,085
Occupied Units   291,946
% with More Than One Person per Room   2.5
% Owner-Occupied   56.7
Median Value of Owner-Occupied Homes $60,800
Average Monthly Purchase Cost $300
Median Monthly Rent $342
New Private Housing Starts   4,039
Value (in thousands) $313,773
% Single-Family   61.2
Nonresidential Buildings Value (in thousands) $409,120

Tallest Buildings	*Hgt. (ft.)*	*Stories*
Bank One Tower (1989)	728	51
AUL Tower (1981)	533	38
Market Tower (1988)	515	32
Indiana Natl. Bank Tower (1969)	504	35
Riley Towers (2 bldgs.) (1963)	427	30
300 N. Meridian Bldg. (1988)	408	28
First Indiana Plaza (1988)	396	31
City-County Bldg. (1962)	375	28

Urban Redevelopment

Urban renewal, administered by the Indianapolis Redevelopment Commission, began in the 1970s and has resulted in a number of impressive projects, including the City-County Building; Riley Center, a complex of high-rise apartment buildings, stores, restaurants, and recreational facilities; a festival marketplace of shops and restaurants in the restored Union Station; the Hoosier Dome, a domed football stadium; the Indiana Convention-Exposition Center; Market Square Arena; Merchants Plaza; Eiteljorg Museum; National Institute for Fitness and Sport Complex; Convention Center Plaza; and the Indianapolis Zoo. Scheduled for the 1990s are the White River Lower Canal Improvement, the Circle Center Redevelopment Project, White River State Park, and the State Office Complex. The Lower Canal Improvement Project is the rebirth of the Indiana Central Canal built in 1836. The Circle Center Redevelopment Project will be the catalyst for downtown redevelopment and will add 786,000 feet of retail space, 225 new hotel rooms, and 3,000 parking spaces.

Crime

In 1991 the crimes known to police consisted of 7,027 violent crimes and 28,933 property crimes.

Crime

Violent Crimes—Total   7,072
Violent Crime Rate per 100,000   732.9
Murder   95
Rape   561
Robbery   2,001
Aggravated Assaults   4,415
Property Crimes   28,933
Burglary   8,732
Larceny   14,970
Motor Vehicle Theft   5,231
Arson   286
Per Capita Police Expenditures $228.81
Per Capita Fire Protection Expenditures $43.96
Number of Police   951
Per 1,000   2.02

Religion

There are more than 600 churches in the city. Of these, 48 are Roman Catholic and the rest belong to various Protestant denominations.

Religion

Largest Denominations (Adherents)	
Catholics	84,033
Christian Church (Disciples)	20,596
Presbyterian	17,990
Black Baptist	56,403
United Methodist	37,027

Religion (continued)	
Assembly of God	10,229
American Baptist	11,483
American Zion	10,328
Church of the Nazarene	8,570
Jewish	6,379

Media

News in Indianapolis is covered by two dailies: the *Indianapolis Star*, published in the mornings and Sundays, and *The Indianapolis News*, an evening newspaper. The electronic media consists of 5 television stations and 8 AM and 11 FM radio stations.

Media

Newsprint

Fishers Sun-Herald, weekly
Indiana Herald, weekly
Indianapolis Business Journal, weekly
The Indianapolis News, daily
The Indianapolis Recorder, weekly
Indianapolis Star, daily
The Northeast Reporter, weekly

Television

WFYI (Channel 20)
WISH (Channel 8)
WRTV (Channel 6)
WTHR (Channel 13)
WXIN (Channel 59)

Radio

WAJC (FM)	WBDG (FM)
WBRI (AM)	WEDM (FM)
WFMS (FM)	WFXF (AM)
WFXF (FM)	WFYI (FM)
WIBC (AM)	WICR (FM)
WNDE (AM)	WNTS (AM)
WSYW (AM)	WTLC (FM)
WTPI (FM)	WTUX (AM)
WXIR (FM)	WTLC (FM)
WXLW (AM)	

Sports

Although there is a dearth of major league sports in Indianapolis (represented only by the Indianapolis Colts football team and the Indiana Pacers basketball team in the four national professional sports), the city is home to a dizzying array of other sports features and events that are highly noted. Chief among these is the Indianapolis 500, held at the Speedway just outside of town; the Pan American Games, of which it was the host in 1987; and the NCAA Final Four, held in 1991 and due to be held in the city again in 1997.

Arts, Culture, and Tourism

Indianapolis's standing in the arts community is on the rise with such groups as the Indianapolis Symphony Orchestra, founded in 1930 and named by the *New York Times* as one of the ten best in the nation; the

Indianapolis Opera, housed at Butler University; Dance Kaleidoscope and the Indianapolis Ballet Theatre, two dance ensembles; and the Indiana Repertory Theatre, the state's only such group, which performs at the Indiana Theatre, a renovated 1927 moviehouse.

Indianapolis is marked by several impressive museums: the Eiteljorg Museum of American Indian and Western Art, a showcase for American Indian and western artifacts; the Children's Museum, the largest of its kind in the world, which offers a hands-on approach for youngsters wishing to learn about science; the Indianapolis Museum of Art; the National Art Museum of Sport, which offers works dealing with sports of all kinds; and the Indiana State Museum, which showcases the state's long history.

Travel and Tourism

Hotel Rooms   14,734
Convention and Exhibit Space (square feet)   302,000

Convention Centers

Indiana Convention Center/Hoosier Dome
University Place Executive Conference Center

Festivals

Indianapolis 500 Festival (May)
St. Benno Feast (March)
Lockerbie Summer A'Fair
Talbot Street Art Fair (June)
Penrod Day (September)
International Festival (October)

Parks and Recreation

Indianapolis has nearly 140 parks. The largest is Eagle Creek Park, which at 3,800 acres is one of the largest municipal parks in the United States. The Garfield Park Conservatory, which honors President James A. Garfield, was opened in the 1860s and is one of the oldest parks in the city. White River State Park on West Washington Street, 250 acres on the banks of the White River, includes as its attractions the Indianapolis Zoo and the aforementioned Eiteljorg Museum.

Sources of Further Information

Indianapolis Convention and Visitors Association
One Hoosier Dome
Indianapolis, IN 46225
(317) 639-4282

The Indianapolis Project, Inc.
One Hoosier Dome, Suite 110
Indianapolis, IN 46225
(317) 639-4773

Indianapolis–Marion County Public Library
40 East St. Clair Street
Indianapolis, IN 46206-0211
(317) 269-1700

Additional Reading

Caldwell, Howard. *Indianapolis*. 1990.
Furlong, Patrick J. *Indianapolis: An Illustrated History*. 1985.
Owen, C. James, and Wilbern York. *Governing Metropolitan Indianapolis: The Politics of Unigov*. 1985.
Winter, Margaret. *Exploring Indianapolis*. 1990.

Jackson

Mississippi

Basic Data

Name   Jackson
Name Origin   From Andrew Jackson
Year Founded   1822 Inc. 1840
Status: State   Capital of Mississippi
      County   Seat of Hinds County
Area (square miles)   109.0
Elevation (feet)   298
Time Zone   Central
Population (1990)   196,637
Population of Metro Area (1990)   395,396

Sister Cities

   Chiayi, China
   Varna, Bulgaria

Distance in Miles To:

Atlanta	399
Boston	1,455
Chicago	745
Dallas	407
Denver	1,198
Detroit	957
Houston	419
Los Angeles	1,818
Miami	912
New York	1,224
Philadelphia	1,106
Washington, DC	973

Location and Topography

 Jackson, the capital of Mississippi, is situated on the western bank of the meandering Pearl River in the south-central section of the state. The city sits on a bluff overlooking the river. Lakes Hico and Larue are to the north, as is Hawkins Field. Jackson International Airport is to the immediate east.

Layout of City and Suburbs

Jackson's imposing grandeur is complemented by a sprawling capitol building occupying a full square block in the northern part of the city. The State Fairgrounds and State Coliseum stretch over much of the city's eastern area. Streets are arranged in the traditional grid pattern of other older cities, although some of the roadways in the western section are at a slant. The suburbs of Jackson include Clinton, Flowood, Ridgeland, and Pearl.

Environment

Environmental Stress Index   3.0
Green Cities Index: Rank   NA
               Score   NA
Water Quality   Alkaline, hard, fluoridated
   Average Daily Use (gallons per capita)   147
   Maximum Supply (gallons per capita)   37.8
Parkland as % of Total City Area   NA
% Waste Landfilled/Recycled   90:10
Annual Parks Expenditures per Capita $28.09

Climate

Jackson has long, humid summers and short, mild winters. In summer, the southerly winds and the accompanying warm gulf air masses predominate, making both days and nights hot and humid. In winter, the colder northern air penetrates the region only occasionally and for brief periods. When this occurs, there are sharp temperature shifts. Annual rainfall is 49 inches, but snowfall is less than 2 inches.

History

 The area that is now Jackson was once occupied by the Choctaw Indians. In 1789 French-Canadian explorer and

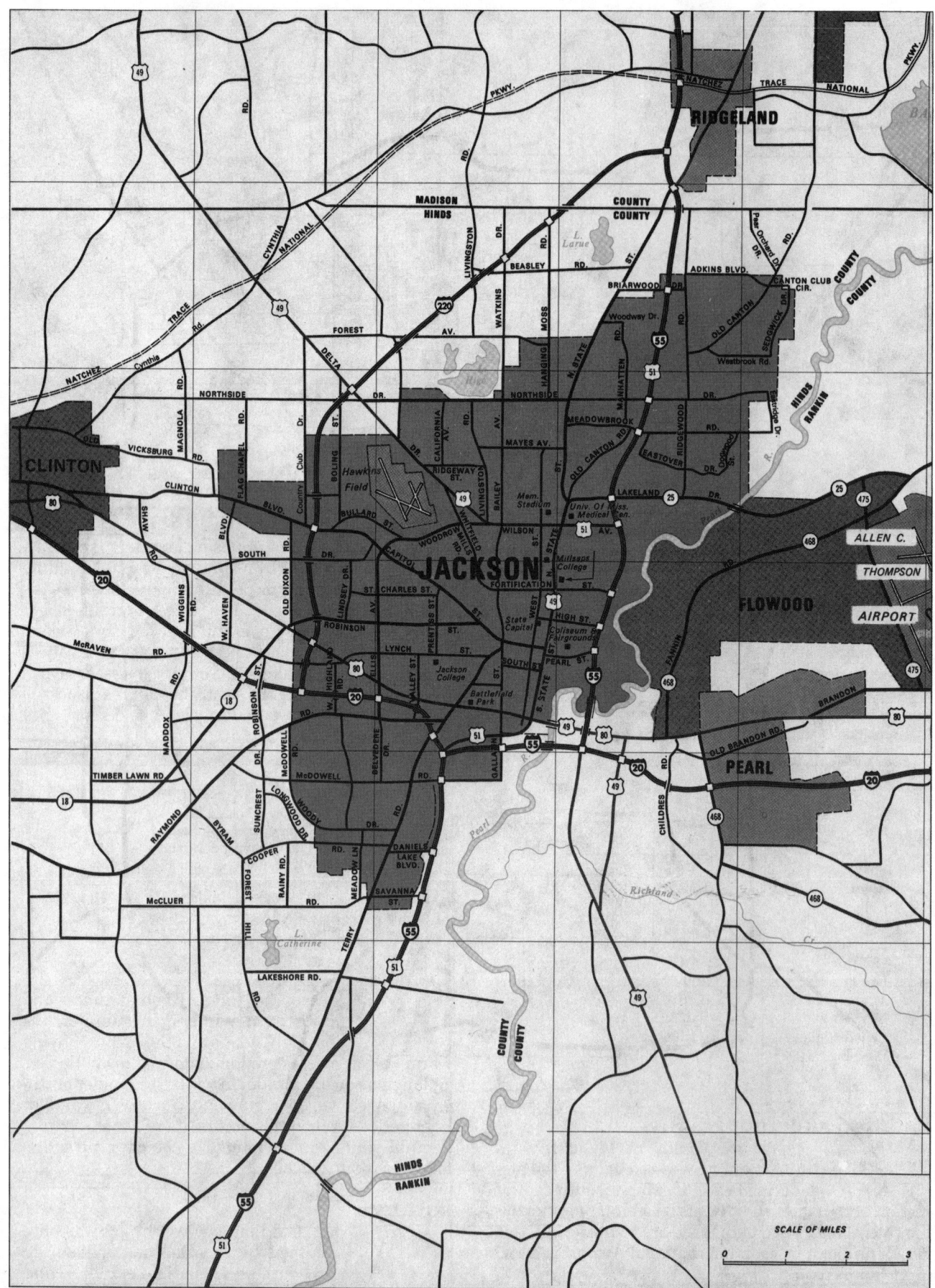

Weather

Temperature

Highest Monthly Average °F   92.5
Lowest Monthly Average °F   34.9

Annual Averages

Days 32°F or Below   47
Days above 90°F   78
Zero Degree Days   0
Precipitation (inches)   49.0
Snow (inches)   1.0
% Seasonal Humidity   75.0
Wind Speed (m.p.h.)   7.6
Clear Days   109
Cloudy Days   148
Storm Days   65
Rainy Days   112

Average Temperatures (°F)	High	Low	Mean
January	58.4	35.8	47.1
February	61.7	37.8	49.8
March	68.7	43.4	56.1
April	78.2	53.1	65.7
May	85.0	60.4	72.7
June	91.0	67.7	79.4
July	92.7	70.6	81.7
August	92.6	69.8	81.2
September	88.0	64.0	76.0
October	80.1	51.5	65.8
November	68.5	42.0	55.3
December	60.5	37.3	48.9

trader Louis LeFleur (the flower) set up his trading post along the bluffs overlooking the Pearl River (now called LeFleur's Bluff). LeFleur soon built up a profitable trade among the Indians and the few whites who dared venture into the region.

By the first decade of the 19th century, immigration by easterners to what is now Mississippi led to increased calls for statehood. In 1817 citizens met at the small community of Washington, near Natchez, and drew up a constitution, naming the new state Mississippi after the huge and mighty river flowing along its western border. Later that year, Congress approved Mississippi as the 20th state, with Natchez chosen as the temporary capital. Soon after, legislators met to select a permanent site for the new capital. But three years passed, and a new site had yet to be chosen. In 1820 Congress appointed Generals Andrew Jackson and Thomas Hinds to negotiate with the Choctaws for land in the northern part of the state. The resulting pact —the Treaty of Doak's Stand, or the Choctaw Purchase—gave the United States most of present-day northern Mississippi. The state assembly appointed a three-man commission—naming Hinds, James Patton, and William Lattimore—to choose a site in this newly gained region for the permanent state capital. On 20 November 1821, the Hinds-Lattimore Report was issued, calling for LeFleur's Bluff to be the site of the new capital. The general assembly accepted the recommendation and named the new city Jackson in honor of the great general and future president of the United States.

The state assembly issued grants to Peter A. Vandorn (an early settler of Jackson), Lattimore, and Hinds to lay out the new town. Thomas Jefferson had advised years earlier that the city be laid out checkerboard fashion like Washington, D.C. The State Capitol building—the first of three—was built in 1822 at a cost of $3,500. The small two-story brick edifice was first used for the opening session of the state assembly on 22 December 1822.

Jackson suffered serious growing pains for the next 40 years. For 20 of those years, its isolated location and poor transportation kept its population from going above 1,000. A constitutional convention in the city in 1832 led to authorization of a new State Capitol building, which was finished in 1840. This "Old Capitol," as it is still known, is now a museum in the eastern section of town.

One guide to Jackson calls the years 1832–1850 the city's "foundation years." The pieces of Jackson's leadership engine—economic, governmental, and cultural—came together at this time. Unfortunately, slavery was leading the city, as well as the South, down a path from which it could not turn back; the result was civil war. With the election of Abraham Lincoln, the Mississippi Seccessionist Convention was held at the Old Capitol in January 1861. For the first two years of the war, Jackson remained the capital of the state. In 1863 General William Tecumseh Sherman besieged the city and burned it to the ground three times. Sherman reported that "Jackson will no longer be a point of danger." The city was dubbed "Chimneyville."

Few buildings survived Sherman's rampage, but those that endured were the basis of a new city. Although there was accelerated growth for the rest of the century, severe yellow fever epidemics stripped the community of citizens; by 1900 the population of Jackson was less than 8,000. In 1903 a third State Capitol building was completed, and remains in use to this day. Economic and governmental growth during the first three decades of the 20th century gave new prominence to Jackson, and it weathered the Depression better than other cities due to the discovery of natural gas in the area in 1930. A diversified economy, an oil strike in 1939, and the opening of the University of Mississippi Medical Center in the mid-1950s served to make Jackson a true state capital.

Historical Landmarks

The State Capitol building, built in 1903, exemplifies the Beaux Arts style of architecture. Topped by a gold-leafed eagle 8 feet high and 15 feet wide, its nearly $1.1 million cost was financed by railroad fees. The Old Capitol building on North State and Capitol streets was in use from 1840 until 1903 and now serves as the State Historical Museum. City Hall, located four blocks south of the capitol, is one of the few buildings that survived three sackings by Union troops during the Civil War. Another survivor is the governor's mansion, built in 1842 and continually occupied by the state's governors. During the Civil War it was used as headquarters by General Sherman and later General Ulysses S. Grant,

Chronology

1789 French-Canadian explorer and trader Louis LeFleur sets up a trading post along the bluffs that overlook the Pearl River.

1820 By the Treaty of Doak's Stand, the Choctaw Indians cede much of northern Mississippi to the federal government. A three-man commission recommends LeFleur's Bluff as the site of a permanent state capital.

1821 The Mississippi General Assembly makes LeFleur's Bluff the permanent state capital. The city is renamed Jackson in honor of General Andrew Jackson.

1822 The opening session of the state general assembly is held at the first state capitol building on 22 December.

1840 The second state capitol building, known as the "Old Capitol," is completed.

1861 The Mississippi Secessionist Convention is held at the Old Capitol.

1863–1865 General William Tecumseh Sherman's troops sack and burn Jackson three times, giving it the nickname "Chimneyville."

1900 Jackson's population is less than 8,000.

1903 The third state capitol building is completed.

1930 Natural gas is discovered in the Jackson area.

1939 An oil strike nearby pumps precious dollars into the Jackson economy.

1950s The opening of the University of Mississippi Medical Center makes Jackson a focal point of medical breakthroughs for the nation.

Population

	1980	1990
Central City	202,895	196,637
Rank	70	78
Metro Area	362,038	395,396
Pop. Change 1980–1990	-6,258	
Pop. % Change 1980–1990	-3.1	
Median Age	30.8	
% Male	46.3	
% Age 65 and Over	11.6	
Density (per square mile)	1,804	

Households

Number   71,865
Persons per Household   2.64
% Female-Headed Households   20.4
% One-Person Households   27.5
Births—Total   3,698
　　% to Mothers under 20   18.5
　　Birth Rate per 1,000   17.7

Ethnic Composition (as % of total pop.)

	1980	1990
White	52.38	43.57
Black	47.0	55.75
American Indian	0.07	0.1
Asian and Pacific Islander	0.31	0.5
Hispanic	0.74	0.45
Other	NA	0.08

Government

In 1985 the city moved from a commission form of government to a mayor-council form. Its seven councilmen are elected by district, while the mayor is elected at large.

Government

Year of Home Charter   1842
Number of Members of the Governing Body   7
Elected at Large   NA
Elected by Wards   7
Number of Women in Governing Body   3
Salary of Mayor $60,000
Salary of Council Members $15,000
City Government Employment Total   3,094
Rate per 10,000   148.5

Public Finance

The annual budget consists of revenues of $151.727 million and expenditures of $123.006 million. Debt outstanding is $314.229 million, and cash and security holdings are $194.069 million.

Economy

Jackson's economy is based in several areas, including government, high technology, and manufacturing. As the seat of state government, Jackson is the site of a $4-billion-a-year industry. Among the larger private businesses in the area are LDDS Communications, Beech Aero-

which helped it avoid the fate of the rest of the city. The Charles H. Manship House was built and owned by the mayor of Jackson who surrendered the city to Sherman in 1863.

Population

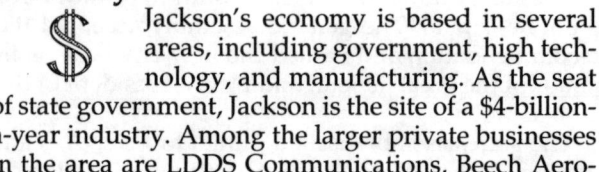

After an impressive 31.8% growth in the 1970s (from 154,000 in 1970 to 202,895 in 1980), Jackson's population dipped slightly in the 1980s, declining 3.1% to 196,637. This drop runs counter to the general growth experienced by southern cities in the 1980s.

Ethnic Composition

Blacks constitute the majority in Jackson with 55.7%. Whites make up 43.6%, American Indians 0.1%, Asians and Pacific Islanders 0.5%, and others 0.1%.

Public Finance

Total Revenue (in millions) $151.727
Intergovernmental Revenue—Total (in millions) $42.06
Federal Revenue per Capita $11.37
% Federal Assistance   7.49
% State Assistance   19.65
Sales Tax as % of Total Revenue   2.65
Local Revenue as % of Total Revenue   61.4
City Income Tax   no
Taxes—Total (in millions) $32.3

Taxes per Capita
   Total $155
   Property $133
   Sales and Gross Receipts $13
General Expenditures—Total (in millions) $111.2
General Expenditures per Capita $533
Capital Outlays per Capita $129

% of Expenditures for:
   Public Welfare   2.9
   Highways   11.5
   Education   0.0
   Health and Hospitals   1.1
   Police   11.6
   Sewerage and Sanitation   21.5
   Parks and Recreation   5.0
   Housing and Community Development   0.3
Debt Outstanding per Capita $1,137
   % Utility   7.5
Federal Procurement Contract Awards (in millions) $97.4
Federal Grants Awards (in millions) $222.7
Fiscal Year Begins   October 1

Economy

Total Money Income (in millions) $2,068.985
% of State Average   132.7
Per Capita Annual Income $9,927
% Population below Poverty Level   18.4
Fortune 500 Companies   NA

Banks	Number	Deposits (in millions)
Commercial	5	9,355
Savings	3	799.8

Passenger Autos   174,950
Electric Meters   154,161
Gas Meters   67,404

Manufacturing

Number of Establishments   220
% with 20 or More Employees   36.4
Manufacturing Payroll (in millions) $207.9
Value Added by Manufacture (in millions) $627.1
Value of Shipments (in millions) $1,252.6
New Capital Expenditures (in millions) $38.6

Wholesale Trade

Number of Establishments   603
Sales (in millions) $2,557.5
Annual Payroll (in millions) $175.749

Retail Trade

Number of Establishments   2,184
Total Sales (in millions)   NA
Sales per Capita   NA
Number of Retail Trade Establishments with Payroll   1,520
Annual Payroll (in millions) $200.6
Total Sales (in millions) $1,714.3
General Merchandise Stores (per capita) $1,307
Food Stores (per capita) $1,195
Apparel Stores (per capita) $347
Eating and Drinking Places (per capita) $713

Economy (continued)

Service Industries

Total Establishments   1,827
Total Receipts (in millions) $821.5
Hotels and Motels (in millions)   NA
Health Services (in millions) $222.4
Legal Services (in millions) $106.4

space Services, Packard Electric, and Miller Trucking, a heavy-moving firm.

In 1990 *Inc.* magazine ranked the city 24th out of 156 communities in the area of economic development. Because of its unique location as "the Crossroads of the South," its past and future serve to make it an attractive spot for future growth and prosperity.

Labor

The combined state and local government is the largest employer in the city. Manufacturing employs only half the number of workers in public employment. There are no heavy industries, and blue-collar workers are in the minority. Five banks and financial institutions are among the top employers.

Labor

Civilian Labor Force   106,948
% Change 1989–1990   1.4

Work Force Distribution
   Mining   600
   Construction   7,100
   Manufacturing   22,400
   Transportation and Public Utilities   13,000
   Wholesale and Retail Trade   43,700
   FIRE (Finance, Insurance, Real Estate)   14,500
   Service   44,300
   Government   40,200
   Women as % of Labor Force   49.0
   % Self-Employed   5.1
   % Professional/Technical   18.0
Total Unemployment   5,732
Rate %   5.4
Federal Government Civilian Employment   4,162

Education

The Jackson Public School District supports 57 schools. More than 50 private and parochial schools supplement the public school system. Among them are the noted Jackson Academy, St. Andrews Episcopal School, Woodland Hills Baptist Academy, and Jackson Preparatory School. The principal institutions of higher learning are Jackson State University, Millsaps College, Mississippi College, Belhaven College, and Tougaloo College. Mississippi College is Baptist, Millsaps is Methodist, Belhaven is Presbyterian, and Tougaloo and Jackson State University are historically black colleges. Mississippi College, founded in 1831, is the second-oldest Baptist college in the country and is considered to be among the best in the nation. The University of Mississippi Medical School manages the state's only medical and dental programs. Four seminaries and one four-year Bible college operate in the metro area. The largest is the Reformed Theological Seminary, and the others are Wesley College, Jackson College of Ministries, and Mississippi Baptist Seminary.

Education

Number of Public Schools   57
Special Education Schools   NA
Total Enrollment   33,546
% Enrollment in Private Schools   15.8
% Minority   79.6
Classroom Teachers   1,651
Pupil-Teacher Ratio   20.3:1
Number of Graduates   NA
Total Revenue (in millions) $110.865
Total Expenditures (in millions) $109.220
Expenditures per Pupil $2,971
Educational Attainment (Age 25 and Over)
   % Completed 12 or More Years   71.3
   % Completed 16 or More Years   24.2
Four-Year Colleges and Universities   5
   Enrollment   10,753
Two-Year Colleges   NA
   Enrollment   NA

Libraries

Number   36
Public Libraries   15
Books (in thousands)   637
Circulation (in thousands)   899
Persons Served (in thousands)   258
Circulation per Person Served   3.48
Income (in millions) $2.42
Staff   95

Four-Year Colleges and Universities
   Jackson State University
   University of Mississippi Medical Center
   Belhaven College
   Millsaps College
   Mississippi College

Health

The University of Mississippi Medical School runs the University Hospital, the premier medical facility in the city. Other facilities include the Veterans Administration Hospital, Humana Hospital, Hinds General Hospital, Mississippi Baptist Medical Center, Mississippi Methodist Hospital and Rehabilitation Center, Riverside

Health

Deaths—Total   1,622
Rate per 1,000   7.8
Infant Deaths—Total   43
Rate per 1,000   11.6
Number of Metro Hospitals   11
Number of Metro Hospital Beds   2,924
Rate per 100,000   1,403
Number of Physicians   1,088
Physicians per 1,000   3.12
Nurses per 1,000   10.26
Health Expenditures per Capita   NA

Hospital, St. Dominic–Jackson Memorial Hospital, Rankin Medical Center, Charter Hospital, River Oaks Hospital, and Women's Hospital.

Transportation

Two major thoroughfares, I-20 and I-55, intersect at Jackson. Interstate 20 extends from South Carolina in the east to Texas in the west, where it connects with I-10 to California. Interstate 55 stretches from Chicago to New Orleans. Further, U.S. highways 49, 51, and 80 fan out in all directions and connect the city with points in the South and the Gulf of Mexico. State highways approaching Jackson include the Natchez Trace Parkway. The MidSouth Corporation handles freight service. Jackson International Airport, located 5 miles east, is served by 4 major airlines with 29 flights daily.

Transportation

Interstate Highway Mileage   9
Total Urban Mileage   522
Total Daily Vehicle Mileage (in millions)   1.854
Daily Average Commute Time   45.5 min.
Number of Buses   33
Port Tonnage (in millions)   NA
Airports   1
Number of Daily Flights   24
Daily Average Number of Passengers   1,106

Airlines (American carriers only)
   Air Wisconsin
   American
   Delta
   Northwest
   United

Housing

Of the total housing stock, 57.3% is owner-occupied. The median value of an owner-occupied home is $54,600 and the median monthly rent $290. Among the fine neighborhoods for which Jackson is noted are Belhaven, South Jackson, Clinton, Brandon, Flowood, and Pearl. Residential developments surrounding Ross Barnett Reservoir are popular because of their marinas. Luxury homes and condominiums are found in North Jackson.

Housing

Total Housing Units   79,374
% Change 1980–1990   4.7
Vacant Units for Sale or Rent   5,977
Occupied Units   71,865
% with More Than One Person per Room   6.2
% Owner-Occupied   57.3
Median Value of Owner-Occupied Homes $54,600
Average Monthly Purchase Cost $332
Median Monthly Rent $290
New Private Housing Starts   271
Value (in thousands) $18,653
% Single-Family   58.3
Nonresidential Buildings Value (in thousands) $23,198

Urban Redevelopment

The Jackson Redevelopment Authority was established in 1968 to reverse the deterioration of downtown. Among its projects are the Municipal Parking Facilities Nos. 1, 2, 3, and 4; Municipal Arts Center; Town Creek Tube and Town Creek Channel Improvements; Federal Building Project; 101 West Capitol Building; Landmark Building; 111 East Capitol Building; One Jackson Place; Hinds County Chancery Court Building; Lynch Street Redevelopment; Barnett Building; King Edward Project; High Tech Park; Elks Club Building; Standard Life Building; Congress Street Corridor; and Jackson Mall Redevelopment.

Crime

Of the crimes known to police in 1991, 1,526 were violent crimes and 27,240 were property crimes.

Crime

Violent Crimes—Total 1,526
Violent Crime Rate per 100,000 1,296
Murder 74
Rape 190
Robbery 1,313
Aggravated Assaults 809
Property Crimes 27,740
Burglary 8,688
Larceny 12,710
Motor Vehicle Theft 3,342
Arson NA
Per Capita Police Expenditures $79.03
Per Capita Fire Protection Expenditures $68.11
Number of Police 401
Per 1,000 1.90

Religion

Jackson has been described as the buckle on the Bible Belt. There are 400-plus churches in the city, of which the majority belong to the main Protestant denominations: Baptist, Methodist, and Presbyterian.

Religion

Largest Denominations (Adherents)

Catholic	7,739
Southern Baptist	79,029
Black Baptist	36,196
United Methodist	22,911
Episcopal	5,778
Presbyterian	5,577
Assembly of God	1,808
Independent Non-Charismatics	3,500
Jewish	450

Media

The press in Jackson consists solely of the *Jackson Clarion-Ledger*, which is published seven days a week. The electronic media consist of 7 television stations and 17 AM and FM radio stations.

Media

Newsprint
  Jackson Advocate, weekly
  Jackson Clarion-Ledger, daily
  Northside Sun, weekly

Television
  WAPT (Channel 16)
  WDBD (Channel 40)
  WJTV (Channel 12)
  WLBT (Channel 3)
  WLBM (Channel 30)
  WMAE (Channel 12)
  WMPN (Channel 29)

Radio

WJDS (AM)	WJDX (AM)
WJNT (AM)	WJTR (FM)
WJXN (AM)	WKXI (AM)
WLIN (FM)	WLRM (AM)
WLTD (FM)	WMPN (FM)
WMPR (FM)	WMSI (FM)
WOAD (AM)	WTYX (FM)
WSLI (AM)	WSTZ (FM)
WZRX (AM)	

Sports

Jackson has no major professional sports team, but the Jackson State University Tigers play at the 60,500-seat Mississippi Veterans Memorial Stadium. The 10,000-seat Mississippi Coliseum at the state fairgrounds is the home of various sporting events.

Arts, Culture, and Tourism

All branches of the performing arts are represented in Jackson. The Arts Alliance of Jackson/Hinds County coordinates performance schedules and offers financial and technical assistance. Ballet is represented by the Ballet Magnificat, Ballet Mississippi, and Mississippi Ballet International. Music performances are highlighted by the Jackson Choral Society, Jackson Community Concert Association, Metropolitan Chamber Orchestra Society, and Mississippi Symphony Orchestra. Opera productions are staged by Opera South and the Mississippi Opera Association. The New Stage Theatre

Travel and Tourism

Hotel Rooms 5,930
Convention and Exhibit Space (square feet) NA

Convention Centers
  Mississippi Trade Mart
  Mississippi Coliseum
  Jackson City Auditorium

Festivals
  Mississippi Arts Festival (April)
  Mississippi State Fair
  Arts, Crafts and Flower Festival (March)
  Festival of Harmony (May)
  Gospel Extravaganza (April)

leads the list of acting troupes, which include the Repertory Theatre of Mississippi, Children's Community Theatre, and Puppet Arts Theatre. Among the leading museums are the Jim Buck Ross Mississippi Agriculture and Forestry Museum/National Agricultural Aviation Museum, Dizzy Dean Museum, Smith Robertson Museum and Cultural Center, Old Capitol Museum, and Mississippi Museum of Natural Science. Among art galleries and exhibitors are the Mississippi Museum of Art and the Municipal Art Gallery.

Parks and Recreation

Major recreational facilities include the Ross Barnett Reservoir, a 30,000-acre waterway named after a recent Mississippi governor; the 305-acre LeFleur's Bluff State Park, the newest of Mississippi's 15 state parks; the 100-acre Jackson Zoological Park; the 79-acre Livingstone Park; and Mynelle Gardens.

Sources of Further Information

Jackson Chamber of Commerce
201 South President Street
Jackson, MS 39225-2548
(601) 948-7575

Metro Jackson Convention and Visitor's Bureau
921 North President Street
Jackson, MS 39215-1450
(800) 354-7695

Additional Reading

Office of the Mayor. *Jackson, the Bold City*. 1988.
Polk's Jackson City Directory. 1991.

Jersey City

New Jersey

complex. It shares the peninsula it sits on with Bayonne, as well as Weehawken, Hoboken, Union City, and Secaucus.

Location and Topography

N

Jersey City, located in New Jersey, is situated on a peanut-shaped peninsula astride Manhattan Island to the east and Newark to the west, and fronted by Newark Bay, the Hackensack River, and the Hudson River. It has benefited financially from its prime location near these major industrial and commercial centers, as well as Bayonne and Staten Island, which are both to the south and west. It is located some 50 miles northeast of the state capital, Trenton.

Layout of City and Suburbs

Connected to the business areas of Manhattan and Newark by bridges, the Holland Tunnel, and Newark International Airport, Jersey City, the second-largest city in the state, is shaped by its peninsular positioning. Its street layout is grid-shaped in the traditional manner, and it is bordered on its eastern side by 11 miles of waterfront area. On its western frontier, across the Hackensack River, is the massive Newark International Airport

Climate

The city has an essentially continental climate tempered by sea breezes. Summers tend to be hot and humid and winters moderately cold. Average temperatures range from 30.6°F in January to 74.6°F in July. The average annual precipitation is 43.77 inches.

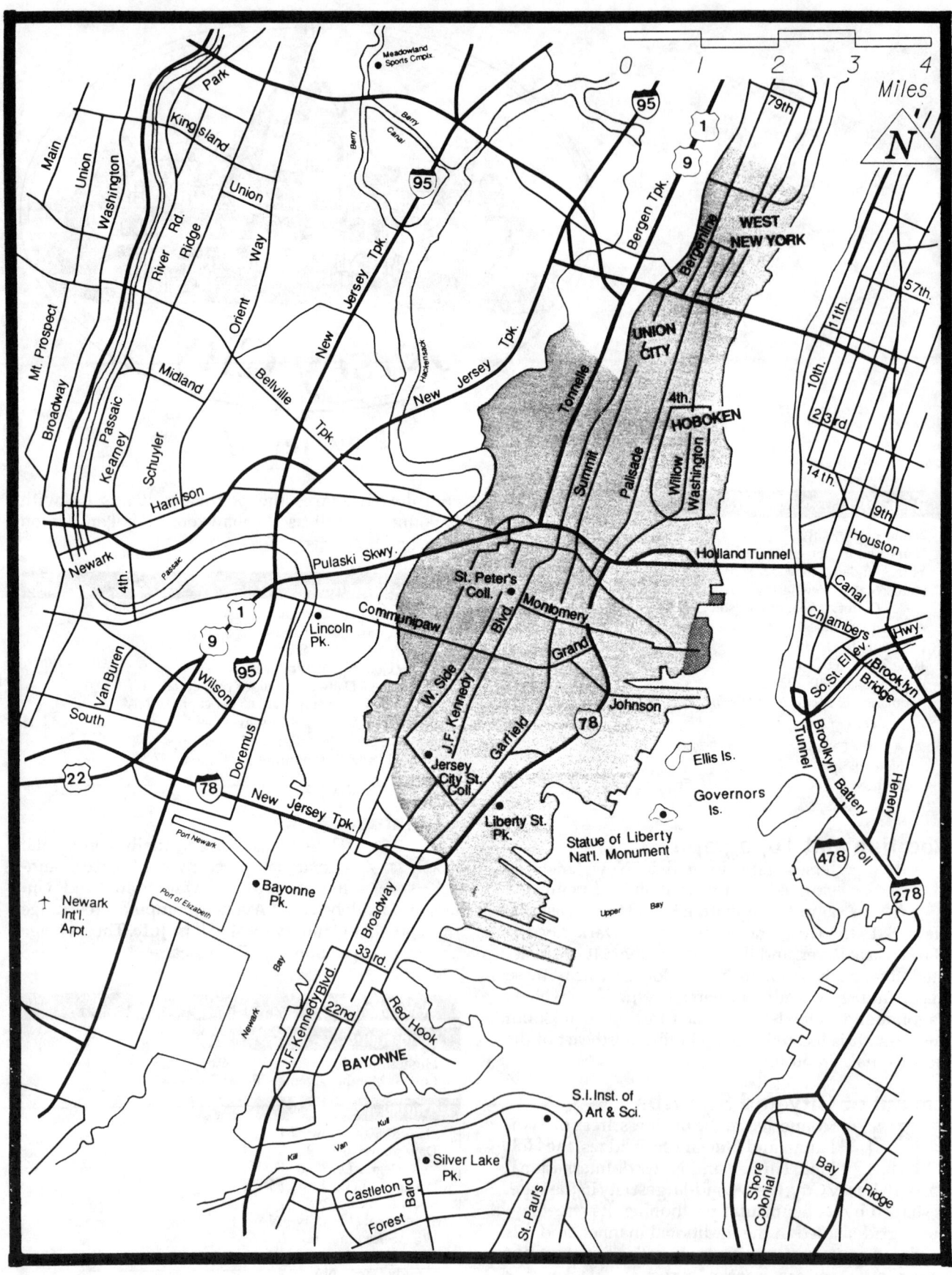

Weather (continued)

Storm Days NA
Rainy Days NA

Average Temperatures (°F)	High	Low	Mean
January	36.7	24.5	30.6
February	38.5	25.5	32.1
March	46.6	33.2	39.9
April	58.1	42.9	50.5
May	68.1	52.6	60.4
June	77.1	61.7	69.4
July	82.1	67.1	74.6
August	80.9	65.7	73.3
September	73.8	58.7	66.3
October	63.3	48.4	55.8
November	52.0	39.0	45.5
December	40.5	28.5	34.5

History

The first permanent settlement by white men was made here in 1630 by Michiel Pauw, an agent of the Dutch West India Company. Cornelius Van Vorst, sent by Pauw to establish a colony called Pavonia, built a house in 1633 near the present Fourth and Henderson streets. Another was built by Michael Paulez, overseer of trade with the Indians at Paulus Hook. The Dutch West India Company bought out Pauw in 1634, but for the next 30 years the settlement, known as Paulus Hook, was harassed by Indian raids. Meanwhile, the village of Bergen was laid out and surrounded by a log palisade. Soon a rowboat ferry service was introduced between Bergen and New Amsterdam across the Hudson River. The transition to English rule took place smoothly in 1664. At that time a rough log church was built for the Dutch Reformed congregation, the first to be erected in the province. In 1668 the settlement was incorporated as a town by Governor Philip Carteret. The town was the scene of at least one engagement between the British and the Revolutionary Army.

After that war, Anthony Dey acquired land and a ferry in Jersey City for a perpetual annuity of 6,000 Spanish dollars. Dey incorporated himself as the Associates of the Jersey Company under a charter that made his organization the effective civil governing body. Steam ferry service began in 1812 with the *Jersey*, built by Robert Fulton. During this time the population consisted mainly of some boatmen and other transients, and the town had no policemen. Efforts to obtain an autonomous government were balked by the Associates, but the city was finally incorporated in 1820, although the Associates retained special powers until 1838. The year 1834 was a turning point in the city's history. A treaty setting the boundary between New York and New Jersey in the middle of the Hudson River gave the city access to its own waterfront. In the same year the terminals of the New Jersey (later the Pennsylvania) Railroad and the Paterson and Hudson (later the Erie) Railroad were established in Jersey City. In 1836 the Morris Canal was extended from Newark to Jersey City. As a result, the city became a very attractive industrial location for such corporate residents as Lorillard Tobacco Company, Colgate-Pal-

molive, Joseph Dixon Crucible Company, Dummer's Jersey City Glass Company, Isaac Edge's fireworks factory, and American Pottery Company. The first stockyards were opened in 1866, and in 1867 the city became the western terminal of the Cunard Steamship Company

Railroad and political battles marked the latter half of the 19th century. Between 1850 and 1860 the population jumped from 7,000 to 29,000. Jersey City was an important station on the Underground Railroad for fugitive slaves. In the 1870s the first paid fire department was hired and the first public high school was opened. In 1909–1910 the Hudson Rail Tunnel was opened, making travel between Jersey City and New York City shorter and easier. The city was the site of the only German terrorist activity in the United States, the Black Tom docks explosion of ammunition-laden railroad cars on the Communipaw waterfront on the night of 30 July 1916, the shock waves of which reached Maryland and Connecticut. A three-decade political era began in 1917 when Frank Hague become the mayor and political boss. His political machine ran the city until 1949. The Colgate Clock was erected in 1924, the Holland Tunnel opened in 1927, and the Roosevelt Stadium opened in 1937. In 1950 Jersey City's population peaked at 299,000, beginning to decline thereafter. City efforts to attract residents back included renovation of the brownstones, the building of Port Jersey, and the opening of the Liberty Harbor, Liberty Park, and Harborside Financial Center. By the late 1980s Jersey City had become an alternative office site for businesses fleeing high rents and crime in New York City. In 1991 Jersey City was being plagued again with political scandals as Mayor Gerald McCann was convicted in a federal court of corruption and financial chicanery.

Historical Landmarks

Jersey City's earliest architectural landmarks are Dutch. A good preservation program has resulted in the renovation of many of the older buildings, such as: the Old Bergen Reformed Church, on Bergen Avenue, one of the oldest churches in the city, dating back to 1680; Van Wegenen House on Academy Street, rebuilt on property once owned by a Dutch family that received its original deed in 1650; Van Voorst House, a brownstone built in 1740; and Grace Van Voorst Church, a Gothic structure built in the mid-1800s. Also renovated were the Ionic House, built between 1835 and 1840, and the Old Hudson County Courthouse, opened in 1910. One of the city's best-known landmarks was the Colgate Clock on Hudson Street, facing the bay. Considered one of the largest in the world, it had a 50–foot-diameter dial and a minute hand weighing over one ton.

Population

The population of Jersey City increased by 5,000 in the 1980s, from 223,532 in 1980 to 228,537 in 1990, although its rank among American cities fell from 61st to 67th place.

Chronology

1633 Cornelius Van Vorst, agent of Michiel Pauw, builds first house. Michael Paulus builds another house at Paulus Hook.

1634 Dutch West India Company buys back the patroonship of Michiel Pauw, known as Paulus Hook, and builds a number of houses in the plantation.

1660 Peace is made with the Delaware Indians, ending decades of strife.

1664 English drive out the Dutch and Paulus Hook is renamed Jersey City.

1668 Jersey City is chartered as a town.

1774 Improved ferry service across the Hudson is introduced.

1776 The British capture Jersey City and remain there until 1779.

1804 Anthony Dey acquires land and a ferry for a perpetual rent, and forms the Associates of the Jersey Company as the effective civil governing body.

1812 Steam ferry service begins with Robert Fulton's *Jersey*.

1820 City of New Jersey is incorporated.

1829 The first police force is formed.

1834 Treaty with New York, settling the boundary between New York and New Jersey along the middle of the Hudson River, enables Jersey City to develop its waterfront. Two railroads make Jersey City their terminal.

1836 The Morris Canal is extended from Newark to Jersey City.

1847 The *Hibernia* docks at Jersey City, the first Cunard liner to do so.

1866 The first stockyard is opened.

1867 Jersey City becomes the western terminal of the Cunard Steamship Company.

1910 Rail Tunnel across the Hudson is completed.

1916 The Black Tom docks explosion of ammunition-laden railroad cars on the Communipaw waterfront by German saboteurs causes damage estimated at $22 million.

1917 Frank Hague becomes mayor, launching a 32-year administration marked by corruption and nepotism.

1927 The Holland Tunnel opens linking Jersey City with Manhattan.

1937 Roosevelt Stadium opens.

1976 Liberty State Park opens.

1991 Mayor Gerald McCann is convicted of corruption and other wrongdoing and forced out of office.

Population

	1980	1990
Central City	223,532	228,537
Rank	61	67
Metro Area	556,972	553,099
Pop. Change 1980–1990 +5,005		
Pop. % Change 1980–1990 +2.2		
Median Age 31.5		
% Male 48.6		
% Age 65 and Over 11.1		
Density (per square mile) 15,338		

Households

Number 82,381
Persons per Household 2.73
% Female-Headed Households 20.4
% One-Person Households 28.7
Births—Total 3,958
   % to Mothers under 20 17.0
   Birth Rate per 1,000 17.7

Ethnic Composition

The percentage of whites in the population has been steadily declining this century; it is now only slightly under 50%. Blacks constitute almost 30%, Hispanics about 15%, and Asians and others the balance. Whites, however, continue to dominate city hall.

Ethnic Composition (as % of total pop.)		
	1980	1990
White	57.13	48.25
Black	27.72	29.69
American Indian	0.12	0.34
Asian and Pacific Islander	4.38	11.36
Hispanic	18.64	24.24
Other	NA	10.35

Government

Since a revision of the charter in 1960, Jersey City has been governed by a mayor-council form of government. The mayor and the nine members of the council are elected for four-year terms. The mayor presides over council meetings, but has no vote except in the case of a tie. Jersey City is also the seat of Hudson County.

Public Finance

The budget consists of revenues of $200.634 million and expenditures of $252.718 million. The outstanding debt

Government

Year of Home Charter   NA
Number of Members of the Governing Body   9
Elected at Large   3
Elected by Wards   6
Number of Women in Governing Body   2
Salary of Mayor $60,000
Salary of Council Members $15,000
City Government Employment Total   9,391
Rate per 10,000   427.9

Public Finance

Total Revenue (in millions) $200.634
Intergovernmental Revenue—Total (in millions) $69.74
Federal Revenue per Capita $0.434
% Federal Assistance   0.21
% State Assistance   34.5
Sales Tax as % of Total Revenue   NA
Local Revenue as % of Total Revenue   53.66
City Income Tax   no
Taxes—Total (in millions) $84.0

Taxes per Capita
    Total $383
    Property $371
    Sales and Gross Receipts $0
General Expenditures—Total (in millions) $379.0
General Expenditures per Capita $1,727
Capital Outlays per Capita $149

% of Expenditures for:
    Public Welfare   1.3
    Highways   1.1
    Education   40.7
    Health and Hospitals   20.5
    Police   7.3
    Sewerage and Sanitation   4.9
    Parks and Recreation   0.7
    Housing and Community Development   0.3
Debt Outstanding per Capita $627
    % Utility   25.9
Federal Procurement Contract Awards (in millions) $5.8
Federal Grants Awards (in millions) $16.8
Fiscal Year Begins   January 1

Economy

Total Money Income (in millions) $1,888.6
% of State Average   65.5
Per Capita Annual Income $8,605
% Population below Poverty Level   21.2
Fortune 500 Companies   NA

Banks	Number	Deposits (in millions)
Commercial	21	5,104
Savings	24	5,915

Passenger Autos   NA
Electric Meters   196,512
Gas Meters   196,480

Manufacturing

Number of Establishments   296
% with 20 or More Employees   46.3
Manufacturing Payroll (in millions) $273.3
Value Added by Manufacture (in millions) $771.3
Value of Shipments (in millions) $1,407.5
New Capital Expenditures (in millions)   NA

Wholesale Trade

Number of Establishments   325
Sales (in millions) $2,551.8
Annual Payroll (in millions) $142.150

Retail Trade

Number of Establishments   1,783
Total Sales (in millions) $1,072.8
Sales per Capita $4,888
Number of Retail Trade Establishments with Payroll   1,108
Annual Payroll (in millions) $113.3
Total Sales (in millions) $1,032.1
General Merchandise Stores (per capita) $375
Food Stores (per capita) $951
Apparel Stores (per capita) $418
Eating and Drinking Places (per capita) $307

Service Industries

Total Establishments   935
Total Receipts (in millions) $390.3
Hotels and Motels (in millions)   NA
Health Services (in millions) $82.5
Legal Services (in millions) $46.4

is $172.386 million and cash and security holdings $70.540 million.

Economy

The proximity to New York City is economically both an advantage and a disadvantage for Jersey City. On the one hand there are spillovers both of capital and skills from the larger city, particularly because of corporations fleeing New York's high rents to relocate across the river. At the same time Jersey City's economy has historically languished in the shadow of New York City, with which it has to compete on very unfair terms. More recently, Jersey City mayors have been pursuing a very aggressive real estate development program, making best use of limited available space and offering extravagant incentives to builders and investors. The result has been a remarkable transformation of the city skyline as well as an expansion of the range of economic activities.

Labor

The largest economic sector is trade (25%), followed by manufacturing, government, and services, each about 18%; transportation and public utilities (14%); and FIRE (finance, insurance, real estate) about 6%. The largest employers include three hospitals, three banks, two manufacturers, and one service firm.

Labor

Civilian Labor Force   102,469
% Change 1989–1990   0.8

Work Force Distribution
    Mining   NA
    Construction   4,800
    Manufacturing   35,500
    Transportation and Public Utilities   29,700
    Wholesale and Retail Trade   60,900
    FIRE (Finance, Insurance, Real Estate)   16,100

Labor (continued)

Service   47,400
Government   40,300
Women as % of Labor Force   44.9
% Self-Employed   2.7
% Professional/Technical   12.4
Total Unemployment   8,494
Rate %   8.3
Federal Government Civilian Employment   6,713

Education

The public school system consists of 5 senior high schools, 28 elementary schools, and 4 special education schools. The Cooperative Education Programs provides an opportunity for students to work in local businesses.

The city's four-year colleges are Jersey City State College, the Jesuit-run St. Peter's College, and a branch of Rutgers, the State University. The Jersey City State College, organized in 1927 as the New Jersey State Normal School, became a college in 1958. St. Peter's College was opened in 1878 as a liberal arts college for men, although it was suspended for 12 years from 1918 to 1930; in 1960 it became coeducational.

Education

Number of Public Schools   37
Special Education Schools   4
Total Enrollment   28,585
% Enrollment in Private Schools   22.4
% Minority   87.4
Classroom Teachers   1,826
Pupil-Teacher Ratio   15.6:1
Number of Graduates   992
Total Revenue (in millions) $190.6
Total Expenditures (in millions) $199.9
Expenditures per Pupil $5,606
Educational Attainment (Age 25 and Over)
    % Completed 12 or More Years   51.2
    % Completed 16 or More Years   11.7
Four-Year Colleges and Universities   3
    Enrollment   10,463
Two-Year Colleges   1
    Enrollment   2,748

Libraries

Number   18
Public Libraries   13
Books (in thousands)   722
Circulation (in thousands)   451.7
Persons Served (in thousands)   722
Circulation per Person Served   0.62
Income (in millions) $5.467
Staff   NA

Four-Year Colleges and Universities
    Jersey City State College
    Saint Peter's College

Health

Jersey City is served by five medical institutions. The largest is the Jersey City Medical Center on Baldwin Avenue. Adjacent are the Margaret Hague Maternity Hospital in Clifton Place and the Berthold S. Pollak Hospital for Chest Diseases. The latter deals chiefly with geriatric diseases, as does the Jewish Hospital and Rehabilitation Center. Christ Hospital on Palisade Avenue was organized in 1883 by Episcopal clergymen. The St. Francis Community Health Center on McWilliams Place is the most modern facility. The smaller facilities are the Fairmount Hospital on Summit Avenue and Greenville Hospital on Kennedy Boulevard.

Health

Deaths—Total   2,436
Rate per 1,000   10.9
Infant Deaths—Total   67
Rate per 1,000   16.9
Number of Metro Hospitals   5
Number of Metro Hospital Beds   1,630
Rate per 100,000   743
Number of Physicians   961
Physicians per 1,000   2.08
Nurses per 1,000   4.57
Health Expenditures per Capita $27.51

Transportation

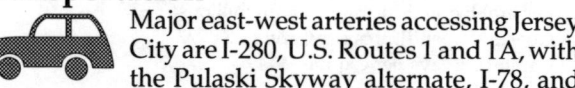

Major east-west arteries accessing Jersey City are I-280, U.S. Routes 1 and 1A, with the Pulaski Skyway alternate, I-78, and the New Jersey Turnpike (I-95) with four exits in the city. New Jersey Highway 440 runs north-south through the city, while I-95 bypasses it to the west. PATH, the local mass transit service, connects Jersey City with Manhattan, Newark, Harrison, and Hoboken. The Holland Tunnel is the most direct link to Manhattan. Thirty bus lines, with a total of 225 buses, operate within the city.

With 11 miles of waterfront on the Hudson River, Jersey City is integrated into the Port Authority of New York. Port Jersey, sometimes called Liberty Harbor because it faces the Statue of Liberty, provides access to the Atlantic Ocean for vessels of all sizes and displacements. The port's Industrial Marine Center has a 100-acre industrial park and a 310-acre port with 17 berths, extensive railroads, and facilities for containerized shipping. Adjacent to the port are Conrail's Greenville Yards. Jersey City is 15 minutes from Newark International Airport and an hour from Kennedy International Airport and LaGuardia Airport in New York City.

Transportation

Interstate Highway Mileage   426
Total Urban Mileage   35,180
Total Daily Vehicle Mileage (in millions)   225.5
Daily Average Commute Time   57.6 min.
Number of Buses   225
Port Tonnage (in millions)   NA
Airports   NA
Number of Daily Flights   904
Daily Average Number of Passengers   84,229

Airlines (American carriers only)
    See Newark and New York

Housing

Jersey City is extremely congested and housing costs are steep. Most of the older houses, like the brownstones in the Hamilton section, are in need of renovation, but new housing units have been built in Newport, Port Liberte, and other places. Newport will eventually have over 9,000 new apartments and condos while Port Liberte will have over 2,250 units, including million-dollar townhouses. In 1989 a $150 million, 1,176-unit condominium community was built beside Newark Bay along Droters Point where Roosevelt Stadium used to stand. Called Society Hill, it was built by K. Hovnanian's Inner City Development Corporation. Many new developments have recently been completed along the waterfront, including Harsimus Cove, a development of townhomes and office space with a 150-slip marina, and the Towers at Portside, two towers of 19 and 25 stories, each with 525 condominiums.

Housing

Total Housing Units 90,723
% Change 1980–1990 3.0
Vacant Units for Sale or Rent 6,831
Occupied Units 82,381
% with More Than One Person per Room 11.4
% Owner-Occupied 29.6
Median Value of Owner-Occupied Homes $127,700
Average Monthly Purchase Cost $391
Median Monthly Rent $464
New Private Housing Starts 171
Value (in thousands) $7,236
% Single-Family 4.1
Nonresidential Buildings Value (in thousands) $101,109

Urban Redevelopment

Three major development projects initiated under Mayor McCann were Harborside, Newport City, and Exchange Place. Since 1985 between $15 and $20 billion has been invested in construction in Jersey City. Harborside consists of three plazas. The Exchange Place Center is a 30-story office tower, the tallest structure in New Jersey. The International Financial Tower is a 19-story structure. In addition, the Science-Technology Center at Liberty State Park, featuring an observation tower, science auditorium, and the world's largest Omnimax theater, opened in the early 1990s.

Crime

Of the crimes known to police in 1991, 4,612 were violent crimes and 16,496 were property crimes.

Religion

Catholics form the majority of those professing religion in Jersey City, but Protestants are well represented in the city.

Crime

Violent Crimes—Total 4,612
Violent Crime Rate per 100,000 1,190
Murder 22
Rape 97
Robbery 2,576
Aggravated Assaults 1,917
Property Crimes 16,496
Burglary 4,610
Larceny 6,494
Motor Vehicle Theft 5,392
Arson 69
Per Capita Police Expenditures $214.72
Per Capita Fire Protection Expenditures $149.42
Number of Police 920
Per 1,000 4.10

Religion

Largest Denominations (Adherents)

Catholic	324,245
Black Baptist	18,680
Evangelical Lutheran	4,780
American Baptist	4,764
American Zion	2,579
Assembly of God	1,806
United Methodist	2,022
Episcopal	2,230
Jewish	15,950

Media

The principal daily is the evening *Jersey Journal*. New York newspapers circulate in Jersey City. No radio or television signals originate in the city, but it does receive all New York stations clearly.

Media

Newsprint
  Jersey Journal, daily
Television
  See Newark and New York
Radio
  See Newark and New York

Sports

Jersey City has no professional sports teams. It shares major sports with New York teams.

Arts, Culture, and Tourism

The city's cultural life revolves around the Majestic Theater, a 1,500-seat concert hall cum theater cum opera house built in 1907. The numerous groups performing here include the American Shakespeare Repertory Company, Hudson Repertory Dance Theater, Hoboken Chamber Orchestra, and the Liberty Center for Performing Arts. The Jersey City Museum is known for its special collections, such as the Otto Goetzke collection of gems.

Art galleries include the Upstairs Gallery, founded in 1964.

Travel and Tourism
Hotel Rooms   1,376
Convention and Exhibit Space (square feet)   NA
Convention Centers
NA
Festivals
Jazz Week (April)
Cultural Arts Festival (July)

Parks and Recreation

Liberty Park, begun under the administration of Mayor Paul Jordan, was formally opened by Governor Brendan Byrne in 1976. Other city parks include Lincoln, Washington, Bayside, and Pershing Field. There also are eight bowling centers, one golf course, and excellent beaches south of the city along Raritan and Sandy Hook Bays.

Sources of Further Information

Jersey City Public Library
427 Jersey Avenue
Jersey City, NJ 07302
(201) 547-4500

Hudson County Chamber of Commerce and Industry
911 Bergen Avenue
Jersey City, NJ 07306
(201) 653-7400

Jersey City Redevelopment Agency
3000 Kennedy Boulevard
Jersey City, NJ 07306
(201) 656-0517

Additional Reading

Economic Profile of Hudson County. Annual.

Kansas City

Kansas

Basic Data

Name   Kansas City, KS
Name Origin   From Kansas River
Year Founded   1843 Inc. 1850
Status: State   Kansas
      County   Seat of Wyandotte County
Area (square miles)   107.8
Elevation (feet)   750
Time Zone   Central
Population (1990)   149,767
Population of Metro Area (1990)   1,566,280

Sister Cities
   Cork, Ireland
   Karlovac, Yugoslavia
   Linz, Austria
   Uruapan, Mexico

Distance in Miles To:
Abilene	150
Leavenworth	29
Topeka	61
Wichita	188

Location and Topography

N

Kansas City, Kansas, is situated at the confluence of the Kansas and Missouri rivers at the easternmost corner of the state. It shares a border with Kansas City, Missouri—in fact, there are no natural borders separating the two communities. North, south, and west of Kansas City are farmlands laced with lakes, streams, and small rivers; the terrain is gently sloping. It is located about 60 miles east of the state capital, Topeka. Among the suburbs of Kansas City, Kansas, are Leavenworth, Lawrence, and Olathe.

Layout of City and Suburbs

The Kansas River bisects the city from the south, creating a ring as it heads north. Because of the flowing terrain, the streets are not arranged in the traditional grid pattern that most cities have. Further, Kansas City is a combination of several former cities that were absorbed in 1886, with annexations that continued until 1966. Greater Kansas City, which encompasses both cities in Missouri and Kansas, spills over irregularly into a number of counties. In the case of Kansas City, Kansas, some of its suburbs, including the two largest of Overland Park and Prairie Village, are in Johnson County.

Environment

Environmental Stress Index   2.8
Green Cities Index: Rank   NA
               Score   NA
Water Quality   Neutral, hard
   Average Daily Use (gallons per capita)   182
   Maximum Supply (gallons per capita)   372
Parkland as % of Total City Area   1.7
% Waste Landfilled/Recycled   NA
Annual Parks Expenditures per Capita $24.32

Climate

Kansas City has a continental climate typical of the heartland. Summers are generally hot, although the nights are mild, with moderate humidity. Winters are moderate, with the monthly mean temperature below freezing point only in January, and an average annual snowfall of 20 inches. Spring is a season of rapid fluctuations. Fall is the most pleasant season, with mild days and cool nights.

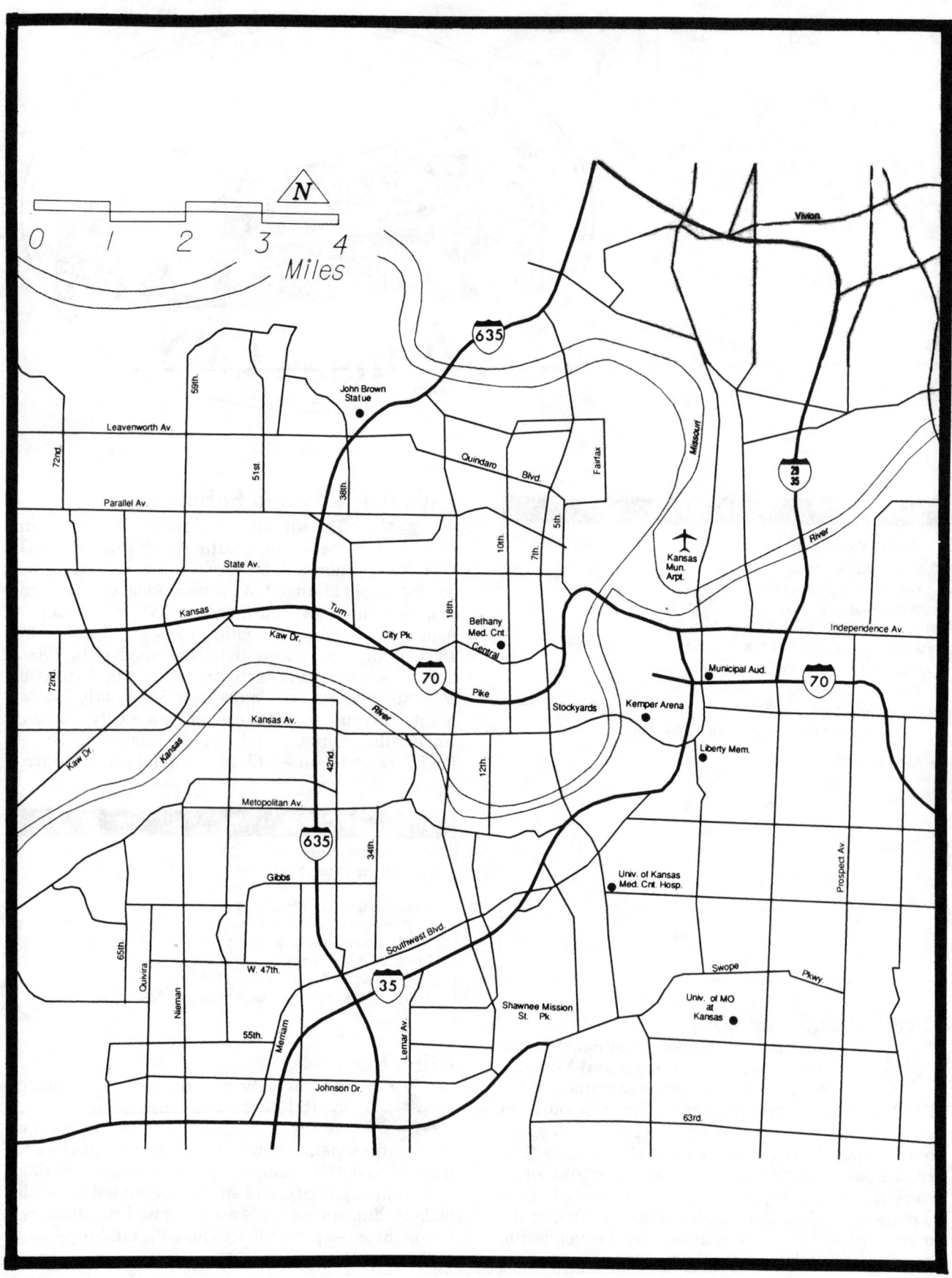

Weather

Temperature

Highest Monthly Average °F 78.8
Lowest Monthly Average °F 27.8

Annual Averages

Days 32°F or Below 105
Days above 90°F 40
Zero Degree Days 5
Precipitation (inches) 37
Snow (inches) 20
% Seasonal Humidity 68
Wind Speed (m.p.h.) 10.3
Clear Days 132
Cloudy Days 148
Storm Days 47
Rainy Days 97

Average Temperatures (°F)	High	Low	Mean
January	36.2	19.3	27.8
February	41.9	24.2	33.1
March	50.5	31.8	41.2
April	64.8	45.1	55.0
May	74.3	55.7	65.0
June	82.6	65.2	73.9
July	88.0	69.6	78.8
August	86.7	68.1	77.4
September	78.8	58.8	68.8
October	68.9	48.3	58.6
November	52.7	34.5	43.6
December	40.4	24.1	32.3

History

The present-day Kansas City region was once the domain of several American Indian tribes, including the Wyandots, Shawnees, and Delawares (all tribes that had been forcibly moved from their homelands in the eastern United States) before the period of exploration by white men. In 1804, and again in 1806, explorers Meriwether Lewis and William Clark passed through the area on their trips to and from the western coast of the present-day United States, but little else happened for the next 12 years. In 1818 the government granted the Kansas City area to the Delaware tribe as part of a reservation. The Delawares inhabited this land until 1843, then sold it to the Wyandots, who plotted a small village called Wyandot City. For the next six years, the Wyandots built schools and a church, and farmed. In 1849, however, Wyandot City became a way station on the road to the California gold rush. As the westward migration increased and the population of the eastern section of the country exploded, more and more pioneers settled in Wyandot City and its surrounding areas. In the decade just before the Civil War, the Wyandots, like other tribes before them, were gradually pushed out.

It was during this period that the Wyandots attempted to make Kansas their permanent home. In 1852 they elected Abelard Guthrie, a white man who had lived among the Indians, to the U.S. House of Representatives as a territorial delegate. In 1853 they created the Kansas-Nebraska Territory and elected William Walker as Kansas's first governor. This set the stage for the fight over whether Kansas should be admitted to the Union as a slave or free state. The resulting controversy led the nation closer to civil war. The Wyandots sided with the North; in return, they were granted the right to sell their lands. This was done in 1855, and the Wyandot nation passed into history. The whites who had purchased the lands renamed the town Wyandotte, incorporating it as a town in 1858, and as a city the following year. Around the new settlement sprang up the cities of Quindaro (founded by Abelard Guthrie) and Old Kansas City.

In 1859 settlers from Wyandotte met and wrote the Kansas constitution, which led the way for Kansas to become the 34th state. Wyandotte was made the seat of Wyandotte County, and the influence of such towns as Quindaro waned.

After the Civil War, former slaves were lured to the area with promises of land. Called "Exodusters," these blacks settled in the area along with immigrant Europeans and people fleeing crowded eastern cities. In 1866 a railway was constructed linking Wyandotte and Topeka. In 1871 Charles F. Adams, a relative of Presidents John and John Quincy Adams, purchased plots of land in Wyandotte and lured huge meatpacking companies to the area. This was the heyday of the Big Four—Armour, Cudahy, Wilson, and Swift—and these companies needed employees and rail lines to produce and ship their product. Thus the economic engine of the area was born.

In 1886 the state legislature combined the cities of Old Kansas City, Wyandotte, Armstrong, and Armourdale (site of the Armour stockyards) into one municipality known today as Kansas City, Kansas. The crash of 1893 left the city economically weak, but new infusions of immigrants served to keep it alive. This second wave included emigrants from eastern Europe, and they settled in ethnically diverse areas, making Kansas City essentially a patchwork of small nations. In the 20th century, Kansas City remains a leading agricultural city, with the largest grain-storing facilities in the world, and the second-largest stockyards (behind Chicago).

Historical Landmarks

The Rosedale Arch, constructed in 1924 as a war memorial to Kansas soldiers who served during World War I, is a 34-foot-tall brick-and-limestone replica of the Arc de Triomphe in Paris. It is located in what was once Rosedale, a town annexed by Kansas City in 1922. The Grinter House, built in 1857, is the restored home of the first white settlers in Kansas City. Moses and Anna Grinter operated a ferry service on the Kansas River from 1831 until the mid-1870s. The Huron Indian Cemetery in the heart of downtown was the burial ground of the Wyandots. Established in 1843, it contains the remains of Wyandot Indians (and their descendants, who are still laid to rest there) and Kansas City's early pioneers.

The historic Granada Theatre, the last movie palace operating in Kansas City, was built in 1929 and restored in 1986. It presents theatrical performances and

Chronology

1804	Explorers Meriwether Lewis and William Clark visit Kaw Point on their way to the Pacific, and again on their return trip in 1806.
1818	The Kansas City area is made part of a reservation granted by the government to the Delaware Indians.
1843	Delaware Indians sell the territory to the Wyandot Indians, who lay out a town named Wyandot City.
1849	The gold rush in California makes Wyandot City a way station for pioneers en route to the Pacific.
1852	The Wyandots petition Congress for territorial status, and elect Abelard Guthrie as a territorial delegate to the 32nd Congress. Congress denies Guthrie his seat.
1853	The Wyandots organize the Kansas-Nebraska area into a provisional territory with William Walker as governor. Guthrie is reelected to Congress, but again fails to be seated.
1854	Congress passes the Kansas-Nebraska Act.
1855	The Wyandots petition for and receive rights of citizenship, including the right to sell property. Most of the town property is thereupon sold to white settlers. The Wyandot nation passes into history.
1857–1859	The new settlers rename the town Wyandotte. It is incorporated as a town in 1858 and as a city the following year.
1859	At the Wyandotte Convention, a state constitution is written by which Kansas becomes the 34th state, with Wyandotte as the county seat of Wyandotte County.
1866	Wyandotte is connected to Topeka by rail.
1871	Charles F. Adams, a relative of Presidents John and John Quincy Adams, buys plots of land in Wyandotte and persuades huge meat-packing companies to locate in the city. Armstrong and Armourdale are founded as towns.
1886	By an act of the state legislature, Wyandotte, Armourdale, Armstrong, and Old Kansas City are consolidated into one city—Kansas City.

silent films with their original music played on the Grande Barton Theatre pipe organ. The Strawberry Hill Museum, a celebration of eastern European culture in Kansas City, is located in a unique structure built in 1887 that was once the St. John the Baptist Children's Home.

Population

Like its Missouri twin, Kansas City, Kansas, has been losing population heavily since the 1970s. In the 1990 census its population was 149,767, compared with 161,148 in 1980 and 168,000 in 1970. Percentage of change was -4.2% in the 1970s and -7.1% in the 1980s.

Population		
	1980	*1990*
Central City	161,148	149,767
Rank	92	115
Metro Area	1,433,464	1,566,280
Pop. Change 1980–1990	-11,381	
Pop. % Change 1980–1990	-7.1	
Median Age	31.5	
% Male	47.6	
% Age 65 and Over	13.0	
Density (per square mile)	1,389	
Households		
Number	57,146	
Persons per Household	2.59	
% Female-Headed Households	16.9	
% One-Person Households	28.0	
Births—Total	2,995	
% to Mothers under 20	19.7	
Birth Rate per 1,000	18.7	

Ethnic Composition

Soon after the Civil War, immigration of former slaves established a strong black presence in the city. Today blacks make up 29% of the population, whites 65%, Hispanics 7%, Asians and Pacific Islanders 1.24%, and American Indians 0.1%.

Ethnic Composition (as % of total pop.)		
	1980	*1990*
White	70.96	65.0
Black	25.34	29.27
American Indian	0.46	0.68
Asian and Pacific Islander	0.44	1.24
Hispanic	4.85	7.15
Other	NA	3.8

Government

Kansas City is governed under a mayor-council-administrator form, established in 1983. The five council members are elected in odd-numbered years for four-year terms; they elect one of themselves as mayor, a titular head

Government	
Year of Home Charter	NA
Number of Members of the Governing Body	5
Elected at Large	5
Elected by Wards	NA
Number of Women in Governing Body	NA
Salary of Mayor	$56,812
Salary of Council Members	$5,000
City Government Employment Total	1,964
Rate per 10,000	121.2

of government. The council appoints an administrator as chief executive of the city.

Public Finance

 The budget consists of revenues of $215.820 million and expenditures of $211.517 million. The debt outstanding is $1.745 billion, and cash and security holdings are $1.679 billion.

Public Finance

Total Revenue (in millions) $215.820
Intergovernmental Revenue—Total (in millions) $24.7
Federal Revenue per Capita $2.95
% Federal Assistance 1.37
% State Assistance 3.64
Sales Tax as % of Total Revenue 2.38
Local Revenue as % of Total Revenue 94.99
City Income Tax no
Taxes—Total (in millions) $46.3

Taxes per Capita
    Total $286
    Property $176
    Sales and Gross Receipts $106
General Expenditures—Total (in millions) $101.5
General Expenditures per Capita $626
Capital Outlays per Capita $64

% of Expenditures for:
    Public Welfare 0.0
    Highways 10.2
    Education 0.0
    Health and Hospitals 1.1
    Police 14.3
    Sewerage and Sanitation 14.1
    Parks and Recreation 3.2
    Housing and Community Development 4.7
Debt Outstanding per Capita $2,895
    % Utility 0.0
Federal Procurement Contract Awards (in millions) $24.3
Federal Grants Awards (in millions) $23.7
Fiscal Year Begins January 1

Economy

 Kansas City's reliance on the waning meat-packing industry was broken by its diversification into other sectors, most notably manufacturing and services. The leading economic sectors include health care, government, railroads, and education. Some of the leading employers are General Motors, University of Kansas Medical Center, Kansas City Board of Education, Santa Fe Railroad, and Colgate-Palmolive.

Economy

Total Money Income (in millions) $1,418.6
% of State Average 82.0
Per Capita Annual Income $8,757
% Population below Poverty Level 14.4
Fortune 500 Companies NA

Banks	Number	Deposits (in millions)
Commercial	20	1,790.6
Savings	5	4,245.9

Passenger Autos 86,870
Electric Meters 63,700
Gas Meters 49,632

Economoy (continued)

Manufacturing

Number of Establishments 282
% with 20 or More Employees 42.2
Manufacturing Payroll (in millions) $467.6
Value Added by Manufacture (in millions) $1,446.9
Value of Shipments (in millions) $3,416.5
New Capital Expenditures (in millions) NA

Wholesale Trade

Number of Establishments 325
Sales (in millions) $3,193.8
Annual Payroll (in millions) $149.281

Retail Trade

Number of Establishments 1,143
Total Sales (in millions) $707.0
Sales per Capita $4,362
Number of Retail Trade Establishments with Payroll 740
Annual Payroll (in millions) $86.3
Total Sales (in millions) $687.3
General Merchandise Stores (per capita) NA
Food Stores (per capita) $909
Apparel Stores (per capita) NA
Eating and Drinking Places (per capita) $443

Service Industries

Total Establishments 759
Total Receipts (in millions) $331.4
Hotels and Motels (in millions) NA
Health Services (in millions) $99.3
Legal Services (in millions) $25.1

Labor

Despite the strength of the manufacturing sector, it ranks only fourth in employment, being preceded by trade, services, and government. The largest manufacturing plant is that of General Motors, followed by International Paper, Certain-Teed, Colgate-Palmolive, and Owens-Corning Fiberglas. Reflecting Kansas City's historic role as a transportation hub, two railroads appear among the top 20 employers: Union Pacific and Santa Fe. Productivity is high as a result of longer working hours. The typical work week is 40 hours in 63% of the firms, as compared to 8.7% of those in New York City.

Labor

Civilian Labor Force 83,150
% Change 1989–1990 -0.8
Work Force Distribution
    Mining 9,800
    Construction 41,600
    Manufacturing 183,900
    Transportation and Public Utilities 65,100
    Wholesale and Retail Trade 268,800
    FIRE (Finance, Insurance, Real Estate) 58,300
    Service 248,400
    Government 219,100
    Women as % of Labor Force 44.3
    % Self-Employed 3.7
    % Professional/Technical 10.9
Total Unemployment 6,608
Rate % 7.9
Federal Government Civilian Employment 1,492

Education

The city's Unified School District supports 50 schools. In addition, there are 12 private and parochial schools. Kansas City does not have a major public university, although the University of Kansas Medical Center is located here. Among private institutions the largest is Donnelly College. The Central Baptist Theological Seminary awards degrees in theology.

Education

Number of Public Schools 50
Special Education Schools NA
Total Enrollment 22,118
% Enrollment in Private Schools 11.3
% Minority 58.7
Classroom Teachers 1,207
Pupil-Teacher Ratio 18.3:1
Number of Graduates 1,212
Total Revenue (in millions) $86.555
Total Expenditures (in millions) $83.840
Expenditures per Pupil $3,497
Educational Attainment (Age 25 and Over)
   % Completed 12 or More Years 61.4
   % Completed 16 or More Years 8.9
Four-Year Colleges and Universities 1
   Enrollment 2,473
Two-Year Colleges 1
   Enrollment 6,353

Libraries

Number 11
Public Libraries 3
Books (in thousands) 388
Circulation (in thousands) 700
Persons Served (in thousands) 166
Circulation per Person Served 4.21
Income (in millions) $2.311
Staff 150

Four-Year Colleges and Universities
   University of Kansas Medical Center

Health

The premier medical institution is the hospital attached to the University of Kansas Medical Center; the Bethany Medical Center also is affiliated with the medical center. Another major facility is the Providence–St. Margaret Medical Center.

Health

Deaths—Total 1,586
Rate per 1,000 9.9
Infant Deaths—Total 51
Rate per 1,000 17.0
Number of Metro Hospitals 4
Number of Metro Hospital Beds 1,213
Rate per 100,000 748
Number of Physicians 1,418
Physicians per 1,000 2.25
Nurses per 1,000 6.84
Health Expenditures per Capita $6.00

Transportation

Because Kansas City, Kansas, essentially shares its border with Kansas City, Missouri, much of the highway system serving the latter serves the former as well. The two main highways that bisect the city are I-35, north to south, and I-70 (the Kansas Turnpike), east to west. Interstate 29, which is a major area highway, joins U.S. 70 in Kansas City, Missouri. U.S. 73 also crosses the area. Both Kansas Cities share Kansas City International Airport, 16 miles north of downtown, across the river in Missouri.

Transportation

Interstate Highway Mileage 180
Total Urban Mileage 6,193
Total Daily Vehicle Mileage (in millions) 27.968
Daily Average Commute Time 48.0 min.
Number of Buses 241
Port Tonnage (in millions) NA
Airports NA
Number of Daily Flights 183
Daily Average Number of Passengers 11,936

Airlines (American carriers only)
   See Kansas City, MO

Housing

Kansas City has affordable housing both within the city and in Wyandotte County. In the western portions of the county, the value of homes ranges from $75,000 to $200,000. The number and value of new residential permits, however, declined in 1990 and 1991.

Housing

Total Housing Units 64,457
% Change 1980–1990 0.0
Vacant Units for Sale or Rent 5,980
Occupied Units 57,146
% with More Than One Person per Room 4.6
% Owner-Occupied 61.9
Median Value of Owner-Occupied Homes $41,200
Average Monthly Purchase Cost $279
Median Monthly Rent $285
New Private Housing Starts 125
Value (in thousands) $8,402
% Single-Family 97.6
Nonresidential Buildings Value (in thousands) $3,715

Urban Redevelopment

Among the major redevelopment projects in recent years are a new General Motors plant, a new $33 million federal building, a high-technology wing for the Kansas City Community College, and new medical office buildings for the Bethany Medical Center and Providence–St. Margaret Medical Center.

Crime

Crime figures are reported for the metro area including Kansas City, Missouri, and Kansas City, Kansas. In 1991, of the crimes known to police, there were 2,790 violent crimes and 15,154 property crimes.

Crime	
Violent Crimes—Total	2,790
Violent Crime Rate per 100,000	1,175
Murder	44
Rape	182
Robbery	1,039
Aggravated Assaults	1,525
Property Crimes	15,154
Burglary	4,170
Larceny	8,469
Motor Vehicle Theft	2,515
Arson	115
Per Capita Police Expenditures	$117.43
Per Capita Fire Protection Expenditures	$109.90
Number of Police	NA
Per 1,000	NA

Religion

Kansas City has a low religious profile in which Catholics constitute the major influence.

Religion	
Largest Denominations (Adherents)	
Catholic	27,912
Black Baptist	10,965
American Baptist	5,487
Christian Church (Disciples)	3,593
Southern Baptist	5,841
United Methodist	5,470
Assembly of God	1,753
Lutheran-Missouri Synod	2,590
Jewish	1,975

Media

The lone city daily is the *Kansas City Kansan*, although the *Kansas City Star*, published in Kansas City, Missouri, is available. The electronic media consist of two television stations, as well as others based in Kansas City, Missouri, and four AM and FM radio stations exclusive to Kansas City, Kansas.

Media	
Newsprint	
Kansas City Kansan, daily	
Wyondotte West, weekly	
Television	
KSMO (Channel 62)	
See Kansas City, MO	
Radio	
KBEA (AM)	KCNW (AM)
KNHN (AM)	KTXR (FM)

Sports

Kansas City, Kansas, has no professional sports teams, but it shares the pride in the major teams across the river: the

Kansas City Royals play baseball at Kauffman Stadium and the Kansas City Chiefs play football at Arrowhead Stadium.

Arts, Culture, and Tourism

The Sandstone Outdoor Theatre in nearby Bonner Springs and Community Theatre at the Kansas City Community College exhibit much of the city's theater and arts. The Granada Theatre, a 1929 movie house restored in 1986, is now a performing arts center and focal point of a silent movies festival. The museums in the area include the Grinter House, home of pioneers Moses and Anna Grinter; the Wyandotte County Historical Society and Museum; the Strawberry Hill Museum and Cultural Center, and, 18 miles west in Bonner Springs, the Agricultural Hall of Fame and National Farmers Memorial.

Travel and Tourism	
Hotel Rooms	18,123
Convention and Exhibit Space (square feet)	NA
Convention Centers	
Constitution Center	
Soldiers and Sailors Memorial Hall	
Festivals	
Renaissance Festival (September)	
Polish Constitution Day (May)	
Festival International (June)	
Piper Prairie Days (May)	
Kansas City Spirit Festival (September)	

Parks and Recreation

Among the largest parks under the direction of the Wyandotte County Parks and Recreation Department are the 1,500-acre Wyandotte County Lake and Park and the Wyandotte County Fairgrounds.

Sources of Further Information

City of Kansas City Kansas City Hall
701 North 7th Street
Kansas City, KS 66101
(913) 573-5000

Kansas City Kansas Area Chamber of Commerce
727 Minnesota Avenue
Kansas City, KS 66101
(913) 371-2070

Kansas City Kansas Area Convention and Visitors Bureau
753 State Street, Suite 101
Kansas City, KS 66117
(913) 321-5800

Additional Reading

Cole's Directory for Kansas City. 1991.
Polk's Kansas City City Directory. 1991.

Kansas City

Missouri

Location and Topography

N

Although called Kansas City, the city lies in Jackson County, Missouri, along the Kansas-Missouri border. Situated about 150 miles from the capital (Jefferson City), Kansas City sits on rolling, hilly country on the southern shore of the Missouri River. It is bordered on the west by Kansas City, Kansas.

Layout of City and Suburbs

Kansas City proper lies partially in Missouri and partially in Kansas, with the bulk of downtown on the Missouri side. Although the river has been an important facet of Kansas City's economic growth, now it is basically a divider of states. The Missouri side of Kansas City has its downtown about 12 blocks south of the Missouri River and is divided by Main Street, which runs from north to south. The rest of the city is a grid that separates the Garment District from the River City Market, Crown Center, Westport, and Country Club Plaza, a Spanish-style shopping center modeled after Kansas City's sister city Seville, Spain. Jackson County suburbs include Independence, the home of Harry S Truman, Lee's Summit, Mission Hills, and Raytown.

Climate

Kansas City has a modified continental climate with frequent and rapid weather fluctuations in spring. Summers are warm with mild nights; fall is the most pleasant season, characterized by many sunny days and cool nights. Winters are only moderately cold and the occurrence of more than 20 inches of snow is rare.

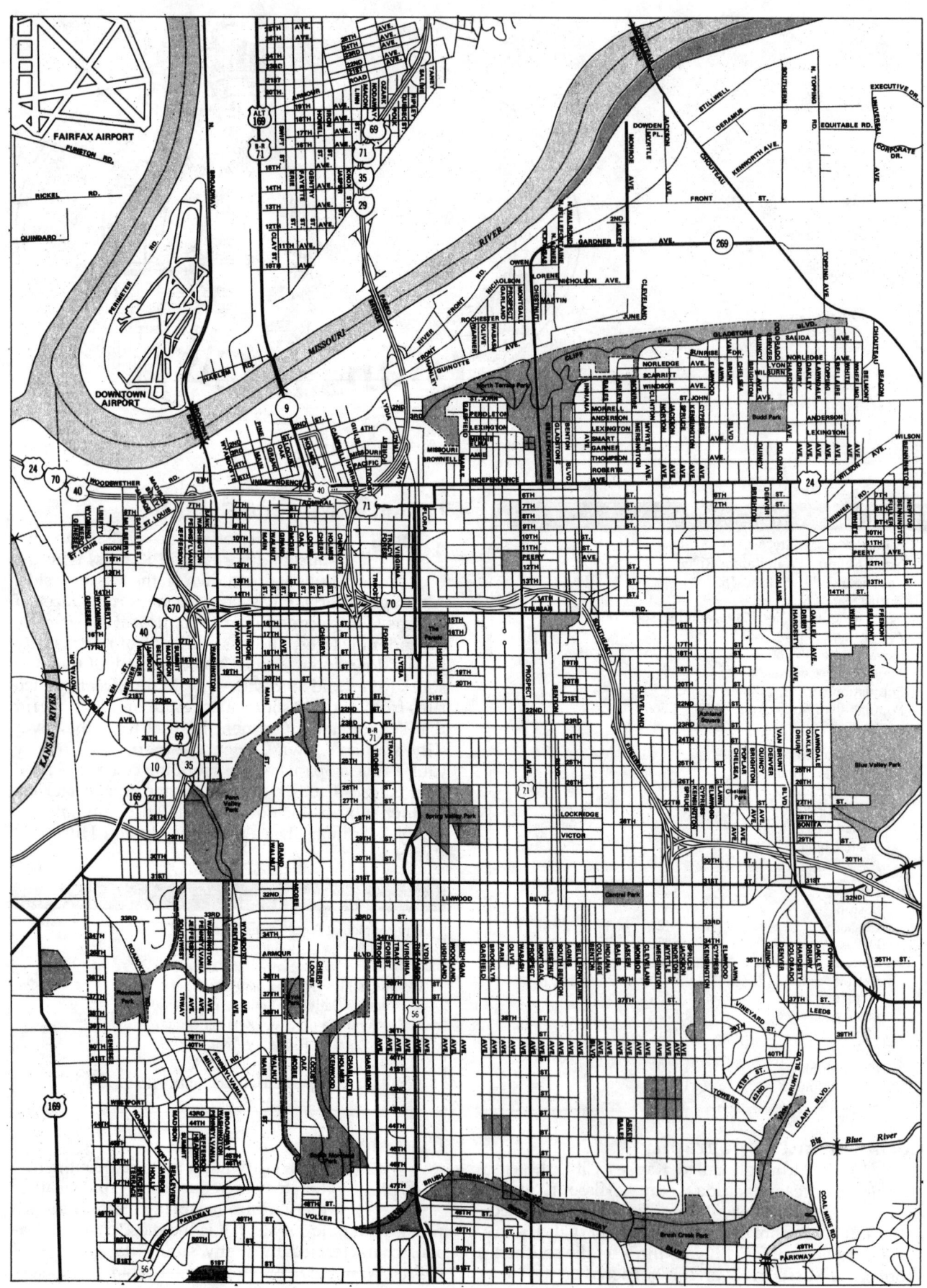

Weather

Temperature

Highest Monthly Average °F 88.0
Lowest Monthly Average °F 19.3

Annual Averages

Days 32°F or Below 105
Days above 90°F 40
Zero Degree Days 5
Precipitation (inches) 37.0
Snow (inches) 20.0
% Seasonal Humidity 68.0
Wind Speed (m.p.h.) 10.3
Clear Days 132
Cloudy Days 148
Storm Days 47
Rainy Days 97

Average Temperatures (°F)	High	Low	Mean
January	36.2	19.3	27.8
February	41.9	24.2	33.1
March	50.5	31.8	41.2
April	64.8	45.1	55.0
May	74.3	55.7	65.0
June	82.6	65.2	73.9
July	88.0	69.6	78.8
August	86.7	68.1	77.4
September	78.8	58.8	68.8
October	68.9	48.3	58.6
November	52.7	34.5	43.6
December	40.4	24.1	32.3

History

The land now occupied by Kansas City was once part of the territory inhabited by the Kansa or Kaw Indians. The first Europeans in the region were explorers Meriwether Lewis and William Clark, who camped at the confluence of the Kansas and Missouri rivers in 1804. Zebulon Pike (for whom Pikes Peak is named) came to the area in 1806, followed by Stephen Long in 1819. Francois Chouteau, an employee of the American Fur Company, came from St. Louis and started a post on the Kaw River to trade with the Wyandotte, Osage, and Kansa Indians.

In 1826 Jackson County was chartered with Independence as the county seat. In 1832 an entrepreneur named John Calvin McCoy arrived in the Kansas City area and set up a trading post and supply station for settlers moving west. The following year he named his post Westport. Meanwhile, Chouteau was flooded out and forced to move his post north of present-day Kansas City, to where Grand Avenue meets the Missouri River, and it was promptly dubbed Westport Landing by the area's residents. In 1838 McCoy organized the Kansas Town Company, bought land around his depot, platted the area, and the following year founded the Town of Kansas on the site of Kansas City, four miles north of Westport.

The population of the town of Kansas grew slowly—by 1846 it still had only 700 people. The Santa Fe Trail and the Gold Rush in 1849 brought visitors and business to the growing settlement. Although cholera broke out later that year, killing about half the

population, the push toward economic vitalization was on. In 1853 the city was chartered as the City of Kansas, streets were built and others widened, and a chamber of commerce was founded. Before the Civil War started in the rest of the country, the state of Kansas was caught up in a brutal fight between proslavery activists and abolitionists. The resulting war caused economic hardship in the city, including a cutoff of trade. Westport saw a major battle in which Union forces held off Confederate units. The war's end in 1865 left the city poor but eager to grow again. That year, the Missouri Pacific Railroad came to town, making it the virtual center of commerce in Missouri. From 1865 to 1870, the population of the city grew from 6,000 to about 32,000. The latter year saw the coming of the stockyards. Westport was annexed in 1889, and the resulting city was named Kansas City.

The stockyards, as well as grain production, dictated much of Kansas City's prosperity for the next half-century. Politics became important as well. In 1911 the A.S.B. Bridge—named after Armour, Swift, and Burlington, the city's three biggest meat packers—opened. The Democratic National Convention nominated William Jennings Bryan for president here in 1900. The Republican party held their national nominating conventions here, as well, in 1928 and 1976. The first two decades of the 20th century brought auto assembly plants and an increasing variety of industries. In the 1920s Kansas City came under the boss politics of Thomas J. Pendergast, which lasted until 1940, when Pendergast was indicted for tax evasion. After World War II, urban redevelopment projects continued to change the skyline. Crown Center, Hallmark Cards' 85-acre city-within-a-city of offices, shops, and restaurants, was one of the most significant architectural projects in the 1970s.

Historical Landmarks

Many of Kansas City's historic sights are tied to its past as a way station to the West. The Alexander Majors House, located on State Line Road, honors the co-founder of the Pony Express. The Pioneer Mother Memorial honors the pioneer women who crossed the American West and the Great Plains. The Shawnee Mission, where the Reverend Thomas Johnson opened his missionary school for Indian children, was a stopping point for those traveling the Santa Fe Trail. The renovated district of Westport includes many original buildings from the early period of Kansas City's history. Other landmarks deal with city history as well. The Lewis and Clark marker on Quality Hill commemorates the site first seen by explorers Meriwether Lewis and William Clark in 1804. The Liberty Memorial on Main Street is a 217-foot memorial tower honoring those who served in World War I; it is also a museum and features a panorama of a war scene. The Vietnam Veterans Memorial pays homage to the 336 Kansas City–area veterans killed in the war.

Chronology

1804– 1819	Meriwether Lewis and William Clark explore the area around present-day Kansas City. They are followed by Zebulon Pike in 1806 and Stephen Long in 1819.
1821	Francois Chouteau, an employee of the American Fur Company, establishes a trading post on the Kaw River to trade with the local Indian tribes.
1826	Jackson County is chartered with Independence as the county seat.
1830	Following destruction of his post in a flood, Chouteau moves his warehouse to Westport Landing, the present site of Kansas City.
1832– 1833	John Calvin McCoy builds a supply store near the Big Blue River crossing to supply travelers heading west on the Santa Fe, California, and Oregon trails. In 1833 he plats the town of Westport.
1839	McCoy founds the Town of Kansas.
1853	The City of Kansas is chartered.
1865	The Missouri Pacific Railroad comes to the City of Kansas.
1870	Stockyards open in the City of Kansas.
1889	Westport is annexed, with the resulting city being named Kansas City.
1900	Democratic National Convention nominates William Jennings Bryan for president.
1911	The A.S.B. Bridge is built.
1928	Republican National Convention nominates Calvin Coolidge for president.
1976	Republican National Convention nominates Gerald Ford for president.
1981	Two skywalks in Crown Center's Hyatt Regency Hotel collapse, killing more than 100 people.

Population

Kansas City ranked 31st among U.S. cities in 1990 (down from 27th in 1980) with a population of 435,146 (compared to 440,028 in 1980). Its loss of population, estimated at 2.9%, is not considered significant.

Ethnic Composition

Whites make up 66.8% of the city residents and blacks 29.6%. In 1940 blacks made up only 9.6%; black migration into the city was a postwar phenomenon.

Population

	1980	1990
Central City	440,028	435,146
Rank	27	31
Metro Area	1,433,464	1,566,280
Pop. Change 1980–1990	-12,882	
Pop. % Change 1980–1990	-2.9	
Median Age	32.8	
% Male	47.6	
% Age 65 and Over	12.91	
Density (per square mile)	1,396	

Households

Number	177,607
Persons per Household	2.40
% Female-Headed Households	15.1
% One-Person Households	32.5
Births—Total	7,749
% to Mothers under 20	16.8
Birth Rate per 1,000	17.5

Ethnic Composition (as % of total pop.)

	1980	1990
White	69.8	66.78
Black	27.38	29.59
American Indian	0.36	0.49
Asian and Pacific Islander	0.78	1.2
Hispanic	3.28	3.91
Other	NA	1.94

Government

Under a home-rule charter adopted in 1925, Kansas City is governed by a mayor and council elected at four-year intervals. The 12 council members elect the city manager, who is the chief executive.

Government

Year of Home Charter	1925
Number of Members of the Governing Body	12
Elected at Large	6
Elected by Wards	6
Number of Women in Governing Body	1
Salary of Mayor	$47,000
Salary of Council Members	$19,500
City Government Employment Total	7,622
Rate per 10,000	172.8

Public Finance

The annual city budget consists of revenues of $620.064 million and expenditures of $570.647 million. The total debt outstanding is $615.905 million, and cash and security holdings are $1.218 billion.

Economy

Kansas City was ranked by *Fortune* magazine as the best city in the United States for business in 1991. It lives up to that reputation as the national headquarters of Hallmark Cards, U.S. Sprint, Merill, Dow Pharmaceuticals,

Public Finance

Total Revenue (in millions) $620.06
Intergovernmental Revenue—Total (in millions) $49.99
Federal Revenue per Capita $24.98
% Federal Assistance   4.03
% State Assistance   3.94
Sales Tax as % of Total Revenue   21.22
Local Revenue as % of Total Revenue   75.33
City Income Tax   yes
Taxes—Total (in millions) $242.2

Taxes per Capita
   Total $549
   Property $71
   Sales and Gross Receipts $262
General Expenditures—Total (in millions) $380.5
General Expenditures per Capita $863
Capital Outlays per Capita $155

% of Expenditures for:
   Public Welfare   NA
   Highways   9.7
   Education   5.2
   Health and Hospitals   6.8
   Police   15.6
   Sewerage and Sanitation   8.4
   Parks and Recreation   6.9
   Housing and Community Development   8.6
Debt Outstanding per Capita $974
   % Utility   5.5
Federal Procurement Contract Awards (in millions)
   $885.4
Federal Grants Awards (in millions) $58.1
Fiscal Year Begins   May 1

Economy

Total Money Income (in millions) $4,918.473
% of State Average   108.5
Per Capita Annual Income $11,153
% Population below Poverty Level   13.2
Fortune 500 Companies   2

Banks	Number	Deposits (in millions)
Commercial	115	13,888.4
Savings	27	5,316.9

Passenger Autos   417,085
Electric Meters   500,000
Gas Meters   400,000

Manufacturing

Number of Establishments   720
% with 20 or More Employees   36.0
Manufacturing Payroll (in millions) $1,329.1
Value Added by Manufacture (in millions) $3,185.1
Value of Shipments (in millions) $5,902.0
New Capital Expenditures (in millions) $140.6

Wholesale Trade

Number of Establishments   1,166
Sales (in millions) $8,248.3
Annual Payroll (in millions) $468.209

Retail Trade

Number of Establishments   4,153
Total Sales (in millions) $3,417.6
Sales per Capita $7,747
Number of Retail Trade Establishments with Payroll   3,077
Annual Payroll (in millions) $439.0
Total Sales (in millions) $3,353.9
General Merchandise Stores (per capita)   NA
Food Stores (per capita)   NA
Apparel Stores (per capita) $508
Eating and Drinking Places (per capita) $1,001

Economy (continued)

Service Industries

Total Establishments   3,787
Total Receipts (in millions) $2,627.6
Hotels and Motels (in millions)   NA
Health Services (in millions) $NA
Legal Services (in millions) $330.9

H&R Block, and Farmland Industries. Its principal economic asset is its location, making it the manufacturing, transportation, distribution, and storage hub for the Midwest. Grain storage and livestock marketing account for a major share of the economic pie. The Kansas City Livestock Exchange is one of the nation's oldest and largest, and the city is the largest winter wheat market in the country. Further, the city ranks second nationally in wheat flour production. It ranks third in car and truck assembly.

Labor

 The labor force declined in 1991 for the first time since 1986—from 793,000 in 1990 to 782,000 in 1991. Manufacturing jobs have held relatively steady, while service jobs have grown, consistently paced by the health-care industry. The unemployment rate hit 6% in 1991 and does not vary significantly from the national average.

Labor

Civilian Labor Force   250,725
% Change 1989–1990   -0.3

Work Force Distribution
   Mining   NA
   Construction   29,800
   Manufacturing   104,900
   Transportation and Public Utilities   63,900
   Wholesale and Retail Trade   194,600
   FIRE (Finance, Insurance, Real Estate)   59,800
   Service   197,200
   Government   122,700
   Women as % of Labor Force   46.3
   % Self-Employed   4.6
   % Professional/Technical   15.1
Total Unemployment   14,521
Rate %   5.8
Federal Government Civilian Employment   19,051

Education

The public school system, District 33, supports 80 schools. The higher education system is led by the University of Missouri–Kansas City with an enrollment of over 12,000. Church-related colleges are prominent in the city: Avila College, Calvary Bible College, Midwestern Baptist Theological Seminary, Nazarene Theological Seminary, and Rockhurst College. Two specialized colleges provide instruction in art and technology: Kansas City Art Institute and DeVry Institute of Technology.

Education

Number of Public Schools 80
Special Education Schools 1
Total Enrollment 34,486
% Enrollment in Private Schools 11.3
% Minority 0.0
Classroom Teachers 2,500
Pupil-Teacher Ratio 13.9:1
Number of Graduates 1,415
Total Revenue (in millions) $241.970
Total Expenditures (in millions) $230.532
Expenditures per Pupil $5,505
Educational Attainment (Age 25 and Over)
   % Completed 12 or More Years 69.6
   % Completed 16 or More Years 16.6
Four-Year Colleges and Universities 4
   Enrollment 17,501
Two-Year Colleges 4
   Enrollment 10,086

Libraries

Number 71
Public Libraries 8
Books (in thousands) 1,633
Circulation (in thousands) 1,861
Persons Served (in thousands) 296.4
Circulation per Person Served 6.27
Income (in millions) $9.8
Staff 168

Four-Year Colleges and Universities
   University of Missouri, Kansas City
   Avila College
   Kansas City Art Institute
   Rockhurst College

Health

Of the city's 19 hospitals the largest are Baptist Medical Center, Bethany Medical Center, Children's Mercy Hospital, Lakeside Hospital, Menorah Medical Center, North Kansas City Hospital, Park Lane Medical Center, Providence–St. Margaret Medical Center, Research Medical Center, St. Joseph Health Center, St. Luke's Hospital, Trinity Lutheran Hospital, Truman Medical Center, University of Kansas Hospital, and Veterans Administration Medical Center.

Health

Deaths—Total 4,454
Rate per 1,000 10.1
Infant Deaths—Total 101
Rate per 1,000 13.0
Number of Metro Hospitals 19
Number of Metro Hospital Beds 4,834
Rate per 100,000 1,096
Number of Physicians 1,700
Physicians per 1,000 2.25
Nurses per 1,000 6.84
Health Expenditures per Capita $33.75

Transportation

The primary highways approaching Kansas City are the north-to-south I-35 and I-29, the latter of which joins U.S. 71. The southerly I-435 links with the east-to-west I-70 from the south. Amtrak runs regular train services.

The site of ten mainline railroads—including Union Pacific, Southern Pacific, Norfolk Southern, KC Terminal Railway, Kansas City Southern Lines, and Burlington Northern—Kansas City ranks nationally as the second-largest rail hub. It is also a major inland port connected by the Kansas and Missouri rivers to the inland water system. Kansas City International Airport, the main airline terminus, lies some 25 minutes to the northwest. Another important terminal is the Kansas City Downtown Airport. Across the river in Kansas is Fairfax Municipal Airport, while to the south of the city is Richards-Gebaur Airport.

Transportation

Interstate Highway Mileage 180
Total Urban Mileage 6,193
Total Daily Vehicle Mileage (in millions) 27.968
Daily Average Commute Time 48.0 min.
Number of Buses 241
Port Tonnage (in millions) 2.127
Airports 2
Number of Daily Flights 183
Daily Average Number of Passengers 11,936

Airlines (American carriers only)
   American
   Continental
   Delta
   Eastern
   Midway
   Northwest
   Southwest
   Trans World
   Continental
   United
   USAir

Media

Kansas City has a single daily newspaper, the *Kansas City Star*, which is published in the evenings. The electronic media consist of 6 television stations and 9 AM and FM radio stations.

Media

Newsprint
   Call, weekly
   Clay Dispatch-Tribune, weekly
   Kansas City Business Journal, weekly
   Kansas City Globe, weekly
   Kansas City North News, weekly
   Kansas City Star, daily

Television
   KCPT (Channel 19)
   KCTV (Channel 5)
   KMBC (Channel 9)
   KSHB (Channel 41)
   KYFC (Channel 50)
   WDAF (Channel 4)

Radio

KBEQ (FM)	KCMO (AM)
KCMO (FM)	KCUR (FM)
KKFI (FM)	KLJC (FM)
KPRT (AM)	KPRS (FM)
WDAF (AM)	

Housing

Kansas City has 201,789 housing units, of which 12,037 are independent one-family homes. Owner-occupied dwellings account for 56.9%.

Housing
Total Housing Units   201,789
% Change 1980–1990   4.9
Vacant Units for Sale or Rent   18,091
Occupied Units   177,607
% with More Than One Person per Room   3.2
% Owner-Occupied   56.9
Median Value of Owner-Occupied Homes $56,100
Average Monthly Purchase Cost $301
Median Monthly Rent $324
New Private Housing Starts   802
Value (in thousands) $83,682
% Single-Family   85.8
Nonresidential Buildings Value (in thousands) $137,356

Tallest Buildings	Hgt. (ft.)	Stories
One Kansas City Plaza	626	42
AT&T Town Pavilion	590	38
Hyatt Regency	504	40
Kansas City Power and Light Bldg.	476	32
City Hall	443	29
Federal Office Bldg.	413	35
Commerce Tower	402	32
City Center Sq.	402	30

Urban Redevelopment

The largest postwar redevelopment project is the Crown Center built by Hallmark Cards. It contains two hotels, stores, offices, and an apartment complex. Near Union Station is another redevelopment project, Pershing Square, on which work began in the 1980s. A third is at Westport Square, four miles south of Pershing Square.

Religion

Kansas City is one of the major centers of Baptist and Methodist denominations.

Religion
Largest Denominations (Adherents)

Catholic	73,120
Southern Baptist	78,997
United Methodist	30,567
Black Baptist	44,996
Presbyterian	13,590
Christian Church (Disciples)	18,777
Assembly of God	10,812
Mormons	4,467
Jewish	7,722

Crime

Of the crimes known to police in 1991, there were 12,413 violent crimes and 45,421 property crimes.

Crime
Violent Crimes—Total   12,413
Violent Crime Rate per 100,000   1,175
Murder   135
Rape   477
Robbery   4,955
Aggravated Assaults   6,846
Property Crimes   45,421
Burglary   13,008
Larceny   22,527
Motor Vehicle Theft   9,886
Arson   540
Per Capita Police Expenditures $157.86
Per Capita Fire Protection Expenditures $85.49
Number of Police   1,114
Per 1,000   2.5

Sports

The two main professional sports teams in Kansas City play at the two ends of the massive Harry S Truman Sports Complex. At one end is Arrowhead Stadium, home of the National Football League's Kansas City Chiefs. At the other is Royal Stadium, home of major league baseball's Kansas City Royals. Other sports events are held at the Kemper Arena downtown.

Arts, Culture, and Tourism

Among Kansas City's many offerings in theater are the American Heartland Theatre, Avenue of the Arts (a downtown arts district opened in 1992), Coterie Theatre, Folly Theatre, Missouri Repertory Theatre, and Starlight Theatre, a 7,862-seat amphitheater in Swope Park. The Kansas City Symphony performs in the Lyric Opera Hall. The Nelson-Atkins Museum of Arts, established in 1933, is Kansas City's largest museum as well as one of the largest in the nation. Its name commemorates William Rockhill Nelson, founder and publisher of the *Kansas City Star*. The Arabia Steamboat Museum exhibits the treasures of the ship, which sank in 1856. The Liberty Memorial Museum includes the 217-foot Liberty Memorial to soldiers from World War I. The Mormon/Latter Day Saints Visitors' Center presents their Missouri history from 1831 to 1839.

Travel and Tourism
Hotel Rooms   18,123
Convention and Exhibit Space (square feet)   186,300
Convention Centers
Kansas City Convention Complex (inc. Bartle Hall, Municipal Auditorium)
American Royal Center (inc. Kemper Arena, Royal Arena and Governor's Exposition Hall)
Festivals
Jazz Festival (August)
Royal Livestock Horse Show and Rodeo (November)
Concert for Champions (November)

Parks and Recreation

At 1,346 acres, Swope Park is the third-largest in the United States. In the midst of its rocky, wooded hills and deep ravines are picnic shelters, an amphitheater where the Starlight Theatre troupe performs, zoological gardens, a large lake and a lagoon, two 18-hole golf courses, and the Kansas City Zoo. Penn Valley Park, which occupies 131 acres from 26th to 31st streets, offers several views overlooking Kansas City. It is the site of the Liberty Memorial as well as the noted sculptures Pioneer Mother and The Scout, the latter a tribute to the local Indian tribes that once occupied the land. Longview Park is located on 930-acre Longview Lake. Wyandotte County Park is nearly 1,500 acres of woodlands surrounding a 330-acre lake.

Sources of Further Information

Convention and Visitors Bureau of Greater
  Kansas City (Missouri)
1100 Main Street, Suite 2550
Kansas City, MO 64105
(800) 767-7700

Greater Kansas City (Missouri) Chamber of Commerce
2600 Commerce Tower
Kansas City, MO 64105

Additional Reading

Ehrlich, George. Kansas City, Missouri: An Architectural History, 1826–1976. 1979.
Grant, William D. The Romantic Past of the Kansas City Region, 1540–1880. 1987.
Sandy, Wilda. Here Lies Kansas City. 1984.

Knoxville

Tennessee

Basic Data

Name   Knoxville
Name Origin   From General Henry Knox
Year Founded   1786 Inc. 1791
Status: State   Tennessee
      County   Seat of Knox County
Area (square miles)   77.3
Elevation (feet)   890
Time Zone   EST
Population (1990)   165,121
Population of Metro Area (1990)   604,816

Sister Cities
   Kaohsiung, China
   Neuquen, Argentina

Distance in Miles To:
Memphis	387
Nashville	178
Little Rock	524
Atlanta	219
Huntsville	217
Bowling Green	230
Chattanooga	114
Cincinnati	285

Location and Topography

N

Knoxville is located on the headwaters of the Tennessee River formed by the union of the Holston and the French Broad rivers. It lies in a broad valley between the Cumberland Mountains to the northwest and the Great Smoky Mountains to the southeast.

Layout of City and Suburbs

The business district is on a small plateau approached by narrow steep streets. The principal thoroughfare is Gay Street, to the west of which is Market Square, the site of the old farmers' market. Industrial plants are scattered all over the city, but principally are found along the riverfront and along railroad tracks. South of the river are marble hills, while the eastern main line of the Southern Railway borders the wholesale district; in the northeast are the lumber yards. The older residential areas are Sequoyah Hills and Holston Hills.

Environment

Environmental Stress Index   3.2
Green Cities Index: Rank   NA
               Score   NA
Water Quality   Alkaline, hard, fluoridated
   Average Daily Use (gallons per capita)   153
   Maximum Supply (gallons per capita)   245
Parkland as % of Total City Area   3.0
% Waste Landfilled/Recycled   NA
Annual Parks Expenditures per Capita $41.53

Climate

Knoxville's mild, temperate climate is due mostly to its two protective mountain ranges. The Cumberland Mountains weaken the force of the cold winter air moving down the northern plains in winter, and the Great Smoky Mountains temper the hot summer winds from the west and south. Snowfall is light, about 12 inches annually, and very little of it remains on the ground for more than a few days. Rainfall is generally limited to winter and late spring. Thunderstorms are quite common in summertime and provide welcome relief from the heat.

History

Knoxville was the domain of the Cherokee—who had displaced the Mound Builders—when it was visited by the first white men. The first recorded journeys through the region were in 1761 by Henry Timberlake, Thomas Sumter, and John McCormack. They were followed 18 years later by Colonel Evan Shelby and a band of

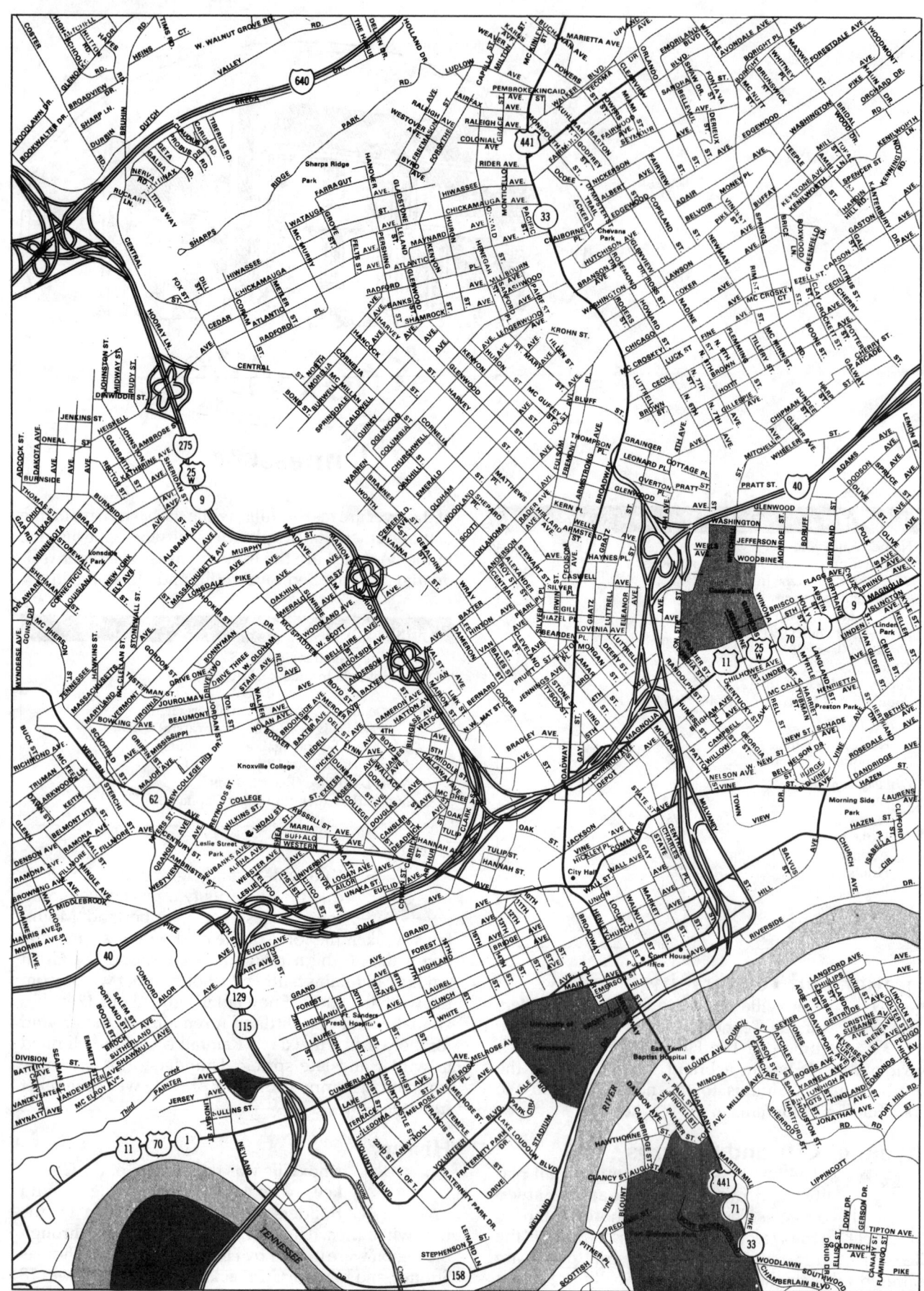

Weather

Temperature

Highest Monthly Average °F 88.0
Lowest Monthly Average °F 32.2

Annual Averages

Days 32°F or Below 71
Days above 90°F 19
Zero Degree Days 1
Precipitation (inches) 46.0
Snow (inches) 12.0
% Seasonal Humidity 71.0
Wind Speed (m.p.h.) 7.3
Clear Days 95
Cloudy Days 163
Storm Days 47
Rainy Days 128

Average Temperatures (°F)	High	Low	Mean
January	48.9	32.2	40.6
February	52.0	83.5	42.8
March	60.4	39.4	49.9
April	72.0	48.6	60.3
May	79.8	56.9	68.4
June	86.1	64.8	75.5
July	88.0	68.3	78.2
August	87.3	67.2	77.3
September	82.0	61.2	71.6
October	71.8	50.0	60.9
November	58.9	39.4	49.2
December	49.8	33.1	41.5

frontiersmen, who are reported to have camped for one night within the present city limits. The following year Colonel John Donelson's flatboat flotilla passed down the river on the way to the Cumberland settlement. In the summer of 1783 James White, Robert Love, and F. A. Ramsey surveyed the region looking for land on which to stake a claim. Two years later the State of Franklin—an independent state formed by the settlers along the Watagua river who were angry at the federal and North Carolina governments when North Carolina ceded their western territory to the federal government—established Sevier and Caswell counties, including the Knoxville area in the latter. This territory would later become Tennessee. In 1785 the Dumplin Treaty between the Franklin government and the Cherokee opened the door to settlers. James White was the first settler to take advantage of the treaty, and he became the first permanent settler of Knoxville. His log cabin was connected with three others by a high palisade of logs, thus making a frontier outpost known as White's Fort. In 1790 William Blount, commissioned as governor of the Territory South of the River Ohio and Superintendent of Indian Affairs, came to Tennessee and established his headquarters in White's settlement. After the Treaty of Holston settled the claims of the Cherokee, Blount had White lay out streets. The new town was named Knoxville, in honor of Major General Henry Knox, the secretary of war. In 1792, Knox County was spun off from Caswell county, and Knoxville was made the county seat. The Knoxville Gazette. was established as a weekly newspaper in 1791. In 1793 a ferry to the southern settlements on the Tennessee River began operation. That same year the first Presbyterian

Church was organized. A post office followed in 1795, the year a wagon road was completed between Knoxville and Nashville. On 1 June 1796, Tennessee was admitted to the Union with Knoxville as the state capital. It remained the state capital until 1812, when the government was moved to Nashville. It was the seat of the legislature again from 1817 to 1819. Despite its prominence as a seat of government, Knoxville was known in the early days as little more than an outpost for outlaws, frontiersmen, woodsmen, gamblers, and flatboatmen. Among the most notorious of the outlaws were the two Harpe brothers, Micajah (Big Harpe) and Wiley (Little Harpe), who terrorized the town for two years until the former was killed and the latter hanged in 1799. Among Knoxville's early industrial establishments were gristmills, sawmills, tanyards, cotton-spinning factories, wool-carding mills, and a brass foundry, all of which were on the banks of the two creeks east and west of the business area. Steamboat navigation to New Orleans was inaugurated in 1828 but was hampered by an obstruction in the channel of the Tennessee River at Muscle Shoals. The growth of the town was slow; in the 1850 census it had a population of only 2,076. The 1850s brought the railways into town: the East Tennessee and Georgia Railroad in 1855 and the East Tennessee and Virginia Railroad in 1858. The Civil War was a particularly painful interregnum for Knoxville. The majority of East Tennesseans were loyal to the Union, and Tennessee was the last to join the Confederate States. To suppress Unionist opposition, a Confederate army of some 10,000 troops was sent to East Tennessee in 1861, and troops were headquartered at Knoxville. Some 1,500 Union sympathizers were arrested and imprisoned, while others fled to Kentucky. When the Confederate troops were withdrawn in August 1863 to be mobilized at Chattanooga, 20,000 Union troops under Major General A. E. Burnside seized Knoxville. Three months later, a Confederate army under General James A. Longstreet tried to recapture Knoxville. The city was besieged, but the Union forces resisted stubbornly. The final Confederate attack on November 29 was repulsed, with heavy losses for the Confederates. The siege was lifted a few days later, but by then the loss in property was enormous. Entire sections of the city had been burned down. When peace was established, however, Knoxville rebuilt rapidly, and the city expanded both in numbers and in industrial resources. With new iron plants, cloth mills, furniture factories, marble quarries, and foundries, Knoxville emerged as a major southern commercial center. In the 20th century Knoxville has gone through a cycle of depression and expansion. By 1917, when the population approached 80,000, the city limits had been expanded from 3.9 to 26.4 square miles. During the Depression Knoxville was hard hit by the closure of banks and industries as well as by inept political leadership, but during the New Deal it shared the general revival of prosperity as the state gained the Tennessee Valley Authority. World War II helped to consolidate these gains with the location here of other mega pro-

Chronology

1761 Henry Timberlake, Thomas Sumter, and John McCormack pass through the area on a goodwill mission to the Overhill Cherokee.

1779 Col. Evan Shelby and a band of frontiersmen camp for one night within city limits.

1780 John Donelson's flatboat flotilla passes down the river on the way to the Cumberland settlement.

1783 James White, Robert Love, and F. A. Ramsey survey the Knoxville region looking for suitable land for settlement.

1785 Knoxville region is included in Caswell County, established by the Franklin State. The Dumplin Treaty with the Cherokee opens the region for white settlement.

1786 James White becomes first permanent settler of Knoxville when he builds a log cabin here. Connected with other log cabins by a palisade, the settlement becomes a frontier outpost called White's Fort.

1790 William Blount, appointed governor of the Territory South of the River Ohio, comes to Tennessee and establishes headquarters at White's settlement. By the Treaty of Holston, Indians cede their lands to the government. On Blount's suggestion, White lays out the streets of a new town called Knoxville after Major General Henry Knox, the secretary of war.

1791 *Knoxville Gazette* debuts.

1792 Knox County is spun off from Green and Hawkins counties with Knoxville as its seat.

1793 Ferry on the Tennessee River begins operation. Presbyterian Church is founded.

1795 Post office opens, and road is built linking Knoxville with Nashville.

1796 Tennessee is admitted to the Union with Knoxville as its capital.

1812 State capital is transferred from Knoxville to Nashville.

1817 State capital returns to Knoxville for two years.

1828 Steam navigation to New Orleans is inaugurated.

1855 East Tennessee and Georgia Railroad is completed.

1858 East Tennessee and Virginia Railroad reaches town.

1861 Tennessee secedes from Union although majority of East Tennesseans were loyal to the Union. A 10,000-strong Confederate army occupies Knoxville. Union sympathizers are arrested.

1863 When Confederate troops are withdrawn, Union troops commanded by Major General A. E. Burnside occupy Knoxville. Confederate army under General James A. Longstreet attempts to retake Knoxville. Union forces successfully withstand the 10-day siege and final assault. The siege is lifted and Confederate troops leave.

1917 The city limits are expanded from 3.9 to 26.4 square miles.

1982 World's Fair is held in Knoxville.

jects, such as the Oak Ridge National Laboratory and companies like Alcoa Alumi-1num. The influx of federal money meant more jobs, more building, and more sales. Despite this, the city entered another period of stagnation in the 1960s. Urban redevelopment programs initiated by a new generation of civic leaders, however, managed to stem the tide. The city's efforts to make a comeback culminated in the World's Fair of 1982.

Historical Landmarks

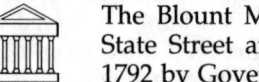 The Blount Mansion on the corner of State Street and Hill Avenue, built in 1792 by Governor William Blount, was the first frame house west of the Alleghenies. The Jackson House on State Street, built in 1800 of red clay bricks made in pioneer kilns, was the home of George Jackson. The Hunter-Kennedy House on Church Avenue, erected in 1820 by James Kennedy of Pennsylvania, was the center of a complete self-sustaining economic community with black slaves producing everything on the property. The First Presbyterian Church on the corner of Gay Street and Clinch Avenue, completed in 1901, houses the oldest church in Knoxville (organized in 1793) and is the third building on the site. It was begun by James White, the city's founding father, who was also the presiding elder. Chisholm's Tavern on Front Avenue was built in 1792 by Captain John Chisholm, soldier of fortune. The Knox County Courthouse is a massive two-story steel-frame structure erected in 1885. Nearby stone markers designate the site of the military blockhouse erected in 1793 and the Treaty of Holston, signed here in 1791. The Cumberland Hotel on Gay Street, erected in 1854 as Schubert's House, occupies the site of John Stone's Log Tavern. The Market House on Market Street is on a tract of land donated to the city in 1853 by William G. Swan and Joseph A. Mabry to be maintained as a free market for farmers. The Park House on Cumberland Avenue was erected in 1798 by John Sevier, first governor of Tennessee. The Dickinson-Atkins House

on Main Avenue was begun by Perez Dickinson in 1830 and completed in 1901 by C. Brown Atkins. Melrose on Melrose Place was built in 1858 with slave labor by John J. Craig, who named it Lucknow. In 1865 it was bought by O. P. Temple, who renamed it Melrose. Longueval, also called Crescent Bend, on Kingston Pike, was built in 1823 as a plantation home by Drury P. Armstrong. Bleak House, on Kingston Pike, named for the novel by Charles Dickens, is a two-story brick structure with a cupola. It was the headquarters of the Confederate General James A. Longstreet during the Siege of Knoxville. James White's Fort with its seven log cabins is still standing on a bluff high above the Tennessee River near downtown.

Population

After peaking at about 175,000, the population of Knoxville has declined in the 1980s. In 1970, 1980, and 1990 its population was 175,000, 175,045, and 165,121, respectively. The percentage of change during the 1980s was -5.7%.

Population

	1980	1990
Central City	175,045	165,121
Rank	77	102
Metro Area	565,970	604,816
Pop. Change 1980–1990	-9,924	
Pop. % Change 1980–1990	-5.7	
Median Age	32.4	
% Male	46.7	
% Age 65 and Over	15.41	
Density (per square mile)	2,136	

Households

Number 69,973
Persons per Household 2.20
% Female-Headed Households 14.3
% One-Person Households 35.5
Births—Total 2,259
  % to Mothers under 20 17.8
  Birth Rate per 1,000 13.0

Ethnic Composition

Whites make up 82.7% of the population, blacks 15.8%, American Indians 0.2%, Asians and Pacific Islanders 1.0%, and others 0.2%.

Ethnic Composition (as % of total pop.)

	1980	1990
White	84.24	82.73
Black	14.62	15.78
American Indian	0.16	0.24
Asian and Pacific Islander	0.53	1.04
Hispanic	0.69	0.67
Other	NA	0.21

Government

Knoxville operates under a mayor-council form of government. The mayor and nine council members are elected to four-year terms.

Government

Year of Home Charter NA
Number of Members of the Governing Body 9
Elected at Large NA
Elected by Wards 9
Number of Women in Governing Body 1
Salary of Mayor $50,000
Salary of Council Members $6,000
City Government Employment Total 5,936
Rate per 10,000 342.7

Public Finance

The annual budget consists of revenues of $468.7 million and expenditures of $447.083 million. The debt outstanding is $302.377 million, and cash and security holdings $376.878 million.

Public Finance

Total Revenue (in millions) $468.7
Intergovernmental Revenue—Total (in millions) $42.46
Federal Revenue per Capita $2.46
% Federal Assistance 0.53
% State Assistance 3.93
Sales Tax as % of Total Revenue 1.69
Local Revenue as % of Total Revenue 25.45
City Income Tax no
Taxes—Total (in millions) $43.7

Taxes per Capita
  Total $252
  Property $213
  Sales and Gross Receipts $26
General Expenditures—Total (in millions) $143.5
General Expenditures per Capita $829
Capital Outlays per Capita $69

% of Expenditures for:
  Public Welfare 0.4
  Highways 1.4
  Education 42.1
  Health and Hospitals 0.0
  Police 9.3
  Sewerage and Sanitation 12.7
  Parks and Recreation 4.7
  Housing and Community Development 3.9
Debt Outstanding per Capita $1,211
  % Utility 21.1
Federal Procurement Contract Awards (in millions) $111.3
Federal Grants Awards (in millions) $38.4
Fiscal Year Begins July 1

Economy

The centerpieces of the Knoxville economy are the Tennessee Valley Authority and the Oak Ridge National Laboratory. These institutions have spawned a host of new technologies that are funneled to private industry, with

Knoxville as a major beneficiary. Called the Energy Capital of America, Oak Ridge supports a network of high-tech facilities. Along with Martin Marietta Energy Systems, TVA, and the University of Tennessee, it has been instrumental in bringing to the area consortiums such as Power Electronics Application Center and the Ceramics Advanced Manufacturing Development and Engineering Center. Between 1980 and 1990 $302 million was invested in 38 new industrial plants. Other key sectors of the economy are transportation and tourism.

Economy

Total Money Income (in millions) $1,634.7
% of State Average 101.6
Per Capita Annual Income $9,438
% Population below Poverty Level 19.6
Fortune 500 Companies

Banks	Number	Deposits (in millions)
Commercial	7	1,594
Savings	7	788.7

Passenger Autos 255,100
Electric Meters 140,685
Gas Meters 23,163

Manufacturing

Number of Establishments 332
% with 20 or More Employees 33.7
Manufacturing Payroll (in millions) $334.7
Value Added by Manufacture (in millions) $944.8
Value of Shipments (in millions) $1,957.1
New Capital Expenditures (in millions) $41.4

Wholesale Trade

Number of Establishments 753
Sales (in millions) $3,129.0
Annual Payroll (in millions) $203.653

Retail Trade

Number of Establishments 2,877
Total Sales (in millions) $2,227.3
Sales per Capita $12,859
Number of Retail Trade Establishments with Payroll 2,008
Annual Payroll (in millions) $255.2
Total Sales (in millions) $2,185.3
General Merchandise Stores (per capita) $1,783
Food Stores (per capita) $2,156
Apparel Stores (per capita) $753
Eating and Drinking Places (per capita) $1,306

Service Industries

Total Establishments 2,142
Total Receipts (in millions) $838.4
Hotels and Motels (in millions) $45.6
Health Services (in millions) $266.8
Legal Services (in millions) $76.4

Labor

The economy is sustained by the availability of a highly skilled and trained labor force. Knoxville has one of the lowest rates of absenteeism and turnover in the nation. A number of local companies have won awards for productivity and quality. Among the largest private employers are Martin Marietta, Levi Strauss, ALCOA, Clayton Homes, and UPS.

Labor

Civilian Labor Force 86,974
% Change 1989–1990 0.4

Work Force Distribution
   Mining 1,300
   Construction 11,600
   Manufacturing 50,900
   Transportation and Public Utilities 10,400
   Wholesale and Retail Trade 71,300
   FIRE (Finance, Insurance, Real Estate) 9,700
   Service 64,400
   Government 52,600
   Women as % of Labor Force 46.0
   % Self-Employed 4.7
   % Professional/Technical 18.7
Total Unemployment 4,156
Rate % 4.8
Federal Government Civilian Employment 6,904

Education

The Knox County Public School System supports 89 regular schools, 2 special education schools, and 2 vocational schools. In addition, there are 20 parochial and private schools. The largest and most influential higher education facility is the main campus of the University of Tennessee, founded in 1794. Associated with the Oak Ridge National Laboratory and the Tennessee Valley Authority, the university is one of the leading 100 research universities in the nation. Other colleges and universities in the area include Carson-Newman College, Knoxville College, and Maryville College.

Education

Number of Public Schools 93
Special Education Schools 2
Total Enrollment 50,750
% Enrollment in Private Schools 4.5
% Minority 14.3
Classroom Teachers 2,919
Pupil-Teacher Ratio 17.3:1
Number of Graduates 3,100
Total Revenue (in millions) $147.347
Total Expenditures (in millions) $148.037
Expenditures per Pupil $2,507
Educational Attainment (Age 25 and Over)
   % Completed 12 or More Years 61.4
   % Completed 16 or More Years 17.4
Four-Year Colleges and Universities 2
   Enrollment 26,680
Two-Year Colleges 3
   Enrollment 6,619

Libraries

Number 38
Public Libraries 17
Books (in thousands) 640.6
Circulation (in thousands) 1,638
Persons Served (in thousands) 343
Circulation per Person Served 4.77
Income (in millions) $3.979
Staff 131

Four-Year Colleges and Universities
   University of Tennessee
   Knoxville College

Health

Knoxville has eight general-use hospitals, of which the largest are the University of Tennessee Memorial Research Center and Hospital of Knoxville with 602 beds, Fort Sanders Park West Medical Center with 350 beds, St. Mary's Medical Center with 530 beds, East Tennessee Baptist Hospital with 425 beds, Fort Sanders Regional Medical Center with 575 beds, and East Tennessee Children's Hospital with 125 beds. Northwest General Hospital provides osteopathic and podiatry services. Lakeshore Mental Health specializes in psychiatric services.

Health

Deaths—Total	1,922
Rate per 1,000	11.0
Infant Deaths—Total	27
Rate per 1,000	12.0
Number of Metro Hospitals	8
Number of Metro Hospital Beds	2,931
Rate per 100,000	1,692
Number of Physicians	1,082
Physicians per 1,000	2.03
Nurses per 1,000	13.98
Health Expenditures per Capita	$20.06

Transportation

Three interstates intersect at Knoxville: the east-west I-40, the north-south I-75, and the north-east I-81. Interstate 640 circles the city to the north. In addition Knoxville is served by U.S. 11, 25W, 70, 129, and 441; and State Highways 33, 71, 127, and 139. Rail freight service is provided by Louisville-Nashville, Norfolk, Southern, and CSX/Seaboard. The Tennessee navigation channel, at whose head Knoxville is located, is an important transportation artery. The river is part of the Interconnected Inland Water System, which links Knoxville with 21 states, the Mississippi River, and the Great Lakes. Six active river terminals handle barge shipments. Knoxville is an inland port of entry and has a Foreign Trade Zone. The principal air terminal is McGhee Tyson Airport, 15 minutes south of downtown.

Transportation

Interstate Highway Mileage	44
Total Urban Mileage	1,431
Total Daily Vehicle Mileage (in millions)	7.950
Daily Average Commute Time	49.9 min.
Number of Buses	50
Port Tonnage (in millions)	0.380
Airports	1
Number of Daily Flights	29
Daily Average Number of Passengers	1,320

Airlines (American carriers only)
Delta
Northwest
Westair
USAir

Housing

Of the total housing stock 49.9% is owner-occupied. The median value of an owner-occupied home is $49,800, and the median monthly rent is $261.

Housing

Total Housing Units	76,453
% Change 1980–1990	4.2
Vacant Units for Sale or Rent	4,788
Occupied Units	69,973
% with More Than One Person per Room	2.3
% Owner-Occupied	49.9
Median Value of Owner-Occupied Homes	$49,800
Average Monthly Purchase Cost	$285
Median Monthly Rent	$261
New Private Housing Starts	452
Value (in thousands)	$19,001
% Single-Family	76.3
Nonresidential Buildings Value (in thousands)	$18,050

Urban Redevelopment

Urban redevelopment is coordinated by Knoxville/Knox County Metropolitan Planning Commission and the Knoxville Community Development Corporation.

Crime

Knoxville ranks very high in public safety, being placed 73rd out of 333 cities in this respect.

Crime

Violent Crimes—Total	2,764
Violent Crime Rate per 100,000	627.9
Murder	35
Rape	123
Robbery	668
Aggravated Assaults	1,938
Property Crimes	12,765
Burglary	3,984
Larceny	6,639
Motor Vehicle Theft	2,142
Arson	172
Per Capita Police Expenditures	$97.01
Per Capita Fire Protection Expenditures	$96.83
Number of Police	288
Per 1,000	1.64

Religion

Knoxville is part of the Bible Belt and is one of the strongholds of the Baptist denomination. Methodists and Presbyterians are also strong.

Religion

Largest Denominations (Adherents)	
Catholic	10,356
Southern Baptist	125,315
United Methodist	30,876
Presbyterian	10,589
American Zion	9,211

Religion (continued)	
Episcopal	4,814
Black Baptist	9,237
Assembly of God	1,250
Jewish	748

Media

The city daily is the *Knoxville News-Sentinel*. The electronic media consist of four television stations and 19 AM and FM radio stations.

Media

Newsprint
    Knoxville News-Sentinel, daily

Television
    WATE (Channel 6)
    WBIR (Channel 10)
    WKCH (Channel 43)
    WKXT (Channel 8)

Radio

WEMG (AM)	WEZK (FM)
WHGG (FM)	WHJM (AM)
WIMZ (FM)	WIMZ (AM)
WITA (AM)	WIVK (AM)
WIVK (FM)	WKCS (FM)
WKXV (AM)	WMYU (FM)
WNOX (FM)	WOKI (FM)
WQBB (AM)	WRJZ (AM)
WUOT (FM)	WUTK (AM)
WUTK (FM)	

Sports

Knoxville has no major professional sports team. The Blue Jays, an AA team in the Southern League, are the local sports heroes along with the University of Tennessee Volunteers, who play at the Neyland Stadium. The new 25,000-seat Thompson-Boling Arena is the home of the basketball team.

Arts, Culture, and Tourism

The hub of cultural Knoxville is the Art Park, located downtown, which includes the Elm Tree Theater. Its companion institution in Oak Ridge is the Oak Ridge Art Center. Musical entertainment is provided by the Knoxville Symphony Orchestra playing in the Tennessee Theater, Knoxville Chamber Orchestra playing in the Bijou Theater, Knoxville Opera Company, Civic Music Association, Oak Ridge Symphony Orchestra, and Oak Ridge Chorus. Dance is represented by the Appalachian Ballet, Metropolitan Dance Theater, Knoxville Ballet, Sidewalk Dance Theater, and the Children's Dance Ensemble. The University of Tennessee's Center for Theater Excellence, including the Clarence Brown Theater and Carousel Theater, and the Maryville College's Playhouse and Orchestra Series are also active in the performing arts. The Knoxville Civic

Auditorium brings outstanding professional theater to town.

Among the historical museums, the most notable are the East Tennessee Historical Center, the University of Tennessee's McClung Museum, Confederate Memorial Hall, and the Beck Cultural Exchange Center for Black History. The Knoxville Museum of Art is the primary art museum, while the American Museum of Science and Energy is one of the world's largest energy exhibitions.

Travel and Tourism

Hotel Rooms 18,866
Convention and Exhibit Space (square feet) NA

Convention Centers
    Knoxville Convention & Exhibition Center
    Knoxville Civic Auditorium and Coliseum
    Lamar House-Bijou Theater

Festivals
    Dogwood Arts Festival (spring)
    Artfest (October)
    Watersports Festival (June)
    Greek Festival (May)
    Statehood Day (June)
    Christmas in the City (December)

Parks and Recreation

Knoxville has over 81 playgrounds and parks. The Great Smoky Mountains National Park, only 30 minutes away, is the nation's most visited park. Other parks and recreational areas in the Greater Knoxville region include the Big South Fork National River and Recreational Area, Frozen Head State Natural Area, Norris Dam State Resort Park, Big Ridge State Park, Cumberland Mountain State Park, Panther Creek State Park, Cove Lake State Recreational Area, and Roan Mountain State Resort Park.

Sources of Further Information

Greater Knoxville Chamber of Commerce
301 Church Avenue
Knoxville, TN 37901
(615) 637-4550

Knoxville Area Council for Conventions and Visitors
500 Henley Street
Knoxville, TN 37901
(615) 523-7263

City Hall
City-County Building
Knoxville, TN 37902
(615) 521-2040

Additional Reading

Deaderick, Lucille. *Heart of the Valley: A History of Knoxville*. 1976.

Dodd, Joe. *World Class Politics. Knoxville's 1982 World's Fair. Redevelopment and the Political Process.* 1988.

Isenhour, Judith C. *Knoxville: A Pictorial History.* 1978.

McDonald, Michael J., and Bruce Wheeler. *Knoxville, Tennessee: Continuity and Change in an Appalachian City.* 1983.

Manning, Russ, and Sondra Jamieson. *Historic Knoxville and Knox County.* 1990.

Lansing

Michigan

Location and Topography

N

Lansing is located on a sloping plateau on the Grand River at the mouth of the Red Cedar. Rolling hills surround Lansing and cup it in a shallow bowl. There are no prominent topographical features.

Layout of City and Suburbs

Lansing is dominated by the State Capitol, illuminated by a battery of lights at night. The Grand, Red Cedar, and Sycamore rivers, spanned by numerous bridges, twist across the city. The Red Cedar from the east and the Sycamore from the south flow together and are joined in midtown by the Grand from the west. The rivers pass within two blocks of the State Capitol, near the business district, and then flow through the residential section. Downtown Lansing streets are laid out on a strict grid system, with the capitol as the center. Inter-

state 496 traverses the city from the south and then turns west, while I-69 and I-96 pass the city to the north and south. Grand River Avenue runs diagonally across the city southeast to northwest. Within downtown the major east-west thoroughfares are Saginaw, Michigan, Oakland, Shiawassee, Ionia, Ottawa, Washtenaw, Kalamazoo, and Lenawee. The north-south thoroughfares are Waverly, Logan, Cedar, Pennsylvania, Washington, and Clemens. Michigan State University is located on the south bank of the Red Cedar.

Environment

Environmental Stress Index   2.2
Green Cities Index: Rank   NA
                  Score   NA
Water Quality   Alkaline, soft, fluoridated
    Average Daily Use (gallons per capita)   157
    Maximum Supply (gallons per capita)   340
Parkland as % of Total City Area   NA
% Waste Landfilled/Recycled   67:33
Annual Parks Expenditures per Capita $52.50

Climate

The main climate influence is the Great Lakes wind system. When there is no wind, the weather becomes continental, with marked variations in temperature; when the winds blow, the climate becomes semimarine. Snowfall is heavy, with an average of 47 inches annually. Thunderstorms and tornadoes are not uncommon. The Red Cedar and Grand rivers tend to flood at least once every three years, causing extensive damage.

History

Lansing happened by accident. Until 1847 Detroit was the capital of Michigan, but the 1835 state constitution required a permanent capital to be chosen in 1847. Detroit's

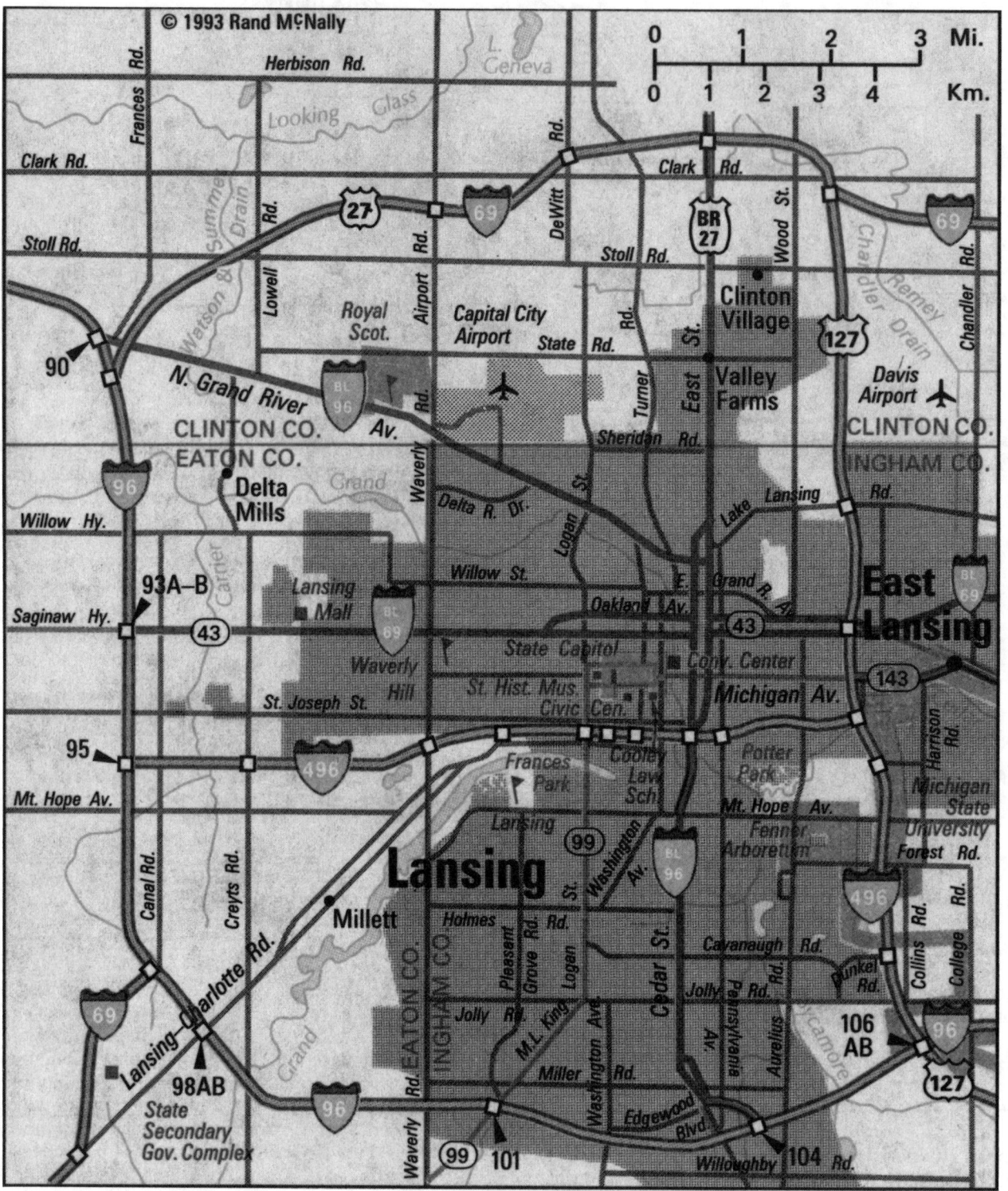

© 1993 Rand McNally

Weather

Temperature

Highest Monthly Average °F   59.1
Lowest Monthly Average °F   38.7

Annual Averages

Days 32°F or Below   149
Days above 90°F   15
Zero Degree Days   5
Precipitation (inches)   30.83
Snow (inches)   47.4
% Seasonal Humidity   85
Wind Speed (m.p.h.)   10.0
Clear Days   65
Cloudy Days   189
Storm Days   37
Rainy Days   134

Average Temperatures (°F)	High	Low	Mean
January	28.1	13.7	20.9
February	37.0	21.8	29.4
March	47.7	27.5	37.6
April	60.0	40.3	50.2
May	75.9	51.5	63.7
June	82.3	56.3	69.3
July	83.0	59.7	71.4
August	81.2	57.4	69.3
September	71.4	45.7	58.6
October	61.7	42.1	51.9
November	43.8	27.1	35.5
December	36.8	20.8	28.8

proximity to Canada and its occupation by the British in 1812 had created legislative concern about retaining the capital in that city. For months the state legislators considered every town in lower Michigan, finally settling on Lansing in desperation. At that time the town had only two buildings—one log house and a sawmill. The township's few families had migrated from the East, most of them from the small village of Lansing in New York, when a shrewd land speculator sold them lots in a city that existed only on paper. Although their dreams were shattered when they arrived at the junction of the Red Cedar and Grand rivers, they decided to stay, naming the place after their hometown in New York. In the 1830s they were joined by another New Yorker, one John Seymour, who bought land for speculation. Seymour successfully persuaded Michigan legislators of Lansing's potential for growth, managing in the process to turn a handsome profit for his land investments. Spurred by its unexpected leap to fame, Lansing grew rapidly. Hotels, stores, and warehouses mushroomed, and one warehouse was converted into a church nicknamed God's Barn. By 1854, when a brick capitol was completed, the town had two potteries, a foundry, a carding mill, and a cooperage. Formal education began as early as 1847 in a rough board shanty, with summer classes held under the trees on the banks of the Grand River. Newspapers were not far behind. The *Lansing Free Press* appeared in 1848. Later it became the *Michigan State Journal* and then *Lansing Journal*. The *Lansing State Republican* was founded in 1855. The first agricultural college was authorized by the state in 1855 and opened in 1857 in

what is now East Lansing under the name of the Michigan Agricultural College. In 1859 Lansing, with a population of 4,000, was incorporated as a city. In 1871 another milestone was the arrival of the railroad. Lansing was a latecomer to manufacturing, being content to rest on its laurels as the state capital. But the arrival of Ransom E. Olds, carriage maker, heralded a new era in the town's industrial history. By 1900 Olds was the world's largest automaker. Soon some 200 manufacturers had established themselves in the area, producing everything from agricultural implements, automobiles, gasoline engines, wheelbarrows, and trucks. Industrial growth led to large-scale in-migration, and by 1930 the city had a population of 80,000.

Historical Landmarks

The State Capitol, between Capitol Avenue and Allegan and Ottawa streets, was built in 1878 in a late Classical Renaissance design. The Michigan Vocational School for Boys on Pennsylvania Avenue was established in 1855 on a 270-acre farm. The Michigan School for the Blind on Grand River Avenue was opened in 1880. The State Office Building on Walnut Street is a seven-story stone structure of neoclassical style.

Population

Reflecting the decreasing number of state employees, Lansing lost population in the 1980s. Its 1990 population was 127,321, a decrease of its 1980 population of 130,414. Lansing is expected to lose population in the next decades, reaching a population of 114,838 in 2010.

Population

	1980	1990
Central City	130,414	127,321
Rank	122	142
Metro Area	419,750	432,674
Pop. Change 1980–1990 -3,093		
Pop. % Change 1980–1990 -2.4		
Median Age 29.7		
% Male 47.4		
% Age 65 and Over 9.6		
Density (per square mile) 3,755		

Households

Number   50,635
Persons per Household   2.50
% Female-Headed Households   16.6
% One-Person Households   29.1
Births—Total   2,566
   % to Mothers under 20   15.3
   Birth Rate per 1,000   20.1

Ethnic Composition

Whites make up 74% of the population, blacks 19%, and Hispanics 8%.

Chronology

1847	Lansing is chosen as the capital of Michigan, although at that time it had only one log house. A wood-frame capitol is erected.
1848	The *Lansing Free Press* is founded.
1854	The wooden capitol is replaced by a brick building.
1855	*Lansing State Republican* is founded.
1857	The Michigan Agricultural College opens.
1859	Lansing is incorporated as a city, population 4,000.
1878	New capitol is erected at a cost of $1.6 million.
1897	Olds Motor Vehicle Company is founded.
1907	East Lansing is chartered as a city.
1955	Michigan State College of Agriculture becomes a university.

Ethnic Composition (as % of total pop.)

	1980	1990
White	80.42	73.94
Black	13.94	18.56
American Indian	0.83	1.02
Asian and Pacific Islander	0.61	1.78
Hispanic	6.32	7.94
Other	NA	4.71

Government

Lansing is governed by a mayor and eight-member council, all elected to four-year terms. The mayor does not serve as member of the council.

Government

Year of Home Charter	NA
Number of Members of the Governing Body	8
Elected at Large	4
Elected by Wards	4
Number of Women in Governing Body	2
Salary of Mayor	$60,661
Salary of Council Members	$10,070
City Government Employment Total	2,459
Rate per 10,000	190.6

Public Finance

The annual budget consists of revenues of $276.859 million and expenditures of $269.875 million. The debt outstanding is $159.271 million, and cash and security holdings are $394.335 million.

Public Finance

Total Revenue (in millions)	$276.859
Intergovernmental Revenue—Total (in millions)	$26.95
Federal Revenue per Capita	$0.859
% Federal Assistance	0.31
% State Assistance	8.39
Sales Tax as % of Total Revenue	NA
Local Revenue as % of Total Revenue	31.13
City Income Tax	yes
Taxes—Total (in millions)	$30.8

Taxes per Capita

Total	$238
Property	$103
Sales and Gross Receipts	$0
General Expenditures—Total (in millions)	$89.3
General Expenditures per Capita	$693
Capital Outlays per Capita	$56

% of Expenditures for:

Public Welfare	0.8
Highways	7.5
Education	0.0
Health and Hospitals	0.0
Police	10.2
Sewerage and Sanitation	20.8
Parks and Recreation	5.1
Housing and Community Development	2.7
Debt Outstanding per Capita	$698
% Utility	15.5
Federal Procurement Contract Awards (in millions)	$6.1
Federal Grants Awards (in millions)	$309.6
Fiscal Year Begins	July 1

Economy

The major economic sectors are manufacturing, services, government, education, finance, and retailing. Lansing is part of the Midwest manufacturing belt, with the bulk of its activity centered in transportation products. General Motors is the region's largest employer, as it has been since 1910 when it took over the Olds Motor Vehicle Company. Other large manufacturing sectors are plastics, nonelectrical machinery, fabricated metal products, food processing, and printing. Among the largest firms are Owens-Illinois, Wyeth-Ayerst, John Henry Co., the Hoover Group, and Dart Container. A small but rapidly growing sector is the medical instruments industry, generated by Michigan State University laboratories. In the services sector the number of firms doubled during the 1980s. The FIRE (finance, insurance, real estate) sector is dominated by the Michigan National Bank and by several insurance companies. Wholesale trade is another large sector

Economy

Total Money Income (in millions)	$1,341.3	
% of State Average	95.4	
Per Capita Annual Income	$10,398	
% Population below Poverty Level	13.1	
Fortune 500 Companies	NA	
Banks	*Number*	*Deposits (in millions)*
Commercial	NA	NA
Savings	21	5,052
Passenger Autos	154,560	
Electric Meters	185,038	
Gas Meters	121,440	

Economy (continued)

Manufacturing

Number of Establishments   150
% with 20 or More Employees   36.0
Manufacturing Payroll (in millions)   NA
Value Added by Manufacture (in millions)   NA
Value of Shipments (in millions)   NA
New Capital Expenditures (in millions)   NA

Wholesale Trade

Number of Establishments   252
Sales (in millions) $1,138.6
Annual Payroll (in millions) $97.665

Retail Trade

Number of Establishments   1,088
Total Sales (in millions)   NA
Sales per Capita   NA
Number of Retail Trade Establishments with Payroll   799
Annual Payroll (in millions) $119.4
Total Sales (in millions) $1,022.5
General Merchandise Stores (per capita)   NA
Food Stores (per capita) $904
Apparel Stores (per capita) $230
Eating and Drinking Places (per capita) $762

Service Industries

Total Establishments   1,009
Total Receipts (in millions) $492.1
Hotels and Motels (in millions)   NA
Health Services (in millions) $NA
Legal Services (in millions) $67.9

due to Lansing's central location and strong transportation network. Of the nearly 600 wholesalers, the largest is the Meijer Distribution Center. Approximately 2,400 retail outlets are dispersed throughout the region. Lansing also is the center of the state's agricultural belt.

Labor

The largest employer in the city is BOC Auto Division, followed by the State of Michigan. Among the top 15 employers only 2 are in manufacturing, while medical, education, and retail employers are more prominent. The metro labor market grew by nearly 8% between 1980 and

Labor

Civilian Labor Force   73,655
% Change 1989–1990   -0.3

Work Force Distribution
   Mining   NA
   Construction   5,900
   Manufacturing   28,900
   Transportation and Public Utilities   6,200
   Wholesale and Retail Trade   47,400
   FIRE (Finance, Insurance, Real Estate)   12,100
   Service   43,700
   Government   69,000
   Women as % of Labor Force   52.2
   % Self-Employed   3.6
   % Professional/Technical   15.3
Total Unemployment   5,309
Rate %   7.2
Federal Government Civilian Employment   1,486

1990, outpacing both Michigan and the nation. Since then, however, employment in government and in the auto industry has fallen and is expected to decline until 2000.

Education

The Lansing School District supports 33 elementary schools, 4 middle schools, 3 senior high schools, and 1 special education school. The metro area has 30 parochial and 5 nonreligious private schools. The largest and oldest institution of higher learning is Michigan State University in East Lansing with an enrollment of over 42,000. The nation's first land-grant institution, it is the only university with three medical colleges.

Education

Number of Public Schools   41
Special Education Schools   1
Total Enrollment   21,390
% Enrollment in Private Schools   7.3
% Minority   44.6
Classroom Teachers   1,428
Pupil-Teacher Ratio   15:1
Number of Graduates   1,106
Total Revenue (in millions) $101
Total Expenditures (in millions) $102
Expenditures per Pupil $4,093
Educational Attainment (Age 25 and Over)
   % Completed 12 or More Years   72.6
   % Completed 16 or More Years   17.3
Four-Year Colleges and Universities   NA
   Enrollment   NA
Two-Year Colleges   1
   Enrollment   22,349

Libraries

Number   22
Public Libraries   3
Books (in thousands)   5,500
Circulation (in thousands)   NA
Persons Served (in thousands)   9,258
Circulation per Person Served   NA
Income (in millions) $1.500
Staff   103

Four-Year Colleges and Universities
   Michigan State University

Health

Six area hospitals serve Lansing's medical needs. The largest is the Edward W. Sparrow Hospital, followed by Ingham Medical Center, St. Lawrence Hospital, and Lansing

Health

Deaths—Total   978
Rate per 1,000   7.6
Infant Deaths—Total   36
Rate per 1,000   14.0
Number of Metro Hospitals   6
Number of Metro Hospital Beds   1,527
Rate per 100,000   1,184
Number of Physicians   626
Physicians per 1,000   NA
Nurses per 1,000   NA
Health Expenditures per Capita   NA

General Hospital (Osteopathic), followed by two smaller hospitals: Clinton Memorial and Eaton Rapids Community.

Transportation

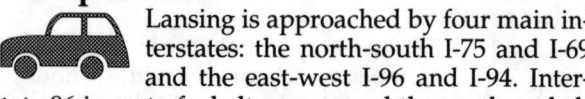

Lansing is approached by four main interstates: the north-south I-75 and I-69 and the east-west I-96 and I-94. Interstate 96 is part of a beltway around the southern half of the city while I-69 completes the beltway around the northern sector. Interstate 496 bisects the downtown area westward from north-south U.S. 127 in East Lansing. Other principal access routes are the north-south U.S. 27 and M-29 and the east-west M-43. The state has all-season green routes, allowing trucks to transport cargo without seasonal load limits or restrictions. The capital city airport is located 15 minutes from downtown. It is served by seven commercial airlines. The nearest international airport is at Grand Rapids, an hour's drive away.

Passenger rail service is provided by Amtrak, with rail freight services accommodated by Conrail, Grand Trunk Western, and CSX Transportation.

Transportation

Interstate Highway Mileage	31
Total Urban Mileage	1,054
Total Daily Vehicle Mileage (in millions)	4.729
Daily Average Commute Time	39.6 min.
Number of Buses	55
Port Tonnage (in millions)	NA
Airports	1
Number of Daily Flights	15
Daily Average Number of Passengers	567

Airlines (American carriers only)
   Air Wisconsin
   Northwest
   USAir

Housing

Most of the residential districts are found in the townships of the Lansing metro region, particularly in East Lansing, Delta, Mason, and Okemos. The average home sale price in Lansing in 1990 was $48,400, and the average monthly rental for a two-bedroom apartment was $460.

Housing

Total Housing Units	53,919
% Change 1980–1990	3.7
Vacant Units for Sale or Rent	2,487
Occupied Units	50,635
% with More Than One Person per Room	3.4
% Owner-Occupied	54.8
Median Value of Owner-Occupied Homes	$48,400
Average Monthly Purchase Cost	$326
Median Monthly Rent	$356
New Private Housing Starts	97
Value (in thousands)	$5,490
% Single-Family	80.4
Nonresidential Buildings Value (in thousands)	$12,094

Urban Redevelopment

Urban redevelopment programs are coordinated by the Industrial Development Institute, the Private Industry Council, and related bodies.

Crime

Of the crimes known to police in 1991, there were 1,768 violent crimes and 8,572 property crimes.

Crime

Violent Crimes—Total	1,768
Violent Crime Rate per 100,000	660.0
Murder	12
Rape	188
Robbery	294
Aggravated Assaults	1,274
Property Crimes	8,572
Burglary	1,759
Larceny	6,218
Motor Vehicle Theft	595
Arson	87
Per Capita Police Expenditures	$107.74
Per Capita Fire Protection Expenditures	$77.70
Number of Police	240
Per 1,000	1.87

Religion

Of the 343 churches in the Lansing region, 61 churches are Baptist, 40 Methodist, 25 Church of God, 24 Lutheran, 17 Catholic, 16 Nazarene, 14 Church of Christ, 11 Pentecostal, 11 Presbyterian, 10 Assembly of God, 9 Episcopalian, 7 Mormon, 21 nondenominational, 9 interdenominational, and 3 Jewish, with the remainder divided among smaller religious groups.

Religion

Largest Denominations (Adherents)	
Catholic	43,976
Black Baptist	9,794
Evangelical Lutheran	4,591
Presbyterian	4,567
United Church of Christ	4,385
Lutheran-Missouri Synod	3,393
American Baptist	4,703
Assembly of God	1,152
Southern Baptist	1,929
Jewish	1,368

Media

The capital's only daily newspaper is the *Lansing State Journal*, published seven days a week. The city's electronic media consists of 3 television channels in the city, four others from Kalamazoo, Battle Creek, and Grand Rapids, and 11 AM and FM stations.

Media

Newsprint
   Lansing State Journal, daily

Television
   WILX (Channel 10)
   WLNS (Channel 6)
   WSYM (Channel 47)

Radio
   KIBM (FM)   WILS (AM)
   WKKP (FM)   WLYY (FM)
   WITL (AM)   WITL (FM)
   WJIM (AM)   WJIM (FM)
   WMMQ (FM)   WVIC (FM)
   WXLA (AM)

Sports

Lansing is represented in football by the Michigan State Spartans, who play their home games at 76,000-seat Spartan Stadium. The Munn Ice Arena is the home of the Spartan hockey team, while the basketball team plays in the Jennison Field House. The Lansing Laurels are considered the nation's premier women's softball team. The Spartan Speedway is the scene of racing on Friday nights from mid-May through September.

Arts, Culture, and Tourism

The premier theater is Boarshead Theater, based at the Center for the Arts. It holds the Winterfare festival of new plays every January. Other local theater companies are the Lansing Civic Players Guild, Riverwalk Players, and the Michigan State University Performing Arts Company. The Greater Lansing Symphony Orchestra presents a season of classical and pops concerts under Gustav Meier. The Wharton Center for the Performing Arts on the campus of Michigan State University, a major cultural resource, offers a full schedule of Broadway plays in the 2,500-seat Great Hall or the 600-seat Festival Stage. Happendance, the oldest troupe in the region, presents contemporary works. Childen's Ballet Theater annually stages *The Nutcracker*. Pashami Dancers present Afro-American performances in traditional dress.

The Historical Center Museum, two blocks southwest of the State Capitol, is a showcase of Michigan history. Michigan history also is on display at the Michigan State Museum. Impressions Five Science Museum is the state's largest participatory museum for children. Lansing's automobile history comes alive at the R. E. Olds Automobile Museum. Michigan Women's Historical Center and Hall of Fame extols the contributions of women to Michigan history. The Lansing–North Lansing Electric Railroad Museum contains models of early–20th-century trolleys and locomotives. Kresge Art Museum on the campus of Michigan State University has an extensive permanent collection and also features changing exhibits. Other museums include the Michigan Museum of Surveying, Nakomis Learning Center, and the Telephone Pioneer Museum.

Travel and Tourism

Hotel Rooms   3,574
Convention and Exhibit Space (square feet)   NA

Convention Centers
   Lansing Center
   Lansing Civic Arena

Festivals
   Boarshead Theater Winterfare (January)
   Sugar Bush Festival (March)
   Lansing Art Fair (June)
   Michigan Festival (August)
   Riverfest (Labor Day)

Parks and Recreation

Lansing has 120 parks with over 2,700 acres of parkland. The largest is the 100-acre Potter Park and Zoo, which was deeded to the city in 1913 by James W. Potter. It contains over 120 animal species. The three-acre Central Park on Capitol Avenue is beautifully wooded with elms and maples. It contains the Reutter Memorial Fountain. The 20-acre Ranney Park on Michigan Avenue was donated by George E. Ranney in 1917. Frances Park on Moores River Drive contains the All-American Rose Garden. River Trail consists of six miles of public parkland along the banks of the Red Cedar and Grand rivers extending to the campus of Michigan State University. Fenner Arboretum and Nature Center has a system of self-guided nature trails. Other natural resources include the 3,000-acre Rose Lake Wildlife Research Center, the 188-acre Woldumar Nature Center along the Grand River, and the Ledges in Grand Ledge, 300-million year-old majestic rock formations jutting from the shore of the Grand River.

Sources of Further Information

Convention and Visitors Bureau of Greater Lansing
  Civic Center
Lansing, MI 48933
(517) 487-6800

Lansing Public Library
401 South Capitol Avenue
Lansing, MI 48933
(517) 374-4600

Lansing Regional Chamber of Commerce
510 West Washtenaw
Lansing, MI 48901
(517) 587-6340

Library of Michigan
735 East Michigan Avenue
Lansing, MI 48909
(517) 373-1593

Additional Reading

Metropolitan Profile. 1991.

Las Vegas

Nevada

Basic Data

Name   Las Vegas
Name Origin   From Spanish for "the meadows"
Year Founded   1867 Inc. 1911
Status: State   Nevada
      County   Seat of Clark County
Area (square miles)   83.3
Elevation (feet)   2,030
Time Zone   Pacific
Population (1990)   258,295
Population of Metro Area (1990)   741,459

Distance in Miles To:

Atlanta	1,979
Boston	2,752
Chicago	1,780
Dallas	1,230
Denver	758
Detroit	2,020
Houston	1,467
Los Angeles	272
Miami	2,570
New York	2,572
Philadelphia	2,481
Washington, DC	2,420

Location and Topography

Las Vegas is located in the center of the Las Vegas Valley, a desert surrounded by the Sierra Nevada and Spring mountains. The valley is in the southernmost section of Nevada, just east of the California boundary, and is bordered on the north by Nellis Air Force Base and on the east by Lake Mead and the Hoover Dam. The terrain is typical desert-flat, with few topographical landmarks.

Layout of City and Suburbs

Las Vegas is known mostly for its main attraction—gambling. Casinos abound on the main thoroughfare, Las Vegas Boulevard, known as the Strip. It is a four-mile glitzy avenue of casinos from the Hacienda in the south to Vegas World at the northern tip. Another thoroughfare, Paradise Road, runs parallel to the Strip and is a two-mile run dominated by such hotels as the Mardi Gras and the Las Vegas Hilton.

The rest of Las Vegas proper is located in an eight-block square ringed by Main Street, Stewart Avenue, Carson Street, and Fourth Street, and is centered by Las Vegas Boulevard. Downtown is made up primarily of a grid system, with the Union Plaza Hotel at the head of Fremont Street, and the Las Vegas History Museum at the northern part of the area near Washington Avenue. The city is intersected by primary roads such as Interstate 93/95, known as the Gragson Highway, and I-15.

Environment

Environmental Stress Index   3.8
Green Cities Index: Rank   59
            Score   38.75
Water Quality   Alkaline, hard
    Average Daily Use (gallons per capita)   300
    Maximum Supply (gallons per capita)   772
Parkland as % of Total City Area   2.8
% Waste Landfilled/Recycled   NA
Annual Parks Expenditures per Capita $48.02

Climate

The mountains surrounding Las Vegas reach elevations of 10,000 feet and act as barriers to moisture from the Pacific Ocean. As a result Las Vegas sees very few overcast or

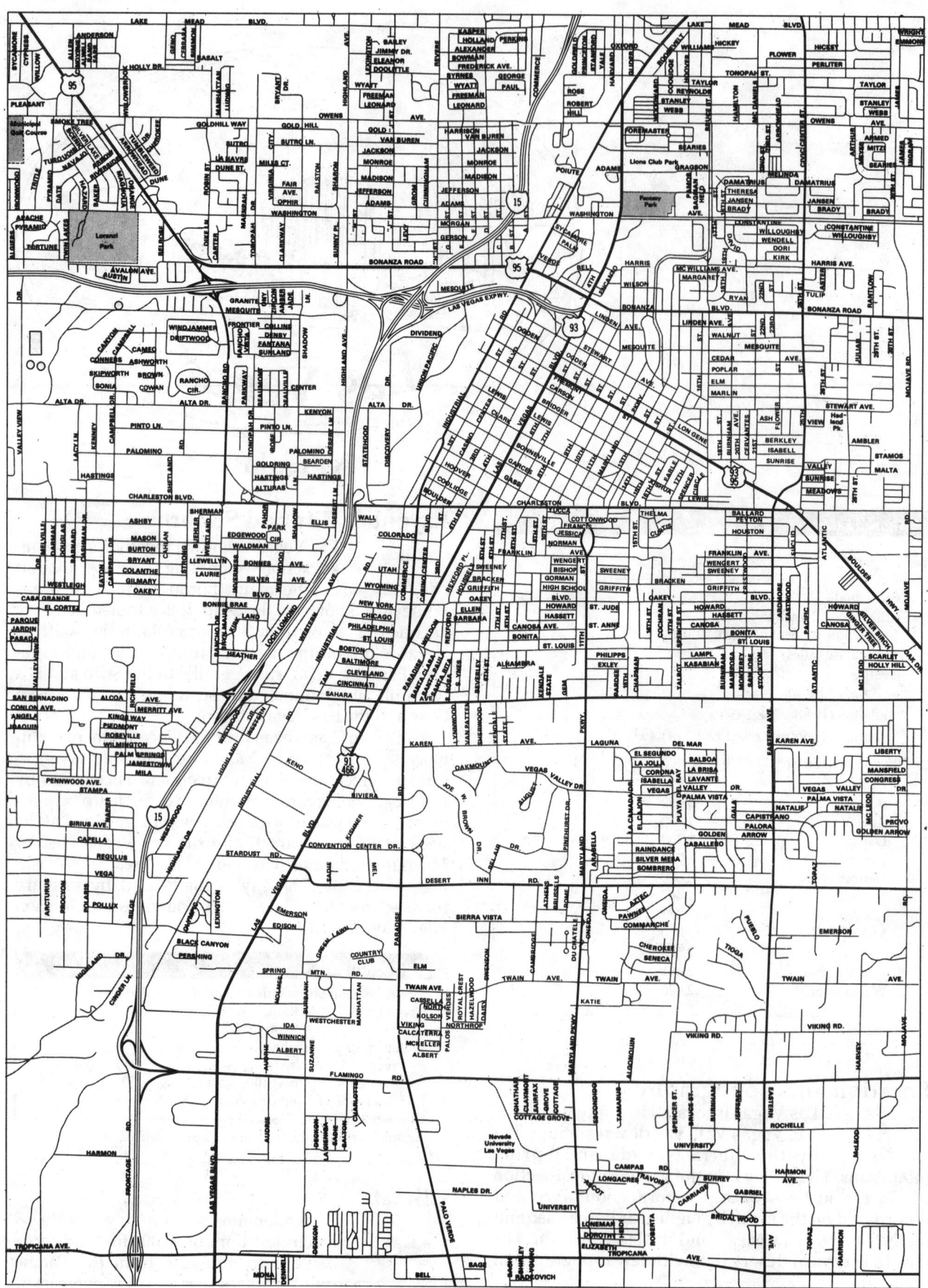

rainy days. The influence of the desert is seen in the hot summer days, when the mercury generally hits 100°F, but the humidity is low and the nights are cool. The winters are mild and snowfall is rare.

Weather			
Temperature			
Highest Monthly Average °F 104.5			
Lowest Monthly Average °F 33.0			
Annual Averages			
Days 32°F or Below 41			
Days above 90°F 131			
Zero Degree Days 0			
Precipitation (inches) 4.0			
Snow (inches) 1.5			
% Seasonal Humidity 29.0			
Wind Speed (m.p.h.) 9.0			
Clear Days 216			
Cloudy Days 65			
Storm Days 15			
Rainy Days 24			
Average Temperatures (°F)	*High*	*Low*	*Mean*
January	55.7	32.6	44.2
February	61.3	36.9	49.1
March	67.8	41.7	54.8
April	77.5	50.0	63.8
May	87.5	59.0	73.3
June	97.2	67.4	82.3
July	103.9	75.3	89.6
August	101.5	73.3	87.4
September	94.8	65.4	80.1
October	81.0	53.1	67.1
November	65.7	40.8	53.3
December	56.7	33.7	45.2

History

The valley has been populated since about 11,000 B.C. by nomadic American Indians. After A.D. 500 the area was taken over by the Anasazi (Navajo word for "ancient ones"). By the year 1000 the Anasazi had simply disappeared from the map, having abandoned the valley. The first white men to visit the valley approached the Paiute Indians in 1776. These men were Franciscan friars, Father Silvestre Escalante and Father Francisco Garces. Fifty years passed before the next white man, fur trapper Jedediah Smith, came through the valley. In 1829 a member of the party of Mexican trader Antonio Armijo came across what he called a grassland meadow—hence Las Vegas (Spanish for "the meadows") became the name of the vicinity.

In 1844 explorer John C. Frémont arrrivd in Las Vegas. He wrote of this camping ground he had found—two narrow streams of water, 4 or 5 feet deep, with a quick current from two singularly large springs. In 1855 Mormon leader Brigham Young sent missionary William Bringhurst and 30 helpers to aid the American Indians in planting crops such as corn, wheat, potatoes, squash, and melons. What Young desired was to make Las Vegas a safe way station on the road from Los Angeles to his outpost in Salt Lake City.

The adobe stockade completed in 1856 was named Bringhurst, but was commonly referred to as the Fort. The Mormons also tried to mine lead, but the enterprise proved economically unfeasible and the mission was abandoned in 1857; a portion of the Fort remains today as the oldest historical landmark in Las Vegas. Following the Mormon departure, the land and water rights were acquired by Octavius Decatur Gass, a gold prospector. In 1864 Fort Baker, a U.S. Army post, was built nearby. In 1867 Las Vegas was detached from Arizona Territory and added to the Nevada Territory. In 1882 the land and water rights to Gass's property were sold to Archibald Stewart, a Scotsman and fortyniner who had made his stake in Gass's camp and later established a cattle ranch about 100 miles north of Las Vegas. In 1903, when the San Pedro, Los Angeles, and Salt Lake Railroad was projected, the Stewart ranch was bought for a townsite and division point by William A. Clark, a former senator from Montana, acting for the railroad company. Near the railroad townsite, another site was acquired by J. T. McWilliams and named McWilliamstown. On 15 May 1905 Las Vegas was born when 1,200 lots in the city were auctioned to prospective settlers for a total price of $225,000. For the next 30 days Las Vegas was a tent town, but soon stores and houses sprouted, roads were laid, and the water supply system was built. With the completion of the railroad from Salt Lake City in 1905, the town became fully established, and the next year it became the seat of Clark County. The town was incorporated in 1911.

In 1931 two events occurred that made Las Vegas what it is today. Construction of the Hoover Dam (Boulder Dam) on the Colorado River began to bring thousands of workers to the city. In the same year casino gambling was legalized, laying the foundation for the emergence of the city as the entertainment capital of the West. The city struggled as a small frontier town until 1946, when Benjamin "Bugsy" Siegel, a mobster from New York, saw Las Vegas's potential for immense profits and opened his Flamingo Hotel. The rest is history. The Strip where Siegel began his own short-lived empire would become the most glittering showplace in the nation, eventually bringing in billions of dollars a year in revenues.

Historical Landmarks

Although mostly a modern city, Las Vegas does have several historical landmarks. Among these are the Old Mormon Fort on Las Vegas Boulevard, which is the only surviving portion of structures erected by Mormon colonists in 1855 and 1856; the Railroad Storehouse Building on Dividend Drive, an original railroad complex built in 1910; the Victory Hotel, the oldest (1910) hotel remaining in Las Vegas; the Union Plaza Hotel, which stands on the former site of the Vegas Depot; the post office on East Stewart, built in 1933 as part of the New Deal's building boom; and the Huntridge Theatre, built in 1944 and once owned by movie star Irene Dunne.

Chronology

500–1000	Anasazi Indians occupy the Vegas valley.
1000–1776	The nomadic Paiute Indians create a culture on the site the Anasazi had abandoned.
1776	Franciscan friars Silvestre Escalante and Francisco Garces become the first known white men to visit the area now known as Las Vegas.
1826	American explorer Jedediah Smith visits the Vegas valley.
1830	A member of Mexican explorer Antonio Armijo's team comes across a grassland meadow, and names the site Las Vegas, Spanish for "the meadows."
1844	Explorer John C. Fremont visits the site of Las Vegas.
1855	William Bringhurst leads a band of 30 Mormons to the site and builds a fort, mission, post office, and school.
1857	Mormons abandon the settlement. Octavius Decatur Gass acquires land and water rights in the settlement.
1864	Fort Baker, a U.S. Army post, is built nearby.
1867	Las Vegas is detached from Arizona Territory and attached to Nevada.
1882	Archibald Stewart acquires land and water rights from Gass and establishes a ranch.
1903	William A. Clark acquires ranch from Stewart's widow on behalf of the San Pedro, Los Angeles, and Salt Lake Railroad, and J. T. McWilliams acquires nearby townsite, now Old Town.
1905	The city is born when 1,200 lots are auctioned. Buildings and stores rise in center of town. Railroad from Salt Lake is completed at Jean, near the California border.
1910	Rainstorm destroys 110 miles of railroad track.
1911	Las Vegas is incorporated.
1931	Construction begins on the Hoover (Boulder) Dam. Gambling is legalized.
1946	Mobster Benjamin "Bugsy" Siegel opens the Flamingo Hotel, paving the way for making Las Vegas the gambling and tourist mecca of the nation.

Population

Las Vegas's demographic growth is a post–World War II phenomenon. From slightly less than 8,500 people in 1940, the population jumped to 25,000 in 1950, 65,000 in 1960, 126,000 in 1970, 164,674 in 1980, and 258,295 in 1990. The rate of growth during the 1970s was 30.9%, and for the 1980s 56.9%. Las Vegas has set a record among U.S. cities for consistent growth.

Population		
	1980	*1990*
Central City	164,674	258,295
Rank	89	63
Metro Area	463,087	741,459
Pop. Change 1980–1990 +93.621		
Pop. % Change 1980–1990 +56.9		
Median Age 32.6		
% Male 50.7		
% Age 65 and Over 10.3		
Density (per square mile) 3,100		
Households		
Number 99,735		
Persons per Household 2.55		
% Female-Headed Households 12.0		
% One-Person Households 26.2		
Births—Total 5,433		
% to Mothers under 20 13.9		
Birth Rate per 1,000 29.7		

Ethnic Composition

Whites make up 78.4%, blacks 11.4%, American Indians 0.9%, Asians and Pacific Islanders 3.6%, and others 5.7%.

Ethnic Composition (as % of total pop.)		
	1980	*1990*
White	81.57	78.42
Black	12.78	11.43
American Indian	0.64	0.88
Asian and Pacific Islander	2.03	3.61
Hispanic	7.77	12.53
Other	NA	5.66

Government

Las Vegas is governed under a council-mayor form of government. The mayor and five council members are elected to four-year terms. Power resides, however, in Clark County rather in the city because all the revenue-producing hotels are in the unincorporated part.

Public Finance

The annual budget consists of revenues of $275.431 million and expenditures of $215.946 million. The debt outstanding is $88.745 million, and cash and security holdings are $153.296 million.

Government

Year of Home Charter   NA
Number of Members of the Governing Body   5
Elected at Large   0
Elected by Wards   5
Number of Women in Governing Body   0
Salary of Mayor $41,621.80
Salary of Council Members $31,682.20
City Government Employment Total   1,471
Rate per 10,000   76.8

Public Finance

Total Revenue (in millions) $275.431
Intergovernmental Revenue—Total (in millions) $90.17
Federal Revenue per Capita $4.816
% Federal Assistance   1.75
% State Assistance   24.28
Sales Tax as % of Total Revenue   4.24
Local Revenue as % of Total Revenue   73.97
City Income Tax   no
Taxes—Total (in millions) $26.5

Taxes per Capita
   Total $139
   Property $48
   Sales and Gross Receipts $41
General Expenditures—Total (in millions) $94.0
General Expenditures per Capita $491
Capital Outlays per Capita $67

% of Expenditures for:
   Public Welfare   0.0
   Highways   9.7
   Education   0.0
   Health and Hospitals   0.0
   Police   22.2
   Sewerage and Sanitation   13.5
   Parks and Recreation   5.1
   Housing and Community Development   2.3
Debt Outstanding per Capita $122
   % Utility   0.0
Federal Procurement Contract Awards (in millions)
   $1,224.3
Federal Grants Awards (in millions) $21.5
Fiscal Year Begins   July 1

Economy

Las Vegas's money machine is the gambling casino. In addition to the hotels, gambling generates heavy tourism, bringing in close to $10 billion annually. Entertainment and gaming also sustain a mammoth construction industry. Gambling and hospitality are also the largest employment sector, but the largest single employer is Nellis Air Force Base. Manufacturing made a late start in Las Vegas, but because of the affordability of space has made considerable gains in recent years. Most of the new corporations moving in are engaged in high technology and research.

Economy

Total Money Income (in millions) $2,110
% of State Average   98.1
Per Capita Annual Income $10,990
% Population below Poverty Level   10.5

Economy (continued)

Banks	Number	Deposits (in millions)
Commercial	10	7,699
Savings	5	2,705

Passenger Autos   396,602
Electric Meters   326,757
Gas Meters   146,859

Manufacturing

Number of Establishments   159
% with 20 or More Employees   19.5
Manufacturing Payroll (in millions) $57.2
Value Added by Manufacture (in millions) $138.5
Value of Shipments (in millions) $257.2
New Capital Expenditures (in millions) $7.4

Wholesale Trade

Number of Establishments   349
Sales (in millions) $1,172.3
Annual Payroll (in millions) $82.498

Retail Trade

Number of Establishments   2,236
Total Sales (in millions) $1,920.9
Sales per Capita $10,030
Number of Retail Trade Establishments with Payroll   1,521
Annual Payroll (in millions) $237.9
Total Sales (in millions) $1,883.2
General Merchandise Stores (per capita) $1,063
Food Stores (per capita) $1,932
Apparel Stores (per capita) $473
Eating and Drinking Places (per capita) $1,025

Service Industries

Total Establishments   2,157
Total Receipts (in millions) $2,121.6
Hotels and Motels (in millions) $937.2
Health Services (in millions) $327.9
Legal Services (in millions) $145.0

Labor

The labor force revolves around the Strip, where the gaming hotels are located. To service the entertainment, tourism, and hospitality industries, the economy is in constant need of workers in support sectors such as trade, transportation, finance, insurance, real estate, construction, public utilities, and communications.

Labor

Civilian Labor Force   137,984
% Change 1989–1990   7.1

Work Force Distribution
   Mining   300
   Construction   28,700
   Manufacturing   10,600
   Transportation and Public Utilities   20,300
   Wholesale and Retail Trade   79,500
   FIRE (Finance, Insurance, Real Estate)   18,800
   Service   185,700
   Government   42,200
   Women as % of Labor Force   42.8
   % Self-Employed   4.1
   % Professional/Technical   10.5
Total Unemployment   7,110
Rate %   5.2
Federal Government Civilian Employment   2,717

The work force distribution is unusual: about 2% in manufacturing and 50% in services.

Education

The Clark County School District supports 106 elementary schools, 21 middle schools, 15 senior high schools, and 4 special education schools. Twenty-one private and parochial schools supplement the public school system. The only four-year higher education institution is the University of Nevada at Las Vegas. Its hotel administration program is naturally one of the best in the country.

Education

Number of Public Schools   150
Special Education Schools   4
Total Enrollment   121,984
% Enrollment in Private Schools   5.1
% Minority   30.6
Classroom Teachers   5,864
Pupil-Teacher Ratio   20:1
Number of Graduates   5,692
Total Revenue (in millions) $383.6
Total Expenditures (in millions) $375.8
Expenditures per Pupil $3,314
Educational Attainment (Age 25 and Over)
    % Completed 12 or More Years   72.1
    % Completed 16 or More Years   11.5
Four-Year Colleges and Universities   1
    Enrollment   18,216
Two-Year Colleges   2
    Enrollment   1,090

Libraries

Number   35
Public Libraries   22
Books (in thousands)   861
Circulation (in thousands)   2,190
Persons Served (in thousands)   651
Circulation per Person Served   3.36
Income (in millions) $10.2
Staff   226

Four-Year Colleges and Universities
    University of Nevada-Las Vegas

Health

Las Vegas has 8 major hospitals and over 150 clinics. The largest are the Southern Nevada Memorial Hospital and the Humana-Sunrise Hospital.

Health

Deaths—Total   1,812
Rate per 1,000   9.9
Infant Deaths—Total   31
Rate per 1,000   5.7
Number of Metro Hospitals   8
Number of Metro Hospital Beds   1,828
Rate per 100,000   955
Number of Physicians   785
Physicians per 1,000   1.40
Nurses per 1,000   8.60
Health Expenditures per Capita $7.04

Transportation

Las Vegas is approached by three major highways: I-15, linking the city with Los Angeles and Salt Lake City; U.S. 95, running into the city from the northwest; and U.S. 93/95, entering the city from the southeast. Rail passenger service is provided by Amtrak and rail freight service by Union Pacific. The principal air terminal is the McCarran International Airport, five miles south of the business district.

Transportation

Interstate Highway Mileage   22
Total Urban Mileage   1,844
Total Daily Vehicle Mileage (in millions)   11,757
Daily Average Commute Time   41.6 min.
Number of Buses   18
Port Tonnage (in millions)   NA
Airports   2
Number of Daily Flights   234
Daily Average Number of Passengers   19,251

Airlines (American carriers only)
    American
    American West
    Continental
    Delta
    Hawaiian
    Midway
    Southwest
    Sunworld
    Trans World
    United

Housing

Las Vegas is spread out and sprawling, and therefore lacks the compact neighborhoods many other cities have. Certain areas are considered chic, such as Roncho Circle, where the entertainers live; Quail Park for executives; and the Spanish Trails, a planned community with golf facilities. Of the total housing stock, 50.4% is owner-occupied. The median value of an owner-occupied home is $89,200, and the median monthly rent $434.

Housing

Total Housing Units   109,670
% Change 1980–1990   38.8
Vacant Units for Sale or Rent   8,370
Occupied Units   99,735
% with More Than One Person per Room   7.9
% Owner-Occupied   50.4
Median Value of Owner-Occupied Homes $89,200
Average Monthly Purchase Cost $467
Median Monthly Rent $434
New Private Housing Starts   9,219
Value (in thousands) $438,044
% Single-Family   51.7
Nonresidential Buildings Value (in thousands) $137,999

Tallest Buildings	Hgt. (ft.)	Stories
Fitzgerald Casino-Hotel	400	34
Landmark Hotel	356	31
Las Vegas Hilton	345	30

Urban Redevelopment

Much of the urban redevelopment since World War II has been in the form of hotels and gaming complexes. Public projects are coordinated by the Las Vegas Department of Economic and Urban Development.

Crime

Las Vegas ranks very low in public safety. Of crimes known to police in 1991, there were 5,661 violent crimes and 43,118 property crimes. Much of the high crime rate is due to the transient nature of the population.

Crime

Violent Crimes—Total 5,661
Violent Crime Rate per 100,000 788.1
Murder 103
Rape 433
Robbery 3,193
Aggravated Assaults 1,932
Property Crimes 43,118
Burglary 10,743
Larceny 25,828
Motor Vehicle Theft 6,547
Arson 481
Per Capita Police Expenditures $151.77
Per Capita Fire Protection Expenditures $121.46
Number of Police 1,021
Per 1,000 2.24

Religion

Religion is not a significant force in public life, and only 20% of the population reports church affiliation. There are a number of older Catholic churches as well as newer Protestant and Mormon churches. Of the total church membership, Catholics claim the majority, followed by Mormons and Episcopalians.

Religion

Largest Denominations (Adherents)

Catholic	109,057
Latter-Day Saints	59,081
Black Baptist	18,815
Southern Baptist	17,667
Evangelical Lutheran	6,138
American Baptist	5,784
Assembly of God	4,272
Presbyterian	2,350
United Methodist	4,355
Jewish	19,000

Media

The Las Vegas press consists of two dailies: the *Las Vegas Sun* and the *Las Vegas Review-Journal*. The electronic media consists of 5 television stations, and 25 AM and FM radio stations.

Media

Newsprint
Las Vegas Review-Journal, daily
Las Vegas Sentinel-Voice, weekly
Las Vegas Sun, daily
Nevada Business Journal, monthly

Television
KLAS (Channel 8)
KLVX (Channel 10)
KRLR (Channel 21)
KTNV (Channel 13)
KVBC (Channel 3)

Radio

KCEP (FM)	KDWN (AM)
KENO (AM)	KOMP (FM)
KEYV (FM)	KFMS (AM)
KFMS (FM)	KILA (FM)
KJUL (FM)	KKVV (AM)
KLAV (AM)	KLUC (AM)
KLUC (FM)	KMMK (FM)
KMTW (AM)	KKLZ (FM)
KNPR (FM)	KNUU (AM)
KORK (AM)	KYRK (FM)
KRLV (FM)	KUEG (AM)
KUNV (FM)	KWNR (FM)
KXTZ (FM)	

Sports

Las Vegas does not have a major professional sports team, but it is the home of the University of Las Vegas–Nevada Running Rebels, a leading college basketball team. The city annually hosts a number of competitions in golf and rodeo.

Arts, Culture, and Tourism

Las Vegas is a tinsel town where the glitz of the Strip overshadows normal city culture. Most of the theatrical, musical, and dance performances take place at the casinos themselves—one can see shows and entertainment at any one of the hotels.

Cultural sights outside the mainframe of casinos include the Majorie Barrick Museum of Natural History on the campus of the University of Nevada–Las Vegas (UNLV), the Nevada Banking Museum on Howard Hughes Parkway, the Las Vegas Art Museum at Lorenzi Park on West Washington Street, and the Liberace Museum on East Tropicana (the most popular non-casino attraction in Las Vegas).

Travel and Tourism

Hotel Rooms 12,947
Convention and Exhibit Space (square feet) NA

Convention Centers
Las Vegas Convention Center
Cashman Field Center

Festivals
Helldorado Days (June)
Great Pumpkin Festival (October)
Greek Festival (October)

Parks and Recreation

 The largest of the municipal parks is the Las Vegas City Park, between Stewart and Linden streets.

Sources of Further Information

Greater Las Vegas Chamber of Commerce
711 Desert Inn Road
Las Vegas, NV 89109
(702) 735-1616 or (702) 457-4664

Las Vegas City Hall
400 West Stewart Avenue
Las Vegas, NV 89101
(702) 229-6241

Las Vegas Convention and Visitors Authority
3150 Paradise Road
Las Vegas, NV 89109
(702) 892-0711

Additional Reading

Castleman, Deke. *Las Vegas.* 1991.

Lawlor, Florine. *Out from Las Vegas.* 1970.

Martin, Don W., and Betty Woo Martin. *The Best of Nevada.* 1992.

Moehring, Eugene P. *Resort City in the Sunbelt, 1930–1970.* 1989.

Paher, Stanley W. *Las Vegas: As It Began, As It Grew.* 1971.

Parr, Barry, and Peter Zimmerman. *Las Vegas.* 1991.

Pearl, Ralph. *Las Vegas Is My Beat.* 1978.

Roberts, Martin S., and John L. Hardy. *Only in Las Vegas.* 1987.

Venturi, Robert. *Learning from Las Vegas.* 1977.

Lewiston

Maine

Basic Data

Name Lewiston
Name Origin NA
Year Founded 1770 Inc. 1861
Status: State Maine
        County Seat of Androscoggin County
Area (square miles) 34.1
Elevation (feet) 210
Time Zone EST
Population (1990) 39,757
Population of Metro Area (1990) 105,259

Distance in Miles To:

Portland	36
Bangor	107
Boston	135
New York	350

Location and Topography

 Lewiston is located in the southwestern section of Maine on the eastern side of the Androscoggin River. Across the river is the city of Auburn, and the two are called the Twin Cities. To the west is Lake Auburn and Taylor Pond. Located among low, rolling hills that slope toward the river, Lewiston is considered the gateway to Maine's lakes and mountainous regions just to the east. Augusta, the state capital, is 30 miles northeast.

Layout of City and Suburbs

The two main thoroughfares are Main and Sabattus streets, which merge downtown at Hulett Square just east of the James B. Longley Memorial Bridge, one of four that connect Lewiston to its twin city, Auburn. Hulett Square was originally known as Haymarket Square, where farmers sold their agricultural goods, including hay; hence its name. In 1915 it became Union Square to reflect the city's patriotic feeling during World War I.

In 1928 the name changed to Hulett Square, honoring the first Lewiston soldier killed in the war. The names of several city streets also reflect the honoring of war dead.

Environment

Environmental Stress Index NA
Green Cities Index: Rank NA
                    Score NA
Water Quality Slightly acid, soft, fluoridated
    Average Daily Use (gallons per capita) NA
    Maximum Supply (gallons per capita) NA
Parkland as % of Total City Area NA
% Waste Landfilled/Recycled NA
Annual Parks Expenditures per Capita NA

Climate

Lewiston has a four-season climate. Summers are comfortable and mild, and the winters generally cold, although not harsh. Prolonged periods of cold weather are rare.

Weather

Temperature

Highest Monthly Average °F 54.7
Lowest Monthly Average °F 36.8

Annual Averages

Days 32°F or Below 57
Days above 90°F 6
Zero Degree Days 12
Precipitation (inches) 45.76
Snow (inches) 80.7
% Seasonal Humidity NA
Wind Speed (m.p.h.) NA
Clear Days NA
Cloudy Days NA

LEWISTON

Weather (continued)

Storm Days NA
Rainy Days NA

Average Temperatures (°F)	High	Low	Mean
January	29.2	12.0	20.6
February	31.6	13.0	22.3
March	39.8	24.0	31.9
April	52.3	34.0	43.2
May	65.1	44.6	54.9
June	74.7	54.5	64.6
July	79.9	60.4	70.2
August	78.0	58.7	68.4
September	69.6	50.8	60.2
October	58.7	40.6	49.7
November	45.3	31.3	38.3
December	32.7	17.9	25.3

History

The original settlers of Lewiston were offered a tract of land in what became Bakerstown Township in New Hampshire. Instead, in 1768 they settled "Lewistown" in the area where Lewiston and Auburn are now situated. These settlements were small and little noticed until 1795, when the town of Lewiston was incorporated. Five years later it numbered only 900 residents.

The first step toward industrialization in this small agricultural village was by Michael Little. Using the power of the Androscoggin River, he opened a carding and woolen mill. By the early 1830s cotton mills also used the river as a power source. Recognizing the river's potential, several town leaders formed the Great Androscoggin Falls, Dam, Lock, and Canal Company in 1836. But within nine years the plan collapsed due to lack of funds, and it was reorganized as the Lewiston Water Power Company.

Between 1845 and 1861 cotton was Lewiston's leading commodity. During the Civil War, the town prospered by selling cotton at a premium price. It also became the home of Bates College, which opened its doors in 1856 as the Maine State Seminary. Renamed in honor of a Boston donor in 1863, it was later established as one of the first coeducational institutions in New England.

Auburn, the town across the river, was incorporated in 1869 and became a leader in shoe manufacturing. The twin cities have been economic partners and rivals ever since.

Money from Boston industrialists funded the construction of dams on the river and new mills to fuel Lewiston's economic engine. The engine roared until the 1930s, when the Great Depression struck. The noted AFL-CIO strike of shoe factories in 1937 led to great friction between Lewiston and Auburn. The Auburn police refused to let Lewiston workers cross the bridges to their jobs.

The modern period has been dominated by a reduction in the textile and shoe manufacturing businesses, forcing the twin cities to diversify their economic base.

Historical Landmarks

City Hall on Park Street is the second such structure to occupy that site; the original burned down in 1890 after standing for 18 years. Consumed in the same fire was the public library, which was also rebuilt. The most impressive structure in the city is the Saints Peter and Paul Church, constructed from 1905 to 1938. Other historic buildings can be seen along the Lisbon Street Historic Commercial District, as well as several of the mills that have been placed on the National Historic Register.

Population

Lewiston's population declined slightly from 40,481 in 1980 to 39,757 in 1990.

Population

	1980	1990
Central City	40,481	39,757
Rank	540	634
Metro Area	99,509	105,259
Pop. Change 1980–1990	-724	
Pop. % Change 1980–1990	-1.8	
Median Age	33.4	
% Male	47.1	
% Age 65 and Over	16.4	
Density (per square mile)	1,165	

Households

Number 15,823
Persons per Household 2.37
% Female-Headed Households 12.6
% One-Person Households 29.7
Births—Total 579
    % to Mothers under 20 15.4
    Birth Rate per 1,000 14.7

Ethnic Composition

Between 65% and 70% of the population of Lewiston is French-Canadian. Whites make up nearly 99% of the population. There is only a sprinkling of blacks and other races.

Ethnic Composition (as % of total pop.)

	1980	1990
White	98.93	98.16
Black	0.32	0.67
American Indian	0.11	0.23
Asian and Pacific Islander	0.33	0.69
Hispanic	0.59	0.71
Other	NA	0.24

Government

Lewiston operates under a city administrator form of government with a mayor and seven councillors elected to two-year terms. It is a strongly Democratic city in a heavily Republican state.

Chronology

1768	The Massachusetts Bay Company grants settlers a piece of land along the Androscoggin River for the "town of Lewistown."
1795	Lewiston is incorporated.
1819	Michael Little opens the first woolen mill, harnessing the power of the Androscoggin River.
1836	The Great Androscoggin Falls, Dam, Lock, and Canal Company is created to plan the industrial use of the Androscoggin River.
1845	The Androscoggin Falls, Dam, Lock, and Canal Company fails because of a lack of money. It is reorganized as the Lewiston Water Power Company.
1856	The Maine State Seminary, later called Bates College, opens in Lewiston.
1861-1865	Lewiston prospers during the Civil War by producing cotton for the Union army.
1893	The *Lewiston Daily Sun*, the city's first newspaper, is published.
1937	A bitter shoe strike by the AFL-CIO leads to friction between Lewiston and Auburn.
1980s	The reduction in textile and shoe manufacturing in the area forces a diversification in the economy.

Government

Year of Home Charter   1972
Number of Members of the Governing Body   7
Elected at Large   NA
Elected by Wards   7
Number of Women in Governing Body   1
Salary of Mayor   NA
Salary of Council Members   NA
City Government Employment Total   1,252
Rate per 10,000   321.2

Public Finance

Lewiston has an annual budget of $75 million.

Public Finance

Total Revenue (in millions)   NA
Intergovernmental Revenue—Total (in millions)   NA
Federal Revenue per Capita   NA
% Federal Assistance   NA
% State Assistance   NA
Sales Tax as % of Total Revenue   NA
Local Revenue as % of Total Revenue   NA

Public Finance (continued)

City Income Tax   no
Taxes—Total (in millions) $16.2

Taxes per Capita
   Total $415
   Property $412
   Sales and Gross Receipts $0
General Expenditures—Total (in millions) $31.6
General Expenditures per Capita $811
Capital Outlays per Capita $90

% of Expenditures for:
   Public Welfare   2.2
   Highways   8.4
   Education   41.3
   Health and Hospitals   0.2
   Police   6.1
   Sewerage and Sanitation   7.6
   Parks and Recreation   1.6
   Housing and Community Development   2.1
Debt Outstanding per Capita $397
   % Utility   16.4
Federal Procurement Contract Awards (in millions) $0.9
Federal Grants Awards (in millions) $2.8
Fiscal Year Begins   NA

Economy

Once known almost exclusively for the manufacture of textiles, today Lewiston has a diversified economy with strong manufacturing as well as nonmanufacturing sectors. Health care in the form of hospitals is the largest employer in the city, with educational facilities at Bates College providing a large share of employment. Other new industries include printing, containers, and engineering products. As is the case with many Maine cities, tourism is an important revenue earner. The Lewiston-Auburn area is also a major retail center for

Economy

Total Money Income (in millions) $351.84
% of State Average   97.3
Per Capita Annual Income $8,796
% Population below Poverty Level   13.3
Fortune 500 Companies   None

Banks	Number	Deposits (in millions)
Commercial	4	73.099
Savings	6	165.514

Passenger Autos   66,995
Electric Meters   40,082
Gas Meters   4,288

Manufacturing

Number of Establishments   84
% with 20 or More Employees   52.4
Manufacturing Payroll (in millions)   NA
Value Added by Manufacture (in millions)   NA
Value of Shipments (in millions)   NA
New Capital Expenditures (in millions)   NA

Wholesale Trade

Number of Establishments   87
Sales (in millions) $267.3
Annual Payroll (in millions) $26.428

Retail Trade

Number of Establishments   429
Total Sales (in millions) $254.9

Economy (continued)

Sales per Capita $6,539
Number of Retail Trade Establishments with Payroll   313
Annual Payroll (in millions) $31.5
Total Sales (in millions) $247.2
General Merchandise Stores (per capita)   NA
Food Stores (per capita) $1,461
Apparel Stores (per capita)   NA
Eating and Drinking Places (per capita) $626

Service Industries

Total Establishments   365
Total Receipts (in millions) $109.8
Hotels and Motels (in millions)   NA
Health Services (in millions) $49.0
Legal Services (in millions) $15.1

the quarter million people living in south-central Maine.

Labor

Following a downturn in the economy of Boston and surrounding areas, workers began moving north in search of employment opportunities. Lewiston is one of the beneficiaries of this movement. Soaring costs of living in Portsmouth, which formerly absorbed much of the labor spillover from Massachusetts, accelerated the trend; consequently, there is a substantial reservoir of skilled labor in Lewiston. The new workers have not moved into the traditional textile mills, but rather have found employment in the growing fields of printing, health and social services, construction, and tourism.

Labor

Civilian Labor Force   19,210
% Change 1989–1990   1.9

Work Force Distribution
   Mining   NA
   Construction   1,600
   Manufacturing   8,100
   Transportation and Public Utilities   1,400
   Wholesale and Retail Trade   9,900
   FIRE (Finance, Insurance, Real Estate)   2,100
   Service   10,500
   Government   4,200
   Women as % of Labor Force   46.6
   % Self-Employed   5.0
   % Professional/Technical   11.7
Total Unemployment   1,404
Rate %   7.3
Federal Government Civilian Employment   102

Education

Lewiston has an elected school committee that oversees its public school system, which includes one high school, one junior high/middle school, and seven elementary schools. The parochial system has three schools, including one high school. Lewiston's most famous educational institution is Bates College, founded by Free Baptists in 1855 as the Maine State Seminary. The

University of Southern Maine maintains a campus in Lewiston-Auburn offering one degree program.

Education

Number of Public Schools   9
Special Education Schools   NA
Total Enrollment   5,200
% Enrollment in Private Schools   9.9
% Minority   NA
Classroom Teachers   NA
Pupil-Teacher Ratio   15:1
Number of Graduates   NA
Total Revenue (in millions)   NA
Total Expenditures (in millions)   NA
Expenditures per Pupil   NA
Educational Attainment (Age 25 and Over)
   % Completed 12 or More Years   49.9
   % Completed 16 or More Years   8.4
Four-Year Colleges and Universities   1
   Enrollment   1,530
Two-Year Colleges   NA
   Enrollment   NA

Libraries

Number   4
Public Libraries   1
Books (in thousands)   84
Circulation (in thousands)   149
Persons Served (in thousands)   40
Circulation per Person Served   3.72
Income (in millions) $0.483
Staff   15

Four-Year Colleges and Universities
   Bates College

Health

The principal medical facilities are the Central Maine Medical Center and St. Mary's Hospital, with a combined capacity of 283 beds.

Health

Deaths—Total   461
Rate per 1,000   11.7
Infant Deaths—Total   5
Rate per 1,000   8.6
Number of Metro Hospitals   2
Number of Metro Hospital Beds   483
Rate per 100,000   1,239
Number of Physicians   178
Physicians per 1,000   NA
Nurses per 1,000   NA
Health Expenditures per Capita   NA

Transportation

The main highway to Lewiston is the Maine Turnpike, which crosses just south of the city. Other roads that serve the Lewiston-Auburn area are Routes 202/100 from Portland to the south, Route 196 from Brunswick to the southeast, and Route 136 from Freeport to the south. The Auburn-Lewiston Municipal Airport is the main air terminus.

Transportation

Interstate Highway Mileage   10
Total Urban Mileage   490
Total Daily Vehicle Mileage (in millions)   1.235
Daily Average Commute Time   35.9 min.
Number of Buses   NA
Port Tonnage (in millions)   NA
Airports   0
Number of Daily Flights   NA
Daily Average Number of Passengers   NA

Airlines (American carriers only)
   Eastern Express

Housing

With the expansion of the work force in recent years, Lewiston has witnessed a housing boom.

Housing

Total Housing Units   17,118
% Change 1980–1990   7.3
Vacant Units for Sale or Rent   1,126
Occupied Units   15,823
% with More Than One Person per Room   1.4
% Owner-Occupied   47.0
Median Value of Owner-Occupied Homes $87,200
Average Monthly Purchase Cost $345
Median Monthly Rent $329
New Private Housing Starts   64
Value (in thousands) $4,732
% Single-Family   84.4
Nonresidential Buildings Value (in thousands) $4,968

Urban Redevelopment

Construction projects in the late 1980s, estimated at $250 million, include expansion and renovation of St. Mary's Hospital and the Central Maine Medical Center, a new L. L. Bean Telecommunications Center, an industrial park near the Maine Turnpike interchange, and a new hydroelectric plant.

Crime

Lewiston has a low crime rate, a feature common to Maine cities. Only 119 violent crimes were reported in 1991 and 2,164 property crimes.

Crime

Violent Crimes—Total   119
Violent Crime Rate per 100,000   147.4
Murder   1
Rape   16
Robbery   39
Aggravated Assaults   64
Property Crimes   2,164
Burglary   519
Larceny   1,582

Crime (continued)

Motor Vehicle Theft   63
Arson   10
Per Capita Police Expenditures   NA
Per Capita Fire Protection Expenditures   NA
Number of Police   67
Per 1,000   1.63

Religion

Lewiston is heavily Catholic, reflecting its French-Canadian heritage.

Religion

Largest Denominations (Adherents)

Catholic	35,130
United Methodist	2,167
American Baptist	2,187
United Church of Christ	989
Episcopal	872
Church of the Nazarene	779
Jewish	500

Media

Lewiston's sole daily newspaper is the *Lewiston Evening Journal*, published seven days a week. There is one television station and three radio stations that directly serve the city.

Media

Newsprint
   Lewiston Evening Journal, daily
Television
   WCBB (Channel 10)
Radio
   WKZN (AM)   WLAM (AM)
   WXGL (FM)

Sports

Lewiston has no professional sports teams.

Arts, Culture, and Tourism

LA (Lewiston-Auburn) Arts was formed in 1973 as a cooperative to coordinate arts in the Twin Cities area. Several arts programs are held at Bates College, which also has the Treat Gallery and the Stanton Museum. In downtown Lewis-

Travel and Tourism

Hotel Rooms   354
Convention and Exhibit Space (square feet)   NA
Convention Centers
   NA
Festivals
   Franco-American Festival (summer)

ton are the Androscoggin Historical Society Museum, detailing the early days of the city, and the Westminster Gallery, which showcases photography exhibits.

Parks and Recreation

Thorncrag Bird Sanctuary is a 230-acre wildlife preserve. Many parks and recreational areas in the Lewiston-Auburn area offer sites for camping, skiing, and boating.

Sources of Further Information

City of Lewiston Development Department
  City Building
Lewiston, ME 04240
(207) 784-2951

Lewiston-Auburn Area Chamber of Commerce
179 Lisbon Street
Lewiston, ME 04240
(207) 783-2249

Lewiston Public Library
105 Park Street
Lewiston, ME 04240
(207) 784-0135

Lexington

Kentucky

Basic Data

Name   Lexington
Name Origin   From Lexington, Massachusetts
Year Founded   1775 Inc. 1832
Status: State   Kentucky
          County   Fayette County
Area (square miles)   284.7
Elevation (feet)   955
Time Zone   EST
Population (1990)   225,366
Population of Metro Area (1990)   348,428

Sister Cities

County Kildare, Ireland
Deauville, France
Shizunai, Japan

Distance in Miles To:

Louisville	79
Nashville	214
Knoxville	173
Frankfort	29
Cincinnati	82

Location and Topography

N

Lexington is located in north-central Kentucky, 20 miles from the capital of Frankfort, on a lush, grassy plateau. The terrain is unbroken bluegrass territory except for the small creeks that encircle the city and empty into the Kentucky River.

Layout of City and Suburbs

The heart of the city is a broad rectangle bounded by Third and High streets, and includes Main and Vine streets. The rectangle is intersected by Broadway, Rose, Jefferson, and Ashland streets. The downtown area is ringed by an inner beltway called New Circle Road (or Kentucky Route 4), and the city's outer reaches are bounded by a partial beltway, Man-O-War Boulevard.

Much of Lexington's finest architecture is in the western part of the city, which is the area of such neighborhoods as Woodward Heights and South Hill. The city suburbs include Versailles, Georgetown, and Nicholasville.

Environment

Environmental Stress Index   2.8
Green Cities Index: Rank   NA
                    Score   NA
Water Quality   Alkaline, medium, fluoridated
     Average Daily Use (gallons per capita)   161
     Maximum Supply (gallons per capita)   293
Parkland as % of Total City Area   2.3
% Waste Landfilled/Recycled   NA
Annual Parks Expenditures per Capita $37.13

Climate

Lexington has a four-season climate. Although temperature extremes are rare, sudden but brief changes of temperature are typical. Rainfall is evenly distributed throughout all seasons, with an annual average of 50 inches. Snowfall is variable and does not remain on the ground long. Fall is extremely pleasant, with clear days and comfortable temperatures.

Weather

Temperature

Highest Monthly Average °F   86.4
Lowest Monthly Average °F   24.5

Annual Averages

Days 32°F or Below   97
Days above 90°F   16
Zero Degree Days   2
Precipitation (inches)   50.0

495

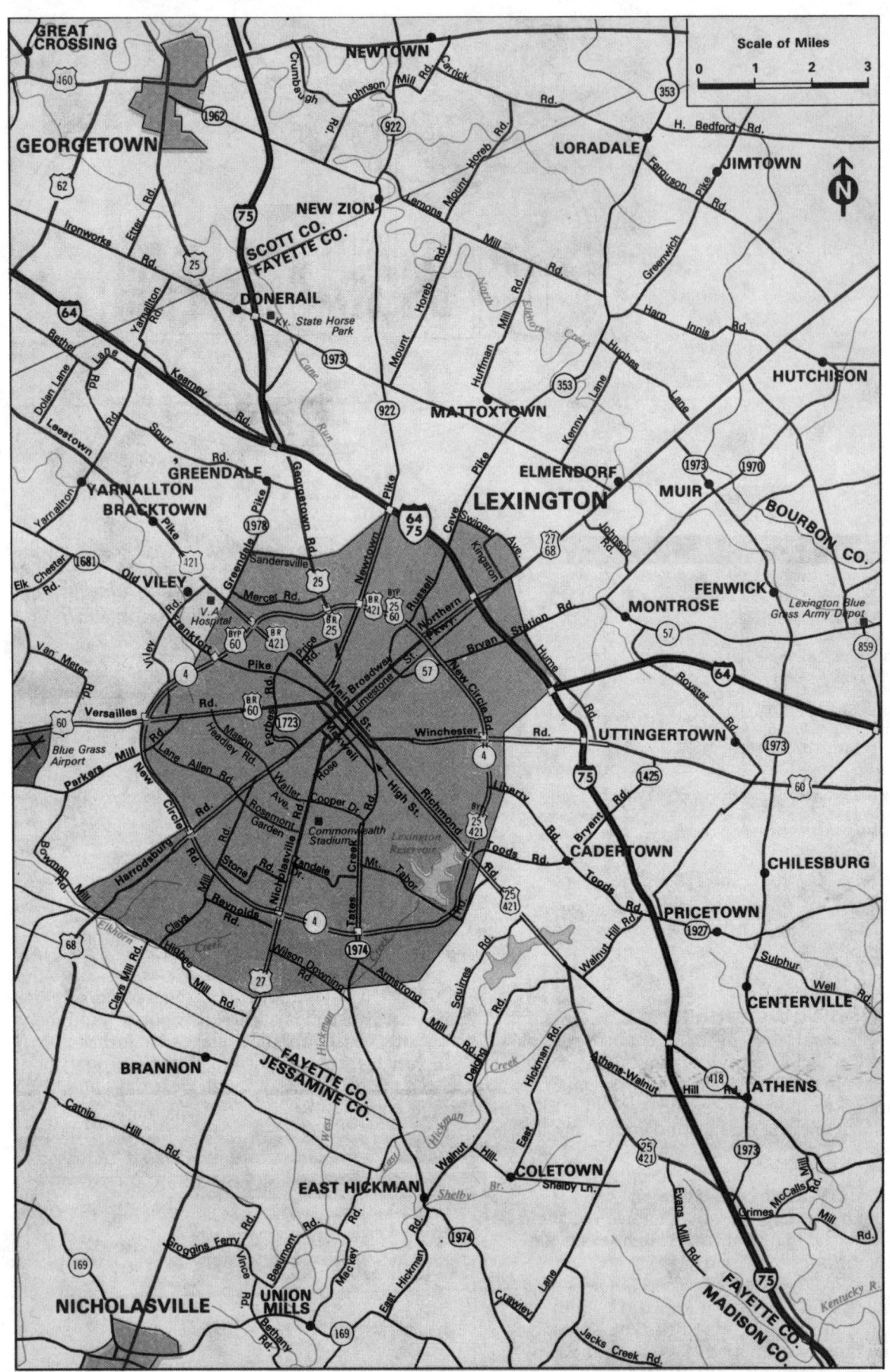

Weather (continued)

Snow (inches)   16.0
% Seasonal Humidity   70.0
Wind Speed (m.p.h.)   9.7
Clear Days   95
Cloudy Days   168
Storm Days   47
Rainy Days   130

Average Temperatures (°F)	High	Low	Mean
January	41.3	24.5	32.9
February	44.3	26.2	35.3
March	53.4	33.7	43.6
April	66.0	44.6	55.3
May	75.5	58.8	64.7
June	83.5	62.5	73.0
July	86.4	65.9	76.2
August	85.5	64.4	75.0
September	79.6	57.6	68.6
October	68.8	46.8	57.8
November	53.9	35.3	44.6
December	43.7	27.2	35.5

History

The area that is now Kentucky was once the hunting grounds of the Shawnee from southern Ohio and the Cherokee from the south. In 1775 a group of hunters including Robert Patterson, John and Levi Todd, and William McConnell set out on a scouting expedition from a fort at Harrodsburg, southwest of present-day Lexington. They camped on the Kentucky River, just to the north of the present downtown area. William McConnell built a small cabin where the Lexington Cemetery is now. Hearing of the famous battle between colonial forces and British troops at Lexington, Massachusetts, the men named the new settlement Lexington in honor of their fellow Americans.

Because Kentucky was not yet a state, Lexington was part of Virginia. Virginia's participation in the American Revolution left the Kentucky wilderness unguarded, and the McConnell cabin was soon abandoned in the name of safety. Three years later, in March 1779, Robert Patterson, now a colonel in the American army, returned to Lexington with a new group of men (including William McConnell and his brother Alexander), and built a stockade at the site. Over the next year, two other parties from North Carolina founded the nearby settlements of Bryant's Station and Grant's Station (named after people in the groups). In 1780, Virginia formed Kentucky out of its western territory with the three counties of Fayette, Lincoln, and Jefferson. Lexington was named the seat of Fayette County. Under this compact of governance, the town was to be laid out in a grid, with half-acre and five-acre plots of land set aside.

In 1782, because of insistent Indian attacks the fort at Lexington asked the Virginia Assembly for the right to expand the settlement into a secure and permanent town. This was done in May 1782, and 710 acres were granted to the people of Lexington. Over the next several years the town grew on the basis of trade, construction, agriculture, and education (the famed Transylvania University opened up in nearby Danville in 1780). In 1790, the population was 835; ten years later it was 1,795. At the turn of the century, it was the largest town in the western part of the country.

In 1792, Kentucky became the 15th state, and a rush was on to choose the new state capital. Although Lexington was named as the provisional capital, Frankfort was eventually chosen as the permanent site. By the third decade of the 19th century, Lexington was known as the principal industrial city in the state with an economy based on the production of hemp and tobacco. Early in the century the city established itself as a center for the breeding of race horses, a tradition that continues today. In 1832 the Lexington and Ohio Railroad was completed to a point six miles west of town, and that same year Lexington incorporated as a city. During the Civil War the cigarette industry was born when soldiers began rolling their own tobacco. The arrival of steamboat traffic gave Louisville, on the Ohio River, an advantage that Lexington did not have; the city suffered an economic eclipse for many years until the railroads restored its prosperity. In 1865 the University of Kentucky was founded and soon became one of the city's major resources. Gradually, as the social and cultural set grew, Lexington took on the reputation as the "Athens of the West" because of its large number of artists, musicians, and cultural facilities.

Historical Landmarks

Ashland, on the corner of Sycamore and Richmond roads, was the home of Senator Henry Clay from 1811 to 1852. Known as the "Great Compromiser," Clay was Speaker of the House of Representatives, U.S. senator, secretary of state, and a three-time candidate for the presidency. Hopemont, the Hunt-Morgan Home, was the estate of millionaire John Wesley Hunt, who purchased it in 1814; his descendants who also occupied the home included Confederate General John Hunt Morgan, who was known as the "Thunderbolt of the Confederacy," and Dr. Thomas Hunt Morgan, who won the 1933 Nobel Prize for medicine. The Bodley-Bullock House was also built in 1814, and served during the Civil War as headquarters for Union Generals Burbridge and Gilmore; today it is the property of Transylvania University. The Mary Todd Lincoln House, built in 1803, was the childhood home of Abraham Lincoln's wife Mary Todd. The Senator John Pope House was designed by famed architect Benjamin Henry Latrobe for Pope, a U.S. senator from 1807 until 1813. The Waveland State Historic Site is an 1847 antebellum mansion designed in Greek Revival style by Joseph Bryant, grandnephew of Daniel Boone.

Population

The population of Lexington has grown at a remarkable rate since 1970. From 108,000 in 1970 the population almost doubled to 204,165 in 1980, and then grew by 10.4% to

Chronology

1775	A party of hunters and explorers led by Robert Patterson, John and Levi Todd, and William McConnell explore the area just north of the Kentucky River; McConnell builds a small cabin. Upon hearing word of the Battle of Lexington in Massachusetts, the men name the new settlement Lexington.
1776	With Indian attacks increasing, McConnell abandons the cabin.
1779	Robert Patterson, now a colonel in the American army, returns to Lexington with McConnell and others, and sets up a stockade.
1782	Lexington asks the Virginia Assembly to form a permanent and secure town.
1792	Kentucky enters the Union as the 15th state; Lexington is named the provisional capital. Frankfort is eventually chosen as the permanent capital.
1832	The Lexington and Ohio Railroad links the town with the rest of the country.
1865	The University of Kentucky is founded.

225,366 in 1990. Much of this growth is the result of merging the county and city after 1970. The consolidated city now ranks 70th among large cities.

Population

	1980	1990
Central City	204,165	225,366
Rank	68	70
Metro Area	317,548	348,428
Pop. Change 1980–1990 +21,201		
Pop. % Change 1980–1990 +10.4		
Median Age 31.3		
% Male 47.8		
% Age 65 and Over 9.90		
Density (per square mile) 791		

Households

Number 89,529
Persons per Household 2.38
% Female-Headed Households 12.2
% One-Person Households 29.1
Births—Total 3,171
  % to Mothers under 20 13.3
  Birth Rate per 1,000 15.1

Ethnic Composition

Whites make up 84.5%, blacks 13.4%, American Indians 0.1%, Asians and Pacific Islanders 1.7%, and others 0.3%.

Ethnic Composition (as % of total pop.)

	1980	1990
White	85.52	84.51
Black	13.28	13.38
American Indian	0.11	0.16
Asian and Pacific Islander	0.67	1.65
Hispanic	0.73	1.13
Other	NA	0.32

Government

In 1974 Lexington and Fayette County were merged into a single governmental structure called the Lexington–Fayette County Urban County Government. The consolidated government operates with a mayor and council. Of the 15 council members, 3 are elected at large and 12 by district.

Government

Year of Home Charter
Number of Members of the Governing Body 15
Elected at Large 3
Elected by Wards 12
Number of Women in Governing Body 3
Salary of Mayor $69,000
Salary of Council Members $14,500

Public Finance

The annual budget consists of revenues of $219.119 million and expenditures of $219.988 million. The debt outstanding is $428.945 million, and cash and security holdings are $437.422 million.

Public Finance

Total Revenue (in millions) $219.119
Intergovernmental Revenue—Total (in millions) $32.67
Federal Revenue per Capita $17.93
% Federal Assistance 8.19
% State Assistance 6.64
Sales Tax as % of Total Revenue 7.10
Local Revenue as % of Total Revenue 78.93
City Income Tax yes
Taxes—Total (in millions) $67.8

Taxes per Capita
  Total $318
  Property $57
  Sales and Gross Receipts $48
General Expenditures—Total (in millions) $128.9
General Expenditures per Capita $606
Capital Outlays per Capita $52

% of Expenditures for:
  Public Welfare 2.4
  Highways 0.0
  Education 0.0
  Health and Hospitals 8.1
  Police 11.2
  Sewerage and Sanitation 7.9
  Parks and Recreation 5.0
  Housing and Community Development 9.1
Debt Outstanding per Capita $1,359
  % Utility 0.0
Federal Procurement Contract Awards (in millions) $63.0
Federal Grants Awards (in millions) $93.7
Fiscal Year Begins July 1

Economy

Lexington forms part of a metropolitan triangle with Louisville, 80 miles west, and Cincinnati, Ohio, 80 miles north. Within this geographic area are a third of Kentucky's population and half of its manufacturing jobs. Lexington's diversified economy and centralized location play to this strength. Situated in the Lexington–Fayette County area are such internationally recognized companies as IBM, General Electric, Rockwell International, and Texas Instruments. Leading employers in the region include Ashland Oil, Central Baptist Hospital, First Security National Bank & Trust, and Kentucky Textiles.

Economy

Total Money Income (in millions) $2,438.5
% of State Average 133.0
Per Capita Annual Income $11,454
% Population below Poverty Level 13.5
Fortune 500 Companies NA

Banks	Number	Deposits (in millions)
Commercial	8	2,331.73
Savings	6	355.92

Passenger Autos 121,719
Electric Meters 86,198
Gas Meters 56,367

Manufacturing

Number of Establishments 250
% with 20 or More Employees 35.6
Manufacturing Payroll (in millions) $481.2
Value Added by Manufacture (in millions) $1,284.1
Value of Shipments (in millions) $2,644.6
New Capital Expenditures (in millions) NA

Wholesale Trade

Number of Establishments 520
Sales (in millions) $3,083.4
Annual Payroll (in millions) $151.253

Retail Trade

Number of Establishments 2,373
Total Sales (in millions) $1,939.6
Sales per Capita $9,110
Number of Retail Trade Establishments with Payroll 1,656
Annual Payroll (in millions) $231.6
Total Sales (in millions) $1,902.8
General Merchandise Stores (per capita) $1,414
Food Stores (per capita) $1,451
Apparel Stores (per capita) $511
Eating and Drinking Places (per capita) $1,082

Service Industries

Total Establishments 1,968
Total Receipts (in millions) $885.3
Hotels and Motels (in millions) $83.5
Health Services (in millions) $280.7
Legal Services (in millions) $64.2

Labor

Lexington's 134,047-strong work force is heavily oriented toward trade, services, and government. Most manufacturers are technology driven. The University of Kentucky is not only a major employer, but a major resource for technical expertise as well.

Labor

Civilian Labor Force 134,047
% Change 1989–1990 0.3

Workforce Distribution
Mining 300
Construction 10,000
Manufacturing 32,800
Transportation and Public Utilities 8,800
Wholesale and Retail Trade 45,100
FIRE (Finance, Insurance, Real Estate) 9,600
Service 50,500

Education

The Fayette County Public School System supports 57 elementary schools, junior high/middle schools, and senior high schools. The parochial system has over a dozen schools. Lexington is home to two universities, both with deep roots in the city's history. Transylvania University, once known as the Harvard of the West, is the oldest educational institution west of the Alleghenies. It grew out of an act of the Virginia Legislature in 1780 setting aside 8,000 acres of confiscated Tory land, to which another 12,000 acres were added in 1783. Transylvania Seminary was opened in 1785 near Danville and later moved to Lexington, where the first building was erected in 1794. In 1798 it became Transylvania University under the auspices of the Disciples

Education

Number of Public Schools 57
Special Education Schools 2
Total Enrollment 32,083
% Enrollment in Private Schools 8.5
% Minority 24.4
Classroom Teachers 1,982
Pupil-Teacher Ratio 15.7:1
Number of Graduates 1,704
Total Revenue (in millions) $105.652
Total Expenditures (in millions) $113.914
Expenditures per Pupil $3,357
Educational Attainment (Age 25 and Over)
    % Completed 12 or More Years 71.6
    % Completed 16 or More Years 25.6
Four-Year Colleges and Universities 2
    Enrollment 23,633
Two-Year Colleges 1
    Enrollment 4,580

Libraries

Number 28
Public Libraries 5
Books (in thousands) 501
Circulation (in thousands) 1,258
Persons Served (in thousands) 226.5
Circulation per Person Served 5.55
Income (in millions) $7.38
Staff 99

Four-Year Colleges and Universities
    University of Kentucky
    Transylvania University

of Christ. Henry Clay was once a professor here, and Dr. Samuel Brown, pioneer in smallpox vaccination, founded the College of Medicine. The University of Kentucky on Limestone Street and Euclid Avenue was established in 1866 as a land-grant college and moved to its present campus in 1878. The university owns a 620-acre experimental farm in Lexington, 15,000 acres at Quicksand, and 600 acres at Princeton.

Health

The medical sector consists of five major hospitals: Central Baptist Hospital, Good Samaritan Hospital, St. Joseph's Hospital, Humana Lexington, and the Albert B. Chandler Medical Center at the University of Kentucky. Shriner's Hospital for Children is one of five specialty facilities.

Health

Deaths—Total 1,517
Rate per 1,000 7.2
Infant Deaths—Total 38
Rate per 1,000 12.0
Number of Metro Hospitals 10
Number of Metro Hospital Beds 3,200
Rate per 100,000 1,503
Number of Physicians 1,168
Physicians per 1,000 3.78
Nurses per 1,000 9.02
Health Expenditures per Capita $43.95

Transportation

Lexington is approached by two interstates: the north-south I-75 and the east-west I-64. New Circle Road, also known as Kentucky Route 4, is a four-lane beltway encircling the city. Rail freight service is provided by the CSX and Norfolk Southern railroads. The principal air terminus is Bluegrass Airport, located about seven minutes from downtown, which handles several major and commuter airlines.

Transportation

Interstate Highway Mileage 14
Total Urban Mileage 549
Total Daily Vehicle Mileage (in millions) 4.242
Daily Average Commute Time 40.5 min.
Number of Buses 39
Port Tonnage (in millions) NA
Airports 1
Number of Daily Flights 27
Daily Average Number of Passengers 915

Airlines (American carriers only)
Air Wisconsin   Delta
USAir

Housing

Of the total housing, 53% is owner occupied. The median value of an owner-occupied home is $73,900 and the median rent $338.

Housing

Total Housing Units 97,742
% Change 1980–1990 16.4
Vacant Units for Sale or Rent 6,427
Occupied Units 89,529
% with More Than One Person per Room 2.3
% Owner-Occupied 53.0
Median Value of Owner-Occupied Homes $73,900
Average Monthly Purchase Cost $354
Median Monthly Rent $338
New Private Housing Starts 1,347
Value (in thousands) $113,135
% Single-Family 94.3
Nonresidential Buildings Value (in thousands) $52,430

Tallest Buildings	*Hgt. (ft.)*	*Stories*
Lexington Financial Center (1986)	410	30
Kincaid Tower (1980)	333	22

Urban Redevelopment

Most urban redevelopment programs since 1970 have been building renovations and conversions of older buildings into shopping malls.

Crime

Lexington ranks below the national average in public safety. In 1991, of the crimes known to police, there were 1,802 violent crimes and 14,134 property crimes.

Crime

Violent Crimes—Total 1,802
Violent Crime Rate per 100,000 711.3
Murder 13
Rape 164
Robbery 453
Aggravated Assaults 1,172
Property Crimes 14,134
Burglary 3,211
Larceny 10,075
Motor Vehicle Theft 848
Arson 100
Per Capita Police Expenditures $84.83
Per Capita Fire Protection Expenditures $84.01
Number of Police 322
Per 1,000 1.53

Religion

Lexington is predominantly Baptist. Other major denominations include Catholic, Methodist, and the Church of Christ.

Religion

Largest Denominations (Adherents)	
Catholic	22,299
Southern Baptist	33,035
United Methodist	15,218
Black Baptist	11,112
Episcopal	3,500
Assembly of God	2,315
Church of Christ	14,178
Jewish	1,294

Media

The lone city daily is the *Lexington Herald-Leader*. The electronic media consist of 4 television stations and 7 FM and AM radio stations.

Media
Newsprint
Lexington Herald-Leader, daily
Television
WKLE (Channel 46)
WKYT (Channel 27)
WLEX (Channel 18)
WTVQ (Channel 36)
Radio
WVLK (AM)   WVLK (FM)
WKQQ (FM)   WLAP (AM)
WLAP (FM)   WRFL (FM)
WUKY (FM)

Sports

Lexington has no professional sports teams. Many of the sporting events in the city involve horses. Racing is held at the Keeneland Association and Red Mile tracks. Other sporting events are handled by the University of Kentucky, which fields several collegiate teams.

Arts, Culture, and Tourism

The arts are organized by the Lexington Arts and Cultural Council. The centerpiece of the Lexington Arts scene is ArtsPlace, a renovated 1904 Beaux Arts Classical building adjacent to the Lexington Opera House. Housed in ArtsPlace are the Lexington Children's Theater; Syncopated, Inc., a dance group; Lexington Philharmonic; Lexington Ballet; Lexington Musical Theatre; and Actors' Guild of Lexington. Other areas of the arts are the Lexington Opera House, Mitchell Fine Arts Center at Transylvania University, and Otis A. Singletary Center for the Arts. Among the museums in Lexington are the American Saddle Horse Museum, Headley-Whitley Museum, Nostalgia Station, University of Kentucky Museum of Anthropology, and Lexington Children's Museum.

Travel and Tourism
Hotel Rooms   6,460
Convention and Exhibit Space (square feet)   46,000
Convention Centers
Lexington Center and Rupp Arena
Festivals
International Festival (October)
American Jazz Festival (March)
Festival of the Bluegrass (summer)
Woodland Arts Fair (summer)

Parks and Recreation

Lexington has over 80 parks, of which the largest are the 274-acre Raven Run Nature Sanctuary, the 660-acre Masterson Station on Lestown Road, the 120-acre Shillito Park on Brunswick Drive, and the 216-acre Jacobson Park on Athens-Boonesborough Road.

Sources of Further Information

Greater Lexington Chamber of Commerce
330 East Main Street
Lexington, KY 40507
(606) 254-4447

Greater Lexington Convention and Visitors Bureau
430 West Vine Street, Suite 363
Lexington, KY 40507
(800) 84LEXKY

Lexington Arts and Cultural Council
ArtsPlace
161 North Mill Street
Lexington, KY 40507
(606) 255-2951

Additional Reading

Polk's Lexington City Directory. 1991.
Wright, John D. *Lexington: Heart of the Bluegrass*. 1982.

Lincoln

Nebraska

Basic Data

Name   Lincoln
Name Origin   From Abraham Lincoln
Year Founded   1867 Inc. 1869
Status: State   Capital of Nebraska
         County   Seat of Lancaster County
Area (square miles)   63.3
Elevation (feet)   1,150
Time Zone   Central
Population (1990)   191,972
Population of Metro Area (1990)   213,641

Sister Cities
   Khodzhent, Tajikistan

Distance in Miles To:
Omaha	58
Sioux City	155
Sioux Falls	210
Cheyenne	445
Denver	485
Des Moines	189
Lexington	166

Location and Topography

N   Lincoln, the capital of Nebraska, is situated in the southeastern section of the state at a conjunction of Salt Creek, Oak Creek, Middle Creek, Antelope Creek, and Haines Branch. South of the Platte River and east of the Big Blue River, the terrain is flat prairie (Platte is the French word for flat). Other water sites in the area are Pawnee and Conestoga lakes to the west, Yankee Hill Lake to the south, Holmes Lake to the east, and Ropers Lake to the north.

Layout of City and Suburbs

Lincoln's skyline is dominated basically by two structures: the huge capitol building at the southern end and the campus of the University of Nebraska at Lincoln at the northern point. The city is laid out in a gridlike fashion, with lettered streets running east and west, and numbered streets running north and south. On the western side of the city is the Haymarket Historic District. Some of Lincoln's suburbs are Walton, Cheney, Waverly, Malcolm, and Denton.

Environment

Environmental Stress Index   2.6
Green Cities Index: Rank   NA
                    Score   NA
Water Quality   Alkaline, hard, fluoridated
   Average Daily Use (gallons per capita)   172
   Maximum Supply (gallons per capita)   427
Parkland as % of Total City Area   13.8
% Waste Landfilled/Recycled   76:24
Annual Parks Expenditures per Capita $42.21

Climate

Lincoln has a true continental climate. Summers are generally hot, with plenty of sunshine and high easterly winds. Humidity is high during summer when the area is exposed to moist, tropical winds. In the winter, occasional foehns or chinooks cause a rapid rise in temperature and a shift to westerly winds. Snowfall may vary from 25 to 55 inches, and much of it does not melt until spring. Three-fourths of the precipitation is received during the crop season from April through September.

Weather

Temperature

Highest Monthly Average °F   89.5
Lowest Monthly Average °F   8.9

503

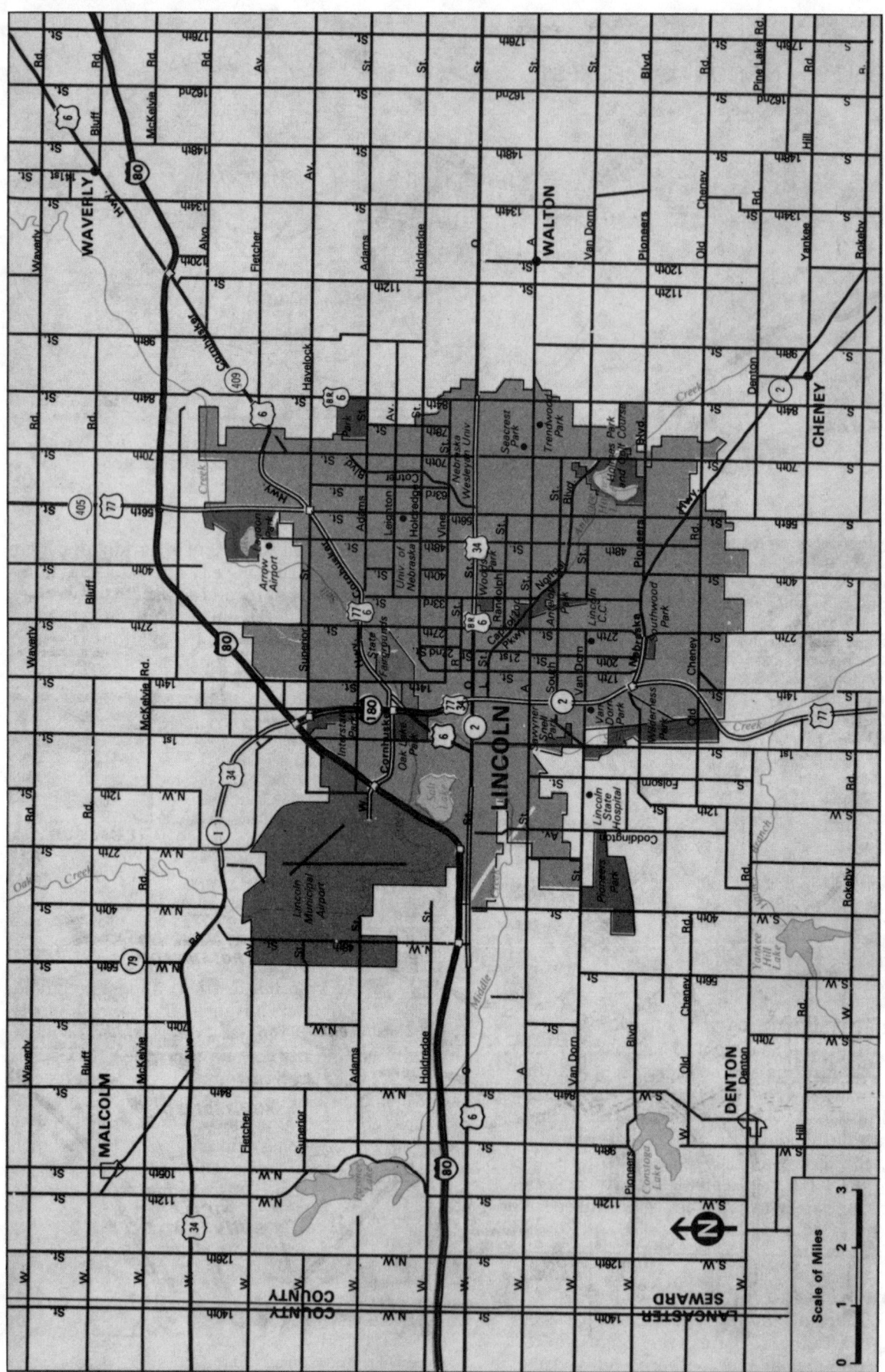

Weather (continued)

Annual Averages

Days 32°F or Below   146
Days above 90°F   43
Zero Degree Days   17
Precipitation (inches)   29
Snow (inches)   26
% Seasonal Humidity   68.0
Wind Speed (m.p.h.)   10.5
Clear Days   115
Cloudy Days   153
Storm Days   9
Rainy Days   88

Average Temperatures (°F)	High	Low	Mean
January	32.8	11.7	22.2
February	38.3	17.4	27.9
March	47.0	26.0	36.5
April	63.4	39.2	51.3
May	73.4	50.6	62.0
June	83.1	60.9	72.0
July	88.9	65.7	77.3
August	87.0	64.2	75.6
September	77.5	53.6	65.6
October	67.6	44.2	54.9
November	50.3	27.8	39.0
December	37.7	16.9	27.3

History

In 1853, an area north of the present city site was explored for salt deposits, although the actual mining of these deposits did not begin until the next decade. The area that contained the brine of underground springs is now under Capitol Beach Lake.

The first settler in what is now Lincoln was John Prey, who settled near the Salt Creek and laid his claim to a spit of land. Others followed, including Captain W. T. Donavan, who in 1856 came to the Lincoln area representing the Crescent Salt Company; he called the area Lancaster after his hometown in Pennsylvania. In 1859 Donavan was a leading member of the group that named the growing town as the county seat. Acceding to Donavan's idea, the group named the town Lancaster. On 1 March 1867, Nebraska became the 37th state, with Omaha as its capital, but Governor David Butler decided to move the state capital to a more central location. The settlers of Lancaster used their influence to have the capital moved to their city, which they renamed Capital City. After an unsuccessful political fight to keep the capital in Omaha, the new capital was named Lincoln in honor of Abraham Lincoln. On 15 August 1867, surveyors Augustus F. Henry and Anselmo B. Smith began to plat the new capital.

The initial sale of land plots was disappointing, and the search for an architect to construct a capitol building was going slowly. Finally, James Morris, an architect from Chicago, submitted his bid and won the contract. The building was completed in December 1868, and the legislature and the workings of state government moved into the building. Lincoln was incorporated in 1869. One of its first acts, in 1869, was to establish the Nebraska State University and Agricultural College, which later became the University of

Nebraska at Lincoln. A year later, the Burlington and Missouri River Railroad constructed tracks from Plattsmouth to Lincoln and points south.

Lincoln suffered from a recession in the 1870s, mainly caused by a depression in land sales following the impeachment of Governor Butler and a grasshopper scourge that wiped out crops. But the 1880s saw an economic boom brought about by the opening of a stockyard and meat-packing plants. Internal improvements such as streets, railways, and sewer lines were constructed. By 1887 the population reached 40,000.

During the last two decades of the 19th century and the first three of the 20th, Lincoln politics was dominated by the Bryan brothers, William Jennings and Charles Wayland. William was elected to Congress as a Democrat from Lincoln in 1890. Just six years later he was the presidential candidate of his party, and was nominated again in 1900 and 1908. Charles Wayland Bryan, at one time his older brother's secretary, served on the Lincoln City Council, as Lincoln's mayor from 1915 to 1917, and as governor of Nebraska from 1923 to 1925 and 1931 to 1935.

The Depression brought Lincoln's economy down, and with it farm credit dried up and unemployment surged. During World War II, Lincoln was the site of a huge base that supplied training facilities for the air force. The present state capitol building was constructed between 1922 and 1932 at a cost of $10 million.

Historical Landmarks

The state capitol, built between 1922 and 1932, is the fifth such building to represent the state. The structure is marked by a 400-foot tower topped by a 27-foot bronze statue of "the Sower," which represents Nebraska's agricultural heritage. In its expansive base are a Great Hall and Rotunda, exhibiting art that details the history of the state, and a legislative hall in which meets a unicameral (one-body) legislature, the only such deliberative body of its kind in the nation. The Thomas Perkins Kennard House on H Street was the home of Nebraska's first secretary of state. Built in 1869, it now honors Kennard, one of three men chosen by the state legislature in 1867 to select a permanent capital site. The Kennard House, now restored, is believed to be the oldest house located in the original 1867 plat of Lincoln. The Historic Haymarket District on the western side of the city is a five-block area of shops, restaurants, and vendors, and is distinguished by the restored Lincoln Station railroad depot. Fairview on Sumner Street was the home of William Jennings Bryan from 1902 until 1922. When he moved to Florida, Bryan made a gift of the building to Lincoln Methodist Hospital.

Population

Lincoln is one of the fastest growing cities in the nation. It grew by 14.62% in the 1970s from 150,000, and 11.7% from 171,932 in 1980 to 191,972 in 1990. It ranks 81st in the nation in population.

Chronology

1853 The area around present-day Lincoln is surveyed for its salt flats.

1856 Captain W. T. Donavan, an agent for the Crescent Salt Company, settles near the Platte River and calls his small village Lancaster after his hometown in Pennsylvania.

1867 Nebraska is admitted to the Union as the 37th state, with Omaha as the temporary state capital. A fight ensues in which Lincoln is chosen as the permanent site. Surveyors Augustus F. Henry and Anselmo B. Smith plat the city. Lincoln's population is 30.

1868 The capitol building is designed by architect James Morris of Chicago and built in record time.

1869 Lincoln is incorporated as a city. In the completed capitol building, the legislature meets and establishes the University of Nebraska at Lincoln.

1870 The Burlington and Missouri River Railroad builds tracks from Plattsmouth to Lincoln. The population of Lincoln reaches 2,500.

1887 The population of Lincoln reaches 40,000.

1890 William Jennings Bryan is elected to Congress from Lincoln. Six years later, he is the presidential nominee of the Democratic party.

1922– 1932 The new state capitol is built at a cost of $10 million.

1929– 1933 The Depression wipes out Lincoln's farm economy.

1941– 1945 Lincoln is the site of a training facility for air force fliers.

Population

	1980	1990
Central City	171,932	191,972
Rank	81	81
Metro Area	192,884	213,641
Pop. Change 1980–1990	+20,040	
Pop. % Change 1980–1990	+11.7	
Median Age	30.3	
% Male	48.6	
% Age 65 and Over	10.9	
Density (per square mile)	3,032	

Households

Number 75,402
Persons per Household 2.40
% Female-Headed Households 9.1

Population (continued)

% One-Person Households 28.8
Births—Total 2,884
　% to Mothers under 20　8.9
　Birth Rate per 1,000　16.0

Ethnic Composition

Whites make up 94.45%, blacks 2.35%, American Indians 0.6%, Asians and Pacific Islanders 1.71%, and Hispanics 1.96%.

Ethnic Composition (as % of total pop.)		
	1980	1990
White	95.48	94.45
Black	2.00	2.35
American Indian	0.54	0.6
Asian and Pacific Islander	0.98	1.71
Hispanic	1.60	1.96
Other	NA	0.89

Government

Lincoln is governed by a mayor and a council of seven members, all of whom are elected to four-year terms on a nonpartisan ballot.

Government

Year of Home Charter　1917
Number of Members of the Governing Body　7
Elected at Large　3
Elected by Wards　4
Number of Women in Governing Body　2
Salary of Mayor　$45,000
Salary of Council Members　$5,000
City Government Employment Total　3,113
Rate per 10,000　170.1

Public Finance

The annual budget consists of revenues of $280.348 million and expenditures of $237.666 million. The debt outstanding is $402.994 million, and cash and security holdings are $255.052 million.

Public Finance

Total Revenue (in millions)　$280.348
Intergovernmental Revenue—Total (in millions)　$23.81
Federal Revenue per Capita　$7.92
% Federal Assistance　2.82
% State Assistance　5.27
Sales Tax as % of Total Revenue　8.39
Local Revenue as % of Total Revenue　47.50
City Income Tax　no
Taxes—Total (in millions)　$39.1

Taxes per Capita
　Total　$214
　Property　$123
　Sales and Gross Receipts　$75

Public Finance (continued)

General Expenditures—Total (in millions) $108.4
General Expenditures per Capita $592
Capital Outlays per Capita $149

% of Expenditures for:
   Public Welfare   0.0
   Highways   14.4
   Education   NA
   Health and Hospitals   27.5
   Police   9.2
   Sewerage and Sanitation   9.6
   Parks and Recreation   6.8
   Housing and Community Development   3.4
Debt Outstanding per Capita $2,282
   % Utility   80.7
Federal Procurement Contract Awards (in millions) $33.7
Federal Grants Awards (in millions) $128.6
Fiscal Year Begins   August 1

Economy

The agricultural way of life in the areas surrounding Lincoln is declining, so other zones of the economy must expand to take up the slack. State government and educational institutions in the form of the University of Nebraska at Lincoln and Lincoln public schools are the city's largest public-sector employers. Leading private employers include Goodyear Tire and Rubber, Burlington Northern Railroad, Bryan Memorial Hospital, Lincoln General Hospital, Ameritas Financial Services (insurance), and Carol Wright Sales (mail order).

Economy

Total Money Income (in millions) $2,154.2
% of State Average   111.6
Per Capita Annual Income $11,772
% Population below Poverty Level   8.9
Fortune 500 Companies   NA
Banks   Number   Deposits (in millions)
   Commercial 11 2,200.7
   Savings 5 2,274.7
Passenger Autos   141,628
Electric Meters   93,317
Gas Meters   72,103

Manufacturing

Number of Establishments   222
% with 20 or More Employees   39.6
Manufacturing Payroll (in millions) $303.2
Value Added by Manufacture (in millions) $809.1
Value of Shipments (in millions) $1,518.7
New Capital Expenditures (in millions) $60.7

Wholesale Trade

Number of Establishments   325
Sales (in millions)   NA
Annual Payroll (in millions)   NA

Retail Trade

Number of Establishments   1,848
Total Sales (in millions) $1,248.4
Sales per Capita $6,820
Number of Retail Trade Establishments with Payroll   1,254

Economy (continued)

Annual Payroll (in millions) $150.1
Total Sales (in millions) $1,229.5
General Merchandise Stores (per capita) $952
Food Stores (per capita) $1,284
Apparel Stores (per capita)   NA
Eating and Drinking Places (per capita) $724

Service Industries

Total Establishments   1,378
Total Receipts (in millions) $600.7
Hotels and Motels (in millions)   NA
Health Services (in millions) $159.7
Legal Services (in millions)   NA

Labor

The three largest employers are Lincoln Public Schools, the State of Nebraska, and the University of Nebraska. Together with the federal, city, and county governments, public services employ one-fourth of the labor force. Services are the next largest sector, employing 23%. Other large employers are three medical facilities; financial services such as Ameritas, Centel, First Federal Lincoln, and FirsTier Lincoln; State Farm Insurance; and Lincoln Telephone. Among manufacturers the largest are Burlington Northern, Goodyear Tire and Rubber, Cushman, Kawasaki, Norden Laboratories, Square D Company, Archer, Daniels Midland, Bruning Hydraulics, and Brunswick Corporation. Value-added rates are above and wages are below the national average.

Labor

Civilian Labor Force   117,094
% Change 1989–1990   4.4

Work Force Distribution
   Mining   NA
   Construction   5,100
   Manufacturing   14,900
   Transportation and Public Utilities   7,400
   Wholesale and Retail Trade   25,800
   FIRE (Finance, Insurance, Real Estate)   8,700
   Service   28,800
   Government   33,100
   Women as % of Labor Force   46.5
   % Self-Employed   4.9
   % Professional/Technical   18.9
Total Unemployment   1,980
Rate %   1.7
Federal Government Civilian Employment   2,460

Education

The Lincoln Public Schools System supports 33 elementary schools, 9 junior high schools, and 4 senior high schools. The principal state university, University of Nebraska at Lincoln, maintains two campuses as well as a law school and dental college in Lincoln. Nebraska Wesleyan University and Union College are private liberal arts institutions.

Education

Number of Public Schools   47
Special Education Schools   NA
Total Enrollment   27,986
% Enrollment in Private Schools   12.3
% Minority   7.7
Classroom Teachers   1,700
Pupil-Teacher Ratio   16.1:1
Number of Graduates   1,619
Total Revenue (in millions) $96.540
Total Expenditures (in millions) $105.343
Expenditures per Pupil $3,917
Educational Attainment (Age 25 and Over)
      % Completed 12 or More Years   81.8
      % Completed 16 or More Years   24.8
Four-Year Colleges and Universities   3
      Enrollment   26,774
Two-Year Colleges   2
      Enrollment   6,917

Libraries

Number   37
Public Libraries   7
Books (in thousands)   534
Circulation (in thousands)   1,709
Persons Served (in thousands)   192
Circulation per Person Served   8.9
Income (in millions) $3.690
Staff   113

Four-Year Colleges and Universities
      University of Nebraska, Lincoln
      Nebraska Wesleyan University
      Union College

Health

Health-care facilities in Lincoln serve the city and Lancaster County. They include Bryan Hospital (the largest), Lincoln General Hospital, St. Elizabeth Community Health Center, Veterans Administration Medical Center, and Lincoln Regional Center, a psychiatric hospital.

Health

Deaths—Total   1,244
Rate per 1,000   6.9
Infant Deaths—Total   31
Rate per 1,000   10.7
Number of Metro Hospitals   7
Number of Metro Hospital Beds   1,459
Rate per 100,000   797
Number of Physicians   332
Physicians per 1,000   1.83
Nurses per 1,000   5.75
Health Expenditures per Capita $19.38

Transportation

Lincoln is on the route of I-80. Interstate 29 provides a north-south connection. U.S. 6 bisects the city from northeast to west, while U.S. 34 runs northwest to south, joining in the center of downtown. U.S. 77 comes from the south, and Nebraska Highway 2 from the southeast. Rail freight service is provided by the Burlington Northern and Union Pacific railroads, with rail passenger service handled by Amtrak. Lincoln Municipal Airport, just to the northwest, is served by six commercial and commuter airlines.

Transportation

Interstate Highway Mileage   9
Total Urban Mileage   848
Total Daily Vehicle Mileage (in millions)   2.786
Daily Average Commute Time   34.8 min.
Number of Buses   52
Port Tonnage (in millions)   NA
Airports   1
Number of Daily Flights   13
Daily Average Number of Passengers   550

Airlines (American carriers only)
      American West
      Continental
      United
      Trans World

Housing

The total number of occupied dwellings in 1990 was 75,402, of which 43,808 were owner occupied. The typical rental for a three-bedroom apartment was $491 and the average selling price of a single-family home was $61,700.

Housing

Total Housing Units   79,079
% Change 1980–1990   12.6
Vacant Units for Sale or Rent   2,826
Occupied Units   75,402
% with More Than One Person per Room   1.6
% Owner-Occupied   58.1
Median Value of Owner-Occupied Homes $61,700
Average Monthly Purchase Cost $378
Median Monthly Rent $323
New Private Housing Starts   2,048
Value (in thousands) $105,999
% Single-Family   46.3
Nonresidential Buildings Value (in thousands), $26,721

Urban Redevelopment

Urban redevelopment was one of the key objectives of StarVenture, a project initiated in 1986 to revitalize Lincoln. The centerpiece of the redevelopment efforts in downtown is a superblock mall that is closed to traffic but linked to other buildings by skywalks. Also included in this project are Centrepointe, a mixed-use facility; Centre Terrace, an office complex; Block 35, a theater complex; and renovation of the Burlington Northern depot.

Crime

Lincoln has a below-average crime rate. In 1991, of the crimes known to police, there were 1,091 violent crimes and 13,863 property crimes.

Crime

Violent Crimes—Total 1,091
Violent Crime Rate per 100,000 519.4
Murder NA
Rape 89
Robbery 112
Aggravated Assaults 890
Property Crimes 13,863
Burglary 2,327
Larceny 11,117
Motor Vehicle Theft 419
Arson 59
Per Capita Police Expenditures $55.34
Per Capita Fire Protection Expenditures $42.51
Number of Police 229
Per 1,000 1.26

Religion

Lincoln is heavily Protestant, and is one of the principal bases of Methodists in Nebraska. Lutherans are also strong in the city.

Religion

Largest Denominations (Adherents)

Catholic	29,297
United Methodist	17,799
Evangelical Lutheran	12,188
Lutheran-Missouri Synod	11,325
Presbyterian	6,890
United Church of Christ	5,032
Black Baptist	1,526
Assembly of God	1,980
Jewish	825

Media

Lincoln's daily press consists of the *Lincoln Journal* and the *Star*, combined as the *Journal-Star* on Sundays. The electronic media consist of 2 television stations, plus three that can be picked up from Omaha, as well as 12 AM and FM radio stations.

Media

Newsprint
  Lincoln Journal, daily
  NEBRASKAland Sun, weekly

Television
  KOLN (Channels 10 & 11)
  KUON (Channel 12)

Radio

KFMQ (AM)	KFMQ (FM)
KFRX (FM)	KFOR (AM)
KKNB (FM)	KLDZ (FM)
KLIN (AM)	KEZG (FM)
KRNU (FM)	KTGL (FM)
KUCV (FM)	KZUM (FM)

Sports

Lincoln has no professional sports team, but the University of Nebraska Cornhuskers' achievements as a leading football powerhouse have given them national prominence. One of the most successful teams in the Big Eight Conference, they play their home games at Memorial Stadium. In the fall, the State Fairgrounds is the scene of thoroughbred racing.

Arts, Culture, and Tourism

In the area of performing arts, the leading institution is the Lied Center for Performing Arts, a 2,210-seat hall that showcases the talents of the Lincoln Symphony, as well as the Lincoln Chamber Orchestra and Lincoln City Ballet/Ballet West. (The latter two also appear at Kimball Hall.) Abendmusik: Lincoln is a concerto troupe that appears at the First Plymouth Church. Rhythm-and-blues and jazz can be heard at the Zoo Bar on 14th Street. The State Museum of History and University of Nebraska State Museum have collections on Nebraska history and archaeology. The Sheldon Memorial Art Gallery and Sculpture Garden, one of the nation's best collections of 20th-century art, is located on the campus of the University of Nebraska. Two ethnic and genealogical museums are the American Historical Society of Germans from Russia and the Lentz Center for Asian Culture.

Travel and Tourism

Hotel Rooms 2,734
Convention and Exhibit Space (square feet) NA

Convention Centers
  Pershing Auditorium

Festivals
  Flatwater Festival
  Nebraska State Fair (September)
  Harvest Festival (September)

Parks and Recreation

The largest park in Lincoln is the 1,455-acre Wilderness Park, a recreational preserve with jogging trails and antique bridges. The 179-acre Antelope Park includes the Sunken Gardens, a landscaped grove with flower arrangements. Holmes Park is a 555-acre park featuring the Hyde Memorial Observatory. Pioneers Park is 600 acres in size and has an exhibit called the Prairie Interpretive Center, which displays animals and fauna from Nebraska's early history. The Folsom Children's Zoo and Botanical Gardens include exotic animals and landscaped gardens.

Sources of Further Information

Lincoln Chamber of Commerce
1221 N Street
Lincoln, NE 68508
(402) 476-7511

Lincoln Convention and Visitors Bureau
1221 N Street, Suite 320
Lincoln, NE 68508
(800) 423-8212

Additional Reading

Cole's Directory for Lincoln. 1991.
Pursell, Donald E., and Jerome A. Deichert. *Economic Impact of the University of Nebraska*. 1984.

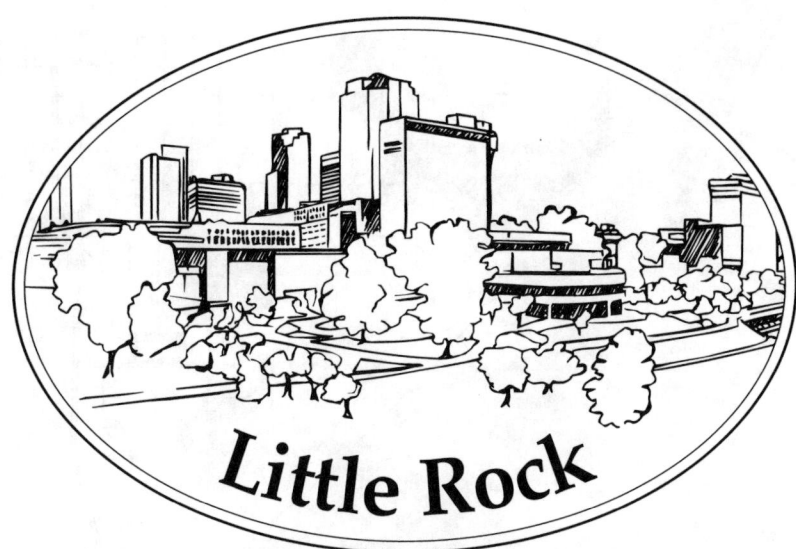

Little Rock

Arkansas

Location and Topography

N

Little Rock, the capital of Arkansas, is situated on the north and south banks of the Arkansas River in the central part of the state. Its central position where, according to one source, "the plains meet the hills" on a bluff, allowed the area to serve as a waystation on the Southwest Trail to Louisiana and Texas. The Ouachita Mountains are to the west of the city, and the Mississippi River valley is to the east.

Layout of City and Suburbs

Little Rock's streets are laid out in a traditional grid pattern. The two main streets are Markham Street, which passes the State Capitol, and Cantrell Road, running parallel to the Arkansas River. To the east of the city at the Arkansas River is the Little Rock Port Industrial Park. To the south are the residential areas, while on Scott Street near MacArthur Park is the Quapaw Quarter District, a neighborhood of restored homes from Little Rock's early days.

Environment

Environmental Stress Index   2.8
Green Cities Index: Rank   NA
                    Score   NA
Water Quality   Neutral, soft, fluoridated
    Average Daily Use (gallons per capita)   140
    Maximum Supply (gallons per capita)   444
Parkland as % of Total City Area   NA
% Waste Landfilled/Recycled   NA
Annual Parks Expenditures per Capita $32.36

Climate

Little Rock has hot and humid summers because of its proximity to the Gulf of Mexico. Winters are mild, but cold snaps can occur when arctic air moves in occasionally from the north. Precipitation is well distributed throughout the year, but about 62% falls during the growing season beginning in early spring. There is little or no snowfall except for an occasional ice storm or freezing rain.

History

An unknown tribe of American Indians flourished on the site of Little Rock 9,000 years ago, first as hunters and then as an

511

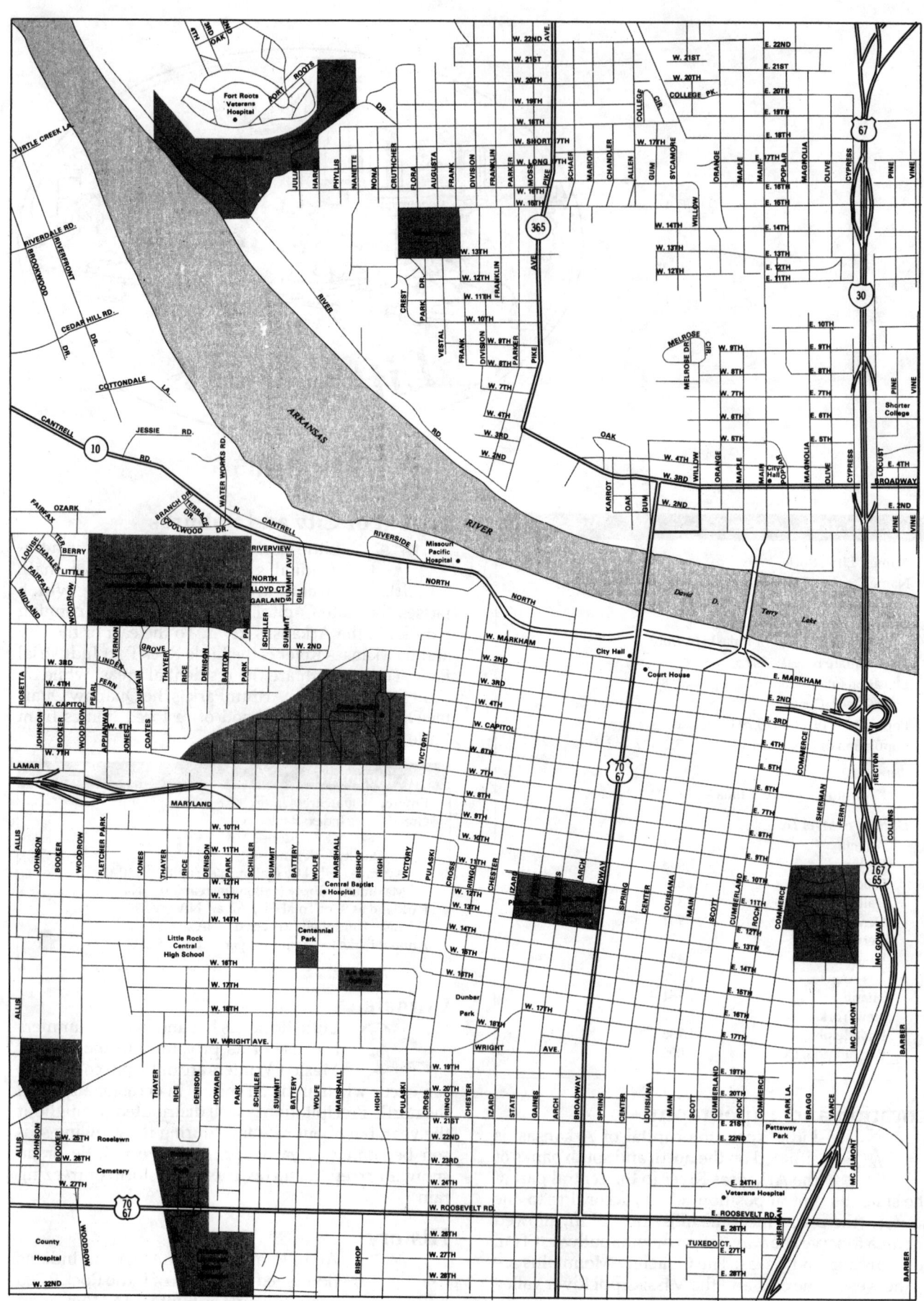

Weather

Temperature

Highest Monthly Average °F   92.7
Lowest Monthly Average °F   29.9

Annual Averages

Days 32°F or Below   63
Days above 90°F   70
Zero Degree Days   0
Precipitation (inches)   49.0
Snow (inches)   5.0
% Seasonal Humidity   70.0
Wind Speed (m.p.h.)   8.2
Clear Days   120
Cloudy Days   145
Storm Days   57
Rainy Days   104

Average Temperatures (°F)	High	Low	Mean
January	50.1	28.9	39.5
February	53.8	31.9	42.9
March	61.8	38.7	50.3
April	73.5	49.9	61.7
May	81.4	58.1	69.8
June	89.3	66.8	78.1
July	92.6	70.1	81.4
August	92.6	68.6	80.6
September	85.8	60.8	73.3
October	76.0	48.7	62.4
November	62.4	38.1	50.3
December	52.1	31.1	41.6

agricultural society. By 1000, a community revolving around small villages near natural lakes had been created, which lasted for about 600 years. In 1541, explorer Hernando de Soto became the first white man to view these peoples. Following his departure, diseases brought by the exploration party devastated the tribe, wiping out most of them. Later explorers to the area found the survivors, the Quapaw tribe, inhabiting the area.

It was almost 150 years before another white man came to central Arkansas. In 1686, Frenchman Henry de Tonti set up a trading post and called it the Arkansas Post. Thirty-six years later, another Frenchman, Benard de la Harpe, wended his way in a canoe on the Arkansas River toward what is now Little Rock. Finding small stones at the site, he called it La Petit Roche—Little Rock. Farther downstream, in what is now the suburb of North Little Rock, he encountered an area of larger stones that he called Big Rock. Even though la Harpe left the area, he had made his imprint.

Arkansas became part of the United States as an outgrowth of the Missouri Territory bought during the Louisiana Purchase in 1803. The first white resident was a hunter named William Lewis, who in 1812 built a cabin on the southern side of the Arkansas River. In 1819, the Arkansaw Territory (spelled with a w) was created. In 1821 state leaders made Little Rock the territorial—and later the state—capital. In 1819 only 14 people lived there, but land speculation gradually took over and the town's population grew; by 1835, the population was 726. Little Rock was incorporated in 1835.

Although at first transportation by river was Little Rock's sole economic lifeline (it shipped cotton, furs, and pelts south and received food and other goods in return), the city grew. A road was built between Little Rock and Memphis in 1827. In 1833, the Little Rock Bridge Company was created to build the first bridge over the Arkansas River. Six years later, the resulting span collapsed into a flooded river.

When Arkansas seceded from the Union in 1861, a federal army under General Frederick Steele occupied Little Rock, which remained his headquarters for the rest of the war. The postwar Reconstruction period witnessed a steady transformation of the city into a modern metropolis. Telephones appeared by 1879, waterworks by 1884, and electric trolleys and streetlights by 1888. The 1880s also saw the expansion of railroads, and with railroads came sawmills. The importance of the river as a chief mode of transportation diminished. The population jumped from 3,727 in 1860 to 25,874 in 1890.

With its emergence into the 20th century, Little Rock became an agricultural hub as well as a center of state government. Two events since then have irrevocably changed the city. The first, in 1957, pitted Arkansas Governor Orval Faubus against President Dwight D. Eisenhower in a fight to keep Little Rock's public schools segregated. The standoff ended when the president called out federal troops to safeguard the entry of black students into the schools. The second event was the election of Governor Bill Clinton as the 42nd president of the United States in 1992, making him the first Arkansan to be elected to the White House.

Historical Landmarks

The restored Old State House, the site of Arkansas's first capitol building, was originally built in 1836 in time for the inauguration of the first state governor, James S. Conway. The building is designed in a classic Greek Revival style, and is noted for its Doric columns. The building now houses various exhibits concerning the history of Arkansas. The new capitol building on Wood Lane, built between 1899 and 1915, was designed to look like the national capitol building in Washington, D.C. Other historical landmarks include the Arkansas Territorial Restoration, which presents restored city buildings from Civil War days; the Saline County Historic Courthouse, built in 1836; the Hernando de Soto Trail Marker, which marks the site of the explorer's visit to Little Rock in 1541; and the Quapaw Quarter District downtown, highlighting the city's preservation district.

Population

Little Rock has grown substantially since World War II, adding to its population with every decade. From a population of 132,000 in 1970, it grew by 19.6% to 159,159 in 1980. By 1990 it had increased by 10.5% to 175,795. The demographic growth reflects the economic upturn and cultural revival experienced by the city during the same decades.

Chronology

1541 Hernando de Soto becomes the first white man to visit what is now Little Rock. After his exploration party leaves, diseases he brought to the area wiped out the native American Indian population, leaving only the small Quapaw tribe.

1686 Frenchman Henry de Tonti sets up the Arkansas Post, a trading post.

1722 Frenchman Benard de la Harpe, traveling the length of the Arkansas River by canoe, comes across a bluff and notes the rocky area. He calls the site La Petit Roche—Little Rock.

1803 Arkansas becomes part of the Missouri Territory bought during the Louisiana Purchase.

1819– 1820 The Arkansaw Territory (spelled with a w) is separated from the Missouri Territory, and Little Rock is named the territorial capital the following year.

1833– 1839 The Little Rock Bridge Company builds the first bridge across the Arkansas River. The bridge collapses in 1839 when the river floods.

1861– 1865 Arkansas secedes from the Union. A federal army under the command of General Frederick Steele captures Little Rock and makes it his headquarters for the rest of the war.

1879– 1889 The city's waterworks system is installed, telephones are introduced, and electric trolleys and streetlights make their appearance.

1957 In a multiday standoff, Governor Orval Faubus attempts to uphold segregation and stop black students from entering Little Rock High School. President Dwight D. Eisenhower ends the siege by sending in U.S. Army troops to safeguard the students and end the crisis.

1992 Arkansas Governor Bill Clinton is elected the 42nd president of the United States.

Population

	1980	1990
Central City	159,159	175,795
Rank	96	96
Metro Area	474,464	513,117
Pop. Change 1980–1990 +16,636		
Pop. % Change 1980–1990 +10.5		
Median Age 32.8		
% Male 46.4		

Population (continued)
% Age 65 and Over 12.6
Density (per square mile) 1,708

Households
Number 72,573
Persons per Household 2.37
% Female-Headed Households 14.5
% One-Person Households 32.1
Births—Total 3,044
   % to Mothers under 20 15.0
   Birth Rate per 1,000 17.9

Ethnic Composition
Whites make up 64.7% of the population, blacks 34%, American Indians 0.3%, Asians and Pacific Islanders 0.9%, and others 0.2%.

Ethnic Composition (as % of total pop.)	1980	1990
White	66.46	64.68
Black	32.24	33.98
American Indian	0.25	0.26
Asian and Pacific Islander	0.57	0.87
Hispanic	0.83	0.76
Other	NA	0.21

Government
Little Rock has a manager form of government. The seven-member board of directors, elected on a nonpartisan basis for staggered four-year terms, elects a largely ceremonial mayor and vice-mayor, but appoints a manager as chief executive.

Government
Year of Home Charter NA
Number of Members of the Governing Body 7
Elected at Large 7
Elected by Wards NA
Number of Women in Governing Body 2
Salary of Mayor $0.0
Salary of Council Members $0.0
City Government Employment Total 2,042
Rate per 10,000 112.8

Public Finance

The annual budget consists of revenues of $140.847 million and expenditures of $144.025 million. The debt outstanding is $301.365 million, and cash and security holdings total $336.189 million.

Public Finance
Total Revenue (in millions) $140.847
Intergovernmental Revenue—Total (in millions) $29.8
Federal Revenue per Capita $4.06
% Federal Assistance 2.88

Public Finance (continued)

% State Assistance 6.5
Sales Tax as % of Total Revenue 10.44
Local Revenue as % of Total Revenue 75.2
City Income Tax no
Taxes—Total (in millions) $28.1

Taxes per Capita
  Total $155
  Property $46
  Sales and Gross Receipts $78
General Expenditures—Total (in millions) $79.2
General Expenditures per Capita $438
Capital Outlays per Capita $39

% of Expenditures for:
  Public Welfare 0.0
  Highways 12.7
  Education 0.0
  Health and Hospitals 0.5
  Police 12.6
  Sewerage and Sanitation 10.7
  Parks and Recreation 6.3
  Housing and Community Development 4.8
Debt Outstanding per Capita $1,217
  % Utility 5.9
Federal Procurement Contract Awards (in millions) $40.8
Federal Grants Awards (in millions) $206.7
Fiscal Year Begins January 1

Economy

Little Rock's economic base is centered in the three areas of state government, federal government, and health-care. As the capital of Arkansas, the city's state government apparatus dominates the economic picture, employing some 20,000 workers. Federal offices, combined with the jobs at Little Rock Air Force Base, account for about 15,000 employees. Nineteen hospitals, led by the Baptist Medical Center (the largest hospital in the state), as well as 43 nursing homes, make the health-care industry the third-largest employer. Other areas, such as education, transportation, and utilities, round out the top fields of employment.

Economy

Total Money Income (in millions) $2,158.4
% of State Average 142.1
Per Capita Annual Income $11,923
% Population below Poverty Level 14.1
Fortune 500 Companies NA

Banks	Number	Deposits (in millions)
Commercial	22	4,278.6
Savings	4	1,563.5

Passenger Autos 187,373
Electric Meters 186,424
Gas Meters 128,275

Manufacturing

Number of Establishments 265
% with 20 or More Employees 38.1
Manufacturing Payroll (in millions) $323.9
Value Added by Manufacture (in millions) $784.2
Value of Shipments (in millions) $1,986.5
New Capital Expenditures (in millions) $59.2

Economy (continued)

Wholesale Trade

Number of Establishments 637
Sales (in millions) $3,161.6
Annual Payroll (in millions) $207.186

Retail Trade

Number of Establishments 2,172
Total Sales (in millions) $1,615.2
Sales per Capita $8,922
Number of Retail Trade Establishments with Payroll 1,538
Annual Payroll (in millions) $190.3
Total Sales (in millions) $1,590.9
General Merchandise Stores (per capita) $1,411
Food Stores (per capita) $1,447
Apparel Stores (per capita) $661
Eating and Drinking Places (per capita) $884

Service Industries

Total Establishments 2,203
Total Receipts (in millions) $998.4
Hotels and Motels (in millions) $41.1
Health Services (in millions) $350.0
Legal Services (in millions) $108.5

Labor

The state of Arkansas and the federal government account for 23,000 jobs, the Little Rock Air Force Base for 6,890, educational institutions for 14,269, medical institutions for 13,726, and public utilities for 5,161. The only private employer with over 2,000 workers is Dillard's Department Store. The work force is drawn from the four-county metro area, including Faulkner, Pulaski, Saline, and Lonoke.

Labor

Civilian Labor Force 94,197
% Change 1989–1990 0.0

Work Force Distribution
  Mining NA
  Construction 11,100
  Manufacturing 33,300
  Transportation and Public Utilities 16,600
  Wholesale and Retail Trade 61,200
  FIRE (Finance, Insurance, Real Estate) 15,600
  Service 68,600
  Government 50,500
  Women as % of Labor Force 47.8
  % Self-Employed 4.7
  % Professional/Technical 20.8
Total Unemployment 5,154
Rate % 5.5
Federal Government Civilian Employment 4,722

Education

The Little Rock School District supports 49 elementary schools, junior high/middle schools, and senior high schools. The city is home for two noted special facilities: the Arkansas School for the Blind and the Arkansas School for the Deaf. A number of parochial and private schools supplement the public school system.

Higher education is offered in one large public university and four smaller colleges. The University of Arkansas at Little Rock is a branch of the main university located at Fayetteville, and it maintains two special graduate institutions in the city: the University of Arkansas for Medical Sciences and the Graduate Institute of Technology. The four colleges are Philander Smith College, affiliated with the Methodist Church; Arkansas Baptist College; Arkansas College of Technology; and Southern Technical College.

Education

Number of Public Schools   49
Special Education Schools   NA
Total Enrollment   25,813
% Enrollment in Private Schools   10.4
% Minority   64.4
Classroom Teachers   1,614
Pupil-Teacher Ratio   15.9:1
Number of Graduates   1,764
Total Revenue (in millions) $86.781
Total Expenditures (in millions) $99.067
Expenditures per Pupil $2,901
Educational Attainment (Age 25 and Over)
    % Completed 12 or More Years   76.2
    % Completed 16 or More Years   25.0
Four-Year Colleges and Universities   4
    Enrollment   14,197
Two-Year Colleges   NA
    Enrollment   NA

Libraries

Number   31
Public Libraries   7
Books (in thousands)   524
Circulation (in thousands)   945
Persons Served (in thousands)   283
Circulation per Person Served   3.33
Income (in millions) $3.289
Staff   86

Four-Year Colleges and Universities
    Arkansas Baptist College
    Philander Smith College
    University of Arkansas, Little Rock
    University of Arkansas for Medical Sciences

Health

Nine hospitals are located in Little Rock. The oldest is St. Vincent Infirmary, founded in 1888, and currently one of the three largest. The other two large hospitals are the

Health

Deaths—Total   1,718
Rate per 1,000   10.1
Infant Deaths—Total   38
Rate per 1,000   12.5
Number of Metro Hospitals   9
Number of Metro Hospital Beds   3,942
Rate per 100,000   2,178
Number of Physicians   1,351
Physicians per 1,000   2.96
Nurses per 1,000   15.81
Health Expenditures per Capita $17.23

Baptist Medical Center and the University Hospital, affiliated with the University of Arkansas for Medical Sciences. The Central Arkansas Radiation Therapy Institute is a combined operation of these institutes. Other medical facilites include the Doctor's Hospital, Arkansas Children's Hospital, Arkansas State Hospital, Riverview Medical Center, Baptist Memorial Medical Center, Baptist Rehabilitation Institute, CPC Pinnacle Pointe Hospital, Charter Hospital, and two Veterans Administration Medical Centers.

Transportation

Little Rock is served by five interstates: I-30 connects the city with its northern suburbs; I-40, located in North Little Rock, heads east toward Memphis; I-430 bisects the western part of the city north to south, crosses the Arkansas River, and heads toward the southern suburbs; I-440 connects Little Rock with I-40; and I-630, also known as the Wilbur Mills Freeway, connects downtown with the suburbs. Little Rock is also served by U.S. Highways 64, 65, 67, 70, and 167, as well as 22 state highways. As a port on the Arkansas River, Little Rock has constructed the McClellan-Kerr Arkansas River Navigation System, a complex of 17 locks and dams in 448 miles of water from 15 miles east of Tulsa, Oklahoma, to Verdigris River. The Fred I. Brown Industrial Harbor was opened in 1987 to store goods moved on barges on the Arkansas River. In addition to Amtrak, Little Rock is served by the Union Pacific Railroad and the Cotton Belt/Southern Pacific Railroad. Located three miles east of the city, Little Rock Regional Airport serves as the main air terminus for the area. A secondary airport is the Worth James private airport just south of the city.

Transportation

Interstate Highway Mileage   57
Total Urban Mileage   1,672
Total Daily Vehicle Mileage (in millions)   7.362
Daily Average Commute Time   43.8 min.
Number of Buses   50
Port Tonnage (in millions)   NA
Airports   1
Number of Daily Flights   42
Daily Average Number of Passengers   2,595

Airlines (American carriers only)
    American
    Delta
    Trans World
    Southwest
    Northwest
    United
    USAir

Housing

Of the total housing stock, 56.2% is owner-occupied. The median value of an owner-occupied home is $64,200 and the median monthly rent $318.

Housing

Total Housing Units   80,995
% Change 1980–1990   20.2
Vacant Units for Sale or Rent   6,639
Occupied Units   72,573
% with More Than One Person per Room   3.1
% Owner-Occupied   56.2
Median Value of Owner-Occupied Homes $64,200
Average Monthly Purchase Cost $322
Median Monthly Rent $318
New Private Housing Starts   472
Value (in thousands) $51,009
% Single-Family   94.5
Nonresidential Buildings Value (in thousands) $61,280

Tallest Buildings	Hgt. (ft.)	Stories
TCBY Towers (1986)	546	40
First Commercial Bank (1975)	454	30
Worthen Bank & Trust (1969)	375	24
Stephens Bldg. (1985)	365	25
Tower Bldg. (1960)	350	18
Union National Bank (1968)	331	21

Urban Redevelopment

Most urban redevelopment programs have been commercial shopping malls, such as the large Metrocentre Mall.

Crime

Little Rock ranks low in public safety. In 1990, of the crimes known to the police, there were 5,290 violent crimes and 23,409 property crimes.

Crime

Violent Crimes—Total   5,290
Violent Crime Rate per 100,000   1,408.9
Murder   46
Rape   268
Robbery   1,459
Aggravated Assaults   3,518
Property Crimes   23,409
Burglary   5,773
Larceny   15,116
Motor Vehicle Theft   2,740
Arson   216
Per Capita Police Expenditures $84.37
Per Capita Fire Protection Expenditures $73.92
Number of Police   328
Per 1,000   1.92

Religion

Little Rock, like the rest of Arkansas, is heavily Baptist and Methodist; these two denominations make up more than 50% of the population. Other major denominations are Assembly of God and Church of Christ.

Religion

Largest Denominations (Adherents)	
Catholic	20,175
Southern Baptist	85,767

Religion (continued)

United Methodist	37,107
Black Baptist	25,321
Church of Christ	9,592
Assembly of God	5,254
Lutheran-Missouri Synod	3,007
Episcopal	4,792
Jewish	993

Media

The lone city daily is the *Little Rock Arkansas Democrat*, which is published in the mornings. The electronic media consist of 6 television stations and 15 AM and FM radio stations.

Media

Newsprint
  Arkansas State Press, weekly
  Arkansas Times, weekly
  Arkansas Business, weekly
  Little Rock Arkansas Democrat, daily

Television
  KARK (Channel 4)
  KASN (Channel 38)
  KATV (Channel 7)
  KLRT (Channel 16)
  KTHV (Channel 11)
  KUTN (Channel 38)

Radio
KAAY (AM)	KABF (FM)
KARN (AM)	KBIS (AM)
KEZQ (FM)	KGHT (AM)
KHLT (FM)	KITA (AM)
KKYK (FM)	KMJX (FM)
KOLL (FM)	KPAL (AM)
KSSN (FM)	KUAR (FM)
WCGM (AM)	

Sports

Little Rock does not have a major professional sports team. The University of Arkansas Razorbacks football team plays at the War Memorial Stadium.

Arts, Culture, and Tourism

The largest initiator of the arts scene in Little Rock is the Arkansas Arts Center. Founded in 1962 in MacArthur Park, it is now considered one of the nation's leading small museums. Other areas in the arts include the Decorative Arts Museum, a restored antebellum house; the Arkansas Repertory Theatre; the Arkansas Symphony Orchestra; Artspree, a series of performances in theater, dance, and music held at the University of Arkansas at Little Rock College of Fine Arts; the Wildwood Park for the Performing Arts; and the University of Arkansas at Little Rock Theatre Arts and Dance Department.

Travel and Tourism

Hotel Rooms 7,366
Convention and Exhibit Space (square feet) 62,150

Convention Centers
   Statehouse Plaza and Convention Center
   University Conference Center
   Robinson Center

Festivals
   Riverfest (Memorial Day weekend)
   Arkansas State Fair and Livestock Show (September)
   Arkansas State Festival of Art (spring)
   Delta Art Exhibit (October)

Parks and Recreation

Of the 56 parks in Little Rock, the 2 largest are the War Memorial Park, which has on its grounds the War Memorial Stadium and the Little Rock Zoo, and Riverfront Park (located near the Old State House), which is a tree-lined walk along the Arkansas River. MacArthur Park, located at Ninth and Sherman streets, is home to the Museum of Science and History as well as the Arkan-sas Arts Center. Other parks include Gillam Park, Boyle Park, East Little Rock Park, and Allsopp Park.

Sources of Further Information

Greater Little Rock Chamber of Commerce
1 Spring Building
Little Rock, AR 72201-2486
(501) 374-4871

Little Rock Convention and Visitors Bureau
Statehouse Plaza
P.O. Box 3232
Little Rock, AR 72203
(800) 844-4781

Additional Reading

DeSpain, Richard. *More Than a Memory: Little Rock's Historic Quapaw Quarter*. 1981.
Wooley, Rita P. *Sketches of Life in Little Rock, 1836–1850*. 1982.

Los Angeles

California

Location and Topography

Los Angeles lies on the southern coast of California, 383 miles from the state capital at Sacramento. The city borders the Pacific Ocean on the southwest, Santa Monica Mountains on the north, and San Gabriel Mountains on the east. The terrain consists of a broad coastal plain broken by low hills. The plain gently slopes northward to the Verdugo Hills.

Layout of City and Suburbs

Los Angeles is more a county than a city. In fact, one guidebook says that Los Angeles is made up of five distinct regions to make "one great city." They are: Downtown, Hollywood, the Westside, the Coastal areas, and the Valleys. Downtown Los Angeles is noted for its ethnic diversity. Olvera Street and its Mexican flavors mark El Pueblo de Los Angeles Historic Park. Oriental visages can be seen in Chinatown, Koreatown, and Little Tokyo. The Music Center of Los Angeles is an arts and culture hub that contains, among other structures, the Dorothy Chandler Pavilion, home of the Academy Awards. The Garment District near Olympia Boulevard is highlighted by the six-floor Cooper Building. Hollywood speaks for itself. From its founding in the early 20th century as a filming location for moving pictures, the city's cinematic splendor has delighted and fascinated millions. On the Westside, Rodeo Drive and Sunset Boulevard set the area aside as one of glitz and glamour. Westside's communities include the cities of Beverly Hills and Bel Air. The Coastal areas are 72 miles of beaches from Malibu in the north to Long Beach in the south. Hugged at its northern end by the Santa Monica Mountains, this strip of land incorporates the cities of Santa Monica, Marina del Rey, and Redondo Beach, and is the home of the Los Angeles

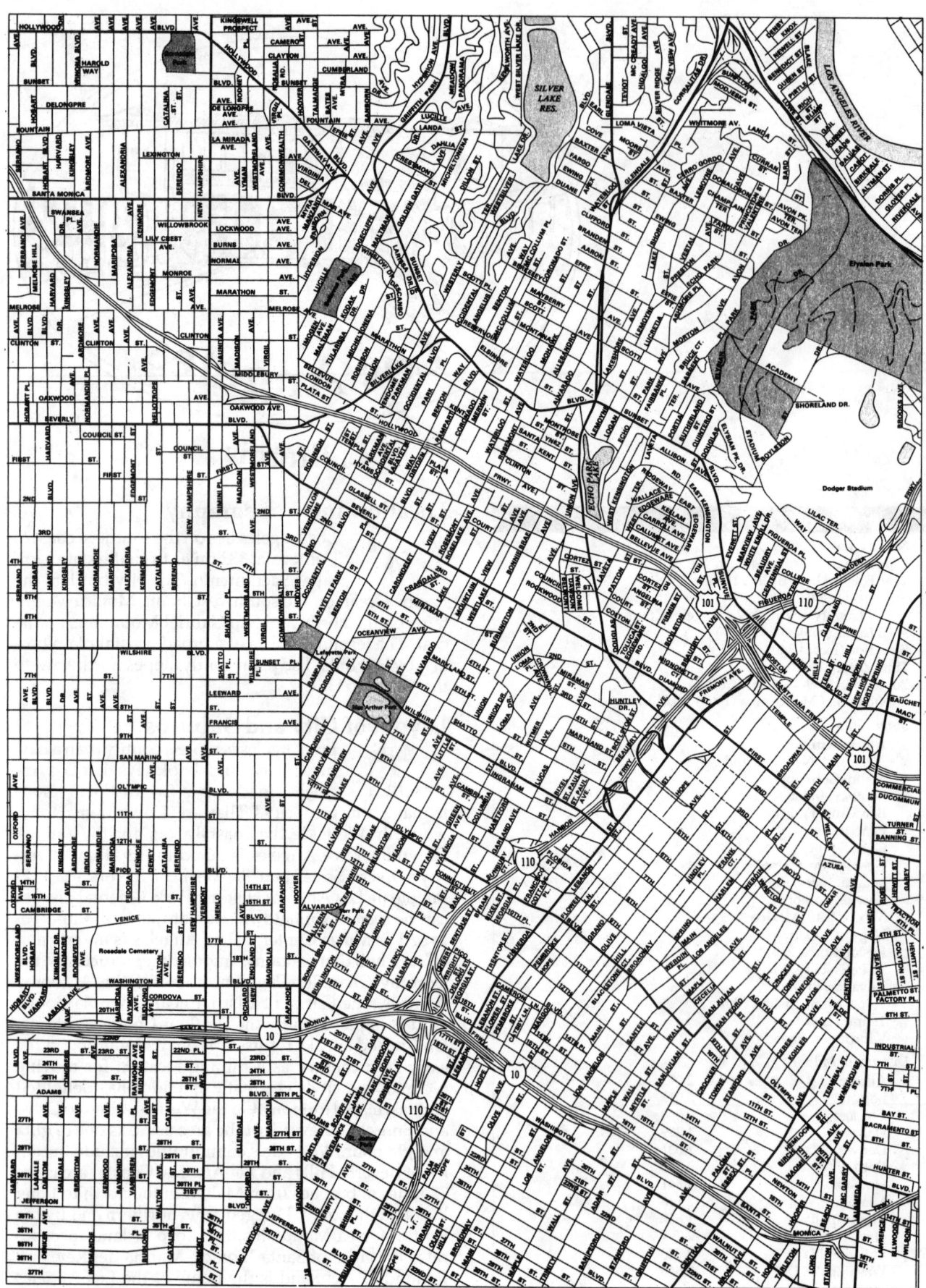

International Airport. The final region is the Valleys. Known in the 1980s for its own teenage language, the San Gabriel, San Fernando, and Santa Clarita valleys ring the rest of Los Angeles County with such cities as Van Nuys and Burbank.

Environment

Environmental Stress Index 3.4
Green Cities Index: Rank 61
                    Score 39.43
Water Quality Slightly alkaline, soft
   Average Daily Use (gallons per capita) 192
   Maximum Supply (gallons per capita) 191
Parkland as % of Total City Area 3.6
% Waste Landfilled/Recycled 85:15
Annual Parks Expenditures per Capita $45.24

Climate

Given its extent and the differences in terrain, the city has diverse climatic conditions. In general, Los Angeles has an inviting two-season climate. The predominant weather influence is the warm, moist Pacific air, keeping temperatures mild throughout the year. Summers are dry and sunny with low clouds at night and in the mornings. Most of the precipitation occurs in the winter months. Unusual weather phenomena include the Santa Ana winds—strong, dusty gales of up to 50 miles per hour blowing from the surrounding mountains—and occasional flash floods in the canyon areas, causing mudslides. When the Santa Ana winds blow, the fire danger rises sharply in the hills and mountains, and late-fall brush fires are a familiar occurrence. Temperatures throughout the Los Angeles basin vary with elevation and distance from the ocean. Because the San Fernando Valley is largely protected from marine influence by the Santa Monica Mountains, it has a warmer and drier climate than the rest of the city, and summer temperatures commonly reach 100°F in some parts of the valley. The city's best-known climatic problem is the smog that results when the surrounding hills hem in the pollution from over 6 million cars. Earthquakes are a potential hazard, although Los Angeles has escaped the kind of destruction that San Francisco suffered a number of times this century.

Weather

Temperature

Highest Monthly Average °F 83.8
Lowest Monthly Average °F 47.7

Annual Averages

Days 32°F or Below 0
Days above 90°F 5
Zero Degree Days 0
Precipitation (inches) 14.85
Snow (inches) 0.0
% Seasonal Humidity 71.0
Wind Speed (m.p.h.) 7.4

Weather (continued)

Clear Days 143
Cloudy Days 107
Storm Days 3
Rainy Days 35

Average Temperatures (°F)	High	Low	Mean
January	63.5	45.4	54.5
February	64.1	47.0	55.6
March	64.3	48.6	56.5
April	65.9	51.7	58.8
May	68.4	55.3	61.9
June	70.3	58.6	64.5
July	74.8	62.1	68.5
August	75.8	63.2	69.5
September	75.7	61.6	68.7
October	72.9	57.5	65.2
November	69.6	51.3	60.5
December	66.5	47.3	56.9

History

By the fifth decade of the 16th century, Spain had sent numerous exploration groups, led by men like Hernando de Soto and Francisco Vasquez de Coronado, into uncharted regions. In 1542, Juan Rodriguez Cabrillo explored the California coast and found the Gabrielino Indians occupying what is now the Los Angeles Basin. However, Cabrillo's men came ashore only at Catalina Island. Sixty years elapsed before another European visited this exact area, although in 1579 Sir Francis Drake explored the southern part of the state and then claimed all of present-day California for England. Two other explorations reached California, but made no record of landings. In 1602, Spaniard Sebastián Vizcaíno was sent to the port of Monterey to see what value it had to the Spanish crown. His report left no doubt that the coast of California was full of riches, but again, little was done about the recommendation.

Up to this time, all of the explorers who had visited the Los Angeles Basin did so from the ocean. In 1769, the expedition of Gaspar de Portolá traveled from San Diego in the south to Monterey, where it was resolved that a Spanish mission would be set up. Accompanying the explorers was Fray Juan Crespi, a Franciscan priest who was the principal diarist of the Portolá expedition. These men named the area Señora Reina de los Angeles de Porciúncula (Our Lady of Los Angeles), with the last name reflecting the Franciscan chapel of St. Francis of Assisi in Italy. Two years later, Franciscan priests Fray Pedro Cambón and Fray Angel Somera traveled the route laid out by the Portolá expedition from San Diego and set up Mission San Gabriel Archangel. Within ten years, the first governor of the Californias, Phelipe de Neve, delivered a Reglamento (loosely translated as a book of laws) in which he spelled out the establishment of several pueblos for habitation by Mexicans. The first was at San Jose and the second was Los Angeles. The first population count showed 44 settlers, a mix of Spanish, Mexican, Indian, and black farmers. By the turn of the century, the population had reached 315.

Chronology

1542 The expedition of Spaniard Juan Rodriguez Cabrillo along the California coast finds the Gabrielino Indians in the Los Angeles Basin area.

1602 Spaniard Sebastián Vizcaíno explores Monterey and writes a report on its value to the Spanish crown.

1769 Spanish explorer Gaspar de Portolá and Fray Juan Crespi, a Franciscan priest and the mission's chief diarist, reach the Los Angeles Basin, which they explore and name Señora Reina de los Angeles de Porciúncula (Our Lady of Los Angeles).

1771 Franciscan priests Fray Pedro Cambón and Fray Angel Somera found Mission San Gabriel Archangel, located near present-day Los Angeles.

1781 Phelipe de Neve, the first Spanish governor of the Californias, selects the site of Los Angeles for settlement. The pueblo of Los Angeles is founded with 44 inhabitants, mostly black and Spanish farmers.

1825 California becomes a territory of Mexico.

1842 Gold is discovered near the San Fernando Mission.

1848 Los Angeles is ceded to the United States under the Treaty of Guadulupe Hidalgo, which ends the Mexican-American War.

1876 The first transcontinental railroad, the Southern Pacific, arrives in Los Angeles. The Santa Fe arrives nine years later.

1910 Hollywood is annexed by Los Angeles.

1932 The IXth Olympiad is held in Los Angeles.

1973 Tom Bradley is elected the first black mayor of Los Angeles. He serves until 1993.

1984 The XXth Olympiad is held in Los Angeles.

1992 Los Angeles experiences one of the worst riots in American history since the Civil War when protests arise over the acquittal of four white police officers accused of beating a black man.

The Mexican period, as the time under command from Mexico is known, lasted from 1825 when California became a Mexican territory until the Mexican-American War in 1846. In this short span, Mexico's leadership was ineffectual at best in encouraging Los Angeles's growth. Commerce in hides brought Americans from the United States and led to a further loss of Mexican influence. The finding of gold near the San Fernando Mission in 1842—six years before the gold rush that forever altered California—completed the rush toward the American transformation of the area. The Mexican-American War ended in 1848 with the signing of the Treaty of Guadalupe Hidalgo, which turned over California (and with it, Los Angeles) to the United States. The city was incorporated on 4 April 1850, and California became the 31st state five months later.

Growth was immediate, but it was accompanied by growing pains. The city remained a seedy town, riddled with vigilante killings, for much of the rest of the century. By 1853 the only newspaper was *La Estrella de los Angeles* (the Los Angeles Star), printed in both Spanish and English. In 1881 the first issue of the *Los Angeles Times*—a newspaper that continues to this day—was published. The first transcontinental railroad, the Southern Pacific, came to town in 1876, and the Santa Fe in 1885. A subsequent real estate boom helped the population to swell from 12,000 to 50,000. The discovery of oil at the turn of the century also helped to sustain the influx of people into the city. In the early decades of the 20th century, the rise of the motion picture industry in Hollywood brought a touch of glamour as well as tourist dollars to the city. Hollywood was annexed in 1910, and the San Fernando Valley in 1915. By the end of World War II, Los Angeles had a population of 1.5 million; by 1960 it rose to 2.5 million despite the emerging problems associated with traffic congestion, smog, crime, drought, earthquakes, and race riots.

The IXth and XXth Olympiads in 1932 and 1984, respectively, made Los Angeles an athletic center, and with this newfound awareness came increased commerce. The city, however, was splintered along racial lines. The Watts riot in 1965 was the first evidence that all was not well with the city that had long prided itself on racial harmony. Increased Asian immigration (mainly Koreans and Vietnamese) and their extensive business success brought other elements into the racial equation. The city's slums and ghettos became tinderboxes, ready to erupt at the slightest provocation. In 1973 Los Angeles elected its first black mayor, Thomas Bradley, but race relations deteriorated. In 1992, Los Angeles experienced a race riot almost as destructive as that of Watts. Thousands of blacks went on a rampage after an all-white jury acquitted four white police officers of beating Rodney King, a black motorist. The four men were later retried on civil rights violations, and two were convicted in 1993.

Historical Landmarks

In Los Angeles, purely historical landmarks are overshadowed by pop cultural landmarks and urban icons, such as Mann's (originally Grauman's) Chinese Theater and the homes of movie stars. Nevertheless, genuine historical landmarks have been preserved, enshrining the city's heritage. The nonprofit Los Angeles Conservancy aids in the restoration, maintainance, and upkeep of these landmarks. The conservancy also sponsors tours of various districts, such as the Broadway Theatres Tour, which includes the restored Million Dollar Theatre and Hollywood apartments from the 1920s and 1930s. At the center of El Pueblo de Los Angeles Historic Park is Olvera Street, on which stands the oldest house in Los Angeles—the Avila Adobe, built in 1818. Along the Hollywood Walk of Fame, which extends along Hollywood Boulevard, are nearly 2,000 star-shaped plaques honoring celebrities and personalities of the silver screen, radio, stage, and television. The Plaza, bounded by Main, Los Angeles, and Marchessault streets and Ferguson Alley, lies southeast of the first plaza laid out in 1781 by Governor Phelipe de Neve, whose statue stands in the circular fountain in the center of the park. Los Angeles's two missions still survive: Mission San Gabriel Archangel and Mission San Fernando Rey de España, although the latter was severely damaged during the 1971 earthquake.

Population

In the heady days after World War II, it was assumed that Los Angeles would keep growing endlessly. Since then the limits to growth have become painfully evident, and the social and environmental costs have taken a heavy toll on the city. With a population of 3,485,398, Los Angeles is the second-largest city in the nation, having passed Chicago in the 1980s. Despite its problems, Los Angeles surpassed its 5.5% growth rate from 2,812,000 in 1970, and grew by 17.4% from its 1980 population of 2,968,528. Housing costs, congestion, unemployment, crime, and other deterrents may finally put the brake to growth and stabilize the population at about 3.5 million.

Population

	1980	1990
Central City	2,968,528	3,485,398
Rank	3	2
Metro Area	7,477,239	8,863,164
Pop. Change 1980–1990	+516,870	
Pop. % Change 1980–1990	+17.4	
Median Age 30.7		
% Male 50.2		
% Age 65 and Over 10.0		
Density (per square mile) 7,426		

Households

Number 1,217,405
Persons per Household 2.80
% Female-Headed Households 13.6
% One-Person Households 28.5
Births—Total 63,267
    % to Mothers under 20 12.5
    Birth Rate per 1,000 20.4

Ethnic Composition

Whites form a bare majority in Los Angeles with 52.8%. Blacks form 14%, concentrated in certain sections. American Indians form 0.5%, Asians and Pacific Islanders 9.8%, and others 22.9%. Hispanics, both black and white, make up 40%. The bulk of Hispanics are of Mexican origin and are estimated to number 800,000. The area around City Hall is considered Little Mexico; Hispanics also dominate the Barrio in East Los Angeles. Adjacent is Little Tokyo, two blocks southeast of City Hall. Chinatown lies a few blocks north of Little Tokyo. Blacks are concentrated in south-central Los Angeles. Among the Asian groups, the largest in order of size are Filipinos, Japanese, Chinese, and Koreans. Most of the whites live in the San Fernando Valley. American Indians live mainly in the Westlake area, near downtown.

Ethnic Composition (as % of total pop.)

	1980	1990
White	61.24	52.83
Black	17.03	13.99
American Indian	0.56	0.47
Asian and Pacific Islander	6.61	9.81
Hispanic	27.51	39.92
Other	NA	22.91

Government

The municipal government is more complex than that of most American cities. Under the archaic 1925 charter, many departments operate independently of the central executive and legislative authorities. The mayor and the 13-member city council are elected to four-year terms, as are the city attorney and the comptroller. Direct policy control over various city departments is by commissions such as Harbor, Airport, and Water and Power; they are also empowered to collect revenues. The county of Los Angeles is governed by a five-member board of supervisors. School districts are governed by citizen boards elected at large rather than by wards.

Government

Year of Home Charter 1925
Number of Members of the Governing Body 13
Elected at Large NA
Elected by Wards 13
Number of Women in Governing Body 3
Salary of Mayor $117,876
Salary of Council Members $90,680
City Government Employment Total 42,771
Rate per 10,000 131.2

Public Finance

Los Angeles has the second highest municipal budget in the nation. The annual budget consists of revenues of $6.585 billion and expenditures of $6.447 billion. The debt outstanding is $6.278 billion, and cash and security holdings are $11.743 billion.

Economy

By sheer population size, Los Angeles dominates the economy of the state of California and, to a lesser extent, the West Coast. No single sector of the economy is dominant.

Public Finance

Total Revenue (in millions) $6,585.2
Intergovernmental Revenue—Total (in millions) $439.3
Federal Revenue per Capita $69.2
% Federal Assistance   1.05
% State Assistance   4.19
Sales Tax as % of Total Revenue   11.74
Local Revenue as % of Total Revenue   48.19
City Income Tax   no
Taxes—Total (in millions) $1,155.5

Taxes per Capita
   Total $355
   Property $115
   Sales and Gross Receipts $170
General Expenditures—Total (in millions) $1,940.5
General Expenditures per Capita $595
Capital Outlays per Capita $114

% of Expenditures for:
   Public Welfare   0.0
   Highways   5.0
   Education   0.2
   Health and Hospitals   0.3
   Police   21.8
   Sewerage and Sanitation   11.5
   Parks and Recreation   5.6
   Housing and Community Development   7.9
Debt Outstanding per Capita $1,126
   % Utility   51.1
Federal Procurement Contract Awards (in millions)
   $4,455.1
Federal Grants Awards (in millions) $704.9
Fiscal Year Begins   July 1

Economy

Total Money Income (in millions) $39,381.756
% of State Average   101.7
Per Capita Annual Income $12,084
% Population below Poverty Level   16.4
Fortune 500 Companies   7

Banks	Number	Deposits (in millions)
Commercial	225	NA
Savings.	78	82,245.7

Passenger Autos   64,788,180
Electric Meters   3,202,004
Gas Meters   3,050,552

Manufacturing

Number of Establishments   8,262
% with 20 or More Employees   32.9
Manufacturing Payroll (in millions) $7,343.0
Value Added by Manufacture (in millions) $16,084.6
Value of Shipments (in millions) $32,108.1
New Capital Expenditures (in millions) $695.1

Wholesale Trade

Number of Establishments   8,683
Sales (in millions) $53,109.5
Annual Payroll (in millions) $2,707.549

Retail Trade

Number of Establishments   32,203
Total Sales (in millions) $20,564.5
Sales per Capita $6,309
Number of Retail Trade Establishments with Payroll
   17,625
Annual Payroll (in millions) $2,576.7
Total Sales (in millions) $19,729.0
General Merchandise Stores (per capita) $604
Food Stores (per capita) $1,224
Apparel Stores (per capita) $428
Eating and Drinking Places (per capita) $767

Economy (continued)

Service Industries

Total Establishments   35,367
Total Receipts (in millions) $25,863.9
Hotels and Motels (in millions) $798.5
Health Services (in millions) $4,034.4
Legal Services (in millions) $3,700.1

Business and management services are most important, followed by tourism, wholesale trade and distribution, and aerospace and high technology. With the end of the cold war, the aerospace industry has been hard hit by layoffs and plant closings. The Port of Los Angeles handles much of the commerce of the West Coast as well as goods to and from Asia and Australia. The city has rich deposits of petroleum, and is a top oil-refining center and producer of oil-field equipment. With Hollywood—the motion picture capital of the world—in its midst, Los Angeles is a major producer of television shows, as well as the center of the U.S. music industry; 50 record companies operate in the area. Tourism is a major industry; in 1991, visitors spent an estimated $7.1 billion in Los Angeles.

Labor

 More than 25% of the work force is employed in services, with trade and manufacturing as close runners-up. One feature of the Los Angeles employment scene is the long commuting time to work places, up to three hours per day from outlying areas. These long commutes also add to highway congestion and air pollution. The work force is younger and has more immigrants than in typical East Coast cities. According to the U.S. Census Bureau, Los Angeles will have a healthy employment climate until 2000.

Labor

Civilian Labor Force   1,792,321
% Change 1989–1990   5.0

Work Force Distribution
   Mining   7,810
   Construction   130,400
   Manufacturing   796,700
   Transportation and Public Utilities   214,700
   Wholesale and Retail Trade   890,700
   FIRE (Finance, Insurance, Real Estate)   272,300
   Service   1,180,600
   Government   539,300
   Women as % of Labor Force   43.4
   % Self-Employed   7.7
   % Professional/Technical   16.8
Total Unemployment   115,830
Rate %   6.5
Federal Government Civilian Employment   33,391

Education

The Los Angeles Unified School District, one of 95 school districts in Los Angeles County and the second largest in the nation, supports 623 elementary schools, junior high schools, and senior high schools. Over 60,000 students attend 225 private and parochial schools. The higher education system is divided similarly between public and private auspices.The former comprises the University of California at Los Angeles, California State University at Los Angeles, and California State University at Northridge. Private institutions include the University of Southern California, Loyola Marymount University, Mount St. Mary's College, Occidental College, Pepperdine University, Woodbury University, and DeVry Institute of Technology.

Education	
Number of Public Schools	632
Special Education Schools	19
Total Enrollment	625,073
% Enrollment in Private Schools	14.0
% Minority	86.3
Classroom Teachers	27,240
Pupil-Teacher Ratio	22.9:1
Number of Graduates	22,811
Total Revenue (in millions)	$3,064.5
Total Expenditures (in millions)	$2,861.0
Expenditures per Pupil	$4,849
Educational Attainment (Age 25 and Over)	
% Completed 12 or More Years	68.6
% Completed 16 or More Years	19.8
Four-Year Colleges and Universities	8
Enrollment	96,855
Two-Year Colleges	6
Enrollment	50,800

Libraries	
Number	243
Public Libraries	63
Books (in thousands)	5,242
Circulation (in thousands)	10,137
Persons Served (in thousands)	3,433
Circulation per Person Served	2.95
Income (in millions)	$42.299
Staff	NA

Four-Year Colleges and Universities
 California State University - Los Angeles
 University of California - Los Angeles
 Loyola Marymount University
 Mount St. Mary's College
 Occidental College
 Pepperdine University
 University of Southern California
 Woodbury University

Health

The medical sector is one of the fastest growing in the city, in terms of both capacity and its impact on the general economy. There are 45 hospitals with 11,075 beds in the metro area. The largest are the Los Angeles County University of Southern California Medical Center with 2,000 beds and the University of California at Los Angeles Medical Center. Other facilities include California Medical Center, St. Vincent's Hospital, Good Samaritan Hospital, Children's Hospital, and Cedars Sinai Hospital.

Health	
Deaths—Total	27,090
Rate per 1,000	8.7
Infant Deaths—Total	694
Rate per 1,000	11.0
Number of Metro Hospitals	45
Number of Metro Hospital Beds	11,075
Rate per 100,000	340
Number of Physicians	20,359
Physicians per 1,000	2.80
Nurses per 1,000	4.35
Health Expenditures per Capita	$2.48

Transportation

Four interstate highways converge on the city: I-5 from the north; I-10 from the southeast; I-15, which intersects with I-10 east of the city; and I-405 from San Diego. State Highway 1 (Pacific Coast Highway) skirts the city along the coast. Los Angeles has one of the world's most extensive freeway systems, comprising nearly 20 freeways totaling more than 700 miles. Rail passenger service is provided by Amtrak through Union Station. Rail freight services are provided by the Santa Fe, Southern Pacific, and Union Pacific railroads. Los Angeles International Airport near Playa del Rey, 17 miles from downtown, is one of the world's busiest, catering to 79 domestic and international airlines. Other regional airports include the Burbank-Glendale-Pasadena Airport, Long Beach Airport, Ontario International Airport, and John Wayne Airport, which serves all of Orange County.

Transportation	
Interstate Highway Mileage	349
Total Urban Mileage	25,188
Total Daily Vehicle Mileage (in millions)	247
Daily Average Commute Time	53.5 min.
Number of Buses	2,209
Port Tonnage (in millions)	45.213
Airports	4
Number of Daily Flights	760
Daily Average Number of Passengers	62,296

Airlines (American carriers only)
 Alaska
 American
 American West
 Continental
 Delta
 Eastern
 Hawaiian Air
 Northwest
 Southwest
 Trans World
 USAir
 United

Housing

Before the 1950s, most houses were single-family bungalows, cottages, and ranch-style homes. These houses generally featured generous windows, patios, atriums, gardens, and swimming pools. Land was plentiful and inexpensive in places like the San Fernando Valley. The construction of single-family homes peaked in the 1960s, and has since declined in favor of apartment houses. By the 1980s homes became unaffordable for the middle class, and Los Angeles became the second most expensive housing market in the nation, after Honolulu. Expensive luxury homes, half a million dollars and up, are found in Burbank, Toluca Lake, Van Nuys, North Hollywood, and Sherman Oaks. Since 1962 more apartments than houses have been built in the city. Of the total housing stock, only 39.4% is owner-occupied, one of the lowest percentages of any city. The median value of an owner-occupied home is $244,500 and the average monthly rent is $544.

Housing

Total Housing Units   1,299,963
% Change 1980–1990   8.5
Vacant Units for Sale or Rent   69,406
Occupied Units   1,217,405
% with More Than One Person per Room   22.3
% Owner-Occupied   39.4
Median Value of Owner-Occupied Homes $244,500
Average Monthly Purchase Cost $420
Median Monthly Rent $544
New Private Housing Starts   11,826
Value (in thousands) $1,357,248
% Single-Family   16.0
Nonresidential Buildings Value (in thousands) $813,458

Tallest Buildings	Hgt. (ft.)	Stories
First Interstate World Center (1989)	1,017	73
First Interstate Bank	858	62
Cal. Plaza 11A	750	57
Wells Fargo Tower	750	54
Security Pacific Plaza	735	55
So. Cal. Gas Center (1990)	733	55
777 Tower	725	52
Mitsui Fudoson (1990)	716	52

Urban Redevelopment

Los Angeles has undergone several cycles of development. After the repeal of a 140-foot height limit on buildings in 1956, there was a spate of new skyscrapers. A new style of architecture, featuring lightweight metal, converted downtown Los Angeles and the nearby Wilshire Corridor into multistoried office and apartment complexes. Today 20- to 40-story government buildings occupy a central mall. Despite the revival of the older downtown area, Los Angeles has witnessed the rise of the urban village, including such planned sections as Century City, Costa Mesa, Encino, Newport Beach, and Westwood. Among the organizations coordinating urban development is Central City Association.

Crime

Los Angeles ranks near the bottom of U.S. cities in public safety. Since 1980, gang activity and drug-related crimes have increased. According to the Federal Bureau of Investigation, in 1991 violent crimes totaled 89,875 and property crimes totaled 256,349.

Crime

Violent Crimes—Total   89,875
Violent Crime Rate per 100,000   1,795
Murder   1,027
Rape   1,996
Robbery   39,778
Aggravated Assaults   47,104
Property Crimes   256,349
Burglary   57,460
Larceny   130,234
Motor Vehicle Theft   68,655
Arson   4,976
Per Capita Police Expenditures $184.26
Per Capita Fire Protection Expenditures $71.61
Number of Police   7,051
Per 1,000   2.21

Religion

Catholics form the largest population in Los Angeles, a city whose early heritage is distinctly Catholic. The city includes a number of churches among its architectural landmarks. The Cathedral of St. Vibiana, the first Roman Catholic cathedral in the city, opened in 1876; it is the seat of the Archdiocese of Southern California. The Church of Our Lady of Lourdes on Third Street is notable for its fine metal and stone grills and the gleaming metal cap of its tower. The Angelus Temple is a relic of the days when Aimee Semple McPherson's brand of Christianity, known as the Foursquare Gospel, achieved immense popularity. The Immanuel Presbyterian Church on Wilshire Boulevard and Berendo Street resembles a Gothic cathedral with its 207-foot tower. The Wilshire Boulevard Christian Church on Wilshire Bouelvard and Normandie Avenue is similar to churches of northern Italy. The Wilshire Methodist Episcopal Church on Wilshire and Plymouth boulevards is of modified Spanish Romanesque architecture. The St. Vincent de Paul Roman Catholic Church on Figueroa Street and Adams Boulevard is an imposing white edifice topped by a 125-foot corner tower and dome. St. John's Episcopal Church recalls the 11th-century church at Toscanella, Italy. The B'nai B'rith Temple

Religion

Largest Denominations (Adherents)	
Catholic	3,077,114
Black Baptist	268,605
Southern Baptist	128,895
Latter-Day Saints	103,286
Assembly of God	55,107
Presbyterian	64,168
United Methodist	70,590
American Baptist	76,010
Episcopal	50,674
Jewish	501,700

with its 135-foot dome, on Wilshire and Hobart boulevards, is the city's largest synagogue.

Media

The Los Angeles press consists of the morning *Los Angeles Times*. In addition, 40 daily community and foreign-language newspapers, as well as numerous underground editions, are published. The electronic media consist of 9 television stations and more than 25 AM and FM radio stations. The three major television networks—ABC, NBC, and CBS—originate many of their programs in Los Angeles.

Media
Newsprint
California Examiner, (2x/mo.)
Eastside Journal, weekly
Eastside Sun, weekly
Herald Dispatch, weekly
Los Angeles Independent Newspapers, weekly
Los Angeles Magazine, monthly
Los Angeles Sentinel, weekly
Los Angeles Times, daily
News-Herald and Journal, (2x/wk.)
Northeast Star Review, (2x/wk.)
Television
KABC (Channel 7)
KCAL (Channel 9)
KCBS (Channel 2)
KCET (Channel 28)
KCOP (Channel 13)
KHSC (Channel 46)
KLCS (Channel 58)
KNBC (Channel 4)
KTTV (Channel 11)
Radio
KABC (AM)   KBIG (FM)
KCDB (FM)   KDLA (AM)
KFI (AM)   KFSG (FM)
KFWB (AM)   KGFJ (AM)
KIIS (AM)   KIIS (FM)
KKBT (FM)   KKGO (FM)
KKHJ (AM)   KLIT (FM)
KLSX (FM)   KMPC (AM)
KNX (AM)   KOST (FM)
KPSC (FM)   KQLZ (FM)
KRLA (AM)   KRTH (AM)
KRTH (FM)   KRXV (FM)
KSKQ (FM)   KTWV (FM)
KUSC (FM)

Sports

Los Angeles is represented by teams in every major professional sport: the Raiders and Rams in football; the Dodgers and the California Angels in baseball; the Kings and the expansion Mighty Ducks in hockey; and the Lakers and Clippers in basketball. Both the University of Southern California and the University of California at Los Angeles field strong teams in sports and athletics. Thoroughbred racing is held in Santa Anita Park and Hollywood Park.

Arts, Culture, and Tourism

Pop as well as traditional culture flourishes in Los Angeles's more than 2,000 theaters, museums, and other cultural establishments. One of 35 performing arts facilities, the handsome Music Center of Los Angeles County symbolizes the city's cultural renaissance. Completed in 1967, the center consists of the Dorothy Chandler Pavilion (recent home of the Academy Awards), the Ahmanson Theater, and the Mark Taper Forum; the latter two showcase various dance and theatrical performances. The Los Angeles Philharmonic Orchestra and Los Angeles Master Chorale perform in the pavilion. The Hollywood Bowl, an open-air amphitheater designed by Frank Lloyd Wright, features performances by the Philharmonic and the Hollywood Bowl Orchestra. Opera is represented by the Music Center Opera and San Gabriel Civic Light Opera. Ballet performances are held by the Joffrey Ballet, UCLA Center for the Performing Arts, and Lewitzky Dance Company. Many dramatic performances take place at the Hollywood Bowl or the Greek Theater in Griffith Park. Other theaters include the aforementioned Mark Taper Forum and Ahmanson Theatre at the Music Center of Los Angeles County, Los Angeles Theatre Center, Shubert and Pantages theatres, Santa Monica Playhouse, Actors' Alley, and International City Theatre in Long Beach.

The Los Angeles County Museum of Art is the largest such museum in the western United States. Others include the J. Paul Getty Museum in Malibu, Museum of African-American Art, Museum of Contemporary Art, Gene Autry Western Heritage Museum, Norton Simon Museum, Huntington Library, Armand Hammer Museum of Art & Culture Center, Pacific Asia Museum, and Santa Monica Museum of Art.

Travel and Tourism
Hotel Rooms   67,193
Convention and Exhibit Space (square feet)   310,000
Convention Centers
Los Angeles Convention Center
Festivals
Tournament of Roses Parade (New Year's Day)
Chinese New Year (February)
California Strawberry Festival (April)
Cinco de Mayo (May)
Calico Spring Festival (May)
Ojai Wine Festival (June)
Playboy Jazz Festival (June)
Parade of Nations (July)
International Surf Festival (July)

Parks and Recreation

Los Angeles has over 200 parks. The largest is the 4,000-acre Griffith Park with 50 miles of bridle paths. Hancock Park, 32 acres near Wilshire Boulevard, is known chiefly for its La Brea pits—bogs of subterranean oil and tar in which Ice Age animals were trapped. The

600-acre Elysian Park on North Broadway and the Los Angeles River includes the Portolá-Crespi Monument commemorating the site where Gaspar de Portolá and Franciscan friar Fray Juan Crespi pitched a tent in 1769. The 32-acre Westlake Park is in the heart of one of the most densely populated areas. Other parks include Echo, Lincoln, Exposition, and Arroyo Seco. The Glendale and Hollywood locales of the Forest Lawn Memorial Parks are not parks per se, but because they are the resting places of such stars as Marilyn Monroe, Errol Flynn, and Clark Gable, they rank among the most frequented "recreation" areas.

Sources of Further Information

Los Angeles Convention and Visitors Bureau
515 South Figueroa Street
Los Angeles, CA 90071
(213) 624-7300

Additional Reading

Acuna, Rudolfo. *East Los Angeles: A Community under Siege.* 1984.

Balderrame, Francisco. *In Defense of La Raza: The Los Angeles Consulate and the Mexican Community.* 1982.

Banham, Reyner. *Los Angeles: The Architecture of Four Ecologies.* 1971.

Bluefarb, Sam. *Set in L.A. Scenes of the City in Fiction.* 1986.

Burnett, William. *Views of Los Angeles.* 1979.

Chapman, Marvey. *A Marmac Guide to Los Angeles.* 1988.

Cleland, Robert G. *Cattle on a Thousand Hills: Southern California, 1850–1880.* 1951.

Comer, Virginia L. *Los Angeles: A View from Crown Hill.* 1986.

Cowan, Robert G. *A Backward Glance: Los Angeles, 1901–1915.* 1965.

Dumke, Glenn S. *The Boom of the Eighties in Southern California.* 1944.

Fogelson, Robert M. *The Fragmented Metropolis: Los Angeles, 1850–1930.* 1967.

Gill, Brendan. *The Dream Come True: The Great Houses of Los Angeles.* 1980.

Glover, Paul. *Los Angeles: A History of the Future.* 1989.

Grenier, Judson. *A Guide to Historic Places in Los Angeles.* 1981.

Henry, Sheila. *Cultural Persistence and Socioeconomic Mobility: A Comparative Study of Assimilation among Armenians and Japanese in Los Angeles.* 1978.

Henstell, Bruce. *Sunshine and Wealth: Los Angeles in the Twenties and Thirties.* 1984.

Kahrl, William L. *Water and Power: The Conflict over Los Angeles's Water Supply in the Owens Valley.* 1982.

Kaplan, Sam H. *L.A. Lost and Found.* 1987.

Kennelley, Joe, and Roy Hankey. *Sunset Boulevard: America's Dream Street.* 1982.

Klein, Norman, and Martin Schiesl. *Twentieth Century Los Angeles: Power, Promotion and Social Conflict.* 1990.

Modell, John. *The Economics and Politics of Racial Accommodation. The Japanese of Los Angeles.* 1977.

Moore, Charles. *The City Observed: Los Angeles.* 1984.

Nadeau, Remi A. *Los Angeles: From Mission to Modern City.* 1960.

Nelson, Howard J. *The Los Angeles Metropolis.* 1983.

Pearlstone, Zena. *Ethnic L.A.* 1990.

Pisano, Jane G. *Los Angeles Two Thousand.* 1989.

Rio-Bustamante, Antonio. *Mexican Los Angeles: A Narrative and Pictorial History.* 1992.

Rolle, Andrew. *Los Angeles: From Pueblo to City of the Future.* 1981.

Romo, Ricardo. *East Los Angeles: History of a Barrio.* 1984.

St. George, Mark. *Los Angeles: City of Dreams.* 1992.

Steiner, Rodney. *Los Angeles: The Centrifugal City.* 1981.

History

Bottles, Scott L. *Los Angeles and the Automobile: The Making of the Modern City.* 1987.

Castillo, Pedro, and Antonio Rios. *An Illustrated History of Mexican Los Angeles.* 1985.

Caughey, John, and LaRee Caughey. *Los Angeles: Biography of a City.* 1976.

Davis, Mike. *City of Quartz: Excavating the Future of Los Angeles.* 1990.

DeMarco, Gordon. *A Short History of Los Angeles.* 1987.

Elias, Judith. *Los Angeles: Dream to Reality.* 1983

Fogelson, Robert. *Los Angeles Riots.* 1969.

Gebhard, David, and Harriet Von Breton. *Los Angeles in the Thirties.* 1989.

Mayer, Robert. *Los Angeles: A Documentary and Chronological History.* 1978.

Nelson, Howard. *The Los Angeles Metropolis.* 1984.

Robinson, W. W. *Los Angeles from the Days of the Pueblo.* 1981.

Romo, Ricardo. *East Los Angeles: History of a Barrio.* 1983.

Louisville

Kentucky

Location and Topography

Louisville is located in the upper northwest section of Kentucky in Jefferson County. Situated on the south bank of the Ohio River, it is about 50 miles west of the state capital of Frankfort. The land is low plain, both hilly and flooded.

Layout of City and Suburbs

Downtown Louisville is cut in half by I-65, which separates the city into eastern and western sectors. The streets are arranged in the traditional grid pattern, and include Muhammad Ali Boulevard and Chestnut, Liberty, and Third streets. Standiford Field, the city's growing metropolitan airport, lies to the south, while the smaller Bowman Field is located to the east. Two beltline roads—the Henry Watterson Expressway and the Gene Snyder Freeway—encircle the city. Some of Louisville's suburbs include Shively, Norbourne Estates, and, across the river, New Albany, Indiana.

Environment

Environmental Stress Index   3.0
Green Cities Index: Rank   34
                   Score   29.69
Water Quality   Fluoridated
     Average Daily Use (gallons per capita)   179
     Maximum Supply (gallons per capita)   446
Parkland as % of Total City Area   3.8
% Waste Landfilled/Recycled   46:54
Annual Parks Expenditures per Capita $55.29

Climate

Louisville has a continental climate with warm summers and moderately cold winters. Both winter and summer bring hot and cold spells of brief duration. Rainstorms of high intensity are common during both spring and summer. A range of hills on the Indiana side of the river serves as a partial barrier against cold winter winds.

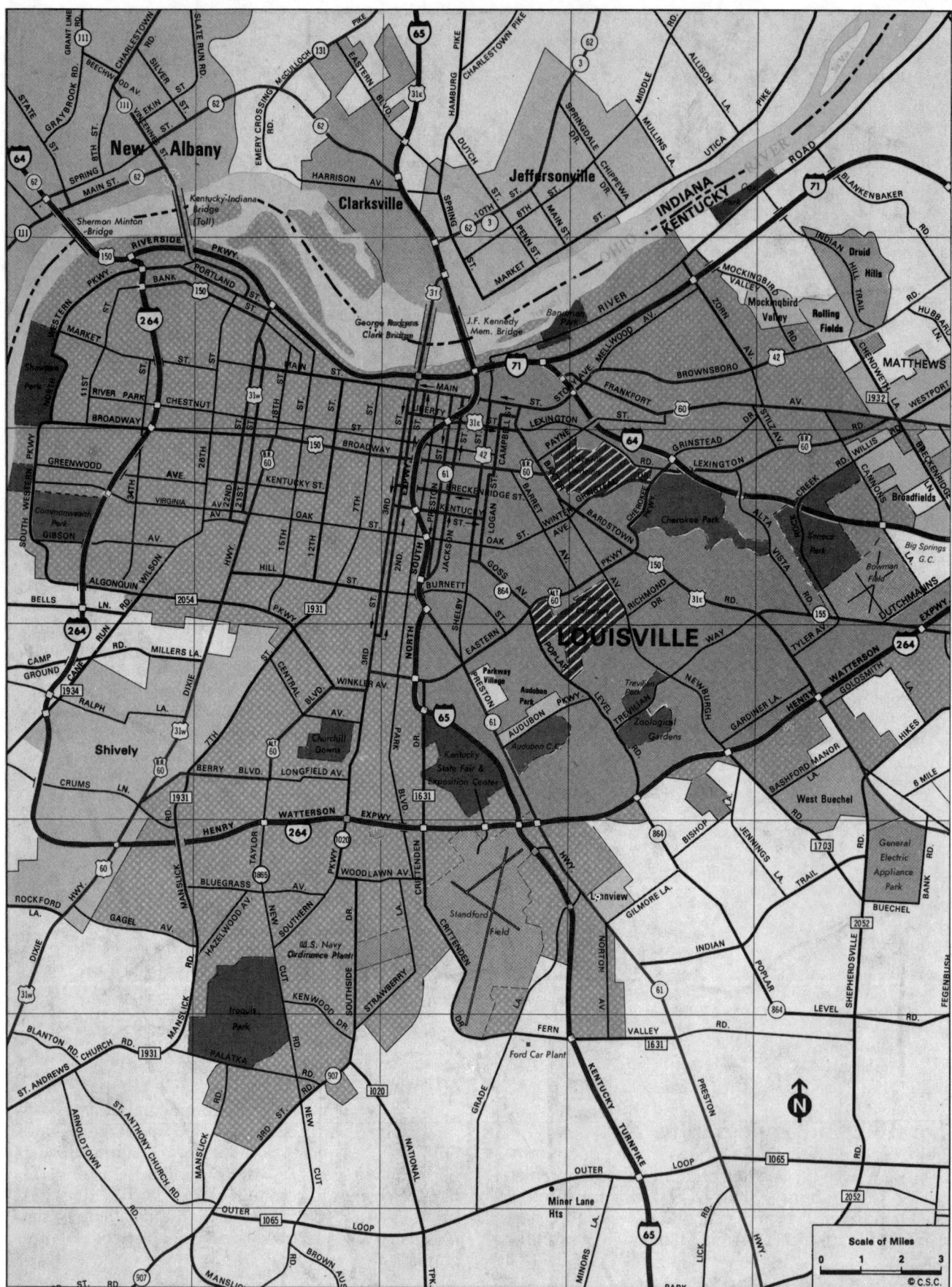

Weather			
Temperature			
Highest Monthly Average °F 87.3			
Lowest Monthly Average °F 24.5			
Annual Averages			
Days 32°F or Below 92			
Days above 90°F 24			
Zero Degree Days 2			
Precipitation (inches) 43.0			
Snow (inches) 17.0			
% Seasonal Humidity 69.0			
Wind Speed (m.p.h.) 8.4			
Clear Days 94			
Cloudy Days 168			
Storm Days 45			
Rainy Days 124			
Average Temperatures (°F)	*High*	*Low*	*Mean*
January	42.0	24.5	33.3
February	45.0	26.5	35.8
March	54.0	34.0	44.0
April	66.9	44.8	55.9
May	75.6	53.9	64.8
June	83.7	62.9	73.3
July	87.3	66.4	76.9
August	86.8	64.9	76.9
September	80.5	57.7	69.1
October	70.3	45.9	58.1
November	54.9	35.1	45.0
December	44.1	27.1	35.6

History

The earliest European visitations to the Ohio River Valley area that is now Louisville were by the French, probably in the late 17th century. Over the next hundred years, a variety of French explorers, traders, and trappers visited the area looking for new riches and bounties. The first opportunity for settlement came after the valley's transfer from the French to the British as part of the settlement over the French and Indian War. In 1773 Dr. John Connolly and Colonel John Campbell received a land patent from the British crown and platted the area in preparation for selling lots. Before they could, however, the American Revolution occurred and the land was confiscated by Virginia.

In 1778, a militia under the command of George Rogers Clark (older brother of famed explorer William Clark) left Pennsylvania with a group of 150 settlers in order to wrest control of the Ohio River Valley from the British. They stopped at what is now Louisville and settled on Corn Island, named for the crop planted that first year. Although Clark and his militia moved on, the pioneers stayed. Within the year they moved to the mainland and constructed a stockade with cabins. In 1779 they named the new and expanding settlement Louisville in honor of French King Louis XVI for his support of the American colonies in their fight with the British. A year later, the state of Virginia granted Louisville a charter.

The first years of Louisville's existence were rough. Because the rest of the lower Mississippi Valley was owned by the Spanish, using the Ohio River to trade with New Orleans was ruled out. The fort's western position made it a constant target of Indian attacks, and several outbreaks of malaria claimed the lives of many of the original pioneers. Two events changed the situation. By 1794, American troops had subdued many of the American Indian tribes in the Ohio River Valley, and the Louisiana Purchase in 1803 made New Orleans an American port. Eight years later, the steamboat *New Orleans* sailed up the Mississippi and Ohio rivers to reach Louisville on its way to Pittsburgh. Trade opened up, making the growing city an important commercial center. Immigrants came, bursting Louisville's population from a little over 4,000 in 1820 to more than 11,000 in 1830, making it the largest city in the state at that time.

In 1830 the Louisville & Portland Canal was completed, bypassing the Ohio Falls and making river traffic possible throughout the year. In 1851, the Louisville & Nashville Railroad (now the CSX Corporation) linked the city with Nashville and opened new areas of trade and commerce. A diversified economy, including factories and shipyards, sprang up. Many historians consider slavery to be the central factor that held Louisville back as a major economic power in the United States. By 1860, the number of slaves in the city had dropped to 7.5% of the population, but as a part of the South, Louisville felt the stigma. However, when the Confederate states began to break away, Kentucky held firm toward the Union. In fact, Louisville sent more men to fight for the Union than for the Confederacy. The city became a substantial base for Union headquarters, had a military supply depot, and was the site of 19 military hospitals. The Louisville & Nashville Railroad, a once-important link for commerce, became a vital connection to the southern cities out of reach of other rail lines. At the end of the war, Louisville stood virtually alone in the South in being physically untouched by the conflict.

The last decades of the 19th century saw improvement in commercial activity and population. The 1883 Southern Exposition allowed the city to highlight its prowess as an industrial power, and the population grew from 100,000 in 1870 to over 200,000 by 1900. Louisville continued to expand in the first two decades of the 20th century, but crashed during the Depression of the 1930s, and the great Ohio Valley flood of early 1937 caused $52 million in damage. The economy turned upward during World War II when Louisville became the center of synthetic rubber production. After the war, a scaled-down military sector gave way to new manufacturing businesses. By the end of the 1980s, Louisville was the home of General Electric and United Parcel Services, the latter with its hub at Standiford Field.

Historical Landmarks

Downtown Louisville exhibits among its historic landmarks the *Belle of Louisville*, an excursion vessel built as the *Idlewild* in 1914, and now preserved as a national historic landmark. The Bank of Louisville, currently the Actor's Theater headquarters, was built in 1837 in Greek Revival style.

Chronology

1773	The British crown grants a land patent to Dr. John Connolly and Colonel John Campbell. Plots of land are readied for sale.
1776	Connolly is charged with being a Tory, and the land is confiscated by the government of Virginia.
1778	A militia under the command of George Rogers Clark, in an expedition to wrest control from the British over the territory northwest of the Ohio River, settles a band of pioneers on Corn Island. Later that year, after Clark and his militia leave, the settlers move to the mainland and build a stockade with cabins.
1779	The pioneers name the new settlement Louisville after King Louis XVI.
1780	The state of Virginia grants Louisville a charter.
1811	The steamboat *New Orleans* makes its way upriver from New Orleans to Pittsburgh and stops at Louisville, opening up the Ohio River to barge and boat traffic.
1830	The Louisville & Portland Canal makes river traffic on the Ohio River possible year-round.
1851	The Louisville & Nashville Railroad links Louisville with Nashville.
1861–1865	Although in a slave state, Louisville remains in the Union and serves as an important military center.
1870–1900	The population doubles from 100,000 to 200,000.
1883	The city's economic engine is showcased at the Southern Exposition.
1937	The Ohio River flood causes $52 million in damage.
1941–1945	Louisville becomes the production center of synthetic rubber for the U.S. military.

The site of Fort Nelson, constructed in 1781 as a military fortification, remains only as a monument on the northwest corner of Main and Seventh streets. On Market Street is the German Insurance Bank and Insurance Company Building, constructed in 1887 with highly decorated columns and balconies. On Jefferson Street is the Jefferson County Courthouse. Started in 1837 but halted because of an economic panic that year, it was completed in 1858, and features a spectacular rotunda. City Hall was built between 1870 and 1873 in Italianate style. The Seelbach Hotel on Muhammad Ali Boulevard opened in 1905 and was reopened in 1982 after a restoration.

Population

Louisville's population has shrunk by nearly 100,000 in the past two decades. From 362,000 in 1970, it declined 17.5% to 298,694 in 1980 and then by 9.9% to 269,063 in 1990. As a result, it ranks only 58th in the nation in size of population.

Population		
	1980	*1990*
Central City	298,694	269,063
Rank	49	58
Metro Area	956,436	952,662
Pop. Change 1980–1990 -29,631		
Pop. % Change 1980–1990 -9.9		
Median Age 34.3		
% Male 46.3		
% Age 65 and Over 16.6		
Density (per square mile) 4,332		

Households
Number   113,065
Persons per Household   2.31
% Female-Headed Households   18.3
% One-Person Households   35.0
Births—Total   4,244
% to Mothers under 20   19.6
Birth Rate per 1,000   14.6

Ethnic Composition

Whites make up 69.2%, blacks 29.7%, American Indians 0.2%, Asians and Pacific Islanders 0.7%, and others 0.2%.

Ethnic Composition (as % of total pop.)		
	1980	*1990*
White	71.07	69.21
Black	28.17	29.65
American Indian	0.11	0.19
Asian and Pacific Islander	0.31	0.73
Hispanic	0.67	0.65
Other	NA	0.22

Government

Louisville has a mayor-council form of government. The mayor is elected to a one-time term of four years, and the 12 members of the council are elected every two years.

Government
Year of Home Charter   1972
Number of Members of the Governing Body   12
Elected at Large   NA
Elected by Wards   12
Number of Women in Governing Body   2
Salary of Mayor $67,376
Salary of Council Members $24,264
City Government Employment Total   4,818
Rate per 10,000   168.2

Public Finance

The annual budget consists of revenues of $277.003 million and expenditures of $369.563 million. The debt outstanding is $359.191 million, and cash and security holdings are $323.475 million.

Public Finance

Total Revenue (in millions) $277.003
Intergovernmental Revenue—Total (in millions) $37.8
Federal Revenue per Capita $123.87
% Federal Assistance   12.79
% State Assistance   3.57
Sales Tax as % of Total Revenue   6.47
Local Revenue as % of Total Revenue   83.63
City Income Tax   yes
Taxes—Total (in millions) $93.0

Taxes per Capita
   Total $325
   Property $102
   Sales and Gross Receipts $39
General Expenditures—Total (in millions) $165.0
General Expenditures per Capita $576
Capital Outlays per Capita $51

% of Expenditures for:
   Public Welfare   3.8
   Highways   4.1
   Education   0.0
   Health and Hospitals   3.7
   Police   17.1
   Sewerage and Sanitation   7.3
   Parks and Recreation   5.3
   Housing and Community Development   5.0
Debt Outstanding per Capita $1,970
   % Utility   45.0
Federal Procurement Contract Awards (in millions) $95.9
Federal Grants Awards (in millions) $62.7
Fiscal Year Begins   July 1

Economy

Louisville's four leading economic sectors are services, trade, manufacturing, and government. Since the 1982 recession, the city has diversified with increased jobs in health care, business services, transportation, and government. The leading private-sector employers include General Electric, Humana Hospitals, United Parcel Service, Ford Motor Company, and the Kroger Company. Tourism accounted for more than $152 million in 1991.

Economy

Total Money Income (in millions) $2,615.2
% of State Average   106.0
Per Capita Annual Income $9,129
% Population below Poverty Level   19.3
Fortune 500 Companies   1

Banks	Number	Deposits (in millions)
Commercial	179	9,316.5
Savings	3	1,951.0

Economy (continued)

Passenger Autos   368,458
Electric Meters   324,529
Gas Meters   246,556

Manufacturing

Number of Establishments   541
% with 20 or More Employees   45.7
Manufacturing Payroll (in millions) $1,519.2
Value Added by Manufacture (in millions) $5,319.0
Value of Shipments (in millions) $11,891.4
New Capital Expenditures (in millions) $187.4

Wholesale Trade

Number of Establishments   826
Sales (in millions) $7,178.9
Annual Payroll (in millions) $267.936

Retail Trade

Number of Establishments   2,894
Total Sales (in millions) $1,793.3
Sales per Capita $6,260
Number of Retail Trade Establishments with Payroll   2,020
Annual Payroll (in millions) $234.3
Total Sales (in millions) $1,754.9
General Merchandise Stores (per capita) $422
Food Stores (per capita) $1,534
Apparel Stores (per capita) $232
Eating and Drinking Places (per capita) $896

Service Industries

Total Establishments   2,834
Total Receipts (in millions) $1,619.0
Hotels and Motels (in millions) $82.6
Health Services (in millions) $604.2
Legal Services (in millions) $179.7

Labor

Louisville has had a long history of strikes and uneasy industrial relations, although efforts are now under way to encourage worker involvement in production policies. The largest employer is General Electric, followed by Humana, United Parcel Service, Ford Motor Company, Kroger Company, Brown and Williamson Tobacco, Blue Cross and Blue Shield, and Delta Dental. Services and trade employ half the work force.

Labor

Civilian Labor Force   143,169
% Change 1989–1990   1.1

Work Force Distribution
   Mining   500
   Construction   22,400
   Manufacturing   86,900
   Transportation and Public Utilities   31,200
   Wholesale and Retail Trade   120,100
   FIRE (Finance, Insurance, Real Estate)   27,400
   Service   127,800
   Government   66,200
   Women as % of Labor Force   46.3
   % Self-Employed   4.6
   % Professional/Technical   15.6

Labor (continued)

Total Unemployment 8,434
Rate % 5.9
Federal Government Civilian Employment 8,502

Education

Jefferson County Board of Education supports 153 elementary schools, junior high/middle schools, and senior high schools. About 20,000 students are enrolled in 85 parochial and private schools. Founded in 1798, the University of Louisville was the first city-owned university in the nation. In 1970 the university faced financial problems, and it was taken over by the state. Other institutions of higher learning include Bellarmine College and Spalding College. Two major theological seminaries are located here: Louisville Presbyterian Theological Seminary and Southern Baptist Theological Seminary.

Education

Number of Public Schools 153
Special Education Schools 7
Total Enrollment 91,450
% Enrollment in Private Schools 17.6
% Minority 32.2
Classroom Teachers 5,267
Pupil-Teacher Ratio 17.3:1
Number of Graduates 4,940
Total Revenue (in millions) $358.444
Total Expenditures (in millions) $346.623
Expenditures per Pupil $3,465
Educational Attainment (Age 25 and Over)
    % Completed 12 or More Years 55.5
    % Completed 16 or More Years 13.3
Four-Year Colleges and Universities 3
    Enrollment 24,941
Two-Year Colleges 3
    Enrollment 3,182

Libraries

Number 41
Public Libraries 16
Books (in thousands) 802
Circulation (in thousands) 3,031
Persons Served (in thousands) 684
Circulation per Person Served 4.43
Income (in millions) $7.8
Staff 290

Four-Year Colleges and Universities
    University of Louisville
    Bellarmine College
    Spalding University

Health

The Humana Hospital and Medical Complex is one of the leading research hospitals in the nation. Louisville is home to 15 other hospitals, including the Louisville Baptist Hospitals, Amelia Brown Frazier Rehabilitation Center, NKC Hospitals, and Veterans Administration Medical Center.

Health

Deaths—Total 3,690
Rate per 1,000 12.7
Infant Deaths—Total 51
Rate per 1,000 12.0
Number of Metro Hospitals 16
Number of Metro Hospital Beds 4,948
Rate per 100,000 1,727
Number of Physicians 2,133
Physicians per 1,000 2.46
Nurses per 1,000 12.21
Health Expenditures per Capita $3.61

Transportation

Louisville is split into eastern and western halves by the north-to-south I-65. Interstate 64 carries traffic both to the southeast and west, while I-71 heads exclusively northeast. Other roads serving the Louisville area include two beltline highways—the Henry Watterson Expressway, close to the city, and the Gene Snyder Freeway, which is further out. As a port on the Ohio River, Louisville handles a major portion of the trade on the waterway. Rail freight service is provided by the CSX Corporation, Norfolk Southern Corporation, Burlington Northern Railroad, Paducah & Louisville Railway, and Conrail. Most commercial airliners use Standiford Field, about five miles from downtown. Bowman Field to the east and Clark County Airport to the north serve smaller planes.

Transportation

Interstate Highway Mileage 111
Total Urban Mileage 2,683
Total Daily Vehicle Mileage (in millions) 18.615
Daily Average Commute Time 48.6 min.
Number of Buses 245
Port Tonnage (in millions) 7.762
Airports 1
Number of Daily Flights 59
Daily Average Number of Passengers 2,493

Airlines (American carriers only)
    American
    Continental
    Delta
    Midway
    Northwest
    Trans World
    United
    USAir

Housing

Louisville is one of the least expensive housing markets in the country. The median value of a single-family home is $62,300 and the median monthly rent is $244. Of the total housing stock, 54.9% is owner occupied.

Urban Redevelopment

Louisville has undergone a wave of rebuilding since the 1960s. The Capital Holding Corporation's $165-million,

Housing

Total Housing Units   124,018
% Change 1980–1990   1.7
Vacant Units for Sale or Rent   6,928
Occupied Units   113,065
% with More Than One Person per Room   3.3
% Owner-Occupied   54.9
Median Value of Owner-Occupied Homes $44,300
Average Monthly Purchase Cost $255
Median Monthly Rent $244
New Private Housing Starts   180
Value (in thousands) $10,288
% Single-Family   55.6
Nonresidential Buildings Value (in thousands) $48,843

Tallest Buildings	Hgt. (ft.)	Stories
First Natl. Bank	512	40
Citizen's Plaza	420	30
Humana Bldg.	350	27
Meindinger Tower	338	26
Brown & Williamson Tower	338	26

35-story headquarters tower is Kentucky's tallest building. The 1-million-square-foot Waterfront Plaza was partially completed by 1991. Commonwealth Insurance has invested $35 million in a three-building headquarters at Fourth and Broadway. The Actor's Theater has expanded its facilities with a $9.5-million addition. Equally striking developments are taking place on the Louisville Waterfront, where $110 million has been invested since 1987, and at Standiford Field Airport, where $300 million has been invested. New corporate building expansion programs include those of Mazda Motor Corporation, Yokohama Tire Company, Zeon Chemicals, Prudential Service Bureau, UPS, Interco, and Amgen.

Crime

 Louisville ranks above the national average in public safety. In 1991, violent crimes totaled 2,245 and property crimes totaled 15,183.

Crime

Violent Crimes—Total   2,245
Violent Crime Rate per 100,000   487.2
Murder   43
Rape   157
Robbery   1,246
Aggravated Assaults   799
Property Crimes   15,183
Burglary   5,007
Larceny   8,446
Motor Vehicle Theft   1,730
Arson   308
Per Capita Police Expenditures $127.70
Per Capita Fire Protection Expenditures $73.74
Number of Police   650
Per 1,000   2.24

Religion

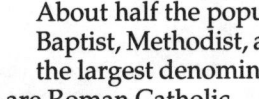 About half the population is Protestant; Baptist, Methodist, and Presbyterian are the largest denominations. Some 40% of the people are Roman Catholic.

Religion

Largest Denominations (Adherents)

Catholic	156,307
Southern Baptist	113,523
Black Baptist	42,477
United Methodist	27,983
American Zion	13,180
Assembly of God	7,596
Churches of Christ	13,477
Episcopal	6,715
Presbyterian	14,486
Jewish	6,990

Media

 Louisville's lone city daily is *The Courier-Journal*, published in the mornings seven days a week. The electronic media consist of 7 television stations and 14 FM and AM radio stations.

Media

Newsprint
Business First, weekly
The Courier-Journal, daily
The Louisville Defender, weekly
The New Voice, weekly
The Newsweek, weekly

Television
WAVE (Channel 3)
WBNA (Channel 21)
WDRB (Channel 41)
WHAS (Channel 11)
WKMJ (Channel 68)
WKPC (Channel 15)
WLKY (Channel 32)

Radio

WAVG (AM)	WLRS (FM)
WDJX (FM)	WFIA (AM)
WFPK (FM)	WFPL (FM)
WHAS (AM)	WAMZ (FM)
WLLV (AM)	WLOU (AM)
WTFX (FM)	WTMT (AM)
WUOL (FM)	WVEZ (FM)

Sports

 Although Louisville has no professional sports team, it becomes a center of sports activity every May with the running of the Kentucky Derby, the first leg of the Triple Crown, at Churchill Downs.

Arts, Culture, and Tourism

 High culture finds expression in numerous theatrical, musical, and dance groups. The Actor's Theater of Louisville, housed in the historic Bank of Louisville, an 1837 landmark, holds the Humana Festival of New American Plays from mid-February to mid-March. Other theater and performing arts groups include the Bunbury Theatre, Derby Dinner Playhouse, Iroquois Amphitheatre at Iroquois Park, Kentucky Contemporary Theatre, Kentucky Opera, Louisville Ballet, Louisville

Orchestra, and Stage One: The Louisville Children's Theatre. There are nine major museums in Louisville. These include the Colonel Harlan Sanders Museum, which highlights the life of the founder of Kentucky Fried Chicken; the Eisenberg Museum of Egyptian and Near Eastern Antiquities; the Filson Club, a private library/historical society; the Howard Steamboat Museum (housed in the former Howard Mansion), which documents 107 years of steamboat building by the Howard Shipyards & Dock Company; the J. B. Speed Art Museum; the John Conti Coffee Factory/ Museum, featuring old-fashioned ways of making coffee; and the Kentucky Derby Museum, which marks the history of one of the three legs of horse racing's Triple Crown.

Travel and Tourism

Hotel Rooms   11,090

Convention and Exhibit Space (square feet)   750,000

Convention Centers

Kentucky Fair and Exposition Center
Commonwealth Convention Center

Festivals

Kentucky Derby Festival (April-May)
Shakespeare in Central Park (summer)
Bluegrass Festival (September)
Corn Island Storytelling Festival (September)
St. James Art Fair (October)

Parks and Recreation

The Metropolitan Park and Recreation Department oversees more than 10,000 acres of parks and recreational spaces in Louisville and Jefferson County including the 73-acre Louisville Zoo; the Louisville Nature Center in Beargrass Creek State Nature Reserve; and Iroquois Park, which includes the Iroquois Amphitheatre. Other nearby state parks include the 375-acre E. P. "Tom" Sawyer State Park located about 20 miles east of Louisville, and the 3,600-acre Otter Creek Park located 30 miles southwest of Louisville in Meade County. The Cave Hill Cemetery and Arboretum features the resting places of George Rogers Clark and Colonel Harlan Sanders of Kentucky Fried Chicken fame.

Sources of Further Information

Louisville Area Chamber of Commerce
1 Riverfront Plaza
Louisville, KY 40202
(502) 625-0063

Louisville and Jefferson County Convention and Visitors Bureau
400 South First Street
Louisville, KY 40202
(502) 584-2121

Additional Reading

Basberg, Lani, and Jean Jennings. *Louisville in Good Taste.* 1989.
Crews, Clyde F. *An American Holy Land: A History of the Archdiocese of Louisville.* 1986.
Morga, William. *Louisville: Architecture and the Urban Environment.* 1979.
Wright, George C. *Life behind a Veil: Blacks in Louisville, Kentucky, 1865–1930.* 1985.
Yater, George H. *Flappers, Prohibition and All That Jazz: Louisville in the 1920s.* 1984.

Lowell

Massachusetts

Basic Data

Name   Lowell
Name Origin   From Francis Cabot Lowell
Year Founded   1686 Inc. 1836
Status: State   Massachusetts
          County   Seat of Middlesex County
Area (square miles)   13.8
Elevation (feet)   100
Time Zone   EST
Population (1990)   103,439
Population of Metro Area (1990)   3,783,817

Distance in Miles To:

Boston	32
Hartford	140
New York	255
Providence	71
Springfield	92
Worcester	41

Location and Topography

Lowell is situated in the northeastern corner of Massachusetts, just south of the New Hampshire border and 32 miles north of Boston. It is located at the confluence of two waterways: the Merrimack River and the Concord River. The elevation of the city is about 100 feet above sea level, rising in a grassy plain while being cut by the mighty Merrimack.

Layout of City and Suburbs

Lowell is settled on the south bank of the Merrimack, as well as being cut into several parts by canals that line the city. Much of the city's downtown is positioned around three main streets: Merrimack Street, Middle Street, and Market Street. Lowell is circled by the Massachusetts suburbs of Dracut, Tyngsborough, Westford, Chelmsford, and Tewksbury.

Environment

Environmental Stress Index   2.8
Green Cities Index: Rank   NA
                         Score   NA
Water Quality   Neutral, very soft, fluoridated
       Average Daily Use (gallons per capita)   NA
       Maximum Supply (gallons per capita)   NA
Parkland as % of Total City Area   NA
% Waste Landfilled/Recycled   NA
Annual Parks Expenditures per Capita $24.02

Climate

Lowell has a typical New England climate with warm, humid summers and cold winters with moderate snow.

Weather

Temperature

Highest Monthly Average °F   59.0
Lowest Monthly Average °F   39.6

Annual Averages

Days 32°F or Below   31
Days above 90°F   10
Zero Degree Days   5
Precipitation (inches)   42.56
Snow (inches)   52.8
% Seasonal Humidity   NA
Wind Speed (m.p.h.)   NA
Clear Days   NA
Cloudy Days   NA
Storm Days   NA
Rainy Days   NA

Average Temperatures (°F)	High	Low	Mean
January	34.7	16.8	25.8
February	36.7	17.9	27.3
March	44.5	27.4	36.0
April	57.3	37.2	47.3
May	68.7	47.0	57.9
June	77.7	56.4	67.1

Weather (continued)			
July	82.8	62.3	72.6
August	80.9	60.4	70.7
September	73.1	52.4	62.8
October	62.7	42.3	52.5
November	50.7	33.7	42.2
December	38.2	21.6	29.9

History

The early history of the region is identified with the town of Chelmsford, of which Lowell was for many years a small part. Chelmsford itself dates back to 1686 when the Pawtucket Falls area was sold by Wannalancet, chief of the Pennacook Confederacy, to English farmers who then named it East Chelmsford. The town grew slowly until the completion of the Pawtucket Canal in 1796. The canal, which bypassed the Pawtucket Falls, was used to carry New Hampshire lumber to Newburyport where it was used in shipbuilding. It lost much of its importance when the Middlesex Canal between Chelmsford and Boston was completed in 1803.

The next chapter in Lowell's history began in 1817, when the Boston Manufacturing Company, founded by Francis Cabott Lowell, came to Pawtucket Falls in search of a site to set up a factory to produce cotton and print calico. Lowell and the other investors were impressed by the water power potential of this junction of the two rivers. 1822 saw the beginning of the construction of textile mills and a series of power canals. By 1823 the Merrimack Manufacturing Company had begun production, and within three years the newly incorporated town was renamed in honor of Lowell. Within ten years the population of the town grew from 2,500 to 17,000, of whom about 7,500 worked in the eight large mills. The Boston and Lowell Railroad arrived in 1835, furthering the city's expansion. In the early years the daughters of New England farmers were recruited to work in the textile mills. They lived in company boardinghouses under a strict regimen. They worked 12 hours a day, six days a week, but nevertheless found time to support churches, lyceums, schools, banks, concerts, and libraries. From 1840 to 1845 they published the *Lowell Offering*, one of the earliest women's literary magazines. Under the editorship of Sarah Bagley, a reformer who organized women to fight for better conditions, they also published the *Voice of Industry* to chronicle their dreary lives.

News of Lowell poured into Europe through mill labor agents who painted glowing pictures of idyllic work conditions on the banks of the Merrimack. Even though working conditions were deteriorating in the City of Spindles, unskilled immigrants came by the shiploads: at first Irish and English, followed by the Portuguese in the 1850s, French-Canadians in the 1860s and 1870s, Greeks and European Jews in the 1880s, Poles in the 1890s, Armenians in the early decades of the 20th century, and Hispanics, Cambodians and Laotians in the post–World War II period.

Lowell occupies a notable niche in the history of industrial relations, especially in the women's labor movement. The operatives, as the mill hands were called, successfully forced a reduction of the workday to 11 hours in 1853 after a number of strikes and walkouts. The first city-wide strike in 1903 was unsuccessful, but in 1912 the workers were successful in their efforts to obtain a wage increase.

Lowell's position as one of the pioneer industrial communities in the United States peaked about 1924 and then began to decline as many of the mills moved south and others were closed down. Thousands were left jobless and homeless. Yet within the next 25 years it began an upward climb to a revitalized economy by diversifying its industrial base.

Historical Landmarks

Lowell has numerous historical sites, many of them well preserved. The Barrett Byam Homestead is the home of the Chelmsford Historical Society Museum. Boott Mills at the foot of John Street was one of the last of the large textile corporations organized in Lowell in 1835. Kirk Street was one of the most popular and fashionable streets until the Civil War. The mill agents lived on this street in princely elegance. The Market Mills is the site of the Lowell Manufacturing Company and other buildings constructed between 1882 and 1902. Merrimack Street, the city's main thoroughfare, is the site of the Old City Hall, St. Anne's church, and the Lucy Larcom Park.

Lining the cobblestoned Shattuck and Middle streets are magnificent examples of 19th-century commercial architecture, including the J. C. Ayer Building, the Mack Building, and the Lowell Institution for Savings. The Lowell National Historical Park houses the Patrick J. Morgan Cultural Center and the Paul E. Tsongas Industrial History Center. The former, located in a restored 1835 boardinghouse, tells the human story of the Industrial Revolution in its Working People Exhibit.

The Birthplace of Whistler (James Abbott McNeill Whistler), the city's most famous son, stands on Worthen Street. The Greek Orthodox Church, established in 1907, was the first Greek Orthodox Church in America. Located in Little Greece, it is a Byzantine structure in yellow brick with a squat red central dome and two lower domed towers.

Population

The population of Lowell in the 1990 census was 103,439, a gain of 11,021 over the 1980 census when the population was 92,418. Lowell is thus among those few cities in the Northeast that have gained population, where most others have lost their residents to the suburbs. The growth was primarily due to the influx of over 10,000 Laotian and Cambodian refugees during the decade. It ranks 188th among all U.S. cities in population.

Chronology

1686 The Pennacook Confederacy sells land along the Merrimack River to English farmers who name the settlement East Chelmsford.

1796 The Pawtucket Canal is completed.

1823 The Merrimack Manufacturing Company builds textile mills along the Merrimack River and begins textile production, thus creating a company town.

1826 The town is renamed in honor of Francis Cabott Lowell.

1835 The Boston and Lowell Railroad arrives.

1840 The *Lowell Offering* is founded.

1853 Workers campaign successfully to reduce daily work hours to 11.

1903 The first city-wide strike is unsuccessful.

1912 Workers lobby successfully for wage increase.

1978 The Lowell National Historical Park is created to preserve the monumental remains of one of America's earliest planned industrial communities.

Population

	1980	1990
Central City	92,418	103,439
Rank	188	186
Metro Area	3,662,888	3,783,817
Pop. Change 1980–1990 +11,021		
Pop. % Change 1980–1990 +11.9		
Median Age 29.4		
% Male 48.7		
% Age 65 and Over 12.1		
Density (per square mile) 7,495		

Households

Number 37,019
Persons per Household 2.68
% Female-Headed Households 17.0
% One-Person Households 27.5
Births—Total 1,721
   % to Mothers under 20 14.4
   Birth Rate per 1,000 18.4

Ethnic Composition

Lowell is predominantly white at 81.07% of the population. Blacks make up 2.39%, Asian and Pacific Islanders 11.11%, and other races the remainder. Compared to the 1980 census, the white population group has lost 4,737 persons while the Asian and Pacific Islanders groups have gained 10,889 persons and others have gained 3,524. Reflecting its immigrant past, Lowell has numerous nationalities represented in its population: English, Irish, French-Canadian, Polish, Portuguese, Jewish, and Armenian. One of the largest groups is Greek. Lowell was one of the favorite destinations of Greek immigrants in the early part of the century, when Lowell was called the Athens of America.

Ethnic Composition (as % of total pop.)

	1980	1990
White	95.86	81.07
Black	1.30	2.39
American Indian	0.11	0.17
Asian and Pacific Islander	0.65	11.11
Hispanic	4.96	10.15
Other	NA	5.26

Government

Lowell runs under a council-manager form of government. The nine members of the council are elected for two-year terms. The council appoints a ceremonial mayor and a salaried professional city manager who serves for an unspecified term.

Government

Year of Home Charter NA
Number of Members of the Governing Body 9
Elected at Large 9
Elected by Wards NA
Number of Women in Governing Body 1
Salary of Mayor $9,500
Salary of Council Members $7,500
City Government Employment Total 2,657
Rate per 10,000 286.1

Public Finance

Lowell's annual budget consists of revenues of $159.789 million and expenditures of $157.365 million. Sound fiscal management has ensured that the property tax rate is kept at a reasonable level. The outstanding debt is $66.069 million and cash and security holdings of $19.468 million.

Public Finance

Total Revenue (in millions) $159.789
Intergovernmental Revenue—Total (in millions) $80.57
Federal Revenue per Capita $7.85
% Federal Assistance 4.9
% State Assistance 45.5
Sales Tax as % of Total Revenue 0.13
Local Revenue as % of Total Revenue 38.8
City Income Tax no
Taxes—Total (in millions) $38.3

Taxes per Capita
   Total $412
   Property $407
   Sales and Gross Receipts $0.0

Public Finance (continued)

General Expenditures—Total (in millions) $93.4
General Expenditures per Capita $1,006
Capital Outlays per Capita $112

% of Expenditures for:
   Public Welfare 0.6
   Highways 2.6
   Education 44.2
   Health and Hospitals 0.8
   Police 8.1
   Sewerage and Sanitation 10.1
   Parks and Recreation 4.7
   Housing and Community Development 0.0
Debt Outstanding per Capita $557
   % Utility 16.8
Federal Procurement Contract Awards (in millions) $561.4
Federal Grants Awards (in millions) $10.5
Fiscal Year Begins July 1

Economy

 Lowell's reputation as a high-tech manufacturing center began with the establishment of the headquarters of the Wang Laboratories in the 1970s. The growth industries include finance, real estate, and government. Textiles are still important, but in terms of value of output, they have long yielded primacy to computer hardware and software, plastics, wire and cable, and printing.

Economy

Total Money Income (in millions) $938.6
% of State Average 80.8
Per Capita Annual Income $10,106
% Population below Poverty Level 13.5
Fortune 500 Companies 1

Banks	Number	Deposits (in millions)
Commercial	78	3,025.8
Savings	8	NA

Passenger Autos 878,212
Electric Meters NA
Gas Meters NA

Manufacturing

Number of Establishments 161
% with 20 or More Employees 43.5
Manufacturing Payroll (in millions) $543.3
Value Added by Manufacture (in millions) $1,735.8
Value of Shipments (in millions) $3,159.0
New Capital Expenditures (in millions) $80.2

Wholesale Trade

Number of Establishments 97
Sales (in millions) $322.5
Annual Payroll (in millions) $33.614

Retail Trade

Number of Establishments 657
Total Sales (in millions) $556.2
Sales per Capita $5,988
Number of Retail Trade Establishments with Payroll 454
Annual Payroll (in millions) $61.8
Total Sales (in millions) $540.2
General Merchandise Stores (per capita) $410
Food Stores (per capita) $871

Economy (continued)

Apparel Stores (per capita) $94
Eating and Drinking Places (per capita) $506

Service Industries

Total Establishments 498
Total Receipts (in millions) $247.5
Hotels and Motels (in millions) NA
Health Services (in millions) $57.4
Legal Services (in millions) $23.9

Labor

 As a former milltown, Lowell has strong labor traditions. The city's labor force has grown dramatically with the influx of Cambodian and Laotian refugees. Average hourly earnings increased through the 1980s but still are below those of the Boston and Worcester areas and the state average. The weekly workload at 42 to 43 hours, however, is among the highest in New England. Like other New England cities, Lowell has been hard hit by the recession of the early 1990s. The unemployment rate, which dipped as low as 4.3% in 1988, reached 8.2% in 1990. Average weekly earnings also have dropped dramatically because of the financial troubles of Wang and other high-tech firms.

Labor

Civilian Labor Force 52,163
% Change 1989–1990 -2.4

Work Force Distribution
   Mining NA
   Construction 3,000
   Manufacturing 30,300
   Transportation and Public Utilities 4,900
   Wholesale and Retail Trade 20,900
   FIRE (Finance, Insurance, Real Estate) 3,300
   Service 20,500
   Government 12,700
   Women as % of Labor Force 44.7
   % Self-Employed 2.7
   % Professional/Technical 13.9
Total Unemployment 4,235
Rate % 8.1
Federal Government Civilian Employment 429

Education

There are two school zones in Lowell: Zone I includes Highlands, Acre, and Pawtucketville; Zone II includes Centralville, South Lowell, Belvidere, the Flats, and Ayer City. The public school system consists of 16 elementary schools, 7 junior high schools, 1 high school, and 2 magnet schools. Eleven parochial schools and the Greater Lowell Regional Technical Vocational High School supplement the public school system. Lowell schools have strong bilingual programs to cater to the large Laotian, Cambodian, Vietnamese, and Portuguese population.

For higher education, Lowell residents look to the University of Lowell, which has two campuses in the city, North and South. North Campus is dedicated to engineering, business administration, and science, while the South Campus is dedicated to liberal arts and health. A third campus, the College of Education, is located in Chelmsford. Boston's two-year Newbury College maintains a campus in Lowell, as does Middlesex Community College, which uses the refurbished Wannalancet Mills in downtown Lowell.

Education

Number of Public Schools   26
Special Education Schools   NA
Total Enrollment   12,500
% Enrollment in Private Schools   8.9
% Minority   NA
Classroom Teachers   NA
Pupil-Teacher Ratio   25:1
Number of Graduates   NA
Total Revenue (in millions)   NA
Total Expenditures (in millions)   NA
Expenditures per Pupil   NA
Educational Attainment (Age 25 and Over)
   % Completed 12 or More Years   57.7
   % Completed 16 or More Years   10.4
Four-Year Colleges and Universities   1
   Enrollment   14,265
Two-Year Colleges   NA
   Enrollment   NA

Libraries

Number   7
Public Libraries   1
Books (in thousands)   210
Circulation (in thousands)   199
Persons Served (in thousands)   94
Circulation per Person Served   2.11
Income (in millions) $0.761
Staff   NA

Four-Year Colleges and Universities
   University of Lowell

Health

Three city hospitals serve the city and all Merrimack Valley: Lowell General Hospital with 293 beds, St. John's Hospital with 254 beds, and St. Joseph's Hospital with 200 beds. Supplementary medical institutions include the Lahey Eye Clinic, the Solomon Mental Health Center, and the Tri-Hospital Paramedic Unit.

Health

Deaths—Total   1,045
Rate per 1,000   11.2
Infant Deaths—Total   20
Rate per 1,000   11.6
Number of Metro Hospitals   3
Number of Metro Hospital Beds   747
Rate per 100,000   NA
Number of Physicians   NA
Physicians per 1,000   NA
Nurses per 1,000   NA
Health Expenditures per Capita $13.69

Transportation

Access to the Merrimack Valley and Lowell can be gained through three interstates: I-93, which runs just east of the city; I-95, which connects to I-93 about 25 miles south of the city; and I-495, which comes from southeastern Massachusetts and cuts east just a few miles south of Lowell. Several smaller roads, such as U.S. Route 3, intersect these highways and bring you closer to the area. The main air terminal is Boston's Logan International Airport, 35 miles to the south.

Transportation

Interstate Highway Mileage   15
Total Urban Mileage   1,017
Total Daily Vehicle Mileage (in millions)   5.878
Daily Average Commute Time   47.3 min.
Number of Buses   36
Port Tonnage (in millions)   NA
Airports   NA
Number of Daily Flights   NA
Daily Average Number of Passengers   NA

Airlines (American carriers only)
   See Boston

Housing

A full-service neighborhood Housing Rehabilitation Program operates within the Division of Planning and Development. Much of the city's housing stock may be described as fairly ancient, making the renovation of old houses and building of new ones a top priority for the city's planning officials.

Housing

Total Housing Units   40,302
% Change 1980–1990   13.4
Vacant Units for Sale or Rent   2,733
Occupied Units   37,019
% with More Than One Person per Room   6.7
% Owner-Occupied   41.9
Median Value of Owner-Occupied Homes $131,100
Average Monthly Purchase Cost $365
Median Monthly Rent $494
New Private Housing Starts   44
Value (in thousands) $2,364
% Single-Family   81.8
Nonresidential Buildings Value (in thousands) $13,431

Urban Redevelopment

The Division of Planning and Development is responsible for all aspects of long- and short-term planning for the city. Lowell is in the midst of a second phase of development in which over $200 million has been spent. A large share of this investment was spent on the redevelopment of the Massachusetts Mills Complex and the Boott Mills Complex. The Lowell Plan, initiated by former U.S. Senator Paul Tsongas and the former city manager Joseph Tully, is a nonprofit private development corporation promoting the ongoing revitalization of the city. Working with the private sector, the Lowell Plan serves as a catalyst between the private and public sectors. The Lowell Development and Financial Corporation, established in 1975, provides low-interest loans to local building owners and tenants for the renovation and restoration of their properties.

Crime

 Lowell is rated as the 79th safest city in the United States on a scale on which Miami is the worst and Beaver County, Pennsylvania, is the best. In 1991, violent crimes totaled 750 and property crimes totaled 3,627.

Crime	
Violent Crimes—Total 750	
Violent Crime Rate per 100,000 4,684	
Murder NA	
Rape NA	
Robbery NA	
Aggravated Assaults NA	
Property Crimes 3,627	
Burglary NA	
Larceny NA	
Motor Vehicle Theft NA	
Arson NA	
Per Capita Police Expenditures $124.23	
Per Capita Fire Protection Expenditures $125.44	
Number of Police 140	
Per 1,000 1.50	

Religion

Lowell has over 60 churches and virtually every denomination is represented in the city. The Roman Catholics and the Greek Orthodox are prominent groups, reflecting historical immigration patterns. More recently, the influx of Vietnamese, Laotian, and Cambodian refugees has brought Buddhism and other Oriental religions and cults to the fore.

Religion	
Largest Denominations (Adherents)	
Catholic	754,988
Armenian Church	12,000
American Baptist	16,200
Episcopal	25,282
United Church of Christ	26,857
United Methodist	19,436
Unitarian	10,916
Black Baptist	9,324
Jewish	86,267

Media

 Lowell's only daily newspaper is the *Sun*, published in the evenings. Lowell residents receive much of their television and radio programs via Boston.

Media	
Newsprint	
Sun, daily	
Television	
See Boston	
Radio	
WCAP (AM)	WJUL (FM)
WLLH (AM)	

Sports

 The *Sun* sponsors the annual Tour de Lowell Bicycle Race on the Sunday of Memorial Day weekend, and the Golden Gloves boxing tournament in January and February each year.

Arts, Culture, and Tourism

The city's major performing arts facilities are the Center for the Performing and Visual Arts at the University of Lowell, and the 2,800-seat Lowell Memorial Auditorium, home of the Merrimack Repertory Theatre, which stages six plays annually. The Merrimack Lyric Opera and the Young American Symphony Orchestra have gained reputations beyond Lowell's borders. Both the Lowell National Historical Park and the Lowell Heritage State Park are dedicated to the preservation of the city's cultural heritage. Many of the exhibits and programs in these parks concentrate on Lowell's heritage as one of the first planned industrial communities in the United States. Also explored are the engineering of canals and locks (a 5-1/2-mile canal is included in the park). Other exhibits feature products of its textile mills. Major museums include the Whistler House Museum of Art, with its collection of 19th- and 20th-century art, the New England Quilt Museum, and the Museum of American Textile History.

Travel and Tourism	
Hotel Rooms 3,077	
Convention and Exhibit Space (square feet) NA	
Convention Centers	
Lowell Memorial Auditorium	
Festivals	
National Folk Festival	
Regatta Festival	

Parks and Recreation

Lowell has over 56 parks of which one of the finest is the Vandenberg Esplanade Riverfront Park along the Pawtucket Boulevard on the north bank of the Merrimack River. It features performances in the Sampas Pavilion. There are two golf courses within city limits. Sailing and other water sports are popular on the Merrimack River.

Sources of Further Information

Merrimack Valley Convention and Visitors Bureau
11 Kearney Square
Lowell, MA 01852-1901
(508) 459-6150

Northern Middlesex Convention and Visitors Bureau
45 Palmer Street
Lowell, MA 01852
(508) 937-9300

Additional Reading

Bender, Thomas. *Toward an Urban Vision: Ideas and Institutions in 19th-Century America*. 1982.
Blewett, Mary H. *Surviving Hard Times: The Working People of Lowell*. 1982.
The Last Generation: Work and Life in the Textile Mills of Lowell, Massachusetts, 1910–1960. 1990.
Malone, Patrick M. *Canals and Industry: Engineering in Lowell, 1821–1880*. 1983.
Miles, Henry A. *Lowell As It Was and As It Is*. 1972.

Madison
Wisconsin

Location and Topography

N Madison, the capital of Wisconsin, is situated in the middle of the southern section of the state surrounding a narrow isthmus of land between Lake Mendota and Lake Monona. To the south are Lake Waubesa and Lake Kegonsa. The confluence of these four waterways is the Yahara River, flowing from the north. Lake Wingra, a smaller body of water, is in the middle of the city.

Layout of City and Suburbs

 Madison is somewhat captive by the waterways that surround it at every side except its southwest and northwest edges. It is, after all, the only city in North America to sit on an isthmus. Madison is located in a hilly area that

is a mixture of what one guide calls "a beautiful collage of wooded hills, lush prairies, and sparkling jewels of water where the Indians [once] fished and hunted, planted corn and squash, and smoked their pipes of peace." The most important structure is the state capitol building, located on the highest hill in the city in the center of the isthmus between Lake Mendota and Lake Monona. Topped by a bronze statue of the state motto, "Forward," this imposing building of Vermont granite can be seen from every vantage point in the city. To the west, on the second-highest hill, is the campus of the University of Wisconsin at Madison. The streets are angled north, east, west, and south from the state capitol building as designed by the city's founding fathers. The largest suburbs surrounding Madison are Middleton, Maple Bluff, Monona, and McFarland.

Environment

Environmental Stress Index   2.2
Green Cities Index: Rank   NA
                    Score   NA
Water Quality   Alkaline, hard, fluoridated
    Average Daily Use (gallons per capita)   163
    Maximum Supply (gallons per capita)   369
Parkland as % of Total City Area   14.6
% Waste Landfilled/Recycled   40:40
Annual Parks Expenditures per Capita $80.74

Climate

Madison typically has a Great Lakes climate modified by its location in the heart of the North American continent. The absolute temperature range is very wide, ranging from -40 in the winter to 110°F in the summer. Cyclones and anticyclones are frequent, but normal summers are pleasant with temperatures ranging in the 60s to 70s. Winter temperatures average 20, with annual snow-

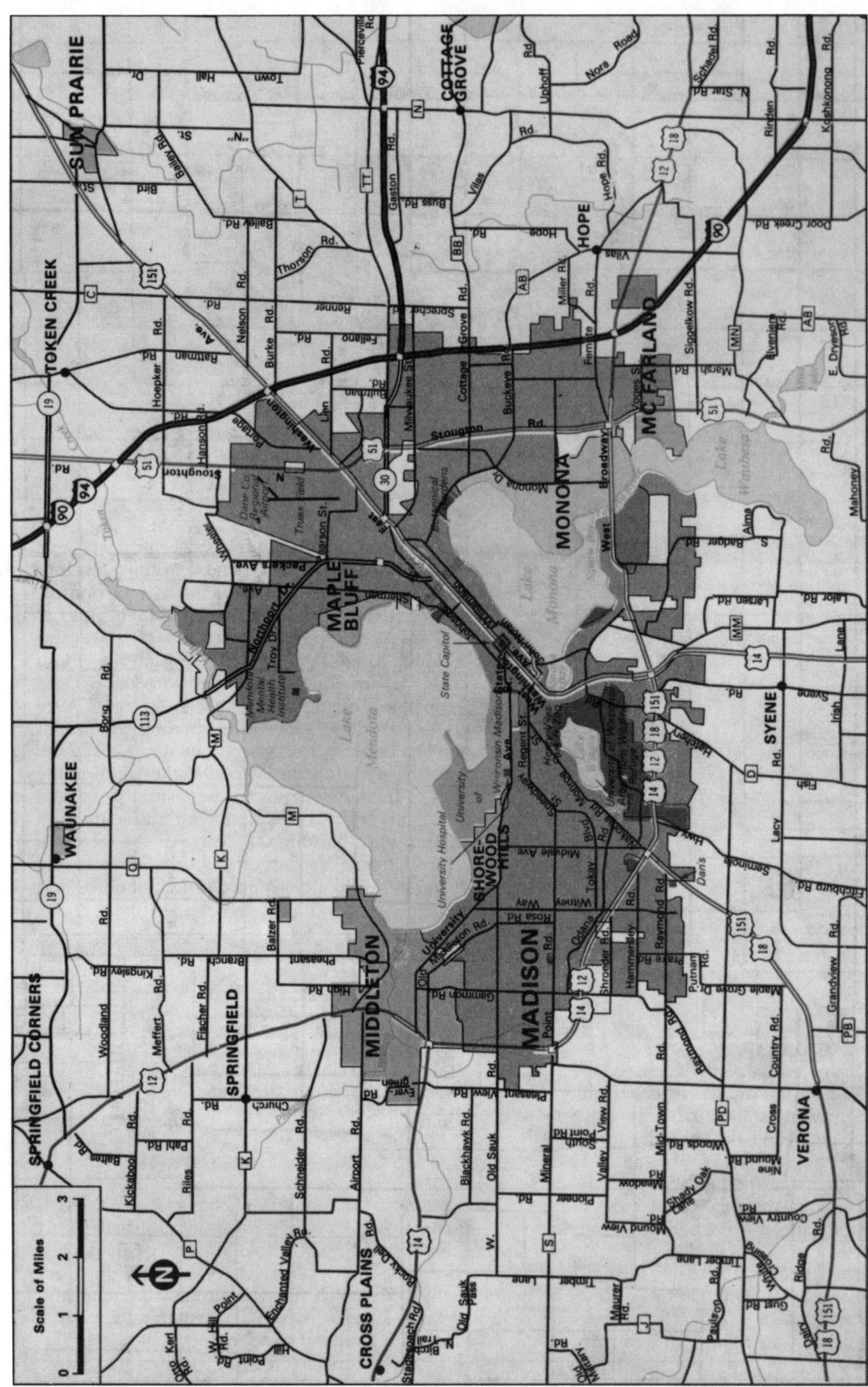

falls rarely below 37 inches. Much of the precipitation falls between May and September.

Weather			
Temperature			
Highest Monthly Average °F	81.4		
Lowest Monthly Average °F	8.2		
Annual Averages			
Days 32°F or Below	164		
Days above 90°F	12		
Zero Degree Days	25		
Precipitation (inches)	30.0		
Snow (inches)	39.0		
% Seasonal Humidity	73.0		
Wind Speed (m.p.h.)	9.9		
Clear Days	94		
Cloudy Days	175		
Storm Days	40		
Rainy Days	117		
Average Temperatures (°F)	*High*	*Low*	*Mean*
January	25.4	8.2	16.8
February	29.5	11.1	20.3
March	39.2	21.2	30.2
April	56.0	34.6	45.3
May	67.3	44.6	56.0
June	76.9	54.6	65.8
July	81.4	58.8	70.1
August	80.0	57.3	68.7
September	70.9	48.5	59.7
October	60.9	38.9	49.9
November	43.0	26.4	34.7
December	29.8	14.0	21.9

History

The Four Lakes Region where Madison now stands was once the home of several American Indian tribes, including the Foxes and Sacs. Dominant in the area were the Winnebago Indians, who called it Taychopera, meaning four lakes. Early visitors to the territory found it to be a place of hills, prairies, and abundant and beautiful waterways—but uninhabitable, at least to a profitable point. These early explorers left no records of their visits, except for Captain Carver, who wrote of his travels in a memoir published in 1768. In 1828, a prospector named Ebenezer Brigham visited the area and camped at what is now Madison to mine lead. He is thought to be the first documented white man to stay in the area. However, it was James Duane Doty, a former federal judge, who visited Taychopera in 1829 and concluded that it was worth substantial investment for habitation. With the help of Steven T. Mason, governor of the Michigan Territory, he paid $1,500 for 1,200 acres of land and began to sell his stake for the site of the capital of Wisconsin Territory. Doty's lobbying led the territorial legislature, located at Belmont, to choose his plot as the territorial capital in 1836, and it was named in honor of former president James Madison.

In 1837 Eben and Rosaline Peck started the Peck Tavern, later called the Madison House, as a place for state legislators to refresh themselves. The state capitol build-

ing was completed in 1844, the state university—the University of Wisconsin at Madison—was created in 1848, and the town received its city charter in 1856. Still, there was a frontier quality about the city. It took the machinations of Leonard James Falwell, a Milwaukee businessman, to make Madison into a true state capital. Buying up much of the land once belonging to James Doty, he built streets and canals, named the lakes surrounding the city after American Indian lore, and became a tireless promoter of Madison. In 1848, when Wisconsin became the 30th state, Madison became the state capital. Between 1851 and 1864 railroads were constructed, linking Madison with other major cities.

During the Civil War, two out of every three Madison men between the ages of 20 and 45 served in the Union army. An encampment at Camp Randall at first housed 70,000 recruits for the Union cause, but was later changed to a Confederate prisoner-of-war camp.

State leaders decided that the capitol building, which leaked when it rained, should be demolished. This task started at the beginning of the Civil War. A second building, finished in 1872, was plagued by tragedy. A wing collapsed in 1883, killing seven people. Although there was a renovation in 1884, a fire in 1904 destroyed much of the building. In 1917, it was torn down and a third capitol building, the present one, was built.

The 20th century saw the bloom of economic development in Madison. Such companies as the French Battery and Carbon Company (the forerunner of Rayovac) and Oscar Mayer, which opened a meat processing plant in the city in 1919 and remains Madison's largest employer, heralded economic improvement. In 1986, Rayovac opened its world headquarters in Madison.

Historical Landmarks

The state capitol dominates Madison. Situated in Capitol Park, it was built between 1906 and 1917 at a cost of $7.2 million. The huge dome, buttressed by 2,500 tons of steel and only several inches shorter than the capitol building in Washington, D.C., is the only one in the United States made of granite. Atop the dome is a gilded bronze statue designed by Daniel Chester French (the man who designed the Lincoln Memorial in Washington) of a lady named "Wisconsin," meant to symbolize the state motto, "Forward." The streets of Madison are also, in a sense, historical. Madison's boulevards were named after figures in American history famous during the time of Judge James Doty, names like Gilman, Carroll, and Dayton (signers of the Declaration of Independence), Hamilton, Monroe, and Langdon. Among the city's noted structures are the Grace Episcopal Church, an 18th-century house of worship; the Keenan House, an 1857 German residence; the Hooley Opera House, Madison's first theatrical establishment; and the Stoner House, an Italian-style dwelling.

Chronology

1828 Lead prospector Ebenezer Brigham camps on the site of Madison, becoming the first documented white man to visit the area.

1829 Judge James Duane Doty and Michigan Governor Steven T. Mason purchase 1,200 acres of land at Taychopera on the Four Lakes isthmus, plat the property, and name it Madison.

1836 Legislators of the newly formed Territory of Wisconsin meeting at Belmont choose Madison as the capital of the territory and site of the future University of Wisconsin.

1837 Eben and Rosaline Peck open the Peck Tavern, known as Madison House, as a place for state legislators to refresh themselves.

1844 First state capitol building completed.

1848 The University of Wisconsin at Madison is opened.

1856 Madison receives its town charter.

1861–1865 Madison is the site of Fort Randall, at first a training center for Union soldiers, later a prison for captured Confederates.

1872 Second capitol building completed.

1884 Second capitol building renovated.

1904 Second capitol building is ruined by fire.

1917 Third capitol building completed.

1919 Manufacturing becomes a major industry as Oscar Mayer opens a major meat processing plant in the city.

1986 Rayovac Batteries opens its world headquarters in Madison.

Population

Population	1980	1990
Central City	170,616	191,262
Rank	83	82
Metro Area	323,545	367,085
Pop. Change 1980–1990 +20,646		
Pop. % Change 1980–1990 +12.1		
Median Age 29.3		
% Male 48.7		
% Age 65 and Over 9.30		
Density (per square mile) 3,309		

Households	
Number 77,361	
Persons per Household 2.30	
% Female-Headed Households 8.3	
% One-Person Households 31.2	
Births—Total 2,580	
% to Mothers under 20 6.1	
Birth Rate per 1,000 15.1	

Ethnic Composition (as % of total pop.)	1980	1990
White	94.33	90.70
Black	2.7	4.24
American Indian	0.25	0.39
Asian and Pacific Islander	1.58	3.91
Hispanic	1.31	2.03
Other	NA	0.75

Government

 Madison runs under a mayor-alderman form of government. Twenty-two aldermen and the mayor, who is not a member of the council, are chosen every two years in nonpartisan elections.

Government	
Year of Home Charter 1856	
Number of Members of the Governing Body 22	
Elected at Large NA	
Elected by Wards 22	
Number of Women in Governing Body 7	
Salary of Mayor $61,522	
Salary of Council Members $4,524	
City Government Employment Total 2,577	
Rate per 10,000 146.6	

Population

Madison is one of the fastest growing cities in the United States. Its 1990 population of 191,262 represents a growth rate of 12.1% over its 1980 population of 170,616. As a result it now ranks 82nd among 195 top cities in the nation.

Ethnic Composition

Whites make up 90.70% of the population, blacks 4.24%, Asian and Pacific islanders 3.91%, Hispanics 2.03%, and American Indians 0.39%.

Public Finance

The annual budget consists of revenues of $152.893 million and expenditures of $160.702 million. The debt outstanding is $118.973 million, and cash and security holdings $138.111 million.

Economy

 Madison was named in 1987 by *Inc.* magazine as one of the 50 fastest growing cities in the United States. A vibrant and expanding economic base is part of this vitality.

Public Finance

Total Revenue (in millions) $152.893
Intergovernmental Revenue—Total (in millions) $49.39
Federal Revenue per Capita $5.87
% Federal Assistance   3.8
% State Assistance   27.16
Sales Tax as % of Total Revenue   1.79
Local Revenue as % of Total Revenue   60.83
City Income Tax   no
Taxes—Total (in millions) $38.2

Taxes per Capita
    Total $217
    Property $200
    Sales and Gross Receipts $9
General Expenditures—Total (in millions) $107.6
General Expenditures per Capita $612
Capital Outlays per Capita $95

% of Expenditures for:
    Public Welfare   7.4
    Highways   12.0
    Education   0.0
    Health and Hospitals   3.6
    Police   16.4
    Sewerage and Sanitation   12.7
    Parks and Recreation   8.2
    Housing and Community Development   6.6
Debt Outstanding per Capita $539
    % Utility   13.9
Federal Procurement Contract Awards (in millions) $69.7
Federal Grants Awards (in millions) $364.5
Fiscal Year Begins   January 1

Economy

Total Money Income (in millions) $2,081.0
% of State Average   114.8
Per Capita Annual Income $11,824
% Population below Poverty Level   13.4
Fortune 500 Companies   NA

Banks	Number	Deposits (in millions)
Commercial	61	NA
Savings	39	NA

Passenger Autos   198,030
Electric Meters   107,115
Gas Meters   77,615

Manufacturing

Number of Establishments   257
% with 20 or More Employees   32.7
Manufacturing Payroll (in millions) $331.9
Value Added by Manufacture (in millions) $662.5
Value of Shipments (in millions) $1,497.4
New Capital Expenditures (in millions) $39.6

Wholesale Trade

Number of Establishments   366
Sales (in millions) $1,373.2
Annual Payroll (in millions) $117.192

Retail Trade

Number of Establishments   2,003
Total Sales (in millions) $1,613.2
Sales per Capita $9,175
Number of Retail Trade Establishments with Payroll   1,547
Annual Payroll (in millions) $200.9
Total Sales (in millions) $1,595.9
General Merchandise Stores (per capita) $1,463
Food Stores (per capita) $1,537
Apparel Stores (per capita) $633
Eating and Drinking Places (per capita) $1,106

Economy (continued)

Service Industries

Total Establishments   1,594
Total Receipts (in millions) $852.7
Hotels and Motels (in millions) $55.2
Health Services (in millions) $247.7
Legal Services (in millions) $86.4

Because it is the state capital, government dominates the employment sector. Second in terms of numbers of employees is education, represented by the University of Wisconsin at Madison. Other areas include services (American Family Insurance Group, CUNA Mutual Insurance), health care (Meriter Hospital, St. Mary's Hospital Medical Center), and manufacturing (Oscar Mayer Food Corporation, Rayovac Batteries, American TV and Appliance).

Labor

 Because Madison has a balanced economy with strong public as well as private sectors, it has remained a healthy labor market even during recessionary times. Unemployment has declined in Madison since 1984 from 5.1% to 2.6%. Because population is growing, the labor pool has been growing as well. Public bodies—including the state and city governments and the university—are among the top employers. The largest private employer is Oscar Mayer Foods.

Labor

Civilian Labor Force   116,816
% Change 1989–1990   -0.3

Work Force Distribution
    Mining   NA
    Construction   8,700
    Manufacturing   25,300
    Transportation and Public Utilities   7,600
    Wholesale and Retail Trade   49,400
    FIRE (Finance, Insurance, Real Estate)   20,600
    Service   50,200
    Government   62,400
    Women as % of Labor Force   47.6
    % Self-Employed   4.2
    % Professional/Technical   26.9
Total Unemployment   3,048
Rate %   2.6
Federal Government Civilian Employment   3,476

Education

The Madison Metropolitan School District supports 27 elementary schools, 8 middle schools, and 4 high schools. Madison also has a strong parochial school system run by the Catholic and Lutheran churches. Higher education is dominated by the University of Wisconsin–Madison, founded in 1848. The university ranks among the top ten in the quality of its doctoral programs and first among all public institutions in its research and development expenditures in science and engineering. The only other college of note is Edgewood College.

Education

Number of Public Schools 39
Special Education Schools NA
Total Enrollment 23,214
% Enrollment in Private Schools 9.7
% Minority 18.8
Classroom Teachers 1,496
Pupil-Teacher Ratio 15:1
Number of Graduates 1,581
Total Revenue (in millions) $117.9
Total Expenditures (in millions) $116.2
Expenditures per Pupil $5,374
Educational Attainment (Age 25 and Over)
   % Completed 12 or More Years 86.3
   % Completed 16 or More Years 38.1
Four-Year Colleges and Universities 2
   Enrollment 44,967
Two-Year Colleges 3
   Enrollment 24,339

Libraries

Number 67
Public Libraries 8
Books (in thousands) 637
Circulation (in thousands) 2,584
Persons Served (in thousands) 191
Circulation per Person Served 13.5
Income (in millions) $5.4
Staff 101

Four-Year Colleges and Universities
   University of Wisconsin, Madison
   Edgewood College

Health

Health care is provided by 7 area hospitals, 100 clinics, a mental health institute, a center for the developmentally disabled, and 5 health maintenance organizations. Among the principal facilities are Madison General Hospital, Meriter Hospital, St. Mary's Hospital Medical Center, the University of Wisconsin Hospitals and Clinics, and Jackson Clinic.

Health

Deaths—Total 1,227
Rate per 1,000 7.2
Infant Deaths—Total 27
Rate per 1,000 10.5
Number of Metro Hospitals 7
Number of Metro Hospital Beds 2,242
Rate per 100,000 1,275
Number of Physicians 1,284
Physicians per 1,000 4.58
Nurses per 1,000 8.75
Health Expenditures per Capita $30.59

Transportation

Two of Wisconsin's three interstates—I-90 and I-94—pass through Madison. Madison also is the hub of five U.S. highways (12, 14, 18, 51, and 151) and two state highways (30 and 113). The West Beltline, formed by U.S. 18, 151, 1, and 14, bypasses the city. There is no passenger rail service direct to Madison. Amtrak passengers may

board in Columbus, 45 minutes from Madison. Rail freight service is provided by the Chicago and Northwestern Railroad, the So/Milwaukee Railroad, and the Wisconsin and Calumet Railroad. The Dane County Regional Airport, owned and operated by Dane County, serves five major airlines and seven commuter airlines.

Transportation

Interstate Highway Mileage 7
Total Urban Mileage 889
Total Daily Vehicle Mileage (in millions) 4.626
Daily Average Commute Time 39.6 min.
Number of Buses 145
Port Tonnage (in millions) NA
Airports 1
Number of Daily Flights 19
Daily Average Number of Passengers 1,052

Airlines (American carriers only)
   Air Wisconsin
   American
   Midway
   Northwest
   Trans World
   United

Housing

Most downtown housing is from 80 to 90 years old on the average. As the demand for student housing increased over the years, older homes were converted into rooming houses and small apartments. The residential density increased and poorly designed buildings created architectural disharmony in neighborhoods. As a result there has been an increase in housing construction in the suburbs.

Housing

Total Housing Units 80,047
% Change 1980–1990 13.8
Vacant Units for Sale or Rent 2,143
Occupied Units 77,361
% with More Than One Person per Room 3.0
% Owner-Occupied 47
Median Value of Owner-Occupied Homes $75,200
Average Monthly Purchase Cost $433
Median Monthly Rent $430
New Private Housing Starts 1,131
Value (in thousands) $66,775
% Single-Family 40.6
Nonresidential Buildings Value (in thousands) $64,887

Urban Redevelopment

Downtown 2000 Report, issued in 1970, is the basis of redevelopment programs within Central Madison. The Urban Design Commission was appointed to monitor the quality of the built environment. A number of development activities followed: the construction of the State Street

Mall, the Capitol Concourse, the Capitol Center constructed west of the square, and the Federal Courthouse.

Crime

 Madison is a relatively safe city. In 1991, violent crimes totaled 770 in 1991 and property crimes totaled 12,114.

Crime

Violent Crimes—Total   770
Violent Crime Rate per 100,000   340.1
Murder   2
Rape   93
Robbery   325
Aggravated Assaults   350
Property Crimes   12,114
Burglary   2,273
Larceny   9,089
Motor Vehicle Theft   752
Arson   65
Per Capita Police Expenditures $123.64
Per Capita Fire Protection Expenditures $95.75
Number of Police   294
Per 1,000   1.72

Religion

 The city's largest congregations are Lutheran and Catholic, reflecting the partly German and Scandinavian heritage of the area, but almost all denominations are represented in Madison. Pentecostals are the third-largest congregation with nine churches. Christ Presbyterian Church on Gorham Street, High Point Church at High Point, and Bethel Lutheran Church on Wisconsin Avenue are the three most active churches in the city. Architecturally, the most famous church is the First Unitarian Society on University Bay Drive designed by Frank Lloyd Wright. Virtually all Catholic congregations are thriving. The Catholic cathedral is St. Raphaels, located on Main Street a few blocks off Capitol Square.

Religion

Largest Denominations (Adherents)

Catholic	102,227
Evangelical Lutheran	47,758
United Methodist	9,368
United Church of Christ	6,586
Lutheran-Missouri Synod	4,714
Presbyterian	4,572
Black Baptist	3,407
Episcopal	2,146
Jewish	4,500

Media

 Madison's press consists of the *Wisconsin State Journal*, published in the mornings and Sundays, and *The Capital Times*, published in the evenings. The electronic media includes 5 television stations (3 commercial, 1 public, 1 independent) and 11 AM and FM radio stations.

Media

Newsprint
  The Capital Times, daily
  Wisconsin State Journal, daily

Television
  WHA (Channel 21)
  WISC (Channel 3)
  WKOW (Channel 27)
  WMSN (Channel 47)
  WMTV (Channel 15)

Radio
WHIT (AM)	WIBA (AM)
WIBA (FM)	WMLI (FM)
WNWC (FM)	WOLX (FM)
WORT (FM)	WTDY (AM)
WMGN (FM)	WTSO (AM)
WZEE (FM)	

Sports

 Madison has no major professional team in any sports.

Arts, Culture, and Tourism

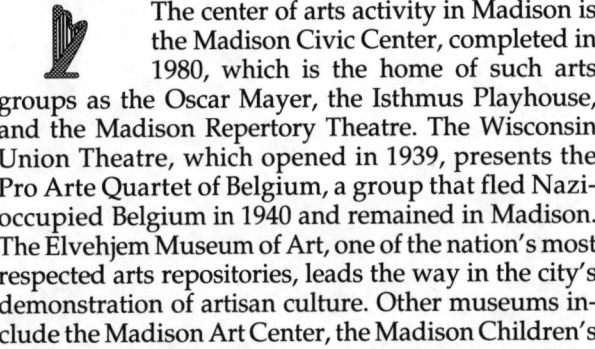 The center of arts activity in Madison is the Madison Civic Center, completed in 1980, which is the home of such arts groups as the Oscar Mayer, the Isthmus Playhouse, and the Madison Repertory Theatre. The Wisconsin Union Theatre, which opened in 1939, presents the Pro Arte Quartet of Belgium, a group that fled Nazi-occupied Belgium in 1940 and remained in Madison. The Elvehjem Museum of Art, one of the nation's most respected arts repositories, leads the way in the city's demonstration of artisan culture. Other museums include the Madison Art Center, the Madison Children's Museum, the Wisconsin Veteran's Museum, and the State Historical Museum.

Travel and Tourism

Hotel Rooms   4,523
Convention and Exhibit Space (square feet)   85,000

Convention Centers
  Madison Civic Center
  The Forum at Dane County Exposition Center
  Dane County Memorial Coliseum

Festivals
  Taste of Madison
  Festival of the Lakes
  Art Fair (July)

Parks and Recreation

 In addition to its lake recreation areas, Madison has 150 parks. Among these are Vilas Park, located on the northern shore of Lake Wingra, which boasts the Henry Vilas Zoo; the University of Wisconsin Arboretum (just

Madison, Wisconsin • 551

across the water from Vilas Park), a conservatory of plants and animals; and the Olbrich Botanical Gardens (on the northeastern shore of Lake Monona), which features various flowers and plants.

Sources of Further Information

Greater Madison Chamber of Commerce
615 East Washington Avenue
Madison, WI 53701-0071
(608) 256-8348

Greater Madison Convention and Visitors Bureau
121 West Doty Street
Madison, WI 53703
(608) 255-0701

Madison Public Library
201 West Mifflin Street
Madison, WI 53703
(608) 266-6300

State Historical Society of Wisconsin
816 State Street
Madison, WI 53706
(608) 262-3266

Additional Reading

Brody, Polly. *Discovering Wisconsin*. 1973.
Gilmour, Stephen. *Index to a History of Madison*. 1985.
Moe, Doug, and Jocelyn Riley. *Greater Madison: Meeting the 21st Century*. 1990.
Urban Land Institute. *Madison, Wisconsin*. 1981.

Manchester
New Hampshire

Location and Topography

Manchester, the largest city in New Hampshire, straddles the Merrimack River in the southern section of the state. It is approximately 20 miles south of the state capital, Concord, and about 20 miles north of the New Hampshire–Massachusetts border. The city is situated in a valley of the White Mountains, where the Merrimack begins its flow southward into Massachusetts. The area is wooded and embraced by several waterways, such as Massabesic Lake to the east and the smaller Baboosic Lake to the southwest. The land rises from 110 feet above sea level at the valley floor to 570 feet above sea level.

Layout of City and Suburbs

Much of downtown Manchester is built around the Amoskeag Millyard area on the east bank of the Merrimack River. Streets such as Market, Stark, West Merrimack, and Kidder radiate eastward from this area. Three bridges over the Merrimack River connect Manchester with its suburbs to the west. The suburbs surrounding the city include North Londonderry, South Hooksett, Severance, Bedford, and Pinardville.

Climate

Northwesterly winds prevail, bringing cold, dry air during the winter and cool, dry air in the summer. The winters are long and cold, but the summers are ideal, with warm, sunny days and cool nights. In an average year, the city has 92 clear days, 113 partly cloudy days, 160 cloudy days, 125 rainy days, 21 storm days, 26 zero-degree days, 176 freezing days, and 11 over-90°F days. The average annual rainfall and snowfall are 36 and 64 inches, respectively.

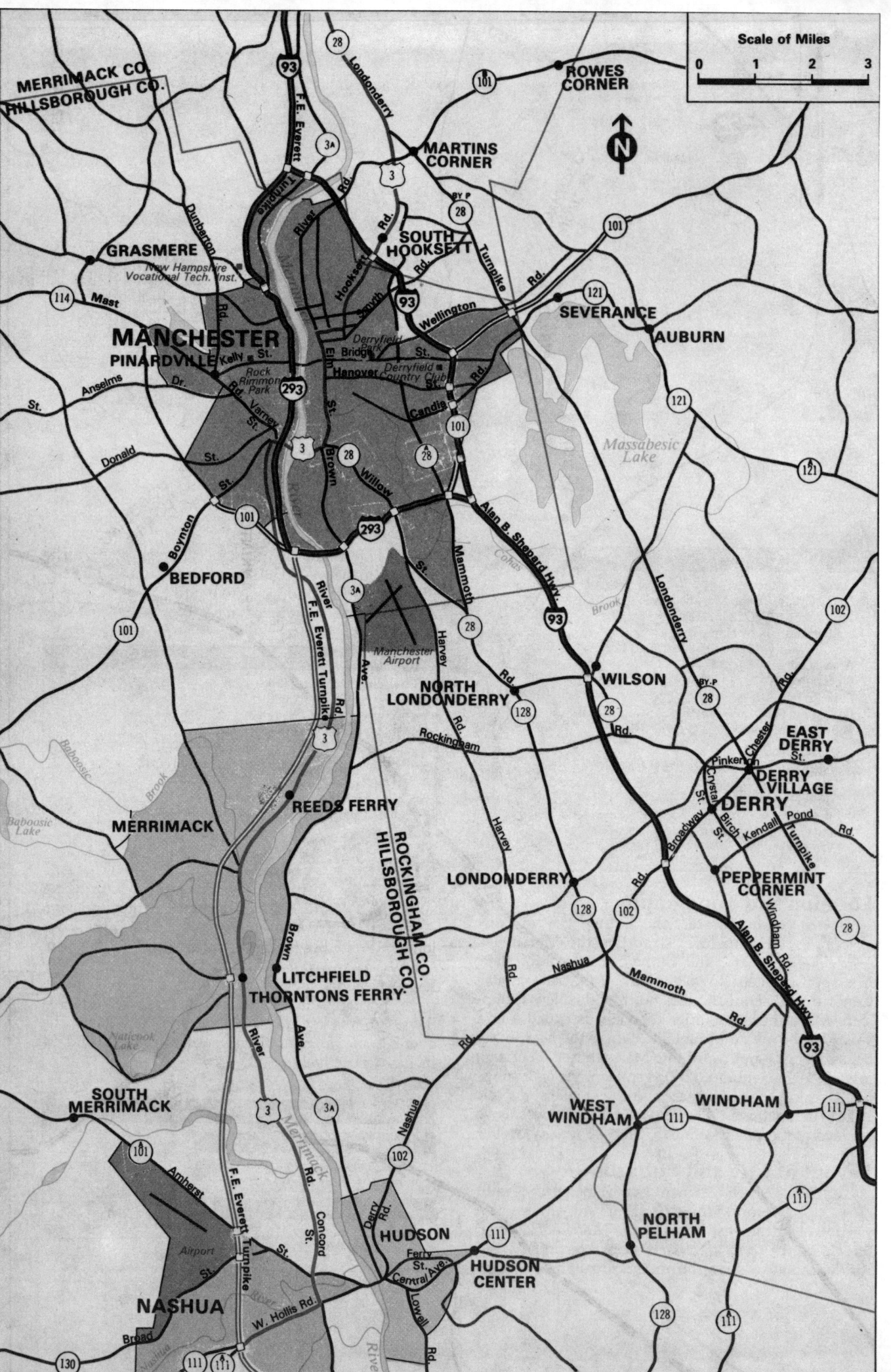

Weather (continued)			
Zero Degree Days 26			
Precipitation (inches) 36			
Snow (inches) 64			
% Seasonal Humidity 73			
Wind Speed (m.p.h.) 6.7			
Clear Days 92			
Cloudy Days 160			
Storm Days 21			
Rainy Days 125			
Average Temperatures (°F)	*High*	*Low*	*Mean*
January	31.3	9.9	20.6
February	33.8	11.3	22.6
March	42.4	22.1	32.3
April	56.7	31.7	44.2
May	68.6	41.5	55.1
June	77.7	51.6	64.7
July	82.6	56.7	69.7
August	80.1	54.2	67.2
September	72.4	46.5	59.5
October	62.3	36.3	49.3
November	47.9	28.1	38.0
December	34.6	14.9	24.8

History

Various American Indian tribes have occupied the Merrimack River area for well over 10,000 years. The last tribe to inhabit the land before the settling by white Europeans were the Pennacooks, led by such men as Passaconaway and Wonalancet. The Pennacooks named the river that cut through the valley Amoskeag, meaning "place of much fish." The first Europeans to see the area were sent by Massachusetts Bay Colony Governor John Winthrop about 1636. Some 14 years later, missionary John Eliot arrived, opened a school, and taught the natives to pray. Over the next 80 years, trappers, hunters, and fishermen invaded this area of natural riches. By 1725, the Indians had moved north to escape the diseases brought by the Europeans.

The Manchester area began to industrialize about 1719. Scotch-Irish immigrants, bringing with them their knowledge and skills in the crafts of wool spinning and weaving, settled in Londonderry, just to the south of present-day Manchester. Three years later, Massachusetts Colony citizens John Goffe, Jr., Edward Lingfield, and Benjamin Kidder established a small settlement and water mill on Cohas Brook. The falls at this spot now bear the name of Goffe.

From 1733 until 1736, some of the most important of Manchester's early immigrants arrived, including Archibald Stark. His home, built in 1736, is now owned by the Molly Stark chapter of the Daughters of the American Revolution. Stark's son John served in the American army at the battles of Bunker Hill, Trenton, and Bennington. In 1735, the settlement was given to a trapper, William Tyng, who had passed through the area in 1703, and named Tyngstown. In 1751, however, a town charter was granted to the settlement's citizens, and the town was renamed Derryfield. In 1810, the name was changed to Manchester in honor of Judge Samuel Blodgett , who constructed a canal between 1794 and 1807 to allow shipping traffic to Concord and Boston. Before his death in 1807, Blodgett had predicted that the city "would rise like Manchester, England" because of the harnessing of the power of the Merrimack River.

Manchester's economic success began in 1828 when Boston investors bought into a failing cotton mill on the Merrimack River and turned the enterprise into the Amoskeag Manufacturing Company. It would later become the largest textile corporation in the world.

The rest of the 19th century and a third of the 20th was the story of textiles. Manchester was the textile king, and this forged the city's economic rise. During the 1930s, however, textiles shaped its demise. The Depression, labor strikes, and increased competition drove the Amoskeag Manufacturing Company out of business in 1936, forcing the city to attract new businesses and diversify the economy. The service industry, as well as a limited revival of the cotton mills and manufacturing, have created a growing base of economic prosperity.

Historical Landmarks

The original Amoskeag Bridge was built in 1842 but washed away by the flowing river sometime after. An 800-foot covered bridge built in its place collapsed in 1920. The present bridge was constructed in 1972. The housing built for the Amoskeag Manufacturing Company on Kidder Street between Canal and Elm streets dates back to 1881 in the southern rows and 1914 in the northern. The Millyard on the east bank of the Merrimack River is the original building that was constructed between 1838 and the company's closing in 1936. The Blodgett Canal is the remains of the waterway built by Judge Samuel Blodgett between 1794 and 1807 to allow shipping traffic between Concord and Boston. City Hall on Elm Street dates back to 1845. The site of the original Manchester Opera House (which was destroyed by fire) is now occupied by shops and apartments. The site of the home of original settler John Stark, as well as his childhood home, the fort built by his father during the French and Indian Wars, and his grave, can be seen in Manchester.

Population

Manchester lies at the population center of New Hampshire. Its population is estimated at 99,567, and it may cross the 100,000 mark before the end of the century. It has a healthy growth rate and its quality of life continues to draw residents.

Population		
	1980	*1990*
Central City	90,936	99,567
Rank	192	197
Metro Area	276,608	336,073
Pop. Change 1980–1990 +8,631		
Pop. % Change 1980–1990 +9.5		
Median Age 32.0		
% Male 47.9		
% Age 65 and Over 13.7		
Density (per square mile) 3,017		

Chronology

1636	An exploration party sent by Massachusetts Bay Colony Governor John Winthrop arrives in the Merrimack Valley.
1650	Missionary John Eliot opens a school for the native Pennacook tribe on a bluff overlooking the Amoskeag Falls.
1703	William Tyng and a band of trappers explore the Merrimack Valley.
1719	Scotch-Irish settlers to the Merrimack Valley bring their knowledge of wool spinning and weaving.
1722	Massachusetts Bay Colony citizens John Goffe, Jr., Edward Lingfield, and Benjamin Kidder establish a settlement and mill at Cohas Brook.
1735	Tyng is awarded the area around the east bank of the Merrimack. The settlement is called Tyngstown.
1751	The governor of New Hampshire grants a town charter to the citizens of Tyngstown, who rename it Derryfield.
1794–1807	Judge Samuel Blodgett of Derryfield constructs a canal on the Amoskeag to create river traffic between Concord and Boston.
1810	Three years after the death of Blodgett, the town of Derryfield is renamed Manchester in honor of his prediction that the town would attain the industrial might equal to that of Manchester, England.
1828	The Amoskeag Cotton and Woolen Factory, a failing enterprise, is sold to Boston investors, who reopen it as the Amoskeag Manufacturing Company. The corporation goes on to become the largest textile company in the world.
1936	The Great Depression, labor strikes, and increased competition drive the Amoskeag Manufacturing Company out of business. Local workers pool their money and purchase the mills for $5 million.
1980s	A slowdown in the New England economy leads Manchester to diversify its economy.

Population (continued)

Households

Number   40,338
Persons per Household   2.40
% Female-Headed Households   11.1
% One-Person Households   29.2
Births—Total   1,477
    % to Mothers under 20   11.0
    Birth Rate per 1,000   15.6

Ethnic Composition

Although considered a Yankee city, Manchester has more ethnic variety than most other cities in New England. French-Canadians make up the largest group and are prominent in business, the professions, and government. The Greeks are the next largest; they have their own schools, churches, and newspapers. The Irish and the Poles rank third and fourth in numerical order. Racially, the city is homogeneous, with whites making up 97%.

Ethnic Composition (as % of total pop.)		
	1980	1990
White	98.90	96.97
Black	0.37	0.97
American Indian	0.14	0.21
Asian and Pacific Islander	0.30	1.1
Hispanic	1.06	2.13
Other	NA	0.75

Government

Manchester operates under a mayor and a 12-member board of aldermen elected to two-year terms. Each alderman represents one of the 12 wards.

Government

Year of Home Charter   1982
Number of Members of the Governing Body   12
Elected at Large   NA
Elected by Wards   12
Number of Women in Governing Body   3
Salary of Mayor $40,000
Salary of Council Members $4,000
City Government Employment Total   2,766
Rate per 10,000   284.3

Public Finance

New Hampshire is the only state with neither an earned income nor a general sales tax. Even interest on bank and credit union savings in the state is tax free. The major items of city revenues are real estate and property tax, auto registration permit fees, boat fees, building permit fees, and municipal licenses. The annual budget consists of revenues of $146.658 million and expenditures of $158.655 million. Total debt outstanding is $80.595 million, and cash and security holdings $33.615 million.

Public Finance

Total Revenue (in millions) $146.658
Intergovernmental Revenue—Total (in millions) $19.9
Federal Revenue per Capita $70.38
% Federal Assistance   4.92
% State Assistance   7.69
Sales Tax as % of Total Revenue   NA
Local Revenue as % of Total Revenue   87.38

Public Finance (continued)

City Income Tax   no
Taxes—Total (in millions) $57.4

Taxes per Capita
  Total $590
    Property $584
    Sales and Gross Receipts $0
General Expenditures—Total (in millions) $79.8
General Expenditures per Capita $821
Capital Outlays per Capita $0

% of Expenditures for:
  Public Welfare   1.4
  Highways   9.8
  Education   37.0
  Health and Hospitals   0.6
  Police   6.4
  Sewerage and Sanitation   7.0
  Parks and Recreation   2.1
  Housing and Community Development   0.0
Debt Outstanding per Capita $480
  % Utility   10.4
Federal Procurement Contract Awards (in millions) $11.4
Federal Grants Awards (in millions) $10.4
Fiscal Year Begins   January 1

Economy

Once a single-industry town dependent on textiles, after 1935 Manchester diversified and developed a broad industrial base. Service-sector companies such as the First New Hampshire Bank and Elliot Hospital account for much of the city's employment. However, an expanding manufacturing base, led by such corporations as the Digital Equipment Corporation, General Electric, GTE, Raytheon, and Velcro USA, has led the way in the creation of new jobs. The nonprofit Greater Manchester Development Corporation serves the city by attracting new businesses to the area.

Economy

Total Money Income (in millions) $1,116.8
% of State Average   98.5
Per Capita Annual Income $11,481
% Population below Poverty Level   10.4
Fortune 500 Companies   NA

Banks	Number	Deposits (in millions)
Commercial	6	702
Savings	2	839.9

Passenger Autos   259,314
Electric Meters   59,726
Gas Meters   18,438

Manufacturing

Number of Establishments   189
% with 20 or More Employees   39.2
Manufacturing Payroll (in millions) $197.1
Value Added by Manufacture (in millions) $484.4
Value of Shipments (in millions) $983.5
New Capital Expenditures (in millions) $24.1

Wholesale Trade

Number of Establishments   263
Sales (in millions) $1,374.7
Annual Payroll (in millions) $110.344

Economy (continued)

Retail Trade

Number of Establishments   1,049
Total Sales (in millions) $1,097.3
Sales per Capita $11,280
Number of Retail Trade Establishments with Payroll   770
Annual Payroll (in millions) $129.0
Total Sales (in millions) $1,078.8
General Merchandise Stores (per capita) $1,974
Food Stores (per capita) $1,505
Apparel Stores (per capita) $707
Eating and Drinking Places (per capita) $969

Service Industries

Total Establishments   1,017
Total Receipts (in millions) $507.4
Hotels and Motels (in millions)   NA
Health Services (in millions) $100.7
Legal Services (in millions) $74.0

Labor

More than 13% of the work force is employed in manufacturing; of the remaining, 80% are engaged in sales, retail, finance, and service. Unemployment is lower than in the region as a whole, remaining until 1991 well below 5%. The largest three employers are in the nonmanufacturing sector: New Hampshire Insurance, New England Telephone, and Catholic Medical Center. Manchester has one of the best records in the nation in terms of hours lost through strikes.

Manchester's economic growth has driven the costs of homes, transportation, health-care, and other services well above the national average.

Labor

Civilian Labor Force   59,406
% Change 1989–1990   3.1

Work Force Distribution
  Mining   NA
  Construction   2,600
  Manufacturing   10,400
  Transportation and Public Utilities   4,200
  Wholesale and Retail Trade   18,500
  FIRE (Finance, Insurance, Real Estate)   8,300
  Service   22,500
  Government   8,500
  Women as % of Labor Force   46.4
  % Self-Employed   4.1
  % Professional/Technical   12.7
Total Unemployment   3,855
Rate %   6.5
Federal Government Civilian Employment   2,039

Education

Manchester has a strong public and parochial education system—the former with 3 senior high schools, 3 junior high/middle schools, and 14 elementary schools, and the latter with 1 senior high, 1 junior high, and 7 elementary schools. In addition, the Derryfield School is a private coeducational school for grades 7–12. The state-funded Manchester School of Technology, founded in 1982, offers training in vocational skills.

There are three higher education facilities: St. Anselm College, Notre Dame College, and the University of New Hampshire at Manchester. The specialized institutes include two business colleges, the four-year New Hampshire College and the two-year Hesser College, as well as the New Hampshire Vocational-Technical College.

Education

Number of Public Schools   29
Special Education Schools   NA
Total Enrollment   14,604
% Enrollment in Private Schools   15.2
% Minority   NA
Classroom Teachers   NA
Pupil-Teacher Ratio   25:1
Number of Graduates   NA
Total Revenue (in millions)   NA
Total Expenditures (in millions)   NA
Expenditures per Pupil   NA
Educational Attainment (Age 25 and Over)   NA
   % Completed 12 or More Years   61.4
   % Completed 16 or More Years   13.3
Four-Year Colleges and Universities   3
   Enrollment   6,303
Two-Year Colleges   1
   Enrollment   2,100

Libraries

Number   14
Public Libraries   2
Books (in thousands)   314
Circulation (in thousands)   335
Persons Served (in thousands)   98
Circulation per Person Served   3.41
Income (in millions) $1.511
Staff   NA

Four-Year Colleges and Universities
   University of New Hampshire
   St. Anselm College
   Notre Dame College
   New Hampshire College

Health

Manchester is New Hampshire's premier health-care center, with four hospitals. The bellwether is the 330-bed Catholic Medical Center, followed by the Elliot Hospital with 296 beds, the Veterans Administration Medical Center with 164, and Lake Shore Psychiatric Hospital with 94.

Health

Deaths—Total   996
Rate per 1,000   10.5
Infant Deaths—Total   17
Rate per 1,000   11.5
Number of Metro Hospitals   4
Number of Metro Hospital Beds   884
Rate per 100,000   912
Number of Physicians   490
Physicians per 1,000   NA
Nurses per 1,000   NA
Health Expenditures per Capita $17.20

Transportation

Manchester is served by its expressway, I-293, also known as the Frederick E. Everett Turnpike. It is linked to Boston in the south and Concord to the north by I-93, and to southern Vermont by Route 101, which is slated for expansion in the next several years. Located south of the city, Manchester Airport serves nine airlines with 1-million people passing through the gateway annually. Port facilities for Manchester are in Portsmouth, some 50 miles away and connected to Manchester by Route 101.

Transportation

Interstate Highway Mileage   19
Total Urban Mileage   509
Total Daily Vehicle Mileage (in millions)   2.322
Daily Average Commute Time   42.5 min.
Number of Buses   26
Port Tonnage (in millions)   NA
Airports   1
Number of Daily Flights   14
Daily Average Number of Passengers   627

Airlines (American carriers only)
   Continental
   United

Housing

Manchester suffered a severe housing shortage in the late 1980s, leading to brisk construction activity. Many new housing projects have been completed, and over 8,000 multifamily units have been built since 1980. Some, like Wall Street, combine residential units with office space.

Housing

Total Housing Units   44,361
% Change 1980–1990   19.1
Vacant Units for Sale or Rent   3,485
Occupied Units   40,338
% with More Than One Person per Room   1.6
% Owner-Occupied   46.0
Median Value of Owner-Occupied Homes $118,600
Average Monthly Purchase Cost $415
Median Monthly Rent $467
New Private Housing Starts   362
Value (in thousands) $23,596
% Single-Family   32.9
Nonresidential Buildings Value (in thousands) $7,686

Urban Redevelopment

Urban redevelopment activities are coordinated by the Greater Manchester Development Corporation, which acts as an umbrella for all groups involved in the economic future of the city. The city has developed a Five-Year Community Improvement Plan that serves as the master blueprint for development projects. There are two other economic development corporations: the Amoskeag Industries, formed in the late 1930s to raise capital to purchase the bankrupt Amoskeag Manufacturing Company, and the Manchester Regional Industrial Foundation. Two recent projects that have changed downtown Manchester are the Center of New Hampshire complex, which houses a hotel, convention center, office building, retail space, and transit facility, and the 20-story headquarters of New England Telephone, the tallest building in New Hampshire.

Crime

The violent crime rate is a low 189.9 per 100,000. In 1991, 240 crimes were violent and 6,773 were property related.

Crime

Violent Crimes—Total 240
Violent Crime Rate per 100,000 189.9
Murder 6
Rape 23
Robbery 165
Aggravated Assaults 46
Property Crimes 6,773
Burglary 2,040
Larceny 4,306
Motor Vehicle Theft 427
Arson 46
Per Capita Police Expenditures $88.45
Per Capita Fire Protection Expenditures $79.01
Number of Police 159
Per 1,000 1.64

Religion

Roman Catholicism is predominant in this partly French-Canadian city, but Greek Orthodox and Protestant denominations are well represented.

Religion

Largest Denominations (Adherents)	
Catholic	117,237
United Church of Christ	9,247
Episcopal	3,693
Latter-Day Saints	1,375
American Baptist	2,457
Presbyterian	1,330
United Methodist	3,873
Unitarian	1,212
Assembly of God	1,093
Jewish	3,500

Media

Manchester's lone daily, the *Union Leader*, is well known nationally as the voice of arch-conservatism. Published only on weekdays, it appears on Sundays as the *New Hampshire Sunday News*. The *Boston Globe* is printed weekly as a New Hampshire edition. Although Manchester receives television and radio signals from Bos-

ton, it also has two television stations of its own and five radio stations.

Media

Newsprint
  New Hampshire Business Review, monthly
  Union Leader, daily
Television
  WGOT (Channel 60)
  WMUR (Channel 9)
Radio
  WFEA (AM)   WGIR (AM)
  WGIR (FM)   WKBR (AM)
  WZID (FM)

Sports

There are no professional teams located in Manchester.

Arts, Culture, and Tourism

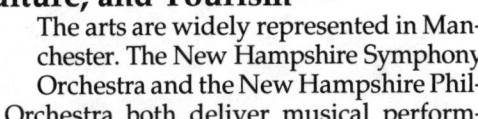
The arts are widely represented in Manchester. The New Hampshire Symphony Orchestra and the New Hampshire Philharmonic Orchestra both deliver musical performances. The Palace Theatre, built in 1915, delivers numerous theatrical and dance exhibitions. The Dana Center at St. Anselm College in nearby Goffstown displays movies and holds lectures. Museums in Manchester include the Art Group Gallery, which exhibits paintings and photographs; the Chapel Art Center at Saint Anselm College, a display of regional artists; the Currier Gallery of Art, featuring American art from the colonial times to the present; and the Manchester Institute of Arts and Sciences Gallery.

Travel and Tourism

Hotel Rooms 2,768
Convention and Exhibit Space (square feet) NA
Convention Centers
  Center of New Hampshire Holiday Inn
Festivals
  Riverfest (September)

Parks and Recreation

Manchester has about 900 acres of parks and nearby recreation areas. Included in the list are four state parks: Bear Brook, Clough, Greenfield, and Pawtuckaway. Several city parks cater to sports and recreation events.

Sources of Further Information

Manchester Chamber of Commerce
889 Elm Street
Manchester, NH 03101
(603) 666-6600

Manchester Historic Association
129 Amherst Street
Manchester, NH 03104
(603) 622-7531

Additional Reading

Fingertip Facts on Manchester. 1990.

Memphis

Tennessee

Basic Data

Name   Memphis
Name Origin   From Memphis, Egypt
Year Founded   1818 Inc. 1826
Status: State   Tennessee
       County   Seat of Shelby County
Area (square miles)   256
Elevation (feet)   275
Time Zone   Central
Population (1990)   610,337
Population of Metro Area (1990)   981,747

Distance in Miles To:

Atlanta	382
Boston	1,341
Chicago	537
Dallas	454
Denver	1,043
Detroit	719
Houston	574
Los Angeles	1,807
Miami	997
New York	1,102
Philadelphia	1,007
Washington, DC	854

Location and Topography

N

Memphis is situated in the extreme south-western corner of Tennessee on the border of Mississippi and Arkansas. It is centrally located in an area ringed by the Mississippi River to the west, McKellar Lake to the southwest, the Wolf River to the north, and Nonconnah Creek to the south. It is elevated and built on a bluff overlooking the Mississippi River.

Layout of City and Suburbs

The most important natural feature of Memphis is its proximity to the Mississippi River. Along its docks is Jefferson Davis Park, named for the only president of the Confederacy. Its streets are wide and expansive, dominated by several thoroughfares: Main, Second, and Third streets running north to south, and Peabody Place, Beale Street, and I-40 running east to west. The original plans laid out the city in a checkerboard pattern, with wide avenues near the center and an unobstructed view of the Mississippi River. President's Island, a large sandbar to the southwest of the city, sits in the middle of the Mississippi River. Memphis's suburbs include Oakville, Shelby Farms, Bartlett, and Benjestown.

Environment

Environmental Stress Index   2.6
Green Cities Index: Rank   41
              Score   31.21
Water Quality   Neutral, hard, fluoridated
    Average Daily Use (gallons per capita)   177
    Maximum Supply (gallons per capita)   276
Parkland as % of Total City Area   2.9
% Waste Landfilled/Recycled   NA
Annual Parks Expenditures per Capita $76.93

Climate

Memphis enjoys an equable climate with few extremes in temperature. The range of temperatures varies from the 40s in the winter to the high 80s in the summer. Rainfall is evenly distributed throughout the year. Although it is not in the normal paths of storms from the Gulf of Mexico or Canada, it is affected by both systems and therefore subject to frequent changes in weather. Fall and spring are extremely pleasant months.

Weather

Temperature

Highest Monthly Average °F 91.5
Lowest Monthly Average °F 30.9

Annual Averages

Days 32°F or Below 59
Days above 90°F 64
Zero Degree Days 0
Precipitation (inches) 49.0
Snow (inches) 6.0
% Seasonal Humidity 69.0
Wind Speed (m.p.h.) 9.2
Clear Days 118
Cloudy Days 148
Storm Days 53
Rainy Days 106

Average Temperatures (°F)	High	Low	Mean
January	49.4	31.6	40.5
February	53.1	34.4	43.8
March	60.8	41.1	51.0
April	72.7	52.3	62.5
May	81.2	60.6	70.9
June	88.7	68.5	78.6
July	91.6	71.5	81.6
August	90.6	70.1	80.4
September	84.3	62.8	73.6
October	74.9	51.1	63.0
November	61.5	40.3	50.9
December	51.7	33.7	42.7

History

The area now called Memphis was known as the Fourth or Lower Chickasaw Bluff when the Chickasaw Indians inhabited it. In 1540 the bluff was visited by explorer Hernando de Soto, who discovered the Mississippi River. After de Soto and his company moved on, the area was not visited again by Europeans until Father Jacques Marquette and Louis Jolliet came to the bluffs in 1673. French explorer Robert Cavelier, Sieur de La Salle, followed Marquette and Jolliet in 1682, and set up Fort Prudhomme on the First Chickasaw Bluff. Several others, including Captain Isaac Guion, who founded Fort Adams, and John Overton, an Indian affairs agent, used the bluffs for forts and trading posts.

In 1819, following the ceding of lands in the western United States from Spain to America, John Overton, James Winchester, and future president Andrew Jackson laid out a city with 362 deeded lots. They envisioned a metropolis with wide streets and an economy based on commerce along the Mississippi River. The town was incorporated in 1826, and within 25 years had become the sixth-largest city in the South. In those years steamboats, railroads, and stagecoaches arrived.

At the start of the Civil War, Memphis became a military fort. In 1862, it was made the emergency state capital. Later that year, the city was taken by Union army forces commanded by Commodore C. H. Davis. Although Memphis was held throughout the rest of the war, and several attempts were made by the Confederacy to retake it, the city was left physically untouched by the war. Its economy, however, was shattered, and took

40 years to recover. Memphis was struck by three successive yellow fever epidemics—in 1867, 1873, and 1878—claiming several thousand lives.

In the 20th century, Memphis has been marked by three distinct events: the rise of Mayor Edward Hill Crump—Boss Crump, whose powerful campaign machine ruled Memphis from 1909 to 1916; the Mississippi floods of 1937, during which thousands of refugees packed Memphis to escape the rising waters; and the assassination of Dr. Martin Luther King, Jr., on 4 April 1968 when he came to the city to settle a sanitation strike.

Historical Landmarks

Memphis is replete with historical landmarks. Beale Street, the home of the city's black community, is noted for being the stomping grounds of composer W. C. Handy, whose inspirational tune "Memphis Blues" is a classic. The Peabody Hotel, built in 1925 and renovated in 1981, is a classic structure with a restored nightclub. The Magevney House, located in the Victorian Village District, is one of the oldest homes in Memphis. The Mallory-Neely House, also in the Victorian Village District, is an Italian-style villa built in 1860. A. Schwab's Dry Goods Store on Beale Street has been serving customers since 1876. The Memphis Belle, a restored B-17 that flew during World War II and was the subject of a recent film, is housed on Mud Island.

Population

Memphis grew in population by 3.6% from 624,000 in 1970 to 646,174 in 1980, but declined in the 1980s by 5.5% to 610,337. However the metro area absorbed much of the shifting population and grew by 7.5% during that period.

Population

	1980	1990
Central City	646,174	610,337
Rank	14	18
Metro Area	913,472	981,747
Pop. Change 1980–1990	-35,837	
Pop. % Change 1980–1990	-5.5	
Median Age	31.5	
% Male	46.7	
% Age 65 and Over	12.2	
Density (per square mile)	2,384	

Households

Number 229,829
Persons per Household 2.59
% Female-Headed Households 21.9
% One-Person Households 28.3
Births—Total 11,407
   % to Mothers under 20 18.5
   Birth Rate per 1,000 17.6

Ethnic Composition

Blacks constitute the majority in Memphis, with 54.8% of the population. Whites make up 44%, American Indians 0.2%, Asians and Pacific Islanders 0.8%, and others 0.2%.

Chronology

1540 Explorer Hernando de Soto visits the Chickasaw Indians located on the Fourth or Lower Chickasaw Bluff. He discovers the Mississippi River on 21 May.

1673 Father Jacques Marquette and Louis Jolliet visit the Chickasaw Indians to trade.

1682 Robert Cavelier, Sieur de La Salle, sets up Fort Prudhomme on the First Chickasaw Bluff. The installation subsequently is contested by the French, Spanish, and British.

1763 Under the Treaty of Paris, signed to end the Seven Years War, France cedes to Britain all of her possessions east of the Mississippi, including the Chickasaw Bluffs.

1782 General James Robertson is asked by John Turner, who is half Chickasaw, to assist the Indians against the growing Spanish influence in the area. Robertson leads a commando force against the bluffs and sets up a post to aid the tribe.

1783 The state of North Carolina grants entrepreneurs John Rice and John Ramsay 5,000 acres of land on the Chickasaw Bluffs. Rice is killed by Indians in 1786, and his share is bought by Indian agent John Overton for $500.

1794 Overton starts a trading post on the Lower Chickasaw Bluff.

1819 Overton, with partners James Winchester and future president Andrew Jackson, sets up the town of Memphis by selling 362 deeded lots. The city is incorporated in 1826.

1850s With its ever-expanding economy, Memphis becomes the sixth-largest city in the South.

1862 Memphis is sacked by the Union army. Although physically untouched by the war, its economy does not recover for 40 years.

1867– 1878 Three yellow fever epidemics strike the city, leaving several thousand dead.

1909– 1916 The city is ruled by Mayor Edwin Hull Crump. Known as "Boss" Crump, he runs the city as his own personal camp.

1937 The Mississippi River floods cause thousands of refugees to seek shelter in Memphis.

1968 Martin Luther King, Jr., is assassinated at the Lorraine Motel in Memphis.

Ethnic Composition (as % of total pop.)

	1980	1990
White	51.64	44.01
Black	47.61	54.84
American Indian	0.08	0.16
Asian and Pacific Islander	0.42	0.79
Hispanic	0.81	0.73
Other	NA	0.20

Government

From 1909 until 1966 Memphis was governed under a commission form of government. In 1966 the city changed to a mayor-council form of government. The mayor and the 13 members of the council serve four-year terms. Six of the councillors are elected at large and seven by district.

Government

Year of Home Charter   1966
Number of Members of the Governing Body   13
Elected at Large   6
Elected by Wards   7
Number of Women in Governing Body   3
Salary of Mayor $82,500
Salary of Council Members $6,000
City Government Employment Total   23,167
Rate per 10,000   355

Public Finance

The annual budget consists of revenues of $1.689 billion and expenditures of $1.587 billion. The debt outstanding is $735.859 million, and cash and security holdings are $1.464 billion.

Public Finance

Total Revenue (in millions) $1,689.100
Intergovernmental Revenue—Total (in millions) $469.4
Federal Revenue per Capita $14.05
% Federal Assistance   0.8
% State Assistance   14.84
Sales Tax as % of Total Revenue   1.72
Local Revenue as % of Total Revenue   28.72
City Income Tax   no
Taxes—Total (in millions) $140.2

Taxes per Capita
    Total $215
    Property $156
    Sales and Gross Receipts $41
General Expenditures—Total (in millions) $560.1
General Expenditures per Capita $858
Capital Outlays per Capita $75

% of Expenditures for:
    Public Welfare   NA
    Highways   2.9
    Education   47.9
    Health and Hospitals   2.1
    Police   9.5
    Sewerage and Sanitation   9.7
    Parks and Recreation   5.7
    Housing and Community Development   1.8
Debt Outstanding per Capita $1,033

Public Finance (continued)

% Utility 25.6
Federal Procurement Contract Awards (in millions) $63.5
Federal Grants Awards (in millions) $78.0
Fiscal Year Begins October 1

Economy

Memphis has turned a diversified economy into a city with a large number of corporate headquarters. Among the companies that do business in Memphis are International Paper, Schering-Plough (toiletries), Great Western Financial Services, Dow Corning Wright, Sharp, Brother Industries, and Kellogg's. Memphis is also the headquarters of Federal Express, and the company's plant as well as the city's airport functions as FedEx Central. Tourism is an important facet, bringing in more than $200 million a year in revenues. Memphis's prosperity, however, was built on King Cotton, and it remains one of the largest cotton markets in the world, boasting such companies as Hohenberg Brothers, Dunavant Enterprises, and the Allenberg Company to handle much of the cotton trading business.

Economy

Total Money Income (in millions) $6,110.0
% of State Average 100.8
Per Capita Annual Income $9,362
% Population below Poverty Level 21.8
Fortune 500 Companies 1

Banks	Number	Deposits (in millions)
Commercial	30	1,966.9
Savings	NA	NA

Passenger Autos 558,110
Electric Meters 363,630
Gas Meters 265,028

Manufacturing

Number of Establishments 853
% with 20 or More Employees 43.3
Manufacturing Payroll (in millions) $988.5
Value Added by Manufacture (in millions) $3,138.7
Value of Shipments (in millions) $6,941.7
New Capital Expenditures (in millions) $180.2

Wholesale Trade

Number of Establishments 1,840
Sales (in millions) $18,447.6
Annual Payroll (in millions) $721.381

Retail Trade

Number of Establishments 5,470
Total Sales (in millions) $4,900.5
Sales per Capita $7,509
Number of Retail Trade Establishments with Payroll 3,875
Annual Payroll (in millions) $559.0
Total Sales (in millions) $4,811.3
General Merchandise Stores (per capita) $985
Food Stores (per capita) $1,143
Apparel Stores (per capita) $394
Eating and Drinking Places (per capita) $638

Service Industries

Total Establishments 4,475
Total Receipts (in millions) $2,255.6

Economy (continued)

Hotels and Motels (in millions) $147.2
Health Services (in millions) $559.9
Legal Services (in millions) $132.4

Labor

Memphis's economy is dominated by service industries. Among these are Federal Express (based in Memphis); Memphis Light, Gas, and Water; First Tennessee Bank; Northwest Airlines; Sears Roebuck; and Wal-Mart.

Labor

Civilian Labor Force 333,822
% Change 1989–1990 0.4

Work Force Distribution
Mining NA
Construction 18,600
Manufacturing 59,700
Transportation and Public Utilities 47,000
Wholesale and Retail Trade 123,300
FIRE (Finance, Insurance, Real Estate) 24,800
Service 120,900
Government 77,000
Women as % of Labor Force 46.2
% Self-Employed 4.7
% Professional/Technical 14.8
Total Unemployment 15,908
Rate % 4.8
Federal Government Civilian Employment 14,383

Education

The Memphis city school system supports 98 elementary schools, 29 junior high/middle schools, 30 senior high schools, and 3 special education schools. These are supplemented by 71 private and parochial schools, including such outstanding ones as St. Mary's Episcopal School, Memphis University School, Briarcrest Baptist School, Presbyterian Day School, and Harding Academy.

The higher education sector has four general institutions. The largest is Memphis State University, with a number of constituent colleges such as the Fogelman College of Business and Economics, Herff College of Engineering, and the Humphreys School of Law. Rhodes College, the oldest Memphis college, was founded in 1848 at Clarksville, Tennessee, and moved to Memphis in 1925. LeMoyne-Owen College was founded in 1870 as LeMoyne College and later merged with Owen College. The University of Tennessee Center for the Health Sciences (UTCHS) has six constituent colleges. Christian Brothers College is a denominational liberal arts college. Memphis is also home to two Bible colleges.

Health

The hub of the medical sector is the William F. Bowld Hospital of UTCHS; it has special programs in rehabilitation engineering and child development. Another acclaimed

Education

Number of Public Schools   160
Special Education Schools   3
Total Enrollment   107,103
% Enrollment in Private Schools   13.2
% Minority   80.7
Classroom Teachers   5,725
Pupil-Teacher Ratio   18.1:1
Number of Graduates   5,177
Total Revenue (in millions) $365.048
Total Expenditures (in millions) $331.240
Expenditures per Pupil $2,978
Educational Attainment (Age 25 and Over)
     % Completed 12 or More Years   63.3
     % Completed 16 or More Years   14.6
Four-Year Colleges and Universities   7
     Enrollment   27,431
Two-Year Colleges   3
     Enrollment   9,473

Libraries

Number   67
Public Libraries   23
Books (in thousands)   1,499
Circulation (in thousands)   2,587
Persons Served (in thousands)   828
Circulation per Person Served   3.21
Income (in millions) $11.41
Staff   370

Four-Year Colleges and Universities
     Crichton College
     Memphis State University
     University of Tennessee – Memphis
     Christian Brothers College
     LeMoyne–Owen College
     Memphis College of Art
     Rhodes College

Health

Deaths—Total   6,317
Rate per 1,000   9.7
Infant Deaths—Total   169
Rate per 1,000   14.8
Number of Metro Hospitals   17
Number of Metro Hospital Beds   6,823
Rate per 100,000   1,045
Number of Physicians   2,248
Physicians per 1,000   2.52
Nurses per 1,000   7.10
Health Expenditures per Capita $8.46

hospital is St. Jude's Children's Research Hospital, supported by the late entertainer Danny Thomas. Other major medical facilities are the Baptist Memorial Hospital, Mid-South (Methodist) Hospital, St. Francis Hospital, Lakeside Hospital, Memphis Mental Hospital, Humana Specialty, LeBonheur Children's Hospital, Veterans Administration Hospital, and the U.S. Naval Hospital.

Transportation

A unique concept called Uniport, utilizing air, water, train, and truck transportation routes for commercial business, has made Memphis one of the nation's top ten distri-

bution centers. The keystone of this effort is Memphis International Airport, just south of the city. The port of Memphis on the Mississippi River has three harbors and complete loading and unloading facilities. Premier rail freight service is provided by the Burlington Northern, Illinois Central Gulf, Louisville and Nashville, Missouri Pacific, Southern Pacific, and Southern railways. I-40 cuts Memphis in half from the east, while the beltway roads of I-240 and I-55 connect the city to points south and west. Memphis is also served by U.S. Highways 51, 61, 64, 70, 72, 78, and 79, as well as seven state highways.

Transportation

Interstate Highway Mileage   72
Total Urban Mileage   3,111
Total Daily Vehicle Mileage (in millions)   16.228
Daily Average Commute Time   48.4 min.
Number of Buses   145
Port Tonnage (in millions)   10.200
Airports   1
Number of Daily Flights   266
Daily Average Number of Passengers   10,930

Airlines (American carriers only)
     American
     Delta
     Midway
     Northwest
     Trans World
     United
     USAir

Housing

Memphis offers a large selection of housing communities and suburbs. Downtown is mostly apartments and condominiums. Midtown contains many of the oldest residential neighborhoods in a variety of architectural styles. East Memphis is the area between downtown and the I-240 loop on the north, east, and south. Poplar Avenue is the vital traffic artery, and most of the houses here were built from the 1940s through the 1960s. North Memphis is a quiet residential section containing some of the oldest residential neighborhoods, one in which the Irish and the Jews were prominent. South Memphis has grown around South Parkway and contains many stately homes. Southeast Memphis is an edge development and is the site of most of the apartments built during recent years. Whitehaven, the site of Elvis Presley's Graceland, has recently spilled over the state line into Mississippi. Germantown, located just east of the city limits, is an executive bedroom community that is 85% residential, with strict laws against industrial and commercial development. Cordova, recently annexed to Memphis, is characterized by large, upscale houses on spacious lots. Bartlett, located northeast of Memphis, is one of the fastest growing suburbs with colonial, traditional, and ranch houses. Raleigh, Fraser, and Millington are other bedroom communities. Of the total housing stock, 55.1% is owner-occupied. The median value of an owner-occupied home is $55,700 and the median monthly rent $282.

Housing

Total Housing Units   248,573
% Change 1980–1990   1.7
Vacant Units for Sale or Rent   15,120
Occupied Units   229,829
% with More Than One Person per Room   5.5
% Owner-Occupied   55.1
Median Value of Owner-Occupied Homes $55,700
Average Monthly Purchase Cost $275
Median Monthly Rent $282
New Private Housing Starts   NA
Value (in thousands)   NA
% Single-Family   NA
Nonresidential Buildings Value (in thousands)   NA

Tallest Buildings	Hgt. (ft.)	Stories
100 N. Main Bldg.	430	37
Commerce Square	396	31
Sterick Bldg.	365	31
Clark, 5100 Poplar	365	32
Morgan Keegan Tower	341	23
First Natl. Bank Bldg.	332	25

Urban Redevelopment

In 1991 the Pyramid, one of the largest urban redevelopment projects in Memphis's history, was completed. It houses a sports and entertainment arena on the downtown harbor. On the riverfront, the River Drive has been reconstructed and Tom Lee Park has been expanded from 5 to 25 acres. South Bluffs and Harbor Town have been developed with new apartment houses and multifamily homes. The National Civil Rights Museum, located in the former Lorraine Motel (site of the assassination of Martin Luther King, Jr.), opened in 1991. The Memphis Cook Convention Center has been renovated and the St. Jude Children's Research Hospital's Danny Thomas Family Research Center was completed. The $23 million Mid-America Mall was completed in 1992.

Crime

Memphis ranks near the bottom in public safety. In 1991, violent crimes totaled 8,818 and property crimes totaled 54,319.

Crime

Violent Crimes—Total   8,818
Violent Crime Rate per 100,000   1,038.3
Murder   169
Rape   653
Robbery   4,504
Aggravated Assaults   3,492
Property Crimes   54,319
Burglary   16,580
Larceny   24,357
Motor Vehicle Theft   13,382
Arson   698
Per Capita Police Expenditures $98.16
Per Capita Fire Protection Expenditures $81.79
Number of Police   1,154
Per 1,000   1.76

Religion

Of the church-going population, 27% are Baptist, 17% are Black Baptist, and 5% are Catholic.

Religion

Largest Denominations (Adherents)	
Catholic	50,000
Southern Baptist	169,276
Black Baptist	103,916
United Methodist	46,357
Churches of Christ	22,839
Presbyterian	11,667
Episcopal	10,439
Assembly of God	7,565
Independent Non-Charismatics	12,747
Jewish	8,417

Media

The two daily newspapers are the *Memphis Commercial Appeal* and the *Daily News*. The electronic media consist of 6 television stations (3 commercial networks, 2 independents, and 1 public) and 26 AM and FM radio stations.

Media

Newsprint
  Daily News, daily
  Memphis Business Journal, weekly
  Memphis Commercial Appeal, daily
  Memphis Magazine, monthly

Television
  WHBQ (Channel 13)
  WKNO (Channel 10)
  WLMT (Channel 30)
  WMC (Channel 5)
  WPTY (Channel 24)
  WREG (Channel 3)

Radio
KWAM (AM)	WBPB (AM)
WPYR (FM)	WBBP (AM)
WBPB (AM)	WCRV (AM)
WDIA (AM)	WEVL (FM)
WEZI (FM)	WGKX (FM)
WHBQ (AM)	WHRK (FM)
WHUL (FM)	WKNO (FM)
WLOK (AM)	WMC (AM)
WMC (FM)	WNWZ (AM)
WODZ (AM)	WRVR (FM)
WPLX (AM)	WQOX (FM)
WREC (AM)	WEGR (FM)
WSMS (FM)	WXSS (AM)

Sports

In the absence of a major professional sports team, most of the sports action is provided by minor teams such as the Memphis Chicks (a farm-league team of the Kansas City Royals) in Double A baseball, and the Memphis State University Tigers in basketball. Major car races are held at the Memphis International Motorsports Park.

Arts, Culture, and Tourism

Memphis, the home of W. C. Handy and Elvis Presley, is justifiably known as the Music City. Noted as hubs of musical and theatrical entertainment are the Memphis Symphony Orchestra, the Opera Memphis, the Memphis Concert Ballet, and the Beethoven Club. Various music renditions are conducted at the Overton Park Shell, a huge arena built during the Depression.

Museums abound in Memphis. Included in the list are the Memphis Brooks Museum of Art and the National Ornamental Metal Museum. Representative of art exhibits are the Dixie Gallery and Gardens and the Memphis State University Art Gallery. In 1990 Memphis began sponsoring an International Cultural Series called Wonders. The series has included exhibitions on Catherine the Great, the Ottoman Empire, the Etruscans, and Napoleon. The Pyramid on the banks of the Mississippi River is a replica of an Egyptian structure with a 22,500-seat arena.

Travel and Tourism

Hotel Rooms   12,514
Convention and Exhibit Space (square feet)   150,000

Convention Centers
   Memphis Convention Center including
   Concourse Hall and Ellis Auditorium

Festivals
   International Children's Festival (May)
   Beale Street Music Festival (May)
   International Fair (May)
   Memphis Cotton Carnival
   Music Heritage Festival (Labor Day weekend)
   Mid-South Fair and Exposition (September)

Parks and Recreation

Memphis has nearly 200 parks covering some 6,700 acres. The largest is the 342-acre Overton Park, which features the Memphis Zoo, Memphis Aquarium, and Memphis Brooks Museum of Art. Other parks include McKellar Park, the King-Riverside Park bordering the Mississippi River, Audubon Park, Firestone Park, and Kennedy Park.

Sources of Further Information

Memphis Chamber of Commerce
P.O. Box 224
Memphis, TN 38101
(901) 575-3500

Memphis Convention and Visitors Bureau
47 Union Avenue
Memphis, TN 38103
(901) 543-5300

Memphis Economic Development Department
P.O. Box 430
Memphis, TN 38101
(901) 528-4171

Additional Reading

Biles, Roger. *Memphis in the Great Depression.* 1986.

Capers, Gerald M. *Memphis: The Biography of a River Town.* 1980.

Dimick, M. T. *Memphis: The City of the White Wall.* 1956.

Hamilton, G. P. *The Bright Side of Memphis.* 1978.

Johnson, Eugene J., and Robert D. Russell. *Memphis: An Architectural Guide.* 1990.

Keating, J. M., and O. F. Vedder. *History of the City of Memphis and Shelby County, Tennessee.* 2 vols. 1977.

Miller, William D. *Memphis During the Progressive Era, 1900–1917.* 1957.

Ornelas-Struve, Carole M., and Frederick L. Coulter. *Memphis, 1800–1900.* 3 vols. 1982.

Roper, James E. *The Founding of Memphis, 1818–1820.* 1970.

Tucker, David M. *Memphis since Crump: Bossism, Blacks and Civic Reformers, 1948–1968.* 1985.

Miami

Florida

Basic Data

Name   Miami
Name Origin   From Indian word "Mayaimi," meaning
   "Big Water"
Year Founded   1836 Inc. 1896
Status: State   Miami
      County   Dade County
Area (square miles)   35.6
Elevation (feet)   10
Time Zone   EST
Population (1990)   358,548
Population of Metro Area (1990)   1,937,094

Sister Cities

   Bogota, Colombia
   Cali, Colombia
   Buenos Aires, Argentina
   Ibiza, Spain
   Lima, Peru
   Kagoshima, Japan
   Kaohsiung County, China
   Nice, France
   Managua, Nicaragua
   Montes de Oca, Costa Rica
   Santiago, Chile
   Santo Domingo, Dominican Republic

Distance in Miles To:

Atlanta	663
Boston	1,520
Chicago	1,397
Dallas	1,343
Denver	2,107
Detroit	1,385
Houston	1,190
Los Angeles	2,716
Minneapolis	1,769
New York	1,334
Philadelphia	1,230
Washington, DC	1,057

Location and Topography

Miami is located at the mouth of the Miami River on the lower east coast of Florida. The city is bordered on the east by Biscayne Bay, an arm of the Atlantic Ocean. Farther east are the islands of Key Biscayne and Miami Beach, which are connected to Miami by a series of bridges known as causeways. A man-made canal connects Miami with Lake Okeechobee. Miami and the cities of Miami Beach, Coral Gables, and Hialeah constitute Greater or Metro Miami.

Layout of City and Suburbs

Miami was designed by the engineers and architects of tycoon Henry Flagler, and reflects his styles and tastes. Its show streets are Biscayne Boulevard, a four-lane motorway paralleling a landscaped park overlooking the bay, and Brickell Avenue. At intervals, broad bridges called causeways reach from island to island across to Miami Beach, Virginia Key, and Key Biscayne. Extending westward from the bay and waterfront park, Miami's shopping and theater district is confined to a dozen blocks centered on Flagler Street. This area is accessible by the Metro-Mover, a public-transportation monorail system. Miami Beach is a sand bar three miles out into the Atlantic, some ten miles long and one to three miles wide. Ringed around Miami are the suburb cities of North Miami, South Miami, Little Havana, Coconut Grove, and Coral Gables.

Environment

Environmental Stress Index   2.8
Green Cities Index: Rank   7
                   Score   20.31
Water Quality   Alkaline, soft, fluoridated
   Average Daily Use (gallons per capita)   238

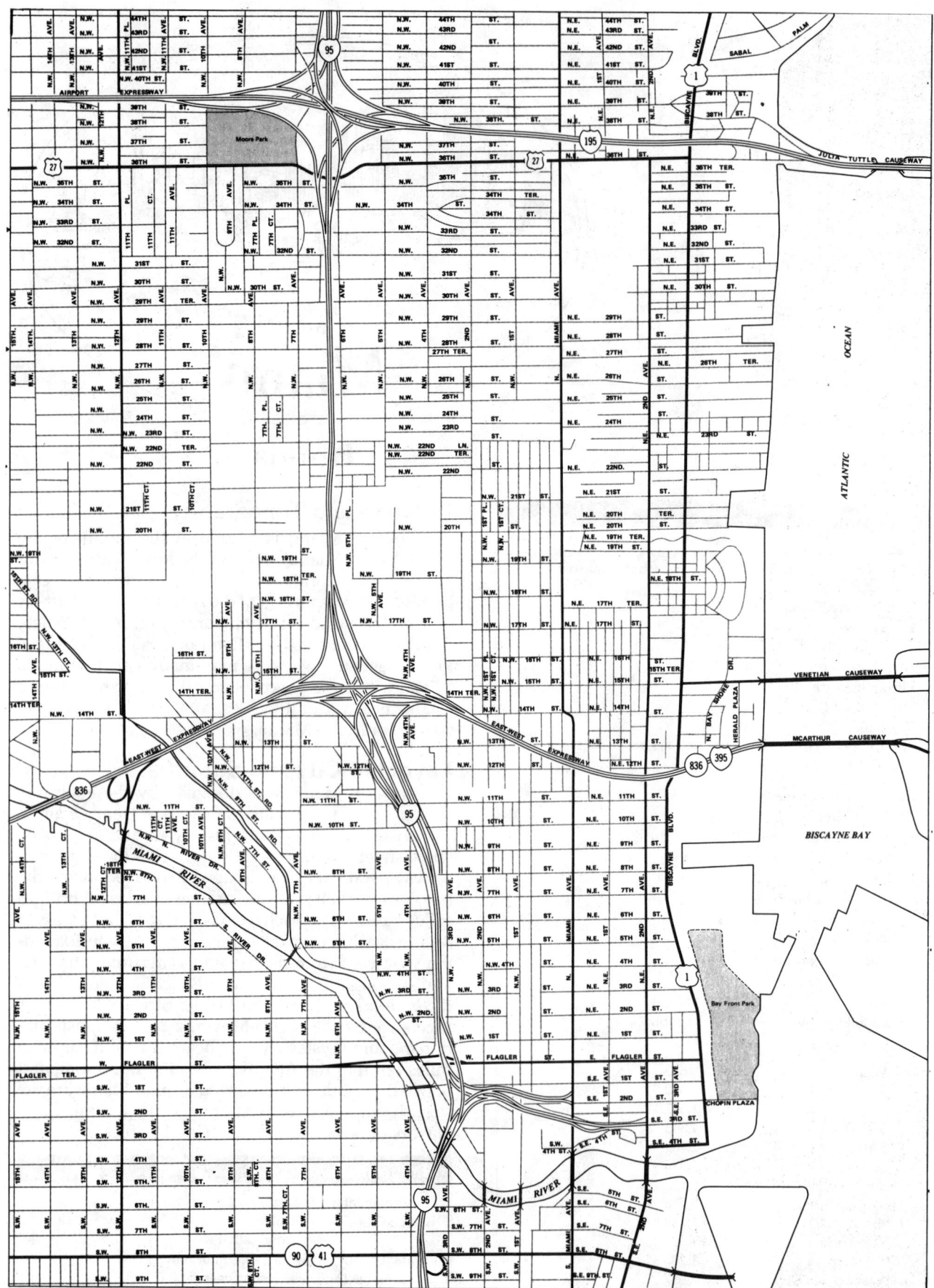

Environment (continued)	
Maximum Supply (gallons per capita)	254
Parkland as % of Total City Area	2.9
% Waste Landfilled/Recycled	NA
Annual Parks Expenditures per Capita	$120.70

Climate

Miami has a typical semitropical climate with a long, warm summer; mild, dry winter; and abundant rainfall. The ocean influences the climate by warming cold air masses. Freezing temperatures may occur occasionally in the surrounding areas, but not in the city. The ocean also helps to cool warm air masses in summer. The city generally records only 30 days over 90°F, while communities a few miles inland may have over 60 such days. Tropical hurricanes are frequent in early fall. Waterspouts are sometimes sighted, but tornadoes are rare. High humidity levels, usually in the range of 86% to 89% in the daytime, make Miami the second most humid city in the nation.

Weather

Temperature

Highest Monthly Average °F	88.7
Lowest Monthly Average °F	59.2

Annual Averages

Days 32°F or Below	0
Days above 90°F	30
Zero Degree Days	
Precipitation (inches)	60.0
Snow (inches)	0
% Seasonal Humidity	75
Wind Speed (m.p.h.)	9.1
Clear Days	76
Cloudy Days	117
Storm Days	75
Rainy Days	129

Average Temperatures (°F)	High	Low	Mean
January	75.6	58.7	67.2
February	76.6	59.0	67.8
March	79.5	63.0	71.3
April	82.7	67.3	75.0
May	85.3	70.7	78.0
June	88.0	73.9	81.0
July	89.1	75.5	82.3
August	89.9	75.8	82.9
September	88.3	75.0	81.7
October	84.6	71.0	77.8
November	79.9	64.5	72.2
December	76.6	60.0	68.3

History

The principal American Indian tribe in present-day Dade County was the Calusas, or Tequestas, who lived in villages along the Miami River. The name Miami or Mayami means "Big Water" in the Calusa language. Although the Spanish never fully succeeded in colonizing the region because of Indian hostility and the prevalence of epidemics, they did make several attempts to settle the present-day Miami area, beginning with a short-lived Jesuit mission on the Miami River in 1567. These epidemics eventually wiped out the Calusas also, and the territory was taken over by the Creeks and Seminoles.

In 1763, during the French and Indian Wars, Spain lost Florida to the British, but regained it after the American Revolution. In 1818, General Andrew Jackson invaded Florida, beginning the First Seminole War. In 1821 Spain ceded Florida to the United States for $5 million under the terms of the Treaty of Paris, signed to resolve matters from the War of 1812.

For the next two decades, attempts at colonization were met with hostilities from the Seminole tribe. In 1825, however, with the help of some "transients" living along the southeastern Florida coast, the U.S. government erected the Cape Florida Lighthouse, the first government structure in Dade County. By 1830, the largest tract of land belonging to a single owner in Dade County was that of Richard Fitzpatrick, who operated a large slave plantation. In 1836, the slave plantation was burned to the ground by the Seminoles.

In an effort to rein in the Indians, the U.S. army built Fort Dallas at the mouth of the Miami River. Fitzpatrick was instrumental in the founding of Dade County, named after Major Francis Langhorn Dade, who was killed in the Second Seminole War. After numerous skirmishes, by 1842 the Seminoles were driven into the Everglades, an area considered unfit for human habitation. That year, Fitzpatrick gave his plot of land to his nephew, William English, who platted "the town of Miami."

In 1849, Fort Dallas was made into a permanent outpost, and remained so until its closure in 1858. However, settlers still avoided the area for the next several years because of a fear of Indian attacks. During the Civil War, many of Miami's inhabitants joined the Confederate cause and became blockade runners, even though the fort at Key West remained in Union army hands. Following the war, Miami was ruled by a carpetbag government. However, it grew into a center of trade and commerce under the auspices of merchants J. W. Ewan, known as the Duke of Dade, and William Brickell, who in 1870 bought the property once belonging to William English and set up a trading post.

The person who changed the map of Miami more than anyone up to this time was Julia Sturdivant Tuttle, widow of a wealthy Cleveland industrialist, who purchased a 640-acre tract of property on both sides of the Miami River shortly after 1870. In 1874 she persuaded Henry Flagler, an associate of John D. Rockefeller, to build the East Coast Railway to Miami. To impress Flagler with the frost-free weather on the east coast, she sent him a bouquet of orange blossoms untouched by frost during the severe freeze of 1894–1895. She gifted 100 acres to Flagler and every alternate lot of her remaining acreage. The Florida East Coast Railroad line was completed in 1896, and on 28 July of that year the city of Miami was incorporated with a population of 1,500.

Chronology

1821 Spain cedes Florida to the United States.

1836 As part of the campaign against the Seminoles, the U.S. army takes over Fort Dallas on the mouth of the Miami River.

1849 Fort Dallas becomes a permanent outpost.

1870 Julia Tuttle buys property on both sides of the Miami River.

1894 Tuttle persuades Henry Flagler to invest in developing her property as a resort and deeds 100 acres for the purpose.

1896 Flagler's Florida East Coast Railway reaches Miami.

1915 Miami Beach is incorporated.

1923–1926 A land boom in the southern Florida area turns Miami into a thriving metropolis.

1959 The rise of Fidel Castro in Cuba prompts a wave of Cuban immigration to Miami.

1980 The famed Mariel boatlift (named after a Cuban port) brings some 125,000 Cuban refugees to Miami. Miami becomes the largest haven to refugees from Cuba.

1992 Hurricane Andrew devastates Miami and much of its western suburbs.

Flagler invested heavily in waterworks and roads—including Flagler Street, a half-mile piece of roadway that today is considered one of the most important areas in the United States for export and import. He also built hotels, including the Royal Palm Hotel.

A series of entrepreneurs followed Flagler in developing the suburbs of Miami Beach and Hialeah. Among these was John Collins, a New Jersey horticulturist and businessman who set out to establish a coconut grove on the so-called barrier islands east of Miami. Even though Collins went broke before the railway bridge connecting Miami to Key West was completed, he did establish these barrier islands as Miami Beach and Key Biscayne. The bridge was completed in 1913 with the aid of Carl F. Fisher, another businessman, who helped Collins in exchange for a piece of his property. Two years later Miami Beach was incorporated as a city.

During the early 1920s, a land boom developed from northern investors who desired to make Miami a tropical paradise. Missouri ranchman James Bright, who was later joined by the noted aviator Glenn Curtiss, founded the suburb of Hialeah. Coral Gables was founded by George Merrick, and Staten Island resident Ralph Munroe formed the city of Coconut Grove. During the three years before the building boom collapsed, Miami was one of the most valuable pieces of real estate in the nation, widely advertised in local and out-of-state newspapers. The boom collapsed in 1926 after a ferocious hurricane hit the area.

A second boom after World War II reshaped the city. Cuban migration following Fidel Castro's rise to power turned Miami into another Havana, marking a large demographic shift and making the city one of the largest on the East Coast. In 1980 the famed Mariel boatlift (named after a Cuban port) brought another 125,000 Cuban refugees to Miami, making Miami one of the largest havens for Cuban refugees.

In 1992 Hurricane Andrew destroyed much of Miami and its western suburbs.

Historical Landmarks

Although Miami is a comparatively young town as far as landmarks are concerned, there are many to be seen. Among them are the 1926 Dade County Courthouse on West Flagler Street, which at one time was the tallest structure south of Washington, D.C.; the Metro-Dade Cultural Center on West Flagler, which consists of the Historical Museum of Southern Florida, the Mediterranean-Style Center for the Fine Arts, and the Miami-Dade Public Library; the U.S. Courthouse on Northeast First Avenue, with its classic columns; Brickell Avenue, where foreign and import-export business is conducted; and the magnificent Villa Vizcaya on South Brickell Avenue, an Italian mansion built in 1914 by farmer-businessman James Deering.

Population

Like most cities in Florida, Miami has been steadily growing in population. From 335,000 in 1970, it grew to 346,681 in 1980 and 358,548 in 1990.

Population	1980	1990
Central City	346,681	358,548
Rank	41	46
Metro Area	1,625,509	1,937,094
Pop. Change 1980–1990 +11,867		
Pop. % Change 1980–1990 +3.4		
Median Age 36.0		
% Male 48.3		
% Age 65 and Over 16.6		
Density (per square mile) 10,071		

Households
Number 130,252
Persons per Household 2.70
% Female-Headed Households 18.6
% One-Person Households 28.9
Births—Total 13,463
% to Mothers under 20 15.5
Birth Rate per 1,000 36.1

Ethnic Composition

Whites make up 65.6%, blacks 27.4%, American Indians 0.2%, Asians and Pacific Islanders 0.6%, and others 6.2%. Hispanics, both black and white, make up 62.4%.

Ethnic Composition (as % of total pop.)

	1980	1990
White	66.6	65.64
Black	25.11	27.39
American Indian	0.09	0.15
Asian and Pacific Islander	0.54	0.63
Hispanic	55.94	62.46
Other	NA	6.18

Government

 Miami has a mayor-commissioner form of government. The four commissioners are elected to four-year terms, and the commissioners elect a mayor to serve a two-year term. Miami is also governed by a metropolitan county government called Metro, headed by a nine-member board of commissioners, created in 1957.

Government

Year of Home Charter   NA
Number of Members of the Governing Body   4
Elected at Large   4
Elected by Wards   NA
Number of Women in Governing Body   1
Salary of Mayor $5,000
Salary of Council Members $5,000
City Government Employment Total   4,423
Rate per 10,000   118.3

Public Finance

The annual budget consists of revenues of $372.067 million and expenditures of $355.389 million. The debt outstanding is $560.208 million, and cash and security holdings $821.654 million.

Public Finance

Total Revenue (in millions) $372.067
Intergovernmental Revenue—Total (in millions) $65.66
Federal Revenue per Capita $29.3
% Federal Assistance   7.88
% State Assistance   8.15
Sales Tax as % of Total Revenue   9.28
Local Revenue as % of Total Revenue   66.95
City Income Tax   no
Taxes—Total (in millions) $138.4

Taxes per Capita
   Total $370
   Property $249
   Sales and Gross Receipts $97
General Expenditures—Total (in millions) $225.8
General Expenditures per Capita $604
Capital Outlays per Capita $82

% of Expenditures for:
   Public Welfare   0.6
   Highways   6.2
   Education   0.1
   Health and Hospitals   0.1
   Police   22.7
   Sewerage and Sanitation   11.5
   Parks and Recreation   10.8
   Housing and Community Development   6.3
Debt Outstanding per Capita $633

Public Finance (continued)

   % Utility   0.0
Federal Procurement Contract Awards (in millions)
   $130.8
Federal Grants Awards (in millions) $108.0
Fiscal Year Begins   October 1

Economy

Historically, Miami's economy was tourism-driven and flourished only in the summer. However, since the 1970s it has been able to leverage its geographical proximity to Latin America and the Caribbean and its excellent transportation facilities into areas of strong commercial and financial leadership. While tourism and the businesses built around tourism continue to be its mainstay, Miami has built up sound institutional bases in international trade and banking. Over 90 banks and foreign agencies are located in downtown Miami, making Brickell Avenue the "Wall Street of the South." The Miami International Airport, the Port of Miami, and the Foreign Trade Center also have played a part in this transformation. In essence, the city is the American gateway in commerce to Latin America and Mexico. Miami is successful in attracting new businesses because Florida has no personal income tax and has one of the lowest corporate income tax rates in the nation. Tourism also has become more vigorous and diversified, with cruise ships providing an added dimension. Miami is the world's largest cruise port and virtually dominates the Caribbean cruise industry. The Design Plaza, with 250 tenants, represents another major industry—interior design.

Economy

Total Money Income (in millions) $3,329.561
% of State Average   79.0
Per Capita Annual Income $8,904
% Population below Poverty Level   24.5
Fortune 500 Companies   1

Banks	Number	Deposits (in millions)
Commercial	66	20,404.6
Savings	43	18,610.0

Passenger Autos   1,362,823
Electric Meters   700,238
Gas Meters   NA

Manufacturing

Number of Establishments   884
% with 20 or More Employees   22.5
Manufacturing Payroll (in millions) $373.6
Value Added by Manufacture (in millions) $942.4
Value of Shipments (in millions) $1,712.2
New Capital Expenditures (in millions) $32.8

Wholesale Trade

Number of Establishments   2,131
Sales (in millions) $6,610.0
Annual Payroll (in millions) $394.895

Retail Trade

Number of Establishments   5,143
Total Sales (in millions) $3,204.9
Sales per Capita $8,571

Economy (continued)

Number of Retail Trade Establishments with Payroll   3,805
Annual Payroll (in millions) $401.7
Total Sales (in millions) $3,149.2
General Merchandise Stores (per capita) $920
Food Stores (per capita) $1,407
Apparel Stores (per capita) $671
Eating and Drinking Places (per capita) $851

Service Industries

Total Establishments   5,329
Total Receipts (in millions) $2,592.2
Hotels and Motels (in millions) $205.7
Health Services (in millions) $466.1
Legal Services (in millions) $823.8

Labor

Miami has a growing labor force, and if workers are not as highly skilled as elsewhere, they are cheaper and protected by right-to-work laws. A high percentage—almost 50%—are bilingual and therefore ideal in an environment where Latin America is the main direction of trade. The warm weather eliminates many of the climate-associated expenditures of other regions. Over 55% of the workers are employed in trade and services bolstered by tourism, while manufacturing contributes only 10%. The recent destruction from Hurricane Andrew in 1992 has for a time depressed the economy, but that is expected to improve in the coming years.

Labor

Civilian Labor Force   207,691
% Change 1989–1990   1.3

Work Force Distribution
Mining   700
Construction   31,900
Manufacturing   84,300
Transportation and Public Utilities   69,700
Wholesale and Retail Trade   226,400
FIRE (Finance, Insurance, Real Estate)   65,300
Service   252,400
Government   124,900
Women as % of Labor Force   46.0
% Self-Employed   5.4
% Professional/Technical   11.0
Total Unemployment   17,203
Rate %   8.3
Federal Government Civilian Employment   13,395

Education

The Dade County Public School District, the fifth largest in the United States, supports 277 elementary schools, junior high/middle schools, and senior high schools. Miami's seven institutions of higher learning operate 13 campuses. They are the University of Miami, Florida International University, Barry University, St. Thomas University, Miami-Dade Community College, Florida Memorial College, and Miami Christian College.

Education

Number of Public Schools   277
Special Education Schools   1
Total Enrollment   292,000
% Enrollment in Private Schools   17.5
% Minority   81.0
Classroom Teachers   16,022
Pupil-Teacher Ratio   18.2:1
Number of Graduates   13,411
Total Revenue (in millions) $1,265.5
Total Expenditures (in millions) $1,269.4
Expenditures per Pupil $4,608
Educational Attainment (Age 25 and Over)
    % Completed 12 or More Years   50.0
    % Completed 16 or More Years   13.0
Four-Year Colleges and Universities   6
    Enrollment   27,035
Two-Year Colleges   4
    Enrollment   51,341

Libraries

Number   75
Public Libraries   30
Books (in thousands)   2,683
Circulation (in thousands)   NA
Persons Served (in thousands)   1,600
Circulation per Person Served   NA
Income (in millions) $31.783
Staff   574

Four-Year Colleges and Universities
Barry University
Florida International University
St. Thomas University
Florida Memorial College
Miami Christian College
University of Miami

Health

Miami's medical sector consists of 20 hospitals. The largest is the Jackson Memorial Hospital, affiliated with the University of Miami School of Medicine. The Veterans Administration Hospital, the second largest, also is a teaching hospital. Other medical facilities include Baptist Hospital, Cedars Medical Center, Bascomb Palmer Eye Institute, Mercy Hospital, Carol Reed Hospital, Highland Park Hospital, North Shore Medical Center, Miami Children's Hospital, Pan American Hospital, Victoria Hospital, Grant Center, and Humana Hospital.

Health

Deaths—Total   4,882
Rate per 1,000   13.1
Infant Deaths—Total   97
Rate per 1,000   7.2
Number of Metro Hospitals   20
Number of Metro Hospital Beds   6,205
Rate per 100,000   1,659
Number of Physicians   5,390
Physicians per 1,000   3.62
Nurses per 1,000   15.25
Health Expenditures per Capita $0.16

Transportation

Miami is approached by three north-south expressways: I-95, State Road 826 (Palmetto Expressway), and the Florida Turnpike. The three east-west routes are Dolphin Expressway (State Road 836), Airport Expressway (State Road 112), and Tamiami Trail (U.S. 4). Miami and Miami Beach are connected by four bridges or causeways: the Julia Tuttle, MacArthur, Venetian, and 79th Street. Other east-west thoroughfares are the Bal Harbor or Broad Street, Sunny Isles (State Road 826), and William Lehman causeways.

Amtrak provides four departures a day, and rail freight is handled by Florida East Coast and Seaboard Coast Lines. Miami has one of the nation's most modern rapid-transit systems—Metrorail-Metrobus. The 21-mile Metrorail is an elevated monorail system that encompasses the downtown area. The Metroloop is a ten station monorail system and the first urban people-mover. Metrorail and Metroloop are connected by the Metrobus. The Port of Miami and the Miami Free Trade Zone are interconnected facilities. The Port of Miami on Dodge Island has 50 steamship lines, is the largest cruise port in the world, and is second only to New York in international commerce. The duty-free zone is located 15 minutes from the port. The principal air terminal is the Miami International Airport—second largest in the nation—15 minutes from downtown. There are five other general aviation facilities, including Opa Locka and Tamiami.

Transportation
Interstate Highway Mileage   24
Total Urban Mileage   5,611
Total Daily Vehicle Mileage (in millions)   32.658
Daily Average Commute Time   52.1 min.
Number of Buses   600
Port Tonnage (in millions)   4.341
Airports   2
Number of Daily Flights   367
Daily Average Number of Passengers   33,528
Airlines (American carriers only)
American
American Trans Air
Continental
Delta
Eastern
Midway
Midwest Express
Northwest
Pacific Interstate
Trans World
Tower Air
United
USAir

Housing

Miami's residential communities are class- and race-oriented. There are exclusive walled-in communities, such as Creek Village, Coral Gables, and Hialeah Gardens, as well as smaller, quiet communities such as South Miami and Surfside. Hialeah and Little Havana are primarily occupied by Cubans, while Overtown and Liberty City are known for their black residents. Overall, Miami is not an expensive housing market. The median value of an owner-occupied home is $79,200 and the median monthly rent $346. The popularity of apartment and condominium living is reflected in the fact that only 33.1% of total housing stock is owner-occupied.

Housing		
Total Housing Units 144,550		
% Change 1980–1990 -0.8		
Vacant Units for Sale or Rent 10,802		
Occupied Units 130,252		
% with More Than One Person per Room 26.9		
% Owner-Occupied 33.1		
Median Value of Owner-Occupied Homes $79,200		
Average Monthly Purchase Cost $318		
Median Monthly Rent $346		
New Private Housing Starts 975		
Value (in thousands) $50,703		
% Single-Family 8.1		
Nonresidential Buildings Value (in thousands) $53,025		
Tallest Buildings	*Hgt. (ft.)*	*Stories*
Southeast Financial Center (1983)	764	55
Centrust Tower (1987)	562	35
Metro-Dade Admin. Bldg.	510	30
Florida National Tower (1986)	484	35
One Biscayne Corp.	456	40
Amerifirst Bldg. (1973)	375	32
Hotel Inter-Continental Miami	366	35
Venitia, 1635 Bayshore Dr.	365	42

Urban Redevelopment

The skyline of Miami is constantly changing, but it is now extending horizontally rather than vertically because skyscrapers have been built on all available land. Most of the big buildings built in the 1980s are on Brickell Avenue in the financial center. They include the 55-story Southeast Financial Center, the 32-story Brickell Bay Office, and the Centrust Tower.

Crime

Public safety is Miami's Achilles heel. It is the most unsafe city in the nation. Of the crimes known to police in 1991, there were 15,645 violent crimes and 52,033 property crimes.

Crime
Violent Crimes—Total   15,645
Violent Crime Rate per 100,000   2,194
Murder   134
Rape   253
Robbery   8,542
Aggravated Assaults   6,716
Property Crimes   52,033
Burglary   12,601
Larceny   30,751
Motor Vehicle Theft   8,681
Arson   322
Per Capita Police Expenditures $216.66

Crime (continued)

Per Capita Fire Protection Expenditures $110.81
Number of Police   1,040
Per 1,000   2.7

Religion

The city's large Hispanic population contributes to the Catholic majority in the city proper. Historically, Jews have settled in the region in large numbers, primarily in Miami Beach. Of the Protestant minority, the largest denominations are Baptist and Methodist.

Religion	
Largest Denominations (Adherents)	
Catholic	364,257
Episcopal	16,741
Southern Baptist	65,582
United Methodist	24,182
Black Baptist	126,236
Evangelical Lutheran	16,741
Assembly of God	8,606
Presbyterian	13,293
Jewish	201,800

Media

The Miami press is bilingual. It is served by a single English-language daily, the *Miami Herald*, and two Spanish dailies, *El Nuevo Herald* (a Spanish version of the *Miami Herald*), and *Diario las Americas*. The electronic media consist of 8 television stations and 18 AM and FM radio stations.

Media
Newsprint
Diario las Americas, daily
El Nuevo Herald, daily
Miami Herald, daily
Miami Monthly/Mensual, monthly
Miami Review, daily
Miami Times, weekly
Miami Today, weekly
Television
WBFS (Channel 33)
WCIX (Channel 6)
WLRN (Channel 17)
WLTV (Channel 23)
WPBT (Channel 2)
WPLG (Channel 10)
WSVN (Channel 7)
WTVJ (Channel 4)

Radio

WAQI (AM)	WCMQ (AM)
WDNA (FM)	WEDR (FM)
WINZ (AM)	WIOD (AM)
WFLC (FM)	WLRN (FM)
WLYF (FM)	WMRZ (AM)
WOCN (AM)	WPOW (FM)
WQAM (AM)	WQBA (AM)
WQBA (FM)	WSUA (AM)
WZMQ (FM)	WZTA (FM)

Sports

The Miami Dolphins of the National Football League have time and again put Miami on the sports map, and are probably one of the city's best-known sporting attractions. They play their home games in the Joe Robbie Stadium. The Miami Heat team of the National Basketball Association plays in the Miami Arena. New teams include the Florida Marlins, set to play their major league baseball games in Joe Robbie Stadium, and the new National Hockey League franchise, as yet unnamed. The University of Miami Hurricanes football team, a consistent national champion in the 1980s, plays at the Orange Bowl. The Hurricanes baseball team plays home games at the Mark Light Stadium on the campus at Coral Gables. Miami also is the site of the Orange Bowl, the annual New Year's Day clash between two top-ranked collegiate football teams. Car racing and horse racing are also popular. The Hialeah Race Track holds thoroughbred racing from March through May with pari-mutuel betting, while Calder Race Course holds thoroughbred racing from mid-May through January. Another major sporting event on the calendar is the Miami/Toyota Grand Prix, held week-long in February in the European tradition: Downtown streets from Biscayne Boulevard through Bicentennial Park are converted into a race track. Jai Alai, a type of indoor handball with intricate hand mitts, is a favorite among the Hispanics and is played at the Jai Alai Fronton from December through April and from June through September.

Arts, Culture, and Tourism

Miami's cultural life has undergone a revival in recent years under both private and public auspices. The Metro-Dade Cultural Center holds free opera, dance, drama, and musical performances on its 34,000-square-foot plaza. Musical entertainment is provided by the Central Miami Youth Symphony, Greater Miami Opera Association, Miami Beach Symphony Orchestra, Miami Chamber Symphony, Pace Concerts, Gusman Concert Hall series, and the Cultural Arts Society of South Florida. The major dance companies are Miami City Ballet, Miami Ballet Company, Dance Miami, Inner City Children's Touring Dance Company, Ballet Concerto, and Momentism Dance Company. Theater is represented by the historic Coconut Grove Playhouse, which stages off-Broadway and Broadway plays, and South of Broadway Company, which brings off-Broadway to Knight Center. Elizabethan drama is staged on the grounds of the Vizcaya by the South Florida Shakespeare Festival. Other theatrical groups include the Spanish-language Acting Together, Ring Theater of the University of Miami, Coral Gables, Ruth Foreman Theater (featuring a children's theater), Theater Afro Arts, and South End Alternative Theater.

Housed in the Metro-Dade Cultural Center is the Historical Museum of Southern Florida. The Cuban Museum of Arts and Culture captures Cuban culture and history in the most Cuban city outside Havana. The Museum of Science and Space Transit Planetarium includes the Animal Exploratorium. The principal art showcase is the Center for the Fine Arts located in the Miami-Dade Cultural Center. The Bass Museum of Art is located in the center of the Art Deco District in Miami Beach. The North Miami Museum and Art Center concentrates on contemporary art with emphasis on Florida artists. Miami Youth Museum caters to a much younger audience. Among the more important galleries are Fabunique, Gideon, Pollack's, Rudolph, and Windsor Arts.

Travel and Tourism

Hotel Rooms   NA
Convention and Exhibit Space (square feet)   250,000

Convention Centers
    James L. Knight International Center
    Miami/Expo Center
    Coconut Grove Exposition Center
    Miami Beach Convention Center

Festivals
    International Folk Festival (May–June)
    Gran Romerio Ponce de Leon Festival
    Orange Bowl Festival
    Miami Film Festival (February)
    Coconut Grove Art Festival (February)

Parks and Recreation

Miami has an extensive park system but, in keeping with its reputation, caters more to water sports and fishing. Scuba and skin diving, waterskiing, swimming, boating, and canoeing activities take advantage of Miami's natural facilities. Diving aficionados may go to Haulover Park and Biscayne National Park, surfers to Haulover Beach in Sunny Isles and South Pointe Beach in South Miami, windsurfers to Hobie Beach in Key Biscayne, and fishermen to Haulover Park and Thompson Park.

Sources of Further Information

City Hall
3500 Pan American Drive
Miami, FL 33133
(305) 250-5300

Greater Miami Chamber of Commerce
1601 Biscayne Boulevard
Miami, FL 33132
(305) 350-7700

Miami Convention Bureau
400 SE Second Avenue
Miami, FL 33131
(305) 579-6341

Miami Economic Development Department
174 East Flagler Street
Miami, FL 33131
(305) 579-3324

Additional Reading

Blum, Ethel. *Miami Alive.* 1981.
Buchanan, James. *Miami: A Chronological and Documentary History, 1513–1977.* 1978.
Cerwinske, Laura. *Miami, Hot and Cold.* 1990.
Didion, Joan. *Miami.* 1988.
Gleason, David K. *Over Miami.* 1990.
Longbrake, David B. *Sunshine and Shadows in Metropolitan Miami.* 1976.
Lotz, Aileen R. *Metropolitan Dade County: Two-Tier Government in Action.* 1984.
Martin, Sidney Walter. *Florida during the Territorial Days.* 1974.
Metrofiles. *Cityfile, Miami.* 1990.
Peters, Thelma. *Lemon City: Pioneering on Biscayne Bay, 1850–1925.* 1976.
Ritz, Stacy, and Marty Olmstead. *Hidden Miami, Fort Lauderdale and Palm Beach: The Adventurer's Guide.* 1990.

Milwaukee

Wisconsin

Basic Data

Name   Milwaukee
Name Origin   From Algonquian, "good land"
Year Founded   1839 Inc. 1846
Status: State   Wisconsin
       County   Seat of Milwaukee County
Area (square miles)   96.1
Elevation (feet)   635
Time Zone   Central
Population (1990)   628,088
Population of Metro Area (1990)   1,432,149

Distance in Miles To:

Atlanta	799
Boston	1,091
Chicago	90
Dallas	1,015
Denver	1,038
Detroit	360
Houston	1,179
Los Angeles	2,069
Miami	1,458
New York	894
Philadelphia	872
Washington, DC	811

Location and Topography

N Milwaukee is located in the southeastern corner of Wisconsin on the western shore of Lake Michigan. The Milwaukee River runs through the city, meeting the Menomonee and Kinnickinnic rivers just south of downtown, emptying as one into Lake Michigan. Milwaukee is located about 90 miles east of Madison, the state capital. The land generally slopes to the east and south.

Layout of City and Suburbs

Milwaukee is a city of bridges. Cut roughly in half by the Milwaukee River, there are 13 bridges downtown connecting the east side, which borders Lake Michigan, to the west side. The streets are laid out in a traditional gridlike pattern, with thoroughfares such as Clybourn Street, Wisconsin Avenue, Mason Street, Wells Street, Kilbourn Avenue, and Juneau Avenue dominating. Among Milwaukee's suburbs along the western shore of Lake Michigan are Shorewood, Whitefish Bay, St. Francis, and Cudahy.

Environment

Environmental Stress Index   2.8
Green Cities Index: Rank   30
                    Score   27.36
Water Quality   Alkaline, medium hard, fluoridated
    Average Daily Use (gallons per capita)   168
    Maximum Supply (gallons per capita)   473
Parkland as % of Total City Area   9.3
% Waste Landfilled/Recycled   90:10
Annual Parks Expenditures per Capita $18.58

Climate

The major effect on the climate is Lake Michigan, which cools the shoreline in summer and warms it in winter. Other influences are storms moving eastward across the upper Ohio River Valley and the Great Lakes region, and large, high-pressure systems moving southeastward from Canada. During winter and summer, weather changes occur almost twice a week. Winters are cloudy, and severe winter storms often produce ten inches or more of snow. Incursions of arctic air leave the city in the grip

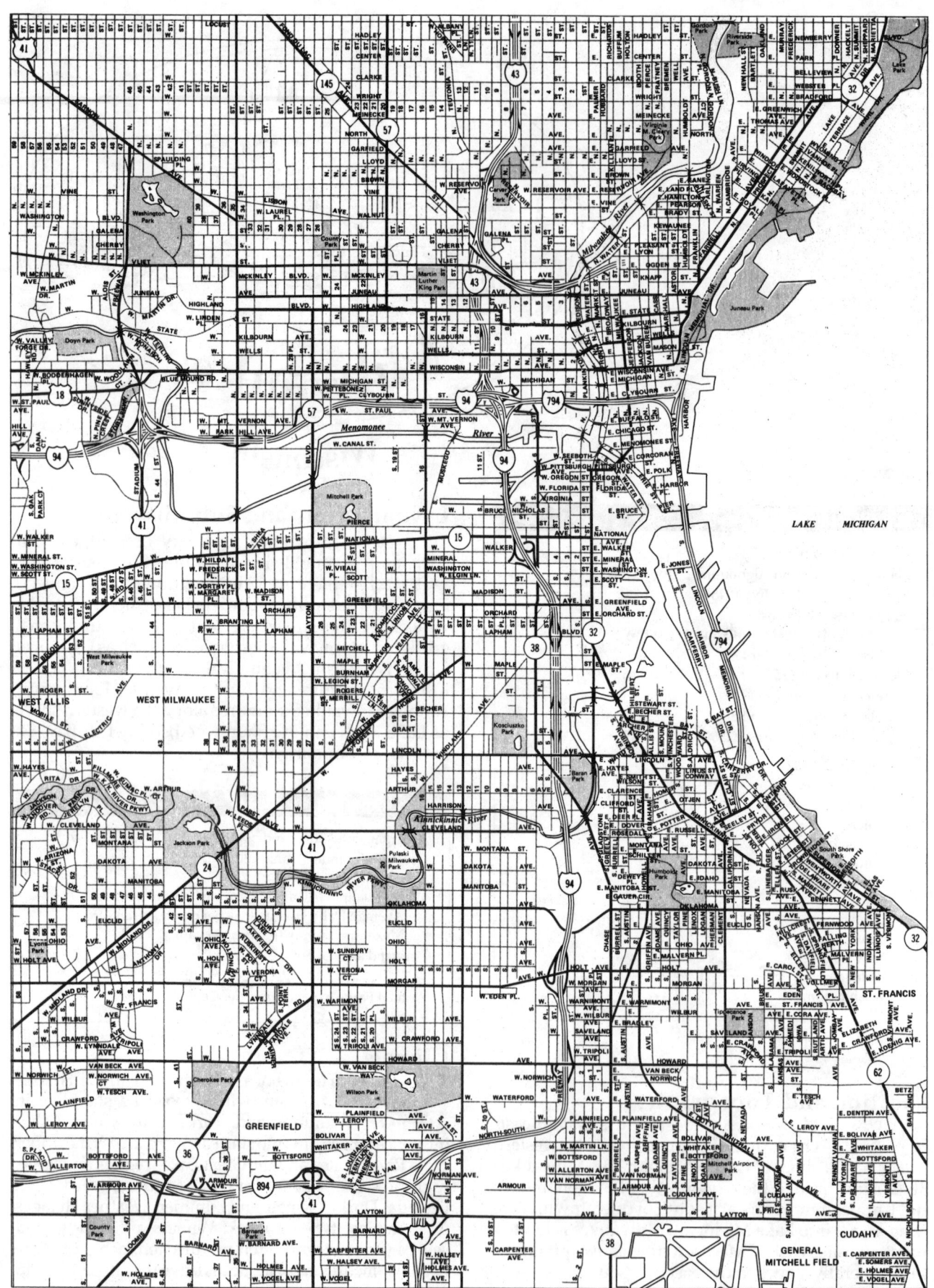

of bitterly cold weather for days. Thunderstorms are less frequent than in regions to the west and south. Summers are bright with occasional high humidity.

Weather			
Temperature			
Highest Monthly Average °F 79.8			
Lowest Monthly Average °F 11.3			
Annual Averages			
Days 32°F or Below 146			
Days above 90°F 9			
Zero Degree Days 16			
Precipitation (inches) 29			
Snow (inches) 45			
% Seasonal Humidity 73			
Wind Speed (m.p.h.) 11.8			
Clear Days 96			
Cloudy Days 170			
Storm Days 36			
Rainy Days 122			
Average Temperatures (°F)	*High*	*Low*	*Mean*
January	27.3	11.4	19.4
February	30.3	14.6	22.5
March	39.4	23.4	31.4
April	54.6	34.7	44.7
May	65.0	43.3	54.2
June	75.3	53.6	64.5
July	80.4	59.3	69.9
August	79.7	58.7	69.2
September	71.5	50.7	61.1
October	61.4	40.6	51.0
November	44.4	28.5	36.5
December	31.5	16.8	24.2

History

The Algonquian tribes who occupied the site of present-day Milwaukee called the area Millioki (gathering place by the waters). Various tribes, such as the Potawatomi, Menominee, Winnebago, Chippewa, Sauk, and earlier the Macoutin and Fox, used the area as a gathering place for tribal meetings. As early as 1764, a French explorer and trader known only as St. Pierre may have settled at the confluence of the three rivers. In 1779, Samuel Robertson reached what he called Millwakey Bay in his ship, the *Felicity*, and came upon St. Pierre. Between Robertson's landing and the dawn of the 19th century, several white traders—among them Jacques Vieau, John Beaubien, Joseph La Framboise, and Laurent Fily—came to the area that is now Milwaukee and its environs.

Feeling threatened by the presence of white settlers, the Indians moved deeper into the woods, but more pioneers came to the three rivers area. In 1818, the American Fur Company took over the local fur commerce from the North West Fur Company (a British concern), and essentially made the area a commercial center for American traders. Beginning in 1831, and continuing for two years, the various Indian tribes, in a series of meetings and conventions, relinquished control of the area. In 1835, when the lands were auctioned off in Green Bay, three men purchased the majority of them. Byron Kilbourn, an Ohio engineer,

purchased a section west of the Milwaukee River that he named Kilbourntown. French fur trader Solomon Juneau bought a tract near Lake Michigan dubbed Juneautown. Virginia-born George H. Walker bought up land south of Juneautown near the Milwaukee River and named it Walker's Point. Juneau lured investors and workers to his small village with money for improvements and the image of a growing, thriving community. Meanwhile, some citizens of Kilbourntown platted their town as Milwaukee in 1835, and the next year founded the city's first newspaper, the *Milwaukee Advertiser*. In 1839, Milwaukee west of the Milwaukee River and Juneautown were consolidated. Although the so-called Bridge Wars sprouted up at this time (over the price of tolls on a bridge Juneau built across the Menominee River), the conflict was settled by 1845. A year later, the city charter was ratified, and Juneau was elected the city's first mayor. Walker, whose village was annexed by Milwaukee in 1845, and Kilbourn followed him into this position.

After 1838, German immigration into Milwaukee served to increase the population and bring to the city an industry that would later make it famous—beer breweries. The Civil War brought new prosperity. After goods from the South were cut off, the Great Lakes shipping lanes became important to the North, and commerce flourished. In 1867 bootmakers formed the city's first labor union, the Order of the Knights of St. Crispin, and the labor movement seemingly found a home. It was in Milwaukee that socialism rose in the last two decades of the 19th century, found in the voices of Victor L. Berger and Emil Seidel among others. In 1898 Berger was instrumental in founding the Socialist party, and was later elected as the first Socialist to the U.S. House of Representatives. In 1910 Seidel became the first Socialist mayor of a major American city.

World War I sharply curtailed German culture and influence. The passing of Prohibition in 1919 hurt the German beer factories and the city's economy as a whole. Socialism, however, reigned supreme, at least in the form of two more Socialist mayors—Daniel Hoan and Carl Zeidler—who ruled from 1916 to 1940. Today, because of its strategic location, Milwaukee is a leader in the manufacture and shipping of goods around the nation and to Canada.

Historical Landmarks

Among the historic sights in Milwaukee is the Northpoint Historic District, a series of older homes listed as national historic landmarks. The Pabst Mansion on Wisconsin Avenue is a restored version of the mansion built in 1893 and owned by Captain Frederick Pabst, who later founded the Pabst beer empire. The Kilbourntown House and the Lowell Damon House, built in the 1840s, represent Greek Revival and Colonial architectural styles, respectively. City Hall, a fine example of Flemish Renaissance architecture, is noted for its iron balconies and glass windows. The Iron Block is a cast-iron structure built in 1860. One of the historic

Chronology

1764? A French explorer and trader known only as St. Pierre is alleged to have settled at the confluence of the Menomonie, Milwaukee, and Kinnickinnic rivers.

1779 Samuel Robertson pilots his ship, *Felicity*, to "Millwakey Bay" and finds St. Pierre already living there.

1780?–1803 Various traders and explorers—among them Jacques Vieau, Laurent Fily, and Joseph La Framboise—visit the Milwaukee area.

1818 The American Fur Company takes over the Wisconsin market from the North West Fur Company, a British enterprise.

1831–1833 Over a two-year period, the various American Indian tribes that inhabited the Milwaukee area relinquish control of their lands to the U.S. government.

1835 Lands around the Milwaukee area are sold at auction in Green Bay; the main investors are Solomon Juneau, Byron Kilbourn, and George H. Walker. Kilbourn founds Kilbourntown west of the Milwaukee River and plats the town of Milwaukee.

1836 The city's first newspaper, the *Milwaukee Advertiser*, is founded by so-called westenders.

1838 Increasing German migration brings German culture and beer making to the city.

1839 Milwaukee and Juneautown are consolidated. The so-called Bridge Wars start over river bridge fees. The conflict is resolved in 1845.

1845 Walker's Point is annexed by Milwaukee.

1846 The city charter is ratified; Solomon Juneau becomes Milwaukee's first mayor.

1867 The city's first labor union, the Order of the Knights of St. Crispin, is founded among bootmakers.

1898 Victor L. Berger brings unions and Socialists together into the Social Democratic party, later known as the Socialist party.

1910 Emil Seidel becomes the first Socialist mayor of a major American city, and Berger becomes the first Socialist member of Congress.

1916 With the country's entry into World War I, anti-German sentiment sweeps the city.

1916–1940 Socialists Daniel Hoan and Carl Zeidler serve as mayor.

1919 Prohibition takes a heavy toll on Milwaukee economy as the breweries are idled.

1980s Milwaukee becomes a leading exporter to other cities around the Great Lakes and Canada.

churches in the area is the St. Joan of Arc Chapel. Originally built during the 15th century in Lyons, France, Joan of Arc supposedly worshiped in it. The building was dismantled in 1926 and shipped to Milwaukee, where it was faithfully put back together; it was restored in 1965. Other noted houses of worship include St. Mary's Church, the Annunciation Greek Orthodox Church, and St. Josaphat's Basilica, the first Polish basilica in North America.

Population

In the 1940s Milwaukee ranked 12th among U.S. cities in population. In the half-century since then, its ranking has fallen steadily. In 1990 its rank was 17th, with a city population of 628,088. Its population was 636,297 in 1980 and 717,371 in 1970. However, the rate of decline has slowed from 11.3% to 1.3%. In age and sex composition, Milwaukee does not differ significantly from the national average.

Population		
	1980	*1990*
Central City	636,297	628,088
Rank	16	17
Metro Area	1,397,020	1,432,149
Pop. Change 1980–1990	-8,209	
Pop. % Change 1980–1990	-1.3	
Median Age	30.3	
% Male	47.3	
% Age 65 and Over	12.44	
Density (per square mile)	6,535	
Households		
Number	240,540	
Persons per Household	2.53	
% Female-Headed Households	19.8	
% One-Person Households	30.5	
Births—Total	11,800	
% to Mothers under 20	17.6	
Birth Rate per 1,000	19.0	

Ethnic Composition

Whites make up 63.4% of the population, blacks 30.5%, and other races 3.4%. Within whites, Germans constitute the largest group with 48%, Polish 14.8%, Irish 12.6%, English 10.4%, French 6%, Italian 3.6%, and white Hispanics 2.5%.

Milwaukee was a diverse community from the very beginning, even before the advent of the Europeans. The Native American tribes included Sauk, Fox, Chippewa, Menomonee, Ottawa, Winnebago, and Potawatomi, a population almost as varied as that of today. Nearly all of the early pioneers were Anglo-Saxons, but German immigration ended their supremacy by the end of the 1840s. By 1890 Germans had a comfortable majority, and German-language newspapers outsold English ones. Irish immigrants began to arrive during the same period, and the Third Ward (now the southeastern section of downtown) housed a large Irish colony.

After 1870 the wave of immigration shifted to groups from southern and eastern Europe. Poles constituted the largest group, and unlike earlier immigrants, the Poles spread outward into suburbs in the south, east, and northeast. Italians, particularly Sicilians, also were prominent among the immigrants of this period. Some settled in the Third Ward and others in Bay View. By the turn of the century, the immigrant stream was enriched by Czechs, Slovaks, Greeks, Hungarians, Jews, Serbs, Croats, and Slovenes. By 1910 every European country was represented in the city and together they made up three-fourths of the population.

Although blacks were active by the 1860s and St. Marks, the earliest black church, was organized in 1869, their migration became significant after World War I and a major demographic factor after World War II. The first Hispanics began to arrive in the 1920s when local tanneries recruited large numbers of Mexicans; they were followed by Puerto Ricans in the 1940s. Many of the Hispanics settled in Walker's Point. In the 1970s and 1980s, Asians arrived in substantial numbers, further intensifying the racial mosaic. Milwaukee has had some serious racial disturbances in the past. In 1967 riots broke out in the black community.

Ethnic Composition (as % of total pop.)		
	1980	1990
White	73.57	63.4
Black	23.1	30.5
American Indian	0.79	0.9
Asian and Pacific Islander	0.57	1.9
Hispanic	4.10	6.3
Other	NA	3.4

Government

Milwaukee is governed by a mayor and a council of 19 aldermen representing 16 districts, known as wards. The mayor (who is not a member of the council) and council members are elected to four-year terms. Milwaukee's elected officials were uniformly Democratic in a heavily Republican state until the 1870s. Republicans were suspect in part because they supported temperance legislation—the political kiss of death in German and Irish wards. The foundations of the city's modern political system can be traced back to the late 19th century when the Social Democrats were organized as a reform movement to throw out the laissez faire administration of Mayor David Rose. The Social Democrats believed in the cooperative commonwealth, but they were less interested in sweeping social change than in good government. They championed causes with a decidedly modern ring: municipal control of utilities, public works projects for the unemployed, a good park system, free textbooks, and services to the disadvantaged.

In 1910 Emil Seidel became the first Socialist mayor of a large American city, and he was backed by a Socialist majority in the Common Council. Seidel lost his bid for reelection, but Socialist Daniel Hoan won the mayoral race in 1916 and served until 1940. During his tenure Milwaukee developed a reputation for honesty and efficiency in public administration, winning numerous awards as the healthiest, safest, and best-policed city in the nation. In 1939 municipal bonds were abandoned as a means of raising money and all city departments were put on a pay-as-you-go basis. In 1943 Milwaukee retired the municipal debt. Hoan's retirement in 1940 was followed by three more Socialist mayors: Carl Zeidler, his brother Frank Zeidler, and John Bohn. Frank Zeidler is remembered for initiating projects in three key areas: public housing, urban renewal, and planning for the central city. When he stepped down in 1960, Socialists had held the office of mayor for 38 years—a record in U.S. municipal history.

Government
Year of Home Charter   1945
Number of Members of the Governing Body   19
Elected at Large   NA
Elected by Wards   16
Number of Women in Governing Body   4
Salary of Mayor $97,661
Salary of Council Members $42,996
City Government Employment Total   9,362
Rate per 10,000   154.7

Public Finance

The annual budget consists of revenues of $781.347 million and expenditures of $648.798 million. The debt outstanding is $515.576 million, and cash and security holdings are $1.944 billion. Milwaukee continues to be a model of fiscal restraint, and is one of the few cities with a consistently high credit rating.

Public Finance
Total Revenue (in millions) $781.347
Intergovernmental Revenue—Total (in millions) $277.4
Federal Revenue per Capita $42.4
% Federal Assistance   5.43
% State Assistance   30.03
Sales Tax as % of Total Revenue   0.52
Local Revenue as % of Total Revenue   36.05
City Income Tax   no
Taxes—Total (in millions) $117.8
Taxes per Capita	
Total $195
Property $183
Sales and Gross Receipts $3
General Expenditures—Total (in millions) $428.7
General Expenditures per Capita $708
Capital Outlays per Capita $113

Public Finance (continued)

% of Expenditures for:
- Public Welfare   0.0
- Highways   10.8
- Education   0.0
- Health and Hospitals   3.8
- Police   19.3
- Sewerage and Sanitation   17.3
- Parks and Recreation   2.1
- Housing and Community Development   7.2

Debt Outstanding per Capita $846
   % Utility   3.6
Federal Procurement Contract Awards (in millions)
   $199.5
Federal Grants Awards (in millions) $110.8
Fiscal Year Begins   January 1

Economy

Milwaukee's image as the beer capital of the world may be outdated, as recent figures show; beer accounts for only about 1% of the city's industrial production. The Milwaukee area is now a national leader in the manufacturing, high-technology, and insurance sectors. With such companies as Johnson Controls, Master Lock, Universal Foods, and Harley-Davidson having major plants in the city, unemployment in Milwaukee is below the state and national averages. Medium- and high-technology equipment, such as iron and steel forgings, gasoline engines, semiconductors, robotics, and X-ray as well as mining machinery, has led to the growth of high-technology companies by 12% from 1977 to 1987. Northwestern Mutual Life, the nation's tenth largest insurance company, is headquartered in Milwaukee.

Economy

Total Money Income (in millions) $5,907.8
% of State Average   94.8
Per Capita Annual Income $9,765
% Population below Poverty Level   13.8
Fortune 500 Companies   4

Banks	Number	Deposits (in millions)
Commercial	80	NA
Savings	31	NA

Passenger Autos   441,017
Electric Meters   803,828
Gas Meters   424,460

Manufacturing

Number of Establishments   1,054
% with 20 or More Employees   39.5
Manufacturing Payroll (in millions) $1,746.0
Value Added by Manufacture (in millions) $3,353.6
Value of Shipments (in millions) $6,502.3
New Capital Expenditures (in millions) $155.2

Wholesale Trade

Number of Establishments   1,006
Sales (in millions) $5,399.6
Annual Payroll (in millions) $345.102

Economy (continued)

Retail Trade

Number of Establishments   4,939
Total Sales (in millions) $3,048.3
Sales per Capita $5,038
Number of Retail Trade Establishments with Payroll   3,419
Annual Payroll (in millions) $392.3
Total Sales (in millions) $2,987.4
General Merchandise Stores (per capita) $551
Food Stores (per capita) $1,065
Apparel Stores (per capita) $260
Eating and Drinking Places (per capita) $726

Service Industries

Total Establishments   3,589
Total Receipts (in millions) $1,920.1
Hotels and Motels (in millions) $79.5
Health Services (in millions) $447.5
Legal Services (in millions) $302.3

Labor

Services now outranks manufacturing as the largest employment sector, while trade ranks third. Within manufacturing, no sector accounts for over 6%. The largest are nonelectrical machinery, electrical machinery, fabricated metal products, printing and publishing, and food and kindred products. Because no broad industry group dominates, the economy is better able to adjust to cyclical fluctuations than other cities with narrow concentrations. Further, the economy is driven by private business. Milwaukee is not a major state or federal center, and has no military base. Approximately 12% of the area's employees are in the public sector, compared to 16% nationwide.

Labor

Civilian Labor Force   312,606
% Change 1989–1990   -2.1

Work Force Distribution
- Mining   NA
- Construction   25,800
- Manufacturing   168,000
- Transportation and Public Utilities   37,100
- Wholesale and Retail Trade   172,100
- FIRE (Finance, Insurance, Real Estate)   51,500
- Service   208,100
- Government   86,400
- Women as % of Labor Force   46.0
- % Self-Employed   2.7
- % Professional/Technical   13.2

Total Unemployment   15,485
Rate %   5.0
Federal Government Civilian Employment   9,411

Education

The Milwaukee public school system, the largest in the state, supports 148 elementary schools, junior high schools, and senior high schools. In addition there are 200 parochial and private elementary schools, and 20 parochial and private junior and senior high schools.

Milwaukee has two universities, eight four-year colleges, and two specialty graduate institutions. The largest is the University of Wisconsin at Milwaukee, founded in 1956 through the merger of two older institutions. Equally prestigious is the Catholic-run Marquette University. The four-year colleges are Alverno College, Carroll College, Cardinal Stritch College, Concordia University, Medical College of Wisconsin, Milwaukee School of Engineering, Mount Mary College, and Wisconsin Lutheran College. The graduate institutions are the Keller Graduate School of Management and Milwaukee Institute of Art and Design.

Education

Number of Public Schools 148
Special Education Schools 4
Total Enrollment 92,789
% Enrollment in Private Schools 20.7
% Minority 68.1
Classroom Teachers 5,366
Pupil-Teacher Ratio 17.2:1
Number of Graduates 3,538
Total Revenue (in millions) $482.832
Total Expenditures (in millions) $491.833
Expenditures per Pupil $5,290
Educational Attainment (Age 25 and Over)
    % Completed 12 or More Years 63.6
    % Completed 16 or More Years 12.3
Four-Year Colleges and Universities 6
    Enrollment 45,584
Two-Year Colleges 2
    Enrollment 21,190

Libraries

Number 97
Public Libraries 13
Books (in thousands) 2,316
Circulation (in thousands) 3,209
Persons Served (in thousands) 602
Circulation per Person Served 5.33
Income (in millions) $16.318
Staff 377

Four-Year Colleges and Universities
    University of Wisconsin – Milwaukee
    Marquette University
    Alverno College
    Cardinal Stritch College
    Mount Mary College
    Medical College of Wisconsin

Health

The Milwaukee area is served by 22 hospitals with a total of 7,170 beds. The largest are Sinai Samaritan Medical Center, Clement J. Zablocki Veterans Administration Medical Center, St. Joseph's Hospital, St. Luke's Hospital, Columbia Hospital, St. Mary's Hospital, St. Francis Hospital, Northwest General Hospital, and St. Michael's Hospital.

Health

Deaths—Total 6,000
Rate per 1,000 9.7
Infant Deaths—Total 168
Rate per 1,000 14.2
Number of Metro Hospitals 22
Number of Metro Hospital Beds 7,170
Rate per 100,000 1,185
Number of Physicians 3,176
Physicians per 1,000 2.62
Nurses per 1,000 7.42
Health Expenditures per Capita $16.37

Transportation

The principal access route to Milwaukee is I-94, which reaches the city from Chicago, then turns west to Madison, while I-43 meets it just south of the city, and continues northward to Sheboygan. Interstate 894 and U.S. 45 serve as a sort of beltway around Milwaukee's southern suburbs. Other highways approaching the city include U.S. 18 and 41, and state highways 24, 32, 36, 38, 57, 59, 62, 100, 145, 181, and 190. Amtrak provides passenger rail service, while three railroads—Chicago and Northwestern, Wisconsin Central, and Soo Line—provide rail freight services. The main airport is General Mitchell International Airport, located just south of downtown, while a smaller commercial and general aviation terminus is the Lawrence Timmerman Airport, north of downtown. As a major city on Lake Michigan, Milwaukee has an extensive port system, which aids in the shipping of products both nationally and across the border to Canada.

Transportation

Interstate Highway Mileage 75
Total Urban Mileage 4,841
Total Daily Vehicle Mileage (in millions) 29.449
Daily Average Commute Time 42.7 min.
Number of Buses 480
Port Tonnage (in millions) 2.289
Airports 1
Number of Daily Flights 98
Daily Average Number of Passengers 5,128

Airlines (American carriers only)
    American
    American Trans Air
    Continental
    Delta
    Eastern
    Northwest
    Trans World
    United
    USAir

Housing

Milwaukee has 254,204 housing units, of which 44.8% are owner occupied. The average resale price is $79,600, which is $14,000 less than the national average. Upscale neighborhoods include East Side and North Shore, while Sherman Park is popular with starting families. Milwaukee's housing stock reflects a great variety of styles.

Before 1900 most homes were built in the Victorian gingerbread style; such homes are most abundant in Walker's Point and Bay View, and on the lower east, near north, and near west sides. The period between 1900 and 1915 was characterized on the one hand by mansions and on the other by basement duplexes favored by Poles and working-class families. Milwaukee has two mansion districts, the lakeshore on the east side and between Wisconsin Avenue and Highland Boulevard on the west side. Basement duplexes are most numerous on the south side below Mitchell Street, but they are also found on Brady Street and Riverwest and in Pigsville. Between 1915 and 1930, bungalows were the most prevalent type, and they are most prominent in the upper west side. After the Depression, the style shifted to two contrasting types: Cape Cod and Period Revival. By 1945 the ranch house replaced the Cape Cod in popularity. After the 1970s condominiums became increasingly popular as the population aged. There also has been a movement in the opposite direction: The architectural treasures of the central city are being rediscovered and many older homes are being renovated.

Housing

Total Housing Units   254,204
% Change 1980–1990   0.3
Vacant Units for Sale or Rent   9,278
Occupied Units   240,540
% with More Than One Person per Room   4.4
% Owner-Occupied   44.8
Median Value of Owner-Occupied Homes $53,500
Average Monthly Purchase Cost $359
Median Monthly Rent $342
New Private Housing Starts   517
Value (in thousands) $25,261
% Single-Family   22.6
Nonresidential Buildings Value (in thousands) $140,045

Tallest Buildings	Hgt. (ft.)	Stories
First Wis. Center & Office Tower	625	42
100 E. Wisconsin	549	37
Milwaukee Center	422	28
Faison Bldg.	417	34
411 E. Wisconsin	385	30
Northwestern Mutual Insurance	350	19
City Hall	350	9
Allen-Bradley Co.	333	17

Urban Redevelopment

One of the city's most ambitious projects is Grand Avenue, a downtown mall that links all buildings between Marshall Fields and the Boston Store. The heart of the project is the old Plankinton Arcade, a spacious, skylighted promenade in the best European tradition. The Grand Avenue's success has created a wave of new construction downtown, the most striking of which is the Milwaukee Center in the shadow of City Hall. The Milwaukee Center is a $100-million project consisting of a 28-story office tower, luxury hotel, and performing arts center. Riverlink is a major riverfront redevelopment project on the Milwaukee River. The East Wisconsin Building is a 37-story riverfront office tower. Riverfront Plaza is a 6-story office building created from the shell of a former warehouse.

Crime

In 1991, 6,228 violent crimes and 51,323 property crimes were reported.

Crime

Violent Crimes—Total   6,228
Violent Crime Rate per 100,000   520.3
Murder   163
Rape   502
Robbery   4.252
Aggravated Assaults   1,311
Property Crimes   51,323
Burglary   9,431
Larceny   28,322
Motor Vehicle Theft   13,570
Arson   419
Per Capita Police Expenditures $190.21
Per Capita Fire Protection Expenditures $94.07
Number of Police   2,041
Per 1,000   3.28

Religion

Constituting 48% of Milwaukee's population, Catholics are the largest church denomination. Black Baptists, Lutheran-Missouri Synod, and Evangelical Lutherans are also well represented in Milwaukee.

Religion

Largest Denominations (Adherents)	
Catholic	304,275
Black Baptist	65,187
Lutheran-Missouri Synod	39,731
Evangelical Lutheran	36,981
Wisconsin Evangelical Lutheran	31,002
American Baptist	7,172
Assembly of God	6,982
Episcopal	6,082
Presbyterian	6,443
Jewish	18,755

Media

Milwaukee has two dailies, under the same management: the *Milwaukee Journal*, published afternoons Monday through Saturday and on Sundays, and the *Milwaukee Sentinel*, published in the mornings Monday through Saturday. The electronic media consist of 9 television stations and 22 AM and FM radio stations.

Media

Newsprint
   Milwaukee Courier, weekly
   Milwaukee Journal, daily
   Milwaukee Magazine, monthly
   Milwaukee Sentinel, daily
   Milwaukee Star, weekly

Media (continued)

Television

WCGV (Channel 24)
WDJT (Channel 58)
WISN (Channel 12)
WITI (Channel 6)
WMVS (Channel 10)
WMVT (Channel 36)
WTMJ (Channel 4)
WVCY (Channel 30)
WVTV (Channel 18)

Radio

WEMP (AM)	WEZW (FM)
WMYX (FM)	WISN (AM)
WLTQ (FM)	WKLH (FM)
WLZR (AM)	WLZR (FM)
WMIL (FM)	WMSE (FM)
WMVP (AM)	WLUM (FM)
WMWK (FM)	WNOV (AM)
WOKY (AM)	WQFM (FM)
WTMJ (AM)	WKTI (FM)
WUWM (FM)	WVCY (FM)
WYMS (FM)	WZTR (FM)

Sports

 Milwaukee is represented by professional teams in two major sports: in baseball by the Milwaukee Brewers of the American League, who play their home games in the Milwaukee County Stadium; and in basketball by the Milwaukee Bucks of the National Basketball Association, based at the Bradley Center.

Arts, Culture, and Tourism

Milwaukee is endowed with many facets of the arts community. Among these are the Milwaukee Performing Arts Center, home of the Milwaukee Symphony Orchestra; Milwaukee Ballet Company; and Florentine Opera Company. Theatrical and musical performances are held in the historic and renovated Riverside Theatre and in the Pabst Theatre, a Victorian structure built in 1895. The Milwaukee Repertory Theatre, housed in the Milwaukee Center Theatre District, stages various plays and arts performances. Other centers include the Milwaukee Riverside Theatre, Milwaukee Chamber Theatre, and First Stage—the Milwaukee Children's Theatre, which spotlights plays and performances for the younger set. Numerous galleries abound in the city, including the Harambee House; John Michael Kohler Art Center, located in an Italian villa built by Kohler in 1882; and Posner Gallery in the historic Third Ward district. The premier museum is the Milwaukee Art Museum, housed in the War Memorial Center, which was designed by noted artist Eero Saarinen. Other major museums include the Charles Allis Art Museum, Milwaukee County Historical Center, Milwaukee Public Museum, Villa Terrace Decorative Arts Museum, Patrick and Beatrice Haggerty Museum of Art, and Wisconsin Black Historical Society and Museum.

Travel and Tourism

Hotel Rooms   10,148
Convention and Exhibit Space (square feet)   NA

Convention Centers

Milwaukee Exposition and Convention Center
and Arena

Festivals

Lakefront Festival of the Arts (June)
Summerfest (June–July)
Bastille Days
State Fair (August)
Festa Italiana, German Fest (July)
Irish Fest, Polish Fest, Fiesta Mexicana (August)

Parks and Recreation

 Milwaukee County has 140 parks and recreational area covering some 14,700 acres. The largest is the Juneau Park area next to Lake Michigan. It includes William O'Donnell Park, Veteran's Park, McKinley Marina, Circus Parade Grounds, and the Milwaukee Art Museum and War Memorial. Other major parks in the metropolitan area inlude Cathedral Square, Red Arrow Park, Pere Marquette Park, and Carl Zeidler Park.

Sources of Further Information

Greater Milwaukee Convention and Visitors Bureau
510 West Kilbourn Avenue
Milwaukee, WI 53203
(800) 231-0903

Metropolitan Milwaukee Association of Commerce
756 North Milwaukee Street
Milwaukee, WI 53202
(414) 287-4100

Additional Reading

Anderson, Harry H., and Frederick I. Olson. *Milwaukee at the Gathering of the Waters.* 1985.
Beckley, Robert M., and Stephen F. Dragos. *Downtown Milwaukee.* 1979.
Brody, Polly. *Discovering Wisconsin.* 1973.
Economic Factbook. *Milwaukee.* Annual.
Fromstein, Ruth. *Milwaukee: The Best of All Worlds.* 1990.
Garber, Randy. *Made in Milwaukee: An Architectural View of the City.* 1984.
Hamming, Edward. *The Port of Milwaukee.* 1953.
Hoan, Daniel W. *City Government: The Record of the Milwaukee Experiment.* 1975.
Perrin, Richard W. E. *Milwaukee Landmarks: An Architectural Heritage, 1850–1950.* 1968.
Slaske, Steve. *Milwaukee: The Cream City Observed.* 1980.
Still, Bayrd. *Milwaukee: The History of a City.* 1948.
Wells, Robert. *This Is Milwaukee.* 1970.
Zimmerman, H. Russell. *Magnificent Milwaukee.* 1987.

Minneapolis

Minnesota

Location and Topography

Situated at the Falls of St. Anthony, Minneapolis lies on both sides of the Mississippi River at the mouth of the Minnesota River. The city spreads over the gently rolling plains on the west, north, and south to join its principal suburbs: Bloomington, Brooklyn Center, Columbia Heights, Coon Rapids, Crystal, Edina, Fridley, Golden Valley, Minnetonka, New Hope, Richfield, and St. Louis Park. There are 22 lakes within city limits, giving the city its nickname of City of Lakes. Twelve miles to the west lies Lake Minnetonka.

Layout of City and Suburbs

The center of the city is Bridge Square, considered the Gateway to Minneapolis. It was at the foot of this square that Minneapolis was born. The present bridge is the successor of the one the early settlers built across the Mississippi to Nicollet Island. The Mississippi River divides the city into two areas, the larger of which is west of the river. The grain-milling district occupies both banks between the Third Avenue and Cedar Avenue bridges. Although most of the large University of Minnesota lies on the east bank, part of its campus lies on the west bank. Downtown Minneapolis, on the west bank, faces the Falls of St. Anthony. Nicollet Avenue, the chief shopping street, features an eight block–long shopping center known as the Nicollet Mall. The law permits cabs and buses, but not other vehicles, to drive on the mall. The Investors Diversified Services (IDS) Center, the city's first tall structure, faces the mall and is connected with other nearby tall structures by the Skyway system. The main financial district is Marquette Avenue, a block southeast of Nicollet Avenue. The upper-crust residential district is found on the hill surrounding Loring Park, in the area of Lake of the Isles, in Lynnhurst stretching back from the east side of Lake Harriet, and along the River Road. The city is laid out on a grid system, with streets south of Grant Street intersecting on a north-south axis and those north of Grant running diagonally northeast-southwest.

Climate

Minneapolis's continental climate is characterized by extremes, with wide variations in temperature, ample summer rainfall, and scanty winter precipitation. Ranked the

589

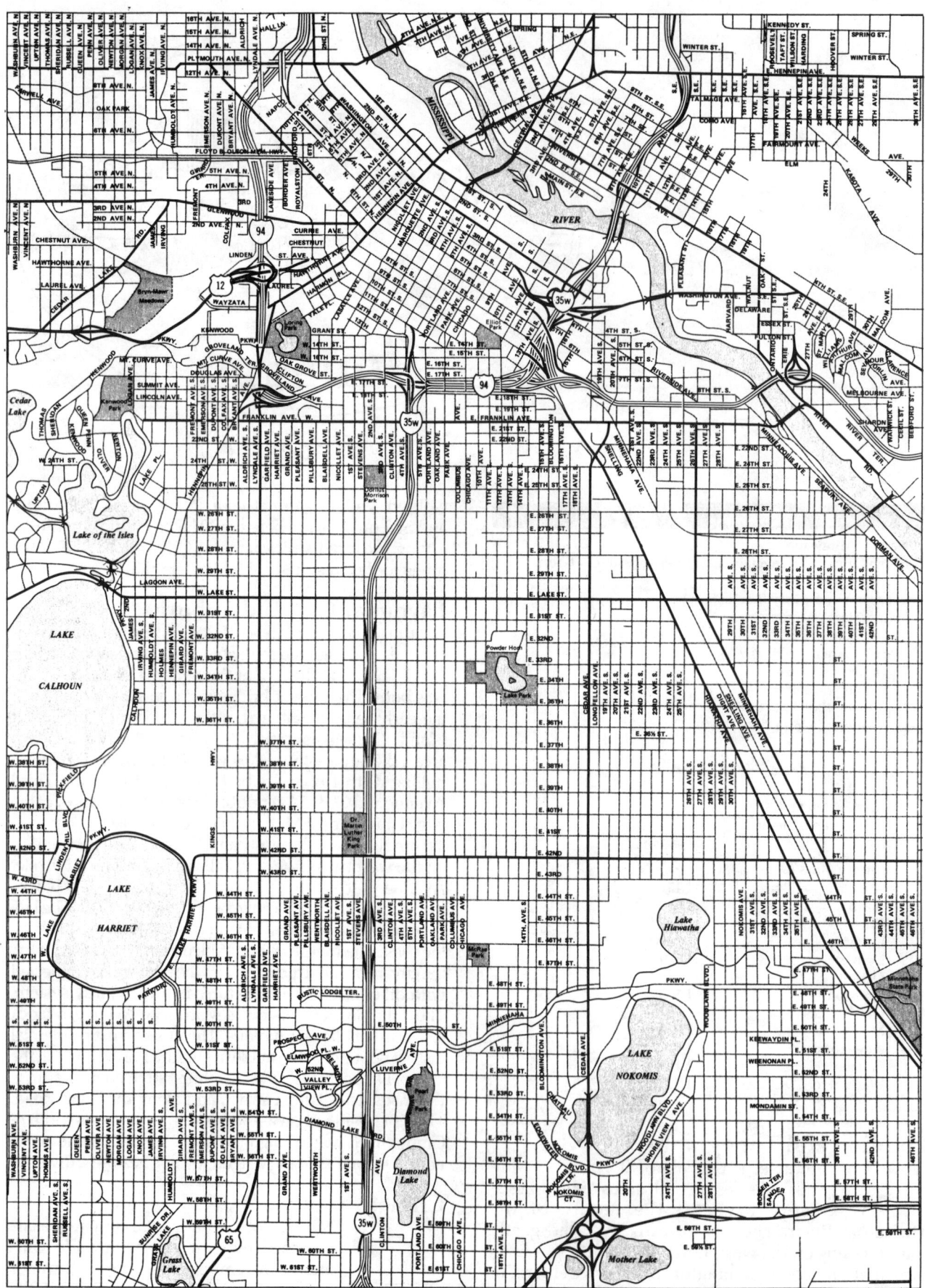

Environment	
Environmental Stress Index 2.8	
Green Cities Index: Rank 31	
Score 28.25	
Water Quality Alkaline, soft	
Average Daily Use (gallons per capita) NA	
Maximum Supply (gallons per capita) NA	
Parkland as % of Total City Area 6.0	
% Waste Landfilled/Recycled 74:26	
Annual Parks Expenditures per Capita $306.50	

second-coldest city in the nation, the city reports an average of 35 days below the zero mark; the average temperature is 44°F. Severe weather conditions—such as blizzards, freezing rain, tornadoes, and hailstorms—are fairly common. Snow on the ground may reach up to 6 to 10 inches, but being dry snow it is ideal for winter sports. Winter snow often exceeds 42 inches annually. Despite all this, Minneapolis is considered a very livable city, with a superior recreational environment.

Weather			
Temperature			
Highest Monthly Average °F 82.4			
Lowest Monthly Average °F 3.2			
Annual Averages			
Days 32°F or Below 158			
Days above 90°F 15			
Zero Degree Days 34			
Precipitation (inches) 26.0			
Snow (inches) 46.0			
% Seasonal Humidity 69.0			
Wind Speed (m.p.h.) 10.5			
Clear Days 100			
Cloudy Days 165			
Storm Days 36			
Rainy Days 113			
Average Temperatures (°F)	*High*	*Low*	*Mean*
January	21.2	3.2	12.2
February	25.9	7.1	16.5
March	36.9	19.6	28.3
April	55.5	34.7	45.1
May	67.9	46.3	57.1
June	77.1	56.7	66.9
July	82.4	61.4	71.9
August	80.8	59.6	70.2
September	70.7	49.3	60.0
October	60.7	39.2	50.0
November	40.6	24.2	32.4
December	26.6	10.6	18.6

History

The site where Minneapolis stands was once occupied by Sioux Indians. The first white man to reach the place was Father Louis Hennepin, a Franciscan priest, who in 1680 explored the Upper Mississippi Valley. Hennepin discovered the falls on the navigable head of the Mississippi River and named it after St. Anthony, his patron saint. In 1819 a fort was established at St. Anthony's Falls by federal troops under Josiah Snelling. Renamed Fort Snelling in 1823, it protected the fur traders from the warring Sioux and Chippewa tribes. St. Anthony's Falls provided the power for lumber and flour milling, two industries for which the place later became famous. Soldiers built the first flour mill in 1823; the first commercial mill began operation in 1841. In 1855 the village of St. Anthony was incorporated, and in 1860 it was chartered as a city. Meanwhile, in 1849, the village of All Saints was founded on the west side of the falls. In 1856 the name of the town was changed to Minneapolis, a hybrid name drawn from the Sioux word *minne* for water and the Greek *polis* for city. It was chartered as a city in 1866. In 1872 the two cities—St. Anthony and Minneapolis—merged under the latter name. Although early settlers were New Englanders, most of the immigrants to the area in the latter half of the 19th century were Swedes. At first the Scandinavian population was almost equally divided between Swedes and Norwegians, but after 1880 the Swedes began to outnumber Norwegians. A mill explosion in 1878 destroyed half the flour-milling district and caused many deaths, but by 1882 Minneapolis emerged as the world's largest flour-milling center. By the turn of the century Minneapolis also was the world's foremost lumber producer, although the lumber industry declined after the great forests were depleted. After World War II Minneapolis found a new industrial niche, emerging as a major producer of computers, electronic equipment, and farm machinery.

Historical Landmarks

Minneapolis has a number of old hotels and inns, the sites of many of which are marked. Among them are the Old Nicollet House on Washington Avenue, an old frontier inn built in 1857; the West Hotel on Hennepin Avenue; and the Old Winslow House on Central Avenue, built in 1857. Other early structures are either still preserved or marked by a tablet. The site of Cheevers Landing is marked by a bronze tablet on a boulder.

Stevens House on Minnehaha Creek was the first frame dwelling on the west side of the falls. It was built by John H. Stevens and was the first meeting place of Hennepin County and its courts and schools. The site of an Indian village is marked by a bronze tablet on East Calhoun Boulevard. The land between Lake Calhoun and Lake Harriet was inhabited by the Island Sioux people. The Godfrey House on Central avenue is the older of the two pioneer structures in the city parks and the first frame dwelling in the village of St. Anthony. It was built in 1848 of lumber from the village's first sawmill. The Alex Coultier House on Second Street also claims to be the first frame building in the city. It was built by Alex Coultier, a French-Canadian who came from Montreal to work for the Hudson's Bay Company. Minneapolis's religious traditions are represented by a number of historic churches. The Basilica of St. Mary on Hennepin Avenue is a striking version of Renaissance architecture. The building was begun in 1906 but was not completed and dedicated until 1926. A statue of Father Hennepin stands in front of the basilica. St. Mark's Episcopal Church on Hennepin Avenue has a

Chronology

1680	Father Louis Hennepin, a French Franciscan missionary, discovers the future site of Minneapolis at a waterfall on the navigable head of the Mississippi River. Father Hennepin names it St. Anthony's Falls.
1820	Federal troops under Colonel Josiah Snelling build Fort St. Anthony on a bluff overlooking the confluence of the Minnesota and Mississippi rivers.
1823	Soldiers, using waterpower from the falls, build the first flour mill. Fort St. Anthony is renamed Fort Snelling.
1841	The first commercial mill begins operation.
1849	The village of All Saints is founded on the west side of the falls.
1855	Settlement around Fort St. Anthony is incorporated as the Village of St. Anthony.
1856	Village of All Saints is renamed Minneapolis.
1860	Village of St. Anthony is incorporated as a city.
1866	Village of Minneapolis is incorporated as a city.
1872	The cities of Minneapolis and St. Anthony merge under the name of former.
1878	Mill explosion destroys half the flour-mill district.

parklike setting similar to many English parish churches. The Hennepin Avenue Methodist Church on Grove and Lyndale avenues is the best example of the Akron plan of church structures. St. Anthony of Padua Church on Main Street is the city's oldest church, founded in 1849. The Russian Orthodox St. Mary's Church on Fifth Street is the religious center of the city's Carpatho-Russian community. Notre Dame de Lourdes on Prince Street was built in 1857 to serve the French-Canadian community. Other notable historic buildings include the Gateway Building on what was once known as the Center Block site of the old City Hall.

Population

In population Minneapolis barely held its own during the 1980s. Its 1990 population of 368,383 was 0.7% smaller than the 1980 figure of 370,951. As a result its rank fell from 34th to 42nd among U.S. cities. One reason for the loss of population is the rise of suburbs, such as Bloomington, which have lured away the affluent with prospects of better amenities and housing.

Population

	1980	1990
Central City	370,951	368,383
Rank	16	17
Metro Area	2,137,133	2,464,124
Pop. Change 1980–1990 -2,568		
Pop. % Change 1980–1990 -0.7		
Median Age 31.7		
% Male 48.5		
% Age 65 and Over 13.0		
Density (per square mile) 6,710		

Households

Number 160,682
Persons per Household 2.19
% Female-Headed Households 12.7
% One-Person Households 38.5
Births—Total 6,301
　　% to Mothers under 20 10.7
　　Birth Rate per 1,000 17.6

Ethnic Composition

Whites make up 78% of the population, blacks 13%, American Indians 3.3%, Asians and Pacific Islanders 4.3%, and Hispanics and others 3%.

Ethnic Composition (as % of total pop.)

	1980	1990
White	87.30	78.4
Black	7.66	13.0
American Indian	2.41	3.3
Asian and Pacific Islander	1.11	4.3
Hispanic	1.26	2.1
Other	NA	0.9

Government

Minneapolis is governed by a mayor and 13-member council, all of whom are elected for four-year terms. The mayor is not a member of the council and is relatively weak vis-à-vis council members. The school board is independently elected. Minneapolis has a long history of citizen involvement and participation through advisory commissions and neighborhood coalitions.

Government

Year of Home Charter 1920
Number of Members of the Governing Body 13
Elected at Large NA
Elected by Wards 13
Number of Women in Governing Body 7
Salary of Mayor $69,000
Salary of Council Members $51,000
City Government Employment Total 5,394
Rate per 10,000 151.2

Public Finance

The annual budget consists of revenues of $729.867 million and expenditures of $715.646 million. The debt outstanding is $1.980 billion, and cash and security holdings are $2.441 billion.

Public Finance

Total Revenue (in millions) $729.867
Intergovernmental Revenue—Total (in millions) $164.5
Federal Revenue per Capita $30.8
% Federal Assistance 4.23
% State Assistance 17.02
Sales Tax as % of Total Revenue 4.71
Local Revenue as % of Total Revenue 58.69
City Income Tax no
Taxes—Total (in millions) $117.7

Taxes per Capita
   Total $330
   Property $274
   Sales and Gross Receipts $35
General Expenditures—Total (in millions) $415.2
General Expenditures per Capita $1,164
Capital Outlays per Capita $135

% of Expenditures for:
   Public Welfare 0.0
   Highways 9.5
   Education 0.0
   Health and Hospitals 1.8
   Police 8.8
   Sewerage and Sanitation 9.3
   Parks and Recreation 6.5
   Housing and Community Development 15.1
Debt Outstanding per Capita $4,410
   % Utility 0.7
Federal Procurement Contract Awards (in millions) $667.7
Federal Grants Awards (in millions) $83.4
Fiscal Year Begins January 1

Economy

 Minneapolis is one of the largest commercial and industrial centers between Chicago and the West Coast. It is also a major financial center as the headquarters of the ninth Federal Reserve District. Seventeen Fortune 500 industrial companies maintain their corporate headquarters in the city and they dominate the economy in such sectors as electronics, milling, machinery, medical products, food processing, and graphic arts. Originally a grain town and the home of the world's four largest grain-milling companies, the city diversified soon after World War II into sunrise sectors, with over 1,200 firms involved in high technology. Driving the economy are such Fortune 500 firms as 3M, Honeywell, General Mills, Control Data, Pillsbury, Bemis,

Economy

Total Money Income (in millions) $4,391.8
% of State Average 110.0
Per Capita Annual Income $12,302
% Population below Poverty Level 13.5
Fortune 500 Companies 8

Banks	Number	Deposits (in millions)
Commercial	191	23,041.2
Savings	5	8,157.4

Passenger Autos 677,996
Electric Meters 459,541
Gas Meters 300,000

Economy (continued)

Manufacturing

Number of Establishments 860
% with 20 or More Employees 39.5
Manufacturing Payroll (in millions) $1,281.2
Value Added by Manufacture (in millions) $2,343.0
Value of Shipments (in millions) $4,032.3
New Capital Expenditures (in millions) $210.4

Wholesale Trade

Number of Establishments 1,123
Sales (in millions) $12,083.1
Annual Payroll (in millions) $485.038

Retail Trade

Number of Establishments 3,368
Total Sales (in millions) $2,349.7
Sales per Capita $6,585
Number of Retail Trade Establishments with Payroll 2,441
Annual Payroll (in millions) $325.0
Total Sales (in millions) $2,316.0
General Merchandise Stores (per capita) $747
Food Stores (per capita) $1,220
Apparel Stores (per capita) $373
Eating and Drinking Places (per capita) $1,031

Service Industries

Total Establishments 3,771
Total Receipts (in millions) $2,837.1
Hotels and Motels (in millions) $124.5
Health Services (in millions) $520.8
Legal Services (in millions) $515.6

Cargill Carlson, Dayton Hudson, and Northwest Airlines. In financial resources Minneapolis ranks seventh, and it is the 12th largest financial center in the nation.

Labor

Minneapolis is noted for its strong work ethic and also a healthy environment. The share of government in employment is much lower than in neighboring St. Paul. The largest employment sectors are services and trade; three of the top five employers are in these sectors. Although blacks are numerically a small minority, they enjoy virtual parity with whites in earning power in many industries.

Labor

Civilian Labor Force 207,165
% Change 1989–1990 1.5

Work Force Distribution
   Mining NA
   Construction 46,900
   Manufacturing 257,800
   Transportation and Public Utilities 77,800
   Wholesale and Retail Trade 326,300
   FIRE (Finance, Insurance, Real Estate) 99,400
   Service 368,000
   Government 189,700
   Women as % of Labor Force 47.6
   % Self-Employed 4.4
   % Professional/Technical 20.2
Total Unemployment 9,415
Rate % 4.5
Federal Government Civilian Employment 10,155

Education

Minneapolis's Independent #1 School District, the largest in the state, supports 38 elementary schools, 9 junior high schools, 7 senior high schools, and 1 special education school. In addition, 345 private and parochial schools offer alternative curricula. More than 77% of the high school graduates go on to college. The main campus of the University of Minnesota, a state institution, is located in the Twin Cities. Although the university dominates the higher education landscape, there are a number of historic private institutions affiliated with religious bodies. Among them are Augsburg College, Bethel College, and Concordia College. In addition, there are six community colleges and three major vocational/technical schools.

Education

Number of Public Schools 55
Special Education Schools 1
Total Enrollment 41,050
% Enrollment in Private Schools 12.5
% Minority 52.1
Classroom Teachers 1,917
Pupil-Teacher Ratio 21.4:1
Number of Graduates 2,021
Total Revenue (in millions) $225.253
Total Expenditures (in millions) $218.117
Expenditures per Pupil $5,248
Educational Attainment (Age 25 and Over)
  % Completed 12 or More Years 74.8
  % Completed 16 or More Years 23.7
Four-Year Colleges and Universities 2
  Enrollment 43,937
Two-Year Colleges 3
  Enrollment 7,284

Libraries

Number 102
Public Libraries 15
Books (in thousands) 1,923
Circulation (in thousands) 3,071
Persons Served (in thousands) 371
Circulation per Person Served 8.27
Income (in millions) $14.414
Staff 334

Four-Year Colleges and Universities
  (See also St. Paul)
  Augsburg College
  University of Minnesota

Health

Minneapolis is noted as the city where HMOs (Health Maintenance Organizations) were born. It is not surprising therefore that it has the highest proportion of population enrolled in prepaid medical plans. The leading medical facility is the University of Minnesota Medical Center, where the first open-heart surgery was performed in 1954. Other major medical centers include: Metropolitan Medical Center/Mount Sinai Hospital, Minneapolis Children's Center, Shriners Hospital, Veterans Administration Health Center, Hennepin County Medical Center, and the Abbott-Northwestern/Sister Kenny Institute.

Health

Deaths—Total 3,935
Rate per 1,000 11.0
Infant Deaths—Total 60
Rate per 1,000 9.5
Number of Metro Hospitals 13
Number of Metro Hospital Beds 5,829
Rate per 100,000 1,634
Number of Physicians 4,964
Physicians per 1,000 2.62
Nurses per 1,000 14.16
Health Expenditures per Capita $27.89

Transportation

Minneapolis is approached by two interstate highways: the east-west I-94, and the north-south I-35, which splits into I-35W to Minneapolis (with I-35E going to St. Paul). A belt loop around the city is called I-494 at its southern end and I-694 at the northern tip, and both connect with I-94. The former Highway 12 is being converted into I-394. The two beltline freeways, I-494 and I-694, provide additional access, while Highway 12 has been converted from I-394 to facilitate travel through the suburbs. Seven federal and 13 state highways provide a network for travel within the metropolitan area.

Rail passenger service is provided by Amtrak, with freight services by the Burlington Northern, Chicago and Northwestern, and Soo Line railroads. Minneapolis–St. Paul International Airport, ten miles from downtown Minneapolis, serves nine airlines, and is the headquarters of Northwest Airlines.

Transportation

Interstate Highway Mileage 194
Total Urban Mileage 9.287
Total Daily Vehicle Mileage (in millions) 43.930
Daily Average Commute Time 44.2 min.
Number of Buses 925
Port Tonnage (in millions) 1.628
Airports 1
Number of Daily Flights 309
Daily Average Number of Passengers 23,178

Airlines (American carriers only)
  Air Wisconsin
  American
  Continental
  Delta
  Midway
  Northwest
  Trans World
  United
  USAir

Housing

The 1990 housing census showed that the city had 172,666 dwellings in 11 neighborhoods. Of these, Powderhorn had 25,082 units, Southwest 21,645 units, Calhoun Isles 17,440 units, Northeast 16,945 units, Nokomis 16,832 units, Central 16,637 units, Near North 13,576 units, Longfellow 13,483 units, Camden 12,177 units, University 11,408 units, and Phillips 7,453 units. The average sale price of single-family homes was $81,427, and the average rent was $390. Minneapolis had a total of 14,792 units of publicly assisted housing, 5,141 units of public housing for the elderly, and 8,052 units of rent-subsidized housing units.

Housing

Total Housing Units 172,666		
% Change 1980–1990 2.2		
Vacant Units for Sale or Rent 9,494		
Occupied Units 160,682		
% with More Than One Person per Room 3.6		
% Owner-Occupied 49.7		
Median Value of Owner-Occupied Homes $71,700		
Average Monthly Purchase Cost $355		
Median Monthly Rent $390		
New Private Housing Starts 823		
Value (in thousands) $46,791		
% Single-Family 14.1		
Nonresidential Buildings Value (in thousands) $360,842		

Tallest Buildings	Hgt. (ft.)	Stories
IDS Center (1973)	787	51
Norwest (1988)	777	57
First Bank Place	774	53
Multifoods Tower (1983)	651	52
Piper Jaffray Tower (1984)	627	42
Dain Bosworth Plaza	550	40
Pillsbury Center (1981)	545	40
Lincoln Centre (1987)	496	31

Urban Redevelopment

The engine of the local economy is urban redevelopment. Since the expansion of the Nicollet Mall in 1982 and the building of the Skyway system, more than $2 billion has been invested in construction projects, and the work is expected to continue throughout the 1990s. The star project is the New City Center, which contains stores, restaurants, a hotel, and the International Multifoods Tower. In 1988 the city invested $9 million in the renewal of Block E on Hennepin Avenue between downtown and the Warehouse District and its conversion into a retail-entertainment complex. Other projects include an arena for the National Basketball Association, and the renovation of two 1920s theaters.

Crime

Minneapolis–St. Paul ranks below the national average in crime. In 1991, of known to police, there were 5,889 violent and 36,226 property crimes.

Crime

Violent Crimes—Total 5,889	
Violent Crime Rate per 100,000 470	
Murder 64	
Rape 744	
Robbery 2,610	
Aggravated Assaults 2,471	
Property Crimes 36,226	

Crime (continued)

Burglary 8,990	
Larceny 22,155	
Motor Vehicle Theft 5,081	
Arson NA	
Per Capita Police Expenditures $147.62	
Per Capita Fire Protection Expenditures $77.63	
Number of Police 677	
Per 1,000 1.88	

Religion

Although of Catholic origins, Minneapolis is a strongly Lutheran city. Nearly 88% of the churches are Protestant.

Religion

Largest Denominations (Adherents)	
Catholic	215,426
Evangelical Lutheran	160,979
Lutheran-Missouri Synod	24,735
Black Baptist	19,596
United Methodist	29,149
United Church of Christ	15,717
Presbyterian	17,903
Episcopal	11,031
Assembly of God	8,825
Jewish	14,034

Media

The daily press consists of the *Minneapolis Star & Tribune.* The electronic media consist of 4 television stations (2 commercial and 2 public) and 35 AM and FM stations.

Media

Newsprint	
Minneapolis-St. Paul City Business, bi-monthly	
Minneapolis Star & Tribune, daily	
Twin Cities, weekly	
Television	
See St. Paul	
Radio	
See St. Paul	

Sports

Minneapolis is represented in three of the four major sports: in baseball by the Minnesota Twins in the western division of the American League, in football by the Minnesota Vikings in the central division of the National Football League, and in basketball by the Minnesota Timberwolves of the National Basketball Association. The NHL Minnesota North Stars have moved to Dallas. The major stadium is the Hubert H. Humphrey Metrodome.

Arts, Culture, and Tourism

The premier cultural center is the Guthrie Theater, which ranks as one of the best regional repertory companies in the nation. Other theater companies include Children's Theater. In music the pride of place goes to the Minnesota Orchestra, followed by the Civic Orchestra of Minneapolis, the Minnetonka Symphony Orchestra, and the Minnesota Opera Company. In dance the city is represented by the Northwest Ballet. Minneapolis has ten major art museums, including the Minnesota Museum of Art, Minneapolis Institute of Arts, Walker Art Center, and the Minneapolis Sculpture Garden. The Walker Art Center, founded in 1879 by millionaire lumberman Thomas Barlow Walker, moved into a new award-winning building in 1971. The American Institute of Swedish Arts, Literature, and Sciences on Park Avenue maintains a turn-of-the-century 33-room mansion containing Swedish immigrant artifacts.

Travel and Tourism
Hotel Rooms   24,250
Convention and Exhibit Space (square feet)   NA
Convention Centers
Minneapolis Convention Center
Festivals
Aquatennial (July)
Heritage Festival (June)
Great Lake Street International Bazaar

Parks and Recreation

Minneapolis's parks are overseen by the Minneapolis Park Board, and include the Minneapolis Sculpture Garden next to the Walker Art Center; Boom Island, a family picnic area on the Mississippi River; Theodore Wirth Park, the city's largest, which has a 13-acre garden; and Minnehaha Park, which features the Minnehaha Falls. Key recreation areas are the beaches on the connected lakes at Brownie Lake, Cedar Lake, the Lake of the Isles, Lake Calhoun, and Lake Harriet.

Sources of Further Information

City Hall
350 South Fifth Street
Minneapolis, MN 55415
(612) 348-3000

Greater Minneapolis Chamber of Commerce
15 South Fifth Street
Minneapolis, MN 55402
(612) 370-9170

Hennepin County Historical Society Museum
2303 Third Avenue
Minneapolis, MN 55404
(612) 870-1329

Minneapolis Convention and Visitors Bureau
1219 Marquette Avenue
Minneapolis, MN 55403
(800) 445-7412

Additional Reading

Borchert, John R. *Legacy of Minneapolis: Preservation Amid Change.* 1983.

Jacob, Bernard, and Carol Morphew. *Pocket Architecture: A Walking Tour Guide to the Architecture of Downtown Minneapolis and St. Paul.* 1987.

Kane, Lucile M., and Alan Ominsky. *Twin Cities: A Pictorial History of St. Paul and Minneapolis.* 1983.

Mickelson, Marlys. *Seat Yourself: A Complete Guide to Twin Cities Areas, Auditoriums and Theaters.* 1990.

Rich, Frieda, and Lael Berman. *Landmarks Old and New in Minneapolis, St. Paul and Surrounding Areas.* 1987.

Rosheim, David L. *The Other Minneapolis.* 1989.

Mobile

Alabama

Basic Data

Name   Mobile
Name Origin   From Mobile Indians
Year Founded   1702 Inc. 1814
Status: State   Alabama
          County   Seat of Mobile County
Area (square miles)   118.0
Elevation (feet)   5
Time Zone   Central
Population (1990)   196,278
Population of Metro Area (1990)   476,923

Sister Cities

   Ashdod, Israel
   Heliopolis, Egypt
   Kaohsiung County, China
   Katowice, Poland
   Malaga, Spain
   Pau, France
   Rostov-on-Don, Russia
   Zakinthos, Greece
   Worms, Germany
   Puertos Barrios, Guatemala

Distance in Miles To:

Atlanta	340
Birmingham	262
Montgomery	170
New Orleans	157
Gulf of Mexico	31

Location and Topography

Mobile is situated in the southwestern corner of Alabama on the west bank of Mobile Bay about 170 miles from the state capital, Montgomery. The city faces Blakely, Pinto, and McDuffie islands, all to the east. Waterways in the area include the Dog River, Montimar Creek, the Mobile River, and the Spanish River. The land is hilly and slopes gently upward from the bay area west.

Layout of City and Suburbs

Mobile streets are platted in a traditional grid pattern and cut only by the thoroughfares of Martin Luther King, Jr. Avenue, Spring Hill Avenue, Canal Street, and Charleston Street. At its southern end, the city is cut in half by the Dog River. Brookley Airport is on the bay to the southeast of the city, while the Mobile Regional Airport is to the west. To the north are the suburbs of Prichard, Chickasaw, and Saraland.

Environment

Environmental Stress Index   2.6
Green Cities Index: Rank   NA
                          Score   NA
Water Quality   Alkaline, very soft, fluoridated
   Average Daily Use (gallons per capita)   NA
   Maximum Supply (gallons per capita)   NA
Parkland as % of Total City Area   2.6
% Waste Landfilled/Recycled   NA
Annual Parks Expenditures per Capita $69.16

Climate

Mobile has a continental climate with mild winters and hot, muggy summers. The temperatures go below freezing for only 19 days a year on average. It is also one of the nation's wettest cities, with thunderstorms almost every other day during July and August, and is subject to hurricanes.

Weather

Temperature

Highest Monthly Average °F   90.6
Lowest Monthly Average °F   41.3

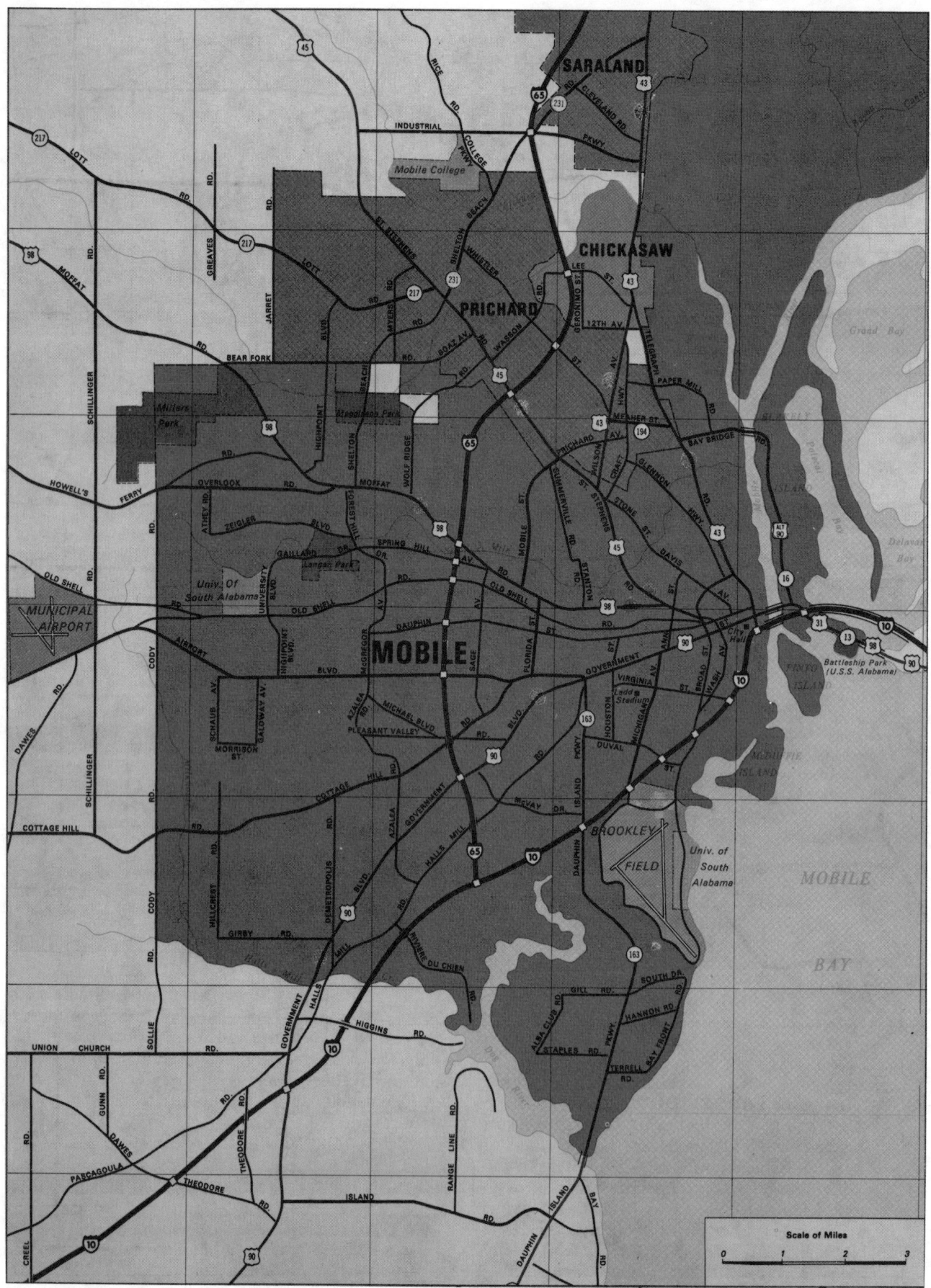

Weather (continued)

Annual Averages

Days 32°F or Below   19
Days above 90°F   81
Zero Degree Days   0
Precipitation (inches)   67.0
Snow (inches)   0.4
% Seasonal Humidity   73.0
Wind Speed (m.p.h.)   9.2
Clear Days   100
Cloudy Days   148
Storm Days   80
Rainy Days   124

Average Temperatures (°F)	High	Low	Mean
January	61.1	41.3	51.2
February	64.1	43.9	54.0
March	69.5	49.2	59.4
April	78.0	57.7	67.9
May	85.0	64.5	74.8
June	89.8	70.7	80.3
July	90.5	72.6	81.6
August	90.6	72.3	81.5
September	86.5	68.4	77.5
October	79.7	58.0	68.9
November	69.5	47.5	58.5
December	63.0	42.8	52.9

History

Mobile Bay appears on the Pineda map of 1520, but the first written record was that of Spanish explorer de Narvaez in 1528. Not until 1559, however, was any attempt made to colonize the area. In that year Tristan de Luna was sent by the viceroy of Mexico to establish a Spanish settlement there, but it was abandoned two years later. Almost a century and a half passed before settlers again came to Mobile Bay.

Two brothers, Pierre le Moyne, Sieur de Iberville, and Jean-Baptiste le Moyne, Sieur de Bienville, were sent by Louis XIV to establish a colony on the gulf in 1699. They passed Massacre, now Dauphin Island, and landed on the flat beaches of Biloxi, where a stockade and cabins were built. Another colony was established on Dauphin Island, and Bienville was appointed governor. He moved the government to Fort Louis de la Mobile—named in honor of both the French king and the Maubila tribe—at the 27th-mile bluff on the Mobile River. The first year was beset with hardships, and the settlers had to depend on store ships from France for their food.

However, new immigrants began arriving. The Pelican arrived from Canada in 1704, bringing soldiers, prelates, missionaries, and nuns, and also 24 girls chosen by the bishop of Quebec to become wives of the colonists. In a month all but one had found husbands, and within a year the first French child was born in the colony. In 1710 floods caused Bienville to move the colony to its present site at Mobile where Fort Condé, later called Fort Charlotte, was erected. Shortly thereafter, Bienville was removed as governor and replaced by the haughty and inept Antoine de la Mothe Cadillac.

Mobile was the capital of Louisiana Territory until 1721, when the capital was moved to New Orleans. Its prosperity was assured when two ships brought 600 slaves in that same year. The town was wiped out in 1733 by a hurricane and an epidemic. Mobile was ceded to the British by the Treaty of Paris in 1763, and Fort Condé was renamed Fort Charlotte. Two years later Mobile was the site of the Choctaw-Chickasaw Congress held among tribal officials and the British.

Mobile fell under its third flag in 1780 when the Spanish commander Bernardo de Galvez brought the Spanish fleet into the harbor, forced its surrender, and occupied the town. Mobile remained under Spanish rule until 1813. Although Alabama, as part of the Mississippi Territory, had been ceded to the United States in 1799, it was not relinquished by the Spaniards until U.S. General Wilkinson, using the War of 1812 as a pretext, seized the town.

Mobile was granted a town charter in 1814 and a city charter in 1819, shortly after Alabama was admitted to the Union. Fort Charlotte was dismantled in 1820. In the early years of the 19th century, Mobile suffered a number of natural disasters and pestilences—fire in 1827 and 1839, and a yellow fever epidemic in 1853. During the Civil War, Mobile was one of the targets of Union naval forces. Mobile Bay was so thoroughly fortified and mined that Admiral David G. Farragut was not able to break its defenses until August 1864. In addition to Fort Morgan at Mobile Point, Fort Gaines on Dauphin Island, and Fort Powell at Grant Pass, the city had three lines of defense consisting of 50 redoubts and 19 bastioned forts. Ten batteries commanded the entrance to the channel. After Farragut established his position in the bay, Fort Morgan continued to hold out until siege guns were brought from New Orleans and a full-scale bombardment subdued it. Mobile finally fell to the Union forces in March 1865. At the end of the war a tremendous ammunitions explosion caused massive destruction.

The post–Civil War history of the city is one of rapid expansion as a port and railroad junction. In 1915 the opening of a system of locks and dams built by the U.S. Army Corps of Engineers—the Tennessee-Tombigbee Waterway—was a major event in the history and economy of Mobile. Cochrane Bridge across Mobile Bay was completed in 1927.

Historical Landmarks

Mobile has preserved several historical areas. The Old Dauphin Way District is a neighborhood of restored cottages and mansions from the 19th century. The Church Street East Historic District suffered from fires in 1827 and 1839 that destroyed much of the Spanish architecture. Nevertheless, a community of structures sprang up in various styles, including Greek Revival and Italianate. An example is the house of Admiral Raphael Semmes. He was the commander of the CSS *Alabama*, which was sunk in Mobile Bay. The Oakleigh Garden Historic District is composed of homes built after the Civil War and

Chronology

1559 Tristan de Luna establishes a Spanish settlement here.

1699 Pierre le Moyne, Sieur d'Iberville, and Jean-Baptiste le Moyne, Sieur de Bienville, are commissioned by Louis XIV to establish a colony on Mobile Bay. Colonies are established in Biloxi and on Dauphin Island.

1702 Bienville is appointed governor of the Dauphin Island colony. He moves his government to Fort Louis de la Mobile on the Mobile River.

1704 The Pelican arrives from Quebec bringing new immigrants, prelates, missionaries, nuns, and 24 girls chosen by the bishop of Quebec to become wives of the colonists.

1710 Floods cause the removal of the colony to its present site in Mobile, where Fort Condé is erected. Bienville is replaced as governor by Antoine de la Mothe Cadillac.

1721 The capital of Louisiana Territory is shifted from Mobile to New Orleans. Two ships arrive, bringing 600 slaves.

1733 Town is hit by a cyclone and an epidemic.

1763 Mobile is ceded to the British by the Treaty of Paris.

1780 Bernardo de Galvez seizes and occupies the town.

1799 Mississippi Territory is ceded to the United States, but Mobile remains in Spanish hands.

1813 U.S. General Wilkinson seizes Mobile.

1814 Mobile is incorporated as a town.

1819 Mobile is chartered as a city.

1827 Fire destroys part of city.

1839 Fire destroys part of city.

1852 Mobile establishes public school system.

1853 Mobile is ravaged by yellow fever epidemic.

1864 Admiral Farragut subdues the Confederate fleet in Mobile harbor.

1865 Mobile falls to Union forces.

1915 Opening of Tennessee-Tombigbee Waterway.

1927 Cochrane Bridge across Mobile Bay is completed.

particularly during Reconstruction. The DeTonti Square Historic District, named for an early French explorer of the Mobile area, is the oldest residential section in Mobile. In addition to these historic quarters, there are other landmarks in the city. Barton Academy is Mobile's oldest educational institution; following the Civil War, it was used as a Union hospital. Fort Condé is a reconstructed French fort built near Mobile from 1724 until 1735. The Magnolia Cemetery was started in 1836 and 30 years later named a national cemetery. Buried there are the bodies of the crew of the Confederate craft *Hunley*, considered the first submarine, and the son of Apache Indian Geronimo. Moored just east of Blakely Island is the USS *Alabama*, which saw service during World War II.

Population

Mobile has suffered a slight decline from its peak population of 200,452 in 1980 to 196,278 in 1990. Demographically, the city experienced its greatest surge in the 1970s when population grew by 5.5%.

Population		
	1980	*1990*
Central City	200,452	196,278
Rank	71	79
Metro Area	443,536	476,923
Pop. Change 1980–1990	-4,174	
Pop. % Change 1980–1990	-2.1	
Median Age	32.5	
% Male	46.4	
% Age 65 and Over	13.7	
Density (per square mile)	1,663	

Households	
Number	75,442
Persons per Household	2.53
% Female-Headed Households	18.3
% One-Person Households	28.4
Births—Total	3,332
% to Mothers under 20	17.3
Birth Rate per 1,000	16.3

Ethnic Composition

Whites make up 59.62%, blacks 38.93%, American Indians 0.23%, Asians and Pacific Islanders 1.01%, and others 0.21%.

Ethnic Composition (as % of total pop.)		
	1980	*1990*
White	62.75	59.62
Black	36.20	38.93
American Indian	0.18	0.23
Asian and Pacific Islander	0.48	1.01
Hispanic	1.13	1.02
Other	NA	0.21

Government

Mobile reverted to a mayor-council form of government in 1985 after being run by a team of three commissioners, each of whom served 16-months of a four-year office term.

Government

Year of Home Charter   NA
Number of Members of the Governing Body   7
  Elected at Large   1
  Elected by Wards   6
Number of Women in Governing Body   2
Salary of Mayor $65,000
Salary of Council Members $1,000
City Government Employment Total   2,170
Rate per 10,000   106.8

Public Finance

The annual budget consists of revenues of $155.143 million and expenditures of $144.901 million. The debt outstanding is $588.552 million, and cash and security holdings $414.084 million.

Public Finance

Total Revenue (in millions) $155.143
Intergovernmental Revenue—Total (in millions) $7.02
Federal Revenue per Capita   NA
% Federal Assistance   NA
% State Assistance   3.28
Sales Tax as % of Total Revenue   42.02
Local Revenue as % of Total Revenue   89.43
City Income Tax   no
Taxes—Total (in millions) $55.7

Taxes per Capita
  Total $274
  Property $25
  Sales and Gross Receipts $179
General Expenditures—Total (in millions) $94.3
General Expenditures per Capita $464
Capital Outlays per Capita $44

% of Expenditures for:
  Public Welfare   0.0
  Highways   4.3
  Education   0.0
  Health and Hospitals   0.4
  Police   12.3
  Sewerage and Sanitation   14.0
  Parks and Recreation   4.6
  Housing and Community Development   0.0
Debt Outstanding per Capita $2,228
  % Utility   14.9
Federal Procurement Contract Awards (in millions) $77.3
Federal Grants Awards (in millions) $27.2
Fiscal Year Begins   October 1

Economy

Mobile survived the collapse of big oil companies in the 1980s by holding onto small businesses and a solid manufacturing sector. The two largest companies in the area are Scott Paper and International Paper. Other companies that do business in Mobile include Ciba-Geigy, Teledyne Continental Motors, and Bender Shipbuilding and Repair. The Port of Mobile, aided by the Tennessee-Tombigbee Waterway, has become a leading harbor of commerce. The 234-mile canal, built by the U.S. Army Corps of Engineers, connects the Tennessee River with the Tombigbee River, which ultimately feeds into the Mobile River. The Port of Mobile is its main terminal.

Economy

Total Money Income (in millions) $1,963.0
% of State Average   111.3
Per Capita Annual Income $9,658
% Population below Poverty Level   18.6
Fortune 500 Companies   NA

Banks	Number	Deposits (in millions)
Commercial	9	17,000
Savings	5	4,000

Passenger Autos   255,842
Electric Meters   205,000
Gas Meters   90,000

Manufacturing

Number of Establishments   228
% with 20 or More Employees   26.8
Manufacturing Payroll (in millions) $354.3
Value Added by Manufacture (in millions) $1,430.8
Value of Shipments (in millions) $2,526.6
New Capital Expenditures (in millions) $100.3

Wholesale Trade

Number of Establishments   607
Sales (in millions) $2,173.4
Annual Payroll (in millions) $153.130

Retail Trade

Number of Establishments   2,303
Total Sales (in millions) $1,816.9
Sales per Capita $8,939
Number of Retail Trade Establishments with Payroll   1,661
Annual Payroll (in millions) $215.6
Total Sales (in millions) $1,787.3
General Merchandise Stores (per capita) $1,298
Food Stores (per capita) $1,506
Apparel Stores (per capita) $497
Eating and Drinking Places (per capita) $833

Service Industries

Total Establishments   1,904
Total Receipts (in millions) $832.8
Hotels and Motels (in millions) $30.3
Health Services (in millions) $332.2
Legal Services (in millions)   NA

Labor

Trade is the largest employment sector and overshadows even services and government. Manufacturing is a smaller sector than in comparable cities. Public employment, including that in the University of South Alabama, is a major stabilizing factor.

Labor

Civilian Labor Force   95,409
% Change 1989–1990   -0.8

Work Force Distribution
  Mining   NA

Labor (continued)

Construction   12,000
Manufacturing   28,400
Transportation and Public Utilities   11,300
Wholesale and Retail Trade   47,500
FIRE (Finance, Insurance, Real Estate)   7,900
Service   45,300
Government   31,400
Women as % of Labor Force   43.3
% Self-Employed   5.2
% Professional/Technical   17.6
Total Unemployment   6,771
Rate %   7.1
Federal Government Civilian Employment   2,321

Education

The Mobile County Public Schools System, the oldest in the state, supports 51 elementary schools, 20 junior high/middle schools, and 15 senior high schools. The public school system is supplemented by an extensive parochial school system consisting of 56 schools in which over 12,000 pupils are enrolled. Higher education is offered in one public institution, the University of South Alabama; one Southern Baptist institution, Mobile College; and one Catholic institution, Spring Hill College (the oldest college in the state and the third oldest Jesuit institution in the nation).

Education

Number of Public Schools   87
Special Education Schools   1
Total Enrollment   67,286
% Enrollment in Private Schools   14.5
% Minority   47.5
Classroom Teachers   3,400
Pupil-Teacher Ratio   19.8:1
Number of Graduates   2,872
Total Revenue (in millions) $178.709
Total Expenditures (in millions) $152.071
Expenditures per Pupil $2,099
Educational Attainment (Age 25 and Over)
    % Completed 12 or More Years   67.1
    % Completed 16 or More Years   17.0
Four-Year Colleges and Universities   3
    Enrollment   14,214
Two-Year Colleges   4
    Enrollment   4,308

Libraries

Number   13
Public Libraries   6
Books (in thousands)   380
Circulation (in thousands)   1,125
Persons Served (in thousands)   389
Circulation per Person Served   2.89
Income (in millions) $4.222
Staff   104

Four-Year Colleges and Universities
    University of South Alabama
    Mobile College
    Spring Hill College

Health

Mobile has eight hospitals. The largest is the University of South Alabama's (USA) Medical Center and College of Medicine, which recently acquired Doctor's Hospital and Knollwood Park Hospital. USA also has a women's and children's hospital and a burn center. Providence Hospital and Health Care Center is a 135-year-old institution run by the Daughters of Charity. Springhill Memorial Hospital was founded in the late 1970s and has expanded its range of services rapidly. Mercy Medical Hospital, located in Daphne, was founded in 1949 by the Daughters of Mercy.

Health

Deaths—Total   1,949
Rate per 1,000   9.5
Infant Deaths—Total   37
Rate per 1,000   11.1
Number of Metro Hospitals   8
Number of Metro Hospital Beds   2,005
Rate per 100,000   986
Number of Physicians   856
Physicians per 1,000   1.95
Nurses per 1,000   11.02
Health Expenditures per Capita $4.36

Transportation

Two interstate highways service Mobile: I-10 comes from the south and, just south of downtown Mobile, heads east across Mobile Bay toward Pensacola, Florida; I-65, an offshoot of I-10, cuts through the heart of the city. U.S. highways 31, 43, 45, 90, and 98 also meet at the city. Two air terminals serve the city: Mobile Municipal Airport to the west, handling several major and commuter airlines, and Brookley Airport in the southeast, from which charter flights originate. Rail passenger service is provided by Amtrak, and freight rail service is by the Burlington Northern, Illinois Central, and Norfolk-Southern railroads, as well as CSX Transportation. The Port of Mobile is the U.S. leader in steel exports.

Transportation

Interstate Highway Mileage   40
Total Urban Mileage   1,688
Total Daily Vehicle Mileage (in millions)   7.166
Daily Average Commute Time   51.7 min.
Number of Buses   39
Port Tonnage (in millions)   36.476
Airports   1
Number of Daily Flights   22
Daily Average Number of Passengers   986

Airlines (American carriers only)
    American
    Continental
    Delta
    Eastern
    Northwest
    USAir

Housing

Of the total housing stock, 58.1% is owner-occupied. The median value of an owner-occupied home is $55,400 and the median monthly rent $248.

Housing

Total Housing Units   82,817
% Change 1980–1990   8.7
Vacant Units for Sale or Rent   5,652
Occupied Units   75,442
% with More Than One Person per Room   3.9
% Owner-Occupied   58.1
Median Value of Owner-Occupied Homes $55,400
Average Monthly Purchase Cost $298
Median Monthly Rent $248
New Private Housing Starts   366
Value (in thousands) $31,088
% Single-Family   100.0
Nonresidential Buildings Value (in thousands) $13,607

Urban Redevelopment

Mobile has witnessed considerable urban redevelopment activity in recent years, including the development of a $50-million convention center, a $45-million county/city government complex, completion of a new airport, construction of a naval station, a commerce park, and replacement of the Cochrane Bridge over Mobile River.

Crime

Mobile ranks below the national average in public safety. It experienced 3,553 violent crimes and 18,165 property crimes in 1991.

Crime

Violent Crimes—Total   3,553
Violent Crime Rate per 100,000   8,090
Murder   40
Rape   151
Robbery   994
Aggravated Assaults   5,307
Property Crimes   18,165
Burglary   5,743
Larceny   11,433
Motor Vehicle Theft   1,882
Arson   44
Per Capita Police Expenditures $89.87
Per Capita Fire Protection Expenditures $62.53
Number of Police   294
Per 1,000   1.42

Religion

There are 388 churches representing 44 denominations. Overall, 69.5% of the residents belong to religious denominations.

Religion

Largest Denominations (Adherents)
Catholic	37,801
Southern Baptist	100,733

Religion (continued)

Black Baptist	39,680
United Methodist	24,401
American Zion	14,694
Episcopal	5,978
Church of God	7,093
Assembly of God	5,881
Presbyterian	4,043
Jewish	873

Media

Mobile's press is represented by a lone daily, the *Mobile Press-Register*. The city's electronic media consist of 6 television stations and 16 AM and FM radio stations.

Media

Newsprint
  Mobile Beacon, weekly
  Mobile Press-Register, daily

Television
  WALA (Channel 10)
  WEAR (Channel 3)
  WEIQ (Channel 42)
  WKRG (Channel 5)
  WMPV (Channels 21 & 45))
  WPMI (Channel 15)

Radio
WABB (AM)	WABB (FM)
WAVH (FM)	WBHY (AM)
WBHY (FM)	WBLX (AM)
WBLX (FM)	WDLT (FM)
WGOK (AM)	WHIL (FM)
WKRG (AM)	WKRG (FM)
WKSJ (AM)	WKSJ (FM)
WLPR (AM)	WMOB (AM)

Sports

Mobile has no major professional sports team.

Arts, Culture, and Tourism

The key arts hub is the Mobile Civic Center, which has a 10,680-seat arena, a 1,937-seat theater, and a 3,500-seat exposition hall to host various arts and musical performances. Other arts centers include the Mobile Theater Guild, the Entertainment Dinner Theatre, the Joe Jefferson Players, the Mobile Ballet, the Mobile Chamber Music Society, the Pixie Playhouse, the Children's Musical Theatre, and the Saenger Theatre. Musical performances are provided by the Symphony Concerts of Mobile and the Mobile Jazz Festival, which is held every April. Museums include the Battleship Alabama Memorial Park; the Museum of the City of Mobile, located in the Bernstein-Bush House, an Italian-style townhouse built in 1872; historic Fort Condé, a restored French fort built between 1724 and 1735; and the Eichold-Heustis Medical Museum, a collection that documents medical history through exhibits and artifacts.

Travel and Tourism
Hotel Rooms   6,869
Convention and Exhibit Space (square feet)   NA
Convention Centers
Municipal Auditorium Complex
Convention Center
Festivals
Mardi Gras
Azalea Trail Festival (winter)
Metro Mobile Allied Arts Festival
Blakeley Battle Festival
Mobile Jazz Festival
Alabama State Shrimp Festival
Greater Gulf State Fair
Mobile International Festival

Parks and Recreation

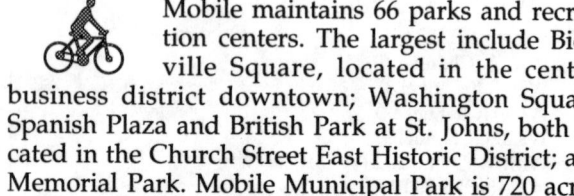 Mobile maintains 66 parks and recreation centers. The largest include Bienville Square, located in the central business district downtown; Washington Square; Spanish Plaza and British Park at St. Johns, both located in the Church Street East Historic District; and Memorial Park. Mobile Municipal Park is 720 acres, while Blakely State Park is located on the site of a Civil War battle. Dauphin Island, an hour south of Mobile, is lined with beaches and has a bird sanctuary.

Sources of Further Information

City Hall
111 South Royal Street
Mobile, AL 36602
(205) 434-7411

Mobile Area Chamber of Commerce
451 Government Street
Mobile, AL 36652
(205) 433-6951

Mobile Convention and Visitors Bureau
1 St. Louis Center
Mobile, AL 36602
(800) 666-6282

Additional Reading

Amos, Harriet E. *Cotton City: Urban Development in Antebellum Mobile.* 1987.
Delaney, Caldwell. *Confederate Mobile: A Pictorial History.* 1971.
Gould, Elizabeth B. *From Port to Fort: An Architectural History of Mobile.* 1988.
Howard, Annie S. *Iron Lace: Mobile.* 1950.

Montpelier

Vermont

Location and Topography

N

Montpelier, the capital of Vermont and the smallest state capital in the nation, sits on both banks of the Winooski (once the Onion) River and along the North Branch River in the north-central part of the state. The city's name apparently comes from the French translation of its topography: Mont (French for hill) and peler (French for to strip or make bald). The main city in the Green Mountains, Montpelier lies in a valley with wooded hills.

Layout of City and Suburbs

Because of its small size, Montpelier has few main thoroughfares. Much of the city's business is conducted on three streets: Main, Elm, and State. The city is laid out like a quaint New England village, with small brick houses lining the streets. The state capitol building is situated on State Street.

Environment

Environmental Stress Index   NA
Green Cities Index: Rank   NA
                    Score   NA
Water Quality   Neutral, hard, fluoridated
    Average Daily Use (gallons per capita)   NA
    Maximum Supply (gallons per capita)   NA
Parkland as % of Total City Area   NA
% Waste Landfilled/Recycled   NA
Annual Parks Expenditures per Capita   NA

Climate

The city enjoys a typical four-season Vermont climate, with average temperatures in the teens in January and in the seventies in July. The average precipitation is 34 inches of rain and 101 inches of snow.

Weather

Temperature

Highest Monthly Average °F   52.0
Lowest Monthly Average °F   32.2

Annual Averages

Days 32°F or Below   173
Days above 90°F   2
Zero Degree Days   29
Precipitation (inches)   33.94

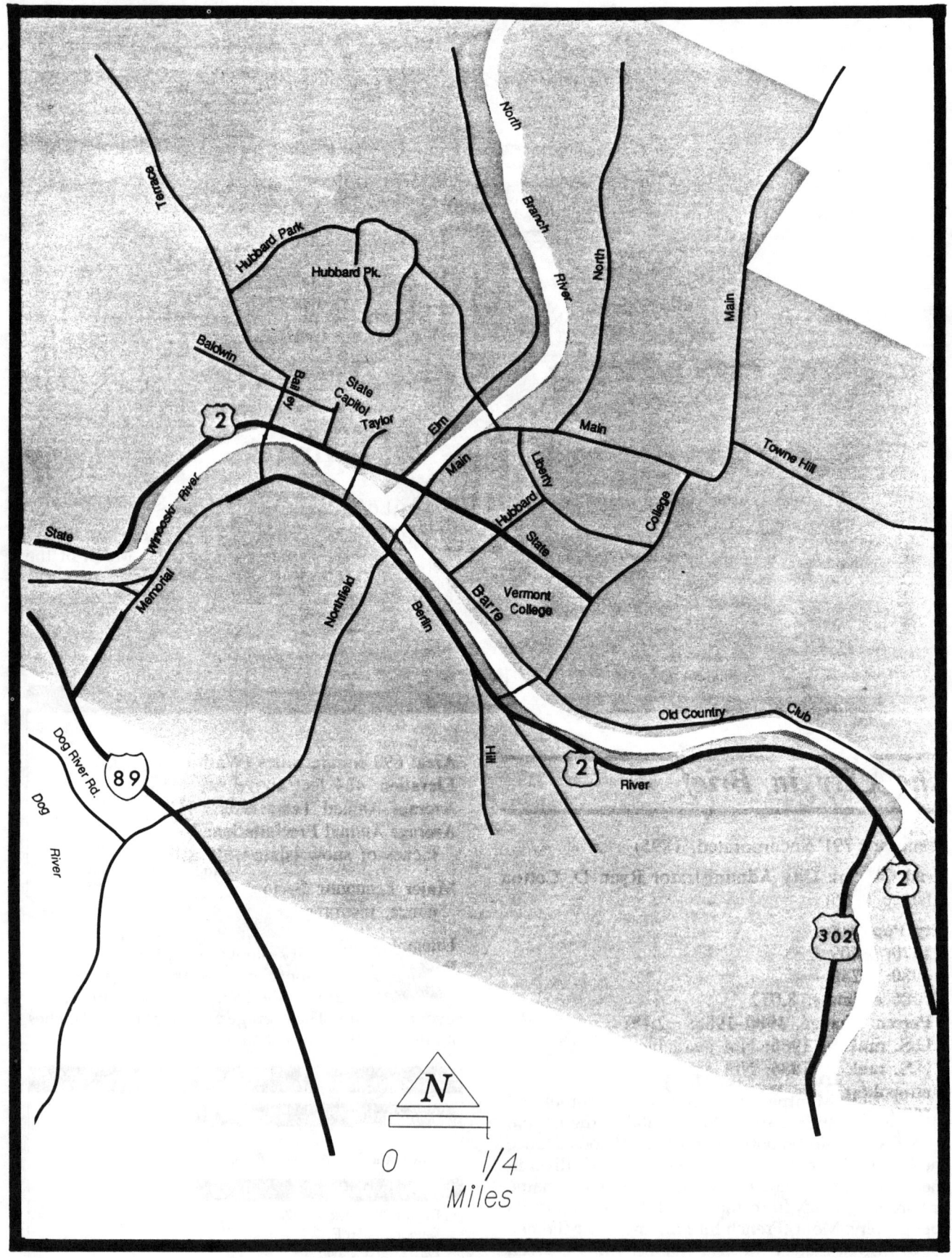

Weather (continued)

Snow (inches)   100.5
% Seasonal Humidity   NA
Wind Speed (m.p.h.)   NA
Clear Days   NA
Cloudy Days   NA
Storm Days   NA
Rainy Days   NA

Average Temperatures (°F)	High	Low	Mean
January	24.9	6.3	15.6
February	27.1	7.7	17.4
March	36.5	19.1	27.8
April	50.5	31.1	40.8
May	64.5	41.6	53.1
June	73.3	50.9	62.1
July	77.9	55.2	66.6
August	75.3	53.1	64.2
September	67.2	45.6	56.4
October	56.2	36.1	46.2
November	42.2	27.1	34.6
December	28.9	12.4	20.6

History

The region that is now the city of Montpelier was once the hunting grounds of the Abnaki Indians, who called the great river that ran through the area Winooski, meaning "wild onion." The waterway was later called the Onion River, although today it has reverted to its original name. The city was the brainchild of Colonel Jacob Davis, a Revolutionary War veteran and pioneer settler in central Vermont. In 1781 Davis received a charter from the colony of Vermont to start two towns, to both of which he gave French names; Montpelier and Calais were born. Over the next several years, he and his family cleared land near the Onion (Winooski) River and down present-day State Street. In 1791, Vermont became the first state (after the original 13) to be admitted to the Union. After some battling, Colonel Davis's struggling pioneer settlement of Montpelier was selected as the state capital in 1805. His son Thomas donated a strip of land on State Street for a capitol building, which was completed in 1808.

Originally, the small town ventured its economic success on the extraction of salt that lay beneath the city, but the removal process proved too unwieldy. The discovery of granite quarries in nearby Barre created vast, profitable opportunities for the area as a whole. In the 1830s, granite by the ton was moved to Montpelier for a new capitol building. This second structure, completed in 1836, suffered a destructive fire in 1857. Surviving portions of the building, primarily the granite walls, were incorporated in the third and present capitol, which opened in 1859.

Montpelier's success during the latter part of the 1800s came from its central location, the granite quarries in Barre, and the coming of the railroads, which heightened business activity. In 1895, Montpelier officially attained the status of a city. The famed Winooski floods of 1927 led to the building of dams along the waterway. The 20th century has seen growth in the areas of insurance, commerce, and government, holding the city together economically but, as one guide explained, discouraging "large city" development.

Historical Landmarks

The capitol building on State Street dominates the skyline of Montpelier. Its 14-carat gold-leaf dome (made of copper-covered wood) is topped by a 14-foot wooden statue of Ceres, the Roman goddess of agriculture. The walls are made of Barre granite, and the building is graced by a Doric portico. Designed in 1836 by Ammi B. Young and based on the Grecian temple of Theseus, the structure was nearly destroyed by fire in 1857; the granite walls were basically all that survived. The present edifice was completed in 1859. The Pavilion Building on State Street is the home of the Vermont Historical Society. Originally a hotel built in the first decade of the 19th century, it has just recently been restored to its original appearance. The boyhood home of Admiral George Dewey, hero of the Spanish-American War of 1898, is located on State Street. Dewey's father Julius, a doctor, was the founder of the National Life Insurance Company of Vermont, which has its offices on State Street.

Population

Montpelier is the least populous of the 50 state capitals, with a 1990 population of 8,247.

Population		
	1980	1990
Central City	8,609	8,247
Rank	NA	NA
Metro Area	NA	55,000
Pop. Change 1980–1990 –362		
Pop. % Change 1980–1990 –4.2		
Median Age 36.3		
% Male 46.1		
% Age 65 and Over 15.34		
Density (per square mile) 778		

Ethnic Composition

The town is racially homogeneous, with whites constituting 98.18%.

Ethnic Composition (as % of total pop.)		
	1980	1990
White	NA	98.18
Black	NA	0.45
American Indian	NA	0.30
Asian and Pacific Islander	NA	0.95
Hispanic	NA	1.42
Other	NA	0.12

Government

Montpelier operates under a council-administrator form of government. Six aldermen, elected to two-year terms, elect a part-time mayor and appoint a city administrator for an unspecified term.

Chronology

1781   Colonel Jacob Davis, a Revolutionary War veteran and pioneer settler of central Vermont, is awarded a charter to found the twin villages of Montpelier and Calais.

1788–
1791   Davis, his family, and other settlers clear the land along the Onion (Winooski) River and along what is now State Street.

1791   Vermont is admitted to the Union as the 14th state. A battle ensues to choose a permanent state capital.

1805   Montpelier is named Vermont's permanent capital. Building commences on a capitol situated on land donated by the Davis family.

1808   The first state capitol building is completed.

1836   Crude and poorly built, the first capitol building is demolished. Architect Ammi B. Young designs the second structure.

1857   The second capitol building is ruined by fire. Portions survive and are incorporated in the third capitol.

1859   Third capitol building completed.

1895   Montpelier attains the status of a city.

1927   The Winooski River floods, causing considerable damage to the city, and leads to the construction of dams along the river.

Public Finance

The 1992 city budget was balanced, with revenues and expenditures of $12.683 million. Propery and school taxes constitute 75% of revenues, and school expenditures account for two-thirds of total expenditures.

Government

Year of Home Charter	1894
Number of Members of the Governing Body	7
Elected at Large	NA
Elected by Wards	7
Number of Women in Governing Body	3
Salary of Mayor	NA
Salary of Council Members	NA
City Government Employment Total	NA
Rate per 10,000	NA

Economy

The economy of the city is dominated by state and local government activities, banking, and the business of the National Life Insurance Company of Vermont. The downtown zone is dominated by small shops and businesses.

Economy

Total Money Income (in millions)	NA	
% of State Average	NA	
Per Capita Annual Income	$10,749	
% Population below Poverty Level	NA	
Fortune 500 Companies	NA	
Banks	*Number*	*Deposits (in millions)*
Commercial	9	NA
Savings	NA	NA
Passenger Autos	NA	
Electric Meters	8,052	
Gas Meters	1,600	

Labor

According to a study conducted by the Corporation for Enterprise Development, Montpelier has a vigorous business climate based on high capital investment, low business failure rate, high percentage of female proprietors, diversified business base, high productivity, and stable employment rates. Most of the new jobs in the 1990s will be in the services sector.

Education

The public school system consists of one high school, one middle school, and one elementary school, all under the direction of the Board of School Commissioners and a superintendent. There is one parochial elementary school. Montpelier is home to the New England Culinary Institute, the Montpelier campus of Vermont State College, Community College of Vermont, and Woodbury College.

Education

Number of Public Schools	4
Special Education Schools	NA
Total Enrollment	1,250
% Enrollment in Private Schools	NA
% Minority	NA
Classroom Teachers	NA
Pupil-Teacher Ratio	16:1
Number of Graduates	NA
Total Revenue (in millions)	NA
Total Expenditures (in millions)	NA
Expenditures per Pupil	NA
Educational Attainment (Age 25 and Over)	NA
% Completed 12 or More Years	NA
% Completed 16 or More Years	NA
Four-Year Colleges and Universities	1
Enrollment	NA
Two-Year Colleges	NA
Enrollment	NA

Libraries

Number	10
Public Libraries	1
Books (in thousands)	50
Circulation (in thousands)	180
Persons Served (in thousands)	8
Circulation per Person Served	17.42
Income (in millions)	$0.267
Staff	5

Four-Year Colleges and Universities
  Vermont College

Health

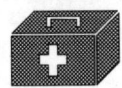

The principal medical facility is the 175-bed Central Vermont Hospital, located in Berlin. Heaton House is a 53-bed nursing facility operated by the Central Vermont Medical Center.

Health	
Deaths—Total	NA
Rate per 1,000	NA
Infant Deaths—Total	NA
Rate per 1,000	NA
Number of Metro Hospitals	NA
Number of Metro Hospital Beds	NA
Rate per 100,000	NA
Number of Physicians	NA
Physicians per 1,000	NA
Nurses per 1,000	NA
Health Expenditures per Capita	NA

Transportation

Montpelier is bisected by two highways, I-89 and U.S. 2. It is served by Amtrak's "Montrealer," which stops at Montpelier on its New York–Montreal run. The main airport is at Burlington, 35 miles northwest.

Transportation	
Interstate Highway Mileage	NA
Total Urban Mileage	NA
Total Daily Vehicle Mileage (in millions)	NA
Daily Average Commute Time	NA
Number of Buses	NA
Port Tonnage (in millions)	NA
Airports	NA
Number of Daily Flights	NA
Daily Average Number of Passengers	NA

Housing

Most construction is in the business sector; housing stock is relatively old and has expanded only modestly in recent years.

Housing	
Total Housing Units	3,769
% Change 1980–1990	NA
Vacant Units for Sale or Rent	NA
Occupied Units	NA
% with More Than One Person per Room	NA
% Owner-Occupied	56.8
Median Value of Owner-Occupied Homes	$96,200
Average Monthly Purchase Cost	NA
Median Monthly Rent	$353
New Private Housing Starts	NA
Value (in thousands)	NA
% Single-Family	NA

Urban Redevelopment

Major redevelopment projects in the 1980s were the $22.5-million expansion of the National Life Insurance Company and $16-million expansion of state government buildings.

Crime

Montpelier has an insignificant crime rate. The city has a 31-employee police department and 45-employee fire department.

Religion

Protestants predominate in numbers, but there is a substantial Catholic minority.

Religion	
Largest Denominations (Adherents)	
Catholic	12,145
United Methodist	3,664
United Church of Christ	2,216
Episcopal	886
Presbyterian	413
Unitarian	537
American Baptist	436
Jewish	500

Media

The printed media in Montpelier consists solely of the daily *Barre-Montpelier Times-Argus*, published in the evenings on weekdays and in the mornings on weekends. The electronic media are made up of two radio stations.

Media	
Newsprint	
Barre-Montpelier Times-Argus, daily	
Television	
None	
Radio	
WNCS (FM)	WSKI (AM)

Sports

There are no professional sports teams in Montpelier.

Arts, Culture, and Tourism

The Onion River Arts Council presents performances by touring companies at City Hall. From September through March, Vermont College holds monthly chamber con-

Travel and Tourism	
Hotel Rooms	NA
Convention and Exhibit Space (square feet)	NA
Convention Centers	
NA	
Festivals	
Vermont Dairy Celebration (June)	
Vermont Apple Celebration (October)	
Festival of Vermont Crafts (October)	

certs. The Vermont Museum is located on the first floor of the former National Life Insurance Company building. The T. W. Wood Art Gallery at Vermont College offers permanent exhibits by Wood, a noted Civil War–era artist.

Parks and Recreation

Montpelier is located in the heart of a ski and mountain resort area, and offers an unusual variety of recreational opportunities. The 134-acre Hubbard Park, a gift to the city in 1899, is noted for its tower.

Sources of Further Information

Vermont Chamber of Commerce
P.O. Box 37
Montpelier, VT 05601
(802) 223-3443

Vermont Department of Travel & Tourism
134 State Street
Montpelier, VT 05602
(802) 828-3236

Additional Reading

Montpelier, the Capital City. 1990.

THE
Little
Country

Other books by

CHARLES DE LINT:

The Riddle of the Wren (1984)

Moonheart (1984)

The Harp of the Grey Rose
(1985)

Mulengro (1985)

Yarrow (1986)

Ascian in Rose (1987)

Jack, the Giant-Killer (1987)

Greenmantle (1988)

Wolf Moon (1988)

Svaha (1989)

Westlin Wind (1989)

The Valley of Thunder (1989)

Berlin (1989)

The Hidden City (1990)

The Fair in Emain Macha (1990)

Drink Down the Moon (1990)

Ghostwood (1990)

The Dreaming Place (1990)

Angel of Darkness (1990)

THE

Little

Country

CHARLES DE LINT

William Morrow
and Company, Inc.

NEW YORK

Library of Congress Cataloging-in-Publication Data

De Lint, Charles, 1951-
The little country / Charles de Lint.
    p.   cm.
ISBN 0-688-10366-9
I. Title.
PR9199.3.D357L58   1991
813'.54—dc20   90-42717
                                                                   CIP

Printed in the United States of America

First Edition

1   2   3   4   5   6   7   8   9   10

BOOK DESIGN BY BARBARA BACHMAN

f o r

DON FLAMANCK and COLIN WILSON
two wise Cornishmen

and for all those traditional musicians
who, wittingly or unwittingly,
but with great good skill,
still seek to recapture that first music

Acknowledgments

Grateful acknowledgments are made to:

Robin Williamson for permission to use a portion of "Five Denials on Merlin's Grave" from the book of the same title published by Pig's Whisker Music Press; copyright © 1979 by Robin Williamson. For further information on Robin Williamson, write: Pig's Whisker Music Press, P.O. Box 27522, Los Angeles, CA 90027; or Pig's Whisker Music Press, BCM 4797, London WC1N 3XX, England.

James P. Blaylock for the use of the quote from *Land of Dreams*, Arbor House; copyright © 1987 by James P. Blaylock.

Paul Hazel for the use of the quote from *Undersea*, Atlantic, Little, Brown; copyright © 1982 by Paul Hazel.

Carrie Fisher for the use of the quote from *Postcards from the Edge*, Simon and Schuster; copyright © 1987 by Carrie Fisher.

Margaret Mahy for the use of the quote from *Memory*, J. M. Dent & Sons; copyright © 1987 by Margaret Mahy.

Hilbert Schenck for the use of the quote from *Chronosequence*, Tor; copyright © 1988 by Hilbert Schenck.

Tom Robbins for the use of the quote from *Jitterbug Perfume*, Bantam; copyright © 1984 by Tibetan Peach Pie Incorporated.

Susan Palwick for the use of the quote from "*The Last Unicorn*: Magic as Metaphor," which first appeared in *The New York Review of Science Fiction*, February 1989; copyright © 1989 by Dragon Press, reprinted by permission of the author.

Russell Hoban for the use of the quote from *The Medusa Frequency*, Viking; copyright © 1987 by Russell Hoban.

Matt Ruff for the use of the quote from *Fool on the Hill*, Atlantic Monthly Press; copyright © 1988 by Matt Ruff.

Ian Watson for the use of the quote from "The Mole Field," *The Magazine of Fantasy and Science Fiction*, December 1988; copyright © 1988 by Mercury Press Inc., reprinted by permission of the author.

Robert Holdstock for the use of the quote from *Lavondyss*, Victor Gollancz Ltd., 1988; copyright © 1988 by Robert Holdstock.

Colin Wilson for the quote from *Beyond the Occult*, Bantam Press, 1988; copyright © 1988 by Colin Wilson.

Jack Dann for the quote from "Night Meetings," *Velocities: A Magazine of Speculative Poetry* #4, Summer 1984; copyright © 1984 by Jack Dann; all rights reserved; reprinted by permission of the author.

Contents

· CONTENTS · 10 ·

Author's Note

T h e novel that follows is a work of fiction. All characters and events in this book are fictitious and any resemblance to actual persons living or dead is purely coincidental.

The tune titles heading each chapter are all traditional, except for "Leppadumdowledum," which was composed by Donal Lunny; "So There I Was," composed by John Kirkpatrick; and "Absurd Good News." Musicians interested in tracking down the tunes should look for them in the usual sources—tunebooks, old and new, but especially in the repertoire of musicians, whether recorded or in live performance and sessions; those tunes credited to Janey Little have been transcribed and can be found in the appendix at the end of the novel for the hopeful enjoyment of interested players.

A work such as this doesn't grow out of a vacuum. *The Little Country* had its origin in sources too exhaustive to list with any real thoroughness, but I can still pinpoint its original spark: many an evening in the early seventies spent listening to my friend Don Flamanck telling stories of Cornwall as he remembered it. When my wife MaryAnn and I finally went to Cornwall in October of 1988 to research this book's settings, we found it to be everything Don had promised it would be, and more.

Thanks are due to Don, first and foremost, for that inspiration, and also to Phil and Audrey Wallis of Mousehole for more wonderful stories and their hospitality; to Bernard Evans of Newlyn for filling me in on the local music scene; to Ben Batten, Christopher Bice, Des Hannigan, John Hocking, Robert Hunt, John and Nettie Pender, Derek Tangye, Douglas Tregenza, Ken Ward,

G. Pawley White, and a multitude of others too numerous to list here for background material; to Colin Wilson for his logical explorations of those things that defy logic; to those many, many traditional musicians, again too numerous to mention, who keep the music alive and give it new life with each note they play; to those musicians who attend the local music sessions here in Ottawa ("All of a Monday Night") and by their enthusiasm keep my own playing in right good fettle; and last, though not least, to my wife MaryAnn, a mean mandolin player in her own right, for her support, both musical and literary, and for her love that I could not do without.

—*Charles de Lint*

myself, a brat who . . .
couldn't figure numbers worth a damn
was always a chancer
and given three lines to add I'd put the middle row
down as the answer
but I could read all day if I could get away with it
and all night too with a flashlight under the covers
of that Green Man . . . or of Merlin of the borders. . . .

— ROBIN WILLIAMSON,
from "Five Denials on Merlin's Grave"

He wanted the sort of book that didn't seem to need a beginning
and end, that could be opened at any page without suffering for
it—slow, candlelight reading.

— JAMES P. BLAYLOCK,
from *Land of Dreams*

PART ONE

THE
Hidden
People

> Man has closed himself up, till he sees all things
> through the narrow chinks of his cavern.
>
> — WILLIAM BLAKE

> Underneath the reality in which we live and have our
> being, another and altogether different reality lies
> concealed.
>
> — FRIEDRICH NIETZSCHE

The Quarrelsome Piper

Like burrs old names get stuck to each other
and to anyone who walks among them.

— PAUL HAZEL,
from *Undersea*

There were two things Janey Little loved best in the world: music and books, and not necessarily in that order.

Her favorite musician was the late Billy Pigg, the Northumbrian piper from the northeast of England whose playing had inspired her to take up the small pipes herself as her principal instrument.

Her favorite author was William Dunthorn, and not just because he and her grandfather had been mates, though she did treasure the old sepia-toned photograph of the pair of them that she kept sealed in a plastic folder in her fiddle case. It had been taken just before the Second World War in their native Mousehole—confusingly pronounced "Mouzel" by the locals—two gangly Cornish lads standing in front of The Ship Inn, cloth caps in hand, shy grins on their faces.

Dunthorn had written three book-length works of fiction, but until that day in the Gaffer's attic when Janey was having a dusty time of it, ferreting through the contents of old boxes and chests, she knew of only two. The third was a secret book, published in an edition of just one copy.

The Hidden People was his best-known work, remembered by most readers with the same fondness that they recalled for *Winnie the Pooh*, *The Wind in the Willows*, and other classics of their childhood. It told of a hidden race of mouse-sized people known as the Smalls, reduced to their diminutive stature in the Middle Ages by a cranky old witch who died before her curse could be removed. Supposedly the Smalls prospered through the ages, living a hidden life alongside that of more normal-sized people right up to the present day. The book was still in print, in numerous illustrated editions, but Janey's favorite was still the one that contained Ernest Shepard's delightful pen and ink drawings.

The other novel was *The Lost Music*, published two years after the first. While it didn't have nearly the success of *The Hidden People*—due no doubt to its being less whimsical and the fact that it dealt with more adult themes—its theories of music being a key to hidden realms and secret states of mind had still made it a classic in the fantasy field. It too remained in print, though there were few children who would find a copy of it under their Christmas tree, illustrated by whichever artist was currently the nadir of children's book illustrating.

Which was really a pity, Janey often thought, because in the long run, *The Lost Music* was the better book. It was the reason that she had taken up with old things. Because of it, she went back to its sources, poring over folktales and myths, discovering traditional music and finding that the references between old lore and old tunes and songs went back and forth between each other. It was a delightful exploration, one that eventually led to her present occupation.

For while she had no interest in writing books, she had discovered, hidden away inside herself, a real flair for the old music. She took to playing the fiddle and went wandering through tunebooks tracked down in secondhand bookshops, the tunes sticking to her like brambles on a walk across a cliff-side field. Old tunes, old names, old stories. So Dunthorn was partially responsible for who she was today—a comment that made the Gaffer laugh when she mentioned it to him once.

"Wouldn't Billy smile to hear you say that now, my robin," her grandfather had said. "That his writings should turn a good Cornish girl to playing Paddy music for a living—not to mention traveling around by her ownsel' with nothing but a fiddle and a set of Scotch small pipes to keep her company."

"*You* like my music."

The Gaffer nodded. "And I don't doubt Bill would have liked it too—just as he liked his own writing. He'd sit up and scribble by the lantern till all hours of the night sometimes—took it all very seriously, didn't he just?—and he'd have admired your getting by with the doing of something you love.

"He always wanted to live by his writing—writing what he pleased, I mean—but all the bookmen wanted was more fairy tales. Bill . . . he had more serious stories to tell by then, so he worked the boats by day to earn his living and did his writing by night—for himself, like. He wouldn't give 'em another book like the one about the Smalls. Didn't want to be writing the same thing over and over again, was what he said."

"*The Lost Music* has fairy-tale bits in it."

"And doesn't it just, my beauty? But to hear him talk, they weren't made-up bits—just the way that history gets mixed up as the years go by. *The Lost Music* was his way of talking about the way he believed that old wives' tales and dance tunes and folktales were just the tangled echoes of something that's not quite of this world . . . something we all knew once, but have forgotten since. That's how he explained it to me, and very serious he was about it too. But then Bill had a way of making anything sound important—that was his gift, I think. For all I know he was serious about the Smalls too."

"You think he really believed in things like that?"

The Gaffer shrugged. "I'm not saying yes or no. He was a sensible lad, was Bill, and a good mate, but he was a bit fey too. Solid as the ground is firm, but ever so once in a while he'd get a funny look about him, like he'd just seen a piskie sticking its little brown head around the doorpost, and he wouldn't talk then for a while—at least he wouldn't say much that made sense. But I never heard a man not make sense so eloquently as Bill Dunthorn could when he was of a mind to do so, and there was more than once he had me half believing in what he was saying."

Dunthorn had also written essays, short stories, travelogues, and poetry, though none of those writings survived in current editions except for two of the short stories, which were constantly being reprinted in storybook collections for children: "The Smalls," which was the original version of *The Hidden People,* and "The Man Who Lived in a Book," a delightful romp about a world that existed inside a book that could be reached by placing a photograph of oneself between its pages. Janey could still remember all the times she'd put pictures of herself between the pages of her favorite books, in the very best parts, and gone to sleep, hoping to wake up in one of those magical realms.

"I could use that trick now," she murmured to herself as she brushed the dust and cobwebs from a chest that was thrust far back under the eaves of the attic.

She still couldn't believe that Alan had left her in the lurch the way he had. Right on the eve of a new tour of New England and California.

Things had not been going well between them this past summer, which just went to show you that one should pay more attention to the old adages because they were all based on a kernel of good solid common sense.

Never mix business and pleasure.

Well, of course. Except having a relationship with one's sideman seemed too perfect to not take advantage of it. Instead of leaving your lover behind, he went on tour with you. What could be better? No more lonely nights while your sideman went out with some guitar groupie and you were left alone in the hotel room because you just wanted to be *away* from the crowds for a change. Away from strangers. Away from having to put on a smiling face when you just wanted to be silly with a friend, or slouch in a corner and simply do nothing at all, without having to worry about what kind of an impression you made or left behind when you traveled on.

But relationships tended to erode if they weren't worked on, and Alan's and hers had been no exception. They'd become grouchy with each other on their last tour of the Continent.

Complaining, not with each other, but about each other. Mostly it was just little things, dissatisfactions and petty differences, but it began to affect the music until it got to the point where they couldn't work up a new arrangement of any sort without a row.

Argumentative was how Alan described her.

Perhaps she was. But she wouldn't see the music compromised. Improvising was fine, but not simply because he couldn't bother to remember an arrangement. And banging his guitar strings like they were horseshoes and his pick the hammer, that was right out. It was still her name on the tour posters. People came to see her play the music, and she meant to give them their money's worth. They hadn't come to see her sideman get soused and have evenings where he made the Pogues sound like brilliant musicians.

And that was the real heart of Alan's problem. They hadn't come to see Alan MacDonald; they'd come to see her.

"Oh, sod him," she said as she dragged the dusty chest out from under the eaves.

Her voice rang hollowly in the attic. She wondered what the Gaffer would think to hear her sitting up here, talking to herself, but she had the house to herself. He was up in Paul, at the King's Arms, having a few pints with his mates. Perhaps she should have gone. Chalkie Fisher would be there and if he'd brought along his box, they could have had a bit of a session. And after a few tunes, Jim Rafferty would take out his wee whistle and ask quietly, "Do you know this one, then?" just before he launched into the version of "Johnny Cope" that was his party piece.

But for once Janey knew she'd find no solace in the music. Not with the tour still looming and her without a sideman. She had an advert in a couple of the papers, but she'd have to go back to Jenny's flat in London for the auditions. *If* anyone even bothered to call. Knowing her luck, she'd end up being stuck with some three-chord wonder that she'd have to teach to play his bloody instrument before they could even start to work on their sets. Because everybody who was decent wasn't available. Unless she wanted to go begging Alan to at least finish this one tour with her.

No thanks.

She creaked open the wooden chest and sneezed at the musty odor that rose from its contents. It appeared to be stacked, from top to bottom, with old journals. She took one out and flipped through the pages, pausing when she came to a familiar byline. "Tom Bawcock's Eve in Mousehole" by William Dunthorn. The article was a brief description of the traditional festivities in Mousehole on December 23rd, when the fishermen gathered to eat "Stargazy Pie"—a pie made with whole fish, their heads sticking out through the crust.

She looked through more of the journals and found brief articles by Dunthorn in each one. Most she'd already seen— the Gaffer had kept all of his mate's writing that he could lay his hands on—but there were one or two she'd never read before, and many of them were in manuscript form as well as published.

Well, this was a find, wasn't it just? Wouldn't it be perfect if down by the bottom there were manuscript pages of some un-completed novel? Or, better yet, a completed novel, just aching to be read. . . .

Her breath caught in her chest as her scrabbling hands came up with a leather-bound book right at the bottom of the chest.

Be still my heart, she thought.

There was some mildew on the cover, but it came off when she rubbed it with the sleeve of her shirt, leaving only a faint smudge. What made her breath catch, however, was the title of the book.

The Little Country. A novel by William Dunthorn.

Fingers trembling, she opened the book. A folded slip of paper fell out onto her lap, but she ignored it as she flipped quickly through the thick parchment pages.

My God. It *was* a novel. A complete, published Dunthorn novel that she'd never heard of before.

She turned to the copyright page, not quite taking in the phrase "published in an edition of one copy" until she'd read it a number of times.

One copy.

This was the only copy.

What was it *doing* here?

Slowly she put the book down on a stack of journals and manuscripts and picked up the slip of paper that had fallen to her lap.

"My dear friend Tom," the letter began.

Her gaze traveled down to the signature. It was a letter from Dunthorn to her grandfather. Blinking once, she went back to the top of the page and read the letter through.

Here is the book you promised to keep for me. Read it if you will, but remember your promise—it *must not* leave your possession. It *must not* be published. Not *ever!!* Its existence must remain secret—not simply the tale told in its pages, but the book itself.

I know you think me mad sometimes, and God knows I've given you reason enough (a good solid bloke, am I?—I smile whenever I hear you describe me so), but you have my eternal gratitude if you will humour me this one last time.

I have a sense of foreboding for this coming year—yes, that famous Mad Bill Dunthorn Gypsy prescience strikes again!—so it is with great relief that I turn over the possession of this book to you and know that it will remain safe with you.

Godspeed, my friend. I wish there was more time.

Janey reread the letter, then her gaze settled on the date under Dunthorn's signature. He'd written the letter just two months before his death.

Gypsy prescience?

A secret book?

Thoughtfully she folded the letter and stuck it back into the book between the front cover and endpaper. Then, sitting there in the Gaffer's dusty attic, she turned to the first page and began to read. Within the first few paragraphs, all her troubles had melted away and she was caught in the spell of Dunthorn's secret story.

Life Is All Chequered

Sometimes I feel like I've got my nose pressed up against the window of a bakery, only I'm the bread.

— C A R R I E F I S H E R ,
from *Postcards from the Edge*

"**I**f our lives are all books," Jodi told Denzil Gossip, "then someone's torn a few pages from mine."

"Tee-ta-taw," the old man replied in a mildly mocking tone. "Listen to her talk."

He was perched on a tall stool at his worktable under the eaves, tinkering with a scaled-down model of his newest flying machine. Squinting through his glasses, he adjusted the last tiny nut and bolt for the third time since Jodi had arrived at his loft that rainy afternoon. Jodi waited patiently as he broke a morsel of Burke cheese from the piece he kept in the pocket of his tweed vest for the purpose of enticing the pair of mice who would be powering the odd little craft—at least they would be if they could be got from their cage and into the two revolving mechanisms that looked like exercise wheels attached to either side of the machine.

Denzil was never one to force an issue, especially not on the creatures upon which his experiments depended.

"They've got to want to do it, you," he'd explained to Jodi when she had asked why he didn't just pick them up and put them in. "Those mice and I are partners in solving the mystery, not master and slaves."

The mice, wiser than many would give them credit for, ignored the bribe and stayed in their cage, peering through its open door, pink noses quivering. Jodi tried to remember which of the pair had been riding in the miniature hot-air balloon that was navigating the length of the loft when she'd dropped by one day last week. She thought it was the one with the brown spot on his left hind leg.

"I don't see much point in any of it," she said.

"What?" Denzil looked up at her. He pushed his wire-rimmed glasses up to the bridge of his nose. "Well, I go to sea! It's the secret of flight, we're speaking of here—the last frontier! And you want to just ignore it?"

"Not really, I suppose," Jodi said. "But what use is a flying machine that you have to run like a madman to keep aloft? You'd be quicker taking the train—and better rested to boot."

"Where's your sense of adventure?"

"I think I left it in my other jacket. Shall I go fetch it?"

Denzil hrumphed and went back to coaxing the mice while Jodi settled back in the fat, stuffed armchair that she'd commandeered from its spot near the hearth and dragged over to the workbench so that she could watch him go about his business in comfort.

"Fetch it," the parrot sitting on the back of the chair repeated. Then he walked back and forth along the top of the padded cushion, mimicking Denzil's hrumphing sounds.

Jodi reached back and ruffled his feathers. "Don't you start, Noz," she told him.

Denzil's loft was a curious haphazard mixture of zoo, alchemist's laboratory, and mechanic's workshop.

In cages along one wall were four more mice, two white rats, a fat, black, lop-eared rabbit, a pair of green lizards, and a turtle. There was also a murky aquarium that presently held two sleepy-looking catfish; Noz's perch, currently in use by a black-eyed crow; and an empty cage where Ollie, the pale brown rhesus monkey, was kept when he started to misbehave. At the moment Ollie was asleep on top of a bookshelf, sharing the spot with Rum, an old orange tomcat with one shredded ear.

The workbench was vaguely divided into two sections: one side a bewildering mess of test tubes, beakers, glass pipes, a gas burner, clamps, ring stands, thermometers, jars, a set of scales, a microscope with a messy tray of slides, and other such para-phernalia; the other side where Denzil was now working pre-sented an equally bewildering display of mechanical tools, wiring, bits of metal, clockwork mechanisms, and the like.

The remainder of the large loft had a small sofa that doubled as a bed on the other side of the hearth, dormer windows, a twin to the armchair Jodi now occupied still in its spot by the hearth, a small kitchen area centered around a black iron stove, and bookcases wherever there was room for them, stuffed with books, folders, and loose bits of paper. Everywhere one tried to walk there were little piles of Denzil's belongings: a heap of scrap metal by the door; a bag of feed leaning against a bookcase; a box filled with rolled-up maps in the middle of the room; little stacks of books, periodicals, and papers.

The room was like its owner, who invariably presented a di-sheveled, half-bemused face to the world, while underneath his worn and patched clothes, bird's-nest hair and beard, and thin, pinched features was secreted a brilliant mind that never ceased to question the world around him. Jodi spent more time with him in his loft, or going on long rambles in the countryside looking for some missing ingredient for his latest experiment, than she did anywhere else in the town of Bodbury.

His company was worth the assault on her nose that the loft always presented—a weird mixture of chemical odors, smells from the cages that she usually ended up cleaning, machine oil, and Denzil's pipe. And though he always appeared totally en-grossed in whatever task was at hand, he was still capable of carrying on conversations on the most diverse series of subjects. There were pauses and lags in those conversations, times when a sentence broken off one morning was completed that afternoon, but the conversations were always worthwhile.

"What sort of pages are you missing?" he asked now.

He put the cheese down between the mice's cage and the flying machine and gave her another glance. Up went his hand to push back his glasses.

"Oh, I don't know," Jodi replied. "I'm just at loose ends and I can't seem to remember anything anymore. I suppose that happens when you get old."

Denzil chuckled. "And you're so very old, you. Seventeen, is it now?"

"Eighteen. And I feel ancient."

"Ancient, is it? My gar. You don't look nearly old enough to be ancient yet. I'd give it a few more years, you."

He pushed the bit of cheese closer to the mice's cage.

"I really do need to *do* something," Jodi said. "I need a Purpose in life."

"Come 'pon that," Denzil said, "I suppose you're right. You can't spend the whole of your life puttering around up here with me. That's not half natural."

"I don't putter. I'm your assistant. You told me so yourself."

"Now was that before or after we decided that it was an assistant's duty to clean up after the animals?"

Jodi grinned. "Before. And it was you that decided it— not me."

"Hmm."

Denzil picked up the morsel of cheese and popped it into his mouth. Reaching into his other pocket he took out a small wedge of Tamshire cheese and put a bit of it near the mice's cage. Both mice regarded it with interest, but neither moved.

"A purpose, you say?" Denzil went on. "And missing pages?"

Jodi nodded. "Great blocks of time. Like this spring. Can my whole life be all so much the same that nothing stands out anymore? *What* did I do this spring?"

"When you weren't helping me?"

Jodi nodded.

"I don't remember, you. What does Nettie say?"

Jodi lived with her Aunt Nettie in a small apartment on the top floor of the bordello that her aunt kept at the edge of town. It was her aunt's greatest disappointment that Jodi hadn't followed the family tradition and taken up the "life of leisure" as the other women in their family had.

"There's those that like 'em scrawny and looking like a boy," her aunt would tell her, which did little to further Jodi's interest in the profession.

Besides, she would tell herself, she wasn't scrawny. Thin, perhaps; lean, even. But never scrawny. Cats were scrawny. Or children.

It didn't help that she was just barely five feet tall, kept her blond hair trimmed short, and went about in scruffy trousers and a shirt like some twelve-year-old boy from the Tatters—the poorer area of Bodbury that was little more than a series of ramshackle buildings leaning up against one another for support in a long tottery row that looked out over the Old Quay's harbour.

"Nettie just says that she doesn't know what to make of me," Jodi said. "Of course, Nettie's always saying that."

"Well, if you're asking me, my advice would be to put it from your mind for now, you."

"And do what? Go quietly mad?"

"No. You could help me convince these obstinate mice to do their part in testing my machine before we all die of old age."

"It's the story of my life," Jodi said as she hoisted herself out of her chair and walked over to the workbench. "Even bloody mice get more attention."

"Tension," Noz repeated from the back of the chair, spreading out his wings and hopping down to the spot Jodi had just vacated.

"Taupin says," Jodi went on as she made a trail of crumbled cheese from inside the mice's cage to the flying machine, "that the world is a book that somebody's writing and we're all in it. That's why I was talking about missing pages. I really do think someone's torn some of mine out."

"Taupin is nothing more than a hedgerow philosopher who wouldn't know an original thought if it came up and bit him," Denzil said. "So what could he know?"

"I suppose. Besides, who'd publish a book as boring as our lives?"

"I don't find my life boring, you," Denzil said.

"'Course you don't. *You've* got a Purpose."

"And I've assigned you yours—convince these mice that this experiment is for the betterment of mankind. And mousekind, too, of course."

The mice had eaten all the cheese that Jodi had put in their cage, but were venturing not a step beyond its confines.

"Oh, bother," she said.

Picking them up, she put one in either exercise wheel.

"I hope you realize that that's coercion," Denzil said.

The mice began to run on their wheels. Cables connected to the wheels spun wooden cogs, which in turn spun others until the propeller at the front of the miniature machine began to turn and the machine lurched forward on the worktable.

"That's got it!" Denzil cried. "By gar, it's a proper job now!"

He lifted the machine from the table, holding it aloft until the propeller was turning at such a speed that it was a blur. Giving Jodi a grin, Denzil cocked his arm. The parrot immediately lifted from his perch on the back of the armchair and took sanctuary on the top of a bookcase. When Denzil let go, the little flying machine jerked through the air, staying aloft for half the distance of the long room until it took a nosedive.

Jodi, already running after it, caught it just before it hit the ground. Setting the machine on the floor, she took the mice out and cradled them in her hands, making "there, there" sounds.

"You've scared them half to death!" she said.

"All in the name of science."

"That doesn't change anything. They could have been hurt."

"Exactly, you! Which is why I was calling for volunteers—not coerced subjects. I wouldn't doubt that their sulking helped weigh the machine down."

"That doesn't make any sense."

But Denzil wasn't paying attention to her.

"Oh, dear," he said, picking up the machine. "Look at this. The cogs on this gear have snapped right off."

Jodi sighed. This, she decided, wasn't where she wanted to be today either. Having already been sent forth from the bordello for her long face, then having wandered up and down Market

Street and skimmed pebbles over the waves on the beach for an hour, she didn't know what she could do to fill up the rest of the hours that remained until supper.

She replaced the mice in the cage by the wall with the others. A glance out the window showed her that though the sky was still grey, the rain had let up. The cobbles of Peter Street were slick and wet.

"I'm going for a walk," she announced.

"Take Ollie with you, would you? He's been a nuisance all morning."

"He seems fine now," Jodi said, glancing at the monkey.

Denzil shook his head. "I know him, you. He's just storing up energy to wreak havoc in here this evening. I won't get a stitch of work done. Go tire him out so that he'll sleep the night away."

Jodi put on her jacket and called Ollie down from the bookcase. He perched sleepily on her shoulder, one arm around her neck, tail wrapped around her arm.

"If you find those pages I've lost," she said when she reached the door.

Denzil looked up from the workbench where he was fussing with the flying machine again.

"I'll send them straight along," he said.

Jodi grinned as she closed the door and started down the rickety stairs that would let her out onto Peter Street. There was a bit of a damp nip in the air, but rather than going back upstairs to fetch the trousers and sweater that the monkey wore in inclement weather—there was something rather too undignified about dressing animals up as people for her taste—she let Ollie nestle inside her jacket before she stepped out on the cobblestones and headed back in the direction of Market Street.

The monkey snuggled against her chest, radiating as much heat as he absorbed, his small head poking out from the jacket, just below her chin. She got the odd curious stare from passersby, but most people in town knew her too well to be surprised by anything she did. Since she was often out and about with both the monkey in tow and Noz perched on her shoulder, his green feathers iridescent against the grey granite houses and cobble-stoned streets, they paid little heed to one pale brown head that appeared to be poking out of her chest.

Come one, come all, she thought as she paused to study their reflection in a store window. See the amazing two-headed woman.

Scratching her second head under his chin, she walked on.

2 ·

Just beyond the row of weather-beaten buildings in the Tatters that faced the sea, the Old Quay of Bodbury's harbour stretched along the shore in a mile and then some length of crumbling stone and wooden pilings. The pilings were rotting and heavily encrusted with dried salt above the waterline, barnacles below. Abandoned piers thrust seaward at right angles, planks missing, greying wood dotted with the droppings of seabirds. The air was heavy with the smell of salt and dead fish swept up against the quay.

At low tide there could be seen, scattered here and there beyond the quay, the hulls of rotting boats and broken spars—a miniature graveyard for that part of Bodbury's small fishing fleet that had fallen victim to the last great storm to hit the town, twenty years ago.

Bodbury's harbouring business was carried out in New Dock now, situated in that part of the town where Market Street opened onto Market Square, and the Old Quay lay abandoned to all but wharf rats, some few old-timers who strolled the stone walkway in the afternoons, reliving memories of other days, and the children of the Tatters who considered the entire area their own private domain.

When Jodi arrived, Ollie asleep in her jacket, a small gaggle of the latter were busily arguing over a game of Nine Men's Morris that two of their company were playing. They had scratched a board on one of the quay's flagstones and were using pebbles and shells for markers. As Jodi approached, they turned grubby faces in her direction.

"Hey, granny," one red-haired boy said, giving her a lopsided grin. "Have you come to throw that ugly babe into the sea?"

To them, anyone over the age of twelve was too old and fair game for their teasing.

"Lay off the poor old woman," another said. Jodi glanced in his direction and recognized Peter Moyle, the son of one of her aunt's working girls. "Can't you see she's got enough troubles as it is, all bent over and ancient as she is?"

A chorus of good-natured laughter spread among them.

"You see?" Jodi asked her sleeping burden. "I'm the low rung on every ladder. Denzil's assistant. Black sheep of the family. Too much the girl to be a boy, too much a boy to be a girl. Relegated to carrying beasts around in my jacket instead of breasts."

"You're not so ugly," another boy said.

"Not like your babe."

"Best drown him quick."

"Time was," Jodi continued to Ollie, "I'd thrash the lot of them, but I'm much too dignified for that now."

"Too old you mean."

"Ah, don't you listen to them," Kara Faull said.

She was a thin gamine, barely eleven, dressed in an assortment of raggedy clothes—shirt and trousers with patched sweater and a skirt overtop the trousers. Her feet were bare, her thin features only marginally less dirt-smudged than her companions. Getting to her feet, she ambled over to where Jodi stood, and reached out to pet Ollie.

"Can I hold him?"

Jodi passed the now-awakened monkey over to her, whereupon Ollie immediately began to investigate the pockets of Kara's skirts.

"Fancy a game?" Peter asked.

"What're the stakes?"

"Ha'penny a man."

"Don't think so, no. I don't feel lucky today."

"Too old," someone remarked. "No time for games."

"Is that true, granny?" another asked.

Jodi laughed at the lot of them. They stood in a ragged circle around her and Kara, eyes twinkling merrily in their dirty faces, hands shoved deep into their pockets. She was about to return their quips when the group suddenly fell silent. They backed to the edge of the quay's low stone wall, studiously not looking in the general area behind Jodi, two of them whistling innocently— separate tunes that were hopelessly off-key, on their own and with each other. Upset by the sudden shift in mood, Ollie pulled free from Kara's grip and jumped into Jodi's arms.

When Jodi glanced casually around and saw who was approaching, her own days of running wild with the children of the Tatters returned in a rush. For no accountable reason, she felt guilty, certain she was about to be accused of some dreadful crime that she hadn't committed, but would suffer for all the same.

The Widow Pender tended to foster such fears in the children of the Tatters. They were all convinced she was a witch and more than one Tatters mother had threatened to punish misbehaving by "sending you to the Widow, just see if I don't."

Silent as the children, Jodi joined their quiet group as the tall, hawk-faced woman dressed all in black went slowly by, walking stick tapping on the quay's stones, back stiff and straight as a board, grey hair pulled behind her head in a severe bun. She gave each of the children a disapproving look, fierce grey gaze skewering each of them in turn, lingering longest on Jodi.

The Widow frowned as Ollie hissed at her. For one long moment Jodi thought the old woman would take her stick to them both, but then the Widow gave her a withering glance and continued on her slow way.

Not until she was well out of hearing did the children relax, loosing held-in breaths in a group sigh. Then they filled the air with whispers of brave talk to take the chill that the Widow had left behind her out of the air.

"Fair gives me the creeps, she does."

"Oh, she doesn't frighten me."

"Didn't see you playing smart with her."

"Someone should give her a shove in."

"Her friends'd just shove her back out again."

It was said that she had caused the storm, twenty years ago, that had drowned the Old Quay and sunk the fishing boats. Called it up because her husband, a fisherman himself, had been gadding about town with a barmaid from the Pintar. Fifteen men were drowned that day, trying to save the boats. The barmaid had left town, though there were those who whispered that she hadn't so much left as been killed by the Widow and buried in a secret grave up on the moor.

Every child in the Tatters knew that the drowned dead were hers to command.

"Ratty Friggens says she's got a Small in that old house of hers—a little wee man that she keeps in a jar."

Jodi turned to the last speaker. "A Small?"

"It's true. Ratty saw it himself—a little man no bigger than a mouse. A Gypsy brought it 'round her house in a wooden wren cage and handed it over right before Ratty's eyes. Told me so himself. Says she'll be using it to creep into people's houses and steal their valuables—once she has it trained."

"She doesn't need valuables," Peter said. "Her whole cellar is loaded with treasure."

Kara nodded. "My da' said that one night, talking to his mates."

"A Small," Jodi repeated.

She looked down the quay to where she could see the Widow, a stiff figure in black, gazing out to sea. Her heart beat quicker. Sensing her excitement, Ollie made a querulous sound. She stroked his head thoughtfully.

Could it be true? If the Widow *did* have a Small, hidden away in that old house of hers . . .

Wouldn't that be something?

And if it *was* true, did she herself have the nerve to sneak in for a look at him?

Not likely.

She didn't have the nerve.

Nor would there really be a Small.

But what if there was?

The Widow turned then and it seemed that, for all the distance between them, her gaze settled directly on Jodi's. The old woman smiled, as though reading her mind.

I know secrets you can't begin to dream of, that smile said. Secrets that will cost you your soul if you'd have them from me. Are you still so willing to learn them?

Jodi shivered. Visions of drowned corpses coming for her flashed through her mind. Bloated white skin, bestranded with wet seaweed. Reeking of death. Dead things lurching into her room while she slept. . . .

Before the Widow returned to walk by them again, Jodi gave the children a vague wave and hurried off, back to Denzil's loft.

The Sailor's Return

―――――――

I would that I were where I wish,
Out on the sea in a wooden dish;
But if that dish begins to fill—
I'd wish I were on Mousehole Hill.

collected from Don Flamanck

Th e old smuggler's haunt of Mousehole in Paul Parish is in the Deanery and West Division of the Hundred of Penwith in southern Cornwall. Its crooked narrow streets and stone-built cottages climb from the western shore of Mount's Bay up the steep slope of Mousehole Hill at a point approximately a quarter of the way from Penzance to Land's End, following the coastline west.

Janey Little's grandfather loved the village, and delighted in regaling his granddaughter's visitors with snippets of its history and folklore that he'd acquired over the years. The source of its name alone could have him rambling on at the drop of a cloth cap.

Some historians, he'd explain, think the village acquired its curious name from the Mousehole, a gaping cavern—now collapsed—that lies south of the village, or that it's a corruption of Porthenys, the Port of the Island, meaning St. Clement's Island, which lies close to the village. Others cite a reference to an old Cornish manuscript that speaks of "Moeshayle," getting its name from the small river that flows through it—"moes" probably being an abbreviation of "mowes," meaning "young women," and "hayle" meaning "river," for a translation of "Young Women's River."

The most dramatic event in Mousehole's history happened in 1595 when the village was sacked by troops from three Spanish ships; it was a Mousehole man who first spied the Spanish Armada seven years earlier. The only surviving building of that period is the Keigwin Arms, which perches on granite pillars above the courtyard where Squire Keigwin killed six Spaniards defending his home. That event is celebrated annually to this day, every July, with a carnival and festivities that end in a commemorative dinner at the Cairn Dhu Hotel where the names of the various dishes serve to tell the story.

Mousehole's other historical claims to fame are far less dramatic. The same back street that houses the Keigwin Arms was also the birthplace of Dolly Pentreath, the last-known native speaker of Cornish whose tombstone is a part of the stone wall of St. Paul's Church overlooking the village, and whose funeral, it's said, was interrupted for a whiskey break. South of the village, along Raginnis Hill overlooking St. Clement's Island in Mount's Bay, stands the Wild Bird Hospital begun in 1928 by two sisters, Dorothy and Phyllis Yglesias, which manages to survive to this day on private donations. Against a mossy wall is a bell with a sign that reads, "Please ring the bell if you have a bird." Each year the hospital tends to more than a thousand sick wild birds brought in by the public.

Mousehole was once the center of Cornwall's pilchard-fishing industry, but though it still retains the flavour of an old Cornish fishing village and there are still fishing boats to be found in its harbour, its principle industry is now tourism. There are few fishermen left, and the only smugglers who remain are in the memories of the older villagers.

Thomas Little remembered the smugglers, though he wasn't thinking of them as he came down Mousehole Lane from the King's Arms in Paul to the home he shared with his granddaughter on Duck Street. A pint of Hick's bitter sloshed comfortably in his stomach. In a brown paper bag he carried a takeout of two brown ales.

The Gaffer, as everyone referred to him, was thinking of Janey at that moment. He'd wanted to show her off to his mates at the local, but she was in one of her moods and hadn't wanted to come. But tonight . . . well, there was a session up at Charlie

Boyd's, at his farm on the road to Lamorna, which was the rambling house of the area where the musicians and storytellers would often gather on a Friday night.

Boyd's farm was on a headland near Lamorna with a good view of the bay. The flat clifftop was bright with the cries of stonechats and gulls that rang above the dull pounding of the surf on the rocks below, the air sharp with a salty tang. The constant pounding of the waves had eaten away at the granite cliffs, but the farm would stand at least a century or two longer before the rock on which it stood completely eroded.

Until then it remained home to Charlie and his family—brother, wife, daughter and two boys, musicians all—and a welcome place to visit on a Friday night for those interested in such entertainments. There weren't that many anymore, not these days—even with the revival of interest in traditional music in other parts of the country—but they usually had a fair crowd, with folk dropping by from as far away as Lizard's Point, across the bay.

Some fine musicians could be counted on at the session tonight, but, the Gaffer thought with pride, his granddaughter would likely still be the best. Hadn't she recorded two phonograph records to date? Wasn't she always on tour—on the Continent and in America, if not in England?

He continued up the street, a short, round man with a balding head and the ruddy features of a fisherman, dressed in old corduroy trousers and a tweed jacket patched at the elbows, smiling to himself, a jaunty lift in his steps, brown ale bottles clinking in the paper bag he carried at his side.

Oh, yes. He was looking forward to showing her off tonight.

When he reached the door to his house—owned outright, thank you, and maintained with his pension and what money Janey sent him while she was on tour—he was whistling one of Chalkie's tunes in anticipation of the evening to come.

"Janey!" he called as he stepped inside. "Do you have a spot of tea ready for an old man?"

For a long moment there was no answer.

2 .

Janey had heard an author describe his writing process once as seeing a hole in the paper that he could step into and watch the story unfold, and that was just how she felt with this new Dunthorn novel. It was like being at a good session when you forgot who you were, where you were, the instrument in your hand, and just disappeared into the music. When the tune finally ended, you sat up and blinked for a moment, the sense of dislocation only momentary, lasting just so long as it took the last echoes of the old tune to fade and a new one to start up.

She looked up from the book now, only vaguely aware of the dusty attic she was sitting in and the book on her lap, her thoughts still wandering the world she'd found within its pages. Then she slipped Dunthorn's letter in between the pages to keep her place and rose from the floor, the book under her arm.

"I'm up here, Gramps!" she called ahead of her as she started down the narrow stairway that would take her to the second floor of the house.

Her grandfather was waiting for her in the small vestibule, the door to the street still open behind him. He looked up to where she came down the stairs. At twenty-two she hadn't yet lost the enthusiasms and energy of a teenager. Her auburn hair hung free to just past her shoulders, except for the bangs in front, and was redder than its natural colour because she'd recently hennaed it. Above her hazel eyes, her brows maintained a slight arch giving her a constant look of questioning surprise that never quite left. Her skin was a good English peaches and cream, nose small and slender, while her smile came so easily and often that it had left dimples in her cheeks.

She was wearing a black leotard under a yellow skirt and a baggy black sweatshirt overtop. Yellow hightop sneakers matched her skirt. Presently the knees of her leotard were dusty and there was a smudge of dirt on her nose. Her cheeks had a healthy ruddy flush of excitement.

"You've got dirt on your nose, my flower," he said as she bounded down the last few steps to join him.

His round Puck's face broke into a smile as she leaned forward to kiss his cheek. But then his gaze alit on what she was carrying under her arm and the smile faltered as he recognized it for what it was.

"Found it then, did you?" he said after a moment.

Janey had the sudden sense of having overstepped her bounds.

"I didn't mean to go prying," she began. She remembered Dunthorn's letter. *Its existence must remain secret. . . .* "You're not cross with me, are you?"

The Gaffer shook his head. "Never with you. It's just . . . ah, well. I meant to give it to you sooner or later, so why not now?"

"It's a marvelous book, isn't it just?"

"Halfway finished it already, are you then?"

"Hardly!"

"Funny you should find it now, though. There was a woman came knocking on our door not three days ago, asking after it. First time that's happened in years. There were lots of crows, circling about when Billy first died, but as the years went by, I'd only see one every year or so, and then not for, what? Five years now? Until this woman came to the door."

"How did she know about the book?"

"Well, she wasn't so much after *it* in particular. She wanted any unpublished writings of Billy's—writings or artifacts. Were hers by right, she said. She was an American woman—about your age—and as unpleasant as Americans can be. Claimed to be the granddaughter of some cousin of Billy's that *I* never heard of before."

"What did you tell her?"

"Well, nothing, my robin. I had a promise to keep, didn't I? Besides, she rubbed me wrong, she did, making some crant the way she was. Offered me money straightway—as though money can buy anything. I sent her packing. Still, it bothered me, her asking like that. It was like she knew there was something. Maybe not so much the book itself, but something, and didn't she just want it?"

"What was her name?"

"She didn't say. Though she did say she'd be in touch—once she'd spoken to her lawyers."

"And you never told me?"

"Janey, my beauty, what was I to tell you? Some daft American comes knocking on my door asking about a book I can't admit to owning. . . . I wasn't ready to tell you about it yet, but I wasn't about to lie to you either. There's no lies between us, am I right?"

Janey nodded.

"Well, there you go."

"And you haven't heard from her since?" Janey asked.

The Gaffer shook his head. "What's to hear? There's nothing she or her lawyers can do. The book doesn't exist."

Janey looked down at the very real book in her hand.

"Yes, well," the Gaffer said. "In a manner of speaking, it doesn't."

"When were you going to tell me about it?" she asked.

"Well, that's the funny thing, my love. I had the feeling the book would choose its own time—and now didn't it just do that very thing?"

She looked for, but couldn't find a teasing twinkle in his eyes.

"Gramps! You don't believe that a book could—"

"Come get your old grandfather his tea and I'll tell you a wee bit more about the Mousehole half of your two Billys."

"Two Billys" was their private joke for her infatuation with the work of Billy Pigg and William Dunthorn. Something very, very good was "almost two Billys' worth of bully."

"I still can't believe you never told me about this," Janey said as she led the way to the kitchen.

"Yes, well"—the Gaffer's gaze settled on the top of Dunthorn's letter marking her place in the book—"I see you've read the letter, too, so you know why I kept it from you."

"I just happened upon it," Janey said, ready to apologize all over again.

"Getting my tea's penance enough, my love," the Gaffer told her.

The center of the Little household was the kitchen—it always had been, especially when Janey's grandmother was still alive and filling it with the tempting smells of her baking and the warmth of her presence.

Janey and the Gaffer had shared equally in the auto accident that had taken the Gaffer's wife and son, Janey's grandmother and father. She was just nudging eight at the time, so that most of her growing up had taken place in this house that she and the Gaffer had made their own special place over the years. Her mother—Constance Little, née Hetherington—had run off with a filmmaker, on holiday from New York, a few years before the accident and remained unheard from since the day the divorce papers became final. Although Janey's mother had reverted to her maiden name for legal purposes, she kept Connie Little as a stage name. Considering the sort of film work she was involved in, Janey's father Paul had remarked in an odd moment of bitterness before his death, she should have used Lingus as a surname.

The Gaffer didn't like to think of the woman. So far as he was concerned, the day she'd walked out on Paul and Janey, she was no longer to be considered a part of the family. She had no place in the life that he and Janey had made with each other.

No matter where Janey's music took her, nor for how long, Mousehole would always be her home—this house on Duck Street where the Gaffer lived, just a half-minute's walk from the harbour from which he'd once set sail in his boat along with the other fishermen of the village. Though the pilchard shoals had ceased at the turn of the century, there was still work for a fisherman when the Gaffer was a young man. That work declined decade by decade until now it was only a shadow of the industry it once was. Most of the boats leaving Mousehole harbour now carried only a crew of tourists.

The first tune that Janey ever wrote was a simple reel on the fiddle called "The Gaffer's Mouzel," and the front cover of her first album jacket was a photo of the village, taken from the ferry that ran between Penzance and the Scillies, out on Mount's Bay. The village was in her blood as much as in her grandfather's.

The Gaffer sat at the kitchen table, rubbing his hand on the cover of the book, while Janey busied herself at the counter making their tea. She brought sandwiches and steaming mugs of tea over, then sat across from him and put her hand on his.

"I've made you sad, haven't I?" she said. "Made you remember sad things."

The Gaffer shook his head. "I could never forget, my robin. Garm, we were a pair, Billy and I, and isn't that God's own truth? Always into mischief. Born a century earlier and I don't doubt we'd both have been smugglers. We knew all the old places where they landed, you know."

Janey nodded. She never tired of rambling the whole countryside around Mousehole with him, the Gaffer full of old bits of lore and stories. He was always ready to tell a tale about these standing stones, that cliff, this old road, that sandbar, that abandoned tin mine. Everything had a story. Especially the stoneworks that riddled Penwith Peninsula. The Merry Maidens stone circle with the two pipers stones just a field over. The Men-an-Tol holed stone east of Penzance. The Boscawen-Un stone circle with its nineteen stones and tilted center pillar just south of Crows-an-Wra. The old Roman Iron Age village on the Gulval downs.

"This letter," she said. "It's so mysterious. . . ."

"Oh, I know. Billy was a real dog in a tayser sometimes—a gruff fisherman with a streak of the old madness in him a league wide and then some. Where do you think I got half my tales from, my queen? The giants and piskies, the saints and smugglers. It was Billy talked of them all, one as real as the other."

"But what's so wrong with him being like that?" Janey asked. "I've heard the old fellows talk down at the local. They're all half-mad with the same kind of stories themselves."

As you are, she added affectionately to herself.

The Gaffer shrugged. "Self-preservation, I suppose. For both of us. We fought in the War together, you know. The other soldiers made enough fun of our country ways as it was without letting them think we might believe in piskies and the like as well. The simplest things, like gulls being—"

"The spirits of dead sailors," Janey said.

"That's what my own dad told me, and I believe it. But there's those you tell that kind of a thing to and they treat you like a half-wit. Or they'll think you're quaint—like the tourists do. Billy didn't much care, but I did. At least I did then. Became sort of a habit since then, I suppose."

"So Billy really believed in what he wrote?"

The Gaffer laughed. "Oh, I don't know, my robin. He'd *tell* you he believed, and in such a way you'd swear he did, but there was always a gleam in his eye if you knew to look."

Just like there was in the Gaffer's, Janey thought, when he started a similar kind of tale. "Do you see that stone there, Janey, my beauty?" he'd begin. "Time was . . ." And off he'd go on some rambling story. Face solemn, not a twitch of a smile, but the gleam was there in his eyes.

"Why do you think Billy didn't want anybody else to see this book?" she asked. "I'm not far into it, but I can tell it's as good or better than the others. And if it's so important that it be kept a secret, why was it published at all?" She opened the book to the copyright page and read aloud, " 'Published in an edition of one copy.' It seems so . . . odd."

She flipped to the title page and glanced at the bottom where the publisher's name was Goonhilly Downs Press, Market Jew Street, Penzance.

"Odd," the Gaffer agreed. "It is that."

"You never asked him about it?"

The Gaffer shook his head.

"Why not?"

"A man's entitled to his secrets if he wants them. A woman, too."

"I suppose." Janey put her finger on the publisher's name. "Maybe we could ask these people. Goonhilly Downs Press. Do they still exist?"

"I've never heard of them before."

The Goonhilly Downs were out on Lizard's Point, across Mount's Bay. It made Janey wonder why a Penzance publisher would take them for the name of his imprint. Well, she could ask them that as well.

"Think of all the people who would love to read this," she said, thinking aloud.

"You mustn't talk about it," the Gaffer said. "I made a promise—a family promise, my flower. You're held to it as well."

"But..." Janey began, but then she nodded. A promise was a promise. "I won't tell anyone," she said.

"Is there more tea?"

Janey rose to get the pot. After first putting a half inch of milk at the bottom of each mug and two spoons of sugar in the Gaffer's, she poured them each another tea.

"Is this book the only secret writing of Billy's?" she asked as she sat down again.

"The only one he had me promise to keep secret. There's some unpublished articles in a folder in the same chest where you found this book—writings about local things—but I never did anything with them. Hadn't the heart, to tell you the truth. It never seemed right to make money from a friend's death. Not to me."

Janey covered his hand with her own again. "Not to me either," she said.

They sat quietly, holding on to the moment of closeness, then the Gaffer shifted in his seat and found a smile.

"Well, then, my beauty," he said. "I think you owe me a favour."

"What did you have in mind?" she asked warily.

"Oh, nothing bad. There's just this session at Charlie Boyd's tonight and—"

"You wanted to show off your granddaughter."

"I only have the one."

Janey smiled with genuine affection. "I'd love to go," she said. "Gives me a chance to show off my granddad."

3 ·

Felix Gavin walked through London's Victoria Station with the rolling gait of the seaman he was. He was a tall, broad-shouldered man, deeply tanned, with dark brown hair cropped close to his scalp, pale blue eyes, and a small gold hoop in the lobe of his right ear. He drew the gazes of women he passed as he made his way to his platform, not so much for his size, or because he was handsome, as that his were features that instilled an immediate trust.

He radiated a sense of strength and calm; the promise that he was a man who could be counted on. He wore loose flannel trousers, a plain white T-shirt with an unbuttoned pea jacket overtop, and sturdy black workman's shoes. In one hand he carried a navy blue duffel bag, in the other a squarish wooden box, painted black and plastered with decals from the ports where his various ships had docked—mostly European and North American, but others from as far away as Hong Kong and Australia.

He'd been a sailor for a good third of his twenty-eight years, most recently as a crewman of the freighter *La Madeleine*, sailing out of Montreal. He'd left the ship in Madrid when he'd received the letter that was now in the front pocket of his trousers. Taking the first flight he could get to London, he'd arrived at Gatwick early this morning, changed his money to British currency, and immediately boarded a train to Victoria Station.

Now he waited at the platform for another train to take him into the West Country.

He set his baggage down at his feet and leaned against a pillar, hands in his pocket. The fingers of his right hand touched the folded letter.

"Oh, Felix," it began, and went on:

I feel terrible writing this. You always send me postcards, when I haven't managed much more than a Christmas card, and it doesn't seem fair. But you said if I ever needed help, I could call on you.

I do need help. Can you come to the Gaffer's?

Please don't hate me. I wouldn't ask, but I'm desperate.

love,
Janey

The letter was typed, even the signature. The postmark was Mousehole, in Cornwall, where her grandfather lived. Where Felix sent his postcards every few months. The cards were never more than just a few lines from whatever port he happened to be—brief condensations of the long one-sided conversations he had with her when he was at sea and she couldn't hear him.

Sighing, Felix prodded the letter with his fingers, folding it into an even smaller square.

Hate her? Never.

His feelings were always mixed. He was happy that he'd known her, sad that everything had fallen apart the way it had, frustrated that they hadn't been able to put it back together, that they hadn't really tried. The good history they had—the two and a half years when everything just seemed perfect—just couldn't seem to defeat the last few months of pointless arguments when things better left unsaid were aired and then regretted too late. Once spoken, those words had taken on a life of their own and couldn't be recalled.

But he never stopped loving her; never stopped hoping that someday, somehow, they'd be together again. Yet now, now that she was finally asking for him, hope was tempered with the fear of what could have happened that was so bad to make her reach out to him.

Not the Gaffer, he prayed. Don't let anything have happened to that sweet old man.

But what *had* happened? The letter was so was vague—so was Janey, in some ways, with her thoughts bouncing every which way.

His train arrived and he thankfully gave up the worry in the bustle of boarding, stowing away his gear, and finding a seat. The carriage was only a quarter full. This time of year—mid-October—the English didn't flock to the West Country for their holidays the way they did in the summer. The area around Penzance was known as the Cornish Riviera, and in the summer, it lived up to its name. Now only the people who lived there, or those who had business there, made the trip out to the Penwith Peninsula.

Settling into his seat, he pulled out a paperback mystery novel and tried to read as the train pulled out of the station. But Janey's features kept intruding on the storyline and he couldn't follow the private eye's narrative for more than a few sentences before he had to go back and begin the paragraph again. Expectations of what he could look forward to were mixing too strongly with an anxiety born of that same anticipation of seeing her again.

Finally, once they left London, he set the book aside and stared out the window, watching the hedgerow-bordered fields flicker by. As memories rose up, one after the other, he simply let them come.

A little more than five hours later, he disembarked at Penzance Station and stood out in the car park, looking over at St. Michael's Mount where it rose like a humpbacked swell from Mount's Bay. It was already dark, the grey skies slating into night. A brisk easterly wind blew in from the water, thick with the tang of salt and the promise of rain.

He turned finally, walking towards a phone booth before changing his mind. He wasn't ready to call her. He didn't want the first contact to be an impersonal communication over a phone line. He thought of taking a taxi to Mousehole—the village lay a few miles west of Penzance, just past Newlyn, the three set all in a row along the shore of Mount's Bay like three gulls on a ship's railing—then decided against that as well.

More memories were waking here. Better to walk through them now, before he reached the Gaffer's old house on Duck Street, he decided, than trying to deal with them in the back of a cab.

Swinging the strap of his duffel bag to his shoulder, he hefted his wooden box and set off, taking the Quay Wharf Road to where it met Battery Road, then following the Western Promenade out of the town and into Newlyn.

Even in the dark, Mousehole was just the way he remembered it. Maybe especially in the dark, because he'd rambled through its benighted streets with Janey often enough to know it as well as he did his own hometown of Deschenes, in West Quebec. Both were fronted by water, but there the resemblance ended.

Deschenes, at least when he was growing up there, was a poverty-stricken village on the wrong side of the tracks that fronted that part of the Ottawa River known as Lac Deschenes. The streets were packed dirt, the buildings ramshackle, some of them little better than tarpaulin shacks. The memories he carried away from it centered around the fighting of his alcoholic parents, his brother Barry who wrapped his Harley around a lamppost, killing himself and his girlfriend, their sister Sue who had her first kid when she was fifteen, and a hundred other unhappy events.

Mousehole was an ancient port, an unspoiled fishing village of narrow streets and alleyways that wound through tiers of cottages and tiny flowered courtyards. If there was poverty here, it didn't show the same underbelly to the world that his hometown did.

He entered by the Parade, passing the Old Coastguard Hotel,

and made his way to North Cliff. There he stood in front of the newsagent's and looked seaward at the two arms of the quay's seawalls that enfolded the village's harbour in a protective embrace. He'd sat on one or another of those walls with Janey on more than one moonlit night, listening to the waves beat at the stone walls, watching the sea, or sitting with their backs to the water and taking in the picturesque view of the terraced village as it climbed the hill, lights twinkling in the windows of the cottages. Those were good nights. They didn't always need conversation. The darkness simply held them in a companionable embrace as comforting as the arms of the quay's seawalls did the harbour.

Felix turned away from the view. He was dawdling, and he knew why. This close to seeing Janey again, all his courage was washing out of him as surely as the tide stole the water from inside the seawalls.

He walked past the newsagent's to where a tiny alleyway separated the buildings on either side of it and walked up its narrow length. This was Duck Street, starting out no wider than a couple of yards, but broadening into a one-lane street by the time it reached Wellington Place, the square just before the Gaffer's cottage on Chapel Place, across from the Methodist Chapel.

A black and orange cat eyed him curiously from the stone wall as he opened the wrought-iron gate that led into the Gaffer's tiny courtyard. There were lights on in the two-and-a-half-story stone cottage.

Janey was in there, he thought. Probably sitting around the hearth with her grandfather. Reading. Or playing a game of dominoes with the Gaffer. She wasn't playing music, because he couldn't hear either her pipes or her fiddle.

He hesitated at the door.

Come on, he told himself.

He lifted the brass knocker on the door, rapping it sharply against the plate screwed into the wood behind it. And suddenly he got a strange feeling.

There was no one home. He could feel the emptiness that anticipation had hidden from him. Neither Janey nor the Gaffer was in. But there was somebody. . . .

He knocked again and heard a crash. Without stopping to think, he let his gear drop to the cobblestoned walk and tried the door. It was unlocked, opening at his touch. He stepped inside, nerves prickling, and sensed the blow coming before it struck.

That momentary warning was enough to give him time to turn aside and take the blow on his shoulder. A figure darted by him, something bulky under his arm. Felix caught his balance and snaked out a hand, snagging the man by the shoulder of his coat. Before he could pull him back into the cottage, the man slammed what he was carrying into Felix's midsection.

Felix lost his grip on the man's shoulder. He buckled over, catching hold of what proved to be a box of papers and magazines. The man struggled for a moment, trying to regain ownership of the box, his features still hidden in shadow. Then a door opened in the cottage next door. At the neighbour's cry, the man shoved the box harder against Felix and fled. By the time Felix regained his balance once more and stepped out into the courtyard, he could see the man fleeing up Duck Street towards Mousehole Lane.

He set the box down on the doorstep and turned to face the Gaffer's neighbour, struggling for a moment before he remembered the man's name.

"Mr. Bodener?" he asked. His voice was husky as he caught his breath.

George Bodener was a few years the Gaffer's senior, and like the Gaffer, he was a Mousehole native, although he'd never traveled farther than Plymouth in the whole of his life. He was thin and grey-haired, but he had a round piskie's face that was rarely without a smile. That smile was missing just now, however. He had a cane upraised in his hand and peered carefully at Felix before he finally brought it down to his side.

"Felix, isn't it?" he asked. "Janey's musician friend?"

Felix nodded. "I surprised a burglar—"

"A burglar? In Mousehole? La, Jey! But I never." He took a few steps closer. "Did you take a hurt, you?"

"No, I'm fine. Just a bit shook up."

But thinking of the moment of violence, he looked worriedly back into the Gaffer's cottage. Had the man hurt Janey or her grandfather?

"Don't you be worrying about them, you," George said. "Gone out, they have, up to Boyd's farm. It's Friday night, isn't it just?"

Friday night meant a session at Charlie Boyd's, Felix remembered. Some things never changed. But what was Janey doing, going to a session, when she was supposed to be in trouble?

Supposed to be? Felix amended. Then what did he call the burglar he'd just surprised? A houseguest?

"My gar," George said as he joined Felix in the hallway and peered inside. "Made a bit of a mess."

Felix nodded. There was a floor lamp lying on the carpet, its glass shade broken. A scatter of books lay on the floor around the hearth. Pillows were pulled from the sofa and the Gaffer's club chair by the window. He looked down at the box he'd rescued from the burglar. It was filled with papers and what appeared to be a book. Who burgled a house for this kind of thing?

"Would you like some tea, you?" George asked him.

Felix shook his head. "I think I'll try to clean this up before Janey and the Gaffer get back—lessen the shock a bit."

"Now there's a kind thought."

"Been much trouble about here lately?" Felix asked, keeping his voice casual.

George blinked in surprise. "Trouble? In Mousehole? It's not London, you. Not even Penzance."

Felix gave him a smile. "I wasn't thinking," he said.

"No crime in that," George said. He gave a last look around the living room. "Well, it's back to the telly for me, Felix. Come 'round in the morning, why don't you just, and tell me a tale of far-off ports."

"I'll do that."

He collected his belongings from the courtyard and brought them and the box of papers inside as George returned to his home. Then he spent a half hour straightening the room and repairing what damage he could before he put on some tea.

An odd thing to steal, he thought as he took the box into the kitchen. He looked through the papers and saw that they were manuscripts and articles by the Gaffer's old mate, Billy Dunthorn. There was a book, too, with a title that wasn't familiar to Felix, but that was hardly surprising. He'd never had much of a head for authors' names or how many books they'd published. He just read what came to hand and either enjoyed it, or didn't.

But he knew Dunthorn because Janey never tired of talking about the man and his work.

Taking his tea into the now-tidy living room, he sat down in the Gaffer's chair with the book and idly flipped through its pages while he waited for Janey and her grandfather to come home.

The Creeping Mouse

Thumbkin, Pointer, Middleman big,
Sillyman, Weeman, rig-a-jig-jig.

—Nursery rhyme

*J*o d i couldn't help herself—she had to know.

Of course there was no such thing as a Small. How could there be? And the Widow Pender wasn't a witch. She had no mysterious powers to wield over the living, nor could she call up the dead. To think otherwise was to live in a fairy tale.

The world was a strange and wonderful place as it was, Denzil never tired of reminding her. What need was there to go prying about, chasing after supernatural oddities that couldn't possibly exist when the mysteries of nature itself were barely understood?

Yes, and of course, and I do agree, Jodi would reply.

But there were always the stories—so many of them. Of ghosts and hauntings and things that went bump in the night. Of fairies and giants and impossible creatures. Where did they come from? Out of our heads, and that was it? Surely something had sparked their authors to imagine the incredible. Surely, somehow, there was some tiny grain of truth to the tale that set it spinning through the author's mind.

What if impossibilities were true marvels?

And what if the moon was made of cheese, Denzil would reply dryly. The question then would be, who ate it, night by night, and how did it come back again, piece by piece, just as good as new?

So Jodi would nod in reluctant agreement, but no matter how sensible she tried to be, she couldn't stop that little voice that whispered in the back of her mind.

What if the marvels were real? What *if*?

She just had to know.

So late that night, when the last of the night's customers was gone and Aunt Nettie and her girls were finally off to bed, Jodi crept out of her window, slid down the drainpipe, and set off through Bodbury's cobblestone streets, heading for the Widow Pender's house.

And it was a night for mystery, wasn't it just? Clouds scudded across the sky, hiding the moon, waking shadows. The sea murmured to itself like an old woman, slapping the pilings of the quay that fronted the Tatters, phosphorus glistening on the tide. There wasn't a light in a single window she passed—not even in Denzil's workshop.

She walked with a swing in her step, breathing in the salty tang of the night air, her soft-soled shoes silent on the cobblestones. She wasn't even a bit nervous—her sense of adventure overriding any such possibility—until she finally reached the outskirts of town and the Widow's cottage came into view. Then she slowed down, pausing when she reached the protective cover of the last cottage before the Widow's.

The two-story stone building that belonged to the Widow Pender rose in gloomy foreboding from its shadowed gardens. A flicker of light came from one ground-floor window. Occasionally a shadow passed the window, as though the Widow were pacing back and forth.

She'd be going out soon, Jodi thought as she settled down by the wall of the neighbouring cottage to wait. In the Tatters it was well known that the Widow went out late each night, when all the town was asleep, and stood on the headland across from her house to watch the sea.

Remembering her husband, the townsfolk said.

Conversing with the sea dead, the children of the Tatters whispered to one another.

The latter seemed all too possible to Jodi as she crouched nervously against the wall, watching the Widow's cottage. The night had changed around her. There was a nasty undercurrent in the murmur of the tide now. The light wind coming in from the water seemed more like breathing than a sea breeze. Trees groaned ominously. Unseen *things* rustled in the hedges.

The warm comfort of her bed seemed very far away, and most appealing, but she chewed at her lower lip and kept to her vigil, refusing to be unnerved. It was a time for bravery, and she was determined to be just that. Yet as she waited there, she couldn't help but think of all the ghostly stories she'd ever heard. Of hummocks, rising from behind hedgerows to frighten travelers with their spectral presence. Of drowned men stumbling from the tide, limbs wrapped with strands of seaweed, water streaming from their rotting clothes. Of the Bagle Wight, a straw-limbed scarecrow of a creature whose head was a large carved turnip; he captured and ate children who snuck out from their houses in the night. . . .

Jodi wished she hadn't thought of him. Now all she could hear was his soft footfall on the street behind her. It was too easy to imagine him creeping towards her, catching her with his knobbly fingers, sharp thorn nails digging into her arms.

She shivered and peered over her shoulder so often that she almost missed the Widow finally leaving her cottage. Jodi watched her go, then rose quickly to her feet. Keeping an eye on the Widow's receding back, afraid to even breathe, she darted over to the lit window and peered in.

And saw nothing out of the ordinary.

She looked in on what appeared to be the Widow's sitting room and what she saw was common enough to make her yawn. A coal fire burned in the hearth. On the mantel above it, two fat white candles sat in silver candlesticks, throwing their flickering light across the room. There were a pair of comfortable chairs by the fire, knitting lying upon the seat of one; a sideboard displaying china plates—mostly with scenes depicting Bodbury and the surrounding countryside; another long table by another wall that reminded her of one of Denzil's worktables as it was littered with various woodworking tools and pieces of wood and cloth; and a bookcase, with as many knickknacks as there were books on its shelves. Paintings and samplers hung on the walls. A cozy thick wool rug lay on the floor.

But nothing magical. None of the paraphernalia associated with witches—no cauldrons bubbling on the fire, no bundles of herbs and odd charms. And of course there wouldn't be, would there? If the Widow was a witch, she'd hide the tools of her trade. In the attic, perhaps. Or the cellar.

Jodi's attention returned to the worktable. At the far end was a square box covered with a piece of velvet. She glanced in the direction that the Widow had taken, but there was no sign of her return yet.

Did she dare? She'd come so far, but to actually enter the woman's house and poke about in her belongings . . .

She hesitated for a long moment, then went 'round by the door and tried the knob. It turned easily under her hand, the door swinging open silently when she gave it a push. She hesitated again on the threshold, before taking a deep breath and stepping in.

She stood there in the hallway, expecting she knew not what. An alarm of some sort, she supposed. A cat to lunge at her, hissing and spitting. A raven to come screeching down the hallway towards her. A black dog to rear up from the floor at her feet, appearing out of a cloud of dense smoke, red-eyed and snarling. But there was nothing.

And why should there be? There were no such things as witches. The Widow Pender was merely a lonely old woman, making do with her loneliness and her pension, and here Jodi was, entering her cottage uninvited and undoubtedly unwelcome.

Ratty Friggens says she's got a Small in that old house of hers. . . .

But Smalls were no more real than witches, were they?

A little wee man that she keeps in a jar.

She moved down the hall towards the sitting room. It appeared as innocuous from her present vantage point as it had from the window she'd peered through. It could be any old woman's room, the fire cheery, a vague scent of dried flowers in the air.

She stepped inside, running a hand along the smooth wooden surface of the sideboard, and moved towards the worktable. She paused when she reached it, looking curiously at what the Widow had been working on.

Doll's furniture.

A little wee man.

There could be a hundred good reasons she was making doll's furniture.

She's got a Small. . . .

Jodi put her hand on the cloth covering the box at the end of the table and slowly pulled the cloth away to reveal an aquarium. But unlike the ones in Denzil's loft, this one was furnished like a doll's house. There was a small table with two chairs; a miniature hearth with a coal in it, the stovepipe rising up the side of the aquarium and escaping from the back through a circular hole in the glass; a wardrobe and a dresser; a tiny woven rug; a bed, complete with bedclothes and pillow. There was even a doll lying under the covers. But then the doll turned around and looked up at Jodi and her heart rose up into her throat and lodged there.

The Small.

Oh raw we, there truly was a little man.

He was no bigger than a mouse; a miniature man, perfectly formed, blinking up at her from his glass prison. He clutched his bedclothes tightly to his throat, eyes wide and a look of alarm on his tiny features.

She bent closer to the glass side of the aquarium, moving as slow as she could so as not to startle him more, when she felt a draft of cold air on the back of her neck. Still moving slowly, but from fear now, she straightened once more and turned to face the doorway.

The Widow stood there, a look of amusement in her dark eyes. She leaned on her cane, the dark folds of her mantle falling about her to the tops of her high, laced boots.

"What have we here?" she said. "Come spying on me, have you, Jodi Shepherd?"

There was no place to hide—it was too late for that anyway—and no place to flee either, so Jodi held her ground, knees knocking against each other as she faced the Widow.

Something moved in the doorway by the Widow's feet, drawing Jodi's gaze. Half-numbed already—both from the existence of the Small and having been caught by the Widow—she could only stare at the little creature that crouched there.

It was no bigger than a cat, or Denzil's monkey, but its body was hairless. Spindly limbs supported its round-bellied torso. It had a triangular face with a wild thatch of dark red hair above it. Ears like clam shells stuck out at right angles from its head. It clung to the hem of the Widow's mantle, staring back at Jodi from its saucer-wide eyes. The flicker of a grin touched the wide gape of its mouth.

Jodi dragged her gaze back to the Widow's face.

"What—what are you going to do to me?" she managed finally.

"Well, that's the question now, isn't it?" the Widow replied.

Her tone was mild, but there was a look in her eyes that made Jodi shiver.

Oh, how could she have been such a fool to come here and no one knowing where she'd gone?

She was doomed to spend the rest of her life as a toad or a newt or whatever the Widow decided to turn her into for trespassing in her cottage and discovering her secrets.

"I—I didn't mean any . . ."

Harm, she wanted to say, but her throat just closed up on her and she couldn't get the word out.

"My little man's so lonely," the Widow said.

By her feet, the odd little creature began to titter. Jodi tried to back up, but there was only the worktable behind her and she was already pressed up against it.

"Please," Jodi tried.

The Widow spoke a word that seemed to hang in the air between them.

It was in no language that Jodi knew, but still, she could almost understand it. She felt queasy, hearing the repetition of its three syllables, as though her body subconsciously inferred its meaning and shied away from its import.

Then the Widow said Jodi's name. She repeated it, and again. Three times in all.

Now Jodi felt light-headed.

I won't faint, she thought as she reeled away from the table.

A stifling sense of closeness came over her, seeming to rush in at her from all sides. At the same time, the walls sped away in the opposite direction.

Dizzy, staggering, and disoriented, Jodi fought to keep her balance, but the floor rose up to meet her all the same.

The Hunt

Proud Nimrod first the bloody chase began—
A mighty hunter, and his prey was man.

— ALEXANDER POPE,
from "Windsor Forest"

*W*est of Mousehole, far west; past the craggy cliffs of Land's End, across the Atlantic Ocean, and farther west still; across the North American continent to the southern tip of Vancouver Island. . . . There, in an immaculately kept Tudor-styled house in the residential section of Victoria known as James Bay, an old man woke from a light sleep and sat up in his bed.

In his late eighties, John Madden was still as fit as he'd been in his mid-sixties, and he'd been fit then—enough so that his doctor had remarked at the time, "If you hadn't been my patient for the past twenty years, John, I'd swear you weren't a day over fifty."

It was true that the shock of black hair belonging to the young man he'd been had turned to grey and thinned some. He moved more slowly now, as well, his lean frame feeling the brittleness of his years so that bones ached in inclement weather, muscles were stiff when he rose in the morning, or from a long session at his desk. But he still saw to his own portfolios, with all the shrewdness that had made him a very rich man many times over, and his mind was as sharp and discerning as it had ever been.

He was a marvel in the circles in which he moved—always a leader, never a sycophant. His associates wondered at his acumen and his uncommon health for his age, though never in his presence. But he could see it in their eyes, more so as year followed year and he remained essentially unchanged while they fell by the wayside, young turks taking their place—the same questions eventually coming into their eyes.

But the secret to his success rested in neither the quick faculties of his mind, nor in the superb condition of his aging body. The key lay, instead, in the small image of a grey dove that was tattooed on the inside of his left wrist, placed just so that his watchband hid it from a casual glance.

Flicking on the light above his bed, Madden pressed a button on the intercom that sat beside the telephone on his night table.

"Sir?"

The response was almost immediate, crisp and alert, even though the recipient of the call had undoubtedly been asleep when it came to his room on the ground floor of the building.

"I'd like to see you, Michael," Madden said.

"I'll be right up."

Madden leaned back against the headboard and closed his eyes.

Thirty-five years ago he'd matched wits with one of his own countrymen, and lost. That loss rankled still, not the losing itself—even then Madden was long past such negligible concerns—but for the irreplaceable prize that had been forfeit.

He'd almost had it in his hands—a secret that couldn't be measured in secular terms—and it had slipped away, as vague and untouchable as mist burned off by the morning sun. It continued to exist, but his adversary had concealed it too well. It slept in some hidden place, the knowledge of which his rival had taken with him to his watery grave.

Madden had sent agents in pursuit of it, time and again, but sleeping, the secret was invisible. Impenetrable. Lost. He'd been through the house and the surrounding area himself—he, with his knowledge and understanding of what he sought, if not the configuration that it presently inhabited—and found nothing, so how could he hope that others would succeed?

Still he had them keep watch.

And he waited.

Because one day, he knew, it would wake again.

And then the secret would be his.

And he would take it into forever.

A knock at the oak door of his bedroom roused him from his reverie. He opened his eyes.

"Come in, Michael," he said.

The man who entered was another secret—suspected, perhaps, only to the world's hermetic community, but its importance went beyond occult concerns. Michael Bett was—Madden had proved it to his own satisfaction, irrefutably and beyond any doubt—a reincarnation of one of the early twentieth century's greatest sorcerers. Born December 5, 1947, his existence was proof, not only that reincarnation was possible, but that a sorcerer's will was strong enough to give him more than one opportunity to walk the world in corporeal form.

Madden had known Bett well in the man's previous life, so well that he could not fail to recognize him when he met him again in his new identity.

The resemblance was not physical. Bett was a wiry, thin man—unlike the man he'd been. He wore his dark hair fashionably long, his features were angular, his cheekbones pronounced, his forehead high, his too bright eyes somewhat sunken. But he had the same powerful will, the tendency towards excess, the incapacity for natural affection, the egotism, and the brilliant mind.

He had been misunderstood in previous lives, and he was misunderstood now. But not by Madden. Madden had nurtured that brilliance.

He'd found Bett ten years ago, stumbled across him as he stood over the corpse of his latest victim in a windy Chicago alleyway, and had known with a flash of insight whose troubled spirit lay behind the man's bright gaze.

Before Bett could turn on him, Madden invoked the Dove—whose symbol both he and now Bett wore on their wrists—and he took Bett away. Groomed him and quelled his insatiable appetite for the suffering of others. Channeled the man's incredible will towards the doctrines of the Order where—given an intellectual outlet for his excesses—he was weaned from the need to wreak havoc on the flesh of others and surpassed all of Madden's already high expectations.

But knowing who Bett was, how could he truly have been surprised?

There were secrets, and there were secrets. This one belonged to Madden and Michael Bett, and to no one else. It was ten years old, but it still brought a glint of satisfaction to Madden's eyes every time he looked on his colleague.

He waved Bett over to his bedside. Crossing the room, Bett sat on the end of Madden's bed.

"You've felt it again?" he asked.

Madden nodded. "Twice in one day. I think it's time you joined Lena."

Bett frowned.

"I know," Madden added. "If she becomes unreliable, or difficult to manage—"

"I'll rein her in."

"But gently. Her father stands high in the Order."

Bett nodded and rose from the end of the bed.

"I'd best go pack my bags," he said.

He turned to go, pausing in the doorway.

"You can count on me," he told Madden, and then he was gone.

Madden nodded to himself. Count on you to bring it to me, he thought. But once the secret is pried from its present configuration and available for our use? Will I still be able to count on you then?

Madden was wise enough to not let his affection for Bett cloud his awareness of the man's avaricious nature. For all that Madden had done for Bett, his colleague's first loyalty would always be to himself.

But then, Madden thought as he gazed across the room, we're not so different in that, are we?

It was what set them apart from the sheep.

What the Devil

Ails You?

It's always good when you come into contact
with other players and you discover you're
not this *freak*, that there are
others ... playing this strange instrument.

— K A T H R Y N   T I C K E L L , on playing
the Northumbrian pipes;
from an interview in *Folk
Roots*, No. 41, November 1986

I t was Manus Boyd—Charlie Boyd's grandfather, a Ker-
ryman from Ballyduff near the Mouth of the Shannon—
who first brought the Irish custom of a rambling house to
the Penwith Peninsula at the turn of the century. Janey had
heard the story so often that, like Charlie's children, she only
rolled her eyes and thought about other things when Charlie
decided to tell it again.

Manus had crossed the Celtic Sea with his wife Anne in 1902
and, one way or another, found himself in Cornwall where he
became a dairyman on a farm near Sennen that belonged to one
of the great Cornish estates. In those days the Estates had trouble
finding tenants for their farms so an established middleman farmer
would rent the unwanted land, stock it with cattle, and lease
the holding to a dairyman of his own choosing. This dairyman
had no responsibility to the Estate; the responsibility of upkeep
lay in the hands of the absentee farmer.

By the time Charlie took over the farm, he no longer dealt
with the middleman farmer, but leased the farm directly from
the estate through a land agent. He was the third generation of

Boyds to work that land, and by the beginning of the Second World War, their taciturn neighbours eventually allowed that it was the Boyd Farm, rather than the Dobson Farm, the Dobsons being the tenants before Manus Boyd.

Manus and Anne had passed on, as had Charlie's own father and mother, but there were still Boyds in plenty on that land, what with Charlie, his wife and three children, and his brother Pat. And the music sessions that had made it a rambling house in his grandparents' time were as popular as ever with those who had an ear for a proper old tune or song.

About the only thing that Janey didn't like about the sessions was that there were so many people smoking; she always came away with her clothes and hair smelling of smoke. It was the same when she played in most folk clubs, but while it was irritating, it was only a minor annoyance considering the grand time she invariably had.

A good crowd was already present by the time she and the Gaffer arrived.

Chalkie was there with his melodeon, sitting next to Jim Rafferty who hadn't taken his tin whistle from the inside pocket of his jacket yet. A couple of members of the Newlyn Reelers— a local barn dance band—had come, as well as Bobbie Wright and Lesley Peake, a professional duo who lived on the other side of Penzance and played guitar and fiddle, respectively.

There were others from the surrounding farms, some with instruments, others with simply their voices, and, of course, the Boyds: Uncle Pat on tenor banjo, Charlie on fiddle, and his wife Molly on piano and Anglo concertina; their daughter Bridget on concert flute and whistle, and their sons, Sean also on fiddle and Dinny who played both the Irish Uillean pipes and the Northumbrian.

It was Dinny who'd tracked down Janey's first set of pipes when she started to talk about wanting to take them up. He taught her both the basics and encouraged her whenever the complexities of the instrument got to be so much that she just wanted to pitch them into Mount's Bay.

Also there that night, sitting beside the two chairs that were waiting for Janey and her grandfather, was Janey's best friend, Clare Mabley. Clare was a dark-haired girl, slender and pale, who worked in a bookstore in Penzance. A blackthorn cane lay on the floor beside her chair. She pulled a small tin whistle from her purse as Janey sat down.

"I got that F whistle," she said. "It came with the post today."

Janey smiled. "And?"

"I'm still getting used to the pitch."

Clare had a good singing voice, but she had always wanted to play an instrument. The trouble was, she couldn't seem to concentrate on learning any one she tried. Finally she took up the whistle and stuck with it when Jim Rafferty assured her it was simple to learn and offered to teach her to play. She was much happier at the sessions now, though whenever her turn came around, she always picked a tune that everyone knew so that she wouldn't have to play it on her own.

As they did every Friday night, they were all gathered in the Boyds' huge kitchen, chairs and stools and crates pulled up into a kind of rough circle around the gas stove and the big kitchen table where was laid out the vast array of cakes, biscuits, and cookies that had been brought along by the various guests. There was always tea steeping in a big ceramic teapot by the stove, though many brought stronger drink, as the Gaffer had with his brown ales, one of which stood under his own chair, the other under Janey's.

The music went 'round the circle. When their turn came up, each person had to offer up something: a tune, a song, a story, a joke—it didn't matter what. If you knew the piece, and it seemed appropriate to do so, you joined in; if you didn't, you merely sat back and enjoyed it.

As always seemed to happen when they arrived, no sooner had Janey sat down than the turn had come 'round to her. Complaining good-humouredly, she lifted her pipes out of their carrying box and buckled the bellows above the elbow of her left arm. Then she attached the air bag with its drones to it, laying the drones across her body so that they rested on her right arm, and connected the tiny chanter. After a few moments of tuning the drones to the chanter, she gave Dinny a grin and launched into a sprightly version of "Billy Pigg's Hornpipe." The tune was a favorite of hers, having been written by Pigg himself.

Playing in the key of F as she was, most of the other musicians couldn't join in. A peculiarity of the Northumbrian pipes was that they couldn't play in the keys of most standard dance tunes. But Dinny, after letting her go through it once on her own, joined her the next time around on his own pipes, as did Clare on her tiny new F whistle, its high sweet tones cutting pleasantly across the bee-buzz of the pipes' drones and the mellower sound of their chanters.

They ended the tune with a flourish to a round of applause, Clare blushing furiously, and then it was the Gaffer's turn to tell one of his improbable tales. After that Chalkie started up a version of "Johnny Cope" on his melodeon and Janey swapped her pipes for her fiddle. By the time Chalkie switched to "Tipsy Sailor"—an Irish variant of the same tune—everyone with an instrument in hand was playing, those who didn't have one were clapping their hands, and the kitchen rang with the sound of the music.

And so the evening went, with tunes and songs and poetry recitations. Whenever her turn or Dinny's came up, they'd both take up their pipes, enjoying the opportunity of playing together. It was what Janey liked best about the sessions.

It was too bad she couldn't get Dinny to come with her on this upcoming tour, she thought as they were in the middle of a particularly sensitive version of the slow air, "The Flowers of the Forest." They played with the melody line, first one, then the other chanter taking up the lead, harmonizing beautifully against the sweet burring of their drones.

But Dinny had no interest in touring. He loved music, but like all his family preferred sessions to organized gigging. It was only after weeks of persuasion that she'd ever gotten them to play on a few tracks of either one of her albums.

At one point the turn in the circle came 'round to Frank Woolnough who had a farm just outside St. Buryan. He didn't play an instrument or sing, but he loved to spin a tale, the more exaggerated the better. Every so often, he and the Gaffer would spend the night seeing who could outdo the other, and since the Gaffer had told his story about the pair of ghostly hummocks he'd seen one night on a country lane near Sennen, didn't Frank have to top him?

"Well," he said. "I got this from my father and it happened down your way, Gaffer, in Mousehole harbour it was. There was a boat from the Lizard docked there and my father was reeling his way from The Ship after a pint too many—wasn't his habit, understand, but he'd had a bit of luck that day and didn't everyone have to stand him a drink?

"Still, drunk he might have been, but 'ark to what he told me. There he was, standing at the rail and looking at the boats all tipping one side or another, it being low tide, and what does he see but a little man come out of that boat from the Lizard. No bigger than a mouse, he were, stepping his way along the mooring line, balanced just as easy as you please.

"Well, my old dad blinks, then blinks again, and somewhere between the two blinks, didn't that little man just vanish?"

By the stove, Uncle Pat gave a laugh. "Back into the bottle he came from, why!"

"Laugh as you will," Frank said, "but my old dad he went down into the harbour to have himself a closer look and what do you think he saw? Tiny footprints leading away from the mooring line across the sand and away to a great heap of netting that was lying there on the stairs."

Frank nodded sagely, one eye turned gravely to the Gaffer.

"Hummocks is one thing," he said. "But could have been was nothing but a mist you saw, Gaffer. No offense, but that's how I see it. But this little man—it was a piskie my old dad saw and that's God's own truth. The footprints there were proof plain for all to see."

"And who else saw them?" Chalkie asked.

"Oh, well," Frank replied. "Tide came up, didn't it, and washed them away. But he saw them plain and, drunk or sober, my old dad wasn't one to make up a tale like that."

Janey had to smile at the story. It reminded her of Dunthorn's work, and of the new book she'd discovered this afternoon that she'd only barely started. But before she could think too much about it, Bridget Boyd, sitting beside Frank, struck up a tune and the music took them all away again.

'Round about midnight, the music wound down and people began to drift off to their homes. Janey and the Gaffer were among the last to leave, the Gaffer having an earnest conversation with Uncle Pat about the door-to-door wet fish business that the Gaffer ran from his home, making his deliveries in a beat-up old Austin stationwagon that was painted a bright yellow with the legend "Fresh Local Fish" painted on each side.

Dinny and Janey were caught up in their own discussion, sitting almost head to head, as they discussed the peculiarities of reeds, particular turns of odd tunes, and other piper talk that had Clare and the others—who'd heard this sort of thing all too often when the pair got together—ignoring them for less esoteric conversation.

When finally it was time to leave, Clare joined Janey and the Gaffer so that they could give her a lift home. Janey packed her instruments in the back of her tiny three-wheeled Reliant Robin—which prompted Dinny to make his usual comment about when was she going to get a *real* car?—and they set off for Mousehole along the winding lanes that ran from Lamorna to the village, the hedgerows rising tall on either side of the narrow roads.

They dropped Clare off at the door of the cottage she shared with her mother on Raginnis Hill, just a few doors down from the Mousehole Wild Bird Hospital. After a promise of getting together tomorrow because it was Clare's day off, Janey gave her friend a wave, the Gaffer adding a "Sleep well, now, my blossom," and they headed on down the hill for home.

2 .

Felix heard the small Reliant before its lights flickered in the Gaffer's living room as it came 'round the corner from Mousehole Lane and parked beside the Gaffer's stationwagon. He set aside the rescued book he'd been reading and leaned forward in the chair, pulse quickening in anticipation.

It's been three years, he thought.

Had she changed? Had he? Would it be awkward?

He ran a hand across the stubble of his hair, listening to their voices outside. He started to rise from the chair, but then the door was flung open and Janey burst into the room in her usual enthusiastic manner.

And stopped dead in her tracks when she saw him sitting there in the Gaffer's chair.

The Gaffer came in behind her more slowly. He was first to speak.

"Felix, my fortune. How *are* you?"

Felix rose from the chair, but before he could speak, Janey had dumped her instruments onto the couch and literally flew across the room to embrace him.

"Felix!" she cried as she hugged him, small arms tight around his body.

Felix's pulse doubled its tempo again. He put his arms around her, touched the familiar shape of her shoulder blades under her jumper, smelled the cigarette smoke that clung to her clothes and hair, but under it the sweet scent that was her.

He couldn't say a word.

Janey leaned a bit back from him so that she could look up into his face.

"This is such a wonderful surprise," she said. "It's been *ages.*"

A surprise? Felix thought.

The Gaffer closed the door to the cottage.

"You should have told us you were coming," he said. "We

would have come by and picked you up at the station."

Janey gave him a last hug and stepped away, face still beaming.

"You big galoot," she said, giving his shoulder a soft punch. "Trust you to show up like this all unannounced."

"But . . ." Felix began.

"It's just wonderful to see you," Janey went on before he could finish. She dragged him over to the couch so that they could sit down beside each other. "You have to tell me everything. Where you've been. What you're doing here." She glanced over at his baggage, gaze settling on the wooden box. "I see you brought your accordion. I hope you've brought some new tunes as well."

"There's no beer," the Gaffer said, "but I can put on a kettle."

Felix shook his head. "No thanks. I just had some tea."

Beside him, Janey took his hand and gave it a squeeze. "How long can you stay?" she asked. "Tell me it'll be weeks."

Felix wanted to just bask in her attention and not say anything, but couldn't.

"Janey," he said. "Why are you surprised to see me?"

She blinked. "Why shouldn't I be? You never said you were coming."

"But the letter—"

"You wrote?" She looked over at the Gaffer. "We never got a letter, did we?"

The Gaffer shook his head.

"It must've got lost in the mail," Janey said. "Where did you send it from?"

"I didn't write to you," Felix said. "You wrote to me."

Janey blinked again. "I didn't never," she said.

Felix disengaged his hand from hers and pulled the folded letter from his pocket. He handed it over to her.

"Then what's this?" he asked.

Janey opened the letter and scanned it quickly.

"I didn't send this to you, Felix," she said.

Felix frowned. "It's not funny," he said. "I came a long way. I . . ."

What could he say? That he'd come because he'd promised

once and promises were sacred to him? Because he'd told her that he'd always be there for her, no matter what? Because the letter had burned like a bright beacon in his mind, awaking dead hopes?

"I honestly didn't write it," Janey repeated. "And I'm not in any trouble, desperate or otherwise."

"But . . ."

"Well, that's not completely true. I broke up with Alan and I've got a tour coming up and I *am* desperate for a sideman, but it's not the kind of thing I'd write to you about." She poked the letter with a finger. "This sounds so . . . so serious."

"That's why I came."

Janey had gone all earnest now. She reached out and took his hand again.

"It means a lot that you did come after getting this," she said.

"Can I see this letter?" the Gaffer asked.

Janey passed it over to him.

"It's a queer sort of game to be playing on someone," the Gaffer said after he'd read it through.

Felix met the old man's steady gaze and saw in it that the Gaffer knew exactly why he'd come—and that he approved. Of course, he and the Gaffer had always got on well. But much as he liked the old man, it was his granddaughter he wanted to get on well with first.

"Did you travel far?" the Gaffer added.

"I got it in Madrid," Felix said, "and came right away."

"I really didn't write it," Janey said. "I don't even own a typewriter."

He wanted to believe her. But if she hadn't sent it, then who had? Who knew him well enough to know that a letter like this would bring him to her, no matter where he was when it reached him? And why would they bother?

It made no sense.

"It's not Janey's sort of prank," the Gaffer said.

"I know."

At least he thought he did. The Janey he'd known would

never have done it for a lark. But who could tell how much she'd changed in three years?

He rubbed the stubble on his scalp again, feeling foolish to have come all this way, to be here, when he wasn't needed.

"It's still *wonderful* to see you," Janey said.

"And better that there is no trouble, don't you think, my robin?" the Gaffer added.

Trouble, Felix thought.

"Well, there has been trouble," he said.

Briefly he described what had happened when he first arrived.

"How could they know?" the Gaffer said when Felix was done.

"Know what?" both Felix and Janey asked at the same time.

The Gaffer glanced at the book where it sat on the arm of his favorite chair. For long moments he said nothing. Then finally he sighed.

"There's a thing about that book," he said. "I don't rightly know what, but there's been people after it for as long as it's been in my possession."

Janey sat forward on the edge of the couch. "That's right! You said some American woman had been asking after it."

"And she's not the first, my gold," the Gaffer said. "When I first got it from Billy. I . . . well, we were mates, Billy and I. Close as brothers, weren't we? I didn't know what it was about the book that made him send it to me, or want me to hide it— I've read it through myself and it's just a tale like the others he's written—but hide it I did.

"First I kept it at Charlie's place, and then later up at Andy Spurr's farm, over near the Reservoir, and a good thing I did, for there were men coming around asking after it, threatening legal action against me—though they didn't have half a leg to stand on—and even coming to the house when neither myself or the missus were home."

"When was this?" Janey asked.

"Oh, years ago—before you were born, my love. But they came and pried and snooped for a few months, never giving me a moment's rest, until one day they were all up and gone. Time to time, I'd get a letter—or a phone call, once we had a line put in—asking after Billy's 'unpublished writings.' They'd be publishers, see, wanting notes or stories that hadn't been published before, or asking after photographs and artifacts, but I could tell the difference between the genuine article and whoever these others were. They weren't publishers, though I can't tell you how I know that, or who they really were. Nor what they really wanted."

Janey shivered. "This is becoming more and more mysterious every moment."

The Gaffer nodded, but he didn't seem very happy about the mystery of it.

"When Andy died last year, his widow had me come take the box of Billy's writings away because she was leaving the farm to live with her son in St. Ives. I put it up in the attic, but I didn't look in it except to see that the book was still there. Didn't open the book."

"Why not?" Felix asked.

The Gaffer shrugged. "Don't know, my gold. It's just a feeling I have that when that book's opened, things start to *happen*."

"But what kinds of things?" Janey wanted to know.

The Gaffer looked as though he was about to say something, then shrugged again and settled on: "That the crows would come sniffing around again."

"I suppose there's money to be made from a previously unknown and unpublished Dunthorn book?" Felix asked.

Neither the Gaffer nor Janey replied.

"Well, wouldn't there be?"

"I suppose," the Gaffer said. "But it wouldn't be right. I made a promise, didn't I?"

"I didn't mean that you should get it published," Felix said. "It's only that it explains why people are coming around looking for it—that they're even willing to steal it. There must be some rumour of the book's existence that gets resurrected every once in a while."

Janey shook her head. "I've got all the biographies on him

and I never came across even a hint of *The Little Country*, or *any* unpublished book, until I found it this afternoon."

"It's more than money," the Gaffer agreed. "There's something odd about the book. I can't put it into words, but it's there. Just a feeling I get."

Felix thought about the book. There *was* a certain feel about it, though he wouldn't have called it odd. The word he would have chosen was comfortable. It was the sort of book that no sooner had he opened it than he felt at ease and among friends. Ready to follow the storyline, no matter how fantastic. And he didn't even care much for that kind of book in the first place.

"What will you do now?" he asked the Gaffer. "Hide it again?"

"I suppose."

"But not until I get to finish reading it!" Janey protested.

The Gaffer smiled. "No. We can wait that long, my queen. But we'll have to be careful and hide it well whenever we go out."

Janey gave another little shiver. "Isn't it all kind of, oh, I don't know, sort of eerie?"

"It's queer, all right," the Gaffer agreed.

Though no more strange than the mysterious letter that had brought him here, Felix thought. He looked at it lying forgotten on Janey's lap, then picked it up and refolded it once more.

"Felix," she began as he put it away in his pocket. "I honestly didn't send that."

"It's all right," he said. "I don't mind having come. It's really good to see you—both of you."

"You're not going to run off again, are you?" Janey asked.

Is that how she saw the way their relationship had ended? Felix wondered. That he'd run off on her?

"No," he said. "I'll stay for a day or so, but then I've got to go."

"But you just got here."

How to explain what it meant to him, being here with her, but not *with* her?

"I used almost all the money I had to get here as quickly as I could," he said. "I have to get back to London and see what ships are in port and if I can get a job."

"You can stay with us," Janey said.

"I'll stay tonight."

"There's lots of room," the Gaffer added.

Felix knew what he meant. It could be like it had been before, when he'd lived here with them. But it wouldn't—couldn't—be what it had been before. And while Felix didn't ever not want to be friends with Janey, right now he was feeling too confused to even think about their getting back together again.

There was that letter lying between them. . . .

"Don't blame me for something I didn't do," Janey began, but the Gaffer shushed her before she could go on.

"Give the man a chance to catch his wits, my love." He glanced at Felix. "You remember your old room?"

Felix nodded.

"Nothing much has changed. You can go on up and use it if you like."

Felix turned to Janey. He wanted to explain the confusion, but while he could speak so eloquently to her when she was only present in his imagination, when he was far out to sea on some freighter, sitting here in the Gaffer's house on Duck Street, with her presence all too real, everything was just a jumble in his head.

"I guess I'll go up," he said.

Janey caught his arm as he got up from the couch and he paused, looking at her.

"I . . ." she began, then sighed. "I just wanted to say good night."

Felix gave her a weak smile. "Good night," he said.

Collecting his baggage, he went upstairs.

3 ·

Janey sat for a long time on the couch after Felix had gone up. As she listened to him moving about in his room, a flood of memories went through her. They were good memories and they made her wonder for the first time in a long time just why their relationship hadn't worked out.

He'd never been jealous of what success she'd found as a musician like Alan, nor had the touring it necessitated troubled him as it did the fellow she'd dated before Alan—probably because Felix's own work took him all over the world. They'd spent weeks together in Mousehole, though, when she wasn't on the road and he was off ship, and when she did tour, he'd often turn up in the oddest places just to spend a few days with her. In New England, once, when his ship had docked in Boston. In California another time, when he took a few months off and hitchhiked across the country to see her. At a festival in Germany. Another in Scotland.

Like Dinny Boyd, he enjoyed playing music, but had absolutely no ambition to turn professional—a fact that constantly irritated her because he was just so bloody good on his box. In the circles that knew about this sort of thing, he was reckoned in the same breath as some of the masters of the instrument—John Kimmel, Paddy O'Brien, Joe Cooley, Tony MacMahon, Joe Burke—and was considered on a par with his contemporaries such as Martin O'Connor, Jackie Daly, and the like. He also played a mean whistle, as well as a little concert flute and guitar. But while he'd sit in with her the odd time, he refused to make the commitment to record or tour.

They used to argue about it—a great deal towards the end of their relationship. In fact, she thought, if she was going to be honest about it, it was the constant pressure she'd put on him about it that had contributed the most to the breakup. They'd start off talking about his reluctance to tour, or about his wanting to settle down—a laugh, since his work took him to the four corners of the world—and somehow that would segue into pointless and often strident arguments that, when she looked back on them, really weren't about anything very important at all.

She could remember his trying to stop them, his calmness in the face of her quarreling, but she had too volatile a temper and his imperturbability just made her more angry. It was silly, really, because five minutes later, she'd forget all about it, but though he wouldn't say anything, he'd still carry the hurt. She could see it in his eyes, or in the cautious way he dealt with her, and that would just set things off again until finally they just called it quits one day. Before she was even fully aware of what they were doing, he'd packed up and was gone.

She'd missed him terribly at first and accepted a long tour on the Continent—one that she'd refused when it was first offered to her because she and Felix had had plans to spend a month traveling around Ireland. Without him, she didn't want to go to Ireland anymore. And she didn't want to stay in Mousehole. All she wanted to do was to try to put it all behind her.

So she'd done just that. But seeing him tonight—feeling her heart lift when she saw him and the way she just fit so perfectly into the circle of his arms—she realized that she'd been too effective. What she should have done was not let him go in the first place.

Sighing, she glanced at the Gaffer who was sitting in his chair by the hearth, pretending not to be watching her.

"He doesn't believe me, does he?" she said.

"Well, it's a strange business, my gold."

"I feel funny seeing him again. It's like we never broke up, but at the same time it's like there's a whole ocean lying in between us."

She tugged at a loose thread at the hem of her short skirt, her gaze fixed on what she was doing, though she wasn't thinking about the thread or her skirt at all. Finally she looked over at her grandfather again.

"Do you think second chances are possible?" she asked.

"Well, that depends," the Gaffer said. "We didn't worry much about that kind of thing in my time. Couples tried to make do, to see each other through the rough spots. I'm not saying that way was right or wrong—there's times when a man and a woman just aren't right for each other and no matter of work can make things better between them—but mostly we stuck to it."

"But what about me and Felix?"

"How do you feel about seeing him?" the Gaffer asked.

"All mixed up."

"Well, my robin, first you have to decide what it is that you want."

"I suppose."

The Gaffer nodded. "It's hard, I know. But know what you want first, my love. If you just try to muddle through, you'll only give each other still more heartbreak."

"But how can I convince him that I didn't send that stupid letter?"

"It's not so stupid, really, is it?" the Gaffer said. "It brought him here, didn't it?"

Janey gave him a sudden considering look. "You didn't send it, did you?"

The Gaffer laughed. "Not a chance of that, my flower. I learned long ago to keep my nose in my own business, *especially* when it comes to family."

"Well, then who did?"

"Don't worry about that so much. Worry about your heart, my love. He won't be here long."

"But he doesn't believe me."

"Give him time to believe."

Janey sighed. "You just said he wasn't going to be here long, and now you tell me I should give him time."

The Gaffer rose from his chair. "Now you know why I like to keep to my own business," he said. "In this sort of an affair, no matter what you say, you're wrong."

"I'm sorry. I didn't mean—"

"That's all right, my dear," the Gaffer said. "Your old grandfather knows you better than you think. Now I'm for bed. Are you staying up?"

Janey shook her head.

The Gaffer picked up the Dunthorn book from the arm of the chair and handed it to her.

"Well, don't leave this lying around," he said.

"I won't. Good night, Gramps."

"Good night, my robin. Things will look different in the morning when you see them with fresh eyes."

"I need a fresh brain," Janey muttered, but the Gaffer was already leaving the room and gave no notice that he'd heard her.

Or maybe a fresh heart, she added to herself. Oh, why did things always have to get so complicated?

She slouched on the couch for a while longer, until at last she got up and collected her instruments. Turning off the lights, she went outside to her own room.

The Gaffer's cottage had a small courtyard in front of it—the same place where Felix had struggled with the burglar earlier that evening. A low stone wall, broken by an wrought-iron gate, closed it in from the road. Flower boxes hung from either side of it, while Jabez, the Gaffer's black and white tomcat, could be found lounging upon the top most days and well into the evening.

Turning right from the front door, the stone patio went through a small archway to a smaller courtyard. Directly facing the arch was the entrance to the cellar where the Gaffer kept the freezers for his fish. Turning right again, one could see a narrow set of stairs that led up to where Janey lived.

She had two rooms.

The outer one had the bathroom directly in front of the door as you came in, and two windows, one looking back into the courtyard, the other overlooking the Gaffer's tiny square of lawn in back of his cottage, which was hedged with blackberry bushes. This was Janey's sitting room and where she practiced her music. The walls were covered with festival posters, including her favorite from the Cornwall '86 Folk Festival in Wadebridge where she'd gotten her first large print billing, as opposed to being lost in among the tiny type or simply listed as "and others." Near the door were two paintings by the Newlyn artist Bernard Evans—one of Mousehole harbour, the other depicting one of the old luggers that used to fish this part of the coast.

The furnishings here consisted of two wooden straightback chairs (Janey couldn't play sitting on a sofa or a chair with arms);

a battered sofa that she'd patched with swatches from a pair of Laura Ashley dresses she'd outgrown; a crate under the back window with a hotplate, kettle, and teapot on it; a dresser filled with records that held her stereo on top, along with a jumble of cassettes; a bookcase filled mostly with tunebooks; and of course her instruments. Two other fiddles and a flat-backed mandolin hung from the wall, her first set of pipes sat in its case in a corner, while various whistles, pipe chanters, spare reeds, and the like were scattered across the low table in front of the couch. A bodhran lay on the couch itself.

The other room was her bedroom. In one corner was the Aquatron shower that the Gaffer had installed for her a couple of years ago, saving her from having to throw something decent on to go next door whenever she wanted to take a shower. There was also her bed, an old wooden wardrobe stuffed with clothes— some of which she'd long outgrown but couldn't throw out— another dresser, and a bookcase jammed with more books than it should have been able to hold. The window in this room also looked out on the inner courtyard.

Leaving her instruments in the first room, Janey wandered into her bedroom. She undressed slowly, only half thinking of what she was doing, then curled up under her comforter, the Dunthorn book held against her chest.

Things were going to look different in the morning, the Gaffer had promised. Which was all well and fine, but how was she supposed to stop thinking about them in the meantime?

She lay there for a long while, listening to the wind outside and the patter of rain that it soon brought with it. After a time she opened the book and let Dunthorn take her away from her troubles until she fell asleep, the book dropping onto the bed-clothes beside her leg.

Off She Goes!

It's not that I'm afraid to die. It's
just that I don't want to be there
when it happens.

—attributed to W O O D Y   A L L E N

J o d i had never fainted before. In the story that was her
life she saw herself as the plucky and brave heroine who—
when some moment of adventurous duress finally arose—
Got Things Done and Made A Difference. She definitely did
not see herself as a light-headed poppet who collapsed at the first
sign of trouble.

But faint she did.

And when she came around, she almost fainted again.

For she found herself lying on top of a bed with a man sitting
beside her on the coverlets who bore an awfully close resemblance
to the little fellow she'd seen inside the Widow Pender's aquarium, except that this man was the same size as she. What made
her almost pass out once more was the realization that he hadn't
become large. No. For she could see past the bed, through the
glass sides of the aquarium, to discover that she was with him
in the aquarium, set up on the worktable in the Widow's giant
sitting room.

The little man hadn't grown large at all.

She'd been shrunk down to his size.

It was impossible, of course. She was just dreaming. Any minute now she'd wake up in her aunt's house to find that she'd
fallen asleep and only dreamt the whole affair. Her midnight
adventure had yet to begin, and given the warning wisdom of
her dream, she'd do the sensible thing for a change and just stay
in her bed until morning.

"Are you feeling a little better?" the small man asked.

She still thought of him as tiny, even though they were now

the same size. He was a pleasant enough looking individual with a countryman's rounded features and a sturdy frame; older than she was—at least in his early twenties—which would make him positively ancient to the children of the Tatters. She gave him a considering glance, then tried to will the whole scene away.

Wake up, wake up, she told herself.

Her surroundings and size remained uncomfortably unchanged.

"Miss?" the little man tried again.

Jodi sat up on the bed, leaning against the backboard when the inside of the aquarium began to do a slow spin around her. She waited a few long moments for her head to settle down, then focused on the little man's face again.

"I'm dreaming, aren't I?"

He shook his head. "No dream—though it is a nightmare."

Well, of course he wouldn't think it was a dream, not when he was a part of it. She tried to place his accent. It wasn't quite the soft burr predominant around Bodbury; instead it had a clipped property about it, which gave it a bit of a formal ring. She wondered what his name was.

"Edern Gee," he told her when she asked.

And that sounded exactly like something she'd make up—not a proper name at all.

"My name's Jodi," she said. "Jodi Shepherd."

Edern nodded. "I know. I heard it when the witch charmed you."

"I didn't find her very charming at all," Jodi said.

"I meant when she used her magic—when she enchanted you."

Magic. Oh raw we. It made her head ache to think about it.

"And you?" she asked. "I suppose you've been enchanted, too?"

Edern gave her a sour look. "Do you think I was born this size?"

"How would I know? We've only just met."

That earned her a smile.

Jodi looked around their glass prison once more.

"So this is . . . real?" she asked.

"All too."

"Did you come snooping about her house as well?"

Edern shook his head. "I only meant to pass through Bodbury and stopped in here to ask if there was any work that needed doing. I never got any farther into town."

"She didn't like the job you did?"

"Didn't want to pay me. She shrunk me down when I argued about it with her. I've been here three weeks, locked up in this glass box like her pet toad."

"*Three* weeks?"

Edern nodded glumly.

"And you didn't try to escape?"

"You try climbing those glass walls."

"But what about over there?" Jodi asked, pointing to where the tin chimney rose up from the stove and climbed up alongside the glass.

"The tin's too hot."

Jodi laughed. "Well, then put out the fire."

For a long moment Edern just stared at her, then he sighed.

"It's not just getting out of the box," he said. "There's that as well."

Jodi looked in the direction he indicated and began to feel all faint again.

Stop this, she ordered herself.

But it was hard, for sitting there on the high back of a chair was the Widow's odd little creature, all fat-bodied and spindly limbs. When it saw it had her attention, it grinned at her, revealing long rows of wickedly sharp teeth. It had been the size of a cat the last time she'd seen it. Now, with her own reduction in size, it had the relative bulk of an elephant.

"Bother and damn," she said.

Not only was this impossible, it wasn't fair either. She could almost hear her aunt's voice as soon as she had the thought. "Fairness is for those what have the money to pay for it," she liked to tell Jodi. "Not for the likes of us."

"It's almost always about," Edern said. "When you can't see it—just a tap on the glass will bring it scampering back to its post."

"What is it?"

"Her fetch."

"But that's like a hummock, isn't it?" Jodi said. "Just another kind of a ghost?"

"It's also a witch's familiar. She calls it Windle. Witches grow them from their own phalanges—usually the ones from their little toe."

Jodi gave him another considering look. Edern Gee might claim to be a simple traveling man, but he seemed to know an awful lot about witches and magic and the like.

"I don't think you're a traveler at all," she said. "I think you've come from the Barrow World. You're a Small—a little piskie man that she caught out on the moors."

"I could say the same about you."

"Ah, but you saw me big. You saw her shrink me down to mouse size."

She found it easy enough to say, but she was nevertheless hedging her bets, mostly because she was still praying that this *was* all a dream.

"You seem to know all about magic and the like," she added.

Edern just shrugged. "Did you never hear the stories of the traveling people in Bodbury? How we're all spellmen and witch-wives?"

"But those are just stories. . . ."

Jodi's voice trailed off. Like Smalls were. Or the fact that a witch could grow an odd little creature from the bones of her baby toe, or shrink someone down to the size of a mole.

"What's she going to do with us?" she asked finally.

"Don't know. Keep us as pets, I suppose. She likes to come in here and talk to me while she makes these tiny furnishings and the like. I don't think she's bad at heart—just lonely."

Jodi couldn't find much sympathy for a lonely witch—at least not for one who'd enchanted her the way the Widow Pender had.

"I can't stay locked up in here," she said. "I'll go mad."

"Does anyone know where you've gone?"

Jodi shook her head. "I'll be missed—sooner or later. Probably later, when either Denzil or my aunt finally goes looking for me at the other's place. But that could take a day or so and they'd never know where to look. How about you?"

"A solitary traveling man? Who's to miss me?"

"Well, I'm not staying," Jodi said.

She got slowly off the bed. Her head still ached, but at least the room stayed in one place. Crossing the aquarium, she leaned against the glass wall and peered out. Windle sat up on the back of its chair and looked at her with interest in its saucer-big eyes.

"Why hasn't she put the cover back on?" she asked Edern.

"She only does that when she goes out."

"And when does she do that?"

Jodi knew about her afternoon walks down by the Old Quay, and her midnight excursions out onto the headland, but that was all.

"Afternoons and late at night—regular as clockwork," Edern replied, adding nothing to what she already knew.

"Then I suppose I'll just have to wait until this afternoon," she said.

She turned from the glass wall to look at her companion.

"Who gets the bed?" she asked.

"It's big enough for two."

"I suppose. But mind you keep yourself to yourself."

Edern laughed. "You're a bit young for me."

Was she now?

"Well, you're far too old for me, geezer," she told him.

Ignoring his smile, she went 'round to the other side of the bed and, not bothering to remove her clothes, crawled under the covers.

Maybe I'll fall asleep and wake up back home, she thought.

Maybe she would. And maybe she'd only dream that she did. How would she ever know?

Thinking about that only made her head ache more, so she tried to think of more pleasant things. But everything merely went around and around in dizzying circles, each of which centered on the impossibility of her present situation.

La, but life could be confusing, she thought as sheer exhaustion finally let her drop off.

2 .

Waking provided no relief.

She was still mouse-sized when she opened her eyes, still trapped in an aquarium like one of Denzil's catfish, though happily, unlike theirs, this one wasn't full of murky water. But dryness was little comfort, all things considered. Her situation was so fanciful that she might as well be in the Barrow World of Faerie— a place she'd longed to visit ever since she read her first fairy tale—as in her native Bodbury. Caught up in the uncomfortable reality of her adventure, however—in reduced circumstances, as it were, she thought with a rueful smile—the wonder of it all had lost much of its previous storybook appeal.

I would settle for my old life, she decided. Pages missing and all. There was no question of it. Unfortunately, the decision of what was to become of her life didn't seem to be hers to make anymore.

"Getting up, are you?"

She glanced over to the other side of the aquarium where Edern was sitting at a table, eating.

"Best hurry up," he added, "unless you don't mind eating in the dark."

"What do you mean?"

"It's past noon and she'll be going out in a bit. It's her habit to feed me—us, now, I suppose—before she leaves."

Rubbing sleep from her eyes and feeling rumpled from having

slept in her clothes, Jodi swung her feet down from the bed and crossed the aquarium to join him. At the mention of food, her stomach had begun to rumble, but the small platter of crumbled cheese and tiny bits of bread didn't seem very appealing. It reminded her too much of what Denzil fed his mice.

She stood there, combing her short hair with her fingers, until Edern motioned her to sit.

"Is this it?" she asked, waving her hand at the food as she sat down.

"I've had worse."

"Maybe you have, and maybe I have too, but this . . . this is what you feed mice. I'm *not* her pet and I *won't* eat it."

Never mind that she liked both cheese and bread. It was the principle of the thing.

Edern laughed. "But that's all we are to the Widow—her pets."

Jodi said nothing.

"Starving won't solve a thing," Edern added.

At Jodi's frown, he pushed one of two ceramic thimbles across the table towards her.

"Have some tea, at least," he said.

"Well, maybe some tea."

She pulled the thimble over to her and took a deep sip. The tea was good, but its container made her feel like Weeman from the old nursery rhyme. She could make up her own bit of verse now:

Now I am small, but once I was big;
I feel like a fool, oh, rig-a-jig-jig.

Without really thinking about it, she put some cheese between two bits of bread and ate it, washing it down with more tea. It was only when she was on her third sandwich that she realized what she was doing. She gave Edern a quick glance, but he was studiously ignoring her.

So she was eating. Well, who cared? Besides, she needed her strength for her big escape.

She finished the third sandwich, then turned her chair so that she could examine the Widow's sitting room.

Windle didn't seem to be about, which was just as well. The witch's fetch made her feel like the Bagle Wight was breathing right upon her neck. And with neither the witch nor her creature in the room, it was a perfect opportunity to do some scouting.

Leaving her seat, Jodi went over to the stove first. The fire was out, so she cautiously touched the stovepipe and found it only warm, rather than hot. Since she'd been climbing about on gutters and roofs from when she was six years old and on, she knew she'd have no trouble navigating the pipe's length. She could even go inside it, which would save her having to try to pry the thing away from the glass when she got to the top. She could just scoot through, then climb down the cloth the Widow would drape over the aquarium when she went out.

Descending from the worktable was another matter again. But she soon spied a roll of twine. If she could open the window, then tie the twine to its latch, she could simply roll the twine over the side and into the garden. And she'd be away.

Then she thought about Edern and studied the stovepipe again. Would he fit? Two could manage both the window and twine more easily than one. But if he couldn't get through . . .

She looked to where the pipe met the glass. It wasn't glued or anything. If she clung to the cloth and gave it a good kick, she might be able to get it away from the glass. It would be easier done from the outside than the inside, at any rate. She turned to share her plan with him, but just then the sitting-room door opened and the Widow came in.

Humming to herself, the Widow took a small pair of tongs from the worktable and used them to extract a coal from the hearth, which she brought over to the aquarium.

Oh, no, Jodi thought. Don't.

She might as well have wished for the moon to come down from the sky and whisk her away.

"And how are you today, my sweets?" the Widow asked as she removed the glass lid of the aquarium.

Her voice boomed like dull thunder. Jodi glared at the Widow's enormous face looming over her, but Edern merely ignored it.

A huge hand came down into the aquarium and shooed Jodi away from the stove. She moved sullenly, wishing she had a large pin. The Widow opened the door to the stove and placed the coal inside, then closed it up again and withdrew her hands.

"There," she said. "Now you'll be warm and snug."

Back went the glass lid. She took the velvet from where it had been hanging over the back of a chair and draped it over the aquarium.

"Now be good," the Widow said before the cloth hid her and the room from view.

It was immediately gloomy inside the aquarium, the only light coming from where the stovepipe met the glass. The cloth had been cut away there so that it wouldn't touch the tin.

As soon as she heard the sitting-room door close, Jodi turned to her companion.

"I've got a plan," she told him.

"This'll be good."

"Do you want to escape or not?"

Edern held his hands out in front of him in mock surrender. "I'm all ears."

"Well, help me get rid of this coal," Jodi said.

They pushed the rug back from the stove, then used the back of a chair to lift the coal up from inside and topple it to the floor where it fell with a shower of sparks upon the glass.

"That's made a fine mess," Edern said.

"Oh, bother and damn," Jodi said. "Will you be quiet?"

Edern listened to her plan and slowly nodded his head when she was done.

"It might work," he said. "But . . ."

"But what?"

"You're forgetting Windle."

"We'll pick up a nail from the Widow's worktable and stab him with it."

"Um-hmm," Edern said dubiously.

Jodi glared at him for a long moment, then turned her back on him and stuck her head in the stove. It was still warm from the coal, but not uncomfortably so. She turned on her back and then squeezed herself up into the stovepipe.

Plenty of room, she thought.

It was just a few moments' work to shimmy her way up the pipe's length. The corner where it made a right-angle turn to leave the aquarium proved a little tricky, but manageable. Grabbing handfuls of velvet cloth, she pulled herself out. With her feet balanced on the lip of the pipe, her hands keeping her balance, she found herself face-to-face with Edern, only the glass wall of the aquarium separating them.

She raised her eyebrows questioningly. When he nodded that he was ready, she took a firmer grip of the velvet and swung out, coming back to kick the pipe with both feet, the force of all her weight behind her. It came loose on the first kick. Edern swayed on top of it, looking as though he was going to drop with it. He only just managed to get hold of the opening before the pipe fell away, back into their prison. It crashed onto the glass floor beside the bed.

They both held their breath, listening. And heard nothing.

"Come on," Jodi whispered.

She made her way quickly down the cloth, lowering herself hand over hand until her feet touched the surface of the worktable. As Edern started his own descent, she crawled out from under the cloth and cautiously peered about the sitting room.

Their luck held, for there was no sign of the witch's fetch.

While Edern manhandled the roll of twine across the tabletop, Jodi clambered up on the windowsill and gave the latch a try. It wouldn't budge.

"I need a hand," she called softly to her companion.

Edern joined her and with his help they got the latch undone and swung the window open. The sharp tang of a salty wind blew in at them.

"La," Jodi said. "I can already taste freedom."

She tied the twine to the latch with a seaman's knot, then

the two of them hoisted the roll of twine up onto the sill and let it tumble out the window where it landed on the ground between the cottage wall and the rosebushes growing up alongside of it.

Edern gave her a flourishing bow. "After you."

Grinning, Jodi scampered down the rope, then held it taut for Edern as he descended.

"Now where to?" he asked when he reached the bottom.

"To Denzil's," Jodi said. At Edern's questioning look, she added, "He's my friend. An inventor."

"An inventor?"

"He's—oh, never mind. You'll see soon enough."

She led the way out from under the rosebush, Edern on her heels. He bumped into her when she came to an abrupt stop.

"What . . . ?" he began, but then he saw what was waiting for them on the Widow's lawn.

Windle was there, saucer eyes laughing, teeth bared in an unpleasant grin. The creature was crouched low and out of sight from a chance passerby on the street beyond the Widow's garden and obviously just waiting for them to move from under the thorny bushes to pounce on them.

"Bother and damn," Jodi muttered. "We forgot our nail."

"Nail?" Edern said softly. "We'd need more than a nail to stop that creature. Look at the size of it!"

He was horribly accurate, of course. Small as mice as they were, the cat-sized fetch appeared to be monstrously huge.

"What are we going to do?" Jodi asked. "The Widow'll be back soon."

Edern nodded glumly, gaze not leaving the creature.

"I'm not going back into her aquarium!" Jodi said.

Brave words. Her legs trembled, knees feeling weak. If only her heartbeat would slow down. The drum of her pulse in her ears made thinking impossible.

"I'm not," she said, as though repeating it would make it true.

Edern nodded again, then touched her arm as the fetch cocked its head and looked towards the low, overgrown stone wall that separated the garden from the street beyond it.

"What's that it hears?"

"The Widow . . . ?"

Edern shook his head.

They could see nothing, but there was a jingling in the air, accompanied by a snuffling sound.

Excitement pushed Jodi's fear aside.

"Edern," she said slowly. "Can you whistle? Whistle really loud and shrill?"

Pull the Knife and

Stick It Again

I don't feel guilty for anything ... I
feel sorry for people who feel guilt.

—attributed to T E D   B U N D Y

M i c h a e l Bett took one of Madden En-
terprises' private jets to London's Heathrow, with only one stopover in St. John's
for refueling. He didn't leave the plane in St. John's, preferring
to keep at his research.

His only true enjoyment in life was discovering what made
things work—to cut through all the frivolities and get to the
heart of whatever particular business currently absorbed his interest. Sometimes that involved research and study, as he was
doing now; sometimes it was a matter of living a certain kind of
life, as he did with Madden's Order of the Grey Dove; sometimes
all it required was to take a knife and see how deeply and often
it could cut before the mystery of life fled.

The first to fall under his knife was the family dog. Body still
aching from the beating his latest "Daddy" had given him, he'd
taken the old hound out into the vacant lot that stood between
two deserted tenements near his mother's house. He stood for a
long time looking down at the dog. There was a curiously empty
feeling inside him as its trusting eyes looked up into his own.
The lolling tongue and the big tail slapping the ground that
always made him laugh couldn't even raise a smile today.

Then he took the knife he'd stolen from the kitchen out of
his jacket pocket, pulled up the dog's head to expose its neck,

and drew the sharp blade across its throat. Blood fountained and he only just stepped back in time to keep it from spraying all over him. Circling around, he came at the dog from behind and brought the knife down again and again, stabbing and hacking away at the poor creature long after it was dead.

He'd been eleven years old at the time.

Other neighbourhood pets followed the first dog's fate. When he was thirteen, he killed his first human—a five-year-old boy whom he kidnapped from a backyard and took away to an empty building where the boy's dying amused him for hours. When he was fifteen, his latest victim—a teenage girl lured away into a deserted tenement with the promise of a party—provided him with a moment of pure epiphany.

Dying, helpless, an inferno of pain flaring in her eyes, she'd croaked out one word: "Why?"

Until then Bett hadn't thought to question what he did, hadn't understood what drove him to such ultimate thievery.

"Because I can," he'd told the girl.

But that wasn't the whole of the truth, just the most obvious part of it. Lying under it was a purpose that, as the years went by, became the focus of his existence: the need to understand, not just the secret of life, but the mystery of its passage into death; how a thing worked, *why* it worked as it did. He never felt a sense of self-recrimination or outrage for his methodology of pursuit for this knowledge. The deaths were only a kind of fuel to feed the curiosity that burned inside him like a smoldering fire.

He lived a kind of controlled autism in the sense that he was always absorbed in one form or another of self-centered subjective mental activity, but he had no difficulty in relating to the world around him. The world and what inhabited it fascinated him. He was disciplined to the degree that he could settle his attention single-mindedly on an object or subject for as long as it took him to understand it, or in the case of the subject, for as long as it took his victim to die.

Everything was important—but only in how it related to him.

Sitting in Madden's jet, his undivided attention was fixed upon the puzzle of Janey Little.

He wore a Walkman on which played a tape containing both of her albums. The small cassette machine was turned to its reverse mode so that the tape played over and over again, stopping only when the batteries wore out. Then Bett replaced them, and the music played on once more.

On the empty seat beside him was a leather briefcase, beside it a Toshiba laptop computer. On his lap was a slender folder of press clippings and a private detective's thirty-seven-page report; the subject of both was the same woman whose music sounded in Bett's ear. He was currently absorbed in the profile of her in an old issue of *Folk Roots* magazine. He'd read it so often that he could have quoted the entire article, word for word. Mostly he studied the photos that accompanied the article, comparing them to those that were attached to the detective's report.

With the material at hand, and the video tapes he had—also provided by the detective agency—he knew as much, if not more, about Janey Little as anyone. Perhaps as much as the woman did herself.

Madden knew nothing of this private research Bett had undertaken—undertaken long before Madden sent him to Cornwall earlier this evening. For Bett had seen, as soon as he learned of the interest that the Order had in Thomas Little, that the answer to what they were looking for lay not in him, but in his granddaughter. She would be the doorway to the old man's secrets. But the approach had to be made subtly—far more so than the Order's own previous bumbling attempts to plunder whatever riddle it was that Tom Little kept.

Ah, yes: the riddle. The secret.

What was it?

Madden wouldn't—perhaps couldn't—say, and no one else knew. And that made it infinitely intriguing to Bett.

He smiled, thinking of John Madden. Sitting together with a glass of sherry before them in the library, Madden loved to repeat the story of how the two of them had met. How he, Madden, had immediately recognized the soul of his old friend Aleister Crowley in Bett's eyes. Madden had a mind that was sharp as a razor, but he let his hermetic studies blind that one part of his logic that would reveal all the occult mumbo-jumbo as drivel.

Bett had another impression of that night in Chicago. All Madden had recognized in Bett was a kindred spirit—the difference between them being that Madden only dreamed of picking up the knife, while Bett allowed himself whatever indulgence pleased him at the moment.

Still this reincarnation business had served Bett well. It amused him to keep up the charade. As soon as he'd realized what could be his if he could convince Madden that he really was the sorcerer who'd called himself the Beast, he'd surreptitiously researched Crowley's life. Utilizing the same thoroughness with which he approached every project, he'd come away with enough obscure details of biographical data that Madden wasn't simply convinced; he *believed.*

Naturally, Bett hadn't been fool enough to give it all out at once. He fed it out, tidbit by tidbit. Haltingly. Unsure of himself—allowing Madden, and his excitement, to "convince" both of them.

This weakness of Madden's—his only weakness—was what made the man so fascinating to Bett. That a man with his hard-nosed common sense and acumen should so readily accept what could only be fairy tales. . . .

If that was what they were.

Bett was blessed, or cursed, with an open mind. Even with such illogical beliefs as those held by the Order, he was still willing to withhold complete judgment. For there were certain anomalies between what could logically be real and what he perceived to be real among Madden and his peers. There was the matter of Madden's longevity—shared by other old guard members of the Order. Their worldly success that couldn't always be put down to simple business astuteness. The curious way in which they invariably attained what they aimed for.

The will is all, the Order said.

Bett knew about will and what one could accomplish with it. What he wasn't ready to make a decision on was whether one's will allowed one to tap into an outside force or entity to gain its potency—as the Order held—or whether that strength came from within one's own self. Or both.

Until he had resolved that to his own satisfaction, Bett would remain a part of this secret order of old men and women who thought they ruled the world.

2 .

A car met him at Heathrow and took him to Victoria Station where he caught the train to Penzance. Madden had been surprised at that decision, arguing against it, but Bett had remained unswayed.

"I need the time to fully assimilate the role I mean to play," he had explained. "Besides, with the time difference, I'll still arrive in plenty of time."

"What role?" Madden asked.

"Allow me to bring you the results first," Bett had countered. "Then I'll explain."

And Madden, the doting mentor, had smiled and nodded. Bett could see the suspicion in the old man's eyes—but it was no more than was always present. He'd yet to fail Madden; so why should he fail him now?

On the train he completed his transformation from Madden's acolyte into his new role. Gone was the businessman's tailored suit, the stiff body language, the expressionless features that gave no inkling as to the thoughts that lay behind them.

He was casually dressed now in corduroys, a light cotton shirt, Nike running shoes, and a dark blue Windbreaker. He'd left his briefcase in the jet, bringing only a Nikon camera in a worn case, the laptop computer and a battered suitcase holding his notes and files and changes of clothing similar in style to what he was wearing.

His body language was relaxed now, his face expressive and open, his whole attitude making him appear ten years younger than the forty-one years he actually was.

When he arrived at Penzance Station, he disembarked looking as fresh as though he hadn't just put in all those many hours of travel. He helped an older woman with her bags, smiling easily with her when she allowed that she wished her own Janet's husband was half as kind with his family, little say a stranger. After he saw her off, a small unsavory-looking individual approached from where Bett had first noticed him sitting outside the bus station.

"Mr. Bett?"

Bett frowned at him. The man was shabbily dressed, his coat patched, shoes worn, a brown cloth cap pulled down low over his ratty features.

"What do you want?"

"Miss Grant sent me to fetch you, uh, sir."

"Give me the address and I'll find my own way."

"But—"

Bett leaned close and his pretense at an easygoing nature fell away as though it had been stripped from him with the blade of a gutting knife.

"Never call me by name," he said. "Never question what I say. Do it again and I'll feed your heart to your mother."

"I—I . . ."

Bett stepped back, smiling pleasantly. "The address?"

Stumbling over his words, the man gave him the name of a hotel on the Western Promenade, overlooking the bay, and a room number. When Bett ascertained that it was within walking distance, he left the man standing there in the station's parking lot and set off on his own.

3 ·

Lena Grant looked the same as she always did—beautiful, spoiled, and bored. Her dark hair was coiffured and swept back from her brow in a stiff wave. Her makeup was Park Avenue immaculate and out of place in this small Cornish town. As was the perfect cut of her designer blouse and skirt; the blouse unbuttoned far enough to show the lacy top of her bra, the skirt slit so that a long stockinged leg was revealed whenever she took a step.

"The Golden Boy," she said as she opened the door of her room to him.

Bett pushed by her and shut the door.

"Where's Willie?" she asked.

"Can I assume it was 'Willie' who met me at the station?"

Lena nodded. "Willie Keel. He's local."

"I don't doubt that."

"You didn't get along?"

"I never get along with fools."

Lena frowned. "One of my father's security men recommended him. Daddy always says that you should use local talent when you're—"

"The operative word there is talent," Bett said, interrupting her.

The perfect lips began a pout that Bett simply ignored. He wasn't in the mood to listen to the perfection of everything and anything associated with "Daddy." He knew all about Daddies.

"Have there been any new developments since yesterday?" he asked before she could go on.

"I did the best I could," Lena said.

He'd give her that. Playing a long-lost relative of Dunthorn's and demanding his personal effects—that was about the limit of her imagination. Or maybe it had been "Daddy's" plan. Roland—"Call me Rollie"—Grant might be a big wheel on Wall Street, but there his expertise ended . . . along with his sense of propriety and his social graces, so perhaps it wasn't all Lena's fault. But Bett had no time for sympathy. About the only interest he had in Lena was in how long it would take her to die and that, unfortunately, was something he was unlikely to find out.

For now.

While the Order was still of interest to him.

"I had Willie go into their house last night," she told him. "He found a box of Dunthorn's manuscripts."

Bett's eyebrows rose with interest and he looked about the room. "Where is it?"

"Ah. . . ." She wouldn't meet his gaze.

"*Where* is it?"

"He got surprised by some thug and only just got away himself."

Wonderful. Now the Littles would be more on their guard than ever.

It was too bad that Madden was so certain that Tom Little would take his friend's secret to the grave, because the simplest solution to all of this would be to just snatch the old man and let Bett have him for a few days. Madden's beliefs notwithstanding, Bett didn't doubt he'd pry the secret from Little. Maybe he could just cut Little's granddaughter in front of him until her bleeding jogged his memory. . . .

He put the pleasant image from his mind.

"A thug, you said?" he asked.

Lena shrugged. "A big man, according to Willie. Arriving with luggage. Looked a bit like a sailor, but then everyone does around here."

"Would he recognize the man from a photo?" Bett tried, but Lena was off on a tangent now.

"I mean, what a dismal place. There's no water pressure in what they call a shower so I can't wash my hair properly. The food's abysmal. There's nothing to do. The air stinks. Everywhere you turn there's—"

"Shut up," Bett said.

He spoke quietly, but with enough force to get an immediate result. She blinked with surprise, then pointed a manicured finger at him.

"If I tell Daddy how you treat me, he'll—"

"Complain to John who'll do nothing. Tell me about this man."

Again the pout. "What's to tell? Maybe they've hired a bodyguard."

Of course she couldn't have taken the initiative to find out who he was and what he was doing at the Littles'. Though if Bett thought about it for a moment, perhaps that was a blessing. Who knew how she'd mess that up.

"You're to have nothing to do with the Littles from now on," he told her. "And you're to act as though you don't know me if we should happen to meet. In fact, it would be better if you simply didn't go out at all."

"I'm *not* staying cooped up in this room."

"Then perhaps you should go home."

She laughed without humour. "I can't. Daddy wants me to do this."

Bett nodded. He'd heard talk among some of the old guard of the Order. They weren't happy with Lena. For all that she carried their mark on her wrist, she was simply too much the debutante to be trusted. Never mind how she lacked the necessary regimen to follow their studies, what they were most afraid of was the possibility of her committing some indiscretion such as having one of her sulks and talking to a tabloid about the Order: revealing what they stood for; who was a member; what they did. With the continuing rise of the Fundamental Christian contingent in business and politics, that could be a disaster.

If her father hadn't been among Madden's oldest confederates—Grant had been one of the founding members of the Order—she probably would have been dealt with a long time ago. As she might still be.

Bett hoped they'd give the job to him.

Until then, he had to deal with her as best he could.

"If you can't go," he said, "then you'll just have to do as I say. I've got the full confidence of the Order behind me and—"

"I know, I know. You're their Golden Boy."

Bett realized that they could continue along this tack forever, so he shifted gears and put on a new mask. He smiled, winningly, charming her despite herself.

"I'm sorry," he said. "I know it's hard for you, all this business. But we're both in the same situation. Do you think I want to be here? Madden insisted that I do it. But if I fail . . . that's it for me."

"What do you mean?"

Her voice was less sulky, betraying her interest.

"You're born to your position," he said. "I have to work at it constantly. If I fail this job, I'm out."

She was unable to resist his false sincerity. "They wouldn't, would they?"

He nodded, eyes downcast. "I don't get a second chance."

"That's horrible. I'll talk to Daddy. . . ."

"That won't do any good."

"No," she said, obviously thinking of the grim old man she knew Bett's mentor to be. "Not with Madden."

Bett glanced at her through lowered lashes. It never ceased to amaze him how easily some people could be manipulated. A moment ago she'd hated him with all her shallow heart. Now they were confederates.

"We could help each other," Bett said. "Let me do this my way—but we'll share the credit. That way we both win out."

"Why would you do that for me?" Lena asked, suspicion finally aroused.

"I'm not just doing it for you—it's for me as well. I can't fail."

Lena sighed. She walked over to him and trailed a hand along the front of his jacket.

"You're such a confusing man," she said. "Sometimes you're just like ice and I'm sure that you hate me, then there are moments like this when you're just so . . . I don't know, vulnerable, I suppose . . . that all I want to do is protect you from the rest of the world."

"This is me," Bett said. "I've got to act cold—that's what Madden wants—but it's hard to do that with you."

"Really?"

He met her gaze, his blue eyes opened wide and guileless. "Really."

She seemed to make a decision and let her hand fall to her side.

"All right," she said. "I'll wait here for you and I won't get in your way. Just promise me one thing."

"What's that?"

"That you won't be mean to me anymore. When it's just us, you don't have to put on a face. I'd like us to be friends."

It was unbelievable, he thought, and so like her. If everyone acted sweet around her, well then, everything was all right, wasn't it? Everyone liked her and would be her friend.

"I'd like that, too," he said.

She leaned forward again and gave him the kind of kiss prevalent among her crowd—bussing the air near his ear.

"I'm glad," she said, then stepped back. "So what do we do?"

Bett straightened his shoulders. "First we get your man Keel to look at some photos to see if he recognizes the man he saw last night."

"And then?"

Bett hesitated.

"I'll stay out of your way," she said. "Honestly. It's just that nobody ever lets me know what's going on."

"All right," Bett said, and he spun her a tale of how he was going to approach the Littles on the pretense that he was a reporter for *Rolling Stone* interested in Dunthorn's work—concentrating his attention not on the old man, but on his granddaughter who was apparently an enthusiast for Dunthorn's work herself.

It was mostly a lie, but Lena was happy with it.

4 ·

Bored as she was, Lena was still relieved when both Bett and Willie Keel had left.

Bett made her uncomfortable. She never knew where she stood with him. Most of the time he treated her like a bimbo, but then he'd turn around and be so nice that she just *had* to like him—even when she knew she couldn't trust him; knew he disliked her; knew that under the calm mask he turned to the world there lurked something infinitely dangerous. Pressed, she couldn't have explained how she could be so sure. She simply *knew*.

Intuition . . . or maybe it was what Daddy called magic.

As for Willie Keel . . . while Jim Gazo might have recommended him—and she trusted her father's security man implicitly—to put it frankly, Keel was uncouth. He looked like a weasel in his disheveled, ill-fitting coat and trousers. His breath smelled of stale tobacco and garlic. His clothes smelled as though they hadn't been washed since the day they'd been handed down to him. And God help her, his body odor was enough to make her gag.

Just thinking about him made her feel queasy.

So it was with relief that she stood at the window of her hotel room and watched the two men go their separate ways on the street below. Once they were out of view, she returned to her bed and picked up the photograph that Willie had chosen from the half dozen or so that Bett had presented to him.

This was the man who'd interrupted his burglary at the Littles' the previous night, he'd assured them, his gaze darting nervously from Lena to Bett, then back again.

Felix Gavin.

A common merchant sailor, Bett had said. Maybe Gavin was, but she liked the look of him. Comparing him to Bett and Willie, she decided that he'd neither smell, nor make her feel uncomfortable.

She turned the picture so that the light didn't glare on its glossy surface. An old lover of Janey Little's, was he? Come back to rekindle his romance with her? An old friend such as he was, mightn't he know something about any Dunthorn heirlooms that just happened to be lying about the Little household? Maybe, at one time or another in their relationship, the Little girl had confided in him . . . confided secrets that were only shared with a lover. . . .

Lena smiled. Perhaps she'd go slumming and show Daddy that she was as good as Madden's Golden Boy. And wouldn't it make Bett frown if she was to succeed where everyone else, Bett included, had failed?

The thought of Bett angry brought a return of uneasiness to her.

Best not to think of that. Think of the glow of pride on Daddy's face, instead.

And she could do it. Like Bett, like Daddy and his cronies with their little tattooed doves—she rubbed the one on her wrist as she thought of the old men's club that called itself the Order— she had her own secrets. Hadn't she been taking her acting lessons, twice a week, for two years now? Didn't her teacher say she was doing as well, if not better, than any of her previous students?

Lena studied herself in the mirror that took up the length of the room's closet door. She could do it: She could make Felix Gavin tell her anything. But not like this. He'd go for class— his kind always did, because normally a woman such as herself was so unattainable for him—but the way she looked at the moment would just make him nervous.

Still, she could easily fix that.

Humming to herself, she changed into a pair of designer-faded jeans, complete with the appropriate tear in one knee, a tight MIT T-shirt, and a pair of hightops. She removed her makeup, then reapplied it, this time going for a casual look. When she was done, she put on a leather bomber's jacket and regarded herself in the mirror.

Yes, she decided. This would do. This would do very well. Felix Gavin didn't have a chance.

Now all she had to do was find him. *Without* Bett being any the wiser.

She put in a call to the front desk and left a message that she was sleeping and wasn't to be disturbed for the duration of the day. Then, feeling deliciously like a spy, she left her room and went to the ground floor by the stairs, waiting until the foyer was empty for a moment before slipping out the front door.

The salty wind tousled her hair as soon as she stepped outside, but rather than irritating her as it had every other time she'd left her hotel, now it just added to the adventure. The skies were grey, promising rain. She turned up the collar of her jacket.

How to find Gavin?

Willie would know.

The Dogs Among

the Bushes

Luck is a very good word if you put a "P" before it.

— MARY ENGELBREIT

*T*h e nice thing about animals, Jodi thought, was that their hearing was so much better than that of people.

Unfortunately, the witch's fetch had an acute sense of hearing as well. Its head turned sharply when Jodi and Edern put their fingers to their lips and the shrill squeaks of their whistling rang out—but by then it was too late. Two dogs came bounding into the garden and Jodi recognized them both.

One was a small mixed breed—part terrier, part who knew what—named Kitey. The other was a border collie named Ansum. Both lived within a few doors of Aunt Nettie's house and had gone for many a long ramble by the cliffs with Jodi and Denzil.

Kitey barked shrilly when he caught sight of the fetch and pounced towards it, Ansum hard on his heels. Windle fled at their enthusiastic approach. The fetch leapt over Jodi's and Edern's heads, over the rosebushes, and went straight through the window, landing with an audible crash on the worktable inside. Kitey ran back and forth in front of the bushes, then burrowed into them through a gap and ran up to the window where he stood on his hind legs, yapping cheerfully. Ansum stayed on the lawn side of the bushes and pushed his head in towards the spot where Jodi and Edern stood.

Edern backed nervously away. When he looked as though he was about to bolt himself, Jodi caught hold of his arm.

"They know me," she told him.

Ansum continued to peer curiously at the two mouse-sized people. A few moments later Kitey left off his vigil at the window and joined the border collie, prancing about on the lawn with barely contained excitement.

"They won't hurt us," Jodi said.

I hope, she added to herself.

As Ansum thrust his nose in towards them, obviously puzzled at the familiar scent coming from such an unfamiliar tiny creature, Jodi moved up to him.

"Hello there, old boy," Jodi said.

She put out a hand to touch his muzzle and was shocked at how tiny her fingers were compared to his nose. Ansum backed nervously away and whined.

"Right," Edern said, his voice betraying his own nervousness. "They won't hurt us at all."

"Oh, do be still," Jodi told him, starting to feel cross. "They're just confused by my size."

"It's more like they're trying to decide whether we're worth eating," Edern muttered. "If you ask me, I'd . . ."

His voice trailed away when Jodi glared at him.

"Come on, then, Ansum," she said. "Hey, there, Kitey."

While the terrier continued to rush about the garden, letting off the odd zealous yap, Ansum lay down on the ground and pushed his muzzle forward until his nose was only inches—by a normal-sized person's reckoning—from Jodi. He made a contented throaty sound when Jodi scratched his muzzle.

"Now what?" Edern asked, still keeping his distance.

"Now we make our escape."

"But the dogs—"

"Are here to help us. Did you never hear of good fortune where you came from?"

Edern sighed. "To be sure. But I've also heard of hungry dogs and I don't much care to—"

This time he was interrupted by the sudden change in pitch and volume of Kitey's barking.

"Evil little creatures," cried an all-too-familiar voice.

"It's the bloody witch," Jodi said.

Ansum started to lift his head, but stopped when Jodi called his name.

"It's now or never," she told Edern as she hurried forward.

Edern could only stare at her as she hauled herself up the border collie's neck, then snuggled in behind his collar so that she was braced between it and his fur.

"You're mad," Edern said.

"Then stay and get turned into a toad. No!" she added as Ansum began to rise again. Then to Edern: "Are you coming? Last chance."

"Go away!" the Widow was crying. "Get out of here, you filthy creatures."

"*I'm* mad," Edern said as he hurried forward.

Moments later he too was hanging on to Ansum's collar. The border collie surged to his feet. White-faced, Jodi and Edern held on for dear life as the dog bolted out of the garden, the yapping Kitey running at his side, head turned back to voice his disdain at the Widow. Jodi caught one glimpse of the Widow's fetch glaring at them from the window, then the Widow's house was lost to sight.

It was a mad, jolting journey for the two of them as the dogs raced through Bodbury's narrow streets, making for the harbour. They clung to Ansum's collar, gritting their teeth against the bounce and jolt of their ride.

"Slow down, slow down!" Jodi tried crying, but neither dog heard her.

Finally they came to a panting halt on the cobbles near the wharves. Crates rose like mountains about them on the dock. Foothills of fish netting lay in untidy piles and heaps. Before the dogs could run off again, Jodi gave Ansum a poke with her elbow. The dog shook his head.

The world spun and her stomach lurched. Frowning, she gripped the collar for all she was worth.

"Will you stop that!" Edern cried as she lifted her elbow to poke the dog again.

"We have to get down, don't we?"

Ansum stood very still at the sound of the tiny voices coming from below his chin. He gave his head another experimental shake, pausing when Jodi shouted at him.

"I'm going to be sick," Edern said.

Jodi knew just what he meant. It was disconcerting and altogether unpleasant to be hanging here from the dog's collar in the first place, without having Ansum try to shake them off as well.

"Down!" she cried as loud as she could. "Lie down, Ansum, there's the boy."

The border collie merely stood there with a puzzled look on his face. Kitey gave a quick yap.

"Don't you start, Kitey!" Jodi cried.

She could feel herself losing her voice from having to shout like this.

"Lie down!" she cried again.

And finally he did.

Before he could change his mind, Jodi and Edern crawled out from behind the dog's collar and scrambled down to the ground. They wobbled about unsteadily on the cobblestones, feeling all off-balance from their wild ride. One of Ansum's enormous eyes turned to solemnly regard them. Kitey yipped and yapped happily.

Edern gave the terrier a nervous look.

"I don't much care for the look of his teeth," he said.

Jodi laughed and pushed him towards a nearby gap in the crates. As soon as they were safely inside, she turned to peer out again. Looking one way and another, she decided that no one had taken any notice of the dogs or their curious cargo.

"We weren't spotted," she said over her shoulder.

Edern slouched against a crate, legs sprawled out before him.

"I can't tell you what a relief that is," he said.

"No need to get all huffy," Jodi told him. "I got us out, didn't I?"

Close at hand, both Ansum and Kitey were still directly beside the crates. The terrier sat with his head cocked, looking at her. Ansum whined and scraped a paw on the cobbles.

"Thank you very much," Jodi told them, "but it's time you were off now."

Neither dog moved.

"Shoo!"

She ran a few steps forward as she shouted and the dogs jumped back, only to return to their stations once Jodi had retreated back between the crates.

"Bother and damn," she said. "They won't go away, which means *we* have to before some nosy tar comes along to see what the fuss is."

Edern gave her a weary look. "Don't you ever get tired?"

Jodi shook her head. She walked by him, stopped long enough to look over her shoulder at him, then continued on. Edern got slowly to his feet. He looked at Ansum and the terrier. When Kitey offered him a shrill bark, he rolled his shoulders to get rid of the shiver that settled in his spine whenever he thought of those dogs, then hurried after his companion.

2 .

It was gloomy in the small spaces between the mountain of crates. The air was heavy with the smell of fish and salt, and little daylight worked itself into the narrow corridors along which Jodi led Edern. After much backtracking and wandering about they finally reached the far side of the mountain and got a look at the sea.

"Well, I don't suppose we'll be leaving by this way," Jodi said.

The crates were stacked right up to the end of the wharf without space for even their mouse-sized bodies to squeeze by. Below, high tide was lapping at the pilings. Out in the harbour, the fishing luggers floated in a careless array, their crews on shore, cleaning fish and mending nets until the next early morning run. Out beyond the shelter of the harbour they could see a freighter approaching.

"What odds these crates are meant for it?" Edern asked.

Jodi shrugged. "It'll take time for it to dock. Then there's paperwork to be done with the harbourmaster and another tide to wait out. We'll be fine."

"I'd rather be out on the open road."

"You're a bit of a tatchy wam, aren't you just?"

"Speak for yourself."

"Well, I'm not gadding about all grouchy and finicky, am I?"

"I'm just not used to this," Edern said. "Give me the hills to walk any day."

"Where some stoat or weasel would have you for its dinner. Wouldn't that be lovely?"

"You know what I mean."

"I suppose. I'm not exactly having the best time of my life either."

She slouched down, letting her feet dangle over the edge of the wharf, not caring if some fisherman spied her or not.

"Where to now?" Edern asked as he settled down beside her.

Jodi shrugged. "We'll wait here until it gets dark, then we'll go off to Denzil's. He'll know how to help us if anyone does."

"Help us?"

"Get back to our proper size, you ninny. Do you think I want to spend the rest of my life as a mouse?"

"I meant to tell you about that," Edern said.

"Tell me what?"

Edern looked uncomfortable.

"Tell me what?" Jodi repeated.

He turned to look at her. "Did you never think about where the rest of you went?"

Jodi blinked, then gave him a blank look.

"One moment you're full-size, and the next you're the height of a prawn. Surely you've thought about the discrepancy?"

"La," Jodi said. "I never did notice."

Edern shook his head. "When the Widow shrunk you down, part of you stayed you—at your present size—but the rest of you was sort of scattered about, into the air as it were. To get those bits back, you need the third part of you, which the Widow kept for herself."

"I don't know *what* you're talking about," Jodi said, feeling uneasy now.

"It's a kind of code of what makes you properly you. A charm, if you will, that will call back the scattered bits when you're ready to go back to your proper size."

"I'm ready now."

Edern shook his head. "Without the charm, you'll never be restored to your rightful size."

"A charm," Jodi said slowly.

Edern nodded.

"That the Widow has?"

Another nod.

"Bother and damn. Why didn't you say something earlier?"

"You didn't give me time."

"I gave you all the time in the world. More than likely you just wanted to get away yourself, and didn't want my head cluttered up with other concerns."

Edern gave her a wounded look.

"Or maybe not," Jodi said. "So what's this charm look like?"

"It's in the shape of a button and it's sewn to the inside of her cloak."

"And yours? What's your charm?"

"I don't know," he said. "I saw her work the spell on you— that's how I know as much as I do. When she worked it on me, I was in the same state as you were. Unconscious."

"So we have to go back?"

"Only if you want to be your proper size."

Jodi shook her head. "I can't believe it. Here it is, my Big Adventure, and how does it turn out? A quest to look for a bloody button on some old woman's cloak. If this were in a book, I'd be embarrassed to turn the page."

"It's not my fault."

"I suppose not. But where's the Romance? Where's the Wonder?"

"Well, you are a Small."

"Oh, yes. What a wonder. To be a mouse. Maybe I'll find some rat prince to rescue the day. Wouldn't that be romantic?"

"There's always me."

"Oh raw we," she said.

"But, of course, I'm too old for you."

"Much too old," Jodi agreed.

And then she sighed—a long, heartfelt exhalation of air that did nothing to settle her gloomy mood.

"I suppose it's my own fault, really," she said. "I was always lumping about, waiting to stumble in upon that Big Adventure of mine. And now that I have—well, it's typical, isn't it?"

Edern looked bewildered.

"That when I *do*," Jodi explained tiredly, "it would be so— oh, I don't know. So laughable. So pedestrian."

"Maybe all adventures are that way and they only seem exciting when they're written up," Edern said. "Though," he added, "when I think of our escape, I could do without any more excitement, thank you kindly."

"You know what I'm saying. I'd just like it to be a bit more meaningful than scrabbling about Bodbury, being no bigger than a mouse and on a quest to find a button. It seems so unremarkable."

"A person being reduced to our size is unremarkable?"

"Don't be a poop."

"Now who's being tatchy?"

"And don't be a bore."

Edern glanced at her and she gave him a grin.

"I'm just being sulky," she said. "And I know I am, so don't lecture. I'll be over it all too soon and then you'll be wishing I was back to sulking again."

"You're not very good at scowling," Edern told her.

"Can't help it. I don't get enough practice." Her grin widened. "Tell me what it's like to be a traveling man," she added. "To pass the time."

"What's to tell? It's walking the roads, up hill and down. . . ."

Jodi pushed her worries to the back of her mind and settled contentedly against the crate, feet still dangling above the steadily rising tide, and closed her eyes. As Edern spoke, she brought up images in her mind to accompany his words—images of roads that wound through wild moorland and down craggy footpaths to the sea, of roads with hedgerows patchworking pastures and fields on either side that wound in and out of stone-cottaged villages in places she'd never been, of roads that were sun-drenched by day and mysterious by night. . . .

It wasn't until the sky darkened beyond their refuge, the long shadows of Bodbury's buildings cast out across the harbour, that she woke up to discover that she'd fallen asleep with her head on Edern's shoulder. He was asleep too, so she stayed where she was, looking out across the water until twilight grew into night. Then she gave Edern a poke with her elbow and sat up.

"Time to go," she said.

"Give me five more minutes."

"I never realized that a traveling man could be so slothful."

"Why do you think we wander about like geese, instead of settling down in one place?"

Jodi merely grinned. She stood up and stretched the kinks out of muscles, then faced him, arms akimbo.

"Ready?"

Edern groaned and made a great pretense of being an old man as he slowly rose to his feet.

"I suppose you have some new amazing plan?" he asked.

Jodi nodded. "We're still off to see Denzil. He might not be able to make us bigger, but I'm sure he'll be able to think of a way for us to get those buttons away from the Widow."

Edern shivered. "Maybe it's not so bad, being a Small."

"Maybe," Jodi agreed cheerfully, "but I don't intend to settle into the life of a mouse until I have to."

The last of her words were thrown over her shoulder as she set off to retrace their path back through the winding maze made by the mountain of crates. Edern followed at a slower pace, wondering how she could move so surefootedly through the dark. It seemed to take forever and he was barely paying attention when she came to a sudden stop ahead of him. He only just stopped himself from bumping into her.

"If you're going to stop like that, the least you could do is warn me so—"

"Whisht!" Jodi said.

"What is it?" he whispered, moving up beside her.

He had time to see the enormous bewhiskered face of a cat staring in at them from beyond the crates, then both he and Jodi were scrabbling back as a clawed paw came shooting in to try to catch them. The cat hissed in frustration, stretching its paw in farther. Jodi and Edern backed up well out of reach.

"Bother and damn," Jodi said. "Now what do we do?"

"Did you never hear of good fortune where you came from?" Edern asked.

Jodi gave him a withering look. "Don't you start," she said.

"You mean you can't charm it?"

The cat made an angry growling sound as it continued to reach for them.

"What do you think?" Jodi asked.

Edern sighed. "I think we'll still be here when the men come to move these crates onto the freighter in the morning."

3 ·

Denzil Gossip was at his worktable, fussing with a small model steam locomotive, as night fell. He was hunched on a stool, back bowed like a victory arch, as he concentrated. His glasses kept slipping down his nose and he'd have to pause in his minute adjustments of the train's clockwork mechanism to push them back up again. Moments later they'd fall back down once more.

It wasn't until it was almost fully dark and he couldn't see a thing that he sat up and looked around his shadowed loft. Seeing that there was finally a chance to gain his notice, the animals immediately began to vie for his attention.

Rum gave a sharp cry and scratched at the door, working new grooves into the wood to join all those he'd already made in days past. Ollie swung down from the top of a bookcase and landed on his shoulder, startling him so much that he dropped the tiny screwdriver he'd been using.

"Now look what you've done," he said.

"Dumb, dumb," Noz cried from his perch and opened his wings to fan the air.

As though he'd planned it from the start of his leap, Ollie continued down from Denzil's shoulder to land on the floor where he stood innocently picking at his nose.

The mice and rats ran back and forth in their cages, excited by the sudden movements. The lop-eared rabbit pressed its face against the mesh of its cage front. The lizards skittered about, before freezing into new positions. The turtle stuck its head out of its shell and stared. The crow gave a loud caw from where it was perched on the top of the window sash. Only the catfish gave no notice, but then they never did to anything except for when bread bits or something equally edible was sprinkled on the surface of their water.

Was it early morning or evening? Denzil wondered.

He got off his stool to search for his screwdriver, but Ollie already had it and was trying to poke it into his ear.

"Give me that," he said.

"Brat, brat," Noz said.

Across the room, Rum added yet another series of scratches to the door.

Denzil stuck the screwdriver into his pocket, took off his glasses and gave them a perfunctory wipe on his sleeve, then crossed the room to the window where he put them back on.

Early evening, he decided. That meant a day had gone by—
only where had it gone? Had he been asked, he would have
assured his questioner that he'd only sat down to tinker with the
clockwork train a half hour ago. Perhaps an hour, tops. Just after
breakfast. . . .

He went to the door and let Rum out, then realized he had
to follow the tomcat down the stairs to open the street door. He
caught Ollie by the shoulder as the little monkey made to follow
Rum out onto the street.

"Don't be bold, you," he said as he swung Ollie up to sit in
the crook of his arm.

He took a look up the street, then down it, before closing the
door and heading back up the stairs. Ollie squirmed in his arms,
but he held on to the monkey until they were inside the loft and
he'd closed the loft door behind them.

The vast room seemed very empty for all the animals. Denzil
lit a lamp, then another. Very empty. And no wonder.

Jodi hadn't been by yet today.

Now that was odd, he thought. Where could she be?

As he went about cleaning cages and feeding the animals, he
tried to remember if she'd said anything about not coming 'round,
because it was quite unlike her not to stop in at least once during
a day. More often a half-dozen times.

All he could remember was talk of missing pages and loose
ends and porpoises—no, that had been purposes. Purposes in
life. She'd mentioned Taupin again—just to irritate him, he was
sure—and then gone out, only to return with some gossip about
a Small being spotted at the Widow Pender's. In short, a typical
day's worth of her cheeky conversation.

But not a word that she wouldn't be by today.

Was she ill?

Unlikely. She seemed to be blessed with a constitution that
didn't know the meaning of the word.

Run off, then?

To where? And from what? For all her talk of boredom and

lacking a purpose in life, she loved her Nettie and she'd never go without first saying good-bye to him.

Kidnapped by thuggees, perhaps? A ludicrous thought, Denzil told himself as he stood by the window, looking out at Bodbury's benighted streets. Still, where *was* she?

Frowning, he thrust his hand into his pocket and immediately impaled it on the sharp end of the screwdriver. He pulled his hand out and sucked at the cut, then made up his mind.

If she wasn't coming here, why then, he'd go looking for her.

He put on his jacket, then a stovepipe hat that canted to one side. From a bamboo holder by the door stuffed with canes and umbrellas, he selected a walking stick topped with a silver badger's head.

Because he was worried.

"Be good, you," he told the animals as he closed the door behind himself.

Awfully worried, really.

When he reached the street, he stood there uncertainly.

The trouble was, he didn't know where to begin to look.

The Unfortunate

Cup of Tea

Courtship consists of a number of
quiet attentions . . . not so pointed as to
alarm, yet not so vague as to be misunderstood.

— LAURENCE STERNE

*J*aney slept late that morning. By the time she got up
and made her way next door for breakfast, the Gaffer was
already back from his morning's deliveries and sitting down
for a cup of tea before lunch, his copy of *The Cornishman* on the
table beside his cup. He took in her sleepy look and gave her a
grin.

"And how are we this fine and sparkling morning, my robin?"
he said.

"Mmm," Janey replied.

She sat down at the table with him. Pouring a half inch of
milk in the bottom of the cup the Gaffer had set out for her
when he had his own breakfast, she pulled the teapot over and
filled the cup up to its lip. The Gaffer went back to his paper
until she'd finished that cup and had poured herself a second.

"Where's Felix?" she asked, eyeing the box of cereal on the
sideboard without much enthusiasm.

"Went out early for a walk."

That woke her up. The clock beside the door leading to the
kitchen told her it was nearing half past eleven.

"Did he say where?"

The Gaffer shook his head. "He borrowed a pair of my old
gum boots, so I'd suppose he went up along the coast path."

"Did he say when he'd be back?"

The Gaffer shook his head again. "Give the lad a chance to get his own thinking done, my love." When she made no reply, he added, "Made a decision, then, have you?"

"No. Yes. Maybe." Janey sighed. "Oh, I don't know. It was so good seeing Felix again; I never realized how much I missed him till he was standing there in front of me. But what's going to change? He still won't want to go gigging, so where will that leave us?"

"Have you asked him?"

"I haven't had much of a chance yet, have I?"

The Gaffer folded up his paper and laid it on the table. "What is it *you* want, my fortune?"

"If I could have anything at all?"

The Gaffer nodded.

"For us to live here with you—both Felix and I—for most of the year. To make records together. To tour a couple of times a year. Have some babies—but not too soon."

"And Felix? What does he want?"

"I . . ." Janey sighed. "I don't know."

"Well, my love, it seems you know your own mind—at least as well as you ever do. So now it's time you sat down with Felix and found out what he wants. But mind you—"

"Don't quarrel with him. I know."

"I was going to say, mind you really listen to him," the Gaffer said. "Half the quarrels in this world come about because one side or the other simply isn't listening to the other."

Though he didn't come right out and say it, Janey knew he was referring to her. She had the bad habit of being so busy getting her own points across that she didn't pay much attention to what anyone else was saying. That, combined with her unfortunate temper, had made more than one important discussion all too volatile.

Rolling up his paper, the Gaffer stuck it in the inside pocket of his jacket.

"Well, I'm off, my love," he said as he stood up. "I promised Chalkie I'd come 'round and give him a hand mending that old wall in back of his cottage. You'll be all right?"

"Just brill. Don't worry about me."

"And you'll remember what I said when you talk to Felix? Lads like an emperent sort of a woman, my flower, but there's a grand difference between cheekiness and simply being wayward."

Janey had to laugh. "Did you ever think of writing an advice column for the paper?"

Out came the rolled-up newspaper to be tapped on her head.

"I'll tell the world that my old granddad beats me," she warned him.

"Old, is it?"

Up came the paper again, but Janey was out of her chair and had danced away before he could reach her with it.

"And cantankerous," she said from across the room. "Or should I say—what did you call it?—wayward?"

"If I didn't have business elsewhere . . ."

He tried hard to sound serious, but the threat was an empty one. Smiling, he put away his paper.

"Come give this old man a kiss before he goes," he said.

When she came, it was cautiously, but he neither tickled nor pinched her as she'd feared.

"When you do talk to Felix," he said, "don't push too hard. And that's the last unasked-for bit of advice I'll give you, my heart. Leave sparking couples to their own, my dad used to say."

Janey watched him go from the front window, then settled back down at the table to have some toast. She took her time, hoping that Felix would be back soon, but finally returned to her own rooms when it got to be twelve-thirty and he still wasn't back. She tried playing some tunes, but wasn't in the mood for music. Picking up the Dunthorn book, she sat down with it by the window overlooking the backyard, but found she wasn't in the mood to read either.

Instead, she idly flipped the pages of the book and stared out at the yard, watching a stonechat hop from branch to branch in the blackberry bushes that hedged the small square of lawn. After a time, she felt the beginnings of a tune stirring inside her.

Usually when she composed, tunes grew out of a practice session. They were rarely planned. A misplaced phrase from one tune might spark the idea for a new one. Or the lift and lilt of a particular set might wake the first few bars of an original piece. Rarely did the tunes arrive, whole cloth as it were. And never did she hear them the way she could hear this one.

It didn't seem to come so much from inside her, as from without, as though she heard someone playing from just over on the other side of a hill, the music drifting across to her, faint, vaguely familiar, but ultimately unknown. And while normally she only needed to hear a tune through once or twice to pick it up, this one remained oddly elusive.

She hummed along with it, her fingers no longer flipping the pages of the book. Setting the book aside, she took her mandolin down from the wall and tried to capture the order of notes. She got one phrase, then another. The third wasn't right. It went more like—

The Gaffer's bell rang next door, breaking her concentration.

Ignore it, she told herself, but when she turned back to her instrument, the music was gone.

"Oh, damn," she muttered as she put the mandolin down.

But then it might be Felix, she thought as she went to see who it was. So don't be cross with him. There was no way he could have known that he'd be interrupting you.

Still, it was a shame. Because the tune had been a good one. Although it *was* odd that she couldn't remember any more than those first two bars of it now.

Keeping a smile firmly in place, she opened the door between her little courtyard and the Gaffer's only to find a stranger standing by the Gaffer's front door.

There was nothing threatening about him. He was slender—no, quite thin rather, she corrected herself—with longish dark hair and that certain kind of pale, but bright eyes that always reminded her of Paul Newman. He wore corduroys and a dark blue Windbreaker, had a camera in its case slung over one shoulder, a couple of cases on the ground beside him.

He could have been anybody, he was undoubtedly innocent of any bad intention, but the first thing Janey thought as she looked at him was, he's after Dunthorn's lost book.

It was too late to undo the smile that had been meant for Felix, and there was—for all her premonition—something too infectious about his own smile for her to stop.

"Janey Little?" he asked.

She nodded warily, for all that she was still smiling like a loon.

"I hope I haven't come at a bad time," he went on. "My name's Mike Betcher; I'm with *Rolling Stone.*"

"What? The magazine?"

Betcher nodded. "I was hoping I could interview you."

For a long moment Janey didn't know what to say. She looked at him, glanced down at his cases to see that one of them was for a portable computer, then met his gaze again.

"You can't be serious."

Betcher laughed. "We don't just do Madonna and the like."

"I know but..."

"If I've come at a bad time, I can come back."

"No, it's just..."

Just what? Ludicrous that *Rolling Stone* would want to do a piece on *her?* That was putting it mildly.

"I'm doing a piece on alternative music, you see," Betcher explained. "I'm over here on holiday and thought I'd like to get a few interviews with some British artists who I admire to round out the article. At the moment it's got too much of a Stateside slant."

"Yes, but..."

"You can't pretend that you don't know you have a following in the States," he said.

"Well, no. It's just that it's so low-key...."

"And that's exactly what I'm hoping to change with this piece," Betcher said. "There are a lot of artists like you— on small independent labels, doing their own music—who re- main relatively unknown to the general record-buying public.

And that's not right. Take yourself. You're a headline act in Europe—"

"In small halls."

"Doesn't matter. And didn't your last tour of California sell out?"

"Yes, but I was only playing in small clubs."

Betcher shook his head. "Maybe I'll run that as the headline: 'The Modest Little.'"

Janey couldn't help but laugh. "That sounds redundant."

He shrugged. "So help me come up with a better one. Look, it can't hurt to give it a go, can it? What have you got to lose? At least give me a chance. I've come a long way."

"You said you were on holiday anyway."

"Okay. But it's still a long way from London. I've been almost six hours on the train."

She should just invite him in, she thought, because, as he'd said, she had nothing to lose and everything to gain. To get some coverage in a national paper like *Rolling Stone* . . . it was as good as being on the cover of the *NME* over here. But something still bothered her about his landing on her door just now.

First that American woman looking for the Dunthorn book.

Then Felix showing up.

Now a reporter from *Rolling Stone*. . . .

It all seemed a bit much. So, no. She wouldn't have him in. But she'd be a complete ass to just send him on his way.

"Just let me get a jacket," she said, "and we can go for a cup of tea. Would that be all right?"

"Absolutely."

She left him there and hurried back upstairs.

A reporter from *Rolling Stone*. Right here in Mousehole. To interview *her*. What a laugh. She could hardly wait to tell someone about it.

A quick glance in the mirror stopped her. God, she looked awful. She put on some eye shadow and lipstick, worried over what might be a pimple but proved on closer inspection to be just a bit of dried skin, then brushed her hair. It took her a few moments to dig up her jacket from underneath the clothes she'd dumped on it last night. As she put it on, her gaze fell on the Dunthorn book that lay on the couch by the window.

It wouldn't do to leave that lying about. She had to hide it, only where?

Looking around her rooms, she realized that there really wasn't any foolproof safe place it could be hidden. So taking her cue from Poe, she merely stuck it on her bookshelf beside his other books. Hidden in plain sight, she thought, pleased with her own cleverness.

Catching up her purse, she went back outside, locking the door behind her and pocketing the key.

Now that felt odd, she thought. She couldn't remember the last time she'd locked her door.

Pushing the feeling aside, she rejoined Betcher by the Gaffer's front door.

"Where to?" he asked.

"Pamela's Pantry. They've got the best cream teas in town."

And 'round about this time of year, she thought, just about the only ones as well, but she wasn't about to admit that to him. Let him think that quaint though it was, Mousehole had as much to offer as any place up country—which was what the Cornish called the rest of England.

"Cream tea?" Betcher asked as he hefted his cases. "What's that?"

"You'll see."

2 .

The Cornish Coastal Path is 268 miles long and runs from Marshland Mouth on the Devon border, around the coast past Land's End, and all the way on to the shores of Plymouth Sound. It is the central part of the 520-mile South West Way, the longest continuous footpath in England.

Much of the Cornish section is based on the tracks marking

out the regular beats walked by Coastguards. In 1947, when a new National Parks Commission first suggested that a continuous pathway 'round the British coast was a possibility, it was seen that Cornwall presented the ideal conditions for it, but it wasn't until May of 1973 that the Cornish Coastal Path was officially opened.

Like the whole of the South West Way, the Cornish Coastal Path is usually walked from north to south, a psychological "downhill" journey that leads the walker southwest from the six-hundred-foot cliffs at Marshland Mouth to the granite shoulders of Land's End, then back east to follow the gentler south coast. When Felix walked it that morning, however, he went the opposite way.

He walked up Raginnis Hill in the west part of Mousehole and past the Wild Bird Hospital and the Carn Du Hotel to where the road turned right. A smaller road continued past a cluster of stone cottages into a narrow lane bordered by blackberry hedges. A handful of cows grazed placidly in the pastures behind the hedges on the left, while beyond them was the sea. When the lane ended, a footpath led on through the fields, heading west to Lamorna.

Felix walked all the way around Kemyel Point and Carn Du to Lamorna's sheltered cove. The path was rugged, climbing up and down the steep cliffs with sometimes no more than two-foot-wide stands of gorse between himself and the drop below. The wind came in from the sea, bringing a salt tang with it. The long grass was bent over, dried and brown from the salt. Gulls wheeled overhead, and except for them, he had the path to himself. As he neared Mousehole on his return, he stopped at a kind of stone armchair that jutted from a granite outcrop just before the Coastguard lookout behind Penzer Point. There he sat and gazed out over Mount's Bay.

Somewhere below him and to the left was the Mousehole Cave that he and Janey had explored on another walk a few years ago. There was a haze in the air so that St. Michael's Mount was only a smudge and the long line of the Lizard coast was completely hidden from view. On a sunny day, and he'd been here on such days, you could see the houses of Marazion and the large dish aerials of the Goonhilly satellite tracking station when the sun caught them just so.

Plucking a long stem of stiff grass, he twisted it between his fingers and thought of Janey, of the letter that had brought him here, and wondered just what he should do. When he thought of how their relationship had ended... He didn't want to go through those last few months again.

But what if it *could* be different? He'd never know if he didn't try, and wasn't Janey important enough to him for him to make the effort?

No question there. He just didn't think he could handle it all falling to pieces around him again.

He sighed, dropped the twist of grass, and plucked another stem.

Talk it out with her, he told himself.

He looked down the path towards Mousehole, his heart lifting when he saw a figure making its way through the fields towards him. It's Janey, he thought. But then the figure's cane registered and he knew it wasn't her. It was Clare Mabley.

He waited patiently through her slow progress until she'd reached him, then stood up and gave her a hug.

"It's been a long time," he said as he stepped back.

Clare lowered herself onto the seat he'd so recently vacated and gave him a smile.

"Hasn't it, though?" she said. "But I got your letters, so I didn't feel as though you'd simply dropped off the edge of the world. You never did visit though—and you promised."

Felix shrugged. "I wasn't ready yet. How'd you know I was in town?"

That ready smile of Clare's reappeared. "Have you been away that long? Mr. Bodener told Greg Lees—he delivers the milk now that his dad retired—and Greg told my mum. Edna next door also heard it from Mr. Hayle who got it from the Gaffer."

"Some things don't change."

"Well, it's a bit of excitement, isn't it?"

Felix nodded. "I suppose."

He sat down on a nearby rock and plucked another grass stem, which he began to shred.

"I thought I'd find you here," Clare said after a few moments of silence.

Felix looked up.

"Well, it's where you used to come the last time you and Janey were having your rows."

"We haven't had a row."

Not really, he thought. Not yet. But that was because they'd barely had a chance to talk.

"Didn't you? That's good. But I saw you walking past the house earlier this morning—by yourself. It didn't seem a good sign."

Clare had been Felix's confidante when he and Janey were breaking up. She was Janey's best friend, but she'd become Felix's as well. Like the Gaffer, she'd hated to see the two of them making a muddle of their lives, but unlike the Gaffer, she hadn't been shy about giving Felix advice when they'd talked. Unfortunately, while he listened attentively and never seemed to mind her concern—he called her "Mother Clare" when she went on too long—he hadn't taken her advice either.

"We haven't got together enough to break up again," Felix said.

When Clare lifted an eyebrow, he looked away across the bay once more. For long moments he said nothing, then finally he began to tell her how his return to Penwith had come about.

"For God's sake, Felix," she said when he was done. "You have to tell her how you feel."

"I know."

"And if she gets angry, be angry back. I don't mean you should start bullying her, but you know Janey. She only really listens to those who talk louder than she does. She doesn't mean to be so bloody obstinate; it's just her nature."

Felix knew that, too. And he'd always been the sort who was willing to accept a friend's faults. But that didn't change the basic differences that underlay all of his disagreements with Janey.

"But why won't you tour?" Clare asked when he brought that up. "You've never told me and you've probably never told Janey either. You love music, so what's so bad about making your living playing it? It must be better than hauling about cargo on a freighter or whatever it is that you do on those ships of yours."

Felix wouldn't meet her gaze.

"Oh, come on, Felix. If you can't tell me, then how will you ever be able to tell her? Is it like the way Dinny feels? That if he plays for money he's going to lose the crack?"

Again, silence. Still he wouldn't meet her gaze.

"Felix?"

He turned finally.

"It scares me," he said. "It scares me so much that I get sick just thinking about it."

He could see the surprise in her eyes and knew exactly what she was thinking: a great big strapping man like himself—scared of something so trivial?

"But . . . you don't have any trouble playing at sessions," Clare said.

"It's not the same."

"Still, people are watching you just as though you were on stage, aren't they?"

Felix shook his head. "It really isn't the same. Believe me, I've tried to get over it. I don't know how many times I've gone to a club on a floor singer's night and given it a go, only to freeze up. Then I can't even get the first note out of my box."

"Well, it's not the end of the world," Clare said.

"Maybe not. But how can I tell Janey about that?"

"She'll understand."

"Do you think so? She thrives on being in the spotlight— that's when her music really comes alive. How could she understand?"

"You believe she'll think the less of you because of it?"

"I know she will," Felix said. "Remember when Ted Praed used to get up to play at The Swan in Truro?"

Clare nodded. "He never got through one song without his voice going all quavery and then he'd leave the stage. . . ." She paused, then went on. "And when we drove home Janey'd have us in stitches mimicking how his voice went."

"Carrying it over with little scenarios of what it must be like to go into a bank or a shop and have his voice break up and then he'd go running out. . . ."

"But we all laughed—you did, too. And we all made jokes about it."

"I couldn't stand her laughing at me like that, Clare."

She nodded. "It wasn't very nice of us, was it?"

"I used to feel like a heel, thinking about it."

"But Ted never knew."

"That still didn't make it right."

"I suppose not."

Felix sighed. "I'd rather have her angry at me than have her laugh at me."

Neither said anything more for a time. They watched gulls circling the ferry that was heading out towards the Scilly Islands. Felix shredded a few more grass stems while Clare poked the end of her cane into the dirt by her feet.

"You'll still have to tell her," she said finally.

"I told you, I couldn't stand to have her—"

"Give her more credit than that, Felix. Maybe she will understand. If she cares about you at all, I *know* she will."

"But when I think of Ted . . ."

"Oh, Ted. He was such a silly ass anyway. So full of himself. The real reason we made fun of him was because he was always going on about what a smashing singer he was and then as soon as he got up on stage, he'd fall apart. It's not the same thing, Felix. If we hadn't laughed at him about that, it would've been something else. It's true," she added before Felix could interrupt, "that it wasn't a nice thing to do, but you have to admit, he did bring it on himself."

"But Janey—"

"Was no worse than the rest of us. If Ted hadn't been such a poppet, she would have been the first to help him get over his stage fright."

She tapped Felix's leg with the end of her cane until he looked at her.

"So you will tell her?"

"If it comes up."

Clare shook her head. "If it comes up! What is it about men that they all feel they have to live up to this silly macho image? I thought you were more liberated than that."

"It's not that," he protested. "It's just . . . well, do *you* like looking like a fool?"

"Of course not."

"Neither do I. It's got nothing about being macho or not."

"But looking like a fool still happens to all of us," she said. "Whether we like it or not. Anyway, we're not talking about me, we're talking about you and Janey. You have to tell her."

"Yes, Mother Clare."

"No, really."

"I will."

"Good. Now you can see me home, like a good gentleman would, and tomorrow you can come by to tell me how it all went."

Felix had to laugh. "Yes, Mother Clare. Will there be an exam?"

She whacked his leg with her cane, then offered him her hand so that he could help her up. She kept her hand in the nook of his arm and chattered about inconsequential things as they made their way back to her house, bringing Felix up-to-date on all the local gossip that might interest him.

Enjoying her company, Felix wondered, and not for the first time, what would have happened if he'd met Clare before he'd met Janey. She was attractive, smart, and they got along famously. She should have been perfect, but she just wasn't Janey. There could only be the one Janey—to which the Gaffer would add, "And thank God for that," if she was in one of her moods.

"Tomorrow, now—don't forget," Clare said as Felix left her at her door.

"I won't. Wish me luck."

"You don't need luck—just be yourself. Nobody could want more than that from you. And *don't* you 'Mother Clare' me again today, or I'll give you such a whack with this cane that you'll be too busy healing to even think about sparking."

Felix gave her a wave, then continued on down Raginnis Hill. Clare was probably right, he thought as he walked. Janey wouldn't laugh—not if she really did care. But how he was ever going to get up the courage to tell her, he really didn't—

He paused in mid-step and stared ahead to where he could see Janey walking in the company of a man Felix had never met. It was hard to tell the man's age, but it was obvious from his cases that he'd only just arrived in Mousehole. Oblivious to Felix, they laughed with each other and went into Pamela's Pantry.

The first thought that came to Felix's mind when he saw the man's cases was, had Janey sent out more than one letter?

He put his hand in his pocket to touch the folded paper that was still there.

But no. She'd denied ever sending it, hadn't she? And he believed her, didn't he?

He had no claim to her, but he couldn't help feeling a little hurt.

You're the one that went off for a walk, he told himself. She didn't. Why should she have to sit around waiting for you?

Because—because . . .

Oh, bloody hell, he thought and went on down the street.

When he reached the harbour, instead of turning up Duck Street to the Gaffer's house, he continued on up Parade Hill until it took him out of Mousehole and onto the coastal road that led to Newlyn.

3 ·

Janey found it easy to relax in the reporter's company—so much so that she had to keep reminding herself that he *was* a reporter and making her feel at ease was part of his job. Because she tended to just talk off the top of her head, she'd had to learn her lesson the hard way when her first interviews appeared and some of her more outrageous, and sometimes unkind, statements lay there on the page, all too accurately quoted. She'd been thoroughly embarrassed by some of the things she'd said in the past and wasn't about to let it happen again.

She'd also made sure that Mike Betcher really was the reporter he said he was.

As soon as they'd sat down at a table in Pamela's and placed their order with the waitress, she'd asked him if he had any ID whereupon he produced a press card, sealed in plastic.

How hard would it be to get something like that? she wondered.

She had no idea. But his looked official enough and she realized that questioning him any further would just make her look like an ass. She knew that there was no conspiracy. The American woman looking for Dunthorn's book, Felix's arrival, and this reporter had no logical connection.

Deliberately, she put it all out of her mind and concentrated on the business at hand. She was determined to be on her best behavior. Did *Rolling Stone* have a million readers? More? If just five percent of them were interested enough to buy her records and come to her gigs, she'd be doing very well indeed.

"This is great," Betcher said after the waitress brought their order.

Janey had always loved the Pantry's cream teas—two scones with jam and thick Cornish clotted cream, served with a pot of steaming tea on the side—but she didn't allow herself the luxury of having them often. If they did, she'd kidded Clare one day, they'd turn into the Amazing Balloon Women.

"I thought you'd like it," she said.

He didn't bring up Dunthorn or his books, lost or otherwise. Instead, he talked about the music, with enough authority that Janey knew that his enthusiasm had to be genuine. She didn't always agree with him, but she made a point of disagreeing diplomatically—not an easy undertaking for her, but good practice, she thought.

"Why do you think there's so many young pipe players on the scene?" he asked at one point.

"Young players? You're forgetting Alistair Anderson, Joe Hutton, Jim Hall—"

"From the Ranters, yes," he said. "I'm not forgetting him, or any of those others, but they don't seem to have the same popularity as the younger players such as yourself, Kathryn Tickell, Martyn Bennet—"

"He plays the Scottish small pipes."

"For the purposes of this piece," he said, "there isn't really enough distinction between the two to make a difference."

"There is when you consider the kind Hamish Moore plays."

"What do you mean?"

Like any piping enthusiast, Janey immediately warmed to her subject.

"Well, there's three kinds of Cauld Wind Pipes," she said. "The Scottish small pipes that we're talking about are related to the Northumbrian, but they use a Scottish style of fingering and tend to be pitched in lower keys. Then there's also the lowland or border pipes, which are more related to the highland pipes, although they're a lot quieter because of the conical bore of their chanter. Nobody much cares for them these days."

"Yes, but—"

"And lastly," Janey broke in, "there's the pastoral pipes, which have a long extended foot joint at the end of the chanter. They also have a regulator and looped bass drone one octave below normal, which gives them a sound that's very much like that of the Irish Uillean pipes." She paused to give him a look. "You're not taking any notes," she added.

Betcher laughed. "That's because you're getting far too esoteric for my readers. Why don't we just stick to the instrument you play?"

"I suppose." She thought for a moment. "You didn't mention Becky Taylor. I did a workshop with her at the Sidmouth Festival in Devon this past summer."

He dutifully wrote that down, then returned to his earlier question. As the interview went on, Janey was surprised at how much he knew of her career, and couldn't help but feel pleased. He avoided all the usual questions, concentrating on the kinds of things that she felt were important but that no one in the press ever seemed to cover in an interview.

"Now what about some of these tunes you wrote yourself?" he asked. "'The Gaffer's Mouzel' is self-explanatory, now that you've told me about your grandfather. But what about some of these others?"

"Which ones?"

"'The Stoness Barn'?"

"It's named after an old barn on a farm in Canada where I stayed for a weekend."

"'The Nine Blind Harpers'?"

Janey laughed. "I've no idea where that title came from. Probably from Felix."

"That's the Felix in 'Felix Gavin's Reel'?"

Janey nodded.

"And the Billy in 'Billy's Own Jig'—that would be Billy Pigg?"

"No," she said. "That one was for Billy Dunthorn."

He wrote that down in his notepad. "Did he play the pipes as well?"

"Not likely. He was a local writer. William Dunthorn. He's the one who wrote *The Hidden People.*"

Betcher frowned, as though trying to catch a thought, then his face lit up.

"Really?" he said. "The one about the Smalls? I read that as a kid and loved it. It's funny he never wrote anything else—or was it just that he was like Grahame or Carroll and we only remember him for the one piece?"

"You never read *The Lost Music?*"

Betcher shook his head.

"But that's his best book—*better* than *The Hidden People* by far. It's all about what I do—traditional music and its magical qualities."

Betcher's eyebrows lifted in exaggerated surprise. "Magic?"

"Oh, you know what I mean. Not witches and things like that—though he's got that in it—but the way the music makes you feel. The magical way it connects you to history. To everything that's gone before. He's one of the main reasons I got into music in the first place."

"Well, I'll have to track down a copy of the book then. Is it still available?"

"They've got it down at the newsagent's on North Cliff—after all, he was born here."

"I'll make sure to pick one up after we're done, then." He referred back to his notes. "So it was Dunthorn who got you interested in music—was that your fiddle playing?"

Janey nodded.

"What brought you to take up the Northumbrian pipes? They're not exactly a traditional Cornish instrument."

"I'll say. It's mostly all choir singing here, like in Wales. Something to do with all the mining, I suppose." Janey grinned suddenly. "Here's an old joke of the Gaffer's: What's the definition of a Cornishman?"

"I don't know."

"A man at the bottom of a mine, singing."

Betcher smiled, then brought the conversation back to its original topic. "What started you on the pipes?"

"Well, that was Dinny's doing—I told you about Dinny?"

Betcher nodded. "He plays on the LPs."

"He got me interested in the pipes, but the only spare set he had at first were these Northumbrian small pipes, so . . ."

The next two hours went by very quickly and all too soon Betcher was putting away his pen and notepad.

"I want to put this in some kind of order," he said, "but would it be all right to come by—say, tomorrow—if I've missed anything?"

"Call first," Janey said, and she gave him the Gaffer's phone number.

"And now . . . two last requests. I'd love to hear you play in person. Do you have any gigs lined up in the next few days?"

Janey shook her head.

"That's too bad."

"I'm on holiday. What's the other thing?"

"I need some pictures. A few of you around your house— wherever it is that you practice, say—and one or two of you somewhere around the village."

Remembering the face that had looked back at her from the mirror this morning, she shook her head again.

"Not today," she said.

She needed to wash her hair, find some decent clothes to wear. . . .

"Tomorrow?"

She sighed. It also meant cleaning up the jumble of her room.

"If you have to. . . ."

Betcher laughed. " 'The Modest Little'—I think I'll stick with that as a title."

"Don't you dare!"

He held his hands up placatingly. "Your wish is my command. Tomorrow it is for the pictures—and maybe a few tunes?"

He looked so earnest that Janey finally had to give in.

"Oh, why not," she said. "But mind you don't ring up too early. I really am on holiday so I'm in my usual slothful state— and don't quote me on that."

"Wouldn't dream of it."

"Where are you staying?" Janey asked. "Maybe I can get a bit of a session together for tonight. If I do I'll ring you up."

"I'm open to suggestions."

"Would a bed and breakfast be all right?"

"Perfect."

Janey put on her jacket and gathered up her purse. "Come on, then, and I'll walk you over to one that's nearby. But after that you're on your own. I've got a friend visiting and here I've gone and spent the whole day ignoring him."

The fact that she'd only just thought of Felix made her feel guilty, but surely he'd realize what this article could do for her career?

Betcher rose with her. He paid their bill, then gathered together his own belongings.

"I hope there won't be a problem," he said. "With your friend, I mean."

"I don't think so. Felix is very understanding."

She hoped.

"This is the Felix Gavin you wrote the tune for? Is he a musician as well?"

She nodded. "And a very good one. But don't try to write him up in an article. He can't stand the business side of things. All he loves is the music."

"You seem very fond of him."

Was that a touch of regret she heard in Betcher's voice? It gave her pause when she realized that she might have been missing the signals. But, now that she stopped to think about it, the signals had been there all along. She just hadn't seen them. It was too bad. He seemed a very likable sort of a fellow, and if Felix weren't here, maybe she would have followed up on this interest of his that apparently went further than the interview.

But Felix *was* here.

"Very fond," she said.

Yes, he was a bit keen on her. She could see his disappointment, for all that he tried to hide it.

Best to just pretend she didn't see it, she decided. Her love life was complicated enough as it was.

"Come on," she said. "If we wait too long, all the rooms'll be gone."

"At this time of year? I thought the tourist season was over."

"It is. But that doesn't mean the B and Bs close down. There's all sorts of folks still traveling about. Hardy hikers. Salesmen. Reporters from American pop papers. . . ."

"I get the picture," he said as he allowed himself to be led away.

4 ·

It never ceased to amaze Michael Bett at how easy it was to manipulate an individual. All one needed to know were the right buttons to push.

Madden liked to think of it as magic, but while Bett agreed it had to do with the strength of one's will, and how able one was to use it to overpower the natural defenses of a subject—the "sheep" as Madden and the other members of the Order liked to call the uninitiated—Bett himself believed it to be simply a form of mesmerism.

He preferred that old term—based on the techniques and theories of Franz Mesmer, which, in turn, had interested Jean Charcot and his peers in the possibilities of "animal magnetism"—to the more contemporary perceptions of hypnotism. For Bett's use of his will *was* a form of animal magnetism, utilizing the same unspoken domination that an alpha wolf held over its pack, the same hypnotic control a snake practiced upon its prey. The difference lay in the fact that Bett's victims were never aware of the control he held over them.

Take Janey Little.

Yes, perhaps he would. But not now. Not yet. Not until she'd given him what he'd come for.

She was a perfect example. Headstrong and bright, she would never dream that she was being manipulated. She was the sort who dominated a group by the sheer exuberance and vitality of her personality, yet by approaching her as he had—offering her a chance at fame, concentrating on her music, feigning a wistful, unspoken attraction for her, in short, giving her what she wanted—she was as easy for Bett to manage as would be the most simpleminded of Madden's sheep.

Given time, he would have her doing anything he told her to do.

Anything.

His will—his "magic," as Madden would put it—was simply that strong.

She would not reveal Dunthorn's secret today. But reveal it to him she would. It was inevitable.

He let her take him to the newsagent's where he bought a paperback edition of *The Lost Music,* then she took him to a bed and breakfast on the east edge of the village. When they'd determined that there was a room for him, he followed her back to the front door where she gave him her easy smile.

"Well, I'm off then," she said.

"Thanks for everything," he told her. "You've been just great. If you—no, never mind."

"If I what?" she had to know.

"I was just going to say, if you do get a session together tonight, or even if you just find you have nothing to do, I'd . . . you know. Love to hear from you."

"I'll see about the session, but I've got—"

"Your friend staying with you. Right. I forgot. Well, maybe the two of you . . . ?"

She laughed. "We'll see. But don't hold your breath. Felix and I have a lot of catching up to do."

"I understand. Well, thanks again for everything."

He saw her off, then went inside to use the phone. When he was connected with Lena's room, a man answered.

"Hello?"

Bett hung up without replying and stared at the receiver.

He'd told her to stay in, but he hadn't told her not to have anyone in, now had he? The stupid cow. Did he have to spell everything out for her?

He needed her now, to get Felix Gavin out of the way. Not to be having a little tête-à-tête with some busboy in her room. He considered calling Willie Keel to have him go around and straighten things out, but then realized it was probably Keel who had set her up with someone in the first place.

He'd just have to do it himself.

5 ·

North of Mousehole, about halfway between the village and neighbouring Newlyn, is the old Penlee Quarry. Though not nearly so busy as it was in its heyday, the quarry's silos still stored the blue alvin stone that was once shipped out in great quantities to many ports, but now only went to Germany. As Felix approached the quarry by the road, he was a little taken aback— as he always was—by the faulted land that presented itself on his left. In picturesque Penwith, with its pleasant winding lanes and hedges and its magnificent sweeps of cliff and moor, the heaps of raw dirt and old scars of the quarry seemed much too out of place.

He stood in the shadow of the silos that loomed over him on the seaside of the road, and looked at the quarry. There was no activity at the moment. Just an old Land Rover parked by a decrepit building, the ruins of other buildings beyond it, and the scarred land. Behind him, enormous disused storage pits were housed beside the silos, stone-walled and metal-roofed, their broad entrances fenced off from the road. Above him, the skies were smudged with grey, promising rain.

It was the perfect place for a murder, Felix thought.

He wasn't in a good mood.

He wasn't angry with anyone—except for himself. Though he loved this part of England, and had a number of friends in and about Mousehole that he'd met through Janey, he hadn't been back since they'd broken up a few years ago. At this moment he wished he hadn't returned.

As the sky so surely promised rain, so his return had seemed to promise something as well. But now he'd found that Janey had never sent the letter that had brought him here. It was all too plain that while she was happy to see him, she had her own life to lead now—one that didn't include him—and he wondered how he could ever have been so stupid as to think it would be otherwise.

It didn't matter who the man was that she'd accompanied to Pamela's Pantry. He could be a boyfriend, an agent, her bloody solicitor—it made no difference. Seeing her with someone else just brought home the undeniable fact that no matter what he wanted, no matter what Clare said, things hadn't changed. And wouldn't change. Why should they? Janey owed him nothing. She had a right to her own life. Just because a mistake had brought him here, didn't mean she had to drop everything and try to take things up again with him.

She fancied him—but as a friend. So grow up, he told himself. Accept her on the same terms and stop mooning about like some lovesick teenager.

You have to tell her, he could hear Clare saying.

But what was the point when he already knew the answer? Why make things uncomfortable? It was better to just spend a couple of days in the village. Better to hang about with her, play some tunes, see Clare again—but not alone, or she'd nag him— maybe go up to the farm and visit with Dinny and his family. . . . Make no waves. Just try to have a pleasant time, and then go.

Say nothing, and just go.

You have to tell her how you feel.

No he didn't. He had his own life to live as well. And if he chose to live it without Janey—well that'd be *his* choice, wouldn't it?

Without her.

With only that ghostly memory of her to talk to at night on the rolling deck of some freighter going from who-cares to what-does-it-matter. Killing time on the ocean.

God, he hated this side of himself.

In most matters he was the sort of person who knew what he wanted to do and then went and did it. He got things done. He didn't have problems with indecision or soul-searching.

Except when it came to Janey.

He picked up a stone by the roadside and flung it into the fenced-off storage pits beside the silos. Time to head back, he thought, irritated with himself for the way his stomach tightened at the idea. Maybe he should go down into Newlyn and find a pub where he could get something to eat before he returned. Except he didn't feel like eating.

Looking down the road, his attention was caught by the figure of an unsteady bicyclist making her way up the graded hill towards the quarry. She wobbled on the narrow shoulder of the road, visibly flinching when a car went rushing by.

A late-season tourist, Felix thought. Not used to these roads. He wondered if she'd been on any of the B-roads yet, because compared to those narrow little lanes, this road was like a four-lane highway.

He started to turn away, but then another car went by the cyclist. Her unsteadiness grew more pronounced in the wake of that car and he could see her wheel catch a stone and the bicycle start to fall almost before it happened. She landed badly, twisting her leg under her. Felix jogged towards her.

"Shit, shit, shit," she was saying when he reached her side.

"Don't try to move yet," Felix told her.

She looked up. Tears made her eye shadow run and her mouth twisted with pain, but neither hid the fact that she was a very attractive woman. Her hair was short and swept back. The leather of her bomber's jacket was scuffed and there was a tear in one knee of her jeans, but the latter appeared to be more a matter of style than caused by her fall. From the MIT T-shirt she was wearing, Felix knew she was an American even before her accent registered.

"Where does it hurt?" he asked.

"My—my ankle. . . ."

"Okay. Just take it easy now."

Gently he helped her disentangle herself from the bike. Once he'd set the bike aside, he helped her up.

"Can you put any weight on it?" he asked.

She gave it a try.

"I think—no!"

She jerked from the sudden pain, trembling as she leaned against him. Felix helped her sit down, then studied her ankle. It was swelling a bit, but was it sprained or broken? He couldn't tell. Lying on the ground nearby was a watch, the links of its bracelet broken.

"Is this yours?" he asked, picking it up.

She put a hand to her wrist, then nodded. As Felix handed it over he noticed what he first took to be a smudge of dirt on her wrist. Then he realized, just before she tugged down the sleeve of her jacket, that it was a tattoo of a small grey bird.

Curious, he thought. When she was wearing the watch, it would be completely hidden. So what was the point of it?

Sitting back, he found her regarding him.

"Hi," she said.

He smiled. "Hi, yourself."

She seemed to be recovering somewhat, now that her weight was off the ankle again and the initial shock of her fall had faded.

"Guess that was a pretty stupid thing to do," she said.

"Accidents happen. Where are you staying?"

"In Penzance. My name's Lena."

She held out her hand.

"Felix Gavin," Felix said as he took her hand to shake.

Lena laughed. "God, we must look silly."

Felix smiled. She gave his hand a quick squeeze, then let go— reluctantly, it seemed.

"Thanks for coming to the rescue," she said.

"You should get that looked after," Felix said, nodding to her ankle. "There was a Land Rover parked back at the quarry. Do you want me to see if they'll give you a lift to the hospital?"

"Oh, it just needs some ice, I think."

"Okay. I'll see about that lift."

She caught his arm as he was about to stand.

"I don't want a big fuss made over me," she said. "Maybe you could just wheel me on the bike? It's mostly downhill."

"You're sure?"

"I feel dumb enough as it is without having a bunch of strangers all gawking at me."

"And we're not strangers?"

"Not anymore—we introduced ourselves, remember?"

Felix couldn't help but return her smile.

"Okay," he said. "I'll give it a go. But if it hurts too much, just let me know."

He retrieved the bike and brought it near to where she was sitting, then leaning it against himself, he reached down and gave her a hand up so that she didn't put any weight on her ankle. It was a man's bike, so he lifted her up onto the crossbar, then wheeled the bike over to the road.

"You sure you'll be all right?" he asked as she grimaced.

She nodded.

When Felix got on the bike, she turned towards him, steadying herself with her arms around his waist, and leaned against him. Feeling awkward, but resigned, Felix started the bike freewheeling down towards Newlyn. The traffic was light and he didn't have to start pedaling until he was down by the harbour, crossing the boundary between Newlyn and Penzance.

6.

The Gaffer and Chalkie were having lunch in the Smuggler's Restaurant in Newlyn, after taking a break from the wall mending that they hadn't actually got around to starting yet. They had stood about in Chalkie's backyard in their wellies, studying the broken-down wall from a number of different angles, but then Chalkie had announced that he was hungry and insisted they eat out, his treat.

"Why dirty dishes, when someone else can do your cooking for you?" he asked the Gaffer.

The truth was, Chalkie always ate out. The highest his culinary skills aimed for was to make the odd bit of porridge or toast for himself in the mornings. And didn't he brew a mean cup of tea?

So they were sitting at a window table in the restaurant at the time that Felix rode by on the bicycle with Lena snuggled against his chest. The Gaffer had to look twice, to make sure he was really seeing what he was seeing. The pair went by so quickly that he could almost doubt who they were—almost, but not enough. He'd recognized them both and it gave him a knotty feeling in the center of his chest.

Poor Janey, he thought.

"Does my heart good to see that," Chalkie said. "A couple out on a single bike like that. Remember when we used to go sparking with our bikes, up Kerris way? What were the names of those sisters again?"

The Gaffer gave him a blank look, then nodded.

"Feena and April," he said.

Chalkie grinned. "That's right. And Feena rode with me on my bike, but April"—his grin grew broader—"she had her own, didn't she just? Had her own bike and you were the loser."

"Wasn't I just," the Gaffer said.

And he was the loser again, he and Janey both. For that woman he'd seen in Felix's arms was the same one who'd come by the house demanding Billy's unpublished writings not four days ago. He would never have thought it of Felix, but now it made sense, his showing up the way he had with that letter of his. Of course Janey hadn't written it—he'd written it himself.

When he thought of how much he'd always liked Felix—he'd

been the best of any lad Janey brought home—it made his heart break.

"Have you gone deaf?"

The Gaffer lifted his head to find Chalkie looking at him, a puzzled look creasing his brow. He hadn't heard a word that Chalkie had said.

"What's that, my beauty?" he asked.

"I said, have you gone deaf?" Chalkie repeated. "Garm, you were lost at sea just now, you."

The Gaffer sighed. "I was thinking."

"Bad thoughts?"

"Well, they weren't good ones," the Gaffer said.

"Comes from getting old," Chalkie assured him. "Always think of the good times, Tom. Makes it easier."

"I suppose."

The good times. Lost times. No, they weren't good to dwell upon. But what did you do when you found out that some of them were lies?

Oh, how was he going to tell Janey?

7 ·

Everything works out in the end, Lena thought, and she hadn't even needed Willie's directions. She had a sprained ankle, and that wasn't fun, but she couldn't have found a better way to meet Felix Gavin than if she'd planned that tumble from the bike herself.

He'd actually carried her upstairs to her room, then seen about getting a pack of ice, which he was now applying to her foot, which was propped up on the bed before her. While he'd gone down to the lobby to get the ice, she'd changed into a big floppy sweatshirt that covered her to her knees. The strained white look on her face from the pain that the change in clothing had cost her hadn't been put on. Just that small effort had almost completely worn her out. And kindhearted hunk that he was, her rescuer had immediately insisted that she lie down when he returned.

He was an interesting man—strong and gentle and she could easily understand what the Little girl had seen in him. What she couldn't understand was why Janey Little had dumped him.

Oh, well, Lena thought philosophically. Her loss, my gain.

She was on her best behavior with him, utilizing everything she'd ever learned in her acting classes. The image she projected was a rather appealing mix, even if she did say so herself.

Demure, but not naive. Hurting, but being brave about it. Open and friendly, a bit lonely, but no hard come on. In short, she was charming the pants off him, without coming off as a tart.

And she could tell that it was working. It wasn't in anything he said or did—he was being the complete gentleman, which rather surprised her, considering his background—but she could tell she was having an effect upon him all the same. It was the way he studied her without really looking. The way he was having an increasingly hard time making ordinary conversation.

"Boy," she said, wriggling a bit as she adjusted her position against the headboard. "What a dumb thing to have done. You'd think I'd never ridden a bike before."

"Do you do a lot of cycling?" Felix asked.

She nodded. "I love it. But I'm not used to these roads and the crossbar on the bike made me feel a bit weird, too. Why do they have those things on men's bikes, anyway? You'd think it'd make guys even more nervous."

Whoops, she thought as he raised an eyebrow. Tone it down. You don't want to scare him off.

"Anyway," she added quickly, "I was lucky to have you be so close to give me a hand. You've been a real angel."

"It was no big deal."

"Not to you maybe."

Felix shrugged and looked about the room.

"Are you here on holiday?" he asked.

A wry smile touched Lena's lips. "You don't really want to hear the whole sorry story of what I'm doing here on my own, do you?"

"I'm a good listener."

I'll just bet you are, Lena thought. And since she wanted to keep him around for as long as possible, she spun out a story of how she was a secretary in Boston, with aspirations to be an actress, and how she'd come here on a sort of business holiday with her new boyfriend—"ex-boyfriend, let me tell you"—who'd claimed he was a film director checking out some locations and did she want to come along just for the fun of it?

"So like a dummy, I agreed," she finished up, "and we're here one day and he dumps me because I wouldn't, you know. Show him a good time."

"What was the film supposed to be about?" Felix asked.

"What film? Everything about it was a big secret before we left and now I know why: There was no film. What I can't figure out is why he brought me all the way over here with him if all he wanted from me was sex, you know? Seems to me that there's cheaper ways to get yourself a girl."

She was tempted to tell him that this "boyfriend" of hers was going around pretending to be a reporter from *Rolling Stone*, but all she had to do was think of what Bett's reaction would be to quickly squelch that idea.

"Maybe there really is a film," Felix said.

Lena nodded slowly. "You're probably right. And since I wouldn't come across, he's found some local bimbo to take my place."

"Don't be so hard on yourself."

"Why not? This whole trip was a mistake from the start and I have to have been a bimbo to fall for it at all." She shook her head. "And I've *still* got nine days before my flight home." She inserted a well-timed sigh. "It's not that there's anything wrong with Cornwall—I *love* it around here—it's just not a whole lot of fun when you're on your own."

"I know what you mean."

Lena gave him a quick smile. "Sounds like you've got your own hard-luck story. Want to talk about it? I know I feel better already."

"I don't think so," Felix said.

"It's a woman—right?"

Felix looked up with surprise to find Lena looking sympathetic.

"It's always something like that," she said. "I think we're cursed to never really find the right partner in life and then, to make things worse, we screw up our lives even more in an endless chase for that perfect someone who's usually not out there in the first place. And when they *are* out there, they're married or won't give us the time of day, or *something.*"

"I can tell you're coming out of the wrong side of a bad relationship," Felix said.

Lena shrugged. "Maybe. I'm not usually so maudlin about this kind of thing—I mean, *he* sure doesn't deserve my spending the time thinking about him—but it starts to wear on you after a while, don't you think?"

"I suppose."

He looked uncomfortable and Lena decided she'd better pull back when he changed the conversation himself.

"That tattoo on your wrist," he began.

"Oh, that old thing. . . ." Self-consciously, she covered it up with her free hand. "I got that done when I was a teenager— one of those things that you regret about ten minutes too late."

Felix laughed. He'd already taken off his jacket earlier. Now he rolled up the sleeve of his T-shirt to show the tattoo he had on his left biceps. It was a full-colour rendition of an old man, sitting on a crate playing an accordion.

"Now that one I like," Lena said. "Do you play one of those things yourself?"

Felix nodded.

"Professionally?"

"Not likely."

"Oh, I bet you're really good at it."

"I get by." Felix indicated her left wrist. "So why a dove?"

"It's the symbol . . . that is, it's supposed to be the symbol of an old . . ."

Now she'd gone too far. If Bett was to hear her now. If her *father* was to hear her now . . .

"An old what?"

"Oh, you know. Peace, love, and flowers, and all that stuff. I was enamoured with the sixties when I was a kid—mostly because I just missed out on them. So when I decided to get the tattoo, I thought I'd get a peace symbol, but I never really liked that circle thing, so when I saw the dove in the tattoo guy's catalogue, I picked it instead."

Was he buying it?

She had no chance to find out because just then the phone rang. Before she could think of a way to stop him, Felix had reached over and picked up the receiver.

"Hello? Hello?"

He gave her a puzzled look.

"There's nobody there," he said as he hung up.

"That's weird."

The actress in her wanted to add, maybe it was my boyfriend checking up on me, just for the drama, but she thought better of it. Felix glanced at his watch.

"I should get going," he said. "Are you going to be okay? Can I get you some takeout or something for dinner before I go?"

She decided not to push it any more today. There'd be another day. She was sure enough of herself to know that. And besides, if that *had* been the Golden Boy on the phone, the sooner Felix was out of here the better.

"No. I can just call room service."

He stood up and retrieved his jacket from the chair where he'd tossed it earlier.

"There is one thing, though," she said. "If it's not too much trouble. . . ."

"What's that?"

"Well, I'm going to need a cane to hobble around with for

the next few days. Is there any chance you could pick one up for me?" As he hesitated, she added, "I'd pay for it, of course."

"It's not that. It's just—" He hesitated a moment longer, then nodded. "Sure. I can do that."

"I know the stores are closed now, so you'd have to go tomorrow."

"No problem. What time will you be getting up?"

"Nine-thirtyish?"

"I'll be by around ten."

She put on an apologetic look. "There's one more thing. I'll take whatever kind you can get, but if there's a choice, could you maybe find something a little funky? Maybe an old one?"

Felix smiled. "No problem. There's some antique shops over on Chapel Street. I don't know what time they're open, though."

"Whatever. I really appreciate this—everything you've done. You've been really great."

Felix nodded. "See you tomorrow, then. And try to stay off that foot."

"Yes, *sir.*"

Laughing, Felix let himself out.

Lena settled back on the bed and smiled to herself. The hooks were in and sinking deep. And if he really was coming off a second rebound with the Little girl, well, that'd just make her job all that much easier, wouldn't it?

So why did what she was doing make her feel a little dirty?

It was an hour later that Bett came by, railing at her. He obviously didn't believe her story about stumbling over the corner of the rug and spraining her ankle, but there wasn't a whole lot he could do except glare at her—that awful promise that if she wasn't protected by her father just simmering in the pale depths of his eyes.

When he gave her his instructions concerning Felix Gavin,

she wanted to rail right back at him. Trust him to take her own idea so that he could get the credit for it. But she said nothing, and did nothing, until he finally left, that unpleasant promise of his still burning in his eyes. Then she picked up the phone and had the operator give her an overseas connection.

"Hello, Daddy?" she said when she got through. She put on her best little-girl voice. "I don't want to sound like a baby or anything, but Mike's beginning to act a little strange. . . . No, he hasn't been threatening me or anything, at least he hasn't *said* anything, but he did give me a push and I fell down and kind of sprained my ankle. . . . No, it's okay; just sore. Oh, would you? Could you send Jim? Have him book into a room here, but he should wait for me to contact him."

Slowly she'd been letting the little-girl voice change to that of a capable woman.

"I think you'll be happy with some developments I've been making on my own, Daddy. There's this man who's very close to the Little girl—no, their surname is Little, remember? She's quite grown up. Anyway, I'm *this* close to having him bring me whatever this secret thing of Dunthorn's is. I thought you'd be pleased. Of course I'll take care. I love you too, Daddy."

There, she thought as she cradled the phone. Her father would tell the other members of the Order that working through Gavin had been her idea and soon she'd have some protection against Bett. Everything was falling neatly into place.

But when she thought of how she was using Felix, she still felt dirty.

Don't be stupid, she told herself. He's just a dumb sailor.

True. But he was a nice dumb sailor, and maybe not so dumb as that. And he'd certainly treated her better than most people in her own social circles did. How many of them would have even stopped if they saw a woman—attractive or not—take a fall from her bike?

She stared across her room. Her ankle was aching again.

"Shit," she said to no one in particular.

Why did everything always have to be so complicated?

8.

There was no one in when Janey got back home. She put on water for tea and went next door to her own rooms to get a sweater. After she'd put it on and checked her mirror to make sure that that thing she'd seen this morning really *hadn't* been a pimple, she went over to the bookcase to make sure that *The Little Country* was still there.

It was right where it was supposed to be.

Taking the book down from the shelf, she flipped idly through a few pages, pausing for a moment when she thought she could hear that music again. But no sooner did she listen for it, than it was gone. Sighing, she closed the book with a snap and went back to the Gaffer's with the book under her arm to call Clare.

"I'm so sorry I didn't ring up earlier," she began when she had her friend on the line, "but the most amazing thing happened." Whereupon she launched into an account of the reporter coming by late that morning and how they'd gone over to the Pantry for the interview.

"What was he like?" Clare wanted to know.

"Oh, very nice. American. I'm not quite sure how old, but not *too* old. He's got Paul Newman eyes and he knows about as much about the music as anyone I've met, so I'm sure the article will be good."

"Because of his eyes?"

"Clare!"

Her friend laughed. "Just teasing. You must be pleased."

"Aren't I just."

"When's it coming out?"

"He didn't say. It probably won't be for a while, though. You

know how these magazines work—they're buying Christmas stories in June."

"Have you seen Felix yet?" Clare asked.

"No. I was just going to ask you the same thing."

"I met him up by the Coastguard lookout about midmorning.
When he left, he was going back to your place. That was only
a bit past twelve."

"I must have just missed him. I wonder where he's gone off
to now?"

"How do you feel about seeing him again?"

"I'm not sure," Janey said. "Both happy and scared, I suppose."

"But you still fancy him?"

"Oh, yes," Janey said before she really thought about what
she was saying, but then she realized it was true.

"He's a wonderful bloke," Clare said. "Make sure you hang
on to him this time."

"I'm planning to have a talk with him when he gets back,"
Janey said. "And this time I won't be the least bit emperent, as
the Gaffer'd say."

"Maybe he likes you cheeky."

"Maybe he does. I hear someone at the door, so I've got to
run. It might be Felix."

"Call me tomorrow."

"I will."

Janey cradled the phone just as the door opened, but it was
the Gaffer. Much as she loved her grandfather, right then Janey
wished it had been Felix instead.

"Not had a good day, Gramps?" she asked when she saw the
grim set to his features.

The Gaffer sighed. "Oh, I've some bad news to tell you, my
gold, and I don't know where to begin."

"Chalkie isn't hurt, is he?"

She could imagine the two old codgers messing about with
that stone wall of Chalkie's and one of them dropping a great
big hunk of granite on the other's foot.

"No," the Gaffer said. "Nothing like that."

He looked so sad.

"Well, what is it?" Janey asked.

The Gaffer sat down at the kitchen table, moving stiffly as though he'd begun to feel the weight of his years for the first time. Seeing that made Janey feel even more concerned.

"It's about Felix, my robin. He's betrayed our trust."

As the Gaffer told her what he'd seen in Newlyn that afternoon, who Felix had been so cozy with on his bicycle, all the blood drained out of Janey's features.

"It's not true," she said in a small voice. "Tell me it's not true."

"I wish it weren't, my love, but I saw what I saw."

All Janey could do then was look at him, her eyes brimming with tears.

The Wheels of

the World

This was the machinery of life, not a clean, clinical
well-oiled engine, monitored by a thousand meticulous
dials, but a crazy, stumbling contraption made up of
strange things roughly fitted together.

—MARGARET MAHY,
from *Memory*

Nettie Shepherd opened her front door to
find Denzil standing on her stoop. He leaned
on his silver-headed cane and peered at her
through his hazy glasses that were fogging up due to the heat
escaping from the house.

Ample was the best description that came to mind whenever
Denzil met Jodi's aunt. She was a large woman, but her largeness
was proportionate. She had enormous thighs, and equally boun-
teous breasts, broad shoulders, a generous face, a waterfall of red-
gold hair—in short, everything about her was larger than life.
The grin that touched her lips at the sight of him was wide and
expansive as well, touched with a cat's knowing satisfaction.

"Well, now," she said. "I never thought to see you here."

"I'm not here for business, you, I'm here . . ." Denzil's voice
trailed off as he realized what he was saying.

"For pleasure? They're one and the same under this roof, Master Gossip."

"Ahem. Yes, well. Actually, I've come 'round about Jodi. Is
she in?"

"You mean she's not been with you?"

Denzil shook his head. "I haven't seen her all day."

Nettie pursed her lips, then opened the door wider.

"You'd better come in," she said.

Denzil hesitated for a moment, looking up and down the street before he followed her inside. Though he hadn't thought it possible, Nettie's grin actually widened.

"Afraid someone would see you entering this den of iniquity?"

"It *is* a bawdy house," Denzil replied somewhat huffily.

"Yes, we do have bodies."

"Please."

Abruptly Nettie looked serious. "You're quite right," she said.

She took his cane and hat, leaning the one against the wall, hanging the other by the door. Denzil snatched the opportunity of having both his hands free to wipe his glasses.

"This isn't much of an evening for bantering," Nettie added.

Denzil soon found out why.

Ushered into her sitting room, he discovered that he wasn't Nettie's only non-paying visitor of the evening. Sitting each to a chair by the window were Cadan Tremeer, Bodbury's chief constable, and the Widow Pender. Tremeer lifted his bulk from his chair and offered Denzil a pudgy hand. The constable smelled vaguely of perfume, which made Denzil wonder if he hadn't been called to duty from one of the rooms upstairs. Once Denzil had shaken the man's hand, Tremeer settled back into his chair with obvious relief.

The Widow merely nodded at Denzil.

"Some tea?" Nettie asked.

Denzil shook his head. He took off his glasses, cleaned them again on the sleeve of his jacket, then set them back upon the bridge of his nose where they promptly fogged up once more. Nettie indicated a chair, but he remained standing.

"Has Jodi got herself mixed up in some sort of misadventure?" he asked.

The Widow hrumphed.

"It's serious this time," Nettie said.

Tremeer nodded, trying to fit a grim look to his jolly features without much success.

"She broke into the Widow's house and stole an heirloom," he said.

He pronounced the word "hair-loom," as though what had been stolen was a tool on which one could weave hair.

Denzil shook his head. "Jodi wouldn't steal a farthing, you."

"The Widow saw her leaving through a window herself. I've been 'round, Master Gossip, and there's a fearsome mess there. Glass broken. Geegaws scattered every which way. It doesn't look good."

Denzil looked to Nettie. "What does Jodi have to say about this?"

"Well, that's what makes it look so bad," the constable said before she could reply. "Young Miss Shepherd's not to be found."

Denzil finally took the chair Nettie had offered him earlier.

Now this was a fine how-to-do, wasn't it just? he thought. It was the last thing he would have expected to discover when he first decided that Nettie's place was where he should begin his inquiries.

"When was the last time you saw her?" he asked Nettie.

"When she went to bed—early for her. Before midnight."

"And?" Denzil prompted her, perceiving that she hadn't told all yet.

Nettie sighed. "Her bed hadn't been slept in and her window was open. Time to time, she thinks she's like your monkey, Master Gossip, and goes climbing about on the drainpipes. Gets her to the ground quickly and without being seen, and then she's off on some kitey lark or another."

"Such as robbing an old woman of her memories," the Widow said, speaking up for the first time.

Her voice was quavery and she was wearing a hangdog expression that Denzil didn't believe for a moment. He'd seen her jaunting about often enough to know that she was as spry as a woman half her years, and as mean as the most curmudgeonly old salt. He'd believe her capable of any nastiness—knowing she'd do it for the pure spite of the deed. What he didn't subscribe to was the so-called magical curses she supposedly could command—no matter what the children of the Tatters claimed.

"How do you know it was Jodi?" he asked. "It was at night, wasn't it? Couldn't you have been mistaken, you?"

"I know that girl," the Widow said. "She eggs on the other children to lampoon me."

Now *that* Denzil could believe.

"Why did you wait so long to report it?" he asked. He glanced at the constable. "I take it she has only just made her complaint?"

Tremeer looked guilty and shot a glance roofward before catching himself.

"I . . . uh," he began. "That is, she . . ."

"It's hard for a woman my age to get about easily," the Widow said. "It's the arthritis."

Now the lies began again, Denzil thought.

Tremeer had recovered his officiousness in the meantime. He took up a notepad and pen from the table beside him.

"And when was the last time you saw her, Master Denzil?"

"Yesterday. When she didn't come 'round today, I got worried." Denzil sighed. "Jodi's not the sort to be involved in this kind of mischief," he added.

Nettie nodded, glad of his support.

"She's a child, isn't she?" the Widow said. "And aren't all children an annoying nuisance?"

Not so much as you are, Denzil thought, but he didn't bother to reply. Rising to his feet, he nodded to Tremeer and the Widow before turning to Nettie.

"Call me if I can help in any way," he told her.

"Thank you. I will."

"And if you should happen to find her . . ." Tremeer began.

"I'll be sure to notify you straightway," Denzil said.

He waved Nettie back into her chair as she rose to see him out.

"I can find the way," he said.

Once he was out in the hall, he collected his hat and cane by the door and quickly made his escape. Outside, his glasses immediately fogged up again, but he ignored the discomfort.

Sometimes it seemed that he spent half his life peering through murky lenses and the other half cleaning them, so he was well used to the burden by now.

Something odd was going on, he thought, and he meant to get to the bottom of it. But first he needed a good stiff drink to take away the taste of the Widow's poor playacting and Tremeer's toadying up to her.

He gave Nettie's house a last considering look, then headed towards the harbour and made his way to the nearest pub, which in this case happened to be The Ship's Inn.

Naturally, to make the night a perfect loss, he found Taupin sitting there with a look about him as though the hedgerow philosopher had been waiting just for him. Or at least waiting for someone to buy him a drink.

He almost turned and walked out again, but Taupin hailed him cheerily and Denzil didn't have the heart to walk the ten blocks or so to The Tuck-Net & Caboleen.

Besides, he thought, the children all liked the old fool. Maybe he'd know where Jodi was.

2 .

It was no use just sitting here, Jodi decided after a half hour had passed and the cat still wouldn't go away. Getting up, she dusted off her trousers and set off to find another way out of the maze of crates. But at each exit they found that the cat, drawn by the whispering sound of their tiny footfalls—and Jodi's running commentary on the dubious ancestry of cats, this one mangy cat in particular—was waiting for them.

"Bother and damn!" Jodi cried.

Picking up a stone, she threw it at the cat, but it had no visible effect. The largest one she could find that she could throw with any accuracy was no bigger than a peppercorn. Still, she kept up a steady barrage until her arm got sore. Then she returned to slouch down beside Edern.

"Why do cats have to be so bloody patient?" she wanted to know.

Edern shrugged. "This friend of yours," he said. "What was his name? Dazzle?"

"Denzil."

"He's a magician?"

Jodi laughed. "Denzil's about as logical a man as you're likely to find, which means he doesn't believe in magic. If it can't be explained by logic, he'd say, then we simply haven't found the proper parameters and reference points."

"Then he won't be much help to us, will he?"

"He's also wise and clever and my best friend."

"Yes, but if he doesn't know anything about magic, there won't be anything he can do for us."

"Do you have a better idea?"

"I think so," Edern said. "What do you know about the stoneworks 'round about the countryside?"

"Bloody little, except they make me feel tingly and sort of— oh, I don't know, touched by mystery, I suppose."

"Did you ever hear that they're supposed to be the places where our world meets the Barrow World?"

Jodi laughed. "Oh raw we. Now you want to call up hummocks and piskies to give us a hand?"

"If a witch can shrink us, then why can't the Little People exist?"

"That's your plan?"

When Edern nodded, Jodi started to laugh again, but she caught herself. Fine, she thought. Let's think this through— logically, as Denzil would have her do it. Magic worked. It obviously existed—they were proof positive of that. So why *not* Smalls?

"Why would they help us?" she wanted to know.

"Maybe we could trade them for their help."

Jodi stuck a hand in her pocket and came out with a piece of twine, some dried pieces of biscuit left over from dinner that she'd meant to give to the first stray dog she ran across, three glass marbles, two copper pennies, a piece of sea-polished wood that had no discernible purpose, two small geared wheels that obviously did have a purpose though Jodi didn't know what kind of a mechanism they'd come from, a small penknife, and some lint. She gave it all a critical look, then held out her hand to Edern.

"What would they like from this?" she asked.

"We could trade services," Edern said patiently.

"What sort of services?"

"We'd have to ask them that, wouldn't we?"

Jodi sighed. "I don't know." She glanced at the cat who continued to eye them with unabated interest. "Besides, first we have to get away."

"But when we *do.* . . ."

Jodi stored the detritus from her pockets back where it had all come from, only keeping out the bits of broken biscuit. She offered Edern a piece and chewed on another herself.

"Stoneworks," she said, mumbling the word as she chewed. She swallowed, wishing she had a drink. "Like the stone crosses and such?"

Edern nodded.

"What if God sends down an angel to see what we're about? I don't think He'd be ready to help me because I rather doubt that I'm in His good books."

"It's unlikely that would happen," Edern said.

"If piskies can exist, then why not God?"

"I was thinking more of a place like the Merry Maidens."

"Oh, I know the story behind them. Some girls were dancing on a Sunday, weren't they? Thirteen of them. And God turned them to stone. There were two pipers playing for the girls and they ran off, but they got turned to stone all the same and stand a few fields over."

"Why all this sudden talk of God?" Edern asked.

"Well, you brought it up."

"The story I know of the Merry Maidens is that they're mermaids who got caught dancing when the sun came up, so they were turned to stone."

"You're thinking of trolls."

"The point is," Edern went on as though she hadn't interrupted, "that there's a sea wisdom in those stones. The sea's full of powerful magic and lore. If we could get Her help . . ."

"I don't think I'm in Her good books either," Jodi said. "At least my family isn't."

Both her father and uncle had been taken by the sea. A year later her mother died of a broken heart, which amounted to the sea being responsible for her death as well. Jodi was quiet for a long moment, thinking of the parents she only knew from the fuzzy memories of the toddler she'd been at the time of their deaths.

"Jodi?"

She shook off the gloom that had started to settle upon her.

"I'm fine," she said. "I was just thinking."

"About the stoneworks?"

She nodded. "I don't think I'm quite ready to accept that the sea could have a bit of a chat with us."

"There's also the Men-an-Tol stone, though that's farther away."

"I've been through its hole the nine times it's supposed to take to wake the charm, but nothing ever happened."

"At moonrise?"

"Not at moonrise. But then—" She gave him a sudden rueful grin. "I can't *believe* we're having this conversation."

"You didn't believe in magic before the Widow enchanted you."

Jodi nodded. "I suppose we could try this stone of yours, but first we have to get the button charms from the Widow's house."

"Better we go to the stone first to find out *how* the spell works. That way, when we do retrieve the charm, we can work it there on the spot."

"And have her shrink us right back down again in the next moment."

"Not if we go when she's not about."

"I suppose. . . ."

"Perhaps the Little People can give us some protection against her magic," Edern said.

Jodi banged the back of her head against the crate in frustration.

"And perhaps," she said, "we can fly away on a leaf and save ourselves the long walk to the stone. Bother and damn! I'm *tired* of perhapses and maybes."

She stood up, chose another stone, and flung it at the cat.

"Get away, you!"

Surprisingly, this time it worked. The cat backed away, looked once to its right, then fled.

Jodi turned to her companion with a grin. "That showed him, didn't it just?"

But Edern didn't look in the least bit pleased. He sat very pale and still, just staring at the gap between the crates through which the cat had been peering at them. With a sinking feeling in the pit of her stomach, Jodi turned to see what it was that he was looking at.

Windle, the Widow's fetch, stared back at her. It had chased off the cat merely to take up the watch itself. And there it would stay, Jodi knew, until the Widow arrived with some new kind of spell to snatch them willy-nilly from their hiding place.

"Found something then have you, my sweet?" a too familiar voice called out.

Or maybe the Widow was already here.

3 ·

It was smoky inside The Ship's Inn, thick enough to be a fog. Those who weren't puffing away on pipes and cigars had cigarettes dangling from their mouths, each exhalation adding to the general haze. Blinking behind his glasses, Denzil navigated his way through to the bar where he resignedly took a stool beside Taupin.

Brengy Taupin looked the part of the hedgerow philosopher he claimed to be. He was thin as a rake and wore an odd collection of raggedy clothes that hung from his frame with about the same sense of style as could be expected from a scarecrow— in other words, it was all angles and tatters. The gauntness of his features was eased by a pair of cheerful and too bright eyes. His hair was an unruly brown thatch in which bits of leaves and twigs were invariably caught. Denzil often caught himself staring at it, waiting for a bird's head to pop up out of its untidy hedgery.

"Can I buy you a drink, you?" he asked.

He signaled to the barman to bring them two pints of bitter without waiting for Taupin's reply.

"This is a kindness," Taupin said after a long appreciative swallow of his bitter, which left a foamy moustache on his upper lip.

"Not to be confused with a habit," Denzil said, still wishing he'd chosen to walk the extra few blocks to the Tuck.

However, if the truth was to be told, for all Denzil's gruffness towards his companion, he and Taupin got on rather well, for they both loved a good philosophical discussion—a rarity in temperate Bodbury—and were each capable of keeping one going for weeks on end.

"Naturally," Taupin replied.

He dug about in one of the enormous pockets of his overcoat as he spoke.

"I've got something for you here," he added as he came up with an odd mechanism that he set on the bartop between them.

Denzil couldn't help but be intrigued.

Taupin knew his weakness for inexplicable machinery and the like. If it was odd, if it appeared useful but couldn't be readily explained, then it became an object of the utmost fascination to the inventor.

What lay on the bartop was most intriguing. It was obviously a clockwork mechanism of some sort, but Denzil could see no way in which it could be wound up. Nor what it would do even if it were wound up.

"What is it?" he asked.

"I haven't the faintest idea," Taupin replied. "But watch."

He gave the thing a shake, then set it back down upon the top of the bar. For a moment nothing happened. Then a cog went rolling down a slight incline, caught another, which made the second cog turn. A small metal shaft rose, returning the first cog to its starting point while the gears of the second turned yet another cog, which in turn set a whole series in motion until a shaft at the far side of the machine began to turn. In the mean-time, the first cog had rolled back down its incline to engage the second once more.

Denzil leaned closer, utterly captivated.

"How long does it run?" he asked.

Taupin grinned. "Well, it's not the perpetual motion machine you're always on about, but it'll go for a good hour."

"With only the one shake to get it started?"

Taupin nodded.

"Where did you get it?"

"In a junk shop in Praed. Fascinating, isn't it? You can keep it if you like."

"How much?"

"Fah," Taupin said, waving aside the offer of monetary return. "You can have me over for dinner some night—but when Jodi's cooking, mind you. I won't eat your idea of a meal."

Regretfully, Denzil pulled his gaze away from the machine that went merrily on about its incomprehensible business. Pushing up his glasses, he turned to Taupin.

"I meant to talk to you about her," he said.

"Who?" Taupin asked. "Jodi? A delightful girl. Quite clever and quick to learn. And oddly enough, considering how the greater part of what she's learned has come from you or my own self, a remarkable cook."

Denzil nodded. "I just wish you'd stop filling her head with fairy tales."

"Why ever for? What can it possibly harm?"

"Her intellect. The logical progression of her reasoning."

Taupin laughed. "Look," he said. "This"—he pointed to the mechanism—"is how you see the world. Everything has its place. It all moves like clockwork, one event logically following the other. When something doesn't fit, it's merely because we haven't understood it yet."

"So?"

Now Taupin reached into one of his voluminous pockets and dumped its contents on the table. Geegaws and trinkets lay helter-skelter upon one another. A small tatty book lay entangled with a length of netting. A tin whistle had a feather sticking out of its mouth hole and what appeared to be a dried rat's tail protruding from its other end. A square of cloth with buttons sewn to it, each oddly connected to the other with startlingly bright embroidery that almost, but not quite, had a discernible pattern. A crab's pincer with a hole in it through which had been pulled a piece of string. Two stones—one with the fossil of a shell upon it, the other with what might be faded hiero-glyphics or simply scratches.

There was more, but it was all too much for Denzil to easily catalogue.

"This is how the world really is," Taupin said. "A confusion in which some things make perfect sense"—he shook the whistle free of its encumbrances and rolled it back and forth on the palm of his hand—"while others may never be explained."

Now he plucked up the stone with its curious markings and offered it to his companion. Denzil took it gingerly, as though afraid it might bite, and gave it a cursory glance. The markings did appear to be some sort of language—though not one he could recognize. And it was very old.

"I found that around by the point," Taupin said. "Washed in from the sea, it was." He pointed back to the bartop. "*That's* the true face of the world, Denzil—all jumbled up with no distinguishable pattern except that, *somehow,* it's all connected to itself and the whole thing muddles through in the end."

"A pretty analogy," Denzil said as he handed the stone back, "but a mistaken one."

"Still, we're not so different, you and I. We both pursue Truth."

"We *are* different," Denzil assured him. "I go about my search for Truth in a rational, scientific manner. You hope to stumble over it through blind luck and tomfoolery."

Taupin raised his glass to him. "Here's to Wisdom, wherever it may be found."

"What I need to find at the moment is Jodi," Denzil said.

"Misplaced her, have you?"

"This isn't a joke, you."

Taupin's grin faltered, his features growing increasingly grave as Denzil explained the situation.

"It makes no sense," Denzil said as he finished up.

"Not a smidgen," Taupin agreed.

"Jodi's simply not like that."

"Not at all."

"And I don't know where to begin to look for her."

Taupin said nothing for a long moment. Brow wrinkled with thought, he slowly moved the contents from his pocket from the top of the bar back into his pocket, then finished the last inch of his bitter.

"There's two ways we can go about this," he said finally.

"And they are?"

"We begin with the Gossip method of logic whereby we search the town from top to bottom, leaving word with the Tatters children and the like as we make our way."

"And the second method?"

"Well," Taupin said, "once we've exhausted the logical route, we'll take the illogical one and start to consider the impossible."

Denzil shook his head. "I haven't the faintest idea what you're on about."

"I smell magic in the air," Taupin said simply.

Denzil snorted. "What a pile of nonsense!"

"It may well be. But I smell it all the same. And after all, rumour has it that the Widow *is* a witch." He held up a hand before Denzil could argue further. "But first we'll take a turn around the town, a-foot and with our eyes peeled for mischief—yes?"

Denzil gave a reluctant nod, which made his glasses skid down to the end of his nose. He pushed them back up again, thinking of Taupin's offer. Denzil knew he needed help. He just wished he could have found it in a more practical corner. Still, a man took what he was offered.

Finishing his own bitter, he pocketed the mechanism that Taupin had given him and got off his stool.

"Let's be on our way," he said.

The Piper's Despair

If you live close enough to the edge of the land and
the edge of the sea, if you listen hard and watch
close, you can get some sense of places that are
different from what most people see and hear.

— HILBERT SCHENCK,
from *Chronosequence*

Felix thought about Lena as he walked back to Mousehole from Penzance. She seemed like a decent sort of person, yet he couldn't help but feel uncomfortable about her obvious interest in him. It wasn't that she was unattractive, or that she'd thrown herself at him. He just didn't need or want any more complications in his life at the moment.

He had enough on his mind already.

But the trouble was, he felt sorry for her. Dumped by her boyfriend in a strange place, unable to even tour about now because of her accident, and then he showed up. . . .

Was it the Japanese who believed that if you saved someone's life you became responsible for that person? His helping her hadn't exactly been a rescue from a life-threatening plight, but he couldn't deny that—now that he knew of her and the unhappy situation she was in—he did feel just a bit responsible for her.

It was probably a case of empathy, because he knew exactly how she had to be feeling. But there was also something else that troubled him about her, some subtext underlying the time he'd spent in her company that had nothing to do with her attraction to him, or his feeling sorry and just a bit responsible for her. Whatever it was, he couldn't put his finger on it. He didn't really want to think about it or her.

He just wished he hadn't met her in the first place. And having met her, he wished he weren't seeing her tomorrow, because that only complicated things more.

Was nothing simple anymore?

At North Cliff he turned up Duck Street towards the Gaffer's house. When he got to Chapel Place and found his bags sitting outside the garden wall, he realized that he hadn't known what complication was yet.

Now what was going on?

Pulse quickening uncomfortably, he left his luggage sitting there, both duffel and accordion case, and knocked upon the door. The grim face of the Gaffer as he answered did little to allay his growing distress.

"Hello, Tom," he began. "What's—"

"Get away, you," the Gaffer said.

"Don't I even get some sort of explan—"

"Is that him?" he heard Janey ask from inside.

"He's not worth your time, my gold," the Gaffer said, but Janey pushed by him in the doorway.

Felix was shocked at her tear-stained face, the hurt in her eyes that grew rapidly into anger the longer she stood there looking at him.

"I hate you for what you've done," she began, her voice deadly calm.

Felix could feel his heart turn to stone at her words. A foggy numbness settled over him, making everything appear to be happening at half speed.

"What—what is it that I'm supposed to have done?"

His own voice, when he spoke, seemed to drone on forever just to get those few words out.

"We know all about you and your—" Her voice cracked, tears welling up anew in her eyes. "You and your little tart."

She meant Lena, he realized.

"But—"

"Don't start lying again!" she shouted. "Gramps *saw* you with her."

Quickly now, Felix told himself. Explain the innocence of your meeting with the woman because this was already getting far too out of hand as it was.

But his voice was still trapped behind the growing numbness that was fogging him. The coldness in his chest deepened. When he spoke, his words seemed distant—unreal even to himself.

"I don't know what he saw, but—"

"And that's not the worst. That stupid lying letter of yours—you wrote it yourself, didn't you? Or did *she* do it for you? You knew—you *knew* how much the book meant to me . . . and the promise . . . the promise Gramps made Billy. . . ."

She couldn't go on. Tears streaming down her cheeks, she turned to the Gaffer who enfolded her in his arms.

"Get away from us," the Gaffer said.

"But—"

He could feel his world collapsing around him like a house made of cards knocked apart by the uncaring sweep of a giant hand.

"Get away," the Gaffer repeated, adding, "or I'll call the law on you."

He turned away, pulling Janey with him, and slammed the door in Felix's face.

Felix stood there, numbly staring at the door. Deep in the pit of his stomach a knot, hard as a rock, was forming. His chest felt tight, heart drumming a wild tattoo.

This couldn't be happening, he thought. They weren't going to shut him out of their lives like this without even giving him a chance to explain that he'd done nothing wrong, were they?

He lifted his hand to knock again, then simply let it fall to his side.

Madness: This whole trip out here had been nothing but madness.

He thought of the letter that had brought him to Mousehole. Janey claimed she hadn't sent it.

He thought of the odd stories the Gaffer had told about strangers trying to steal his old mate's writings.

What had turned such kind and gentle people as the Littles into a pair of raving paranoids?

Those stories—were any of them even true? There was the theft he'd stopped. . . .

He lifted his hand a second time, then slowly turned away. What was the use? They weren't going to listen to him.

His own eyes were burning now. He let the tears fall as he collected his bags and stumbled off to the only sanctuary he might still have in the village.

"Oh, no," Clare said when she opened the door. "It didn't go well, did it?"

"It went bloody awful," Felix said. "It didn't go at all."

His head had cleared a little on the walk over to her place, but the coldness was still there inside him. He didn't know if it would ever go away. He could think a little more clearly again; he just couldn't believe that the scene that had played itself out on the Gaffer's doorstep had actually happened. He kept wanting to go back, to prove to himself that it had all been a mistake, something he had only imagined, but then he'd see Janey's face again, the hurt and the anger in it, he'd see the Gaffer's rage, and know it had all taken place.

Clare ushered him inside. Her mother was already in bed, but Clare had been sitting up reading. She took him back into the kitchen and poured him a cup of tea from the pot she'd just made for herself. Felix accepted it gratefully, almost gulping the scalding liquid down. He was trying to warm the coldness that had lodged inside him, but the tea didn't help. Maybe nothing ever would.

"Do you want to talk about it?" Clare asked.

Felix lifted his head slowly from the whorls of wood grain on the kitchen table that he'd been staring at.

"There's nothing really to tell," he said. "I never got to say a thing. I got back from Penzance to find my cases sitting outside by the wall and when I knocked on the door, all she did was yell at me. She was crying and shouting all at the same time. The Gaffer said he was going to call the cops if I didn't leave."

Clare listened with mounting horror. "What did you *do?*" she asked.

Felix laughed bitterly in response. It was an ugly sound that grated even on his own ears.

"That's just it," he said. "I didn't do anything except . . ."

Slowly he told her of what he'd done since he'd seen her to her door earlier in the day.

"I swear there was nothing going on between us," he said, finishing up. "I mean, what was I supposed to do? Leave her lying there by the side of the road?"

"Of course not. You did the decent thing."

"Maybe it looked bad, when I was taking her back to her hotel on her bike, but, Jesus, shouldn't I at least get the chance to tell my side of it?"

Clare nodded. "There's got to be more to it than just that."

"She thinks I wrote this letter she sent," Felix said. He pulled the crumpled paper from his pocket and tossed it onto the table. "Or that Lena wrote it for me," he added.

"Oh, no," Clare said. "She's wrong. That's not at all what—"

"And then there's all the Gaffer's crap about people coming around trying to steal William bloody Dunthorn's precious writing." Felix shot her an anguished look. "They've gone off the deep end—both of them."

He shoved his seat away from the table and stood up.

"I can't stay here," he said.

There was a wild look in his eyes, like that of a caged animal.

"Felix, you can't just go."

"You're wrong. I can and I will. I've *got* to."

"At least stay here for the night."

Felix shook his head. "I'll find a place in Penzance, get the stupid cane for Lena, then I'm going to hitch back to London and find myself another job. I spent almost everything I had just to get here as quickly as I did. If Janey wants to talk to me, she can just show up at whatever dock my next ship happens to land in."

Clare caught his hand before he could walk away.

"The stores are closed tomorrow," she said. "It's Sunday."

"The antique shops . . . ?"

"It's not the tourist season anymore."

"Shit."

"I can lend her one of my canes. There's some business cards beside the typewriter in the study with the store's address on them. You can tell her to drop it off there when she's done with it. No sense in spending the money on a new one."

She let go of his hand and Felix moved to the doorway, pausing on its threshold.

"You believe me, don't you?"

Clare nodded. "I just wish I'd known earlier you fancied girls with canes." She obviously regretted saying that as soon as it was out of her mouth. "I'm sorry. This isn't a time for teasing."

"That's okay," Felix said. "I know you mean well. I'll keep in touch with you. And I'll come visit. I should have sooner, but I . . ." He sighed. "I shouldn't forget what friends I *do* have."

"Don't write Janey off so quickly," Clare told him. "Things can still work out."

Felix merely shook his head. The coldness hadn't left him. He was still numb and shaken, but reality had settled in.

"There was never anything to work out," he said. "I see that now."

"You can't believe that."

"If there *had* been," Felix said, "she'd have heard me out."

"But that's just her temper. You know Janey, she's—"

"That's right. I do know Janey. Or at least I know her now. I . . ." He shivered. "I have to go, Clare. I just have to get out into the air. I feel like my head's going to explode if I don't. Where's that cane?"

"Beside my desk."

She followed him out of the kitchen into the study where he picked up the cane and a business card.

"Felix," she began when they were by the front door. "About that letter."

He shook his head. "I don't want to talk anymore. I'll call you before I leave Penzance tomorrow, okay?"

"But—"

"Thanks for the cane." He bent down and gave her a kiss. "I love you, Clare. Always have. You were always there for me. I'll try to make it up to you sometime."

He saw the tears starting up in her eyes. Before she could say anything more, he gave her a quick hug, then collected his luggage and went out the door.

2 .

That's what you get for meddling, Clare thought as she watched Felix head back down Raginnis Hill towards the harbour.

She sighed and looked out over the rooftops to where Mount's Bay lay dark and brooding in the Cornish night. There were no stars visible over the water tonight, the sky being overhung with a cloud cover that promised rain. She looked back down the road, but Felix was gone now. The street was empty, except for the inevitable Mousehole cat. This one was the small calico female that lived a few doors down. She was prowling along the side of the road, stalking who knew what.

Clare watched her for a few moments longer, remembering the old story about the red cats of Zennor.

Between the two World Wars, a woman came to the village of Zennor, which lay on the north coast of Penwith Peninsula, and announced that she was going to breed tigers. The local authorities, needless to say, forbade her to do so, whereupon the woman promptly announced that if she couldn't breed tigers, then she would breed a red cat as fierce as a tiger. Now, if one was to go anywhere from St. Ives to Zennor, it was the oddest thing, but nearly every cat one would see would have a tinge of red about it.

When the calico disappeared into a garden across from the

Wild Bird Hospital, Clare went back inside her own house and closed the door.

Meddling, she thought.

She'd always been a meddler.

It dated from when she was very young—just after her accident down by the cave—when the doctors told her parents that she'd never walk again. She'd been playing above Mousehole Cave and followed some older children who were clambering down the rocky fields to where the cave lay; only where their longer limbs took them easily down, with her smaller size, it was all she could do just to keep them in sight. She scrambled after them and one misjudged step later, she was tumbling straight down a twenty-foot drop.

She'd been lucky to come out of it alive, though that wasn't how she viewed things in the first bleak months of her convalescence.

The bones of one leg sustained multiple fractures, and to this day that leg remained thinner and weaker than the other as it had never healed properly. She could sense the weather in it, as an old sailor could in his bones. But there had been damage done to her spinal column as well.

For two years she'd had no use of her lower limbs. But she was determined to walk again and whether it was through the sheer persistence of her will—"Never seen a child with such heart," the doctor told her parents when, after an initial depression, she simply refused to give up her dream of walking again—or whether it was a miracle, eventually the nerves and muscles healed. She was in a wheelchair for three years after that, a walker for another six months, the crutches for far too long, but finally she could get about with a cane as she still did to this day.

The muscles never fully recovered, and she still had her bad days when her leg gave her such trouble she could only walk after taking a painkiller against the hurt, but what did she care about that? Compared to being a bedridden invalid for the rest of her life, her present mobility was a gift from heaven.

Janey had been her best friend before the accident, and stayed her friend after. While Clare was still bedridden, she came by after school to share her lessons, or just to gossip, and once Clare was mobile again—if only in her wheelchair—Janey pushed her about all over the village, struggling up the steep roads, hanging on the back as they played daredevil in places where the inclines weren't too steep.

Still, for all Janey's companionship, Clare had far too much time on her own. It was during this period that she began a lifelong love affair with the written word. And it was also then, when it appeared that she would only be able to sample a great deal of life vicariously, that she began her meddling.

It was Clare who convinced her mother to go back to school when Father died. She was the one who pushed Jack Treffry into trying out for the local rugby team where he did so well that he eventually turned professional. She, along with Dinny, kept after Janey when she was first starting up the pipes because Clare understood long before any of them that, while a fiddler was welcome at any session or barn dance, one needed something a bit more exotic to make a mark for oneself in the folk circuit where fiddlers were a penny a dozen.

It became such a habit that when she *could* take up the reins of her own life again, she continued to meddle in the affairs of others all the same. As she had with Janey and Felix.

But how, she asked herself, could she do anything but meddle when it came to them? They were the two friends she loved most in the world. And she *knew* they were right for each other. They were just each too thick-headed in their own way to put what was needed into their relationship to keep it together.

So she'd done what she could, only now it had backfired on them all.

Clare sighed.

She'd do anything for Janey. And when it came to Felix . . .

Her only real regret with Felix was that she hadn't met him

before Janey had, but she knew she'd kept her feelings well hidden about that over the years—except for the stupid remark she'd blurted out to him just before he left.

Fancying girls with canes.

She wished.

But he and Janey were never to know and she could only hope that feeling as he had, Felix would simply forget her momentary lapse.

Time to set matters right, she thought as she put on a jumper her mum had knit for her last winter. Over that, she wore a yellow nor'wester against the coming rain and stuck a matching yellow rain hat in its pocket.

Leaving a note for her mum, in case she should wake up and wonder where her daughter had gone off to when she said she was staying in for the evening, Clare let herself quietly out the front door and set off down the hill towards the Gaffer's house, her cane tap-tapping on the road by her side.

3 ·

Felix wished he were back at sea.

Mousehole, the closeness of its cottages and houses, its narrow streets and its sense of close-knit community, had none of its usual charm for him tonight. The lit windows behind which families went about their business were only reminders of what he didn't have. The buildings appeared to lean towards him, making him feel claustrophobic. The noisy revelry inside The Ship's Inn when he went by, the cheerful faces of its patrons, laughing and chatting as they kept one another company, was something he felt he'd never share.

And in his loneliness, the sea called to him. As it always did. It was what had kept him sane the last time he and Janey had broken up.

He walked past the harbour, listening to the tide murmuring, but even over its calming sound, all he could hear were Janey's

accusations, the grim set to the Gaffer's voice, and Clare. Trying
to explain it all away again.

Clare.

I just wish I'd known earlier you fancied girls with canes. . . .

Oh, Clare, he thought. I never knew.

He'd never seen past the friendship, past her warmth and
gentle teasing, that he might have meant more to her than just
a friend. But lost in his own anguish as he'd been, heart open
and hurting, he'd been privy to her innermost longings in that
one moment before she realized what she'd said and quickly
covered it up.

Why couldn't he be like everyone else? Felix wondered, and
not for the first time.

It wasn't just his stage fright that stood between Janey's and
his happiness. He knew that, subconsciously, a part of him sab-
otaged their relationship for fear that it would be no different
from that of his own parents. That was why he never opened
himself up completely—it wasn't just the fear of ridicule.

He'd never even told Clare that.

And how kind had he been to her? How much of a friend?
Writing, oh, yes, lots of long letters, but—never mind what he'd
discovered tonight—all he seemed to do was lean on her, borrowing her strength because his love life wasn't going well, and
all the time she'd loved him. From afar, as it were. Talking him
through his problems with no hope of her own needs being
fulfilled. . . .

He was outside of the village now, on the road to Newlyn and
nearing the quarry. The sea still spoke to him and he made his
way down the stairs by the old silos to the concrete wharf below
by the sea where the ships used to dock to collect their loads of
blue alvin stone. He put down his cases and Clare's cane. Sitting
on the edge of the wharf, he looked out across the water.

What was he going to do with himself?

Run away again? Because that was what he *had* done the last
time. Never mind that he and Janey had called it quits. He'd
been as much a part of their quarreling as Janey had, but the

old adage was true. It took two to argue. And for all that he'd tried to see things through, to stay calm and keep the dialogue going, had he really tried hard enough? Or had he simply given up, leaned on Clare until even her support could no longer sustain him, then simply run away?

He just didn't know anymore.

Why couldn't he just fit into a normal nine-to-five slot, instead of traipsing all over the world, looking for a heart's peace he was never going to find anyway? Marry, raise some kids, have friends in one place instead of scattered halfway across the planet. Not worry about whether he was going to turn out to be the same kind of a shit as his parents had been, just carry on with life. Not worry about playing on stage, just keep the music as a hobby. . . .

But, of course, it wasn't that simple. Nothing was. And no one's life was free of complications.

How many times hadn't he listened to friends, tied down to some office job by their mortgages and families, thinking he was such a lucky stiff for being footloose and free? How many times hadn't he heard about lost loves, and might-have-beens and if-onlys from them? What was so different between them and him? It was only details.

The woman he loved hated him, as did her grandfather.

He had some secretary-cum-struggling-actress interested in him because her boyfriend had dumped her and she was bored.

A woman he'd thought of as his best friend had been hiding romantic feelings for all these years.

The one thing he did well—playing music—was denied him as a career because he was too much of a chickenshit to fight a little stage fright.

He worked in a thankless job with no future, because the freedom of movement it gave him kept him from making too many lasting ties and the sea was the only thing that kept him sane. . . .

He was no more screwed up than anybody. He just hadn't learned how to deal with it properly. Other people's problems?

He was always willing to listen and was all too good at handing out advice that could solve them if they only gave what he offered a try. His own? Don't think about them seemed to be his motto, and maybe they'll just go away.

But they never did.

They just got worse.

They got so bad that no matter where you turned, something was screwing up.

Felix watched the lights of a boat go by across the bay.

That was him, alone in the darkness. But didn't it only take his coming out into the light to make all his troubles go away? Wouldn't that at least be a start?

He just couldn't think about it anymore. Not right now.

He couldn't go back to Mousehole, to either the Gaffer's where he wasn't welcome anyway, or to Clare's where he was perhaps too welcome. Neither did he want to go into Penzance where Lena was sitting bored and alone in her hotel room.

Instead, he tried to give the sea an opportunity to calm the turmoil in him. That's what worked best. When he had the late watch on ship, or when he was in a place like this—that secret territory between sea and shore—he could almost step outside of himself and become part of some hidden otherworld where time moved differently and the familiar became strange. Then he understood how the sailors of old could have seen mermaids and sea serpents and ghost ships, how they could hear a music in the waves that could only be the beckoning of sirens.

For there was a music in the sea that Felix could hear at times like this. Not the obvious music of wave on shore, rattling stones on shingle beaches, waves lapping quietly against wharf and pilings, breakers thundering in desolate coves. But another, more exotic music that went deeper. That had its source in the hidden lands undersea and came to the ears of men from how it echoed with the movement of their heart's blood, rather than by phys- ically vibrating against their eardrums. A music that called up tunes from his own fingers, to join its singular measures.

He reached behind him and took his button accordion from

its case, setting it on his knee while he undid the bellows straps. It was a vintage three-row Hohner that he'd bought in a little shop in the old part of Quebec City. Its grillwork was battered, the instrument's casing scratched and worn, the bellows repaired so often they probably didn't have a bit of original material left to them. But the action on the buttons was still perfect, the reeds were true, and he'd yet to run across an instrument he fancied more, though the opportunity had come up often enough.

Felix loved rummaging about in old music shops, loved tracing the history of a particular box, or even just the instrument in general. Its origin was fascinatingly peculiar, coming about by happenstance rather than design.

A cousin to the mouth organ, the accordion was a free-reed instrument that was invented by a German named Christian Buschmann in the course of his development of the mouth-blown instrument. He produced a device that had twenty reeds on a brass table, powered by a leather bellows, which he called a "hand-aeoline." Further improvements were made by Demian of Vienna in 1892, who coined the name "accordion," but the first serious commercial production of diatonic accordions, or melodeons, was the work of the M. Hohner harmonica factory, situated in the Black Forest's Trossingen some fifty years later.

Felix had often suffered the ignorance of those unfamiliar with the instrument to whom the word "accordion" conjured up painful versions of "Lady of Spain"—a far cry from the music that Felix and his peers played. Those same souls, once they heard what could be done with both the piano and button accordion in traditional music, were, more often than not, won over with only a few tunes. And they were surprised at the instrument's heritage.

For before zydeco and rock 'n' roll, before Lawrence Welk and Astor Piazzolla, the "squeeze box" was being used in traditional music—to accompany Morris dancers in England and clog dancers in Quebec and on the Continent, and to give an unmistakable lift to the jigs and reels of Ireland and Scotland. Without the pedigree of the harp, the flute, the fiddle, or the various kinds of bagpipes, it had still developed a surprisingly large number of virtuoso players who were only just beginning to be acknowledged as some of the finest proponents of the folk tradition.

Their music could make the heart lift, the foot tap, and, as Felix had found so often, bring consolation to him when he was feeling depressed. The only thing better than listening was playing.

He slipped one shoulder strap over his right shoulder; the other went over the biceps of his left arm. Thumbing down the air-release button, he opened the bellows and ran through an arpeggio of notes, fingers dancing from one row to another as he went up and down the three-row fingerboard. He didn't touch the accompaniment buttons, just played a freeform music with his right hand to loosen up his fingers.

Then, still looking out across the choppy waters of the bay, he let the secret music hidden in its dark water mingle with the jumble and confusion inside him and he began to play.

It was a plaintive, disconsolate music that he called up that night. It neither cheered him nor eased his problems. All it did was allow him the expression of his sorrow and cluttered thoughts so that he could at least face them with a clearer mind.

The wounds of his heart ran too deep for an easy cure; healing would take more than music.

Two hours later, he finally set his instrument aside. A surreal calm touched him as he stored the accordion back into its case and then slowly rose to his feet.

He knew what he had to do now.

He would drop the cane off with Lena, but that was as far as he'd let her complicate his life. Then he'd go. He needed money, needed a job. But this time when he worked the ships, he'd save his money. He wouldn't moon over what was lost, or what couldn't be. He'd look ahead to what could be. He'd finally do something with himself; face life, rather than avoiding it.

Thinking of Janey still hurt—would always hurt, because it was impossible to simply put her aside as if she'd never had any importance—but he couldn't let his need for her continue to steer the course of his life.

And he would come back.

To Penwith. To Mousehole. Because he wouldn't let what couldn't be with her affect his friendship with Clare and Dinny and the others he knew in the area.

Not anymore.

Easy to say, he thought as he gathered up his duffel bag and slung it to his shoulder.

He picked up his accordion case and Clare's cane and started back up the stairs to the road that would take him into Penzance. He paused at the top to look back towards Mousehole. The village was mostly dark now. Above him the clouds let fall the first misty sheet of a drizzle that would probably continue throughout the night. His chest was tight again as he turned from the village and started to walk away.

His hard-won resolutions clotted like cold porridge inside him, sticking to one another in a tangle that no longer made the sense he'd thought he'd resolved them into only a few moments ago. It was all he could do to not turn around and go back.

Goddamn it, Janey, he thought. Why couldn't you have just *listened* for a change?

There was a wet sheen on his cheeks as he steeled himself to continue down to Penzance. Most of it was due to the light drizzle that accompanied him on his way.

But not all.

4 ·

All Janey wanted to do after the Gaffer had sent Felix off was crawl away and die. A numb, sick feeling settled over her. She sat slumped in an easy chair by the hearth, her arms wrapped around the Dunthorn book as though it were a life ring that would keep her from drowning. She stared at Jabez washing himself on the throw rug by her feet, not really seeing the cat, not really aware of anything except for the emptiness that had lodged inside her.

It was really true, she thought. You never knew what you wanted until you lost it.

She started when the Gaffer laid his hand on her shoulder.

"Don't blame yourself, my gold," he said. "It was none of your fault."

She nodded, not trusting herself to speak.

The Gaffer sighed. Giving her shoulder a squeeze, he went over to his own chair and sat down, the same unhappy look in his features.

"But who would have thought," the Gaffer began. He shook his head. "He seemed the best of men. . . ."

"He—he wasn't always . . . like this. . . ." She couldn't go on.

"No, my love," the Gaffer agreed. "I do suppose what hurts the most is being three scats behind to find out just what sort of a man he'd become since last we saw him."

Janey nodded again. There should have been some hint, shouldn't there? she thought. Surely a bloke couldn't change that much without it showing somehow? But he'd been just the same old Felix—the little she'd seen of him.

Bloody hell. Why did he have to go and do it?

To be fair, she had no claim on his heart. What he did with his love life was his own business, for all that it hurt. But to betray their trust by siding with those who were basically trying to rob Billy's grave. . . .

"We'll have to hide that book again," the Gaffer said, as though he were reading her mind.

"I—I just want . . ."

The Gaffer nodded. "You go ahead and finish it, my queen. But then it has to go away."

Trust things to go all awful like this, Janey thought. It had just been too perfect to last. Finding the book, Felix coming back, the reporter from *Rolling Stone* wanting to do a piece on her. . . . Trust it to turn all horrible. It was the story of her life. Surely she should have learned by now: Don't get too happy, or someone would come along and pull the carpet out from under her. Like bloody Alan making a mess of their upcoming tour. Like Felix arriving to wake a promise in her heart, only to stab her in the back.

She just wished she could feel angry instead of so lost.

"I have to go to bed," she said.

"Sleep in my room," the Gaffer said. "I don't want you next door on your own."

"I . . . I'll be all right. . . ."

"It's not your heart I'm thinking of, my gold; it's these bloody vultures out to pick Billy's bones. Best we stick together, you and I."

"All right," Janey said.

Still clutching the book, she went up to his room. She didn't bother to undress, just crawled under the comforter where she curled up in a fetal position and tried not to think. When Mike called a little later, she asked the Gaffer to tell him that she was sick and couldn't speak to him.

"Maybe you should see him," the Gaffer said. "It might take your mind off things."

"I—I can't see anyone, Gramps."

"Perhaps it's too soon," he agreed.

Any time, period, was going to be too soon, Janey thought as he went back downstairs. Oh, Felix, why did you have to come back? I was doing just fine not remembering you until I saw you again yesterday.

She tried sleeping, to no avail. All she could do, when she wasn't crying, was lie there in the dark and stare up at the ceiling. When she heard the doorbell ring downstairs, she sat up in bed, half hoping it was Felix, half dreading it. But when the visitor spoke, asking for her, she recognized Clare's voice and let out a breath she hadn't been aware she was holding. A pang of disappointment cut across her relief.

"She's not feeling well, my heart," she heard her grandfather say.

"She's still going to see me," Clare replied, "and you're both going to listen to me. Pardon my rudeness, Mr. Little, but you and Janey have been acting like a pair of twits tonight and I'm not leaving until I talk some sense into the both of you."

Janey burrowed back under the comforter. She couldn't face Clare's well-meaning, but this time misguided, attempts at getting her and Felix to reconcile. Not tonight.

"Now see here, you," the Gaffer began.

"No," Clare interrupted him. "You *will* listen to me." Louder, she called up the stairs: "Janey! I know you're here. Will you come down on your own or do I have to go up and drag you down here?"

Couldn't she be left alone with her grief?

"Janey!"

"I don't know rightly what's got into you, Clare Mabley," the Gaffer said, "but if you don't leave off your shouting, I'll—"

"You'll what? Call the police to come take me away? Go on and do it then, but I'll still have my say before they arrive."

"You don't understand," the Gaffer tried to explain. "What happened with Felix was—"

"No, you don't understand." Again a loud cry up the stairs: "Janey!"

Was the whole world going mad? Janey wondered. First Felix betraying them, now Clare carrying on, sounding angrier than Janey had ever heard her before.

"Janey!"

"You'll stop that shouting!" the Gaffer cried back.

Janey dragged herself out of bed. Still hugging the Dunthorn book to her chest, she shuffled out into the hall and stood at the head of the stairs, looking down at the pair of them. The Gaffer had gone all red in the face. Clare stood by the door, an equally angry look in her own features.

"Please don't fight," Janey said.

They turned like guilty children, then they both tried to speak at once.

"It's about time—"

"She wouldn't go—"

Janey held up her hands. She looked from Clare to the Gaffer, loving them both, wondering how things could have deteriorated to the point that they should all be at one another's throats.

"Why don't we make a pot of tea, Gramps," she said, "and then we can see what Clare wanted to talk to us about."

It felt decidedly odd to Janey to be acting as a mediator—especially between the Gaffer and Clare. Her grandfather was so good-natured that he was everybody's mate, and Clare was normally so even-tempered that Janey felt she could count on the fingers of one hand the number of times she'd seen her friend angry. But mediating helped keep at bay the bleak feeling that was inside her and she wanted to hear what Clare had to say—hoping, she had to admit to herself, that Clare would somehow be able to defend Felix's behavior, however unlikely that seemed.

It took a while, but when Janey and the Gaffer had heard her out, the three of them sitting in the kitchen with a pot of tea, Clare's story did exactly that. At the first mention of Lena, the Gaffer interrupted to explain who the woman was—that she'd come around earlier, sniffing after Dunthorn's secrets.

"I never knew," she said. "And neither did Felix."

Before the Gaffer could take the conversation off on a tangent, she went on with her story, refusing to be interrupted again until she was done. Then she let them speak.

"But I *saw* him and that American woman," the Gaffer said. "The two of them together on that bike, looking for all the world like a pair of lovers."

"And how else was he supposed to get her back to her hotel?"

"Did he never think of an ambulance?"

"And did you ever give him a chance to explain?" Clare shot back. "He'd only *just* met her. Would you rather he'd left her there by the side of the road?"

Janey found herself nodding, then realized how spiteful she was being. Besides, if what Clare was saying was true, then Felix couldn't have known who this Lena was in the first place.

"That's well and fine," the Gaffer said, "but it still all rests on our taking Felix at his word."

"And did he ever lie to you before?" Clare demanded.

Janey shook her head. But the Gaffer nodded.

"There was that letter," he said. "Janey never sent it. I *believe* her."

"Of course she didn't send it," Clare replied. "I did."

Janey's eyes went wide. "You?"

Clare nodded. "Someone had to get the two of you back together again."

"So—so Felix had nothing to do with—with any of it . . . ?"

Janey felt about an inch tall. She turned to the Gaffer, the anguish plain in her eyes. The Gaffer looked as mortified as she felt.

"Of course he didn't! For God's sake, how could you even *think* Felix would be involved in anything that would hurt you?"

He wouldn't, Janey realized. And if she'd given it even a half moment's thought, instead of going off half cocked the way she had, she would have seen that.

Oh, Felix. Talk about betraying a trust. . . .

"I'm awful," Janey said. "I'm an awful, horrible person. How—how could I have treated him like that?"

"We both did," the Gaffer said bleakly.

"Well, it's partly my fault," Clare said. "I shouldn't have sent that letter. It just seemed like such a good idea at the time. . . ."

"It was a very good idea," Janey said.

Because seeing Felix again had made the world seem better. She'd been a little confused about her feelings at first, but that was only natural. Once she'd had a chance to think things through, she'd realized just how much she'd missed him. Yet now . . .

"Is he—is he at your place?" she asked.

Clare shook his head. "I lent him a cane that he was going to drop off with that Lena woman—I wonder if she even *did* sprain her ankle—and then he was going to hitch to London to get a job."

"How long ago did he leave?" the Gaffer asked.

Clare looked at the clock. "It took me a half hour to get here, and we've been talking for almost two hours. . . . I'm not sure. Say three hours all told?"

"What hotel was she staying at?"

"Felix never said."

"He'll be gone now," Janey said. Tears were welling up in her eyes again. "Bloody hell! Why couldn't I have listened to him?"

"You didn't know," the Gaffer began, reaching over the table to pat her arm.

She refused to be comforted.

"That's right," she said. "But I should have."

She rose from the table.

"Where are you going?" the Gaffer asked.

"To look for him—what do you think?"

"I'll come with you."

Janey shook her head. "This is something I have to do myself, Gramps." She turned to her friend. "Thanks, Clare. I mean that."

"If I hadn't sent that—"

"I'm *glad* you did," Janey said fiercely. "Now I have to see if I can't salvage something from what you started for me."

She went next door to get a jacket and her car keys and came back to find Clare and the Gaffer outside. Clare was just buttoning up her nor'wester. She was wearing a matching yellow hat against the light drizzle that had started up. The whole outfit made her look like one of the lifeboat Coastguards.

"Do you want a ride?" Janey asked her.

Clare shook her head. "You just go on and find Felix. I'll be fine."

"Clare, my gold," the Gaffer said. "I don't know how to say I'm sorry."

"We've all got things to be sorry about tonight," she told him. "Go on, Janey. I'll talk to you both tomorrow."

Janey waited a few heartbeats. Clare gave her a small smile, then started off for home. The Gaffer waved Janey to her car.

"Bring him back," he said.

Janey nodded. "I will, Gramps."

5 ·

Chapel Place, the small square on which the Gaffer's house stood, took its name from the old Methodist Chapel on its northeast corner. The chapel had a small yard, separated from the square by a low stone wall, the base of which was slightly raised from the street, for the village still climbed the hill towards Paul here where Duck Street became Mousehole Lane.

Sitting behind the wall, hidden from view and apparently listening to a Walkman, was Michael Bett. He wore a low-brimmed hat that hid his features and what appeared to be a pair of sunglasses but were in fact specially treated infrared lenses that served the double duty of both disguising him further from a chance glance and allowing him better night vision. He was bundled against the night's damp chill with a heavy sweater under his lined raincoat, thick denim trousers, and rubber shoes with a thick sheepskin insulation.

Removing the earplugs from his ears, he waited to hear the Gaffer's door close and for Clare's footsteps to fade. Not until the sound of Janey's three-wheeled Reliant Robin had died away as well, did he finally sit up.

When he'd hired the private eye Sam Dennison, part of Dennison's surveillance had included the installation of a state-of-the-art microphone/transmitter remote eavesdropping system.

Four miniature wireless transmitter microphones had been placed in the Gaffer's house—one each in the kitchen, living room, and main bedroom upstairs, the fourth in Janey's rooms. At Bett's request, Dennison had left the microphones in place when he'd completed his surveillance.

The microphones had a transmission range of fifteen hundred feet—far more than Bett required in his present position, though he would have appreciated a greater range so that he could have remained in the comfort of his B and B, instead of crouching here in the drizzle. But then, he thought, he wouldn't be in such a perfect position to take immediate action, now would he?

Storing the receiver in the inner pocket of his coat, he hopped over the wall to the street below and made his way to the red box of a telephone booth he'd noted near the post office when he'd explored the village earlier. Fishing coins from his pocket, he put through a call. Lena answered on the second ring.

"Did anyone ever tell you that you have a beautiful telephone voice?" he asked her.

"What do you want?"

"Well, it's an odd thing, but I was listening in on a conversation that the Littles were having earlier with their good friend Clare Mabley, and what do you think I found out?"

"I'm not in the mood for games, Bett."

"Neither am I. I told you to *stay* in your hotel room this afternoon."

There was a momentary pause that Bett didn't fill. Let her think about it, he decided.

"I can explain," she began.

"Don't bother. Surprisingly enough, you didn't screw up." He filled her in on what he felt she needed to know about what he had recently learned, then finished up with, "He's going to be showing up at your room any minute now."

"Oh, shit."

"Do I detect a certain reluctance in your voice, dear Lena?"

"No. I..."

She was just regretting the trouble she'd brought into Gavin's life, Bett realized with surprise. Now there was one for the books. The Ice Queen was worrying about somebody else for a change. That was just what he didn't need now—to have the Ice Queen turn into a soft-hearted cow. Bad enough she was so stupid.

"Here's what's going to happen," he told her in a voice that would brook no further discussion. "He's going to show up at the hotel and you're going to keep him there, in your room, and you're not going to let him leave."

"But—"

"I don't care how you do it, just make sure that you don't screw it up. You see," he added, "if I find him wandering around the streets tonight, the next time he shows up in public will be when the tide washes his body in. Am I making myself clear?"

"What are you planning?"

"I've got some business with another of Janey Little's friends. Like you, she's been sticking her nose into what doesn't concern her. Unlike you, she's not going to get a second chance."

There was another moment of stiff silence as Lena digested that.

"Daddy said this was supposed to be a low-key operation," she finally said.

Bett laughed into the receiver. A low-key operation. Christ, she had the terminology down pat, but she didn't have the first clue as to what she was really talking about.

"This isn't some spy novel," he told her.

"But Daddy—"

"*I'm* in charge here. Just do it." He hung up before she could whine any more.

She was seriously getting on his nerves.

Opening the door to the telephone booth, he stepped out into the drizzle and took a few steadying breaths, hands opening and closing at his sides. It had been a long time since he'd taken someone apart to see how they worked and the more he listened to her whiny voice, the more he wondered just how long she'd last under the knife.

She'd squeal. She'd beg and plead. She'd—

Forget it, he told himself.

He couldn't touch her. Not without Madden's okay. Just as he couldn't touch the Littles—at least not until they'd coughed up what the Order was looking for.

Fine. He could handle that. But no one had said anything about the Littles' friends.

Take the Mabley woman.

Yes, thank you. I do believe I will.

She was an interfering whore who couldn't be allowed to go around making everything hunky-dory anymore. He wasn't going to have the time to do her right, but he'd still get a little satisfaction out of throwing her off a cliff. He didn't like meddlers. And he didn't like cripples.

According to the file Dennison had compiled on her, she'd taken a fall once when she was a kid. Those cliffs out past her house were dangerous places for a crip. It'd be a real shame if she took another fall.

Poor Clare Mabley.

And poor Janey Little, losing a friend like that, hard on the heels of screwing up things with Gavin who—if Lena knew what was good for her—would soon be found in a compromising position with the "enemy."

Janey was going to need a friend. She was going to need comforting. And he knew just the man for her—Mike Betcher, ace reporter for *Rolling Stone*.

Bett felt calmer now, enough so that he cracked a smile as he set off to find the Mabley woman before she hobbled her way back to the supposed safety of her home.

He'd do her inside, if he had to.

It'd just make things that much easier if he could save himself the trouble of having to break in.

Lonely streets. Dark streets. Anything could happen on them. Even in a quiet little village like this.

6.

The Gaffer returned inside and shut the door behind him. He looked slowly about the room, feeling a constriction that he'd never experienced before in its cozy limits.

Came from doing the wrong thing, he thought. Clare had been correct in that much. They'd never given Felix a chance to explain himself at all. They'd treated him unfairly, as though he'd proved himself unworthy of their trust long before today's incident, and the Gaffer knew that he himself was the most to blame for that.

He wondered if Felix would forgive them. Wondered if they would be allowed the chance to find out. He could be anywhere, and the Gaffer didn't hold much hope that Janey would simply run across him. That smacked too much of chance, and chance, of late, had proved to be working against them.

His gaze settled on the copy of *The Little Country* that Janey had brought downstairs with her, but then left on the sofa when they had all gone into the kitchen to have their talk with Clare.

Whether Felix was innocent or not—and the Gaffer was inclined now to give Felix the benefit of the doubt—he still couldn't shake the feeling that Billy's book was at the center of the web in which all the events of the past few days had become entangled.

He picked up the book and took it to his chair by the hearth. He didn't have to open it to remember the story—for all that he hadn't dipped into its pages since that time, years ago, when he'd first read it. A time when, he recalled, another series of baffling events had made their presence felt in the Little household. It hadn't just been the vultures, out scavenging for anything that had belonged to Billy. There'd been other occurrences, less easily explained, but evident all the same.

Music heard, when it had no visible source.

Movement sensed from the corner of one's eye, but nothing being there when one turned to look.

An uncommon restlessness in himself and his young wife, Adeline, that was even less easily explained.

And their son Paul—starting and crying with night-fears late at night, when normally he slept through the dark hours and had no fear of the shadows under his bed, or in his closet.

All gone when the book was safely hidden once more.

"What did you do, my robin?" he asked the ghost of his old friend who he could sense hovering near. "What did you hide in this book?"

Nothing that the Gaffer could see.

True, it was odd that it should have been published in an edition of only one, but that explained little. And the story— while told in Billy's remarkable prose—was no more remarkable than that of either of his previous books, though the Gaffer had liked it the best of the three.

He had particularly appreciated one of the lead characters who was the captain of a fishing lugger called *The Talisman,* back before the end of the pilchard industry. He became the best friend of the book's heroine, an emperent young orphan who had disguised herself as a boy and worked on *The Talisman* until she was found out. And wasn't there a row about that, for having a woman on board ship was bad luck, as any fisherman knew— nearly as bad as having a dog, or, worse, a rabbit or a hare. The fishermen wouldn't even use the common names of animals while at sea, calling them two-deckers instead.

Billy had set their story in an imaginary town, but it had been easily recognizable to the Gaffer as a combination of Penzance, Newlyn, and Mousehole—the three rolled up together into one fanciful harbour town. There was a bit of the familiar Dunthorn magic in the book as well: the Smalls whose miniature craft was found in the harbour one morning at low tide, and the hidden music that could grant any one wish, could one but remember its odd phrasing and repeat it. Both were details that Billy had used in his previous two books.

That had surprised the Gaffer some, for Billy hadn't been one to repeat himself, but the story itself had been a new one, and a good one. A story that the Gaffer had felt spoke directly to him when he was reading it, and became more so as he grew older and he could find parallels between his own life and that of *The Talisman*'s captain in the book.

Still, none of that explained why it should be of such interest to this Lena woman and her friends. Nor why they'd been searching for it for so long, for the Gaffer was convinced that this new interest was merely a renewed interest, though why he thought so, he couldn't have explained.

Thirty-five years it had been, now, since the crows had first come 'round looking for it.

He flipped through its pages, trying to fathom what it was about the book that made it more than merely a literary curiosity, but still nothing came to mind.

He paused for a moment, head cocked and listening, thinking he had heard something. Janey returning perhaps, or . . . he didn't know what. It was gone now.

Just the wind, he thought. Or a scatter of earnest rain, in among the drizzle.

He glanced at the clock to find that Janey had only been gone twenty minutes. He was tired, but knew he couldn't sleep until she returned—with Felix, or without him. He had to know.

Opening the book again, he decided to reread it while he waited. He smiled at the opening lines and was soon caught up in the familiar story, humming an old, half-familiar tune under his breath as he read.

The Moving Bog

From ghoulies and ghosties
and long leggety beasties,
And things that go bump in the night,
Good Lord, deliver us.

—CORNISH PRAYER

"Don't look into her eyes!" Edern cried as the fetch moved aside to allow the Widow to bend down and peer in between the crates to where he and Jodi were hiding.

But his warning came too late.

That one enormous eye of the Widow's, staring at her with its unblinking magnetic gaze, had already pinned Jodi to the spot where she stood. It mesmerized her, called to her.

Come to me, come to me. . . .

Jodi took a step forward.

"Jodi, don't!" Edern called.

He might just as well have tried to catch water in a sieve, for the Widow's spell was already taking root in Jodi's mind. All she could hear was that warm, friendly voice, beckoning her to its promised safety.

Come to me, my pretty. . . .

As Jodi took a second step, Edern grabbed her by the arm and shoved her roughly against the side of a crate. The jolting movement was enough to momentarily break the Widow's spell.

"What . . . ?" Jodi began.

Edern's face was inches from her own.

"*Don't* look into her eyes," he warned again, "and don't listen to what she says."

Before Jodi could argue, he caught her arm again and hauled her deeper into the labyrinth between the crates. Freed now from the Widow's mesmerizing gaze, Jodi shivered. Behind them, the

Widow called after them, her words dripping honey, promising them their heart's desire if they would only return. Will she, nill she, Jodi found herself starting to turn back until Edern gripped her arm again and began to sing. His clear tenor voice cut through the Widow's enchantment leaving her words to lie bare and be revealed for the lies they were.

But if she didn't listen to Edern's voice, it was so easy to just believe. . . .

Edern, as though sensing how she was weakening again, sang louder as he reached the chorus:

"*Hal-an-tow,*
Jolly rumble-o,
We were up, long before the day-o—"

"Sing with me!" Edern cried.

Jodi hesitated for a heartbeat, then joined in on the familiar song.

"*To welcome in the summer,*
To welcome in the May-o,
For summer is a-coming on
And winter's gone away-o."

Forgoing a verse that she might not know, Edern launched straight into a repeat of the chorus. He kept a hand on Jodi's arm, pulling her along when she seemed to falter in her step.

Singing at the top of their lungs, they retreated to where the wharf ended and they could go no farther. They could still hear the Widow's voice, but now the stretch of the massed crates between them and the sound of the tide as it washed the pilings below stole away its enchantment.

Finally, the Widow gave up and fell silent.

Jodi slumped against a crate. "Oh raw we," she said. "Wasn't that close?"

"Too close," Edern agreed.

"How can she do that with her voice? She must be able to get anything she wants from anybody."

Edern shook his head. "She needs to have a piece of you, first. Your name called three times, or a pinch of your soul, the way she's got that one of yours sewn up in her cloak. Can you imagine having a conversation with someone who, just before they ask you something, calls you by your full name three times? It wouldn't be long before they knew her for what she was and brought out all the old charms to ward off her spells."

"Still, we're safe for now, aren't we?"

"Not for long. And don't forget, they'll be loading these crates soon and then where will we hide?"

"Maybe we can get inside one of them?" Jodi tried.

"And end up where?"

She nodded glumly. "Bother and damn. You'd think—" She paused to lift her head, smelling at the air. "What's that awful pong in the air?"

She couldn't really make out Edern's features in the gloom, but she could sense his sudden tension.

"Edern," she said. "What's the matter?"

"She has more power than I gave her credit for," he replied.

"*What* are you talking about?"

Jodi stood up as she spoke because the wood planking of the wharf under her was becoming damp. The smell grew worse: It was like the stink raised from disturbing stagnant waters. Standing, she wiped at the seat of her trousers and wrinkled her nose. The planking underfoot was acquiring a definite spongy feel to it.

"Have you ever heard of a sloch?" Edern asked.

"No," she said, shaking her head. The motion was lost in the darkness. "Why do I get a bad feeling about what you're going to tell me?" she added.

"Because they're terrible creatures—especially to folk our size."

Jodi could hear something approaching now—more than one something, each moving with a wet, sucking sound.

"Normally a witch will use them like a fetch," Edern explained, "but they are only temporary fabrications. They rarely live out the night in which they were created."

Jodi stared back the way they had come, into the shadows. In the distance she could make out a dull green grow, but that was all. The reek was truly awful now and there was a chill in the air that had nothing to do with the normal damp of an autumn night in Bodbury.

"What *are* they, Edern?"

"They're made from materials collected in a bog—fouled mud and rotting twigs, bound together with decaying reeds and rushes. Stagnant water runs in their makeshift veins like muddy blood. Their eyes glow with the marsh gas that the witch combines with a spark of her own soul when she animates them."

Jodi could see the ghostly pinprick glow of those eyes as he spoke—small malevolent sparks that shone brightly in the sickly green glow that preceded the creatures. The stench was so bad now that she had to breathe through her mouth.

"What are they going to do to us?" she asked. "What *can* they do?"

By the glow that seemed to emanate from their skin, she could see the shape of them now as the sloch shuffled wetly forward. Stick-thin limbs attached to fat-bellied torsos, squat heads atop, connected without the benefit of necks. Jodi gagged, nausea roiling in her stomach, as a new wave of their stench rolled towards her. Underfoot, the wharf's planking had become as soggy as the soft ground of a bog.

"They can take us back to the Widow," Edern replied bleakly.

"No," Jodi said. "I won't go back."

"They can pull us to pieces, those things," Edern said. "They're far stronger than their origins would lead you to believe."

"There must be something we can do."

But there was nowhere left to go, no place to turn. They were backed up to the edge of the wharf now. Below lay the sea. On either side, crates blocked their way. And in front of them, approaching slowly but inexorably, came the Widow's reeking creatures.

"There's nothing," Edern said. "Unless. . . ." He turned to look at the dark waters below. "Can you swim?" he added.

"Yes, but the size we are . . . How would we ever make it all the way to shore?"

"It's the chance you'll have to take—the only one left to you. The brine of the sea will protect you."

"What do you mean, protect *me?*"

"Witches are like hummocks in that way," Edern said. "Neither can abide the touch of salt. That's something the travelers know, if others have forgotten it."

"I meant," she said, "the way you just said me. What about you?"

The sloch were close enough so that their faces could be made out in the feeble light that their bodies cast. Jodi wished they had stayed in the shadows. They had heads like turnips, featureless except for leering grins that split the bottom parts of their faces and those ghastly glowing eyes. The very lack of other features made them that much more horrible to her. This close, their reek was unbearable.

"I can't swim," Edern told her.

"I'll help you—Taupin showed me how to swim while towing someone along with you. It's not so hard."

"You don't understand—it's not just that I can't swim. I would sink to the bottom of the ocean as soon as I touched the waves."

"That's nonsense. Why would you—"

"Trust me in this."

"I'm not going without you."

Edern took a step away from her, towards the horrible creatures.

"You must," he said. "Remember the Men-an-Tol. Go nine times through it at moonrise."

"I'm not—"

But she had no more chance to argue. Edern ran at the creatures, ramming into them as though he were a living battering ram. The foremost sloch went tumbling down, falling into the ones behind. A weird hissing arose in the air that sounded like an angry hive of bees.

"I want them alive!" Jodi could hear the Widow faintly cry from beyond the crates.

Jodi danced nearby the struggling figures, trying to get a kick in, but Edern was blocking her way. The passage between the crates was so narrow that only a pair of the creatures could get at him at one time.

"Let me help!" Jodi cried.

But "Go!" was Edern's only response, made without his turning his head towards her.

He grabbed the arm of the closest creature and pulled it from its torso. Black, muddy blood sprayed about. A drop splattered against the back of Jodi's hand, stinging like a nettle. And Edern, who took the brunt of the spray—

Jodi started to gag.

His features seemed to be melting. Where once had been his somewhat handsome face, now there were runnels of dripping skin, like wax going down the side of a candle.

"Y-you—" she began.

He pulled the limb from another of the sloch and a new spray of the stinging blood erupted. The bee-buzz of the creatures grew higher pitched and angrier now. The sloch in the rear began to clamber over their fallen comrades to get at Edern.

"No!" Jodi heard the witch cry. "You'll ruin them!"

Jodi nodded dumbly in agreement.

"Don't hurt him . . ." she said in a small voice.

Him? she thought. Was he even a person?

She took a hesitant step forward. Edern turned towards her, his face melted now to show metal not bone under the skin. The polished steel gleamed in the light that came from the creatures' bodies. Jodi put a hand to her mouth, too shocked to even speak. A sloch punched a hole in the little man's chest. When it withdrew its arm, clockwork mechanisms spilled forth, gears and little wheels and ratchets rolling across the soggy planks of the wharf.

Frozen in place, Jodi stared at what Edern was revealed to be: a clockwork man.

Like something she might find on Denzil's worktable.

But he'd walked and talked like a real person. Clockwork mechanisms moved with stiff, jerky motions. They couldn't speak. They couldn't feel. They...

"You..." she began. "You can't...."

This couldn't be real.

The sloch pushed him aside. More cogs and tiny geared wheels spilled from his chest as he hit the soggy wharf planking.

None of this was real.

But he looked up at her, life still impossibly there in his eyes.

"Remember," he said. "The stone. Nine times through its hole...."

His voice had a hollow ring to it now.

"Remember," he repeated.

She nodded numbly. At moonrise.

"You fools!" she heard the Widow cry.

She backed away from the shuffling creatures, gaze still locked on Edern's ruined face. When the light finally died in his eyes—no, the eyes simply changed from a real person's eyes to ones made of glass—she turned and ran towards the edge of the wharf.

The creatures followed. The air was filled with their bee-buzz anger. Their reek was almost a physical presence in the air. She could hear the Widow shouting, caught a glimpse above her of Windle peering down at her through a crack in the crates, then she reached the edge and launched herself out into the air.

Moments later, the dark waves of the sea closed in over her head.

2 .

Denzil and Taupin traveled back and forth through Bodbury for hours, but could find no trace of Jodi. It was as though she had simply vanished into thin air.

Early in their search, Taupin had enlisted the help of Kara Faull, one of the Tatters children, by the simple method of tossing pebbles at her window until she came down to see what they wanted. Once the situation had been explained to her, she set off on her bicycle and soon there was a whole gaggle of Tatters children scouring the town as well. From time to time, one of them would pedal up to wherever Denzil and Taupin were to give a report.

"She hasn't been seen on the Hill."

"No sign of her in old town."

"We've been up and down New Dock, but didn't see a thing except for the Widow walking with what looked to be the ugliest cat I ever did see."

"It had no fur, I'll swear."

"Garm, yes. And such a pong there near the wharves."

Well past midnight, the children had all returned to their beds and only Denzil and Taupin remained to continue the search, neither of them knowing how to proceed now.

"Well," Taupin said finally, sitting on a low stone wall by the Old Quay. "We've done it logical, haven't we?"

"Why do I not want to hear what you're going to tell me next?" Denzil asked.

Taupin smiled. "All the same, it's time we considered the impossible now." At Denzil's frown, he added, "We did agree to that."

"You decided that."

"Have you got a better idea?"

"We could take another turn around by..." Denzil's voice trailed off as Taupin shook his head.

"To what purpose?"

"To find Jodi, you!"

"Will you give me a chance to explain?"

Denzil sighed. "All right. But I'm worried, Brengy."

"I am, too."

"What did you have in mind?"

Taupin pointed with his chin over to the far side of the Tatters where a number of old warehouses stood.

"We'll go ask Henkie."

"Now I know you're mad," Denzil said.

Hedrik Whale was the town reprobate. As his surname hinted, he was an enormous man, standing six feet three and weighing some three hundred pounds. He had a beard that came down to his waist, portions of which he wore in tiny braids, and hair cropped so short he might as well have simply shaved his scalp. He gadded about town in paint-stained dungarees and old workboots, a knee-length jersey and an ever-present scarf.

Years ago, when the pilchard died out, he had used the immense inheritance left him by his father—Rawlyn Whale, of Whale Fisheries—to buy up a few of the old Tatters warehouses, which he peopled with the derelicts of the town. One he kept for his own use and in it he stored an immense library and the enormous canvases upon which he worked. His paintings were invariably of beautiful women—who for some unknown reason were attracted to him in droves for all that he almost always smelled as though he hadn't washed in a week—and his style was stunning. His canvases seemed to literally breathe—not just with life, however, but with lewdness and debauchery as well.

His real notoriety—if one discounted the mural of the town council depicted in various states of inebriation and undress that he'd painted on the side of one of his warehouses—was the curious case of a missing corpse. When one of his derelict friends, a certain John Briello of no fixed age nor address, died a few years ago, Henkie, rather than giving the fellow a proper funeral, had followed Briello's instructions and had his friend stuffed.

He'd kept the body propped up in a corner of his studio until the authorities got wind of its existence, but when the constables arrived en masse at the studio, the body wasn't to be found. Nor was it ever heard of again, save in rumour.

For all Denzil's admiration of the man's craft—or at least the stylistic excellence of his craft, for Denzil, if the truth be told, was somewhat of a prude—he'd never been able to spend more than a few minutes in the man's company. Henkie smelled bad and, for all his artistic ability, was himself an obese eyesore. He was brash, unreasonable, crude, offensive, belligerent . . . in short, not an easy man to like.

"You only have to get to know him," Taupin argued.

"That," Denzil said, "is what I'd be most afraid of, you."

"He can help us," Taupin insisted.

"Tee-ta-taw. About as much as the Widow could."

"No," Taupin said. "But he has some of her rumoured talents."

Denzil rolled his eyes. "I suppose he can scry with a glass ball?"

"Better. He can speak with the dead."

"You really are mad, you."

Taupin stood up from the wall and made a great show of dusting some nonexistent lint from the sleeve of his coat.

"It makes no sense," Denzil said.

Taupin studied his nails, then dug into his pocket until he came up with a penknife that he used to clean one.

"It would be a complete waste of time," Denzil tried, obviously weakening.

Taupin began to whistle a bawdy pub song and turned to look out at the harbour.

Denzil sighed. "I know I'll regret this," he said.

Turning to face him again, Taupin gave Denzil a hearty clap on the back.

"That's the spirit, old sport," he said. "Optimism. One can do wonders with optimism. Bottle it up and serve it as a tonic, I wouldn't doubt, if we could only find a way to distill its particular—"

Denzil straightened his glasses, which had gone all askew on the end of his nose, and pushed them back until they were settled in their proper place once more.

"Can we just get this over with?" he asked.

"—healing properties." Taupin gave him a grin. "You won't regret this."

"I already regret it," Denzil assured him as they set off along the Old Quay towards Henkie's warehouse.

The woman who answered their knock was a breathtaking brunette whose only clothing was a sheet that she'd obviously only just halfheartedly wrapped about herself for the express purpose of answering the door, for it was also obvious, from the light that shone behind her, that she wore nothing underneath it. Denzil recognized her and couldn't help being surprised to find her in this place.

Her name was Lizzie Snell, and by day, she was the mayor's secretary.

"Hello, Brengy," she said. "And Mr. Gossip. What brings you by at this time of night?"

"Is Henkie still up?" Taupin asked.

Lizzie blushed. "Well, he was when I left him."

"I meant, can he see us?"

"Oh. I'll see. Do you want to wait inside?"

She closed the door behind them once they'd come in, then wandered off into a labyrinth of bookcases leaving them in the company of a fifteen-foot-high painting of herself in which she wore no sheet to disguise her undeniably generous charms.

"Beautiful," Taupin said.

"Yes," Denzil said after one quick eye-popping look. He turned away and studiously looked at a pamphlet that he picked up from the table by the door. "He's a gifted artist."

Taupin laughed. "I meant Lizzie."

Denzil read the title of the pamphlet—"The Care and Spiritual Welfare of the Penis: A Study by Hedrik Whale"—and hastily returned it to the table.

This night was proving far too long, he thought.

"Perhaps we should go," he said to his companion. "It's obvious we're rousing him from his, ah, bed, and—"

"Go?" a deep voice boomed out. "Bloody hell. But you've only just arrived."

Denzil blinked for a moment as he turned, thinking a bear had come trundling out from between the bookcases where Lizzie had disappeared earlier, but then he realized it was only their host—all three hundred pounds of him, wrapped in a bearskin. His own hairy legs protruded from underneath, appearing oddly thin. Lizzie came up behind him, dressed now in a loose Arab-styled robe.

"Tea for everyone?" she asked.

"Or something stronger?" Henkie boomed.

His voice, Denzil remembered as he fought the impulse to rub his ears, was always this loud.

"Tea would be fine," Denzil said. "Wonderful, really."

"I'll have the something stronger," Taupin said.

A half hour later they sat around a potbellied coal stove that stood in a corner of the warehouse given over to be a makeshift sort of kitchen. Lizzie and Denzil were both on their second cups of tea. Denzil had lost track of how much whiskey Taupin and their host had consumed. Amenities had taken up most of that half hour as Henkie and Taupin brought each other up-to-date on what they'd been up to since the last time they'd gotten together, but finally Taupin got around to relating the reason behind their visit.

"Oh, I never liked that Widow," Lizzie said. "She's always about his lordship's office, complaining of this, wanting that."

"Not to mention what a pissant Tremeer is," Henkie added. "Bloody stupid constables."

"Had another run-in with them?" Taupin asked.

Henkie nodded. "Don't start me on it."

Yes, Denzil thought. Don't.

Happily, after a moment of dark brooding, Henkie turned to Denzil.

"Brengy's got the right of it," he said. "There's the stink of magic in the air tonight."

Not to mention the odor of unwashed bodies, Denzil thought. He stole a glance at Lizzie. How could she sleep with the man?

"But I think we can help you," Henkie added.

"You see?" Taupin put in.

"How can you help?" Denzil asked.

"Well, it won't be me, directly," Henkie said. "We'll have to ask Briello."

Denzil could only stare at him. "Pardon?"

"My mate, John Briello."

"The *dead* John Briello?"

"Who else?"

Denzil turned to Taupin. "I really think we should go, you."

"Don't be so hasty to judge what you don't bloody well understand," Henkie told him.

"Dead men don't talk," Denzil said flatly. "But whiskey does."

Henkie's eyes went hard. "Are you calling me a liar?"

All of Denzil's instincts told him to back down, but that simply wasn't his way. He pushed up his glasses with a stiff finger and met Henkie's gaze, glare for glare.

"If you tell me that I can get advice from a dead man," he said, "then yes, I'm calling you a liar."

Henkie glared at him, then burst into a sudden laugh. "Oh, I like you, Denzil Gossip. You've a dry wit, and that's rare in bloody brain-dead Bodbury, isn't it just?" Turning to Taupin, he added, "But we'll have to blindfold him."

"Denzil won't mind," Taupin replied. "After tonight he'll realize he's been going all through his life with blinders on."

Denzil shot him a hard stare and got to his feet. "I've got a friend to find and I don't have time to—"

"Oh, do sit down," Henkie boomed.

"Don't take it so hard," Lizzie said. "They're just teasing you."

"I'm not in the mood for jokes tonight," Denzil said stiffly.

"Oh, but it's no joke," she assured him. "Briello really will be able to help you. I've heard him talk myself."

"But—"

"I know it doesn't make sense, but then not much does in this world, does it?"

"No more talk," Henkie said. "Lizzie, get us a scarf to blindfold our friend here—you will allow yourself to be blindfolded?"

"Well, I don't—"

"Good."

"Don't worry," Lizzie said as she came up behind him. She took off his glasses and stuck them in the breast pocket of his jacket, then drew the scarf across his eyes. "I'll make sure you don't take a tumble."

She took him by the arm and then led him off before he could frame another protest.

They walked across wood first—Denzil could hear their footsteps on the planking—then, after the creak of a door of some sort, they were outside, on cobblestones. Denzil could smell the sea in the air. The wind tousled his hair. Moments later they were in another building, then descending a stone stairway. Many stairs and turns later, he heard the creak of another door, and then the scarf was removed. He stood blinking in lantern light, feeling a little disoriented as he fished his glasses from his pocket.

He found himself in a cellar of some sort, only it had been fashioned after a Victorian sitting room. Taupin held the lantern, which cast a bright glow over the furnishings. The walls, not surprisingly, were festooned with Henkie's artwork. Lizzie stood beside him, the scarf hanging from her hands, a reassuring smile on her lips. And Henkie—Henkie stood, still barefoot and wrapped in his bearskin, beside the preserved corpse of a derelict that was leaning up against the far wall.

Except for a somewhat withered look about its skin, and the stiff posture of its limbs, the corpse could almost pass as a living man, Denzil thought. Except a living man didn't have a silver coin in each eye.

Denzil swallowed dryly, sure now that he'd got himself caught up in the clutches of a group of Bedlamites. He gave the door behind him a surreptitious glance, but while it didn't appear to be locked or barred, he doubted he'd be able to get it open and flee before one or another of his captors brought him down.

He turned to Taupin, an admonishment taking shape on his tongue, but before he could speak, Henkie, who had been explaining Denzil's problem to the corpse all this while, was just finishing up.

"So, old mate. Can you tell us where she's gone and bloody well lost herself?"

Denzil, unable to help himself, had to look at the corpse. And then his jaw fell slack.

For the corpse moved. The coins in its eyes blinked eerily in the lantern light as the dead man slowly turned its head towards him. The jaw creaked as it opened and the sound that issued forth was like the wind from an open grave.

But it *was* a voice.

The corpse *could* speak.

"I can see her," it said. "She seems very small."

"La, Jey," Denzil murmured in a hoarse voice. He felt decidedly faint.

"I do believe the sea has her in its grip," the corpse went on. "Out by New Dock. But she's very small. The size of a mouse, seems, but that can't be, can it?"

It turned its head towards Henkie, silver-coin eyes flashing again, and gave a dusty-sounding laugh.

"I'm one to talk about what can or can't be—aren't I just, Henkie?"

It was done with mirrors, Denzil was trying to convince himself. Or they'd drugged him. Hypnotized him. Driven him bloody mad. . . .

"You're sure about that?" Henkie was asking. "She's the size of a bloody wee mouse and floating in the sea?"

"Oh, yes," that dry voice replied.

"In a boat?"

"No, she's wet and shivering and won't last long."

Ventriloquism, Denzil decided. That's how it was being done. And there was someone behind the wall, manipulating the corpse in some manner to make it look as though it could move.

"Thank you," Henkie was saying.

"Do you have something for me?" the corpse asked.

"A new painting—it's almost done."

Now those dry lips actually smiled. Denzil couldn't tear his gaze away from the sight.

"That will be wonderful," the corpse said.

And then it went still.

"We'll have to hurry if you want to rescue your friend," Henkie said.

Lizzie started towards Denzil with the scarf, but he shook his head and crossed the room until he stood directly in front of the corpse.

"Rubbish," he said, lifting a hand towards its face. "The thing's not real. The dead can't—"

Suddenly the corpse's arm lifted up and dead fingers gripped his wrist.

"The size of a mouse," it said, blowing a grave-cold breath in his face. "Now how do you suppose *that* came about?"

Denzil shrieked and jumped back. His glasses flew from his nose. He tripped over a table and would have fallen, except that Henkie caught and steadied him. In that moment of confusion, the corpse returned to its initial position. Denzil stared at it.

Lizzie, who had caught his glasses, handed them to him. With trembling fingers, Denzil got them back into place. He couldn't seem to stop his hands from shaking, so he stuck them in his pockets.

"Come along," Henkie said. "We don't have long to help your friend."

"But—but . . ."

The scarf came over his eyes, blessedly removing the corpse from his sight. Moments later they were leaving the room and beginning the trek up the series of stairways once more.

"It just couldn't be," Denzil kept muttering as he let himself be led along. "*How* could it be?"

It couldn't. It was that simple. He'd imagined—been made to imagine—the whole ridiculous affair. There was no other logical explanation.

But he could still feel the grip of those dead fingers on his wrist.

Four Bare Legs Together

And, after all, what is a lie? 'Tis but
The truth in masquerade.

—LORD BYRON,
from *Don Juan, canto XI*

*L*e n a listened to the dead phone for a few moments after Bett had cut the connection, then slowly cradled the receiver.

This wasn't the way things were supposed to go, she thought.

She got up and hobbled over to the window to look outside. A misting rain was sprinkling on the Promenade, giving the surface of the street a shiny wet sheen under the streetlights. Beyond the stone wall separating the sidewalk from the rocky beach below, the waters of Mount's Bay swelled and dropped on the timeless wheel of the tides.

Daddy had made a mistake, she realized. She really shouldn't be here.

It wasn't that she didn't think she could get the job done. And for all her lack of success so far, not to mention the stupid accident with the bike, it was kind of fun. Just *like* a spy novel, never mind what Bett had to say about it.

But to be a part of a murder . . . to have foreknowledge, and not do anything about it. . . .

That didn't sit right.

She didn't know Clare Mabley, except from the files she'd read on the woman. She owed Mabley nothing. But that didn't make a shred of difference to the way she felt at the moment. The woman didn't deserve to die—not simply because she was

Janey Little's friend and she was interfering with Bett's plans for Little.

She wondered if Daddy even knew what Bett was up to here. It was one thing to be ruthless in business. She could even condone a little strong-arming, if it became necessary and there was no other option, but not when it was directed at an innocent party. And it made her a little sick to understand just how much Bett would enjoy it.

Because he *would* enjoy it. She knew that much. Whenever she was in his presence, she could sense that core of controlled violence that lay just below the surface in him, straining to get loose. She knew enough about men to recognize that aspect in them when it was present. There were those who talked the tough talk, and then there were those who just did it, and they were the ones you really had to look out for. Because their violent impulses owed nothing to common anger. Instead they were born out of either an amoral view of the world or, worse, a sick need to hurt others.

In Bett, it was probably both.

Maybe the Order, through Madden, had made a mistake in sending him here.

She could still remember the night that her father had initiated her into the secrets of the Order. She was seventeen and had thought the whole idea of this secret group of old men and women who wanted to rule the world to be both goofy and terrifying. But it hadn't just been old men and women waiting for her the night that the Order of the Grey Dove welcomed her into their ranks.

There were three generations represented in that church in upstate New York where they had gathered, men and women both. People old enough to be her grandparents—though her own, from both sides of the family, were dead and Daddy would never tell her which of them, if any, had been members. Then there was her father's generation. And lastly, teenagers, only one of them younger than she was herself.

They were all masked—costumed, she'd thought at the time,

like the members of some Elk Lodge getting ready for a parade, though if the Order was a lodge, then it was a sinister one. There had been blood, and she still didn't know if it had been human as one of the other younger initiates had told her later, and there had been a ritual. And there had been the tattoo.

It would all have seemed ridiculous if it hadn't been so deadly serious. And then, as years went by and she was initiated into the deeper mysteries, when she found that you could get any-thing—*anything*—you wanted, just through the use of your will, it hadn't seemed frivolous at all anymore.

Did you want to live forever?

The Order claimed it was possible. Many of the older members avowed to be well over a hundred, though not one of them seemed more than sixty.

Was it prosperity you desired?

They were all wealthy and even though Lena had been born into wealth herself, who didn't want more?

Did you want to wield power over others?

Through the proper use of your will, the Order's secrets taught you how to control the sheep. And if sometimes more physical manipulations—such as the surreptitious use of drugs or other external machinations—were necessary, there was a kind of magic needed to utilize them to their fullest potential as well.

Lena had thrived in that environment, for all that she main-tained a somewhat distant and decadent attitude towards the Order. Why give them the satisfaction of thinking they con-trolled her as well? For she saw that as another aspect of the Order, how the elder members lorded it over the younger; viewed them, in fact, as another kind of sheep.

In many ways the Order was no different than society at large. One rose through its ranks the same as one did in the business world, or in the whirl of society.

Lena preferred to take what she could use, but played their game as little as possible. She had other uses for the knowledge that she'd acquired. Rather than being on the Order's lower rungs, she elected to create her own little circles of power, making sure only that they didn't interfere with any of the Order's.

It only backfired at times like these, when her father, frustrated at his lack of control over his own daughter—and undoubtedly embarrassed when in the company of other members of the Order because of that same lack of control—sent her off on a chore such as this to prove that he could still govern her.

Usually she made the best of it, getting through the task as quickly as possible so that she could return to the social rounds of Boston in which she was a leader, rather than a sycophant. Unfortunately, this time Felix Gavin had to come along to complicate matters.

In some way that she still didn't quite understand, he'd cut through the shield of debutante bullshit by which she held the world at bay, and walked straight into her heart. Making her actually care what happened to someone else for a change. And the worst of it was, it didn't feel bad. Except for the hopeless feelings she had for him.

So what was she supposed to do?

Sighing, she took her gaze from the world outside her window and looked down at her wrist. The grey dove, symbol of her father's precious Order. Were those old men and women at all aware of the dark malicious streak that ran through Bett?

Probably.

But she still felt she should call her father.

She limped back to the bed and had the receiver raised in her hand, before she cradled it once more, the call unmade. Another realization had come to her.

Daddy was sending Jim Gazo over to serve as her bodyguard, but there was no way Jim would make it here before tomorrow morning at the earliest. Until then, she was on her own. If she called her father, and Daddy got Madden to call Bett off, Bett would come by to take it out on her. He'd probably go ahead and kill Mabley anyway, then come back and hurt her, and damn the consequences. Just like he really would kill Felix if she didn't find a way to keep him here tonight.

Michael Bett was just that kind of man.

Until tomorrow, she was on her own. Neither Daddy nor the Order could help her until then. Which brought her circling back to that same question: Just what the hell did she do now?

Self-preservation came first. No question there. But the Mabley woman . . . Could she really just stand by and let Bett kill her? And what about Felix? She was having very weird feelings when it came to him. She found she didn't want to lie to him. God help her, she wanted a chance to win him away from Janey Little, honestly and without subterfuge.

It wasn't going to work. None of it was. So she was going to have to settle for a trade-off. Mabley's life in exchange for the lie that would keep Felix here. And maybe, when it all came out in the end, he'd understand. Because Mabley was Felix's friend as well, wasn't she?

She picked up the phone again.

"Hello, Willie?" she said when the connection was made. "No, don't worry. He's not around. Yeah, I don't much care for him either. Listen, this is important. Remember that friend of Janey Little's that Gavin was with this morning? That's right, the Mabley woman. Someone's going to try to kill her tonight.

"No, I don't know who," she lied. "It's just important that she isn't hurt. Can you call that friend of yours in Mousehole and have him deal with it? No, right now. The last I heard, she was on her way home from the Little house. There's a thousand dollars in it for you"—let him figure out the exchange rate—"if she makes it through the night—the same again for your friend.

"Thanks, Willie. I kind of thought you'd be interested. Just make sure you don't screw this up, because—"

There was a knock at her door.

"I'll talk to you later, Willie," she said and hung up.

She ran a hand through her hair and looked nervously across the room.

"Who's there?" she called.

"Felix."

Okay, she thought. I've done my part, now it's up to you to do yours, Felix. Because if you blow it, we're both screwed.

"Just a sec," she called.

She gave herself a quick look in the mirror as she hobbled over to the door, wincing when she put too much weight on the bad ankle. The pained look on her face when she opened the door owed nothing to acting.

"I'm sorry to be coming by so late," Felix began, "but—"

"God," she said, interrupting him. "You look terrible."

He gave her a faint smile, but she didn't miss the pain that was lodged there in his eyes. He was soaking wet, short hair plastered to his scalp, clothing drenched. He had a duffel bag over one shoulder, a square black box on the floor by his side. In his hand he held a cane.

Got it from Clare Mabley, she thought, with a twinge of uneasiness. Willie, you'd better come through for me.

"Come on in," she added.

"I can't stay. . . ."

"That's okay. Just come in for a moment. What did you do, go for a swim?"

"No. It's just that it's raining—"

"I can see that." She took the cane from him and used it to step back from the door. "That's better. You're an angel, Felix. Really. Where did you find it? Come in," she added when he hesitated out in the hall.

"I really can't stay." He dug about in his pocket and handed her a business card. "The cane belongs to a friend of mine—"

"*The* friend?"

He shook his head, the pain deepening in his eyes. "No. But I saw her tonight. She—that is we . . . I don't really want to talk about it."

"So don't. It's okay. You don't have to do anything you don't want to, Felix."

"I just came by to give you the cane. I got it from the woman whose name is on the card. If you could just drop it by the shop when you're done."

"No problem. It was kind of her to lend it."

"Yeah, well, Clare's a good person."

"I'll look forward to meeting her."

Don't screw up, Willie, she thought.

"I'm heading on to London," Felix added. "I just have to get away."

Lena nodded. "Sometimes that's all you can do." She gave him a sympathetic look, then added, "Will you *come* in? Just long enough to dry off a bit, at least. You look like—well, now I know what they mean about something the cat dragged in."

"I don't think—"

"I won't bite."

When he still hesitated, she moved forward—putting on a good show of how much the movement hurt her—and reached for the black case by his foot.

"Okay," he said, picking it up for himself. "But just for a moment."

Lena moved back to clear the doorway. "Why don't you hang your coat on the chair by the window where the heater can dry it off a bit? I'll put on some tea. It's nice the way English hotels have a kettle and the makings in each room, don't you think?"

She kept up a cheerful chatter as he hung up his coat and then lowered himself onto the sofa. Little puddles formed on the carpet around his shoes. Outside, the drizzle had turned into a real downpour. A gust of wind drove a splatter of rain against the window.

"Listen," Lena said after she'd put on the water and sat down on the edge of the bed. "It looks to me like you're on the road because you don't have a place to stay."

"I'll be all right."

"I'm sure you will, but why don't you stay here tonight? No strings. You take the couch, I get the bed. The trains aren't running at this time of night anyway, are they?"

Felix shook his head. "I just have to get out of town."

Would that be enough? Lena wondered. She ran Bett's conversation back.

You're going to keep him there, in your room, and you're not going to let him leave. . . .

No, she realized. It wasn't going to be enough. Because when it came to Bett, she didn't trust what could happen.

She glanced at Felix who was staring at his shoes, shoulders drooped.

Shit. And *he* wasn't going to stay.

That didn't leave her any other choice.

She wore a ring on either hand. Each had a small storage space under the gem. The settings were fixed in such a manner that only using the one hand, it was just a moment's work to twist the ring around, open the secret compartment, and spill its contents into a drink. The powder in each was completely tasteless. The one in the right was a knockout drug. The one in the left was something a little more special. It was based on a variation of thiopentone that had been developed by a member of the Order, and worked not only as a general muscle relaxant and reflex suppressor, but simultaneously broke down the will, leaving the target utterly susceptible to suggestion.

Lena considered which to use. The new feelings that Felix had woken in her told her that rendering him unconscious was all she needed to do to fulfill her bargain with Bett. But considering that she wasn't going to have another chance—not like this, not ever with him. . . .

If he'd only loosen up.

But he wouldn't.

She felt both guilt and excitement as she made her decision. With her back to him, she emptied the contents from the ring on her left hand into a teacup, then poured the tea over it.

"Milk? Sugar?" she asked.

"A little of both."

She added the two and stirred vigorously. Felix appeared at her shoulder, startling her, but he'd only come over to save her the awkward trip back to where he was sitting.

They talked some more, Lena eyeing him surreptitiously, waiting for the drug to take effect. She didn't have that long to wait. Very soon Felix began slurring his words. His movements grew more languid, until finally he just sat there with a glazed look in his eyes.

"Felix?" Lena said.

"Mmm . . . ?"

"How are you doing?"

"Uhmm. . . ."

"You must be feeling a little uncomfortable in those wet clothes. Why don't we hang them there with your jacket and let them dry out."

She got up and, using the cane to keep the weight off her ankle, went over to help him stand. She started him on the buttons of his shirt, and soon he was removing it, and the rest of his clothes, on his own.

"You've got a very nice body," Lena said. "Have you ever done any weight lifting?"

"Uhmm. . . ."

The drug didn't do much for conversation, but Lena wasn't in the mood for conversation anyway. It had been developed for one of the Order's rituals that she wasn't yet privy to, but she knew it was of a sexual nature—something dreamed up by one of the elder members, no doubt, who used it to get their rocks off with some sweet young things that they couldn't otherwise get close to. Sex magic wasn't an aspect of the Order's teachings that Lena had explored to any great extent, preferring to keep that aspect of her life as entertainment.

And she was being entertained now; the last of her guilty feelings fled as she led Felix to the bed. Removing her own clothes, she got up beside him and ran her hands up and down the hard length of his body.

How much was he even going to remember of this? she wondered as she began to stroke his penis and felt it stiffen under her manipulations. Not much, if her previous experiences with the drug were anything to go by.

But she'd remember.

And he'd have such dreams, never imagining their source. . . .

2 .

It was a dark and stormy night, Clare said to herself as she made her slow way home. Not a creature was stirring, not even a mouse; but hark, what light through yonder window shines . . . ?

A faint smile touched her lips.

You do read too much, Mabley, she thought.

The trouble really was that she remembered everything she read—especially clichés and homilies and the like. She liked to string them together into nonsense sentences and paragraphs—a habit picked up from too much time spent on her own when she was young. Other similar amusements included taking the top thirty songs from the current music charts, or the headlines from the various newspapers in the newsagent's while she was queued up to be served, or titles from a row of books on one of the shelves in the shop, and seeing how they read, all bunched and tumbled together.

Take Thomas Hardy.

Under the greenwood tree, far from the madding crowd, a pair of blue eyes. . . .

Did what? Juded the obscure?

She shook her head. Adding the "D"—that wasn't quite fair.

Perhaps if she included poem titles.

Under the greenwood tree, far from the madding crowd, the ghost of the past, god-forgotten, weathers the return of the native.

Not bad. There was almost a kind of poetry in the way it—

She paused and peered back down the steep incline of Raginnis Hill, aware of the sudden sensation that she was no longer alone. But there was no one there. Turning, she had the wind in her face. She wiped the rain from her eyes and cheeks with the back of her hand and continued up the hill, the titles of Thomas Hardy's books and poems forgotten.

The night's damp chill had got under her nor'wester and jumper, but that didn't account for the unexpected chill she felt. There was an odd feeling in the air—an electricity that owed nothing to what lightning there might be lurking in the storm clouds above her. Everything seemed a bit on edge—or it had ever since this whole business with Felix and Janey and the Gaffer had come about. People skulking around Mousehole, looking for old William Dunthorn manuscripts. The burglary.

Shakespeare, she thought, trying to take her mind from the peculiar turn it had taken.

Much ado about nothing . . . the tempest. . . .

Bloody hell.

She looked back again, the skin on her back crawling, but could still see nothing out of the ordinary. Just peaceful Mousehole, mostly dark now because it was getting late and no one stayed up much past closing time anyway—even on a Saturday night. The narrow dark street, unwinding steeply behind her between the houses, slick with rain. The shadows thick in the alleyways. . . .

She was spooking herself and she knew it, but couldn't stop herself because nothing felt right.

Don't be a silly goose, she told herself.

Chiding didn't help either.

She tried to hurry, but with the damp in her bones and the steepness of the road, she could only go so fast. A turtle could walk faster. A slug could crawl more quickly. She simply wasn't an efficient walking machine, and that was all there was to it.

The wind quickened, buffeting the rain against her with such force that she had to bend her head, her free hand pulling the neck of the nor'wester more closely to her chin. Under her hat, the skin of her neck was prickling in unhappy anticipation of something horrible—the feeling growing so strong that she finally had to turn again only to find—

She jumped, she was so startled, and nearly lost her balance.

"My God," she said to the muffled figure who had come up behind her. "You gave me quite a turn, coming up on me like . . ."

Her voice trailed off as she took in the long raincoat, the hat with the goggles peering at her from just below its low brim, the scarf pulled across the lower part of the face, effectively hiding all features. Her heart jumped into a double-time rhythm as the stranger took his left hand from his pocket and brought out a large folded knife. As though by magic, the knife's blade came out of its handle with a quick snap of the man's wrist.

"N-no," Clare said. "Please. . . ."

"We're going for a walk, you and I," the man said, his voice muffled by his scarf. "Up by the cliffs, I think."

Cold fear paralyzed Clare's muscles for long moments, then she gathered her wits about her and swung her cane. The man dodged the blow easily. Clare wasn't so lucky when he struck her with his free hand. The blow knocked her cane from her grip and sent her down to the road where she scraped her hands on the pavement. Her bad leg offered up a protesting flare of pain at its mistreatment.

Before she could scrabble away, the man was down beside her, right hand on her shoulder, forcing her down, the knife held up near her face.

"We can do this pleasantly," he said. "A stroll up by the cliffs and no pain. Or I can drag you up there by your hair and we'll see if the rain can wash away the blood as quickly as I can make it flow."

The goggles stared at her, soulless bug-eyes that offered up no hope.

"It could take some time," he added.

Clare opened her mouth to scream, then closed it with a snap as the point of the knife touched her cheek just below her left eye. The rain streamed onto her face, making her vision blur.

"No cries." The voice was so damned conversational. "No screams. Wouldn't do you any good, anyway. There's no one to hear you—not tonight."

The knife pulled back a bit, floating in the air between them.

The man held it with a casual familiarity. Clare stared at its menacing point. Dimly she took in the nightmarish image of the man—just a shadowy bulk, featureless with his hat, goggles, and scarf. She had an odd moment of total objectivity. She noticed the crease in the brim of the hat, as though it had been folded in a pocket for too long. The missing button at the top of the raincoat's right lapel. The odd little tattoo on the man's left wrist.

Then he hauled her to her feet and gave her a shove in the direction of the coast path. He closed the knife and returned it to his pocket.

"My—my cane. . . ."

"Do without it," the man said.

"But—"

The knife appeared again, the blade flicking open with a snap.

"You're beginning to bore me," the man said. "Don't bore me. You wouldn't like me when I'm bored."

The knife moved back and forth in front of her face. She took a staggering step back, but he closed the distance again easily.

"You wouldn't like me at all," he said softly.

3 ·

Janey was having a miserable time of it. The wipers of her little Reliant Robin had decided to work only at half power, which left them less than effective in clearing the heavy rain from her windshield. The defrost wasn't working properly either, so she had to drive with the driver's side window open. By the time she was halfway to Newlyn, her left shoulder and arm were soaked.

And then there was the reason she was out on the road tonight in the first place. . . .

She drove through Newlyn and Penzance, going too fast, but not really caring. Her attention was divided between keeping the Robin on the road, trying to spot Felix on either side of the verge, and roundly cursing herself for the fool she'd been when he'd come by the Gaffer's house earlier. Why couldn't she have *listened* to him, instead of going off half cocked the way she had.

It was her bloody temper.

She banged her fist on the steering wheel in frustration by the time she was on the far side of Penzance. The buses and trains weren't running at this time of night, but what if he'd been hitching? He might have already gotten a ride. . . .

She cruised back through Penzance, crisscrossing through the town and going slower now, without any better luck. Finally, she pulled over to the side of the street just before she reached the Newlyn Bridge at the end of the North Pier. She stared morosely out the windshield. The wipers went feebly back and forth, pushing the rain about more than clearing the window.

This was pointless. He could be anywhere.

Then she remembered Clare saying something about Felix planning to drop off a cane to that Lena woman before he left. On a night like this, he'd be mad to try hitching out of town. Maybe he was still in the woman's room.

Janey's spirits lifted slightly. The American would be staying in a hotel.

She made a U-turn and started east again on the Promenade.

A hotel. Of course. Then her spirits sagged again. Only which one?

She got lucky at the third hotel she tried. Ron Hollinshead, an old schoolmate of hers, was behind the counter. He looked up from the magazine he was reading as she came in. Pushing back his dark hair from his brow, he stood up, a smile crinkling his features. On his feet he only topped Janey by a few inches.

"Hello there, Janey," he said, peering past her to where her car was pulled up to the curb. "Car giving you a bit of agro?"

"Don't talk to me about that car."

Ron came around the counter. "Want me to take a look at it?"

"No. It's not that. I just—do you have an American woman staying here? All I know is her first name: Lena."

Ron nodded. "Lena Grant. She's been here a few days. Thinks she's a bloody princess. What do you want with her?"

"Has she had any visitors this evening?" Janey asked.

"About a half hour or so ago—rough-looking bloke. Looked like he'd been swimming in the bay."

"Did he have any baggage?"

"A duffel and a case of some sort. What's this all about, Janey?"

"What room's she in?"

"I can't tell you that."

"It's important."

Ron looked uncomfortable. "But it's privileged information. I could lose my job if I let people go about bothering the guests. Be fair, Janey."

"I'm not going to bother anyone," Janey said. "Honestly. I just want to talk to the fellow who's visiting her."

"I don't think so," Ron said. "This time of night, there's not much guesswork needed to know what they're up to."

Janey did an admirable job of keeping down the sudden flare of anger that rose up in her.

I sent him away, she told herself. If he's in bed with her, it's my fault. I'm going to stay calm. I'm just going to talk to him. And maybe tear out all of *her* bloody hair. . . .

"I'm sorry, Janey," Ron said. "But there's rules and I've got to stick to them."

Janey sighed. "You won't tell me?"

"Not won't—can't."

"Then I'll just have to find out for myself."

Ron caught her arm as she started for the stairs. "For Christ's sake, Janey. Don't cause a scene."

"I won't. Just tell me what room they're in." She found a disarming smile to charm him with. "Come on, Ron. It's really very important."

"Bloody hell."

"No one has to know who told me," she assured him.

"You won't start shouting and carrying on?"

"Promise," she said and crossed her heart.

I'll kill her quietly, she added to herself.

"If I lose my job . . ."

"You won't, Ron. I'll be up to have a quick bit of a chat and out again, quiet as a mouse. No one'll even know I was here."

He sighed heavily and looked around the lobby as though expecting to find his employer lurking about, just waiting for him to break the rules before she booted him out and then he'd be on the dole again.

"All right," he said. "Room five—top of the stairs on your right. But mind you don't—"

Janey nodded. "I'll be quiet as a ghost."

A ghost of retribution, she thought, then forced that thought away. She was going to stay calm—no matter what she found in the bloody woman's room. She was *not* going to cause a scene.

"Thanks, Ron," she said.

She gave his arm a quick squeeze, then hurried up the stairs before he could change his mind. She looked back down when she reached the first landing to find him staring up at her, obviously still distressed. She put a finger to her lips and tiptoed exaggeratedly on up until she was out of his sight.

I'm going to be calm, she reminded herself as she reached the door with the brass plate that read "Number Five."

Easy to say. Her pulse was drumming wildly as she reached up to rap on the door with her knuckles and the last thing she felt was calm. She paused before knocking and put her ear to the wood paneling. She could hear an odd sound, but the thickness of the door made it impossible to identify.

Maybe they were asleep. Together in the same bed. Exhausted after a frenzied bout of lovemaking. . . .

She was going to kill that woman. She was going to tear out her—

Calm, she warned herself. Be calm.

She knocked, and got no response. But she could sense that they were in there. Empty rooms had a different feel about them. And there was that faint, rhythmical sound.

She knocked a second time, then tried the handle when there

was still no answer. It turned easily under her hand. She flung the door open and stepped into the room where her worst fears were realized.

A naked woman was astride Felix on the bed, riding him as though he was some thoroughbred stallion, hands on his shoulders, breasts bobbing as her hips went up and down. She turned wide, startled eyes to Janey, pausing in midmotion with Felix's penis still halfway inside her. Felix never moved, never turned.

"What the hell are *you* doing here?" the woman demanded.

Janey looked around the room for the nearest thing with which to hit her.

4 ·

Davie Rowe buttoned his shirt across his broad chest and stepped into his trousers, right leg first.

Two bloody hundred quid, he thought as he tucked in his shirttails and then zipped up his trousers. And for doing something legal in the bargain. Wasn't that just something.

"Is that you, Davie?"

Davie glanced at the wall separating his bedroom from his mother's.

"Yes, Mum."

"Who was that on the phone, then?"

Her voice was closer now.

Oh, do stay in bed, Davie thought. But there wasn't much chance of that.

"Just a mate," he said.

His mother appeared in his doorway, a worn, old flowered housecoat wrapped around her thin body.

"Not that Willie Keel, was it?"

Davie shook his head. "It was Darren Spencer. He got himself a flat up by the quarry and needs a hand."

"Because I don't like that Keel chap," his mother went on as though she hadn't heard him. "He's the one what got you in trouble before and he'll do it again, give him half a chance. You mark my words, Davie, he's a bad sort and—"

Davie cut her off with a quick kiss on the cheek.

"I really must go, Mum. Darren's waiting."

"Yes, well. It's important to stand by your friends," his mother said. "Not that I saw Darren stand by you when you went to prison. Where was he then, I ask you? But now, when he needs himself a spot of help at—what time *is* it?"

"Time for me to go. You get back to bed, Mum. I won't be long."

His mother nodded. "Mind you take a coat and hat, now. It's a proper flood out there tonight."

"I will."

He found his boots by the door where he'd dropped them when he came in earlier and quickly laced them up. His mother continued to prattle as he shrugged into a thick raincoat and pushed a fisherman's cap down over his unruly brown curls.

"A big lad like you," his mother said as he opened the front door, "can still catch his death of cold."

"I'll be careful, Mum."

He closed the door and stepped gratefully into the street, preferring the physical discomfort of the rain to his mother's nagging. She meant well, he knew, but her incessant nattering got on his nerves something fierce. Of course it was his own fault, wasn't it? Almost thirty and still living at home with his mum. And didn't that give Willie a laugh, just? Still, what else could he do? He couldn't afford his own lodgings and if he didn't look after the old woman, then who would? Not his father— God rest his soul—and they had no other family since the cousins moved to Canada.

A fine how-do it was when the only Rowes left in Mousehole were a grumbling old woman and her half-arsed crook of a son. Such times. Things were better when Dad was alive, bringing in the odd bit of contraband to augment the family's poor fishing income. And in his grandfather's day . . . time was the Rowes were the best smugglers this side of up country.

But that was in days long past, when the pilchard still ran and men used the wind, not motors, to propel their ships. This was now. At the moment his only concern was the two hundred quid he had riding on finding Clare Mabley and keeping her alive.

Two hundred quid!

As he hurried across the village through the rain to Raginnis Hill, Davie wondered how much Willie was keeping for himself. And he wondered as well about who would want to hurt Clare. He'd done some bad things in his own time, and would undoubtedly do more, but he could honestly say that he'd never hurt a disabled person, nor stolen from one either.

He couldn't understand a man who would.

Because of the heavy rain, Davie was almost upon the two figures before he saw them. Clare was hobbling painfully up the hill without her cane, while the man with her kept shoving her when she slowed down.

"Here!" Davie cried. "Lay off her, you!"

The man turned. His left hand dipped into the pocket of his overcoat and came back with a knife. Davie took in the man's odd muffled appearance and the knife with a touch of uneasiness. Bugger was decked out like the villain in some bad American movie, he thought. But the knife was no joke. Nor the assured way the man held it, cutting edge up.

Davie couldn't help but picture that blade plunging into his belly and then tearing up his chest until it was stopped by his breastbone. . . .

Still he held his ground.

Two hundred quid, he thought.

And besides, he rather liked Clare.

"Got yourself a knife, have you?" he said. "Makes you feel grandly brave, I'll wager."

The man's only reply was a sudden lunge forward. The knife cut through Davie's coat, but missed the skin as Davie sidestepped the attack. Before the man could swing about, Davie struck him squarely in the side of the head with one meaty fist and dropped his attacker in his tracks.

Those knuckles were going to hurt come morning, Davie thought as he moved in to make sure the man stayed down.

Shaking his head, the man made it to his feet before Davie could reach him. He held the knife between them, effectively keeping Davie at bay. Then Davie spied Clare's cane lying where it had fallen on the wet pavement earlier.

Right, he thought. We'll end this quickly now.

He feinted towards the man, dodged the sweeping blow of the knife, and kicked the man's feet from under him. As Clare's attacker went tumbling to the pavement, Davie stepped quickly over to where the cane lay. He turned with it in hand, just as the man was rising.

"Fun's over, mate," Davie said. "Why don't you bugger off before you get seriously hurt."

The man roared inarticulately and charged. Davie swung the cane twice. One blow knocked the knife from the man's hand. Sidestepping out of the way, Davie delivered the second blow to the man's shoulder as he went by. The man stumbled against a low garden wall, turning quickly. His right arm now hung loosely at his side.

Broken, Davie thought. Or maybe the nerves had simply been struck numb. Either way, the man was in no shape to continue the fight.

Davie raised the cane again.

"I'm serious, mate," he said. "Bugger off or there'll be some real pain."

He could feel the man's hatred burning from the eyes hidden behind those odd goggles. It was a venomous rage that had no need for words to express itself. Davie had lost his cap in their brief struggle and the rain was plastering his curls to his head, running into his eyes. But he didn't move, didn't even blink, until the figure by the wall slowly sidled towards the left, then fled off down the hill.

Davie bent down and retrieved the man's knife, which he

pitched off into the darkness behind the nearest house below the road. He collected his sodden hat and shoved it into his pocket, then went to where Clare was crouching wide-eyed on the road.

"Oh, God, Davie," she said as he came near. "He was going to kill me."

Davie didn't quite know what to do now. He helped Clare to her feet, feeling stupid and awkward once she was standing on her own, holding her cane again.

"Yes, well . . ." he started, then he ran out of words.

"You saved my life, Davie."

"It's just, uh, lucky I happened by when I, uh, did."

Clare stepped a little closer and leaned against his arm. He could feel her trembling.

"I've never been so frightened before in all my life," she said.

"Well, he's, uh, gone now."

A new tremor went through Clare. "What if he comes back?"

"I doubt that."

It was getting a little easier to talk to her now.

"But if he does?" she asked. "We'd better call the police."

"No police," Davie said.

"But . . ." Clare turned to look up into his face. She blinked away rain, and then nodded. "Of course," she said. "You don't exactly get along with them, do you?"

Davie sucked on his bruised knuckles. "Not exactly. Did he hurt you?"

"No, I'm just a little shaken still—that's all."

"I'll walk you home," Davie said.

"This is very kind of you."

"You could call the police from your house," Davie went on. "Just don't mention me, that's all."

Clare nodded, letting herself be led on up the hill, past the bird hospital, to her front door.

"What could they do anyway?" she asked. "He's long gone now."

"Long gone," Davie agreed.

"But I should report it all the same, just so he doesn't attack someone else. Unless . . ." Her voice trailed off.

"Unless what?" Davie asked.

Clare shivered. Her fingers shook as she tried to fit her key to its lock. Davie took them from her and unlocked the door for her.

"I had the oddest feeling that he was after me in particular."

"Why would anyone want to hurt you?" Davie asked.

But he was thinking about two hundred quid as he spoke, and of Willie Keel. Someone had told Willie that this attack was going to happen. Someone who was willing to pay at least two hundred quid—probably double that when you took in Willie's share—to make sure that it didn't happen.

The only person Davie could think that would fit that bill was the American woman who was staying in Penzance. But why? And why Clare?

"I don't know," Clare said. "But someone does."

She stepped inside, then looked back at him.

"Will you come in for a bit?" she asked. "You've gotten all drenched. I could put on some tea."

"I suppose I could," Davie said. "Just so long as you don't phone the police while I'm here."

She gave him an odd look. "What've you been up to, Davie?"

"Nothing. I swear. I was just out walking, that's all. But if I'm here when the police come, they'll take me in all the same."

"Well, I can't have that happen," Clare said. "Not after you've helped me. But walking in the rain?"

"It helps clear my mind."

"There's a lot of that needed around here," Clare said.

"Pardon?"

"Nothing. Would you like that tea?"

"Please."

"I'll put the kettle on."

She hung up her coat by the door and started off down the hall to the kitchen. Davie hung up his own gear, then stood awkwardly by the coat rack until she called him into the kitchen.

"I feel better with you here," she said. "Safer. Did you see his face?"

"Not much to see, what with the goggles and scarf and all."

"That's just it. It fairly gives me the creeps just thinking about him."

Davie nodded and took a seat at the kitchen table. It *had* been creepy. And hurt or not, the man was still out there. He could come back. If he did, and Davie wasn't there to stop him, then Davie knew he could just kiss away his two hundred quid. Not to mention that Clare would be dead. . . .

"Do you have a phone I could use?" he asked.

Clare raised her eyebrows. "Are *you* going to phone the police now?"

"Not likely. I just wanted to call a mate I was supposed to be seeing to tell him I won't be by." The questioning look remained in her eyes. "I thought I should, uh, stay a bit," he added. "In case the bloke who attacked you decides to come back. The police wouldn't leave a man here with you, you see."

"That's a kind thought."

"Unless you'd rather I went . . . ?"

"No. I could make up a bed for you on the couch, if you like."

"I don't need much." He paused, then added, "The phone?"

"It's in the study," she said, pointing the way.

"Thanks."

As soon as he got to the telephone, Davie rang up Willie's number.

"You were spot on the money about that attack," he said when Willie answered.

"You had no trouble?"

"None to speak of. Do you know who he was?"

"No."

"Do you think he'll be back?"

"I hadn't thought of that," Willie said. "Is there a place nearby where you can watch Mabley's house?" He was quiet for a moment, obviously thinking, then added before Davie could speak,

"Of course there's this bloody weather, isn't there?"

"It's all right," Davie said. "I'm in Clare's house at the moment. She invited me in when I rescued her."

"Can you stay?"

"That's not a problem. What I want to know, Willie, is, what's this all about?"

"Haven't the faintest idea, mate. I just take the money and do the job. That's how you get ahead in this world."

"I'll remember that," Davie said, and then he rang off.

He looked around the room, at the books lining the walls, and wondered if Clare had actually read them all. He remembered her in school. She was still in primary when he was taking his exams to go to the comprehensive school in Penzance—exams that he'd failed. But he could remember how after the accident she'd been home for so long, and then going to school in her wheelchair, Janey Little always at her side.

She would have had plenty of time to have read all of these and more, he decided. He pulled a book at random from the shelves and flipped through its pages. He wondered what it was like to read something like this. As a boy, reading the weekly *Beano* was about the most he could manage. The most he ever read now were the soccer scores—and that was only after he'd had a good eyeful of the page-three girl. But books . . . give him a good film anytime—preferably one of the old ones where black was black and white was white and a man didn't get confused between the two the way it was so easy to in real life.

He hefted a volume, enjoying the feel of it in his hand. Films were all well and fine, but something like this. It had a good weight in your hand.

Clare was clever—had to be after reading all these books. And pretty, too. Funny how he'd never really thought of that before. You saw the cane and then that was as far as you looked.

"Ready for that tea?" Clare called from the kitchen.

"I'm on my way," he said.

Clever and pretty and easy to be with. And now someone was trying to kill her.

He put the book back.

Well, not if he had his say about the matter.

5 ·

"Felix, how *could* you?" Janey cried.

To find him in bed with this woman was the final slap in the face. The ultimate betrayal. Because she'd been willing to listen to him. She'd *believed* Clare when she had argued for his innocence. But to find him like this . . . to know that all the time he really had been playing her for a fool. . . .

The red tide of her anger lashed against the false calm that she'd held desperately in place for the past few hours.

"Felix!" she cried again. "Will you at least *look* at me?"

You drove him to this, a part of her protested, so why are you so angry? You sent him away into her arms.

That was bloody rubbish.

She'd sent him away—that much was true enough—but if he was really so innocent would he have rushed here to the American's bed?

"Felix!" she cried a third time, her voice going shrill.

Lena was very cool. She rose from her awkward position— Felix's penis slapping against his stomach as she got off him— and calmly covered her nakedness with a bathrobe.

"Get out of here," she told Janey as she belted the robe.

Her voice was pitched low, but there was iron behind it. It was a voice used to being obeyed. A voice reserved for servants.

Janey ignored her, all her attention on Felix.

He never moved. He never turned his head towards her. He just lay there on the bed, staring at the ceiling, his penis shrinking and soft. He looked ridiculous, but Janey could feel her heart breaking all over.

She took a step towards him. Lena moved forward, favouring her hurt leg, and stood between the bed and Janey.

"I said—" she began.

The woman's movement broke the spell that Janey had been under. Without even thinking about what she was doing, she shaped a fist and hit Lena in the stomach as hard as she could. She stepped aside as Lena buckled over, gasping. Lena's leg gave way under her and she fell to the carpet. Janey closed the distance that separated her from the bed. She moved her hand back and forth in front of Felix's face, waiting for his gaze to track the motion, but all he did was continue to stare at the ceiling.

Comprehension dawned on Janey, if not understanding.

"You've drugged him," she said, turning from the bed.

Realizing that, her anger didn't so much flee as it was redirected. But riding above it now was an awful fear for Felix. What had the woman given him? Would he recover?

Lena was recovering. Using the side of the bed for leverage, she pulled herself up from the floor and leaned against the bed. She flinched when Janey took a step towards her.

"Don't think . . . you can get away with this," Lena said. "I'll have you charged with assault, you stupid little—"

"You drugged him!" Janey cried, overriding the threat. "What did you give him?"

As she stepped closer still, Lena took a swing at her, fingers spread like a claw, long polished nails arching towards Janey's face. Janey dodged the feeble attack and slapped Lena, her hand leaving its imprint behind on the woman's cheek—sharp red against the pale skin. Lena winced. She put up her own hand to cover the stinging cheek, her own attack forgotten.

"*What* did you give him?" Janey demanded.

She made another threatening gesture with her hand when Lena didn't reply that quickly had the woman talking.

"He'll be fine. It's just a drug to leave him open to suggestion. It'll wear off in a few hours."

Her voice was surly, angry, but Janey didn't much care. She'd bully the woman right out of Cornwall if she could.

Keeping half an eye on Lena, she returned to the side of the bed.

"Felix?" she said. "Can you hear me?"

"Uuuh. . . ."

She caught up his hand and gave his arm a pull, which brought him sitting up in bed like a robot that could move stiffly on its own, but couldn't generate the locomotion without prompting. Janey glanced around the room until she spied his clothes lying on the floor. She gathered them up and gave them to him.

"Put these on," she said.

He held them on his lap, but stared numbly into some unseen distance.

Janey looked at Lena. All the fight seemed to have gone out of her except for a dark spark of anger that flashed deep in her eyes. Satisfied that she wouldn't complicate matters, Janey helped Felix dress. It wasn't much different from how she thought it would be clothing a mannequin. But she finally had him standing by the door, his duffel and accordion case standing out in the hall. Janey picked up Clare's cane as well. Let the woman crawl around on her knees.

"You're going to be sorry," Lena said suddenly.

"Oh, really?"

Janey was quite proud of the way she was keeping her temper in check.

"You don't have any idea of who I—"

"That's where you're wrong," Janey said. "I know exactly what kind of a person you are, *and* what you're here for."

She smiled coldly as Lena registered surprise.

"That's right," she added. "And maybe you can get anything you want with a snap of your fingers wherever it is that you come from, but it's different here. Here we take care of our own. The best thing you can do is hop on the first train to London and fly back home, because if you come 'round bothering us again, you'll have more than just me to deal with. I have a lot of friends in this area, Lena Grant, and we really do take care of our own."

"You don't—"

But Janey just shut the door on whatever the woman was about to say. She gave Felix a push down the hall, then lugging his duffel and accordion case, Clare's cane awkwardly stuck under her arm, she followed him to where he'd stopped at the top of the stairs.

"Down we go," she said and gave him another little nudge to get him mobile once more.

Ron met them at the bottom of the stairs, his anxiety almost comical. He looked closely at Felix who had paused once more, standing as still as a machine that had been switched off, then turned his questioning gaze towards Janey.

"I heard shouting," he began.

Janey nodded wearily. "Sorry about that. Did we wake anybody up?"

"No. It's just . . ." He looked at Felix again. "What's wrong with him?"

"She drugged him. Nice clientele you have staying in this place, Ron."

"We don't exactly pick and choose. Are you taking him to the hospital?"

Janey shook her head. "I'm taking him home."

"But—"

"About now," she said firmly, "it's the best place for him to be. I don't want him waking up in some hospital room not knowing how he got there."

Ron looked as though he had more to say, but then he just shrugged.

"Here," he said, taking the duffel and case from her. "Give me those."

He stowed them in the car while Janey led Felix out into the rain and got him to fold his bulk into the Reliant's small passenger seat.

"There's nothing more I can do?" Ron asked.

"No," Janey told him. She started up the car. "Thanks ever so much. You'd better get in out of the rain."

She flicked on the headlights and wipers. The latter were still misbehaving and pushed the water halfheartedly about on the windshield. Sighing, Janey rolled down her window and the rain came in. Ron stood watching them in the open door of the hotel.

Giving him a wave, Janey turned the car about once more and headed back towards Mousehole.

If she'd ever had a more miserable night, she couldn't think of when it had been.

6.

Lena watched the door close behind them. She lifted a hand to her cheek, which was still stinging. Her stomach hurt too. Opening her robe, she looked down to see a bruise forming.

She was not in good shape.

Slowly she rose to her feet and hobbled over to the window where she watched Janey Little's bizarre three-wheeled car pull away from in front of the hotel. She held a hand across her stomach, gently stroking the soreness, not caring that she stood with her robe open in the window where anyone passing by outside could see. But finally she belted it closed once more and sat down in a chair.

It was karma, she thought. She had been trying to do the right thing, but because she hadn't gone about it properly, it had all fallen apart. There had been a singular lack of focus. She hadn't drawn on the clean sharp strength of her will, but had let her body's pleasure centers rule her mind.

"Never think with your groin," Daddy had told her more than once. "That's the first rule of business and it goes for women as well as men—don't you forget it. Use your logic, not your libido. I've seen more comedowns brought about by business associates thinking with their brains in their groins instead of in their heads where they belong. . . ."

It made sense. It was good advice.

But she'd gone and broken that rule. She'd let her libido drag her into a situation where common sense would never have taken her. If she had just given Felix the knockout drug . . . rolled him up on the couch and then gone to bed . . . none of this unpleasantness would have happened.

But now that it had . . .

And when she thought of that little bitch waltzing in here like she owned the world . . .

Anger didn't solve anything either, but she indulged herself in it for a few moments all the same until she finally sighed. With an effort, she put it aside.

Don't get mad, get even.

But that just meant losing him forever. Not that she had a ghost of a chance in patching things up with him in the first place. Not that she even wanted to. He was just some big dumb sailor, wasn't he?

Except and but and damn it all. . . .

She considered the alien sensibility that had brought her to this present situation and realized, with a maudlin regard that was also unfamiliar, that her feelings for Felix Gavin hadn't changed. Not one little bit. He'd put a crack in the walls that she had raised so protectively around herself, squeezed his way through, into her heart and head, and now he wouldn't leave.

It wasn't just the way he'd dropped everything to help her this afternoon, where anyone in her own circle would have nodded sympathetically and just gone on, if they even bothered to notice in the first place. Nor was it the simple honesty that just seemed to shine out of his pores, or the attentiveness with which he'd listened to her blather on. Nor was it the fact that he had a terrific bod. . . .

She didn't know what it was. And what she didn't understand, upset her. Because it left her open to weakness. Because it had her sitting here feeling lost and lonely like all the rest of the stupid sheep in the world who couldn't have what they wanted. . . .

She remembered the feel of his skin against hers. The gentle strength of his hands. How she'd drawn his hardness deep inside her. Because of the drug, he hadn't been very energetic without prompting, it was true. If you stopped to think about it, it was almost a kind of necrophilia . . . but it had all felt so good. . . .

Her hand dropped between her legs and she leaned her head

against the back of the chair, closing her eyes as she imagined that it was his fingers, rubbing back and forth, his touch, his caring for her that fueled the hot flash that grew deep in her belly and began to spread through her in a wave.

But then she remembered Janey Little. And Felix's disconsolate face when he'd come by to drop off the cane. . . .

Her hand stilled. The desire fled, if not the need.

She opened her eyes and stared across the room. Pulling her robe closed, she wrapped her arms tightly around herself.

Don't get mad, get even.

There had to be a way that she could make good for Daddy and the Order and *still* get everything that *she* wanted at the same time. She just hadn't worked it all through yet.

This isn't over, Janey Little, she thought. Not by a long shot, it isn't.

7 ·

For Clare, it was a matter of control.

When her assailant first attacked her, out there in the rain, just the two of them, she'd been afraid. Of being hurt. And then of dying. But underlying it all, reaching right to the heart of the primordial core that made her who she was—that differentiated her from the billions of other souls with whom she shared the planet—was the fear of losing control.

What her assailant took from her at that moment violated her very essence. He had stolen what had kept her sane through the bedridden years and the years of physical therapy.

Control.

She had been dealt a bad hand—or dealt it for herself, some might say, though it was hard to think in those terms considering how young she'd been at the time she'd taken her fall. She had lost motor command of her body and fought with all the inner strength and will she could summon to regain it. And regain it she did. She didn't recover it all, but she'd been far more successful than the doctors had allowed she ever would be.

What was the secret?

Control.

When she was finally mobile once more, she swore she'd never give it up again. Not over any aspect of her life.

So when her assailant stole it away—as casually as some horrible little child pulling the wings from a fly, simply plucking it from her with his brute strength and a knife—it undermined everything that had kept her strong through the years. Just like that. And even now, sitting in the kitchen sharing a pot of tea with Davie Rowe, the memory of that theft entangled her like a swimmer caught in a snarl of seaweed, caught and dragged down from the surface of the ocean, down into the depths, losing air, losing strength, losing control. . . .

Control.

What frightened her the most was how easily her assailant had stripped it away.

She glanced across the table at her companion who was trying manfully not to slurp his tea. Davie Rowe. With his severe acne scars, pug nose, and oversize chin; the one large ear and his basically kind eyes that were unfortunately too small and set too closely together; the purple blotch of a birthmark that smeared the left side of his brow. . . .

It was a face only a mother could love, and from what Clare knew, only his mother did.

Like Clare herself, Davie Rowe had been dealt a bad hand as well, one over which he could never have had any influence. Based on his looks, he'd never had many friends. When he looked for employment, the doors closed in his face. He'd had little schooling and his only virtue, if it could be called such, was that he could handle himself well in a fight—he'd had a whole childhood and adolescence perfecting that skill. Unfortunately it wasn't marketable. Was it any wonder that he'd taken up nicking wallets and the like from the rooms of the tourists who flocked to Penwith every summer? What else was he supposed to do?

Everyone knew him in the village. He wasn't so much Mousehole's village idiot as its black sheep and locally he was viewed with a certain amount of wary affection, though no one cared to spend much time in his company.

But never mind his looks, or his history. At this moment Clare felt a pronounced fondness for him. And an odd sense of affinity.

She considered—as a way of taking her mind away from that bleak feeling that had settled deep inside her and refused, point-blank, to be dislodged—what it must be like to be him.

He wasn't crippled, because physically his body performed all its functions in the manner they were supposed to, but he was disabled all the same. Because where people looked no further than her limp and her cane when they met her, with him they looked no further than his face. The principle difference between them was that she'd forced herself to overcome the limitations that society put on her while he either hadn't been able, or been given the opportunity, to try to do the same for himself.

"Have you read all those books?" Davie asked suddenly.

Clare blinked and brought her thoughts back to earth.

"What did you say?"

"Those books in your study," Davie said, nodding with his head down the hall. "Have you read them all?"

Clare smiled. "Not likely. But I've read a lot of them. Why do you ask?"

"I just wondered what it was like."

"What, reading that many books?"

"No. Reading a book. All the way through, like, from start to finish. One without pictures."

"You've never read a book?" Clare asked, trying to keep the incredulity out of her voice.

Davie shrugged. "Never really had the time. . . ."

"But what do you do with your time?" She regretted what she had said the moment the words were out of her mouth. "I'm sorry," she added quickly. "It's really none of my business."

"I don't mind your asking. I like to walk. I go for long walks. And I have a bicycle now that I got from Willie. Sometimes I'll pedal all the way up to St. Ives and back in a day. I listen to the radio a lot and in the evenings Mum and I watch the telly. And I love to go to the cinema. But I look at all those books in your study and I get to thinking that you can't half help being clever after you've read so many of them."

"It takes more than reading to be clever," Clare said.

Lord knew, she saw that every day in the shop where they sold more romances and bestsellers than anything that had a bit more literary worth or insight. She couldn't remember the last time they'd sold a copy of Joyce that wasn't to a student.

"It's understanding what you read," she added. "And it's challenging your mind. I've no quarrel with entertainment, but I like to mix my reading about so that I get a bit of every-thing."

Davie nodded, but she saw that he was only going through the motion of understanding.

"You play music, too," he said. "Up at Charlie Boyd's, don't you?"

"Most Friday nights," Clare said. "I haven't seen you there, though."

Davie shrugged. "Sometimes when I'm walking by, I hear the music and I stop outside for a bit of a listen."

"Why don't you come in?"

"I can't play an instrument or carry a tune."

"You could tell a story, then, like some of the old gaffers."

"Don't know any stories. I . . ." He shifted uncomfortably in his chair. "It's just that everything changes when I come in a room. Goes all quiet like and then people are always looking at me. When I go 'round to the local, the only way I can get any company is by playing the fool. Then I can have a crowd around me, buying drinks or letting me play billiards with them, but . . ." His voice trailed off.

Clare was at a loss as to what to say.

"I just get tired of it sometimes," he added after a few mo-ments.

Clare nodded. "It's not easy being . . . different. I know that well enough."

"You're not that different," Davie said. "You're pretty and clever and—"

He broke off suddenly and finished his tea in one long swallow.

"It's getting late," he said, standing up from the table. "If you could bring me a blanket and pillow, I can make my own bed on the sofa."

Clare started to say something commiserating, but then left it unsaid. If he was anything like she was, it would just sound like pity, and she hated to be pitied.

"I'll just go get them," she said.

Later she looked in on her sleeping mother—as she had when she'd first come home—but her mother was still sleeping. She left a note on her mother's night table briefly explaining Davie Rowe's presence downstairs, then went into her own room. She changed for bed, but then found she couldn't sleep. Instead she spent the remaining hours of the night staring out the window, watching the rain die to a drizzle, then give away altogether until only an overcast sky remained as a reminder of the night just past.

The gulls were wheeling about the roof of the house when she finally fell asleep in the chair where she was sitting. She dreamed of a masked man stalking her down narrow, winding streets where she could only flee by crawling painfully along the cobblestones because she'd lost her cane. Rain made the cobblestones slick and hard to grip. The goggled face of her pursuer loomed over her. He held a long shining blade upraised in his hand, the incongruously peaceful image of a dove tattooed on his wrist. Laughter spilled from behind the scarf that hid his features.

She woke with that hideous laughter in her ears, then realized it was only the raucous cries of the gulls. Feeling stiff, she limped over to her bed and crawled under the covers where she immediately fell asleep once more, this time without dreams.

8.

The Gaffer awoke with a start when the front door banged open. The Dunthorn book fell from his lap and he only just caught it before it tumbled to the floor. He looked over, then quickly rose to his feet as his much bedraggled granddaughter came in bringing with her an equally bedraggled Felix who also appeared to be in a somewhat somnambulant state.

"You found him!" he said. "Felix, I can't tell you how sorry I am about—"

"Doesn't do any good to talk to him, Gramps," Janey said.

The Gaffer peered closer and saw that while Felix's eyes were open, he saw nothing. The only reason he was moving at all was because Janey was nudging him along.

"What's happened?" the Gaffer asked. "Was he in an accident?"

Janey shook her head. "No. I'd say this was brought about very deliberately. Will you help me get him to bed?"

It took a while to get Felix upstairs, undressed, and in bed. Some more time was spent in fetching his gear from the Reliant, but finally everything was done. Janey and the Gaffer sat down in the living room, sitting together on the sofa, and it was then, as she started to explain what had happened, that the finely held control Janey had kept in place all evening unraveled. She burst into tears and buried her face against the Gaffer's shoulder.

It took him a while to get the story out of her. Then he merely held her, close to him, stroking her hair and murmuring in her ear. What he said made no real sense. There were promises of everything getting better, and that they'd get to the bottom of things, just you wait and see, my robin, and the mystery would soon be solved, wouldn't it just, when they all put their minds to it together, and how she wasn't to worry.

But it was all just words.

He looked across the room as he spoke, at the Dunthorn book where it lay on the chair.

It was uncomfortably apparent that whatever they had become involved in was just beginning, though the Gaffer couldn't have said how he knew that. It was just a feeling he got.

When he looked at the book.

When he listened to the wind outside the house, rattling the shutters as it went hurrying up the street.

When he remembered the last time the strangeness had come into his home.

He knew it was only beginning.

And that this time it would be worse.

Silly Old Man

Philosophers have argued for centuries about how
many angels can dance on the head of a pin, but
materialists have known all along that it
depends on whether they are jitterbugging or
dancing cheek to cheek.

—TOM ROBBINS,
from *Jitterbug Perfume*

Th e water of the harbour punched Jodi like a fist.
Stunned, she sank deep into its shadows, propelled down by the momentum of her long drop.
Moments later she bobbed back to the surface, brought up by
the natural buoyancy of the salt water. The shock of its coldness
immediately numbed her. Already suffering from the trauma of
discovering that Edern had been no more than some enchanted
clockwork man, this second shock on her system left her barely
aware of her predicament.

The sea ran cold around Bodbury in late autumn. More than
one fisherman had died in its waters as the cold seeped into their
muscles, stealing away the sweet heat of life. Then the undertow
would pull them under.

If they were washed ashore, their grieving families would have
their swollen blue corpses to bury. A small comfort, but comfort
nonetheless, for most were dragged out to sea, their bodies never
seen again. For all their closeness to the sea—day in and day
out upon its waters—given a choice, most fisher-folk would
choose to leave their bones on land, buried deep in the solid
earth, rather than know that they'd become nothing more than
the playthings of the tide and currents.

Jodi was only dimly aware of the cold and the heat it was
stealing from her body. She kept herself afloat with haphazard

flutterings of her arms and legs, but her mind was locked on a stark impossible image:

Edern Gee. . . .

The spraying blood of the bog creatures as it melted his skin and made it flow like hot candle wax. . . .

The hole punched in his chest and the bewildering spill of cogs and gears and spoked wheels rolling across the boggy planking of the wharf. . . .

The memory stuck in her mind like a waterwheel snagged on a branch and locked in place. Movement frozen. The moment captured and held fast, looped like a cat's cradle string, so that no matter how much you turned it, there was no beginning and no end. Just the endless parade of that one instant, splayed across her mind, that she couldn't escape.

Until her head fell forward and a trickle of salt water exploded in her lungs. She lifted her face, choking and coughing. And then the first shivers began.

Swim, she told herself. Swim or you'll drown here.

But the shivers turned to trembling, which in turn became an uncontrollable shaking. Her head dipped into the water again, too heavy to keep aloft, but she managed to raise her face before she took another breath of water.

The current had already taken her some distance from the pier. She could see its dark bulk towering up behind her. Perched on a crate was Windle, the witch's fetch, gibbering angrily at her. There was no sign of the Widow herself. Farther away still was the length of the Old Quay—the distance between it and her multiplied a thousand times because of her present diminutive size.

She closed her eyes—

. . . and there was Edern, his face melting, his torso burst open, spilling out its clockwork mechanisms. . . .

—and opened them quickly again.

Swim, she told herself again.

But her arms and legs had grown too heavy. They felt so thick—cold and prickling with numbness. Her face sank into the water again and she had barely the strength to lift it. The current turned her so that she was no longer facing shore. When a wave lifted her to its crest, she could see out across the endless wash of its dark waters, then she dropped into another trough.

Hope died in her. Her movements were no more than minimal now.

Why fight the cold? she asked herself. Why fight the waves?

The sea had never been her friend, stealing Mother and Father as it was now stealing her life as well. But she could sense a kind of peacefulness waiting for her deep beneath the waves. A promise of warmth and solace if she just let herself sink. . . .

The wave crest lifted her again, but this time there was more than the never-ending vista of dark water to be seen. Something darker still was moving through the water towards her, leaving a V-shaped wake behind it.

Shark, Jodi thought, a new surge of panic hurling adrenaline through her body. It had to be one of the small blue sharks that the fishermen caught with their baited lines of mackerel and pilchard just outside the harbour.

A moment or so ago she'd been ready to give up, to simply allow herself to sink and let the waves claim her. But self-preservation—kicked awake by the immediate threat of being some shark's late-night snack—had her struggling to live once more.

She splashed frantically in the water, trying to get away, then realized that she was just going to draw it to her all the more quickly with her thrashing about. The swell of the waves drew her down into a trough.

It wasn't fair, she thought, and never mind what Aunt Nettie had to say about fairness. There weren't even supposed to *be* sharks about at this time of year.

Back she rose on the crest of another wave, to find her assailant had vanished.

Oh raw we, she thought with relief, then screamed as something came up from the waters underneath her.

She pounded her tiny fists against the thing, shrieking all the while, until she realized that she wasn't inside a shark's mouth, nor was it a shark's smooth skin that she was pummeling, but rather the wet-slicked fur of a seal's head. Her cries died and she grasped the fur with both hands.

"Oh, thank you, thank you, thank you," she mumbled against the fur.

Her teeth started to chatter against one another again. Her limbs shook as though palsied. She held on tightly, fingers wound into the short fur, as the seal streamed through the waves, bearing her shoreward. And then, improbably as it might seem, she immediately fell into a comalike stupor, still clinging to the seal as she slept.

Exhaustion and trauma had finally taken their inevitable toll.

2 .

An hour or so after he was led blindfolded from the hidden underground room that housed John Briello's animated corpse, Denzil still couldn't be sure if the odd turn that the night had taken was all a part of some incomprehensible hoax or not. If it was a hoax, it had been most elaborately planned. And was being most elaborately maintained. For here they were now, the four of them, an incongruous grouping if ever there was, out on the harbour in a rowboat, scouring the dark water with lanterns at bow and stern.

Henkie Whale put his bulk to good use, sitting amidships and bending his back to the oars as they rowed back and forth across the harbour. The big man had forsaken his bearskin for dungarees and jersey, the inevitable scarf wrapped about his neck and fluttering in the wind. Taupin sat in the bow, hanging over the hull with one lantern as he studied the water before them, both to look for Jodi and to call out warnings against the various abandoned ship masts and hulls they might otherwise run into. Denzil had the other lantern and sat in the stern with Lizzie Snell.

Lizzie had changed her clothes as well, decking herself out like a pirate of old from one of the costume chests Henkie maintained for his models—when he had them wear anything at all. She leaned into the starboard quarter, a long bangled sleeve trailing in their wake as she peered out at the water behind them. Denzil sat in the port quarter.

They were looking for Jodi.

Who had supposedly been enchanted and shrunk down to the size of a Weeman from the old nursery rhyme and was now helplessly adrift in the harbour.

According to a dead man.

Not bloody likely, Denzil thought.

The whole affair was absurd from start to finish. Except Jodi *was* missing. And he could still feel the touch of the cadaver's hands on him, could still hear Briello's ghostly voice, issuing forth from between his dead lips with its cold, raspy tones. . . .

"What's that?" Lizzie cried, pointing off to one side where the light from Denzil's lantern had momentarily illuminated something floating on the swell of the waves.

Taupin shone his own lantern in that direction. Henkie paused in his rowing to have a closer look, then took up the oars once more.

"It's too big," Taupin said.

"Just a seal," Henkie agreed.

"Maybe we should ask it to help us, you," Denzil said, unable to keep the sarcasm from his voice.

But Henkie appeared to give the idea serious consideration.

"Oh, no," Denzil said. "Now you go too far. . . ."

The seamen around Bodbury—fishermen in their pilchard luggers and sharking boats, sailors and Coastguard, smugglers and crabmen, anyone who worked the water—were a superstitious lot. And their notions were a motley and dizzying collection of nonsense and old wives' tales.

They disliked anything being stolen from their vessels—not only for the obvious reasons, but because they believed that a part of the ship's luck had gone with it. Strong steps were taken, or high prices paid, to get it back. For the same reason, anything lent from one ship to the other detracted from the lender's luck, unless the object was first damaged a little, however slightly, before being handed over.

They considered it unlucky to have a clergyman on board, or even to mention a minister, so "fore and after," with its reference to the clerical collar, was used. Another substitute, used by others, was "white choker."

Once on board ship, it was unlucky to return home to fetch some forgotten thing.

Women aboard brought bad luck.

To eat a pilchard by starting from the head was the same as driving away the shoals of fish.

And a hundred other strange and illogical assertions that the fisher-folk clung firmly to, for all that many of them were deeply religious.

Such as their beliefs when it came to the souls of the dead.

Never mind heaven and hell. They said that gulls embodied the souls of dead fishermen and sailors, while seals embodied the souls of dead piskies. The small became large; the large, small, was how they put it. And they firmly believed that to harm either would bring on such an incursion of bad luck as to make a broken mirror a joke.

So the gulls raided the fishermen's wharves and wheeled and spun freely above Bodbury. And the local colony of seals, whose rookery was by the Yolen Rock south of the town, could swim directly into the harbour with impunity, for who would dare harm them? And didn't they help the fishermen—steering them to pilchard shoals, or guiding their luggers back to harbour in deep fog?

There were no tales of selchies in Bodbury—those creatures who were seals in the water and men on the land. Such stories were saved for those who lived farther north. No, here the seals were ancestrally akin to the Good Neighbours, and treated with the same cautious respect as the country-folk extended to the piskies.

It was all superstitious poppycock, of course, Denzil thought. A great load of rubbish, pure and simple.

But Henkie paused in his rowing once more. He cupped his hands together and called out across the water to where the seal rose from a trough to the crest of another wave.

"It's got something on its head," Lizzie said.

"A hat, I don't doubt," Denzil muttered. "Is it a bull or a cow? I hear you can tell by the kind of headgear they assume when they take a turn about the harbour at night."

"It's a cow," Henkie said in the kind of voice that stated a plain fact.

And of course, Denzil thought, being the philanderer he was, Henkie would know.

"Keep that light on her," Henkie said as he started to turn the boat and row towards the seal.

Denzil rolled his eyes and glanced back at shore. His gaze caught and then focused on a figure that stood on the wharf of New Dock, watching them. Because of the distance and the dark, it was hard to make out more than a silhouette framed by a light in the market behind it, but that silhouette bore an uncanny likeness to the Widow Pender.

A shiver went through Denzil and he couldn't have said why. He looked away, then back again, but the figure was now gone.

"My soul and body!" he heard Taupin exclaim.

Feeling tired and irritable, and more than a little put upon with the night's strange goings on, Denzil turned once more to see what had excited Taupin. And then his jaw went slack for the second time that night.

3 ·

Jodi was having the oddest sort of a dream.

It was a late summer's afternoon and the sea was quiet. She was in the bay near Yolen Rock, floating on the gentle waves in a carker—one of those little boats that the boys in the Tatters made from cork with a piece of slate or hoop-iron for a keel. When you were a Small, a carker was just the right size.

All around her, in the sea and on the rocks about the craggy island of blue alvin stone that was the rookery, were the seals of Yolen Rock. Better than a hundred of them. Mated bulls and cows, bachelors and young females and pups. Sunning themselves. Floating as dreamily in the water as she did in her carker. And making such a racket. Barks and yelps filled the air—a kind of conversation that Jodi almost felt she could understand if she tried a little harder.

She'd often come here when she was her proper size, Ollie snuggled in her jacket when it was cool, perched on her shoulder or rambling about on the ground in front, behind and on all sides when the summer sun shone warm. Sometimes she'd come here with Denzil, and they'd talk the hours away, or with Taupin, and they would sit up on the headland across from the Rock, sit there for hours, not saying a word, while they watched the herd.

She'd never been this close to them before.

A pod of the young pups had a slide near the water and were playing on it like otters—carrying on like a pack of Tatters children as they filled the air with their squeals and shouts. Her carker drifted closer to them, but then was intercepted by a bachelor. His sleek fur streamed water as he lifted his head to look at her.

The stone, he said.

When he spoke, the words sounded in Jodi's ears—a sweet bell-like sound as unlike a seal's vocal barking as a forest is lit by the sun and then the moon. It seemed familiar as well, as though she'd heard just that particular cadence before, that country burr—but with her ears, not in her mind.

Trailing a hand lazily in the water, she looked at Yolen Rock where it rose from the water.

"What about it?" she asked.

Don't forget the holed stone.

An uncomfortable sensation awoke in the pit of her stomach. A dark memory stirred under the stimuli of sun and fair weather that had been warming her.

"No," she said.

Nine times through.

The feeling grew, spreading up to constrict her chest, bringing a shiver that traveled the length of her body. The memory expanded as well . . . something to do with the inner workings of clocks. . . .

"Don't talk like that."

At moonrise.

A dull throbbing started up behind her eyes, a pinprick of pain that whistled into a shriek between her temples.

"Please, don't. . . ."

But it was too late. Already she was remembering. The Widow and her creatures and what they'd done to Edern. What the little man was. A clockwork mechanism that had been smashed to pieces. Cogs and gears scattered all about while she plunged into dark water and drowned. . . .

When you wake, the seal said, his huge liquid eyes engulfing her. *Don't forget the stone.*

"I don't want to wake up."

Because being a Small here was lovely, but waking meant she'd be in a place where everything was horrible. Witches and their fetches. Bog creatures and little clockwork men who got torn to pieces. And the sea, always the dark waters of the sea, closing over her head the way they'd closed over her father's. . . .

"You can't make me wake up."

But her surroundings were already smearing as though they'd only been so much condensation on glass and a huge hand was now wiping the glass clean.

"I won't!" she cried.

But we need you.

Now she recognized the voice's familiarity.

She floated in darkness—not the sea, but in a place where there was no up and no down, just that sensation of floating. And the darkness. But these shadows held no menace.

I need you.

She remembered the old seamen's tales then—how seals carried in them the souls of dead piskies.

She remembered a small man.

Her clockwork man.

Dead now.

All too dead—if he'd ever even been alive in the first place.

"Edern?"

There was no reply.

"Edern?" she tried again. "Were you real?"

Too late now, for she was waking up in earnest and now even the floating sensation and the darkness were going away and she was waking to a bruised and aching body, and a light that shone so bright it stung her eyes and made them tear.

4 ·

"She's so tiny," Lizzie said, her eyes wide with astonishment. "Like a doll."

Henkie only grunted. He'd had a quick look himself, but now he concentrated more on keeping the boat steady to allow the seal with its odd little burden an easier approach than on the burden itself.

Beside Lizzie, Denzil could only stare at the tiny figure carried through the waves on the seal's head—tiny, but recognizable, God help him—and consider how either he had gone entirely mad, or else he needed to reconsider his complete outlook on the world. He took off his glasses to dry the salt spray that had splashed onto them from a particularly enthusiastic wave and set them back on the bridge of his nose.

Everything had changed.

What could be and what couldn't. What was, what was probable, and what was impossible.

Absolutely nothing made sense anymore and he no longer knew *what* to think. Relief at Jodi's safety—no matter her size— warred with utter bewilderment at how she could be such a size in the first place. And he felt like a fool. Like such a silly, foolish old man. He could hear his own mocking "tee-ta-taw" at every mention of what he considered a scientifically unsound principle.

How completely mortifying to know he'd been wrong all this time. But at the same time, an indefinable excitement was rising up inside him.

That such a thing could be. It opened whole new worlds of possibilities and study.

Denzil's only consolation was that—except for Henkie who seemed to grow grumpily taciturn whenever he was in the middle of something delicate and obviously approached any wonder in a matter-of-fact fashion—he wasn't alone in his astonishment. Taupin and Lizzie seemed just as dumbfounded as he was himself.

Dumbfounded and enchanted.

For what could be so enchanting as the perfect tiny size that Jodi had become?

Lizzie lifted her carefully from the seal's head. Wrapping the tiny shivering body in a kerchief, she held her close to the lantern, murmuring cooing sounds that, Denzil knew, would drive Jodi mad if she were awake to hear them.

Denzil leaned closer to have a look.

"Is she . . . ?"

"She's had a terrible soaking," Lizzie said, "and the poor little thing is trembling from the cold, but I think she'll be all right. What do you think, Henkie?"

The big man, working the oars again as he rowed them back towards his warehouse at the end of the Old Quay, gave yet another grunt that could have meant anything. Denzil decided to take it as an affirmative. He was just as happy that Henkie kept his mind on the business at hand. It was a tricky business, navigating a way through the graveyard of ship masts and hulls that protruded from the water all along the Old Quay.

Taupin was shining his lantern towards Lizzie, half standing to try to get a better look himself. The boat rocked back and forth.

"Will you sit!" Henkie said.

Taupin sat.

Denzil tore his gaze away from the tiny figure and looked for the seal, but it was gone.

"What an amazing thing," he said softly. "You've my thanks, you!" he added, calling out over the water.

Henkie gave him a look and a smile, but said nothing. The muscles of his arms rolled under his jersey as he rowed them across the harbour with long steady strokes. Denzil turned back in his seat and returned his attention to Jodi.

There was a bump as they reached the shore. Denzil glanced up, surprised that they'd made the trip so quickly.

"Changed your mind then, have you?" Henkie asked him as he stowed the oars.

"About what?"

"About everything."

"I suppose I have."

"Oh, look," Lizzie said, her voice rising in pitch a few notes. "She's coming around."

They all leaned forward to see the tiny eyelids fluttering open.

"It's a bloody miracle," Henkie said. "Pity she doesn't have wings, though. I'd love to see how real working wings would look."

"She's not some Victorian fairy, you," Denzil said.

"But she's a bit of magic all the same, isn't she?"

"Will you be *quiet*," Lizzie hissed.

They looked to see Jodi's tiny features scrunched up, her hands over her ears.

"Let's bring her inside," Henkie said as he moored the rowboat.

He tried speaking quietly, but even his whispering had a booming quality about it.

"Softly," Lizzie said.

Henkie nodded, muttering, "Bloody hell," under his breath as he led the way into the warehouse.

The others trooped in after him. Denzil was last and paused in the doorway to look down the dark stone walkway that spilled the length of the Old Quay all the way to New Dock.

He looked for the Widow and saw no sign of her, but he couldn't shake the feeling that something out in the night was watching them all the same. There was a perplexing scent in the air, which he likened to disturbed bog water, but he could find no source for it either.

He stood there for a few moments longer, then finally shook his head and followed the others inside.

5 ·

Once she got over the initial shock of having all those huge faces peering at her where she sat on the tabletop, and was warmed with a set of dry clothes taken from a doll that Henkie dragged out from somewhere in the vast confusion of boxes and shelves and crates that filled his warehouse, Jodi sipped from a thimbleful of tea and told her story. She was hoarse by the time she was done, even with the tea—laced with rum added to it a careful bead at a time from an eyedropper—to soothe her throat. Thankfully, the giants—which was how she'd come to think of her rescuers—spoke only in whispers so her ears had mostly stopped their ringing.

"Makes me feel like we're a band of conspirators," Taupin remarked.

"I suppose we are, in a way," Henkie said.

Of the four of them, his was the only voice that still made her ears ache. His idea of whispering was a dull, low-pitched growl that rumbled like distant thunder. Whenever he spoke, Jodi could feel the bones in her chest resonating with his deep bass tones.

Like anyone who grew up in the Tatters, she was familiar with the eccentric painter, though this was the first time that she'd actually been inside his warehouse. It was everything that it had promised it would be from the spying glances that she and the other Tatters children had stolen through its dirty windows. She could easily spend hours in its cavernous depths—its immensity magnified still more due to her own present size.

Which reminded her of the first problem at hand.

"How can I get back to my own size?" she squeaked hoarsely.

"First off," Henkie said, "we'll march straight over to the bloody Widow's place and get that button."

"That won't necessarily be so easy, you," Denzil said.

"And why would that be?" Henkie asked.

"Because when we were out in the harbour, I saw her spying on us from New Dock. She'll be warned and have the button well hidden by now."

"And she's such an old grouch," Lizzie added, "that she'll never tell us where she's gone and hidden it."

"Then we'll bloody well beat the secret from her," Henkie growled.

"La," Taupin said. "And won't the constables take that in stride?"

Denzil nodded. "Some of us aren't exactly the most respected members of this community."

"Tremeer would jump at any chance to run you in," Lizzie said.

"There must be *something* we can do," Henkie said.

Jodi winced as the volume of his voice rose.

"What about the stone?" she piped up. "The Men-an-Tol?"

"That's just a fairy tale," Denzil said. "There's about as much magic in a piece of stone, carved by the ancients or not, as there is in—in . . ."

"In what?" Taupin asked with a grin.

"Never you mind, you," Denzil told him grumpily.

Even Jodi had to laugh, though she put her hands over her ears when Henkie joined in.

"Henkie," Lizzie warned.

He glanced at her, then at Jodi, and broke off immediately. Though he said nothing, Jodi saw his lips mouth the words, "Bloody hell." It appeared to be his favorite expression.

"This little man," Taupin said. "You say he was actually a clockwork mechanism?"

Jodi's good humour drained away as she nodded.

"And then you dreamed his spirit was in the body of a seal?"

Another nod.

"I thought only gods and angels spoke to one in a dream," Denzil said, still unable to keep the sardonic tone from his voice.

"Only if it's a true dream," Henkie said.

"Perhaps that's a potential of the piskies that we've not heard of before," Taupin said thoughtfully.

"What is?" Henkie asked. "Speaking in dreams?"

"That, and the fact that they can slip their minds out of their own bodies and into the minds of others—borrowing the bodies of animals and inanimate objects when the need arises and their own bodies can't fulfill the necessary task."

Denzil hrumphed, but said nothing.

Taupin gave him a smile and added, "Surely, every time one turns about, the world proves to be a more marvelous place than it was the moment before."

Lizzie nodded. "Did you ever think of the way a cat just sits there sometimes, looking for all the world as though it was hanging on to your every word?"

Taupin nodded. "It makes you think, doesn't it just?"

"So," Denzil said a little wearily, "you think we should take Jodi to the stone and pass her nine times through its hole?"

"At moonrise," Jodi said.

Denzil sighed. "But what will it *do?*"

"There's only one way to find out, isn't there?" Henkie said.

"But we'll have to be careful of the Widow," Jodi added. "She's got that Windle to spy on us. Who knows what would happen if she followed us out to the stone."

"Now that fetch creature is something I'd like to paint," Henkie said. He glanced at Jodi. "And you as well, all tiny as you are. I never knew Nettie had a daughter in the first place, little say one so pretty."

"I'm her niece," Jodi said.

"And she doesn't want to be painted, you," Denzil added.

He shot a glance at the full-length portrait of Lizzie that was still on the artist's easel, then quickly looked away. The movement earned him another of Henkie's laughs.

"I didn't say in the buff," the big man said.

"It might be kind of fun," Jodi said. "No one's ever painted me before."

"And best it remain that way," Denzil said. "What would your aunt say if—"

"That creature," Lizzie broke in. She'd been looking nervously around the warehouse. "Could it be spying on us at the moment?"

They all fell silent and peered into the shadows that lay beyond their little circle of light.

"Well, we've been whispering," Henkie said, "so I doubt it's heard anything."

"There's also those sloch," Jodi said. "The bog creatures. But Edern said that they won't last out the night, and besides, we would have smelled them by now."

"Smelled them . . . ?" Denzil sat up straighter in his chair and adjusted his glasses, which had gone a little askew. "I did smell a terrible stink when we were coming inside. . . ."

Henkie stood up so quickly that his chair fell to the floor behind him. The loud crash it made brought Jodi's hands back to her ears once more. In a few long strides, the artist had crossed the open space to the door and flung it wide. He stood there for a long moment, taking in the grey dawn that was breaking over the town, then bent down to look at something that lay on the ground near the door.

"What is it?" Taupin asked.

"See for yourself."

They trooped over, Denzil carrying Jodi carefully in his cupped hands, to see the small puddles of marsh mud and vegetation that Henkie was crouched over.

To Jodi, the smell was unmistakable. The horrible memory of Edern's dying reared up in her mind and she turned away, holding tightly on to Denzil's thumb.

"How much do you think they heard?" Lizzie asked.

"Depends," Henkie replied, straightening up, "on how keen their hearing is."

He shooed them all back inside and closed the door firmly behind them.

"What we need is a plan," he said, his voice pitched so low that they all had to lean in close to hear him, "and I've got just the one to leave that bloody witch's mind reeling in confusion. And it won't"—he glanced at Lizzie—"get us in trouble with the law, either."

"And this plan is?" Denzil asked in a voice that made it apparent that he'd just as soon not know.

"Consider Tatters children on their bicycles," Henkie began. "A whole pack of them, wheeling about like so many hornets. . . ."

The Conundrum

Now o'er the one half-world
Nature seems dead; and wicked dreams abuse
The curtained sleep. . . .

— WILLIAM SHAKESPEARE,
from *Macbeth*

I f the Order of the Grey Dove was a pool of secret water, hidden deep in the forest of the world, then John Madden could be likened to the dropped stone that causes waves of consequence to flow in concentric circles from the center of its influence.

The line of authority was simple to follow to its source, if one knew how and where to look: There was the world, there was the Order, there were the various branches of the Order's Council of Elder Adepts, there was the Inner Circle, and finally, at the center of it all, there was Madden himself, tugging the strands of his spiderwebbed will to govern them all. Like the dropped stone in water, his influence caused a ripple effect that spread, first through the various levels of the Order, then out into the world of the sheep that he knew he had been born to rule.

What he wanted, he invariably got. And he was patient.

He had only known one failure—one absolute failure—and the ripples of *its* effect were still being felt. Such as tonight, when the Inner Circle of the Order met and he was reminded of it yet again.

The theatrics invoked for other aspects of the Order were not present in this suite where they had gathered. There were no masks nor robes nor candles nor rituals. It was a Spartan yet tastefully furnished boardroom, thirty stories above the streets of Manhattan. It gleamed of glass and steel, teak and burnished leather. Five seats, each occupied, were set at one end of a long wooden table. There were no notepads, nor pens with which to

write upon them; no recording devices, nor secretaries to tran-
scribe the proceedings. The walls were unadorned, except for a
tapestry depicting the grey dove of the Order that hung behind
Madden's chair at the head of the table.

To Madden's right sat Roland Grant who *Forbes,* the American business weekly, said was the world's seventh richest non-
monarch. He was a large, burly man, a Paul Bunyan of the North
American business world, tamed in a three-piece tailored suit,
still dark-haired for his years, and trim for all his weight. His
assets were a who's who of major corporations and he sat on
more boards than a Monopoly game had squares.

If he had one weakness, it was his daughter, Lena.

Beside Grant was James Kelly "J.K." Hale, a slender, tanned
man with the lean features of a hawk who was the Hong Kong
legal counsel for a number of Western corporations. Madden was
presently grooming Hale to enter the American political arena
in an advisory capacity, though if Hale had been asked about
his planned career change, he would have thought the idea to
be his own.

To Madden's left sat Eva Diesel, the West German author and
political rights activist who used her considerable reputation as
one of Europe's great humanitarians to influence public and government to the aims of the Order. She was a formidable woman,
both in appearance and temperament, and Madden had yet to
decide how much of her propaganda was actual conviction and
how much was simple rhetoric to further the Order's aims when
it required the nature of public and state support that she could
gain for them.

Beside her, completing the inner circle, was Armand Monette,
the French business magnate whose head offices were based in
Paris. Like Grant, his world-scale corporate holdings were centered primarily in the fields of shipping, transport, fuels, and
various media. Giving lie to the image of a suave Frenchman,
he invariably appeared in rumpled suits, tie askew and hair
mussed, red-eyed and in need of a shave, but his mind was as
sharp as his appearance was disheveled and if his businesses were

not as prosperous as Grant's, it was only because Madden didn't trust the man as much and therefore kept a careful—if surreptitious—curb on his successes.

Of the five, not one was under sixty, though that information would have surprised more than one gossip columnist.

They met once a month to assess the viability of the Order's ongoing strategies and ventures, and to discuss private projects—undertakings that only they were privy to in their entirety. General endeavors were reported, in turn, to the branch leaders of the Council of Elder Adepts by the member of the Inner Circle responsible for that particular branch, but the Adepts were told only enough to keep them compliant. The Order as a whole knew little or nothing of the Inner Circle's long-term goals, except in the vaguest of terms.

That was how it should be, Madden had realized long ago, because for all their dedication to his doctrines, the general members of the Order were still just another kind of sheep, subject, in the end, to his will, not their own.

And sometimes he thought—especially on a night like tonight—that the Inner Circle also required a lesson in who ruled and who was ruled. It was important, at least in terms of their continued usefulness to him, to allow them a sense of free will, so he was subtle in his manipulations, but the bottom line remained: He was in charge.

No other.

The Order of the Grey Dove had been created through *his* vision and perseverance. All the others—members of the Inner Circle and of the Council of Elder Adepts alike—were Johnny-come-latelies. Without him, the Order simply would not exist.

So he let them question him tonight; he let them bring him to task for his failure to acquire Dunthorn's secret. But he waited until the end of the meeting to give them their opportunity, and he allowed them only a few moments before he broke the discussion off.

He ruled them.

The underlying vision of the Order was his vision.

"À *bien*," Armand Monette began—and of course it would be him, Madden thought. "We have yet to discuss the matter of this secret of yours, John. *Le mystère* in Cornwall. How is it progressing?"

"We have two of our best agents working on it now."

Madden was aware of Grant's grateful look for his including Lena in such a positive light, but he gave no indication of his observation.

"But it has been the better part of two weeks," Monette continued. "Surely you have some results?"

"Yes," Eva Diesel said in her clipped, formal English. "You have tantalized us with it for years. Has anything new been learned?"

How to explain that there was a bond between himself and the hidden power that Dunthorn had guarded, that he knew each time it woke and stretched its influence, but that he could gain no sense of what shape it wore, or what it actually was, only that it was a power beyond imagining.

Better yet, he thought, *why* should he explain?

He had long ago regretted ever mentioning its existence in the first place.

"We know only that it has finally surfaced again," he said. "And that we are very close to acquiring it."

J. K. Hale straightened in his seat. "I have to ask you again, John: Why all this pussyfooting around? Why don't we just walk in and take it?"

"We had Dunthorn for two days," Madden said. "He told us nothing. If we move too soon, we're just as liable to lose it for another thirty-five years."

"We have better interrogation methods now," Hale said. "The tongs have been developing some very interesting drugs over the past few years—"

"Not to mention your own government," Monette broke in.

Hale shot him an irritated look. "We could make them talk," he said. "Give my people just one day with them."

"I'm well aware of the pharmaceutical advances made in both

America—which is *not* my country, Armand—and abroad," Madden said. "But I know these people. They have a stubborn streak that goes beyond the reach of the most sophisticated methods of interrogation that we could bring to bear on them. And remember, they might well not even *be* aware of what we are looking for."

"But you said the secret has been woken," Diesel said. "Surely, then, someone must have woken it?"

All Madden needed to do was still that inner conversation that all men and women carry on inside themselves and he could feel Dunthorn's hidden legacy, awake and powerful, reaching out across the vast range of the Atlantic to speak to him. And this time, more than ever before, he was realizing a sense of the thing that offered him a far clearer understanding of just exactly what it was that he had pursued for so long.

"It might even not be an object," he said softly. "It might be a . . . place. All we need is the key that will unlock its secret. And soon. . . ."

"A place?" Monette asked.

Madden frowned, annoyed with himself for having said as much as he had, and with Monette for pressing him. But he couldn't help himself. More and more he found Dunthorn's legacy whispering to him, waking odd longings, undermining the usual clarity of his thought process.

"What do you mean?" Diesel asked as well, her eyes bright with interest.

Hale nodded, his own eagerness apparent. "You've learned something?"

Only Grant remained silent and for that Madden was grateful.

Madden stood up. "If you can't feel what I feel," he said, falling back on the mystical to end the probing questions, "then perhaps you aren't yet ready for the secret's gift. It will be a gift, yes, but one that must be earned."

He held up a hand to forestall any further conversation.

"Think about it," he added, then left the boardroom.

2 .

Madden was sitting in his private office when Grant joined him a little later. Here thick shag carpeting lay underfoot and the leather furniture was thickly padded, built more for comfort than appearance. A ceiling-to-floor bookcase lined one wall; another was completely given over to one enormous window. The drapes were open and the New York skyline lay outside, dark and lit with jeweled lights. His desk was an antique rolltop, polished until the wood glowed. Original paintings by three different Impressionists hung on another wall. In one corner was a small bar; in another a computer system tied by modem into Madden's own commercial empire.

He looked out the window to the Manhattan skyline, but was seeing past it, away beyond the man-made mountains and their constant hurly-burly of lights and glitter; away beyond the dark reaches of the Atlantic to a small peninsula, its shores rocked by waves, its land cloaked in a darkness that New York City might once have known, but would never know again; away to that place where Dunthorn's legacy hummed and throbbed with a power that Madden yearned to hold in his grip and that had never seemed so close within his reach as it did now.

Grant said nothing when he entered the office. He poured himself a neat whiskey, then sat down on the leather sofa by the bar and sipped thoughtfully at his drink, patiently waiting until Madden finally turned to face him.

"They don't understand, Rollie," he said.

"I don't understand either."

Madden nodded. "I know. But you're willing to wait for enlightenment and that's what sets you apart from the rest of them. If we didn't need them . . ."

Grant set his drink down on the glass table in front of the sofa.

"They could be replaced," he began.

Madden smiled. "And then we'd have to train a new group and that's something neither of us has the time to do. Nor do we have the time to assume their responsibilities. Besides, at least we *know* these wolves."

"Too true."

Grant picked up his drink again and took another sip before replacing the glass exactly on the outlined ring of condensation it had made earlier on the table's clear surface.

"What do you see, John?" he asked. "When you look out at the night, what is it that you see that we can't?"

From another, Madden might consider this prying. But Rollie Grant wasn't only his oldest business partner: He was also the closest Madden had to what others might call a friend.

"More than power and glory," Madden said. "I see a mystery, a kind of mystical purpose that grows more obscure the further you follow it, but each step you take, the more your spirit grows. Swells. Enlarges until one day, you feel as though it will encompass the whole of the world. But best of all, even then you know the mystery will go on, unexplained, and you can keep following it forever. Past life. Past death. Past whatever lies beyond death."

He looked out the window again, a half smile touching his lips, the distance thrumming in his eyes when he turned to Grant once more. Wild energy and a monumental peace, commingled, played there in Madden's gaze until he blinked.

"True immortality," he said, his voice soft.

"In Dunthorn's legacy?" Grant asked.

Madden nodded. "Enough for us all, but it will only be offered to those we know are worthy. To those who earn it."

He saw anxiety rest fleetingly in Grant's eyes, then it fled before his searching gaze.

"I wouldn't worry, Rollie," he said. "You're on the right road. You've earned the right to taste the secret."

"That's not what's important," Grant said. "Not so much as your achieving it."

If it had been anyone else, Madden would have considered the man to be just toadying up to him, but he knew Grant well enough to know that he sincerely meant what he said. If history was to prove Madden an aviator—as eventually Madden knew it must—then Grant would be ranked foremost among his disciples. Even above Michael Bett, for Bett's present body housed the soul of the Beast, and the Beast, for all his expertise and wisdom, could never be trusted. Not in his past incarnations; not in his present one.

Grant was his John. Simple and steadfast, and he would remain true to the last.

"Whatever Dunthorn's legacy is," Madden said, "it has finally broken free of its constraints once more. Now I can feel its presence in the air, wherever I turn. There isn't a moment when it isn't present."

"Could you track it down?"

"I think so," Madden said with a nod. Then, firmer: "Yes. I'm sure I can."

Grant rubbed his hands together. "So when do we leave for Cornwall?"

Madden laughed. "Just like that?"

His laughter died when Grant didn't join in with it.

"What's wrong, Rollie?"

Grant hesitated.

"No secrets between us," Madden lied. "Remember?"

Grant nodded. "It's Michael," he said. "I spoke to Lena earlier this evening. From what she tells me, I think Bett is losing it."

"Ah, Lena. . . ."

"I know what you think of her, John, but she can be competent when she sets her mind to the task."

"She's just so easily detoured," Madden said.

He held up a placating hand before Grant could defend his daughter.

"I spoke to Michael before the Circle met," he said. "He seemed . . . distraught. I think, that in this case, Lena is very close to the mark. I don't think Michael's out of control—not yet, at any rate. But if we leave him there on his own, he soon will be."

"So we are going?"

Madden smiled. "Of course we are, Rollie. This close to finally putting our hands on Dunthorn's legacy, how could we not?"

"I sent one of my security people over to look after Lena," Grant added. "I was worried about her. Bett—apparently he threatened her. The trouble is, Gazo won't get there until morning at the earliest."

"You did the right thing," Madden said, "if only to set your own mind at ease. But Michael won't trouble her again tonight. Tonight he discovered that not only do sheep have teeth, but sometimes they bite with them as well."

"He's been hurt?"

"Bruised," Madden replied. "And mostly just his pride." He looked out the window again; felt the mystery calling to him, whispering. . . .

"See about our flight, would you, Rollie?" he said, his voice gone soft once more.

He didn't hear Grant's reply, nor did he hear the man leave. His head thrummed with the promise hidden in Dunthorn's lost legacy: lost once, and now awake again. Almost found. Calling to him; calling and calling. . . .

Madden had never heard such a sweet sound before.

3 ·

Madden wasn't alone in feeling the presence of William Dunthorn's legacy. Like a fog creeping up from the sea, that same presence touched those sleeping in Mousehole and Paul, in Lamorna and Newlyn, and as far as Penzance.

To some it was merely a feeling of something brighter or darker in their dreams. It called up memories of those who had emigrated or moved up country, or merely to another part of the West

Division of the Hundred of Penwith; called up those who had died and gone on—a beloved wife, a missed friend, a cherished child, a husband or brother or cousin stolen by the sea; called up hopes and fears and all the tangled emotions in between; called up the absent and the dead and walked them through the sleepers' dreams.

Some greeted their spectral visitors with awe and joy and love.

Some were merely confused.

Others could know nothing but dread. . . .

Clare Mabley relived her experience from earlier in the evening, only this time there was no Davie Rowe present to help her.

In a heavy rain, she crawled down Mousehole's narrow, twisting streets, relentlessly pursued by her masked assailant, his switchblade transformed into a butcher's knife that would have done Jack the Ripper proud. Its blade glowed with its own inner fire and sparked and sizzled when the raindrops hit its polished steel. He finally caught her up by the Millpool, his blade lifting high, his face behind its goggles and scarf more than ever like some monstrous bug, but before the knife could plunge down, she clawed away his mask to find—

She woke, shivering in her chair, and shook her head.

"No," she whispered. "Never Felix."

One room over, Lilith Mabley met her husband in her dreams.

They sat, the two of them, as they had sat so many times before, on the stone stoop of their cottage, Mount's Bay spread out before them in the mist. He draped his hand over her shoulders and if there was a briny scent about him, Clare's mother didn't mind, for she had so much to tell him, and he to tell her. . . .

* * *

Davie Rowe was in a place where everyone was more disfigured than he was, their faces swollen until they seemed more like children's drawings come to life than humans. But it was also a place of miracles—a grotto, hidden away under the granite cliffs near the village.

The sea pounded outside, but inside, the water was as still as a sheet of glass and glowed with phosphorus. Beside a mirror set into the stone above the ledge that ran along the far side of the grotto, there was a candle that gave off more light than a candle should. One by one, in an orderly queue, the people approached it for their share of the miracle.

For in its light, their disfigurements fell away and their inner selves were revealed. That monstrous child, now an angel. That man suffering from neurofibromatosis, now as handsome as a matinee idol. That woman with her deformed facial bones and the grey tumors that spread like a blight across her features, now a beauty. . . .

And finally it was his turn.

He trembled with eagerness as he approached, legs barely sturdy enough to support his massive frame. But the weakness didn't matter, because it was finally his turn.

His turn to bathe in the candle's light and then look into the burnished mirror with its brass frame, only to find that his true self—

(No! he howled.)

—was even more monstrous than the face he presently turned towards the world.

He woke on the sofa in Clare's study and sat up, tangled in blankets and hyperventilating, disoriented by his surroundings until he remembered where he was and how he'd come to be here.

He'd rescued Clare. He'd proved he was really a good person, just like Bogart and Eastwood and the hundred other cinema idols whose exploits filled his waking thoughts.

(Never mind the two hundred quid, hey, Davie?)

He would have done it anyway.

(Of course you would have. But only so you'd have a chance to get into her knickers. . . .)

It wasn't like that.

(And a fine bloody pair the two of you will make—the cripple and the freak. . . .)

He shook his head. It wasn't like that at all.

(A cripple and a freak. . . .)

She's not a cripple.

(And you're not a freak, are you, Davie boy? Not bloody much, you aren't. When was the last time someone looked you in the face without gagging?)

Clare. She—

(Is a bloody cripple.)

Davie shook his head again, trying to shake the voice out from between his ears.

(When was the last time you didn't have to pay for it, Davie boy? Do you think Cary Grant had to pay for it, then? Or does Redford?)

"Stop," he whispered.

(And even then you can see it in their eyes: For all your money, they still wished you'd put a bag on your head. . . .)

Davie rocked back and forth on the sofa, moaning softly, refusing to listen to any more. When the dawn came, smudging grey across the eastern skies, he stole out of the house and away to home, but the voice followed him.

He couldn't escape it.

It was always there in his head.

Sometimes it was just harder to ignore.

Down Raginnis Hill, in the village proper, the Gaffer lay sleeping in his house on Duck Street.

His dream took him out past the protective arms of Mousehole harbour in a rowboat. He sat in the stern with Adeline—sweet, gentle Addie, her arm nestled comfortably into the crook of his arm from where it should never have strayed—while their son

Paul rowed them out past Shag Rock and St. Clement's Isle, his back bent easily to the task, that familiar smile of his that lit his whole face, beaming and shining.

On the island, hidden at first by the rocks, the Gaffer's old mate Billy sat up from where he'd been reading and waved to them as they went by, his book tucked under his arm. The oddest thing was that Dunthorn wasn't the young man now that the Gaffer remembered from old photos and his memories, but rather he appeared as he would have had he lived to this day.

"Billy!" the Gaffer cried.

"Did a proper job 'mazing you, didn't I just?" Billy called back. "Thought I was dead, did you?"

The Gaffer turned in his seat. "Wait a bit, Paul," he said.

But Paul kept rowing and the island fell away, Billy still waving on its rocky shore.

"Don't fuss so," Addie told the Gaffer. "Now tell me, how's it been with our Janey?"

"Our Janey . . . ?"

Anxiety rode high and wild through the Gaffer until he looked into Addie's gently smiling face, and then the turmoil washed away and he settled back in his seat.

"Our Janey's a musician now," he began, smiling to see how Paul leaned forward to catch every word as well.

Janey Little's dream was of neither her grandmother nor her father, but it did involve a member of her immediate family— the forgotten lost soul that was her mother.

Janey found herself walking at night through an enormous city that she'd never been in before, but she immediately recognized it as New York when the thoroughfare she was on dropped her into the mad hubbub bustle of Times Square. Neon screamed, passersby pushed her aside in ever-increasing numbers; she was offered drugs, sex, to be bought, to be sold, all in the space of a half-dozen moments. Her senses were assaulted with the hurly-burly and felt like they were going to overload until she finally found a quieter side street to duck into.

There she stood, leaning against the dirty wall, the stink of garbage and urine making her stomach queasy, the end of the street still spitting its noise and confusion at her. But at least it was quieter. She pushed off the wall and moved farther down the street, starting when something stirred in a nest of newspapers near her feet. Light from a window above fell down on the dirty face that looked up at her. Through the grime, looking past the multiple layers of filthy clothes and the greasy hair, she realized with a shock that this was her mother, lying there, looking up at her.

"Didsha never shink I *wandud* chew come hum?" her mother asked.

Her voice was thick and alien, muffled from the night's drinking and her missing teeth.

"I mished muh baby. . . ."

The grubby fingers reached for her—skeletal, like a bird's claws—and Janey backed away.

"Pleash. . . ."

Guilt reared up in Janey, but she continued to back away from the woman. Her mother staggered to her feet. As she stood and stumbled after Janey, hanging on to the wall to keep her balance, urine leaked down one leg. Unheeding of it, she continued after Janey who turned tail and ran back the way she'd come.

She was pushed back and forth between the angry pedestrians until sheer desperation brought her out of sleep and gasping for air. She sat up in bed, shivering from the chill as her damp body met the cool night air, and tried to slow her breathing. She looked down at Felix who was moving back and forth, caught in his own dream. She started to reach for him—to comfort, to be comforted—but then a final memory from her own nightmare rose up in her mind, staying her hand.

It was her mother's voice, clear and sober, that had followed her out of the grey reaches of sleep.

"Forgive me," she'd said, just as Janey was waking.

Her final words had been . . .

Forgive me.

With a kind of sick uneasiness, Janey realized that she never thought of the woman—couldn't even remember her. Could barely put the word "mother" to her.

The woman had abandoned them; it was like she was dead. But what if she'd realized that it was all a mistake? What if years ago she realized the mistake she'd made, and regretted it, but by then it was too late?

Forgive me.

Hadn't Janey made her own mistakes in the past? Mistakes that seemed just as final, decisions made in the heat of the moment that could almost never be recalled?

She looked down at Felix, still stirring restlessly beside her in the bed.

Forgive me.

She shook her head. It was just a dream, that was all. A bad dream.

Forgive me.

She owed her mother nothing. Her mother owed her nothing.

Forgive me.

Tears welled in her eyes as she shook her head again, but neither helped to dislodge the memory of the New York City bag lady from her dream. Nor did it quiet the echoing refrain of her voice that whispered on and on through Janey's mind.

Forgive me.

"I don't know if I want to," Janey said.

Forgive me.

"I don't know if I even can. . . ."

Felix Gavin had been hanged.

He didn't know what his crime had been, nor who had judged him, but they had put the noose around his neck and he'd dropped the long drop, his neck broken, his limbs twitching, and now he was dead. Still in his body, but it was no longer his to command. He was a passenger now, on a trip that went to nowhere. He merely swung back and forth in the rain, hanging from the makeshift gallows—a huge old tree on a crossroads.

He became aware of a woman approaching him through the rain, cloaked and hooded against the weather. Holding a knife in her teeth, she hoisted her skirts and climbed the oak. When she could reach the rope, she cut him down and he fell into the mud, but he didn't feel the impact.

His nerve ends were all dead. He was dead. A ghost, jailed in its own corpse, dispassionately observing what became of the shell he'd worn while still alive.

Death wasn't what the church had taught him it would be, but he was used to being lied to by figures of authority. The world he'd left with his death was full of lies. But he discovered that one thing he'd heard about hangings was true: You did get a hard-on when the rope hit its limit and your neck was broken— a finger to the world, as it were. A final "Screw you all."

How he knew this to be true was that after the woman had stripped his clothes off, she hoisted her skirts again and rode him there in the mud and rain, drawing his last inadvertent statement to the world deep inside herself, closing her warmth around its dead, cold length.

This was wrong, Felix thought. It was sick. Perverted.

She began to make small noises in the back of her throat and moved faster, moaning and twitching, which struck Felix—in his curious dispassionate state—as odd. So far as he could see this brutal bouncing up and down held about the same amount of excitement as butter being churned.

But then what did he know? He was dead. While she—

Her hood fell back as she arched her back. If Felix had had a throat at that moment, his breath would have caught in it.

She . . .

That dark hair . . .

Those familiar features . . .

She shuddered as she reached her climax, her entire body

shaking and trembling. She lay down across his chest, still holding him inside her, and brushed his cold cheek with her lips.

Physically, he felt nothing. But in his heart, in the spirit that lived on, he could feel something dying.

"I'll do anything for you," she said. "Anything it takes to make you mine."

She bit at his lip, hands cupped on either side of his face, then slipped her tongue into his mouth.

No, he wanted to shout at her. But he had no voice. Could feel nothing.

"And if I can't have you when you're alive . . ."

She ground her hips against his.

No, he cried soundlessly again. This is wrong.

He struggled to be heard, to move the dead limbs that had once been his, to push her from him.

". . . then I'll have you when you're dead."

She pushed up, hands against his chest, and began to move up and down once more.

This time when Felix fought to be heard—

—he woke instead.

He felt flushed and cold, all at once. A headache whined like a dentist's drill behind his eyes. The contents of his stomach roiled acidly around and he knew he was going to throw up, but he still couldn't move.

That was because he was dead. . . .

But he could feel his body again, the sheets against his skin, someone in bed beside him. So he wasn't dead. He just couldn't move. All he could do was open his eyes and stare at a shadowed ceiling that seemed vaguely familiar and make a kind of strangled noise.

"N-nuh . . ."

The bedsprings gave as that someone in bed with him shifted position. He tried to turn his head to see who it was, but even that simple motion was denied him. Vomit came burning up his throat.

I'm going to choke on my own puke, he thought. I'm going to—

But whoever it was who was beside him lifted, then turned his head. He had a momentary glimpse of Janey's worried features above him before his body hurled up the contents of his stomach into the wastepaper basket that she had brought up from the side of the bed.

He heaved until his stomach was empty, then heaved some more, a rancid taste in his throat, his chest hurting. But finally it was over. Finally, he could lay his head weakly on the pillow and take small shallow breaths that didn't make his chest ache. But he still felt queasy. The dentist's drill was still whining inside his head.

He tried to concentrate on Janey, on what she was saying, but for a long time all he could hear was just the wordless soothing sound of her voice as she brought him water to rinse his mouth and wiped his face with a damp cloth.

He tried to understand what he was doing back here—for now he could recognize the bedroom as the one he'd been staying in at the Gaffer's house—and why Janey was taking care of him.

The last thing he remembered . . .

He was a hanged man, being cut down from an oak tree and then—

No. That had been a dream.

The last thing that he could remember was . . .

But that, too, seemed to involve a woman sitting astride him, his hardness drawn deep inside her. . . .

Another dream.

The last real thing he could remember, he decided, was the Gaffer and Janey sending him off. Playing music by the old quarry—a duet with the tide. The storm. Lena. Drinking tea. . . .

"Felix, can you hear me?"

Finally something Janey said registered.

He tried to speak, then settled for nodding his head.

"You're going to be all right," she said. "You were drugged, by that woman—"

Lena. The tea. So that much was real. But drugged? She'd drugged him?

"H-h-how . . . ?" he managed.

"I came and got you. Oh, Felix. . . ."

A flickering image came into his mind. A naked woman. Riding him. Not in the rain and mud. But in a bed. . . .

A dream?

"Can you remember what happened to you?"

The whine in his head grew sharper. He squinted, tried to push past the pain to where his memories lay tangled up with dreams, to sort through which were real, and which were not. But he couldn't get past the pain.

"N-nuh . . ." he tried. "Nuh . . . ing. . . ."

Janey bent down and wrapped her arms around him.

"I'm so sorry I didn't give you a chance to explain," she said. "I'm an awful person sometimes."

No, he wanted to tell her, but it only came out, "N-nuh . . ."

"I love you, Felix."

"Luuv . . . too. . . ."

She gave him a squeeze. He could see the tears in her eyes. His own vision blurred. As she started to draw away, he tried to move his hand to stop her, but couldn't.

Don't go, he wanted to say. Don't leave.

"Nuh . . . nuh . . ." was all he could say.

But she understood and lay down beside him once more. The whining ache in his head wound into a dart that sped deep into the back of his mind and he followed it down, leaving Janey to hold his sleeping body until she finally fell asleep again herself.

Felix didn't dream again. But Janey. . . .

This time her dreams took her into a more familiar setting.

She found herself standing at the bottom of the stairs in the Gaffer's house, looking across the room to where William Dunthorn's *The Little Country* lay on the Gaffer's favorite chair. It remained there as the Gaffer had left it earlier, its leather covers sealing in the magic of its words, the light behind the chair spilling a soft halo of light upon it as though the chair were a stage, the book a thespian.

And as though Janey's presence had signaled the opening of the curtains for the first act, the book's bindings made a faint crackling sound and the cover flipped open. The pages rustled as if they were being turned, one by one, ruffled as though by the breath of a wind, or an invisible hand flipping through them.

She took a step forward, then paused as music rose up around her—a wash of mysterious notes that played a tune both familiar and strange. It spoke of hidden places, secrets long lost that waited to be found. Her fingers twitched at her sides, searching for the fingerboard or air holes of an instrument that wasn't at hand.

The pages stopped moving as the music grew stronger. Figurines on the mantel, picture frames on the wall, and glasses and dinnerware in the kitchen cupboards trembled, then clattered as deep bass resonances echoed through the small house. She could feel the floor trembling underfoot, and swayed slightly, moving in time to the curious rhythm.

She took another step forward, then a third, pausing again when she saw something moving on top of the book.

No, she realized. Not moving on top of it. Rising from it. A Lilliputian man stepping from its pages to lift his head and look about the room, his gaze tracking the giant furnishings until it caught, then rested, on Janey's own gaze.

He was no bigger than the little mice or moles that Jabez occasionally deposited on the Gaffer's back doorstep with that smug pride of his species. Janey could have held the man in the palm of her hand—the whole of him, from toe tip to the top of his head.

She found she couldn't breathe as the light behind those tiny eyes locked on her own.

The music continued, a kind of slow reel, but played on instruments she couldn't recognize. They had a certain familiarity with ones that she knew, but something remained odd about them all the same, differences that made their pitch alien, for all their familiarity. There were plucked string sounds and bowed string sounds. An underlying drumming rhythm like that woken from the skin of a crowdy crawn—the Cornish equivalent of a bodhran. Free reed instruments and others with oboelike tones. A kind of psaltry or harpsichord and distant piping that sounded like a chorus of Cornish pibcorns—the ancient native instrument that had a single reed and two cow's horns at the end of a cedarwood pipe and was much like a Breton bombarde.

She knew this music—knew it down to the very core of her being—but she had never heard it before. Unfamiliar, it had still always been there inside her, waiting to be woken. It grew from the core of mystery that gives a secret its special delight, religion its awe. It demanded to be accepted by simple faith, not dissected or questioned, and at the same time, it begged to be doubted and probed.

There was wonder in its strains, and bright flares of joy that set the heart on fire, but there was a darkness in it as well, a shadow that could reach into the soul and cloud all one's perceptions with a bleak grey shroud. The path between the two was narrow and treacherous, like the winding track that old folk songs claimed led one into Faerie.

Janey knew those songs, knew the lessons of the hard road to Heaven, the broad easy road to Hell, and the dangers of Faerie that lay in between, onion-layered with the world of the here and now into which she had been born, now lived, and would one day die. Given a choice, she would always take the winding road to Faerie, because Heaven was too bright. There were no secrets there, for none could withstand the judgmental glare of its light. And Hell was too dark.

But Faerie. . . .

This music seemed to show the way to reach that realm. It led into secret glens where hidden wonders lay waiting for those brave enough to dare to follow it home.

Janey couldn't help herself. She had to go.

The key to where she should put her first foot forward lay there in the music, but it was tantalizingly just out of reach at the same time.

"How can I . . . ?" she began.

A new wash of the music, a sudden swell, rising to a crescendo, made her lose her train of thought, and then died down again.

If you must ask, it seemed to say, *then you will never find the way.* . . .

"But . . . ?"

She looked to the little man on Dunthorn's book for help.

Dark is best, the music whispered. *Dark is all.*

The tiny man looked back at her with a sense of alarm that she shared.

The music had settled into a deep drone. The entire house vibrated with its bass tones, wooden beams cracking, foundation stones shifting against one another. Heaven's awe, Faerie's wonder, faded from its strains.

Janey took another step forward all the same.

An eerie wail rose out of the drone, shrieking across the back of the music like a fingernail drawn across a blackboard. The little man sank back into the book—flailing his arms as though he were being drawn into the quickening mire of a bog.

Janey moved quickly closer, but this time a scratching at the window stopped her. She looked out to see a hundred tiny leering goblin faces staring in at her. The creatures clawed at the glass, slit eyes burning with a yellow light.

The music was a horror soundtrack now.

She caught movement from the corner of her eyes and turned to look back at the book. Its pages were flipping once more, rapidly turned by invisible hands. When they stopped this time, the music shrieked to another crescendo and a dark mist rose from the open pages of the book.

There were monstrous shapes in the mist. The stench of old graves dug open and corpse breath haunted the air. Childhood night terrors came to life: a Pandora's box of horrors and fears;

specters of death and pestilence—visited on friends and family.

Her grandfather, stumbling out of the dark fog like a corpse, animated, but the soul was long fled, mouth full of squirming maggots, the eyes dead. . . .

Felix, reduced to a skeletal frame and covered with running sores, reaching for her with bleeding hands. . . .

Clare, dragging herself across the carpet towards her with fingers transformed into eagle's talons, her body ending at the waist, her mouth a horror of barracuda teeth, dripping blood from its corners. . . .

The *Rolling Stone* reporter shuffling forward, eyes milky and unseeing, trailing a ragged stream of his own entrails behind him. . . .

And more, so many more, all converging on her.

All reaching for her. . . .

Hands upon her now, a hundred hands, clawing at her arms and legs and torso, tearing long runnels of bleeding skin from her flesh, dragging her back into the heart of that dark mist where worse horrors waited for their chance to feed on her. . . .

At the windows outside, the goblins screeching their nails on the glass. . . .

The room stinking like an abattoir, reeking of blood and excrement, of burning hair and open graves. . . .

The music a rhythmical electronic drone on which rode the sounds of grinding teeth. . . .

And wet burbling.

Hateful whispers.

And a long pitiful moan that she—when she finally woke—realized was crawling up from her own throat. . . .

It was a very long time before, emotionally exhausted, she finally fell asleep again.

In his small room in the bed and breakfast, just a hop, skip, and a jump away from the Gaffer's house on Duck Street, Michael Bett lay alone, brooding.

He'd dreamt as well—of sunlit fields that were thick with the sweet scent of violets and anemones, and the hum of bees. Steep hillsides that ran down to a cove below where the surf washed against ancient granite. The sky was clear and there was a gentle music in the air—the soft sound of a set of Northumbrian pipes playing a tune that was familiar to him because it was on Janey Little's second album.

Bett had never been in such a peaceful place before.

It sickened him, enraged him.

This wasn't the way the world was. The world was all sharp edges and looking out for number one and take what you can get while you can.

Not this lie.

He took up a stick and began hacking at the flowers, cutting the heads from them with vast sweeps of his arm, but his one shoulder felt as though it had almost been dislocated and the bee-buzz/bird chorus sound of the pipes was getting under his skin until he could barely think and all he wanted was to kill whoever was playing them.

Janey Little.

He wanted to rip her lungs out of her chest.

He spun in a circle, flailing with the stick, trying to find the source of the music, a primordial howl building up in his chest, wailing for release.

He woke with that howl in his throat and only just muffled it in the nest of bedclothes in which his limbs had become entangled. His shoulder throbbed with pain.

He remembered his failure with Clare Mabley earlier this evening.

He remembered Lena Grant's newfound independence.

He remembered having to explain to Madden how things had become unraveled.

He wanted to lash out at something, someone, anything, but all he could do was lie there in the dark room, his shoulder aching, and stare up at the ceiling.

Patience, he told himself. Be patient. Everything's going to come together. And then the hurting was going to start. He was going to find out how they worked, every one of them. What arteries were connected to what veins. How long they could breathe with a hole in their lungs. How loud they could scream as he peeled away their skin. . . .

He could be patient.

But he wasn't going to try to sleep again tonight.

In her hotel room in Penzance, Lena Grant was also awake.

Her dream had been mundane compared to those that had visited others on the Penwith Peninsula tonight. She had simply been confronted by an angered Felix and had tried to explain herself to him. But he wouldn't listen. And her heart was breaking. And she wondered why she was even concerned about explaining anything to him, but she went on trying all the same, over and over again. And still her heart was breaking. Until she finally woke, alone in her room, to find her cheeks wet with tears and an emptiness lying there inside her that she'd never experienced before.

She didn't try to go back to sleep. Instead, she sat up, knees drawn to her chin, rocking back and forth against the headboard, and tried not to let the emptiness overcome her. She turned her mind back to Boston, to what the peers of her social circles would be up to this weekend, but her thoughts came continually spiraling back to Penzance.

Sitting alone in this hotel room, heart breaking.

Wishing . . . wishing. . . .

Trying not to think. . . .

Of Felix and of Janey Little and of what they were thinking of her right now. Of how she could ease this ache inside. She wondered if Willie had got to Clare Mabley before Bett had. She thought of her father's call that she'd just taken, how he and Madden would be arriving in England on one of Madden's private jets first thing tomorrow morning.

Like Michael Bett, she also felt that everything had come

apart, but she lay the blame solely on herself. She was the one who was changing. Who had changed. And she couldn't understand why.

How could one brawny sailor do this to her?

But failing her father, and indirectly the Order, and worrying about Bett—these were all secondary concerns at the moment. What she wanted to know was what had happened inside her to turn her world upside down.

If this was love, she'd rather do without, thank you very much.

Unfortunately, no one was asking her for her preference in the matter.

She was finally learning a truth that her father and Madden had yet to learn: For some things, you didn't get a choice.

And so the long night wound on, and those gifted or cursed with the influence of William Dunthorn's legacy journeyed through its seemingly endless hours, with joy and with sorrow, with fear and with anger.

For some the morning came too soon.

For many it seemed as though it would never come.

PART TWO

THE

Lost

Music

Music is the one incorporeal entrance into the higher
worlds of knowledge which comprehends mankind,
but which mankind cannot comprehend.

—attributed to
LUDWIG VAN BEETHOVEN

Originally, the function of songs was devotional.
Then in the balladeering centuries, they became a
vehicle for the spreading of information, stories and
opinions. Now in the 20th century, they have become
a way of making money and achieving fame. I think
the other two purposes were better.

— MIKE SCOTT;
from an interview in *Jamming*, 1985

When Sick Is It Tea You Want?

I do not know how I may appear to the world, but to myself I seem to have been only a boy playing on the sea-shore, and diverting myself in now and then finding a smoother pebble or a prettier shell than ordinary, whilst the great ocean of truth lay all undiscovered before me.

—attributed to
SIR ISAAC NEWTON,
in Brewster's *Life of Newton* (1831)

Morning came to the Cornish Riviera, blustery and heavy with dark grey skies when it reached Mount's Bay. It was what the locals called black eastly weather—bad, but not storming. In the fishing days, the men would take extra care to watch for the sudden storms that the Atlantic could throw up at them, seemingly from nowhere. But now the trade was mostly tourism, and the season over, so the weather was something one remarked on sitting over the morning's tea, rather than a force that could affect their livelihood.

And if this morning many were quieter than usual, or spoke in subdued voices of their unusual dreams the night before, out-of-doors the tide still rumbled against the shore, the wind still rattled the shutters and spun weather vanes around in dizzying circles as it shifted from one quarter to another, and there were the gulls, sailing like kites and filling the air with their rowdy cries from the first promise of light in the eastern skies.

They were still swooping and diving above the houses on

Raginnis Hill when Lilith Mabley came into her daughter's bedroom, the note Clare had left for her late the previous night
held in one hand. Once she'd had Clare's same dark hair, but
now it was turning to grey; she didn't believe in touching it up
or in dyes. The grey added to her stately bearing—straight-
backed and head always held high. She carried herself with the
pride of a duchess, but then to the people of Penwith, a fisherman's widow was no less the lady than one born to a manor.

"Clare?" she called softly from the door.

Clare woke, heartbeat quickening, then calmed herself when
she saw it was only her mother.

"Hello, Mum."

"This note . . . ?"

"I can explain."

"But there's no one downstairs."

Clare sat up and combed her hair with her fingers. Her mind
was still muddy from the poor bit of sleep that she'd managed
to steal from the first few hours of the morning.

"No one . . . ?" she repeated.

Had it all just been part and parcel of the night's awful dreams?

"Well now," her mother said. "There's a blanket and pillow
folded up on the sofa in your study, but no one sleeping on
it."

No, it hadn't been a dream, Clare thought as she swung her
feet to the floor. For her leg ached something fierce. As did her
head. And she had only to close her eyes to see that bug-face
with its goggle eyes and scarf.

And the knife. . . .

"Davie's gone?" she said.

Her mother nodded. "Davie Rowe," she said in a tone that
showed her surprise. "Whatever were you thinking, bringing the
likes of him into our home?"

"I . . ."

Clare tried to remember what she'd said in the note. Nothing
more than a vague explanation. Her mother obviously wanted
more now.

"I took a fall out in the rain last night," she said, "and Davie happened along to give me a hand home. The rain was so bad by then that I made him up a bed on the sofa. I suppose he left as soon as the weather cleared."

"The last I remember, before going up to my bed," her mother said, "was you sitting in your study, reading."

Yes, but then Felix came by, and she'd gone to Janey's, and some madman had come after her with a knife. . . . But she couldn't tell her mother all of that, not and have anything of the day left to herself. Had Janey found Felix? Had anyone else been attacked?

"I got tired of my book," she said, "so I went 'round by Janey's."

"So late," her mother said, shaking her head. "You were lucky that the Rowe boy came along when he did."

It was obvious from her tone of voice that for all his help she still disapproved of any commerce with Davie Rowe.

"He's not so bad," Clare said.

Her mother nodded. "Of course not. That's why they sent him to prison—because he's such a decent sort of a chap."

"You know what I meant."

"Janey should have given you a lift home," her mother said to change the subject.

"Janey had an errand to run."

"At that time of night?" Her mother shook her head. "What *is* the world coming to?"

Clare wondered that herself.

"I'd better get dressed," she said.

"You're going out?"

"I promised Janey I'd go 'round again this morning."

"I was hoping we could work on that puzzle. . . ."

Her mother loved jigsaw puzzles, the more complicated the better. After they were done, she glued the finished puzzle to a stiff piece of cardboard and displayed it on the mantel until the next one was done. At the back of her closet, there was a stack of mounted puzzles some four feet high. The latest one was a particularly daunting project—a bewildering landscape reproduction of a small lugger with a grey-blue sail, adrift on blue-grey water, the skies blue-grey above, the cliffs grey-blue behind, all the similar shades running confusingly into one another.

Sometimes in the weekday evenings after Clare got home from the shop, and almost invariably on Sunday mornings, they'd sit together at the table in the parlour where the puzzles were laid out, and work together on them. Clare enjoyed that time, for they would bend their heads together, ostensibly concentrating on the task at hand, but more simply enjoying the relaxed conversation that neither of them seemed to have as much occasion for during other times of the week.

"I'm sorry, Mum," she said. "Really I am. But it's important."

Her mother smiled, hiding her disappointment well.

"It's that Felix, isn't it?" she asked. "The pair of them need you to referee another of their arguments, I don't doubt."

"Something like that," Clare allowed.

Her mother tched. "And he back for no more than a day. You think they'd learn. Well, get yourself dressed, Clare. You'd best get over there quickly before there's nothing left to be saved."

"It's not so bad as all that."

"Perhaps it wasn't so bad last night, but you've told me enough of how that pair carried on the last time they had troubles to know you can't leave them alone for long." She shook her head and stuffed Clare's note into her pocket. "Though what they'll do when they get married," she added, "well, I *don't* know. We'll let that be their worry."

All Clare could do was laugh, but that was enough to clear the last cobwebbed distress of the previous night from her mind. She was finally beginning to feel more like her normal self. Now if only Janey had been able to find Felix. . . .

"Do get dressed, Clare," her mother repeated as she left the room. "Your breakfast will be ready in just a minute or so."

"I love you, too!" Clare called after her.

2 .

Felix awoke alone in bed, his headache gone. The experiences of the previous night, real events and dreams alike, tumbled through his mind in a confusing muddle, but clearest of all was the memory of Janey and the Gaffer sending him off.

He thought for one moment that it had all been a dream—for here he was, back in the Gaffer's spare bedroom as though he were just waking on his first morning back in the village—but no, they *had* sent him away. That had been real. The memory was too sharp, and too painful, to have been a dream.

And last night, waking to find Janey beside him again?

He looked around the room. If he was here—though not entirely sure how he came to *be* here—then that hadn't been a dream either.

He sat up, feeling a little groggy, though otherwise no worse for the wear.

So how had he come to return?

His duffel and accordion case stood near the door, Clare's cane leaning against them. His jacket was hanging from the back of a chair, his clothes in an untidy hoard on its seat.

He tried to remember what he could. After the argument, he'd gone up to Clare's. Then there'd been the walk from her house; playing his accordion by the sea; the storm; going to Lena's hotel room to lend her Clare's cane. And then . . . then it all became confusing. Nightmare images. He'd been dead—executed. Cut down from the oak tree to lie in the mud where the woman—

That had been a dream.

He shivered, remembering her features.

She'd been making love to his corpse. And superimposed over that memory was the image of Lena also making love to him, but on the bed in her hotel room. The similarities were shrill—

from the symmetry of the two women's positions to his own forced immobility. It had been as though he were an outsider sitting inside the shell of his own body. . . .

Had that been real, or was it the trace memory of yet another dream?

Last night, Janey had said something about him having been drugged.

Lena drugging him.

Try though he did, Felix couldn't remember any of it. Not clearly. Only as vague troubling images that flickered behind his eyelids whenever he closed his eyes.

Sighing, he got out of bed and put on his clothes. He started to wash up in the bathroom, but his legs began to feel weak, his stomach queasy, and he got no further than washing the sour, cottony taste from his mouth before he had to go lie down again.

But not back in his room. He felt sick, but not sick enough to forgo some answers.

He made it downstairs where he found both Janey and the Gaffer sitting at the kitchen table having their breakfast. They shot him identical looks of worry mixed with guilt. If he hadn't been feeling so nauseated, he might have teased the pair of them, but it was all he could do to make his way back out to the living room and lie down on the couch before his legs gave way from under him. He lay there, waiting for the room to stop spinning, hoping he wouldn't throw up.

Janey followed him out and sat down on the couch, the movement of her weight on the cushions making his stomach lurch.

"Felix?" she asked.

"I . . . I'll be okay. . . ."

"You don't look okay."

He tried to find a smile without success.

"Actually," he said, "I feel awful."

"Perhaps we should take you into Penzance," the Gaffer said. "To the hospital."

He'd followed Janey into the living room and now stood near

the stairs, leaning against the banister, obviously hesitant to come much closer.

Felix shook his head—and immediately wished he hadn't. Every movement made him want to hurl.

"No hospital," he managed.

If he hated being sick, he hated hospitals more. As far as he was concerned, they were designed solely to make you feel worse than you already did, though how he could feel any worse than he did at the moment, he couldn't imagine.

"It might be a good idea," Janey said. "We've no idea what kind of drug that woman fed you."

"She *did* drug me?"

Janey nodded.

"And you brought me . . . here?"

"All on her own she did, my robin," the Gaffer said.

Felix looked from one to the other, moving only his eyes.

"You both believe me now?" he asked. "That I had nothing to do with these people. . . ."

Janey laid a hand on his shoulder. "Of course we believe you. We were rotten not to have given you the chance to explain."

"We went a bit mad, I suppose," the Gaffer added. "I'm sorry, Felix. Sorrier than I could ever say."

For all his nausea, that made Felix feel a hundred times better. Deep in his chest, a tightness eased. An ailing part of his spirit began to heal.

"That's okay," he said. "We all screw up."

"But not this badly," Janey said.

"It's okay," Felix repeated. "Really it is."

"About that hospital," the Gaffer began.

Felix shook his head again, sending up a new wave of nausea.

The Gaffer eyed him for a long moment. Some of the heaviness that had been lodged behind his eyes had faded while they spoke. He straightened his back and nodded.

"Then you'll be wanting some tea," he said.

That brought a real smile momentarily to Felix's lips. Trust

Tom Little. If it needed a cure, why then, it was tea that would cure whatever the ailment. The Cornishman's answer to chicken soup.

"Tea would be great," he allowed.

"You should just rest now," Janey said as the Gaffer went to put a new pot on.

Felix closed his hand about hers as she started to get up to leave as well.

"I don't want to be anywhere but here," he said.

Smiling, Janey remained sitting on the couch beside him.

3 ·

Willie Keel appeared at Lena's door, bright and early. He stood out in the hallway, cap in one hand, the other hand extended towards her.

"Got the job done," he said. "Just like you wanted."

The sleepless night had left Lena in a foul mood, but she kept a rein on her temper. Depending on how things went, she might still need Willie's help again.

"I don't have cash," she said. "Can I give you traveler's cheques?"

"Are they in sterling?"

"Of course."

Lena looked in her purse to see how much she had left in traveler's cheques. Just a little under six hundred pounds.

"How about if I give you five hundred today and we can go together to the bank for the rest on Monday morning?"

Keel considered that for a moment.

"Well, now," he said with a frown. "That wasn't our bargain, as I recall it. You were the one who called me up in the middle of the bloody—"

"Are you having some trouble, miss?"

Lena looked up to find Jim Gazo standing in the hallway no more than a few steps away—not a flicker of recognition in his eyes, just as she'd asked. He'd come upon them so quietly that neither she nor Keel had been aware of his approach.

If Keel reminded Lena of a weasel, then Gazo was a grey-eyed bull. He was broad-shouldered and tall, his features handsomely chiseled except for a nose that had been broken once and never set properly. He kept his dark hair short, and with the care he took of his physique, whatever he wore looked good on him. Considering his size, his ability to be unobtrusive and next to silent on his feet was one of his major assets. No one wanted a bodyguard's presence constantly screaming protection—unless that was a necessary part of the job, and then Gazo could handle that equally well.

Lena glanced at Keel who was trying to surreptitiously place the newcomer without being obvious about it. He wasn't having a great deal of success.

"I . . ." she began.

"There's no problem," Keel said quickly. "Traveler's cheques would be perfect."

With Keel's back to him, Gazo allowed a flicker of a smile to touch his lips before he gave Lena a nod and continued on down the hall to his room. Keel followed her back into her room where she sat down by the dresser. She dug about in her purse for a pen, then signed over the required number of cheques and handed them to him.

"I'll ring you tomorrow morning," he said as he stuffed them quickly in the pocket of his jacket. "Unless you've got other work for me today?"

"Tomorrow will be fine," Lena told him.

She hobbled back to the door with him and closed it firmly behind him. She started to lock it, then reconsidered. She hadn't asked Willie *how* he'd managed his success with the Mabley woman, but it *had* been done, and knowing Bett, she knew that Bett would be in a worse mood than ever after having been thwarted. She waited a few moments to give the hallway time to be cleared, then limped painfully down to Gazo's room. He opened it on the first knock, gaze shifting quickly left and right, down either length of the hall, before it settled on her.

"Bad move?" he asked.

Lena shook her head. "No, it was just the right one."

Gazo glanced down at her leg and noted the swelling. "Did Bett do that to you?"

"Would you believe I fell off a bike?"

"Coming from you? Yes. You don't know the meaning of doing things halfway. Do you want to come in?"

Lena nodded. "I got in Bett's way last night and though I'm not sure if he knows it or not, I'd just as soon be somewhere he can't find me."

When Gazo offered her his arm to lead her into the room, Lena couldn't help but remember Felix and all of his small kindnesses. She could feel her eyes start to well up with tears, and blinked fiercely.

Damn him.

Damn this whole situation.

When Gazo showed concern, she pretended more pain in her ankle than she actually felt as an excuse for the shiny glisten that thinking of Felix had brought to her eyes.

"Daddy's flying in today," she said once she was sitting and had her emotions under a little better control. "With John Madden."

Gazo, moving like a panther for all his bulk, sat down on the bed.

"So what's going on?" he asked. "Or do I even want to know?"

Lena shook her head. "You don't want to know."

This is what it's like to have no friends, Lena thought, astonished at the realization. She'd never really thought of it before. She had employees, from Jim Gazo here to her maids and gardeners at home. She had every kind of person willing to spend time in her company, trying to impress or waiting to be impressed, but no friends. Not one.

Right now she would give anything to have someone with whom she could share the turmoil that tore at her heart. Someone who would understand. Unfortunately, the only person she could think of who fit the bill was Felix Gavin, and she'd closed the book on his ever giving her a moment of his time again.

Last night's bad dreams came roiling back through her mind.

Put them aside, Lena, she told herself. Put it all aside. It was time to carry on. Get that mask in place and don't let it slip again.

Imagine Bett sniffing out her present weakness. . . .

"So tell me, Jim," she said. "What's new in Boston?"

"Other than the Celtics being in top form?"

4 ·

Like Felix, Janey had her own troubling memories to deal with— both real and dreamed—but unlike him, there was no vagueness in her sense of recall. It wasn't something for which she felt grateful. Images circled around and around in her mind, as though they were spliced together on a tape loop. . . .

The scene outside on Chapel Place, when she and the Gaffer had sent Felix off.

Driving through the rain.

Felix in the American woman's bed.

Her mother as an alcoholic bag lady.

Forgive me.

And the secret Dunthorn book, spilling out its music, so magical at first, until the shadows closed in and then it turned so very, very dark. . . .

She was happy to be with Felix, sitting on the couch with him to keep him company, but she didn't like the silence. Because it gave her too much time to think. It made it too easy to start the tape loop spinning its captured images through her mind and then all she wanted to do was just hit something . . . any-thing, but preferably the woman who'd drugged Felix, because—

She jumped when the doorbell rang.

Now who . . . ? she started to think, but then she remembered the *Rolling Stone* reporter who was supposed to be by today and thought for one horrible moment that it was him coming to take his photos, and here she was, looking like death warmed over. But when the front door opened, it was Clare who stepped inside.

"Who's that then?" the Gaffer asked, coming out of the kitchen.

Seeing Clare, he smiled.

"Decided to forgive me?" Clare asked.

"You were right and we were wrong, my flower," he replied. "*We* should be the ones asking for your pardon. If you hadn't . . ."

His voice trailed off as Clare waved a hand at him.

"It's done," she said. "Let's not worry over it anymore."

She turned to step into the living room, her gaze sliding past Janey to where Felix lay on the sofa. Relief settled over her features. It wasn't until that moment that Janey realized just how anxious Clare had been. As Clare looked at Felix, a tightness eased from around her eyes and the corners of her mouth.

"You *did* find him," Clare said.

She came farther into the room to have a closer look at him and some of her worry returned.

"Is he all right?" she asked.

"Well, the woman did drug him," Janey began, but then Felix cracked open an eye and looked at the pair of them.

"I wish you wouldn't talk about me like I wasn't here," he said.

"Feeling better then, are we?"

Her tone was teasing, for all that the question was serious. She gave his hand a squeeze.

Clare sat down on an ottoman that she pulled over closer to the couch. The Gaffer came into the room as well and, after moving the Dunthorn book, settled into his own chair.

"A bit," Felix replied. "I'm not ready to go body surfing out on the bay or anything."

Janey didn't hear him for a moment. She stared at the book that the Gaffer had moved, the memory of its music—both the glad and the dark—moving through her mind before she turned back to Felix and found a smile to offer up.

"No," she said. "There's been quite enough excitement around here as it is, without us having to call out the lifeboat to rescue some daft sailor who's decided he's in Hawaii instead of Cornwall."

"Excitement?" Clare asked.

So Janey launched into an account of what had happened last night, editing out just what sort of a compromising position she'd found Felix and the woman in. If Felix couldn't remember, well then she bloody well wasn't going to drag it up herself.

"I had a bit of excitement myself on the way home," Clare said when Janey was done.

And then it was her turn to relate how a simple walk up Raginnis Hill had turned into a scene from one of those slasher films that the tabloids liked to dwell on when there isn't any real news for them to either uncover or make up.

"Oh, that must have been awful," Janey said.

Felix looked grim.

"Did you call the constables, then, my love?" the Gaffer asked.

Clare shook her head. "Davie doesn't get along well with them and—"

"No surprises there," Janey interrupted.

"And by the time I got up this morning," Clare went on, "well, I just felt sort of stupid. I mean, what would I say when they asked why I'd waited so long to report it?"

"The truth," the Gaffer said.

Clare shook her head. "That wouldn't be fair to Davie."

"He was probably out looking for someone to rob himself," Janey said.

"And that's not fair either," Clare said. "If it weren't for him, I wouldn't be here talking to you right now."

"I suppose. But Davie Rowe." Janey shook her head. "And then you invited him *in* to your house?"

"What should I have done? Sent him off, back into the rain, without so much as a thank you? Besides, I was still scared. At least with him there, I felt safe."

"But Davie Rowe. . . ."

"I think she gets the picture," Felix said.

Janey turned to him. "I suppose. But you don't know him, Felix. He's been to prison and everything."

"What she means," Clare said, "is that he's not the most handsome bloke you're likely to meet."

"What difference does that make?" Felix asked.

"It shouldn't make any," Clare said.

Janey threw up her hands. "I give up. You know what I meant, Clare. I don't have anything against Davie Rowe."

Clare nodded. "I know."

Janey looked at her friend, sitting there on the ottoman, as unruffled as though she hadn't almost been killed the previous night. How did she do it? How did she stop her own tape loop from replaying its images through her mind?

"You seem so calm," Janey said to her. "If it had happened to me, I'd still have the jitters."

Clare nodded. "I do have them—but they're hidden away, deep down inside me. Sort of locked up and secreted because I feel that if I let them out, then I'll lose control and I won't be able to ever stop shivering. So I act calm, and somehow acting calm makes me feel calm."

"Did you get much of a look at the man?" Felix asked.

"Not really. It's all sort of blurry, and then he was wearing those goggles and the scarf. . . ." She paused as though remembering something. "But there was something. He had this tattoo, right about here—" She lifted her wrist and pointed.

"What kind of a tattoo?" Felix asked.

Janey gave him an odd look. His tone had been sharp, almost cross. He'd raised himself up on one elbow and was staring at Clare with an intensity that was disturbing.

"A dove," Clare said.

Felix sank back against the sofa, seeming to shrink like a deflating balloon.

"A dove," he repeated slowly.

Clare nodded. "Well, it was a stylized kind of a thing. I thought of a dove when I saw it, but I only saw it for a moment. It was definitely a bird."

"Do you have a pencil and some paper?" Felix asked Janey.

The Gaffer got up and fetched some. He started to hand them to Clare, but Felix shook his head.

"No," he said. "Let me see them."

He lay on his side when he had them and made a quick drawing that he held up to show to Clare.

"Did it look like that?" he asked.

Clare went white. "How did you . . . ?"

"I've seen that tattoo before."

"You *know* the man who attacked Clare?" Janey asked.

Felix shook his head. "Lena Grant has a tattoo just like it on her own wrist."

Janey's eyes widened. If Lena and the man who had attacked Clare last night were connected . . .

"It's the book," she said.

The Gaffer picked up *The Little Country*, three pairs of eyes tracking the movement.

"Lena Grant was after the book," Janey went on. "There was the burglary, then she tried to drug Felix while her friend went after Clare. . . ."

She closed her eyes, trying to follow it all through, but her train of thought ran up into a tangled knot that wouldn't unravel.

"Why?" she said. "What could drugging Felix or trying to hurt Clare have to do with that book?"

"Better yet," Felix said, "what is it about the book that's so important?"

Janey nodded. "They can't just want to publish it."

"There'll be more to it than that, my queen," the Gaffer said. "There's something odd about this book of Billy's."

Clare held up a hand. "Everybody wait a minute. You've lost me. I know that there are people trying to get hold of some of Dunthorn's unpublished writings, but what is this book you're all talking about? You don't mean to tell me that there's an unpublished novel . . . ?"

The Gaffer handed it over to her. Clare read the spine, gave Janey a questioning glance, then turned back and opened the book before anyone could speak. She read the title page, flipped to the copyright page. Janey could see her fingers trembling.

"An edition of one," Clare said wonderingly.

She flipped a few pages, read a few lines, flipped a few more pages. As though she was back in her dream, Janey heard a faint trace of music that was abruptly cut off when Clare closed the book. She blinked to find Clare regarding her with an unfamiliar look in her eyes. It took Janey a few moments to realize that it was anger. A sad kind of anger, but anger all the same.

"You know how much I love Dunthorn's work," Clare said. Disappointment lay heavy in her voice. "I'm as mad for it as you are, Janey—maybe more. How could you keep this from me?"

"It's not what you think."

"I thought we were friends."

"We *are* friends," Janey said. "But I only just found it and—and..."

"And what? You couldn't trust me to keep the secret?" Clare shook her head. "I don't understand any of this. *Why* is it a secret?"

"You can't blame Janey, my robin," the Gaffer said. "She was only keeping a promise that I made to Billy when he first gave me the book."

"But..." Clare was holding the book close to her, one hand lying possessively over it, the fingers of the other running along the top of the binding. She looked at Felix.

"You knew?"

"Only since yesterday," he replied. "I found it when I was waiting for Janey and Tom to come home from the session. Then they told me it was a secret—their secret. It wasn't mine to tell."

"It was my secret to keep," the Gaffer said. "The book's been hidden for years, but recently I had to store it in the attic and then Janey found it...."

He looked as uncomfortable as Janey was feeling. She'd been so caught up in finding the book, and then there'd been all those curious events since she'd found it, that she'd never thought about how much Clare loved Billy's writing. It hadn't been her secret to share, but she felt awful for not asking her grandfather to let Clare in on it. They both knew that Clare would never break a trust.

"Everything's been so mad lately," Janey said. "I never thought to ask Gramps if you could see it."

"I made a promise to Billy," the Gaffer repeated.

"A promise?" Clare asked.

Janey glanced at her grandfather, who nodded.

"It's in the letter there that I'm using for a bookmark," she said. "Go ahead—read it."

Clare took out the letter, leaving a finger to mark the place, and read Dunthorn's brief note.

"This only makes things *more* mysterious," she said when she'd read it.

Janey nodded. "That's exactly what I felt when I read it."

"Did Dunthorn really have any paranormal abilities?" Clare asked, looking over at the Gaffer.

The Gaffer blinked. "What do you mean?"

" 'That famous Mad Bill Dunthorn Gypsy prescience strikes again,' " she read from the letter. "That makes it sound as though he had foretold the future on more than one occasion, and foretold it correctly, I'd assume, or why bring it up at all?"

"Well, Billy had a way about him," the Gaffer began.

Janey glanced at him. He was obviously feeling uneasy discussing this sort of thing. She shot him an encouraging look when he turned her way for a moment.

"What sort of a way?" Clare asked.

"Well, my flower, he seemed to *know* things, that's all. Not the marvels he wrote about in his stories, but odd things all the same. Unlucky ships, good times coming, and bad. He didn't talk about it much—for who'd listen to a young lad like he was, spouting off that sort of nonsense?—but he talked to me, and I listened."

The Gaffer hesitated again.

"And?" Janey asked.

The Gaffer sighed. "And he was right more often than not."

"And the book?" Clare asked. "What is it about the book that makes it so important?"

The Gaffer shook his head. "Billy never said, my flower. But things—odd things—seem to just *happen* whenever it's not hidden away. I can't rightly explain what I mean. It's not so much that the book makes these things happen as that it gives them a push to get them started."

"You mean it's like a catalyst?" Clare asked.

"That's the word."

"But why? What could possibly be the purpose in that?"

"Does it need a purpose?" Felix asked. "Maybe it's just enough to know that there's something marvelous still in the world, that all the mystery hasn't been drained out of it by those who like to take a thing apart to understand it, then stand back all surprised because it doesn't work anymore."

That made Janey think for a moment—both about what Felix had said and the fact that he'd said it. She'd always considered Felix to be a very practical, down-to-earth sort of a person—but then that's how her grandfather described Dunthorn as well. She supposed a person could be practical and still have a fey streak.

That was what music was like, she'd always thought. You'd see some old lad like Chalkie Fisher, about as commonsensical a man as you'd care to meet, all plain talk and plain facts, but when he brought out his box and woke a tune from the buttons and bellows, well then it was just a kind of magic, wasn't it?

You didn't try to understand it. You just appreciated it.

Music.

Magic.

The tape loop of her memories brought up that moment in her dream when the book lay open and the music first started to spill out of it. A music so similar to what she'd thought she'd heard when Clare had been flipping through its pages. . . .

"What kind of things happen?" Clare asked, bringing Janey's concentration back to the conversation at hand.

The Gaffer shrugged. "Just . . . odd things, my gold. Sounds and noises where there shouldn't be any. Movement caught from the corner of your eye when there's nothing there. Everyone filled with a certain unexplained restlessness. The village getting a . . . haunted feeling to it. And then the dreams. . . ."

Janey thought she heard a catch in his voice as his words trailed off, but then she was remembering her own odd dreams of the previous night. When she looked about the room, everyone appeared thoughtful, and she wondered what kind of dreams they'd had. If theirs had been anything like her own. . . .

The Gaffer shifted in his chair and cleared his throat.

"But that's neither here nor there," he said.

Felix nodded. "We've got a more basic problem to deal with."

"But where do we begin with it?" Janey asked.

"I think it's time we called in the constables, my love," the Gaffer said.

Janey nodded.

"And tell them what?" Clare asked.

"That you were attacked for one thing," Janey said. "And the house was burgled."

"And that we believe it's all part of some conspiracy by a secret society that's looking for a hidden talisman that just happens to be this old book?" Clare tapped *The Little Country* with a short fingernail. "They'd think we'd all gone bonkers."

Janey leaned forward. "That's it, isn't it?" she said. "That dove tattoo—it must be the symbol of a secret society, like the Freemasons or something like that."

"Could be," Felix said. "Though it seems a little farfetched."

Janey ignored him. "So how do we find out what society uses that symbol?"

"Would it even be possible to find out?" the Gaffer asked.

"What do you mean?" Janey asked.

"Well, if they're known, my treasure, then they wouldn't be very secret, would they?"

"There's people that study that kind of thing," Felix said. "I've got a friend in California who's made a life's study of the weird and the wonderful. The odder the better; the more secret, the more he wants to know about it."

"We have someone like that right around here," Clare said. "Peter Goninan. He's forever putting the strangest books on order—all kinds of obscure historical and hermetic texts—and I don't doubt that he does as much or more by private mail order."

"I know him," the Gaffer said. "He still lives on the family farm out by St. Levan. Billy and I went to school with him when we were all boys and he was an odd bird then."

Janey shivered. "I've run into him along the coast path a few times," she said. "He gives me the creeps."

"I've never met him," Clare said. "He usually makes his orders by phone, then has a neighbour fetch the books for him. At least I suppose she's his neighbour—she's a tall, gangly woman who always rides about on an old boy's bike."

"I've seen her about," Janey said.

The Gaffer nodded. "Chalkie's met her. Her name's Helen something or other and I think she rents a cottage from Goninan."

"Then she's been doing it for a few years," Clare said, "because Tommy knew her from when he worked at W. H. Smith's—before he opened his own shop."

"Do you really think Peter Goninan could help?" Janey asked.

She was reluctant about going out to Goninan's place, but then she realized that just as Davie Rowe's looks gave her one impression, Peter Goninan's gave her another. He was tall and ungainly, skeletal thin and bald, with a way of looking at a person that a medieval peasant would have put down as the evil eye. He dressed in tattered clothing, usually black, so that he looked like some odd sort of crane hopping about the fields whenever she'd seen him.

But since looks weren't everything, as Clare had so recently reminded her, he was probably the kindest of souls.

She smiled to herself. Right. And bloody Davie Rowe had never been to prison. . . .

"It's worth a try," Clare said.

"There's this to think about if you go to talk to him," Felix said. "If there is some secret society that uses a dove as their symbol, who's to say he's not one of their members?"

Clare grinned. "Well, we'll just have to have ourselves a quick look at his wrist before we tell him anything, then won't we?"

Felix smiled back. "Fair enough. So let's go talk to him."

He started to sit up, but immediately lay back down again, his face pale.

"Felix?" Janey began.

He shook his head, then grimaced at the movement.

"I can't go," he said. "Not unless you promise to stop every few feet along the way so that I can throw up. I'm fine when I lie down, but as soon as I sit up, or move at all . . ."

"Janey and I'll go," Clare said.

Janey nodded. She wasn't enamoured with the idea, but Clare couldn't go on her own.

"Will you stay with Felix, Gramps?" she asked.

"I don't like it," the Gaffer said.

"We'll be fine," Clare assured him.

"Fine," the Gaffer replied in a voice that plainly said he thought they'd be anything but. "With madmen running about, attacking people with knives, and who knows what other mischief brewing? Who's to say you won't be attacked on the way? Come 'pon that, who's to say that when you get there, it won't be as Felix said and you'll find Goninan himself in the thick of it?"

"We'll be very careful," Clare said.

"Unless you want to drive Clare over and I'll stay with Felix," Janey said.

She could see her grandfather weighing the danger between the two. The house was in the village, but that hadn't stopped the enemy before. Here, they knew where to find her. Down the coast, they might not be able to find her as quickly. . . .

"Go on, then," he said. "But don't be too long about it."

Janey leaned down to give Felix a kiss.

"You'll be careful?" he asked.

"Very," she promised.

"Can I take this?" Clare asked, picking up the rough drawing of the dove that Felix had made.

Felix nodded.

Janey fetched her jacket and just got to the door where Clare was waiting for her when the phone rang.

"It's for you, my gold," the Gaffer said, holding it out towards her.

Janey sighed, and went back into the room to take the call.

5 ·

Michael Bett's lack of sleep the previous night left him clear-headed and alert when morning finally came.

The deprivation made little difference to him. He hated sleep anyway, normally allowing himself only the bare minimum amount that his body required. To his mind, sleep bred complacency. It took you away from the edge where everything was clear-cut and precise; that edge where you could make an instantaneous decision and not have to second-guess the consequences. The mind automatically correlated all available data and spat it up so that you could concentrate on getting the job done, not worrying about whether or not you could pull it off or if it was the right thing to do.

On the edge, you just *knew*.

And that was something that Madden's sheep would never experience. Because they were soft-bellied and slothful, their heads stuffed with cotton. When he walked the edge, he was more than a wolf to them; he was an alien species. A man such as he knew himself to be could do anything—so long as he was operating on the edge.

With a man like him, the sheep didn't stand a chance.

Take Janey Little and whatever secret of Dunthorn's it was that she and her grandfather were hiding from the world.

He'd been approaching the problem like a sheep would, soft-stepping around them, playing by the rules. Madden's orders: Don't make waves. But there were no rules—not on the edge—and standing there, with the world in sharp focus all around him, his mind honed as keen as the cutting edge of a razor, he knew exactly how to handle her now.

Madden was still important to him. Bett hadn't finished with the Order and Madden remained his link to it. So he'd accommodate Madden's wishes for the moment. He wouldn't take the knife to either of the Littles. He wouldn't even hurt their friends. There were other ways to cut their world off from under them.

Leaving his room, Bett went downstairs. He'd heard the owner of the B and B go out a few minutes ago, then watched him head off down the street from his window. With the place to himself, he sat down in the man's sitting room and pulled the phone over onto the fat arm of his chair. It took a few minutes before the operator could make his overseas connection, but finally he could hear the phone ringing on the other end of the line in New York.

"Dennison Investigations," a voice answered.

"Sam? Michael Bett here."

"What can I do for you, Mr. Bett?"

"I'm in Cornwall and things are winding up to a head. It's time for you to work off the final part of our contract."

"Let me get a pen. Okay, shoot."

"First thing you do is contact a man named Ted Grimes." He gave Dennison the particulars of an Upper West Side address and the phone number of Grimes's office there. "Then you're to pick up the woman and the three of you are going to take the first flight over here. I want you all in Penzance, ASAP."

"The woman's coming voluntarily?"

"She's on salary, the same as you."

"I'll get right on to it, Mr. Bett."

Bett cut the connection and stared at the phone for a moment before calling the operator again. He made a half-dozen other long-distance calls, then finally dialed a local number. Tom Little answered and put his granddaughter on the line.

"Janey? Mike Betcher here."

"Oh, hello, Mike. Did you sleep well?"

Bett put a smile in his voice. "Sure. I slept great. Listen, about our getting together today . . ."

"Something's come up and I was just on my way out. Can I ring you up a little later in the day?"

"I wanted to cancel myself," Bett said. "Actually, I didn't want to so much as I have to."

"Is something wrong? Are you all right?"

"It's not me—I'm fine. It's . . . Christ, I don't know how to tell you this, Janey. It's the strangest thing. I got a call from my editor canceling your participation in the article. He wouldn't talk to me about it, he just said he didn't want you in the piece, period."

There was a moment's silence on the other end of the line, then Janey asked, "But . . . why?"

"That's what *I* want to find out. I'm heading back to London today to see if I can't straighten this all out. You haven't been making any enemies lately, have you?"

"What?"

"The thing is, he seemed pretty pissed—my editor, that is. The last time I heard him in a mood like this was when he got a lawsuit thrown at him by that guy in—well, never mind who. It got settled out of court. But he's not happy with you, Janey, and I can't figure out why. I'm kind of pissed off myself—not at you, naturally—and I'm going to go to bat for you, but if there's anything you can tell me about what's going on that could help . . . ?"

"I—I don't know anything about this."

"Yeah. I didn't think you did. Look, I'm going to straighten this out, but it might take a few days. Can I call you when I get back in town?"

"Of course. But—"

"I have to get going, Janey. I'm sorry to hit you with all of this, but I figured that if you didn't know, then you should."

"I appreciate that, Mike. Only could you—"

"That's the thing I hate about this business," Bett went on. "All these feuds and vendettas and crap. You'd think people could carry on their business with a little maturity, but it's worse than dealing with toddlers in a day care sometimes, you know what I mean?"

"Not really. I—"

"I've really got to run. I'll call you in two days—three at the max. Don't worry, Janey. We'll get this all straightened out. In the meantime, you take care of yourself, okay? And try not to worry."

"But—"

Bett cradled the receiver and thought about what he'd said.

Try not to worry.

He smiled to himself.

Like she was just going to forget about this call. And when the other pieces of the puzzle started to fall into place and she found out just how easy it could be to lose it all . . .

A mind, he thought, was almost as much fun to take apart as a body.

Replacing the phone where he'd found it, he went back up to his room to get dressed.

Time to pay a little social call on the Ice Princess, he thought. Maybe play a few games with the tiny excuse for a mind that she had. Apologize for last night. Come on all sweetness and light. Vow to help her get back together with her sailor, if that was what she really wanted.

By the time he was done with her, she'd be telling him how sorry she was that *she'd* screwed things up. And when Madden and "Daddy" showed up, well Lena and he'd just be the best of pals, now wouldn't they?

Sure they would.

Everything was going to go his way again because he was back on the edge.

Back on the edge and looking good.

6.

Janey slowly cradled the telephone receiver, her face paling as what Betcher had told her sank in.

It made no sense.

Not a smidgen.

"What is it, my robin?" the Gaffer asked.

"That was Mike—Mike Betcher," she replied.

"The *Rolling Stone* writer?" Clare asked.

Janey nodded. "He said that his editor canceled the article. No, that's not right. He just canceled my part of it. Mike asked me if I have any enemies; he said that the editor was mad at me. . . ." She looked from her grandfather to Clare and Felix. "I don't even *know* the man."

"There must be some sort of a mistake," the Gaffer said.

"Or maybe it's just the opposite," Clare said.

"What do you mean?"

"Maybe it was deliberate. If we're postulating conspiracies . . ."

Janey gave a halfhearted laugh, but no one else joined in.

"Oh, come *on*," she said. "Think about what you're saying. It doesn't make any sense."

"I don't know," Felix said. "Maybe Clare's got something there. So far they've already tried to alienate you from me and to kill Clare. That sounds to me like they're trying to cut you off from your friends. Now they're working on your career. . . ."

"I can't believe Mike's involved in it as well," she said. "He just told me that he's going up to London to argue my side of it with his editor."

"His editor's in London?" Clare asked.

"Well . . . I don't know. That's just what he said. Maybe they have a branch office or something there." She shook her head. "It doesn't make sense that he'd be involved. Or his paper."

"People can be bought," Felix said.

"But . . . ?"

Clare took her arm. "The sooner we see if we can find out something about these people, the better, Janey."

Janey looked at Felix.

"She's right," he said.

"I don't know what Peter Goninan can do to help," the Gaffer added, "but we'd best get to the bottom of this quickly, my gold."

"I suppose. Gramps, would you ring up Kit and ask her if she's heard anything?"

Kit Angelina was Janey's booking agent who worked out of London.

"Her number's in my little red phone book," she added.

"I'll ring her straightway," he replied.

"Ta."

Janey hesitated a moment longer, but then Clare took her arm again, so she followed her friend out to the car.

As she got in behind the wheel, she looked around at the familiar sight of Chapel Place—her grandfather's garden, the Methodist Chapel, the friendly houses all leaning close to the street. Suddenly everything seemed distant, strange. As though they were all part of one world, and she was in another.

It was a horrible, lost feeling.

"Janey?" Clare asked.

She looked at her companion, not seeing her for a moment, then slowly nodded and started up the car.

But as she pulled away, she couldn't help but wonder, why was this all happening to *her*?

7 .

Davie Rowe was sitting in the King's Arms, waiting for Willie Keel to arrive. The pub was in Paul, across Mousehole Lane from St. Paul's Church. Silver-haired Harry was in his usual spot behind the bar, talking to a pair of old lads who farmed up Trungle way. Their gum boots were still muddy, but both men were wearing their Sunday best—cloth caps and clean jackets and trousers, ties knotted under their chins. Other than them, Davie had the pub to himself, although the dining room next door was rapidly filling up. Snatches of conversation and laughter spilled through the open partition behind the bar that led to the other bar in the dining room.

But on this side it was still quiet. The inevitable Fruit machine was silent for a change. Davie was tempted to play it for a while, but he never won much with the gambling machines and he was low on cash, with no more than the price of another half in his pocket until Willie came 'round with his money. So he sat on a bench by the billiards table and nursed his pint.

And waited another half hour.

Willie showed up just after Davie had finally finished his pint and ordered a half of Hicks bitter from the barman. He was returning to his table when Willie came in, grinning expansively. Keel got himself a pint of bitter from the bar and brought it over to where Davie was sitting. He took a long swig from his pint, draining the glass by a third, then set it down on the table between them.

"How's the lad, then?" he asked.

"I've been better."

"Well, this'll cheer you up."

Keel glanced towards the bar, then drew a folded sheaf of ten-pound notes from his pocket that he handed over to Davie. Davie pocketed them quickly, not bothering to count them. Whatever extra Willie might have made on the deal himself—taken out of Davie's share, to be sure—Willie wasn't one to go back on a deal. If he'd promised Davie two hundred quid, then the bills he'd just handed over would amount to two hundred quid, not a farthing more nor less.

"Not bad for a quick spot of work, eh?" Keel said.

"Not bad at all," Davie agreed.

It was very good money.

"And I don't doubt that there'll be still more where that came from," Keel added.

Davie leaned forward on the table. "What's this all about, Willie?"

"Well, now, you know my feeling on that. You do the job and you collect your pay, but you don't ask questions."

"I know that," Davie said. He'd learned that and a great deal more from the time he'd spent in prison. "But this woman—what could she want with Janey and Clare?"

"What do we care? Just so long as she pays."

"Yes, but—"

"I'll tell you this." Keel leaned closer as well. "Our Miss Grant isn't alone in this business. There's not just money behind her, but more manpower as well. Now we have the in, Davie my lad. It's our backyard, as it were, and the Americans can't move about as freely as we can. But"—he tapped the table with a finger for emphasis—"I'll tell you this. If we go about talking out of turn and shoving our noses in where they don't belong, they'll step in themselves, and then how will we profit?"

"But you just said that they can't get about the way we can."

"And it's true. But there's others'd like a cut of this easy money, Davie. And come nightfall, who can tell the difference between a local man and some American? They may want to step easy, but they're not above doing a little dirty work their own selves. And maybe, the first bit of work they'd take on would be to quiet a flapping gob, if you get my meaning."

Davie shook his head. "I'm not looking for trouble. It's just that . . . well, Clare. Why would anyone want to harm her?"

"There's a thing you need to learn," Keel said, "and that's the plain and simple truth that everyone has their secrets. Some are darker than others, but we all have them. You might have known Clare Mabley all your life—"

"I have."

"But that doesn't mean that you *know* her. I could tell you tales . . ."

"What? About Clare?"

Keel laughed and shook his head. "Not about her. But there's many a fine and upstanding citizen in these parts that's done worse than either you or I could even think of, Davie. I tell you, I know a secret or two."

"Like what?"

"Now that would be telling and then what sort of secrets would they be?"

"That's easy to say."

"Then think of this: Why is it that I've never been sent up to prison, my lad?" Keel patted his upper arm. "That's because I *know* things that important people would rather not see made public."

Davie was still curious, but he let his questions ride. It was true that the law never seemed much interested in Willie Keel, but he doubted that it was due to any hold the little man held over various and sundry important citizenry. Who'd listen to, little say believe, tale-telling when it came from the likes of him? It was far more likely that Keel was simply an informer.

Keel finished his bitter and stood up.

"Well, Davie," he said. "I've work still to do."

"Anything for me?"

"Maybe, maybe not. Stay near a phone and I'll give you a ring if something comes up."

Davie didn't want to leave it at that. He wanted to know more about the American woman—how she could know that Clare was in danger and, more important, *who* the threat was coming from. If Willie wouldn't tell him, straight out, then tagging along with him would have been the next best thing. Because Willie liked to talk and sooner or later, over the course of the afternoon, he'd let some tidbit or another slip. But he also knew he couldn't push.

"Fair enough," he said. "I've got an errand or two to run myself, but then I'll be at home."

Keel gave him a broad wink. "Here's to Americans and their money," he said and made for the door.

Davie watched him leave the pub, then settled back on his

bench. He finished his half. Fingering the money in his pocket, he thought of buying another, then decided against it.

It felt wrong to spend this money. Wrong to even have it.

Oh, he'd earned it, no doubt about that. He'd saved Clare and sent her attacker running. He'd done his job.

His job: That was exactly what bothered him. Clare had never been unkind to him—not like some others he could name. Helping her shouldn't have been a job. It should have been something he'd do simply because it needed doing. Because she was in trouble and needed help. Not because there was money to be made.

It was an odd thought, he realized, coming as it did from a man who made his living nicking what he could from the tourists who flocked into the area every summer. But they were different. They were rich, or at least richer than he was. They weren't anybody he knew. They . . .

They weren't Clare.

A couple of local lads came in then and started up a game of billiards. He watched them play until the one who was losing began to complain in a loud voice that he was missing his shots because a certain ugly face was throwing off his concentration. His friend grinned and Davie could feel the red anger come rising up inside himself when he looked into their smirking faces.

He stood up and both lads backed up a little at his size, holding their pool cues more tightly. Davie's hands formed meaty fists at his sides and his eyes narrowed. He started to take a step towards them, but then he glanced at the barman, he thought of Clare, and he let his fists unclench. Nodding stiffly to Harry, he left the pub, laughter ringing in his ears.

They knew he wouldn't fight. Once he had—every time they sniggered or called him names—but not anymore. He couldn't. Not if he didn't want the law on him again. And not fighting made him feel better than them. But it didn't stop the hurt, nor the anger.

As he walked back down the lane towards Mousehole, hands

thrust deep in his pockets, he allowed himself the pleasure of imagining how it would feel to smash those smug grins of theirs, but that only made him feel worse.

Think of something cheerful, Davie, he told himself.

The first thing that came to mind was sitting with Clare at her kitchen table. He wondered what it would be like to hold her. If they made love. . . .

What kind of strength did she have in that lame leg of hers? Was it strong enough to wrap around him, holding him tight against her, drawing him in deeper?

You'll never find out, he told himself.

But that didn't mean they couldn't be friends. Perhaps he could go over and borrow a book from her.

He fingered the wad of ten-pound notes in his pocket.

Or he could just talk to her. About what he knew. Perhaps she was in trouble and she could use his help. It would be the two of them against her enemies—just like in the films. He'd be Dennis Quaid and she'd be his Ellen Barkin. And when her enemies were defeated, she would be so grateful. . . .

He could feel himself get hard, his penis pressing painfully against his trousers.

No, he told himself. You'd only be friends.

But that would still be something, wouldn't it? To have a real friend?

He thought of what Willie had said, back in the King's Arms.

Everyone has their secrets.

What were hers?

Some are darker than others. . . .

How dark could hers be?

What did it matter? He knew that however dark her secrets might be, they would never be so black that they would make him turn away from her.

Bloody hell, he thought. The whole thing was hopeless.

But when he got to Regent Terrace, he took the right-hand turn all the same—the one that would lead him across the back of the village to Raginnis Hill where Clare lived.

Touch Me

If You Dare

Yield not to evils, but attack
all the more boldly.

— VIRGIL ,
from *Aeneid, Book VI*

The Tatters children began to arrive while Henkie, Taupin, and Lizzie were blocking off the windows of the warehouse. The three of them took turns standing on a rickety ladder, covering the panes with squares of cardboard that they then taped into place. Window by darkened window, the warehouse took on a gloomy air as the only light inside now came from the handful of oil lamps that Henkie had hung about the cavernous room.

Taupin had gone out earlier to leave word with Kara Faull about how they needed the help of the Tatters children and she was now the first to arrive, flinging the door open without so much as a knock and marching inside. Sunlight streamed in through the door, cutting a bright swath of light down the center of the warehouse while deepening shadows beyond.

"Hello!" she cried, blinking in the doorway. "Shall I bring in my bike?"

"Shut the bloody door!"

Henkie's voice boomed from the far side of the warehouse— loud enough to make Jodi wince. She sat on Denzil's right shoulder, because that was the best way for her to stay out of the way, yet still make herself heard to at least one of her co-conspirators. She hung on to his collar to keep her perch, grumbling whenever

Denzil bent too far over the table to work on the task that Henkie had assigned to him.

"Does he always have to shout so?" she asked Denzil.

"Actually," he replied, "I rather feel he's been on his best behavior."

"I can't believe that."

"Well, from all I've heard—"

"Will you shut the door!" Henkie repeated, his voice booming louder.

Kara merely smiled at him, now that she could make him out in the gloom.

"The others are just coming," she said, "so we might as well keep it open. What about my bike?"

"Toss it in the bay for all I care."

Kara's lips shaped a practiced moue. "You're not being very friendly," she announced. "*Especially* seeing as how we're here to help *you*."

Henkie glared down at her from the top of the ladder.

"Well, it's true," she added.

"Fine," Henkie told her. "Leave the bloody door open. *Let* the witch's creatures in so they can spy out all our secrets. We've only spent the last bloody hour blocking off these windows so that they can't peer in, so naturally we're delighted that you plan to leave the door wide open so that they can simply waltz in. Shall I put on some tea for them, do you think?"

"What's he on about, then?" Kara asked Taupin.

"Never mind him. We're happy to see you. Just do keep an eye on that doorway and make sure nothing comes in."

"What sorts of nothing?"

Taupin shrugged. "I'm not sure. To be safe, how about nothing larger than a fly?"

Kara's gaze panned from him to Henkie and Lizzie, then to where Denzil was sitting at a table, sewing doll's clothes.

"Nothing larger than a fly?" she repeated.

Taupin nodded. "Just to be safe."

"*Will* you send up another square of cardboard?" Henkie asked from above.

Taupin reached down to the stack by his foot and passed another piece up to Lizzie who stood on a rung about halfway up the ladder. She handed it on to Henkie.

"You've all gone mad, haven't you?" Kara said.

"Not really," Taupin said. "It just seems odd. Give us a few moments to finish up with this here and we'll explain the whole business to you."

"That's all right," she told him. "I like things when they get a bit mad."

"Who's mad?" a new voice asked.

Peter Moyle had come up behind Kara. He peered into the warehouse, over her shoulder.

"Hello there, Denzil," he called. "What's that you've got there on your shoulder—a new kind of monkey?"

"I'm going to give him such a thump," Jodi said. "Once I'm a bit bigger, that is."

"That's not a monkey," Kara said, her voice suddenly all aglow with wonder. "It's a Small."

They both stepped closer.

"No, it isn't," Peter said. "It's Jodi!"

"The door!" Henkie shouted.

Peter glanced up at him. "It's still there," he called back.

"Shut. It."

But neither of the children paid him any mind. They approached the table where Denzil was working, mouths open to form wondering O's.

"However did you turn her into a Small?" Kara asked.

"Can you do me next?" Peter added.

"Bloody hell," Henkie muttered. "See to the door, would you, Brengy?"

"But the ladder . . . ?"

"We'll be fine."

As Henkie turned back to lay the new sheet of cardboard over the window, Taupin went to shut the door only to be confronted by a gaggle of Tatters children who trooped in, all in a group, and were soon clustered around the table where Denzil was now holding court, speaking as though he'd known magic was real all his life and not in the least embarrassed by his abrupt about-face.

Taupin gave a quick glance outside. The children's bicycles lay in a litter of metal and wheels all around the door, but that was all he could see. Or at least it was, until he turned his gaze a bit farther from the area directly in front of the warehouse. Then he caught a glimpse of someone in a black mantle ducking out of sight behind the seawall—there one moment, gone the next.

"She's still out there," he called inside.

It was quieter now, Denzil having admonished the children for their excited cries by explaining how their loud voices were hurting Jodi's ears.

"Any sign of her wee beastie?" Henkie asked. "What's its bloody name? Willow? Whimple?"

"Windle," Lizzie supplied.

"Nothing that I can see," Taupin called back.

"Then shut the bloody door!"

"Henkie," Lizzie said. "Must you shout so?"

He looked down at her.

"Now don't you start in on me," he began, wagging a finger at her. "Ever since Brengy dragged us into this, it's been nothing but 'Henkie, don't do this,' and 'Henkie, don't do that'—"

He broke off as the ladder began to sway.

"Steady now," he cried. "Steady."

But it was his shifting his weight that was making it wobble and as he tried to compensate for the sway, he leaned too far over in the other direction. The ladder tottered for a moment, then pitched to one side. Lizzie jumped and landed on an old mattress that lay nearby, but Henkie was on the top and all he could do was hold on and ride the ladder down.

All conversation stopped in the warehouse as they watched

him topple into a stack of paintings. The ladder skidded out across the floor, bouncing once or twice before coming to a stop. Henkie plunged into the paintings and the whole stack tumbled down in a cloud of dust. When the air finally cleared, it was to show Henkie sitting stunned amid the paintings.

He'd poked his hand through one, his foot through two others, but what made the Tatters children hoot with laughter was the painting that his head had gone through. It was a nude of a busty woman and hung before him like an apron, his head having gone through exactly where the model's head had initially been painted.

He tugged it off with a steady stream of curses and lumbered to his feet, whereupon everyone fell still. There was something more than a little intimidating about an angry man his size.

"Right," he said. "You and you"—he pointed to a pair of the children—"finish blocking off the windows. You"—his finger jabbed the air again—"listen by the door. The rest of you can help Denzil—you *do* know how to sew, don't you?"

"I can."

A gamine half the size of Kara stuck up a dirty little hand as she answered. She couldn't have been older than seven. Her face was round and her hair a mop of tightly wound curls.

Henkie's glare softened. "Can you now?"

The small girl nodded.

"And what's your name?"

"Ethy."

"Well, then, Ethy, you'll be Denzil's special helper."

Her little face beamed.

"As for the rest of you," Henkie went on.

"Wait up a minute," Peter said. "We came to help—not to be ordered about like you were the law or something. We can get enough of that at home."

"If you came to bloody help," Henkie started, "then you can bloody well begin by listening to what I have to bloody tell you, or you can just bloody well bugger off and leave us to our . . ."

His voice trailed off as Lizzie gave him a kick in the shin.

"Have you gone mad, woman?" he demanded.

"They're all mad," Kara confided to the other children.

"Listen to yourself," Lizzie said.

A rumbling growl began deep in Henkie's chest.

"Listen," Lizzie repeated.

For a moment it looked as though he was going to smash something. Everyone, except for Lizzie, took a step back. But then he sighed and nodded.

"I'm going to sit down in that chair over there," he said, pointing to a corner, "and I'm going to quietly drink a great bloody big glass of whiskey. Call me when the planning can begin."

Lizzie stepped up on her tiptoes and bussed him lightly on the cheek before he went off.

"Ta," she said.

The children parted like the Red Sea before Moses as Henkie stalked towards them, closing up again when he'd gone by. They watched him pour a full glass of whiskey and then sit down in the chair where he swallowed half the whiskey without so much as his eyes watering. Having tried the foul liquid themselves at various times—as children will—they were suitably impressed and more than a little awed.

When they turned their grimy faces back to Lizzie, she faced them and smiled.

"We're very grateful to have your help," she told them, "and though some of what needs to be done is boring, there'll still be some fun at the end of it all."

"What needs to be done?" Peter asked, obviously as charmed by her as he'd been put off by Henkie's attempt at ordering them about.

Lizzie explained how they needed to finish blocking off the windows. There were any number of identical doll-sized outfits to be sewn. Wigs needed to be cut and pasted to dolls' heads. A watch had to be kept against spying eyes and ears.

"What's it all about?" another of the children asked.

Glancing over from her perch on Denzil's shoulder, Jodi identified the speaker—Harvey Ross. He was a big, strapping boy who'd give Henkie a run for his money when he finally stopped growing. At twelve years old, he was already getting odd jobs on the fishing luggers, working side by side with the men.

"Do you know the Widow Pender?" Taupin asked.

"She's a witch," a boy replied.

Jodi didn't have to look to recognize Ratty Friggens's voice. As big as Harvey was for his age, Ratty was small. He was a year younger than Jodi, but topped tiny Ethy by no more than a pair of inches. His real name was Richard, but because of his twitchy nose, pointed features, and the way he liked to skulk about using his size to its best advantage, he'd been dubbed "Ratty" years ago and the name stuck.

"Exactly," Taupin said to a chorus of in-drawn breaths from the children.

It was one thing to suppose there were such things as witches and Smalls, but quite another to find that they truly *were* more than tales.

"What we have to do is hide Jodi from her long enough to get her to the Men-an-Tol without the Widow being aware of what we're up to."

"What if she turns us all into Smalls for helping you?" Kara asked.

"She needs to know your name and repeat it three times before she can work her spells," Taupin explained. "Surely you could run away from her in that time? Or at least block your ears?"

"And it has to be your true name, doesn't it?" Ratty asked.

"The one that makes you who you are," Taupin agreed. "The one that, in your mind, encompasses all that you see yourself to be. So if she was to try to enspell you, Ratty, she'd have to call you Ratty Richard Friggens, because I'm guessing that's how you think of yourself."

Ratty nodded.

"She can't possibly know all your names," Taupin said.

"But she could learn them, couldn't she?" Ethy asked.

"I . . ."

Taupin looked helplessly at Lizzie who then took over once more. She went on to explain the rest of Henkie's plan. By the time she was done, the children were grinning from ear to ear.

"This *will* be fun," Kara said.

Then it was a matter of setting everyone to their task. All the children wanted to volunteer to help Denzil, because then they could look at the tiny Jodi perched on his shoulder and listen wide-eyed to her story, not to mention giggle at her high-pitched squeaky voice. There were a number of arguments—along the lines of "I had first dibs" and "She couldn't sew if her life depended on it" and "Sod you, too"—but soon it was all sorted out fairly by the simple expediency of allowing everyone to have their turn at the sewing.

By the time everything was prepared—the plans laid out and every contingency that they could foresee argued out to a suitable solution—it was midafternoon and time to begin.

"Remember," Taupin told the children as they all gathered by the door. "If worse comes to worst, you can always jump in the bay and neither she nor her creatures can touch you."

"What about the drowned dead?" Ratty asked.

Various children nodded nervously.

Taupin glanced at Jodi. "Do you know anything about this?"

Jodi shook her head, fed up with how the children all giggled whenever she spoke. She was going to thump more than one of them when she was finally her own size again.

"It's just what I've heard," Ratty said. "That she can call up the dead from the sea and they come shambling out, dripping water and seaweed, to chew on the flesh of the living."

"We have it from a very good source," Taupin said, "that witches can't abide the touch of salt."

"Yes, but the sea dead won't be touching *her*," Ratty said.

Henkie rose from his chair like a bear leaving its den in the spring.

"If you don't want to go, boy," he said, "just bloody come out and say so."

"I'm not scared," Ratty said.

"Me either," Ethy added. "I'm not scared at all."

"Then let's see what we can do," Henkie said.

Kara was closest to the door. At a nod from Lizzie, she turned the knob, threw it open, and went outside to where her bicycle lay in the dirt.

2 .

The Widow Pender wasn't always a widow, nor a Pender.

She was born at that exact moment that lies equidistant between the last sliver of the old moon and the first sliver of the new. Her birthing took place in the bed of a donkey-pulled cart drawn up in back of a hawthorn hedge when the first winds of winter were shivering the trees and the hoarfrost lay black on the frozen ground.

It was an auspicious time for a birth—at least, it was deemed auspicious by her people, for they believed that it was by hardship that a spirit was tempered and made strong.

Her mother's midwife had been a witch, and she was born into a family of witches, the third and last of three daughters to bear the surname of Scorce. Her people were considered travelers by those who knew no better; the traveling people themselves, however, knew exactly what the Scorces were and avoided them when they could, leaving their secret signs scratched into the dirt to warn the other traveling clans of the Scorces' whereabouts.

The new babe was named Hedra in a curious ceremony a few weeks later, for that was the old word for October, the name of the month in which she was born. Her family gathered about a tall, craggy standing stone set high on a cliff overlooking the sea, and had there been observers to view the proceedings, they would have seen much gadding about in the raw, wordless chanting and mad dancing, the burning of small straw figures and charms in fires made of bones, and the crafting of fetishes that were each bound to the new babe's name and her future. Each participant in the ceremony left with one such fetish that they would keep safe through the years to preserve the newly named child's luck.

Under her stiff blouse, the Widow Pender still wore her fetish in a tiny leather pouch. She wore it to remind herself of those days when she had been Hedra Scorce and the world was a merry place of bright wonder, when shadows were only shadows and she had no knowledge of what hid behind their darkness, watching her every move, glittering eyes heavily lidded with cobwebs.

But she didn't wear it for luck, because all her luck had long since fled.

The Scorces had traveled the country for many years—mother, aunt, and grandmother riding in the donkey cart, the girls walking alongside. Like other traveling people, they did odd jobs and mending, picking potatoes and other vegetables in season, selling the besom brooms and baskets that they made and the charms that, unlike those of the other travelers, were potent in and of themselves, requiring no belief to work their magic. They loved the road, the long road that unwound underfoot that had no beginning and no end, carrying them from one town to another, through one village and beyond, up into the lonely places, the moors and rock-strewn clifftops that were anything but lonely to those who lived as close to the earth as they did.

But times changed. They grew harder for all the traveling people as the constables shifted them from town and village green, until only the moors and cliffs were theirs; but they could gain no sustenance from those desolate reaches. The natural beauty and wonder sustained the spirit, but the body required more secular nourishment, and that they could only earn in the villages and towns.

Hard times.

Sometimes now, she could see those eyes, watching her from the shadows. And she'd hear a voice, whispering. And then a whole chorus of them.

"Don't listen," her grandmother told her when she asked about what lay in the shadows. "The mischiefs and evils of the world wait in the shadows to prey on children innocent as you. They will promise you anything. Follow their advice, accept their gifts, and your soul will grow bitter. It will shrivel and wither until you can no longer feel the Mother's presence. When you leave her light, all that will remain for you is the shadows and I'd wish that on no one, not friend, not enemy."

"But they say they can help us."

"The sweeter the promise," Grandmother replied, "the surer the lie."

"But—"

"Remember the lesson that the Christians have forgotten: When Adam and Eve made their choice in Eden, it concerned neither blind obedience nor righteous piety. It was a choice of self over God, arrogance over faith."

"We aren't Christians," Hedra objected.

"True. But our Mother of Light and their Christ are not so different—in our hearts we both follow the light; only the names differ. What speaks to you from the shadows is that same Eden serpent, child."

"I like snakes."

Her grandmother smiled. "So do I. But there's a world of difference between the small cousin we can catch in the grass and the one whose voice tempts us from the shadows. Promise me you won't listen to it."

She had never seen her grandmother so serious, so solemn.

"I promise," she said.

And she did try to follow her grandmother's advice, to keep her promise, but it was hard not to listen when the world was as it was, when the light seemed to die, no matter where you turned, and all that was left was shadows.

Hard times.

Kerra was the first to leave, marrying a shoemaker in Peatyturk. Grandmother died. Aunt married into another traveling family. Mother took sick, but recovered. Gonetta stayed on until they passed through Rosevear, marrying the son of a shopkeeper.

Then there was only herself and Mother left, following the road with their donkey and their cart.

Hard times.

The whispers in the shadows grew stronger and she couldn't help but listen. But she remembered her promise to her grandmother and did nothing with the secret knowledge that they breathed into her ear.

Not when the constables sent them from town before they could buy a few meager provisions and they were reduced to grubbing for roots and scavenging along the shore.

Not when they were jeered at by those who went to church, those fine upstanding townsfolk who listened piously to the teachings of the light spoken of within the holy stone halls, but left with less charity in their hearts than the cold winter winds.

Not when the children pelted them with stones, or the dogs were set on their heels. For fun.

Hard times.

Mother died on a night as cold and lonely as the one on which Hedra had been born. They were camped in back of a different hedge, but the hoarfrost lay as black on the ground, the wind was as cold. Fifteen years old, Hedra sat up all night, rocking her mother's corpse in her arms. Come morning, she buried the unfamiliar object that her mother had become. It was an empty thing, its soul fled, and bore no more resemblance to her mother than did a stone.

But she could remember comforting arms, a sweet high voice that sang lullabies to the counterpoint of the wind outside their canvas tent, a smile as warm as sunlight in summer.

The shadows drew close to her, whispering, whispering.

She huddled by her mother's grave, arms wrapped around her chilled body, shivering and trying not to listen, but it was hard, hard. As hard as the times. She crooned one of her mother's lullabies, closing her ears to the voices, rocking back and forth again, but this time the burden was in her heart, not in her arms.

And that was how Edwin Pender found her.

He brought her home. He made her his wife. He gave her order and love and comfort and kept the shadows at bay. The donkey grew old and lived out its life in content. The cart stood behind the Pender cottage, its bright paint fading in the rough weather, grass entwined in the spokes of its wheels, its bed home now to leaves and debris while sleepy cats lay on its driver's seat when the sun was warm on the wooden slats.

But Hedra didn't mind, for Edwin Pender had driven the hard times away and filled the emptiness inside her. He worked the sea and she kept their home. If he was disappointed that she never gave him a child, he never once mentioned it. They went to church together and Hedra was content to exchange her Mother of Light for their Christ, because hadn't Grandmother said they were one and the same—that only the names differed?

Hard times fled.

Until she learned of her husband's mistress.

He laughed when she confronted him with her knowledge. A man such as he needed more than one woman, he told her, but she wasn't to worry. Her home was here and he had more than enough love still left over for her, didn't he just? So come to his arms now. . . .

She had backed away from him, but she hadn't said a word.

Her rage was a silent storm.

For as her world went dark, the shadows came back in a rush, eyes glittering in the dark corners of the room where they hid, voices whispering, and she remembered all the secret knowledge that they had ever told her.

When her husband went to sea, she called up a storm. If it drowned the Old Quay and sank the fishing boats, if fifteen men had lost their lives, what did it matter, so long as Edwin Pender was in their number?

Her husband's mistress she gave to the shadows. High on a clifftop, on a moonless night, she fed the barmaid a length of steel, then buried the corpse in an unmarked grave where its moldering bones remained to this day.

She felt no regret.

She felt no regret because her spirit belonged to the shadows now and they bled all such softness from her spirit, embittering and withering it. In return, they gave her yet more of their secret knowledge.

She spent the years toying with the folk of Bodbury, working small unpleasantries that could never be traced back to her, setting into motion complex patterns of bad luck that took years to be fully realized and were all the more appealing to her for the invisible machinations of her own hand in their intricate making.

She created the approximation of a child for herself, from herself, giving it birth as surely as other women nurtured children from their womb. Her fetch. She named it Windle. Together they lived in the borderland between the world as common folk knew it and the secret world that hid in the shadows. Spying and playing their games, they were like a pair of spiders who made an invisible web encompassing the lives of every man, woman, and child in Bodbury.

And she was content.

The bright child she had once been was as forgotten as though she had never existed.

Hedra Scorce? Who was she? There was only the Widow Pender now.

And the years went by.

Twenty years since the storm, since she accepted the shadows.

Those years stole the lives of fishermen on sea. Others died on land, men and women both. Children were born. The wheels of the world turned. And the Widow Pender grew older, her spirit no more than a smear of darkness inside her, as black as the hearts of the shadows.

But as she grew older, she found herself remembering a time when the world was a brighter place, when she bore a different name and the shadows didn't rule her. The memories came first as small nagging thoughts that she simply ignored. But as time passed, she'd see faces.

Her sisters; her aunt. What had become of them?

Her mother. Her grandmother.

Edwin Pender.

How could so much good have gone wrong? she would find herself wondering. Had there been another manipulator—one such as she was now—who had pulled the marionette stringed web that was the heart of her life and that of her family?

The shadows hissed and spat when she thought such thoughts. Windle grew distant.

She found her birth fetish lying in the back of a drawer, and took to wearing it again. She thought of luck, bad and good, found and lost.

She remembered an old song she had heard once, verses of which returned to haunt her at odd times of the night or day:

> *You took what's before me and what's behind me,*
> *You took east and west when you wouldn't mind me;*
> *Sun, moon, and stars from my sky have been taken,*
> *And God as well, or I'm much mistaken.*

Her husband had given her everything, and then taken it all away again. She would have done anything for him, but even that had not been enough.

> *O black as a sloe is the heart that's in you;*
> *Black as a coal is the grief that binds me;*
> *Black as a boot print in shining hallway—*
> *'Twas you that blackened it, forever and always.*

That dark, shriveled stain that was her spirit began to ache, deep in her chest. She thought more and more of what her grandmother had told her, of how the shadows lied, of how they could manipulate the innocent. . . .

She tried hard to remember, but she couldn't imagine what it would be like to be any way other than how she was now. Considered so, how could she know if she'd made the right choice in her life? How could she know that the choice hadn't been made *for* her?

To find out, she needed to be free of the shadows and they

wouldn't let her go. Not unless she could give them a secret that they didn't hold themselves. That was the price—a simple, impossible price.

Until she remembered the child she had been and the tales her grandmother and mother both had told her of the Barrow World—the otherworld of the piskies. The shadows had no hold there. If she could give them its key . . .

She bought a mechanical toy man and, with wax and charms, made it appear so lifelike that one would expect it to sit up and talk at any moment. Then she woke the one spell concerning piskies that the shadows knew. The enchantment sped through the air one moonless night like a fisherman's hook and line, whirring through the darkness until it snagged and caught the dreaming mind of a little moor man and brought it back to her cottage.

Animated now, her mechanical toy man would still not speak. Would reveal no secrets.

The shadows laughed.

Windle watched, an unfamiliar grin on its lips.

But the Widow was undaunted. Like a child with a new toy, she made a home for her captive in an old aquarium and became engrossed in fashioning furniture and clothing to his size. While she worked, she considered and put aside a hundred plans on how to wrest the little man's secret from him, thought until her head hurt and she began to realize that she was defeated. She would never discover his secrets. She would never be free of the shadows.

In the end, it was the arrival of the snooping Tatters child that gave her a workable plan. She had meant to let Jodi stew for a few days—just long enough for despair at never regaining her own size to settle in—then she would strike a bargain with the girl. If Jodi stole the necessary secret from the little man, then the Widow would set her free.

It was that simple.

Except the miserable girl, and piskie both, had escaped and now she was back where she'd begun, with only one hope left—

that the little man had told the girl something useful while they were together.

It was clutching at straws, but clutching at straws was all that the Widow had left. The pain in her chest ached fiercely. And the whispering laughter from the shadows was driving her mad. Worse still, understanding had come—riding on the back of those selfsame memories that tormented her so—that when she died, she would join the shadows.

If truth be told, she had always known. But it hadn't seemed so important once. Now she grew old, and with age came a fuller realization of what being part of the shadows meant.

Never being free of pain.

Never knowing peace.

Never joining her family in the beyond.

Losing all that was hers not simply once or twice, but forevermore without any hope of reprieve. . . .

The irony of what she was doing—attempting to regain lost innocence through tormenting another—simply never occurred to her at all. She was blind to all but her own need. Had she stopped to consider, she would have understood exactly what it was that made the shadows laugh as they did.

But her strength was her single-mindedness and it was for that reason that she crouched by the seawall of the Old Quay, spying on Hedrik Whale's warehouse, while her fetch scurried about its roof and walls, attempting a closer look. She cared nothing of what the townsfolk would think of her behavior. She wanted only to understand what Whale and the others were up to. She knew they had Jodi in there with them. But what were they going to *do* with her?

They were such an improbable collection of individuals that they made an impossible group to second-guess. Each on his or her own could be odd enough, but collected together, they were literally capable of any mad scheme. And when one added the gaggle of Tatters children that had arrived earlier . . .

The Widow was sure that certain disaster lay ahead.

She shifted uncomfortably from foot to foot, utterly sick of staring at the weather-beaten side of the warehouse. Then she saw a small spidery shape swing down from the roof to come scuttling along the base of the seawall towards her.

Something was up. She could feel it brewing in the air.

Windle began chittering away to her, so fast that she could barely make out a word of the creature's odd language. She finally realized that it was merely telling her what she already felt—that the waiting had ended.

As though on cue, the door to the warehouse was flung open and the whole crowd, adults and Tatters children, came streaming out. The Widow closed her eyes and reached out with her witch-sight—a kind of seeing that looked beyond what could be seen by the naked eye, for it stripped the world down to its basic components.

Blood called to blood.

The Widow had taken the precaution of taking a few drops of blood from Jodi when she was unconscious and swallowing them. The taste of them fired sharply against her palate now as her witch-sight reached for, found, and locked on the first child to come through the door.

That little Tatters girl. She was carrying Jodi, the Widow knew. She could taste Jodi's blood so near the girl that she had to be carrying her.

She started to straighten up and open her eyes, but then she realized that the second child was carrying Jodi as well. As was the third and fourth—they were all carrying her, children and adults alike.

Which was impossible.

She focused her witch-sight more sharply and her head began to ache from the effort.

She felt old and tired.

The bright sun made pockets of shadow at the base of the seawall and she could hear sniggering laughter coming from those dark patches.

Fine, she thought. They've either cut her up and they're all carrying a bit of her, or they've managed some other trick, but it won't help them. She'd merely track them all down, each and every one of them. One way or another, she meant to regain hold of the Small she'd created.

The sniggering of the shadows grew louder.

Laugh all you want, she told them. You'll still not have me in your ranks.

At that, the laughter came long and sharp.

Not ever, the Widow said.

In front of the warehouse, the children were all on their bicycles now. They sped off in a dozen directions, little legs pumping the pedals for all they were worth. The adults also took different directions, only they moved more slowly. The Widow sent Windle after one of the children, then marked and set off after another herself.

Not ever, she repeated.

There was no reply from the shadows, but that was only because she had stepped out into the sunlight where they couldn't follow her.

3 ·

When she heard her parents complaining, when she saw what it was like to be even a few years older than she was, Kara Faull would think that there couldn't be a grander age to be than eleven. She hated the idea of growing any older. There was the odd adult like Denzil and Taupin who might as well still be children for the way they carried on, or those like Jodi and Ratty who were still in that undefined stage between being normal and adult, but mostly, growing old just seemed to be a steady progression of doors being shut.

On magic.

On wonder.

On just plain having fun.

She was thinking about that as she pedaled away from Henkie's warehouse. If you couldn't go off on a mad lark like this, any which time you pleased, then really, what was the point?

For this *was* a lark. And more, it pointed true to all those things that adults said couldn't be real. For when you saw it with your own two eyes, how could you doubt it? The old stories weren't lies. There truly *were* witches and Smalls and every manner of wonderful thing. They were *real*. And if that wasn't the best thing she'd learned in weeks, she didn't know what was.

Her legs pumped furiously to maintain her speed up the incline that was Weaver Street. When she reached its crest, she grinned as she coasted down the far side of the hill—fat bicycle wheels humming on the cobblestones, the wind in her face, the skirt of her sundress flapping against her thighs, laughter bubbling up inside her.

Tucked away in a pocket of her dress was one of the dolls that they had made in the warehouse. Not one of them looked anything like Jodi, but that wasn't the point, Taupin had told them. It was the size, and the flash of hair colour, and all the clothing being alike. And it was the tiny drop of Jodi's blood that was carefully dripped onto the head of each doll, the blood that was immediately absorbed by the thirsty cloth.

Kara hadn't liked that part—and neither had Jodi, judging by the grimace on her miniature face when she had to prick her finger with a pin and then give a bit of herself to each doll.

Privately, Kara was sure that even a witch couldn't be so stupid as to mistake any of these dolls for the genuine article, but Taupin had insisted, quoting tales of enchantment and witcheries where just that sort of trick was not only considered clever, but proved to be successful as well.

We'll see, she thought, as she leaned into the corner at the bottom of the hill where Weaver Street briefly met Tinway Walk, crossing over and changing its name to Redruth Steep as it climbed another rise.

She chanced a glance behind as she turned the corner, but the way was clear. Still grinning, and only narrowly avoiding a collision with a pedestrian who shouted angrily after her, she stood up on her pedals at the bottom of Redruth Steep and began the new ascent. Halfway up the hill, she shot into the mouth of Penzern Way—a crooked narrow alley that would take her back to the harbour by a circuitous route as it wound its way between the backs of the close-set stone buildings that clustered in this part of the town.

Well, I'm away, she thought, slowing her pace to avoid a run-in with someone's untidily stacked garbage. The witch and her fetch—whatever *that* was—had chosen someone else to follow, which only proved her point.

The dolls simply weren't the clever trick that Taupin had made them out to be. Now if he'd only listened to her plan of borrowing a fisherman's net with which they could catch the witch and then toss her into the bay, why then they'd all be laughing by now, because—

Something the size of a cat landed on her back and dug its claws into her shoulders.

Kara shrieked and lost control of her bicycle. Its front wheel turned awkwardly on a cobblestone and she was tossed over the handlebars. All that saved her from a terrible collision with an all-too-rapidly approaching wall was that the hem of her skirt caught on the end of a handlebar. The thin cloth ripped, but its momentary hold had been enough to break the momentum of her flight so that she landed in a pile of refuse—winded and shaken—rather than cracking her head on the wall.

But she had no time to consider her good fortune. The thing on her back was clawing at her skin and all she could do was to continue shrieking as she rolled about in the garbage, trying to dislodge it. When she succeeded, it immediately scampered around in front of her and swiped at her face with its talons. Kara jerked her head back so quickly that she pulled a muscle in her neck.

"If," Taupin had told them, "you feel that you're in any sort of danger at all, for God's sake, *give* up your doll. That's what they're after. Give it up, and when they see what it is they've been chasing, they'll hurry off after another one of us."

Taupin's words rang in Kara's mind as she stared with horrified fascination at the creature that was perched so near her face.

Jodi's description had been all too accurate. It looked like a hairless caricature of Denzil's monkey, but there the resemblance ended, for Ollie didn't have claws like the fetch's, nor those rows of sharp teeth that would do a shark proud. Nor did Ollie's throat produce the awful chittering sound that escaped from the creature—akin to drawing a fingernail across a chalkboard.

Kara's earlier curiosity about the creature had utterly vanished. All she wanted to do now was to escape its presence, but the fetch crouched too closely by her. There wasn't a move she could make that would allow her to avoid those sharp teeth and claws.

The fetch's saucer-wide eyes glared with malevolence and she shivered as the creature's gaze locked onto her own. There was a brutal rage in those eyes—and also the promise that the fetch would enjoy the violence that would ensue when that rage was released.

Kara didn't want to hang about to see that happen.

She scrabbled in her pocket for the doll. Trembling fingers took a moment to get a grip on the thing, but then finally she was pulling it free and offering it up to the little monster facing her.

It tore the doll from her hand, rage glittering sharper as it saw what it was. Its chittering rose into a high-pitched crescendo that made Kara's eardrums feel as though they would burst at any moment.

"Th-that's all I've g-got," she managed.

Her throat felt thick and dry and she could barely croak the words out.

The fetch glared at her. It opened its mouth wide and bit off the head of the doll, chewing the cloth and fabric stuffing, throat working as it swallowed the mess down.

Kara could only continue to stare, fascinated and repulsed by its every motion.

When it had finished swallowing the doll's head, it tossed the body away and leaned closer to Kara, grin widening. It swung its paw at her and panic loosened her throat's constriction to let wail another shriek. The creature snickered as she fell back in the garbage in her attempt to get away, then it swung onto a drainpipe and scrambled quickly up to the roof. Two breaths later, it had disappeared.

For a long moment Kara simply lay where she'd fallen. Her every muscle ached. She felt as though she were bruised from head to foot. The stench of the garbage made her stomach queasy and she wanted to throw up.

But she was alive.

The creature hadn't killed her.

She sat up slowly, wincing at the pain the movement brought her. A nervous look at the rooftops surrounding her showed no saucer-eyed face peering down at her still. It was gone now—after one of the others.

Well, that was their problem, she thought. She was just happy to be alive. As far as she was concerned, all the fun had gone out of the day's lark.

But then she thought of Ethy. Little Ethy, with her own doll hidden under her shirt. If the fetch went after her . . .

We were all bloody fools, Kara thought as she hobbled over to where her bicycle lay. We should have stood up against them together, sitting in great vats of seawater, armed with salt-water balloon bombs. . . .

Balloon bombs. Now that was absolutely brill.

She opened the little purse attached to her belt and counted her pennies. She had barely enough to buy what was needed—but it was enough.

She righted her bicycle and got on. Setting off down Penzern Way towards the market, she couldn't help but groan as every bump she hit reminded her poor body of the recent abuse it had undergone. Tears of pain sparkled in her eyes, but she kept on, her mouth set in a tight line, and ignored the way the bumps made her want to lie down in a corner somewhere and not move for weeks.

She was determined to give back as good as she'd gotten.

And then some.

4.

It was the Widow who tracked down Ratty Friggens.

Like the others, he'd left Henkie's warehouse on his bicycle, but he went on afoot as soon as he reached Market Square. Hiding his bicycle behind a stack of crates that he knew wouldn't be shipped out for a few days, he continued on through the maze of warehouses and shipping docks until he reached the beginning of one of New Dock's long piers. There he swung down to where the storm drains emptied into the sea. He gave a last quick look out across the bay, then slipped inside and began to make his way back through town—underground.

Find me here, he thought with a happy grin. If you can.

Ratty knew every hidden nook and secret cranny to be found, in and around and under Bodbury. Like his namesake he could squeeze into the tiniest openings, wriggling his way through narrow drains that others would swear were too narrow for a cat, little say a boy from the Tatters, no matter how small he might be. But if Ratty could get his head in, then it was just a matter of drawing his shoulders in close to his body until they appeared to be folded across his chest. And then he would simply slither his way along.

Today he kept to the larger drains. Once his eyes adjusted to the poor light, it was easy for him to walk along at a steady pace. The only illumination came from the odd grating that opened up onto the streets above, but it was enough for him to make do. He kicked at pebbles and the odd bit of debris, pausing to unstop the more complex entanglements that might otherwise dam up a drain.

Ratty kept his underground passages clear for his own convenience, but he was also providing an unknown service to those above whose homes might otherwise be flooded out during a big enough storm. They didn't know and he didn't care if they did or didn't. Below, it was his kingdom.

His plan was to follow the drains right up to the top of the town. From there he meant to go across country for as far as he got before it became dark. He'd been nervous when Taupin first talked about the witch, but then he had made his own plan of what he'd do and where he'd go, and his nervousness had fled. No one was going to follow him down here.

He took his time to reach the far end of the last drain, emerging from it cautiously, but there was no one about. This high above the town he could look out across the rooftops, all the way across the bay. It was one of his favorite places. He could spend hours sitting up here, just watching the boats out on the water, the gulls wheeling above them.

He settled the grating back into place and went to sit on a low wall that backed onto a hedge for a bit of a rest before he continued.

It was amazing really, when he thought about it. He'd spread about the tale that the Widow Pender had got herself a Small just for the fun of it, never dreaming there was any truth in the matter. How could there be? Smalls and witches were part and parcel of fairy tales and had no part in the real world. If there was magic, if there was wonder, then it remained well hidden. So well hidden that it might as well not even exist in the first place. But now . . . oh, yes, now. . . .

Well, he'd seen the miniature Jodi Shepherd with his own two eyes, hadn't he just? *She* was real. There was no denying that. And if she was real, then—

"Ratty Richard Friggens."

His heart stopped cold in his chest at the sound of the Widow's voice. He turned slowly to find that she'd crept up on him as if from out of nowhere—stepping now from the shadows by Kember Cottage, the last building in Bodbury before the hedge-bordered fields began their walk across the hills. She was no more than the length of a half lane from where he was sitting.

She regarded him with an amused smile on her tight lips, dark eyes flashing dangerously.

How could she . . . ? he thought in panic, but the answer came before he could even complete the question.

She was a witch, wasn't she?

"Ratty Richard Friggens," she said again.

He started at the repetition of his name. Remembering what Taupin and Jodi both had told him about witch's spells needing a name spoken three times to work, he hastily pulled the doll he was carrying from his pocket and offered it to her.

"H-here," he said.

Just don't turn me into a toad, he added to himself.

"I don't want that," the Widow said.

"But..."

"I want the girl. The Small."

"I—I don't have her."

"Then who does? Who carried her out?"

Ratty swallowed dryly. He couldn't tell because there was no knowing what the witch would do to Jodi when she had her in her power once again. But if he didn't tell, there was no knowing what she'd do to him either.

He just knew it would be something horrible.

"Come, boy. I don't have all day."

"I—I..."

The name was on the tip of his tongue, burning to be set free into the air, but he couldn't do it. He just couldn't break faith. Not and still live with himself after.

He straightened his shoulders and met the Widow's gaze with his own, trying to stay steady, though his legs were trembling so much that if he hadn't been sitting down, he would have fallen down.

"I won't tell you."

"Ratty Richard Friggens," the Widow repeated for the third time. "Are you so brave, then, boy?"

Brave? He was frightened out of his wits. But by now his throat was so constricted that he couldn't have given her the name if he'd wanted to.

He shook his head.

"Bah," the Widow said.

She added some words in a language that Ratty couldn't understand and the world went all fuzzy on him.

She's turning *me* into a Small, he thought.

His panic lessened somewhat. That wouldn't be so bad. He could prowl about in places that he'd never been able to reach before. He could...

It was growing hard to think. Dizziness rose up in waves. There was a metallic taste on his tongue and he realized that he'd bitten his own cheek. That was his own blood he tasted.

His own blood.

He thought of Jodi pricking her finger, putting a drop of blood onto the head of each doll.

Jodi who was the size of a mouse.

But he didn't seem to be shrinking. Instead, he seemed to be fading away. He was...

His thoughts grew too fragile to hold on to anymore. They flitted about through his head like flies, humming and buzzing, but he couldn't snag even one of them.

What—

He looked down at his hand. It had grown so gossamer that he could see right through it.

—was she—

The doll fell from his grip—no, fell *through* his grip to land splay-limbed on the road.

—doing—

Terrified now, he stared at his hand. It was coming apart like smoke. A breeze touched him, took away a finger in a wreath of pink mist.

—to . . .

He never did get to finish the thought.

5 ·

The Widow smiled humourlessly as the last parts of Ratty Friggens were dissipated by the wind. All that remained was a small bone button on the wall where he'd been sitting. That, and a distant fading cry that sounded very much like his voice, before it too was taken away by the wind.

He'd thought she was going to change him into a Small as well, she had realized towards the end. She'd seen it in his eyes.

Instead, she'd simply unmade him.

Because that had been his real fear. He was the sort who could find fortune in any size he might be. But to be nothing . . .

She smiled and scooped up the button. Needle and thread appeared from her pocket and she quickly sewed it to her cloak where it joined a dozen or so others already sewn there. With the button in place, needle and thread returned to her pocket. She stooped and picked up the doll he'd dropped, her smile fading.

Clever.

Which of them had thought of this?

She lifted the doll to her mouth and licked the spot stained with Jodi's blood.

Too clever.

But she'd have the miserable girl yet. And she'd have gifts as well for the whole gaggle of fools who'd tried to help her. She would change them and unmake them. She would . . .

She sighed. Closing her mind, she reached out with her witch-sight until she found and marked the presence of another one of the carriers. Did this one bear another doll, or the girl herself? The bothersome thing was that there was only one way to find out. She might well waste the entire day tracking them all down.

Unless . . .

She glanced skyward. The early afternoon was aging, the day steadily wearing into the evening. Night would be here soon. She could call up helpers then.

From the marshes.

From under cairns.

From sea graves.

Wrapping her cloak more closely about her, she fingered the newest addition to her collection and set off after the next Tatters child whose position she had noted moments ago.

Behind her, where the shadows were thickening at the base of the wall, shadows laughed softly to themselves. The Widow heard them, as they knew she would, but she paid them no mind.

6.

The animals went mad when Denzil finally returned home in the early afternoon.

Ollie flung himself onto his shoulders as soon as he opened the door, and happily hugged him. Noz gave a complaining squawk from his perch and ruffled his feathers, while the raven swooped down to circle once around Denzil's head, before flying back to its own perch on the bookshelf. The mice scurried about in their cages and Rum wound back and forth in between his legs, tripping him up as he tried to close the door, deal with Ollie, and get into the room.

"That's enough, you!" he cried, straightening his glasses with an angry shove of his thumb and forefinger.

Silence descended. Movement stopped.

"I'm sorry I left you so long, but there were important matters to attend to."

"End to," Noz repeated gravely.

Denzil had to laugh.

He propped up his own Jodi doll by the flying machine on his workbench and spent the next half hour grumbling good-naturedly as he set about feeding them all, then cleaned cages and the mess in the box of sand in one corner where the birds, Ollie, and Rum had been trained to relieve themselves.

Rum scratched to go outside as soon as he was fed, but the other animals followed him about—Noz and the raven with their unblinking gazes, Ollie tagging along like an errant child, making more of a mess in trying to help Denzil clean up than if he'd left well enough alone. But finally order was restored, routines brought back onto track, and Denzil could sit by the window and stare out at Peter Street to consider the past night's odd occurrences.

"Utter madness," he told Ollie who cuddled close to him on the chair. "That's what it is. All the world gone topsy-turvy."

His gaze traveled across the room to where the Jodi doll was sprawled on his workbench.

Nothing was the same anymore. New equations had entered into the calm, if complex, natural world he thought he had come to somewhat understand. Not well, mind you. He'd barely scratched its surface in the better part of the lifetime that he'd spent attempting to unravel its mysteries. But he'd had the basic tools necessary for the task, the scientific demeanor that told him how to best go about his studies, the understanding of the underlying logic that bound the unknown to the known.

And now everything was changed.

Smalls and witches and dead men who could still move and speak. . . .

Tee-ta-taw. *Utter* madness.

His gaze shifted from the Jodi doll to his bookshelves where the raven was now grooming its feathers. He had a wealth of scientific texts, research notes—those of his own, and of colleagues—and every manner of useful tract on every manner of useful subject, from mechanics to astronomy, philosophy to natural history. But not the one of them was of any use in his present situation. He would have to go down to the library and pore through their collections of folklore and myth to learn what he now needed to know. To understand it all. Understand, and correlate it to what he already knew so that he could fashion some kind of a working plan as to what he would do when this immediate crisis was over.

He sighed.

Correlating madness to what he already knew.

Bother and damn, as Jodi would say.

How could he know what to keep and what to throw out? Piskies were real, but did that mean dragons were as well? The dead could walk and talk, but did that prove the existence of demons? Witches could shrink people down to the size of a mouse, but could they fly through the air on a broomstick?

It made his head hurt to think of it all.

And then there was Jodi.

It made sense that he couldn't bring her home with him. This was perhaps the first place the Widow would look for her. But he didn't much care for her to be out of his sight. To have to sit here and wait and wonder until it grew close enough to moonrise so that they could make their way out to the holed stone on which Jodi, Henkie, and Taupin all put so much faith.

Too much faith, if you asked him.

Yes, he told himself, but come 'pon that, twenty-four hours ago you didn't believe there was such a thing as a Small, either, you.

Another sigh escaped him and Ollie reached up to touch his cheek, trying to comfort him.

"I just don't know," Denzil said aloud.

He had his misgivings about this plan that had been concocted in Henkie Whale's warehouse. For all that he could no longer deny the existence of magic, the reality of myth, he still found it difficult to accept that someone like Henkie carried the kind of wisdom they needed. The only sensible one of the lot of them—himself included, he had to admit—was Lizzie Snell.

She was a clever, down-to-earth, practical jewel of a woman. And utterly wasted on the likes of Henkie. What did she see in him? It was easy to see what he saw in her. . . .

Now don't start that kind of thinking, you, he told himself. You're too old a man to think about sparking with the ladies.

But he hadn't always been so old. There'd been a time, when he was a young man—

He shook his head. No, he'd made a choice then and it was far too late to change his mind about it now. He had his studies and nothing had really altered from the time he had made his decision to the present day. What woman would put up with the likes of him anyway—what with his odd hours and animals, the studies that swallowed his life, and he so set in his ways?

A woman like Lizzie Snell.

Or the woman that Jodi would grow up to be.

It was his own fault that he'd given up any hope of finding such a companion for himself.

Too late, too late, the past whispered.

The present agreed.

Fair enough. He would just have to make do with the surrogate daughter that Jodi had become. He'd done so for years, loved her as though she really *were* his daughter. But that didn't stop regrets bittering up against the corners of his mind.

He shook his head again, trying to dislodge this train of thought. Think of something different, he told himself. But then only worries arose—for Jodi; for the Tatters children that they'd involved in their troubles. If anything happened to them . . .

The afternoon leaked slowly away as he sat there, staring out at Peter Street, at the folk who went about their business below him without any concern or care for the hidden world that he'd discovered lying all about them, all about each and every one of them. He stroked Ollie's fur, smiling vaguely as the monkey fell asleep in his arms, and waited for the time to pass.

7 ·

Ethy Welet was really too young for the task at hand, but she would never have admitted it, and no one was about to deny her her chance to take up her part in the trick they meant to play on the Widow. In the Tatters, it simply wasn't done. The children accepted one another for what they were, for what they said they could and would do, and judged one another only on how they kept their word and how well they accomplished the promised task.

So Ethy left with the others, her own Jodi doll tucked under her shirt, and pedaled her small bicycle away, a brave grin on her grimy face, waving cheerfully to the others. But once they were out of sight and she was on her own, the nervousness came.

She thought of the Widow. Even without magic, the old woman was a towering fearsome figure—at least four times Ethy's size and easily capable of far more strength than was hidden in her tiny frame. Whatever would she *do* if the Widow confronted her? And then there was this fetch creature that Jodi had described. It sounded as though it was even more awful.

Maybe they wouldn't come after her. Maybe they'd chase one of the others instead.

She could hope. . . .

But that wasn't a kind thought.

Ethy lived with her father in a small shabby room deep in the Tatters. Caswal Welet was an absolutely brilliant darts and billiards champion. Unfortunately, after Ethy, they were his only loves, so while they had any number of trophies neatly lined up, row upon row, in their room, there was rarely much to eat because Caswal couldn't keep a job if his life depended on it, and one change of clothes each was all they had. When Ethy outgrew what she owned, it was the other children in the Tatters who helped her find new garb. Her father simply couldn't muster enough interest in any job to keep it for more than a week.

Ethy's mother had left them because of that and the people of Bodbury considered him, as they did so many who made the Tatters their home, to be nothing more than a lazy layabout. Caswal, in moments of honesty, would have been the first to agree with them. But Ethy didn't see him like that at all.

The man she knew was kind and thoughtful, if a bit silly. But he always made sure that she had enough to eat, even if he didn't, and they had time to walk about together and he taught her how to play both darts and billiards—moving the crate she had to stand upon around the table when it was her turn for a shot. But best of all were his stories.

He knew any number of them. Wise and wonderful stories. Funny ones and sad. And the heroes—they were always brave and strong, yes, but they were kind as well.

"Kindness is important, my little wren," he would tell her. "Doesn't matter how poor you are, you can still be kind. Doesn't

cost a tuppence, and maybe those you're kind to won't be kind
back, but at least you'll have the satisfaction of knowing that
you tried to leave the world a bit of a better place, even if all
you had to spare was a smile."

She wasn't that strong, Ethy thought as she pedaled along,
but at least she could try to be brave and kind. But the former
was easier thought than done. As she took a shortcut through
an alley 'round back of the butcher's on Weaver Street, the
Widow's fetch dropped on her back and knocked her from her
bicycle.

She stared horrified at the creature, trying not to cry from the
bumps she'd taken in her fall, and clutched the Jodi doll under
her shirt tight against her skin.

The fetch was ever so much worse than Jodi had described
it—all teeth and claws and those huge evil eyes. It made a
chittering sound that rose *click-clicking* from the back of its throat,
a sound like the same harsh words being repeated over and over
again. Ethy knew she wasn't really understanding them, but she
couldn't help but hear them as—

Killyoukillyoukillyoukillyou . . .

Taupin had said to hand over the doll if she was in danger,
but that didn't seem to be a very brave thing to do, no matter
how badly she wanted to do it right at this very moment. Because
if she handed over the doll, then the fetch would just go after
one of the others.

And maybe kill her anyway, just for fun.

She trembled as it advanced on her, and hugged the doll more
tightly.

Killyoukillyoukillyou . . .

"D-daddy . . ." she cried.

The fetch's grin widened.

Ethy didn't want to look, but couldn't unlock her gaze from
that of the horrible little creature. It crouched low, gathering its
muscles to spring at her. A voice stopped it before it could attack.

"Hey, you!"

Ethy looked up and relief went through her. It was Kara.

The fetch turned to look as well and hissed as though it recognized the older girl.

"Come on, you little bugger," Kara said. "You and I, we haven't finished our own dance yet."

Ethy stared wide-eyed at her friend. Kara was scratched, her sundress torn, but she stood as tall as a heroine from one of her daddy's stories, eyes shining, voice firm, just like some knight all in armour, holding up a great heavy sword. Except that Kara didn't have any armour or a sword. All she had was a balloon full of water.

The fetch shrieked and flung itself towards Kara, who promptly let fly her water bomb. Neither of the girls was prepared for what next ensued.

The balloon burst, soaking the fetch with water.

That'll never stop it, Ethy thought.

But the water had been drawn up from the bay, salty seawater filling not only the balloon that Kara had just thrown, but the half-dozen others that she was lugging about in the satchel at her side.

The fetch howled. Steam hissed up from its skin, like water dropped onto a hot griddle. The creature fell to the ground, howling and wailing.

Ethy's fingers went up to her mouth. A moment ago she would have given anything to be able to fend off the creature. Now she felt pity for its pain. Her gaze went to Kara's face to find her own shock mirrored there.

The fetch stopped its thrashing, only to lie still. It whimpered, saucer-eyes filled with pain, its malevolence fled. Its limbs twitched. Its skin was the red of a lobster, steam still hissing from it.

Kara walked slowly around it, never taking her eyes from the creature. She helped Ethy to her feet.

"G-get your bike," she said.

Ethy blinked. "But it's so hurt. . . ."

"It got only what it deserved," Kara replied, but she seemed none too sure of that herself as she spoke. "We have to go."

"We can't leave it," Ethy said. "The poor thing."

She approached it cautiously, holding out one nervous hand. The fetch snapped its teeth feebly at her, but didn't seem to be able to move much otherwise. Ethy looked back at Kara.

"We can't."

Kara hesitated. "What will we do with it?"

"Take it to the Widow's house."

"While she's off attacking our friends?" Kara said, her perspective on the situation returning. She patted the satchel at her side. "We have to help *them* with these."

"You go, then," Ethy said. "I'll take it 'round."

"I . . ." Kara began, then she sighed. "Oh, bother."

She looked about in the refuse that littered the alleyway until she found a relatively dry newspaper. Moving gingerly, she wrapped the fetch in it, her own heart going out to the little creature as it whimpered in pain at the touch of the paper. The fetch tried to bite her, but it had no strength in its jaws. Its whimpering was enough to bring tears to Ethy's eyes.

"Oh, be careful," she said, hovering nearby.

"I *am* being careful."

Kara lifted the fetch. It made a tiny bundle, easy enough to carry in the crook of her arm. Ethy got her bicycle for her, then the two set off for the Widow's house, Kara walking her bike and carrying the Widow's creature, Ethy fluttering along beside her pushing her own bicycle.

8.

The Widow Pender had Peter Moyle backed up against the wall of an alleyway in another part of Bodbury. She had just repeated his name for the second time when she suddenly doubled over, a sharp cry of pain escaping from between her lips. Her missing toe—the one from which she'd taken the bone to grow Windle— came ablaze with pain.

Gasping, she stumbled forward. Peter ducked away to one side and dashed for his bike. He was on it and wheeling for the end of the alley when he stopped to peer back. The Widow was hunched against the wall, moaning, the tears streaming from her eyes.

Shivering, Peter pedaled quickly off, his Jodi doll still tucked safely away in his belt.

The Widow remained behind in the alley. Once the pain struck, she had been no more aware of his presence when he'd been there than she was of his departure when he left. All she knew was Windle's pain.

Burning as though he'd been boiled alive.

His agony was hers, the pain so sharp, so anguished.

So *raw*. . . .

What had they *done* to him?

She was slow in straightening up from the wall. Her leg could scarcely support her weight, the pain in her missing toe was so fierce. Every inch of her skin felt burned and raw. Cramps threatened to buckle her over again, but she stayed upright. She closed her eyes, not against the pain—there could be no surcease from its fire—but to use her witch-sight to track the position of her fetch.

The agony stretched like a wire between them, making it child's play to place him.

It took a moment longer for her to judge her own position in relation to his, but then she hobbled off, a fire burning in her heart as fiercely as the pain wracked her body.

They would pay, she vowed. Every last one of the monsters would pay for what they had done.

Border Spirit

No magic can change something into something it is
not; the imaginative transformation at the heart of
magic is recognition, not creation. . . .

— S U S A N   P A L W I C K ,
from "The Last Unicorn: Magic as
Metaphor," in *The New York Review
of Science Fiction*, February 1989

*J*aney's Reliant Robin was admirably suited to the narrow back lanes of Penwith Peninsula—lanes so confining that in most places they were only wide enough to allow one car egress at a time. But the Reliant's tiny three-wheeled body took to them like a ferret, low-slung and quick, whizzing along at a happy putter between the tall hedgerows that rose on either side, darting by other vehicles, even where the road hadn't been widened for passing.

While Clare had ridden with Janey more times than she could possibly begin to count, she could never help but feel just a bit nervous on a trek like this. As far as she was concerned, the little Reliant was simply too small, its three wheels much too precarious, and Janey's driving, especially when she was in a mood like this, far too impetuous. Any moment she expected them to come smack upon a lorry, or to have the car tip over on some particularly sharp corner that she was certain Janey took far too fast.

It didn't help today that ever since they'd set off from the Gaffer's house, neither of them had spoken so much as a word to each other. It made Clare feel somewhat put upon. After all, none of this was her fault. She hadn't found some rare book that a gang of thugs were bent upon stealing. When it came right down to it, if it weren't for the Littles, she herself would never have been attacked last night. She was the innocent in all of this. All she'd been trying to do was help.

She shot a sidelong glance at Janey and was surprised to see unshed tears glistening in her friend's eyes. She immediately felt guilty for the turn her thoughts had taken. She really wasn't being very fair.

It wasn't Janey's fault either.

"Janey," she began, but then was at a loss as to what to say next.

Janey slowed the Reliant's headlong pace and gave Clare a quick sad look.

"It's all gone so awful," she said. "Finding that book . . . having Felix come back. . . . Everything should have been all wonderful and happy, but it's not. It's horrible."

Clare stifled a sigh. Trust Janey to simply feel sorry for herself. But the next thing Janey said made her realize that she'd misjudged her friend once again.

"I never meant to hide the book from you," Janey said. "I would have asked Gramps if you could borrow it. But everything went so odd, all in a sudden, and I never had a chance to even think about it in the first place." She shot Clare another quick glance. "I'm really sorry that I never told you, Clare. Honestly I am."

"That's all right," Clare said, feeling somewhat chagrined.

"I only found it on Friday," Janey went on, "and there's been ever so much going on since then. . . ."

"I really do understand," Clare said.

And she did. Janey had a mind like a sieve and it wasn't because she didn't care that she'd let something like telling Clare about the Dunthorn book slip her mind. It was just that as soon as something new came up, whatever Janey had been thinking of earlier would find itself put away into a little box and then stored off somewhere in the muddle that was her mind, haphazardly stacked up with all the other boxes of ragtag odds and ends by which Janey compartmentalized her memories.

"I wish I had a brain that worked like a normal person's does," Janey said as though she'd been reading Clare's mind.

"Who's to say what's normal?" Clare replied.

"You know what I mean."

"I do. But if you were any different, then you wouldn't be you."

"Sometimes," Janey said, "I think that might not be such a bad thing."

Clare shook her head. "Don't start."

Every once in a while, Janey would decide that everything in her life was wrong and after long soul-searching talks with Clare would attempt to set it all straight. It never worked. Her intentions were good, but as Clare endlessly pointed out, why try to be someone she wasn't?

Janey's personality was so strong that she simply couldn't change. She had strong views on everyone and everything—not always informed ones, unfortunately—and she could easily rub a person the wrong way. But the other side of that coin was that the very strength of her convictions was part and parcel of her charm. She could wax eloquent on any number of passions, which was far more entertaining than listening to gossip along the lines of who so-and-so's sister was dating, or have you heard about the Hayles taking in a boarder?

She envied Janey's easy geniality and if not her quick temper, then at least her ability to forgive just as quickly. The envy that was hardest to deal with was how Janey always seemed to come out ahead, no matter what the situation.

Sometimes Clare wondered why she didn't hate Janey for that. Janey always got what she wanted, and got it first.

Got the music.

Got the new Dunthorn book.

Got Felix. . . .

Best not to think of that, she told herself. She glanced at Janey again and stifled yet another sigh. For all the times Janey drove her mad, there were a hundred others when she'd rather not be with anyone else. Hating Janey would be like hating a part of herself.

"We turn here," she said.

Janey steered them through a gap in the hedgerows onto a narrow bumpy track that drifted down to Peter Goninan's cottage. It had been a lane once, but now it barely held back the encroaching woods on one side, or the fields on the other, most of which had grown over into moorland since the land had stopped being farmed. No more than a quarter kilometer along, the track gave out completely, ending at a jumble of rock that had once been a stone fence. A gate in it led over a stream that had dammed into a pool a few yards down the slope because the density of the weeds blocked its flow.

Two paths led from the stream. One wandered down to the cliffs that dropped in a jungle of thorns, gorse, elderberry trees, and thick couch grass that formed a series of broad steps to the small bay below. The other led across an unkempt field to the cottage. Around the cottage, which was itself in good repair, were a scattering of roofless outbuildings and tumbled-down stone walls, covered with brambles. Blackthorn grew in abandon; brushwood and gorse bushes littered the fields in unruly tangles.

"It looks abandoned," Janey said, gazing out at the rampaging vegetation.

Clare merely pointed to the thin tendril of smoke that rose from the cottage's stone chimney.

As they crossed the stream, stepping from stone to stone, an orange and black cat rose suddenly from the grass. Clare, having to move more slowly for fear her cane would slip off a stone, brought up the rear. She paused when the cat appeared. The cat watched them with an unblinking gaze for a long moment, apparently fascinated by their crossing, then vanished into the woods. It had no tail.

Another of that Zennor woman's Cornish tigers, Clare thought with a smile as she continued on across the stones.

No sooner had they both set foot on the dry ground than a

chorus of barking started up. They looked nervously at each other as a pack of five or so tattery dogs came bounding towards them from the outbuildings.

"Do we stay or run?" Janey asked.

"I can't run," Clare said needlessly.

"They won't hurt you."

At the sound of a stranger's voice, both women started and turned so quickly they almost lost their balance. The newcomer had appeared out of the woods as silently as the cat had disappeared into them. So sudden and quiet was her appearance that Clare had the odd fleeting thought that the cat had merely changed into a woman once it was out of their sight.

Clare recovered before Janey, recognizing Helen Bray from her visits to the bookshop The Penzance. She was a gangly, coltish woman in her mid-twenties, at least six feet in height and slender as a rail. Her red hair was as tangled as the gorse thickets about them, her cheeks flushed from the weather. Her clothes were those of a man and bore the look of many mendings—tweed sports jacket, blue jeans that were worn and had a tear in the right knee, and a navy blue beret that did little to tame her unruly hair. On her feet were green gum boots, besmirched with mud.

As Janey and Clare looked at the woman they realized that the dogs were almost upon them and showed no sign of stopping their charge. Helen gave a shrill whistle, just as the lead dog— a terrier-collie cross—seemed ready to fling himself upon Janey. The dogs stopped in their tracks and all sat down in a half circle, tongues lolling, eyes fixed on the two newcomers.

"The dogs won't hurt you," Helen repeated. "Not if you leave straightway."

Clare cleared her throat. "We're here to see Mr. Goninan."

"He doesn't much care for visitors."

"Yes, well," Clare began, but Janey broke in.

"Why don't you let him decide for himself?" she asked.

Helen had odd pale eyes that were each a different colour—

one grey, the other blue. At the question, she turned her intense gaze on Janey.

"That's not really the point," she said.

"Well, what is the point?" Janey asked. "It's not as if we could call ahead—he doesn't have a phone."

"He doesn't like to be bothered by people."

"We're not here to bother him," Janey said. "We're here to ask his advice about something."

Helen got a feline look of curiosity in her eyes.

"What kind of something?" she asked.

Janey smiled. "Never you mind." She turned to look at the dogs. "I'm going to walk to the cottage and knock on the door. If one of those dogs bites me, you're going to be very sorry."

Oh, Janey, Clare thought. Don't push so.

But as Janey set off, a determined set to her shoulders, Helen finally gave another sharp whistle and the dogs streamed back towards the cottage and disappeared behind the outbuildings. By the time the three women reached its door, there wasn't an animal to be seen except for an old great black-backed gull that was pecking at something by the stones of the chimney, up on the cottage roof.

Giving Helen one of her patented fierce looks, Janey rapped sharply on the door with her knuckles.

"It's open," a voice called from within.

2 .

By the time he reached Clare's house, Davie Rowe knew just what he was going to do. He had his hands in his pockets and fingered the roll of ten-pound notes that Willie had given him.

He couldn't very well hand over a portion of the money to Clare, for all that it would make him feel better. She'd just ask where it had come from and he wasn't about to lie to her about it. That would make the whole exercise pointless. But so that she would get a share of it, he'd decided that he would offer to take her out for dinner tonight.

Just the two of them.

They could go to the Smuggler's Restaurant over in Newlyn for the special Sunday night Feast—a roast-beef dinner with Yorkshire pudding and all the trimmings. They could even have some wine with their dinner, just as the posh folk in the films did.

Davie was pleased with himself for the idea and looked forward to the evening. There was always the chance, he realized, that she wouldn't want to go. Perhaps she and her mother did something special for themselves on Sunday nights. Well, then. He'd invite Clare's mum and his own too. Surely she wouldn't say no to that?

What he hadn't considered was that she might not even be home to say yes or no in the first place.

"I'm sorry," her mother said when she answered the door, "but Clare's gone out for the day."

There was a look in the woman's eye that plainly said, and what makes you think she'd be so blind as to go out with the likes of you? My daughter may be crippled, but she's not daft.

"Do you—ah—can you tell me when she'll be back?"

"She didn't say. Would you like to leave a message?"

"No. I . . . Just tell her I was 'round."

"I'll tell her when she gets in."

The door closed on him before he could say anything more.

Bloody hell, he thought as he trudged off. They were all the same—the lads up at the King's Arms or this woman here in the village. They never gave a bloke a chance. Lilith Mabley would probably have a good laugh about this with Clare when she came home.

He clenched his fists at the thought of Clare laughing at him.

No, she wouldn't do that. She'd ring him up and ask him what he'd wanted, and then he could still ask her out for dinner.

He hurried off home to wait for her call, but when he got

there, he found a stranger sitting outside on the front stoop. The man rose up at Davie's approach.

"The name's Bett," he said, not offering his hand. "Michael Bett."

The American accent registered.

"Uh . . ."

"I want to have a word with you, Davie. Is there somewhere private where we can talk?"

There was something familiar about the man, but Davie couldn't pin it down.

"There's the pub," he said, vaguely waving in the general direction of Mousehole harbour.

"I was thinking of somewhere even more private," Bett said. "Isn't there some kind of scenic walk along the coast nearby?"

Davie nodded.

"Why don't we go take in its sights?" Bett said. "I'm in the mood for a nice walk, and I think you will be too, once you hear the proposition I have for you."

"I really can't go," Davie began. "I'm expecting a call. . . ."

Bett pulled a hundred-dollar bill from his pocket and stuffed it into the breast pocket of Davie's shirt.

"All I'm asking for is an hour of your time," he said.

Davie glanced at his house. Should he tell his mother that he was expecting a call from Clare? No. That would just take too long to explain. Clare might not even ring him up. She probably *wouldn't*. But if she should and he wasn't here to take the call . . .

"I . . ."

"C'mon," Bett said. "What've you got to lose?"

"An hour, you said?"

"Tops. Guaranteed."

"All right," Davie agreed. "But that's all the time I have."

"I understand," Bett said. "Time's a precious commodity—especially for a busy guy like yourself."

Was the American making fun of him? Davie wondered.

"Which way do we go?" Bett went on.

Davie pointed back the way he'd just come and the two set off, the American chatting on about how pretty the village was and had Davie lived here all his life and what did a fellow do around here for excitement?

Long before they reached the beginning of the Coastal Path, Davie was sorry that he'd ever agreed to listen to what the man had to say. But he was curious. It was Americans that had something to do with the trouble plaguing the Littles, the trouble that had spilled over onto Clare. Reckoning it so, there might be something useful he could learn from this Bett—if the man ever came out with something even remotely worth listening to.

Davie stopped when they reached the Coastguard lookout and turned to his companion. They had the place to themselves. Bett scraped some mud from his shoe and looked around.

"Nice place," he said.

Now Davie knew he was being mocked. The path itself was beautiful, even in this season. But the same couldn't be said for the station. On its weather-beaten white walls the paint was peeling. In places, flat stones held loose shingles down on its level roof. A ratty chicken-wire fence encircled the building. There was a wrought-iron porch facing the bay, its metalwork rusting. Leaves floated in the rain barrel by its door. Dried ferns crouched against the side of the building, sheltering from the sea winds.

"What do you want with me?" he demanded of the American.

"Well now."

Bett reached into his pocket. When his hand came out again, it held a small automatic pistol, muzzle pointed at Davie.

"You and me," he said. "We've got some unfinished business left over from last night. . . ."

Now Davie understood why the man had seemed vaguely familiar.

The trouble was, as happened so often in his life, the knowledge had come too late.

3 ·

Peter Goninan's cottage, Janey discovered, was surprisingly bright—the extra light coming from a skylight that had been built into the roof facing the ocean. The interior was all one large room with a kitchen area on one side and stairs leading up to a small sleeping loft on the other. A potbellied cast-iron coal stove sat by one of the many support beams that islanded the ground floor. Set near to it was an old sofa and a pair of club chairs with tattered upholstery.

Goninan sat in one of those chairs. He stood up when they entered, a tall, gaunt man with a bald head that gleamed in the sunlight. While Helen Bray reminded Janey and Clare of a cat, Goninan was more like a bird. His eyes were small and set close to a narrow nose. His cheeks were hollow. His age was indefinable—somewhere between late forties and early seventies, if Janey had to hazard a guess. As it was, he radiated a sense of timelessness.

His birdishness was accentuated by the avian motif that filled the cottage. There were paintings and sculptures of hawks and kestrels. And masks—a dozen or more, from crudely carved wooden ones to one that was ornately decorated with hundreds of tiny feathers. There was a stuffed owl on one bookcase, a raven on another, a pair of stonechats on a third. A heron stood in one corner. An egret and two gulls were by the window. Hanging from the support beams like shamanistic fetishes were dozens of bundles of feathers and birds' feet tied together with leather thongs.

There were books everywhere—on shelves, in boxes and crates, stacked in unruly piles wherever there was space. But what fascinated Janey more were all the oak and glass display cases filled with odd old coins, fossils, ancient clay whistles in the shape of birds and flint artifacts, pieces of bone and tiny wooden dolls with feather skirts, clay pot shards and things that she couldn't readily recognize. Each piece was meticulously identified by a little square of white card set near the appropriate item, the information written on the card in a tidy neat hand.

He really is like a bird, Janey decided, sitting here in his nest with everything he's collected over the years like some kind of magpie.

"They wouldn't go away," Helen said.

Goninan smiled. "That's all right. I've been expecting a visit from Janey Little."

Janey blinked with surprise. "You were?"

"I've seen you any number of times out on the cliffs by the bay—toodling your tunes, piping, and pennywhistling. You make fine music. I believe I even have copies of your recordings . . . somewhere in here."

He waved a hand negligently about the cluttered room. Except for the display cases with their neatly organized contents, Janey could easily see how something could get lost in this room. Lost forever.

"Sooner or later I knew you would come 'round for a visit."

Janey had trouble following the logic of that statement.

"Would you like some tea?" Goninan added.

"Ah . . ."

"Would you put the water on, Helen?"

The tall woman nodded and moved gracefully through the clutter to the kitchen area where she filled a kettle.

"Do take a seat," Goninan said, ushering them both to the sofa facing his chair.

None of this was going as Janey had expected it to, but then again, she hadn't known what to expect.

"And you are?" Goninan asked Clare.

At least he doesn't know everything, Janey thought as Clare introduced herself.

They made their way carefully to the sofa and sat down. Janey perched on the edge of the cushion, unable to stop herself from staring around the room. No matter which way she turned, something odd or wonderful caught her eye.

She could spend weeks in here, she thought.

Goninan smiled at her as he took his own chair again.

"We were wondering if you could help us," Clare said. "You're considered an expert in . . . I guess you could call it arcane subjects. . . ."

"I prefer to call myself a theurgist."

"What's that?" Janey asked.

"A magician," Clare said.

Goninan smiled. "Of a sort."

Janey stifled an urge to roll her eyes.

"Theurgy," Helen said, sitting down in the other club chair. She leaned forward a bit, her disconcerting gaze fixed on Janey. "From the Latin, *theurgia,* meaning a miracle worker. A theurgist is one who is intimate with the spirits that oversee our world."

"And I guess you're his apprentice, right?" Janey said, refusing to let the other woman daunt her.

Clare jabbed Janey with her elbow, the meaning clear: Behave.

"We were more interested in your knowledge of secret societies," Clare said.

Goninan's eyebrows rose questioningly, but he said nothing, so she went on.

"We were wondering if you could identify a symbol we have, if you could perhaps tell us if it's a motif associated with any particular society."

Janey thought about Felix's rough sketch of the dove, then looked around at all the avian material in the cottage and wondered how good an idea this was. The old homily drifted through her mind—*Birds of a feather* . . . —but by then it was too late because Clare had already taken out the sketch and passed it over to their host.

"Ah," he said.

"Is there anything in your library that can tell us something about the people who use this for their symbol?" Clare asked. "They wear it on their wrists—tattooed there."

"Yes. I know. And there's no need for me to look it up. I'm quite familiar with these people."

Bloody hell, Janey thought. We're doomed.

"They call themselves the Order of the Grey Dove, dedicating themselves to hermetic principles, something along the lines of the Golden Dawn and their like. I've followed their growth over the years with considerable interest." He smiled. "Not least because of the symbol they have chosen for their motif."

"Their bird and your birds?" Clare asked.

Goninan nodded. "Mine—if I can use a possessive term such as that for such things—are my personal key to the invisible world of the spirits that surrounds us. My totem if you will."

"And that's what this Order does?" Janey asked. "They . . . ah . . . talk to spirits through a dove?"

"They seek knowledge—as do we all—but their methodology has been known to employ, at times, activities that could be considered to be, shall we say, questionable?"

"What kinds of knowledge?"

Goninan smiled again. "Oh, the usual: Longevity. Power. Even understanding, though that's somewhat rarer among this particular Order's membership."

"That's not all they're looking for," Janey mumbled, forgetting herself.

"How so?" Goninan asked.

Janey gave Clare a glance, but Clare only shrugged as if to say, we're here to get information.

"They seem to think we have something that they want," Janey said finally, "but it's nothing very important. It's not something that can let you live forever or give you power. At least it doesn't seem like that kind of a thing."

Except she remembered what her grandfather had told her about the odd occurrences that had come about the last time the book had been read. And then there was the music.

And her dream.

"The most innocent thing can hold immense power," Goninan said. "To those who know how to use it."

"What do you mean?" Janey asked.

"It's all got to do with magic," Goninan explained.

"Magic?"

Janey wanted to roll her eyes again, but stopped herself in time.

"Oh, not spells and incantations and that sort of thing. More like the beliefs of, say, George Gurdjieff—the Russian philosopher."

Clare nodded. "I know him," she said. "Well, not personally," she added when Janey shot her a curious look, "but I know his work. We've carried his books in the shop—*Beelzebub's Tales to His Grandson* and things like that."

Now it was Goninan's turn for curiosity.

"Shop?" he asked.

"I work at The Penzance Bookshop on Chapel Street."

"Ah, yes. That new one. Your people have acquired a text or two for me."

Clare glanced at where Helen was getting the tea ready.

"That's where I've seen Helen before," she said.

Goninan nodded. "Yes, she's usually kind enough to fetch the books for me. I don't get into town much anymore."

"You were talking about magic," Janey said.

"No, I was talking about Gurdjieff. He says that there are three levels of consciousness. There is sleeping"—he counted them off on his fingers—"there is sleeping wakefulness; and then there is awareness. Sleeping is just that. Sleeping wakefulness is when you walk around—" He suddenly pointed at Janey's hand where it was tap-tapping against her knee. "You didn't even realize you were doing that just now, did you?"

Janey looked down at her hand, which now lay still, and shook her head.

"That is sleeping wakefulness. We all walk through the world barely aware of what our bodies do, or what goes on around us. Awareness is when you are informed—utterly *aware*—of it all. Yourself and your environment. It's akin to being an aviator— the sort of awareness of a Christ or a Buddha.

"For most of us, those moments of true awareness are very rare. They come at high points in our lives, such as the moment before one pronounces one's wedding vows, or just before death—brief moments of complete awareness that encapsulate everything that we are in relation to, everything that is. Do you understand what I mean?"

Janey and Clare nodded slowly.

"Now imagine that you are always in such a state. To constantly recognize everything for what it truly is, and then to have such absolute control over your will that you aren't capable so much of transforming your surroundings or the wills of those around you, but you *can* influence them to such extent that it might as well be considered magic.

"We humans have so much untapped potential that it literally boggles the mind. Consider the amazing things of which we are already capable in moments of need or duress—such as the woman whose child has been run over by a car and she goes over and lifts that immense weight so that the child can escape.

"People will explain this away as being the result of adrenaline, or psychic phenomena, or some such thing. What they don't say is that the basic underlying truth of any such incident is the fact that in our moments of utter awareness, we are capable of things that defy our understanding of our accepted range of capabilities.

"We can literally do anything."

"That . . ." Janey began. "That's what the people of this Order are like?"

"No—but it is what they strive for; it is their magic. And many of them are, if not fully aware all of the time, at least in such a state far more than the rest of the world's population. They have acquired great talents—woken gifts that are inherently present in each one of us—but they have twisted them to dark uses. Selfish uses."

"And . . . this thing they're looking for?" Janey asked. "The thing that they think we've got?"

"It will be a talisman of some sort. A catalyst. For see: Although we are all capable of waking from the sleep through which we live our lives—through perseverance and study and much practice and labour—there have always been objects of power that will facilitate the waking. In the Western tradition they center around relics such as the Spear that pierced Christ's side, or the Fisher King's Grail; there are others less familiar and also less powerful, though no less effective. The trouble with taking such a route is that one acquires the 'magic,' but not the wisdom to use it with any moral enlightenment. Following such a prac- tice—the left-hand path, if you will—results in amorality."

"And this thing we have—is it one of those artifacts?"

"I would have to see it to make that judgment."

"Ah . . ."

Right, Janey thought. All sorts of weird people had been after the Dunthorn book for years and they were supposed to simply bring it by to show it to Goninan as though it were some old ring that they wanted appraised. She had that done with a piece of jewelry once and the old lady in the shop had tut-tutted over the piece, telling her, "I'm afraid it's not gold, love. More like pinchbeck—what the poor people used in place of gold in Vic- torian times. It was invented by a Mr. Pinchbeck, but the secret died with him."

So they could pop by with the book and Goninan would pooh- pooh its value and offer to take it off their hands for a tiny sum— as the old shoplady had done—and then later they'd find out that it had been worth a fortune—as her pinchbeck pendant had been.

Not bloody likely she'd fall for that a second time.

Except Goninan surprised her again.

"But I don't think that I *have* to see it," he said. "Not to know what it is."

Janey just looked at him, feeling nervous all over again.

"What do you mean?" Clare asked.

"I knew Bill Dunthorn as well as Tom Little ever did—in some respects better, for we shared a common interest that"— he glanced at Janey—"your grandfather never did."

"Gramps always says that Billy was a practical kind of a bloke,"

Janey said. "He didn't belong to any mystical orders."

"Absolutely. But he did seek after hidden knowledge. And he found it."

The line from that letter that Janey had found in Dunthorn's *The Little Country* returned to her.

That famous Mad Bill Dunthorn Gypsy prescience . . .

"Magic?" Janey said slowly. "Is that what you're saying he found?"

Goninan nodded. "Though I think he would have preferred to describe it as a kind of enchantment. He found it and put it in a book. Not the books he had published, but a special book of which only one copy has ever existed. And that, I believe, is what the Order of the Grey Dove seeks from you."

"You know about the book?"

"Of course. Bill and I talked about it a great deal."

"Then how come you never wanted it for yourself?" she asked.

"There are as many different paths to enlightenment as there are people in this world. The path Bill took wasn't mine. I already knew my path. I had, and have, no interest in following another."

"And your path is . . . talking to bird spirits?"

"That is one way of putting it, yes."

"What does the book do?" Clare asked.

"You might call it a gate to knowledge. To understanding. To the invisible world of the spirits."

"Well, how does it work?" Janey asked.

"And where does it take you?" Clare added.

"To both questions, I must reply: I don't know. It was Bill's path, not mine, and though we spoke of our studies to each other, there are always elements to such work that cannot be understood without first being experienced. I had no wish to dilute my own work by testing another's and Bill felt the same way about my studies. We compared results—not tangible results, but spiritual ones."

Janey sighed. "This is making my head hurt," she said.

Helen came over with a tray at that moment, laden with mugs

of tea, a plate of scones, and small clay jars of clotted cream and jam. When she put it on a crate of books that stood between the sofa and club chairs, Goninan motioned to the tray.

"We'll break for tea," he said, "and give your subconscious minds a chance to assimilate what I've told you. After we've eaten, I'll tell you about John Madden."

"Who's he?"

"The leader of the Order of the Grey Dove and a very dangerous man."

Janey thought of how Clare had been attacked and Felix had been drugged and nodded.

"I'll say he is."

A somber look touched Goninan's features.

"I hesitate to say this, for fear of spoiling your appetites," he said, "but I must warn you that whatever unpleasantness has already fallen your way, I'm afraid that things will only get worse."

"Don't say that," Janey groaned.

"Why?" Clare asked Goninan.

"Because you've opened the book. I've felt its enchantment working these past few days. And if I can feel it, then you can rest assured that Madden feels it as well. He's been searching for that book for the better part of his life."

"But there's nothing magical *in* it," Janey protested. "It's just a story. There's no secret knowledge—at least there isn't so far. I'm not quite done reading it yet."

Goninan indicated the tray again. "Drink," he said. "Eat. We'll talk again later. But this time we'll talk outside."

"Why outside?" Janey wanted to know.

But Goninan only smiled and helped himself to a scone.

4 ·

When the knock came at Jim Gazo's door, Lena started to rise from her chair until Gazo waved her back to her seat. He took a small revolver from his pocket and, holding it at his side, out of sight, stood to one side of the door.

"Come on in," he said.

The door swung open and Willie Keel stepped inside.

"Miss Grant," he began when he saw Lena. "I've just come 'round to—"

Gazo stepped from the side of the door. He closed the door with his foot and lifted the revolver until the muzzle was touching the back of Willie's neck. The small man froze.

"Th-there's no need for this," he said.

"How did you know to find Ms. Grant in here?" Gazo demanded.

"That's all right, Jim," Lena said. "You can put away the gun."

Willie relaxed visibly when the muzzle was removed from his skin. Gazo replaced the revolver in his pocket and leaned against the wall.

"I still want to know how you knew," Gazo said.

"Do you mind if I sit?"

Willie directed the question to Lena who nodded in acquiescence.

"I'd like to know, too, Willie," she said.

"Well, now," Willie said once he was seated. "The game of strangers you two played this morning didn't wash with me, so when there was no reply at the door to your room, I just came down here to the room your friend went into this morning."

Lena nodded. That seemed reasonable enough.

"What did you want, Willie?" she asked.

"It's about my money. . . ."

"I told you we'd get it to you tomorrow. Don't you trust me?"

Though why he should, Lena didn't know.

"It's not that," Willie assured her. "It's just that things have changed." He glanced at Gazo, who still stood by the door, arms folded across his chest. "Your other, ah, associate—the one I met at the station for you?"

Lena nodded.

"Well, he was by my flat this morning. Threatened to kill me unless I told him who it was that stopped him from hurting the Mabley woman last night."

"And you just told him?" Gazo asked.

Willie tugged his shirt from his trousers and pulled it up so that they both could see the welter of blue-black bruises that covered his sides and chest. Lena's eyes widened.

"Take a look at this, mate," Willie said to Gazo. "Your friend doesn't have much patience, and I wasn't getting enough money to risk my life, I'll tell you that straight up and no word of a lie. The man would've killed me"—he turned back to look at Lena— "I could see it in his eyes."

He tucked his shirt back in, wincing as he brushed against a bruise. Lena grimaced in sympathy.

"You did the right thing," she said. "Did you warn your friend?"

Willie shook his head. "There was no answer at Davie's place—both he and his mum were out."

Lena indicated the telephone. "Do you want to try him again?"

"No time. I've got a ride waiting for me outside. This time tomorrow I'll be so far from the West Country that your friend will never find me. And it's there I'm staying until he's gone."

"So you want the rest of your money," Lena said.

"If you have any you can give me."

He started to reach into his pocket, stopping when Gazo stepped away from the wall.

"I'm just getting a wee slip of paper with an address on it," he said. His gaze went to Lena. "Is that all right?"

When she nodded, he extracted a folded piece of paper and handed it over to her.

"That's where you can send what you owe me," he said. "I won't be there, and the lad whose address it is doesn't know where I'll be either, but you can leave the money or a message with him and be sure I'll get them."

"I'm sorry about this," Lena said. "Jim, do you have any money?"

"Only traveler's cheques."

"Will you sign some over to Willie?"

Gazo nodded, obviously unhappy about the situation, but not willing to argue with his employer—especially not in front of a third party.

"There . . . there's one more thing," Willie said when Gazo had signed over the cheques.

Willie stood by the door, ready to go.

"What's that?" Lena asked.

"He also made me tell him who'd hired us to protect Clare Mabley—'confirm' was the word he used. He wanted it confirmed. I'm sorry, Miss Grant."

Before either she or Gazo could move, he slipped out the door and was gone.

"That little weasel," Gazo muttered.

He started for the door, pausing at Lena's call.

"At least he came by and warned us," she said. "He didn't have to do that."

"He just wanted his money."

"I suppose."

Why hadn't she thought of that? Lena wondered. Normally, cynic that she was, it would have been her first thought.

"Bett was going to find out anyway," she added. "One way or another."

"No denying that."

Lena glanced at the clock. The afternoon was winding down.

"Daddy'll be here soon. He'll get Madden to call off Bett."

Gazo had crossed the room and was looking out the window, watching Willie Keel's car pull away from in front of the hotel. Once the car was gone, his gaze shifted to the bay where the afternoon sun was gleaming on the water.

"I wouldn't mind dealing with Bett before either of them arrive," he said.

Lena shook her head. "Only if he comes here."

"I know. I was just wishing aloud."

You and me both, Lena thought, but she knew enough not to try to take on Bett—even with Gazo at her side. That was a last resort, because the trouble with Bett was that he was crazy. She could see that now. And how did you deal with a madman?

"What really makes me feel bad," she said, "is thinking about that friend of Willie's that Bett's gone after."

Gazo gave her a curious glance, caught what he was doing, and quickly looked away again. But Lena knew what he'd been thinking.

The Ice Queen was getting a heart.

And it was true. Felix had opened the gap in her walls and now she couldn't seem to close it up again. She found herself worrying about Willie's friend, about what might happen to Jim if Bett showed up here, about all the people whose lives had gotten tangled up with Michael Bett's viciousness.

There was no stopping it, no matter how much she tried.

And oddly enough, she wasn't even sure that she wanted to try.

It hurt. And she didn't like the pain. But she did find herself wondering why she would want to build up those walls again. She couldn't deny the aching, deep hurt that she felt at the moment. It cut so deeply through her that it felt as though it would never go away again. But there was something else as well. Something unfamiliar.

It was what people called compassion.

And she found that it gave her hope. That caring for what happened to others actually made her feel better about herself. It went against everything that the Order had taught her, it might prove to be only a false promise, a momentary aberration in her character, but she found herself growing more and more determined to not go back to being the kind of person she'd been before.

It wouldn't help her with Felix.

But it might bring her peace—something that she'd never even realized she was looking for until she'd tasted it in Felix's company.

"Can people change?" she asked Gazo.

He turned with a puzzled look.

"I mean, can they really change," she said. "Not just their appearance, or the face they turn to the world, but in here"—she touched her chest—"where it really counts?"

Gazo looked uncomfortable. "I don't think I'm sure what you mean. . . ."

"Just be honest," Lena said. "Forget the employer/employee business for just a few minutes and tell me what you think."

Gazo didn't say anything for a long moment, but then finally he nodded.

"It depends on how big a change it is that we're talking about," he began. He was couching it in vague terms, but they both knew he was talking about her. "But if it was a big one—a major change in someone's personality—well, I don't think it'd be easy, and it'd take time and a lot of patience, but I think people can do anything they want—so long as they really set their minds to it."

Which, Lena realized, was a kind of paraphrase of the Order's basic tenets.

And then something sparked in her mind.

This was what enlightenment must feel like, she thought. A moment like this when everything falls neatly into place in one's mind and there's nothing, not one little thing, that's out of place or misunderstood.

It wasn't the Order's teachings that were at fault. It was what one did with them.

"Thank you, Jim," she said.

5 ·

"John Madden is a very powerful man," Goninan said.

After they'd had their tea, he took Janey and Clare out into the fields overlooking the small cove below his property. They were far from the cottage and its outbuildings—far from any man-made object. Here the unruly vegetation had been given free rein and returned to its natural wild state. They all sat on stone outcrops, the rocks weathered smooth and grey like old bones.

"His magical abilities aside, Madden has enormous business interests. His own fortune is vast enough to deny easy calculation. Other members of the Inner Circle of his Order are also in high positions of influence and power—together they have formed a global network that encompasses the entire sphere of international commerce and politics."

"Why is it," Janey interrupted, "that the current villains in the world are always businessmen or politicians?"

Goninan smiled. "That has never changed. What else can they do but acquire power? And power has always lain in the fields of politics and commerce."

"And religion," Clare said.

"And religion," Goninan agreed. "Hence Madden's Order of the Grey Dove."

"What do they worship?" Janey wanted to know. "This grey dove? Madden?"

"Religion involves worship," Goninan said, "but like anything concerned with spiritual matters, its strictures vary according to how its followers approach it. Some seek solace, others a promise of hope in the hereafter; some enter into it as a means to enlightenment, still others view it as a road to power. It need not necessarily involve worship. A better word for it, perhaps, would be Way. And the Ways of our world are as varied as the road taken by a Taoist, or that followed by a man such as, say, Aleister Crowley."

"Who's he?" Janey asked.

"A Cornishman, actually—originally from Plymouth—who is reviled or exalted, depending on the person who is discussing him."

"He was evil," Clare said. "Anybody who'd follow his teachings would have to be as bad or worse."

Goninan shook his head. "That is like condemning all Christians for the Inquisition or the Crusades—or for present-day Fundamentalism. Crowley himself was certainly somewhat depraved, but as in all teachings, there are truths and insights in his work that are relevant to all people. L. Ron Hubbard is an excellent contemporary example."

"And who's he?" Janey asked.

"The founder of Scientology."

Janey had heard of Scientologists before. They'd often stopped her on the street in London, asking her if she wanted to take a personality test—whatever that meant.

"I never heard of Hubbard being depraved," Clare said.

"I didn't mean to imply that he was," Goninan said. "I use his teachings as an example of how a body of work can be reviled—mostly by those who have no knowledge of its workings—and yet still carry elements of what can only be considered eternal truths. What Hubbard merely did was couch them in more contemporary terms—not a particularly innovative methodology, I might add. A part of every religion's genesis is the modernizing of old truisms."

"So what you're saying," Janey said, "is that it's not the work or the personality of the founder of a religion that's important, but what its followers do with what they learn?"

"Exactly. Which brings us back to John Madden and his Order of the Grey Dove. The underlying tenets of the Order deal with many of the same universal truths as do other orders and religions, but it is the personality of its followers, *particularly* its founder Madden in this case, that makes it an extremely dangerous sect."

"What makes these people go bad?" Janey asked. "Not just this Order, but all the people you were talking about."

"Human nature, I'm afraid. We seem cursed with the need to acquire control over each other and our environment. To rule. To change everything we can possibly meddle with."

"Yes," Clare said, "but if we didn't do that, we'd still be living in caves and chewing on bones."

Goninan laughed. "I'm no Luddite," he said. "I agree with you completely. The advances we make in technology and the sciences are very important to our development as a race. But, like religion, science depends on what one brings to it. Were we only seeking cures for cancer and world hunger and the like, I would have no complaints. What I condemn is this narrow-minded quest for the most devastating weapon or the years of research that go into a better deodorant or shampoo. It's madness. It has no heart—no care for the spirit, be it ours, or that of the earth itself. Thousands of acres of rain forests are destroyed every day—*every* single day—the ozone layer is being rapidly worn away, yet our world leaders are more content to argue about how many weapons they can stockpile.

"They remind me of primary school bullies, vying for dominion of the school yard, while an entire world—a real world—lies just beyond its confines. A world of far more sacred importance that they cannot see for their blindness."

As he spoke, his face had reddened, his voice growing cross, eyes flashing. He paused suddenly and looked away, over across the bay, silently watching the dip and wheel of seabirds over the water until the timeless image had calmed him enough to continue.

"Your pardon," he said when he finally looked back at Janey and Clare. "I've lived through one World War only to watch the world grow worse instead of better when we finally put down that madman's Reich."

He laid a hand on the stone on which he sat, stroking its smooth surface with his fingers.

"I love this world," he added. "That is what rules my life. When I die, I want to have done all in my power to leave it in a better state than it was when I found it. At the same time I know that this can never be. The world has grown so complex that one voice can do little to alter it any longer. That doesn't stop me from doing what I can, but it makes the task hard. The successes are so small, the failures so large and many. It's like trying to stem a storm with one's bare hands."

Janey felt a little embarrassed listening to him. It wasn't that she didn't agree with what Goninan was saying; it was more because she did agree, only she never did anything about it except for the odd benefit gig.

"My quarrel with Madden," Goninan went on, "is that he has the opportunity to make a difference, yet he does nothing with it. His entire life is channeled towards self-gain."

"You seem to know as much as he does," Janey said. "Why didn't you start your own Order?"

"I thought of that," Goninan said. "When I was young. But to acquire the position of power that Madden presently holds, I would have to become as ruthless as he. And then I would be no better than he."

"But if you could make a difference . . . ?"

Goninan shook his head. "I expect that once I reached such a position of influence, I'd no more care for the world than does Madden himself. It may sound trite, but using the weapons of the enemy, no matter how good one's intentions, makes one the enemy."

He spoke then at length of Madden's rise from obscurity and the forming of the Order, sketching in a fuller, if still incomplete, picture of the man.

"So his magic," Janey said. "It's a sham? It's just manipulating people and knowing when to make the best deal?"

"No. The magic is real."

"But . . . ?"

"Consider legend and myth," Goninan said.

"You mean how they're all based on some kernel of truth, no matter how obscure?" Clare asked.

"In part. Legend and myth are what we use to describe what we don't comprehend. They are our attempts to make the impossible, possible—at least insofar as our spirits interact with the spirit of the world, or if that's too animistic for you, then let us use Jung's terminology and call it our racial subconscious. No matter the semantics, they are of a kind and it is legend and myth that binds us all together.

"Through them, through their retellings, and through those new versions that are called religion while they are current, we are taught Truth and we attempt to understand Mystery. How many brave or chivalrous deeds have come about through a young boy's fascination with childhood stories of King Arthur and his Knights of the Round Table? Or how many injustices were attacked by those who learned of right and wrong from tales of Robin Hood?

"Teaching a child the correct moral choices he or she should make is simple, but not always effective. The young rebel—not because they're amoral, but because it is in their nature to do so. The words of an elder are always suspect—especially here in what is traditionally called Western society. It is through legend and myth, through the young spirit's connection with the old spirit that lies at the heart of this matter, that the lessons are learned without being deliberately taught.

"The lessons lie in the subtext of the stories, as it were.

"Today, children are given toys to look up to as heroic figures. Rock performers and movie stars form their pantheon—an amoral pantheon where the performer who eloquently speaks out against drugs is arrested two weeks later for possession of heroin. Where the stalwart heroic figure from the silver screen is discovered to be a wife beater.

"The subtext here is that one may do anything one wishes—one need only make certain not to get caught."

"And the magic?" Janey asked when Goninan fell silent.

She'd been having trouble making the connection with what he was saying to what she had supposed they were talking about.

"Is real," he said. "It is your perception of it that makes it true—our recognition of the true shape or spirit of a thing. But like legend and myth, magic fades when it is unused—hence all the old tales of elfin kingdoms moving further and further away from our world, or that magical beings require our faith, our *belief* in their existence, to survive.

"That is a lie. All they require is our recognition."

"And the book?" Clare asked. "Where does it fit in?"

"I spoke of totems before we had our tea—do you remember?"

Janey and Clare both nodded.

"Your birds," Clare said.

"Yes. They are a symbol—a talisman, if you like, but a personal one, which is what a totem is. A symbol that sets one in the proper frame of mind to work one's magic. How such totems differ from Bill's book is that they require sacrifice and much study for one to acquire one's appropriate symbology.

"Bill did that study, he made the sacrifices of time and ostracism that such work requires—hence the book's magic worked for him. It was his totem. But, unknowingly, he also created a talisman when he crafted it—a universal symbol so that it is now a catalyst as well as the personal totem it was for him.

"The artifact he created now has a twofold existence."

"I'm not sure I know what you mean," Janey said.

"Every book tells a different story to the person who reads it," Goninan explained. "How they perceive that book will depend on *who* they are. A good book reflects the reader, as much as it illuminates the author's text."

Clare nodded in understanding.

"Now," Goninan said, "imagine a book that literally *is* different for each person who reads it."

Janey frowned. "Do you mean that the story I'm reading in *The Little Country*—I'm the only person who will read that particular story?"

"Exactly."

"But that's not possible."

Goninan smiled. "No, of course it isn't. It's magic."

"But Gramps has read it and he never said . . ."

Janey's voice trailed off as she realized that she'd never actually talked to anyone about the story that was in the book—not her grandfather nor Felix—while Clare hadn't read it yet.

"So," Goninan said, "the book's first purpose is to reflect the reader's spirit—somewhat along the lines of an oracle."

"Would it be the same every time I read it?" Janey asked.

"I can't say for certain. But it's not likely. For see, as you change, so will the story that reflects your spirit change with you."

"But it's following logically along at the moment," Janey said. "The plot's following a logical progression."

"For this story," Goninan said.

"Are they Dunthorn's words that we're reading?" Clare asked.

"It's not likely—although there will be a part of Bill in each story, because it was his creation."

Janey found this a bit much to swallow. But then, everything she was hearing today seemed farfetched. None of it could be possible.

Of course it's not, she could hear Goninan saying again. *It's magic.*

Magic.

Legend and myth.

Her heart wanted to believe. Her logic told her it was poppycock.

The kinds of things that Goninan was talking about simply couldn't fit into the real world—the world she knew. But at the same time, his words awoke resonances inside her that were naggingly familiar, as though when he spoke she was remembering, rather than hearing.

"And the second purpose?" Clare asked.

"Is as a talisman," Goninan said. "An artifact. And I would warn you that to wield such an object, one must be very, very careful. It is a grave responsibility. Every time one uses it, the world changes. One can hide an artifact, but one can't hide one's responsibility to it. The only way that can be done is if the artifact is willingly passed on to another."

"The world . . . changes?" Janey said.

"The more such a talisman is employed, the more pronounced its effects become. Eventually, if it is used long enough, it will remake the world."

"How?" Janey asked.

"Into what?" Clare added.

"Into whatever is possible."

Janey thought again of the little that her grandfather had told her of what had happened when he first got the book, before he hid it away—of the ghosts and odd sounds and how people changed. . . . She remembered her own dream last night. Of the music that came from the book. How it changed.

She thought of that lost tune that she'd been trying to recover and realized she had only heard it when she had the book open, on her lap. . . .

"Does it change forever?" Clare asked.

"That depends on how long it is used. And by whom. Wielded by its proper guardian, it can only do good. Wielded for the sake of personal gain—as Madden plans—it could eventually destroy the world."

"How do we know who its proper guardian is?" Janey asked. "Is it my grandfather? Is it me?"

"I don't know," Goninan said. "But it's not likely. Neither of you follow a Way. You don't have the background, nor the knowledge."

"But you do?" Janey said, suddenly suspicious again.

Goninan only laughed. "I have both," he agreed, "but it's too late for me to take a new road. My birds have brought me as far as I can go and now I stand in a borderland—half in this world, half in the otherworld. Sooner, rather than later, I will be crossing over."

"What do you mean?" Clare asked.

But Janey knew. In the same way that Goninan's words seemed more memory than new.

"You're dying," she said.

Goninan nodded.

"I'm sorry. I . . ." She didn't know what to say.

"Don't be," Goninan said. "I've had a long full life and I have seen where I am going next. My only regret is what I told you before—that I won't be leaving the world a better place than it was when I entered it."

They were quiet for a time then, until Janey stirred. She took her gaze from the small stonechat that she'd been watching as it hopped from thorn branch to thorn branch in the field above them and turned to Goninan.

"And Helen's your . . . nurse?" she asked.

"Great-niece. A kindred spirit. She has long had a similar

bent of mind to mine, so I've been teaching her, while she takes care of me."

"And that's why you can't guard the book."

"Exactly."

Janey frowned, thinking.

"What I don't understand is . . . we haven't done anything with the book. We haven't"—she looked a little embarrassed—"you know, chanted above it or lit candles around it or anything. All we've done is read it."

"That's all it requires to come awake—to be opened."

"Well, I'm going to hide it away," Janey said. "Someplace far and safe where no one will ever find it."

"If you can find such a place."

"And I won't read another word."

Goninan shook his head. "You must finish the story," he said. "If you leave it incomplete, the book will remain open—not much, but enough so that someone like Madden will be able to track it down and find it."

"Why didn't Billy *warn* Gramps?"

"I don't think he knew."

"Why didn't you tell him? You seem to know a lot more about it than you said you did back in the cottage."

"I've just been thinking about it these past few days," Goninan said. "Since I first felt it wake. And I didn't speak more of it then, because I was waiting to speak of it now."

"Oh."

Janey picked at a frayed bit of her jeans and sighed.

"What can I do?" she asked finally.

"Finish reading the book," Goninan said. "Your subconscious already knows what you must do. Perhaps you'll find that answer reflected in the book as you read on."

"Why can't you just tell me?"

"Because I don't know."

Goninan rose stiffly to his feet.

"I should go back," he said. "It's time for my medicine and Helen will have my hide if I'm much later."

Janey and Clare rose with him.

"Why did we have to talk about all of this outside?" Clare asked as they walked back towards the cottage.

"As my totems are my birds," Goninan replied. "So Madden's lie in shadows—the shadows cast by man-made objects. He can see through them, hear through them, speak through them . . . perhaps even move through them. They give him his health; they feed on his magic."

"Can't your birds help you?" Janey asked.

"How so?"

"You know—to cure you."

Goninan smiled. "Why should I ask them to? Dying is a part of living—a natural progression. Should I ignore the natural order of my life, twist it to my liking and thereby become something I was not meant to be?"

"That sounds so fatalistic—" She put her hand across her mouth the moment she spoke. "I'm sorry," she added quickly. "I didn't mean . . ."

"I know what you meant," Goninan said. "You feel that such a way of living lacks free will."

Janey nodded.

"You forget that I made the *choice* to live in such a way."

There was nothing more that could be added to that. When they reached the cottage door, Helen was waiting for them, a frown vying with worry in her features.

"Thank you for your time," Clare said.

"For everything," Janey added.

Goninan nodded. "I enjoyed the chance to meet and talk with you both."

"Peter," Helen said. "You have to come in."

She motioned for him to enter the cottage. Goninan gave Janey and Clare a wink.

"She's ever so strict."

"We won't take any more of your time," Janey said.

Goninan caught her arm before she could turn away.

"One more word of warning," he said. "Madden has arrived

in this country. I can *feel* his step on the land."

"We'll be careful," Janey assured him.

"I hope you will be. Especially of what you say when shadows can hear you speak. Godspeed and good luck."

Janey smiled. She looked at him, seeing the birdishness still in his stock-thin frame and his shining eyes, but seeing the illness now as well.

"You *are* leaving the world a better place," she said.

Before he could reply she hurried off, leaving Clare to follow at a slower pace.

6.

"I guess you're wondering how I tracked you down," Bett said.

A thin smile touched his lips as he watched Davie Rowe. The big man stood as still as the stone outcrops that dotted the clifftop around them, his own gaze not meeting Bett's, but fixed rather on the muzzle of the automatic that Bett held.

Christ, he was an ugly one, Bett thought. Killing him was doing the world a favour.

"I . . ." Rowe began.

Walking on the edge as he was, Bett felt he could see right down into the big man's soul and taste the fear that cowered there. He knew there was no mercy in his own features. All Rowe would see in Bett's eyes was his death. Old Mr. D., staring right back at him, a big death's-head grin laughing in the face of the man's terror.

Bett shrugged.

"Guess you'll just have to take that question down to your grave," he said.

And pulled the trigger.

The automatic's report was loud in the still air. Rowe jerked back as the bullet punched his chest. He went tumbling from the path into the long couch grass at the lip of the cliff. Bett stepped closer, the muzzle of his revolver tracking the man's fall for a second shot. His finger tightened on the trigger.

"Hey!"

Bett turned as sharply as though he'd been shot himself at the sound of the new voice. Coming around the corner where the Coastal Path dipped past an outcrop of rocks that had the appearance of a stone armchair was a young, blond-haired man in jeans and a Windbreaker, a small knapsack on his back.

Shit, Bett thought. Just what I needed. A hiker.

He ducked away into the undergrowth, worming his way deep into its thickets on his stomach, pulling himself along on his elbows.

"What is the matter here?" the stranger cried.

German, Bett realized from the accent. And he was no dummy.

The man had stopped near the stone armchair. Keeping a cautious distance, he peered in the direction where Bett had first disappeared into the thick vegetation. But Bett had already worked himself parallel to the path so that he was well away from the spot where he'd disappeared.

Bett smiled.

The man was no dummy, but he didn't have a chance.

He wasn't walking the edge.

The hiker took a few more tentative steps forward, pausing again to rake the landscape with his gaze. Bett ducked as the man's gaze tracked past his own hiding place. He waited for a count of five, then crawled farther along the route he'd chosen, still parallel to the path, but above it now, for here the land rose steeply above the outcropping of rocks of which the stone armchair was a part.

When he chanced another look, it was to find himself behind and above the hiker who was now gingerly approaching the place where Davie Rowe had fallen. The stranger paused again before reaching the Coastguard lookout and called out once more.

Bett shoved the revolver back into his jacket pocket and rose as silently as a ghost from his hiding place. He crept forward and was about to jump down upon the stranger when the man turned and saw him.

Too late.

Bett landed like a cat beside him and gave him a shove. The hiker went over the edge of the path with a scream, pinwheeling his arms as he fell to the rocks some two hundred feet below. When Bett bent over the lip of the cliff to look down at him, all he could see was the hiker's splayed figure lying still—a splash of colour against the grey. Waves lashed the rocks. The hiker didn't move.

"You picked a bad time to drop by," Bett said.

A shame, really. Walking along this treacherous path all by yourself. One misstep and—

Well, it was a long fall.

Dusting off the dirt from his clothes, he pulled out his revolver again and went over to where Rowe had fallen.

The body was gone.

Frowning, Bett looked over the edge of the cliff here, but there were no rocks below to catch the body. Just the sea, washing against the face of the cliff, ragged waves breaking into white foam as they hit the rocks. If the body had fallen all the way down, Bett knew that he wasn't going to spot it now.

He crouched down and studied the place where Rowe had first dropped. Bett wasn't any kind of a tracker—at least not outside the city. Hunting humans was a game he liked to play in a forest of steel and concrete. The only kind of tracking it involved was some detective work in picking a victim. Then it was just the stalk and, if he had time, a little knife work to see what made the sucker tick. If there wasn't time, then the skinning knife could be used just as effectively for the kill.

Rowe had stolen his knife last night, but it wasn't like Bett didn't have another couple of blades stashed away in his luggage. But he hadn't wanted to use the knife today. Rowe was just too big and Bett's shoulder still hurt from their encounter the previous night. So he used the gun, but he didn't like it.

It wasn't personal enough. A gun didn't let you get up close and see the life-light die.

But you made do.

When time was tight, you just made do with whatever came to hand. But you liked to have a chance to check out the results. You liked the opportunity to stand back and admire your own handiwork.

You liked to make sure the sucker was dead.

So he looked for clues as to what had happened to the body. He'd never had much experience or inclination to play Davy Crockett. But he spotted Rowe's blood where it stained the dirt and grass. And he'd seen the big man take a hit, right in the chest.

He spent a few more moments, combing the undergrowth nearby, then put away his automatic once more and headed back towards the village.

Rowe had fallen over the edge and the sea had taken him. It was as simple as that.

And if last night's failure hadn't exactly been remedied yet, Bett had at least been compensated for it. Now it was time to get on with the rest of the day's projects.

He still had a lot of other business to take care of before his work here was done. Next on the agenda was finding a nice out-of-the-way place, something with four walls that was remote, but not so remote that he couldn't get away from it easily. And thinking back on his walk from Mousehole to where he'd run down Lena's slimy little friend, Willie Keel, he thought he knew of just the place.

He'd go check it out now.

Staying on the edge.

Letting it all fall into place.

Doing it for himself, because if whatever it was that the Littles had stashed away was important enough for Madden to actually make the trip over here today, then it was worth Bett's keeping it for himself. If he couldn't figure it out, if he couldn't get the girl or her grandfather to show him how it worked . . . well, he'd always liked puzzles.

He liked taking things apart just to see how they worked.

It was what he did best.

7.

Janey waited for Clare at the first stile. She leaned against the tumbled-down stone wall beside it, looking off into the woods on their left.

"Why did you run on ahead like that . . . ?" Clare began.

She broke off when she saw the tears glistening in Janey's eyes.

"It's just so sad," Janey said. "He seems like such a dear old man and it's so sad that he's going to die."

Clare nodded. "I know."

"And what makes me feel worse," Janey said, "is all those times I've seen him up on the cliffs and either laughed at the way he looked, or ran off scared. I could have *known* him all this time. . . ."

She looked about in her pockets for a handkerchief, then wiped her eyes on her sleeve. Clare dug about in her own pockets and came up with a tissue that Janey accepted with a nod of thanks. She blew her nose.

"He had such . . . odd things to say," she said finally, still sniffling a bit.

"Very odd."

"Did you believe him?"

Clare sighed. "I don't know. Logically, I know that a lot of it can't be true—not the bits about Gurdjieff or how you can use your will and that sort of thing. I've heard of all that before. But those other things. . . ."

"The *real* magic," Janey said.

Clare nodded.

"There's only one way to find out," Janey said.

"Compare what you've read in the book to what Felix and your grandfather have read," Clare said.

"Because," Janey agreed, "if that's true, then maybe the rest of it is, too."

They started to walk slowly back to where they had left the car. The tailless cat wasn't near the stream when they crossed over. The whole of their surroundings, fields and wood, seemed still, as though the land were holding its breath. Even the babble of the stream was muted.

"You know what Mr. Goninan didn't talk about?" Janey said.

"What's that?"

"Music. That's part of the old legends as well, but it's not something that got written down until during the last century or so. And it's probably never been written down the way it *really* was. Every transcriber you hear about prettied it up, took the modal keys and fit them into minor ones—that kind of thing."

"But it doesn't pass on the same sorts of things that Mr. Goninan was telling us about," Clare said.

"It just doesn't teach it in words," Janey replied. "But you can still find traces of it in things like old mummers' plays and Morris dancing. The Hobby Horse Fool—he's really the trickster. The antlered man—he's Robin Hood. Not the storybook Robin Hood, but the Robin in the Wood. The Green Man."

"I suppose."

"No, really," Janey said. "Think about it. We remember ancient rituals in mumming and dancing. It's like Mr. Goninan said: We don't forget anything."

Clare nodded slowly. "We just forget why."

"I really think that's true. We go through the motions, and it stirs something in us and we feel good, but we don't know why it does. I think that's a real kind of magic—how nothing is ever really lost. Just hidden."

She smiled. "That's what draws us to the old tunes, I think. That's why we always want to learn as many as we can and why they've survived for as long as they have the way they are. Not the tunes in books, but the ones we get from memory, the ones we learn from the living tradition. And that's why we don't change them. We do new twiddles here, and arrange them with any number of modern instruments, but the bones of the tunes, the heart of the music—we keep *it* the same."

When they reached the car, she leaned on its hood and looked back the way they'd come. The sadness came back to her, riding an intangible breeze that washed through her without touching a hair on her head. It went to the heart, ignoring secular concerns. It wasn't the ache she'd felt last night when she'd thought that Felix had betrayed her, but a gentle sadness, like the breath expended into the mouthpiece of a whistle as it called up the bittersweet notes of a slow air.

Her fingers itched for an instrument, but there was none at hand. And this was neither the time nor the place. They had so much still to do. But she still wished she could play a music, something that would carry across the fields to the cottage where Peter Goninan nested with his bird totems and niece, something that he would hear and know by it that she had understood what he'd been trying to tell them. Understood not with her mind, but with her heart. She wanted to show her gratitude to him and knew that the best thanks the old man would ever ask for was the knowledge of that understanding.

She hoped there'd be time to come back.

She glanced at Clare, wanting to share the feeling with her, but Clare, she believed, for all her interest in the old tunes, didn't see them, didn't *feel* them in the same way.

But Felix would understand. She'd bring him to meet Peter Goninan, she decided. The two of them would get along famously. If they all only lived long enough. . . .

Sighing, she got into the car where Clare was already waiting.

"Felix would like that old man," she said as she started up the Reliant.

Clare nodded. "In a way, they're of a kind."

Maybe she'd been wrong, Janey thought. Maybe Clare did understand.

"What do you mean?" she asked.

"They both follow the road that their own hearts tell them to follow and give never a mind to what the rest of the world thinks about it."

"I never thought of it like that."

The track was too narrow to turn around in, so Janey carefully backed the car out onto the lane. Shifting into first, she set off for home at a far more sedate pace than they had left at earlier that day.

"I wanted to talk to you about Felix," Clare said.

"I think we'll be okay," Janey said. "I'm going to try really hard to make it work."

"I know you will. It's just that—"

She broke off and looked out through the side window at the hedges blurring past.

"Just what?" Janey prompted her.

"It's something he should probably tell you himself, but knowing him, he'll never get around to it. And it's important."

Janey's heart sank. What was she going to learn *now?*

"It's about how you want Felix to play with you on stage."

Janey's relief came as suddenly as her worry had.

"I won't push him," she said. "I think I've learned my lesson about trying to do that. If he doesn't want to, then he doesn't want to."

"That's good. Not that it's my business, really. . . ."

Janey laughed. "We're all mates, Clare. And we've always appreciated the way you've made us your business."

"That's nice to know," Clare said.

Janey heard a wistfulness in her friend's voice, but before she could think of a way to ask what was bothering her, Clare was speaking again.

"But I think it's important that you know *why* he won't do it."

"I know why," Janey said. "He just doesn't like it."

Clare shook her head. "He's scared to death of the idea."

All Janey could do was laugh at the very notion.

"Scared?" she said. "That big lug? I doubt he's scared of anything. And besides, I've seen him play in front of people a thousand times. At sessions, on street corners, backstage at festivals. . . ."

"But not *on* stage."

"No," Janey agreed. "Not on stage. Still, what's the difference?"

"I don't know. But I've been reading up on phobias since he first told me about this a few days ago, and while there's usually some hidden root to the problem that can be dealt with, very often there simply *is* no reasonable answer. What he suffers from is called topophobia—stage fright."

"But—"

"I know what you're going to say: Why doesn't he just deal with it? Get on stage a few times and simply work *through* his problem."

Janey nodded. "Well, isn't that how you deal with that kind of thing?"

"Unfortunately, it doesn't seem to be that simple. What happens is a panic syndrome sets in and if you've ever had a panic attack, you'll know it's not fun."

"I guess. . . ."

"I can still remember that last operation I had for my leg," Clare said. "I was panicking so badly—and it's a *horrible* feeling—that I fainted before they could give me the anesthetic."

"Saved them having to give it to you, I suppose."

Clare shook her head. "No, they can't do that. It's too dangerous. Your heartbeat and blood pressure go all irregular and none of their equipment can monitor you properly. They had to bring me around again first, and then give me the needle."

"So you're saying that Felix could faint if he got up on stage?"

"I was reading about the symptoms and they're really odd. You start off feeling sick, then your heartbeat becomes very fast and erratic; your chest gets tight and you start to breathe too fast.

The rapid breathing actually causes chemical changes inside you that make your hands and feet feel numb—that awful tingling when they've fallen asleep, you know?"

Janey nodded.

"The nausea then gets worse and is followed by headaches and cramps. And those are just the physical symptoms. Your brain also goes a bit mad. Everything begins to seem unreal. Apparently there can be the sensation of an out-of-body experience, or peculiar changes in the quality of light so that you lose your sense of depth and perspective. . . ."

"It sounds horrible," Janey said. "Is that what happened to you?"

"No. I just fainted, straightway."

"Lovely."

"And if all of that isn't bad enough," Clare went on, "there's also something called anticipatory anxiety that comes from just thinking about a panic attack. It apparently brings on a lot of the same symptoms as the actual attack. I saw a bit of that in Felix when he was telling me about it."

Janey was quiet for a long moment.

"I wish he'd told me this when we used to argue about him touring with me," she said.

"He was too scared to."

"Scared? Of me?"

Clare nodded. "Of your laughing at him—as you did when I started telling you about this a few moments ago."

"Well, I didn't really mean to laugh. It's just . . ."

"I know. It's hard to imagine Felix being frightened of anything. But he didn't want you to laugh at him and he also thought that you wouldn't think as much of him if you knew about his fear. A male ego thing, I suppose, since stage fright isn't something that many people take very seriously. It's always an 'Oh, get on up there; you'll feel better before you know it' sort of a thing, isn't it?"

"I suppose."

Janey was thinking about all the times she'd bullied people to get up and play on a stage and began to feel horrible about it.

"He thought you'd think he was like Ted Praed," Clare said. "Remember him?"

Janey started to giggle at the thought of Ted and his quavery voice, but then she realized what she was doing.

"We weren't very nice to him, were we?"

"Well, as I told Felix, Ted wasn't exactly the nicest person himself to begin with."

"But still. . . ."

"But still," Clare agreed. "Think of all the jokes—and Felix was there to hear them all."

"But he used to laugh, too."

Clare nodded. "He laughed, but if you think back, he was never the one who started the jokes, or told any himself."

"I could never think of Felix as being anything like Ted Praed—stage fright or no stage fright."

"Neither can I," Clare said. "But I did want to tell you so that you'd know why he feels the way he does, *before* you brought it up."

"I won't bring it up unless he does," Janey said, "and then I'll certainly not press him to get up on stage."

"That's good."

They were very near the village now, just coming on the south side of Raginnis Hill.

"How did you get him to tell *you?*" Janey asked.

Clare smiled. "I don't have the same things at stake as do the two of you, so I just browbeat it from him."

Janey laughed.

"Trust you," she said as she pulled the car up in front of Clare's house. "Did you want to be let off here," she added, "or are you coming on down to the house?"

"I'd like a chance to see the book," Clare said. "Before it's hidden away forever."

Janey smiled. "We'll read it together," she said.

Taking her foot from the brake, she steered the car on down into the village proper.

The Bargain Is Over

Power without abuse loses its charm.

— PAUL VALÉRY

A s their train crossed the Tamar River at Plymouth, John Madden sat up straighter in his seat. This was why he'd opted to return to the land of his birth by train, rather than by one of the more expedient methods of transportation that he could so easily have afforded.

The same *clackety-clack* rattle of the carriage's wheels against the tracks that had helped put him into a half-waking, half-dreaming state now rang with the heartbeat of the land for him and set his pulse drumming to ancient rhythms. A music sang inside him. A native music—that of crowdy crawn and pibcorn. He felt more alert, more *awake* than he had all day, and he knew it was due to the enchantment of the venerable countryside through which they journeyed.

This was Arthur's land.

Tintagel lay to the north, craggy and majestic; Arthur's birthplace, standing now in ruins above the mysterious depths of Merlin's cave. Dozmary Pool was on Bodmin Moor, where the Lady of the Lake had reclaimed Excalibur from Bedivere's hand. There was an Arthur's Chair, where the king was said to have sat and watched the sea. An Arthur's Cave, where he and his knights still slept. . . . The Once and Future King had been a West Country man—Madden had always believed that and over the past few decades the work of modern archaeologists supported that claim.

But there were older mysteries than Arthur hidden in this countryside.

Lyonesse, the drowned land, once stood between Land's End and the Isles of Scilly. The Scillies, and St. Michael's Mount near Penzance, were all that remained of that land today, though one could still hear the tolling of its bells beneath the sea.

And older still . . .

The land was riddled with Bronze Age stone circles, standing stones and other prehistoric relics.

There were the Merry Maidens near St. Buryans.

One tale held that the stones of its circle, and the two solitary menhir standing nearby, were dancers and musicians turned to stone for dancing on a Sunday. An older tale held that they were mermaids, caught by the sun one dawn and turned to stone like trolls, "merry maiden" being an old sailor's name for the women of the sea.

And Gwennap Pit between Redruth and St. Day.

The Methodists claimed it was an irregular mining sink that John Wesley was instrumental in having remodeled into its present form in 1806, but folklore told another story: Of how when Mervin the harper of Tollvaddon cracked his skull, he played his harp until his fingers were worn to the bone. The harp god Larga showed pity on him then, removing his wound and transferring it to the earth. So those who preferred the folktales called that great pit "the hole in the harper's head."

And the Men-an-Tol near Morvah.

The largest tolmen in the British Isles, archaeologists believed that it could be all that remained of the entrance to an ancient barrow or tomb. But tradition had it that passage through the holed stone brought healing to those who were ill and that it marked not the entrance to a barrow, but to the Barrow World, the land of the *muryan*, or piskies.

But beyond legend, beyond stone relics, Madden knew that the land itself was enchanted.

He was not alone in this understanding. Crowley, a native son, had known it. Dylan Thomas had been drawn to this countryside, living in Newlyn and Mousehole, a poet rather than a magician, but then again, at one time there was no difference perceived between the two. Dennis Wheatley had lived in the West Country as well.

And others, modern as well as the old:

Colin Wilson, whose career Madden had been following since his remarkable theories were first aired in *The Outsider*, now lived in Gorran Haven where he continued to study the Mysteries with a scientist's precise documentation. And Peter Goninan, the reclusive theurgist with whom Madden had crossed swords on occasion.

The land gave them birth, or drew them to it. Its hold ran deep, far beyond its simple pastoral beauties or coastal splendors. It ran as profound as the ancient granite backbone of the land, as instinctive as the inexplicable urges that first drew a man or a woman into the Mysteries, so that there was no choice involved, only inevitability.

An untapped wealth remained in the heartbeat of this land and every time Madden returned, he wondered anew why he had ever left in the first place. The secular concerns that drove him to live in other parts of the world seemed insignificant whenever he again set foot here.

"Kernow," he breathed.

Rollie Grant turned to him when he spoke. "What's that?"

Madden smiled. "The ancient name of an ancient country—this country."

"What, Cornwall?"

Madden nodded.

"I thought it was just like a state of the U.K.—you know, like Rhode Island or Connecticut."

"It's a state of mind," Madden said, remaining deliberately oblique.

Grant looked past him out the window for a long moment, then shrugged and returned to the business papers he was reading. They didn't speak again until they reached Penzance where Grant wanted to call a cab to take them from the train station to the hotel.

Madden laughed. "This isn't New York," he said. "We can walk."

"Walk?"

"Yes, walk," Madden said, still chuckling. "It's not far."

He glanced at a couple who were arguing a few carriages down from where they had disembarked, then hefted the small overnight case he'd brought and set off along the ocean front. Grant collected his own bags and hurried after him.

It was a fifteen-minute walk at Madden's slow pace to where the Queen's Hotel stood at the corner of Morrab Road and the Western Promenade Road, but it took them longer because Madden kept stopping along the way. Near Battery Rocks, he stood at the site of the old gun battery and looked out across the bay for a long time, breathing in the salt tang of the sea air, watching the waves spray against the rocks below, listening for the sound of bells. Across the road, he admired the St. Anthony Gardens and dawdled in front of the shop windows along the way, for all that most of them were closed and only carried tourist souvenirs anyway.

When they finally reached the Queen's Hotel, Grant looked up at it and sighed.

"This is the best the town's got?" he asked.

"No, but it's charming, don't you think?"

Grant smiled. "You're really in your element here, aren't you?"

"I've come home."

"I thought it was your father—John Madden Sr.—who was born in Cornwall."

"It was," Madden lied. "And my grandfather as well—in the 1850s." Another lie. "But it still feels like coming home."

Grant nodded and gave the hotel another look. "Well, I did tell Lena to keep a low profile. Looks like she's actually been listening to me for a change."

"When you come to another country," Madden said, "even one that in many ways is similar to your own, what's the point of staying in a Holiday Inn?"

"Comfort. Security. You know what you're getting."

Madden shook his head. "What you're speaking of is complacency, Rollie, and that will simply put you to sleep." He led the way towards the door. "Shall we register?"

They went to their own rooms after registering, meeting a few minutes later in Madden's when they had both had a chance to freshen up. There was a little confusion in reaching Lena, for she didn't answer her door when they knocked, but a request to the desk had their call transferred to where she was, and soon they had joined her in Jim Gazo's room. Madden settled into one of the chairs by the window, Grant in the other. Lena perched on the edge of the bed after giving her father a welcoming hug. Gazo stood by the door.

"Do you want me to go for a walk, Mr. Grant?" he asked.

Grant glanced at Madden who shook his head. As Gazo started to lean against the doorjamb, Madden indicated the head of the bed.

"You might as well be comfortable, Jim," he said. "It *is* your room."

Madden could read Gazo's thoughts easily. Sure, it was his room, but Grant was paying for it. Gazo was just on the payroll and being in Madden's company made him nervous, though if Gazo had been pressed he wouldn't have been able to say why he felt that way.

Which was how it should be, Madden thought. The nervousness of sheep was something that he cultivated. It kept them alert—or at least as alert as sheep could be—and stopped them from having too many thoughts of their own because they were so busy trying to stay in Madden's favour.

"Why don't you tell us how things have gone?" Madden said to Lena.

She spoke for some time, obviously choosing her words carefully because she knew that Michael Bett was Madden's protégé, but laying out all the facts. Madden was impressed with her delivery. He felt she was holding something back—something to do with this Felix Gavin—but it didn't appear to have any bearing on his own immediate concerns, so he didn't press her on it. But while she was tactful in how she spoke of Bett—making no judgments, but rather allowing Madden to make up his own mind from what she had to report—her father had no such reservations.

"He's out of control," Grant said when Lena was done.

"Perhaps," Madden said.

"I'm sorry, John, but we've got to face the facts. He's working on something for himself."

Madden nodded slowly. "I expected this," he said.

Only not so soon. He'd known all along that the reincarnated spirit of Crowley would eventually turn against him. Crowley had always been a leader, as witness his altercations with MacCregor Mathers and the like, but Madden had still expected to have some time before it was necessary to deal more firmly with Bett. He had thought to squeeze a few more years of service out of the man and then, depending on his loyalty, decide whether he would be discarded or rewarded.

He had half imagined Michael as a son. . . .

"What are we going to do about Michael?" Grant asked.

"That will require some thought," Madden replied. "First we must discover exactly what it is that he is up to."

"That's simple," Grant said. "He wants what you want. He wants whatever it is that Dunthorn hid from us."

Madden nodded. "If that is true, then I'm afraid we will just have to deal with him before he has the chance to find it."

But what a waste that would be. Michael had such potential.

His mistake, Madden realized, was in thinking of Michael as a kind of tabula rasa—as though he could create whatever he wanted from the blank slate of Michael's spirit, when all along that spirit had already been formed and shaped and fired in an iron will of its own—not through merely one lifetime, but through many. It was easy to forget that he wasn't teaching Michael; he was helping him remember.

The danger had been in allowing him to remember too much.

Madden wasn't terribly worried about that, however. Mistakes were unfortunate, but if caught in time, they were only temporary setbacks. They could be corrected. Not always easily, not necessarily without regret, but they could be corrected.

And Madden had no compunction about seeing that it was done. None whatsoever.

His only loyalty had always been to himself.

2 .

Sam Dennison was in a foul mood.

He was feeling punchy and red-eyed from a lack of sleep and wished, not for the first time that day, that he'd known Bett was going to call him this morning. He wouldn't have had quite so many drinks the night before if he had. Hell, he wouldn't have had any. He would've turned in early and been all bright-eyed and bushy-tailed for this gig. As it was, his patience level was right on the edge and he had to catch himself from wanting to hit someone just to ease the tension.

It wasn't so much the flight over, nor the wait for their train and the subsequent five-and-some-hour journey to the West Country, as the traveling companions with whom he'd been thrown together on this job. The woman was bad enough.

Connie Hetherington was a good-looking woman—at least Dennison thought she was, somewhere under all that makeup and the teased peroxide hair. She had an hour-glass figure that would do a college kid half her own age proud, and legs that just didn't stop, but she carried herself like a tramp. Not to mention dressing to fit the role: skimpy skirt and high-heeled pumps, low-cut blouse and cheap fur jacket.

She was a looker, but Dennison was embarrassed to be in her company. And not just because of the way she dressed and came on to just about anything wearing trousers that got within taking distance of her. She chewed gum with her mouth open, chain-smoked, and hadn't stopped whining since they'd left Kennedy Airport first thing that morning. Baby-sitting her was like being trapped in the opening frames of a porn flick—unending hours of inane conversation and double entendres that had him gritting his teeth by the time they finally arrived at Penzance Station.

Ted Grimes was the opposite end of the spectrum.

He was dressed in a tailored dark suit and didn't look in the least bit rumpled from the hours of travel. His black hair and dark complexion placed the source of his genes in the Mediterranean, but Dennison didn't figure him for a wise guy, never mind the way that Grimes moved with the ice-cool easy cruising style of one of the Cerone Family's enforcers. He didn't have the size—coming in a half head under Dennison's own six-one—but there was something of a shark about him all the same and Dennison could tell, the moment he laid eyes on the man, that if Grimes wasn't a hitman, he'd still done his share of killing for hire.

He might not be connected, but he had the flat, dead eyes of the type, and Dennison figured that his own baby-sitting duties didn't include looking after Grimes. They hadn't exchanged more than two words since Dennison had collected him. Grimes had ignored Connie as well after giving her one cool look when they picked her up. He hadn't even batted an eye when she pointed to his prosthetic hand and asked him, "Hey, you got a vibrator attachment to go with that thing?"

Dennison had wondered about the hand, too, but hadn't said a thing about it. Wasn't his business. He'd learned that long ago. Never mind the white knight PI crap that TV and paperbacks foisted off on the public, the only way you got ahead in this business was by sticking strictly to the job. Leave the crusades for those who didn't have to make a living.

What he didn't like about having Grimes tagging along was that if Grimes *was* setting up a hit, then that left Dennison himself as an accessory. Maybe he wasn't a white knight, but

Dennison still had drawn lines between what was kosher and what wasn't, and being involved in a hit was definitely stepping way over the line.

As soon as they left the train, Grimes vanished.

"We'd better be getting a hotel room soon," Connie complained. "I'm sick of traveling. I feel like shit, you know what I'm saying? I need to wash up and get beautiful, pal."

Dennison ignored her and took care of getting their luggage out on the platform.

"Hey, where's poker-face?" she went on. "I thought we were, like, a big happy family."

Dennison was wondering that as well. He scanned the platform, but except for some French hikers with their knapsacks, a family of four with luggage enough for twice that number, who were obviously also tourists, and a pair of older gentlemen—probably businessmen—they had the area to themselves.

"You know I'm getting kind of sick of the silent treatment from you guys," Connie said. "It'd be nice if you acted like I was here. I mean, just because you've got a pickle up your—"

"Shut up," Dennison told her.

The few people present were all staring at her. He threw his raincoat at her, which she caught awkwardly.

"And put this on," he added.

She started to throw it back at him. "Hey, don't go getting all prissy on me, Mr. Big Shot Private Det—"

She broke off at the glare in his eyes. He didn't say a word, just continued to give her a long hard stare until she slowly put the coat on. It was far too big for her and made her look like a bit of a clown with her high heels and stockinged calves underneath it and her teased blond hair and painted face above, but it also made her look the best she had since he'd first collected her at her Lower East Side apartment where she'd met him at the door dressed in a baby-doll nightie right out of the pages of a Fredricks of Hollywood catalogue.

He stepped over to her and spoke in a voice pitched just loud enough for her to hear.

"Let's get something straight," he told her. "We're both on a payroll. You screw up, and it looks bad on me, and I don't like looking bad, got it?"

"Sure, I—"

"I don't know what the hell Mr. Bett has got planned for you, but you can be damn sure it doesn't include parading your ass all over town so that everybody who happens to be within a hundred yards of you will never forget you. So keep a lip on it and keep that coat on until we get a hotel room and then you're going to change into something a little less—well, let's be polite and only call it trashy."

"C'mon," Connie said. "Give me a break. It's not like—"

"If Mr. Bett is paying you anything like he's paying me, you owe him this much." He lifted a fist between them. "I'm sick of your whining and I'm not one of those candyasses who wouldn't lay a hand on a woman—not if that's what it takes to shut 'em up."

Her lip curled, but Dennison spoke before she could get a word out.

"I'm not jiving you, lady."

Connie shrugged. "Screw you, too," she said, but there was no force behind her words.

She lit up a cigarette and studiously ignored him.

Dennison sighed. He didn't feel particularly proud about threatening her, but he was way beyond his usual limit of patience.

What the hell made her tick? He could see kids getting into the skin trade because it looked like a fast track to the good life, but surely a woman her age would have seen through the lie by now? What the hell made her still play out the party-girl image?

Getting old doesn't mean you get smart, he answered himself. She probably just didn't know any better.

Happily, Grimes chose that moment to reappear.

The guy moved like a ghost, Dennison thought, as Grimes collected his small traveling case from where Dennison had placed it on the platform.

"You missed our PI here playing the tough guy," Connie said.

Grimes gave Dennison a glance. For a moment Dennison thought he saw a trace of humour behind the man's flat gaze, but it was gone before he could be sure.

"What happened to you?" Dennison asked him.

"Saw someone I'm not ready to do business with yet," Grimes replied.

So it was a hit, Dennison thought. He'd have to talk to Bett about this. No way he was going to be a part of this kind of a thing.

"Ready to find a hotel?" he asked.

Grimes shook his head. "Bett knows how to get in touch with me when the time's right."

"Do you need to know where we're staying?"

"Can't see why."

Maybe things were going to work out after all, Dennison thought. With Grimes on his own track and if he could keep Hetherington quiet until Bett needed her, maybe he could salvage a little something for himself out of all of this. He'd enjoyed his previous trip here, but he'd only been playing the tourist then. Maybe he could fit in some real sight-seeing time before he had to head back to the States.

"Well, good luck," he said.

Grimes smiled. "I've been waiting a long time to settle some unfinished business and I'll tell you right now, it's going to be a real pleasure finally getting the job done, but luck's not going to have anything to do with it. Just patience."

Dennison didn't look at the prosthetic hand, but he knew that whatever Grimes was talking about had something to do with it. He gave Grimes a nod, then handed Connie her overnight case and picked up their other two cases.

"Let's go, sunshine," he said.

Connie butted her cigarette under the toe of her shoe and followed him with unfeigned reluctance.

Yeah, me, too, lady, Dennison thought. But we're stuck with each other for the moment. He wasn't going to say let's make the best of it. All he wanted to do was get this crummy job over with.

Leppadumdowledum

*For the moon's shining high
and the dew is wet;
and on mossy moor,
they're dancing yet.*

—CORNISH RHYME

*J*o d i had suffered through her fair share of long, boring afternoons before, but she couldn't remember one as tedious as this one that she spent tucked away for the most part in the pocket of the mayor of Bodbury's secretary.

It made sense, of course, for her to go with Lizzie. Of all the conspirators to gather in Henkie Whale's warehouse earlier that morning, Lizzie was the most likely candidate to take on the responsibility of hiding the Small that Jodi had become from the Widow Pender. It seemed logical that the Widow would pursue Denzil or Taupin, or any of the Tatters children, before she would think to confront Lizzie in her tiny office at the back of the town hall.

The logic was impeccable, everyone had agreed—especially Taupin whose idea it had been. But logic didn't make the hours go by any more quickly; nor did it relieve the boredom.

When they first arrived, Jodi had insisted that she be given the freedom of the desktop at the very least. As Lizzie rattled away on her typewriter, Jodi had wandered about the oversize desk, investigating common objects made strange by her new size: giant pens, a wooden letter opener as large as an oar, enormous sheets of paper as large as bedsheets and the like. She walked up and down the mayor's correspondence, amused at reading words composed of letters that were each as big as her hand, and played soccer with a wadded-up bit of paper and two erasers as goalposts, but the novelty of it all soon palled.

She ended up sitting on Lizzie's thesaurus, swinging her heels against its leather spine and wishing she were anywhere but where she was—until she was nearly caught by one of Lizzie's coworkers, and Lizzie insisted that she remain out of sight. Then Jodi spent a half hour in a drawer, which was too dark, even with the slat of light that came through the crack that Lizzie had left open, and even more boring.

Eventually she went back into Lizzie's pocket where she divided her time between dozing and peeking up over the edge of the pocket to look at the clock on the wall and gauge how much time had passed since the last time she'd looked. It was invariably less than ten minutes.

"Bother and damn," she muttered. "What's the point of being magical if this is all it gets you? Where's the glamour and romance? Where's the adventure?"

But then she thought of Edern—her Small who had turned out to be a clockwork man when he died, and then, in a dream, spoke to her from the mind of a seal. . . .

Oh, Edern. Why did you have to go and die? Were you ever even real in the first place?

That line of thought just made her feel depressed. And it brought back memories of the Widow, and the creatures at the witch's command. Adventure? She realized that she could do without the adventure, thank you all the same.

But this endless monotony. . . .

"I wish I could *do* something," she said and kicked out against the fabric of the pocket in frustration.

"What are you doing?" Lizzie whispered.

Jodi stuck her head out of the pocket and stared up at Lizzie's enormous face.

This is the world as a mouse sees it, she thought. Oh raw we. What if she was stuck like this forever?

"I'm going all kitey," she shouted back in her high piping voice. "Desperately kitey."

"Well do try to keep it down," Lizzie replied, still whispering. "What if someone hears you?"

"Tell them it's your stomach rumbling and you must go home for an early supper."

Lizzie shook her head, which was a disconcerting gesture. It was like the top of a mountain moving back and forth. Her blond hair cascaded about her shoulders like a waterfall unable to make up its mind as to which course it would follow. It made Jodi's head ache to watch.

"Stomach squeaking, rather," Lizzie said.

"It's not my fault I sound like this. Are you almost done for the day?"

Again the mountaintop moved back and forth. "We agreed it was best for us to stay here where the Widow won't dare start a row—remember?"

All too bloody well, Jodi thought.

"I really am going mad," she told Lizzie.

"You'll survive."

"Yes, but without a brain. It'll have all turned to porridge in another few hours—truly it will. How can you stand to work here, day in, day out?"

"I like it. It gives me a chance to—"

"Who are you talking to, Lizzie?"

Jodi dropped back into the pocket as Lizzie started nervously and looked to the doorway where one of her coworkers stood.

"Just thinking aloud," Lizzie replied.

The woman in the doorway smiled and shook her head. "That's the first sign of madness," she said, "talking to yourself."

"I thought it was when you answered yourself," Lizzie said.

"That, too."

The woman went on to her own office and Lizzie looked down at her pocket.

"Do you see what I mean about keeping hidden?" she hissed. "You almost gave it all away."

Jodi peeped above the top of Lizzie's pocket again.

"I'm ever so frightened," she said sulkily.

"Be good," Lizzie said, "and I'll leave early. We can get some ices and walk along the Old Quay before we meet the others."

"Don't . . ." Jodi began, then sighed.

Don't talk to me as though I'm a child, she had been about to say, but she realized that Lizzie was only treating her like a child because she was acting like one. Lizzie was using the same tone of voice that Jodi did when she talked to Denzil's monkey.

Bother and damn.

I'm even smaller than Ollie, she thought. And not nearly so well behaved.

"I think I'll have another nap," she said and dropped back into the pocket.

Lizzie went back to her typing.

Ten minutes later Jodi popped her head up to check the time once more. Only six minutes had passed.

Bother and damn, she thought as she sank back down into the pocket again.

2 .

This was utter foolishness, Kara thought as she and Ethy approached the Widow's cottage. They were supposed to be avoiding the Widow and her creatures, yet here they were bringing the wounded home to be tended. The Widow would probably work a spell with the snap of her fingers to heal the little beastie and then they'd simply have to deal with the fetch all over again.

That was if they didn't run into the Widow at her home first. . . .

When Kara glanced at her companion, she could see that Ethy was having second thoughts as well, now that they were so close. What they should do was just drop the fetch right here within sight of the Widow's cottage, lay it on the cobblestones, bundled up and all, and pedal off while they still had a chance.

That was the sensible thing to do.

Windle moved in her arm and made a piteous sound.

Kara sighed. Unfortunately, she wasn't so hard-hearted as to be able to do it. Not now, after having come this far. Not with the little creature so helpless. They'd given up the opportunity to be sensible from the moment they first set off with the wounded fetch in hand.

When they reached the last cottage before the Widow's, Kara leaned her bicycle up against its garden wall and turned to Ethy.

"Wait for me here," she said.

"What are you going to do?"

"Lay it on her doorstep."

"I can help."

"There's nothing for you to do," Kara explained.

She left unsaid the fact that there was no need for them both to be at risk when one could do the task as well as two.

"But—" Ethy began.

"You can watch our bikes," Kara said.

Keeping a careful grip on the fetch in its newspaper bundle, she crossed the road and darted into the Widow's garden. From there it was only a few steps to the cottage stoop where she knelt and laid down the fetch.

Was that a sound from inside the cottage? she wondered nervously.

No. Just a shutter rattling somewhere.

She gave Windle a comforting pat and the fetch snapped feebly at her hand.

Wonderfully grateful creature, she thought. Wasn't it just?

She straightened up and began to back away when she heard Ethy's warning shout.

"Kara!"

She turned to see the Widow in the road, Ethy cowering near the garden wall where their bicycles were leaning.

"Monsters!" the Widow cried. "Murderers!"

"Get away!" Kara shouted to Ethy, but the little girl was too frightened to move.

"I'll fry you both," the Widow said, her voice dropping to a menacing growl. "I'll cook you in a pie and feed you to the crows. I'll pull off your fingers, one by one, and make a necklace of them that I'll hang about my neck."

"W-we—we brought him back," Kara stuttered.

The Widow was standing directly by her gate now, blocking Kara's escape. Kara glanced at Ethy, willing her friend to flee, then looked about the garden for another gate, but there was none. Still, the hedgerow wasn't that thick. Perhaps she could squeeze through and give the Widow the slip. Only that left Ethy, frozen by their bicycles. . . .

The Widow was still cataloging the terrible fates she had for the pair of them.

"I'll pop your eyes and boil them in a soup. I'll make shoes of your skin and laugh as I dance in them."

Kara was so frightened that she almost forgot the satchel hanging at her side. But when she took a nervous step towards the hedge, the satchel banged against her knee. With trembling fingers she took out a balloon and held it up in her hand.

"You—you just keep back," she said, advancing towards the gate.

The Widow's eyes narrowed. "What have you got there, girl?"

"Keep back or I'll throw this," Kara replied.

"What have you *got*?"

But Kara could tell that the Widow already knew. She backed up as Kara continued to move forward, gaze fixed on the balloon filled with seawater that Kara held in her hand.

When she reached the road, Kara edged around so that she was still facing the Widow, but each step brought her closer to where Ethy was standing near their bicycles.

"Kara Faull," the Widow said.

Kara shivered. Three times named was what it took for the witch to work her spells—that's what Taupin had told them this morning. So the Widow had just spoken the first third of a spell.

"You shut your gob," Kara cried, hoisting the balloon higher, "or I *will* throw it."

"I have you marked," the Widow said. "You, and Ethy Welet, there, and all your miserable friends. Don't think that I haven't."

Kara had reached the bicycles now. She nudged Ethy with her foot, but got no response, so she gave the smaller girl a light kick on the shin with her toe.

Ethy blinked and shivered.

"Get on your bike," Kara told her.

"I'll bake you in an oven until your heads pop open and your brains spill out," the Widow said. "I'll crack your bones and suck out their marrow."

Kara got on her own bike.

"Go," she told Ethy. "I'll be right behind you. She won't harm you."

"Harm her?" the Widow cried. "I'll unarm her. I'll pull off her legs and use them to stir a stew."

"Go," Kara repeated.

Straddling her own bicycle, she held it upright with her knees and gave Ethy a push with her free hand. Ethy's bike wobbled as she set off down the hill, but soon picked up speed. With the balloon still in one hand, her other gripping the handlebar of her own bicycle, Kara backed up, wheeled her bike farther away from the Widow.

"I'll have you all," the Widow told her. "There'll be no escape."

Shuddering, Kara quickly turned her bicycle about and whizzed off down the hill herself. She dropped the balloon back into its satchel and bent low over her handlebars, trying to catch up to Ethy who was still far ahead of her. Behind her she could hear the trailing fade of the Widow's curses. She heard her name a second time, but before she could hear it repeated for the third time that Taupin had said would give the spell its potency, she was beyond hearing distance and safe.

Safe.

Her pulse drummed with fear. How could she ever be safe again when she knew that from now until forever she was carrying a witch's enmity along with her wherever she went? She and Ethy might have escaped for the moment, but sooner or later the Widow would track them down, each and every one of them—just as she'd promised—and then what would they do?

What *could* they do?

They would have to push her into the sea, Kara realized. They would have to become murderers in truth.

The day had begun as a lark. Now it felt so grim that Kara wondered if she'd ever feel lighthearted again.

She finally caught up with Ethy and the two of them pedaled on across town until they reached Peter Street. There they threw their bicycles by the door that led up to Denzil's loft and pelted up the stairs to tell him what had happened.

3 ·

The Widow stood in the middle of the road until the two girls were out of sight. She saw a curtain move in the window of a neighbouring house and turned in its direction. Whoever had been watching from the window had now ducked out of sight.

"You, too," the Widow said. "I'll ruin you all. I'll bring down such a storm on this town that there won't be anyone left after its tempest and roar to remember it."

But first she would deal with this ragtag gaggle of miserable urchins and the like who thought they could prove any sort of a match for her.

Faint laughter spilled from the shadows alongside the hedge as she entered her garden, but she ignored it. She knelt down by the stoop and unfolded the newspapers from around her fetch. Her eyes teared as she took in the damage that the small creature had sustained.

"There, there," she crooned, gently lifting Windle from the papers. "Mother will have you well again, my sweet."

Her heart broke at the pitiful whimpers that even her gentle handling drew out of the fetch.

This would be redressed, she swore.

"On the graves of my mother and grandmother," she said, looking into the shadows where they collected against the side of the cottage. "Do you hear me? Let them never know rest if I fail to keep my vow."

We hear, the shadows whispered.

"Will you lend me what I need?"

Whatever you need.

And then the shadows rang again with that too familiar laughter, hollow and mocking.

The Widow merely regarded them for a long moment, then opened the door to her cottage and carried Windle inside.

4 ·

High on Mabe Hill, overlooking the town of Bodbury, were the ruins of an old church called Creak-a-vose after the ancient barrow mound upon which it had been built. A rambling affair, its bell tower had fallen in on itself and one of its walls had tumbled down. Its roof was open to the air. The remaining three walls were covered with vines and ivy and home to birds and one owl. It was there that the conspirators met as evening fell, straggling into the ruins by ones and twos until all, except Ratty Friggens, were gathered.

"I fear the worst," Denzil said when another half hour had dragged by and the Tatters boy still hadn't made an appearance. "After what the girls told me . . ."

Henkie nodded grimly. "The bloody Widow must have got to him."

Jodi's happiness at finally being freed from the confines of Lizzie's office had taken a downward turn as she learned of the narrow escapes made by Kara and Ethy. Ratty's absence simply made her feel worse.

It was still an hour's walk across farmers' pastures and moorland to the field where the Men-an-Tol stood with its two outriding

standing stones, one on either side of its hole. Taupin had reckoned that if they left Creak-a-vose come dusk, they would reach
the tolmen just as the moon was rising. The argument now was
as to who would go.

"The children must be sent back to town," Denzil said. "We
can't be responsible for harm coming to any more of them, you."

The other adults nodded in agreement, but Kara shook her
head.

"We're coming," she said.

"Don't start," Henkie told her.

But Kara stood her ground.

"It will be too dangerous," Lizzie said. "You've done your share
already—more than your share."

Taupin had also reckoned that they'd had such an easy time
of it for the later part of the afternoon because the Widow had
been lying low, seeing to the wounds of her fetch.

"We're not scared," Ethy said, though even in the dim light
they could all see her trembling.

"You don't understand," Kara added. "It's not that we *want*
to come; we just don't have any other choice."

Ethy nodded.

"We have to stick together," Peter said.

"None of us wants to be on our own when the Widow sends
her creatures out to hunt us down," Kara said.

"I hadn't thought of that," Taupin said.

But Denzil still disagreed. "She'll be too concerned with us to
trouble anyone else tonight," he said.

"How can you be sure?" Kara asked.

"I . . ." Denzil looked to the others for help, but no one could
offer any. "I can't," he finished lamely.

"So there you have it," Kara said firmly. "We all go."

"If we're going," Taupin put in, "then it'll have to be quickly.
If we're to make it to the stone by moonrise, that is."

Denzil looked around one last time at the other adults, hoping
that someone could think of a better solution than bringing the

children along with them, but there was still no help to be found. Lizzie sighed and shook her head. Taupin shrugged. Henkie grumbled into his beard.

"No other way about it that I can see," the big man said.

"Maybe we shouldn't go at all," Jodi piped up. "Any of us. We could sit out the night in a boat, out on the bay where she can't get near us."

"Sea dead," Peter muttered.

"She didn't call up any sea dead last night," Jodi said.

"It was probably too late at night," Kara said, "or it all happened too quickly for her. Perhaps it takes time to call them up."

"Perhaps there's no such thing," Denzil offered.

Taupin smiled. "Still begrudging what lies at the end of your nose?"

"Just because one mad thing is true, it doesn't mean it all is," Denzil replied.

"How can you look at Jodi and not accept—"

"I accept she's a Small, you," Denzil said. "But the secret to science is that one should be able to arrive at the same set of results every time one has set up a specific experiment or set of conditions. It has to be repeatable—nothing else will do. I can see Jodi is a Small, and she remains a Small, therefore such a thing can be."

"And the Widow's magics?"

"I can accept that she's capable of turning a normal-sized being into a Small and I will remain open to her other powers for safety's sake, but that doesn't necessarily mean she can do all that a witch from the folktales can."

"Like raising the dead?" Henkie asked.

"Exactly."

"Can't be done?"

Denzil nodded firmly.

"Then what do you have to say about my mate Briello who you were gabbing with last night?"

"I . . ."

"It grows late," Lizzie interrupted.

Denzil blinked at her for a moment, then nodded. "We should go."

They trooped outside and stood in a bunch.

"Seawater works against the Widow and the creatures she makes," Henkie said, "but what about these sea dead? What'll we do if we run into them?"

They each had satchels carrying balloons filled with salt water, or watersacks filled with the same. They were heavy, but no one complained.

"We'll have to hope that we're going too far inland for them to come," Taupin said. "Come along now, and watch your step."

With the moon still below the horizon, it was dark out in the fields. Henkie complained about the lack of light. He had a big hammer stuck in his belt and had also carried up an oil lamp.

"It's not like she won't track us down," he said.

"Only why make it easier for her?" Lizzie asked him.

The big man's reply was a wordless sound that rumbled deep in his chest.

"If we should get separated," Denzil said, always the worrier, "should we plan to meet back here—at the church?"

With that agreed upon, they finally set off.

Taupin led the way cross country, following trails that only he knew, acquiring his knowledge of them from his constant traveling about the countryside that surrounded the town. He knew which fields had boggy patches that needed to be avoided, which hedgerows could be slipped through with the least amount of effort, where there were nettles and where there weren't.

The fields opened up into ragged moorland as they neared the Men-an-Tol. Sweeps of heather, dried ferns, and prickly gorse spread out on all sides of them, but were soon lost to easy view as ragged mists rose up from the ground with the cooling of the night air.

"Good weather for hummocks," Peter whispered.

"Don't even mention anything to do with ghosts," Denzil warned him.

He was holding Ethy's hand and could feel her trembling beside him at the very thought of some ethereal hummock rising up from the gorse to pluck at her clothing.

They reached the holed stone just as the moon was peeking over the horizon, giving the mists an even ghostlier air. Photographs and etchings gave the tolmen a height and majesty that it didn't have in real life. The circular stone came to just barely above Henkie's waist, but the hole was large enough for even Peter to crawl through, and there remained an air of mystery and ancient riddles about it despite its small size. The rising mists added to its sense of otherworldly glamour.

Shivering, they all gathered about the stone and looked at one another.

"What do we do now?" Kara asked.

"I have to go nine times through the hole in the stone," Jodi piped.

Her throat was getting sore again from constantly having to shout to be heard.

"Do the rest of us do anything?" Peter asked as Lizzie stepped towards the stone with Jodi cupped in her hands.

"Watch, I suppose," Jodi said.

"Should we make a circle of seawater around the stone to protect us from the witch's creatures?" Henkie asked.

"That would kill the vegetation," Taupin said.

"Who's to mind?"

"Maybe what we're calling up from the stone?"

"There's that," Henkie agreed.

He set his oil lamp down on the ground at his feet and fingered the haft of his hammer.

"Are you ready?" Lizzie asked Jodi.

"What's to do?" she replied, sounding cockier than Denzil knew she must be feeling.

Lizzie passed her through the hole in the stone.

"That's one," Henkie said.

Nothing happened, except that the mists continued to deepen, hanging low to the moors, while the moon climbed steadily up in the sky. As Lizzie continued to pass Jodi through the hole in the Men-an-Tol, one voice, then another, joined Henkie's counting until they were all counting with him.

"Seven."

Denzil cocked his ear, thinking that he had heard something. He sensed something approaching, *felt* it deep in his bones. It wasn't the Widow, or any of her creatures. It was more a sound. A strange sort of music, distant and eerie. Unfamiliar, but he felt as though he'd known it all his life.

"Eight."

The music grew until he could begin to pick out the instruments. He could hear harping in it and fiddle, the hollow drumbeat of a crowdy crawn and a breathy flute. But there were no musicians, just the moor.

He could tell that the others also heard it now as they lifted their heads and tried to peer through the mists that surrounded them. A faint light caught Denzil's eye. He turned back to look at the tolmen where a glow like the last ember of a fire hovered in the center of the stone's hole.

Lizzie brought Jodi through the hole and around the outside of the stone again. As she started to put her through for the final time, the music swelled around them.

"Nine," Henkie breathed, his voice alone, the others all hushed.

Light flared from the hole, piercing and bright. The music had risen to a crescendo with the flare, then faded to dying echoes as the light died, winked out, was gone.

Henkie fumbled with a match, muttering to himself until he finally got his oil lamp lit. The lamp's light cast a dim glow over the stone where Lizzie stood staring down at her empty palms.

"She's gone," Lizzie said. "She simply vanished. . . ."

With the light, Denzil thought. With the music.

Deep in his chest he felt a pang of loss.

"Jodi . . ." he whispered.

Would he ever see her again?

"Oh, bloody hell," Henkie said.

Denzil looked up to see what had agitated the artist this time and his own heart sank. Coming out of the mists on all sides of them were shambling man-shapes. A bog-reek was in the air, low and cloying. Cutting above it came the sharp scent of the sea: salt and brine; the smell of wet seaweed and rotting fish.

Why did he have to be wrong again? Denzil asked.

But wrong he was.

For these were drowned men that encircled the stone, drowned men called up from the sea graves that marched across the moors and fields to confront them here in this place.

The Widow *could* call up the sea dead.

5 ·

From the dark night on the moors outside Bodbury, the ninth passage through the stone's hole plunged Jodi into a world of bright light.

Daylight, she realized as her eyes adjusted to the glare.

A sunny day.

In a different world.

Oh raw we. . . .

She found herself to be the same tiny size she'd been in the other world. She was sitting in a bed of dried ferns and looking straight at the Men-an-Tol, which had either come with her to this world, or existed here as well. The sunlight gleamed on its stone.

How could this be real?

And that made her want to laugh—hysterically, perhaps, but laugh all the same. For here she'd just spent the better part of two days the size of a mouse and she was thinking that magical otherworlds were impossible?

But still. . . .

"Jodi."

She turned at the sound of that familiar voice to find a stranger facing her—but a stranger with eyes she knew, whose body, for all its physical unfamiliarity, stood in the same stance that someone else's body had often stood, who stepped towards her with a step that was also familiar.

And she had never seen him before in her life.

He was small, just as she was, which made him exactly the right size, she supposed. His ears tapered to small points at their tops, small gold hoops in each lobe; his hair was curly and golden and also swirled up to form a bit of a point at the top of his head. His eyes were familiar, his face merry, his body slender in a shirt, jacket, and trousers of mottled moorland colours. He was barefoot.

She knew him. She didn't know him.

"Edern . . . ?" she asked.

The stranger nodded.

"I'm grateful for your coming," he said.

Constant Billy

The stories are always waiting, always
listening for names; when they hear
the names they're listening for they
swallow the people up.
—RUSSELL HOBAN,
from *The Medusa Frequency*

*J*aney wasn't ready for more bad news, but that was what
was waiting for her when she and Clare finally got back
to the house on Duck Street.

"I'm sorry, my fortune," the Gaffer said. "I rang up Kit as you
asked me to do and she told me she was about to call you herself.
It's about your American tour."

Janey could feel her heart sinking.

"What about it?" she asked.

"It's been canceled."

"Canceled? But . . . ?"

She looked to Felix for help, but found only sympathy.

"Oh, Janey," Clare said, laying a hand on her arm. "That's
awful."

"How can it be canceled?" Janey asked. "Did she say
why?"

The Gaffer shook his head. "She had no idea. She said she
would look into it, but couldn't expect to have any word back
until tomorrow, it being Sunday and all. I'm sorry, my love. I
know you were looking forward to it."

"It's not just that. It . . ."

First that odd message from the *Rolling Stone* reporter this
morning about how his editor had canceled her participation
in his article, and now this. It wasn't coincidence. Someone
was out to make her life as miserable as they possibly could.
And now, after the talk she and Clare had had with Peter

Goninan, she could make an educated guess as to who that someone was.

"It's Madden," she said. "It's that John Madden."

Clare nodded in slow agreement. "If what Mr. Goninan told us about him is true, then I think you're right. He's set upon getting the book from you and until you give it to him, he's going to keep after you until you don't feel you have any choice *but* to give it to him."

"I think we're missing something here," Felix said.

Janey looked at the confusion on his and her grandfather's features. Sighing, she plunked herself down on the sofa beside Felix.

"We learned an awful lot from Peter Goninan," she said.

The Gaffer hrumphed. "I hope you listened with a grain of salt. The man *is* half-daft."

"But the other half," Clare said with a smile as she took a seat, "is fascinating."

"I like him," Janey added. "I like him an awful lot."

The Gaffer shook his head. "Now that do belong," he said. "Peter Goninan charming anyone, little say you."

"I'm easy to get along with," Janey protested. At the raised eyebrows that statement called up from everyone in the room, she added, "Well, in a manner of speaking."

"I wasn't thinking of you so much, my love," the Gaffer said, "as I was of Peter. He's such an odd bird"—Janey couldn't stop a little smile at that description of Goninan—"sticking to himself up on that farm of his the way he does. Gives new meaning to the word recluse, doesn't he just? I'm surprised he even spoke to you at all."

"He's dying," Janey said.

The Gaffer fell silent, considering that.

"Maybe the reason he keeps to himself is because there's never been anyone else interested in the kinds of things he is," Janey added. "That doesn't make him bad—just eccentric. He probably got into the habit of being alone when he was younger and now he just prefers it that way."

"I never thought of it quite like that," the Gaffer said. "He was always—standoffish. Seemed to hold himself to be better than the rest of us. Didn't care for games or fishing or anything that the rest of us did, just his books and his birds. The only ones of us who had any time for him were Billy and Morley Jenkin—but the Jenkins moved up country just before we all took our O levels and Billy never seemed to spend that much time with him—not that I ever saw."

"Maybe he just seemed standoffish," Clare said. "It's not easy to be mates when you don't think you have anything in common with the rest of the blokes."

The Gaffer nodded.

"That woman," Janey said. "Her name's Helen Bray and she's his niece. She's nursing him."

"And he's dying, you say?"

Janey nodded.

"Makes me feel a bit of a rotter."

"I know exactly what you mean, Gramps. When I think of how I used to laugh at his stick figure out by the cliffs, I just feel awful."

"You couldn't know," Felix said.

The Gaffer nodded. "But we should have been more charitable."

Janey sighed, then sat up a little straighter.

"Anyway," she said, "he knew all about the tattoo. It belongs to a hermetic order called the Order of the Grey Dove and the head of it is this John Madden who's so mad keen to get his hands on Billy's book."

She and Clare went on to relate what Goninan had told them of Madden's background, of the different states of consciousness, and how an artifact or talisman like *The Little Country* was a kind of shortcut to attaining higher planes of being and the subsequent power that came with them.

"The years of study are what prepares a person to be responsible when they finally attain those higher states," Clare finished up.

"Without it, they have power, but not the wisdom to use it properly. Responsibly."

Neither Felix nor the Gaffer had much to say and Janey knew exactly why. It all sounded a bit mad. Laid out as they had just presented it, she wasn't all that sure herself anymore as to how true any of it was. It made a kind of sense—but first you needed to take that quantum leap forward that accepted the fact that paranormal abilities were possible in the first place.

"He also told us about Lena," Janey said. "Apparently her father, Roland Grant, is a big-shot American businessman who also just happens to be a member of the Order's Inner Circle."

She went on to name the other three.

"I've heard of Eva Diesel," Felix said. "She doesn't seem to fit in with what you're telling us. So far as I can tell, from what I've read by her, she's heavily into humanist causes and environmental concerns."

"It's supposed to be a facade," Clare said. "Mr. Goninan said that if you took the time to thoroughly document all the various causes she's supported, together with the eventual ramifications of those that were implemented, you'd find that her hands are just as dirty as the rest of them."

Felix shook his head. "You know what this sounds like? One of those nutty conspiracy fantasies. Paranoia running out of control. It doesn't seem to fit the real world."

"I can't help that," Janey said.

She could feel her back getting up and tried hard to stay calm.

"What about things like the Christine Keeler affair or the American Watergate?" Clare asked. "They seemed just as Byzantine and improbable when news of them first surfaced."

Felix smiled. "But they didn't involve magic."

"You're just being obstinate," Janey said.

"No, I'm not. I'm just trying to put it into perspective, that's all. I mean, it's like seriously considering Elvis still being alive."

"It's not like that at all," Clare told him, "and you know it."

"Okay," Felix said. "I stand corrected. But how's this Goni-

nan, living way out in the sticks the way he does, supposed to
have the inside line on all this stuff?"

Maybe his birds tell him, Janey thought.

"That's not really the point, my gold," the Gaffer said.

Felix turned to him. "What do you mean?"

"Well, there's the book itself."

Janey nodded. "We can prove it with the book. You've read
it, Gramps. What's it about?"

"I was just looking at it again last night," he replied, "but I
remember the story well enough that I didn't need to read it
again. It takes place in an imaginary town, very much like Penzance, but set around the turn of the century, or perhaps even
a bit before that."

Janey and Felix both nodded in agreement, but their features
grew increasingly more puzzled as the Gaffer went on to relate
his version of *The Little Country*, of the captain of a fishing lugger
called *The Talisman* and the orphan girl who'd disguised herself
as a boy to work on the boat with him.

Clare, not having read the book herself, could make no comment, but Janey and Felix were both shaking their heads when
the Gaffer was finally done outlining the novel for them.

"That's not the story I'm reading," Janey said finally.

"And it's not the one I'm reading either," Felix said. "Mine's
about a sailor, all right, but he works on a freighter. He comes
to the same town, and he meets a girl with the same name, but
she's older than your orphan, Tom, and it looks to me like the
book's going to be a romance as much as it is an adventure story."

Janey felt an odd tingle start up in the base of her neck and
travel down her spine.

"There aren't any sailors in the one I'm reading," she said,
"but there's lots of magic. The story's just thick with it."

Clare looked at them one by one. "This is weird," she
said.

"Very weird," Felix agreed. "I think I'm ready to listen to what
your Peter Goninan had to say about all of this."

"Can I see the book?" Clare asked.

Janey fetched the copy of The Little Country and brought it over to where Clare was sitting. She perched on the arm of the chair as Clare opened the book to the first page of text and started to read.

"What's the first line say?" Janey asked.

" 'She hadn't always been crippled, but she might as well have been,' " Clare read.

Janey shook her head. "That's not what I see."

She read out the opening line that was there for her, then looked up at the others. It wasn't even remotely the same. Her version opened with a line of dialogue.

The tingle in her spine grew stronger.

"It isn't possible—is it?" she asked.

The Gaffer only shrugged helplessly. Felix crossed the room to where the two women were sitting and, looking over Janey's shoulder, read the opening line of his own version aloud.

"It's really true," Clare said in a voice as quiet as a whisper. "It really is different for everyone. . . ."

"Listen," Janey said suddenly. "Can you hear it?"

As shadows sometimes seemed to move when viewed from the corner of one's eye, so she could hear—from the corner of her ear, as it were—a faint hint of music. She couldn't pick out either the melody line or the instrumentation. It was too vaguely defined for that. But she could hear it. She knew it was there.

And she'd heard it before. It was that same music that she'd been trying to pick out yesterday afternoon when the Rolling Stone reporter had come 'round and interrupted her.

"Music," the Gaffer said. "It's like music. . . ."

Janey reached over to Clare's lap and gently shut the book.

The sound disappeared as soon as the cover was closed, vanishing as though a turntable arm had been lifted from the spiraling matrix of a record's grooves. But the tingling sensation that Janey felt was still with her.

"Magic," she said.

The others nodded in agreement. For a long time none of them could speak, each of them lost in the wonder of the moment.

Janey hugged the reality of the book's enchantment to her like the precious secret it was.

Magic was real.

Smalls and . . . that music . . . the hidden music that was the title of Billy's second book . . . the music that she'd always wanted to hear. To be able to play it. . . .

It was all real.

And then another reality pressed to the fore of her mind. If the magic was real, then so was John Madden's Order of the Grey Dove. And the danger they presented lay on more levels than simply the physical world.

"Mr. Goninan said the book is a talisman," she said. "A talisman that should only be wielded by its proper guardian. And that if none of us was that guardian, then we should hide it—keep it safely in trust for when that guardian would come for it."

"That guardian won't be John Madden," Clare said.

Janey shook her head. "And I don't think it's any one of us, either, except . . ." Her voice trailed off.

"Except what, my flower?" the Gaffer asked.

"I feel so close to its music. . . ."

"Where can we hide the book?" Clare asked, ever practical.

"I don't know. I . . ." Janey looked around the room. "I can't think of *any* place that would be safe."

"Mr. Goninan said the book would tell us," Clare reminded her.

Janey nodded. "That's right. He did. Only if it does, I haven't got to that bit in it yet."

"We should hide it quickly," the Gaffer said.

"We have to finish reading it first," Janey said.

"Now is that wise, my robin?"

"That's what Mr. Goninan said. Until we finish reading it, a crack of its magic will stay open and Madden will be able to use it to track the book down."

"Tom's already finished it," Felix said. "That leaves the three of us. We could sit together on the couch."

"Ta," Clare said.

Felix's eyebrows rose quizzically. "What for?"

"For including me."

"There was never any question," Janey said. "It's just . . ." She shook her head at the look that came over her friend's features. "Oh, no," she added. "I wasn't changing my mind about your reading it. I was just wondering if we shouldn't go through the rest of Billy's manuscripts and the like first. He might have made notes on the book—written something that would explain things to us better."

"Want me to get them?" Felix asked.

Janey nodded. "There's the box in the kitchen that we almost lost to that burglar, and then more in the open chest in the attic."

She went to help him bring down the chest. The Gaffer set about making some tea while Clare prepared a plate of sandwiches. By the time it was all ready, the living room of the Gaffer's house looked as though a bomb had hit it with manuscripts, papers, magazines, and the like piled every which way one turned.

It was Clare who found the second piece of magic, hidden away in Dunthorn's chest.

"Look at this," she said, holding up an old photograph.

It was tinted in sepia tones, the image area fading near the edges. The surface of the photo was wrinkled from having been bent sometime in the past, but the image was still easy to make out.

"That's my Addie when she was a girl," the Gaffer said.

"Can I see?" Janey asked, reaching for it.

The photo showed a young girl of about eleven sitting in an old fat-armed easy chair. She was dressed in an old-fashioned dress and brown lace-up shoes and her hair hung in ringlets. There was a cheerful smile on her face and her gaze was fixed on something just over what must have been the photographer's shoulder—probably her father, making a face at her to get her to smile, Janey thought.

Most of the rest of the photo was blurry, but she could make out curtains and a picture on the wall behind the chair, a door directly to the right of it, while on the left—

Janey's breath went short.

There on the left arm of the chair was the ghostly image of a little man. He was dressed in a white shirt and dark trousers. His head was bald, but he had a full, trimmed beard. And he was playing a fiddle, hunched over the instrument that was in the crook of his shoulder.

A Small.

Janey's tingling sensation intensified as she looked at the little man. She could almost hear the music he was playing.

"What is it?" Felix asked.

"There," Janey said. "On the left arm of the chair."

"Looks like a smudge of light—there was probably a window open behind the chair and the light coming through it reflected on the camera's lens. They didn't exactly have the best equipment in those days."

But Janey was shaking her head. "*Look* at it," she said. "Take a *really* close look at it."

So Felix did, with Clare and the Gaffer peering over his shoulder.

"What am I supposed to be seeing?" Felix asked.

Janey pointed. "If that's an arm . . ."

"It's a little man!" Clare cried. "Oh, my God. There's a little man sitting there, playing a fiddle."

Felix started to laugh, but then both he and the Gaffer saw the Small as well.

"Garm," the Gaffer said. "I never."

"That's unbelievable," Felix added. "Even if it's just a trick of the light, it's just fabulous."

"It's a Small," Janey said. "That's where 'The Smalls' and *The Hidden People* came from. *That* picture."

"Or maybe," Clare said with a mischievous gleam in her eye, "it only confirmed something he already knew."

"I'll bet you're right," Janey said.

"I've seen that photo a hundred times," the Gaffer said, "but I never noticed the little man in it before."

"You've got another copy?" Felix asked.

The Gaffer nodded.

"Can we see it?" Janey asked.

"I'll see if I can find it, my love."

He rummaged about through some photo albums in the bottom of the bookshelf near the hearth until he finally found the one he was looking for.

"Here it is," he said, holding the album open so they could all see it.

"And the Small's there as well," Janey said. "I wonder if he's in any more photos?"

She started to reach for the album, but Felix touched her shoulder.

"It's starting to get on," he said. "Maybe we should get to the book. If Madden's already in town as your friend Goninan said he was, we probably don't have a whole lot of time."

Clare nodded. "I'm a fast reader so I'll be able to catch up with the rest of you quickly."

"And in the meantime," the Gaffer said, "I'll continue to look through all of this."

He waved his hand at Dunthorn's papers and manuscripts that were littering the room. True to his word, he sat himself down in his reading chair and picked up another sheaf of papers. The others made themselves comfortable on the sofa, Felix in the middle, Janey and Clare on either side of him, and started to read.

"It's not his usual style of writing, is it?" Clare said as she turned the page to the second chapter. "It's not as well written as his other books."

"I thought that, too," Janey said. "I suppose it's because *we're* telling the story to ourselves."

Felix tapped the book with his finger.

"Let's just read and save the critiques for later," he said.

"Spoilsport," Clare said.

"Bully," Janey added.

Felix smiled at the pair of them and shook his head.

"Just read," he said.

2 .

John Madden sat quietly in the chair by the window in Gazo's hotel room and watched the movement of the waves on Mount's Bay, his mind far from the view that his eyes took in. Behind him, Gazo was still sitting on the bed, reading a magazine. Grant was in the other chair, his daughter sitting by his knee. They had been conversing with each other in soft voices for a time, but now the only sound in the room was that of Gazo turning the pages of his magazine.

Madden appreciated the quiet. It let him still his own thoughts. It let him put to rest all the inner conversation that the mind will always amuse itself with if given free rein, allowing the antiquity of the land to soak into his soul.

From the westernmost tip of Land's End to where the Tamar River followed the Devon-Cornwall border, almost making an island of Cornwall, the familiar spirit of the countryside spoke to him. Its quiet murmur filled him with its presence, whispering ancient stories and secrets, unlocking riddles, replenishing his store of its hidden wisdoms that had slowly leaked away since he had last walked its shores.

Time stole all—even from one such as Madden who hoarded these secret resources as a miser might his gold. So now he filled the holes in his memory, renewed his bond with the past and the unaging mysteries that history carried into the present. This was the real magic to which he was heir: the understanding that neither logic nor emotion on their own was enough to keep a man's soul pure, and thereby at the peak of its power. The mind narrowed and blocked the world into understandable packages with which it could deal, but the soul required a broader view, one that encompassed both the microcosm of the mind's perceptions as well as the macrocosm of the world as a whole with which it must interact. Less than a perfect harmony of the two left one crippled.

So Madden drank in the sweet secret that was the underlying heartbeat of the land. He let the rhythm of his own pulse join with its ancient rhythm until the two hearts beat as one.

The one dissonance was the trail of his protégé as he walked heedlessly across the land's mystery, disturbing and unraveling its harmony with his unconsidered intrigues and scheming.

Heavy footsteps; a thoughtless tread.

From the vantage point of perception that he now inhabited, Madden could read every irresponsible move Michael had made, every tenet of the Order that he had set aside.

For, Madden realized now, Michael had forgotten the first rule of dealing with the sheep. The trick to ruling them was to not let them know that they were being ruled. Treat them well, and they were as happy as their wool-bearing cousins in the fields, contented with their lot. One needed to cull the odd dissident, or firmly yet subtly deal with the odd disguised wolf that might creep in among the innocents.

It was plain common sense. Happy sheep were sheep that did what they were told and caused no disharmony or inconvenience. They let the gears that run the world turn freely, without need for repair. Sometimes patience was necessary, for subtle control required equally subtle solutions to problems that did arise, but the rewards were proportionate to the effort one expended.

Michael's present methods gained immediate results, but they also required far too great an expenditure in time and resources *after* the fact to tie up the loose ends. The point Michael missed was that, certainly, he could remove an interference such as the Mabley woman had proven to be, but then he had to deal with the ramifications of that act as well as continue with his principal course of action. Too many such deviations from the central project and one lost one's control of the situation.

As witness the present state of affairs.

Madden sighed.

A great deal of work lay ahead in bringing some semblance of order back to what Michael had mismanaged. For at the heart of it all lay the secret that Dunthorn had hidden away: the key.

Madden was still undecided as to whether or not it was an artifact of some sort, a physical talisman that would unlock a mystery of which he still lacked a full understanding, but he knew he must have it. He had also come to realize that the key must be acquired with the least amount of coercion. It could be stolen, but the cost must not be in blood.

He had fallen victim to that same erroneous mismanagement when first confronting Dunthorn; and he had paid for that mistake. Paid with decades of lost time—years in which, if he had had the key, he would have been that much further along in his ambitions.

The lost time nagged at him, like a heartache that came and went, and had no cure. But it had taught him patience, and he wouldn't make the same error twice.

He doubted that the key would ever be willingly handed over to him—which would be the optimum method of acquisition. But he could see to it that when it finally came into his possession, it did so with the least amount of harm to its present guardian.

To do that, he must first deal with Michael.

There was no indication on his features as to what went through his mind. To all intents and purposes, it appeared as though he was merely watching the view from the window. But that was another part of Madden's magic: control. He was aware of every thread of movement about him, yet gave no sign that he was even paying attention in the first place. So it was that he could sense the almost imperceptible movement of Lena shift-ing her position slightly and knew that she was about to speak before she ever said a word.

"I've been thinking about the Littles, Daddy," she said.

Madden glanced over at her.

"What about them?" he asked before her father could reply.

"Well, shouldn't we warn them—about Bett, I mean."

"And what do we tell them about *how* we know?" Madden shook his head. "No. Much as I will regret it if any harm comes to them, we must play this out without warning them."

But he looked more carefully at Lena, and wondered. It was odd how her question had cut so close to the turn his own thoughts had taken, but then he realized that her concern grew not from the same source as his own. He worried about despoiling the key by acquiring it through violence. She worried for the Littles themselves; and their friends. Most of her worry was prob-ably for this Felix Gavin.

And that was odd as well, he thought. In all the years he'd known her—watching her grow from the child she had been to the woman she was today—he had never sensed in her an interest for anything other than a fulfillment of her own desires and amusements. Her trip here had softened her, made her care for others—and it wasn't simply her libido driving that concern; her compassion was selfless.

Had the land touched her?

But if that was so, then why had it not left its mark on Michael as well? The reincarnated soul that his body carried had its roots in this countryside from a previous life. Surely the ancient mys-teries the land carried, the heartbeat that Madden's own pulse still twinned, would have spoken to Michael as well?

Perhaps they had.

And Michael had heard only the darker tones in its music.

"We could say Bett and we represent rival publishers," Lena was saying. "You know. We've heard a rumour of a rare man-uscript and each company would consider it a coup to be the first to acquire . . ." Her voice trailed off as she took in Madden's sudden intent interest in her proposal.

"A manuscript," Madden said. "Of course."

That was where the secret lay—in an unpublished manuscript. What better place to hide it than somewhere in among Dunthorn's papers and manuscripts? And to think he'd only wanted that paperwork for the clues it might afford him.

He had spent years trying to guess the key's secret—its physical shape, did it even have one. He had thought it would be small, and something that could be easily carried—a coin, an earring, a tie pin. And it would have something of the land in it—tin was his best guess, considering how much the tin mines had once been a part of Cornwall's economy. But it could have been bone, too, from one of the animals indigenous to the area; a simple fishbone. Or even a pebble. A chip of granite. A sliver of blue alvin stone.

The years of frustration had finally led him to consider his current pet theory: that it might not even be something tangible at all. It might be a phrase. A snatch of music.

And he knew now—absolutely *knew*—that he'd been partially right. The key was hidden in a manuscript. But it was only by reading it aloud that the key would be activated, the door unlocked. . . .

"Why did I never think of that before?" he murmured.

He probably had. But the concept, the idea, had simply evaded him. Was that another part of its enchantment? That the very *idea* of it would be hidden, so that just thinking about the talisman's shape or its whereabouts made it all the more secret?

"Think of what?" Grant asked.

But as Madden was deciding how much he cared to tell his associate, Lena was already replying.

"It's hidden in a manuscript," she said. She glanced at Madden. "That's it, isn't it?"

"It seems likely," Madden admitted. "All things considered."

Lena sighed. "And I almost had my hands on a whole box of them. . . ."

"Maybe it's just the directions to find the thing that are in a manuscript," Grant said.

"Either way, we need to acquire them," Madden said.

But he already knew that somewhere in Dunthorn's paperwork the key itself lay hidden, or else how could the Littles—knowingly or unknowingly—have woken it? How else could he sense its call?

"So what do we do?" Grant asked. "Do we still wait for Bett to show up, or do we go after the papers ourselves?"

Madden wished it were that simple.

"Let me think about it," he said.

3 ·

Although they still had a handful of chapters left to read, they all decided to take a break around five. Felix stood up to stretch while Janey sat down on the floor beside the Gaffer to look at the other photos he'd found scattered in among the manuscripts and magazines. She studied each one carefully, but there was no little man in any of them. Nor anything else remarkable either. They were just old sepia photographs, fascinating in their own right for the windows they opened onto Mousehole's past, but of no more help than any of the manuscripts that the Gaffer had skimmed through proved to be.

Clare remained on the couch, holding *The Little Country*, rubbing her thumb against its leather cover.

"Did you find anything useful in the storylines you read?" she asked the others.

Felix shook his head. "Not really. Mine's turned into a murder mystery. Hasn't got any magic in it at all."

"That's probably because you don't go for that kind of thing in the first place," Clare said.

"I read his other books—and enjoyed them both."

"But you don't normally go for that kind of book, do you?"

"Not really."

Clare turned to Janey. "How about you?"

"I'm not sure," Janey said. "Is the Men-an-Tol in either of yours?"

Clare and Felix both nodded.

"But I don't think it's in the same spot as it is in our world," Felix said. "At least in respect to Penzance, if the town in the book is even supposed to be Penzance."

"Is the stone closer?" Janey asked.

"Just an hour's walk."

"It's the same in mine," Clare said.

"And is there a high hill behind the town with a ruined church on it?"

Again Clare and Felix nodded.

"They were both in the story I read as well, my treasure," the Gaffer said.

"How did he do it?" Clare asked. "How could all the stories have the same elements, the same characters and settings, and still be so different?"

"It's like one of those books you hate," Janey said with a grin. "What are they called again?"

"Interactive fiction," Clare replied with a look of distaste.

"Maybe the book's really a magical computer," Janey said. "We all open the same program, but we each use it differently."

"Why were you asking about the Men-an-Tol?" Felix wanted to know.

"Because it gave me an idea," Janey said. "A daft sort of an idea, but then again the whole situation's a bit mad, isn't it?"

"I don't think I'd blink at anything anymore," the Gaffer said.

Janey nodded. "Did you ever hear of the Men-an-Tol being the entrance to a prehistoric barrow?"

"Of course," her grandfather replied.

Clare nodded in agreement.

"Well, what if it's not?" Janey said. "What if it's the entrance to the Barrow *World*."

"Do you mean a different world entirely?"

"Where the piskies live," Janey agreed, smiling.

"That's just a story . . ." the Gaffer began, then he slowly shook his head. "What am I saying?"

"Nine times through the hole," Janey said. "Folklore says that will cure your ills. But my version of the book says that if you do it when the moon's rising, it will open a door to the Barrow World."

"And then what?" Felix asked.

"We put the book in and close the door."

Clare laughed. "You're right, Little. That is a daft idea."

"Maybe not," Felix said. "The rules have all changed now. Magic works."

Clare nodded. "Yes, but . . ." She looked from one to the other and then sighed. "It just seems too much."

"There've always been odd tales about moorland," the Gaffer said. "Hummocks and piskies and old barrow mounds. If enchantments are real, then it stands to reason that there would be a whole unseen world waiting to be discovered."

"I've sometimes felt that long before we learned about the book," Felix said.

"I know exactly what you mean," Janey said. "There've been times when I've been out toodling tunes by the cliffs when I've had the uncanniest feeling that there was more listening to me than the rocks and the grass, only there's never anyone, or *anything*, to be seen."

Felix nodded. "I've had that feeling, too. Especially when I'm playing near water."

"Music's magic anyway," Janey said. "Always has been. Why wouldn't it call to Smalls and the like if there really are such things?"

There came a knock at the door just then, interrupting their conversation.

"Tonight," Janey said as she went to get the door. "After we've finished the book, we'll go to the Men-an-Tol tonight and see. Oh, hello, Dinny," she added as she opened the door.

Dinny Boyd gave her an awkward smile. "Didn't know you had company, Janey. Maybe I should come back another time?"

But Janey was already pulling him inside. One look at him had told her that something was up, and considering how odd the past few days had been, she didn't doubt for a moment that it had something to do with all the other mad goings-on that had already disrupted her life.

"Hello, then," Dinny said, nodding to the others as Janey closed the door. "Lovely day it's been, hasn't it just?"

He looked, Janey thought, as though it had been anything but. She'd never seen him in such a sad state.

Tucking her arm in his, she walked him to a vacant chair where she sat him down.

"What's happened, Dinny?" she asked.

"I . . ." His gaze shifted from hers, returned as quickly. "Is it that obvious?"

" 'Fraid so."

"It's just—I don't know where to begin."

"I'll put on some tea," the Gaffer said.

Janey sat on the arm of the chair and took Dinny's hand. He looked up at her and gave her a vague smile that never quite reached his eyes.

"We've lost the farm," he said.

"Oh, no!" Clare cried.

Dinny nodded. "Dad got the oddest call from a man who said he'd bought out our lease and was evicting us."

"But they can't do that, can they?" Janey asked.

"I don't know. Dad rang up our solicitor, but he said there was nothing he could do until Monday morning. He's going to ring us back first thing."

Janey could feel her heart sinking. This had an uncomfortably familiar ring about it. First her participation in the *Rolling Stone* article, then her tour. . . .

"But if your solicitor can't do anything until Monday," Clare said, "than neither can this man, I should think."

Dinny sighed. "That's what Mum said. But this man—he

never did give us his name—seemed very knowledgeable and sure of himself. He knew all the details of our lease and . . ."

He glanced at Janey.

Here it came now, she thought.

"He said it was because of you, Janey. He said you could stop the whole thing from being finalized. What did he mean?"

This was awful, Janey thought. How could she begin to explain?

"I've made myself an enemy," she said finally. "A very powerful one, it seems."

"I don't understand."

"Neither do I—not really. I . . ." She glanced at Clare. "I think you should ring up your mum," she said. "And, Gramps," she added to the Gaffer who'd just come in from the kitchen where he'd put on the kettle, "when Clare's done, perhaps you should ring up Chalkie and some of your other mates."

As Clare nodded, Janey gave Dinny a much edited version of the past few days. She left out any reference to the paranormal, concentrating instead on Madden and the apparent wide sphere of his influence.

"It doesn't make any sense," Dinny said. "What would this man want with an old book?"

"I think he stands to make a great deal of money from it," Janey replied.

It wasn't wholly a lie. Because money was power—an unpleasant reality that they were now having driven home to them. She just didn't know what else to say that wouldn't make Dinny think they'd all gone a bit bonkers. She certainly wasn't going to let anyone else start reading the book—not at this late date.

"Though Lord knows why he would need more," she said. "Any luck, Clare?" she added as her friend put down the receiver.

Clare shook her head. "Mum's fine. But there were two messages for me. Davie Rowe was by the house earlier today and Owen from the bookstore left a message for me to call him. I'm going to ring them both up now."

The others went back to their discussion as she picked up the receiver once more. The first call was short, the second longer.

"Well?" Janey asked.

Clare gave the Gaffer her seat by the phone so that he could make his own calls and returned to the sofa.

"Davie's mum hasn't seen him since he left the house late last night," she said. "And that doesn't bode well."

"Didn't know you were mates with him," Dinny said.

"Don't start her on him," Janey said.

Dinny shrugged. "Seems like a nice enough bloke to me."

"What about Owen?" Janey asked.

"Well, Owen," Clare said. "A man called him and told him that if he didn't give me the sack, he'd make sure that there wasn't a publisher that would supply him with a single other book until he did."

"How can they *do* this?" Janey cried. "Where's the bloody justice in it? I don't doubt that first thing Monday morning, we can call up the bank to find that the bloody bastards have managed to do something to our bank accounts as well."

She started to pace back and forth across the room, kicking a stack of manuscript pages across the carpet before Felix got her to sit down. By then the Gaffer was off the phone, his face grim. Janey buried her face in her hands.

"I don't want to know," she said, her voice muffled.

"That was Chalkie," the Gaffer said. "Someone killed Sara— his cat"—he added for Felix's sake—"and nailed her body to the tree 'round back of his house."

"Oh, no!" Janey cried. "What if they've got Jabez?"

She jumped from her seat and ran to the door. Flinging it open, she called out for the Gaffer's cat who came sauntering in after a few anxious moments and gave Janey an uncomprehending look as she swept him up into her arms to give him a hug. Janey kicked the door shut with her foot and returned to her seat on the sofa, still holding the cat.

"What do we *do?*" she asked.

Felix took charge. "There's not much *anyone* can do until Monday morning," he said, "so as I see it, we have to go on with our plan. We finish the book, then we hide it."

"But what's the point?" Janey said. "Even if we hide it so well that no one could ever find it, that still won't stop them from ruining our lives and that of every one of our friends."

"We'll fight them," Felix said.

The Gaffer shook his head. "That will cost money, my beauty. They'll take it to the courts and solicitors cost money—money that none of us have to spare. We're not rich folk like this John Madden."

"If the book's gone—gone forever," Felix said, "then there'll be nothing left to fight about, will there?"

"Unless they just want revenge," Janey said morosely.

"I still don't understand," Dinny said. "What's so special about this book? Why would a man want to ruin the lives of people he has never met, just for a book?"

"Greed," Clare said.

"Spite," Janey added.

"We'll stand up to him," Dinny said. "All the Boyds will. And our friends will stand by us, just as we'll stand by you."

"We appreciate that," the Gaffer said.

Dinny nodded, looking grimmer by the moment. "We should go to the police as well. There must be laws to protect us."

"But we can't prove anything against these people," Clare said. "We don't even know what they look like—except for that Grant woman in Penzance."

Janey glared. "And *don't* start me on her, either," she said.

"Then we'll just have to maneuver them into a position where we can prove it," Felix said.

"What do you mean?" Dinny asked.

Felix started to explain, but Janey shook her head.

"Don't talk," she said.

"Why not?"

She pointed to the shadows that had been growing in the corners of the room as the day drew to its end.

"Remember what we told you about what Mr. Goninan had to say about Madden and the shadows cast by man-made objects?" She shook her head. "We've been bloody fools. He'll have heard everything we've already talked about."

"What's old Peter have to do with this?" Dinny asked.

"It's too long to explain just now," Janey said. She turned back to Felix. "Maybe it's not true, this thing about the shadows and Madden; maybe it's impossible, but the magic in the book's real, isn't it?"

Dinny looked from one to the other in confusion. "Magic?" he said.

"It's a mad sort of a story," Janey told him.

Dinny stood up, obviously ill at ease.

"Perhaps I should be going," he said.

Janey nodded and saw him to the door. "I'm sorry that any of this had to come on you and your family."

"It wasn't your fault."

"We'll try to get things sussed out," she told him. "Don't worry about the farm. We'll think of something to stop this man before anything else happens."

"If you need any help . . ."

"We'll make sure to call you straightway," Janey said.

When she returned to the living room, the others were still arguing about magic and shadows and the like.

"If Mr. Goninan wouldn't talk about it in his house," Clare said, "and this Madden isn't even looking for *him* . . ."

The Gaffer pointed to a spot just above the front door where a small brass figurine of a piskie stood on the door frame—placed there for luck.

"Jan Penalurick will keep us safe from any kind of magical spying and harm," he said. "So long as we stay in the house."

"It's not really the same thing," Clare said, but the Gaffer merely shushed her.

"If you can accept unkind magics, my love," he said, "then you'll have to accept kindly ones as well."

Felix looked at Janey who simply nodded.

"I suppose," she said.

She picked up a worn photo of William Dunthorn and looked at those familiar features that she knew only through other photos.

It all centered around him.

Oh, Billy, she thought. Didn't you think about what you were doing when you magicked your book?

The Man Who Died and Rose Again

> Christ's image is just the perfect symbol for our civilization. It's a perfect event for us—you have to die to survive. Because the personality is crucified in our society. That's why so many people collapse, why the mental hospitals are full. No one can survive the personality that they want, which is the hero of their own drama. That hero dies, is massacred, and the self that is reborn remembers that crucifixion.
>
> —LEONARD COHEN,
> from an interview in
> *Musician,* July 1988

When Bett pulled the trigger of his automatic, the normal flow of time ceased to have meaning for Davie Rowe. He could almost see the bullet leave the muzzle of the revolver, the spark of light deep in the bore that had ignited the propulsion, the bullet's passage through the air that left a streaming trail of afterimages in its wake. The report of the shot was like a clap of thunder.

And then the bullet hit him, dead in the chest.

The pain started—sharp and central, first just above his heart where the bullet impacted, then in his shoulder, then in a wave that exploded through the remainder of his body.

He knew he was dead.

The fall to the ground took an age to complete—time enough for a thousand regrets to flood his mind, riding the pain.

That he'd never had a real friend.

That he'd never had a sweetheart.

That he'd never once looked in a mirror without cursing God or fate or whoever it was who was responsible for the ravaged features that looked back at him from his reflection.

That he'd never had the strength of will to make something of himself, never mind the hand that fate had dealt him.

That he'd never be the hero he'd imagined he could be, if he was just given half a bloody chance; a hero like those larger-than-life celluloid idols of his who stalked across the screen in the cinema down in Penzance.

That he'd die and not be missed, not be grieved for.

Except by his mother. And would she miss *him,* or merely the body that brought in what money it could to support them, the heart that was there for her to wound with her nagging and thoughtless words?

"If you didn't have such an evil mind, Davie," she would tell him, "God wouldn't have punished you with that face."

Davie Rowe didn't believe in God.

But he couldn't help but wonder if what she said was true. For he did have evil thoughts. Ugly thoughts of hurting those who mocked him. Of simply taking what he wanted because the world bloody well *owed* him, didn't it? Of having his will with someone like Clare. . . .

They weren't the thoughts of a hero.

There was no bravery in them. No decency.

He had lived in a constant state of rage. All that let him suppress the worst of his impulses was the knowledge that giving free rein to them would put him right back in prison. Locked in a cage like the animal he was in the eyes of the world.

It hadn't been compassion that stayed his hand; it had been the simple fear of returning to that cage.

And now he was dying.

He lay here dying as meaningless a death as his life had been with no chance to make good. Shot down like a dog, lying here in his own pooling blood. Unable to move, unable to feel anything but the pain and the wash of regret that was drowning him.

Like a dog; not a hero.

Every dog has its day. . . .

But, like all else in this world, he'd soon realized that the old homily was a lie as well for this hound never got his day.

Last night he'd done the one good and important thing he'd ever accomplished in his life—saving Clare from Michael Bett—and his only reward was this: lying here with Bett's bullet in him, helplessly watching Bett approach to finish off.

Because of the odd change in Davie's sense of perception, Bett appeared almost comical as he moved closer. It was as though the air had turned to honey and Bett could barely make his way through the cloying thickness of it that impeded his progress.

But there was nothing humourous about the weapon in Bett's hand.

And dying was no joke—though maybe God, sitting up there in his great sky and looking down, was having a good laugh.

Bett leveled his weapon—slowly, slowly—and Davie braced himself for the second bullet.

It never came.

Bett turned away, distracted, and then through that same endless drag of time, like a slow-motion sequence in a cinema, moved off, away and out of Davie's range of vision.

Relief came in a flood that washed away the regrets and pain. Davie felt as though he were floating. The blue of the sky had never seemed so sharp. His ears had never been so attuned to sound—the waves lashing the rocks below, the rustle of the ferns and couch grass in the wind, a bird's call . . . all came to him with a clarity he had never experienced before.

He glanced at a dried fern and knew that the fern was a part of the clifftop moor, which was in turn a part of the land, which was part of Britain, which crouched in the sea, a part of the earth, which was part of the sky, and beyond, beyond . . . the stars, the galaxies, the universes . . . all connected . . . each an integral part of the other. . . .

And he was a part of it all as well. No better or worse than that singular frond of dried fern. As important as the queen in

Buckingham Palace, as important as a vole rooting about at the base of a hedgerow.

Dying, he had never felt more alive.

And then he realized that he wasn't dying.

He lifted a hand to his chest and winced at the pain. But his searching fingers found no open wound. Instead, they connected with the small silver flask he carried in his inside jacket pocket. He had nicked it from a tourist at Land's End this summer just past and, when he could afford to, liked to fill it with the dark rum he so loved.

He wasn't a tippler, nor a drunk, but there were times when he would sit out on the rocks, overlooking the bay, and have a swig or two, imagining himself to be one of those old smugglers who once haunted the coast, tippling a bit of his swag. The flask had been empty today—it often was—but he still liked to carry it about with him. And now it had saved his life.

He could feel the dent in the metal from where the bullet had struck it and then careened off, leaving his chest bruised, but the skin unbroken.

Then where did all the blood come from . . . ?

He winced again as his fingers explored farther and found where the bullet had ricocheted up from the flask and gone through his shoulder.

He could have shrieked with agony as his probing finger touched the wound—but the pain was sweet, for it carried a message that made his heart sing.

He was going to live.

But Bett . . . where was Bett and his revolver? Surely the man wouldn't him here, still alive, with the possibility that he would survive to tell the tale?

He reached for Bett's presence—thinking that he was lifting his head—but then the oddest thing of all occurred, for he realized that it was his mind that was reaching out to Bett, not his physical senses. As he'd felt the connection with the whole of the world and the stars that lay beyond, a connection that he could not retain because it was simply too vast for one mind to encompass, he now felt a connection with his would-be murderer. He still lay there on the ground, but he knew exactly what Bett was about. It was as though he sat on the man's shoulder, or rode along in the back of his mind.

He followed Bett, crawling through the thick undergrowth, stalking . . . stalking . . . a hiker.

He wanted to shout a warning to the unsuspecting man, but couldn't get his throat to work properly. And then his own sense of self-preservation cut in.

Get away, it told him. Get away while you can.

So he crawled into the undergrowth on his own side of the path, burrowing deeply into its tangles, his mind still connected to Bett. The pain, as he moved, was so fierce that he fell in and out of consciousness. But the odd flow of time continued so that what he thought of as long minutes were only the briefest of seconds. He swept feebly at the trail he was leaving behind him with a stiff bit of brush that he managed to pull from a dead thorn thicket.

And on he went, nesting deeper into the wild jungle of vegetation that ran riotously along the clifftop. He paused when Bett pushed the hiker from the cliff. His connection to Bett widened suddenly, encompassing the hiker as well so that he followed the man in his plummet to the rocks below. He almost shrieked when the hiker hit the rocks; he was left shivering afterward.

His mind was slow in returning to his own head. His strength was waning. It took most of what remained to tear a strip from the bottom of his shirt, using his good arm and his teeth, and then awkwardly binding it about his wound.

The bullet had gone straight through. If he could keep the wound clean and have it properly looked after . . .

He sensed Bett looking for him and lay very still. Through his connection to the man, he could sense Bett's puzzlement. Bett searched for a while, but his heart didn't seem to be in the task. His mind was on other matters that Davie could sense— seething there in the turmoil that was Bett's mind—if not quite grasp. But the connection remained, even when Bett finally walked back along the Coastal Path towards Mousehole.

The connection remained.

He followed Bett through the village, and out again along the road to Newlyn.

I can find you, Davie thought as he laid his head wearily in the grass, too exhausted to move anymore. Wherever you go, I can find you now.

And when he did . . .

Every dog has its day.

Willie had a stash in a crib that was part of a farm up back of the village. Davie had been up there with Willie often enough, and knew exactly under which floorboard Willie had hidden his spare handgun, wrapped up in plastic and oilskin to protect it from the weather.

Davie would make his way up there and then he'd do his second good deed in as many days. He'd rid the world of one Michael Bett and bugger the consequences.

Unconsciousness rose in a wave to cloud his mind and drag him down into its dark depths. Davie let himself go, but there was a smile on his lips when he finally let the darkness swallow him.

So There I Was

Under the earth I go,
On the oak-leaf I stand,
I ride on the filly that never was foaled,
And I carry the dead in my hand.

—SCOTS TRADITIONAL,
collected by Hamish Henderson

"We can't leave our land anymore," Edern said, "except in dreams—our dreams, your dreams. . . ."

"Seal dreams?" Jodi asked.

Edern smiled and nodded. "Even seal dreams." Then he sighed. "But dreams are not enough."

His smile and body language, like his voice, remained familiar. But it was odd for Jodi to see what she thought of as Edern's mannerisms being used by a stranger. A familiar stranger, but a stranger all the same.

They sat, the two of them, in the shade of the tolmen in the world to which the hole in the Men-an-Tol had carried her. Edern leaned against the stone, legs stretched out in front of him, crossed at the ankles. Jodi was perched on another stone across from him where she sat swinging her legs lightly, kicking her heels against the rough granite.

Edern had brought out a kind of old-fashioned leather knapsack from which he drew bread and a spread made from crushed nuts to go on it, sticky buns and cheese. For afters, there were candied fruits and something that tasted remarkably like chocolate, though Edern told her that it was actually made from another kind of nut. Completing the meal was a waterskin full of cold tea with which they washed it all down.

"There was commerce once between our worlds," Edern went

on when they'd finished eating. "An interchange of poetry and song, of art and ideas. We were almost one world, divided only by a thin onion-skin thickness of wall. Passing through it was like stepping through a thick mist—a clammy feeling, but not unpleasant.

"Still, that was long ago."

"What happened?" Jodi asked.

"Cold iron."

She shook her head. "I don't understand."

"Your world took to metalwork in a fierce fashion. The soft metals were no longer enough—gold and silver, copper, bronze, and tin. You needed iron, for its strength. But iron was anathema to us, and remains so up to the present day.

"That soft onion-skin border thickened. Layer upon layer was added to it until now only a poet's dreams can cross from one to the other."

"Are you a poet?" Jodi asked. "I met one once—in the Tatters. His rhymes were fine, even if the lines didn't scan as well as they might. But they were funny poems. What kind do you write?"

"I use the word in its old sense," Edern said. "Words have power, and power is the realm of magic."

"I thought magic lay in names."

"They do," Edern said. "And what are names, but words? They are the first words—the ones we learn as babes to make sense of the world around us. They lose their power as most of us grow older; only for poets do they retain their potency."

"Are you a poet? I mean *that* kind of a poet. Are you a . . . magician?"

"Of a sort."

"Then how come you didn't magic your way out of the Widow's place when she caught you?"

"Because she bound me in a body constructed of metal."

"And there was iron in the alloy?"

Edern nodded.

"She caught my dreaming mind," he said. "Caught it and

pulled it from my world to yours, then confined it in that body with its iron bindings so that I could not escape back home again to where my body lay sleeping."

"So you were never a traveling man? She never turned you into a Small—like she did to me?"

"No."

"Why did you lie to me?"

"I didn't know if I could trust you."

"But you trust me now?"

"I would trust you with my life," he said.

Jodi shook her head. "I don't understand. What changed?"

"I came to *know* you," he replied simply. "Had we more time together in your world, I would have told you there."

Easy to say now, Jodi thought. But then she realized that she believed him. She couldn't have explained why that was. Maybe she'd just come to *know* him, whatever that entailed. Or maybe it was just that she wanted to trust him.

"Why did you want me to come here?" she asked finally.

"Our worlds need each other," Edern said. "They grow too far apart now and we suffer for it—both our worlds suffer. Their separation makes for a disharmony that reflects in each of them. Your world grows ever more regimented and orderly; soon it will lose all of its ability to imagine, to know enchantment, to be joyful for no other reason than that its people perceive the wonder of the world they are blessed to live in. Everything is put in boxes and compartmentalized and a grey pall hangs over the minds of its people. Your world will eventually become so drab and drear that its people will eventually destroy it through sheer blindness and ignorance."

"And your world?"

"Grows too fey. Magics run amuck. Anything that can be imagined, is, and if left unchecked, my world will simply dissolve into chaos."

"This sounds like Denzil's two-minds theory," Jodi said with a smile.

"How so?"

"Well, he says that each side of our brain has a different"—
she paused to search for the word—"physiology. The left side is
sort of like the captain of a lugger. It handles all the day-to-day
aspects of our lives." Her voice took on the cadences of Denzil's
theorizing as she spoke. "It sees everything up close, like through
a microscope. The right side holds the hidden self. It's nondom-
inant and that's where our feelings and instincts come from. It
gives a wide view of the world, connects everything instantly,
instead of you having to figure it out through trial and error; it
does it intuitively. The trouble is, you can't just call on it like
you can the left side—that's why Denzil calls it the hidden half.
But if you *don't* use it, it gets lazy.

"We need to use both, Denzil says, because both are necessary
for a fully rounded personality."

"That's exactly it," Edern said. "Your world is becoming a
place without light—an opaque and joyless place that is almost
no longer real—while my world has too much light, so much so
that it will eventually consume us. We both—the peoples of
your world as well as my own—have knots in our minds that
need to be untied and the only way we can do that is by bringing
the worlds closer together again."

"But what you're saying isn't true," Jodi said. "There's people
in my world who make the most beautiful things—painters and
sculptors and artists and musicians. . . . If they don't have any of
this light of yours, then how can they do that?"

"Are there many of them—in relation to the rest of your
population, I mean?"

Jodi shook her head.

"It's the same in my world. We have our logicians and the-
orists, but they are few in number and while they are respected
by the general populace, no one truly understands them. Not
what motivates them, nor exactly what it is that they are sharing
with us."

Jodi nodded slowly. "I suppose it's the same thing with the
artists in my world," she said. "Sometimes I think that *they* don't
even know what they're doing, they're just driven to do it."

"They are reaching out for the Barrow World," Edern said, "just as my people reach for the Iron World—your world."

This, Jodi thought, seemed a perfect opportunity to find out something that she'd been curious about ever since she'd arrived in the Barrow World.

"Where *are* your people?" she asked.

"They knew you would be arriving soon, so they stayed away," Edern explained. "They didn't want to meet you."

Jodi scowled. "That's not very nice."

"No, no," Edern said. "Don't think ill of them. It's for a very good reason that they stay away and it doesn't reflect on you personally. The danger with meeting an Iron Worlder for us is that we can never forget that meeting. Forever after we yearn for that other half of ourselves. That sense of wanting something more—of reaching to your world—is always present in us, but it becomes unbearable once we have had the actual experience.

"It can drive us mad."

"Like mortals crossing over into Faerie," Jodi said.

Edern nodded.

"Our folktales say the same thing," she added. "That the experience leaves a man mad . . . or a poet." She looked more closely at Edern. "Is that what happened to you?" she asked.

Edern nodded again. "I dreamed too long in your world."

"Oh raw we. Is it going to happen to me?"

"I don't know. I'm hoping we can do something about it—you and I."

"But I don't have any magic," Jodi protested. "I'm nobody important."

"It doesn't require either importance or magic," Edern explained. "Only sympathy . . . and music."

Jodi laughed. "You certainly picked the wrong person then. I don't know the first thing about playing an instrument and whenever I try to sing, people applaud—but only because I've stopped."

"You don't need to know how to play an instrument or sing," Edern said. "You just have to be able to take the music into your heart and carry it back into your world with you."

"But how?"

"We all carry that music inside us," Edern said. "Here"—he tapped his chest—"in our hearts. It's the pulse of our heartbeat."

"If it's already there, then why do I have to carry it back with me?"

"Because you have to learn to recognize it—and then teach others to do the same. It's not difficult. That's the real magic of the world—its truths are far simpler than we make them out to be."

"Yes, but—"

"Let me explain. How much do you know about music?"

"I know a good tune when I hear it."

Edern smiled. "People composing music—and I speak of the true artists now—are only trying to recapture the strains of a first music—the primal music that shaped the world and gave it its magic. That is what drives them. The closer they get, the more they are driven to seek further. Then there's the old music—the jigs and reels that have always seemed to be around. Are you familiar with them?"

Jodi nodded. "I like them best."

"Most people do; it's because they set up a resonance—an echo to things lost—in the listener. The reason those old tunes retain that resonance is that they haven't been tampered with as much, they haven't really been changed. The musicians who play them retain the heart of the music, layering new instrumentation or arrangements over them, but the bones are always there.

"Those tunes are played now as they were played then—a hundred years ago. A hundred hundred years ago. They come very close to that first music, but they're still wrong. They still remain only echoes of the first song that the snake taught Adam and Eve—an old dance, the oldest dance of all.

"What I want to teach you is that first music. I want you to learn how to recognize it in yourself, in others, in your own world. Wake it, and the borders will grow thin once more."

Jodi shook her head. "I don't understand. If you know it, then why don't you do all of that?"

"We all know it in this world," Edern said. "We know it too well. It's the underpinning to the magic that runs rampant in the Barrow World. Where it *isn't* remembered is in *your* world. It must sound in both."

"But I told you—I can't carry a tune."

"If you'll let me," he said, "I will teach you how."

"Will it be hard or . . . hurt?"

Jodi didn't know why she was asking that. She supposed it was just because it seemed that it couldn't be that simple—never mind what Edern said about that being the magic of the world. *Its truths are far simpler than we make them out to be.*

"It will hurt some," Edern said. "It's an old magic. Remembering calls up both sides of the coin—the storm and the sunny day."

"And will it help me get back to my own size?"

Edern shook his head. "That you must accomplish as I told you. The Widow has a part of you that you need to regain from her. But the music will help you once you have done so."

"Why is it that her magic still works in my world? I thought you said it was all gone."

"I didn't say it was gone," Edern replied. "Only that it was going. But most of it *is* gone. Will you help me, Jodi?"

"I . . ."

She was frightened now. And again, she couldn't have said of what. But there was a hollow feeling deep inside her. Her throat was dry and felt like sandpaper. Her chest felt too tight; an enormous stone had settled in the pit of her stomach.

Bother and damn, she thought. Wasn't this what she'd been aching for? Hadn't she been complaining about just this sort of thing to Denzil not two days ago? How she wanted to do something that was important. Something that had meaning.

She swallowed dryly.

"I . . . I'll try," she said.

She thought she'd feel better with the decision made, but the hollow feeling only grew worse.

"But I'm scared," she added.

"I'll be by you," Edern assured her.

And that brought some comfort.

She wondered if what she was feeling—all these instinctual trusts and suspicions, the sudden fluctuation of her emotions—had something to do with the Barrow World itself. If it was like Denzil's two-minds theory, and this world was her world's subconscious, then didn't it stand to reason that it would have her own intuition working at full tilt? Except then, why didn't she already *know* this first music that Edern was talking about? *Know* it the way she *knew* him . . . ?

Her head started to ache the more she tried to think it all through.

"When do we start?" she asked.

"As soon as you're ready."

Jodi took a deep breath. She looked around at the sunny moorland about her—the sweeps of heather and dried ferns, the gorse all still in bloom, yellow flowers bobbing on their prickly stems.

She'd stepped from night in her world to this.

From the Iron World into the Barrow World.

By magic.

And hadn't there been a music playing, just before the light took her away and brought her here? A wonderful, heart-stopping music that brought tiny chills mouse-pawing up her spine when all she did was just think about it? A music that when you heard it, you realized you'd been sleeping through your life, because what it did was it woke you up. Suddenly and completely.

If that was the music he was going to teach her . . .

If he was going to show her how to always know it . . .

She smiled at Edern. He smiled in return, his unfamiliar features growing more familiar the longer she sat with him here.

Not because she was growing used to them, she realized, but because she was learning to *know* him.

"I'm ready," she said.

2 .

Denzil's first thought was for the children. He should never have let himself be talked into allowing the children to accompany them here. They'd been mad to let them come.

But then the whole affair was mad, wasn't it?

Witches and bogies and walking dead men.

Jodi vanishing in a wash of music and light. . . .

Despair stalked his heart and he turned to his companions, but they were more concerned with practical matters.

"Bugger them," Henkie grumbled. "The seawater won't do us any good with this bloody bunch, will it?"

"Not likely," Taupin said. "They'll be mostly seawater themselves—corpse flesh and bone, seawater and weed."

"I thought the bloody Widow couldn't abide the stuff," Henkie said.

"Maybe she can't," Kara said. "But these things can."

Ethy huddled near Denzil, her small hand creeping up to clasp his.

"I am scared now," she said in a small voice.

Denzil nodded. "No less than I, you."

For they were monstrous figures, these sea dead. Their eyes were flat, swallowing the light that spilled from Henkie's oil lamp, rather than reflecting it. Their pale flesh gleamed wetly, seaweed hanging from their tattered clothing in long, damp streamers. Behind them, other shapes moved in the darkness that lay beyond the circle of light cast by the lamp—long, thin shadowy figures that seemed to caper and prance with glee.

They moved, not as might normal shadows cast by some flickering light, but with a movement all their own. Their dance mesmerized Denzil, sending new shivers through him to join the fear that was already lodged deep in his chest.

There was a boggy smell in the air—that same unpleasant odor that Denzil had smelled last night when the Widow's spies were near. But they had been just tiny things, hadn't they? That was what Jodi had told them. The sloch that she and Edern had faced had been tiny and about as swift-moving as these slow drowned men with their shuffling gait.

But these shadowy creatures . . .

What new deviltry had the Widow called up with her witcheries?

Nowhere could Denzil spy the Widow herself, but then what need was there for her to make the trek out here? She wanted them all dead, but it need not be by her own hand. Her drowned dead and giant sloch would be more than up to completing the task on their own and the end result would be as final.

At least Jodi was safe from them.

It was small comfort, but it would have to be enough.

"What can we do?" Lizzie said.

The Tatters children were clustered near the tolmen, all except for Peter and Kara who stood their ground with the adults.

"Well, now," Henkie said. "Mostly made of seawater, are they?" He turned to grin at Taupin, teeth flashing white. "What is it you do when you get a soaking?"

The dead men came shuffling closer. Denzil looked for something he could use as a weapon, but nothing lay at hand. Their only weapons were the hammer in Henkie's belt and the small penknife that Peter had produced from his pocket and was now holding, blade outward, in a trembling hand.

"Why, you dry yourself off," Henkie went on, answering his own question. "You sit near the fire and steam the bloody damp from you, don't you just?"

He stepped suddenly forward and, opening the top of the lamp, swept it in a half circle in front of him. The oil caught fire as it sprayed outward, splashing over the nearest creatures. In moments their clothing was afire and patches of oil burned on white flesh, set thatches of limp hair aflame. The night air, already

fouled with the boggy smell of the sloch that capered beyond
the sea dead, now filled with the stench of burning hair and
cooked flesh.

A dull wet roar gurgled and spat from the drowned men as
they burned. Henkie howled and tossed his lantern at another
pair. The only light now came from the oil burning on the flesh
of the sea dead.

"Have at them!" Henkie roared.

He charged forward, brandishing his hammer. The first blow
struck one of the sea dead square in the chest and the drowned
man's flesh literally exploded from the blow. Salt water sprayed
from the wound and the monster collapsed into a limp, shapeless
bundle to the moor.

Denzil stared, aghast. He held Ethy's head against his side so
that she couldn't see. All that remained of the drowned man
were his bones and the pale white folds of his skin that had
covered them.

"They can die!" Henkie cried, attacking another.

A second fell, then a third.

Now there was an opening in their ranks.

"Come along," Denzil cried, pulling Ethy and another of the
children in Henkie's wake.

"Get your balloons ready," Taupin said.

He and Lizzie ushered the rest of the children ahead of them
and then took up the rear. Kara took a saltwater bomb from her
satchel.

"What good will they do?" she asked. "They *come* from the
sea."

"It's not for the sea dead," Lizzie said. "But for *them.*"

She pointed to where the thin shadowy figures of the sloch
were gathering to attack Henkie ahead of them.

Kara nodded and flung her balloon. Her arm was strong, her
aim true. The saltwater bomb flew over Henkie's head and burst
against the foremost sloch. Salt water sprayed over it and its
nearest companions. Wails and shrieks filled the air. As Kara

reached for another balloon, the other children began to throw theirs as well.

"That's it!" Henkie cried. "Drown the buggers!"

The stench in the air was something awful. Moans and shrieks and a terrible caterwauling rose in a deafening cacophony. Sea dead and sloch both gave way to the little company as it forged forward.

"I think we might actually have a chance," Denzil muttered.

He looked down at what was left of the first sloch that Kara had dropped with her bomb. The stink was worse here than it had been so far. The thing was a little taller than Ethy, which made it almost four feet tall. It seemed to be made of equal parts bog mud, rotting weeds, thin twisted bits of wood and shadow. Luminous eyes stared up at Denzil as he stepped around it, the light dying in them.

"Don't look," he told Ethy.

"Come along then," Henkie called from up ahead. "Quick march, unless you want to be dinner for the bloody things."

They hurried after him, holding their water bombs ready. The sloch kept their distance for the moment, merely pacing them, keeping them hemmed in on either side. And while their quick pace was leaving the sea dead behind, the drowned men were still following.

"Where's the Widow?" Lizzie said worriedly.

"That's what I want to know," Taupin muttered.

Denzil didn't even want to think about her.

"Hedrik Henkie Whale," a sharp voice called from out of the night ahead of them.

With the moon at her back, the Widow stood on the moor, her arms raised as though she meant to enfold the sky with them.

"Shut her gob!" Taupin cried.

Denzil nodded. Three times named and the Widow would be able to enchant the strongest member of their small company. And then what would they do? But how could they hope to stop her?

She had magic—and powerful magic it had proved to be. And the bogies she had called up from bog and sea easily outnumbered them. Her sloch rose in a wave from the moorland around her, more than they could ever hope to combat with their rapidly diminishing supply of saltwater bombs.

"Don't listen to her," Lizzie said. "Stop your ears."

There was no chance to retreat, Denzil realized, for the sea dead were rapidly closing in on them from behind. No chance to go forward. And how could one not listen to the Widow? How could they *not* hear what she cried?

But then Denzil remembered Jodi's story—how the Small had stopped the Widow from enspelling her by singing.

He started to sing then, as loudly as he could—that same old song that Edern had sung with Jodi.

> "Hal-an-tow,
> Jolly rumble-o,
> We were up, long before the day-o;
> To welcome in the summer,
> To welcome in the May-o,
> For summer is a coming in,
> And winter's gone away-o. . . ."

His was not a marvelous voice, but it was enough to carry a tune, and he put volume behind it to make up for his lack of skill. The others joined in, a ragged chorus, but surely loud enough to drown out the Widow's voice?

The Witch merely laughed—a cackling sound that brought an answering clap of thunder from the sky above. The singers faltered over their words and the Widow called out Henkie's name for the second time.

Again she laughed. Clouds came rolling in on the heels of the Widow's laughter, rapidly hiding the moon and stars. Darkness deepened on the moor. Lightning licked the sky, followed by more thunder. Above it and their tattered voices, they could still hear the Widow's voice as she cried out Henkie's name for the third and last time.

The singing faltered again and this time Denzil couldn't save it from dying out completely.

"Be stone," the Widow told Henkie.

And stone he became.

Denzil saw Henkie stiffen. His hands fell to his side, the hammer dropped from numbed fingers to the ground. His neck arched back, his head turned to the sky, and then he was gone. All that remained was a tall, fat standing stone where once he had stood.

"No!" Lizzie cried.

Peter flung a balloon at the Widow, but the distance was too great and it fell short. The balloon burst uselessly on the moor. Lizzie started forward to where the stone now stood, but Taupin caught her arm. One of the children began to wail in fear. Denzil bundled Ethy up in his arms.

"Run!" he told them all. "Run as best you can."

But it was too late, he realized.

It had been too late from the first moment that the Widow's drowned men had encircled them at the Men-an-Tol. For while the Widow had transformed Henkie from man to stone, the sea dead had approached them silently from the rear. Before the small company could scatter, the dead were in among them— the dead drowned men, reeking of weed and salt, catching hold of them with their pale corpse hands, gripping them hard so that no matter how they might struggle, they couldn't break free.

Only Kara evaded their first onslaught. She dodged in between them and caught up the hammer where it had fallen from Henkie's grip. She swung it wildly against the knee of a drowned man. His skin burst, gushering seawater, and then he collapsed in an untidy heap of bones and skin and rotted clothing. Before Kara could swing the hammer again, another of the sea dead had wrested it from her hands and held her in a grip she couldn't escape.

The Widow named her three times and turned her into

stone—a small menhir to stand beside the larger bulk of the stone that had once been Henkie.

"No!" Denzil cried. "Leave the children alone. They've done no harm."

"No harm?" the Widow said. "Ask my Windle how harmless they are."

Ethy whimpered in Denzil's arms as one of the sea dead tore her from his grip. He fought the iron grip of his own captor with a desperate fury as the Widow spoke the child's name three times and transformed her into a tiny standing stone as well.

Denzil went limp in his captor's arms and despaired. He remembered the small hand in his, the trusting face turned to his for protection. Now she was stone. All her vibrant life stolen from her while he had been helpless to do a thing to stop the change.

One by one the Widow transformed first the other children, then Taupin and Lizzie, until only Denzil was left. He cursed her with an eloquence that would have put Henkie to shame, but she only laughed. Above them, the storm grumbled and shot the thick clouds with streaks of lightning.

The Widow stepped close to Denzil. He looked from her features to those of the evil little fetch that clung to her shoulder. There was no difference between them. The same hate lived in each of their eyes. Behind them the sloch pressed near—dozens of the creatures, filling the air with their bog reek and chittering voices.

"I can still spare you," the Widow said. "Who knows, perhaps you can find a cure for your stony friends. All I require is the girl. Give me the Small and you can live."

Denzil knew she lied. And even if she didn't, he still would never give her Jodi.

"Fool," she said, and she spoke his name.

Once, then twice.

"Bravery doesn't become you, Denzil Gossip," she said, completing the charm with the third voicing of his name. "You won't reconsider?"

He spat in her face.

She never moved, gave no indication of her anger except that the coals that were eyes glimmered a touch more brightly. The spittle ran down her cheek touching the corner of her mouth as she smiled.

"Be stone," she said.

And Denzil felt the greyness of granite come over his limbs.

3·

Above the moor, the clouds grew thicker still. Thunder cracked, lightning spat. But the Widow Pender was calm. She surveyed her handiwork—the new scattering of standing stones that littered this part of the moor—and was partly content. Had Jodi Shepherd been in their company, the moment would have been perfect, but as it was, she was as satisfied as might be expected.

She sought the missing Small with her witch-sight, but it was as though the diminutive girl had been spirited away from the world itself. Turning to look at the Men-an-Tol, she couldn't help but wonder what it was that the girl's friends had hoped to accomplish out here on the moors tonight. Had she come just a few moments earlier, she would have known.

Now she must continue her search again.

The shadows would help her. Just as they had lent her their strength for the large sloch that she had called up from the bogs, for the drowned dead that had marched up from their sea graves, for the storm that had grown from the red fire of her rage to cloud the sky with her anger so that her own mind would remain calm.

She would find the girl.

But first she would deal with Bodbury.

She had only this one night of borrowed power and she didn't mean to waste it. The shadows were generous, but the cost was dear. If she failed them, it was very dear.

But she wouldn't fail them.

She would give them Bodbury, just as she had given them the girl's miserable friends.

Darkness stirred at the bases of the newly made longstones.

We want more, they told her.

"I will give you the Barrow World," the Widow said. "But first Bodbury."

Give us more.

"Oh, you will feed well tonight, never fear."

Open the door between the worlds for us.

The Widow glanced back at the Men-an-Tol once more and wondered what part it had played in the girl's disappearance. She had walked this moorland in day and in night, searching for the Barrow World's entrance. She had poked and pried into every hollow and dip of the land, dug around the bases of the stoneworks, tipped one or two over on their sides, but all in vain. She'd never found so much as a hint of a gate to that otherworld.

She looked at the Men-an-Tol once more. She had searched long and hard, coming back time and again to that holed stone, for around it, the mystery seemed to lie thickest. The very air resonated with it.

But the stone never gave up its riddles. Not before—

The tolmen mocked her with its silent mystery.

—not now.

What *had* the girl's friends been up to?

We want, we want, we want, the shadows chanted.

The Widow nodded. "I know what you want."

She thought she could see eyes flickering in their depths, vague disembodied smiles.

We want it all. . . .

The first pinprick of uneasiness went through the Widow at that. They wanted it all?

"First Bodbury," she said.

She turned to face the sea where it lay hidden by moor and hill. Putting the mystery of the Men-an-Tol at her back, she set off for the town, the sea dead shuffling in her wake, the sloch capering along either side.

What did they mean by *all?* she couldn't help but wonder.

As though reading her thoughts, behind her, on all sides and before her, the shadows laughed in response.

4 ·

"So what do I do?" Jodi asked.

Edern pointed to the hole in the Men-an-Tol. "That would be a good place to sit."

Jodi looked up. If she'd been her normal size, getting up to the hole would have presented no difficulty. All she'd have had to do was bend over and scrunch herself in. But mouse-sized as she was...

"Here," Edern said.

He lifted his lanky frame from the ground and stood underneath the stone, cupping his hands to give her a step up. Jodi gave him a dubious look.

"I don't know," she said.

"There are handholds."

And so there were, she realized, as she gave the stone a closer scrutiny. It was only the first bit that looked hard.

"All right," she said.

She stepped into his cupped hands and gave a startled little gasp as he lifted her up, up, above his shoulders. She held on to the stone to keep her balance, wondering at his strength.

More magic, she supposed.

"I can't hold you up all day," he said.

She found a handhold, then another. A few moments later she had scrambled the rest of the way up and could sit down in the Men-an-Tol's hole. With an enviable skill that would have put Ollie to shame, Edern made his own quick way up until he had joined her. He sat at her side and gave her a reassuring smile.

"Now what?" she asked.

"Empty your mind."

Jodi laughed. "Do you think it's so full of wise thoughts? It's empty most of the time, I'm afraid."

Edern shook his head. "I mean, stop thinking. Let your mind clear until all you can feel is quiet, until you are drifting, without thought, without that constant burr of conversation that murmurs in your mind, day and night."

"Are you going to hypnotize me?"

Again he shook his head. "Just try."

So Jodi did.

She sat there, looking out over the moorland, enjoying the feel of the sun and the rare clear skies. She wondered what it was going to feel like to find this secret music—this first music. What would it sound like? She thought of all the old tunes she could, wondering which came the closest.

"What are you thinking of?" Edern said.

"Of music," Jodi replied.

"Well, don't. Think of nothing. *Don't* think at all. Just be."

Jodi found that it was harder to do than she had expected. The more she tried, the more quickly this thought or that popped into mind. One led to another, then to another, to yet more until her head was filled with a long connected parade of observations and memories and little commentaries, all tangled together in a noisy confusion in her head.

And suddenly she'd be aware of them, and remember what she was *supposed* to be doing. She'd sigh, and start all over again.

And back would come the parade.

"I can't do it," she said finally.

Edern smiled. "You've hardly tried."

"I've been trying for ages."

"You've been trying for ten minutes."

"Honestly?"

He nodded.

"Bother and damn. I'll never be able to do it."

"Try listening to your heartbeat. Don't think about listening to it, just focus on it, on its rhythm, on how it moves the blood through your arteries and veins. If some extraneous thought comes to mind, don't worry at it, don't be impatient with it; just set it gently aside and return to your contemplation of that steady rhythm of your heartbeat."

This was a little easier, Jodi discovered after a few moments of following his advice.

Whoops, she realized. That was a thought.

Back she went to concentrating.

Dhumm-dum. Dhumm-dum.

Odd bits of memory and the like continued to float up from the pool of her mind, but she found it easier and easier to set them aside. She did it gently—as Edern had told her to. She didn't allow herself to become frustrated by them. Didn't worry about how she was doing, whether she was doing well or poorly.

She just listened.

Dhumm-dum.

And drifted.

Dhumm-dum.

Until she felt as though she were floating away, out of her body.

Dhumm-dum.

Away and away—or was it deeper and deeper within herself? It didn't matter. She just followed that steady rhythm . . .

Dhumm-dum. Dhumm-dum.

. . . away and down . . .

Dhumm-dum.

. . . deeper and farther. . . .

Dhumm-dum.

At some point she passed between awareness of what she was doing and simply doing. At that moment, in that place, she found the first music waiting for her.

It was born of harp string and flute breath, fiddle note and drumbeat.

Dhumm-dum.

But it had no sound.

It was a place where lives end, where lives begin. Where lost things could be found, where found things could be lost. A forbidden place, fueled by that forgotten music. A place of shadows and echoes. A place that encompassed every landscape that she had ever viewed or imagined.

But it had no physical presence.

Dhumm-dum.

It consisted of pure logic. It showed her how everything that existed in the world, no matter how large, no matter how small, was all connected to each other, could not exist without each other.

At the same time, it made no sense whatsoever.

Dhumm-dum.

The individual disappeared into its vastness, into the greater whole, linked together so that there was no division between where one began and the other left off.

The whole was divided into individuals, each so separate and distinct from the other that their unity was incomprehensible.

Impossibility abounded.

It all made perfect sense.

It was a mystery, and all the more revered for that.

An old magic.

She knew such unthinkable joy at discovering it that she thought her heart would burst. No. Not at discovering it, but at *rediscovering* it, for she knew now that it had always been there. In the world around her. Inside her. . . .

And then that part of her that was still her recalled what Edern had said about the music. How remembering called up both the storm and the sunny day.

And she wept.

For all the things that were lost because of the segmentation in the world, the divide that had created an Iron World and a Barrow World. Species extinct. Hopes extinguished. Heartlands ravaged. Wastelands and barren lands that lay both in the world and in the hearts of its inhabitants.

Some could be found again—just as she had found the music. Some would be found again.

But there were so many that could never again be reclaimed. Lost forever. . . .

She was still weeping when she returned to Edern's side in the hole of the Men-an-Tol. He was shaking her—not hard, but firmly.

"Stop," he was saying. "Let the music be still."

She regarded him through eyes blurred with tears.

"But all that's lost . . ."

"Would you lose the rest as well?"

He pointed then, beyond their vantage point in the tolmen. She saw the moorland heaving and moving like an angry tide. Waves of heathered hills rose in crests to cascade down again. There was a roaring in the air, a shrillness of grinding stone, a thunder of rumbling earth.

The peaceful calm of the Barrow World had changed into a place of mad chaos.

"I—I . . ."

She was doing this, she realized. Here in the Barrow World where magic ran rampant. Her calling up the first music had let it run free, pulling the world into chaos.

But she didn't know how to stop it.

The tolmen shook and she clutched at Edern for balance. He braced himself so that they wouldn't topple over into that seething mass of earth, but the effort to do so grew rapidly more difficult with each buffeting wave of earth that rocked the stone.

A heaviness lay inside her—a deep sorrow that even the remembered joy that the music had also brought could not take away.

"H-help me," she asked Edern.

Braced against the stone, holding her firm, he gave her a grave, considering look—the worry plain in his features.

"Please. I—I can't stop it. . . ."

And he tickled her.

Her first thought was that he'd gone mad. They were going to fall into the roiling flood of earth that lashed and beat against the tolmen.

"Stop it!" she cried.

But then her body betrayed her and she couldn't help but squirm. And giggle. Try to push his hands away, but he wouldn't stop until she almost fell from their perch and then finally lay still. Exhausted. And became aware of the silence.

She lifted her head weakly to see that the world had returned to what it had been. There were no waves of earth, washing across the moorland. No thunder under the ground. No shrieking of stone.

Only stillness.

Quiet. And—

Dhumm-dum.

—the sound of her heartbeat, echoing on inside her.

She remembered her experience, but already it was fading into a vague, disconnected series of images and emotions that she would be hard put to frame into coherent thought, little say words. But the joy was remembered. And the sorrow.

Both were bearable now.

"What—what happened?" she asked.

"It was my fault," Edern said. "I hadn't realized what your Iron World blood would call up when you remembered the music."

"I almost destroyed your world, didn't I?"

Edern shook his head. "I told you, the magic is too thick here. All you did—with the sorrow the music woke in you—was give it something to focus through."

"I can't call it up again," she told him. "I can't chance it."

"It won't be the same in your world," he said. "There it will be a quiet murmur of mystery that will set hearts beating to the old remembered dance—but gently."

"There's so much lost," she said. "So much gone forever."

"But there's still much we can reclaim," Edern said. "So much that is now in peril that we can yet rescue."

"And . . . and that's all I do?" Jodi asked. "I just follow my heartbeat down to the music when I'm back in my own world?"

Edern nodded.

"It seems too easy."

"The magics of the world," he began.

"Are far simpler than we make them out to be," Jodi finished for him. "I remember." She was quiet for a moment, then asked, "Why do you call it music?"

"What would you call it?"

Jodi thought about that and realized music was as close a word as could come to describing it. Except for perhaps—

"What about mystery?"

"Or magic. It has a hundred thousand names and is sought after in a hundred thousand ways, but it can't be named. That is its magic. Men have borrowed pieces of it for their own use, but they can't tame *it*, only those pieces that they steal away, and the cost of doing so is dear. What's saddest of all is that they didn't need to take or steal those pieces in the first place— they had their own echoes of it inside themselves all along."

"Could an instrument play that music?" Jodi asked.

Edern shook his head. "But it can come so close as to almost make no difference. It can come so close that the resonances it sets up call the first music to it."

Jodi said nothing for a long time, then. She just sat, thinking. Remembering. Until Edern finally spoke.

"You should go," he said.

Jodi nodded. "How do I get back?"

Edern stood up and called through the hole in the stone, called something in a language that Jodi didn't recognize, though she did hear a phrase that was repeated three times. She gave a little start as a cool draft of air wafted over her and she could see the night of her own world from where she stood.

It made for a very disconcerting experience. Looking one way, she could see the sunlit moorland of the Barrow World; the other, and she was looking into the benighted moors of her own world.

Edern clasped her shoulder and gave it a squeeze, but Jodi wasn't going to leave it at that. She stepped close to him and hugged him fiercely for a long moment.

"Thank you," he murmured into her hair.

"No. Thank you."

She moved from his arms and took a step across the odd border, pausing when she stood with one foot in her own world, one in his.

"Will I see you again?" she asked.

"If we can thin the borders, we'll see each other whenever we choose."

"And if we don't? If it takes a long time to work—longer than we have years to live, or at least than I do. I suppose you live forever."

"For a long time," Edern agreed.

"Well?"

"Then we'll see each other in dreams."

Jodi sighed. Dreams weren't going to be nearly enough.

She started to step through once more, then paused for a second time.

"Edern," she asked. "Will the music stop the Widow's magics? Can I use it to get back to my proper size?"

He shook his head.

"Only salt will work against her," he said.

"Like seawater?" Jodi asked, remembering Kara's saltwater bombs.

Edern nodded. "But tears work best."

She had more she wanted to ask him. A dozen more things, a hundred. She knew she could stay here forever, just talking, but also knew she shouldn't. Her friends were waiting for her, back in her own world. They might be in danger. And she had a message to bring, as well—a secret song to sing in the quiet places that would hopefully ripple away through the world and bring it closer to its cousin, here on the other side of the Men-an-Tol.

So she smiled, gave Edern a wave that was far jauntier than she felt, and stepped all the way through.

She shivered at the chill in the night air of her own world, blinking as her eyes adjusted to the darker light. When she turned to look back, Edern and the Barrow World were gone. She saw only the moorland of her own world through the hole in the stone where once they'd been.

Oh raw we, she thought. What a tale I have to tell.

But when she looked for her friends, she found herself alone here. The area around the Men-an-Tol was deserted.

She had a sudden fear. She found herself remembering all those tales of mortals straying off into Faerie—gone for an hour or a day or a week, only to find that years had passed in their own world while they were gone.

Had this happened to her?

She wrapped her arms around herself, shivering at the thought. And then she caught the boggy smell in the air and another kind of fear overrode the first.

The Widow's creatures had been here.

Had they harmed Denzil or any of the others?

Thunder rumbled and she turned in the direction of the town. The skies were beclouded here, but a true storm hung over Bodbury. Lightning flickered in the dark clouds above it. And then Jodi's gaze fell on something that lay in between the town and the tolmen. Standing stones.

They hadn't been there before, she thought.

Had years and years passed since she stepped from one world to another?

But there was something familiar about their number. And their heights. Their stone surfaces, even viewed from a distance, seemed too unweathered. Too new. She counted them off. The one large stone. Three more almost as tall, but not so thick. All the small ones. . . .

And then she knew.

Clearly, immediately, with an intuition that echoed the magic of her experience in the Barrow World when she touched the hidden music.

They were her friends. Turned to stone by the Widow.

And that storm hanging over Bodbury. . . . She remembered the stories of the Widow and the storm she was said to have brought some twenty years ago.

That storm was also her doing.

She had to get to town. She had to stop the Widow. She had to rescue her friends, regain her size. . . . But it was so far and she was so small. The journey would take her *days* at her present size.

What was she going to *do?*

The answer was taken out of her hands.

Fingers closed around her, tightly, fiercely.

Jodi shrieked with alarmed surprise.

She was hoisted into the air and found herself face-to-face with Windle, the Widow's fetch, left behind to watch the holed stone. Chittering with pride, the evil little creature clutched her to its breast and bounded from the tolmen, heading for Bodbury, ignoring the blows that Jodi rained on it with her tiny fists.

Those blows, she soon realized, had about as much of a chance of hurting the fetch as a man might have trying to swab out his boat with a piece of netting.

But she kept hitting it all the same—all the way across the moorland and into the town. And once in town, she began to shriek for help. But her voice was a tiny piping thing, barely audible at any distance in normal times. It was utterly useless now with the winds of the storm whistling down the streets and the thunder rumbling above.

Tottering Hame

You must understand that our lives
were raw, red bleeding meat.

—CAITLIN THOMAS,

from an interview in *People*,

June 1987

"So how do I look?"

Connie stood in the doorway of Sam Dennison's room, leaning casually against the doorjamb as she tried to gauge a reaction from the private investigator's taciturn features. He gave back nothing, just sat by the small desk in his room, tapping an envelope against his knee.

She wondered why she bothered looking for his approval—she didn't even like the man. But looking for approval was a habit. She couldn't come near a man without trying to get a reaction. It had always been that way, getting worse instead of better as the years went by. If she didn't get what she was looking for the first time, then all she did was keep shifting gears until she did. It was the unfortunate story of her life—she saw her own worth only in how it was reflected in a man's eyes.

She didn't want them, but she needed them. Needed the confirmation.

So she'd done what Dennison had asked—toned down the makeup and hair and squeezed her bod into some sucky threads that she'd brought along at Bett's request: a narrow tweed skirt with a hem that fell just below the knee, a white blouse with only the top button undone, and, yessir Mr. Uptight, a bra underneath so we don't go too bouncy-bouncy. Completing the look was a snappy little businesswoman's jacket worn overtop, sensible stockings, and flat-heeled shoes. What more did he want?

Personally, she thought she'd have a lot more effect on the

Gaffer and her kid looking the way she usually did. But what the hell. When you took the money, you played the gig their way. The least Dennison could do was appreciate the effort.

"C'mon," she said, pouring on the charm. "You've made your point. Everybody knows you're a hard case, so why don't you lighten up a bit."

Dennison nodded. "Okay. You look good."

"Yeah, but do I look great? I feel like I've got a pickle up my ass in this getup."

A smile touched his eyes, there and gone, and she knew that was all she was going to get. But it was enough. She had him figured now. It wasn't that he didn't like women, he just liked the packaging to hide more of the product, that was all. He wanted to imagine, before he got to see.

Well, lookee but no touchee, big guy.

Knowing now that she could turn him on, she lost interest in him and settled down on the edge of his bed. He handed her the envelope he was holding.

"Mr. Bett dropped this by for you," he said.

The envelope wasn't sealed. Connie slid its contents out onto her lap and found herself looking at a photocopy of a legal document, the last will and testament of one Paul Little.

"I still can't figure out why Bett flew me all the way in to hand this over to them," she said. "Don't they have lawyers over here?"

"You tell me—you're the native."

Connie shook her head. "That was a whole other person, pal. I'm not from here anymore. When you live in a city like New York, it doesn't matter where you come from, *that's* where you belong."

"I know the feeling," Dennison said.

She didn't doubt that for a moment. Born and bred in the Bronx, this was probably the first time he'd ever been away from home in his life.

She tapped the papers again. "Seems to me having a lawyer deliver these would make it more official. Save Bett some dough, too. I don't come cheap and then there's expenses. . . ." She looked around the room. "Not that Bett's going all out on us. Economy class tickets and this dump. I've met bigger spenders in my time, let me tell you."

"I think Mr. Bett is pushing for the psychological edge."

Connie thought about what her reappearance might mean to her father-in-law and daughter. How long had it been since they'd seen each other? Fifteen, twenty years?

Never bothering to think about it, she'd lost count long ago.

"I'm not really looking forward to it," she said.

She'd spoken before she really thought about what she was saying, but it was true. She was surprised at the realization. It was going to be unpleasant—she'd known that from the first time Bett had approached her with his proposition—but she'd been sure she could handle it. She was still sure. But when she thought about how this was going to hurt the old man and Jane . . . She might never see the kid, but she was still *her* kid.

"Then why are you doing it?" Dennison asked.

Connie put her uneasiness aside, her tough mask slipping easily back into place.

Screw 'em both. It wasn't like they'd ever had time for her either.

"For the ten grand Bett's paying me," she said. "What did you think—that I'd be doing it for charity?"

Dennison didn't say anything, but she read disapproval in his silence.

"It's not like you're doing this just for your health," she added.

"Didn't say I was."

No, he was just sitting there thinking that he was better than she was because it wasn't so up close and personal for him. Like he'd never done a sleazy thing in his life.

Asshole.

Connie sighed. Why did guys like Dennison always rub her the wrong way?

"So what do you think?" she asked finally. She held up the will. "Is this thing legit?"

Dennison shrugged. "Beats me."

"The way I figure it, Paul would've changed his will as soon as the divorce went final."

"Doesn't much matter whether it's legal or not," Dennison said. "Not for Mr. Bett's purposes. Like I said, he's playing head games with them and you can bet that this is just one more move on the board. Mr. Bett doesn't strike me as the kind of guy who'd do anything halfway."

Connie nodded. "He's got money to burn, all right."

She stuffed the will back into its envelope and stood up, hiding a smile when she caught Dennison staring at her legs.

"What is it?" she said. "About dinnertime? I'm so screwed up with these time changes."

Dennison checked his watch. "Just going on six-thirty, English time."

"Well, then. I guess we might as well get this over with."

How did that old Shangri-las' song go? Something about how you could never go home again?

Well, it wasn't true, she thought as she rode in the back of the cab with Dennison.

You could go back—there just wasn't much point in it. When you left for the reasons she had, because you wanted to see the frigging world instead of being caged up in the past, coming back was just putting yourself back into the cage again and shutting the door.

She didn't need this.

The familiar sights of her childhood flooded her mind with memories; some bad, some good. There'd been changes, but not so many as she had expected. She'd rarely thought of her ex-husband, because there was nothing in her life to remind her of him. But here, where they'd both lived, where they'd gone through the whole shmear—growing up together, falling in love, getting married, having a kid—it was hard not to remember him.

He'd never understood what she needed.

They'd talked of leaving—Paul just as eager as she was—of seeing more than what Penwith had to offer, but it never happened. The past hooked Paul, just like it had God knew how many generations of Littles. Whenever she brought up the idea of moving—to London, say, or anyplace where the twentieth century had a stronger hold—it kept getting put off. When the farthest you went was a day-trip to Plymouth, you just lost patience after a while. Hooked on to the first ride out you could get—in her case, a sleazebag film producer—and made your escape.

She had to smile at the idea of calling Eddie Booth a film producer. That was like calling herself an actress. But what the hell. She was up there on the screen, and she made good dough, and she couldn't really complain. She'd known what she was getting into as soon as Eddie came on to her in the pub where they'd first met.

He was her way out of the cage—and that was it. He set it up so that she got her green card without a hassle, got her some dancing gigs, and then the film work. Sure he was connected, but then who in the industry wasn't? And it wasn't so bad. You could make out fine. Just stay clean—no drugs, no booze—and they didn't have a hold on you. You could walk, anytime you wanted to.

The time just hadn't come for her yet.

She was in her late forties now, but so long as her bod held out, she was going to hang right in there. Because she liked the action. She liked the idea of all those little weenie men sitting in dark theatres or renting video cassettes, getting hot because of what she could put out. If they only knew what went into those films. Like making them was anything but a chore.

She had to work a little harder than all the fresh young talent the sleazebags like Eddie "discovered," but then she had the experience. She could do more in five minutes on the screen than most of those kids could in a whole reel.

Maybe she was an actress after all.

She watched Mousehole approach through the front window of the cab.

Not like anybody here would understand—or even care.

She wondered what Bett's game was. What the hell could the Littles of Mousehole have that was so important? About the most they had going for them was the ability to bore you to tears without half trying. Still it had to be something, something big, because Bett was throwing around an awful lot of money to get it.

There was a bonus waiting for her and Dennison if they could get it themselves. Whatever "it" was. Kinda hard to imagine them collecting that bonus when they didn't even know what it was that Bett was looking for in the first place. She got the idea that he didn't know either, but that just made it more interesting.

The cab pulled up in front of the newsagent on North Cliff. Connie got out, leaving Dennison to handle the cabbie, and looked out at the harbour.

Now this hadn't changed a bit. It gave her the creeps to think of how she might have spent the whole of her life in this dead-end hole.

Thank you, Eddie, she thought. Maybe I owe you more than I thought I did.

"Ready?" Dennison asked as the cab pulled away.

Connie nodded. "The sooner we get this over with and I can get out of this place, the happier I'll be."

"What's wrong with the town?"

"Village," Connie corrected him. "Over here, they're very set on what's a village and what's a town and get insulted when you screw it up."

"That still doesn't tell me what's wrong with it."

"*Look* at it. The place hasn't changed for five hundred years, I'll bet. It's got nothing going for it."

"I think it's pretty."

Connie sneered. "Or quaint?"

"Yeah, that too."

"Christ. You should try living here." She laughed. "Wouldn't that be something? Mousehole with its own hotshot private dick. Be a lot of work for you here, I'll bet."

"You don't much care for the place, I take it."

Connie gave him a hard stare. "You wouldn't understand," she said.

"Try me."

She shook her head. "Let's just get the job done, okay? We can socialize later."

Her humour returned at the frown that settled on his features. That was supposed to be his line. She licked a finger and made a mark in the air with it.

"Score one for the gal," she said.

2 .

So far, Ted Grimes had no complaints about the way Bett had handled things. It showed he was serious, and Grimes appreciated that in a man.

Bett had booked him into the kind of room he wanted, away from the tourist areas—although at this time of year that wasn't hard to manage. With the tourist season over, it looked like everything was away from where the sightseers liked to hang out. The package was waiting for him on his dresser, as well. After stowing his bag in the closet, Grimes cut the string and unwrapped the brown paper from the parcel to find a nice snubnosed Colt .38 Detective Special and a box of shells.

Grimes didn't much care how Bett had gotten hold of the goods. All that was important was that they were here. Onehandedly, he took the gun apart, cleaned and oiled it in record time, then loaded it up with one shell. He snapped the cylinder back into place and gave it a spin with his prosthetic hand.

The Colt had a comfortable heft in his left hand as he held it, weighing in at a clean seventeen ounces. Six shots. More than enough for the job.

If there was a job.

Everything else Bett had promised had turned out just the way he said it would, but Grimes wasn't sure about the job itself. It didn't figure that Madden would head over here without a single member of his security force in tow—not when you considered the way he lived at home. His place in Victoria might not look it, but the damn place was a fortress.

Grimes knew.

His missing hand ached with the memory.

Of course the thing about Madden was that maybe he never needed guards. He sure hadn't needed them that night.

The ache in his missing hand deepened.

Wasn't that a thing? Frigging hand had been gone now for the better part of two years, but he could still feel the sucker sitting there on the end of his stump.

Grimes gave the cylinder another spin.

It's *Wheel of Fortune* time, he thought. Round and round and round she goes, and where she stops, nobody knows.

He spun it again, then lifted the gun to press its muzzle up against his temple.

Okay, Madden, he thought. Here's your chance. Work your hoodoo. Finish what you did to me—just like you should have done before.

Adrenaline pumped through him as he slowly squeezed the trigger. The world turned sharp—every object in the room going suddenly into a deeper focus than it had been moments ago.

The hammer clicked against an empty chamber.

No go.

Grimes brought the gun down again and snapped open the cylinder. Holding the gun between his prosthetic hand and his chest, he loaded the chambers until all six carried a load.

You had your chance, Madden. Now it's my turn.

He laid the gun on the table within easy reach and tucked the box with its remaining shells into his jacket pocket. Then he sat and waited for the phone to ring, heartbeat still quick-stepping from the adrenaline charge he'd given it a moment ago.

Russian roulette: the game of champions.

He'd been playing it with Madden ever since that night Madden had stepped inside Grimes's head with those hoodoo eyes of his and made Grimes cut off his own hand.

Madden didn't know about the game, but he was going to find out.

Real soon now.

It was that, or Michael Bett was going to be one sorry sucker before this night was through.

Fortune My Foe

One of the bugbears of modern life is too much
rationalism, too little easy interplay between the world
of the unconscious and the unseen.

—ROBERTSON DAVIES,
from an interview in
Maclean's, October 1987

J a n e y got up from the sofa when she was finished reading
and went to stand by the window. She looked out at
Chapel Square where the last light of the day was leaking
away. Shadows thickened in doorways and clung to the walls.
She shivered, looking at them, remembering the shadows in the
story she'd just finished reading, remembering what Peter Goninan had told her and Clare about shadows and John Madden.

*He can see through them, hear through them, speak through
them . . .*

Perhaps even move through them.

Was he out there in those shadows? Watching? Waiting?

"Did you finish?"

She turned from the window to see her grandfather standing
in the door to the kitchen. The smell of frying fish lay heavy in
the air and her stomach rumbled. She hadn't even thought of
eating a moment ago, but now she was starving.

"I finished it," she said.

On the sofa Felix was just closing the book. Clare was sitting
beside him, head leaning back, eyes closed. She'd finished that
last page before either one of them.

"Was there something . . . wrong about it?" the Gaffer asked.

Janey shrugged. She was feeling unaccountably irritable all of
a sudden, but she was determined not to take it out on either
her grandfather or her friends.

Good practice for the new and improved Janey Little, she

thought. Just saying Madden let them live that long.

"It just didn't end like I was expecting it to," she said.

Clare opened her eyes. "How did it end?"

"I'm not sure. I mean, I know how it ended, I'm just not sure what it means. I need a bit of time to suss it all out."

"I know what you mean," Felix said.

"I feel like doom's just hanging over our heads," Janey went on. "It's like no matter what we do, we're going to do the wrong thing."

"What you have," Clare said, "is an attitude problem."

Janey scowled at her, forcibly reminding herself not to come back with some sharp-tongued retort.

"And just what is that supposed to mean?" she asked.

Despite her good intentions, there was still a bit of an edge to her voice.

Clare smiled to take the sting from her words. "It's just that if you expect things to go wrong, they usually will."

"*I* didn't bring this all down on us," Janey protested. "You can blame Bill Dunthorn for that. I only found the book after *he* wrote it." She frowned as she said that. "Or whatever he did to make it."

"That's not what I meant."

Janey took a moment to answer, then sighed.

"I know," she said. "But it's hard feeling positive when everything feels so bleak. I expect this Madden bloke to come bursting through the door with a gang of thugs any minute."

"You've been watching too many American movies," Clare said.

"I suppose. But I swear, if one more thing goes wrong, I'm going to do more than scream. I'm going to bash someone. I really am."

So much for the new and improved Janey Little, she thought.

"Remind me to keep out of her way," Felix said to Clare in a loud stage whisper.

"She's a frightful bully, isn't she just?" Clare replied in a similar voice.

Janey shook her head and couldn't help a smile. It felt good.

"All right," she said. "But you have been warned."

Felix and Clare started shaking with mock fear until Janey started to laugh. She collapsed into the Gaffer's reading chair, unable to stand.

"Feel any better?" Clare asked when Janey's laughter had finally subsided.

Janey nodded. "Much."

"Dinner's ready," the Gaffer said.

"I could eat a horse," Felix said as he got up from the couch to follow the Gaffer into the kitchen.

"You are a horse," Clare told him.

"Would that make me a cannibal, then?"

"Don't know. Aren't horses vegetarian?"

Felix put two fingers on either side of his mouth and assumed a very poor Boris Karloff imitation.

"Not vher vhe come from, mine dear."

Clare made a cross with her own fingers and brandished it fiercely in his face whereupon Felix began to moan.

They were being silly, Janey thought, and it felt good. It was just like old times. She could almost forget all the mad things that had been going on, not to mention the perplexing end to the book. . . . Unfortunately, none of their problems were going to go away as easily as her irritable mood just had.

"So do you still want to go to the Men-an-Tol?" Felix asked a little later while they were still eating.

"More than ever," Janey said.

Felix nodded. "It's worth a try, I suppose. But I wouldn't hold my breath expecting that we really are going to call up some magical world full of piskies and the like."

"I know."

If she did that, she'd soon turn blue and asphyxiate. But she knew she had to try.

"Before we go," Felix went on, "we should wrap the book in plastic. That way we can still hide it somewhere out in the fields."

"Won't Madden just track it down?" Clare asked.

"Well, we've all finished reading it now, haven't we? Didn't your friend say that that would close off its magic?"

Both Janey and Clare nodded.

"The last time odd things occurred because of that book," the Gaffer said, "the effects remained for some time afterward."

"Doesn't change anything," Felix said, "because here's what we're going to do. We'll hide the book as best we can, then when we get back here, we'll call Lena Grant and tell her that we'll give it to her for a price."

Janey's brow furrowed.

"But—" Clare began.

"No, hear me out. We'll arrange to meet at a certain place— you can figure out where, Janey, but someplace fairly public would be best. . . ." His voice trailed off.

"And then what, my robin?" the Gaffer asked.

Felix looked around the table at each of them.

"I don't know," he said finally. "I haven't worked it all out. We want them to incriminate themselves, but I can't figure out how we'll do that."

"They won't do anything in a public place," Clare said. "They've already proved that they're too smart for that."

"But hiding the book's a good start," Janey said.

She laid down her utensils, her meal done. She'd been so hungry that she hadn't even been aware that she'd polished off everything on her plate until she was done. She looked down at it ruefully.

"I'm sorry, Gramps," she said. "I didn't taste a thing."

"Understandable, my treasure."

"We should go," Janey said.

"I'm too old for that kind of a trek," the Gaffer said.

"But will you be safe here by yourself?" Janey asked.

"They won't do anything in the middle of the village when everyone's still awake," her grandfather replied.

"And we'll be back soon," Felix said.

"Should we call Dinny?" Janey asked. "He did ask us to."

Felix shook his head. "And when he asks *why* we're going out to the Men-an-Tol? We'll call him when we get back."

"But I'm coming," Clare announced. "I promise I won't slow you down."

"That's all right," Janey said. "I know the farmer there—we can drive most of the way up his track."

They stood up from the table.

"Leave the dishes," the Gaffer said as Felix started to clear the table. "It'll give me something to do while I'm waiting for you."

"If you're sure . . . ?"

The doorbell rang, halting any further conversation. With the day they'd just had, no one wanted to answer it.

"It's more bad news," Janey said. "I can feel it in my bones. Why don't we just duck out the back and ignore it?"

"That's brave," Clare said, trying to make light of the nervousness that she was feeling as much as Janey was.

"Well, you go answer it then."

"I'll get it," Felix said.

2.

John Madden's spirit traced the pattern of the countryside surrounding Penzance like a cloud of birds.

He was a sharp-eyed kestrel, hovering high in the still air, missing nothing of what went below. A hook-beaked fulmar petrel that stalked the strand line along the coast. A long-legged curlew wading in boggy moorland. A stonechat in the furze, hopping closer to where two old men sat on a stone wall with their cloth caps and gum boots, gossiping as they rested. A jackdaw catching a vagrant breeze above a reservoir.

His spirit soared high, sailed low, and the patchwork countryside was laid bare to his view. He traced ley lines, rediscovered old secret places, marked new ones: stone crosses and standing stones; barrow mounds and old battlefields; smugglers' caves and deserted tin mines; pools where salmon wisdom lay dreaming and graves where old spirits stirred at his passing.

And central to it all, like the hub of a spider's web from which its emanations spread out in patterning threads, he was always aware of William Dunthorn's secret key, thrumming to its own rhythm, a rhythm that twinned and was yet apart from the heartbeat of the land. A hidden wisdom that whispered and promised and had lain central to his thoughts for longer than he cared to remember.

Soon to be his.

Soon to—

He started and opened his eyes.

"What is it?" Grant asked.

Madden lifted a hand for silence as he concentrated.

The gate that Dunthorn's key had opened was closing, withdrawing. It was recalling its secrets—all the untutored enchantments to which it was heir—and locking the door on them once more.

It wasn't possible.

The Littles should have had no knowledge of what it was that they held. They could open it—for the door to such secrets could easily be opened by accident. But they should have no understanding as to how to close it once more.

Yet it *was* closing.

Senses stretched taut, he could already feel its presence fading.

The process was slow. Residual traces would remain for weeks in the area. But the gate itself that the key unlocked was closing. When it was shut, he would be returned to the same moment of frustration as he had been some thirty-five years ago.

That he wouldn't allow. Before he let Dunthorn's secret slip away from him again, he would risk a tide of blood to acquire it.

He turned to Grant.

"I need a car," he said.

Grant nodded and glanced at Gazo who had laid aside his magazine and was looking at them.

"I don't know what I can find at this time of day on a Sunday," he said, "but I'll see what I can do."

He stood up and headed for the door, pausing when Madden called after him.

"I don't care how you get it, or who you get it from, but I'll pay well for its use. Perhaps the clerk at the desk can provide us with something."

Gazo nodded. "I'll get right on it."

"Where are we going?" Grant asked when the door closed behind him.

"Not we," Madden said. "Only I."

"But—"

"I appreciate your wanting to help, but this is something I must do on my own, Rollie. I'm afraid that there will be a price paid for what must be done; a price paid inside"—he touched a closed fist to his chest, just above his heart—"and you are still not far enough along the Way to disperse the inevitable effects that will result from tonight's work."

It must be *mine*, Madden thought. He'd learned the lesson that Michael's treachery had taught him. First it must belong to him alone. If there were aspects he could share with others of the Order, tidbits he could pass out to those he favoured, he would do so. But first it must belong to him. Heart and soul.

"What about Bett?" Lena asked. "What do we do if he comes back?"

"There's no more time to wait for Michael."

"But if he *does* come back?" Lena pressed.

"Have your man Gazo restrain him. But I don't think we will be seeing Michael here tonight. I can sense his hand in this."

Grant shook his head. "I don't understand. In what?"

"The Littles have found a way to undo the spell that woke Dunthorn's secret. It's fading away again."

"But—"

Enough, Madden thought.

Though he rarely used the influence of his will in such an undisguised manner with members of the Order, his patience had run out. Time was speeding by, almost out of control—time he could not afford to waste with explanations.

He locked gazes with them—first Grant, then his daughter.

You will do as I tell you, he told them. *There will be no further discussion.*

When he let them go, Grant squeezed his eyes shut and rubbed at his temples.

"Maybe it's best you go on alone," Grant said. "I've got a migraine coming on."

"Do you want me to get you something for it?" Lena asked, all her concern now focused on her father.

Grant shook his head. "I think I'll just go back to my room and lie down for a while."

Madden and Grant had worked in such close proximity for so long, with Madden constantly influencing him, that Grant didn't have a chance to fight the older man's will. Grant would never even begin to suspect how he had just been manipulated. Madden's control over his colleague was absolute, though he was usually far more judicious in his display of it.

The daughter was another matter. For all the years he had known her, she was still an unknown quantity that Madden suspected had far more natural affinity for the Order's teachings than anyone suspected. She might present a problem.

Madden could see questions lying there behind her eyes, but either the force of his will was holding strong for the moment, or she was wise enough to keep silent. That would have to do for now. If she did remember this incident and raised a fuss about it later, he would deal with her at that time.

But for the present moment . . . He caught her gaze again and locked his will to hers. Knowing her preoccupation with the pleasures of the body it was a simple matter to influence her, and then Gazo when he returned with word of the car that he'd found, to busy themselves once he was gone.

The questions faded in her eyes, and he smiled. He had set the desire so firmly upon them that they might well be at it before her father even had a chance to leave the room.

Madden stopped in his own room long enough to put on an overcoat. When he stepped outside the hotel a few minutes later, the car was right where Gazo had promised it would be. It was a small red Fiesta—smaller than Madden would have preferred, but beggars couldn't be choosers, he told himself, and considering the narrow back roads and lanes of this area, it was probably the most appropriate vehicle Gazo could have acquired for him.

He had a few awkward moments, getting behind the wheel on what felt like the wrong side of the car for him, but he adjusted almost immediately and was soon on his way along Penzance's seafront, heading for Mousehole.

3 ·

Felix opened the door to a pair of strange faces. One belonged to a well-dressed woman, the other to a hulking man in a cheap suit who for some reason reminded Felix of a bodyguard. It was something about the careful way the man held himself. He stood a bit behind the woman and off to one side, measuring Felix with as watchful a gaze as Felix was studying him.

The woman was holding an envelope in her hand. She seemed calm, but her fingers were nervously fidgeting with the envelope.

"Can I help you?" Felix asked.

But then the Gaffer and the others were there. Janey stood at her grandfather's shoulder and peered at the woman, struck by her familiarity. She struggled to place the face.

"Hello, Tom," the woman said to the Gaffer. "It's been a long time, hasn't it?" She turned her attention to Janey. "And you must be Jane. You've grown."

The accent was American. The clothing, the fresh face with just a touch of makeup, was nothing like what Janey remembered from her dream, but then that had been a dream. Not real.

But this didn't feel real either.

"Mother . . . ?" she said.

The Gaffer stood stiffly at her side, his anger a palpable presence that seemed to spark from him.

"You . . ." he tried. He could barely speak, he was so enraged. "You dare. . . ."

Felix moved to one side so that the Littles could directly confront their visitor. He and Clare exchanged worried looks. Clare's hand crept to Janey's who clasped it with a grip so tight it hurt.

"I want to talk to you," the woman said.

The Gaffer pointed a stiff finger to the street beyond his garden gate.

"Get away from this house!" he demanded. "Take your whorish—"

"Now wait a minute," the woman's companion began.

He took a step forward, pausing when Felix straightened up from the doorjamb where he'd been leaning. The stranger held his hands out in front of him, palms outward.

"We don't want any trouble," he said. "We just want to talk to you for a minute, Mr. Little, and then we'll be on our way."

"I've nothing to say to the likes of her," the Gaffer told him. "Nor to you, if you're her friend."

Janey could only stare at the woman. She'd always wondered how she'd feel if she ever met her mother. A hundred scenarios had gone through her mind—her mother would come back to Penzance for a holiday and they would run into each other by chance on Market Jew Street, or they would meet at one of Janey's American gigs, her mother coming to listen to her talented daughter whose career she had been following with pride from afar. Or maybe on a plane, or on a bus. On a crowded city street somewhere. Always a chance meeting. Always they would find they had so much in common. . . .

Never like in last night's dream.

But the sentiment would be the same. Her mother would turn

to her and whisper softly, with tears welling in her eyes, *Forgive me.*

Janey laid a hand on the Gaffer's arm. "Wait a minute, Gramps. Can't we see what they want?"

She drank in her mother's presence, memorizing her features. They had the same nose, the same cheekbones. Her mother's carriage was different—smaller bones probably—but they had the same peaches and cream complexion. The same long fingers.

"Thank you, Jane," her mother said. "May we come in?"

"We can hear you well enough from where you are," the Gaffer said stiffly, the anger in his voice almost raw.

Janey started to say, oh, let her come in, but the words died unsaid at what she heard next.

"It's about Paul's will," her mother said.

Janey thought of the man who had attacked Clare. Of her canceled tour. Of how the Boyds' farm was being taken from them. Of the woman who had drugged Felix. . . .

Forgive me.

Her mother wasn't here to be forgiven. She wasn't here to return to the fold.

"It seems Paul never made a new will after the divorce," her mother was saying. "My lawyer tells me that . . ."

Janey couldn't concentrate on what was being said. All she knew was that her mother was here because John Madden had sent her.

She could feel the Gaffer's anger deflating—turning to despair as her mother spoke of Paul Little as though his only legacy was nothing more than a commodity. There was no room for memory, for the warmth and kindness that had been so much a part of her father. Didn't her mother understand how much she and Gramps had *cared* for him?

"Naturally, it would be more convenient for us all to settle out of court, but we're quite prepared . . ."

How could her mother be doing this? Didn't she see what it was doing to Gramps? What kind of a hold did Madden have on her? Didn't she have a bloody heart?

Would a compassionate woman have left the way she did?

"Get out of here," Janey found herself saying.

Her mother turned her gaze from the Gaffer to Janey. "I don't think you really know what—"

"Don't talk to me like I'm a child," Janey said.

The new and improved Janey dissolved under a wave of anger that ran far deeper than the Gaffer's.

"But—" her mother started.

"You just tell Madden that he's not getting it," she said. "I don't care *what* he does, I'll destroy it before I'd ever let him get his hands on it."

"Now don't go off half cocked," the man who accompanied her mother began.

"Shut your gob," Janey told him.

"We don't know any Madden," her mother said.

"Oh, really? You don't know John Madden—the old bugger who sits around in an office somewhere getting a kick out of thinking up new ways to ruin people's lives? Too bad. I guess you can't pass the message on to him that we know what the secret is and we know how to destroy it. So why don't you just piss off."

She gave Felix a little push to get him out of the way and started to close the door.

"All right!" her mother cried, putting her own hand up to stop the door. "I'll admit we're here to get whatever it is that Dunthorn left you, but we're not working for any John Madden."

"You *aren't?*" Janey said in a sweet voice that bore a dangerous underpinning edge to it. "Then who are you working for?"

"I can't tell you."

"Too bad."

She started to push against the door again. She wanted it closed. She wanted the woman out of her life, just as she'd been for most of it. She wanted her to have never come, because if it was possible, she felt worse now than she had before. And poor Gramps. . . .

Felix started forward to put an end to the shoving match that

had developed between Janey and her mother when Janey suddenly shouted: "I hope you rot in hell!"

The vehemence in her voice startled her mother. With the
slight ease of her pressure on the outside of the door, Janey put
all her weight behind her own side and slammed it shut. She
had time to lock it before she turned and almost fell into the
Gaffer's arms, tears streaming down her cheeks.

Felix started to reach for her, then turned towards the door.
Clare caught his hand before he could unlock it and step outside.
He started to shake her off.

"Don't," she said. "It'll only make it worse."

"But—"

"It's not worth it, Felix."

Felix turned to where the Gaffer was trying to comfort Janey.
The old man's eyes were shiny.

"How . . . how can she be my mother?" Janey wept against her
grandfather's shoulder. "How can she be so awful? I don't ever
want to be like her."

"You aren't, my love," the Gaffer said, stroking her hair.
"You're your father's daughter and as fine a young woman as I've
ever known. Your father would have been proud of you."

"But she . . . she . . . How could she . . . ?"

"It's that man's doing—your John Madden. I'm sure he paid
her well."

Janey finally stood back. She wiped at her eyes with the backs
of her hands. Felix got a box of tissues from the kitchen and
brought them back to the front door where he handed her one.
She blew her nose and daubed at her cheeks. She took a long
ragged breath, slowly let it out.

She felt worse than awful.

"But *why* would he pay her to do it?" she asked. "What was
the point?"

"To make you feel like this," Clare said.

Felix pulled back the lace from the window in the door and
looked out.

"They're gone," he said.

Janey sniffled and blew her nose again.

"And we have to go, too," she said. "Before something else happens. I can't bear any more."

Felix nodded, then turned to the Gaffer. "You'll have to come with us now, Tom. There's no telling what they'll do."

"They're not chasing me out of my own home," the Gaffer said.

"Will you at least call someone to stay with you while we're gone?"

"I don't need baby-sitting."

"Please?" Janey put in.

The Gaffer sighed. "All right. I'll ring up Dinny. But don't you wait for him to come. You just go on and do what you can with the book."

"But—"

"I won't budge in this, my robin. I'll be fine."

Janey looked to Felix for help but he only shook his head.

"We don't have much time," Clare said. "The moon will be rising soon."

"Oh, Gramps. . . ."

The Gaffer gave her a hug. "Go on then, my gold. No one will be bothering me here."

He went to the phone as he spoke and dialed the Boyds' number.

Full of misgivings, Janey collected the Dunthorn book that they'd wrapped, first in a plastic bag, then in a waterproof oilskin satchel. She waited until the Gaffer had finished his call, refusing to leave until she could at least be sure that Dinny was going to be staying with him.

"There, my treasure," the Gaffer said as he got off the phone. He tried, but didn't quite manage, a smile. "It's all arranged."

Janey could see that her grandfather felt about as much like smiling as she did, but she loved him for trying.

"We should go," Clare said.

Janey nodded. "I love you, Gramps," she said.

"I love you, too," he told her.

Blinking back new tears, Janey reached for the tissue box again. It was sitting on the back of the sofa, beside her purse. She blew her nose, then stuffed more tissues into her purse. Her Eagle tin whistle, the kind that came in two parts so that it was easy to carry around, was in the way. She started to take it out, then just stuffed the tissues around it, and hung her purse from her shoulder.

She gave the Gaffer one last look. "Don't let anyone in," she said, "unless you're sure it's Dinny. And if it's not, if *anything* happens, promise me you'll ring the police straightway."

"I will."

Plainly unhappy at leaving him behind, she finally let Felix and Clare hurry her out to the car. The little Robin started first time around and moments later they were chugging up the hill to Paul.

4 ·

"Well, that's that," Connie said after a moment's stunned silence.

She and Dennison stared at the door that had been slammed in their faces. Connie couldn't help shivering as she remembered the look on her daughter's face just before the door closed.

I hope you rot in hell.

Connie had been cursed before, but never with such conviction. Coming from her own flesh and blood seemed to lend more weight to it. She suppressed another shiver.

"I guess I blew it," she said, turning to her companion.

And she felt like shit for trying.

Think of that ten grand, she told herself. Bett's still going to pay up. All she'd lost was her shot at the bonus.

And her self-respect.

"I don't think so," Dennison said.

Connie just shook her head. "Where were you when all this was going on? Didn't you see the look she gave me?"

"But that's exactly what Mr. Bett hired you to do—shake them up. Put them even more off their stride."

"So how come I feel so bad?"

Dennison gave her a considering look, then shrugged. "I didn't say what you did was right—I just said you'd done what Mr. Bett hired you to do."

"Thanks for caring."

Christ, she thought as soon as she said it. Like she should talk about caring after what she'd just done.

I hope you rot in hell.

She probably would. And living as she had for the better part of her life, she knew just who'd be keeping her company down there. All the sleazebags and lowlifes and losers.

Dennison took her arm and steered her out of the Littles' tiny yard.

"Let's see if we can find a phone booth and call ourselves a cab," he said.

Connie shot a lingering glance at the Gaffer's house and suppressed a sudden desire to go back and apologize, then she shook her head.

Like they'd even listen.

As though even if she'd known exactly how she'd be feeling right this moment when Bett had first asked her, she wouldn't still go right ahead and do it all the same.

She knew herself too well. She needed that money. She needed whatever she could get.

"Connie?" Dennison said.

She turned from the house and let him lead her back down to the harbourfront.

5 ·

It was Lena's sprained ankle that saved her.

She had the faint buzz of a headache in the back of her head, but it wasn't enough to stop the wave of pure animal hunger that had her shivering every time she looked at Gazo. As soon as Madden left she could barely hold on for her father to leave the room before she started to peel off her clothes.

Her jacket dropped to the floor, quickly followed by her skirt. A glance at Gazo showed her that he already had his pants off, his penis standing at stiff attention as he crossed the room towards her. She fumbled with the buttons on her blouse in her hurry to get it off but then Gazo was standing in front of her. He tore it open, popped buttons spraying across the room.

Pushing her bra up from her breasts, he pressed his face in between them and started backing her towards the bed. Lena could hear herself making small moaning sounds in the back of her throat. She reached down and grabbed his penis, wanting it inside her, wanting—

Her ankle twisted badly as Gazo backed her up—the sudden sharp pain momentarily clearing her mind.

"Wha—"

Gazo pushed her back onto the bed. His hands were all over her.

Her ankle felt like it was on fire.

She tried to push him aside.

He had his penis in his hand and was roughly pushing its head against her vagina.

That hurt too. Her need for him had fled and she wasn't wet enough. It felt like he was trying to stick a roll of sandpaper up inside her.

"Stop it," she said, trying to wriggle out from under him.

But he was too big for her. His weight alone was enough to keep her pinned to the bed, never mind his superior strength.

Panic set in.

"Stop it!"

She drummed her fists against his back, but that just seemed to excite him more. And then he was inside her and she shrieked from the agony. Her arms flailed. One hand brushed up against the lamp on the night table beside the bed. Her fingers grabbed hold of it and smashed the lamp alongside his head.

He stiffened, pulling partway out of her.

She hit him again. This time the lamp broke.

He rolled from on top of her to lie on the bed, curled up now, hands clutching his head.

Lena backed up against the headboard, still clutching what remained of the lamp. Her breathing came in short, ragged gasps. Pain moved in waves from the hollow in between her legs and her ankle. She lifted the broken base of the lamp as Gazo straightened up and turned his face towards her.

"Don't touch me!"

But his eyes were different. The blow to his head had cleared his mind as well. He sat up, looking shocked and confused, but no longer dangerous.

"What . . ." he began. He shook his head and winced at the pain. "What the hell . . . happened?"

Lena started to shake her head as well. How should she know? One moment they were all sitting around in the room and everything was normal. The next . . .

She remembered Madden's eyes.

The low buzz of a headache sharpened in the back of her head to join the rest of the pain.

And then she knew.

"Madden," she said.

"What?"

"Madden—he did this to us."

Gazo just looked more confused.

"His will's that strong," Lena said.

A dull anger was building up inside her. He'd used her and Gazo like they were his sheep. She thought of her father's sudden migraine. That had been Madden's doing as well. If it suited his purposes, he'd use even his most trusted colleague as though he were nothing more than a servant—less than a servant. Servants at least got paid. It was a job, for them. They *knew* what it entailed before they ever hired on.

But this. . . .

When she thought of all of Daddy's migraines, she realized

that they must have come from exactly this kind of a situation. Madden forcing his will on Daddy. Who did Madden think he was, playing around with their heads like this? With *her* head.

Lena knew exactly what he was. A monster disguised as an old man. But a very dangerous old man.

"What do you mean his will?" Gazo asked.

Lena looked up at him.

Of course, she thought. He wouldn't know. He wasn't an initiate. He was part of Daddy's security force. He knew all about the cutthroat practices of the business world, stood in as a bodyguard sometimes, but he knew nothing of what the Order really stood for. That secret wasn't trusted to outsiders. If Gazo knew about it at all, he would simply think of it as some kind of an exclusive country club, though what he'd thought of some of the conversations he'd overheard—like when Madden and Daddy were discussing this thing of Dunthorn's—Lena didn't know.

Maybe it was time he learned, then. Time everyone learned.

"He got inside our heads," she said. "Got in there and manipulated our thoughts so that we'd do whatever he wanted."

"You mean . . . this . . . ?"

Gazo indicated their state of dishabille.

Lena nodded.

"He hypnotized us?"

"That's one way of putting it."

Gazo shook his head slowly.

"I don't know," he said. He looked around the room at where their clothing lay scattered on the floor. "Jesus, I'm sorry, Lena. I . . ."

He got up and collected her skirt, jacket, and what remained of her blouse. Passing them to her, he went to put his pants on. Lena dressed as best she could. Her ankle screamed when she was slipping her skirt on. She pulled her bra down. With the buttons torn off her blouse, all she could do was tie it closed. She put her jacket on overtop and buttoned it up.

Being dressed helped—but not enough. When she thought of

what Madden had done to them, how he had manipulated them . . .

Suddenly an intense feeling of revulsion came over her.

Felix.

My God. When Felix thought of her . . .

Knowing how she now felt about Madden, she realized that Felix must really hate her. And there was nothing she could do to make it up to him. It wasn't the kind of thing that could be forgiven, that you could make better, because the memory of it was always going to be there, sitting in the back of your head just like this headache was sitting in the back of her own mind.

He would never forgive her.

She didn't deserve to be forgiven.

But she could warn him. About Madden and Bett and the kind of power they had behind them. Not just their wealth and influence, but this other thing. The ability to crawl right inside your head and manipulate your thoughts.

She'd never dreamed that the Order's tenets concerning the power of the will could be taken so literally. She'd always thought of it as a kind of psychological edge. Not a physical reality.

It was like magic.

"Maybe I'd better go," Gazo said.

She looked up to find him watching her. His features were guarded, embarrassed.

"It wasn't your fault," she said. "Madden *made* you do it."

"Maybe. But maybe I . . . maybe I've always been . . . interested in you. In that way. Not forcing myself on you," he added quickly. "But, you know. Attracted to you."

"There's no law against being attracted to someone," Lena said.

"Yeah, but I'm supposed to be working for you. Your father hired me to protect you. Instead—"

"Read my lips," Lena said firmly, "I'm telling you it wasn't your fault."

"Yeah, but—"

"Maybe I've thought that way about you, too. Are we supposed to feel bad every time we see someone that turns us on a little?"

"I suppose not."

Lena smiled wearily. "Could you bring the phone over? I need to make a call."

She had the operator connect her with the Little household. A man's voice answered, but it wasn't Felix. It was an older man—probably Janey Little's grandfather.

"May I speak to Felix?" she asked him.

"He's just stepped out."

Tom Little's voice was heavy with suspicion. Must be the American accent, Lena thought. She couldn't really blame him. With all that had been going on lately, he wouldn't be feeling too kindly towards Americans at the moment.

"Can you tell me where he's gone?" she asked.

"He didn't say."

"It's very important. When will he be back?"

"He didn't say."

Wonderful. Tom Little's voice sounded like a recording.

"Could I leave a message then? Would you tell him that—"

Tell him what? That Lena Grant called? That would certainly make Felix eager to get back to her.

"Yes?" Tom Little prompted her.

"Never mind. I'm sorry to have bothered you."

She hung up.

"What were you just trying to do?" Gazo asked her.

She set the phone aside and gave him a considering look. "Warn Felix about Madden."

"He wasn't in?"

"No. That was Tom Little I was talking to."

"So why didn't you just warn him?"

Lena sighed. "I didn't think he'd listen to me. Felix might. I'm sure he hates me, but I think he'd still listen. Especially about something that might hurt Janey."

"Do you want to drive over and wait for him?" Gazo asked.

"I don't think so. I think we should tell Daddy about what Madden's been doing to him."

"I'm still not sure about that myself," Gazo said. "This hyp-notizing business . . . I thought they had to, you know, move a watch back and forth in front of you until you fell asleep—or something along those lines. I've never heard of someone being able to do it just"—he snapped his fingers—"like that. It's like . . . I don't know . . . like . . ."

"Magic."

Gazo smiled. "Yeah, right."

"It takes a leap of faith," Lena told him, "but that's about the best description I can come up with."

"Magic."

Lena nodded. "Would you help me up? I want to go talk to Daddy."

"He's going to be angry when he finds out."

"I hope so," Lena said.

6.

Bett arrived at his vantage point behind the wall fronting the Methodist Chapel a little later than he had planned. He'd had a lot to take care of and it all took longer than he'd thought it would. The whole damn country seemed to close up on a Sun-day.

He settled down where he could see the house easily and tuned in his radio transmitter just in time to hear the Little woman and her friends saying good-bye to the old man. He removed his earplug when they came outside so he could hear what they were saying.

"How far is the Men-an-Tol?" Gavin was saying.

"Just a little ways past Madron," the Mabley woman replied. "It won't take us that long to get there."

Gavin said something else that Bett couldn't hear over the sound of them opening their car doors.

"I doubt we'll get lost," the Mabley woman said. "There's a footpath that goes all the way from the track. Didn't Janey ever take you out there?"

"Yeah, but not at night."

The doors closed and the Little woman started up the car, effectively muting any further conversation that Bett might have been able to overhear.

Maybe he should have had Dennison wire the cars, too, he thought.

He ducked down out of sight as the car's headbeams washed over the chapel's low wall, lighting up the side of the chapel itself with a bright glare. He waited until the car had passed him and was going up Mousehole Lane to Paul before lifting his head again. He saw the Reliant's taillights going up the hill, then they disappeared as the car went around a corner.

The Men-an-Tol, Bett thought. That was one of those stoneworks that Madden was so keen on. Now why the hell would they be going out there at this time of night?

He looked back at the house.

Didn't matter. He needed only one of them—the old man or his granddaughter. Made no never mind which of them he got. The woman would have been fun, but a man screamed just as shrilly as a woman if you knew how to coax it out of him.

He stowed away his earplugs and the radio receiver in the knapsack that hung from his shoulder by one strap and started to rise, only to be forced to duck down again as another set of headbeams hit the wall. These came from a small red Fiesta that rolled up from the harbour. It stopped in front of the Little house, its engine idling, the headlights no longer aimed at the chapel. With the cover of darkness, Bett peered above the wall. When he dropped back down behind the wall this time, it was with a curse on his lips.

Madden was in that car.

Bett had been hoping to get the night's work done without

Madden's interference, but he'd prepared to deal with his mentor if the need arose.

He looked above the wall again to see Madden just sitting there in his car, eyes closed. When Madden lifted his head suddenly, Bett was sure that his mentor had spotted him, but Madden wasn't looking in his direction. Instead, Madden gazed up the hill to where Janey Little and her friends had driven off. Putting his car into gear, Madden drove off in the same direction.

Bett waited until the Fiesta's taillights had disappeared around the same corner that the Littles' car had before he stood up and brushed himself off.

Looked like Madden was walking on the edge tonight as well, he thought. Got himself locked onto Janey Little's wavelength and he wasn't going to let go.

Bett wasn't happy with the complications this was going to bring to his own carefully orchestrated plans.

He jumped down to the street and crossed over, slipping in through the hedge behind the Littles' house so that he was approaching the building from its own tiny backyard. He could see Tom Little in the kitchen, cleaning up dishes.

That made it nice and easy.

He pulled a gun from his knapsack, then slipped the loose strap over his other shoulder so that the knapsack was hanging against his back.

He didn't have to do this himself. He could have hired someone to pick up the old man or his granddaughter for him. But the more people you brought into this kind of thing, the more problems you made for yourself. Besides, he *liked* the look of shock that came over a victim's face when they knew they were screwed.

It sharpened the edge and brought everything into focus.

He didn't waste time pussyfooting around. He just kicked in the door and leveled the gun at the old man. The look on Tom Little's face was everything he could have hoped for.

"Hi there, pops," he said. "Mind if I use your phone?"

The old man was holding a pot and looked like he was ready to throw it.

Bett shook his head. "Uh-uh. That'd be a bad move. Just put it down."

"I don't have what you're looking for," the old man said.

"Maybe, maybe not. But you're going to tell me where I can find it."

The old man's face just shut in on itself.

Bett smiled. Like the old geezer wasn't going to tell him anything Bett wanted him to. Not now, maybe. Not here, for sure. Bett was saving that bit of fun for when they had a bit more privacy. For when the old man could scream his head off and nobody would interrupt them.

And he was going to scream. No question of that.

"The phone," he repeated.

He stepped in close, the gun never wavering in his hand. Giving the old man a rough shove, Bett spun him around and walked him into the living room where he spotted the telephone. He sat the old man down in a chair.

"This won't take long," he assured Little as he dialed.

Grimes completed the connection on the other end of the line halfway through the first ring.

"Yeah?"

"The job's on," Bett told him. "Madden's driving a red Fiesta." He gave him the license plate number. "Last time I saw him he was driving up to the Men-an-Tol stone."

"What the hell's that?"

"Some kind of old rock stuck in a field somewhere."

"I need more than that."

"It's near Madron," Bett said, remembering what the Mabley woman had told Gavin earlier.

"Jesus, Bett. Why don't you make it a little easier?"

"Would if I could. There's some topographical maps in the glove compartment of the rental car I got you. Look it up on one of them. I'm kind of busy right now."

"You're a real sweetheart, Bett. If I didn't want Madden this bad, I'd just—"

Bett hung up, cutting him off. He took a folded piece of paper from his pocket and laid it on the mantel where it could be easily seen as soon as someone entered the room.

"Okay," he told the old man. "Time to get our show on the road. On your feet."

When Tom Little refused to budge, Bett just sighed. He stepped over to the chair and, holding the gun against the old man's stomach, hauled him to his feet and shoved him back towards the kitchen.

"We're going to have some fun, you and me," Bett told him as he steered him into the yard, back through the hedge, then down the lane to where Bett's own rental car was parked.

He walked close to the old man, shielding his weapon from the chance view of anyone looking out a window. When they reached the car, he opened the passenger's door and pushed Little inside.

"Scoot all the way over," he said. "You're driving. And don't think of playing any games on the road. You might think you're feeling real brave and decide to kill us both in a crash, but if something happens to me . . . well, I'm not alone in this deal. Be a shame if my friends had to take it out on your grand-daughter. . . ."

"I won't do anything foolish," the old man said.

Bett smiled. "That's what I like to hear."

But the possibility still hung there between them, and Bett relished it.

It made the edge he was walking all that much sharper.

7 ·

"What if there really *are* two different groups after the book?" Clare asked from the back seat of the Reliant Robin.

Janey and Felix were sitting in the front, Janey actually driving carefully for a change. They entered Newlyn from a back road, turning left at the A3077 that they followed until it connected with the A3071 that would take them northwest to Tremethick Cross. There they turned right, heading north to Madron. They passed the National Trust gardens of Tregwaiton House on their left, the Boscathnoe Reservoir on their right, before they reached the village where they made another left onto the B3312.

"Doesn't make any difference for what we're doing now," Felix said.

Clare nodded. "I'd just like to know."

"Mr. Goninan didn't say anything about another group of people," Janey said.

"Doesn't mean there isn't," Clare said.

"I suppose."

The road they were on now would take them all the way to the village of Trevowhan if they kept following it. A little farther past the village and they would be at the Morvah cliffs where, far below, the Atlantic washed against the tiny islands of Manakas and Wolf Rocks. They'd often picnicked on those cliffs in the years before Janey and Felix broke up—sometimes just the three of them, other times with Dinny and his sister Bridget joining them.

There was good music at those picnics—little sessions with the sound of the wind and the waves adding their own counterpointing rhythms to the sounds of fiddle and accordion, whistle, flute, and the two sets of pipes, Northumbrian and Uillean, that Janey and Dinny invariably brought. Janey was half inclined to go there now and never mind all the mad things that had come along to turn their lives topsy-turvy. But when they reached the Men-an-Tol print studio, housed in the old Bosullow schoolhouse, she dutifully turned the little Reliant up the dirt track that would take them across Bosullow Common and most of the distance to the Men-an-Tol itself.

The holed stone wasn't the only stonework in this area—

just the most famous. It was the largest tolmen in the British Isles, which often surprised visitors who were expecting something along the scale of Stonehenge. Instead, what they got for their twenty-minute walk from the B3312 was a round wheel of a stone with a large hole in its center, two short menhir on either side of the hole, with a third stone lying flat on the ground beside the easternmost longstone. The hole in the tolmen was large enough for a grown man to crawl through, although someone with shoulders as broad as Felix's might have some trouble.

Besides the Men-an-Tol, there were only two other major stoneworks nearby: the Boskednan, or Nine Maidens, stone circle to the east, and an inscribed stone known as the Men Scryfu to the north. But the area was riddled with smaller stoneworks, both ancient and more modern. A little farther north of the Men Scryfu was a point called the Four Parishes, a large slab of rock bearing an incised cross-hole where one could stand heel and toe with the parishes of Gulval, Madron, Morvah, and Zennor. There were also any number of cairns and crosses, solitary stones and hut circles, tumuli and all the remnants of the old tin mines: shafts, pits, and the disused mines themselves.

Janey stopped the car when the track finally gave out and they could go no farther. They all got out, Felix rooting about in the glove compartment for the flashlight that he knew Janey kept there. The night was quiet, the moon still below the horizon, but they could see its glow. As their eyes adjusted to the dark, Felix thrust the flashlight into his pocket in case they needed it later.

"We should get moving," he said.

"Just a minute," Janey said.

She was looking back down the track towards the Coronation House farm that lay on the other side of a privet hedge that they had passed earlier.

"We don't have long," Felix reminded her.

"She knows," Clare said. "She's just waiting for Kempy."

"Who?"

"You'll see."

Janey put her fingers to her lips and let a shrill whistle sound out across the land. A few moments later they all heard an answering bark.

"Kempy?" Felix asked.

Clare nodded.

Kempy was a mad border collie that invariably followed any visitor on their walk to the Men-an-Tol. His biggest thrill was to have stones tossed for him that he would then fetch and bring back to lay at the thrower's feet, a lunatic grin on his face as he barked for the game to begin again.

Janey had always loved the name of the moorland here—the Ding-Dong Moors. It was an old name, and she knew that the inspiration for it couldn't have been taken from Kempy, but she couldn't help but believe that if it hadn't been named for Kempy's antics, then one of the border collie's forebears had had that dubious honour of being responsible for it, which was "Almost the same difference," as Chalkie liked to say.

The name actually came from the bottle or bell mines from which the ancient Romans had excavated rich lodes of ore, particularly from the one known as the Ding-Dong Mine on the eastern edge of the moor where during the last century a loud bell was rung to summon the miners to work.

Kempy himself came charging up just then. Janey bent down to accept an enthusiastic faceful of licks before she finally stood up.

"Want to go for a walk, Kempy?" she asked.

The dog barked happily. He went and danced about Felix, sniffing at him, tail wagging, then tried to stick his head up Clare's skirt. She pushed him away with a laugh.

"Pervert," she muttered.

Janey threw a stone that rattled off farther down the narrowing track when it landed. Kempy raced after it, charging through the darkness, leaving the others to follow at a slower pace. About fifty yards on they came to a stile on their right that took them directly onto the moor. From there a path led off through the thick gorse, ling, and bell heather to the holed stone.

8.

Madden had no trouble tracking the artifact that was Dunthorn's secret—and it was an artifact, he had decided by now. A talisman of some sort. He could almost see it. It occupied space, had physical weight. All he lacked now was an understanding of its actual shape.

But although he could track the artifact as Janey Little ferried it across the countryside, his unfamiliarity with the area itself slowed him down. He knew exactly where the object was at all times, but found himself going down too many dead ends where he had to back up and start again, or following narrow lanes that after leading him in the correct direction for a time, unaccountably veered off, taking him out of his way.

When he eventually reached the Men-an-Tol print studio, the moon was already rising. He turned up the lane, following it until he reached a Reliant Robin that had been parked there ahead of him. He pulled in behind what he assumed was Janey Little's car and stepped out onto the lane. Closing his eyes, he turned slowly in one spot until he had the object's position fixed once more.

He was about to start off down the narrowing track when he heard a call from the direction of the Coronation House farm he had passed earlier. He turned to see the beam of a flashlight bobbing along the dirt. The man following it was short and stout. He had a Cornishman's round face, wellie boots on his feet, a rain slicker, and the unavoidable cloth cap on his head.

"You there," the farmer called out as he approached. "What do you think you're doing?"

"Parking my car."

The farmer shook his head. "Not allowed. This is private land. You'll have to move it."

"But this other vehicle . . . ?"

"That belongs to a friend of mine—she can park there anytime she likes—but you'll have to park back at the road."

Madden had no patience for this sort of nonsense—not now, not when he was so close. He locked gazes with the farmer, his annoyance making him use far more force than was necessary. The man staggered back, clutching at his head with one hand. The beam of his flashlight pointed skyward, weaving back and forth as the man fought for balance against the fierce, sharp fire that was hammering behind his eyes.

"You don't mind if I park my car here, do you?" Madden asked.

The farmer shook his head slowly. He didn't glance at Madden; he simply pressed his hands against his temples in a vain hope to alleviate the pain.

"Perhaps you should lie down—get to bed a little early tonight," Madden suggested. "You appear as though you could use the extra hours of sleep."

"Think I will," the farmer said.

His voice was dull with pain.

A dim-witted sheep, Madden thought as he watched the farmer walk slowly back the way he'd come. That was all the man was. That was all any of them were—the world teemed with them.

He sighed, flexed his fingers, then turned to look across the dark moorland once more.

He concentrated for a moment, marking the location of Dunthorn's artifact, then set off along the narrowing track that he'd been about to follow before the farmer had interrupted him. He knew this area. He could even guess, when he reached the stile that would let him out onto the moor, where Janey Little and her friends were going.

To the Men-an-Tol.

What he couldn't comprehend was why.

And that troubled him more than he would care to admit to anyone—including himself.

9 ·

The moon was peeping over the horizon when Janey and the others finally reached the Men-an-Tol. As always happened when she found herself in an ancient site such as this, she couldn't help but shiver with its sense of mystery—no matter how small or insignificant the stonework might be, no matter if it was out on a moor like this, or stuck in a farmer's field with cows placidly chewing their cuds around it.

The moor around this tolmen was one of her favorite spots—and it had obviously been one of William Dunthorn's as well, considering how much it had played a part in his writing, not only its significant role in *The Little Country,* but also in a number of articles he'd written for various journals. She'd often brought her pipes up here, enjoying the mood that their music woke in her when it mingled with the antiquity of the place. She smiled as she remembered the face of more than one tourist who'd followed the sound of her music to the stone. She was never sure if they were disappointed or relieved to find that it was only her toodling tunes by the tolmen and not some faerie piper.

"Well," she said.

She looked at Felix and Clare who were both waiting for her to make the first move. Kempy lay at the edge of cleared ground that surrounded the stone, smack dab in the middle of where the path from the lane joined it. His tongue lolled from his mouth and she couldn't shake the feeling that he was grinning at her.

If he was, she knew why.

The tingly feelings she got from places like this, that sense of old mysteries lying thick in the air just waiting to be called up, that was one thing. What had brought them tonight . . .

"I feel kind of dumb," she said.

"You have to give it a try," Felix said.

"I know. It's just . . ."

She sighed, taking the satchel with the book in it from her shoulder.

"Is there anything we should do?" Clare asked.

Janey smiled. "I don't even know what *I'm* supposed to do."

But she did. Hadn't Dunthorn told her, his counsel crossing the boundary of the years by way of the book? Maybe it was her story that she'd read in *The Little Country*, her phrasing, her voice, but it was still Bill Dunthorn speaking to her.

Nine times through the hole at moonrise.

"Better get to it," Felix said.

Janey nodded and walked over to the stone. "Give me a hand?"

He stepped over to the opposite side of the hole. She looked at him through the gap in the stone, still feeling foolish. He smiled reassuringly.

"Here goes nothing," she said.

She passed the satchel through to him. He took it and handed it back to her. She put it through the hole again.

That was twice.

And she felt more than dumb: She felt downright harebrained. But she kept passing the satchel through, counting off the times softly under her breath.

Six.

What if there really *was* another world on the other side of the stone? Who would end up guarding the book, then? Some little pointy-eared piskie?

The whole situation was mad. But the book itself—there *was* a magic in it. They'd proved that, because they'd each read a different story in it.

Seven.

She paused as she got the satchel back from Felix, thinking she'd heard something. She cocked her head, listening. The sensation grew in her that something was approaching. She felt it, not in the rational part of her mind, but in the intuitive side: an odd, inexpressible feeling that crept into the marrow of her bones and resonated there.

A sound.

She remembered what had happened in the Dunthorn book and then, as though that memory was a catalyst, she recognized what it was that she heard.

A faint trace of music, distant and eerie.

And familiar.

It was the same music that she'd heard coming from the book. . . .

She looked at Felix, wanting to ask if he heard it too, but she didn't need to ask. She could tell by the look on his face that it wasn't just her imagination. There was a look of wonder in his eyes, a slight loosening of his jaw.

It had to be real, because he was hearing it as well.

She passed the satchel through again.

Eight, she counted to herself.

And now she could pick out individual instruments: whistle and pipes; the clear ring of harp strings and the long, slow notes of a bow drawn across a fiddle's strings; the soft rhythm of a drumbeat—

Dhumm-dum. Dhumm-dum.

—that seemed to twin her own heartbeat.

And there, in the center of the Men-an-Tol's hole, a pinprick of light. A faint glow. A glimmering.

Her breath caught in her throat and she found it impossible to take another. She was numbed with awe.

It's real, she thought. There was a real magic here. . . .

Beyond the tolmen, mists were rising from the moorland. Slowly Janey took the satchel that held the Dunthorn book and passed it through the hole for the last time.

Nine.

Light flared, blinding her. The music rose to a crescendo. Janey let the satchel go. The flare died down, fading on the last strains of the music that seemed to be moving away, over one hill, over another, until it was gone. The silence around the stone lay heavy and deep, sweet with wonder.

When Janey could see again, she found Felix looking at her through the Men-an-Tol's hole. His hands were empty.

"The—the book . . . ?" he asked haltingly.

"Gone," Janey said.

Her heart sang. She could still hear the music—the memory of it—inside her, its rhythm still twinning her heartbeat. She fumbled in her purse for the tin whistle that she'd brought with her, her fingers trembling as she put the two parts together and then brought the mouthpiece up to her lips.

"It was unbelievable," she heard Felix say.

His voice seemed to come from a great distance. Clare was kneeling on the grass beside her, one hand reaching out to touch the stone. Janey felt aware of everything and nothing in that moment. She started to blow into the whistle, wanting to capture that music, or at least what she could of it, before the memory was completely gone, but then Kempy barked, and the moment of wonder came thundering down in a crash.

She turned to look at the path leading up to the stone. Kempy was backing up into the clearing, still barking. Standing there on the path was a tall figure; an angry figure. His eyes seemed to glow with his rage. They were red coals that caught the moonlight and took it inside them, swallowing it.

"What have you *done?*" he cried.

The voice was like ice, promising pain. Power crackled in the air around the man. He shot a gaze at the dog and Kempy abruptly stopped barking. Whining, the dog crawled on its belly away from the dark figure.

It didn't take much insight for Janey to realize that they were finally face-to-face with John Madden.

IO .

Grimes was in a foul mood by the time he finally pulled up across from the Men-an-Tol print studio on the B3312. He looked at the darkened building, then over to the signpost on the other side of the road that indicated the beginning of a public footpath to the Men-an-Tol.

It had taken him longer than he'd expected to get here. The maps that Bett had left in the glove compartment of the rental car had been more than adequate. It was matching them up to the often unmarked roads that had been a bitch. Especially at night.

He looked past the signpost, off into the darkened moorland. So how far was this stone anyway?

Turning on the interior light, he pulled the map up from the seat beside him and spread it out across the steering wheel.

Not too far. Close enough so that he could leave the car here and walk up. That'd save the sound of the engine carrying across the moor.

He didn't want to give Madden any more of a warning than he could possibly help. When he thought of the man's eyes—

His missing hand started to ache again.

Uh-uh, he thought. This time it ends differently.

He parked his car over in the small lot near the print studio and crossed back over to the lane that led up to the Men-an-Tol. Removing his .38 from his pocket, where the cloth might snag against its trigger if he had to get it out quickly, he thrust it into his belt, under his jacket. Then he started up the lane.

He walked at a steady clip, reaching a pair of parked cars in under fifteen minutes.

Bingo. One red Fiesta.

Thank you, Bett. I owe you one.

The other vehicle was one of those weird three-wheeled Re-liants. He wouldn't ride in one of those if you paid him to. Damn thing looked like it'd tip over the first time it went around a sharp curve.

He studied the surrounding landscape, trying to decide where Madden and the owner of the other car might have gone, then figured he'd just stay put. Wandering out on those moors, who knew where the hell he'd end up? Getting lost he didn't need— not when he was this close. Sooner or later Madden would be coming back for his car. He'd just wait here for him.

Grimes stepped over into the deeper shadows of the hedgerow on the west side of the lane and leaned up against a stone. He slowed his breathing, relaxing until a deep calm settled over him. It was a simple hunter's trick. You just melted into the background—*became* a part of the background. Until you made your move.

For this kind of a thing, all you needed was patience.

And Grimes had that in spades.

I I .

Dinny Boyd arrived at the Gaffer's house to find no one home. The front door was locked, and though he rang the bell a number of times, there was no reply. His pulse quickened as he tried peering in through the lace-curtained window above the door, but he couldn't make out very much.

It wasn't like Tom Little to say one thing, then do another. If the Gaffer planned to meet a body somewhere, then he would be there for that meeting.

Unless he'd run into trouble.

There was something decidedly odd going on—Dinny had no doubt about that. This business with the farm and then the things that Janey had told him earlier this afternoon . . .

He went around back, his pulse quickening still more as he took in the state of the kitchen door.

Someone had broken in.

He stepped nervously inside, stilling his first impulse to call out.

What if whoever had done this was still inside?

There were dirty dishes piled up near the sink. Taking a bread knife from where it lay on the counter, he moved cautiously into the living room. A thorough search of the house let him know that he was alone in it.

Janey, Clare, and Felix were gone.

And so was the Gaffer.

Then the phone rang.

Dinny went back into the living room.

That'd be one of them ringing up to explain matters, he thought as he picked up the receiver. But he couldn't still the prickle of uneasiness that had lodged in between his shoulder blades—an uneasiness that only increased when he answered the phone.

"Hello?"

"Who's this?" an unfamiliar voice asked. The accent wasn't quite American.

"Dinny Boyd."

"Sorry. Wrong number."

The line went dead.

Dinny slowly cradled the receiver. He looked around the room again, searching for some clue as to what was up. His gaze settled on a piece of folded paper that was propped up on the mantel. He crossed the room, read the note, then returned to the phone.

"Dad?" he said when the connection was made. "I think you'd better meet me at the Gaffer's."

"What's the matter, then, Dinny?"

"I'll explain when you get here. Bring Sean or Uncle Pat with you, just don't leave Mum and Bridget alone."

He went to the front door and unlocked it, standing on the Gaffer's small stoop while he waited for his father to come. The early evening lay quietly upon the village, giving no indication of the danger Dinny could feel closing in on him, his family, and his friends.

Kick the World

Before You

I seem to be a verb.

—attributed to
BUCKMINSTER FULLER

Bodbury seemed a strange and furious place to Jodi when the Widow's fetch carried her through it.

The wind howled and leapt through the narrow streets in a hundred different directions at once, whirling and spinning like a mad pack of dervishes. It crept in between the glass panes and metal frames of the gaslit street lamps, blowing out the flames, making the dark streets darker still. Litter danced and tumbled in its wake. Shutters rattled. Red clay shingles were torn from the rooftops to shatter on the cobblestones. Windows were blown open, curtains billowing inward, until the owners of the houses had a chance to shut them again.

The fetch chittered happily to itself as it scampered down the steep streets towards the harbour, careening from side to side to keep its balance as the wind buffeted it. The creature seemed utterly in its element, its fearsome mouth split from ear to ear in a grin as it ran.

When they reached Peter Street, Jodi shrieked as loud as she could in the hope that she'd been wrong about those new long-stones out on the moor near the Men-an-Tol. Surely they weren't her friends, enchanted by the Widow the way that legend told that the wicked young women who danced on a Sunday had been changed into the Merry Maidens or Boskednan stone circles in times long past and gone.

The fetch paused to look up as the window to Denzil's loft rattled and then flew open. Jodi's heart lifted high with hope at the thought of rescue, then plummeted again when she saw it was only Ollie, peering curiously out into the stormy night from the windowsill. Denzil's monkey clung to the curtains as the wind tried to blow him from his perch. Jodi opened her mouth to call again, but then Windle hissed and she realized that while Ollie could easily swing down from the upper story to the street, she doubted that he was any match for the Widow's fetch.

She kept silent, allowing the fetch to bear her off down to the harbour. Ollie remained behind on the windowsill, playing tug-of-war with the wind as he tried to close the window once more. The last view Jodi had of the monkey, before the fetch bore her around a corner, was of him hanging from the window as it was swept back and forth by the battering wind.

Now they were nearing the waterfront. The waves lashed up against the shore, spraying in enormous white spumes as they struck the wood and stone of the piers. By New Dock, fishermen were struggling with their luggers and boats—to little avail. Jodi saw that some of the boats were already wrecked; others were breaking free to smash against the stone quay.

And then there was the Widow.

She stood well back from the washing spray of the seawater, a tall forbidding figure in a dark mantle with eyes that seemed to glow with their own inner light. On either side of her, shadowy sloch capered and flittered in the wind. Between where she stood and the wild sea itself were rank upon rank of drowned men— corpses dragged up from their sea graves to serve her. They paid no mind to the battering waves that lashed them. Seawater streamed from their limp hair, their tattered rags and the seaweed that clung to their limbs.

It was all some horrible nightmare, Jodi prayed. Please let that be what this was. Don't let it be real.

But the grip of the fetch's bony fingers was too solid to be a dream; the storm too wild. The Widow too imposing. The sloch and sea dead . . .

Yammering happily to itself in its high grating voice, Windle bore her forward and presented her to the Widow. Jodi shivered as the Widow's cold fingers closed around her and took her from Windle's grip. She lifted Jodi to the level of her eyes.

The fires in them burned like hot coals and Jodi remembered Edern's warning.

Don't look into her eyes.

The memory came too late. Jodi tried to look away, to block the crackle of power that leapt from the Widow's gaze into her own eyes, but the Widow's witcheries tore down the feeble walls Jodi tried to raise and easily entered her mind.

The fingers squeezed painfully, rubbing Jodi's ribs against one another. It was growing impossible to breathe.

No, Jodi realized mournfully. It wasn't a dream.

It was all too real.

The Widow's witcheries stirred about in Jodi's mind as though they were a ladle, her mind a cauldron. Jodi's memories churned and roiled in confusion until, as though from a great distance, she heard a vague rhythmic sound.

Dhumm-dum.

"You've led me a pretty chase," the Widow was saying, "but now you're mine, you miserable little wretch."

Her eyes glittered with promises of the torments she had in store for her diminutive captive.

But Jodi was beyond fear now. The Widow's witcheries had called up a trace of that sense of unity that Jodi had shared with the Barrow World, a sliver of memory that had still remained lodged inside her. It echoed to her heartbeat—

Dhumm-dum. Dhumm-dum.

—and distanced her from the moment at hand. It took her past her terror into a place where a numbness spread throughout her limbs, separating her from her body and the pain that the Widow was inflicting upon it until she could look on what was happening to her and the town with the dispassionate gaze of a simple observer.

She was still aware of her danger, still afraid. But the part of her that was an observer was now able to consider the situation from a more objective point of view. She took in the fury of the storm that the Widow had called down. The monstrous creatures...

Yesterday the Widow had been hard put to raise a few miniature shambling sloch and send them after one clockwork man and Jodi herself. And failed. But today... today her sloch were tall and moved like quicksilver, the sea dead answered her call, and she seemed to rule the elements.

How had she become so powerful?

"I want the secret," the Widow went on. "You will give me the secret to the Barrow World."

Jodi merely looked at her, thinking, what secret? It lay all around them, separated only by an invisible boundary of onion-layered thickness. With her sympathy to the Barrow World still thrumming powerfully inside her—

Dhumm-dum.

—Jodi could almost see that otherworld superimposed over the storm-wracked view in front of her. It was that close.

"Each time you refuse," the Widow said, "I'll pluck a limb from your body. I'll keep you alive until you're nothing more than a bodiless head, pleading for death. And don't think you can trick me. I can smell the stink of a lie."

The pressure of the Widow's witcheries in Jodi's mind was like a dull, throbbing headache.

"Lie...?" Jodi asked.

Her voice was still hoarse from when she'd cried for help on the mad journey from the Men-an-Tol to Bodbury in the fetch's grip.

Lie, she thought dreamily. She would like to lie down if she could.

For everything had become increasingly bewildering. It was as though she were here, but not here. Viewing a droll from the safe anonymity of an audience, rather than from the stage itself. The world about her was now a surreal blending of two worlds— on one hand, the storm-tossed bay at Bodbury's harbour; on the other, the clear, still water of the Barrow World. The night here with its thunder and shocks of lightning set against the Barrow World's bright blue skies. The Widow, her monstrous sea dead and sloch and the struggling fishermen compared to a strange array of the Barrow World's creatures who had gathered near the shore of their own world—mermaids and piskies; a man with a raven's head, another with a stag's antlers sprouting from his brow; creatures that appeared to be small trees that had pulled their roots from the ground and gone walking; a woman with a round face like the moon, whose hair was green, whose eyes were golden, whose hips disappeared into the shoulders of a grey-backed horse so that the two disparate segments were a part of the same body. . . .

In this world, the Widow and her creatures threatened; in that world, the folk were listening to that music—

Dhumm-dum. Dhumm-dum.

—that echoed inside Jodi.

"You *will* tell me," the Widow said.

Her voice seemed to come from very far away—a vague murmuring sound against the deep richness of the first music.

"Tell you . . . ?" Jodi asked dreamily.

She saw that Bodbury's fishermen had given up their struggle with the sea and were gaping openmouthed at the Widow and her creatures. One or two, more attuned to secrets and hidden things than their fellows, were pointing at cottages and buildings that flickered, were replaced by the green swards of the Barrow World, only to blur and disappear again.

Dhumm-dum.

And now Jodi saw more than a blurring blend of the two worlds. She saw the past and present mingled: Old Bodbury mixed with the new. All was changed—the same but different. There were fewer buildings in the town, there were more. New Dock existed; it was gone as though it had never been. The ruin of the Old Quay appeared as it had been in its former heyday; it returned to disrepair.

She saw the fishermen exclaiming as they saw their ancestors walking the streets towards them—flickering images that winked in and out of existence.

And always the music, haunting and echoing, sounding to the echo of her heartbeat, the drum of her pulse, the heartbeat of the town, of the bay, or the moorland that lay beyond. . . .

Dhumm-dum.

Jodi felt herself expanding to become a part of it all, of both worlds, of the past and of the present, drifting further and further away from the moment at hand, from its danger, from the Widow and her creatures. . . .

Dhumm-dum.

The Widow shook Jodi until her teeth were rattling in her head.

"*Tell* me!" the Widow cried.

The shaking brought Jodi somewhat back to earth. She stared deep into the fires that lay at the back of the Widow's eyes and was surprised to find that all her fear of the woman had gone. The pressure of the Widow's witcheries was gone from her mind.

"I can't tell you," she said.

The Widow's eyes glittered dangerously.

"I can only show you . . ." Jodi said.

Something sparked between their locked gazes—a fire more ancient than anger.

And then the Widow was drawn into seeing the world as Jodi perceived it; hearing the heartbeat rhythm:

Dhumm-dum.

Two worlds flickering between each other, past and present mingling.

In one moment she knew all that Jodi had ever been. And Jodi knew her. Jodi met Hedra Scorce—the girl the Widow had been before she'd lost her innocence, before she'd changed. Jodi saw Hedra's life unfold, heard the whisper of the shadows that had turned the Widow from what she'd been into who she was now.

Those awful shadows who approached so eagerly now. Not the capering figures of the sloch that surrounded the Widow, but older shadows: the dark voices that whispered to every man's and woman's heart, that fed on jealousy and anger and hatred.

"I'm so sorry," Jodi said.

And she was. Tears welled in her eyes and spilled down her cheeks.

"No," the Widow said in a small voice.

The winds had died. Above, the sky was still dark with clouds, but the lightning had ceased, the thunder was silenced, the rain still held back.

The sea dead shambled back towards the sea. The capering oversize sloch that the Widow had made from bog and shadow and parts of herself collapsed in upon themselves into heaps of putrefied mud and rotting vegetation.

The Widow fell to her knees.

Dark things crept from the sides of the buildings and walls where the night lay thickest. Old shadows. Evil things.

A witch cannot cry, Jodi thought. And she knew why. Tears, with their salt content, were anathema to them. It made sense that a witch would lay a spell on herself, some form of a defense mechanism to ensure that she physically *could not* weep.

But the Widow was no longer just herself now. A part of her was Jodi Shepherd; a part of her was Hedra Scorce, the innocent child that she had once been. That part of her wept at the knowledge of what she had become.

Tears welled in her eyes, blinding her. They ran like lava down her cheeks, stripping the skin to the bone. Her flesh smoldered and filled the air with an awful reek. On her knees, the Widow bowed her head until her brow rested against the cobblestones. The muscles of her hands went limp and Jodi slipped free.

Jodi backed away from the Widow, but couldn't go far. The old shadows that had ringed the Widow completely blocked her escape. They whispered and snickered among themselves. Their greedy eyes drank in the Widow's pain, her defeat. Forgotten for now was the Barrow World and its secret gate. Sweeter by far was the immediate moment.

The Widow whimpered. Her fetch stroked at her hair and made mewling sounds.

The tears continued to burn from the Widow's eyes. Her skin smoked. She opened her mouth to scream, but the tears ran down her throat and only smoke issued forth. Her throat worked involuntarily and now she burned from the inside as well as the out.

The shadows tittered.

"Fight them!" Jodi cried.

She didn't think it at all odd that her sympathy lay now with her former enemy, for when the first music had taken her through the Widow's history, Jodi had understood that the blame lay not wholly with the Widow herself. The Widow had been weak, she had listened to the evil whispering of the shadows and allowed her own disappointment and sorrow to blind her to the wrongness of what she did, but it was the shadows themselves that were the real enemy.

Their incessant whispering.

How they trapped those whose despair and weakness left them susceptible to the endless chattering of their voices.

And their false promises. . . .

Jodi could hear them as she stood there watching the Widow die; their whispering battered against her mind. It crept in under her thoughts, tempting her with a dark power. No longer need she be victim to any other, they told her. Hers would be the mastery. Hers the control. Let others beware *her*. . . .

But Jodi could ignore their voices. She could push them aside. Not because she was stronger than the Widow had been when her name was still Hedra Scorce, and not because she was necessarily a better person, but because she had the first music thrumming inside her.

Dhumm-dum. Dhumm-dum.

Its rhythm showed the whispers to be the lies they were. In its harmony there was no room for their untruth. They brought only pain and suffering while the first music healed.

"Listen to it," Jodi told the Widow.

She knew the Widow could hear the music—it was there inside her the same way that the Widow's memories were in Jodi.

"Let the music heal you," she added.

The Widow lifted her head to look in Jodi's direction. Her ruined features made Jodi's stomach churn. Bone showed through the flesh. Skin hung in tattered strips from cheeks and chin. The blind eyes fixed sightlessly on her.

For one moment Jodi saw another face there—that of Hedra Scorce, the sweet and gentle face of an innocent child—then the ruined mask returned.

"It . . . is . . . too . . . late . . ." the Widow said.

Her voice was a rasping croak. More tears streamed from her eyes as she spoke, burning their way through her flesh.

"Try!" Jodi cried. "Oh, please try!"

"I . . . can't. . . ."

The shadows tittered with great good humour as the Widow collapsed on the cobblestones again. Smoke wreathed from her flesh. Her fetch howled and threw itself upon her as an unearthly blue-green fire flared up, consuming them both.

Jodi stared horrified, unable to turn away. She watched until the flames died away and all that remained of the Widow and her fetch was an untidy heap of her empty clothes. All else was gone—flesh, skin, and bones.

With the Widow gone, the shadows turned their full attention on Jodi, but she barely heard them. She stumbled forward, and fumbled about the Widow's mantle until she came upon the buttons that were sewn there. Unerringly, steered by the rhythm of the first music that still rang inside her, she reached for the button that was her own.

When she touched it, a fiery pain flared through her body. She dropped to her knees, blinded by its raw fury. She couldn't breathe, couldn't think. All she knew was that unending hurt that seemed to go on and on forever.

It was a very long time before she could finally lift her head again. She found herself crouched upon the Widow's empty clothes. The first music was gone, though she could still hear its echoes. The shadows were fled, back into their dark corners, though she could still hear them, too, as a faint annoying bee-buzz in the back of her head.

She sat up slowly.

"Do you need some help there, girl?" a voice asked.

She looked up to find a burly fisherman offering her his hand. He was so matter-of-fact, so plainly here and now, of this world, that Jodi could only look at him with confusion. Others stood nearby and she heard snatches of their conversation.

"Strange wind, no doubt o't."

"Come like a tempest, gone as quick."

"Well, now, autumn's the time for odd weather."

"My old granddad had a tale about a night like this. . . ."

They didn't remember anything about the Widow or her creatures, Jodi realized. Nor the strange shifting between the worlds. Nor the ghosts of times past and people long dead who had flickered to life all around them.

"Up you come then," the fisherman said as he gave her a hand up. "Were you hurt at all by the wind?"

Jodi shook her head.

"Well, you've dropped your laundry," the fisherman said. "Basket's long blown away, but you could wrap it up in this mantle."

Jodi let him bundle up the Widow's clothes and hand them to her.

"Do you need some help finding your way home?" he asked.

"No. I . . . thank you."

"You look like you've taken a chill," the fisherman said. "Best get yourself home for a cup of something hot."

Jodi nodded. "I . . . will."

She found a faint smile to give him and walked unsteadily off, not really sure where she was going until she was up at the top of Mabe Hill, above the town, standing near the ruins of the Creak-a-vose. She let the bundle she was carrying drop to the ground and sat on a nearby stone.

She lifted her hands up to her eyes and studied them carefully, comparing their size to the dried blackberries on a bush beside the stone.

She was her own size again.

Unless . . .

Oh raw we. Had she ever been a Small in the first place? Perhaps she'd gotten herself a thump on the head in the middle of this odd storm and only dreamed the whole affair?

No, she thought. It had all seemed far more real than a dream. And if she listened hard, she could hear the faint rhythm of the first music, still twinning her heartbeat, but it was a far and distant sound now.

It had all happened. She was sure of that. Only something was making her forget—just as the fishermen on the waterfront had already forgotten.

Well, she *wouldn't* forget. That was the promise she'd made to Edern, wasn't it? To wake the first music in her own world, to bring the two worlds closer together again. But how was she supposed to do that when people could stare something magical straight in the face—as the fishermen had done—and then simply turn away from it as though it had never happened?

The thought of it just made her feel depressed.

But at least she was her own size again. And the Widow wasn't a threat anymore.

That didn't make her feel any better. It was a relief to feel like herself again and know that she was safe from the Widow, but she got no pleasure from having defeated the old woman. It seemed to her that the only winners were those whispering shadows. If they fed on pain and despair, then they had fed well on the Widow tonight.

Jodi sighed.

She looked down at the bundle of clothes. Reaching down, she unwrapped the bundle until she could shake the mantle free from the rest of the clothes. Sewn there, on the inside of it where that piece of her had been sewn, were a double handful of buttons. She touched one and the image of one of the Tatters children rose in her mind. Another, and she saw Henkie Whale.

She thought of the new set of longstones out by the Men-an-Tol.

Magic *was* real, she reassured herself yet again.

The good with the bad. Which meant one really did have to beware of the whispering in the shadows. But there was the first music—

Dhumm-dum.

Just thinking of it made it seem closer. Where she'd felt a bit of a chill thinking of what watched from the shadows, now a comfortable glow started up in the center of her chest and spread out to enclose her in a soft cocoon of warmth.

The one helped to balance the other, she supposed.

Standing up, she slung the Widow's mantle over her shoulder and set off across the moorland to where her friends stood like so many stones in the gorse, waiting to be rescued.

The Eagle's Whistle

The thing to remember, is that artists are magical
beings. They're the only people other than the gods
who can grant immortality.

—MATT RUFF,
from *Fool on the Hill*

*F*elix smiled as Janey pulled her whistle from her
purse and put its two pieces together. The sheer
beauty of the music that seemed to rise up from all
around them had his fingers itching for an instrument as well.

Capture the magic, he thought, watching Janey bring the
whistle to her lips. For it *was* magic.

He looked at his hands, then at the hole in the stone where
the satchel had disappeared in a flare of light. If he hadn't seen
it with his own two eyes . . .

His heart was singing. There was a foolish grin on his face
and he didn't care who saw it. The world had changed, in one
moment, into a place of infinite possibilities. Every wonder was
possible. Every mystery could be revealed.

On the back of that music . . .

And then it all came crashing down with John Madden's
appearance.

Music fled: and with it, the wonder. The magic.

For a long moment Felix could only stare at Madden and curse
his intrusion. He was only barely aware of the glow in the man's
eyes, of the way the border collie fled their eerie gaze. He rose
to his feet, anger tightening the muscles of his shoulders until
his own gaze locked with Madden's.

He thought he was falling.

Madden's gaze swallowed him whole and then the ground
opened up underfoot and he was plummeting some unguessed

distance, stomach lurching at the speed of his descent, head dizzy, muscles all gone weak.

It's just a trick, he told himself. The man's just putting the evil eye on you—like he did the dog.

But then all logic fled. He was caught in the sudden flare of a spotlight and he was no longer falling. He was seated on a stool, on a stage. His box was on his knee; before him an ocean of faces.

Im-impossible. . . .

But he could feel the hard wood of the stool under his buttocks, the familiar weight of his accordion, the sweat that broke out over his face under the onslaught of that piercing spotlight. The audience was vast. He couldn't make out individual faces—just a presence in the darkness beyond the stage. An animal crouching, waiting for him—

To play.

His hands shook. Gone was all memory of how he'd come to be here, or any question of where here was. There was only the feral presence of the audience and his own panic—a gibbering, howling panic that settled on him like a too familiar nightmare. There was a dull pressure on his chest. He felt feverish and sweaty cold. The restless noises from the audience as they stirred impatiently in their seats faded away in one moment, became overly bright in the next.

His chest was tight now, heart speeding up, its beat ragged. Simply breathing was a labour. The restless sound of the audience pressed in on him, beating at his ears in a shrill cacophony of overly loud coughs, fabric rustlings, foot tappings.

Snickering.

They know, he thought. They know I can't. . . .

A stifled chuckle to the left—a stagehand, with his hand up against his mouth, the taunting laughter still bubbling in his eyes.

Felix shook his head numbly. His voice was trapped in his throat. He spoke with his eyes.

Please. I . . .

A great big bloke like you, a mocking voice whispered in the back of his mind. *Where's your courage?*

I . . .

Play or die, that voice whispered.

No. I . . .

His legs trembled uncontrollably. His box would have tumbled from his knee were it not for the death's grip his hands had on its straps.

Play.

The laughter was spreading through the audience and he could feel his soul curling up inside himself into a fetal position, thumb in its mouth. . . .

Play—

I c-can't. . . .

—or die.

He was bent over his box, sweaty brow pressed against the cool surface of its plastic casing. He wrapped his arms around it, hugging it to his chest.

The laughter grew into a wave of ridicule, wailing inside his head, shrieking behind his eyes. His heart was hammering an explosive tattoo. Sharp, whining pains pierced his chest. His bowels grew loose.

Play—

The laughter was like thunder. He moaned, trying to shape words, if only in his mind.

I . . .

—or die.

Thousands of heads tilted back, roaring at his discomfort, their laughter thick with derision as they pointed their fingers at him. Individuals all melded together into a lumbering beast, galvanized by his panic, drinking in his terror like greedy vampires.

I . . . can't. . . .

It's show time, kid, that awful voice inside him mocked. *Time to play or—*

He'd just have to—
—*die*.

2 .

Charlie Boyd took the note from his son's hands when he arrived at the Gaffer's house. He'd come alone, leaving Sean and his brother at home with Molly and Bridget. He took out a pair of glasses and settled them on the bridge of his nose, his face growing grimmer with each terse line he read:

> Dear survivor,
> Here's the game plan. You got something I want and I got something you want. We do a straight exchange. No muss, no fuss. And no cops. Screw up, and what I got comes back in pieces. And then I'm coming after you. Hang loose now. You'll be hearing from me real soon.

When he had read it through a second time, Charlie laid the note down on the table by the door. He put away his glasses.

"Where did you find it?" he asked.

"On the mantel."

"And the Gaffer?"

"There was no sign of him, Dad. Just the back door—broken in."

"And someone rang up?"

Dinny nodded. "A wrong number. The accent was American—or close enough to it to make no difference."

"It was an American that rang us up earlier," Charlie said thoughtfully.

"It must be the same man."

"So it would seem."

"What do we do now, Dad?"

Charlie sighed. "We've no choice," he said. "We have to ring up the police."

"But the note said—" Dinny began.

"I know what the note said, son. But what can we do? I'm not bloody John Steed."

"It's just that . . . if something happens to the Gaffer because of what we've done . . ." Dinny turned pained eyes to his father. "How could we face Janey?"

"Where *is* Janey?"

"Gone off somewhere with Felix and Clare."

Charlie glanced at his wristwatch.

"We can't wait for them to come back," he said. "We have to turn this over to the professionals, son. We'll tell them what Janey told you—about this Madden man and all—and let them deal with it."

Dinny nodded glumly. His father crossed the room to where the phone stood. He had no sooner put his hand on the receiver than the phone rang, its sudden jangle startling them both.

3 ·

Clare leaned on her cane and almost didn't feel the need of its support. The music that washed around the Men-an-Tol made her want to throw it away and dance—really dance, with complete freedom, with utter abandon. With the liquid movement of a ballerina, or the animated spontaneity of a modern jazz artist, not the laggard shuffle of a slow dance that was the best she could manage.

As it was, she swayed where she stood, marveling at the magic. Of the music. Of the flare of light that had swallowed Dunthorn's book. Of the sheer wonder of it all.

She grinned when Janey took her whistle from her purse and wished she'd thought to bring along one of her own. But then she'd never be able to come close to capturing this magic. Not like Janey could.

So she just closed her eyes, her body moving in an easy swinging rhythm, back and forth in one spot, letting the wonder wash
through her—

Until a sudden coldness bit into her with the force of a knife
thrust and everything changed.

She turned to see John Madden standing at the end of the
path, his eyes glowing. Kempy fled his gaze, whimpering. Janey's
music faltered before it even had a chance to really begin. Felix
rose from the other side of the stone. He took two steps towards
Madden, then crumpled to the ground, moaning and curling up
into a fetal position.

Clare took a half step towards him. "Felix, what . . . ?"

But then she made the mistake of looking into Madden's glowing eyes herself. His gaze locked on to hers and then she was
falling too, just like Felix had. She sprawled onto the ground,
but she couldn't move. Though it had been years since she'd
known this feeling—that emptiness in her legs where there
should be feeling—she could never forget it.

That lack of feeling was there now. Her nerves were dead,
muscles unresponsive. Corpse limbs attached to her body.

Madden had paralyzed her, but not just her legs.

"Nuh . . . no . . ." she moaned, her voice no more than a
whimper.

Oh, no. Not just her legs, but her whole body. Paralyzed from
the neck down. With that one fiery glare from his eyes, he'd
turned her . . . not back into a paraplegic.

No. That was too simple a horror.

Instead he gave her her worst fear: He'd made her a quadri-
plegic.

And that she couldn't bear. That was *all* possible control stolen
from her. Better to take her life. Better to just die now than to
try to live with this horror.

Because she couldn't.

She'd been strong. All her life she'd had to be strong. But she
wasn't this strong. Nobody could be this strong. Nobody could
go through all she'd had to go through, recover as much as she

had, and then have it taken away like this.

"Puh-please. . . ."

All she could do was turn her head towards him, begging him. Her body was some monstrous mound of dead flesh, attached to her only by flesh and bone. There was no connection with meaning. No nerve. No muscle. There was nothing there.

She couldn't live with it.

"Nuh-not . . . this. . . ."

But he was already turning his attention away and looking towards Janey.

4 ·

Bett grinned at his captive. They were hidden from sight and from hearing both at the bottom of one of the silos of the bay side of the quarry that lay almost midway between Mousehole and Newlyn. Apparently they still used these old silos to ship the stone out to Germany and the like. But they didn't use them at night; they certainly weren't using them tonight. Bett had made sure of that.

And all he needed it for was the one night.

He'd tied the old man to a chair that he'd brought along for that purpose and now it was just the two of them, here on the edge. Walking the thin line.

"It's you and me, old man," he said.

He'd tried to impose his will on his captive, without success. He had to give the old man credit. Tom Little proved to have far more resistance to Bett's mesmerizing than Bett had ever imagined he would. But it didn't matter. It would just take a little longer, that was all.

And they had all night.

"Be a shame if I got hold of that cute little granddaughter of yours," Bett said. "She already likes me—I can tell. Thinks I'm her step up to the big time."

"You . . . you're the reporter?"

Bett laughed. "In the flesh. To tell you the truth, I was hoping to grab her instead of you. I figure she'd squeal quicker and I do like to hear them squeal."

The Gaffer spat at him, but that only made Bett laugh louder.

"Now here's the game," Bett said. "We're going to make one more call to your sweet little granddaughter. She comes across with the goods, we're all going to leave this place as friends. But if she doesn't . . ."

He patted one of the three jerricans of gasoline that he had sitting beside him on the loose stones.

"If she doesn't, you and I are going to have ourselves a weenie roast, old man."

"You—"

"And then I'll *still* go after her."

"If I—"

"Yeah, yeah. If you were free. If I faced you like a man. Grow up, you old jerk. That's not the way the game goes. Uh-uh," he added as the Gaffer opened his mouth again. "Time to make our little phone call."

He took the portable phone from the knapsack that lay beside the jerricans and punched up the number for the house on Duck Street.

"There," he said. "It's ringing. Scream all you want now. It's just going to add to the . . . validity of the call."

He smiled at the tight line that the Gaffer's lips made.

"Who's this?" he said into the receiver when the connection was made.

"Charlie Boyd," came the reply.

"Wrong answer," Bett said.

He hung up and put away the phone. With an exaggerated sigh, he rose to his feet and shook his head.

"Gee, I'm real sorry about this, old-timer. But the ball's really in your court now."

He unscrewed the top of the jerrican and stepped over to the chair, pouring the gasoline over one of the Gaffer's legs. With a show of great care, he took the can back across the small space and put it next to the others, then returned to stand in front of his captive.

"Anything you want to tell me?" he asked as he pulled a lighter from his pocket.

The Gaffer's eyes were round with fear, but he shook his head.

Bett sighed again. The old coot had balls. No doubt about that.

He really wished that he did have the girl instead. There's no way she'd've lasted out fifteen minutes of this. Splash a little gas on her face and explain how pretty she was going to look when the fire got to her skin. . . .

Guys always had to prove how tough they were—even an old bird like this one here.

"You're not being brave," he told the Gaffer as he flicked the lighter into life. "You're just being stupid."

The Gaffer's gaze locked on the light's flame. Bett could see the whole world narrowing in for the old man, focusing on that one spot of flickering light.

He brought the flame close to the gas-soaked pant leg, laughing when the Gaffer shut his eyes and flinched. Bett snapped the lighter shut.

"Hey, but we're having fun—right?" he said when the Gaffer's eyes opened to glare at him.

Bett fed on his captive's fear, drinking it in.

"Okay," he said. "This time it's for real."

He opened the lighter again, spun its steel wheel against the flint.

The flame leapt up from the wick, an inch and a half high.

5 ·

Janey had a forewarning that neither of her companions did.

Her version of the Dunthorn novel had predicted this very situation, from the magic of the Men-an-Tol through to Madden's arrival. Not perfectly—the details were different. But all the same, she could almost smell the stink of a bog in the air . . . could almost see the Widow's sloch, twisting and writhing on the moorland behind the intruder's tall figure.

The whistle tune faltered on her lips, fell still.

She saw Felix go down—curling up into a ball like a threatened hedgehog—rapidly followed by Clare who looked as though all her muscles had just turned to jelly on her. She started to take a step towards them, but then Madden's eerie gaze was turning on her. The magnetic intensity of his will bore down on her, sending a knife-blade chill up her spine, turning her heart to stone, until she heard a small voice, coming to her as if from far away, from a dream.

Don't look in his eyes. Don't listen to what he says.

And she remembered the little man in the Dunthorn book. The Small. . . .

Before Madden's magnetic gaze could lock fully on her will, she managed to turn her head away and lift the whistle up to her lips again.

She'd never been that fond of this particular Eagle brand tin whistle; she'd bought it on a whim, for the way it came apart in two pieces, which made it easy to tote about in a pocket or purse, rather than for its tone. It was fine in the lower register, but the upper one always sounded as though the instrument was being overblown, no matter how much she controlled her breath. It was hard enough to control its tone, little say play a tune.

But at the moment what was important was that it *did* play a tune, no matter how faulty the upper register notes sounded. All she needed was its music. It wouldn't have the magic of that other music—the first music, she thought, naming it as the characters had named it in the Dunthorn book—but so long as it kept her from hearing Madden, from looking into his eyes, it would be magic enough.

She started up a version of "The Foxhunter's Jig"—a slip jig in 9/8 that rang out far jauntier than she was feeling at the moment. She leaned into the long B notes in the second part, wishing she had her pipes with her so that she could really bend the note, and then realized it was working.

Madden's presence was a buzz that lay behind the music. He spoke, but she couldn't hear what he was saying, and so long as she didn't look into his eyes. . . .

The tune faltered as it skirled into the high notes of the third part. It was partly the whistle's fault—making her overblow the notes—but all the blame couldn't be laid on the instrument.

There was Madden.

She couldn't hear him. She refused to look at him. But she could feel him approaching her. His presence was a dark shadow in her mind—an ugly buzz. It set up a discordance—not only in the music, but in the night itself. Because she could feel him, drawing nearer, step by step.

And she didn't know what she was going to do.

She fumbled the run in the fourth part of the tune that took it back into the lower register. And heard—

"—at me. You *will* look—"

She centered all her attention on the music, circling around the stone, away from his approaching presence. But there was a crack in her concentration now. A hole in the music.

She could feel his eyes boring through it.

She tried to imagine sheet music in front of her.

The eyes burned through it.

She switched to a faster 4/4 tempo, same tune title, but a different tune. "The Foxhunter's Reel."

His eyes were the hounds and she was the fox; his will was the hunter's gun, its muzzle bearing down on her.

The tune grew ragged and she began to flub notes.

She could hear his voice again—a wordless sound that prodded and pushed at her. Her fingers faltered on the whistle's finger holes. The tune came tumbling to a halt.

Her gaze locked on Felix, lying almost at her feet, still curled up in a fetal position. Clare was lying like a dead fish a little farther away. Vaguely, in the back of her mind, she could hear Kempy whimpering, but she had no idea as to where the border collie had hidden himself.

She still couldn't hear what Madden was saying, but the tone of his voice was slowly turning her face towards him, his eyes drawing her gaze to them like a shark snagged on a mackerel-baited hook and hauled towards the sharking boat.

The mouthpiece of the whistle was still at her lips, but she couldn't seem to draw the breath needed to blow it awake again. Her throat was dry, raspy as sandpaper.

She could run. Off across the moor, into the darkness. He'd never catch her because she had to be faster on her feet than he could ever be, and fear would fuel her.

But Felix—and Clare—she couldn't leave them.

She bowed her head and looked at the ground as her traitorous body turned completely around and faced Madden. She refused to look up.

Think, she told herself. What happened in the book?

So much of what had befallen in its storyline was happening to her now that there had to be a clue in it. But the Small's voice was silent.

Salt, she thought. They'd used salt.

But she didn't have any, and whatever paranormal powers Madden had, she doubted very much that salt would do anything to stop them.

Her head was slowly lifting.

Tears, she remembered then. The music had been called up and the witch's own tears killed her. But that was back to salt again and she wasn't sharing Madden's memories. Neither could she call up the music. That needed calm, a relaxed mind. A twinning of her heartbeat to the music's ancient rhythm—

Dhumm-dum. Dhumm-dum.

—only her heart was jackhammering the blood through her veins. Quick tempo. No old slow dance tune this, but some mad Eurobeat rhythm.

Slow down, she told herself.

She forced her foot to tap on the packed earth around the Men-an-Tol.

Pat-pat. Pat-pat.

That was almost the beat. A simple rhythm—deceptively simple, because now that she was starting to get it, she couldn't understand how she might ever have forgotten it. Was it the Small from the Dunthorn book or Peter Goninan who had said . . . something about . . .

The magics of the world are far simpler than we make them out to be.

She could hear the voice in her head. And with it, a hint of music. *That* music. Thrumming to its hoofbeat rhythm.

Dhumm-dum. Dhumm-dum.

It put a brake to the jackhammering of her heart, slowing her pulse until it was beginning to twin the music's own stately rhythm. But it came far too late.

Her head had been lifting higher all the time until she was looking at Madden's chin, the thin frown of his lips, the hawk's nose. . . . Every detail, every tiny hair, every pore of his skin, stood out in sharp clarity—never mind the darkness. She could almost see below the skin, to the blood moving through his veins and arteries below it, the pull of his muscles as his jaw worked, the fiery webwork of his nerves. . . .

The heartbeat rhythm of the first music steadied inside her. The strains of its melody were whispering in the distance. It lay just over that gentle sweep of land on the Men-an-Tol's moor. Just around that corner of her mind. Coming from the deep well of magic that was the Barrow World, into this Iron World where its enchantment was almost forgotten.

She tried to shut her eyes, to let the magic fill her, but her lids wouldn't close. It was as though they'd been locked open.

And then Madden's gaze connected with her own and her head filled with a babble of voices that drowned out the music.

Tell me, tell me, tell me. . . .

What have you done. . . .

Tell me. . . .

Give me the secret. . . .

TELL ME.

Madden's voice ringing in her head multiplied a hundredfold

into a deafening jabber. Amplified and ringing. Drilling through her mind. Pulling her into him.

Tell me, tell me. . . .

She tried to fight him, but it was like trying to stem a storm on the bay with a sieve. The waves of his voice lashed against her mind with a gale force—raging, demanding. Allowing her not a moment's respite.

She dropped to her knees, never feeling the jarring impact with the ground. Her head tilted up, gaze still trapped, still locked on his. The music was lost now, somewhere under the roar of his thundering voice as it stormed through her. And with it hope.

All that remained of herself was a tiny core of being, crouched in a corner of her mind. Hidden, as Madden's will smashed through her feeble defenses. Buried in those few memories that Madden had not yet overturned in his raging search, secreted away as Dunthorn's riddle had been hidden from him for all those years. But not for long.

She knew it couldn't last.

So she let herself go. Let herself fall into him, as the heroine of the Dunthorn book had let herself become a part of the witch that was tormenting her. And found . . .

Not his life, laid out before her in all its layers of memory as the witch's had been for Jodi, but the world as Madden perceived it through his heightened senses. She became a part of how he connected to the ancient heartbeat of the land, and saw how the webwork of the land's secrets and mysteries shaped a pattern, even in its apparent confusion; how it created a harmony despite its differences—*because* of the differences.

Floating there, a disembodied spirit trapped in another's mind, she finally understood what Peter Goninan had meant about the discrepancy between being asleep and awake. If this . . . if this was how it felt to *almost* be awake . . . a wide-awake equivalent of that moment that lies between sleep and waking when anything was possible. . . .

What more can you want? she asked her captor.

The secret, Madden demanded. *Dunthorn's secret.*

But you already have it, she said.

For she saw what he did not, that for all his manipulations and self-interest, he was ignoring the real truth to this mysterious patterning that underlay the world. It was the sheet music to the first music, there to be read for any who could perceive it.

Listen, she said.

To what?

It was unbelievable, Janey thought. Madden was tuned in to the existence of the hidden meaning that resonated to the first music, had been for years, but he couldn't hear it. He took bits and pieces and used them to override other people's wills, to give himself power, but he never once saw it for what it was, never guessed, never heard—

The music.

So she called it up.

Dhumm-dum. Dhumm-dum.

The deep bass rhythm boomed like ancient thunder on the first day of the world. Harp strings plucked an ethereal counterpoint against a skirling wash of fiddles and flutes and whistles. And there, taking the melody and imbuing it with a power that Janey could never have duplicated, was a set of pipes; drones, deep and rumbling, like the speech of mountains, stone grinding against stone, rock faces speaking from the sides of time-rounded hills; the chanter wailing like all the winds of the world blown through its bore with perfect control—the melody both bitter and sweet, quick tempo and slow air, all music distilled into one flawless sound.

She had no fear of giving the first music to Madden for she knew that no matter how he might have manipulated the bits and pieces of it that he'd borrowed or stolen over the years, it was impossible for any one being to control. It required the joint accord of every being, of every single part of the world.

Perhaps of worlds.

Like the world that lay through the hole in the Men-an-Tol.

Loosing the music inside Madden was like waking magic in

the Barrow World. The music ran wildly through him. The more he fought it, the stronger it grew, unbalancing him.

But Janey, by letting it simply flow through her, by accepting it, and, rather than attempting to control it, by merely welcoming it, she shivered with the gift of its beauty.

At first she floated there in Madden's mind and remained unaffected by the storm that he fought. But after a time, she visualized herself in her own body and went walking through the dark corridors of shifting shadows that was Madden's mind. In the rooms that led off from the corridors—which were pockets of memory or thought, she realized—she came upon knots and dark, twisting patterns that she loosened and set free.

In one such pocket, she found Kempy's spirit. The border collie was trapped in a dream. Men surrounded him and whenever he tried to move, to break free of their circle, the men's booted feet would lash out at him, driving him back into the center again.

Janey slipped in between the ghost figures of the men and lifted the dog in her arms. When she turned to leave the circle, the men had vanished and there was only the moor surrounding them. She set Kempy down.

"Go on," she said.

But the dog merely pushed his head against her leg and followed her as she went on down the corridor.

And found Clare.

Her friend lay in an absolutely featureless place, sprawled on the floor, limbs splayed out around her. She looked as though she were dead. But her gaze tracked Janey's movement as Janey stepped closer and then crouched down by her head. Janey stroked Clare's head, brushing the hair from her brow.

"What's the matter, Clare?" she asked.

"I—I can't move. Not just my . . . legs. But nothing. Only—only my head. . . ."

The ancient wisdom of the first music still sang through Madden's mind, still filled Janey.

"It's not true," she said. "Madden's just making you think it is."

Clare blinked back tears. "I can't *move!*"

Janey continued to stroke Clare's hair, her touch tender.

"Listen," she said. "Listen to the music."

"I can't. . . ."

"Listen," Janey repeated, softly but insistently.

Then, as Clare finally heard the ancient strains, Janey helped her friend to her feet. Clare wasn't even aware of what she was doing until she was standing beside Janey.

Clare moved her hands in front of her eyes, touched her upper arms, hugged herself.

"I . . ."

But words failed her.

Janey smiled at her and put an arm around her shoulder for support.

"Come on," she said. "We've still got to find Felix."

They came upon him, sitting alone on a vast stage, an enormous audience jeering at him and throwing beer cans and rotting fruit at where he huddled on his chair, arms wrapped around his accordion. Kempy growled at the audience as the three of them picked their way through the litter on the stage, but that only made the audience laugh more.

Janey handed Clare her whistle.

"Play a tune," she said. "Something simple. Something old."

Clare looked at the audience, her eyes blinded by the spotlight. Her gaze turned back to Felix and in that moment Janey saw Clare's love for him reflected. A deep, hopeless love.

"But . . ." Clare began.

The first music stirred its wisdom inside Janey.

"I'm sorry," she said. "I never knew. But he loves you, too, Clare. Not in the same way, but . . ."

Even the first music's wisdom failed here.

Clare blinked back tears and nodded slowly. "I know."

She brought the whistle to her lips and began "The Trip to Sligo," a jig that was one of Felix's favorites. Its bouncing rhythm was almost lost as the audience ridiculed her. Clare faltered on the tune. The whistle, with its faulty upper register, didn't make it any easier. But Janey nodded encouragingly to Clare as she bent down beside Felix.

So Clare played on.

The tune changed on her as she kept at it. Her playing grew more assured as the first music took hold of her instrument and sang through it.

Janey pressed her lips close to Felix's ears and began to murmur soothingly. She pried his hands away from his instrument, took them in her own. She told him what strong hands they were, how she loved their gentleness when he touched her. He was better than the whole audience combined, she said, and reminded him that the music was important for how he wanted to play it, not how others wanted to hear it. She assured him she didn't care if he never played on even the smallest stage, just so they could be together. Just so that they couldn't lose what they'd so recently regained.

"Listen," she said. "Listen to Clare play."

She laid her arm around his shoulder and pulled him in close to her. He trembled—a feverish shiver that ran through his entire body.

"J-Janey . . . ?" he murmured.

"I'm here."

"They . . . they . . . I can't. . . ."

"This is all a lie," she said. "There's no stage. No audience. It's just Madden."

As she spoke the sound of the audience was finally overwhelmed by the music. Clare stood straight and tall, her fingers dancing on the small whistle. Janey had never heard the instrument sound so good. She'd never heard Clare play so well. She took her arm from around Felix's shoulder. Picking up his accordion, she took it from his lap and set it down on the floor. Then she tucked her hand in the crook of his arm and gave him a gentle tug.

"Come on," she said. "We're going to leave this place."

Felix finally lifted his head.

"*Why* does this happen to me?" he asked.

"I don't know, Felix. It doesn't matter. This isn't real."

He shook his head. "It's just as real as what . . . as what happens to me anytime I get on a stage."

"But this time it's just Madden's doing. Let's go, Felix. These people don't matter."

She nodded towards the audience who sat utterly silent now— so still that in the darkness beyond the spotlight they might just as well not have existed at all.

"I could play that music," Felix said. "Any other place. On ship, at a session, on a bloody street corner. . . . Why can't I play it *here*?"

"I don't know," Janey said. "It really doesn't matter."

"It does matter," Felix said.

He disengaged his arm from her grip and picked up his box.

Janey started to protest, to tell him he shouldn't try again, but she stopped herself. She knew he could do it. There was just something inside him that blocked him. Trying again now might make things worse, but she knew she couldn't stop him from the attempt. Maybe the first music would help him. Maybe nothing would change. It seemed an awful lot to expect that a lifetime's fear could be dissolved in just a few moments like this. Whatever the root of his problem was, it had to be far more complex than what a few bars of music could cure.

But then she remembered: *The magics of the world are far simpler than we make them out to be.*

"I love you, Felix," she said as he strapped on his box.

She stepped back from his chair. He lifted his head, stared into the spotlight's glare, trying to look past it to the darkness beyond. He's trying to focus on just one person, Janey realized. Trying to convince himself that he was playing just for that one person, that there's no one else out there.

She'd done the same thing herself when she first got stage jitters at the beginning of her career.

He put his left hand through the wrist strap near the accompaniment buttons, rested his left hand lightly on the fingerboard. Thumbing down the air release button, he stretched out the bellows.

Oh, do it, Janey wished.

But he couldn't play. Sweat broke out on his already glistening face. His hands started to shake. He tried to play along with Clare, but the notes came out in a discordant jumble. They were all wrong.

Janey couldn't bear to watch it happen to him again.

Before the audience could react, before he froze up completely once more, she stepped in behind his chair and pressed her chest in close to its rungs. She put her arms around him.

"Listen," she breathed in his ear. "To the music. To what Clare's playing."

"I . . ."

"Don't try to play. Just listen. Let the music fill you. Close your eyes. You're not here. You're not anywhere. There's just the music. Feel the rhythm—it's the same as your heartbeat. The tune's as simple as breathing."

She stroked his temples.

"Who cares about who's listening?" she said. "It's the music that's important. And this music . . ."

"This . . . music . . ." he repeated slowly.

"It's magic."

Haltingly, he worked the bellows and played a simple two-note chord with his right hand on the melody buttons. Incomplete as it was, it didn't matter if the tune Clare was playing was in a minor or a major key. The partial chord fit.

"That's it," Janey encouraged him as he drew the chord out, shifted to another as the tune required it.

He fumbled the next chord change, but caught it quickly.

"Magic," Janey whispered.

"Magic," he said, repeating the word as though it were a talisman.

The next change went more smoothly. As did the next. He added some accompanying notes to fill in the space between the chords. Janey could feel the tension in his shoulders. His muscles were locked tight as braided wire. She kneaded them, feeling them loosen as much from her ministrations as from his growing confidence.

He was playing along with the melody now—tentatively, catching two notes in three the way one might play at a session when the tune was unfamiliar and you were learning it as you went along with the rest of the musicians, letting them carry the bulk of the melody while you were still picking it up.

Felix straightened in his chair. His box began to bounce on his knee as he tapped his foot. The notes came more quickly, the music changing, catching up both accordion and whistle and pulling them along into the brisk 4/4 measures of a high lilting tune.

Janey recognized the tune, and smiled. It was "Miss McLeod's Reel," but both she and Felix knew it as "The May Day." A spring tune, to call in the summer, like the old "Hal-an-Tow" song. A promise of new beginnings. Of the wheel turning, the cycle of the year beginning anew.

And the first music was a part of it—as it was a part of all tunes. It sang a counterpointing harmony of wonders and wisdoms . . . and magic.

Of hope found.

Music was immortal—but it needed the players to keep it alive. Just as the world itself needed those who walked it to keep its heartbeat singing.

Someone whistled in the audience. A few people near the front began to clap along. By the time the three-part reel came 'round to the first part again, the whole audience was clapping in time to its infectious rhythm.

When the tune ended, they broke into a thunderous applause. The spotlight dimmed. Janey looked out over Felix's shoulder to see the thousands of cheerful faces and she hugged Felix proudly.

"I . . ." he began.

"You did it," Janey said.

He set the accordion down and turned to grin at her. He got up from his chair and lifted her to her feet to return her hug. Behind him, the applause was dying down.

No, Janey realized, it was fading. As was the stage. There was just her and Felix here now. Clare stood nearby, the Eagle whistle in her hand, Kempy sitting at her feet. She felt Felix's body grow insubstantial in her arms. Clare and Kempy fading. Felix fading. And she was—

She opened her eyes to find herself kneeling in the dirt by the Men-an-Tol. The silence, after the constant presence of the first music inside her, after the thunderous applause in the concert hall, seemed almost deafening. She lifted a hand, touched her shoulder, ran the hand down her arm.

Had any of it been real?

But then she saw John Madden, hunched on his knees by the tolmen, face pressed against the stone, one hand reaching through its hole and dangling limply out the other end. She turned to find Felix sitting up, staring around himself in confusion. And Clare—Clare was now holding the tin whistle that Janey had had in her own hand before Madden took her into his mind.

Impossible as it seemed, it had to have been real.

"What—what happened?" Clare said. "I was having the most horrible dream, but then it turned . . . all golden. . . ."

"We won," Janey said.

She collected her purse from where it lay in the dirt in front of her and got to her feet.

"We hid the book so it can't ever be found," she went on, "and though Madden tried to use his mind powers on us, they didn't take hold. We proved we're stronger than him."

Except there was still her canceled tour. And the Boyds' farm. And—

No, she told herself. Don't think about any of that right now.

Hang on to the victory and face the rest of it when it comes.

Clare and Felix were looking at Madden, but the man never stirred from beside the stone.

"Is he . . . dead?" Clare asked.

"I don't know," Janey said.

She gave Kempy a pat as he came out of the nearby gorse where he'd been hiding and pressed his face anxiously against her leg.

"And I really don't care," she added.

"But we can't just leave him here. . . ."

"Why not?" Felix said. "We don't owe him anything."

He was remembering what Madden had done to him, Janey thought.

She moved closer to Clare and took her arm.

"Let's just go home," she said.

"We really did beat him, didn't we?" Clare said as she let herself be led away.

"We beat him," Janey said.

"Together," Felix added.

Janey nodded. "Together," she agreed. "The three of us—all right, four," she added as Kempy pushed against her leg again. "The four of us and the music."

"The music," Felix and Clare breathed in unison, remembering.

None of them spoke again as they followed the path back to where they had left Janey's car.

6.

Madden couldn't move. He leaned against the Men-an-Tol, face pressed against its rough surface, one arm still hanging through its hole. The world had closed in on him. He tried to shut off his mind, but the secret—

Dunthorn's secret that the Little woman had so casually handed over to him—

That damned music—

It fed back through his mind, overloading his mind's ability to process the information. He was aware of everything. Every sound, scent, sight, taste, emotion that existed in the world and beyond it was flooding into his mind.

He could no more control the vast torrent of input than a man could cease to breathe and still live.

He was aware of it *all*.

From molten rock flowing deep under the earth's crust to a whisper of conversation halfway around the world.

From the sugar-heavy cereal that some snotty-nosed child was consuming in a suburb of Chicago to the fall of a tree in a Brazilian rain forest.

From a deep-space panorama of uncharted stars, far beyond the scope of earth's most powerful telescope, to a bug crawling along a water-logged wooden post on a Cambodian riverbank.

From a high Himalayan wind to the brain-dead mind of a drunken man lying in a Melbourne alley.

It was the detail, the vast wealth of unfocused detail, flooding him.

From the lumbering tread of a Kenyan elephant to the whine of a mosquito in a Florida everglade.

From a marital dispute in one of the stately houses near his home in Victoria to the ear-piercing shriek of a heavy metal band in a small London club.

From the vast sweep of the empty silent spaces between the stars to—

He caught that tiny fragment of input and held to it.

Be calm, he told himself. Be calm. Still your mind. Hold that silence.

He wanted to scream.

Hold the silence. Let it spread. Here and here, and over there. . . .

Slowly he regained control of his ability to focus and channel external stimuli. When he could finally rise, he looked out across the moor and almost laughed.

He had been a fool.

It was true. Dunthorn had unlocked a gateway to unlimited power, but of what use was it when it couldn't be controlled? When all one could do was apportion small parts of it to one's needs—as he had been doing all along?

But the Little woman—why hadn't *she* been affected? How had *she,* untutored as she was, learned to deal so easily with it?

There had to be more to it than what he had taken from her mind: a book in which each person created their own story; a gateway through the hole in the tolmen to another world; tiny people the size of mice. . . .

These were fairy tales.

But if they were real? Dunthorn had to have had some reason to let himself die before allowing his book to fall into Madden's hands. And this Janey Little . . .

He knew he had to leave that puzzle for another day. Tonight he could barely keep his balance leaning on the tolmen. Tonight it was enough that he had survived to learn the lesson.

But the waste. All those years, searching for Dunthorn's secret, following his own arcane paths, only to find that what he sought couldn't be had. To find that it was merely the harmonic vibration to which every element of the universe vibrated.

Such a simple skein of knowledge. A high school student knew as much. That student couldn't control it any more than Madden himself could, but at least he *knew.*

Madden shook his head.

The waste.

He was too old now to begin anew. And with Michael turned against him, he no longer even had an heir to whom he might leave the heritage of this knowledge that he had so painfully acquired tonight.

And the real irony was that by forcing his hand as he had, he was now left in a position where he was unable to even utilize those strengths that he had gained on his own. He couldn't open his mind, couldn't let down his defenses for a moment, without having the flood of the world come rushing back in. He had to fare deaf, dumb, and blind through the world, along with all the other sheep.

He thrust his hands deep into his pockets and slowly made his way back along the path that led from the Men-an-Tol to the lane where he'd left his car.

He had to find a way to regain what he had lost. The Little woman would be of no help. Dunthorn was dead. But there was Peter Goninan. He seemed, from what he'd taken from Janey Little's mind, to know far more than Madden had ever supposed he did. Like Little's grandfather, Madden had never even realized that Goninan and Dunthorn had been such close friends.

He would speak to Goninan. But without his power to *make* Goninan tell him what he needed, he would be reduced to accepting only those tidbits that Goninan deigned to hand him. . . .

Madden sighed.

The simple truth was, he could plan and scheme all he wanted, but it changed nothing. He had opened a door that must not be opened—not as *he* had opened it—and like all the other feckless meddlers in the history of those who studied the hermetic secrets, now he, too, had to pay the price.

The devil would be getting his due.

Madden didn't believe in either a benevolent deity, or his evil opposite.

But he believed in Hell.

Hell was knowing that he would be spending the remainder of his life as much a sheep as the rest of those who inhabited this sorry world.

No, it was worse than that. They slept, never knowing that they slept.

But he knew. He had been awake, and now must sleep.

It was that or go mad.

7 ·

Ted Grimes straightened up by the hedgerow where he was standing when he heard the voices coming down the lane. He marked them—three voices and not one belonged to his quarry. Unless Madden was keeping silent, he wasn't with them.

But there was a dog.

Invisibility was another hunter's trick Grimes knew well. It was easy with people and most animals. You just stayed still. You never looked at them—some sixth sense warned them when they were being watched. You just melted into the background and *belonged* there.

He wasn't so sure how that was going to go over with the dog. But at least the wind was blowing from their direction. If he didn't move, didn't look at them . . .

"I still don't think we should have just left him there," a woman was saying.

"Would you want to touch him?" another woman's voice asked.

"Not likely."

Grimes almost gave himself away. They were talking about Madden. If something had happened to Madden, if they'd taken away his revenge, he'd hunt them down one by one. . . .

Standing out here in the dark as long as he had, his night vision was about as perfect as it was going to get. There was enough moonlight that he could easily make them out now, studying them from the corner of his eye. Indirectly. Not making waves. Not even breathing.

There was a woman with a cane, being supported by a shorter woman. The man was big—a broad-shouldered, hefty sucker. And the dog. . . .

The dog never even looked in his direction.

Stupid mutt.

"I feel like letting the air out of his tires," the man said.

"Why bother?" the shorter woman said. "We've already let the air out of *him.*"

"What really happened, Janey?" the woman with the cane asked.

Yeah, Grimes thought. What happened?

But Janey's reply was muffled by the opening of the car door.

They all got into the little three-wheeled job, including the dog. The car's muffler coughed twice, then the engine caught and the quiet moor was suddenly awash with the intrusive rumble of its motor. Grimes closed his eyes when the headbeams came on, not wanting to lose his night sight.

He tracked them with his ears, listening to them head back down the lane towards the road. When they paused halfway there, he looked down the road after them to see that they were only letting the dog out at that farmhouse he'd passed earlier. They pulled away again, going on until they were out of sight, though he could still hear the car's engine as they drove on down to the road.

When they reached the end of the lane and turned onto the road, Grimes looked back up the way they'd come from the moor.

I'll give you ten more minutes, Madden, he thought. And then I'm coming to look for you.

He didn't bother worrying about what he'd just heard, didn't think at all. Madden would come, or he'd go find him. It was that simple. He just let himself sink back into the invisibility of the night.

Ten minutes hadn't quite gone by when he heard footsteps coming from the direction of the stile that led onto the moor.

He was careful now, far more careful than he'd been when the other three had been approaching.

His missing hand ached, reminding him of just how much Madden was capable. One look in that sucker's hoodoo eyes, even in the dark, and it was game over. No way Grimes was letting that happen to him again.

He gave Madden all the time he needed to make his slow way down the path, not moving until he was opening his car door.

And then Grimes drifted across the space between them like a ghost—swift and silent. He had his right arm around Madden's neck, the prosthetic digging into the old man's flesh, and slammed him up against the side of the car before Madden could have possibly guessed he was there. His left hand rose and brought the muzzle of his .38 up to Madden's temple.

"Hello, John," he said. "Remember me?"

He felt Madden stiffen.

"You . . . you're Sandoe's man."

"Yeah, and whoever you sent after him took care of old Phil just fine. I appreciated not having to pay back my advance for screwing up. But I didn't"— he shoved the prosthetic harder against Madden's skin—"appreciate *this.*"

"What do you want?"

His coolness enraged Grimes and it took all his willpower to not just pull the trigger right then and there.

"I know you like games, John—like the one where you made me cut off my own hand. Well, I've got a game for you now that goes by the name of Russian roulette. Feel like playing?"

"It doesn't matter."

What the hell did he mean, it doesn't matter? Did the sucker think he had some ace up his sleeve? Did Madden think he was going to turn him around and let him have a chance to use those hoodoo eyes of his? Maybe Madden figured he was going to just hand the gun over and let Madden pull the trigger himself.

Hang loose, Grimes told himself. You've got the advantage. He's just trying to spook you.

And doing a damn good job of it, too.

"This gun's got six chambers," Grimes went on, his voice only slightly betraying his nervousness, "but only one of them's got a bullet in it. I gave her a little spin after I loaded her up earlier tonight, so even I don't know which one it's in."

"Fine."

"You just might be dying right here," Grimes said.

Come on, he thought. Give me a reaction.

"It doesn't matter," Madden said again.

Screw this, Grimes thought.

He pulled the trigger. Madden bucked in his arms. The bullet made a small hole in the old man's left temple and took out most of the right one on its way out.

Grimes stepped back and let the body fall. Then he fired again, emptying the gun into Madden's body.

"About that one bullet," he said to the corpse, "I lied."

He stared down at the corpse and heard only a whispering echo of the old man's voice.

It doesn't matter.

He's dead, Grimes told himself. You said you'd get him for what he'd done and you kept your word.

But he didn't feel anything.

It doesn't matter.

Only an empty feeling inside.

Two years of waiting for this day, of imagining how it was going to go, coming up with a hundred different scenarios until Bett finally got in touch with him and told him to be patient, he'd deliver Madden to him, no problem. So he'd been patient. Waiting for Bett to come through.

And Bett had come through.

It doesn't matter.

And now here he was. The sucker was dead and all he felt was zip. Nada.

There had to be more.

He wiped down the gun and stuck it in Madden's hand.

Suicide, he thought with a smile. Maybe the local yokels will actually believe it, too.

He straightened up, still waiting for that sense of accomplishment to hit him, but the emptiness just sat there inside him.

It doesn't matter.

It was like the sucker had wanted to die. Like he hadn't cared. . . .

It doesn't matter.

Grimes's missing hand still ached. There was no relief of the burning need inside him.

Bastard won, he thought as he trudged off down the lane towards his own car.

I kill him and he still comes up on top.

It doesn't matter.

Because he'd wanted to die.

Grimes paused to look back, his prosthetic hand held against his chest, its ache deepening.

Go figure it, he thought.

He continued on down the lane.

The Touchstone

A church is a stone tooth in the jawbone of the ground. That's why the cold bites. The toothache of antiquity, the twinges of time. A church gets you ready for your coffin.

—I A N   W A T S O N ,
from "The Mole Field,"
*The Magazine of Fantasy and
Science Fiction*, December 1988

S o m e h o w Jodi wasn't surprised at how quickly the memory of the Widow's magics faded from her friends' minds. She'd already had some forewarning with the fisherman down at the waterfront the night of the storm and while it took longer for Denzil and the others to forget, in the end it was less than a week, all told, before their memories were gone as well.

That Denzil put it so easily from his mind was the least surprising. His thoughts worked along such logical byways that any twisty path that might lead to something out of the ordinary was immediately suspect. She had expected more from Taupin, but he was less inclined to whimsy now than he had been before the whole affair began. And while she didn't know Lizzie well enough to form much of an opinion as to how she might react, Jodi was amazed that Henkie Whale—who, after all, kept the body of his dead friend somewhere in the catacombs under his warehouse and was known to talk to that corpse—should also be able to forget so easily.

The Tatters children still talked about it—but they spoke of it as though it were a story that they had heard, not as something that had happened to them personally. Only Ratty Friggens—whom the Widow's button charm had called back from the air itself, rather than from a longstone like the others—still seemed affected by his ordeal, but he wouldn't speak of it. When he was about at all, it was with a haunted look in his eyes; mostly he kept to himself.

As time passed, Jodi found it increasingly difficult to remember it all herself. Details kept shifting in her mind, fading out, getting tangled up with bits of fairy tales that she'd heard as a child, until there were times when she doubted much of it herself.

For even the music had left her. She remembered the *fact* of it; she just couldn't call it back up. When she listened to her heartbeat, all she heard was the *thump-thump* in her chest. There was no answering rhythm, no twinning of her pulse with that ancient rhythm.

She didn't see much of Taupin in those days. His wanderings took him farther afield from Bodbury than usual—and for longer periods of time. Neither Henkie nor Lizzie seemed to do more than vaguely recognize her when she passed one of them on the streets, and the Tatters children were strangely quiet around her. Denzil, when she tried talking about it with him, had less patience than ever for what he termed "Complete and utter nonsense. If you keep filling up your head with such tomfoolery, soon you won't have a speck of room left for common sense, you."

Jodi took to wandering the streets of Bodbury at all hours of the day and night, searching for something that grew more vague in her mind with every passing day. She often found herself standing outside the Widow Pender's cottage that was boarded up and presented the only mystery that the people of Bodbury had the inclination to gossip about.

Where had she gone? What had become of her?

They had a hundred theories, each more preposterous than the next, but not one came close to what had actually taken place.

Only Jodi knew, but no one wanted to listen to her.

So she would stand there in front of the cottage, remembering her and Edern's descent from the windowsill and their mad ride through the town, dangling from Ansum's collar. She no longer worried about what had been real, and what not. She just appreciated the memories she still had, for day by day they became less defined, so vague that at times she felt like one of the Tatters children, remembering a story rather than something that had actually happened to her.

The boarded-up windows of the cottage depressed her—they reminded her too much of the boarded-up minds of her friends and the way her own mind was being boarded up. It was as though she'd spent her whole life half asleep and had woken for just a moment before drifting off again, her memories fading like dreams in the morning light.

The Widow's cottage was the best place to bring those memories all clearly to mind again—or at least as clearly as she could recall them. She would stand there, remembering and thinking. Of being a Small. Of Edern and the Barrow World and the first music. Of the Widow and how the poor choices she had made had created such a ruin of her life.

Jodi would always turn away then, feeling sorry for the Widow and pretending that she didn't hear a whispering in the shadows along the garden hedge and close in to the walls of the deserted cottage itself. She would see the Widow's ruined features, the innocent child that the old woman had been superimposed on her features for just a moment before she died, and tears would well in Jodi's eyes.

She wondered sometimes how she could be so sympathetic toward someone as evil as the Widow had been, and yet have so little patience for her own friends. She knew it wasn't their fault that they forgot. It was this world that they lived in that made magic fade and logic rise to the fore; just as logic was absent from the Barrow World. But she couldn't help but be angry with them.

It wasn't as though they hadn't *seen* the magic with their own eyes. It wasn't as though they hadn't been enchanted themselves. . . .

One day, after a particularly frustrating morning spent arguing with Denzil, she found herself walking up Mabe Hill to where the ruins of Creak-a-vose lay in a jumble of stone under the afternoon sky. The Widow's clothes were no longer where she'd dropped them after taking the mantle with its the buttons that she'd needed that night; someone had stuffed them—dress, stockings, and all—into the hedgerow where they were now grey with dust. She stood and looked at them for a long moment, then went into the old ruined church and sat down on a fallen pillar.

She felt depressed. She'd been moping about for days now and she knew the real reason. It wasn't anything to do with how everyone else was forgetting the magic, nor even how she herself was losing her own memories of it, thread by tattered thread.

It was the promise she'd made to Edern Gee about the first music—about keeping it alive in this world so that both it and the Barrow World would grow closer together again.

She'd defeated the Widow, rescued both herself and her friends, but the most important thing was still undone. In the great scheme of things, in her memories of the music that she could still recall, she remembered what was lost with the music. Not just magic, or wonder, or mystery. But the perfect symmetry of the land itself that was slowly unraveling as the worlds drew further and further apart. If she closed her eyes, she could remember the feeling—

Species extinct.

Hopes extinguished.

Heartlands ravaged.

Waste and barren lands lying both in the world and in the hearts of its inhabitants.

—but she could no longer *feel* it.

Edern would just have to find someone else, she thought. He'd have to go into somebody else's dreams.

But what if he couldn't? What if she'd been his last chance?

Thinking that just made her feel worse.

I'm where I should be, she thought. In a ruined church with a barrow underneath it. A forsaken place of worship built up on the bones of those long dead. A place where hopes die.

She sank lower and lower into her depression. She looked around herself and everything had a dull pallor about it, as though someone had draped the gauze of a corpse shroud over her head and she was only able to see through its dimming fabric. There was such an utter pointlessness to everything, she realized.

The first music? Better to call it the lost music: the forever lost music.

And what if she did find it again? Of what use would it be? Who would hear it—who would even remember it long enough for it to do any good? If she, caught up in its thundering measures as she had been in the Barrow World, living and breathing its rhythm and the power of its cadences . . . if she could forget *that*, if it had changed inside her from something she felt and *knew* to something she could only vaguely recall, the way she could remember the first time she met Denzil's menagerie, but not how she *felt* at that moment, then how could she expect anyone else to remember it? All she'd be able to call up would be some faint echo.

And what good could that possibly do?

She'd had the chance to do something important with her life—just like she'd always wanted. To do something that had real *meaning*. And she'd let it slip away.

Lost.

Like the music.

It was so frustrating, to remember but not *remember*. She could call up the logic of what she'd experienced, but not the emotion of it. It was like the proverbial word on the tip of one's tongue— so close, but it might as well be a thousand miles away.

If only . . .

She lifted her head, hearing a sound. Her heart lifted for a moment, thinking that the music had returned, but it wasn't that. Nor was it the wind. It was more a soft, snickering whisper of dark laughter coming from the shadows. . . .

She looked at those places where the shadows lay deepest.

"Go ahead," she told them. "You might as well laugh. After all, you've won. . . ."

Won, won, won. . . .

The echoes mocked her.

And then she stopped to think about what she had just said. The shadows had won. Won what?

It wasn't the shadows that were at fault here—as they had been with the Widow—but her own self. The shadows didn't mock her because they'd won, but because she'd simply given up.

The insight shivered through her.

She stood up from where she'd been sitting and walked out of the gloom inside the ruined church's walls to stand in the sunshine outside. The step she took, from shadow to light, was like a switch being thrown in her head. She looked around herself, *truly* looked around and wondered how she could have let herself sink into such a morbid mood.

No matter which way she turned, everything looked marvelous. The hedgerows, the moorland behind them, the rooftops of the town, the old ruins of Creak-a-vose . . . they all had a crystalline clarity about them that simply took her breath away. Why did men worship in churches, locking themselves away in the dark, when the world lay beyond its doors in all its real glory?

Bother and damn. The only pointlessness at work here was her own moping about. So what if Denzil and the others didn't remember anymore. She still did, didn't she? Not everything, but enough to keep it alive.

She couldn't change the world all at once. But she could change a bit of it—her bit, at least. It might not be much, but something was better than nothing.

It seemed so childishly simple. She could almost hear Edern's voice.

The magics of the world are far simpler than we make them out to be.

The music wasn't lost. How could it be lost when it was there inside her all the time? She hadn't discovered it in the Barrow World, she had *rediscovered* it.

"Thank you!" she called to the shadows that lay inside the ruins.

There was no response from them as she slipped through a hedge and headed off across the moor towards the Men-an-Tol, but then she probably wouldn't have heard it if there had been a response. Her heart was bubbling over, too full with the simple joy of being alive. She couldn't have begun to explain to anyone how it was that she could be so depressed one moment, and so alive in the next. She only knew, as she skipped through the yellow-flowering gorse, that she'd been walking through the past days like one deaf, dumb, and blind.

But she could finally hear again—the rustle of her trousers against the gorse, the skip of her step on the ground, the distant sound of a birdsong, the breath of the wind as it rattled dried ferns, one against the other; she could sing—wildly off-key, but full of enthusiasm as she made up her own words and her own melody to propel her along her way; and she could see—the rolling sea of yellow and green gorse, brown ferns and the dusty-rose blooms of the heather.

When she finally reached the tolmen, she was out of breath and giddy. She collapsed on the ground beside the holed stone, and lolled back against it to stare up at the sky where a kestrel was silhouetted against a dusting of white cloud, islanded in a surrounding ocean of blue.

"Hello, up there!" she called, waving up at the bird.

And didn't it seem to dip its wings—just for a moment there—in response, or was it only her imagination?

She didn't care. Wasn't that half of what life was all about—imagining possibilities and then following through on them? And what she was going to imagine—what she was going to *do*—was make the Men-an-Tol sing. Out here, on the moor. It would sing and never stop singing, and whoever came by would hear that music and take it away with them. The wind itself would carry it to other lands until one day the whole of the Iron World would hear and recall that music.

The first music.

She got up from where she was sitting and clambered up onto the stone, straddling it so that her stomach was pressed against it, her elbows in front, propping up her head, her legs dangling down either side. She lay very still then, quieting her mind—

Think of nothing. Don't think at all.

—trying to soak up the ancient stillness that was hidden deep in the stone below her, a stillness that was like—

an old dance

—focusing on her heartbeat, on its rhythm, on how the blood that moved through her twinned that—

hidden music

—until she was drifting in that state between sleep and wakefulness when all things are possible.

And then she heard it.

Dhumm-dum. Dhumm-dum.

A distant, far-off sound like a hoofbeat. Coming closer. And she was floating, floating away. . . .

Edern's features drifted up in her mind. He was in the Barrow World, a look of worry making him frown.

"What are you doing?" he asked.

"Dreaming," she said. "Dreaming magic."

Dhumm-dum. Dhumm-dum.

His worry deepened into alarm.

"You won't ever be the same again," he warned.

"I know. But the music will go on."

"The Barrow World will be closed to you as well—because of your Iron World blood."

"I know."

Dhumm-dum.

"I'll become the music," she added, "and I'll never let it fade again."

He shook his head. "That's too steep a price—"

"I won't die," Jodi interrupted him. "I'll go on forever."

"But changed," he said.

"But changed," she agreed.

"I didn't mean for you to do this."

Dhumm-dum.

"I chose to do this," Jodi told him.

"But—"

Dhumm-dum. Dhumm-dum.

The music was taking her away now. Parts of her dissolved to fuel it. It sang with her voice now—not the off-key voice with which she normally tried to sing songs, but with the pure, clear tones that lay inside her, echoing her heartbeat. She felt as though she were unraveling into the Men-an-Tol, becoming part of it. She followed the roots of its mystery as they spread away from the center of the hole in its stone, deep into the heartbeat of the land. The wind carried her across the moorland, through forest and over Bodbury to the sea.

"Good-bye, Edern," she said. "Remember me."

"How could I forget?" he asked as the crack between the worlds faded and he could see her no more.

But the music went on, echoing and echoing forever, through the Barrow World and beyond. And this time it raised no tempests. It soothed the land, bringing the gift of logic to his world just as it brought the gift of magic to hers.

Sustaining the Mystery, so that it echoed and echoed, on into forever.

2 .

Denzil couldn't concentrate that afternoon. He kept thinking of Jodi and the pointless argument that had sent her storming out of his loft earlier that day. The animals had been restless ever since she'd gone and that restlessness translated into a nagging feeling inside himself that he could no longer ignore.

Finally he set his work aside.

He'd been too harsh, he realized. She was still young and wasn't youth allowed its fancies? Who was he to rein in her sense of wonder? The world itself would do that to her all too soon on its own. And then she might discover that there was a different kind of wonder in the world—not magic like in fairy tales, but a magic all the same. For what were the wonders of nature, but a magic?

But she had to come to that realization herself. And until she did, what sort of a friend was he proving to be by constantly pointing out the errors of her thinking? There came a point when helpfulness merely became a kind of fussing criticism that would do neither of them any good.

"Come along then, you," he told Ollie as he put on his coat and hat.

The monkey jumped from the back of the chair where he had been mournfully plucking at a bit of loose stuffing and crawled in under Denzil's jacket.

"We'll see if we can't find her," he added.

But once he was on the street below, he was at a loss as to where to begin. That odd nagging sensation returned, but this time it was a feeling of his having done this all before.

There was a dream he'd had—one he should never have shared with Jodi because all she did now was talk was of it—of when the Widow Pender had turned her into a Small and how they'd all gone to the old tolmen out on the moorland behind the town. . . .

The certainty came to him then that that was where she had gone.

Grumbling a little to himself, he set off up Mabe Hill. When he reached the moors beyond the old ruins of Creak-a-vose, Ollie grew increasingly restless where he was tucked away under Denzil's jacket.

"Stop your fussing, you," Denzil told him, but he was beginning to feel a little light-headed himself just then.

There was the sense of a storm approaching in the air, yet that was patently impossible for the sky was clear as could be except for a small desultory smear of ragged clouds to the west. Ollie pushed himself out from under Denzil's jacket and sat up on his shoulder, chattering urgently, tugging at Denzil's hair as though to make him hurry. There was a sound in the air, an odd sort of thrumming like a drum playing a heartbeat tempo over a wash of wind that was almost like music.

And Denzil thought he could recognize a melody in it—it was one he remembered from when he was a boy, an old tune that his father used to sing. It had always been Denzil's favorite song. Today it filled him with foreboding.

He stepped up his pace, feeling that same urgency as Ollie obviously did—an insistent need to reach the Men-an-Tol as quickly as he could.

When he got there, he wished he'd never come.

Ollie shrieked and bounded from his shoulder to scamper across the last few yards separating them from the holed stone. He bounded up to the top of the stone and turned a mournful eye to Denzil.

"Oh, Jodi," Denzil said. "What have you done?"

Ollie plucked at the clothing that lay there on top of the stone, pushing his face against the all-too-familiar shirt and trousers that Jodi had been wearing when she'd stormed off earlier that day. Her jacket lay on the ground beside the stone. One shoe on either side of it. But of her there was no trace.

The monkey whimpered, holding out the shirt to Denzil, but he was frozen where he stood, listening to the music.

Remembering.

A mad time: a night, a day, and then another night—of magic. Of Smalls and reanimated corpses. Of witches and stone.

Especially stone.

A longstone.

He had *been* a longstone, enchanted by the Widow. . . .

"Oh, Jodi," he said again, his voice a bare mumble.

The unearthly music sang all around him now and he swayed in time to its rhythm, tears blurring his sight. He could hear Jodi in that music, knew that she'd sacrificed herself to wake it.

It's got to be heard, she'd tried to explain to him more than once in the past week or so. *Without the music, both worlds are doomed.*

He'd told her that was nonsense. There was no Barrow World.

Can't you remember anything *about what happened?* she had shouted. *How can you be so blind?*

"I'm not blind," he had replied. "I can see how the world is perfectly well, you."

All you see is the world the way a sleepwalker would, she had replied this morning in the latest installment of their ongoing argument.

And then she'd stormed out, leaving only the echo of her words behind.

The way a sleepwalker would.

The tears streamed down his cheeks. He didn't know how she had done it, but she had *become* the music. To prove it was real. To him. To all the rest of the sleepwalkers. . . .

A hand fell on his shoulder, but he never started. He only turned slowly to find Taupin standing beside him.

"She . . . she's gone," Denzil said. "Into the music."

Taupin's eyes were shiny as well. He nodded slowly.

"I know," he said. "I was . . . walking nearby . . . thinking. And then I heard it. And remembered. . . ."

"I was wrong," Denzil said. "I treated her poorly—without respect. But it seemed so mad, what she was saying. . . ."

"I treated her worse," Taupin said. "I always knew, but some-how . . . somehow I forgot. . . ."

"And now it's too late. She's gone."

Taupin laid his arm across Denzil's slumped shoulders.

"Into the music," he said softly.

His voice was filled with wonder, with sorrow.

Into the music, Denzil repeated to himself.

They stood and listened, arms around each other for comfort, as the sound washed over them. It reverberated in the marrow of their bones, sung high and sweet, heartbreakingly mournful, quick as a jig, slow as the saddest air. Their hearts swelled with its beauty, its mystery. With all it revealed, and all that it hid.

They couldn't move, couldn't speak. They could only hold on to each other and stare at the holed stone with its scattering of clothing that lay upon it.

They could only listen.

And then slowly the music faded, faded to a soft murmur that became the wind breathing through the hole in the Men-an-Tol. A wind that still held an echo of that music, but allowed them to move once more, to stir and sadly sigh.

Finally Denzil could lift a sleeve and wipe at the tears that spilled from his eyes. He looked at the stone where Ollie sat clutching Jodi's shirt. The monkey's thin little arms pulled the fabric close to his chest and rocked sadly back and forth. Denzil moved forward to collect the rest of Jodi's clothes from where they lay.

Then suddenly Ollie peered over the side of the Men-an-Tol that was hidden from Denzil's and Taupin's view. He tossed aside the shirt and jumped off the stone, landing on its far side with an excited chatter.

"Jodi . . . ?" Denzil asked.

His heart leapt as he rounded the stone, dropping when he saw no sign of her there. But Ollie had something in his hand. It looked like a little pink mouse that was squealing and flailing its limbs about. . . .

But a mouse never had limbs like that, Denzil thought. Nor a shock of blond hair. And now he could make out what the little creature was saying.

"Put me down. Put me *down!*"

He knelt down quickly and pried Ollie's paw open. A tiny nude Jodi Shepherd spilled out onto his palm. She immediately covered herself up with her hands. Denzil turned away, blushing, until Taupin shook the lint from a handkerchief that he pulled from one of his voluminous pockets and offered it to the diminutive Jodi. Denzil looked back at her, once she'd wrapped herself up in it.

"*Now* do you believe me?" she asked in her high piping voice.

Denzil nodded slowly. "What . . . what happened to you? I thought the Widow was dead."

"So you *do* remember."

"Ever since I heard the music," Denzil said.

"Well, the Widow is dead," she told him.

"Then how . . . ?"

"Did I get this way?" Jodi said. "I gave up part of myself to make the music live. All that's left of me now is a Small."

"But . . . that is, can you . . . ?"

She shook her head. "I can't change back. It's not like when the Widow shrank me down. She kept that other part of me in her cloak. But I've given it away."

"To the music," Taupin said.

Jodi smiled. "To the music," she agreed.

"But what will we *do* with you?" Denzil asked.

"Take me home, I hope. Otherwise I'll have a very long walk ahead of me."

Ollie put a paw tentatively out towards her and she gave it a playful whack.

"But don't you dare think of exhibiting me at some scientific meeting," she warned.

"Or worse," Taupin added with a grin, "a circus."

Jodi proved her new maturity by sticking her tongue out at him.

"We can't tell people," she said. "Not about me—just about the stone. Everyone should come and listen to the music in the stone."

"But your aunt," Denzil began.

"Oh, we can tell *some* people, of course," she allowed. "We'll just have to be careful as to who."

Denzil could only shake his head.

"Just think how much I can help you with your experiments now," Jodi said. "Or I can go traveling about in Taupin's pocket. There's hundreds of things I can do."

"You're daft, you," Denzil said as they set off back across the moor towards Bodbury. "How could you do such a thing to yourself?"

"Listen," Jodi said, pointing back towards the stone.

Denzil and Taupin paused and turned back, doing as she'd asked. They found that they could still hear the wind in the stone. And borne on it was an echo of the first music—just a whisper, it was true, just a hint, but enough. Enough for the wind to carry, away across the moor and perhaps, in time, across the world.

"Don't you think that's worth it?" Jodi asked.

Both Denzil and Taupin nodded.

"Just don't let them build a church around it or something," Jodi said. "It needs to be free to work its magic."

Some Say the Devil

Is Dead

Gods that are dead are simply those that no longer
speak to the science or the moral order of the day...
every god that is dead can be conjured again to life.

—JOSEPH CAMPBELL,
from *The Way of the Animal Powers*

Charlie Boyd cradled the receiver and turned to his son.

"That was himself," he said.

"The same man that rang us up at the farm this afternoon?" Dinny asked.

Charlie nodded. "Considering what he had to say to me, I wouldn't soon forget that voice."

"What did he say?"

Charlie told him.

"What does he mean by 'wrong answer,' do you think?" Dinny asked.

"That it's time for us to ring up the constable," Charlie said.

"But the note said—"

"I know, son. It's not a decision I care to make. But Janey's not here and it has to be made."

Dinny sighed and went over to the front door as his father called the police. He looked out at the night. Chapel Place was quiet, except for a cat that was sitting in the middle of the street, washing its face. The windows of the cottages that lined the narrow street cast squares of light out onto the pavement—there the soft yellow glow of a reading lamp, a little farther down the blue-white flickering of a telly.

To all intents and purposes, it was merely another peaceful night in Mousehole. Life went on. Except somewhere out in that same night a madman had taken their friend hostage.

Dinny shook his head. This was a situation one might expect in Northern Ireland or the Middle East. Not here, not in Mousehole.

His father joined him at the door after he'd made his call and laid a hand on his shoulder. He seemed about to speak, but then sighed as Dinny had. They just stood there, waiting. Trying not to think of the Gaffer or what they must tell Janey.

Dinny felt his heart sink as he saw a familiar set of headbeams come down the steep hill from Paul. Moments later Janey had parked her Reliant Robin beside the Gaffer's yellow delivery wagon.

"I think our troubles are all over," Janey said as she got out of the little car.

She had a cheerful bounce to her step that faltered as she took in the Boyds' glum faces.

"What's wrong?" she said. "Gramps . . . ?"

"It's not good," Charlie said.

But before he could explain, the local constable arrived. The policeman stopped Charlie before he could get too far into his tale to call the assistant chief at the subdivision station in Penzance to send for more help. When he finished his call, he turned back to Charlie.

"All right," he said. "Let's take it from the beginning again, shall we?"

2 .

The Gaffer had been in tight situations before—during the war, of course, and too many times out on the bay when gales drove the sea against the cliffs, and sometimes boats with them. He didn't consider himself a particularly brave man. He just did what needed doing, when it needed doing. When the Penlee

Lifeboat, the *Solomon Browne*, went down in '81, attempting to save the crew of the *Union Star* that had run up on the Boscawen Cliffs, he'd been out there with the rest of the men of the village, not considering the danger nor whether he was brave or a coward, simply doing what needed to be done.

If he had ever been brave, it was carrying on after the deaths of Addie and his son. That took more courage than he'd needed on either the beaches of Dunkirk or Mount's Bay. Janey had seen him through that time. And it was only by thinking of Janey that he could face his present straits.

For her sake, he must hold out. Because the longer his captor was busy with him, the longer it would be before he could turn his attention to her. By that time, he hoped that she would have had the good common sense to ring up the police.

They would protect her.

But until then, he needed to buy time and the coin was dear.

The reek of petrol was strong in the air. His pant leg was soaked with the fluid. His arms ached from the rough way that he'd been tied to the chair. By the light of the electric lamp that the American had brought with him, he could see the strange gleam in the man's pale eyes as he brought the lighter forward a second time.

They were not the eyes of a sane man. They were the eyes of a man who took pleasure in pain—another's pain. Pain that he inflicted upon them.

The Gaffer couldn't hold back a cry as the gas on his pant leg burst into flame. The gas ignited with a *whoof* of blue fire, the heat searing his eyebrows and hair as he whipped his head back. He pulled at his bonds, arching his back against the chair for leverage, but the ropes binding his arms and legs allowed him to do no more than feebly jerk against their tethering. There was a sudden cloud of black smoke and the stink of charred fabric and burnt hair. He could feel the heat on his leg. The skin blistering—

Bett threw a blanket onto his leg, suffocating the flames.

But the pain was still there.

And the promise of more to come lay in Bett's eyes.

With a sense of shame, the Gaffer realized that his bladder had emptied, soaking his pants. Sweat glistened on his brow. His shirt clung damply to his back. His fear sent a fever heat through his limbs, but it was also like ice, tightening in a cold grip on his chest.

He trembled uncontrollably from the hot and cold flashes.

He blinked sweat from his eyes, not wanting to look at his captor, but unable to look away.

And the fear continued to compound—not simply for himself. Mostly it was for Janey. For what this madman would do to her.

And he *would* go after her. No matter what happened here tonight, Bett would go after Janey next.

The Gaffer couldn't bear the thought of it. If he went after her too soon, before she'd had a chance to call the police . . .

"I tell you, we don't have it anymore," he tried once more.

Bett shrugged. "Maybe, maybe not. But you know where it is."

"It—"

But the Gaffer had to close his mouth as Bett upended a jerrican above his head and the gasoline poured all over him. It burned at his eyes. The fumes made him choke and his stomach twisted with nausea. He shivered with a sudden chill as a waft of cool air blew up against his wet clothes.

Bett tossed the empty jerrican aside and fetched another. He unscrewed its cap, then paused as the sound of a siren went screaming by, out on the Newlyn Road to Mousehole. He looked at the Gaffer and slowly shook his head.

"Someone's doing what they're not supposed to," he said.

"What—what do you mean?"

The Gaffer stumbled over his words, trying to hide the relief he felt. At least Janey would be safe.

"I said no cops," Bett said. "But people never listen, do they? It's just like you, old man. I'm giving you a choice, but do you hear me?"

"I . . ."

"You know what I think? I think you *want* to burn."

Please God, the Gaffer thought. If I have to die in such a way, then let me at least take this madman with me.

He pulled against his bonds again, but the knots held too firmly.

Bett laughed. He set the second jerrican down.

"I think you're juiced up enough for what I've got in mind," he said.

He stepped over to where the Gaffer struggled helplessly in his bonds.

"How long do you think you'll last? Will the pain get you first—maybe make your old ticker kick out? Or do you think it'll be from sucking those flames into your lungs?"

He took the lighter out of his pocket.

"Only one thing's going to save you and that pretty little granddaughter of yours," he said. "You've got to tell me—"

There was a sudden boom. The Gaffer flinched, closing his eyes to the roar of the gas igniting.

But there was no increase in his pain.

No heat.

He opened his eyes to see that the lighter had fallen from Bett's hand. Bett himself was lying in the loose stones, clutching his leg. Blood seeped out from between his fingers. He was looking up at the top of the ladder that leaned against the stone wall of the silo.

"Y-you . . ." Bett said through clenched teeth.

The Gaffer followed Bett's gaze with his own. The poor light cast by the electric lamp made it difficult for him to identify the man standing up there. The stranger was a big man, pale-skinned and wild-haired. A rude, bloodied bandage was wrapped around one shoulder, the arm held in close to his chest, the hand tucked into his belt. The other held a gun.

"You're . . . dead," Bett said.

Awkwardly, the man started down the ladder. He came down, facing outward, leaning back against the wood frame. The gun centered on Bett, but wavering.

It was Davie Rowe, the Gaffer realized as the man came farther down into the light. He appeared to be on his last legs. What had Bett said about his being dea—

Bett reached into his pocket and Davie fired again. Bett howled as the bullet tore into his other leg.

The shot's report boomed and echoed, louder still now that Davie had descended deeper into the silo's confines.

"Followed . . . you . . ." Davie said to Bett. "You're in my . . . head . . . can't get you . . . out. . . ."

His speech was slurred and it was obvious to the Gaffer that he was in a great deal of pain. Davie winced as he made it down the last few rungs, then leaned weakly against the ladder for support once he reached the bottom. He turned slowly to the Gaffer.

"I . . . I'll have you . . . free in . . . in no time . . . Mr. . . . Litt—"

He shouldn't have looked away.

The sound of the gunshot was like a thunderclap.

The bullet hit Davie high in the chest and smashed him back against the ladder. A second shot spun him away from its support, but though he lurched, he didn't fall.

Bett had pulled his own revolver from his pocket. His features were twisted with pain, his eyes livid with anger, mad lights dancing in their pale depths. He fired a third time.

"Die, damn you!" he cried.

He lay on the ground, propped up on an elbow. Both legs were useless, blood pumping from their wounds to spread in a widening dark stain over his pants. His third shot took Davie straight in the chest, but still the man didn't fall.

"Why won't you die?" Bett screamed.

"C-can't . . ." Davie mumbled.

His chest was a ruin. Blood seeped from the corners of his mouth where he'd bitten down on his tongue. He staggered one step, another, moving towards Bett, the gun raising slowly in his hands. The Gaffer couldn't understand how Davie could still be on his feet, little say moving, but mobile he was. Before Bett could fire a fourth time, Davie's gun bucked in his hand. A hole appeared beside Bett's nose where the bullet went in and then the back of his head exploded outward.

Davie simply stared at him, swaying there on his feet.

"E-every . . . dog . . ." he said, choking on blood as he tried to shape the words. "Has his . . ."

He emptied his weapon into the body. The corpse twitched as each bullet struck, but it was only from the impact of the bullets. Bett had died from that shot in the head.

"My . . . day now . . ." Davie mumbled.

He continued to pull the trigger of his weapon, long after his ammunition was spent. The Gaffer's ears rang with painful echoes, but he could still hear the dry click of the gun's hammer until Davie finally dropped the weapon onto the loose stones.

He moved towards the Gaffer, fumbling a clasp knife from his pocket. He dropped to his knees when he reached the chair, his upper torso falling across the Gaffer's lap. Slowly his hand brought up the knife, but he didn't have the strength to cut the ropes. He coughed up blood. His body shook with violent tremors against the Gaffer's legs.

"Always . . . wanted . . ." he began.

And then he died.

It took the Gaffer a long time to move Davie's body from his lap. His every movement woke flares of pain in his burnt leg, but he put the pain aside as best he could. He pushed with his feet against the loose stone until the chair was finally shoved back far enough for the corpse's weight to do the rest of the work.

The Gaffer tipped the chair over then, wincing at the pain as his shoulder hit the stones. The seared nerve ends in his legs screamed. For long moments all the Gaffer could do was lie there, choking on the gas fumes. Then slowly he pushed the chair around, infinitesimal inch by inch until eventually his hand closed on the clasp knife. It was another age before he got it open, longer still to saw through the ropes.

When he was finally free, he didn't climb out of the silo. He crawled to where Davie Rowe lay and cradled the man's head on his unhurt leg, gently stroking the hair from Davie's brow.

"I'll tell them, my robin," he said. "Be sure, I'll tell them all you were a good man."

He was still holding the body when the police arrived.

3 ·

Peter Goninan was the only person to whom Janey told the whole story.

The days following that Sunday night were miserable. Janey and the others spent hour upon hour being questioned by the police—the local constables, the C.I.D., and even Scotland Yard. They were interviewed separately and had to repeat their stories over and over, ad nauseam. At one point, because he was unemployed, a foreigner, and the only suspect with a reasonable motive, the police were set to arrest Felix for Madden's murder, but a sergeant of the Devon and Cornwall Constabulary—a nephew of Chalkie's who knew Felix from when he'd stayed in Mousehole before—interceded on his behalf. They finally let Felix go and eventually left them all in peace. Madden's murder remained unsolved.

The Gaffer only had to spend a half day in the hospital—his burns, while painful, were mostly superficial. If Bett had waited only a few seconds more before dousing the fire . . . But none of them wanted to even think about that.

The threat against the Boyds' farm never fully materialized; nor did the one against Clare's job at the bookstore. Janey's tour was as mysteriously restored as it had been canceled, but she had it postponed. She could no more face a gig at that point than she could bear dealing with even one more of the crowd of Fleet Street vultures who descended on the village and pried into their lives with such obvious relish.

It was a week after the night of the murders when she, Felix, and Clare drove out to the Goninan farm. Janey still felt she needed some explanation as to exactly what had occurred and she could think of no one else to turn to.

As it was, Goninan was expecting them. A considerably less sulky Helen ushered them into the little cottage and, with Felix's help, saw about readying tea for them all.

"Was it real?" Janey asked when she finished relating what had happened by the Men-an-Tol.

"It depends on what you mean by real," Goninan replied.

"No, I'm serious. He just hypnotized us all—out there by the stone. Didn't he?"

Goninan smiled. "Aleister Crowley defined magic as 'the science and art of causing change to occur in conformity with the will.'"

A moment's silence followed as they all waited for him to expand upon his statement, but Goninan merely sipped at his tea.

"Are you saying it *did* happen?" Felix asked at last.

Goninan shook his head. "I wasn't there, so I can't tell you what did or didn't happen. All I can tell you is that Madden—like Crowley whom he so admired, and many others besides—*were* great magicians. They could work what we can only perceive of as miracles."

"And you . . . ?" Janey asked.

"I'm not a great magician."

"Why are they all evil?" Clare wanted to know.

"But they're not," Goninan said. "There are a great many magicians who have worked only for the good of the world and its people. Men such as Gurdjieff, whom we spoke of before, and Ouspensky. Rudolf Steiner . . . the Native American, Rolling Thunder . . . or Spyros Sathi, the Cypriot better known as Daskalos. They do only good work. They seek to lift mankind's spirit to a higher destiny. And they accept no reward for what they do."

Clare shook her head. "Those aren't magicians—they're philosophers."

"The best magicians are, for it's not the magic that draws them to their studies, but their need to understand the world and their own place in it. That is where they differ from men like Madden. Madden thought only of himself—worked only *for* himself. So his downfall, like that of so many other great magicians who have been led astray, was his egoism. He couldn't conceive of a normal man or woman being his peer, and for that reason underestimated those he thought of as 'sheep.'"

"It seems awfully tidy," Janey said, "the way everything worked out in the end."

"That's the beauty of magic," Goninan said. "It thrives on coincidence and synchronicities. That's the way the world's subconscious—what Jung called the racial memory—tries to wake us from our sleep. It teaches men like Madden that there is a harmonic balance, and it teaches the untutored—in this case, yourselves—that there is more to life than the gloom most people feel boxes them in."

"But then why does it fade?" Janey wanted to know. "Why can't we have real proof? I've got nothing—just little bits of memory and mist, and I'm even losing them. Everything's starting to feel like it was only a part of a dream. If magic's here to teach us something, why does it fade?"

"It doesn't," Goninan said. "Your interest in it does. This is a practical world we live in—or I should say, we have *made* it a practical world. It leaves little room for ancient wonders or magical phenomena. We're so busy with the practical day-to-day aspects of our lives that we don't have time to pay attention to whatever else might be around us as well.

"Yet if you immerse yourself in their study . . . The more time you spend in that sort of an atmosphere and with such beliefs, the more you yourself will become subject to unusual experiences and encounters. If you keep your distance, then the phenomena will do the same and eventually fade.

"It will still exist—it just won't exist for you."

"It all sounds kind of . . . spacy," Janey said with an apologetic smile.

Goninan laughed. "I suppose it does. To tell you the truth,

in some ways, magic is irrelevant. As are our concerns over life after death, spiritualism . . . all that sort of thing. What is important is that we utilize our potential as human beings—and we have *great* potential—to the utmost of our abilities."

"To be awake," Janey said.

Goninan nodded. "And then you will discover—truly *comprehend*—that *everything* is connected. The past, the present, the future. Ourselves as individuals, and the world in which we live. This life and whatever lies beyond it when we leave it. There is no end to our potential.

"The trouble is we tend to concentrate on what we don't have, rather than on what we do. We must learn to recognize what we already possess to its fullest potential."

"That sounds like Buddhism," Clare said.

Goninan smiled. "Everything is connected," he repeated. "I think it was Colin Wilson who pointed out that we accept the present moment as if it were complete in itself. But the present moment is always incomplete and the most basic achievement of our minds is in completing it. In making all the connections.

"If you don't want the magic to fade, then learn to wake up and stay awake."

"But *how* do you do that?" Janey asked.

Goninan swept a hand around his cluttered cottage, taking in the tangle of bookcases, stuffed birds, and display cases with the gesture.

"You might try watching birds," he said.

4 ·

They hadn't been back at the house on Duck Street for more than an hour before the doorbell rang. With everyone sitting about in the kitchen having the second tea of the afternoon— this one provided by the Gaffer, complete with thick clotted cream and homemade scones and blackberry jam—they took a quick vote as to who would answer the door and Janey lost. She was smiling good-humouredly as she opened the door, but scowled when she saw who was standing there on the stoop.

"You," she said.

Lena Grant nodded. "I don't expect a welcome," she said.

"That's good."

The new and improved Janey was having a hard time remaining civil, little say friendly. She wanted to slam the door in the woman's face, but she kept a rein on her temper. It wasn't easy.

"What do you want?" she asked.

"To apologize."

Janey couldn't help but laugh. The sound was harsh even to her own ears.

"There's nothing you can say to make up for what you've done," she said after a moment.

"I know."

That gave Janey pause. She gave Lena a long considering look. There was something subdued about the woman that didn't at all fit in with Janey's mental image of her.

"Then what do you want?" Her voice was softer now. Still not friendly, but the new and improved Janey was at least trying to listen.

"I told you, just to say I'm sorry. It's not enough to say I didn't know what I was doing. I did. I just didn't think about it. I'm going to change myself and I just wanted to . . . thank you, I suppose."

Janey blinked with surprise.

"Thank me?"

"You and Felix—for showing me how people *can* conduct their lives."

"You're the one who fixed things—aren't you?" Janey asked. "The tour, the Boyds' farm . . . ?"

Lena nodded. "When we woke up, really *woke up*—"

Janey heard Peter Goninan's voice in her mind.

Learn to wake up and stay awake.

"—to what Madden was doing, not just to us, but to everyone around him, and then what we in turn were doing to those around us. . . . Let's just say that Daddy and I are going to make sure that there's some changes."

"In the Order?" Janey asked.

Lena shook her head. "You can't change something like that— not from inside. It just sucks you in. We've left the Order. Now we're going to do what we can to discredit it and its influences."

"I don't envy you," Janey said.

She saw in Lena's eyes that she read a double meaning into that simple statement.

"Felix," Lena began. "He . . . would you apologize to him for me?"

Janey relented. She couldn't help herself.

"He doesn't know what you did," she said. "Just that you— you drugged him."

"Why didn't you tell him?"

"For his sake at first," Janey said. "And now . . . there's really no point to it, is there?"

"Who's at the door?" Felix called from inside.

Janey studied Lena for a long moment, then she sighed.

"You might as well come in," she said. "I can't pretend I'll be your friend, but if you want to say you're sorry to him . . ."

Lena shook her head. "I couldn't face him," she said. "I can hardly . . . face you."

She took a business card from her pocket and pressed it into Janey's hand.

"If I can ever help you," she said, "with *anything* at all, just call me."

She turned and walked away then, just as Felix came to join Janey at the door. Her step showed only a slight trace of a limp now.

"Janey . . ." he began, then he saw Lena's retreating figure. "Is that . . . ?"

"Lena Grant," Janey agreed.

Felix's eyes narrowed, but Janey just gave him a tug and steered him back inside.

"She came by to say she was sorry," she said.

"Sorry?" Felix said. "How can she expect us to believe that?"

"She didn't."

Janey looked at the business card again, then stuck it in the back pocket of her jeans.

"But I think she really meant it," she said as she closed the door.

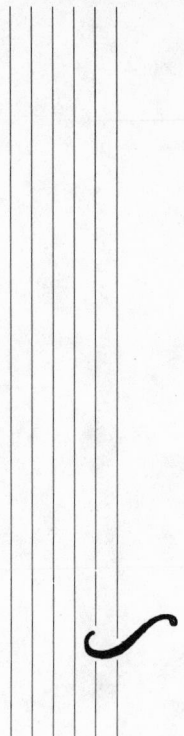

Coda

All things are known, but most things are forgotten.
It takes a special magic to remember them.

—ROBERT HOLDSTOCK,
from *Lavondyss*

The road that will take us forward is
also the road that will take us inward.

—COLIN WILSON,
from *Beyond the Occult*

Absurd Good News

His playing, to me, seemed to typify the wild hills and
moorland.

—BILL CHARLTON, founder of
the Northumbrian Gathering,
referring to Billy Pigg

"I wonder what happened to them after that," Jodi said as Denzil closed the book.

She was sitting on the windowsill, comfortably ensconced in a tiny beanbag chair that Denzil had made for her at the height of the sudden enthusiasm for miniature furniture that had taken hold of him in the first few weeks since the mouse-sized Jodi had come to live in his loft. His worktable was littered with more half-finished pieces, while all about the loft his handiwork made life easier for Jodi's diminutive size.

He'd taken a wooden crate and built a private bedroom for her that was now set on a lower shelf on one of the bookcases. A multitude of ladders provided her access to various tabletops and the windowsill and he was currently at work on an elevator device that would allow her to come and go from the loft at her pleasure, though he worried constantly under his breath about her being out on the streets alone. He was afraid of some normal-sized person stepping on her—not to mention Bodbury's all-too-many cats.

As it was, when she went outside now, it was in the pocket of one of the Tatters children, or with either Denzil or Taupin. Her days were full, filled with such excursions, or in helping Denzil with his work; she had the eye and size for the most painstakingly tiny craftsmanship—although not, much to Denzil's dismay, the proper enthusiasm. What she liked best was lolling about in the evenings and having Denzil read to her as he had done tonight.

The book they'd just finished was an old leather-bound volume that Taupin had found out on the moors near the Men-an-tol and subsequently presented to Denzil and Jodi since they were, as he put it, "the only ones he knew who would fully appreciate its preposterous conceits."

And then he had winked.

"I hope they lived happily ever after," Jodi said.

"Maybe some of them did."

"Taupin says that the stories go on forever, whether we're a part of them or not. They have their own lives. When we open a book, it freezes the tale—but only for so long as we're reading it."

Denzil hrumphed. He and the hedgerow philosopher continued to have their long—and to Jodi, pointless—arguments; only now they centered around the particulars and specifics of certain aspects of folkloric wonders and their properties rather than the reality of magic itself.

Two nights ago, which was the last time Taupin had been over, they'd gone on for hours about whether or not whiskey was an actual cure, or if calling it "the water of life" was merely symbolic of the altered state of mind into which the alcohol led the tippler.

"The pair of you are like two peas in one pod," Jodi told him. "I don't know which one's worse than the other."

"Watch it, you, or I'll put you in a jar."

Jodi smiled, then cocked her ear to the open window.

"Listen," she said. "There it is again. Can you hear it?"

"I hear something. . . ."

But what was vague for him was clear as crystal to her. The wind was bringing a strain of the first music down from the moorland near the Men-an-Tol. In its measures, lifting high above the rest of the ethereal instruments, was the lilting voice of a set of small pipes, humming like a bird's chorus against the bee-buzz of their drones.

"I wonder if Taupin managed to remember to take it to the stone yet," Jodi said.

Denzil knew just what she spoke of—she'd talked of little since they'd finished making the small tin brooch that was a perfect replica of the cover of the book that Taupin had found by the stone.

"Brengy does what he says he'll do," he admitted. Ollie was curled up on his lap, fast asleep. He scratched the little monkey between the ears. "He may forget for a week or two, but eventually he gets done everything he said he would."

"I wonder what she'll think when she gets it," Jodi said.

"Maybe she'll write a book to tell you," Denzil said.

Jodi smiled. "Maybe she'll write a tune, instead."

Outside the window, where the night lay thick on Bodbury's narrow streets, the wind continued to bring a fey music down from the hills and take it through the narrow streets of the town and out to sea. In its measures were the steps of an old dance— the whisper of a mystery, echoing and echoing, across the moors, across the sea, hill to hill and wave to wave, on into forever.

Contentment Is Wealth

I met you long ago,
but you couldn't have known,
for you weren't there.
Only your ghost.

The ghost that slid out of one
of your books and met me. . . .

—JACK DANN,
from *"Night Meetings"*

A year later Janey Little stood again on the moor by the Men-an-Tol, the small box in which she carried her Northumbrian pipes tucked under her arm. She often came out here, sometimes at night, sometimes during the day; sometimes with Felix, sometimes alone. She'd sit nearby the stone and play her whistle, trying to clear her mind, trying to remember. Tonight, on its first anniversary, she looked at the tolmen and regretted more than ever her inability to recall that night with the clarity and detail she tried to re-capture every time she found herself here.

But it remained obscure. She could remember John Madden and all he had put them through. She could remember what her grandfather had told her about his ordeal with Michael Bett and poor Davie Rowe. But the magic and the music . . . Memories of them stayed vague and distant. Especially those of the music.

It was just like it had happened in the Dunthorn book—in *her* version of what lay between its boards.

No one remembered, not really. It had all taken on a dreamlike quality for them as the months went by and one by one the various aspects of the sheer *wonder* of what had taken place were forgotten. Except by her.

Sometimes she'd take out that photo of her grandmother and

stare at the Small perched on the arm of her chair. It *was* a little man—she'd swear to that, and he was playing a fiddle—or at least it had been that night when they'd first come across it. But all too often these days it looked like just a smudge of light.

There was a session at the Boyds' farm tonight—in honour of her and Felix's return from a fall tour of California. Felix didn't play on stage yet—except for adding a bit of rhythm on the crowdy crawn towards the end of an evening. Mostly he worked the soundboard—and Janey knew she'd never sounded as good as with him on it—and played at the sessions afterward.

But he was getting closer. She could tell. If he didn't get up with his box this next tour they already had booked, then it'd be the one afterward. She could be patient—the new and improved Janey Little still holding firm to all her resolutions.

And he had played on almost every track of her third album—so much so that the only real argument they'd had this past year was in her wanting him to share the billing for the album, while he refused, saying that people would then expect him to be playing up there on stage with her on subsequent tours. He'd much rather just be listed in the credits with the other guest musicians, like Clare and Dinny and the other regulars of the sessions that had sat in on a tune or two. The new and improved Janey hadn't pushed him after he brought that up.

The LP had done well—racking up pleasant sales both domestically and abroad, where they sold it off the stage in between sets and after the shows. They'd called it *The Little Country*, naturally enough. A reviewer in *Folk Roots* magazine opined that the title came from her surname, or from the "little country" that Cornwall might seem to some, but only those who had been involved with the Dunthorn book knew the real origin and they kept it a secret.

There had only been one other major change in Janey's life over the past year: her mother had begun to write to her. Janey had ignored the first letter, complete with its muddle of confused apologies—after all, what did she owe the woman? But the correspondence continued to arrive, once a month. There was never a reprimand for her not replying to them, hidden there in her mother's untidy script. They were merely gossipy letters, talking about the changes in her mother's life. How she'd moved from New York. How she'd finally become involved in repertory theatre in New England as she'd always wanted to. How she was poor, but finally happy. How she'd bought all of Janey's albums and was so very proud of her.

The paraph of each was a flourishing, "your loving mother, Connie."

That afternoon Janey had finally sat down and written back. She sealed the envelope and took it up to the post office for a stamp just before tea. As she sent the letter off on its way, a weight that she hadn't been aware she was carrying slipped from her shoulders.

She'd felt a little light-headed and that was when she'd decided to come up to the Men-an-Tol tonight before the session.

By herself.

At moonrise.

With her pipes.

Kempy had been delirious to see her again, bounding about with great good enthusiasm. He lay now near the tolmen, tongue lolling, as he watched her fuss with her pipes. Opening their carrying box, she took them out and put them together, bellows attached to the air bag by one tube, chanter by another. But before she blew them up, she lay them down on the lid of their case and, giving Kempy a small embarrassed smile, walked over to the stone.

The moon was just rising.

She looked about the dark moor. Satisfied that there was no one watching her except for the border collie who was half mad himself anyway, she squeezed through the hole in the stone. Walking around, she went through again. And again. Nine times, all told.

She wasn't trying to find her own way into that otherworld. She just wanted to *see* it. To know that it was real.

But the mist never rose from the surrounding moorland. There was no flare of light.

No music.

Just the quiet of the night. The stars glimmering high above in a sky that was surprisingly clear for this time of night. The moon steadily rising.

She had to laugh at herself for even trying. Standing on the far side of the Men-an-Tol after her ninth passage through its rounded hole, she brushed the stone dust from her jacket.

That was desperation for you, she thought.

She was disappointed with her failure, but not surprised by it. After all, if the magic could be so simply called up, why then anybody could simply waltz up to the stone and prove that there was such a thing. And as Peter Goninan had told her, the magic was more secret than that.

It was—

She paused as her fingers touched an unfamiliar object pinned to her jacket. Fumbling in her pocket, she took out the torch that she'd brought from the car with her and shone its light onto her chest.

There was a brooch pinned to the fabric that hadn't been there when she'd left the house earlier this evening. She touched it with wondering fingers. It seemed to be made of heavy tin—like the hefty little souvenir cottages and lighthouses that used to be on sale in Penzance and the village two summers ago. It was the shape of a book and the design of its cover . . .

She traced the words of its title with a finger, wonder growing in her mind.

The Little Country.

An eerie warmth spread through her. Looking at the stone, she half imagined she saw a man sitting there on the top of the Men-an-Tol, swinging his legs so that his heels tapped against the stone. And she recognized him. William Dunthorn. Not as she knew him from her grandfather's old photos, but the way he'd look if he'd lived to this day. Smiling at her, mysteries brimming in his penetrating gaze.

She blinked, and the image was gone—but not the warmth. Nor the memory of him sitting there on the stone.

And not the brooch.

She flicked off the torch and picked up her pipes. She buckled on the bellows and arranged the small drones so that they lay across her left forearm. Then she blew up the air bag with a squeezing motion of her elbow. The drones hummed their quiet buzz. Inspired, she woke a new tune from the chanter, composed on the spot. For its title, she took that feeling of two Billys' worth of Bully that was singing through her veins, following the deep rhythm of her heartbeat—

Dhumm-dum. Dhumm-dum.

—that seemed to echo in the ground underfoot and off, away, across the moor.

She felt as dizzy as though she'd just received some absurd good news and needed to shout it out to the world in a tune.

A simple bit of a jig that was an echo of the first music. In its measures were the steps of an old dance—the whisper of a mystery, echoing and echoing, across the moors, across the sea, hill to hill and wave to wave, on into forever.

The session at the Boyds' that night was a rousing success, so much so that friends of theirs claimed to have heard the music spilling out of the Boyds' kitchen from as far away as St. Ives and Land's End.

But Janey knew what music it was that they'd really heard.

It had been an echo of the first music, she had explained to Felix and Clare the next day.

The music of the Little Country that every person had hidden away inside them.

Appendix I:

A Selection of

Janey Little's Tunes

The following tunes were written on the fiddle, but have proved admirably suitable for a wide variety of instruments. All tunes are copyright (c) 1991 by Charles de Lint; all rights reserved.

ABSURD GOOD NEWS

ALL OF A MONDAY NIGHT

BILLY'S OWN JIG

FELIX GAVIN'S REEL

THE GAFFER'S MOUZEL

THE GIRLS OF EDMONTON

HER TWO CHAIRS

JOHN WOOD'S MAZURKA

THE MEIKLEJOHN JIG

THE MEN-AN-TOL WALTZ

THE NEW TASSELED SHOES

THE NINE BLIND HARPERS

SHE'S TOO FAST FOR ME

STARGAZY PIE

THE STONESS BARN

THE TINKER'S BLACK KETTLE

Appendix II:

A Brief Glossary

of Unfamiliar Terms

I'm indebted to conversations with Phil and Audrey Wallis, as well as Douglas Tregenza's *Departed Days: Mousehole Remembered* (Dyllanstow Truran, 1984) and Ben Batten's *Old Newlyn Speech* (self-published, 1984) for the following terms:

agro—short for aggravation
ansum—handsome
bagle—a troublemaker
brill—short for brilliant
caboleen—rounded stone used as an anchor
carker—little cork boat with a slate or iron keel
come 'pon that—so far as that goes
dog in a tayser—square peg in a round hole
emperent—cheeky, pert
fore and after—clergyman
garm—expression of surprise, wonder
kitey—a bit loony
la Ley!—exclamation
making some crant—creating a fuss
oh raw we—exclamation
sparking—courting
tatchy—irritable

tee-ta-taw—a vaguely critical or mocking comment

that do belong—that's unusual

three scats behind—too slow, late

tuck-net—small net used to lift up pilchard in a seine

two-deckers—any four-footed animal; sailors call them this rather
    than by their common names to ward against bad luck

up country—the rest of England

wam—very finicky person

well, I go to sea—surprise, astonishment

white choker—clergyman

3/10
11 - Gar toto